FACT, FANCY, AND FABLE:

FACT, FANCY, AND FABLE:

𝔄 𝔑𝔢𝔴 𝔥𝔞𝔫𝔡𝔟𝔬𝔬𝔨

FOR

READY REFERENCE ON SUBJECTS COMMONLY OMITTED FROM CYCLOPÆDIAS;

COMPRISING

PERSONAL SOBRIQUETS, FAMILIAR PHRASES, POPULAR APPELLATIONS, GEOGRAPHICAL
NICKNAMES, LITERARY PSEUDONYMS, MYTHOLOGICAL CHARACTERS,
RED-LETTER DAYS, POLITICAL SLANG, CONTRACTIONS
AND ABBREVIATIONS, TECHNICAL TERMS,
FOREIGN WORDS AND PHRASES,
AMERICANISMS, ETC.

COMPILED BY

HENRY FREDERIC REDDALL.

"TRIFLES MAKE THE SUM OF HUMAN THINGS."

CHICAGO:
A. C. McCLURG & COMPANY.

REPUBLISHED BY GALE RESEARCH COMPANY, BOOK TOWER, DETROIT, 1968

PREFACE.

IN the words of John Dryden, " Some will think this book needs no excuse, and others will receive none ; " but for those who belong to neither class, and who judge the work on its merits, a few words of introduction and explanation seem necessary.

Not the least of the problems connected with the compilation of a work having a distinct plan, and bearing such a title as " Fact, Fancy, and Fable," is to decide what to admit and what to exclude. Occasionally there must needs be a deviation from the set rule ; yet in the main the lines of selection will be found to be clearly laid down and closely adhered to. Approximately, our " Fact " embraces Americanisms, Memorable Days, Pseudonyms, Political Nomenclature, Foreign Words and Sentences, and Contractions and Abbreviations ; " Fancy " deals with Personal Sobriquets and Nicknames of all kinds, and with Familiar Phrases and Folk-Sayings ; while the realm of the purely mythological belongs to " Fable."

The wholly fictitious characters of satires and novels and of romance and poetry, which consume so large a portion of the works of Wheeler and Brewer, and must ever be of secondary popular interest, have been reserved for a future compilation, should the same be deemed advisable. Only where a nominally fictitious character is a portraiture or a burlesque of a real personage has the reference been admitted here.

A glance at the scheme of " Fact, Fancy, and Fable," outlined on the titlepage, will enable the reader to form some idea of the scope of the work. Briefly stated, the aim of the author has been to amass a great amount of useful or curious information which has hitherto been either inaccessible to the general reader or so widely scattered among a score or more of different volumes as to be practically unattainable when most needed. Thus, for pen-names the anxious inquirer has had to turn to Frey's " Initials and Pseudonyms " or some kindred work ; for mythological characters and events, to the various classical dictionaries ; for Americanisms, to Bartlett's admirable compilation ; for personal sobriquets, to Wheeler's " Noted Names of Fiction ; " for every-day and folk sayings, to Brewer's " Dictionary of Phrase and Fable," to the same author's " Reader's Handbook," Wheeler's " Familiar Allusions," or to Edwards's " Words, Facts, and Phrases." Much information pertaining to our Red-Letter Days may be gleaned, amid a mass of other data, from Chambers's " Book of Days ; " but this fruitful subject is only partially treated therein. Political nomenclature must also be sought for in divers channels ; and not until one has essayed to run to earth some apparently self-explanatory phrase does it become apparent how little has been done to catalogue such matters. The interesting subject of Geographical Nicknames is nowhere else treated at the length it deserves. Contractions and Abbreviations, and Foreign Words and Phrases, may be found appended to any good dictionary ; but in no case, it is believed, have these ever been set forth so fully as in the present instance. It will be admitted that there is a distinct advantage in having all these matters grouped under one alphabet.

The books above enumerated may be said to constitute the bibliography of the various topics, and to all of them grateful acknowledgment is made in so far as the writer has profited by their contents. But in addition thereto many other works of reference, indirectly related to the subjects involved, as also modern history and biography, both English and foreign, have been ransacked for references, and much correspondence carried on with friends and authorities at home and abroad.

The departments embracing Geographical Nicknames, Red-Letter Days, and Political Nomenclature are thought to be noteworthy in that they deal with subjects never before adequately treated ; in all other directions the constant aim has been to include every entry likely to be sought for. While it would be folly to claim or expect that complete success in this respect has been attained, the author indulges in the modest hope that in the following pages much will be found that has never before been collated. For instance, in none of the works mentioned above is there to be found an explanation of the allusion contained in the phrase " Legislature of a Thousand Drinks." It occurs in Dana's " Two Years before the Mast," and refers to an episode in the early annals of California. To Mr. Hubert Howe Bancroft, the historian of the Pacific coast, the writer is indebted for an account of the origin of the nickname. So with the sayings " Between the Devil and the Deep Sea," " Angel Gabriel Riots," " Gladstone's Umbrella," " Spellbinders," " Nigger in the Woodpile," " Cain of America," " Gossamer Days," " California Column," " Cockerel Church," and a hundred others. It may easily be that the world is not actually suffering for lack of such " hole and corner" information, but the inquiry-columns of the periodical press afford ample evidence that there is no little popular interest therein.

It remains to be said that scattered throughout the dictionary will be found many entries gleaned from the author's previously published writings during the past decade. The articles on " Caspar Hauser," " Junius," " The Man of the Iron Mask," and the " Wandering Jew," are condensed from his little book " Who Was He?" published in 1887.

H. F. R.

New York City, 1889.

FACT, FANCY, AND FABLE.

A.

A. When written as an indorsement on the margin or face of a document, *A* signifies *Approved* or *Accepted* or *Audited*, as the case may be. The small *a* indicates *one*, or *unity;* as, "one dollar a pound," — meaning one dollar for each pound. When written @, it signifies *at;* as, "12 lbs. at 50 cts."

A 1. First quality; the registry mark of underwriters, indicating first-class. American vessels are registered A, and afterward distinguished by figures in descending grade; as, A 1, A 1¼, A 1½, A 1¾, A 2, etc. In the English Lloyds "A 1" denotes that the vessel is well built and seaworthy, the figure 1 indicating that her rigging, anchors, cables, etc., are in good condition. A 2 indicates that the equipments are unsatisfactory. The ordinary expression as to the highest mercantile standing is "A No. 1."

A. or Ans. Answer.

A. A. A. G. Acting Assistant Adjutant-General.

A. A. G. Assistant Adjutant-General.

A. A. P. S. American Association for the Promotion of Science.

Aaron's Serpent. England has been so named because she absorbed the various petty states of India; Germany, because she did likewise for the smaller German states. The allusion is to Ex. vii. 10–12.

A. A. S. *Academiæ Americanæ Socius.* Fellow of the American Academy (of Arts and Sciences).

A. A. S. S. *Americanæ Antiquarianæ Societatis Socius.* Member of the American Antiquarian Society.

A. B. *Artium Baccalaureus.* Bachelor of Arts.

A. B. That is, "able-bodied," — the rating on board ship of all skilled or able seamen. A ship's "boys" are unskilled mariners, no matter what their age.

Ab. The fast of Ab, or "Black Fast," as it is sometimes called among the Jews, occurs annually about Aug. 10, and lasts from sunset to sunset. This fast is one of the most solemn occasions in the Hebrew worship, and is scrupulously observed by orthodox Jews. It commemorates the destruction of the two temples of Judæa. The temple of Solomon was destroyed by Nebuchadnezzar, king of Babylon, which sad event of Jewish history occurred in the month of Ab. The second temple was destroyed by Titus the Roman. This happened on the 9th of Ab. Hence the season of fasting and lamentation which marks the event as each year goes by.

Abactu ad posse valet consecutio. (Lat.) Inference by induction from what has been to what may be.

Abaddon. The Hebrew designation of the fallen angel or evil spirit who is called Apollyon in Greek.

Ab agendo. (Lat.) From acting or doing.

Abandannad. A slang sobriquet for the purloiners of pocket-handkerchiefs; *i. e.*, bandannas. Supposed to be a corruption or contraction of "a bandanna lad."

Abandon fait larron. (Fr.) Negligence makes the thief.

Ab ante. (Lat.) Before; previously.

Ab antiquo. (Lat.) From olden time.

Abaris. In classic myth a priest of Apollo to whom the deity presented a golden arrow on which to traverse the air, and which also rendered him invisible. Hence the allusion to the arrow, or dart, of Abaris.

A bas. (Fr.) Down; down with.

Abaster, Abatos, and Æton. The three horses of Pluto (*q. v.*).

Abb. Abbott's U. S. Circuit and District Court Reports.

Abbot of Misrule. The master of revels, especially of Christmas festivities, in the Middle Ages.

Abbot of Unreason. A mediæval personage who held sway in the houses of the nobility during the Christmastide festivities. The same as "Lord of Misrule."

Abby Willey. The stage-name of Mrs. R. B. Chamberlain.

Abcedarian. One who teaches or is learning the A B C.

Abcedarian Hymns. Those in which each verse, from the first to the last, began with successive letters of the alphabet in regular progression.

A. B. C. F. M. American Board of Commissioners for Foreign Missions.

Abdallah. (Pseud.) Otway Curry, a writer for the American press.

Abderitan. Another name for an idiotic or foolish person. The natives of Abdera, in Thrace, were famed in ancient times for their dense stupidity.

Abderite. The nickname for a scoffer. *See* LAUGHING PHILOSOPHER.

Abdiel. The angel who defied Lucifer when he urged the angels to revolt.

Abdiel. (Pseud.) (1) Joshua William Brooks. (2) Samuel Hull.

A beau jeu beau retour. (Fr.) One good turn deserves another.

Abel Keene. A village schoolmaster, afterward a merchant's clerk. He was led astray, lost his place, and hanged himself.

Abel Shufflebottom. (Pseud.) Robert Southey (1774–1843).

Aberdeen. (Pseud.) Hugh D. McIntyre.

Abessa. The impersonation of abbeys and convents, represented by Spenser in the "Faerie Queene" as a damsel.

Ab extra. (Lat.) From without.

Ab hoc et ab hac. (Lat.) From this and that; confusedly.

Abiali. An African deity, wife of Makembi. She is invoked in time of pestilence.

Ab identitate rationis. (Lat.) "From identity of reason." For the same reason.

Abigail. Another name for a lady's or waiting maid. Abigail, in 1 Sam. xxv. 3, repeatedly styles herself David's handmaid. The term was also much used by the Queen Anne novelists, — probably in allusion to Abigail Hill, afterward the famous Mrs. Masham, who was woman-in-waiting to her royal mistress.

Abigail Perkins. (Pseud.) James Otis Kaler in the "Boston Globe."

Abingdon Law. Summary punishment without trial. In 1645 Lord Essex and Waller held Abingdon, a town in Berks, against Charles I. The town was unsuccessfully attacked by the Royalists in 1644 and 1645. On these occasions the besieged put every Irish prisoner to death, without the semblance of a trial. Hence the origin of the term "Abingdon Law."

Ab inconvenienti. (Lat.) From the inconvenience.

Ab incunabulis. (Lat.) From the cradle; from childhood.

Ab initio. (Lat.) From the beginning.

Ab integro. (Lat.) Anew; afresh.

Ab intestato. (Lat.) Without a will; intestate.

Ab intra. (Lat.) From within.

A bis et à blanc. (Fr.) "From brown to white." By fits and starts.

Abl. Ablative.

Abnormis sapiens. (Lat.) Wise by natural good sense; endowed with good sense.

Aboard. The extent to which in the United States the nautical term "aboard" has extended its meaning to land affairs, is quite amusing. Travellers by rail are urged to *go aboard the cars*, as railway carriages are called, the conductor finally crying out, "All aboard!"

Abolitionists. A term, denoting the Anti-Slavery party in the United States, which appeared soon after the founding of "The Liberator" by William Lloyd Garrison in 1831. Garrison, Wendell Phillips, John Brown, E. P. Lovejoy, Joshua R. Giddings, John P. Hale, Salmon P. Chase, and Charles Sumner were avowed Abolitionists.

There never was a time when all Americans acquiesced in slavery. The Society of Friends — the original English settlers of Pennsylvania — opposed it, and so from time to time did others; but the acrimonious contest over slavery, out of which grew the term "Abolition" and its derivatives, dates from 1829, when William Lloyd

Garrison began the severe arraignment of slave-holders as criminals. In 1831 he started his paper, "The Liberator." The next year a society was formed in Boston for the purpose of promoting the cause of emancipation; that was the New England Anti-Slavery Society. The American Anti-Slavery Society was formed at Philadelphia in 1833, Beriah Green, president, and John G. Whittier one of the secretaries. Their number was small; but in 1840 they divided into two wings, one favoring abolition within the Union, the other denouncing the Constitution as a bulwark of slavery. Wendell Phillips, the chief orator of the cause, was especially virulent in denunciation of the Constitution. The cause of anti-slavery grew much more rapidly than the party which was its highest embodiment. There was never any very large number of American citizens who were, prior to the civil war, avowed Abolitionists. Gradually the principle of emancipation gained ground, however. At the South, and largely in Democratic circles North, the Republicans were called Abolitionists, — often with the epithet "Black" prefixed. After the war, a majority of the Northern people took pride in claiming to have been Abolitionists. In 1844, when the Abolitionists polled 62,300 presidential votes, the Whigs attributed the defeat of Clay by Polk to the defection of Anti-Slavery Whigs. The ticket then was Birney and Morris. In operating the "underground railroad" the Abolitionists took the lead, as they did in all anti-slavery movements. Their first martyr was Elijah P. Lovejoy, of Alton, Ill., who was killed by a mob in 1839. John Brown was the most famous of the list. John Quincy Adams, Joshua R. Giddings, John P. Hale, Salmon P. Chase, and Charles Sumner were conspicuous in Congress for boldly avowing Abolitionism before the formation of the Republican party. It was not until emancipation had become an accomplished fact that the party finally disbanded. The Colonizationists, who wanted to do away with slavery by returning the negroes to Africa, were bitterly hostile to the Abolition movement. They never went into politics. — HALE.

A bon chat bon rat. (Fr.) "To good cat good rat." They are well matched; tit-for-tat.

A bon marché. (Fr.) Cheap. The *Bon Marché* in Paris is an immense establishment, where everything is sold, much frequented by foreign shoppers and bargain-hunters.

Abonnement. (Fr.) Subscription.

Ab origine. (Lat.) From the beginning.

Aborigines. This word is explained in every dictionary, English, Latin, or French, as a general name for the indigenous inhabitants of a country. In reality it is the proper name of a peculiar people of Italy, who were not indigenous, but were supposed to be a colony of Arcadians. The error has been founded chiefly on the supposed derivation of the word from *ab origine*. Never was a more eccentric

etymology, — a preposition with its governed case made plural by the modern final *s!*

Abou Hassan. A rich merchant, transferred during sleep to the bed and palace of the Caliph Haroun-al-Raschid. Next morning he was treated as the caliph, and every effort was made to make him forget his identity. The same trick was played on Christopher Sly in the induction of Shakspeare's comedy, "Taming of the Shrew."

Abou-Jahia. In Mohammedan mythology, the angel of death.

Above Par, Below Par. These are common Americanisms. "Par" is a commercial term signifying that certain stocks or shares can be bought on the Stock Exchange at their nominal value; as when £100 worth of London and Northwestern Railway stock can be bought for £100, there being neither premium nor discount. "Par," therefore, may be taken to mean level, or average. It is used in America to denote the state of health or spirits of a person. "Below par" means low in health or spirits; "above par" signifies in better health or spirits than usual.

Ab ovo. (Lat.) "From the egg." From the beginning.

Ab ovo usque ad mala. (Lat.) "From the egg to the apples." From the beginning to the end of anything. At a Roman entertainment eggs were the first and apples the last dish served.

Abp. Archbishop.

A. B. Philologer. (Pseud.) Laurence Sterne, author of the "Sentimental Journey," etc.

Abr. Abridgment, or abridged.

Abracadabra. A famous ancient formula, to which was ascribed mysterious powers, said to be of Persian origin. No other combination of letters was regarded with so great veneration, and it was thought to be an infallible preventive of fevers and agues. Here are the directions for its preparation and use given by an old writer: —

Write the letters of the word so as to form a triangle, capable of being read many ways, on a square piece of paper. Fold the paper so as to conceal the writing, and with white thread stitch it into the form of a cross. This amulet wear in the bosom, suspended by a linen ribbon, for nine days; then go in dead silence, before sunrise, to the banks of a stream that flows eastward, take the amulet from off the neck, and fling it backward into the water. If you open or read it, the charm is destroyed.

```
A B R A C A D A B R A
  A B R A C A D A B R
    A B R A C A D A B
      A B R A C A D A
        A B R A C A D
          A B R A C A
            A B R A C
              A B R A
                A B R
                  A B
                    A
```

See OM MANI PADMA HUM.

Abraham Newland. A colloquial term for a Bank of England note. For many years in the early part of the present century Abraham Newland was cashier, and signed all the notes. To counterfeit these was a capital offence; whence arose the famous couplet: —

"I have heard people say, sham Abram you may,
But you must not sham Abraham Newland."

Abrahamic Covenant. The covenant made by God with Abraham that Messiah should spring from his seed.

Abraham's Bosom. The repose of the happy in death. The figure is taken from the ancient custom of allowing a dear friend to recline at dinner on one's bosom. Thus the beloved John reclined on the bosom of Jesus.

Reclining on the *triclinium*, or dinner-bed, the guest lay usually upon his left side, leaving his right hand free to reach the food. His head would thus easily come into contact with the breast of the person on his left. It was in this way that John leaned on the bosom of Jesus while at supper. This is also mentioned in John xiii. 25; xxi. 20. A figurative use of the custom referred to is made in Luke xvi. 22, 23; John i. 18. — FREEMAN.

Abram Man. A slang term for a begging impostor. The name is derived from the occupants of the Abraham Ward in Bedlam, who used to solicit alms of charitable visitors. The phrase "to sham Abram" means to feign sickness or distress in order to shirk honest labor. See ABRAHAM NEWLAND.

A bras ouverts. (Fr.) With open arms.

Abrax. In classic myth, one of Aurora's horses. See AURORA.

Abraxas, or **Abracax.** In Persian mythology, the Supreme Being.

Abraxas Stones. Stones with the word "Abraxas" engraved on them, used as a talisman. The word symbolizes the mystic number 365 and the number of intelligences between earth and deity.

Abrégé. (Fr.) Abridgment.

A. B. S. American Bible Society.

Absalom. In Dryden's poem, "Absalom and Achitophel," the former character stands as a nickname for the wayward son of Charles II., the Duke of Monmouth (1649–1685).

Absence d'esprit. (Fr.) Absence of mind.

Absens hæres non erit. (Lat.) "The absent will not be the heir." Out of sight, out of mind.

Absente reo. (Lat.) The defendant being absent.

Absit invidia. (Lat.) Let there be no ill-will.

Absit omen. (Lat.) May it not prove ominous.

Absolutism tempered by Assassination. Count Ernst Friedrich Münster, Hanoverian envoy at St. Petersburg, discovered that Russian civilization is "merely artificial," and first published to Europe the epitomization of the Russian Constitution, that it is "absolutism tempered by assassination."

Absquatulate. To run away, or abscond. An American word, compounded of *ab, squat*, to go away from your squatting. A "squatting" is a tenement taken in some unclaimed territory without purchase or permission. The persons who take up a squatting are termed "squatters."

Absque argento omnia vana. (Lat.) Without money all is vain.

Absque hoc. (Lat.) Without this.

Absque ulla conditione. (Lat.) Unconditionally.

Absyrtus. In classical mythology a brother of Medea who fled with her from Colchis. Being nearly overtaken by her father, she slew Absyrtus and divided his body into fragments, which she dropped behind her, that her father might be hindered in his pursuit by stopping to pick up the remains of his son.

Abundat dulcibus vitus. (Lat.) He abounds with pleasant faults.

Ab uno disce omnes. (Lat.) "From one learn all." From a single example you may have an idea of the whole.

Abusus non tollit usum. (Lat.) Abuse is not an argument against proper use.

A. C. *Ante Christum.* Before the birth of Christ.

A. C. Arch-chancellor.

Acacians. (1) Followers of Acacius, bishop of Cæsarea in the fourth century, who held peculiar doctrines respecting the nature of Christ. (2) Partisans of Acacius, patriarch of Constantinople, promoter of the Henoticon (482–484).

Acad. Academy.

Acad. Nat. Sci. Academy of Natural Sciences.

Academic City. A name given to Worcester, Mass., in allusion to the number and excellence of its educational institutions. *See* HEART OF THE COMMONWEALTH.

Academics. Followers of Plato, who taught in the Academy, a garden planted by one Academos.

Academicus. (Pseud.) (1) Rev. Aula Macaulay, who contributed to " Ruddiman's Weekly Magazine " under this signature. (2) Charles Seager, M. A. (3) William Pulteney Alison. (4) John Loveday, D. C. L., in his contributions to the "Gentleman's Magazine."

Academy Figures. Drawings in black and white chalk, on tinted paper, from living models used by artists. So called from the Royal Academy of Artists.

A cader va chi troppo alto sale. (Ital.) Who climbs too high, goes to fall.

Acadia, or **Acadie.** The original name, but now the poetical designation, of Nova Scotia. It was granted by Henry IV. of France, Nov. 8, 1603, to De Monts, a Frenchman, and a company of Jesuits, who were finally expelled from the country by the English governor and colonists of Virginia, who claimed all that coast by virtue of its prior discovery by the Cabots in 1497. In 1621 Sir William Alexander, a Scotchman, applied to and obtained of James I. a grant of the whole peninsula, which he re-named Nova Scotia, in honor of his native land. The country frequently changed owners during the next century, and in 1713 was finally ceded to England. In 1755 the French residents were forcibly expatriated by the English, which event forms the subject of Longfellow's poem, "Evangeline."

A capite ad calcem. (Lat.) From head to foot ; thoroughly.

A capriccio. (Ital.) At will; agreeably to the fancy. (Mus.)

Acariâtre. (Fr.) Ill-natured; cross; crabbed.

A causa persa, parole assai. (Ital.) When the cause is lost there is enough of words.

Acc. Accusative.

Accedas ad curiam. (Lat.) You may come into court.

Accelerando. (Ital.) Gradual quickening of movement. [Mus.]

Accepta. (Lat.) The receipts in accounts.

Accessit. (Lat.) He came near.

Acciacatura. (Ital.) A species of arpeggio. (Mus.)

Accoltellatori. Literally, " gladiators." A name given to secret assassins who infested Ravenna and other places in Italy in 1874.

According to Gunter. In the United States this phrase is used as the equivalent of the English " According to Cocker." Gunter was an English mathematician of great eminence, who died 1626. He invented " Gunter's scale " and the surveying chain universally known as " Gunter's chain."

Acct. Account.

Accueil. (Fr.) Reception; greeting; welcome.

Accusare nemo se debet, nisi coram Deo. (Lat.) No one is bound to accuse himself, unless before God.

Accusative, The. A nickname conferred on John Calvin by his mates in college.

Ace Clubs. (Pseud.) J. C. Loftin.

Aceldama. A field of battle, or any place where much slaughter has taken place. The name is derived from the locality to the south of Jerusalem, so called, which the priests purchased with the thirty pieces of silver paid to Judas for the betrayal of Christ.

Acephalites. Literally, "without a head." (1) Certain of the Eutychians who in the fifth century were " deprived of Mongus, their head," through his renunciation of his errors. (2) A body of reformers in the reign of Henry I. who "acknowledged no leader." (3) Another name for the mythical Blemmyës, a people said to inhabit the interior of Africa, who had no heads, their mouth and eyes being placed in their chests.

Acerrima proximorum odia. (Lat.) The hatred of the nearest relatives is most intense.

Acervatim. (Lat.) By heaps.

Acestes. In classical mythology a son of the river-god Crinisius, who in a trial of skill at archery shot an arrow into the air with such velocity that it took fire, and left a flaming path until it was wholly consumed.

Ac etiam. (Lat.) And also.

Achæan League. A federation between the twelve cities of Achaia. Alexander the Great dissolved it; but it was revived in 280 B. C., only to be finally broken up by the Romans in 147 B. C.

A chaque saint sa chandelle. (Fr.) To every saint his candle; that is, conciliate every source of possible favor.

A charge. (Fr.) At expense.

Acharius. (Pseud.) Fredrik Wilhelm Scholander.

Acharné. (Fr.) Bloodthirsty.

Achates. In classical mythology the companion of Æneas, whose fidelity has given us the phrase *fidus Achates*, — faithful Achates.

Acheron. In classical mythology a son of Sol and Terra, who was changed into a river in Hades. The word is sometimes used as a synonym for hell itself.

Acherontian Books. The celebrated books of augury which the Etruscans received from Tages, grandson of Jupiter.

Acherusia. A chasm or abyss in Pontus, said to communicate with the nether world, and through which Hercules hauled Cerberus to earth.

Acheta, or **Acheta Domestica.** (Pseud.) Miss L. M. Budgen, an American poet.

A cheval. (Fr.) On horseback.

Achilles. In classical mythology son of Peleus and of Thetis, a Nereid. He was the chief personage of Homer's Iliad, and was famed more than all the Greeks in the Trojan war for bravery, strength, and personal beauty. At birth his mother immersed him in the River Styx, and he was thus made invulnerable, save in the heel by which she held him; but he was killed by Paris, to whom Apollo discovered his weak spots.

Achilles. Albert III., Margrave of Brandenburg, was so named. *See also* ULYSSES.

Achilles' Heel of England. (1) Ireland has been so named. A legend has

it that Achilles was vulnerable only in the heel, and that in consequence of a wound in that part he died. In allusion to the almost constant disaffection existing in Ireland during the last two centuries, and from the fact that foreign invasion has more than once descended on her shores, the "sister isle" has come to be regarded as the spot where England might be most easily assailed should she ever be embroiled in an extensive foreign war. (2) Carlyle so named Hanover, which, he said, was "liable to be strangled at any time for England's quarrels; the Achilles' heel to invulnerable England."

Achilles of England. The Duke of Wellington (1769–1852) was thus frequently referred to.

Achilles of Germany. Albert, Elector of Brandenburg (1414–1486).

Achilles of Rivers. The Columbia River, the largest American river that enters the Pacific Ocean. It is a noble stream, remarkable for grand and picturesque scenery. Like the famous Homeric hero, it may be said to be vulnerable at its heel, for a treacherous and constantly shifting bar obstructs navigation at its mouth; though, this passed, the largest steamers can ascend 115 miles to Vancouver.

Achilles of Rome. A sobriquet for Sicinius Dentatus (flourished 405 B. C.).

Achilles' Puzzle. This is an argument that Achilles could never catch a tortoise, because while the man was running the intervening distance, the tortoise would still get some distance ahead, and so on to infinity. It was invented by Zeno the Eleatic, 455 B. C.

Achilles' Spear. Telephus tried to stop the march of the Greek army on its way to Troy, and received a wound from Achilles. The oracle told him, as "Achilles gave the wound, only Achilles could cure it." Whereupon Telephus went to the tent of the hero, and was cured, — some say by an herb called "Achilles," and others by an emplastrum of rust scraped from the spear. Hence it was said that "Achilles' spear could both hurt and heal."

Whose smile and frown, like to Achilles' spear,
Is able with the change to kill or cure.
        SHAKSPEARE, 2 *Henry VI.*, act v. sc. I.

Achilles' Tendon. The sinew running from the heel to the calf of the leg.

Achitophel. The Earl of Shaftesbury is thus satirized in Dryden's "Absalom and Achitophel." Achitophel was the treacherous friend and adviser who deserted David and fled to Absalom, and who afterward hanged himself. 2 Sam. xvii.

Achor. The god of flies. He was adored by the Cyrenians, in the belief that they thereby secured immunity from annoyance by those insects.

Achtequedjams. In Hindu mythology the eight colossal elephants who sustain the earth on their heads.

Acis. In classical mythology a Sicilian shepherd, beloved of Galatea, but crushed under a rock by Polyphemus, the Cyclops, in a fit of jealousy. Galatea, when his life-blood gushed forth from under the stone, changed it into a river.

Ackland von Boyle. The stage-name of Mr. A. Boyle.

Acknowledge the Corn. An expression which means "to confess or acknowledge a charge or imputation." The following is the origin of the phrase : —

Some years ago a raw customer from the upper country determined to try his fortune at New Orleans. Accordingly he provided himself with two flat-boats, one laden with corn, and the other with potatoes, and down the river he went. The night after his arrival he went up town to a gambling-house. Of course he commenced betting, and, his luck proving unfortunate, he lost. When his money was gone, he bet his "truck;" and the corn and potatoes followed the money. At last, when completely cleaned out, he returned to his boats at the wharf, when the evidences of a new misfortune presented themselves. Through some accident or other, the flat-boat containing the corn was sunk, and a total loss. Consoling himself as well as he could, he went to sleep, dreaming of gamblers, potatoes, and corn. It was scarcely sunrise, however, when he was disturbed by the "child of chance," who had arrived to take possession of the two boats as his winnings. Slowly awakening from his sleep, our hero, rubbing his eyes and looking the man in the face, replied : "Stranger, *I acknowledge the corn,* — take 'em; but the potatoes you *can't* have, by thunder!"

A cœlo usque ad centrum. (Lat.) "From heaven as far as the centre." From the sky as far as to the centre of the earth.

A cœur ouvert. (Fr.) "With heart open." Openly; frankly; with the most perfect candor.

A compte. (Fr.) On account; in part payment.

A contre-cœur. (Fr.) Against the heart; against the grain; against one's will; reluctantly; grudgingly.

Acorn. (Pseud.) James Oakes.

A corps perdu. (Fr.) With might and main; desperately; headlong.

A coup sûr. (Fr.) With certainty; certainly; sure to win.

A couvert. (Fr.) Under cover; protected.

Acrasia (Feebleness). In Spenser's "Faerie Queene," an enchantress who lived in the "Bower of Bliss," situate in "Wandering Island." She transformed her lovers into monstrous shapes, and kept them captive. Sir Guyon crept up softly, threw a net over her, and bound her in chains of adamant; then broke down her bower and burnt it to ashes.

Acrates (Incontinence). Called by Spenser the father of Cymochles and Pyrochles.

Acre Fight. The conflicts of the Scottish border were so named because they were fought in the open field, — Lat. *ager*, a field.

A. C. S. American Colonization Society.

Act. Active; acting.

Actæa. (Pseud.) Mrs. Elizabeth Cary Agassiz.

Actæon. In classical mythology a mighty hunter who, having intruded on Diana while bathing at a fountain, was changed by her into a stag, and in that shape was killed by his own dogs.

Actian Years. Augustus founded athletic games at Actium to commemorate his naval victory over Antony. Hence Actian years were those in which the contests took place, — every fifth year.

Acti labores jucundi. (Lat.) Finished labors are pleasant.

Act of Faith. *See* AUTO DA FÉ.

Act of Uniformity. This Act, which was passed in 1661, for regulating public worship, etc., obliged all the clergy to subscribe the Thirty-nine Articles. Upwards of two thousand conscientious ministers left the Church of England and became dissenters rather than submit.

Acton Bell. (Pseud.) Anne Brontë, sister of Charlotte Brontë (1820–1849).

Actum est de republica. (Lat.) It is all over with the commonwealth.

Actum et tractatum. (Lat.) Done and transacted.

A. D. *Anno Domini.* In the year of the Lord.

Ada Bartling. The stage-name of Mrs. Gustavus Levick.

Ada Boshell. The stage-name of Mrs. J. W. Grath.

Ada Cavendish. The stage-name of Mrs. Frank Marshall.

Ada Clare. (Pseud.) Mrs. Jane McElhinney.

Ada Gilman. The stage-name of Mrs. Leander Richardson.

Ada Gray. The stage-name of Mrs. Charles A. Watkins.

Ada Hall. The stage-name of Mrs. T. S. Dare.

Ada Harland. The stage-name of Mrs. Brander Mathews.

Ada Melville. The stage-name of Mrs. J. H. Hazleton.

Ada Newcomb. The stage-name of Mrs. Paul Hamlin.

Ada Rehan. The stage-name of Ada Crehan.

Ada Stanhope. The stage-name of Mrs. A. Bothner.

Ada Vernon. The stage-name of Mrs. E. A. Taylor.

Ada Wilkes. The stage-name of Mrs. J. F. McLeod, *née* McCoffery.

Ad absurdum. (Lat.) To an absurdity.

Adagio. (Ital.) A very slow degree of movement, demanding much taste and expression. (Mus.)

Adagio assai or **molto.** (Ital.) Very slow and expressive. (Mus.)

Adagio cantabile e sostenuto. (Ital.) Very slow and sustained. (Mus.)

Adam. (Pseud.) Arthur Hugh Clough, an English writer.

Adamastor. The spirit of the Stormy Cape (Good Hope), described by Camoens in the "Lusiad" as a hideous phantom.

Adam Bede. This famous portraiture in George Eliot's novel of the same name represented the author's father, Robert Evans.

Adam Bell. A famous outlaw who roamed the forests of northern England. Such was his skill with the long bow that his name has become a synonym for an expert archer.

Adam Cupid, — *i. e.,* Archer Cupid; so called from Adam Bell, the celebrated archer. See *supra.*

Adam's Ale, or **Adam's Wine.** Water as a beverage; from the supposition that Adam had nothing but water to drink.

Adam's Apple. The name colloquially given to the swelling in the forepart of the male throat, because of the old saying that a piece of the forbidden fruit stuck there and left the mark on all of Adam's descendants.

Adam's Needle. In Gen. iii. 7 we are told that Adam and Eve sewed fig-leaves together and made themselves aprons. If they did this, the bayonet-like leaves of the Yucca would have made admirable needles; whence the nickname of this plant.

Adam's Peak. (Port., *Pico de Adam.*) A fanciful name given by the Portuguese to a mountain in Ceylon. The Arabs say that Adam stood thereon on one foot bewailing his expulsion from Paradise, till Jehovah forgave him.

Adam's Profession. Gardening, agriculture. Adam was appointed by God to dress the Garden of Eden and to keep it; and after the fall he was sent out of the garden "to till the ground."

There is no ancient gentleman, but gardeners, ditchers, and grave-makers; they hold up Adam's profession. — *Hamlet,* v. 1.

Adams and Clay Republicans. In 1825 the Federalist party was of no influence; the Democratic-Republican was the only real party. In it there were two factions, — the supporters of President John Quincy Adams and his lieutenant, Henry Clay, known as above; and the followers of Andrew Jackson, known as Jackson Republicans, or Jackson Men. The Adams and Clay Republicans ultimately became Whigs.

Ad aperturam libri. (Lat.) "At the opening of the book." As the book opens; without study or preparation.

Ad arbitrium. (Lat.) At pleasure.

Ad astra. (Lat.) "To the stars." To heaven, or an exalted state.

Ad astra per aspera. (Lat.) To the stars through difficulties.

A. D. C. Aide-de-camp.

Ad calendas Græcas. (Lat.) "At the Greek calends," — that is, never; the Greeks having no calends.

Ad captandum vulgus. (Lat.) To catch the rabble : to please the multitude.

Addendum. (Lat.) An addition, or appendix.

Addie. (Pseud.) Adelaide J. Cooley.

Addie Glenmore. (Pseud.) Mrs. Alice McClure Griffin, an American poet.

Adding insult to injury. A fly bit the bare pate of a bald man, who, endeavoring to crush it, gave himself a heavy blow. Then said the fly, jeeringly, " You wanted to revenge the sting of a tiny insect with death : what will you do to yourself, who have added insult to injury ? "

> Quid facies tibi,
> Injuriæ qui addideris contumeliam?
> PHÆDRUS, *The Bald Man and the Fly.*

Addison of the North. Henry Mackenzie (1745–1831), author of " The Man of Feeling" and " The Man of the World."

Addled Parliament. The Parliament which sat from April 5, 1614, to June 7, 1615, was so named because, although it remonstrated with the king because of his levying " benevolences," it passed no enactments.

Adelaide. (Pseud.) Miss Elizabeth Bogart, an American poet.

Adelaide Moore. The stage-name of Mrs. Valentine.

Adelaide Neilson. The stage-name of Mrs. Lee.

Adelaide Randel. The stage-name of Mrs. Atwood.

Adelaide Thornton. The stage-name of Mrs. Paul Nicholson.

Adele Belgarde. The stage-name of Adele Levy.

Adele Bray. The stage-name of Mrs. F. M. Kendrick.

Adele Giuri. The stage-name of Madame Pizzarno.

Adele Measor. The stage-name of Mrs. J. C. Buckstone.

Adelina Patti. The stage-name (and also the maiden name) of Madame Nicolini, formerly the Marchioness de Caux.

Adeline. (Pseud.) Mrs. E. F. A. Sergeant.

Adeline Hynes. The stage-name of Mrs. Henry DeLorme.

Adeline Stanhope. The stage-name of Mrs. Nelson Wheatcroft.

Adelphagia. In classic myth the goddess of Gluttony. She possessed a shrine in Sicily.

Ademar, in Tasso's " Jerusalem Delivered," is intended to portray the Archbishop of Poggio, an ecclesiastical warrior who, with William, Archbishop of Orange, besought Pope Urban on his knees that he might be sent on the Crusade. He took four hundred armed men from Poggio, who sneaked off during a drought, and left the Crusade. Ademar was not alive at the time, having been slain at the attack on Antioch by Clorinda; but in the final attack on Jerusalem his spirit came with three squadrons of angels to aid the besiegers.

A Deo et rege. (Lat.) From God and the king.

Adeste Fideles was composed by John Reading, who also wrote " Dulce Domum," the famous song of Winchester College. It is miscalled the " Portuguese Hymn " from being heard at the Portuguese Chapel by the Duke of Leeds, who supposed it to be a part of the Portuguese service.

Ad eundem. (Lat.) To the same (rank or class).

A deux. (Fr.) } For two voices or
A duo. (Ital.) } instruments. (Mus.)

A deux mains. (Fr.) With both hands ; two-handed.

Ad finem. (Lat.) At or toward the end.

Ad gustum. (Lat.) To one's taste.

Ad hominem. (Lat.) " To the man; " that is, to the interests or passions of the man.

Adhuc sub judice lis est. (Lat.) The matter in question is still undecided.

Adiaphorists, *i. e.,* " indifferentists." A name given to those of the adherents of Melanchthon who held that certain of the tenets of Luther were matters of no moment to salvation.

Adieu jusqu'au revoir. (Fr.) Good-by till we meet again.

Adieu pour toujours. (Fr.) Farewell forever.

Adina. (Pseud.) Rev. Joseph H. Ingraham, author of " The Prince of the House of David."

Ad infinitum. (Lat.) To infinity ; without end.

Ad inquirendum. (Lat.) For inquiry.

Ad interim. (Lat.) In the meanwhile.

Ad internecionem. (Lat.) " To destruction ; " to extermination.

Adirondack. (Pseud.) L. E. Chittenden, an American *littérateur.*

Adirondack Murray. W. H. H. Murray, American author and clergyman, born in Guilford, Conn., 1840, author of " Camp Life in the Adirondacks," " Adirondack Tales," etc.

A discrétion. (Fr.) At discretion; without restriction.

Adj. Adjective.

Adjt. Adjutant.

Adjt.-Gen. Adjutant-General.

Ad lib. *Ad libitum.* (Lat.) At one's pleasure or taste; at will or discretion, implying, as in music, that the time is at the pleasure of the performer, or that he is at liberty to introduce whatever embellishments his taste directs. Another musical meaning of this term is where one or more accompanying instruments may be introduced at pleasure.

Ad litem. (Lat.) For the action (at law).

Ad literam. (Lat.) "To the letter." Letter for letter.

Ad longum. (Lat.) At length.

Adm. Admiral; admiralty.

Adm. Co. Admiralty Court.

Ad medium filum. (Lat.) To the middle line.

Admetus. In classical mythology a beauteous youth, beloved of Venus and Proserpine, who being killed by a wild boar while hunting, was changed into an anemone by Venus.

Administration Resorts. A name given to Frenchman's Bay and Bar Harbor, Me., and the vicinity, from the fact that several members of President Cleveland's cabinet passed the summer there in the years 1885–1888.

Admirable Crichton. James Crichton (1551–1573), a Scottish scholar who took the degree of M. A. at the early age of fourteen.

Admirable Doctor. Roger Bacon (1214–1292) was so named.

Admiral of the Red. A slang sobriquet for a tippler, whose nose or face is often of a fiery tint.

Admire. Americans retain the old English use of this word in the sense of "wonder at." Shakspeare speaks of "most admired disorder," which sounds like nonsense to modern English ears, but which an American would understand to mean "in a wonderful or extraordinary state of disorder." They also use the word in the sense of "to desire very much." Thus, in New England it is not uncommon to hear such phrases as "I should *admire* to go to Paris," etc. It is still used in some parts of England in the sense of "to wonder at." Not long ago an old woman in Oxfordshire told a clergyman that "if he saw her husband he would quite *admire* him, he looked so ill."

Ad modum. (Lat.) After the manner of.

Admonitionists. In 1571 a number of Puritans sent a written "admonition" to Parliament, in which they denounced everything in the doctrine and usage of the Church of England which did not chime with the Geneva tenets.

Admr. Administrator.

Admx. Administratrix.

Ad nauseam. (Lat.) "To disgust." To an extent to make one sick.

Adonaïs. A poetical name applied by Shelley to Keats in the famous line:

Oh, weep for Adonaïs! he is dead.

Adonists. Hebrews who believe it a sin to speak the name of Jehovah. Instead, they say "Adonai," from the Hebrew *adon*, lord.

Adoptian Controversy, The. An echo of the Arian dispute, originating in Spain near the close of the eighth century,— the land in which the doctrines of Arius longest survived. Elipandus, the archbishop of Toledo, advanced the opinion that "Christ, in respect of his divine nature, was doubtless by nature and generation the Son of God;" but that as to his human nature he must be considered as only declared and adopted through the divine grace, as with all other holy men. *See* ARIAN CONTROVERSY.

Ad quod damnum. (Lat.) To what injury.

Adrammelech. The deity of the people of Sepharvaim,— supposed to personify the sun. To him living infants were burned in sacrifice.

Adrastus. In classical mythology a king of Argos and the founder of the Nemæan Games.

Ad referendum. (Lat.) For further consideration,— much the same meaning as the Scotch law term, *avizandum*.

Ad rem. (Lat.) To the point or purpose.

Adrian. (Pseud.) James L. Cole (1799–1823), an American poet.

Adrienne. (Pseud.) Miss Susan C. Hooper, a contributor to the "Magnolia Weekly," of Richmond, Va., in wartimes.

Ad summam. (Lat.) On the whole; to sum up the matter; in conclusion.

Ad summum. (Lat.) To the highest amount or point.

Adullamites. An attempt, in the year 1866, by the Government of Earl Russell and Mr. Gladstone to carry a measure which would have brought about a sweeping reduction of the elective franchise, gave occasion to a large number of the more moderate Liberals to secede from the Whig leaders and vote with the Conservatives. The designation of "Adullamites" was fastened on the new party in consequence of Mr. Bright having in the course of debate likened them to the political outlaws who took refuge with David in the cave of Adullam (1 Samuel xxii. 1, 2), — a comparison taken up by Lord Elcho, who humorously replied that the band congregated in the cave was hourly increasing, and would succeed in delivering the House from the tyranny of Saul (Mr. Gladstone) and his armor-bearer (Mr. Bright).

Ad unguem. (Lat.) "To the nail." With perfect accuracy; nicely. A phrase borrowed from sculptors, who, when modelling, give the finishing touch with the nail.

Ad unum omnes. (Lat.) All to a man.

Ad utrumque paratus. (Lat.) Prepared for either alternative.

Ad v. *Ad valorem* (Lat.) See *infra.*

Adv. Adverb.

Ad valorem. (Lat.) "According to the value." Thus, an *ad valorem* duty of twenty per cent. means a duty of twenty per cent. upon the value of the goods.

Advent, or Time of Advent. (Lat. "the approach," or "coming.") A term applied by the Christian Church to certain weeks before Christmas. In the Greek Church the time of Advent comprises forty days; but in the Romish Church and those Protestant Churches in which Advent is observed, only four weeks. The origin of this festival as a Church ordinance is clear. The first notice of Advent as an appointment of the Church is found in the Synod of Lerida (A. D. 524), at which marriages were interdicted from the beginning of Advent until Christmas. The four Sundays of Advent as observed in the Romish Church, the Church of England and its offshoots, and in the Protestant Episcopal Church in the United States, were probably introduced into the calendar by Gregory the Great.

Adversary, The. Another name for Satan. See 1 Pet. v. 8.

Adversity Hume. A nickname bestowed on Joseph Hume (1777–1855) in the time of "Prosperity Robinson," and as a foil to him, because of Hume's gloomy predictions of trouble and disaster in store for the English nation. *See* PROSPERITY ROBINSON.

Ad vitam aut culpam. (Lat.) "For life or fault." For life or till fault. Said of the tenure of an office only terminable by death or delinquency.

Ad vivum. (Lat.) To the life.

Advt. Advertisement.

Æacus. In classical mythology the son of Jupiter and Ægina, famed for his mercy and probity, and who after death was appointed one of the three judges in Hades.

Ægeon. In classical mythology a monster having a hundred arms and fifty legs, who, together with his brothers Cottus and Gyges, vanquished the Titans by hurling upon them three hundred rocks at once.

Aeger. In Scandinavian mythology the god of the ocean. Rana is his wife; they had nine daughters, clad in white robes or veils, who represented the white-capped billows.

Ægeus. In classical mythology a king of Athens, after whom the Ægean Sea was named.

Ægina. In classical mythology a daughter of the river-god Asopus, and a favorite of Jupiter.

Æginetan Sculptures. Sculptures excavated by a company of Germans, Danes, and English (1811), in the little island of Ægina. They were purchased by Ludwig, Crown Prince of Bavaria, and now ornament the Glyptothek at Munich.

Ægis. (1) The wonderful shield worn by Jupiter. (2) The short cloak or mantle worn by Minerva, covered with scales and fringed with serpents.

Ægrescit medendo. (Lat.) "He becomes sick by the doctoring." The remedy is worse than the disease.

A. E. I. O. U. The initials of a motto devised by Frederick, Emperor of Germany, — *Austriæ est imperatura orbi universo*, or, in English, "Austria's empire is over all universal." It was satirically paraphrased so as to read:

"Austria's empire is obviously up-set;" and Frederick the Third in the fifteenth century made another motto reading: *Austria erit in orbe ultima,* — "Austria will one day be lowest in the scale of empires."

Ælia Lælia Crispis. The subject of a famous inscription in Bologna, dating from mediæval days, which has long puzzled the learned. It runs thus: "Ælia Lælia Crispis, neither man, nor woman, nor hermaphrodite; neither girl, nor boy, nor old woman; neither harlot nor virgin, but all of these; destroyed neither by hunger, nor sword, nor prison, but by all of them; lies neither in heaven, nor in the water, nor in the ground, but everywhere; Lucius Aga-tho Priscus, neither her husband, nor her lover, nor her kinsman; neither sad, glad, nor weeping, but all of these at once; knows and knows not what he has built, which is neither a funeral pile, nor a pyramid, nor a tomb, that is, a tomb without a corpse, a corpse without a tomb, for corpse and tomb are one and the same." Some have doubted whether the riddle has any meaning; but many very ingenious explanations have been put forth. Some hold that it signifies "rain-water," others the "reasoning faculty," others "the philosopher's stone," others "love," others "a shadow," others "hemp," others "an embryo." Professor Schwartz thinks it means "the Christian Church," and quotes in support of his opinion Gal. iii. 28. Yet other writers have denied its antiquity, and regard it as emanating from the fancy of some modern author; but this last theory is not well established.

Æmilia Julia. (Pseud.) Miss Emily Clarke.

Æmonia. An ancient name for Thessaly, noted for its magic.

Æmonian Art. Magic; the "black art." So named from Æmonia, as Thessaly was anciently called, noted for its sorcerers.

Æmonian, The. Another name for Jason (*q. v.*), who received this title because his father was king of Thessaly. See *supra.*

Æneas. In classical mythology a Trojan prince, son of Anchises and Venus, renowned for his loving care of his father. He is the hero of the "Æneid."

Æquam servare mentem. (Lat.) To preserve an equable mind.

Æquo animo. (Lat.) With an equable mind.

Ære perennius. (Lat.) More enduring than brass.

Ærians. Followers of Ærius, a presbyter of the fourth century, who maintained that bishops and presbyters were alike in order and office; that Lenten and other fasts should not be observed; and that prayer should not be made on behalf of the dead.

Æschylus of France. Prosper Jolyot de Crébillon, 1674–1762.

Æsculapius. In classical mythology the son of Apollo, and the deity who presided over the art of healing.

Æsop. (Pseud.) Mrs. Lillie Devereux Blake used this pen-name in the "New York Evening Telegram."

Æsop of England. John Gay (fl. 1688–1732).

Æsop of France. Jean de la Fontaine (fl. 1621–1695).

Æsop of Germany. Gotthold Ephraim Lessing (fl. 1729–1781).

Æsop of India. Bidpai, or Pilpai, who fl. about three centuries B. C.

Æt. Ætatis. Of age; aged.

Ætatis suæ. (Lat.) Of his age, or Of her age.

Æthiopem lavare. (Lat.) "To wash an African." To wash a negro white, — labor in vain.

Ætians. Followers of Ætius, an Arian heretic who flourished about 351.

A. F. or **A. Fir.** Firkin of ale.

A. F. B. S. American and Foreign Bible Society.

Affaire d'amour. (Fr.) A love affair.

Affaire d'honneur. (Fr.) "An affair of honor;" a duel.

Affaire du cœur. (Fr.) An affair of the heart.

Affetuosamente. (Ital.) With tenderness and pathos. (Mus.)

Affetuoso. (Ital.) With tenderness and pathos. (Mus.)

Afflatus. (Lat.) Inspiration.

A fin. (Fr.) To the end.

A fortiori. (Lat.) "With stronger or greater reason." Arguments drawn from consequences or facts are so called.

Afr. African.

Afric. A diminutive appellation of Africa.

> So geographers in Afric maps
> With savage pictures fill their gaps,
> And o'er unhabitable downs
> Place elephants for want of towns.
> SWIFT, *Poetry, a Rhapsody.*

Africa, Head of. *See* HEAD OF AFRICA.

After-cast. A throw of dice after the game is ended; anything done too late.

> Ever he playeth an after-cast
> Of all that he shall say or do. — GOWER.

After-clap. An after-clap is a catastrophe or threat after an affair is supposed to be over. It is very common in thunderstorms to hear a "clap" after the rain subsides and the clouds break.

> What plaguy mischief and mishaps
> Do dog him still with after-claps.
> *Hudibras,* pt. i. 3.

After us the Deluge. This was a saying of Madame de Pompadour. It is generally attributed to Metternich.

Aft-meal. An extra meal; a meal taken after and in addition to the ordinary meals.

A. G. Adjutant-General.

Ag. *Argentum* (silver).

Agag. Under this name Sir Edmondbury Godfrey, the justice who received the famous deposition of Titus Oates, is satirized in "Absalom and Achitophel," Dryden's great satire. See I Sam. xv. Godfrey was murdered and his body cast into a ditch near Primrose Hill, London.

Agamemnon. In classical mythology a brother of Menelaus, king of Mycenæ, and commander of the Grecians in the Trojan war.

Aganippe. In classical mythology a fountain at the foot of Mount Helicon, in Bœotia, consecrated to Apollo and the Muses, and believed to possess the power of inspiring those who drank of its waters.

Agar-Town. *See* ENGLISH CONNEMARA.

Agate. (Pseud.) Whitelaw Reid, American correspondent and editor "New York Tribune" (b. 1837).

Agatha Singleton. The stage-name of Mrs. Graham Earle.

Age. *See* GOLDEN AGE; SILVER AGE; IRON AGE, etc.

Agelasta (Joyless). The stone on which Ceres rested when worn out by fatigue in searching for her daughter.

Agenda. (Lat.) Things to be done.

Age quod agis. (Lat.) "Do what you are doing." Finish what you have in hand; attend to what you are about.

Agitato con agitazione. (Ital.) With agitation; anxiously. [Mus.]

Agla. A cabalistic title for the Deity, composed of the initials of the Hebrew words Attâh, Gibbor, Leholâm, Adonâi, and signifying, "Thou art strong forever, O Lord!"

Agläus. (Pseud.) Henry Timrod, a Southern poet, contributor to "Southern Literary Messenger" (fl. 1829–1867).

Agl. Dept. Department of Agriculture.

Agnes. The heroine of "David Copperfield," by Charles Dickens. A sort of female Verdant Green, who is so unsophisticated that she does not even know what love means. Also the name of a character in Molière's "L'École des Femmes."

Agnes Booth. The stage-name of Mrs. John Shöffel.

Agnes Ethel. The stage-name of Mrs. Tracy.

Agnes Herndon. The stage-name of Mrs. Joseph A. Jessel.

Agnes Hewitt. The stage-name of Mrs. Lytton Sothern.

Agnes Leonard. The stage-name of Mrs. F. C. Bangs.

Agnes Robertson. The stage-name of the first wife of Dion Boucicault.

Agnes Wallace. The stage-name of Mrs. Samuel B. Villa.

Agnoitæ (from the Greek ἄγνοια, ignorance). (1) A sect founded by Theophronius of Cappadocia about 370, who doubted God's omniscience. (2) Followers of Themistius of Alexandria, about 530, who held peculiar tenets respecting Christ's body, and doubted his divinity.

Agnostic. This is derived from a Greek word γνωστός with a privative, and means "not made known." Originally the sect of the agnostics arose among the Christians of the third and fourth centuries. Its belief was that God does not know all things, and cannot be known. Nowadays an agnostic does not call himself a Christian; he pretends to no knowledge of God, and claims that He cannot be known, and that nothing can be known, save by experience. He says his mind is receptive, open to conviction; but his passiveness is always defensive, and often offensive.

A gorge déployée. (Fr.) At the top of one's voice ; to an immoderate degree.

Agr. Agriculture.

A grands frais. (Fr.) At great expense ; very expensively.

Agricola. (Pseud.) (1) Rev. Percival Stockdale, who in 1779 wrote several communications in the " Public Advertiser " over the above signature. (2) William Elliott, American author. (3) James Anderson, author of numerous essays in the " Bee." (4) Philip Norborne Nicholas (1773–1849) in the " Richmond Enquirer." (5) John Young, a Canadian agricultural writer (1773–1837) in the " Halifax Recorder," 1818.

A. G. S. S. American Geographical and Statistical Society.

Agt. Agent.

Aguecheek. (Pseud.) Charles Bullard Fairbanks,who contributed sketches of travel to the " Saturday Evening Gazette," of Boston, *circa* 1859.

A. H. *Anno Hegiræ*, in the year of the Hegira.

Ahasuerus. The patronymic of several monarchs of Persia, similar to the Pharaoh of the Egyptian kings, and equivalent in meaning to the French *Cœur de Lion.*

Ahmed, Prince. Noted for the tent given him by the fairy Paribanou, which would cover a whole army, but might be carried in one's pocket ; and for the apple of Samarcand, which would cure all diseases. See *infra.*

Ahmed's Apple. A cure for every disorder. This apple the prince purchased at Samarcand.

A. H. M. S. American Home Missionary Society.

Aholibamah. A granddaughter of Cain, in Lord Byron's drama of " Heaven and Earth," loved by the seraph Samiasa. She is a proud, ambitious, queen-like beauty, a female type of Cain. When the Flood comes, her angel-lover carries her under his wings to some other planet.

Ahriman, in the Magian system the spirit of darkness or evil. *See* ORMUZD.

Aide-de-camp. (Fr.) Assistant to a general.

Aidenn. An Anglicized form of the Arabic word for Eden, often used as an equivalent for the celestial paradise.

Tell this soul with sorrow laden, if, within the distant Aidenn,
It shall clasp a sainted maiden whom the angels name Lenore. POE, *The Raven.*

Aide-toi et le ciel t'aidera. (Fr.) Help thyself, and Heaven will help thee.

Aiken Dunn. (Pseud.) Thomas C. Latto in the " Brooklyn Times."

Ain. (Pseud.) William Stevens. *Ain* is the Hebrew word for " nobody."

Air Écossais. (Fr.) A Scotch air. (Mus.)

Air Martyrs. *See* PILLAR SAINTS.

Aitiaiche. (Pseud.) Annie T. Howells, an American writer.

Ajax. In classical mythology a son of Telamon, king of Salamis, and next to Achilles the bravest, the most renowned, and the most beautiful of all the Greeks who fought at Troy. Another Ajax, son of Oïleus, is called the Lesser Ajax.

Akuan. In Persian mythology the giant slain by Rustan.

Al. Aluminium.

Al, All', Alla. (Ital.) To the, or, in the style of. (Mus.)

Ala. Alabama.

Alabama. The name is derived from a Creek word meaning " Here we rest."

A l'abandon. (Fr.) Unprotected or uncared for.

A la belle étoile. (Fr.) Under the stars ; in the open air.

A la bonne heure. (Fr.) That 's right ; excellent ; very well ; as you please.

A l'abri. (Fr.) Under shelter ; under cover.

A la campagne. (Fr.) In the country.

A la Chinoise. (Fr.) After the Chinese fashion.

Aladdin's Lamp. The source of wealth and good fortune. After Aladdin came to his wealth and was married, he suffered his lamp to hang up and get rusty.

Aladdin's Window. The phrase " To finish Aladdin's window " means to attempt to complete something begun by a great genius, but left imperfect. The London " Times" applied the illustration to Earl Russell's attempt to patch up the vacancy made in the ministry by the death of Lord Palmerston. The genius of the lamp built a palace with twenty-four windows, all but one being set in frames of precious stones; the last was left for the sultan to finish; but after exhausting his treasures, he was obliged to abandon the task as hopeless.

A la dérobée. (Fr.) By stealth.

Aladine. The sagacious but cruel old king of Jerusalem in Tasso's epic, "Jerusalem Delivered." This is a fictitious character, inasmuch as the Holy Land was at the time under the dominion of the caliph of Egypt. Aladine is slain by Raymond.

A la Française. (Fr.) After the French fashion.

Alako. Son of Baro-Devel, the supreme god of the gypsies.

A la lettre. (Fr.) Word for word; literally; to a tittle.

A l'Américaine. (Fr.) After the American fashion.

A la mode. (Fr.) According to the custom; in fashion.

Alamo Massacre. During the Texan war of independence 140 Texans were besieged in a fort called the Alamo, near San Antonio, by two thousand Mexicans. Santa Anna finally stormed the place, and six Texans who survived the conflict were subsequently murdered after surrendering under a promise of protection. "Remember the Alamo!" was ever after a thrilling Texan war-cry.

Alan Fairford. (Pseud.) John Kent, editor of the "Canadian Literary Magazine" about 1834 *et seq*.

A l'Anglaise. (Fr.) After the English fashion.

A l'antique. (Fr.) According to the old fashion or way.

A la Parisienne. (Fr.) After the Parisian fashion.

A la portée de tout le monde. (Fr.) Within reach of every one.

Alaric Cottin. A satiric name conferred by Voltaire on Frederick the Great of Prussia, who was famed alike for his military conquests and for his dabbling in literature. The name has reference to Alaric the Visigoth, whose valiant deeds Frederick was supposed to have emulated, and to the Abbé Cottin, an obscure scribbler of the seventeenth century. *See* TRISSOTIN.

Alastor. (Greek, "not to forget.") The evil genius of a house. Cicero says: "He meditated killing himself

that he might become the Alastor of Augustus, whom he hated." Shelley has a poem entitled "Alastor; or, the Spirit of Solitude."

Alb. Albany.

Alba. (Pseud.) Alexina B. White, an American writer.

Albani, Madame. The professional name of Mrs. Ernest Gye, whose maiden name was Marie Emma Lajeunesse. The name "Albani" is derived from Albany, N. Y., the city where she made her *début* as a singer.

Albanian Gates. A defile in the Caucasus, formerly closed on the north by a massive iron gate near the city of Derbend.

Albano. (Pseud.) Count Carl August Adlersparre, German poet and novelist.

Albany, Albin, or **Albainn.** An appellation often used by the mediæval chroniclers and romancers for the Highlands of Scotland. It may indeed be safely assumed that Albion, or Albany, was the original name of Britain among its Celtic inhabitants, — on account, it is supposed, of the gleaming whiteness of the south-coast cliffs, from Latin *albus,* white.

Albany Beef. The flesh of the Hudson River sturgeon is so nicknamed. It is a staple commodity of food among the population of the river towns. *See* BLOCK ISLAND TURKEY.

Albany Congress. A body which met at Albany in 1754 with the object of drawing up a plan of union for the Thirteen Colonies.

Albany Controversy. In 1698 Hendrick Van Rensselaer bought from the Schaghticoke Indians a tract of six square miles on the Hoosac River, and secured a patent therefor. This purchase interfered greatly with the growth of the city of Albany, N. Y., and Van Rensselaer refusing to sell, the dispute became a state affair. In 1699 the controversy was amicably settled, and he passed his patent over to the city.

Albany Regency. A term given to the cliques, both Whig and Democratic, which, centred at Albany, ruled the politics of New York for many years, — the term "Albany Regency" applying to each, but more particularly to the Democratic factions from 1820–1854.

Albert. (Pseud.) Rev. John Armstrong, a Scottish poet (1771–1797).

Albert J. Booth. (Pseud.) Cecil Burleigh, contributor to various periodicals.

Albert Welser. The stage-name of William P. Graw.

Albertazzo. The hero of "Orlando Furioso," who married Alda, daughter of Otho, duke of Saxony. His sons were Hugh or Ugo and Fulke or Fulco. From this family springs the royal family of England.

Albiazar, in Tasso's epic, "Jerusalem Delivered," was one of the leaders of the Arab host which joined the Egyptian armament against the Crusaders.

" A chief in rapine, not in knighthood bred."

Albion. *See* ALBANY, *supra.*

Albion. The signature of George James Stephenson, M. A. (d. 1888), an English religious author and correspondent of the New York "Christian Advocate." One of his most useful works is a volume of nearly seven hundred pages, entitled "The Methodist Hymn-Book, Illustrated with Biography, History, Incident, and Anecdote." He also wrote "Memorials of the Wesley Family," "The Life and Work of Pastor C. H. Spurgeon to his Forty-third Birthday," "Hymns and Hymn-Writers of every Age and Nation," "The Methodist Hymn-Book and its Associations," "The History of City Road Chapel, London," "The Origin of Alphabetical Characters," and many others.

Albion, New. *See* NEW ALBION.

Alcestis, in classic mythology a daughter of Pelias and wife to Admetus, to save whose life she died. She was brought back to the upper world by Hercules.

Alcibiades. (Pseud.) (1) James Anderson, editor of the "Bee" (1790), and author of numerous essays therein over the above signature. (2) Alfred Tennyson in sundry communications to "Punch," *circa* 1846.

Alcibiades' Tables represented a god or goddess outwardly, and a Silenus, or deformed piper, within. Erasmus has a curious dissertation on these tables, emblematic of falsehood and dissimulation.

Whoso wants virtue is compared to these
False tables wrought by Alcibiades;
Which noted well of all were found t 've bin
Most fair without, but most deformed within.
WM. BROWNE, *Britannia's Pastorals.*

Alcides. Another name for Hercules (*q. v.*).

Alcinous. In classic mythology a king of Drepane, or of Phæacia, who succored the Argonauts on their return from Colchis, and Ulysses when he was wrecked.

Alciphron. (Pseud.) Rosina Doyle [Wheeler], Lady Lytton.

Alcofribas Nasier. The anagrammatic pseudonym of François Rabelais, the French satirist (1495–1553).

Alcoran. Another name for the Koran, the sacred scriptures of the Mohammedans, written by Mohammed.

Alcyone. In classic mythology a daughter of Æolus. When she heard of the death of her husband, Ceryx, by shipwreck, she cast herself into the sea, and was changed by the gods into a kingfisher.

Ald. Alderman.

Alderman. A cant term in England for a half-crown. An alderman, as a magistrate, may be termed half a king (or crown). A turkey is called an alderman, both from its presence in aldermanic feasts and also because of its red and purple colors, which make it a sort of poultry alderman. An "alderman in chains," by a similar effort of wit, is a turkey hung with sausages.

Alderman Rooney. (Pseud.) D. O. C. Townley, an American *littérateur.*

Aldiboronte Phoscophornio. A nickname given by Sir Walter Scott to his schoolmate, printer, partner, and confidential friend, James Ballantyne, because of his habitually grave and somewhat pompous manner.

Aldingar, Sir. The steward to Queen Eleanor, wife of Henry II. He impeached her fidelity, and submitted to a combat to substantiate his charge; but an angel in the shape of a child established the queen's innocence.

Alecto. In classic myth one of the Furies (*q. v.*). Her head was entwined with snakes.

Ale-draper. A tapster. Ale-drapery is the selling of ale, etc.

No other occupation have I but to be an aledraper.—H. CHETTLE.

Aleka. Wife of Pangeo. Idols of the Oroungou tribes in Africa, the special protectors of kings and governments.

Alere flammam. (Lat.) "To feed the flame." To nourish the love of learning.

Ale-Silver. A yearly tribute paid to the corporation of London as a license for selling ale.

Ale-Stake. The pole set up before ale-houses by way of sign. A bush was very often fixed to its top.

> A garland had he set upon his head
> As great as it werin for an ale-stake.
> CHAUCER.

Alethes. (Pseud.) Thomas H. Baird in the Pittsburg " Commercial Journal " about 1851.

Ale-Wife. The landlady of an ale-house or ale-stand.

Alex. Alexander.

Alexander of Persia. Sandjar, one of the Seljuke sultans (fl. 1117–1158), renowned for his conquests.

Alexander of the North. The sobriquet of Charles XII. of Sweden (fl. 1682–1718), and which was conferred on account of his prowess in military affairs.

Alexander the Coppersmith. A nickname applied to Hamilton by those who were dissatisfied with the copper cents coined in 1793 at his suggestion while Secretary of the Treasury.

Alexander the Corrector. A title self-conferred on Alexander Cruden (fl. 1701–1770), author of the famous " Concordance," and who always carried with him a moistened sponge with which he erased every scurrilous scrawl which met his gaze. He petitioned Parliament to appoint him " Corrector of the People."

Alexandrian School. An academy of literature founded by Ptolemy, son of Lagos, and especially famous for its grammarians and mathematicians. Of its grammarians the most noted are Aristarch, Harpocration, and Eratosthenes; and of its mathematicians, Ptolemy and Euclid.

Alexandrine Age. The epoch 323–640 A. D., during which Alexandria in Egypt was the metropolis of learning.

A l'extremité. (Fr.) At the end; at the point of death; at the last gasp; without resources.

Alf. Alfred.

Alfa Pease. The stage-name of Mrs. Charles E. Crouse.

Alfader (Father of all). In Scandinavian mythology the parent of the Asen, and the oldest and most revered of the Norse deities.

Alfheim (home of the genii). In Norse mythology a celestial city inhabited by the elves and fairies.

Alfred. (Pseud.) (1) Dr. Girardin, author of some of the essays in Wirt's " Old Bachelor," 1812. (2) Grenville A. Sackett, a well-known American poet in the periodical press of New York and vicinity. (3) Samuel Adams wrote a communication to the " Boston Gazette," Oct. 2, 1769, over this signature.

Alfred Ashton. (Pseud.) William Henry Forman.

Alfred Ayres. (Pseud.) Dr. Thomas Embly Osmun, author of " The Orthoëpist," New York, 1880.

Alfred Burton. (Pseud.) John Mitford, R.N.

Alfred Coudreux. (Pseud.) Honoré de Balzac in his sketches in " La Caricature."

Alfred Crowquill. (Pseud.) Alfred Henry Forrester, an English caricaturist, 1806–1872.

Alfred Dubois. (Pseud.) James Stuart Bowes, a London playwright.

Alfred's Scholars. A number of learned men are grouped under this name, who flourished in the reign of Alfred the Great and were patronized by him. The chief were Grimbald, a Frenchman; Asser, a Welshman; Plegmund, Ethelstan, and Werwulf, three Mercian priests; and Werfrith, bishop of Worcester.

Al fresco. (Ital.) In the open air.

Algernon Sidney. (Pseud.) Gideon Granger, an American lawyer and writer, 1767–1822.

Alguazil. (Span.) A constable.

Alias. (Lat.) Otherwise.

Ali Baba. (Pseud.) Alberigh Mackaye, an Anglo-Indian author, 1849–1881.

Alibi. (Lat.) Elsewhere, not present.

Alice Atherton. The stage-name of Mrs. Willie Edouin, formerly Mary Alice Hogan.

Alice Dunning. The stage-name of Mrs. William Lingard.

Alice Eliot. (Pseud.) Sarah Orne Jewett, in " Country Byways," 1881.

Alice Harrison. The stage-name of Alice Metz.

Alice Irving Abbott. (Pseud.) Miss H. H. Burdick.

Alice King. (Pseud.) Mrs. Alice King Hamilton, an American miscellaneous writer.

Alice Marriott. The stage-name of Mrs. R. Edgar.

Alice May. The stage-name of Mrs. Lewis Raymond.

Alice Oates. The stage-name of Mrs. Tracy Titus.

Alice Placide. The stage-name of Mrs. Charles E. Emmett.

Alice Sherwood. The stage-name of Mrs. Charles A. Haslam.

Alice Thorne. The stage-name of Mrs. James Craythorne.

Alice Vane. The stage-name of Mrs. John Templeton.

Alicon. In Mohammedan mythology the seventh or highest heaven.

Alida. (Pseud.) Mrs. Catherine Stratton Ladd, in her contributions to various periodicals.

Alieni temporis flores. (Lat.) Flowers of another or past time.

Alifanfaron. Don Quixote attacked a flock of sheep, which he declared to be the army of the giant Alifanfaron. Ajax in a fit of madness fell on a flock of sheep, which he mistook for Grecians.

Alilat. The name by which the Arabs adore Nature, which they represent by a crescent moon.

A l'improviste. (Fr.) Suddenly; unawares.

Alio sub sole. (Lat.) Under another sun; in another climate.

Aliquid inane. (Lat.) An indescribable kind of silliness; silly trifling.

Alis volat propriis. (Lat.) She flies with her own wings. The motto of the State of Oregon.

A l'Italienne. (Fr.) In the Italian mode.

Aliud et idem. (Lat.) One and the same thing; the same thing under different aspects.

Aliunde. (Lat.) From some other quarter or person.

Al Kader. A particular night in the month Ramadan, when, the Arabs say, angels descend to earth, and Gabriel reveals to man the decrees of God.

Alkali Desert. Wide stretches of land in Colorado and Nevada, the surface of the soil being covered with a deposit of alkali.

Alla capella. (Ital.) In churchly style. (Mus.)

Allah. The Mohammedan name for the true God.

Alla militaire. In a military style. (Mus.)

Allan Field. The stage-name assumed by Lester Wallack (d. 1888) during his early career in England.

Allan Grant. (Pseud.) William Wilson, for many years a writer for the American press.

Alla Polacca. (Ital.) In the style of a Polish dance. (Mus.)

Alla Russe. (Ital.) In the style of Russian music. (Mus.)

Alla Scozzese. (Ital.) In the Scotch style. (Mus.)

Alla Siciliana. (Ital.) In the style of the Sicilian shepherds' dance. (Mus.)

All' attava. (Ital.) In the octave. An expression often met with in orchestral scores, to indicate that one part is to play an octave above or below another. (Mus.)

Alla zoppa. (Ital.) In a constrained and limping style. (Mus.)

Allegremente. (Ital.) With quickness. (Mus.)

Allegretto. (Ital.) Somewhat cheerful, but not so quick as *allegro*. (Mus.)

Allegretto scherzando. (Ital.) Moderately playful and vivacious. (Mus.)

Allegrezza. (Ital.) Joy. *Con allegrezza* means joyfully, animatedly. (Mus.)

Allegro. (Ital.) Quick, lively. A musical term implying a rapid and vivacious movement, but which is often modified by the addition of other words, as: —

Allegro agitato. Quick; with anxiety and agitation.

Allegro assai. Very quick.

Allegro comodo. With a convenient degree of quickness.

Allegro con brio. Quick, with brilliancy.

Allegro con moto. Quick, with more than the usual degree of movement.

Allegro con spirito. Quick, with spirit.

Allegro furioso. Quick, with fury.

Allegro molto or **di molto.** Very quick.

Allegro vivace. With vivacity.

Allegro vivo. Quick, with unusual briskness.

Allemande. (Fr.) A dance peculiar to Germany and Switzerland.

Allen Grahame. (Pseud). George Arnold, comic poet and humorist.

Allevato nella bambagio. (Ital.) Brought up too tenderly, or as an infant.

Allez-vous en. (Fr.) "Go you away." Away with you.

All-Hallow. A church feast on the first day of November, in honor of all saints; also called All Saints' Day (*q. v.*).

All' improvista. (Ital.) Extemporaneously; without premeditation. (Mus.)

All' Inglese. In the English style. (Mus.)

All is lost save Honor. It was from the imperial camp near Pavia that Francis the First, before leaving for Pizzighettone, wrote to his mother the memorable letter which, thanks to tradition, has become altered to the form of this sublime laconism: "Madame, tout est perdu fors l'honneur." The true expression is, "Madame, pour vous faire savoir comme se porte le reste de mon infortune, de toutes choses ne m'est demeuré que l'honneur et la vie qui est sauvée." — MARTIN, *Histoire de France.*

All' Italiana. In the Italian style. (Mus.)

All Quiet along the Potomac. This phrase became proverbial during the fall of 1861 and the beginning of 1862. The weather at that time seemed favorable to a campaign, and McClellan's army, of about two hundred thousand men, was in excellent condition; and yet no advance was undertaken. McClellan's policy at that period is sometimes referred to as a policy of "masterly inactivity."

All Saints' Day. The day following "Halloween," in old English All-Hallows, All-Hallowmas, or simply Hallowmas, originally a festival of the Roman Catholic Church, introduced because of the impossibility of keeping a separate day for every saint. The festival of All Saints was first regularly instituted by Gregory IV. in 835, and appointed to be celebrated on November 1. It was admitted into England about 870. The choice of the day was doubtless determined by the fact that November 1, or rather the eve or night preceding it, was one of the four great festivals (February 1, May 1, August 1, and November 1) of the heathen nations of the North; for it was the policy of the Church to supplant heathen by Christian observances. " In the South of Germany the old and venerable custom of adorning the graves in the burying-grounds on the first and second day of November with garlands and lamps is still kept up. It is an affecting festival, which the survivors prepare for their deceased relations and friends. On those days the whole population of the town assemble in the churchyard, and gaze with melancholy recollection, or joyful confidence in the future, on the adorned death-feast, and pray, while the priest, using the requisite forms, draws from the holy well the sacred flood with which he is to sprinkle the graves in order to consecrate them. Death, then garlanded with flowers, becomes a friendly teacher; the lamps and tapers are images of the everlasting light; and the passing from the joys of summer and autumn to the quiet Advent time involves a very peculiar preparation. This festival is celebrated nowhere so beautifully as at Munich. On the morning of All Saints' Day the families greet each other over the resting-places of those they loved, arranging, adorning, and praying in faithful hope, or weeping in sad remembrance. There are but few signs of mourning to be seen. Light and life reign everywhere; the loveliest flowers and plants bloom on the graves; cypresses and weeping-willows wave and rustle in the breeze; and if anything reminds us of the chilliness of death or the gloom that we dread, it is the lifeless forms of the hired male and female grave-watchers, who stand near the mounds to tend the lamps and flowers, mechanically repeating their rosary, contemplating sullenly and indifferently the imposing spectacle around them, and longing for the evening, when the reward which has been promised them is to be paid. In the evening these repugnant figures leave the garden, but they take away with them the flowers and lights, and the feast is at an end. The variegated lamps are hung up again in the rooms, and the flowers and plants are taken to the gardeners' hothouses, to the milliner's shop-counter, or to the boudoir of some lovely maiden." All Souls' Day customs on the Continent are not merely confined to visiting and adorning the graves of friends and relatives. In Belgium poor children erect rude altars before their cottage doors, duly decked with figures of the Madonna and candles, and stand patiently there all the evening begging the passers-by to give them money "to buy cakes for the poor souls in purgatory." Cakes and All Souls' Day are also inseparably connected in childish minds throughout the Tyrol, where the little ones are given sweet biscuits in the shapes of horses or hares, called "soul-pieces;" while in Bavaria they receive long cakes, pointed at each end, called *Seelenspitze.*

All Saints' Summer. November 1, Halloween, — equivalent to the American "Indian Summer" (*q. v.*).

All - the - Talents Administration. The cabinet of Lord Grenville, 1806, was so nicknamed because of the real or fancied ability of its members. It contained Lord Henry Petty, Lord Erskine, Charles James Fox, and Sir Charles Grey. Fox's death, Sept. 13, 1806, led to numerous changes.

All we ask is to be let alone. This phrase occurred in the message of Jefferson Davis to the Confederate Congress in March, 1861. He referred to Northern preparations to oppose secession.

Ally Sloper. (Pseud.) Charles H. Ross, an English humorist and author, (b. 1836.)

Alma Calder. (Pseud.) Mrs. A. C. Johnston, author of "Miriam's Heritage" (1878).

Almack's. A suite of assembly-rooms in King Street, London. They were built in 1765 by Almack, a tavern-keeper, and were hence called Almack's Rooms; they were afterward known as Willis's Rooms, from the name of their subsequent proprietor. The name of Almack's is chiefly associated with the balls that were held there under the management of a committee of ladies of high rank, and has become synonymous with aristocratic exclusiveness.

Almain. A mediæval English name for Germany.

I have seen Almain's proud champions prance.
Old Ballad.

It is supposed that it was derived from *Alemanni,* the tribal designation of many ancient confederated peoples settled in the valley of the Main.

Alma Mater. (Lat.) "A gentle or benign mother," — applied by students to the university at which they are or have been educated.

Alma Murray. The stage-name of Mrs. A. W. Pinero.

Alma Stuart Stanley. The stage-name of Mrs. Charles De Garmo.

Almaviva. (Pseud.) (1) Clement Scott, an English dramatic critic. (2) Harry St. Maur, a contributor to the Chicago "News-Letter."

Almighty Dollar. In this phrase, coined by Washington Irving, we have a personification of the supposed object of American worship. It is intended as a satire on the mad race for wealth that has at different times and in divers places characterized the American people.

The almighty dollar, that great object of universal devotion throughout our land, seems to have no genuine devotees in these peculiar villages. — *The Creole Village.*

Almond-tree. Gray hairs. Ecclesiastes xii. thus describes old age : —

"In the day when the keepers of the house [the hands] shall tremble, and the strong men [the legs] shall bow themselves, and the grinders [the teeth] cease because they are few, and those that look out of the windows [the eyes] be darkened, . . . and the almond tree shall flourish [gray hairs on a bald pate], and the grasshopper shall be a burden, and desire shall fail, . . . or ever the silver cord [the spinal marrow] be loosed, or the golden bowl [intellect] be broken, or the pitcher be broken at the fountain [the pulse of the heart stopped]."

Al Moshtari. The Arabian name of the planet Jupiter.

A. L. O. E. "A Lady of England." (Pseud.) Miss Charlotte Tucker, English writer of Sunday-school fiction (b. 1830).

A l'ordinaire. (Fr.) In the ordinary manner.

Alpha and Omega. The names of the first and last letters of the Greek alphabet, A, Ω. These words occur in the Revelation of Saint John as a title of the Christ. They were also used by the early Christians as symbols of faith, and were engraved on tombs, ornaments, coins, etc.

Alpheos. In classic myth a river-god who became enamoured of the nymph Arethusa. She fled from him, and midway in his pursuit he was changed into a river, and she into a fountain.

Alphonse. The name given by the Parisians to those despicable fellows who subsist on the earnings of abandoned women.

Alpin. (Pseud.) William Wilson, for many years a writer for the press.

Al più. (Ital.) At most.

Alp of Literature. The Bible has been so named.

Alsatia. A former name of Whitefriars (*q. v.*), a district of the city of London, where, in the seventeenth century, criminals were permitted to find sanctuary. This immunity was abolished in 1696 or 1697. The locality is described in Scott's "Fortunes of Nigel." Shadwell's comedy, "The Squire of Alsatia," has for its scene this place. As regards the origin of this name, antiquarians hold that the frontier province of France, on the left bank of the Rhine, long a cause of contention, often the seat of war, and familiarly known to many British soldiers, suggested the application of the term "Alsatia" to the precinct of Whitefriars.

Al seg. *Al segno.* A musical sign signifying that the performer must return to a similar sign in the course of the movement, and play from that place to the word *fine.*

Al-Sirat. In the Mohammedan system the bridge over Hades, no wider than the edge of a sword, over which all who essay to enter heaven must pass.

Alt. Altitude.

Alter ego. (Lat.) "Another, or second I." A name conferred on Spanish viceroys when exercising royal power.

Alter idem. (Lat.) "Another the same;" another precisely similar.

Alter ipse amicus. (Lat.) A friend is another self.

Alternativo. (Ital.) Alternating; proceeding alternately from one movement to another. (Mus.)

Alternis vicibus. (Lat.) Alternately; in turn.

Alterum tantum. (Lat.) As much more.

Althæa's Brand. The Fates told Althæa that her son Meleager would live just as long as a log of wood then on the fire remained unconsumed. Althæa contrived to keep the log unconsumed for many years; but when her son killed her two brothers, she threw it angrily into the fire, where it was quickly consumed, and Meleager expired at the same time.

> The fatal brand Althæa burned.
> SHAKSPEARE, 2 *Henry VI.*, act i, sc. 1.

Alton Riot. The disturbance known to American history by this name occurred in Alton, Ill., on the night of Nov. 7, 1837, and grew out of an attempt to destroy the printing-office of the "Observer," an Abolitionist sheet. The editor, Rev. E. P. Lovejoy, was shot and killed, but the leaders of the mob were acquitted.

A. M. *Anno mundi.* In the year of the world.

A. M. *Ante meridiem.* Before noon; morning.

A. M. *Artium Magister.* Master of Arts.

Amadis of Gaul. The hero of a romance in prose, of the same title, originally written in Portuguese in four books, translated into Spanish by Montalvo, who added a fifth. Subsequent romancers added the exploits and adventures of other knights, so as to swell the romance to fourteen books. The French version is much larger still, — one containing twenty-four books, and another running through seven volumes. The original author was Vasco de Lobeira, of Oporto, who died in 1403.

Amadis of Greece. A supplemental part of the romance called "Amadis of Gaul," added by Feliciano de Silva.

A main armée. (Fr.) By force of arms.

Amalfian Code. An eleventh-century compilation of maritime laws collated by the merchants of Amalfi.

Amalgamationists. During the antislavery struggle in the United States the pro-slavery men asserted that the Abolitionists and the Republicans were in favor of miscegenation between the whites and blacks, — a charge utterly baseless.

Amalthæa, Amalthæa's Horn. In classic mythology Amalthæa was the name of the goat on whose milk the infant Jove was fed, and one of whose horns he was said to have broken off. This horn he endowed with the power of becoming filled with whatever its possessor might desire; hence it was called the cornucopia, or horn of plenty. *See* AMMONIAN HORN.

Amanda. The impersonation of love in Thomson's "Spring," the original of which was Miss Young, afterwards married to Admiral Campbell.

Amanda. The pen-name of Miss Amanda E. Dennis. *See* POET OF WICOMISCO.

Amanga. The Indian love-god.

Amantium iræ. (Lat.) The quarrels of lovers.

Amaryllis. A pastoral sweetheart. The name is borrowed from the pastorals of Theocritus and Virgil.

Am. Ass. Adv. Sci., or **Am. Assn. Sci.** American Association for the Advancement of Science.

Amateur Casual. (Pseud.) James Greenwood in the "Pall Mall Gazette," London. He made a name in reportorial literature by passing a night in the "casual ward" of a London workhouse, among tramps and outcasts, and then detailing his experiences in print, signed as above.

A maximis ad minima. (Lat.) From the greatest to the least.

Amazon. A horsewoman; a fighting or masculine woman. The word means "without breasts." According to Grecian fable, there was a nation of women in Africa of a very warlike character. There were no men in the nation; and if a boy was born, it was either killed or sent to his father, who lived in some neighboring state. The girls had their right breasts singed off, that they might the better draw the bow.

Amb. Ambassador.

Ambrose. (Pseud.) Rev. James Ambrose Wight, Bay City, Mich., in his letters to "The Evangelist."

Ambrosia. In classic myth the food of the gods. *See* NECTAR.

Âme de boue. (Fr.) "A soul of mud." A debased creature.

Amelia. A model of conjugal affection in Fielding's novel of the same name. It is said that the character is intended for a portraiture of his own wife.

Amelia Somerville. The stage-name of Mrs. Frederick Runnels.

Amen Corner. Before the Reformation the clergy walked annually in procession to St. Paul's Cathedral on Corpus Christi Day. They mustered at the upper end of Cheapside, and there commenced to chant the *Paternoster*, which they continued through the whole length of the street, thence called Paternoster Row, pronouncing the *Amen* at the spot now called Amen Corner. Then commencing the *Ave Maria*, they turned down Ave Maria Lane. After crossing Ludgate Hill, they chanted the *Credo* in Creed Lane. Old Stow mentions Creed Lane, and adds that Amen Lane "is lately added thereto," from which it may be inferred that the processional chant-

ing ended at that spot. Amen Lane no longer exists.

Amende. (Fr.) Compensation.

Amende honorable. (Fr.) A full apology for insult or injury.

Amendment-Mongers. A name applied to the Anti-Federalists.

A mensa et thoro. (Lat.) "From table and bed." From bed and board, — a judicial separation of husband and wife short of divorce.

Amer. American.

Amer. Acad. American Academy.

American Addison, The. Joseph Dennie (1768–1812).

American Baden-Baden. Sharon Springs, a fashionable pleasure and health resort of New York, about sixty miles west by north of Albany. There are four springs, — chalybeate, magnesia, white sulphur, and blue sulphur. Twenty miles in a southeasterly direction is situated Howe's Cave, after the Mammoth Cave of Kentucky one of the most remarkable caverns known.

American Blackstone. Chancellor James Kent, LL.D., was so named.

American Cato. Samuel Adams was so named.

American Christmas. *See* THANKSGIVING.

American Cicero. *See* CICERO OF AMERICA.

American Fabius. George Washington, whose military policy was similar to that of Fabius, the Roman general, who wearied Hannibal by marches and countermarches, and avoided a general action. *See* FRENCH FABIUS.

American Gibraltar. *See* GIBRALTAR OF AMERICA.

American Girl Abroad. (Pseud.) Miss Trafton, an American *littérateur*.

American Party. More generally known as Know-Nothings, which appeared in 1854. It was based on a widely spread secret society, and advocated twenty-one years' residence as a qualification for citizenship, and native-born citizens as office-holders. It swept the country like a tornado, carrying nearly every State. In 1888 another party arose bearing this name, and nominated General Curtis for the Presidency.

American Prodigy. A sobriquet bestowed on Sauvelle Lemoine, governor of Louisiana, 1699–1701, on account of his mental attainments.

American Rhine. The Hudson River, "unrivalled among American rivers for picturesque and magnificent scenery." Though destitute of the numerous architectural remains of bygone ages that crowd with interesting reminiscences the banks of its Old World namesake, the Hudson is equally enriched by Nature, and is not without its share of legendary lore.

American Sappho. Sarah Wentworth Appleton, American poet (1759–1846), was so named by Robert Treat Paine, Jr.

American System. In the debates which resulted in the tariff law of 1824 Henry Clay called his plan of protective duties and internal improvements the "American System." The term is usually restricted, however, to denote the policy of protection to home industries by means of duties on imports.

American Titian. *See* TITIAN OF AMERICA.

Americans' Paradise. The city of Paris. American travellers congregate there, and it has been jocularly said that the good American hopes to go to Paris when he dies.

Americanus. (Pseud.) Robert Baird, D.D., in his European correspondence in the New York "Commercial Advertiser."

Americus. (Pseud.) Dr. Francis Lieber, German-American historian and political writer (1800–1872).

Amicus. (Pseud.) Charles Wildbore in "The Ladies' Diary."

Amicus curiæ. (Lat.) A friend of the court.

Amicus Curiæ. One of the pen-names attributed to Junius (*q. v.*).

Amicus humani generis. (Lat.) A friend of the human race.

Ami du peuple. (Fr.) Friend of the people.

Amiel. An anagrammatic rendering of the name Eliam, "friend of God," and conferred on Sir Edward Seymour by Dryden in his satire, "Absalom and Achitophel." Amiel, or Ammiel, is called Eliam in 2 Sam. xi. 3.

Aminadab. A Quaker. The Scripture name has a double *m*, but in old comedies, where the character represents a Quaker, the name has generally only one. "Obadiah" is used also to signify a Quaker, and "Rachel" a Quakeress.

Amistad Case, The. "In June, 1839, the schooner 'L' Amistad' sailed from Havana for Principe with a number of slaves that had been kidnapped in Africa. The slaves overpowered the whites, and killed all but two. These white men steered the vessel northward instead of to Africa as directed, and soon the vessel was seized and taken into New London, Conn., by Lieutenant Gedney, of the United States brig 'Washington.' The Spanish minister requested the delivery of the slaves, to be taken to Cuba for trial. President Van Buren was desirous of granting this request as a matter of comity, but the Anti-Slavery Society procured counsel, and the District Court of the United States decided that even by the Spanish laws the slave trade was illegal, and the negroes were free men. The Circuit Court affirmed this decision, and so, in March, 1841, did the Supreme Court, where John Quincy Adams devoted himself to the cause of the negroes without remuneration. The negroes were sent back to Africa in an American vessel." — BROWN AND STRAUSS.

A. M. M. *Amalgama.* Amalgamation.

Ammon. An Ethiopian or Libyan god who has been identified with the Greek Zeus.

Ammonian Horn. The cornucopia. Ammon, king of Libya, gave to his mistress, Amalthæa, mother of Bacchus, a tract of land resembling a ram's horn in shape, and hence called the "Ammonian horn" from the giver, the "Amalthæan horn" from the receiver, and the "Hesperian horn" from its locality. Amalthæa also personifies fertility.

Amnesty, General. In May, 1865, a proclamation of pardon to the great mass of Southerners recently in arms against the United States was issued by President Johnson. Later, the policy of general amnesty was advocated by the best minds in and out of Congress, and finally prevailed in the various Reconstruction Acts.

Among the Gods. This expression had its origin in the fact that the ceiling of Drury Lane Theatre was formerly painted in imitation of a blue sky and fleeting clouds, among which great numbers of Cupids were disporting themselves. As the ceiling extended over the gallery, its occupants were said to be "among the gods."

Amoret. A lady brought up by Venus in the Court of Love, in Spenser's "Faerie Queene." "She is the type of female loveliness, — young, handsome, gay, witty, and good; soft as a rose, sweet as a violet, chaste as a lily, gentle as a dove, loving everybody, and by all beloved." She becomes the loving, tender wife of Sir Scudamore. Timias finds her in the arms of Corflambo (sensual passion), combats the monster unsuccessfully, but wounds the lady.

Amor nummi. (Lat.) Love of money.

Amoroso, Amorevole, or **Con amore.** (Ital.) Affectionately, tenderly. (Mus.)

Amorous, The. Philippe I. of France (fl. 1061–1108). So named because he put away Berthe, his wife, in order to marry Bertrade, who was already wedded to Foulgues, Comte d'Anjou.

Amor patriæ (Lat.) Love of native country.

Amour-propre. (Fr.) "Self-love." Vanity.

Amphibious Regiment. The 21st Regiment — afterward the 14th — in the Revolutionary War, — one of the best and bravest in the Continental army, composed almost entirely of fishermen; whence its nickname.

Amphilogist. (Pseud.) Robert C. Sands in the New York "Commercial Advertiser."

Amphion. In classic mythology a son of Jupiter and Antiope, who built a wall around Thebes by the music of his lyre. It is said that when he played, the stones moved of their own accord, and fitted themselves together to form the rampart.

Amphitrite. Wife of Neptune (*q. v.*), goddess of the sea, and mother of Triton (*q. v.*).

Amphrysian Prophetess. Another name for the Cumæan sibyl. See SIBYL.

Amri. Heneage Finch, Earl of Nottingham and Lord Chancellor, is satirized under this name in Dryden's "Absalom and Achitophel."

Amrita. "Immortal." In Hindu mythology the elixir of immortality, made by churning the milk-sea. Sir William Jones speaks of an apple so called because it bestows immortality on those who partake of it.

Amsanctus. A fabulous Italian lake, said to communicate with the infernal regions.

Amt. Amount.

A multo fortiori. (Lat.) On much stronger grounds.

Amyclæan Brothers. A title of Castor and Pollux, who first saw the light at Amyclæ.

Amyclæan Silence. "The inhabitants of Amyclæ were so often alarmed by false rumors of the approach of the Spartans that they made a decree that no one should ever again mention the matter. When the Spartans did actually come against the town, no one durst speak of it, and the place was captured." — BREWER.

Amy Ames. The stage-name of Mrs. Augustus Hennessy.

Amy Lothrop. (Pseud.) Miss Anna B. Warner, an American writer (b. 1825), sister of Elizabeth Warner.

Amy Roselle. The stage-name of Mrs. Arthur Dacre.

Amy Steinberg. The stage-name of Mrs. John Douglas.

An. *Anno.* In the year.

An. or **Ans.** Answer.

Anabaptists. "Twice baptized." A nickname of the Baptists, who are so called because, in the first instance, they had been baptized in infancy, and were again baptized, on a confession of faith, in adult age. Of course, nowadays there is no "infant" baptism among Baptists.

An. A.C. *Anno ante Christum.* In the year before Christ.

Anacharsis, or **Anacharsis among the Scythians.** A wise man among fools; "good out of Nazareth." The opposite proverb is "Saul among the prophets," *i. e.*, a fool among wise men. Anacharsis was a Scythian by birth, and the Scythians were proverbial for their uncultivated state and great ignorance.

Anacharsis Clootz. A self-conferred title of Baron Jean-Baptiste Clootz (fl. 1755–1794), an enthusiast who adopted and preached the doctrines of the French Revolution. He also dubbed himself "The Orator of the Human Race."

Anacreon Moore. Thomas Moore, the poet (fl. 1779–1852), so named because his poems resembled those of Anacreon, the Greek singer of wine and love.

Anacreon of France. Pontus de Thiard (fl. 1521–1605), one of the "French Pleiads."

Anacreon of Painters. Francesco Albano (fl. 1578–1660), a noted painter of female loveliness.

Anacreon of Persia. Mohammed Hafiz (fl. in the fourteenth century).

Anacreon of Sicily. Giovanni Meli (fl. 1740–1815).

Anacreon of the Guillotine. Bertrand Barère de Vieuzac, the president of the National Convention (fl. 1755–1841), thus nicknamed on account of the florid, jesting tone he adopted toward the victims of the popular fury.

Anacreon of the Temple. A sobriquet conferred on Guillaume Amfrye (fl. 1638–1720), Abbé de Chaulieu. He was also called the "Tom Moore of France."

Anacreon of the Twelfth Century. A sobriquet of Walter Mapes (fl. 1150–1196), a famous poet. He was also nicknamed "The Jovial Toper," because he wrote many drinking songs.

Anagrams. The construction of anagrams is at once the most easy and the most entertaining form of word-jugglery, and for these reasons perhaps has been most widely indulged in, rising at times to the dignity of a popular craze. The passion for anagrammatizing proper names reached its height in the sixteenth and seventeenth centuries, when it was a fashionable amusement of the witty and learned. At court it became a mania; the little persons flattered the great ones by inventing complimentary anagrams for them. In the reign of Louis XIII. we find mention of Thomas Billon, who enjoyed a pension of 1,200 livres as anagrammatist to the king. The term "anagram" in its proper sense means the letters of one or several words written backward, being derived from two Greek words, — ἀνά, "backward," and γράμμα, "letter;" but generally it denotes simply a transposition of the letters of a word or sentence so that a new word or sentence is formed, of which the following are simple examples : —

Astronomers	{ Moonstarers.
	{ No more stars.
Democratical	Comical trade.
Gallantries	All great sins.
Lawyers	Sly ware.
Misanthrope	Spare him not.
Monarch	March on.
Old England	Golden land.
Punishment	Nine thumps.
Presbyterian	Best in prayer.
Penitentiary	Nay, I repent it.
Radical reform	Rare mad frolic.

Revolution	To love ruin.
Telegraph	Great help.
The calceolaria	Eat coal, Charlie.
Geranium	Ear in mug.
Heliotrope	Hit or elope.
The nightingale	High gale in tent.
The turtle-dove	Eve, let truth do.
Congregationalist	Got scant religion.
Crocodile	Cool'd rice.
Impatient	Tim in a pet.
Masquerade	Queer as mad.
Matrimony	Into my arm.
Melodrama	Made moral.
Midshipman	Mind his map.
Parishioner	I hire parson.
Parliament	Partial men.
Sweetheart	There we sat.

Some of the foregoing transpositions are very apt. For a perfect anagram no new letter should be interpolated and no letter dropped; and some applicability to the person or subject involved, either complimentary or satirical, an allusion to an event, or a hit at some personal trait, is always desirable. The letters *I* and *J*, and *U* and *V*, are interchangeable, as was formerly the case in writing and printing. Here is a batch of more or less clever personal anagrams : —

Marie Antoinette : Tear it, men ; I atone.
Selina, Countess of Huntingdon : See, sound faith clings to no nun.
James Watt : Wait, steam.
Lord Palmerston : So droll, pert man.
William Ewart Gladstone : A man to wield great wills.
Léon Gambetta : Able man to get.
Alfred Tennyson, Poet Laureate : Neat sonnet or deep tearful lay.

Anagrams are of very ancient origin. "The Cabalists were professed anagrammatists ; they pretended to discover occult qualities in proper names, — an Oriental practice adopted by the Greeks. Thus, the Hebrew characters for the name "Noah" form by transposition the Hebrew word "grace," and in like manner the name "Messiah" becomes "He shall rejoice." Among the Romans two kinds of anagrams were in use, — one formed as in *Roma : amor ; Corpus : porcus ;* and the other by merely dividing the word selected into several parts, the god *Terminus* becoming *ter minus,* and *sustineamus* being *sus tinea mus.*"

Two classic anagrams have come down to us from Lycophron, who lived B. C. 280, — one on Ptolemy Philadelphus, and the other on his queen, Arsinoë :

Πτολεμαῖος — ἀπὸ μέλιτος : Of honey.

Ἀρσινόη — Ἥρας ἴον : Juno's violet.

Another ancient anagram is formed of the question put by Pilate to the

Saviour, out of which was evolved its own answer. Pilate asked, *Quid est veritas ?* — "What is truth?" The anagrammatic reply is, *Vir qui adest !* "The man who stands before you ! "

Before leaving the subject of personal anagrams, we may not omit several on Napoleon I. and some of his greatest antagonists. Probably the former was the subject of more lampoons of this sort than any other man of ancient or modern times. Here are a few of them, — and it should be premised that they were mostly of English origin. When he ended the French Revolution with the consulate, the words *Révolution Française* were transposed, forming, *Veto ! un Corse la finira.* But when the arch-conqueror was forced to yield his throne to Louis XVIII., the letters were arranged to read, *La France veut son roi.* On the return from Elba the following imperfect but appropriate anagram was circulated : " Napoleón Bonaparte ! — No, appear not at Elba ! " as also, " Napoleon Bonaparte ! — *Bona rapta leno pone :* Rascal, yield up your stolen possessions ! "

On Arthur Wellesley, Duke of Wellington, the Frenchman's great foe, this was made : " Let well-foiled Gaul secure thy renown." The naval hero, Horatio Nelson, has two, — " Lo ! nation's hero ; " and *Honor est a Nilo :* "There is honor from the Nile," referring to Nelson's celebrated victory over the French fleet off Alexandria.

An anagram on the occasion of the death of Princess Charlotte, daughter of George IV., is also worthy of record : "Princess Charlotte Augusta of Wales : P. C., her august race is lost ! O fatal news ! " In the " Curiosities of Literature," compiled by the elder Disraeli, there are several most amusing anagrams, and the author had a thorough appreciation of the points of a good one. It is to be hoped that this trait was transmitted to his descendant, the Earl of Beaconsfield, so that the ingenuity which, after the stinging defeat of 1880, converted his title into the phrase, " Self-fooled ; can he bear it ? " was duly appreciated.

The virtue attaching to an anagram in the sight of the superstitious is well exemplified in the case of Charles James Stuart, the Pretender. The loyal Scotch squandered blood and treasure in his behalf because of their faith in the prophetic significance of two anagrams

on his name, — the first being "Charles James Stuart : He asserts a true claim ; " the second, "James Stuart : A just master." But no more appropriate or beautiful anagram was ever devised than that on Florence Nightingale : "Flit on, cheering angel ! " — worthy, as has been said, of being chiselled on her tomb, in letters of stone, as her epitaph.

Anak of Publishers. John Murray (1778-1843) was so called by Lord Byron.

Anal. Analysis.

Anarchy Poles. A derisive name for liberty-poles.

Anastasius Grün. (Pseud.) Anton Alexander von Auersperg, the German poet (b. 1806).

Anat. Anatomy.

Anc. Ancient ; anciently.

Ancæus. In classic mythology a son of Neptune, who, having set down a flagon of wine untasted, that he might pursue a wild boar, was slain by the beast ; whence arose the proverb, " There's many a slip between the cup and the lip."

Anchor. (Pseud.) J. Watts De Peyster, American antiquarian author (1821–1873).

Ancienne noblesse. (Fr.) "The old nobility," — that is, before the French Revolution.

Ancien régime. (Fr.) An antiquated system of government. This phrase, in the French Revolution, meant the monarchical form of government, or the system of government, with all its evils, which existed prior to that great change.

Ancient Mariner of the Wabash. A name applied to Richard W. Thompson, of Indiana, Secretary of the Navy in the Hayes cabinet (b. 1809).

Ancile. The Palladium of Rome. It was the sacred buckler which Numa said fell from heaven.

And. Andrew.

Andalusia, Frying-pan of. *See* FRYING-PAN OF ANDALUSIA.

Andante. (Ital.) A musical term implying a movement somewhat slow and sedate, but in a gentle and soothing style. This term is often modified, as to time and style, by the addition of other words, as : —

Andante affetuoso. Slow, but pathetically.

Andante con moto. Slow, but with emotion.

Andante grazioso. Slowly and gracefully.

Andante maestoso. Slowly and majestically.

Andante ma non troppo e con tristezza. Not too slow, but with pathos.

Andante non troppo. Slowly, but not too much so.

Andante pastorale. Slowly, with pastoral simplicity.

Andantino. (Ital.) Somewhat slower than *Andante.* (Mus.)

Andantino sostenute e simplicimento, il canto un poco più forte. (Ital.) In a sustained and simple style, with the melody somewhat louder than the other notes. (Mus.)

Andare stretto. (Ital.) "To go in a narrow line." To go about anything in a miserly manner.

Andrea Ferrara. Another name for a sword or rapier, after a famous maker of these weapons.

Andrew Philopater. (Pseud.) Robert Parsons, an English Jesuit (1546–1610).

Andromache. In classic mythology the most bewitching female character in Homer's Iliad. She was the daughter of Eëtion and the loving wife of Hector, to whom she bore Astyanax.

Andromeda. In classic mythology a daughter of Cepheus, king of Ethiopia, and of Cassiopeïa. Her mother having boasted that her beauty equalled that of the Nereids, Andromeda was delivered to a sea-monster, but was discovered by Perseus, who rescued and married her.

Anfriso. (Pseud.) Manuel Maria de Navarrete, a Mexican author (1768–1809).

Angel. In theatrical slang "an angel" is the nickname for an unseen financial backer.

Angel. This was the name of an ancient English coin, originally of the value of 6*s.* 8*d.*; but for a long period its value was 10*s.* The coin was so called from its obverse bearing the figure of the Archangel Michael overcoming the dragon. An old verse in which its name appears is a very convenient "ready reckoner." It runs thus:

"Compute but the pence
Of one day's expense ;
So many pounds, angels, groats, and pence
Are spent in one whole year's circumference."

So that if a penny a day be spent, the amount at the end of the year will be equal to one pound, one angel, one groat, and one penny; or £1 10*s.* 5*d.* Twopence a day is equal to two pounds, two angels, two groats, and two pennies, or £3 10*d.* ; and so on.

Angel-Beast. A favorite round-game of cards, which enables gentlemen to let the ladies win small stakes. Five cards are dealt to each player, and three heaps formed,— one for the king, one for play, and the third for Triolet. The name of the game was *La Bête* (beast), and an angel was the stake.

Angel Gabriel Riots. Disturbances in Brooklyn, N. Y., caused by the street preaching of a lunatic who called himself the angel Gabriel. They were put down by the Fourteenth Regiment, commanded by Gen. Jesse C. Smith.

Angelical Stone. The speculum of Dr. Dee. He asserted that it was given him by the angels Raphael and Gabriel. It passed into the possession of the Earl of Peterborough, thence to Lady Betty Germaine, by whom it was given to the Duke of Argyle, whose son presented it to Horace Walpole. It was sold in 1842 at the dispersion of the curiosities of Strawberry Hill.

Angelic Doctor. A sobriquet conferred on Thomas Aquinas, the learned Schoolman, because he debated the question, "How many angels can dance on the point of a needle ? "

Angelic Hymn. Another name for the canticle otherwise known as the *Gloria in excelsis,* — so called because the opening lines were sung by the celestial host that visited the shepherds on the plains of Bethlehem.

Angelici. Certain heretics of the second century who advocated the worship of angels.

Angelites. A branch of the Sabellian heretics ; so called from Angelius, in Alexandria, where they used to meet.

Angel of the Schools. Thomas Aquinas, the most famous metaphysician of the Middle Ages.

Angels' Visits. Norris of Bemerton (1657–1711) wrote of those joys which

" Soonest take their flight
Are the most exquisite and strong,—
Like angels' visits, short and bright."

Robert Blair, in 1743, wrote in his poem called the "Grave ": —

" In visits
Like those of angels, short and far between."

Campbell, in 1799, appropriating the simile, but without improving it, wrote : —

" Like angels' visits, few and far between."

Anglicè. (Lat.) In English.

Anglo-American. (Pseud.) Sir Brenton Halliburton, who contributed some articles on the War of 1812 to the Halifax "Recorder."

Anglomania. Generally applied to a French or German imitation of the manners, customs, etc., of the English. It prevailed in France some time before the First Revolution, and was often extremely ridiculous.

Angry, The. Christian II., king of Denmark, Sweden, and Norway, was so named because of his fiery temper (b. 1513, d. 1559).

Ang.-Sax. Anglo-Saxon.

Anguillam cauda tenes. (Lat.) "You hold an eel by the tail." You have to deal with an active and slippery antagonist.

Anguis in herba. (Lat.) "A snake in the grass." A lurking danger.

Anguwadel. In Scandinavian mythology the sword of Frithiof, engraved with runes which blazed in war-time, but only gleamed with a pale light in time of peace.

Aniles fabulæ. (Lat.) Old wives' stories.

Animal implume bipes. (Lat.) A two-legged animal without feathers, — Plato's definition of man.

Animals, Symbolism of. The ant, frugality and prevision; ape, uncleanness; ass, stupidity; bantam cock, pluckiness, priggishness; bat, blindness; bear, ill-temper, uncouthness; bee, industry; beetle, blindness; bull, straightforwardness; bulldog, pertinacity; butterfly, sportiveness, living in pleasure; cat, slyness, deceit; calf, lumpishness; cicada, gift of poetry; cock, vigilance, overbearing insolence; crow, longevity; crocodile, hypocrisy; cuckoo, cuckoldom; dog, fidelity, dirty habits; dove, innocence, harmlessness; duck, canard; eagle, majesty, inspiration; elephant, sagacity, ponderosity; fly, feebleness, insignificance; fox, cunning, artifice; frog and toad, inspiration; goat, lasciviousness; goose, conceit, folly; gull, gullibility; grasshopper, old age; hare, timidity; hawk, penetration; hen, maternal care; horse, speed, grace; jackdaw, vain assumption, empty conceit; jay, senseless clatter; kitten, playfulness; lamb, innocence, sacrifice; lark, cheerfulness; lion, noble courage; lynx, suspicious vigilance; magpie, garrulity; mole, obtuseness; monkey, tricks; mule, obstinacy; nightingale, forlornness; ostrich, stupidity; ox, patience, strength; owl, wisdom; parrot, mocking verbosity; peacock, pride; pigeon, cowardice; pig, obstinacy, dirtiness; puppy, emptyheaded conceit; rabbit, timidity; raven, ill luck; robin redbreast, confiding trust; serpent, wisdom; sheep, silliness, timidity; sparrow, litigiousness; spider, wiliness; stag, cuckoldom; swallow, a sunshine friend; swan, grace; swine, filthiness, greed; tiger, ferocity; tortoise, chastity; turkey cock, official insolence; turtle-dove, conjugal fidelity; vulture, rapine; wolf, cruelty.

Animis opibusque parati. (Lat.) Ever ready with our lives and fortunes.

Animo et fide. (Lat.) With courage and faith.

Animo facto. (Lat.) Really and truly.

Animo non astutia. (Lat.) By courage, not by craft.

Animus furandi. (Lat.) Felonious intent.

Anita Alameda. The stage-name of Annie E. Gleason.

Ann. *Annales.* Annals.

Annabel, in Dryden's satire of "Absalom and Achitophel," is designed for the Duchess of Monmouth. Her maiden name and title were Anne Scott, Countess of Buccleuch, — the richest heiress in Europe. The duke was faithless to her, and after his death the widow, still handsome, married again.

Anna Holyoke. (Pseud.) Mrs. A. H. C. Howard in "The Household," published at Brattleboro, Vt.

Anna Katherine Green. (Pseud.) Mrs. Rohlfs, an American writer of fiction (b. 1846).

Anna Matilda. (Pseud.) Mrs. Hester Lynch (Salusbury) Piozzi, an English novelist (1740–1821).

Anne Frances Randall. (Pseud.) Mrs. Mary Robinson, an English poet and actress (1758–1800).

Anne Hathaway. (Pseud.) Mrs. W. A. Ingham, in the Cleveland "Herald."

Annie Boudinot. The stage-name of Mrs. Joseph Sendelbach.

Annie Boyd. The stage-name of Mrs. Harry Morris.

Annie Carroll. The stage-name of Mrs. Edward Snow.

Annie Edmonstone. The stage-name of Mrs. Frederick Warde.

Annie Helen Blancke. The stage-name of Mrs. James Neill.

Annie Mack. The stage-name of Mrs. Berlein.

Annie Melvin. The stage-name of Mrs. Samuel Lucas.

Annie Myrtle. (Pseud.) Miss Annie M. Chester.

Annie Pixley. The stage-name of Mrs. Robert Fulford.

Annie Russell. The stage-name of Mrs. G. W. Presbrey.

Annie Shindle. The stage-name of Mrs. L. W. Tupper.

Annie Suits. The stage-name of Mrs. Henry Maddock.

Annie Sutherland. The stage-name of Mrs. Richard M. Carroll, Jr.

Annie Ward Tiffany. The stage-name of Mrs. Charles H. Green.

Annie West. (Pseud.) Mrs. Annie [Adams] Fields.

Anniversary Day, or **May Walk.** An annual festival of the Sunday-schools of Brooklyn and New York, consisting of singing, feasting, and a street parade.

Ann Jane. (Pseud.) Mrs. Ann Jane Morgan.

Anno ætatis suæ. (Lat.) In the year of his or her age.

Anno Domini. (Lat.) In the year of our Lord.

Anno lucis. (Lat.) In the year of light.

Anno mundi. (Lat.) In the year of the world.

Annot Lyle. (Pseud.) Mrs. A. L. Saxon, in the Philadelphia "Courier."

Anno urbis conditæ. (Lat.) In the year of founding the city, namely, Rome, B. C. 753.

Annuit cœptis novus ordo sæculorum. (Lat.) "The new order of the ages smiles on our undertakings," — the motto on the U. S. mail-cars.

Annunciation Day. The 25th of March (also called Lady Day), on which the angel announced to Mary that she was to become the mother of the Messiah.

Annus mirabilis. (Lat.) "A wonderful year." A year of wonders. *See* YEAR OF WONDERS.

Anobium Pertinax. (Pseud.) William Hand Browne, in "The Nation," New York, 1883.

Anomœans. A fourth-century sect who held that the nature of the Son is wholly unlike that of the Father. The word means literally "Unlikists."

Anon. Anonymous.

Anonyma. A lady of the demi-monde. *See* INCOGNITA.

Another County heard from. During the excitement incident to the Presidential campaign of 1876 this phrase gained currency. The returns were very slowly received from some of the doubtful States, especially in Florida, and each addition to the uncompleted vote was hailed as above.

Ans. Answer.

Ansarian. The Moslems of Medina were called Ansarians (Auxiliaries) by Mahomet, because they received him and took his part when he was driven from house and home by the Koreishites.

Anselmus. (Pseud.) Samuel Willoughby Duffield, American clergyman (1843–1887), in "The Evangelist."

Ansted Hope. (Pseud.) Miss Burdett in the "Family Herald," London.

Ant. or **Antiq.** Antiquities.

Antæus. In classic mythology the son of Neptune and of Terra. He was a giant of fabulous powers, whose strength remained unimpaired so long as he maintained contact with his mother (Earth). Hercules discovered the secret of his strength, raised him from the ground, and crushed him in mid-air.

Ante barbam doces senes. (Lat.) You teach old persons before you have a beard.

Ante bellum. (Lat.) Before the war.

Ante lucem. (Lat.) Before light.

Ante meridiem. (Lat.) Before noon.

Anteros. In classic mythology the deity or power who opposes Eros, or Love, and represented as perpetually warring against him.

Anth. Anthony.

Anthony Absolute, Sir. A warm-hearted, testy, overbearing country squire in Sheridan's play of the "Rivals."

Anthony Grey. (Pseud.) Henry Carl Schiller, an English writer (b. 1815).

Anthony Harmer. (Pseud.) Rev. Henry Wharton, an English antiquary (1664–1695).

Anthony Pig. A pet pig; the smallest of a litter. Saint Anthony was originally a swineherd, and became the patron saint of that class.

Anthony Poplar. The pen-name used by the editors of the "Dublin University Magazine."

Anthony's Fire, St. Another name for erysipelas, — so called because of the tradition that those who invoked the aid of Saint Anthony during the pestilential erysipelas which prevailed in 1089 invariably recovered.

Anthony's Nose. (1) A popular name for the extremity of a hill called the Klips (*i. e.*, rock, or cliff), on the right bank of the Mohawk, in Montgomery County, N. Y. It resembles a nose, and is three or four hundred feet long. (2) A bold promontory on the east bank of the Hudson River, projecting from the south side of Breakneck Hill, at the northerly entrance to the Highlands, fifty-seven miles from New York city.

Anthroposophus. The nickname of Dr. Vaughan, rector of St. Bride's, in Bedfordshire, — so called from his "Anthroposophia Teomagica," to show the condition of man after death.

Anti-Belial. One of the pen-names attributed to Junius (*q. v.*).

Antichrist, or the **Man of Sin,** expected by some to precede the second coming of Christ. Saint John so calls every one who denies the incarnation of the Son of God.

Anti-Erastian Party. Those who wish the church to have the power of punishing ecclesiastical offenders.

Anti-Federalist Party. This party arose in the United States during the discussion of the ratification of the Constitution. Its principles were based on opposition to the centralization of power in the general Government. It was also known as the Republican party; and this name Mr. Jefferson, its greatest leader, was anxious to retain. But its members became known as Democrats, and the other titles were dropped. Its first success was the election of Thomas Jefferson in 1801. Mr. Jefferson transferred at once the chief offices to members of the party; internal revenues were abolished; and the Alien and Sedition laws were repealed. He was elected a second time in 1805; and on the expiration of his term, the sympathy of the Democrats with France and their enmity toward England, whose conduct on the seas had rendered her obnoxious, caused the election of James Madison to the presidency in 1809, who was again chosen in 1813. The successful issue of the War of 1812 continued the power of the party, and James Monroe became President in 1817, followed by a second term in 1821. In the election of 1824 there were four candidates for President, namely, John Q. Adams, Andrew Jackson, Henry Clay, and W. H. Crawford, all of whom claimed to be Democrats. None having a majority, the election was thrown into the House of Representatives, when Mr. Adams was chosen President, John C. Calhoun being Vice-President by the votes of the electoral college. In 1828 Andrew Jackson was elected President after a struggle with the advocates of Adams, no principle being at stake; and he was again chosen in 1832. The acts of General Jackson caused strong opposition, and it was during his administration that the Whig party was formed. And as the lines were drawn and men ranged themselves on either side, the Democrats took the name of the Democratic party, and claimed to be the successors of the old Jeffersonian party.

Anti-Federal Junto. "When it was proposed in the Pennsylvania Legislature to issue a call for a convention to ratify the United States Constitution, nineteen of the members withdrew, leaving the House without a quorum. Enough of these were, however, dragged to the House to allow business to be transacted. In September, 1787, sixteen of these same members signed an address against the Constitution; this address contained so many misstatements that it soon became an object of ridicule. To the signers and their followers the name of Anti-Federal Junto was given." — BROWN AND STRAUSS.

Anti-Fox. One of the pen-names attributed to Junius (*q. v.*).

Antigone. In classic mythology the daughter of Œdipus by his mother, Jocasta. She was famed for her filial affection.

Antigone, The Modern. *See* MODERN ANTIGONE.

Antilles, Queen of the. *See* QUEEN OF THE ANTILLES.

Anti-Masonic Party. In 1826 W. Morgan, who was preparing a revelation of the secrets of freemasonry, suddenly disappeared. It was rumored that he had been foully dealt with by members of the order, and intense excitement was the result, followed by the establishment of a political party based on opposition to the order. It cast in New York, in 1828, 30,000 votes; in 1829, 70,000; and about 128,000 in 1832. In 1832 it nominated William Wirt for President, but carried only one State, — Vermont. The excitement gradually died out, and the party disappeared. *See* GOOD-ENOUGH MORGAN.

Anti-Monopoly Party. "The Anti-Monopoly Organization of the United States met at Chicago, May 14, 1884, and nominated Benjamin F. Butler, of Massachusetts, for the Presidency. It adopted a platform demanding economical government and the enactment and enforcement of equitable laws, including an Interstate Commerce Law (one has since been enacted), establishing Labor Bureaus, providing Industrial Arbitration, a direct vote for Senators, a graduated income tax, payment of the national debt as it matures, and 'fostering care' for agriculture; while it denounced the tariff and the grant of land to corporations. Its nominee was also selected by the Greenback Labor party, the joint ticket being known as the People's party. It polled 130,000 votes." — BROWN AND STRAUSS.

Anti-Nebraska Men. A name applied to the Northern Whigs that opposed the Kansas-Nebraska Bill in 1854. These were joined by Democrats of similar views, and together they controlled the House in the Thirty-fourth Congress. The Republican party sprang from them.

Antinomians. A sect who, it is alleged, denied an obligation under the Gospel to obey the moral law of the Old Testament.

Antiope. In classic mythology the favorite of Jupiter, by whom she became the mother of Amphion and Zethus.

Antiquarius. (Pseud.) John Loveday, D.C.L., in his contributions to the "Gentleman's Magazine."

Anti-Rent Movement. The explanation and history of the anti-rent movement in New York State, given concisely, is as follows: Large portions of Columbia, Rensselaer, Greene, Delaware, and Albany counties in the State belonged to manors, the original grants of which were made to "patroons" by the Dutch Company, and renewed by James II., the principal being Rensselaerswyck and Livingston manor. The tenants had deeds for their farms, but paid annual rental in kind instead of a principal sum. This arrangement caused growing dissatisfaction among the tenants after 1790. When Stephen Van Rensselaer, who had allowed much of the rent to remain in arrears, died in 1839, the tenants, who longed to become real landowners, made common cause against his successor, refused to pay rent, disguised themselves as "Injuns," and began a reign of terror which for ten years practically suspended the operations of the law and the payment of rent throughout the district. An attempt to serve process by militia aid, known as the "Helderberg War," was unsuccessful. In 1847 and 1849 the antirenters "adopted" a part of each party State ticket, and thus showed a voting strength of about five thousand. This was not to be disregarded in a closely divided State, and in 1850 the Legislature directed the Attorney-General to bring suit against Harmon Livingston to try title. The suit was decided in Livingston's favor in November, 1850; but both parties were then ready to compromise, the owners by selling the farms at fair rates, and the tenants by paying for them. Most of Rensselaerswyck was sold; and of the Livingston manor, which at one time contained 162,000 acres of choice farming land, very little now remains in the possession of the family. Another anti-rent movement arose in Ireland in 1884 and succeeding years.

Anti-Rent Riots, Anti-Renters. See *supra*.

Anti-Slavery Men. The terms "Anti-Slavery" and "Abolitionist" are frequently confounded, In reality there was a wide difference; for many of the anti-slavery party repeatedly disclaimed being in favor of abolition. *See* ABOLITIONISTS.

Antisthenes. Founder of the Cynic School in Athens. He wore a ragged cloak, and carried a wallet and staff like a beggar. Socrates wittily said he could "see rank pride peering through the holes of Antisthenes' rags."

Anti-Stuart. One of the pen-names attributed to Junius (*q. v.*).

Antonio Aguaverde. (Pseud.) Alfred Trumble, a contributor to the New York "Boys' and Girls' Weekly."

Anton Strelezki. The professional name of Arthur Burbank, a native of Detroit, Mich., a well-known pianist and composer.

Antrustions. The vassals of the Frankish kings, who held land in trust. These lands were subsequently hereditary.

Anubis. In Egyptian mythology a divinity, the son of Osiris (*q. v.*), who accompanied the spirits of the dead to the nether world. He is usually worshipped in the shape of a dog, or as a human being with a dog's head.

Aor. Aorist.

A. O. S. S. *Americanæ Orientalis Societatis Socius.* Member of the American Oriental Society.

A outrance. (Fr.) Combat to the death.

Ap. Apostle; Appius.

Ap. *Apud*, in the writings of; as quoted by.

A pas de géant. (Fr.) With a giant's stride; rapidly.

Ape. The signature of Carlo Pellegrini, the celebrated English caricaturist. He adopted his well-known signature because he "apes" the peculiarities of his subjects when quizzing them with his pencil.

Aperçu. (Fr.) A brief sketch of any subject.

A perte de vue. (Fr.) Beyond one's view.

A. P. G. or **Ast. P. G.** Professor of Astronomy in Gresham College.

Aphrodite. In classic mythology the Greek name of Venus (*q. v.*).

Aphrodite's Girdle. The ancients believed that whoever wore the magic girdle of Aphrodite became the object of love.

A piacere, A piacemento. (Ital.) At the pleasure of the performer. (Mus.)

A pied. (Fr.) On foot.

Apis. The chief deity of the ancient Egyptians, worshipped in the guise of a bull.

A plomb. (Fr.) "To the lead." Perpendicularly.

Apo. Apogee.

Apocalypse. One of the names applied to the last book (Revelation) in the Christian Bible. It means "discovery," "disclosure."

Apocalyptic Number. The mystic number 666. See Rev. xiii. 18. *See* NUMBER OF THE BEAST.

Apocr. Apocrypha. Certain books in the Christian Bible whose divine inspiration is considered doubtful.

A point. (Fr.) "To a point." At the right moment; exactly right.

Apollinarians. An ancient sect founded in the middle of the fourth century by Apollinaris, bishop of Laodicea. They denied that Christ had a human soul, and asserted that the Logos supplied the place of the reasonable soul. The Athanasian Creed condemned this heresy.

Apollo. In classic mythology son of Jupiter and of Latona, and brother of Diana. He was the god of song, music, prophecy, and archery.

Apollo of Portugal. The poet Luis Camoens (fl. 1527–1579), author of the "Lusiad."

Apollyon. The Greek form of the Hebrew Abaddon, an evil spirit, described in Rev. ix. 11 as "the angel of the bottomless pit."

A posse ad esse. (Lat.) From possibility to reality.

Apostate, The. Julian, Emperor of Rome (fl. 331–363), was so named because he abjured the Christian faith and returned to paganism.

A posteriori. (Lat.) From the effect to the cause.

Apostle of Ethiopia. Saint Frumentius. *See* APOSTLE OF THE ABYSSINIANS.

Apostle of Free Trade. Richard Cobden (fl. 1804–1865).

Apostle of Germany. Saint Boniface (fl. 680–755).

Apostle of Hungary. Saint Anastasius (fl. 954–1044).

Apostle of Infidelity. Voltaire (fl. 1694–1778).

Apostle of Molasses and Moonshine. A nickname conferred on Matthew Arnold, the English man of letters (d. 1888).

Apostle of Ireland. Saint Patrick.

Apostle of Silence. Thomas Carlyle has been so nicknamed, satirically.

Apostle of Spain. Saint James the Greater, who died 44.

Apostle of Sweetness and Light. So Matthew Arnold, the English poet and critic, was named (d. 1888). See *supra*.

Apostle of Temperance. Father Mathew (fl. 1790–1856).

Apostle of the Abyssinians. Saint Frumentius, who flourished in the fourth century of our era.

Apostle of the Alps. Felix Neff (fl. 1798–1829).

Apostle of the Ardennes. Saint Hubert (fl. 656–730).

Apostle of the Armenians. Gregory of Armenia (fl. 256–331).

Apostle of the English. (1) Saint Augustine, who died 607. (2) Saint George has been so named.

Apostle of the French. Saint Denis, who lived in the third century.

Apostle of the Frisians. Saint Wilibrod (fl. 657–738).

Apostle of the Gauls. (1) Saint Irenæus (fl. 130–200). (2) Saint Martin (fl. 316–397).

Apostle of the Gentiles. Saint Paul.

Apostle of the Highlanders. Saint Columba (fl. 521–597).

Apostle of the Indians. (1) Bartolome de las Casas (fl. 1474–1500). (2) Rev. John Eliot (fl. 1603–1690).

Apostle of the Indies. Francis Xavier (fl. 1506–1552).

Apostle of the Netherlands. Saint Armam, bishop of Maestricht (fl. 589–679).

Apostle of the North. (1) Saint Ansgar (fl. 801–864). (2) Bernard Gilpin (fl. 1517–1583).

Apostle of the Peak. William Bagshaw (fl. 1628–1702), an English Nonconformist divine, the scene of whose labors was around the Peak of Derbyshire.

Apostle of the Picts. Saint Ninian.

Apostle of the Scottish Reformers. John Knox (fl. 1505–1572).

Apostle of the Slavs. Saint Cyril, who died 868.

Apostle of the Sword. Mohammed (fl. 570–632) was so named because he enforced his creed by means of the sword.

Apostle of Unitarianism. William Ellery Channing (fl. 1780–1842).

Apostle of Wales. Saint David (fl. 480–544).

Apostle of Yorkshire. *See* APOSTLE OF THE PEAK.

Apostle Spoons. Spoons presented to an infant at its christening,—so named because the figure of one of the Apostles was engraved on the handle. Sometimes twelve spoons were thus presented; at others only four, when the four Evangelists were depicted.

Apostle to the Blind. Abbé Valentine Hawy (fl. 1745–1822), who invented the art of printing with raised letters.

Apostolic Fathers. The five great Christian teachers who were contemporary with the Apostles,—Clement, Barnabas, Hermas, Ignatius, and Polycarp.

Appeal of Battle. By the ancient law of England a man might fight with his accuser, thereby to make proof of his guilt or innocence according as he became victor or vanquished. The law was not repealed till 1819.

Appiades. In classic terminology a grouping of five deities, whose temple graced the vicinity of the fountain of Appius, in Rome. They were: Vesta, Venus, Concord, Pallas, and Peace. They were represented by five equestrian statues.

Apple of Discord. The story of the Apple of Discord forms the theme of one of the most charming legends of classic mythology. It is related that at the marriage of Peleus and Thetis, the Goddess of Discord, not being invited to the entertainment, showed her displeasure by throwing among the gods, at the celebration of the nuptials, a golden apple, on which were written the words, " To be given to the fairest." All the goddesses claimed it as their own; but only Juno, Venus, and Minerva were allowed to dispute the right to the apple. The gods appointed Paris to adjudge the prize of beauty. The goddesses appeared before him without any ornament, but each tried to influence his judgment. Juno promised him a kingdom; Minerva, military glory; and Venus, the fairest woman in the world for his wife. Paris at length adjudged the prize to Venus. This decision drew upon him and his family the resentment of the two other goddesses. Paris then equipped a fleet, with the pretended motive of rescuing Hesione, whom Hercules had carried away and obliged to marry Telamon. He recollected that he was to have Helen, the fairest woman of the age, whom Venus had promised him. On these grounds he visited Sparta, the residence of Helen, who had married Menelaus, and was received kindly; but he abused the hospitality of Menelaus, and while the king was absent in Crete, carried off Helen to Troy, where Priam received her in his palace. Upon this all Greece took up arms. Agamemnon was chosen general of the combined forces, and a regular war was begun. Paris armed himself, with his brothers, to oppose the enemy, but is said to have fought with little courage, and at the sight of Menelaus he retired from the front of the army. In a combat with Menelaus he would have perished, had not Venus protected him from the resentment of his adversary. He nevertheless wounded in another battle Machaon, Euriphilus, and Diomedes, and according to some killed the great Achilles. Others of the poets relate that he fell by one of the arrows of Philoctetes, which had formerly belonged to Hercules, and was tended in his last moments by his wife, the nymph Œnone.

Apple of Perpetual Youth. In Scandinavian mythology the apple of Idun, wife of Bragi. By tasting this apple the gods preserve their perpetual youth.

Apple of the Eye. Probably a corruption of "pupil."

Apple-pie Bed. A name for a bed so made that a person cannot lie in it at full length, the sheets being folded like an apple turnover. But a more probable derivation is from the French *à plis*, folded in plaits.

Apple-pie Order. Perfect order; probably a corruption of *cap à pied*, — said of a knight when completely armed from head to foot. Another not improbable derivation is from the French *à plis*, folded in plaits.

Apples of Istkahar are "all sweetness on one side, and all bitterness on the other."

Apples of Paradise, according to tradition, had a bite on one side, to commemorate the gripe given by Eve.

Apples of Pyban, says Sir John Mandeville, fed the pygmies with their odor only.

Apples of Sodom (called by Witman "oranges") are the yellow fruit of the osher or ashey tree. Tacitus (History, v. 7) and Josephus both refer to these apples. Thevenot says, "The fruit is lovely [externally], but within is full of ashes."

The fruit of the osher or ashey tree, called "apples or oranges of Sodom," resembles a smooth apple or orange, hangs in clusters of three or four on a branch, and is of a yellow color when ripe. Upon being struck or pressed, it explodes with a puff, and is reduced to the rind and a few fibres, being chiefly filled with air. — *Gallery of Geography.*

> Like to the apples on the Dead Sea shore,
> All ashes to the taste.
>   Byron, *Childe Harold.*

Appogiatura. (Ital.) A note of embellishment, written in a smaller character than other notes. (Mus).

Apr. April.

April Fool's Day. The custom of sending one upon a bootless errand on the first day of April is perhaps a travesty of the sending hither and thither of the Saviour from Annas to Caiaphas, and from Pilate to Herod; because during the Middle Ages this scene in Christ's life was made the subject of a Miracle Play at Easter, which occurs near the 1st of April. It is possible, however, that it may be a relic of some old heathen festival. The custom, whatever be its origin, of playing off little tricks on this day, whereby ridicule may be fixed upon unguarded individuals, appears to be universal throughout Europe. In France one thus imposed upon is called *un poisson d'Avril* (an April fish). In England and the United States such a person is called an April fool; in Scotland a "gowk." The favorite jest is to send one upon an errand for something grossly nonsensical, or to make appointments which are not to be kept, or to call to a passer-by that his latchet is unloosed, or that there is a spot of mud upon his face. It is curious that the Hindus practise precisely similar tricks on the 31st of March, when they hold what is called the Huli Festival. There is a tradition among the Jews that the custom of making fools on the first of April arose from the fact that Noah sent out the dove on the first of the month corresponding to our April, before the water had abated. To perpetuate the memory of the great deliverance of Noah and his family, it was customary on this anniversary to punish persons who had forgotten the remarkable circumstance connected with the date, by sending them on some bootless errand similar to that on which the patriarch sent the luckless bird from the windows of the ark.

A priori. (Lat.) From the cause to the effect.

A propos. (Fr.) "To the point." Pertinently; seasonably.

A propos de bottes. (Fr.) "Seasonably of boots; with respect to boots." Not to the purpose; without reason; *à propos* of nothing.

Aq. (*aqua*). Water.

A. Q. M. Assistant Quartermaster.

A. Q. M. G. Assistant Quartermaster-General.

Aquarist. (Pseud.) Nicholas Jeffery Andrew in the New York "Courant."

A quatre mains. (Fr.) For four hands; a pianoforte duet. (Mus.)

Aqua vitæ. (Lat.) "Water of life." Brandy or other spirits.

Aquilo. In classic mythology a personification of the north wind; the same as Boreas (*q. v.*).

Aquinian Sage. Juvenal was so named. He lived at Aquinium, a Volscian town.

A. R. *Anna Regina.* Queen Anne.

A. R. *Anno regni.* Year of the reign.

Ar. *Argentum.* Silver.

A. R. A. Associate of the Royal Academy.

Ara. Arabic.

Arabici. A sect, originating in Arabia about 207, maintaining that the soul dies with the body and will rise again with it.

Arabs, or Street Arabs. Children of the street in our great cities; so named because, like the Arabs, they lead a nomadic life with no settled home.

Araby. A poetical diminutive for Arabia.

> Farewell, farewell to thee, Araby's daughter.
> MOORE, *The Fire Worshippers.*

Arachne. A Lydian maiden who was so vain of her skill in weaving that she challenged Minerva to a competition. She was successful in the contest, but being slighted by the goddess, she hung herself in despair, and was turned into a spider.

Arachne's Labors. Spinning and weaving. See *supra.*

Araf, Al (lit. "the partition"). According to the Koran, a middle kingdom or region, situate between Gehenna and Paradise, and reserved for those neither good nor evil in a moral sense, such as babes, lunatics, or idiots. The inmates of this realm will be allowed to hold intercourse with both the lost and the blessed: to the former their abode will appear a heaven; while to the latter it will seem a hell.

Aranearum telas texere. (Lat.) "To weave spiders' webs." To indulge in sophistry or quibbling.

Arbiter elegantiæ. C. Petronius was appointed dictator-in-chief of the imperial pleasures at the court of Nero, and nothing was considered *comme il faut* till it had received the sanction of this Roman Beau Brummel.

> Behold the new Petronius of the day,
> The arbiter of pleasure and of play.
> BYRON, *English Bards and Scotch Reviewers.*

Arbiter elegantiarum. (Lat.) A judge in matters of taste.

Arbor Day. Throughout the United States this has come to be more or less observed, not as a public holiday, but as an occasion for the planting of trees and for beautifying the streets and open squares of cities. It is a movable festival, according to climate, but usually falls in April or May. In 1889 thirty-four States and two Territories observed it. For the purpose of encouraging arboriculture in sparsely timbered regions, many of the States offer bounties for a certain number of shade-trees planted, whether by the roadside or in plantation. In some of the treeless regions of the great West, Arbor Day has come to occupy a leading place among the red-letter days of the year.

Arcades ambo. Both fools alike; both "sweet innocents;" both alike eccentric. There is nothing in the character of Corydon and Thyrsis (Virgil's Eclogues, vii. 4) to justify this disparaging application of the phrase. All Virgil says is, they were both "in the flower of their youth, and both Arcadians, both equal in setting a theme for song or capping it epigrammatically;" but as Arcadia was the least intellectual part of Greece, an "Arcadian" came to signify a dunce, and hence *Arcades ambo* received its present acceptation.

Arcady. Another form of Arcadia, — the middle and highest part of the Peloponnesus, derived from Arcas, the son of Callisto.

Arcana cœlestia. (Lat.) Heavenly secrets.

Arcana imperii. (Lat.) The secrets or mysteries of government.

Arcanum. A secret.

Arc-en-ciel. (Fr.) "The arch in the sky." The rainbow.

Arch. (1) Archibald. (2) Architect; architecture.

Archcarnifex. Thomas Norton, the persecutor (1532–1584).

Archd. Archdeacon.

Arches, The. Sailor men have nicknames for nearly every port or haven in the navigable globe. They always speak of archipelagoes as "the arches." The story goes that an officer of the deck on board a United States man-of-war saw a knot of sailors listening intently one night to the yarns spun by a grizzled old tar about his adventures in "going through the arches." A young sailor after a while said, with a puzzled and sheepish air, "The arches of what?" To which the old salt responded, with a look of withering contempt, "The arches of Pelago, of course, you lubber!"

Archeus. (Pseud.) John Sterling, in "Hymns of a Hermit," in "Blackwood's Magazine."

Archilochian Bitterness. Ill-natured satire; so named from Archilochus, the Grecian satirist (fl. 714–676 B. C.).

Archimage. The name given by Thomson to the demon Indolence.

Arch-Monarch of the World. Napoleon III. of France.

Arctic Sahara. In 1883 Baron Nordenskjöld explored the interior of Greenland, and found it to be a gigantic ice-field, destitute of vegetation and devoid of life. He named it the "Arctic Sahara."

Arcturus. (Pseud.) Mrs. Catherine Stratton Ladd (b. 1809), in her contributions to various periodicals.

Ardentia verba. (Lat.) Glowing words.

Ares. In classic mythology the god of war; the same as Mars (*q. v.*).

Arethusa. In classic mythology one of the Nereids, and an attendant on Diana.

Arg. *Argumento.* (Lat.) By an argument drawn from such a law.

Argan. A miserly hypochondriac. He reduced himself to this dilemma: If his apothecary would not charge less, he could not afford to be sick; but if he swallowed fewer drugs, he would suffer in health.

Argent comptant. (Fr.) Ready money.

Argo. In classic mythology the name of the fifty-oared ship in which Jason and his heroes made their voyage to Colchis in search of the Golden Fleece. *See* ARGONAUTS.

Argonauts. (1) Legendary Greek heroes of antiquity who undertook a voyage to unknown seas in a vessel called the Argo, under the command of Jason. After four months of peril and adventure they returned to Iolchus, and Jason dedicated the Argo to Neptune at the Isthmus of Corinth. The common interpretation of the legend is, that Jason's expedition was simply a voyage of discovery. The reputed search for the Golden Fleece (*q. v.*) is probably a later appendage to the tale. (2) The name Argonauts has become proverbial, and is often applied to those early pioneers who emigrated to California about the year 1849, during the gold fever.

Argo Navis (the Ship Argo). A constellation of the southern hemisphere containing sixty-four stars, two of which (Canopus and Miaplacidus) are of the first magnitude. This constellation commemorates the mythological story of Jason's expedition to Colchis to recover the Golden Fleece.

Argosy. A merchant's freight, — so called from the ship Argo, which went to Colchis to fetch away the Golden Fleece.

Argot. (Fr.) Slang or flash language.

Argumentum ab inconvenienti. (Lat.) An argument to prove that a proposition will not meet the intended purpose, and is therefore fruitless.

Argumentum ad absurdum. (Lat.) An argument to prove the absurdity of a thing.

Argumentum ad crumenam. (Lat.) An argument directed to the purse or pocket.

Argumentum ad fidem. (Lat.) An appeal to faith.

Argumentum ad hominem. (Lat.) "An argument to the man." An argument deriving its force from its direct personal application.

Argumentum ad ignorantiam. (Lat.) "An argument to ignorance." An argument founded on the ignorance of facts shown by an opponent.

Argumentum ad invidiam. (Lat.) "An argument to envy." An appeal to low passions.

Argumentum ad judicium. (Lat.) An appeal to the common-sense of mankind.

Argumentum ad populum. (Lat.) An appeal to the people.

Argumentum ad verecundiam. (Lat.) An appeal to modesty.

Argumentum baculinum. (Lat.) Club law.

Argus. In classic mythology a creature endowed with a hundred eyes, and of enormous strength. Juno sent him to guard Io (*q. v.*); but Mercury killed him, and transferred his eyes to the tail of the peacock.

Argus. (Pseud.) Irwin Willes, a sporting writer on the staff of the London " Morning Post " (d. 1871).

Argus-eyed. Jealously watchful. According to Grecian fable, Argus had a hundred eyes, and Juno set him to watch Io, of whom she was jealous.

Argus the Exile. (Pseud.) Another signature of Irwin Willes ; see *supra.*

Ari. Arizona.

Aria buffa. (Ital.) A comic song. (Mus.)

Aria d' abilita. (Ital.) A song of difficult execution. (Mus.)

Aria di cantabile. (Ital.) An air to be sung in a graceful and flowing style. (Mus.)

Arian Controversy, The, raged from the fourth to the seventeenth century with more or less virulence. The Arians denied the divinity of Christ. They were condemned by the Council of Nice (325 A. D.); but their doctrine long prevailed, and so late as 1614 Leggatt, an Arian, was burned at Smithfield. *See* ADOPTIAN CONTROVERSY.

Ariel. (Pseud.) Rev. Stephen Fiske, 1828–1864, in his contributions to the New York " Leader."

Arion. In classical mythology an ancient Greek bard and musician.

Arioso. (Ital.) In the manner of an air ; vocal, melodious. (Mus.)

Aristæus. In classic mythology an ancient Greek divinity, the protector of vines and olive gardens and of hunters and herdsmen.

Aristeas. In classical mythology a fabulous creature, known as " the Wandering Jew of Ancient Greece," who figures in widely separated ages and places and in very different characters. Herodotus says he was a magician whose spirit could leave his body and return at will.

Aristophanes of Caricature. Henri Daumier (b. 1810), the French caricaturist, was so named by critics.

Aristotelian Unities. Aristotle, the Greek philosopher, laid it down as a rule that every tragedy, properly constructed, should contain but one catastrophe ; should be limited to only one scene ; and be circumscribed to the action of one single day. These are called the Aristotelian unities.

Aristotle of China. Tschuhe, who died A. D. 1200, called the " Prince of Science."

Aristotle of the Nineteenth Century. George Cuvier, the great naturalist (1769–1832).

Arith. Arithmetic.

Arizona. This is an Indian word, meaning " blessed sun."

Ark. Arkansas. So much uncertainty exists as to the proper pronunciation of the name of Arkansas (Indian, *kansas*, "smoky water," and the French prefix *arc*, "a bow") that it may not be out of place to give a brief account of the origin of the name and define the correct usage. The proper pronunciation is " Ar'kahnsah'," accented on the first and last syllables. This was the old Indian pronunciation, which the early French traders expressed in letters as "Arkansas." The French *a* is always broad, and the final *s* is silent ; so "Arkansas" to the French was pronounced " Ar'kahnsah'." Congress, in the Act organizing the Territory, spelled the name "Arkansaw," and for some years the name continued to be so spelled. Finally, as every one knew the pronunciation, the original spelling was brought again into use. Then, however, came a generation who knew not the history or the pronunciation of the word, who called it " Arkan'zass," with the accent on the second syllable ; and this mispronunciation throve, and was accepted by many. In 1880 the State Historical and the Eclectic Societies jointly investigated the name and its pronunciation, and on their report, the substance of which is given above, the Legislature of the State decided that the legal pronunciation was " Ar'kahnsah'."

Arkansas Toothpick. A bowie-knife of a peculiar kind, the blade of which shuts up into the handle.

> Straightway leaped the valiant Slingsby
> Into armor of Seville,
> With a strong Arkansas toothpick
> Screwed in every joint of steel.
> BON GAULTIER, *American Ballads.*

Arm. Armenian.

Armed Neutrality. The compact formed by Russia, Sweden, and Denmark against England in 1780, and which fell to pieces in 1781. It was renewed in 1800. The British Cabinet remonstrated, war ensued, and Nelson and Parker destroyed the Danish fleet before Copenhagen, April 2, 1801.

Armed Soldier of Democracy. Napoleon I. was so named.

Armes blanches. (Fr.) Steel weapons; cold steel.

Armiger. One bearing arms; an esquire.

Arm-in-arm Convention. A name given to a convention of Republicans that supported President Johnson's policy on reconstruction. It met in Philadelphia in August, 1866. Its name arose from the fact that the members from Massachusetts and from South Carolina entered the convention together at the head of the delegates.

Armor. Armoric.

Arnoldists. The partisans of Arnold of Brescia, who raised his voice against the abuses and vices of the papacy in the twelfth century. He was burned alive by Pope Adrian IV.

Arod. Designed for Sir William Waller, in the satire of "Absalom and Achitophel," by Dryden and Tate.

Aroostook War. *See* NORTHEAST BOUNDARY.

Arouet. (Pseud.) Joseph Brown Ladd, American poet (1764–1786), who wrote a volume of poetry to "Amanda" signed "Arouet."

Around. This word is used in America in the sense of "near." An American "Police Gazette" quotes a witness as saying, "I was standing *around* when the fight took place;" and Bartlett, in his "Dictionary of Americanisms," says, "A friend assures me that he has heard a clergyman in his sermon say of one of the disciples that "he stood *around* the cross."

Arpeggio. (Ital.) Those passages which are formed of the notes of regular chords played in rapid succession, after the manner of a harp. (Mus.)

A. R. R. *Anno regni regis.* In the year of the reign of the king.

Arr. Arrive; arrival.

Arria. (Pseud.) Mrs. Eliza Lofton (Phillips) Pugh (b. 1841), in various daily papers of New York City.

Arrière-garde. (Fr.) The rear-guard.

Arrière-pensée. (Fr.) Mental reservation; a thought kept to one's self.

Arrow Festival. Instituted by Zoroaster to commemorate the flight of the arrow shot from the top of the Peak of Demavend, in Persia, with such miraculous prowess as to reach the banks of the Oxus, causing the whole intervening country to be ceded to Persia.

Arrow of Acestes. In a trial of skill, according to the Roman fable, Acestes the Sicilian discharged his arrow with such force that it took fire.

> Like Acestes' shaft of old,
> The swift thought kindles as it flies.
> LONGFELLOW.

A. R. S. A. Associate of the Royal Scottish Academy.

Ars est celare artem. (Lat.) "Art is to conceal art." The perfection of art is to conceal art.

Ars longa, vita brevis. (Lat.) Art is long, life is short.

A. R. S. S. *Antiquariorum Regiæ Societatis Socius.* Fellow of the Royal Society of Antiquaries.

Art. Article.

Art and Part. A Scotch law phrase, — an accessory before and after the fact. A man is said to be art and part of a crime when he contrives the manner of the deed and concurs with and encourages those who commit the crime, although he does not put his own hand to the actual execution of it.

Artemis. The same as Diana (*q. v.*).

Artemisia. Lady Mary Wortley Montagu was satirized under this name by Pope.

Artemus Ward. (Pseud.) Charles F. Browne, American humorist and lecturer (1834–1867).

Arthur Bitter. (Pseud.) Samuel Haberstitch, German author.

Arthur Dudley. (Pseud.) Charlotte Campbell, Countess of Bury (1775–1861).

Arthur Sketchley. (Pseud.) George Rose, English humorous writer (1830–1883).

Arthur Venner. (Pseud.) William McCrillis Griswold, in the magazines of the United States.

Artil. Artillery.

Artotyrites. Certain heretics from among the Montanists, — so called because they offered bread and cheese to the priesthood.

Art preservative of all Arts. Printing is so named. The phrase is from the inscription upon the façade of the house at Haarlem formerly occupied by Laurent Koster, or Coster, who is credited, among others, with the invention of printing. Mention is first made of this inscription about 1628 : —

MEMORIÆ SACRUM
TYPOGRAPHIA
ARS ARTIUM OMNIUM
CONSERVATRIX.
HIC PRIMUM INVENTA
CIRCA ANNUM MCCCCXL.

Arts d'agrément. (Fr.) Accomplishments (in ladies' schools) ; music and dancing.

Arturi, Mademoiselle. The professional name of Miss Ada Arthur.

Aruna. The phaeton of Indian mythology.

Arvakur. One of the horses of the sun, in Scandinavian mythology.

A. S. Anglo-Saxon.

A. S., or Assist. Sec. Assistant Secretary.

As. Arsenicum.

A. S. A. American Statistical Association.

Asa-Loki. The same as Loki (*q. v.*).

Asa-Thor. In Scandinavian mythology the first-born of mortals.

Asa Trenchard. (Pseud.) Henry Watterson, American journalist (b. 1832).

Ascalaphus. In classical mythology a son of Acheron who was transformed into an owl by Ceres for mischief-making.

Ascension Day. The fortieth day after Easter Sunday. *See* HOLY THURSDAY and MAUNDY THURSDAY.

Ascræan Sage. Hesiod (eighth century B. C.) is so named by Virgil in his Sixth Eclogue. He was born in Ascra, in Bœotia.

Asgard. In Scandinavian mythology the Norse celestial abode of the gods, situated in the centre of the universe, and reached only by the bridge Bifrost (the rainbow).

Ashtaroth. The Biblical name of Astarte (*q. v.*).

Ash Wednesday. This is the first day of Lent in the modern Christian calendar. In ancient times Lent began on the Sunday now called the first Sunday in Lent. Pope Felix II. in 487 added the four days preceding the old Lent Sunday, in order to raise the number of fasting days to forty. Gregory the Great, about 590, introduced the sprinkling of ashes, on the first of the four additional days ; hence the names of *Dies Cinerum*, or Ash Wednesday. At the Reformation this practice was abolished, "as being a mere shadow of vain show." It is said that the ashes were obtained from the burning of the Christmas greens which had adorned the churches since Christmastide, and which in turn formed a relic of an old Pagan custom.

Asinum tondes. (Lat.) "You are shearing an ass." There is a great cry, but little wool.

Asir. In Scandinavian mythology the twelve gods and twelve goddesses, — Odin, Thor, Baldur, Niord, Frey, Tyr, Bragi, Heimdall, Vidar, Vali, Ullur, and Forseti.

Ask and Embla. The Adam and Eve made by Odin, — one from ash-wood, and the other from elm.

Aslo. One of the horses of the sun, in Scandinavian mythology.

Asmodeus. In Hebrew mythology the evil spirit of Vanity, called in the Talmud "King of the devils." In modern literature he is often pithily referred to as the destroying angel of marital happiness.

Asmodeus of Domestic Peace. Asmodeus falls in love with Sara, daughter of Raguel, and causes the successive death of seven husbands, each on his bridal night. After her marriage to Tobit he was driven into Egypt by a charm made by Tobias of the heart and liver of a fish burned on perfumed ashes, and being pursued, was taken prisoner and bound.

Asopus. In classical mythology a son of Oceanus who was changed into a river for revolting against Jupiter.

Aspasia. A courtesan. She was the most notorious of the Greek Heteræ, to whom Pericles attached himself; after the death of the latter she lived with Lysicles, a cattle-merchant.

Asp for the Breast of the Poor. The sewing-needle has been so named.

Asphaltic Lake. The Dead Sea, where asphalt abounds both on the surface of the water and on the banks. Asphalt is bitumen, from the Greek ἄσφαλτος.

Asrafil. The angel who will sound the resurrection trumpet, according to the Koran.

Ass., or **Assn.** Association.

Assai. (Ital.) Very; extremely. A word appended to some other musical term, as *Adagio assai,* very slow; *Allegro assai,* very quick. (Mus.)

Assassination Plot. The name by which a conspiracy to assassinate William III. is known in English history. The Earl of Aylesbury and others planned to take his life near Richmond as he returned from hunting; but the plot was discovered Feb. 15, 1696, the day before that fixed for its consummation.

Assaye Regiment. The Seventy-fourth English foot, — so named because they first distinguished themselves in the battle of Assaye, India, in 1803.

Assiento Treaties. Contracts entered into by Spain with Portugal, France, and England, to supply her South American colonies with negro slaves. England joined in 1713, after the peace of Utrecht.

Assinego. (Port.) A young ass; a simpleton.

Associated Youth. A name given in 1798 to associations of young Federalists, who drew up addresses in favor of the Federalist party and its principles, and in other ways supported and aided it. They were largely instrumental in spreading the custom of wearing black cockades.

A. S. S. U. American Sunday-School Union.

Assumpsit. It is assumed, or taken for granted.

Assumption Day. August 15, — so named in honor of the Blessed Virgin, who, according to the Greek and Roman Churches, was received into heaven without dying, in the seventy-fifth year of her age.

Assunta Howard. (Pseud.) Miss Edith A. Salter.

Astarte. The Punic form of the name of the Syrian deity known in the Bible under the name of Ashtaroth.

Astor Place Riots. Incited by Edwin Forrest's friends to hinder Macready's acting at the Astor Place Opera House in New York, May 10, 1849.

Astra castra, numen lumen. (Lat.) The stars my camp, the Deity my light.

Astræa. In classical mythology the goddess of justice, daughter of Jupiter and of Themis. During the Golden Age this goddess dwelt on earth; but when sin began to prevail, she reluctantly left it, and was metamorphosed into the constellation Virgo.

Astræa. (Pseud.) Mrs. Aphra Behn, English authoress (1640–1689).

Astral Spirits. The spirits of the stars. According to the mythology of the Persians, Greeks, Jews, etc., each star had its special spirit, which may be termed its soul, or vital principle. Paracelsus maintained that every man had his attendant star, which received him at death, and took charge of him till the great resurrection.

Astrol. Astrology.

Astron. Astronomy.

Astrophel. "Star-lover." A name by which Sir Philip Sidney refers to himself. "Phil. Sid." he took as being at once a contraction of his name and of the Latin *philos sidus;* and the Latin *sidus* being exchanged for the Greek ἄστρον, he obtained "astronphilos," — hence "Astrophel." The "star" he adored was Penelope Devereux, whom he named "Stella," and to whom he was affianced.

Astyanax. In classical mythology the only son of Hector and Andromache. To prevent the fulfilment of an oracle that he should restore the kingdom of Troy, the Greeks hurled him from the walls of the city.

Asylum of the Oppressed of every Nation. This phrase is used in the Democratic National Platform of 1856, referring to the United States.

A. T. Arch-treasurer.

Atalanta. In classical mythology a princess of Sayros, or of Arcadia, famed for her beauty. She agreed to marry that one of her suitors who should outrun her, those whom she outstripped to suffer death. In this manner many perished; but Hippomenes, by dropping at intervals three golden apples, which Atalanta stopped to pick up, arrived first at the goal, and claimed her hand.

Ate. In classical mythology a daughter of Jupiter and goddess of discord.

A tempo, or A tem. (Ital.) In time. Used to indicate that after an *ad libitum* passage, or a variation in the regular time of a piece, the performer must return to the regular time. (Mus.)

A tempo giusto. (Ital.) In strict and equal time. (Mus.)

A tergo. (Lat.) "From behind." At one's back.

Athena. The ancient name of Athens (Gr. 'Αθῆναι), by which it is often referred to in modern literature. Minerva (in Greek, Athene) was regarded as the tutelary goddess of the city.

Age shakes Athena's tower, but spares gray
    Marathon.
            BYRON, *Childe Harold*, canto ii.

Athene. In classical mythology one of the chief female deities of the Greeks, corresponding to Minerva among the Romans.

Athenian Aberdeen. George Hamilton Gordon, Earl of Aberdeen (b. 1784), was thus named by Byron. He made a tour through Greece, which was commemorated in the following line: —

" The travelled thane, Athenian Aberdeen."

Athenian Bee. Plato the philosopher was so named because of the honeyed sweetness of his words.

Athens. *See* MODERN ATHENS; NORTHERN ATHENS.

Athens of America. Boston, Mass.; celebrated as a centre of polite literature.

Athens of Ireland. (1) The city of Cork, the domicile or the birthplace of many erudite and eminent Irishmen. (2) The city of Belfast has also been so named.

Athens of the East. The city of Sheraz, capital of the province of Fars, in Persia. It has numerous colleges, and anciently was the home of poetry and the arts. It gave birth to more distinguished Persian poets than any other Persian city.

If Mohammed had tasted the pleasures of Sheraz, he would have begged of Allah to make him immortal there. — *Persian Saying*.

Athens of the West. (1) A mediæval name of Cordova, in Spain; under its Mohammedan rulers it attained great eminence in the domain of letters.

(2) Jacksonville, Ill. It has numerous colleges, schools, and academies.

Atherton Gag. This was a resolution seeking to have all petitions and papers relating to slavery " laid on the table without being printed, debated, or referred," introduced by C. G. Atherton, of New Hampshire, and passed by the United States House of Representatives Dec. 11, 1838. It was repealed in 1845.

Athor, in Egyptian mythology, answers to the Venus of classic myth.

Atlantean Shoulders. Shoulders broad and strong, like those of Atlas, which support the world.

Sage he [Beëlzebub] stood,
With Atlantean shoulders, fit to bear
The weight of mightiest monarchies.
            MILTON, *Paradise Lost*.

Atlantis. Nine thousand years before Plato lived and wrote, there existed, he tells us in his Timæus, in the ocean that separates the Old World from the New, an island larger than Asia Minor and Northern Africa combined, densely peopled by a powerful race. He locates it in what is now a watery waste, midway between the westward projection of the desert coast of Africa and the corresponding indentation by the Gulf of Mexico of the " paradise of America." On its western shores were other and smaller islands, by way of which access might be had to a vast continent beyond. Its civilization was as advanced as that of ancient Egypt. Its people were descended from Neptune and mortal women, and by force of arms their warriors penetrated into Africa as far eastward as Egypt, and into Europe as far as the shores of the Tyrrhenian Sea (the western coast of Italy). Their conquests were checked by the Greeks after the Atlantean sea-kings had attempted to subjugate Europe, Africa, and Asia, and the deed was accounted one of the glories of Athens. At length, however, the people became so desperately wicked that the island with all its inhabitants was swept away by a deluge. In a day and a night Atlantis disappeared beneath the waves. Another account, slightly varied, says that after the defeat of the islanders a terrific earthquake, attended by inundations of the sea, caused the island to sink, and for a long time thereafter the ocean was impassable by reason of the muddy shoals. Such is the substance of a legend, first communicated to Solon by an Egyptian priest, and perhaps founded on fact, that has existed from a very early date. On old Venetian maps Atlantis was placed to the westward of the Canaries and the Azores. To the ancients the unknown was always gigantic or terrible ; so they represented Atlantis as being larger than either Europe or Africa, though the great extent assigned to the island may have only signified one very large in proportion to the smaller isles of the Mediterranean, — the only islands with which the ancients were familiar. Diodorus Siculus tells us that " over against Africa lies a very great island in the vast ocean, many days' sail from Libya westward. The soil there is very fruitful, a great part whereof is mountainous, but much likewise champaign, which is the most sweet and pleasant part, for it is watered by several navigable streams, and beautiful with many gardens of pleasure, planted by divers sorts of trees and an abundance of orchards. The towns are adorned with stately buildings and banqueting-houses, pleasantly situated in their gardens and orchards." The inhabitants of Venezuela and of Guiana retained traditions of a convulsion " which swallowed up a vast country in the region now covered by the Atlantic ocean." The Toltecs, the ancient inhabitants of Central America, have a tradition of the "cataclysm of the Antilles ; " among the Indians of North America there is a similar legend. The tribes located farther southward have a circumstantial narrative to the effect that the waves of the ocean were seen rolling in like mountains from the east, and that of the millions of people who fled toward the hills for refuge, only one man (seven in other accounts) was saved, from whom descended the present Indian races. A religious festival was instituted to commemorate the dread event, and to beseech the Almighty not to revisit the earth with such terrors. In this catastrophe it is claimed that an area greater in extent than France was engulfed, embracing the peninsulas of Yucatan, Honduras, Guatemala, and the Lesser Antilles, together with the magnificent cities of Palenque and Uxmal, with most of their inhabitants ; and it is supposed that "the continent has since risen sufficiently to restore many of these ancient sites." The Greeks, the Egyptians, the Gauls, and the Romans possessed traditions on this subject, and all the accounts substantially agree

with each other. These traditions were collected by Timagenes, the Roman historian, who flourished in the century preceding the birth of Christ. He represents Gaul as having been invaded from a distant island to the westward, by which many understand Atlantis to be meant. Another writer, Marcellus, mentions that the inhabitants of seven islands lying in the Atlantic Ocean near the coast of Europe (probably the Canaries) kept alive the memory of a much greater island, named Atlantis, which terrorized over the smaller ones. At the date of the existence of Atlantis, according to Humboldt, what is now the Strait of Gibraltar was probably bridged by a solid isthmus at least as wide as that of Suez, thus closing the Mediterranean and making of it an inland sea. The same convulsion of Nature which engulfed the island also established communication between the Atlantic and the Mediterranean. Charles Frédéric Martins, the French botanist, says that " hydrography, geology, and botany agree in teaching us that the Azores, the Canaries, and Madeira are the remains of a great continent which formerly united Europe to North America." The ancient writers found this a most captivating subject upon which to expand their conjectures, as is proved by the many comments upon Plato's narrative which have descended to us moderns. Nor have there been wanting scientists in our own day to view with favorable eyes the possibility of the existence, at a time now remote, of a mid-Atlantic island. Although Humboldt, Unger, and Goeppert, the Abbé Brasseur, Winchell, Foster, Wild, Heer, and others equally eminent found nothing startling or improbable in the idea, the story is now considered to be mythical.

Atlas. In classical mythology one of the Titans, son of Iapetus and Clymene, who for punishment was condemned by Jupiter to bear on his head and hands the world he had attempted to destroy.

Atonement, Day of. The Jewish day of national expiation for sin, kept on the tenth day of the month Tisri, corresponding to our October, five days before the Feast of Tabernacles. · Its origin and commemorative signification are generally thought to date from and refer to the remembrance of the day when Moses came down from the mount with the second tables of the law, and proclaimed to the people the divine forgiveness of their sin in worshipping the golden calf.

A tort et à droit. (Fr.) Right or wrong.

A tort et à travers. (Fr.) At random; without discretion.

Atossa. A nickname conferred on Sarah, Duchess of Marlborough, by Pope, because she was the friend of Lady Mary Wortley Montagu, whom he likewise christened Sappho.

A toutes jambes. (Fr.) As fast as one's legs can carry.

A tout propos. (Fr.) At every turn; ever and anon.

Atropos. In classical mythology one of the three Fates, — she who cut the thread of life.

A. T. S. American Tract Society.

Ats. At suit of.

At spes non fracta. (Lat.) But hope is not broken.

Attacca, Attacca subito. (Ital.) Implies that the following movement is to be immediately begun or attacked. (Mus.)

Attic Bee. Sophocles, the Athenian poet; so named from the sweetness and melody of his compositions.

Attic Bird. Another name for the nightingale.

Attic Hercules. Theseus, who went about, like Hercules, his great contemporary, destroying robbers and achieving wondrous exploits.

Attic Homer. Sophocles was so named by the ancients.

Attic Muse. Xenophon, the historian, was so named. He was a native of Athens, and his style was a model of elegance.

Attic Salt. Elegant and delicate wit. Salt, among the Greeks and Romans, signified wit or sparkling thought cleverly expressed. *Scipio omnes sale superabat* (Scipio surpassed all in wit). The Athenians were noted for their wit; hence Attic salt means wit delicately expressed, as by those of Athens, the capital of Attica.

Atticus. *See* the prefixes CHRISTIAN, ENGLISH, IRISH, etc.

Atticus. (Pseud.) (1) William Maccall, English author (b. 1812). (2) One of the pseudonyms commonly attributed to Junius (*q. v.*).

Attila of the Piano. Thalberg was so named.

Attingians. Heretics of the eighth century, who solemnized baptism with the words, " I am the living water."

Attorney-General to the Lantern. A title adopted by Camille Desmoulins (fl. 1762–1794), one of the earliest promoters of the French Revolution and of the excesses which culminated in the hanging of inoffensive persons to the lamp-ropes which crossed the streets of Paris.

Atty. Attorney.

Atty.-Gen. Attorney-General.

A. U. A. American Unitarian Association.

Au bout de son Latin. (Fr.) " At the end of his Latin." Having exhausted his knowledge.

Aub. Theol. Sem. Auburn Theological Seminary.

A. U. C. *Anno urbis conditæ*, or *Ab urbe condita*. In the year from the building of the city (Rome).

Au contraire. (Fr.) On the contrary.

Au courant. A French phrase which means " well acquainted with." In English composition it is used in such sentences as, " He kept himself *au courant* of all that was passing around him."

Auctor pretiosa facit. (Lat.) The giver makes the gift more precious.

Audaces fortuna juvat. (Lat.) Fortune favors the bold.

Au désespoir. (Fr.) In a state of despondency.

Audhumla ("the nourishing power"). In Scandinavian mythology the cow created by Surt to nourish Ymir. " She supplied him with four rivers of milk, and was herself sustained by licking the rocks."

Audi alteram partem. (Lat.) "Hear the other side." Hear both sides, and then judge.

Au fait. (Fr.) Acquainted with; having a thorough knowledge of.

Au fond. (Fr.) To the bottom, or main point.

Aug. August.

Augean Stables. A phrase borrowed from antiquity, and signifying an accumulation of corruption almost beyond the power of man to remove. Augeas, king of Elis, kept a herd of three thousand oxen in his stables, which had not been cleansed in thirty years. Hercules performed the task of renovating these in one day by turning into them the rivers Alpheus and Peneius. *See* TWELVE LABORS OF HERCULES.

Augeas. In classical mythology king of Elis, and one of the Argonauts. The cleansing of the filthy stables of this king formed the fifth of the twelve labors of Hercules (*q. v.*). *See* AUGEAN STABLES.

Augur. (Pseud.) (1) Another of the pseudonyms attributed to Junius (*q. v.*). (2) Henry Mort Feist, a sporting writer and racing "prophet" in the London "Life."

Augusta Dargon. The stage-name of Mrs. Dr. Piercy.

Augusta J. Evans. (Pseud.) Mrs. Augusta J. Evans Wilson, author of "Beulah."

Augusta Raymond. The stage-name of Mrs. Edward E. Kidder.

Augustan Age. The best, most prolific period. The term "Augustan" is from Augustus, emperor of Rome in the palmy days of Latin literature.

Augustan Age of England. The Elizabethan period. That of Anne is called the "Silver Age."

Augustan Age of France. That of Louis XIV. (1610–1740).

Augustan Age of Germany. The nineteenth century.

Augustan Age of Portugal. The reign of Don Alphonso Henrique. In this reign Brazil was occupied; the African coast explored; the sea-route to India was traversed; and Camoens flourished.

Augustinians. Divines who maintained, on the authority of Saint Augustine, that grace is effectual absolutely, quite independent of the person who receives it.

Augustus. A surname conferred on (1) Philip II. of France (fl. 1165–1223), because he was born in the month of August; (2) Sigismund II. of Poland (fl. 1520–1572).

Augustus Dunshunner. (Pseud.) William E. Aytoun, British critic and poet (1813–1865).

Au jour le jour. (Fr.) Day by day; day in, day out.

Auld Ane, or **Old Clootie,** or **Auld Hangie.** Colloquial names among the Scotch for the devil. *See* AULD HORNIE.

Auld Brig and **New Brig,** of Robert Burns, refer to the bridges over the river Ayr in Scotland.

Auld Hornie. The heathen deities were degraded by the Christian Church into fallen angels; and Pan, with his horns, crooked nose, goat's beard, pointed ears, and goat's feet, was transformed to his Satanic majesty, and called Old (Scotch, "Auld") Hornie.

Auld Reekie. The city of Edinburgh; so named on account either of (1) its filthy and ill-smelling thoroughfares, or (2) the canopy of cloud or smoke that seems to overhang the city when viewed from a distance.

Au naturel. (Fr.) To the life; in its natural state; simply cooked.

Aunt, Aunty, Uncle. The peculiar American use of these personal terms is really of Old England origin, though now obsolete in the mother-country. In 1793 some one gave a list of local expressions as belonging to Cornwall, and in regard to "aunt" writes: "It is common in Cornwall to call an elderly person 'aunt' or 'uncle' prefixed to their names. The same custom is said to prevail in the island of Nantucket, in North America." "Aunt" and "uncle" as familiar terms, it may be remembered, are as common among colored people as in Cornwall.

Aunt Abby. (Pseud.) Abby Skinner, an American author.

Aunt Adna. (Pseud.) Mrs. J. M. Dana, American author of juvenile tales.

Aunt Carrie. (Pseud.) Mrs. Caroline L. Smith, an American writer.

Aunt Carry. (Pseud.) Mrs. C. E. S. Norton, author of sundry poems for children, 1847.

Aunt Charity. (Pseud.) Mrs. Sarah C. [Smith] Yeiser, a well-known Southern writer. *See* AZELÉE.

Aunt Effie. (Pseud.) Mrs. Harkshaw.

Aunt Fanny. (Pseud.) Mrs. F. D. B. Gage, a charming writer for children.

Aunt Friendly. (Pseud.) Mrs. Sarah S. Tuthill Baker.

Aunt Hattie. (Pseud.) Mrs. H.W.W. Baker.

Aunt Kitty. (Pseud.) Maria J. MacIntosh, an American writer (b. 1803).

Aunt Lucy. (Pseud.) Mrs. L. E. B. Bather.

Aunt Maggie. (Pseud.) Mrs. Raymond Blaythwait.

Aunt Maguire. (Pseud.) Mrs. Frances Miriam Berry, in " Godey's Lady's Book."

Aunt Margaret. (Pseud.) Miss Margaret Buchan, in " St. Nicholas."

Aunt Mary. (Pseud.) Miss Mary A. Lathbury, American author and artist.

Aunt Sophronia. (Pseud.) Mrs. Julia McNair Wright, author of temperance literature for the young.

Au pied de la lettre. (Fr.) Literally.

Au pis aller. (Fr.) At the worst.

Aur. *Aurum.* (Lat.) Gold.

Aura popularis. (Lat.) The gale of popular favor.

Aurea mediocritas. (Lat.) The golden mean, or middle way.

Au reste. (Fr.) " To the remainder." In addition to this ; besides.

Au revoir. (Fr.) Good-by ; farewell.

Au rez-de-chaussée. (Fr.) On the ground-floor.

Auri sacra fames. (Lat.) The accursed thirst for gold.

Aurora. Early morning. According to Grecian mythology the goddess Aurora, called by Homer " rosy-fingered," sets out before the sun, and is the pioneer of his rising.

Aurora's Tears. The morning dew. These tears are shed for the death of her son Memnon, who was slain by Achilles at the siege of Troy.

Aus. Austria ; Austrian.

Ausonia. The ancient classic name for Italy, derived from Auson, son of Ulysses, and father of the Ausones.

> Romantic Spain,
> Gay-lilied fields of France, or, more refined,
> The soft Ausonia's monumental reign.
> CAMPBELL, *Gertrude of Wyoming.*

Auster. A wind pernicious to flowers and health. In Italy one of the south winds was so called ; its modern name is the " Sirocco."

Austin Stannus. (Pseud.) Clotilda Greaves, an American writer for the stage.

Austrian Hyena. An epithet given to Julius Jakob von Haynau (fl. 1786–1853), an Austrian general, execrated for his cruelty to the political prisoners who were unfortunately committed to his charge during the risings under Kossuth and Gorgei.

Austrian Lip. The thick under-lip characteristic of the members of the house of Hapsburg, said to have been derived from Cymburgis, niece of a former king of Poland.

Austrian Succession. Charles VI. died Oct. 20, 1740. His daughter, Maria Theresa, succeeded him. The succession was, however, disputed by Charles Albert, Elector of Bavaria, and August III. of Poland and Saxony. Spain claimed a part of the Austrian dominions, and Frederick the Great demanded the cession of Silesia, his invasions of which began what is known to history as the " War of the Austrian Succession."

Aut Cæsar aut nullus. (Lat.) Either Cæsar or nobody.

Authentic Doctor. Gregory of Rimini (d. 1357).

Author of " The Task." Cowper (fl. 1731–1800) is so named from the title of his principal poem.

Auth. Ver., or **A. V.** Authorized Version (of the Bible).

Auto da Fé. (Port., literally " an act of faith ; " from the Latin *actus,* act, and *fides,* faith.) A day set apart by the Inquisition for examining heretics, who, if not acquitted, were burned. The Inquisitors burned their victims, being forbidden to shed blood ; the Roman Church holding *Ecclesia non novit sanguinem* (The Church is untainted with blood).

Autolycus. In classic mythology one of the Argonauts. He was a very daring and successful robber, and possessed the power to metamorphose both his plunder and himself.

Automedon. Another name for a coachman. He was charioteer to Achilles.

Au troisième. (Fr.) On the third floor.

Aut vincere aut mori. (Lat.) Either to conquer or die.

Aux armes. (Fr.) To arms.

Auxilium ab alto. (Lat.) Help from on high.

Av. Average ; avenue.

Avant-coureur. (Fr.) A forerunner ; one sent before to announce the approach of another.

Avant-garde. (Fr.) The vanguard.

Avant-propos. (Fr.) The preliminary matter ; the preface.

Avatar. The incarnation of deity in Hindu mythology, or the appearance of a god in a visible form. It properly means "out of the boat," and the allusion is to the wide-spread tradition of Noah coming out of the ark.

Avdp., or **Avoir.** Avoirdupois.

Avec nantissement. (Fr.) With security.

Avec permission. (Fr.) With permission.

Ave Maria. A Roman Catholic form of prayer to the Virgin Mary. The name is derived from the first two words in Latin, which signify "Hail, Mary!" The word *Ave* is of two syllables, and is pronounced "A-ve."

Avenger of Blood. The man who had the birthright, according to the Jewish polity, of taking vengeance on him who had killed one of his relatives.

> The Christless code,
> That must have life for a blow.
> TENNYSON, *Maud.*

A verbis ad verbera. (Lat.) From words to blows.

Avernus. (Gr., "without birds.") A lake in Campania, so called from the belief that its sulphurous and mephitic vapors killed any bird that happened to inhale them. Poets call it the entrance to the infernal regions.

Avertin, Saint. The patron saint of the insane. From this comes the French cant-word *avertineux*, lunatics.

Avesta. The sacred scriptures of the Magians, composed by Zoroaster.

A vinculo matrimonii. (Lat.) From the bonds of matrimony.

A volonté. (Fr.) "At will." At pleasure.

A votre santé. (Fr.) To your health.

Axe. An Americanism. The dismissal of Government employees is figuratively spoken of as being guillotined, or beheaded. *See* BLUE ENVELOPE.

Axenus. *See* INHOSPITABLE SEA.

A. Y. M. Ancient York Masons.

Ayrshire Poet. Robert Burns, who was born near the town of Ayr.

Azamat Batuk. (Pseud.) Napoleon L. Thieblin, a miscellaneous writer and correspondent (d. 1888). *See* RIGOLO.

Azazel. The scapegoat. So called by the Jews because the high-priest cast lots on two goats. One lot was for the Lord, and the other lot for Azazel, or Satan; and the goat on which the latter lot fell was the scapegoat.

Azaziel. In Lord Byron's "Heaven and Earth," a seraph who fell in love with Anah, a granddaughter of Cain. When the Flood came, he carried her under his wing to some other planet.

Azazil. In Paradise Lost, Azazil is the standard-bearer of the infernal host. According to the Koran, when God commanded the angels to worship Adam, Azazil replied, "Why should the son of fire fall down before a son of clay?" and God cast him out of heaven. His name was then changed to Eblis, which means "despair."

Azelée. (Pseud.) Mrs. Sarah C. [Smith] Yeiser in her contributions to the New Orleans "Crescent."

Azor's Mirror. Zemira is the name of the lady, and Azor that of the bear, in Marmontel's tale of "Beauty and the Beast." Zemira entreats the kind monster to let her see her father, if only for a few moments; so, drawing aside a curtain, he shows him to her in a magic mirror. This mirror was a sort of telescope, which rendered objects otherwise too far off distinctly visible.

Azrael. In Hebrew and Mohammedan mythology the angel who watches by the dying and separates the soul from the body.

B.

B. Born; Boron.

B. A. Bachelor of Arts.

Ba. Barium.

Baal. A name applied by the Hebrews to the gods of the heathen nations by whom they were surrounded, but used with more particular reference to the chief male deity of the Phœnicians, the sun-god.

Baalbec of Ireland. Kilmallock, in Limerick, noted for its ruins.

Bab, Lady. A waiting-maid on a lady so called, who assumes the airs with the name and address of her mistress. Her fellow-servants and other servants address her as "Lady Bab," or "Your ladyship."

Babylon. *See* MODERN BABYLON and MYSTICAL BABYLON.

Babble Brook. (Pseud.) John H. McNaughton, of Caledonia, N.Y., author of the famous poem "Belle Mahone."

Babbler. (Pseud.) (1) Alfred Trumble, in his articles in the New York "Sunday News." (2) Hugh Kelley, in the "Weekly Chronicle," etc.

Babes of the Wood. Bands of outlaws who infested the hills of County Wicklow, Ireland, at the end of the eighteenth century, and who were charged with acts of great iniquity.

Babeuf's Conspiracy. "Gracchus" Babeuf was editor of the "Tribune du Peuple" in Paris. In 1796 he plotted against the Directory with a view to obtaining a division of property. He was condemned to death, and killed himself May 27, 1797.

Babington's Conspiracy. A plot to assassinate Queen Elizabeth and make Mary Queen of Scots queen in her stead. It was approved by a number of the Catholic gentry of the realm, among whom was Babington, who believed that Mary out of gratitude would marry him, should the scheme prove successful. But the plot was discovered, and fourteen of the conspirators were executed Sept. 20, 21, 1586.

Baboon. Arbuthnot, in his "History of John Bull," satirized Louis XIV. of France under the name "Lewis Baboon," and Philip, Duke of Anjou, grandson of that monarch, under the name "Philip Baboon."

Baby Charles. A nickname conferred by James I. on his son Charles, afterward Charles I.

Bacchanalia. Festivals in honor of Bacchus, characterized by their licentiousness and debauchery. Plato says he has seen the whole population of Athens drunk at these festivals.

Bacchant. A person given to habits of drinking, — so called from the "bacchants," or men admitted to the feasts of Bacchus.

Bacchante. A female winebibber, — so called from the "Bacchantes," or priestesses of Bacchus.

Bacchus. In classic mythology the god of wine, son of Jupiter and Semele; usually described as a beautiful but delicate youth.

Bachelor Bluff. (Pseud.) Oliver Bell Bunce, an American author.

Bachelor President. James Buchanan was the only unmarried President of the United States, and was consequently called as above. President Cleveland was at the time of his inauguration unmarried; but he married during his term of office, June 2, 1886.

Backbone of the Continent. The Cordilleras, forming the Andes in South America, and the Rocky Mountains in North America.

Back-stair Influence. Intriguing or manœuvring. The palaces or mansions of the great were usually built with a staircase for those state visitors who came publicly, and with another for persons desiring to see the great man privately. Hence it was often desirable to be in favor with the guardians of the back stairs, who could admit or exclude at pleasure.

Backwoodsman. (Pseud.) Thomas D'Arcy McGee, Canadian author and statesman.

Bacon of Theology. Bishop Butler (fl. 1692–1752), author of the "Analogy."

Bacon's Rebellion. Nathaniel Bacon, "The Virginia Rebel," in 1676, raised a force to chastise the Indians, for which Governor Berkeley proclaimed him a rebel, and sent a force against him. He was captured, tried, acquitted, and restored to all his honors and rights.

Bactrian Sage. Zoroaster, the founder of the Magian religion. He was a native of Bactria, the modern Balkh.

Bad, The. Charles II. of Navarre (fl. 1332–1387).

Baddeley Cake. The annual cutting of the Baddeley Cake forms a curious custom at Drury Lane Theatre, London, on Twelfth Night, January 6. William Baddeley, the last actor to wear the uniform of "His Majesty's servants," left £100 in bank stock, the income from which was to purchase a Twelfth Cake, with wine and punch, which the ladies and gentlemen of the company were requested "to partake of every Twelfth Night in the great green-room."

Baden-Baden, The American. *See* AMERICAN BADEN-BADEN.

Badge-men. Paupers or inhabitants of almshouses, because they frequently wore a badge or an emblem of some sort. *See* BLUE-GOWNS.

Badger. This word, applied to a trader, is common in old plays and books. In the "State Papers, Domestic Series," 1547–1580, is the following: "Dec. 17, 1565. Note of certain persons upon Humber side, who buy up great quantities of corn, two of whom are authorized *badgers*." By 5 Eliz. c. 12, badgers are to be licensed annually under penalty of £5. The word means "corn-dealer."

Badger State. Wisconsin, — a representation of which animal appears on its coat-of-arms.

Badinage. (Fr.) Light or playful talk.

Badinguet. A nickname given to Napoleon III. It was the name of the man whom he shot in the Boulogne affair, and was conferred by his enemies in memory of that event.

Bad Lands. "In the arid region of the western portion of the United States there are certain tracts of country which have received the name of *mauvaises terres*, or bad lands. These are dreary wastes, naked hills with rounded or conical forms, composed of sand, sandy clays, and fine fragments of shaly rocks, with steep slopes, and, yielding to the pressure of the foot, they are climbed only by the greatest toil, and it is a labor of no inconsiderable magnitude to penetrate or cross such a district of country." — POWELL, *Exploration of the Colorado of the West.*

Bad Old Man. Gen. Jubal Early was thus nicknamed by the Confederate soldiery under his command.

Bætica, or Bætic Vale. Granada and Andalusia, or Spain in general. So called from the river Bætis, or Guadalquivir.

> While o'er the Bætic vale,
> Or through the towers of Memphis [Egypt], or the palms
> By sacred Ganges watered, I conduct
> The English merchant.
> AKENSIDE, *Hymn to the Naiads.*

Bagatelle. (Fr.) A trifle.

Baggage-car, or **Luggage-van.** These are the synonymous terms in vogue respectively on American and English railroads. Similarly what we call "baggage" the English term "luggage." *See* FREIGHT.

Bagman. A commercial traveller, who carries a bag with specimens to show to those whose custom he solicits. In former times commercial travellers used to ride a horse with saddle-bags sometimes so large as almost to conceal the rider.

Bairam. The name given to two movable Moslem feasts. The first, which begins on the first day of Lent and lasts three days, is a kind of Paschal feast. The second occurs seventy days later, and is not unlike the Jewish Feast of Tabernacles.

Baker Poet. Jean Reboul, French versifier, who published a volume of *Poésies* in 1836.

Baker's Boy of Anduze. Jean Cavalier (1679–1740), a brilliant and successful French Protestant leader in the religious wars of the seventeenth century.

Baker's Dozen. Strictly, thirteen for twelve; but often used colloquially to denote good measure, running over. The phrase arose out of the custom of English bakers, when a penalty was inflicted for short weight, giving an extra loaf, so as to be on the safe side. The thirteenth loaf was named the "vantage loaf."

Baker's Light Bobs. The Tenth Dragoon Guards in the English army are thus nicknamed after their former colonel, Baker Pasha.

Bal. Balance.

Bal abonné. (Fr.) A subscription ball.

Balak, in the second part of "Absalom and Achitophel," a satire by Dryden and Tate, is meant for Dr. Burnet, author of "Burnet's Own Time."

Balance of Power. An ideal condition of affairs aimed at by the statesmen of Europe, whereby no one nation attains such preponderance of strength as to endanger the existence of the others.

Balance of Trade. The money-value difference between the exports and imports of a nation.

Baland of Spain. A man of herculean strength, who called himself Fierabras.

Bal champêtre. (Fr.) A ball held in the open air, or out of doors.

Bald, The. Charles I. of France, son of Louis le Débonnaire (fl. 823–877).

Bald Eagle of Westchester. James William Husted, a legislator of the State of New York (b. 1833), and a power in the politics of the Empire State.

Baldur. In Scandinavian mythology the second son of Odin and Frigga, the god of the summer sun. His untimely death typifies the disappearance of the sun below the horizon during the winter months.

Baldwin, in Tasso's "Jerusalem Delivered," is the restless and ambitious duke of Bologna, leader of twelve hundred horse in the allied Christian army. He was Godfrey's brother.

Baldy Smith. The army sobriquet of Gen. William Farrar Smith (b. 1824), who performed gallant service in the Army of the Cumberland.

Balham Mystery, or **Bravo Case.** On April 18, 1876, Mr. Charles D. T. Bravo, an English barrister, died under suspicious circumstances at Balham, in Surrey. Suicide was at first suspected, but later developments pointed to poisoning. Verdict rendered, "Wilful murder by administration of tartar emetic;" but the guilty parties were never discovered.

Balios. One of the horses given by Neptune to Peleus on his wedding-day. It afterward belonged to Achilles.

Balitsama. The realm of Bali, the Indian Pluto.

Ballet. (Fr.) A theatrical representation of a story or fable by means of dancing and music. In England the *ballet* is the closing piece of an evening's performance.

Balloon Tytler. James Tytler, a Scottish scholar, who emigrated to America in 1796; he gained his sobriquet because he was the first in Scotland to ascend in a fire-balloon on the Mongolfian principle. He died in Salem, Mass., 1805.

Balmung. The sword of Siegfried, forged by Wieland, the Vulcan of the Scandinavians. Wieland, in a trial of merit, clove Amilias, a brother smith, through steel helmet and armor down to the waist; but the cut was so fine that Amilias was not even aware that he was wounded till he attempted to move, when he fell into two pieces.

Balt., Balto. Baltimore.

Baltic Question. A controversy of long standing between the Baltic Provinces and the Russian Government concerning the rights and privileges confirmed to their inhabitants by Alexander II., February, 1856.

Bambocciades. Grotesque scenes in low life, such as country wakes, penny weddings, and so on. They are so called from the Italian word *bamboccio* (a cripple), the nickname given to Pieter van Laer, the first Dutch painter of such scenes, distinguished in Rome.

Bamboozle. (Ital. *bamboccio*, an old dotard, or a babyish gull.) To cheat by cunning, or daze with tricks. It is a gypsy word, meaning to dress a man in bamboos to teach him swimming. Like the bladders used for the same purpose by little wanton boys, the apparatus is dangerous and deceitful.

Bampton Lectures. These lectures are named in honor of their founder, the Rev. John Bampton, canon of Salisbury, who left estates originally worth £120 (= $600) per annum to the University of Oxford for the endowment of eight divinity lectures to be delivered at Great St. Mary's yearly, and to be published at the expense of the estate within two months of their being preached. "The preacher is to lecture on one of the following subjects: The Confirmation of the Christian Faith, and the Confutation of all Heretics and Schismatics; The Divine Authority of the Scriptures; The Authority of the Primitive Fathers in Matters of Christian Faith and Practice; The Divinity of Christ; The Divinity of the Holy Ghost; The Apostles' and Nicene Creeds. No person is qualified to preach these lectures who has not taken the degree of M.A. either at Oxford or

Cambridge, and the same person shall never preach them twice." The first course was delivered in 1780.

Banbury Cakes are of great antiquity. In "A Treatise of Melancholy, by T. Bright, Doctor of Physic, 1586," is the following paragraph : "Sodden wheate is a grosse and melancholicke nourishmente, and bread, especiallie of the fine flower unleavened : of this sorte are bagge puddings, or panne puddings made with flower, frittars, pancakes, such as we calle *Banberrie Cakes*, and those greate ones confected with butere, egges, etc., used at weddings ; and howsoever it be prepared, rye and bread made thereof carrieth with itte plentie of melancholie."

Bandanna. *See* RED BANDANNA.

Banded Peak. Another name for Mount Hesperus, a peak of the San Juan Mountains in Southern Colorado. It is composed mainly of volcanic rocks, trachyte, and shale, and at a distance its sides appear banded, or streaked.

Bande Noire. A name conferred on the capitalists who bought up the church property during the French Revolution. The term means "Black Band." They pulled down many shrines and destroyed many sacred relics.

Bangorian Controversy. This famous theological dispute was occasioned by Dr. Benjamin Hoadly, bishop of Bangor, preaching a sermon before George I., March 31, 1717, upon the text, "My kingdom is not of this world" (John xviii. 36), in which he demonstrated the spiritual nature of Christ's kingdom. He drew upon himself the general indignation of the clergy, who published hundreds of pamphlets in refutation.

Banian Days. Days when no meat is served to a ship's crew. The term is derived from the Banians, a class of Hindu merchants who carried on a most extensive trade with the interior of Asia, but being a caste of the Vaisya, abstained from the use of meat.

Banker Poet. Samuel Rogers, author of "The Pleasures of Memory." *See* BARD OF MEMORY.

Bankers' Case, or **Case of the Bankers.** The petition of Hornblee and others to the Barons of the Exchequer, in 1691 (14 How. St. Tr. 1), for the payment of certain annuities granted by Charles II. to repay money originally loaned to him on the security

of the revenues. On appeal, the House of Lords decided that the grant was binding upon his successor, and continued a charge upon the revenue.

Bank Holidays. England and Ireland : Easter Monday, Monday in Whitsun week, first Monday in August, and December 26 (if a week-day). Scotland : New Year's Day, Christmas Day (if either falls on Sunday, the following Monday to be a bank holiday), Good Friday, and first Monday in May and August. United States : Christmas and New Year's Day, February 22, May 30, July 4, and all other legal holidays of the States in which banks do business. *See* SAINT LUBBOCK.

Banks's Horse. A learned horse, called Marocco, belonging to one Banks, in the reign of Queen Elizabeth. It is said that one of his exploits was the ascent of St. Paul's steeple, London.

Bannatyne Club. A literary club which took its name from George Bannatyne, to whose industry we owe the preservation of very much of the early Scotch poetry. It was instituted in 1823 by Sir Walter Scott, and had for its object the publication of rare works illustrative of Scotch history, poetry, and general literature. The club was dissolved in 1859.

Banshee. In Irish folk-lore a species of female evil genius called "the wife of the fairies," who is believed to herald an approaching death by uttering unearthly shrieks and wailings.

Baptiste. "Jean Baptiste" is a collective nickname for French Canadians, on account of its commonness among them as a Christian name.

Bar. Barometer ; Baruch.

Barataria. Sancho Panza's island-city, over which he was appointed governor. His table was presided over by Dr. Pedro Rezio de Augero, who caused every dish set upon the board to be removed without being tasted, — some because they heated the blood, and others because they chilled it ; some for one ill effect, and some for another ; so that Sancho was allowed to eat nothing. The word is from *barato*, cheap.

The meat was put on the table and whisked away like Sancho's inauguration feast at Barataria. — THACKERAY.

Barbadoes Leg. A disease characterized by hypertrophy of the skin and of the subcutaneous areolar tissue, which seems to be identical with the *elephan-*

tiasis of the Arabs. Notwithstanding its name, it may affect the arm, female breast, etc. It begins with acute febrile symptoms, and inflammation of the superficial lymphatic vessels. The part swells, and becomes uneasy from tension, the glands being especially large and hard. The skin varies in appearance, being sometimes white and shining, and in other cases of a dark color, and studded with projecting veins. The swelling is sometimes very great and quite hard. In some parts of the body, skin which would naturally weigh less than a couple of ounces is thus converted into a tumor weighing from one hundred to one hundred and fifty pounds. The disease is endemic in the tropics ; and in the cases which we see in this country, it always appears that the disease commenced in a hot country.

Barbançons. Troops of adventurers and free-lances in the twelfth century, who made war a trade, and lent themselves for money to any one who would pay them. So called from Brabant, whence many of them came. *See* VARANGIANS.

Barbarossa. *See* RED BEARD.

Barbary Pirates. "The countries on the Mediterranean coast of Africa from Egypt to the Atlantic, namely, Morocco, Algeria, Tunis, and Tripoli (which are known collectively as the Barbary Powers), had been in the habit of preying on the commerce of nations that refused to pay a tribute to them. Shortly after the Revolution these pirates directed their operations against American commerce, to protect which, treaties were negotiated with the Barbary States, — in 1786–87 with Morocco, in 1795 with Algiers, in 1796 with Tripoli, and in 1799 with Tunis. By these treaties the United States purchased immunity for its commerce by gross sums or yearly tributes. This shameful course was made necessary by our lack of an effective navy. But the Government was now forced to organize a small navy, which was found useful against Tripoli. That country, becoming dissatisfied with the tribute, declared war in 1801. In 1803 some half a dozen American vessels were despatched to the Mediterranean. In October the frigate 'Philadelphia' ran aground in the harbor of Tripoli and was captured. Decatur in the following February sailed into the harbor at night, boarded the 'Philadelphia' under the guns of the enemy, killed or forced overboard every one of her defenders, set fire to the vessel, and escaped without losing a man and with only four wounded. A land expedition conducted by General Eaton, the American consul at Tunis, terminated the war and forced Tripoli to make peace in June, 1805. In 1812 Algiers declared war against the United States. As soon as the war then commencing against England had been brought to an end, our Government turned its attention to Algiers. In the spring of 1815 Commodore Decatur was sent with nine or ten vessels to chastise the pirates. In June he captured the largest of their frigates, and soon after took another vessel. He then dictated a treaty to the Dey of Algiers, which was signed June 30, 1815, relinquishing all claims to tribute in the future. Tunis and Tripoli were next forced to pay an indemnity for permitting British men-of-war to seize American vessels in their ports during the War of 1812. Thenceforth there was no more tribute paid to the Barbary States, and their depredations on American commerce ceased. The troubles with these countries had forced the formation of a navy on the country, despite the wishes of the Republicans, and thus prepared the United States for the war with England. They also led to a slight increase in customs duties in 1804 and following years for the purpose of forming the Mediterranean Fund, as it was called, to protect American commerce." — BROWN AND STRAUSS.

Barbecue. (Span., *barbacóa*.) A term used in the Southern States and in the West Indies for dressing a hog whole, which, being split to the backbone and laid flat upon a large gridiron, is roasted over a charcoal fire. A writer in the "Westminster Review" supposes the word to be a corruption of the French word *barbe à queue*, i. e., from snout to tail. In former times, especially in the presidential campaign of 1840, immense open-air meetings were held for political discussion and speech-making, at which roasting an ox whole and other rude diversions were indulged in.

Barber Poet. Jacques Jasmin (1798–1864), the "last of the troubadours." He was a barber of Gascony.

Barber, The. A severe storm, accompanied by intense cold, peculiar to the Gulf of St. Lawrence. Sometimes with a high wind the air becomes much colder than the open water. The latter, being relatively hot, begins to smoke, and the vapor freezes into peculiarly sharp spicules. The *poudre* snow-crystals of the Northwest are usually small, dry, and six-sided, and though penetrating as sand, they are soft, and when driven by a gale, nearly cut the skin of the face ; hence the name "barber" is applied to this phenomenon. The name is also applied to a phase of cold along the coasts of Nova Scotia and New England. When a vessel is caught by a gale of wind in a cold Arctic current, the spray freezes the moment it touches the deck or rigging. Every block is turned into a lump of ice, men become coated with it like an icicle, and sometimes such a weight of ice forms on the bow that the stern is lifted out of the water, and the ship becomes unmanageable for want of steering power.

Barber's Pole. Anciently barbers performed minor operations in surgery, and in particular when bleeding was customary, it was to the barber that the patients applied to be bled. " To assist this operation, it being necessary for the patient to grasp a staff, a stick or pole was always kept by the barber-surgeon, together with the fillet or bandaging he used for tying the patient's arm. When the pole was not in use, the tape was tied to it, so that they might be both together when wanted, and in this state pole and tape were hung at the door as a sign. At length, instead of hanging out the identical pole used in the operation, a pole was painted with stripes round it in imitation of the real pole and bandage, and thus came the sign." Lord Thurlow, in a speech in the House of Lords, July 17, 1797, said that "by a statute still in force barbers and surgeons were each to use a pole [as a sign]. The barbers were to have theirs blue and white, striped, with no other appendage ; but the surgeons' — which was the same in other respects — was likewise to have a galley-pot and a red rag, to denote the particular nature of their vocation." The last barber-surgeon in London was a man named Middleditch, of Great Suffolk Street, in the Borough. He died there in 1821. Mr. Timbs, in his "Autobiography," says, " I have a vivid recollection of his dentistry."

Barcarolle. (Ital.) A song sung by the gondoliers of Venice.

Bardesanists. Followers of Bardesanes, of Mesopotamia, who denied the resurrection, incarnation, etc., of our Lord (about 175 A. D.).

Bard of all Time. William Shakspeare. *See* BARD OF AVON.

Bard of Arthurian Romance. Alfred Tennyson, the poet-laureate of England.

Bard of Avon. William Shakspeare, who was born and buried at Stratford-on-Avon.

Bard of Ayrshire. Robert Burns, who was a native of Ayrshire.

Bard of Hope. Thomas Campbell (1777–1844), author of "The Pleasures of Hope."

Bard of Memory. Samuel Rogers, author of " The Pleasures of Memory." *See* BANKER POET.

Bard of Olney. Cowper, who resided at Olney, in Bucks, for many years.

Bard of Prose. Boccaccio.

Bard of Rydal Mount. William Wordsworth, whose home was Rydal Mount, in the English Lake Country. *See* POET OF THE EXCURSION.

Bard of the Imagination. Mark Akenside, author of " The Pleasures of the Imagination."

Bard of Twickenham. Alexander Pope, who resided at Twickenham, on the banks of the Thames.

Bards of Epworth. (Pseud.) Samuel Wesley, Sr., Samuel Wesley, Jr., Charles Wesley, and Maria Wesley. There was published in London in 1856 a work entitled " Gems from the Wesley Cabinet," by the Bards of Epworth.

Barebone's Parliament. The " Little Parliament," summoned by Oliver Cromwell, which met July 4, 1653, was so called from Praise-God Barebone, a leather-merchant, and one of its members. It consisted of about one hundred and forty men of good position and of well-approved life and religion, but most of them of very destructive social principles. They proceeded to abolish the Court of Chancery, and were also about to abolish tithes, to the alarm of Cromwell himself and the more moderate men, when the Parliament dissolved itself, December 12 of the same year.

Barguest. A fairy hobgoblin, armed with teeth and claws, and much dreaded by the superstitious in the North of England.

Barker. A vociferous touter employed at the entrance to a cheap theatre, a dime museum, or a mock auction, to apprise passers-by of the entertainment or proceedings going on within.

Barking up the Wrong Tree. *See* TREE.

Bark of Peter The Roman Catholic Church has been so named, in allusion to the claim of its priesthood that the Apostle Peter was its founder.

Bark-peelers. Woodsmen of Sullivan County, N. Y., who strip hemlock bark for tanning.

Bar'l. A slangy abbreviation for the word "barrel," used in politics to denote that which the "barrel" is supposed to contain; namely, money. Any rich politician who opens his coffers for the benefit of his party is said to "tap his bar'l."

Barlamm and Josaphat. One of the most widely current religious romances of the Middle Ages, "relating to the conversion of the Indian prince Josaphat by the hermit Barlamm, and thereby illustrating the power of Christianity to overcome temptation, and proving its superiority over all other creeds. The story has been discovered to be a Christianized version of the legendary history of Buddha, agreeing with it in all essentials and many details."

Barmecide, Barmecide's Feast. The word "Barmecide" is used to express the uncertainty of things on which we set our heart. As the beggar looked forward to a feast, but found only empty dishes, so many a joy is found to be mere illusion when we come to partake of it. The story of Barmecide's Feast is told as follows in the "Arabian Nights": "A prince of the illustrious family of the name, which flourished at Bagdad contemporaneously with the Caliph Haroun-Al-Raschid, ordered rich viands for a famished beggar named Shacabac, and, before they could be brought, called upon him to help himself to the different dishes, naming them one after another. The beggar humored the joke, pretending to eat, and praising the entertainment, and even protesting that he could eat no more. In the end, the eccentric host, pleased with the patient complaisance of his guest, ordered a real and sumptuous entertainment for him, in place of that of which he had previously partaken only in imagination."

It is, to be sure, something like the feast which the Barmecide served up to Alnaschar

[Shacabac] ; and we cannot expect to get fat upon such diet. — SIR W. SCOTT.

The Barmecide's dinner to Shacabac was only one degree removed from these solemn banquets. — THACKERAY.

Barnabas Day. June 11. Saint Barnabas was a fellow-laborer of Saint Paul.

Barnabites. An order of monks so called because the church of Saint Barnabas in Milan was given to them to preach in. They are also called "Canons of Saint Paul," because the original society made a point of reading Saint Paul's Epistles.

Barnacle. (Pseud.) A. C. Barnes, American *littérateur*.

Barnacles. (1) Chronic office-holders. Dickens has held the Barnacle family up to everlasting ridicule. (2) This word is often used by old people to signify "spectacles." It may have been formerly the common name for them. (3) The word "barnacles" is used by farriers as the name of an instrument by which they hold a horse by the nose. As spectacles are supported by the nose, there is some analogy.

Barnburners. (1) Lawless individuals who secretly set fire to the barns of the great landed proprietors in the State of New York in the first half of the nineteenth century. (2) A nickname formerly given to the more radical and progressive section of the Democratic party in the United States, who aimed at removing the abuses connected with banks and corporations, — in allusion to the story of an old Dutchman who relieved himself of rats by burning his barns, which they infested.

Barney Maglone. (Pseud.) Robert A. Wilson, in the Boston "Republic."

Barney Williams. The stage-name of Barney O'Flaherty.

Barnwell. (Pseud.) Robert Barnwell Roosevelt in his "Game Fish of North America," 1862.

Barons' War. *See* WAR OF THE BARONS.

Barrel Mirabeau. (Fr., *Mirabeau-Tonneau.*) A nickname given to Boniface Riquetti, Viscount Mirabeau (1754–1792), brother to the great tribune, on account of his girth and the amount of liquor he could consume.

Barrel-of-Butter Island. A fanciful name given to a skerry or islet off the south coast of Pomona, one of the Orkneys. The tenant pays the proprietor a barrel of butter annually for the privilege of killing the seals on it.

Barrels Blues. The English Fourth Regiment of the Line is so nicknamed.

Barrens. Wild land bearing neither timber nor grass.

Barrier Treaty. That by which the Low Countries were ceded to the Emperor Charles VI. It was signed by the English, Imperial, and Dutch governments, Nov. 5, 1715.

Barry Cornwall. (Pseud.) Bryan Waller Procter, English poet (1787–1874).

Barry Gray. (Pseud.) Robert S. Coffin, American printer and poet (1797–1857).

Bart., or Bt. Baronet.

Bartender, Barmaid. Whereas in England attendants at bars and refreshment counters are women, termed "barmaids," in the United States the same place is invariably filled by a man, who is called a "bartender."

Bartholomew Bouverie. According to a book about Eton, by the Rev. A. E. L'Estrange, it appears that in 1827 Mr. Gladstone (then presumably in the sixth form) edited the "Eton Miscellany," under the assumed name of "Bartholomew Bouverie."

Bartholomew Pig. A coarse nickname for a very fat person. One of the chief attractions at Bartholomew's Fair, London, was a prize pig roasted whole.

Bartholomew, Saint, the Hibernian. See HIBERNIAN SAINT BARTHOLOMEW.

Barton Gray. (Pseud.) George H. Sass in "The Independent," New York.

Barzillai. In Dryden's "Absalom and Achitophel," the Duke of Ormond, the faithful friend of Charles II., is portrayed under this name. The allusion is to 2 Sam. xvii. 27–29.

Bas Bleu. (Fr.) A blue-stocking; a literary lady. See BLUE-STOCKING.

Bashaw. An arrogant, domineering man; so called from the Turkish viceroys and provincial governors, each of whom bears the title of *basch*, pacha.

Bashibazouk. (Pseud.) William Harding, a sporting writer on "The Clipper," New York.

Basin States. A recent name for those States and Territories lying in the great depression or basin of the United States west of the Rocky Mountains. They are Utah, Idaho, Nevada, and Arizona.

Basis virtutum constantia. (Lat.) Constancy is the foundation of all virtues.

Basochians. French lawyers. When the French Parliament ceased to be the council of the king, and confined itself to the administration of justice, a distinction of name became imperative; so the nobles, or court party, called themselves "courtiers," and the lawyers took the name of "basochians," or king's men.

Bastard of Orleans. Jean Dunois (fl. 1403–1468), a natural son of Louis, Duke of Orleans, brother of Charles VI. "He was one of the most brilliant soldiers France ever produced."

Batavia, formerly the name of Holland, is often used in modern times as a poetical designation of that country. It is derived from the Batavi, a Celtic tribe who dwelt there.

> Flat Batavia's willowy groves.
> WORDSWORTH.

Bateau. A long light boat.

Bates's Case. An English prosecution (1606) of a merchant, in which the claim of James I. to impose duties as a personal prerogative was sustained, — a question afterward settled the other way under Cromwell. Also called the "Case of the Impositions."

Bath-Kol. "Daughter of the Voice." A sort of divination common among the ancient Jews after the gift of prophecy had ceased. When an appeal was made to Bath-Kol, the first words uttered after the appeal were considered oracular.

Bathsheba. In "Absalom and Achitophel" the Duchess of Portsmouth, a favorite court lady of Charles II. The allusion is to the wife of Uriah the Hittite, criminally beloved by David. The Duke of Monmouth says: —

> "My father, whom with reverence I name,
> Charmed into ease, is careless of his fame;
> And, bribed with petty sums of foreign gold,
> Is grown in Bathsheba's embraces old."

Batrachomyomachia. A storm in a puddle; much ado about nothing. The word is the name of a mock-heroic poem in Greek, supposed to be by Pigres of Caria, meaning "The Battle of the Frogs and Mice."

Battle of Spurs. (1) The name given to a fight between the French and English in 1513 at Guinegate, in which the former were defeated. It was so named because the French, running away, used their spurs more than their swords. (2) At the battle of Courtrai, Belgium, in 1302, Robert of Artois was vanquished by the Flemings. This conflict received its name from the number of gilt spurs assembled.

Battle of the Barriers. A desperate struggle under the walls of Paris, March 30, 1814, between the forces under Napoleon and the allies. The latter were victorious, and the capitulation of Paris and the abdication of Napoleon followed.

Battle of the Books. A satirical pamphlet by Dean Swift, called " The Battle between the Ancient and Modern Books in St. James's Library," and alluding to a bitter controversy among the literary lights of his time as to the respective merits of ancient and modern literature.

Battle of the Frogs and Mice. The theme of a mock-heroic poem designed to travesty the Iliad and the Odyssey. *See* BATRACHOMYOMACHIA.

Battle of the Gauges. A famous controversy in the early days of railroads in England (1833). Brunel, Stephenson, and Locke, all famous engineers, favored different widths of track, and much discussion ensued.

Battle of the Giants. A fight at Marignano (now Malignano), North Italy, in which Francis I. of France defeated the Duke of Milan and the Swiss, Sept. 13, 14, 1515.

Battle of the Herrings, fought Feb. 12, 1429, when the English were besieging Orleans, obtained its name from the attempt of the Duc de Bourbon to intercept a convoy of salt fish on the road to the English camp. He was beaten.

Battle of the Kegs. The title and theme of a mock-heroic poem by Francis Hopkinson (1738–1791), based upon a real incident. During the Revolutionary War the patriots set afloat a number of explosive machines shaped like kegs, in the hope of destroying the British fleet at Philadelphia. The danger being discovered, the troops of the latter assembled on the wharves and shipping, and fired at every floating object during the ebb-tide.

Battle of the Moat. A famous engagement between Mohammed and Abu Sofian before Medina. Most of the fighting took place in a ditch or moat dug by Mohammed before the city to keep off the enemy.

Battle of the Nations. The battle of Leipsic, Oct. 16, 18, 19, 1813, between the French army and its numerous allies (160,000 strong) and the Russians, Prussians, and Austrians (240,000 strong). The French were defeated, owing, in part, to the flight of their Saxon allies in the heat of the fight.

Battle of the Poets. The title and theme of a poem by the Duke of Buckingham (1725), in which he arrays all the rhymesters of the time against one another.

Battle of the Standard, fought between the English and Scotch at Northallerton, Yorkshire, Aug. 22, 1138, was so named because the English bore a high crucifix on a wagon as their ensign. The Scots were defeated.

Battle of the Thirty. One of the most renowned conflicts in the days of chivalry. It took place March 27, 1351, half-way between the castles of Josselin and Ploermel, in France, between thirty English and thirty French knights, headed respectively by Bemborough and Beaumanoir, who had agreed to decide certain differences in this way. At first the English were successful, but, Bemborough being killed, the French were ultimately victorious.

Battle of the Three Emperors. Austerlitz, Dec. 2, 1805. So called because the Emperor Napoleon, the Emperor of Russia, and the Emperor of Austria were all present. Napoleon won the fight.

Battles, Fifteen Decisive. Under this name Professor Creasy enumerates the following fifteen great conflicts as affecting the destiny of mankind : —

	B. C.		A. D.		A. D.
Marathon	490	Teutoburg	9	Blenheim	1704
Syracuse	413	Châlons	451	Pultowa	1709
Arbela	331	Tours	732	Saratoga	1777
Metaurus	207	Hastings	1066	Valmy	1792
		Orleans	1429	Waterloo	1815
		Sp. Armada	1588		

Baucis. In classic mythology an aged woman of Phrygia, who, with her husband Philemon, entertained Jupiter and Mercury after every one else had refused to receive them. The enraged gods sent upon the country a flood that destroyed the inhabitants save this couple and their house, which latter was changed into a beautiful temple, of which they were made priest and priestess. Having asked that they might die together, they were by Jupiter metamorphosed into two trees in front of their temple.

Bavarian Succession. In 1778-1779 Austria attempted to enforce her claim to a portion of the Bavarian dominions, in which she was opposed by Prussia. This is what is known to history as the " War of the Bavarian Succession."

Bayard of the Revolution. John Laurens, an American soldier (1756-1782), who, on account of his daring, was thus named by his comrades in arms.

Bayardo. The famous steed of Rinaldo, which once belonged to Amadis of Gaul.

Bayardo's Leap. A locality near Sleaford, England. Bayardo was the famous steed of Rinaldo. The legend has it that rider and horse were once passing near Sleaford when the foul spirit of the spot sprang behind Rinaldo. The horse, in terror, took three tremendous leaps, which unhorsed the fiend. These strides are marked by three great stones, about thirty yards apart.

Bayou. A name derived from the early French settlers, and applied to those inland lagoons so frequent on the shores and margins of rivers of the Gulf of Mexico.

Bayou State. Mississippi, whose southern coast abounds in swamps, bayous, and creeks.

Bbl. Barrel.

B. C. Before Christ.

B. C. L. Bachelor of Civil Law.

B. D. *Baccalaureus Divinitatis.* Bachelor of Divinity.

Bdls. Bundles.

Bds. or bds. Boards (bound in).

Bds. Bonds.

Beacon Hill. A famous locality in Boston, Mass. " The old beacon, shown in all the early plans of the town, and which gave the name to Beacon Hill, was erected in 1634-1635 to alarm the country in case of invasion. It stood near the present State House, the exact spot being the southeast corner of the reservoir formerly standing on Temple Street. It was a tall mast, standing on cross timbers placed upon a stone foundation, supported by braces, and was ascended by treenails driven into it; and, sixty-five feet from the base, projected a crane of iron, from which an iron skeleton frame was suspended, to receive a barrel of tar or other combustibles. When fired, this could be seen for a great distance inland. It was newly erected in 1768, having fallen from some cause unknown; and in 1789 it was blown down. The next year a monument of brick, sixty feet high and four in diameter, was erected on its site to the memory of those who fell at Bunker Hill ; and in 1811 this was taken down, the mound being levelled." — KING.

Beak. A slang term for a magistrate, supposed to be a corruption of the Saxon *beag*, the gold collar worn formerly by magistrates. Mr. W. H. Black, in a note to his " Ballad of Squire Tempest," says this term was derived from a Mr. Beke, who was formerly a resident magistrate for the Tower Hamlets. *See* HOOKEY WALKER.

Bean Feast. Much the same as " Wayz-goose " (*q. v.*), a feast given by an employer to those he employs.

Bean in the Cake. A phrase signifying " to meet with some unexpected good fortune." It refers to the custom of the Romans, in their Saturnalia, of placing a bean in a cake, the finding of which, when cut and distributed, constituted the fortunate one king of the festivities. The custom was perpetuated in more modern days on Twelfth Night and at weddings, when a ring or a jewel was often substituted for the bean.

Bean King A king elected by ballot. The Greeks used beans in voting by ballot.

Bean King's Festival. Twelfth Day, when he who secures the bean in the cake is king for the night.

Beans are in Flower (" les fèves fleurissent "), and this will account for your being so silly. Our forefathers imagined that the perfume of the flowering bean was bad for the head, and made men silly or light-headed.

Bear, The. Albert, Margrave of Brandenburg (fl. 1106-1170). *See* FAIR, THE.

Bearded, The. (1) Constantine IV., Emperor of Rome. (2) Geoffroy the Crusader. (*See* HANDSOME BEARD.) (3) Johann Mayo, the German artist. His beard swept the floor when he stood erect.

Bearded Master. So Persius styled Socrates, under the notion that the beard is the symbol of wisdom.

Bear Flag Republic. In the summer of 1846 a number of California settlers from the United States set up a movement for independence, and tried to establish a government, which was known as "The Bear Flag Republic."

Bear-garden. A noisy, quarrelsome assembly. Formerly bear-gardens were maintained in many cities, where the unfortunate creatures were baited for the delectation of the populace.

Bearing the Bell. A phrase which signifies "to take the lead or first place in any event, or to carry off the prize." The idea arose from the custom of placing a bell around the neck of the oldest wether in a flock of sheep, called the bell-wether, and who always marched in front of the flock.

Bear-leader. One who undertakes the charge of a young man of rank on his travels. It was once customary to lead muzzled bears about the streets, and to make them show off in order to attract notice and gain money.

Under favor, young gentleman, I am the bear-leader, being appointed your tutor. — G. COLMAN, *Heir-at-Law.*

Bearnais, Le. Henry IV. of France. His native province was Le Bearn.

Bears and **Bulls.** Words often used in connection with the purchase and sale of stocks. The "bears" are those who seek to depress the value of stocks and securities, while the "bulls" are those whose interests prompt them to act in the other direction.

Bear State. Arkansas has been so dubbed, from the fact that bears formerly roamed in great numbers through its thinly settled timber-lands.

Beastly Drunk. The ancients believed that men in their cups exhibited the vicious qualities of beasts. Seven kinds of drunkards were enumerated: (1) The ape-drunk, who is jovial and musical; (2) The lion-drunk, who is quarrelsome; (3) The swine-drunk, who is sleepy and stupid; (4) The sheep-drunk, conceited but mute; (5) The martin-drunk, who drinks until sober again; (6) The goat-drunk, wanton; (7) The fox-drunk, crafty in his cups.

Beating the Bounds. Once a year in certain London parishes a queer custom is observed. This is known as "beating the bounds." The boys of the parish "Union," or workhouse, clad in their corduroy trousers, blue jackets with brass buttons, and a very broad expanse of white collar, their faces glistening and radiant from a vigorous application of yellow soap and hard towel, march in double file around the boundary of the parish. They are headed by a pompous beadle of the genus Bumble, and each boy carries in his right hand a long peeled willow wand. In old London the parish lines were plainly marked by streets or lanes or alleys; but the march of modern improvement has frequently obliterated these, and not seldom some great palace of trade or line of industry stands half in one parish and half in the next. But Bumble and the boys laugh at such obstacles. The "bounds" must be traversed; so away they go, the beadle in front, the boys shrilly singing school songs, and with their wands smiting the walls they pass. First on one side of the street, then on the other, crossing the roadway diagonally, disappearing for a moment under a gloomy archway, winding around two sides of a mouldering churchyard, deflecting from a straight path to skirt a pump, a milestone, or some other ancient landmark, and even invading a business office, a bank, a shop whose walls happen to stand upon the dividing line. The ceremony over, the youngsters troop back to the "Union," where the London boy's regulation "treat," consisting of buns and milk, is dispensed. The origin of this old observance dates back many hundreds of years, to the day when the 'prentice lads of the city were a formidable body, who played an active part in the petty disturbances of the time. Although these youths might be relied on to act as a unit in defence of their common liberties or privileges, conflicts between the apprentices of adjoining parishes were frequent, and quarter-staff and single-stick were often wielded with fatal effect. Hence the lads of each parish were interested in keeping its boundary lines well defined; and they, it is said, inaugurated this quaint ceremony, which in modern days has been left to the workhouse boys.

Beatrice Gold. The stage-name of Belle Dunnigan.

Beatrix Phipps. The stage-name of Mrs. Maurice F. Kemp.

Beau. & Fl. or **B. & Fl.** Beaumont and Fletcher.

Beau Brummel. George Bryan (fl. 1778-1840), a noted man about town in London.

Beauclerc (lit. "good scholar "). Henry I. of England (fl. 1068–1135), who possessed scholarly attainments extremely rare in the age in which he lived.

Beau désordre. (Fr.) Beautiful disorder.

Beau D'Orsay, Le. The father of the Count D'Orsay. Byron nicknamed him *Jeune Cupidon*, "Young Cupid."

Beau Fielding. Fielding the novelist. King Charles II. dubbed him " Handsome Fielding."

Beau idéal. (Fr.) " Beautiful ideal." An imaginary standard of absolute perfection ; the true realization.

Beau monde. (Fr.) The fashionable world ; people who make up the coterie of fashion.

Beau Nash. *See* KING OF BATH.

Beau Neill. The army sobriquet of Thomas Hewson Neill, an American soldier (1826–1885), on account of his handsome person and dashing manners.

Beau Sabreur, Le (" the handsome swordsman "). The name given to Joachim Murat (fl. 1767–1815) by his comrades in arms.

Beau Tibbs, noted for his finery, vanity, and poverty, is a famous character in Goldsmith's " Citizen of the World," and a skit on Beau Nash (*q. v.*).

Beautiful, The. In the days of the Italian republics the chiefs of the sisterhoods of cities were known by some special epithet, supposed to be descriptive of their peculiar charms or of the idiosyncrasies of their inhabitants. Thus we have Naples, the Beautiful ; Rome, the Eternal City ; Genoa, the Superb ; Lucca, the Industrious ; Padua, the Learned ; Bologna, the Fat ; and Florence, the Gentle.

Beautiful Corisande. Diane d'Andouins (fl. 1554–1620), Countess of Guiche and Grammont, and widow of Philip de Grammont.

Beautiful Daughter of Rome. Florence was so named by the early writers.

Beautiful Gardener. A nickname given to a famous mistress of Henry IV. of France.

Beautiful Parricide. Beatrice Cenci (d. 1599). She conspired to kill her father in revenge for his violation of her person.

Beautiful Ropemaker. A sobriquet bestowed on Louise Labé (fl. 1526–1566), a French poetess. She married a rich ropemaker named Perrin. She was noted for her bravery at the siege of Perpignan.

Beau Trap. A loose or rocking paving-stone from beneath which mud or water squirts upward when trodden on, to the ruin of the clothing of the smartly dressed.

Beauty of Buttermere. Mary Robinson, a lovely English maiden, married to a villanous impostor named John Hatfield, who was executed for forgery at Carlisle in 1803.

Beauty only Skin deep. The first-known, if not the original, use of this phrase occurs in Ralph Venning's " Orthodoxe Paradoxes," third edition, London, 1650, p. 41 : " All the beauty of the world tis but skin-deep, a sunne-blast defaceth it."

Beaux esprits. (Fr.) Gay spirits ; men of wit.

Beaux yeux. (Fr.) " Beautiful eyes." Handsome eyes ; attractive looks.

Bedchamber of New York. The city of Brooklyn.

Bedfordshire. A punning allusion to the land of sleep, akin to " the land of Nod."

Bed of Justice. Literally, the seat or throne occupied by the French monarch when he was present at the deliberations of Parliament. Historically, a Bed of Justice signified a solemn session, in which the king was present, to overrule the decisions of Parliament, and to enforce the acceptance of edicts or ordinances which it had previously rejected. The theory of the old French constitution was that the authority of Parliament was derived solely from the crown ; consequently, when the king, the source of authority, was present, that which was delegated ceased. Acknowledging such a principle, the Parliament was logically incapable of resisting any demand that the king in a Bed of Justice might make, and decrees promulgated during a sitting of this kind were held to be of more authority than ordinary decisions of Parliament. Monarchs were not slow to take advantage of this power to overawe any Parliament that exhibited signs of independence. The last Bed of Justice was held by Louis XVI. at Versailles in September, 1787, on the brink of that Revolution which abolished the despotism of the old French monarchy.

Bed of Ware, or Great Bed of Ware.
The great bed at Ware, in Hertfordshire, is one of the curiosities of England, referred to in the "Twelfth Night" of Shakspeare : "Although the sheet were big enough for the Bed of Ware in England." This famous bed, still seen in one of the inns at Ware, measures twelve feet square, and is said to be capable of holding a dozen persons.

Bedouins of London. The London "Times" so named the ragged and homeless street-boys of the great metropolis. *See* ARABS.

Beds. Bedfordshire.

Bee. The significance borne by this word in the United States constitutes a pure Americanism. The new settler generally built his log-cabin without help; but when he proposed to erect a house he had a "raising," as the setting up of the timbers was called. All the neighbors gave their aid, calling it a "building-bee," or a "raising-bee." In like manner we find the phrases "chopping-bee," "husking-bee," "quilting-bee," and even "spelling-bee."

Beefeaters. Another name for the Yeomen of the Guard in the English service. In former times they used to watch the buffet, and were in consequence named *buffetiers* or *boufitiers,* — *i. e.* "waiters at the side-board," — which became corrupted into "beef-eaters."

Beefheads. A nickname applied to the people of Texas, in allusion to the cattle raised there.

Bee-line. The American bee-hunter has enriched our every-day English with the phrase "to strike a bee-line." An energetic pursuit, or rapid direct course toward a certain goal, is called "making a bee-line" for that point. The English "as the crow flies" conveys the same idea.

Beelzebub. In Hebrew mythology the chief of the evil spirits.

Been. Referring to the difference in the pronunciation of this word in England and America, one writer says : "But to me the most interesting connection between Lincolnshire and New England pronunciation is the little word 'been.' It has long been a wonder to me how and why that word should be pronounced, not only in New England, but throughout the United States, so differently from what it is in England and in all her many colonies. In England, Scotland, Ireland, Canada, Australia, Nova Scotia, South Africa, it is made to rhyme with 'seen' and 'between,' whereas in our country it is made to rhyme with 'sin' and 'din.' It was all explained when I came to Lincolnshire and found that the old local usage there was to call it 'bin;' and that is not yet entirely driven out to this day."

Bee of Athens. Sophocles, the tragic poet (fl. 495-405 B. C.).

Beetle-crusher. A slang name for a large flat foot. The term was coined by "Punch." London is largely infested with black beetles, — a species of cockroach.

Befana. "The good fairy of Italian children, who is supposed to fill their stockings with toys when they go to bed on Twelfth Night. Some one enters the children's bedroom for the purpose, and the wakeful youngsters cry out, 'Ecco la Befana.' According to legend, Befana was too busy with house affairs to look after the Magi when they went to offer their gifts, and said she would wait to see them on their return ; but they went another way, and Befana every Twelfth Night watches to see them. The name is a corruption of *Epiphania.*" — BREWER.

Begging the Question. A term frequently used in debate or controversy, and meaning "to assume without proof."

Beginning of the End. Fournier asserts, on the written authority of Talleyrand's brother, that the only breviary used by the ex-bishop was "L'Improvisateur Français," a compilation of anecdotes and *bon-mots,* in twenty-one duodecimo volumes. Whenever a good thing was wandering in search of a parent, he adopted it ; among others, "C'est le commencement de la fin."

> To show our simple skill,
> That is the true beginning of our end.
> SHAKSPEARE, *Midsummer-Night's Dream.*

Beheaded. *See* AXE.

Behesth. The Elysian fields of Persian mythology.

Behmenists. A sect of visionary religionists, so called from Jacob Behmen, their founder (1575–1625).

Behram. The most holy kind of fire, according to Parseeism.

Bejan. A freshman, or greenhorn. This term is employed in the French and Scottish universities, and is evidently a corruption of *bec jaune* ("yellow

beak "), a French expression to designate a nestling or unfledged bird. In
the University of Vienna the freshman
is termed *beanus.*

Bel. The same as Baal (*q. v.*).

Belcher. Slang for a pocket-handker-
chief — one having a blue ground and
white spots — much affected by London
roughs. So named from Jim Belcher,
the pugilist, whose colors it was.

Bel esprit. (Fr.) A vivacious wit;
a man or woman of quick and lively
parts, ready at repartee.

Belfast Kidney. A cobble-stone, —
a formidable missile in the street riots
which have too often disgraced the city
of Belfast.

Belg. Belgic; Belgian; Belgium.

Belgravia. An embodiment of the
ultra-fashionable district, including Bel-
grave Square and the adjacent streets
in London. It adjoins Mayfair (*q. v.*).

Belial. A Hebrew word meaning
"worthlessness," but in the Scriptures
used as an appellative of Satan, the embodiment of all evil.

Bella donna. (Ital.) A fair lady. The
name was given to the deadly nightshade
from a practice once common among
ladies of touching their eyes with it to
make the pupils large and lustrous.

**Bella femina che ride, ruol dir,
borsa che piange.** (Ital.) When a
handsome woman laughs you may be
sure her purse cries.

Bella! horrida bella! (Lat.) Wars!
horrid wars!

Bella matribus detestata. (Lat.)
Wars by mothers detested.

Bell Battle. The *casus belli* was this:
Have the local magistrates power to allow parish bells to be rung at their discretion, or is the right vested in the
parish clergyman? This squabble was
carried on with great animosity in the
parish of Paisley in 1832. The clergyman, John Macnaughton, brought the
question before the local council, which
gave it in favor of the magistrates; but
the court of sessions gave it the other
way; and when the magistrates granted
a permit for the bells to be rung, the
court issued an interdict against them.

For nearly two years the Paisley bell battle
was fought with the fiercest zeal. It was the
subject of every political meeting, the theme of
every board, the gossip at tea-tables and dinner-
parties, and children delighted in chalking on the
walls, "Please to ring the bell" (May 14, 1832, to
Sept. 10, 1834). — *Newspaper paragraph.*

Bell, Book, and Candle. A ceremony of excommunication belonging to
the Church of Rome. The above name
is taken from certain peculiar phrases
or gestures which occur in the rite:
"Cursed be they from the crown of the
head to the sole of the foot. Out be
they taken of the book of life. [Shuts
the book.] And as this candle is cast
from the sight of men, so be their souls
cast from the sight of God into the
deepest pit of hell. [Casts the candle
on the ground.] Amen." The rubric
adds: "And then the candle being
dashed on the ground and quenched,
let the bell be rung," the bell being
tolled as for one dead.

Bell City. Racine, Wis.

Belle Archer. The stage-name of
Mrs. Herbert Archer, *née* McKenzie.

Belle Boyd. (Pseud.) Mrs. Belle
Boyd Hardinge.

Belle Brittan. (Pseud.) Hiram
Fuller.

Belle étage. (Fr.) The second floor
of a house.

Belle France, La. A popular poetical designation of France, similar to
the nickname "Merry England."

Belle Gabrielle, La. The daughter
of Antoine d'Estrées, Grand-Master of
Artillery and Governor of the Ile de
France. Henry IV. fell in love with
her.

Bellerophon. In classical mythology
a son of Glaucus, who, aided by the
winged horse Pegasus, killed the Chimæra. He was subsequently thrown
from his steed, and became lame and
blind, so that he roamed alone and forsaken of men up and down the Aleïan
field.

Bellerus. A famous Cornish giant.

Belles lettres. Polite literature.

Bellona. In classic mythology the
goddess of war among the Romans.
She was described by the poets as "the
companion, sister, wife, or daughter of
Mars; she was also represented as
armed with a bloody scourge, and as
inspiring her votaries with a resistless
enthusiasm in battle. In the temple of
Bellona the senate gave audience to em-
bassies from foreign powers, and also
to consuls who had claims to a triumph
which would have been nullified by entrance into the city. The priests of
the goddess were styled *Bellonarii*, and
practised sanguinary rites."

Bellona's Day. March 24. On this day the votaries of the Roman war-goddess gashed themselves and quaffed the blood as an act of homage to the deity. Called in Latin *Dies Sanguinis.*

Bellona's Handmaids. Blood, Fire, and Famine.

The goddesse of warre, called Bellona, had these thre handmaids ever attendynge on her: BLOOD, FIRE, and FAMINE, which thre damosels be of that force and strength that every one of them alone is able and sufficient to torment and afflict a proud prince; and they all joyned together are of puissance to destroy the most populous country and most richest region of the world. — HALL, *Chronicle* (1530).

Bell Smith. (Pseud.) Mrs. Louise Kirby Piatt, an American writer (1812–1864).

Bell-the-Cat. A nickname bestowed on Archibald Douglas, Earl of Angus. James III. capriciously chose several men of low birth as favorites; one of them, a mason, he elevated to be Earl of Mar. The enraged nobles held a council for the purpose of devising means to put down the upstarts. "But who will bell the cat?" inquired Lord Gray. "That will I," answered Douglas; and he courageously slew, in the presence of the king, the hated individuals.

Bellum internecinum. A war of extermination.

Bellum lethale. A deadly war.

Bell-wether of the Flock. A jocose term applied to the leader of a party. Of course, the allusion is to the wether or sheep which leads the flock with a bell fastened to its neck.

Beloved Disciple. Saint John. See John xiii. 23.

Beloved Merchant. A title given by Edward III. of England to Michael de la Pole, an eminent London merchant, who in the next reign became Lord Chancellor and Earl of Suffolk.

Beloved Physician. Saint Luke the Evangelist. See Col. iv. 14.

Bel paese. (Ital.) A beautiful land or country.

Belphegor. A Moabitish deity, whose rites were celebrated on Mount Phegor, and were noted for their obscenity.

Belted Will. Lord William Howard (fl. 1563–1640), Warden of the Western Marches.

Beltein (from *Bel*, the name of the chief Gaelic deity in pagan times). An ancient votive festival still observed in the remote Highlands of Scotland. "On the day of the festival the inhabitants of several hamlets resort to a certain hilltop provided with provisions and victuals of all sorts. The younger among them, with spades, remove square patches of turf, with which they construct a sort of altar; they cover it with a thick layer of peat, to which they set fire. As soon as it is thoroughly alight, they place on this blazing hearth a large open kettle, in which the bystanders throw all the butter, eggs, and honey they have brought with them. When the mixture has boiled a sufficient length of time, each of those present fills his glass and empties the contents in a circle around him with a loud adjuration to the invisible spirits of the universe. At the conclusion of these libations, which are only the preliminary part of the ceremonies, the pilgrims take from their satchels votive cakes, kneaded out of oatmeal and shaped to form nine knots; standing with their backs to the blazing altar, they break off one knot after another, and throw them in succession over their left shoulder into the fire, accompanying each gesture with special thanks to the guardian spirits: 'To thee, for preserving my horse!' 'To thee, for preserving my oxen!' and so on, till the whole cake is disposed of. When the first litany is exhausted, fresh cakes are produced, and the ceremony is repeated in exactly the same manner, but the invocations are made this time to the evil spirits, to mollify them or turn aside their wrath. It is only then, when the fire is burnt out, that the votaries gather together and amicably consume the remainder of the provisions."

Belus. The same as Baal or Bel. *See* BAAL.

Ben. (Ital.) Well; as, *Ben marcato*, well marked. The phrase denotes that the passage or air must be delivered in a clear, distinct, and firmly accented manner. (Mus.)

Benaiah, in "Absalom and Achitophel," is meant for Gen. George Edward Sackville. As Benaiah, captain of David's guard, adhered to Solomon against Adonijah, so General Sackville adhered to the Duke of York against the Prince of Orange (1590–1652).

Nor can Benaiah's worth forgotten lie,
Of steady soul when public storms were high.
DRYDEN AND TATE.

Benauly. (Pseud.) A sort of triple-headed literary partnership is contained herein: *Ben*jamin, *Au*stin, and *Ly*man Abbott.

Bender. In New York, to "go on a *bender*" is to go on a spree. In this case a man comes under spiritual influences so potent that, not being able to stand straight under them, he must *bend*.

> I met her at the Chinese room;
> She wore a wreath of roses,
> She walked in beauty like the night,
> Her breath was like sweet posies.
> I led her through the festal hall,
> Her glance was soft and tender;
> She whispered gently in my ear,
> "Say, Mose, ain't this a *bender*?"
> *Putnam's Monthly*, August, 1854.

Bender. The slang or colloquial name for the English silver sixpence. It is rather thin, and when worn may be easily bent.

Bend Sinister. This phrase is applied to any one born out of lawful wedlock. In heraldry, a band running from the upper right-hand corner to the lower left-hand corner is called a bend-sinister, and indicates bastardy.

Benedick. A newly married man. The reference is to the character of the name in Shakspeare's "Much Ado about Nothing." It is often written "Benedict," from the Latin *benedict-us* (a happy man), and a skit on the order of Saint Benedict, famous for their ascetic habits, and rigidly bound to celibacy. Shakspeare avails himself of this joke in making Benedick, the young lord of Padua, "rail against marriage," but afterwards marry Beatrice, with whom he falls in love.

Benedict. (Pseud.) Edward Walter Dawson, an American writer.

Benedict Cruiser, M. M. (Pseud.) George Augustus Sala (1858). "M. M." signifies "married man."

Bene exeat. (Lat.) Let him depart with a good character.

Benefit of Clergy, and **Neck Verse.** "Benefit of Clergy" (*Privilegium Clericale*) arose in the regard paid by Christian princes to the Church, and consisted of (1) an exemption of places consecrated to religious duties from criminal arrests, which was the foundation of sanctuaries; (2) exemption of the persons of clergymen from criminal process before the secular judge in particular cases, which was the original meaning of the *privilegium clericale*. The *bene-fit of clergy* was afterwards extended to every one who could read; and it was enacted that there should be a prerogative allowed to the clergy, that if any man who could read were to be condemned to death, the bishop of the diocese might, if he would, claim him as a clerk, and dispose of him in some places of the clergy as he might deem meet. The ordinary gave the prisoner at the bar a Latin book, in a black Gothic character, from which to read a verse or two; and if the ordinary said, "Legit ut clericus" ("He reads like a clerk"), the offender was only burned in the hand; otherwise he suffered death (3 Edw. I. 1274). The privilege was restricted by Henry VII. in 1489, and abolished, with respect to murderers and other great criminals, by Henry VIII. (1512). Each prison had its particular "Neck Verse;" and although a criminal might roll off glibly that of Edinburgh or Carlisle, it by no means followed that he would be equally successful elsewhere. Most of these have now become extinct, and so far search for them has only ended in failure. The authentic "Neck Verse" used at Newgate is, however, extant; it was the first verse of Psalm li., technically known as David's prayer for remission of sin: "Miserere, mei Deus, secundum magnam misericordiam tuam. Et secundum multitudinem miserationum tuarum dele iniquitatem meam." ("Have mercy upon me, O God, according to thy loving kindness; according unto the multitude of thy tender mercies, blot out my transgressions.") This Newgate "Neck Verse" is the only one recorded as belonging especially to that prison. Very often the selection of a passage of Scripture to be used in this way depended upon the whim of the acting magistrate, who had the right to open the psalter at random and put before the culprit any sentence he might select, though generally this office fell upon a proper ordinary, appointed by the Church. In the reign of Queen Anne the "benefit of clergy" was still in use, though modified somewhat, and extended to all persons convicted of clergyable offences; nor was it finally abolished until the time of George IV.

Bene placito. (Ital.) At will. (Mus.)

Bengal Tigers. The Seventeenth Foot Regiment in the British army. Their crest consists of a green tiger.

Benicia Boy. John C. Heenan, the American pugilist, was so named. He was born in Benicia, Cal.

Benignant Hulda. The German goddess of marriage and fecundity, who sent bridegrooms to maidens and children to the married.

Benigno numine. (Lat.) By the favor of Providence.

Benj. Benjamin.

Benjamin's Mess. The largest share. The allusion is to the banquet given by Joseph to his brethren. "Benjamin's mess was five times so much as any of theirs."

Benj. F. Johnson of Boone. (Pseud.) The name under which James Whitcomb Riley, the "Hoosier Poet" (b. 1852), issued his "The Old Swimmin' Hole and 'Leven more Poems" in 1883. *See* HOOSIER POET.

Ben Jochanan, in the satire of "Absalom and Achitophel," by Dryden, is meant for the Rev. Samuel Johnson, who suffered much persecution for his defence of the right of private judgment.

> "A Jew of humble parentage was he;
> By trade a Levite, though of low degree."

Benton's Mint Drops. So Philadelphians named gold dollars. The term was given to them because they were first coined in accordance with a resolution offered by Senator Benton of Missouri.

Ben trovato. (Ital.) Well feigned or invented.

Benzine. A colloquial term for strong drink in the Eastern States. *See* POISON.

Berecynthian Goddess. Cybele is so called from Mount Berecynthus, in Phrygia, where she was held in especial adoration. She is represented as crowned with turrets, and holding keys in her hand.

> Her helmèd head
> Rose like the Berecynthian goddess crowned
> With towers.
> SOUTHEY, *Roderick.*

Berecynthian Hero. Midas, the Phrygian king. He was so named after Mount Berecynthus in Phrygia.

Berengarians. Followers of Berenger, Archdeacon of Angers, the learned opponent of Lanfranc (eleventh century). He said that the bread by consecration did not become the very body of Christ "generated on earth so many years before, but becomes to the faithful, nevertheless, the blessed body of Christ."

Berenice. The sister-wife of Ptolemy III., who vowed to sacrifice her hair to the gods, if her husband returned home the vanquisher of Asia. She suspended her hair in the temple of the war-god; but it was stolen the first night, and Conon of Samos told the king that the winds had wafted it to heaven, where it still forms the seven stars near the tail of Leo, called Coma Berenices. See *infra*.

Berenice's Hair. A beautiful cluster of forty-three stars in the northern hemisphere, about five degrees east of the equinoctial colure; its principal stars are between the fourth and fifth magnitudes.

Bergelmir. In Norse mythology a frost-giant, father of the Jotuns, or second dynasty of giants.

Berg Folk. In Scandinavian mythology heathen spirits doomed to a wandering existence on the hills and mountains till Ragnarok.

Berkeley's Seat. A rock near Newport, R. I., is known by this nickname. It was a favorite spot for meditation with George Berkeley, Bishop of Cloyne (1684–1753), during his two years' sojourn in Newport (1728–1730).

Berks. Berkshire.

Berkshire Hogs. A nickname conferred on the Sixty-sixth Regiment of the English service, "because the regiment was principally recruited in the country of prize pork."

Berkshire White Horse. *See* WHITE HORSE OF BERKSHIRE.

Berlin Decree. A decree issued at Berlin by Napoleon I., forbidding any of the nations of Europe to trade with Great Britain (1806). This mad fancy was the first step to the great man's fall.

Berliner. (Pseud.) Rev. Joseph Parrish Thomson, D.D., in his letters home from Berlin (1873), *et seq.*

Bermoothes. The Spanish pronunciation of the name of Bermudez, the discoverer of the Bermuda group (1527), frequently used in literature to designate these islands.

Bermudas. The slang name once given to a disreputable portion of London, lying north of the Strand, used as a place of concealment by insolvent debtors, civil offenders, etc.

Bernard the Little. Solomon Bernard, a Lyonnese engraver, who flourished in the sixteenth century.

Bernard the Poor. Claude Bernard (fl. 1588–1641), the philanthropist of Dijon.

Bernesque Poetry. Serio-comic poetry, so called from Francesco Berni, of Tuscany, who greatly excelled in it (1490–1536).

Bernouilli's Numbers. A system of algebraic formulas first used by James Bernouilli (fl. 1654–1705), Professor of Mathematics at Basle.

Bersaglieri. A name for the sharpshooters of the Sardinian army, first employed about 1848.

Berserker. Grandson of the eight-handed Starkader and of the beautiful Alfhilde, called *boer-serce*, " bare of mail," because he went into battle unharnessed. See *infra*.

Berserker Rage. The champions of the ancient Scandinavians were called berserkers, from their custom of fighting with no armor save a sark or shirt; hence, literally, *bare-sark-er* = berserker. They were at times seized with fits of martial frenzy, during which they could perform prodigious feats of valor, and were invincible against any foe. After the rage or spasm was over, reaction ensued, and then a child might lead them.

You say that I am berserker. And . . . baresark I go to-morrow to the war. — *Hereward the Wake*.

Bertha M. Clay. (Pseud.) The works of Charlotte M. Braeme were published under this name in America.

Bertha of the Great Foot. Mother of Charlemagne, and granddaughter of Charles Martel. Said to have been so named because she had one foot longer than the other.

Berwick. (Pseud.) James Redpath, correspondent and editorial writer on the " Tribune," New York.

Berwickshire Sandie. (Pseud.) Alexander Brown, who printed a volume of poems in the Scottish dialect early in the present century.

Beryl Carr. (Pseud.) L. Ella Byrd, in her " Marston Hall," New York, 1881.

Berzak (lit. " the interval "). In the Koranic system, the gap between death and the resurrection.

Besieged Resident. (Pseud.) Henry Labouchere, English journalist and author (b. 1831), who wrote letters from Paris during the siege (1870–1871) over this signature.

Bessie Bernard. The stage-name of Mrs. Bernard G. Shields.

Bessie Burt. The stage-name of Mrs. Imson.

Bessie Chandler. (Pseud.) Mrs. Elizabeth [Chandler] Parker.

Bessie Darling. The stage-name of Mrs. Charles Berry.

Bessie Sudlow. The stage-name of Mrs. Michael Gunn.

Bess o' Bedlam. A nickname among the common people for a female maniac. The corresponding term for a male lunatic is Tom o' Bedlam. Bess and Tom are common English names, while Bedlam is a comprehensive term for all mad-houses.

Best-abused Man in England. See ZOILUS.

Bête noire. (Fr.) " Black beast." Bugbear; an object of aversion.

Better to wear out than to rust out. When a friend told Bishop Cumberland (1632–1718) he would wear himself out by his incessant application, " It is better," replied the Bishop, " to wear out than to rust out." — BISHOP HORNE, *Sermon on the Duty of contending for the Truth.*

Betty. A nickname for a man who interferes with the tasks of female domestics, or affects pursuits relegated to women. Also named a " Molly."

Between Hay and Grass is a proverbial expression in America, equivalent to the English word " hobble-de-hoy," — that is, a youth between boyhood and manhood.

Between the Devil and the Deep Sea. This expression is used by Colonel Munroe in his " Expedition with Mackay's Regiment," printed in London in 1637. The regiment was with Gustavus Adolphus's army, and was engaged in a battle with the Austrians. The Swedish gunners did not elevate their guns sufficiently, and their shot fell among the ranks of this Scottish regiment, so that " we were between the devil and the deep sea."

It may be that the phrase has an earlier origin. Some date it as far back as the Hebrew Exodus, when the chosen people had the Red Sea in front and Pharaoh's hosts behind. Others think it refers to Scylla and Charybdis (*q. v.*). Yet another derivation ascribes it to an unknown skippper, caught in a gale of wind on a rocky lee-shore, trying to " claw off " and work his ship out to sea. The vessel being leaky, her crew might with justice be said to be " between the devil and the deep sea."

Beulah. That land of rest which a Christian enjoys when his faith is so strong that he no longer fears or doubts. Sunday is sometimes so called. In Bunyan's allegory (" The Pilgrim's Progress ") the pilgrims tarry in the land of Beulah after their pilgrimage is over, till they are summoned to cross the stream of Death and enter into the Celestial City.

After this I beheld until they came unto the land of Beulah, where the sun shineth night and day. Here, because they were weary, they betook themselves awhile to rest; but a little while soon refreshed them here; for the bells did so ring, and the trumpets sounded so melodiously, that they could not sleep. . . . In this land they heard nothing, saw nothing, smelt nothing, tasted nothing that was offensive. — BUNYAN, *The Pilgrim's Progress.*

Beverley. (Pseud.) Mrs. S. B. Hughes Cox, a writer in the Southern press.

Beware of a Man of one Book. When Saint Thomas Aquinas was asked in what manner a man might best become learned, he answered, " By reading one book."

The *homo unius* is indeed proverbially formidable to all conversational figurantes. — SOUTHEY, *The Doctor.*

Bezaliel, in " Absalom and Achitophel," by Dryden, is meant for the Marquis of Worcester, afterward Duke of Beaufort.

" Bezaliel with each grace and virtue fraught,
  Serene his looks, serene his life and thought;
  On whom so largely Nature heaped her store,
  There scarce remained for arts to give him more."

Bezonian. An epithet often applied by old English writers as a term of reproach, signifying "a beggar, a cheat, or a vulgar fellow." It is derived from the Italian *bisogno*, " need, want."

B-Flats. Another name for bedbugs; derived from *B*, the initial letter, and *flat*, in allusion to the flatness of the insect. *See* NORFOLK HOWARDS.

Bi. Bismuth.

B. I. British India.

Bianchi and Neri (" Whites " and " Blacks "). (1) Political factions in Florence in 1300, the Bianchi, headed by Vieri di Cerchi, opposing the Neri, headed by Corso di Donati. The former favored the imperial party (the Ghibellines), but were banished by the Neri in 1302. (2) Bianchi were also male and female penitents who roamed Italy, and were suppressed by Boniface IX. in 1400.

Bib. Bible; biblical.

Bibbiena, Il. A name given to Cardinal Bernardo (fl. 1470–1520); he wrote a number of comedies, and resided at Bibbiena in Tuscany.

Bible-clerk. A sizar of Oxford University; a student who gets certain pecuniary advantages for reading the Bible aloud at chapel. The office is almost a sinecure; but the emolument is given to the sons of poor gentlemen, either as a gift or as the reward of merit.

Bible of the British Aristocracy. Burke's " Peerage," a biographical register of all the titled families of the kingdom, has been so named.

Bible Orchard; Bible Thursday. Names arising out of a curious custom in the parish church of St. Ives, Hants, on the last Thursday in May. On a table in the church at the chancel steps are placed six Bibles, and near them a box and three dice. Six boys and six girls, solemnly watched over by the vicar and a crowd of parishioners, throw dice each three times to see which shall have the six Bibles. This remarkable custom dates from 1678, when Dr. Robert Wylde bequeathed fifty pounds, of which the yearly interest was to be spent in buying six Bibles, not to cost more than seven shillings sixpence each, to be cast for by dice on the communion-table every year by six boys and six girls of the town. A piece of ground was bought with the money, and is now known as Bible Orchard. The legacy also provided for the payment of ten shillings each year to the vicar for preaching a sermon commending the excellency, perfection, and divine authority of the Holy Scriptures. The will of the eccentric Doctor was exactly observed, and for more than two hundred years dice were regularly cast upon the communion-table. Lately a table erected on the chancel steps was substituted, the bishop of the diocese having considered that the communion-table was not for throwing dice.

Bibles, Peculiar. Because of various typographical and other peculiarities, there are a number of editions of the Scriptures known by curious nicknames. For notices of these the reader is referred to their respective titles; as, BISHOP'S BIBLE, BREECHES BIBLE, BUG BIBLE, CAXTON MEMORIAL BIBLE, CRANMER'S BIBLE, DOUAY BIBLE,

EARS-TO-EAR BIBLE, GENEVA BIBLE, GREAT BIBLE, GUTENBERG BIBLE, HE-AND-SHE BIBLE, KNAVE BIBLE, MAT-THEW'S BIBLE, MURDERER'S BIBLE, PLACE - MAKERS' BIBLE, PRINTERS' BIBLE, ROSIN BIBLE, STANDING-FISHES BIBLE, THUMB BIBLE, TO REMAIN BI-BLE, TREACLE BIBLE, VINEGAR BIBLE, WICKED BIBLE.

Biblia Pauperum. *See* POOR MAN'S BIBLE.

Biblicus. (Pseud.) Alexander Til-loch, LL.D., in the "Star" newspaper.

Bibliophile. (Pseud.) Samuel Aus-tin Allibone, American bibliographer (b. 1816).

Bibliophile Jacob. A nickname con-ferred on Paul Lacroix, a French author (fl. 1807–1884).

Biddenden Maids. This name, says Wheeler, was given to two unmarried sisters, named Mary and Elizabeth Chulkhurst, born at Biddenden, Kent, England, in 1110, and joined together, as tradition relates, by the shoulders and hips. They lived together thirty-four years; when one died the other persistently refused to be separated from the corpse of her sister, and suc-cumbed six hours after. They are said to have left twenty acres of land, called "Bread-and-Cheese Land," where, on the afternoon of Easter Sunday, six hundred rolls are distributed to stran-gers, and two hundred and seventy loaves, weighing three-and-a-half pounds each, with cheese in proportion, are given to the poor of the parish, — the expense being defrayed out of the rental of the land. So runs the legend. But Halsted, in his "History of Kent," ridi-cules this story as fabulous; he does not dispute the existence of the "Bid-denden Maids," but says the "Bread-and-Cheese Land" was bequeathed by two maiden ladies named Preston.

Bidding-prayer. The prayer for the souls of benefactors said before the ser-mon; a relic of this remains in the prayer used in cathedrals, churches, etc., in England.

Bideford Postman. Edward Capern, the poet, was thus nicknamed. At one period of his career he was a letter-carrier in Bideford.

Bidi. A Malabar deity, correspond-ing to the classic Destiny.

Biel. In Scandinavian mythology the deity of the forests.

Bienséance. (Fr.) "Civility." De-corum; decency.

Bienséances. (Fr.) "Decencies." The proprieties of life.

Bifrons. One of the pen-names com-monly attributed to Junius (*q. v.*).

Bifrost. In Norse mythology the bridge between heaven and earth; the rainbow may be considered to be this bridge, and its various colors are the reflections of its precious stones.

Big Ben at Westminster. The great bell in the clock-tower, weighing 13 tons 10 cwt., named after Sir Benjamin Hall, Chief Commissioner of Public Works when the monster was cast. Its note can be heard for many miles in calm weather.

Big Head. A phrase — a pure Ameri-canism — by which it is intended to sig-nify that the person suffering therefrom is puffed up with vanity. A *swelled head* refers to the consequences of a drinking-bout.

Big Knife. A name applied to Gen. Andrew Jackson by the Southern In-dians in recognition of his military successes against them.

Big Thursday. The chief day of the State Fair at Waverly, N. J., in Septem-ber of each year. It is made the occa-sion of a great political pow-wow, and the party leaders assemble in force to see and be seen, exchange opinions, and make plans.

Big Trees of California. The large trees in California are specified by Has-well as follows: The Keystone State, in Calaveras Grove, is 325 feet in height. The Father of the Forest, felled, is 385 feet in length, and a man on horseback can ride erect 90 feet inside of its trunk. The Mother of the Forest is 315 feet in height, 84 feet in circumference (26.75 feet in diameter) inside of its bark, and is computed to contain 537,000 feet of sound one-inch lumber. These measure-ments appear to be exceeded by some trees in Australia, as is set forth in the report of the Intercolonial Exhibition of 1870 (p. 639), published from the Gov-ernment Printing Office at Sydney in 1871. Here is the statement: The average height to which the Eucalypts attain in this colony may be stated at 100 to 120 feet, with a stem of from three and a half to five feet in diameter. All above these dimensions must be re-garded as exceptional. In jungle forests they have been known to reach a height of

200 feet, or more. But these heights sink into insignificance compared to those given of some allied species of the same genus indigenous to Victoria, Tasmania, and western Australia. The Tasmania "blue gum"(Eucalyptus globules) is said to reach to a height of 300 feet; and Dr. Von Mueller states, in the official record of the Melbourne Intercolonial Exhibition, that a "Karri tree" (Ecolossa) of western Australia was measured by Mr. Pemberton Walcot, which reached 400 feet in height; and a Mr. Boyle measured a fallen tree of Eamygdalina in the deep recesses of Daudanong, near Melbourne, 420 feet in length; further, that a Mr. Klein took the measurement of a Eucalyptus ten miles from Thalesville, 480 feet high; and that a Mr. G. W. Robinson ascertained the circumference of a tree of the Eamygdalina to be eighty-one feet.

Big-wig. A slang name for a judge, from the custom prevalent among occupants of the bench of wearing large wigs.

Bijou Heron. The stage-name of Mrs. Henry Miller.

Bill Arp. (Pseud.) Charles H. Smith, American humorous writer; one of the editors of the Atlanta "Constitution."

Billet-doux. (Fr.) A love letter.

Billets d'état. (Fr.) "Notes of State." Government paper; bank-notes.

Billingsgate. A wharf and fish-market a little below London Bridge on the Middlesex shore. It is the chief wholesale fish-market in London, and fish of every kind is admitted free of duty if taken by British subjects in British vessels. The vulgarity and scurrilous talk indulged in by the hucksters who frequent the locality has given rise to the proverbial use of the name.

Bill Nye. (Pseud.) E. W. Nye, a well-known humorist and lecturer, and a contributor to the Detroit "Free Press" (b. 1850).

Bill of 1800. A law introduced in that year by Senator James Ross, of Pennsylvania, to regulate the electoral count. It provided for a "grand committee" of six Senators, six Representatives, and the Chief-Justice. These, sitting in secret, were to settle all disputes concerning electoral votes. The bill was amended in the House so as to give to the committee the power merely to take testimony, doubtful returns to be rejected only by a concurrent vote of both houses; this was amended by the Senate so as to cause returns to be rejected unless accepted by a concurrent vote. The bill was lost. The bill is memorable as the first open attempt on the part of Congress to arrogate to itself the duty assigned by the Constitution to the President of the Senate of counting the electoral votes. — BROWN AND STRAUSS.

Billy Barlow. A Merry-Andrew. So called from a half-idiot of that name, who fancied himself some great personage. He was well known in the east of London, and died in Whitechapel Workhouse.

Billy Florence. The stage-name of William J. Conlin.

Billy Patterson, Who struck? The origin of this once famous phrase is as follows: About forty years ago, at one of the medical colleges of this country the students had a trick of hazing every new man who entered the institution. They would secure him hand and foot, carry him before a mock tribunal, and there try him for some high crime with which they charged him. He would be convicted, of course, and sentenced to be led to the block and decapitated. A student named William Patterson came along in time, and was put through the court and sentenced in the usual solemn and impressive manner. He was blind-folded and led to the block, and his neck placed in position. The executioner swung his axe and buried it in the block, allowing it, to be sure, to go nowhere near Patterson's head. The students laughed when the trick was at an end, but Patterson was dead. He had died from what medical men call shock. All the students were put under arrest, and the question arose, "Who struck Billy Patterson?" On the trial it was shown that nobody struck him; but the medical students retained the expression, and it has come down through them to the present day.

Billy Sedgwick. The stage-name of of S. W. Putnam.

Billy Wix. An owl. "Billy" is a play upon the beak, or bill, which is very striking in the owl; and "Wix" is the German *weck*, "a wig," alluding to the judge-like appearance of the "wise bird."

Bingham's Dandies. A nickname for the Seventeenth Lancers in the English army. Lord Bingham was once their colonel, and their uniform is noted for its almost foppish trimness.

Biog. Biography; biographical.

Bion. (Pseud.) Robert Southey.

Bird of Washington. The bald eagle, the American emblem.

Birkbeck. (Pseud.) Henri Beyle.

Birmingham of China. The city of Fat-Shan, in Quang-Tong, China. It has large iron-works, whence its sobriquet.

Birmingham Poet. John Freeth, the English versifier, who died in 1808, aged seventy-eight, was so named. He was a publican as well as a poet, and something of a wit. He set many of his lyrics to music, and sang them well.

Bis. (Lat.) "Twice." A term indicating that a passage distinguished by a curved line drawn under or over it is to be played or sung twice. (Mus.)

Bisc. Biscayan.

Bis dat, qui cito dat. (Lat.) "Twice he gives who quickly gives." He who bestows a favor promptly and with little fuss, greatly enhances its value.

Bishop Bunyan. John Bunyan (fl. 1628–1688) was thus named because he visited his religious brethren in various parts of England, preaching and exhorting.

Bishop of all the Denominations. The Rev. Dr. Fraser, Bishop of Manchester (d. 1885), was so named in allusion to his broad spirit of toleration to all sects.

Bishop of Hippo. Saint Augustine.

Bishop's Bible. An edition of the Scriptures which appeared in 1568. It was prepared under the supervision of Archbishop Parker. *See* TREACLE BIBLE.

Bismarquer. One who cheats at cards or billiards. The word, it is said, is coined from the name of Prince Bismarck, whose shifty statecraft in 1865–1866 awoke honest indignation throughout Europe. *See* BITE.

Bis peccare in bello non licet. (Lat.) To blunder twice is not allowed in war.

Biss. Bissell's Circuit Court Reports.

Bistonians. The Thracians. So called from Biston, son of Mars, who built Bistonia, on the lake Bistonis.

So the Bistonian race, a maddening train,
  Exult and revel on the Thracian plain;

With milk their bloody banquets they allay,
  Or from the lion rend his panting prey;
On some abandoned savage fiercely fly,
  Seize, tear, devour, and think it luxury.
    Statius, book ii.

Bis vincit, qui se vincit in victoria. (Lat.) "Twice he conquers who conquers himself in victory." He conquers twice who conquers himself in the hour of victory, — *i. e.*, his enemy by his valor, and himself by his moderation.

Bite. A cheat; one who bites us. "The biter bit" explains the origin. We say "a man was bitten" when he meddles with something which promised well but turned out a failure.

Bitter End. "This phrase is nearly without meaning as it is used. The true phrase, 'better end,' is used properly to designate a crisis, or the moment of an extremity. When, in a gale, a vessel has paid out all her cable, her cable has run out to the 'better end,' — the end which is secured within the vessel and little used. Robinson Crusoe, in describing the terrible storm in Yarmouth Roads, says, 'We rode with two anchors ahead, and the cables veered out to the better end.'" — BARTLETT.

Bizarre. (Pseud.) John Russell Young in the "Washington Chronicle."

B. Jon. Ben Jonson.

Bk. Bark; book.

Black, The. *See* LOCHIEL.

Black Abolitionists. A Southern nickname for the Northern abolitionists during the anti-slavery agitation.

Black Act. A law passed in the ninth year of George I. to punish armed poachers who at that day used to blacken their faces, and were popularly known as "Blacks."

Black Acts. A series of enactments of the Scots' Parliament between the accession of James I. and the year 1587, because they were printed in Saxon, or "black" characters.

Black Assize. During the sitting of the court held at Oxford in 1577, judges, lawyers, and jurymen were stricken with the plague. The plague has been called the "Black Assize."

Blackbeard. Edward Teach, the notorious pirate, was so named.

Black Brunswickers. Name given to a body of about seven hundred hussars commanded by Frederick William, Duke of Brunswick, in the Napoleonic wars. They were called " Black " because they wore mourning for the deceased duke.

Black Captain. A nickname given to Col. Dennis Davidoff, an officer in the Russian army, by the French during the French invasion.

Black Cockade. A black cockade worn on the hat was an emblem adopted by the Federalists during the troubles with France in 1797, when war seemed imminent. Its meaning lay in the fact that it had been a part of the Continental uniform during the Revolution, and moreover it served as a contrast to the tricolor cockade of France which the Republicans had affected. " Black Cockade Federalist " was a term of reproach applied to Federalists during the days of the party's decline.

Black Codes, Black Laws. Certain enactments passed in many of the Northern States before the abolition of slavery, requiring certain acts to be performed by free negroes conditional to their residence in those States.

Black Country. A certain district of Staffordshire, England. " In this region occurs," says Mr. Moncrief, " the argillaceous or clay and black band ironstone of the coal measures, and the geological formation known as the Oölite and Lias. It occurs in such quantities, and in such close proximity to the fuel necessary for smelting it, that it has altogether altered — we might almost say begrimed — the face of the country in the neighborhood of its manufacture. As most folks know, it has given to a great part of Staffordshire the name of the Black Country." But the truth is, many people do not know this. Londoners think all colliery and iron districts come under this designation; and many persons in Birmingham have to learn that the black band of ironstone of the local coal measure is the foundation of the name " Black Country," though the funereal pall of smoke and the general grimy appearance of the great mining and manufacturing district that has made Birmingham populous and rich would be a sufficient reason for the designation.

Black David. David Forman, an American soldier (d. 1812), so named from his excessive cruelties toward the loyalists of New Jersey during the Revolutionary War.

Black Death. The name bestowed by the populace on a terrible sickness that raged in Asia, Europe, and Africa in the fourteenth century. It took its name from the black blotches, symptoms of putridity, that appeared on the skin of its victims immediately after death.

Black Diamonds. (1) Coal. Diamonds and coal are both carbon. (2) A name given in England to " smart " fellows of the lower classes.

Black Dick. Richard Earl Howe, the English admiral (fl. 1725–1799).

Black Dog. A fiend still dreaded in many country places.

Black Douglas. William Douglas, Earl of Nithsdale (fl. fourteenth century).

Black Douglas. Introduced by Sir Walter Scott in " Castle Dangerous," is a portrait of James, eighth Lord Douglas, who twice took Douglas Castle from the English by stratagem. The first time he partly burned it, and the second time he razed it to the ground. The castle, says Godscroft, was nicknamed " Dangerous " because every one who attempted to keep it from James was in constant peril.

Black Douglas. Frederick Douglas, the colored orator and philanthropist, was so named to distinguish him from Stephen A. Douglas.

Black Dwarf. (Pseud.) Thomas Jonathan Wooler, English political writer (1791–1859).

Black Eagle. In the National Republican Convention of 1884 Gen. John A. Logan, who had been proposed as the Republican candidate for President, was referred to by Judge West, the blind orator of Ohio, as " that grand old Black Eagle of Illinois."

Black Friars. The Dominicans are so called from the color of their habit.

Black Friday. (1) Dec. 6, 1745, the day on which the news arrived in England that the Pretender had landed. (2) May 11, 1866, the culmination of the commercial panic in London, when Overend, Gurney & Co. stopped payment. (3) Sept. 24, 1869, in Wall Street, New York, when a group of speculators forced the price of gold to 162½, creating a serious crisis.

Black Hawk War. In 1832 the Sacs, the Foxes, and the Winnebagoes of Wisconsin Territory began a war, incited thereto by the famous chief Black

Hawk, who, like many of his predecessors, believed it possible to form a confederacy of Indian nations sufficiently strong to arrest the westward progress of the white man. The lands of the Sacs and Foxes, lying on the Rock River, Illinois, had been purchased by the United States a quarter of a century previously; but since there was no immediate urgency for white occupancy, the Indians had been allowed to retain possession of the ceded lands. When at last possession was demanded, they refused to comply, and cavilled at the conditions of the treaty. The government insisted that its provisions should be carried out, and hostilities were forthwith commenced. The United States troops under General Scott, aided by the Illinois militia, defeated the Indians in several actions, and captured Black Hawk. He was escorted to the East, where the extent and power of the nation his people had foolishly sought to withstand became fully apparent to his understanding. Returning to his people, he told them that resistance was hopeless, and the disputed lands were then abandoned.

Black Hole. An appellation familiarly given to a dungeon or dark cell in a prison, and which is associated in the public mind with a horrible catastrophe in the history of British India; viz., the cruel confinement of a party of English in an apartment called the "Black Hole of Calcutta," on the night of the 18th of June, 1756. The garrison of the fort connected with the English factory at Calcutta having been captured by the Nabob Suraja Dowlah, he caused the prisoners, one hundred and forty-six in number, to be confined in an apartment twenty feet square. This cell had only two small windows, and these were obstructed by a veranda. The crush of the unhappy sufferers was dreadful; and after a night of excruciating agony from pressure, heat, thirst, and want of air, there were in the morning only twenty-three survivors.

Black Horse. The Seventh Dragoon Guards, the "facings" of whose uniforms are black. Other names for this corps are "Princess Royal's Dragoon Guards," "Strawboots," and "The Blacks."

Black Horse Cavalry. A name given to those legislators that act together for the purpose of exacting money from the friends of any measure under consideration, and threaten its defeat in case of non-compliance. Their number is frequently great enough to be of considerable influence.

Black Indies. A name given by English people to their vast system of coal-mines, which have contributed perhaps even more than the Indian colonial possessions to swell the surprising wealth of the United Kingdom.

Black Jack. Miners call blende, or sulphide of zinc, "Black Jack," the occurrence of which is considered a favorable indication. The blende usually precedes a lode of good ore.

Blackjack. A nickname given to General John A. Logan, of Illinois. The name is usually written "Black Jack," and is supposed to point to his swarthy complexion; but this is an error. The blackjack oak is the knottiest and toughest wood growing in the Western country, and during the Civil War the Confederates dubbed him the "Blackjack Colonel" because of his toughness as a commander.

Blackleg. An English slang term for a race-course swindler.

Black Letter. The Gothic or German type, because of its black appearance.

Black-letter Day. An unlucky day, — one to be recalled with regret. The Romans marked their unlucky days with a piece of charcoal, and their lucky ones with chalk.

Black-letter Dogs. Bibliomaniacs who delve in out-of-the-way corners to unearth black-letter copies of old books.

Black-mail. Tribute of cash, corn, or cattle annually paid in North Britain to certain bands, allied to robbers, to be by them protected from plunder. BLACK RENT: Rent paid in grain or flesh. GRASS-MAIL: Rent paid for pasturage.

Black Monday. (1) On Easter Monday, April 14, 1360, Edward III. was encamped before Paris with his army, and many of his men and horses perished from the intense cold. The Monday after Easter Sunday is so nicknamed in memory of this fatal day. Says Lancelot, in "The Merchant of Venice": "It was not for nothing that my nose fell a-bleeding on Black Monday last at six o'clock in the morning." Another account traces the origin of the name to the massacre of the English by the Irish at Cullen's Wood, near Dublin, on Easter Monday, March 30, 1209.

The English were merrymaking, when the Irish fell on them and slaughtered men, women, and children. *See* BLUE MONDAY. (2) Feb. 27, 1865, was so named in Melbourne, where a terrible hot wind from the N. N. W. wrought much havoc.

Black Money. Spurious coin was so first named in 1335.

Black Monks. The Dominican friars were so named.

Black Museum. A collection of burglar's tools and other implements of crime at Scotland Yard, London, is so named.

Black Parliament. Convened by Henry VIII. in the London Bridewell.

Black Prince. Edward, Prince of Wales, son of Edward III., so styled, according to Froissart, "by terror of his arms;" according to others, because he wore black armor. The last derivation is probably without foundation.

Black Rent. *See* BLACK-MAIL.

Black Republicans. A name of reproach bestowed by the pro-slavery men in the United States upon the Republican party, certain of whose members resisted the extension of slavery into any State where it was not already an "institution."

Blacks, or Neri. *See* BIANCHI.

Blacks, The. *See* BLACK HORSE.

Black Saturday. The 4th of August, 1621, upon which day the Scottish Parliament agreed to certain articles admitting Episcopalian customs into the church, — a highly obnoxious measure to the Presbyterians. A violent storm that darkened the heavens was thought to be a mark of God's displeasure.

Blacksmith Astronomer. Lawrence J. Ibach (1818–1888), a resident of Pennsylvania, was so named. He followed the trade of a blacksmith nearly all his life. When a boy he lived with a relative who had a knowledge of astronomy. Young Ibach devoted himself to the study of the science, and for thirty-five years was one of the leading almanac calculators in this country. Mr. Ibach made his calculations at night after working at his trade in the daytime.

Black Snake. The sobriquet given to Anthony Wayne (1745–1796) by the Indians, in allusion to his success in warfare. The black snake will attack any other species, and is rarely worsted.

Black Swan. The sobriquet of Elizabeth Taylor Greenfield, a negro singer (1808–1876). She was born in slavery, but developed great ability as a vocalist.

Black Thursday. The name given in the colony of Victoria, Australia, to Thursday, Feb. 6, 1851, when the most terrible bush fire known in the annals of the colony occurred. It raged over an immense area. One writer in the newspapers of the time said that he rode at headlong speed for fifty miles, with fire raging on each side of his route. The heat was felt far out at sea, and many birds fell dead on the decks of coasting vessels. The destruction of animal life and farming stock in this conflagration was enormous.

Black Watch. Armed companies of the loyal clans, — Campbells, Monroes, etc., — employed to guard the Highlands of Scotland from 1725 to 1729, when they were mustered into the famous Forty-second Regiment, "the Royal Highland Black Watch." They wear dark tartans, whence the name.

Blanche. (Pseud.) Mrs. E. B. Field, a story-writer in the "Saturday Night."

Blanche Corelli. The stage-name of Madame Blanche Crillae.

Blanche Manning. The stage-name of Mrs. Daniel C. Manning.

Blanche Meda. The stage-name of Mrs. James Delphin, *née* Pratt.

Blanche Miller. The stage-name of Mrs. Niel Florence.

Blanche Roosevelt. The stage-name of Madame Machetta.

Blanche Webster. The stage-name of Mrs. D. Birom.

Blanche Wilson. The stage-name of Madeline Le Baron.

Blaney's Bloodhounds. *See* ROLLICKERS.

Blanketeers, Blanket Meeting. On March 10, 1817, a number of suffering operatives met in St. Peter's Field, near Manchester, many of them having blankets or rugs rolled and strapped to their backs. They essayed to march on London, but were dispersed by the magistracy. Their object was believed to be the commencement of a great insurrection. Eventually the leaders obtained an audience with the Cabinet ministers, and better feeling prevailed.

Blarney Stone. A relic of the ancient castle of Blarney, in Ireland. It is a triangular stone suspended from the north angle of the castle about twenty feet from the top, and bearing this inscription : "Cormack MacCarthy fortis me fieri fecit, A. D. 1446." According to a tradition of the country the castle was besieged by the English under Carew, Earl of Totness, who, having concluded an armistice with the commander of the castle on condition of its surrender, waited long for the fulfilment of the terms, but was put off from day to day with soft speeches instead, until he became the jest of Elizabeth's ministers and the dupe of the Lord of Blarney. From that day "kissing the Blarney Stone" has been synonymous with flattery and smooth, deceitful words.

Blasphemous Balfour. Sir James Balfour, a Scottish judge, who died in 1583, was so nicknamed because of his apostasy.

Blatch. Blatchford's Circuit Court Reports.

Blaze, Blazing. In Virginia crown grants were commonly *blazed out*, or *blazoned*, by cutting some marks in the bark of a tree. The word (from the French *blason*) has grown into an Americanism; a new-comer *blazes out* his pre-emption right on the tree-trunks, or he *deadens* the tree for the same purpose by belting or *ringing* it, — *i. e.*, cutting off a circular piece of bark, so as to prevent the sap from rising.

Blear-eyed. Aurelius Brandolini, the Italian poet (fl. 1440–1497).

Bleeding Kansas. Kansas was so named because much of the sanguinary strife of the anti-slavery agitation immediately preceding the civil war took place within its borders.

Blind, The. (1) Luigi Groto, Italian poet (fl. 1541–1585). (2) Ludwig III, Emperor of Germany (fl. 880–934).

Blind Half Hundred. *See* DIRTY HALF HUNDRED.

Blind Harper. John Parry, a famous performer, who died 1739.

Blind Harry. A famous Scottish minstrel who flourished in the fifteenth century. He composed an epic on William Wallace over eleven thousand lines in length.

Blind Leaders of the Blind. A sect of the Pharisees who were in the habit of walking with their eyes closed, and often ran against a wall or into a roadside ditch. Matt. xv. 14.

Blindman's Holiday. The twilight hour, when it is too dark to work and too light to kindle gas or candles. All are then in the condition of blind men, who for the most part enjoy perpetual holiday.

Blind Preacher. (1) Timothy Woodbridge (1784–1862). (2) James Waddel (1739–1805). (3) William Henry Milburn (b. 1823). All were Americans.

Blind Singer. Oliver Shaw (1776–1849), an American song-writer and vocalist, is referred to by this name by Dr. Ritter.

Blind Traveller. Lieut. James Holman (fl. 1787–1857).

Blizzard. A modern American word, probably more or less onomatopoetic : suggestive words are *blow*, *blast*, *blister*, *bluster ;* the Fr. *blesser*, to wound, has also been conjectured, but there is nothing to indicate a French origin. As applied to a bitter snow-storm, the word became general in the American newspapers during the severe winter of 1880–1881 ; but according to the "Milwaukee Republican," March 4, 1881, it had been so applied in the "Northern Vindicator," Esherville, Ill., between 1860 and 1870.

"Blizzards are cold snaps which come with a high wind, as opposed to the calm frost of anticyclones. They are the result of the passage of the rear of cyclones or of V depressions in the winter months. Then we get high, strong northwesterly winds, blowing off a frozen continent, with a temperature many degrees below zero, and with surroundings which are very destructive to life. The wind drives the cold into the bones, even through fur clothing, and raises a blinding dust of powdery snow. Under these circumstances only are the Western voyagers ever lost. If wood cannot be found Nature can only resist the cold for a certain number of hours, and the men are frozen to death if no shelter can be reached. A very curious circumstance attends these deaths. In almost every case the victims are found to have begun to strip themselves. When the body is nearly reduced to an icicle, only a very little blood continues to circulate languidly through the brain. Then delirium sets in, with a delusive sensation of heat, under the influence of which the traveller begins to divest himself of his clothes."

Blizzard Monday. March 12, 1888, on which day the Eastern States were visited by a snow-storm of unparalleled severity, lasting two days, and which paralyzed travel and business for a week.

Block Island Turkey. A colloquial name for salted codfish. *See* ALBANY BEEF.

Blondin, M. The professional name of Emile Gravelet, the famous tight-rope walker.

B.LL. *Baccalaureus Legum.* Bachelor of Laws. Same as LL.B.

Blood Bath (1520). A massacre of the Swedish nobles and leaders, which occurred three days after the coronation of Christian II., king of Denmark, Sweden, and Norway. The victims were invited to attend the coronation, and were put to the sword, under the plea of being enemies of the true church. In this massacre fell both the father and brother-in-law of Gustavus Vasa. The former was named Eric Johansson, and the latter Brahe.

Blood, Field of. *See* FIELD OF BLOOD.

Blood is Thicker than Water. "Many think that this saying originated with Commodore Tatnall, of the United States Navy, who assisted the English in Chinese waters, and, in his despatch to his government, justified his interference by quoting the phrase. It is, however, an old English proverb, and it is to be found in Ray's 'Collection of English Proverbs,' published in 1672. Walter Scott, too, makes Dandie Dinmont say, 'Weel! *blude's thicker than water;* she's welcome to the cheeses and the hams just the same.' It is a protest against modern cosmopolitanism and universal benevolence that 'spreads as far and is as weak and useless as the threads of summer gossamer.' A brother is better than a stranger, is the pith of the saying. Blood stands for traceable, admitted consanguinity ; water, for the colorless and chilled fluid that flows through the veins of the rest of mankind, who are *homines homini lupi*, and take but cold interest in the happiness of a stranger, and thus cause the fluid coursing through their hearts to appear as one with water to the proverb-maker. Water, too, in our early writers was symbolic of looseness, inattachment, falsity. 'Unstable as water' is the scriptural phrase. Thicker signifies greater consistency and substance; hence closeness of attachment, adhesiveness. 'As thick as thieves,'—as close as bad men when banding for evil enterprise. Blood is always thought binding. Conspirators have signed their bonds with their own blood, as martyrs have their attestation of the truth. 'He cemented the union of the two families by marriage,' is a stock phrase with historians. Quitting metaphor for physical fact, we find that the blood as well as the hair of oxen has been used to bind mortar together and give greater consistency than mere water, as is reported of the White Tower of London. The proverb may also allude to the spiritual relationship which, according to the doctrine of the Roman Catholic Church, is created between the sponsor and the child whom he brings to the waters of baptism. The relationship by blood would probably be more thought of than one originating in water."—LIPPINCOTT.

Bloodless Lambs, or **Peacemakers.** A nickname given to the Sixteenth Regiment of the line, because it is the only regiment in the British service without the names of battles inscribed on its flags.

Blood of the Martyrs the Seed of the Church. "Plures efficimur, quoties metimur a vobis ; semen est sanguis Christianorum."—TERTULLIAN, *Apologet.*

In a note to this passage in "Tertullian" (ed. 1641), is the following quotation from "Saint Jerome": "Est sanguis martyrum seminarium Ecclesiarum."

Blood's Conspiracy. Colonel Blood, a cast-off member of the Protector's household, with a number of confederates, seized the Duke of Ormond's coach, Dec. 6, 1670, and carried the duke to Tyburn, where he would have been hanged but for the timely arrival of some friends. Blood afterwards tried to steal the royal crown from the Jewel-room in the Tower, May 9, 1671. For neither of these offences, strange to say, was he punished.

Blood-tubs. A set of rowdies in Baltimore, chiefly butchers, who got their epithet from having on an election day dipped an obnoxious German head down in a tub of warm blood, and then driven him running through the town. The following is from the song of the Irish Legion, written after the attack on the Union soldiers while passing through Baltimore, in 1861 :—

"Blood-tubs and Plug-uglies, and others galore,
Are sick for a thrashing in sweet Baltimore ;
Be jabers ! that same I'd be proud to inform
Of the terrible force of an Irishman's arm."

Bloody, The. Otho II., Emperor of Germany (fl. 955–983).

Bloody Angle. In the fighting at Spottsylvania in 1864 there was a sharp salient between the troops of Hancock and Lee, where the fighting was as fierce as any during the war, and the carnage correspondingly severe.

Bloody Assize. The state trials held by the notorious Jeffreys in 1685 after the defeat of Monmouth at Sedgmoor. Three hundred persons were executed; numbers were whipped, fined, or imprisoned, and nearly a thousand were transported to the American plantations.

Bloody Bear, in Dryden's poem, "The Hind and Panther," means the Independents.

" The bloody bear, an independent beast,
    Unlicked to form, in groans her hate expresses."

Bloody Bill. A name given to a statute of King Henry VIII., which prescribed hanging or burning as the penalty to be visited on all who should deny the doctrine of transubstantiation.

Bloody Butcher. The Duke of Cumberland, second son of George II., who was so dubbed because of his enormities in suppressing the rebellion of the partisans of the Young Pretender.

Bloody Eleventh. An English regiment, so nicknamed from the fact that they were on more than one occasion nearly annihilated, as at Fontenoy and Salamanca.

Bloody Mary. Queen Mary of England, whose reign is notorious for the burnings and beheadings of Protestants throughout the realm.

Bloody Meadow. A field in the outskirts of Tewksbury, England, where the battle of Tewksbury was fought, May 14, 1471.

Bloody Rump. Another and a later name for the Rump Parliament (q. v.).

Bloody Shirt. We know of no better explanation of the origin of this phrase than that given by Roscoe Conkling in a speech made in New York, Sept. 17, 1880. Referring to the "bloody shirt," he said : " It is a relief to remember that this phrase, with the thing it means, is no invention of our politics. It dates back to Scotland, three centuries ago. After a massacre in Glenfruin, not so savage as has stained our annals, two hundred and twenty widows rode on white palfreys to Stirling Tower, bearing each on a spear her husband's bloody shirt. The appeal waked Scotland's slumbering sword, and outlawry and the block made the name of Glen-

fruin terrible to victorious Clan Alpine, even to the third and fourth generation." The "ensanguined garment" is a euphonious rendering of this now historic phrase.

Bloody Sweat. *See* STIGMATA.

Bloody Wedding. The massacre of Saint Bartholomew, 1572, has been so named because it occurred during the nuptial festivities attending the union of Henry IV. and Marguerite, daughter of Catherine de' Medici.

Blouses. A collective name for a mob in Paris. French workmen uniformly wear the blouse.

Blow a Cloud. A term as old as the reign of Elizabeth for the act of smoking a cigar or pipe.

Blowzelinda. A country maiden in Gay's pastoral called "The Shepherd's Week."

" Sweet is my toil when Blowzelind is near;
    Of her bereft, 't is winter all the year.
            .   .   .   .
    Come, Blowzelinda, ease thy swain's desire,
    My summer's shadow and my winter's fire."

Bls. Bales.

Blue-apron Statesman. An English lay politician ; a tradesman who interferes with the affairs of the nation. The reference is to the blue apron once worn by almost all tradesmen, but now restricted to butchers, poulterers, fishmongers, etc.

Bluebacks. The Southern paper currency during the civil war was so named to distinguish it from the Greenbacks (q. v.) of the North.

Blue Blood. The old families of Spain traced their pedigree beyond the time of the Moorish conquest, and claimed that their blood was blue, while that of common people was of a muddy hue.

Blue Bonnet. (Pseud.) Rev. Thomas Fenwick, a Canadian clergyman and miscellaneous writer.

Blue-bonnets. The Scotch. *See* BONNET LAIRDS.

            England shall many a day
                Tell of the bloody fray
    When the blue-bonnets came over the border.
                        SCOTT.

Blue-bottle. A policeman. So named from the color of his uniform.

Blue-coat School, Blue-coat Boys. The name colloquially given to Christ Hospital and its scholars, Newgate Street, London, in which the boys wear long blue coats or gowns.

Blue-devils, or A Fit of the Blues. Melancholy or low spirits. It is affirmed that indigo-dyers are especially subject to moodiness.

Blue Dog. *See* ONCE IN A BLUE MOON.

Blue Envelope. Some of the great American railroads use various colored envelopes for different branches of their business. On some of these a blue envelope contains a notice of dismissal; hence the use of the phrase "to get the blue envelope" signifies a loss of one's employment. A yellow envelope is sometimes used.

Blue Fear, Blue Funk. *See* ONCE IN A BLUE MOON.

Blue-gowns. The name popularly given to a class of privileged mendicants in Scotland. Their proper designation was "King's Bedesmen," or "Beadsmen." "Each of the beadsmen on his Majesty's birthday received a gown or cloak of blue cloth, with a loaf of bread, a bottle of ale, and a leathern purse containing a penny for every year of the king's life. Every birthday another beadsman was added to the number, as a penny was added to each man's purse."

Blue-grass State. A name popularly bestowed on the State of Kentucky, and derived from the so-called "blue-grass" which has made the State so noted as the breeding-ground of fine cattle and horses. Of course the grass is not blue; the name refers to the underlying strata of blue limestone.

Blue-hen State. Delaware. This name arose from the fact that cock-fighting was at one time very popular in the State. One of the devotees of this sport, a Captain Caldwell, used to say that no bird could be really game unless hatched by a blue hen.

Blue Jacket. (Pseud.) Admiral John Adolphus Bernard Dahlgren, U.S.N.

Blue Laws. A derisive name given to the laws of the early colonists in Connecticut. It is related that "the strict enactments of the Puritans were recounted in England and in the other colonies with many laughable exaggerations and malicious additions; and some of the satirical statements of contemporary writers, taken literally, have given rise to the erroneous opinion that the Blue Laws actually existed as a legal code."

They assumed the right to regulate the expenditures of the people, even for wearing-apparel, according to their several incomes. The General Court of Massachusetts on one occasion required the proper officers to notice the "apparel" of the people, especially their "ribands and great boots." Drinking of healths, wearing funeral badges, and many other things that seemed improper, were forbidden. At Hartford the General Court kept a constant eye upon the morals of the people. Freemen were compelled to vote under penalty of a fine of sixpence. The use of tobacco was prohibited to persons under twenty years of age, without the certificate of a physician; and no others were allowed to use it more than once a day, and then they must be ten miles from any house. The people of Hartford were all obliged to rise in the morning when the watchman rang his bell. These are but a few of the hundreds of similar enactments found on the records of the New England courts. In 1646 the Legislature of Massachusetts passed a law which imposed the penalty of a flogging upon any one who should kiss a woman in the streets. More than a hundred years afterward this law was enforced in Boston. The captain of a British man-of-war happened to return from a cruise on Sunday. His overjoyed wife met him on the wharf, and he kissed her several times. The magistrates ordered him to be flogged. The punishment incurred no ignominy, and he associated freely with the best citizens. When about to depart, the captain invited the magistrates and others on board his vessel, to dine. When dinner was over, he caused all the magistrates to be flogged, on deck, in sight of the town; then, assuring them that he considered accounts settled between him and them, he dismissed them, and set sail. — LOSSING.

Blue-light Federalists. A name given to those Americans who were believed to have made friendly "blue-light" signals to British ships in the War of 1812.

Blue Monday. Those whose affairs of business occupied them on Sunday were considered to have a right to a holiday on Monday. The name is said to be derived from a custom of decorating European churches with blue the Monday before Lent. *See* BLACK MONDAY.

Bluenoses. A collective nickname for Nova-Scotians, in allusion to the effect of their bleak climate upon that part of the face.

Blue-peter. A flag with a blue ground and white square centre, flown from the fore, in token that a vessel is about to sail. "Peter" is a corruption of the French *partir*, to leave.

Blue Ribbon of the French Turf. The Grand Prix de Paris.

Blue Ribbon of the Turf. The stakes for the English Derby were so named by Lord Beaconsfield. When Lord George Bentinck quitted the turf for the House of Commons, he sold his stud. On the 22d of May, 1848, his protectionist resolutions were negatived in the House, and on the 24th Surplice, one of the horses he had parted with, won the Derby. "All my life," he groaned, " I have been trying for this, and for what have I sacrificed it!" The sympathizing Disraeli in vain strove to console his friend. " You do not know what the Derby is," rejoined Lord George. " Yes, I do," said Disraeli ; " it is the Blue Ribbon of the English Turf." *See* ISTH-MIAN GAMES OF ENGLAND.

Blue-ruin. Gin is so named in England ; *blue* from its tint, and *ruin* from its effects.

Blues. *See* BLUE-DEVILS.

Blues, The, of Constantinople. A political party in the reign of Justinian, opposed to the Greens of Anastasius. Ever afterward blue was the emblem of royalty at Rome.

Blueskin. The surname or nickname given to Joseph Blake, the English highwayman, executed Nov. 11, 1723. His complexion was very dark.

Blueskins. A nickname given to Presbyterians, because of their alleged grave demeanor.

Blue-stocking. A female pedant. In 1400 a society of ladies and gentlemen was formed at Venice, distinguished by the color of their stockings, and addicted to literary pursuits. Similar societies sprung up all over Europe. In England they did not become extinct till 1840, when the Countess of Cork, who, as Miss Moncton, was the last of the clique, died.

Bluff City. Hannibal, Mo. It is built on rising ground on the bank of the Mississippi.

Bluff Harry or **Hal.** Henry VIII., "who was famed for his bluff and burly manners."

B. M. *Baccalaureus Medicinæ.* Bachelor of Medicine. Same as M. B.

Boanerges (" sons of thunder "). A name given to James and John, sons of Zebedee, because they desired to call down fire from heaven to consume the contemptuous Samaritans. See Luke ix. 54. The name in modern times has been given to a preacher who delivers "rousing" sermons, and expounds the doctrines of election and punishment with emphasis.

Boar, The. Richard III. was so nicknamed from his armorial device. *See* BRISTLED BAPTIST BOAR.

Bob. A colloquial nickname for a shilling in England. It is thought to be a corruption of the Scotch *bawbee.*

Bobadil. A military braggart. Captain Bobadil is a character in Ben Jonson's comedy of " Every Man in his Humor." This name was probably suggested by Bobadilla, first governor of Cuba, who sent Columbus home in chains.

Bobbing John. John Erskine, eleventh Earl of Mar (1675-1732).

Bobby. An English nickname for a policeman, because Sir Robert Peel first introduced them into the realm. They are dubbed " peelers " for the same reason.

Bob Hart. The stage-name of Robert Sutherland, a " minstrel," and later a revival preacher (d. 1888).

Bob White. Nickname for the American quail (*Ortyx virginianus*), whose note of warning closely resembles those words in sound.

Boden See. The German name for the Lake of Constance in Switzerland, — so called because the *bodmanno*, or royal messenger, of the Carlovingian kings used to reside near by.

Body of Liberties. The first code of laws established in New England, compiled for the colony of Massachusetts in 1641, by Rev. Nathaniel Ward.

Bœotian. An epithet current among the ancients to denote a supremely stupid person. The natives of Bœotia were famed for their dulness.

Bœotian Ears. Ears unable to appreciate music and rhetoric.

This is having taste and sentiment. Well, friend, I assure thee thou hast not got Bœotian ears. — LESAGE, *Gil Blas.*

Bogle Swindle. A gigantic swindle concocted in Paris by fourteen persons, who expected to net at least a million sterling. It was exposed in the London " Times."

Bogomili. A religious sect of the twelfth century, whose chief seat was Thrace. So called from their constant repetition of the words, " Lord, have mercy upon us," which in Bulgarian is *bog milui.*

Bog-trotters. A colloquial term in Ireland for vagrants or tramps, in allusion to their skill in crossing the bogs from tussock to tussock.

Bogus. The most plausible explanation of this common term is that the assumed name of a remarkably successful swindler, "Borghese," was in course of time not only reduced to "bogus," but finally applied to everything false and fraudulent. It spread rapidly over the whole Union, and is now one of the most familiar of Americanisms.

Bohem. Bohemian.

Bohemia. A slang sobriquet for those localities in the great cities of Europe and America frequented by adventurers in art or literature, and who lead an unsettled, gay, and often questionable existence. Bohemia, in Europe, was long thought to be the original home of the gypsies.

Bohemian. "A term of mild reproach bestowed on persons of unconventional habits. But a 'Bohemian' in the real sense of the word is a person, man or woman, who does not go into 'society;' who is happy-go-lucky, unconventional, now 'flush,' now 'short' of money; who, having money, spends it freely, enjoying it, and having none, hopes for it in the future; who makes the best of everything, and takes life as it comes. Your true Bohemian is a philosopher, and in spite of his unconventionality he is at least as apt to be respectable as a leader in conventional society."

Bold Bean-hiller. The sobriquet borne by John Durkee (1728–1782), the American Indian-fighter. His place of residence in Windham, Conn., gave rise to the odd title.

Bolerium Promontory. Land's End, Cornwall, is so called.

Bolero. A Spanish dance with castanets.

Bolingbroke. Henry IV. of England (fl. 1366–1413) is often alluded to by this name. He was born at Bolingbroke, in Lincolnshire.

Bolingbroke. (Pseud.) Nicholas Amherst (*circa* 1726), as editor of the "Craftsman."

Bolivar, Patsy. *See* PATSY BOLIVAR.

Bolognese School. There were three periods to the Bolognese school of painting, — Early, Roman, and Eclectic. The first was founded by Marco Zoppo in the fifteenth century; and its best exponent was Francia. The second was founded in the sixteenth century by Bagnacavallo; and its chief exponents were Primaticcio, Tibaldi, and Niccolo del Abbate. The third was founded by the Carracci at the close of the sixteenth century; and its best masters have been Domenichino, Lanfranco, Guido, Guercino, and Albani.

Bolt, Bolter. To secede from the political programme laid down by one's party is to "bolt" the ticket; those who do so are named "bolters."

Bolton Row. (Pseud.) Hon. Spencer Cecil Brabazon Ponsonby, author of "Peril," etc.

Bolton Rowe. (Pseud.) (1) Clement Scott. (2) B. C. Stephenson, a dramatic writer of the present day.

Bolus. An apothecary, so called because he administers boluses. George Colman adopts the name for his apothecary, who wrote his labels in rhyme, one of which was —

> "When taken,
> To be well shaken; "

but the patient, being shaken instead, died.

Bomba. Ferdinand II., king of Naples, was thus nicknamed in consequence of his wanton attack on Messina in 1848, during which many innocent lives were lost and much property destroyed. His son, Francis II., was nicknamed "Bomba II." for his bombardment of Palermo in 1860; he was also dubbed "Bombalina; " *i. e.*, Little Bomba.

Bombardinio. (Pseud.) William Maginn in "Fraser's Magazine."

Bombastes Furioso. One who talks big and uses long words; the hero of a burlesque opera, so called, by William B. Rhodes.

Bombastus. The family name of Paracelsus, who was believed to keep a small devil prisoner in the pommel of his sword.

Bomb City. A nickname conferred on Chicago, Ill., on account of the "Haymarket Riots," May 4, 1886, on which occasion dynamite bombs were thrown at the police, five of whom were killed.

Bona Dea. Literally, "The Good Goddess." A mysterious Roman divinity, variously described as the wife, sister, or daughter of Faunus. She was worshipped at Rome from the most ancient times, only by women, however, even her name being concealed from men. Intercession was made for the whole Roman nation. "The solemnities were performed generally by aristocratic vestals. At this celebration no males were allowed to be present; even portraits of men were veiled. The wine consumed was called milk, in order that its name might not be discovered; and the vessel in which it was served, *mellarium*. The symbol of the goddess was a serpent, indicating her healing powers, and certain herbs were sold in her temple."

Bona fide. This phrase is frequently pronounced by imperfectly educated people as though the latter word were one syllable only. Its proper division into syllables is *bo-nâ fi-de ;* the accent is on the *fi.* The literal meaning is "in good faith." *Bona fides* is "good faith."

Bon ami. (Fr.) Good friend.

Bonanza. A Spanish term, of similar meaning to Placer (*q. v.*). It is a nautical word, and means "fair weather at sea." If the reader will refer to Matthew viii. 26, he will read that, after the Lord rebuked the wind and the sea, "there was a great calm." And if reference is next had to the Spanish version of the New Testament, he will find the phrase there given, "una grande bonanza." It is easy to understand how the word came into its figurative use as meaning a happy calm and good hope after a weary search.

Bonanza Kings. James Clair Flood, W. S. O'Brien, John W. Mackay, and James G. Fair, four men of Irish parentage who acquired vast fortunes from the gold and silver mines on the Pacific coast. They had various imitators and successors who shared the name, but these four men were the "only original" Bonanza Kings.

Bona-roba. An Italian nickname for a courtesan, in allusion to her gay attire.

Bon-bon. A sweetmeat.

Bon bourgeois. (Fr.) "Good citizen." A citizen of substance.

Bon chevalier, etc. *See* GOOD KNIGHT.

Bone to pick. It is the custom in Sicily for the father of a bride to hand the bridegroom a bone, saying, "Pick this bone ; you have undertaken a more difficult task."

Boney. A diminutive nickname for Bonaparte, current in England in the first part of this century.

Bonfanti, Mlle. The professional name of Mrs. Hoffman, daughter-in-law of the late ex-Governor Hoffman of New York.

Bon Gaultier. (Pseud.) W. E. Aytoun and Theodore Martin, literary collaborateurs.

Bon gré, mal gré. (Fr.) "Good will, bad will." With a good or bad grace; willing or unwilling.

Bonhomie. Good-natured simplicity.

Bonhomme. The French peasant is nicknamed "Jacques Bonhomme;" *i. e.*, "James Goodfellow." More particularly, however, the name is given to those of the common people who meddled in politics. The uprising of the peasantry in 1358 is known as "La Jacquerie."

Bon Hommes ("Good Men"). An order of hermits of gentle and simple lives who first appeared in France about 1217, and in England about 1283. The prior of the order was named "Le Bon Homme" by Louis VI. *See* JACQUES BONHOMME.

Boniface. This name is probably applied to publicans from the legend mentioned in the "Ebrietatis Encomium," which relates that Pope Boniface instituted indulgences for those who should drink a cup after grace, to his own memory, or to the Pope for the time being, which cup is proverbially called Saint Boniface's Cup.

Boni principii finis bonus. (Lat.) A good ending comes from a good beginning.

Bonis nocet quisquis pepercerit malis. (Lat.) He hurts the good who spares the bad.

Bon jour. (Fr.) "Good day." Good morning.

Bon mot. A witty saying.

Bonne. (Fr.) A nurse or governess.

Bonne bête. (Fr.) "Good beast." Good-natured fool.

Bonne bouche. (Fr.) Literally, "a good mouth." Used in England as equivalent to *tit-bit*, or in reference to some rare old wine; as, "Now I'll give you a *bonne bouche.* This is a bottle of the celebrated Comet Port of 1811."

Bonne et belle. (Fr.) "Good and beautiful." Good and handsome.

Bonne foi. (Fr.) Good faith.

Bonne fortune. (Fr.) Good fortune; a piece of good luck.

Bonnes gens. (Fr.) "Good people." Civilized beings; men of the right stamp.

Bonne table. (Fr.) A good table.

Bonnet de nuit. (Fr.) A nightcap.

Bonnet Lairds. Country magnates who wore the old Scotch cap, or *braid bonnet.*

Bonnet rouge. (Fr.) The red cap; the cap of liberty.

Bonnie Chevalier. Charles Edward, the "Young Pretender" (1720–1788).

Bonnie Meyer. The stage-name of Mrs. J. H. Thorne.

Bono Johnny. A nickname for the English throughout the East.

Bon soir. (Fr.) Good evening.

Bon ton. (Fr.) High fashion; first-class society.

Bon vivant. (Fr.) A jolly fellow; a high feeder or liver.

Bons vivants. (Fr.) Good companions.

Bon voyage. (Fr.) A pleasant journey or voyage, as the case may be.

Booby. A dunce; a spiritless fellow. Among the Bahama Islands there is a sort of pelican, called a booby, which suffers itself to be attacked by other birds, and without resistance gives up the fish it has caught for itself.

Boodle Aldermen. In 1884–1886 certain New York aldermen were believed to have been bribed to vote away a certain railroad charter on Broadway, and the accused were dubbed "Boodle Aldermen," *boodle* being a slang term for "money." One writer suggests that the word "boodle" is doubtless derived from the Dutch word "boedel," which means "property or goods." A "boedelster," he says, is the attorney or other person who finally possesses the "boedel."

Book of Books. The Bible; Greek βίβλος, book.

Book of the Four Kings. (Fr., "Livre des Quatre Rois," a pack of cards.) In a French pack the four kings are Charlemagne, David, Alexander, and Cæsar, representatives of the Franco-German, Jewish, Macedonian, and Roman monarchies.

Bookworm. One always poring over his books, in allusion to the insect that eats holes in books, and lives in and on its leaves.

Bookworm. (Pseud.) Thomas F. Donnelly, American *littérateur.*

Boötes ("the ox-driver"). In classical mythology the son of Ceres, and the inventor of the plough. He was translated to the heavens, where he was made a constellation.

Border, The. In the history of Great Britain a popular designation of the boundary between England and Scotland. From the end of the tenth century until that of the seventeenth this frontier was the scene of constant conflict, the details of which abound in and inspire both song and story. It was not until the union of the kingdoms in 1707 that these disturbances became of less frequency, but during the Jacobite excitement they were revived with great frequency.

Border Minstrel. Sir Walter Scott (fl. 1771–1832), poet and novelist, who reckoned his descent from the great Buccleuch family, the powerful border magnates.

Border Ruffians. Southern settlers from Missouri who went into Kansas to combat the anti-slavery men about 1854.

Border States. In *ante-bellum* times in American history a popular name for those States lying next to the line of the free States; viz., Missouri, Kentucky, Virginia, Maryland, and Delaware. Upon the abolition of slavery the term passed into desuetude.

Border-thief School. The name given to Sir Walter Scott and his imitators who sung the praises of various freebooting chiefs of the Scottish border.

Border War. A name applied to the hostilities that took place between the Free-State emigrants to Kansas and the slaveholders from Missouri, when, in 1854, the Kansas-Nebraska Bill left the question of slavery in that Territory to be settled by the inhabitants. Bloody encounters were frequent, and several pitched battles were fought.

Boreas. In classical mythology the north wind, son of Astræas and Aurora.

Borough English. The law of succession where the youngest son inherits instead of the eldest. It is of Saxon origin, and is so called to distinguish it from the Norman custom. It obtains in the manors of Lambeth, Hackney, part of Islington, Heston, Edmonton, etc.

Borrowing Days. The last three days of March are so named in Scotland and in parts of England. The popular notion is that these days are borrowed or taken from April, and may be expected to consist of wet or stormy weather. Although this belief dates from a period before the change of the style, a few days of broken and unsettled weather at the end of March often give color to this old superstition.

Boscawen. (Pseud.) Nathaniel Greene in his various editorial capacities from 1817 to 1852.

Bosphorus, The Cimmerian. *See* CIMMERIAN BOSPHORUS.

Boss = MASTER, EMPLOYER, LEADER. The word "boss" is derived from the Dutch *baas*. Originally used in its primitive meaning of "master or overseer," it became customary to speak of a *boss tailor* or a *boss carpenter*, meaning a mechanic who employed several *hands* or workmen. Soon the word became widely popular. It has even been turned into a verb, and to "*boss* a job" is a common expression for undertaking a business. The word, harmless in itself, has passed into politics and become part of the history of the United States. The head of a party, the manager of an intrigue, the patron of a bill in Congress, each is called the *boss*. The term is current from the Gulf of St. Lawrence to the Gulf of Mexico, from the Narrows to the Golden Gate.

Bossuet of the American Church. Archbishop Napoleon Joseph Perché, of New Orleans (1805–1883), was so styled by Pope Leo XIII.

Bost. Boston.

Boston Bard. (Pseud.) Robert S. Coffin, American poet (1797–1827).

Boston Massacre. A street affray in Boston, March 5, 1770, in which a sergeant's guard fired into a mob of people who had pelted them with snowballs. Three men were killed and several wounded.

Boston Rebel. (Pseud.) John Lowell, LL.D., American lawyer and political writer (1769–1840).

Boston Sydney Smith. Thomas G. Appleton, a brother-in-law of Longfellow, received this appellation.

Boston Tea-Party. A name popularly conferred on the historic gathering of citizens in Boston, Dec. 16, 1773, who met to carry out the resolution of the colony respecting the non-importation of goods from England. Disguised as Indians, they boarded three English vessels, and emptied their cargoes of tea into the waters of the harbor.

Not long ago the "Boston Transcript" published the names of fifty-eight persons who were in the "Tea-Party," quoted from Thatcher's "Traits of the Tea-Party," published in 1835, at which time nine or ten of the parties immediately interested were alive and attested the correctness of the list. The names were as follows : George R. T. Hewes, Joseph Shed, John Crane, Josiah Wheeler, Thomas Urann, Adam Collson, S. Collidge, Joseph Payson, James Brewer, Thomas Bolter, Edward Proctor, Samuel Sloper, Thomas Gerrish, Nathaniel Green, Benjamin Simpson, Joseph Eayres, Joseph Lee, William Molineux, Paul Revere, John Spurr, Thomas Moore, Samuel Howard, Matthew Loring, Thomas Spear, Daniel Ingoldson, Richard Hunnewell, John Horton, Jonathan Hunnewell, Thomas Chase, Thomas Melville, Henry Purkitt, Edward C. Howe, Ebenezer Stevens, Nicholas Campbell, John Russell, Thomas Porter, William Hendley, Benjamin Rice, Samuel Gore, Nathaniel Frothingham, Moses Grant, Peter Slaper, James Starr, Abraham Tower, William Pierce, William Russell, T. Gammell, —— McIntosh, Dr. Thomas Young, Joseph Wyeth, Edward Dolbear, —— Martin, Samuel Peck, Lendall Pitts, Samuel Sprague, Benjamin Clarke, Richard Hunnewell, Jr., John Prince. To these names have been added the following, on the strength of family tradition. The list is not to be accepted as absolutely accurate : Nathaniel Barber, Samuel Barnard, Henry Bass, Edward Bates, Nathaniel Bradlee, David Bradlee, Josiah Bradlee, Thomas Bradlee, Seth Ingersoll Brown, Stephen Burce, Benjamin Burton, George Carlton, Gilbert Colesworthy, John Cochran, Gershom Collier, James Foster Condy, Samuel Cooper, Thomas Dana, Jr., Robert Davis, Joseph Eaton, —— Eckley, William Etheridge, Samuel Fenno, Samuel Foster, John Fulton, Samuel Hammond, John Hicks, Samuel Hobbs, Thomas Hunstable, Abraham Hunt, David Kennison, Amos Lincoln, Thomas Machin, Archibald MacNeil, John May, —— Mead, Anthony Morse, Eliphalet Newell, Joseph Pearse Palmer, Jonathan Parker, John Peters, Samuel Pitts, Henry Prentiss, John Randall, Joseph Roby, Phineas Stearns, Robert Sessions, Elisha Story, James Swan, John Truman, Isaac Williams, David Williams, Jeremiah Williams, Thomas Williams, Nathaniel Willis.

Boswell Butt. (Pseud.) Charles H. Ross, English humorist (b. 1836).

Boswell Redivivus. (Pseud.) William Hazlitt, in the "New Monthly Magazine," 1826–1827.

Bot. Botany.

Botany Bay of American Colleges. Union College has been so named because of the fact that many students who for various reasons failed to graduate from other institutions of learning were there allowed to complete their college studies.

Botheration Primus. The college (Princeton) sobriquet borne by Nathaniel Niles, the American lawyer (1741–1828).

Botherers, The. A by-name for the King's Own Borderers (Twenty-fifth Regiment) in the English service, growing out of the manner in which the Scotch pronounce the name "Borderers."

Bothie System. The Scottish mode of grouping all the outbuildings of a farm, with the dwellings of the laborers, in a sort of barrack. A *bothie* is a cot or hut, and answers to the English "booth."

Bottle-holder. One who gives moral but not material support. The allusion is to boxing or prize-fighting, where each combatant has a bottle-holder to wipe off blood, refresh with water, and do other services to encourage his man to persevere and win.

Lord Palmerston considered himself the bottle-holder of oppressed States. He was the steadfast partisan of constitutional liberty in every part of the world. — *The Times.*

Bottle Imp. *See* CARTESIAN DEVIL.

Bottle of Hay. To "seek a needle in a bottle of hay" is a common expression. Shakspeare makes Bottom (Midsummer's Night's Dream, act iv. sc. 2) say, "I have a great desire to a bottle of hay." The phrase originally signified a quantity of hay tied in a bundle, to be carried out for foddering cattle. The word comes from the French *boteau*, a bundle.

Bottle Riot. An *émeute* at the theatre in Dublin, Dec. 14, 1822, arising out of the intensely bitter feeling against the Marquis of Wellesley. So named because, among other missiles, a bottle was hurled into his box.

Bottle Trick, The. Notice was given in the public prints that, to settle a wager, a man would undertake to jump into a quart bottle, at the Haymarket Theatre, London, Jan. 16, 1749. An immense crowd assembled inside and outside the house, and the pickpockets reaped a rich harvest. When the crowd realized that it had been duped, it nearly tore the house down.

Bottomless Pitt. A vulgar nickname given to William Pitt, who was of a spare habit.

Bottoms. The richest land commonly lies along the course of a stream, or, as it is termed, in the "river-bottom."

Boudoir. A small private apartment.

Bounty-jumper. During the civil war a term applied to men who received a bounty when enlisting, then ran away, enlisted in another State, and received a second bounty. Instances are known where men received many bounties in this way.

My song is of a fast young man whose name was
    Billy Wires;
He used to run with the machine, and go to all
    the fires:
But as he loved a soldier's life, and wished strange
    things to see,
So the thought struck him that he would go and
    jump the bounti-ee.
        Song of the Bounty-Jumper.

Bourbon. A dyed-in-the-wool Democrat; "one who never learns and who never forgets."

Bourgeois. A citizen of the trading class.

Bourgeoisie. The body of citizens.

Bourgeois of Calais. *See* SIX BOURGEOIS OF CALAIS.

Boustrapa. A nickname for Napoleon III., and containing an allusion to various notorious episodes in his career. The word is composed of the first letters of the words *Bou*logne, *Stra*sburg, and *Pa*ris.

Bow Bells. *See* COCKNEY.

Box Days. Two days in spring and autumn, and one at Christmas, during the English law vacation, in which pleadings may be filed. This custom was established in 1690, for the purpose of expediting business. Each judge has a private box with a slit, into which informations may be placed on box days, and the judge, who alone has the key, examines the papers in private.

Box Harry. To "box Harry," among commercial travellers, is to avoid the usual *table d'hôte*, and take something substantial at tea-time, in order to save expense.

Boxing-day. The name popularly given in England to December 26, the day after Christmas. It is generally observed as a holiday, and is made the occasion of much giving of gratuities from employers to employed, which are dubbed "Christmas boxes" or presents. On Boxing-night, too, the metropolitan theatres all open, and present their Christmas pantomimes.

Boy. In the South the house and stable servants were universally called "boys," no matter what their age. From this arose the custom of dubbing the male help in American hotels "boys," as bell-boy, waiter-boy, though they may be gray-haired men.

Boy Bachelor. William Wotton, D.D. (fl. 1666-1726), who was admitted to St. Catherine's Hall before he was ten years old, and secured his degree of B.A. when he was twelve.

Boy Bishop. From a very early time the custom of choosing a Boy Bishop on St. Nicholas' Day has been in vogue in Catholic countries, and in England seems to have prevailed in almost every parish.

Although the election took place on St. Nicholas' Day (December 6), the authority lasted to

Holy Innocents' Day (December 28). The Boy Bishop was chosen from the children of the church or cathedral choir, or from the pupils at the grammar-school. He was arrayed in episcopal vestments, and, attended by a crowd of subordinates in priestly dress, went about with songs and dances from house to house, blessing the people, who, as Bishop Hall says, "stood grinning in the way to expect that ridiculous benediction." The ceremony, or rather saturnalia, contained so much that was derogatory to the dignity of religion, that it was abolished in the reign of Henry VIII.; it was revived during the reign of Mary, but finally sank into oblivion near the close of the sixteenth century. — CHAMBERS.

Boyle Controversy. *See* BATTLE OF THE BOOKS.

Boyle Lectures. They were founded by the Hon. Robert Boyle, who left an annuity for "some preaching minister, who shall preach eight sermons in the year for proving the Christian religion against Atheists, Deists, Pagans, Jews, and Mohammedans, not descending to any controversies among Christians themselves." The first was preached in 1692 by Richard Bentley.

Boy Merchants. John, William, and Robert Kelly, of New York, who, although under age, successfully carried on their father's business after his death in 1825.

Boy Preacher. (1) Crammond Kennedy (b. 1842). (2) Thomas Harrison. (3) Joshua Soule, the Methodist Episcopal bishop (1781–1867).

Boys in Blue. Soldiers in the United States army, — so named on account of the color of their uniforms. Similarly the soldiers of the Southern Confederacy were named "Boys in Gray."

Boythorn. (Pseud.) William S. Robinson, in the Worcester (Mass.) "Transcript" (1857–1860).

Boz. (Pseud.) Charles Dickens, English novelist (1812–1870).

"Boz, my signature in the 'Morning Chronicle,' was the nickname of a pet child, a younger brother, whom I had dubbed Moses, in honor of the 'Vicar of Wakefield,' which, being pronounced 'Bozes,' got shortened into 'Boz.'"

> Who the dickens "Boz" could be
>   Puzzled many a learned elf;
> But time revealed the mystery,
>   For "Boz" appeared as Dickens' self.
>   *Epigram in the "Carthusian."*

Bozzy. James Boswell, the biographer of Dr. Johnson.

Bozzy and Piozzi. James Boswell and Mrs. Hester Lynch Piozzi.

Bo3. This seems to have been formerly used as a contraction for bushel; the symbol 3 being the same mark of contraction as used in "vi 3" (which see). In a bill of charges for a dinner given by Lord "Leiyster," as Chancellor of Oxford, Sept. 5, 1570, is the following item: "For ij bo3, a pecke and a haulfe pecke of flower, to Mr. Furnes, at ij*s* vii*d* the bo3, vi*s* iiij*d*."

Bp. Bishop.

B. R. *Banco Regis* or *Reginæ.* The King's or Queen's Bench.

Br. Brig; bromine; brother.

Brabançonne. A Belgian patriotic song, composed in the revolution of 1830, and so named from Brabant, of which Brussels is the chief city.

Braddock Field. (Pseud.) Charles Patton Dimitry.

Bradlaugh Case. A prolonged controversy (1881–1886) over the claim of Charles Bradlaugh to take a seat in the House of Commons without taking the oath required of members, he declaring that he did not acknowledge or believe in its obligation; and later, to have the oath administered. Two notable legal decisions were reached in the course of the controversy. In 1884, in the case of Charles Bradlaugh *v.* Francis R. Gossett, sergeant-at-arms of the House of Commons, arising out of a resolution excluding plaintiff from the House until he should engage not to disturb its proceedings by demanding to take the oath as a member, it was held that courts cannot control the House in its administration of laws relating merely to its internal procedure, nor inquire into the propriety of a resolution restraining a member from doing in the House what he had a lawful right to do, and that action will not lie against the sergeant-at-arms for obeying such resolution. In 1885, in the Court of Appeal, the case of the Attorney-General *v.* Bradlaugh, for penalties under the Parliamentary Oaths Act, for voting in the House without having been sworn as a member, it was decided that a member who does not believe in a Supreme Being, and upon whom an oath is binding only as a promise, is incapable of taking the prescribed oath; but if he goes through the form of taking it (as Bradlaugh did by administering the oath to himself at the bar of the House), he is liable for violation of the Act.

Braggadocio. A braggart; one who is valiant with his tongue, but a coward at heart; a barking dog that bites not. The character is from Spenser's "Faerie Queene."

Bragi. In Scandinavian mythology the son of Odin and Frigga, husband of Iduna, and the patron of poetry and eloquence.

Brahma. In Hindu mythology the supreme deity, forming, with Vishnu and Siva, the Trimurti, or triad of the Brahmanical faith.

Brains. *See* OLD BRAINS.

Brain-Picture Hoax. A scientific hoax gotten up by George G. Rockwood, photographer, and published in the New York papers in 1887.

Brain Street. A sobriquet conferred on Fleet Street, London, by George Augustus Sala. It is the centre of the metropolitan newspaper press.

Bramine, The. An endearing epithet bestowed by Sterne on Mrs. Elizabeth Draper, a young Englishwoman, for whom he contracted an ill-advised passion. The name contains a reference to the place of her birth, — India; and by his reference to himself in the same connection by the term " The Bramin " he evidently sought to indicate his clerical calling.

Brandenburg Lucky Star. The history of this star — so named because it appeared on the night in which Elector Sigismund of Brandenburg was born — is as follows : In 945, during the reign of Emperor Otho I., say the German papers, a new and brilliant fixed star was seen in the constellation Cassiopeia, which has the shape of a W. In 1264 a similar star was seen in the same place; and again on Nov. 11, 1572, when Tycho Brahe noticed a brilliant star of unusual magnitude in a spot where he had only seen small ones until then. It had no tail, nor was it surrounded by a haze, that might cause observers to take it for a comet. It resembled, on the contrary, the other fixed stars, and shed a more brilliant light than the stars of the first magnitude, excelling in this respect Sirius, Jupiter, and Vega. It could only be compared to Venus, and was visible also in the daytime, even at noon. At night, with a covered sky, while all the other stars are invisible, it was repeatedly distinguishable through the clouds. Tycho was convinced of its complete immovability. Its light began to fade in November, 1572; and after having shone for nearly seventeen months, it disappeared entirely in 1574. In vain the astronomers have looked for it in its wonted place since.

Brandy Nan. Queen Anne of England, who was very fond of ardent spirits.

Bras-de-fer. *See* IRON ARM.

Bras de Fer. (Pseud.) Comyns Cole, in the London " World."

Brave, The. (1) Alfonso IV. of Portugal (fl. 1290–1357). (2) John Andreas van der Mersch, "the brave Fleming " (fl. 1734–1792).

Bravest of the Brave. Marshal Ney (fl. 1769–1815) was so named by the Friedlanders on account of his intrepid courage.

Bravo Case. *See* BALHAM MYSTERY.

Bravura. (Ital.) An air requiring much spirit, fire, and facility of execution. (Mus.)

Braz. Brazil ; Brazilian.

Brazen Age. In classical mythology one of the four eras into which the ancient bards divided the history of mankind. The Iron Age preceded, and the Silver Age followed it.

Brazilian Humboldt. Alexander Rodrigues Ferreira, the Brazilian traveller (1756–1815).

Bread-and-Butter Brigade. Those who seek office solely for the sake of its emoluments, without regard to party honor or allegiance, are thus nicknamed.

Breakbone Fever. "A term commonly used to denote the *dengué*, a malarious fever of the South. It is so called either from the 'pain in the bones,' of which the patients complain, or from the great debility which follows the attack. Both reasons have been assigned for the appellation." — BARTLETT.

Breaking on the Wheel. A barbarous mode of inflicting capital punishment, formerly in vogue in Germany and France. It consisted in stretching the victim upon a wheel or upon a wooden frame in the shape of Saint Andrew's cross, and then breaking his limbs by blows from iron bars. The sufferer was then left to die slowly from fever, thirst, and exhaustion.

Break Priscian's Head. To violate the rules of grammar. Priscian was a famous Roman grammarian.

Fair cousin, for thy glances,
Instead of breaking Priscian's head,
I had been breaking lances.
PRAED.

Breeches Bible. The Geneva Bible (*q. v.*) is also so named because of its peculiar rendering of Gen. iii. 7: " Made themselves breeches out of fig-leaves."

Breeches Review. A nickname for the " Westminster Review " among the booksellers, owing to the fact that a Mr. Francis Place, a weighty contributor, was at one time a leather-breeches maker and tailor at Charing Cross, London. *See* GRANDMOTHER'S REVIEW, MY.

Breidablik. In Scandinavian mythology the palace of Baldur, in the Milky Way. The word signifies " wide-shining."

Brent Winwood. (Pseud.) John Thomas Denny, a famous English writer.

Bret Harte. Francis Bret Harte, the American novelist.

Breveté. Patented.

Brevi manu. (Lat.) " With a short hand." Off-hand ; without delay ; summarily.

Brewer of Ghent. Jacob van Arteveld.

Briareus. In classical mythology a giant with a hundred arms and fifty heads, son of Cœlus and Terra. He aided the giants to storm Olympus, and was buried alive under Mount Etna as a punishment.

Briareus of Languages. Cardinal Mezzofanti (fl. 1774–1849), who knew fifty-eight different tongues. Byron dubbed him "a walking polyglot, a monster of languages, a Briareus of parts of speech."

Briareus of Music. Händel.

Brick. The phrase " A perfect brick," or " You are a brick," is one very frequently heard, and if tradition speaks truly, boasts a very respectable origin and antiquity. Plutarch, in his life of Agesilaus, king of Sparta, tells this story : —

" On a certain occasion an ambassador from Esperus, on a diplomatic mission, was shown by the king over his capital. The ambassador knew of the monarch's fame, knew that though only nominally king of Sparta, he was ruler of Greece, and he had looked to see massive walls rearing aloft their embattled towers for the defence of the town, but he found nothing of the kind. He marvelled much at this, and spoke of it to the king, when the following conversation took place : —

" ' Sire,' he said, ' I have visited most of the principal towns, and I find no walls reared for defence. Why is this ? '

" ' Indeed, Sir Ambassador,' replied Agesilaus, ' thou canst not have looked carefully. Come with me to-morrow morning and I will show you the walls of Sparta.'

" Accordingly, on the following morning, the king led his guest out upon the plain, where his army was drawn up in full array, and pointing proudly to the serried hosts, he said, —

" ' There thou beholdest the walls of Sparta, — ten thousand men, and every man a brick.' "

Brick-and-Mortar Franchise. A Chartist phrase for the £10 household system of voting in vogue some time ago in England.

Brickdusts. A nickname for the Fifty-third Foot Regiment, from the color of their facings. They are also dubbed the "Five-and-Threepennies," in allusion to their number and to the daily pay of the ensigns.

Brick Pomeroy. (Pseud.) Mark M. Pomeroy, American journalist (b. 1840).

Bricktop. (Pseud.) George G. Small, an American writer.

Bride of Syria. A name given by Arab geographers to the ancient city of Askelon, on the Mediterranean.

Bride of the Sea. Venice, so named from the ancient annual ceremony of throwing a ring into the sea by the doge. In the year 1177 it is said that the Pope of Rome presented to the Doge of Venice a ring, saying, " Take this as a pledge of authority over the sea, and marry her every year, you and your successors forever, in order that all may know she is under your jurisdiction, and that I have placed her under your dominion as a wife under the dominion of her husband." Hence arose the strange custom of " Wedding the Adriatic." When the yearly marriage-day came round, Venice kept the anniversary in the most festive robes. All her officers and wealthy citizens might be seen in their gondolas, each boat and its occupants striving to outdo all others in wealth of adornment and brilliance of display. The gondolas formed in procession, the doge leading, and at a certain part of the procession a well-known and often-repeated formula was recited, claiming for Venice authority over the sea ; the emblematic ring was then dropped into its depths, and the marriage was considered as complete. But the Venice of the doges is a thing of the past, and the custom has long been obsolete.

Bridge of Sighs. The bridge connecting the palace of the doge with the state prison of Venice, over which prisoners were conveyed from the hall of judgment to the place of execution.

> I stood in Venice on the Bridge of Sighs,
> A palace and a prison on each hand.
> BYRON, *Childe Harold.*

Bridgewater Treatises. Eight celebrated works on "The Power, Wisdom, and Goodness of God," by eight of the most eminent authors in their respective departments, published under a bequest of the last Earl of Bridgewater, whereby each writer received £1,000, and the copyright of his own particular treatise.

Bridled Bear. A young nobleman under the control of a travelling tutor.

Brig. Brigade; Brigadier.

Brig.-Gen. Brigadier-General.

Brigians. The Castilians, one of whose ancient kings was named Brig or Brixus.

Brillante. (Ital. and Fr.) A term denoting a brilliant and showy style of performance. (Mus.)

Brilliant Madman. Charles XII. of Sweden (fl. 1682–1718).

Brimstone Corner. Park Street Church, Boston, is so known, in vulgar nomenclature, on account of the extreme Calvinism taught there.

Brindamour. (Pseud.) Jacques Albin Simon Collin de Plancy, contributor to various French journals.

Briny, The. The ocean, in allusion to its saltness.

Brio, Brioso, or **Con brio.** (Ital.) With brilliancy and spirit. (Mus.)

Brise. (Fr.) Broken, or sprinkled. Said of chords split into arpeggios. (Mus.)

Brissotins. A nickname given to the advocates of reform in the French Revolution, because they were "led by the nose" by Jean Pierre Brissot. The party was subsequently called the Girondists.

Bristled Baptist Boar. So Dryden denominates the Anabaptist sect in "The Hind and Panther."

Bristol Boy, or **Bristol Poet.** Thomas Chatterton (fl. 1752–1770), the poet. He was also named the "Marvellous Boy."

Bristol Diamonds. Brilliant crystals of colorless quartz found in St. Vincent's Rock, near Bristol, England.

Bristol Man's Gift. A present of something which the giver pronounces to be of no use or no value to himself.

Bristol Milk. Sherry punch, formerly given by Bristol people to their friends.

Britain, Lesser. *See* LESSER BRITAIN.

Britain, Little. *See* LITTLE BRITAIN.

Britannicus. (Pseud.) One of the signatures of Adam Thorn, in the Montreal "Herald" (1837–1838).

British Aristides. Andrew Marvell (fl. 1620–1678) was so named on account of his justice and probity.

British Bayard. Sir Philip Sidney.

British Cicero. William Pitt, Earl of Chatham.

British Homer. Milton, the great Puritan poet.

British Legion. The name given to a body of soldiery raised by Lord John Hay, Col. DeLacy Evans, and others, to assist Queen Isabella of Spain against the Carlists in 1835. The legion defeated them at Hernani in 1836 and at St. Sebastian in October of the same year.

British Lion. The spirit or pugnacity of the British nation, as opposed to John Bull, which symbolizes the substantiality, obstinacy, and solidity of the British nation, with all its prejudices and national peculiarities. To rouse John Bull is to tread on his corns; to rouse the British Lion is to blow the war-trumpet in his ears. The British Lion also means the most popular celebrity of the British nation for the time being.

> Our glorious constitution is owing to the habit which the British Lion observes of sitting over his wine after dinner. — WILLIAM JERDAN.

British Pausanias. William Camden (fl. 1551–1623) was so named. He was among the greatest scholars and antiquarians of his time.

British Samson. Thomas Topham, son of a London carpenter (1710–1753). He lifted three hogsheads of water, weighing 1,836 pounds, in the presence of thousands of spectators assembled in Bath Street, Cold Bath Fields, London, May 28, 1741. Being plagued by a faithless woman, he committed suicide.

British Soldiers' Battle. The battle of Inkerman, Nov. 5, 1854.

> For stubborn valor, for true old English resolution to fight it out to the last, amid every disadvantage and against almost overwhelming odds, men will for ages point to Inkerman, "the British Soldiers' Battle." — SIR EDWARD CREASY, *The Fifteen Decisive Battles.*

British Subject. (Pseud.) Sir Francis Bond Head, English soldier and author (1793–1875).

Brit. Mus. British Museum.

Britomartis. A Cretan nymph, very fond of the chase. King Minos fell in love with her, and persisted in his advances for nine months, when she threw herself into the sea.

Broad Arrow. A government mark, stamped, cut, branded, or otherwise affixed to all solid materials used in English ships or dockyards and on government stores generally in order to guard against embezzlement. Brewer says that all attempts to trace the origin of this mark have been fruitless. It is said that trees fit for shipbuilding in the forest of Dean, during the reign of James I., were commonly marked or "blazed" with a crown and arrow.

Broadaxe. (Pseud.) Martin Knapp in the Rockland County (N.Y.) "Press."

Broadbottom Ministry. In English political annals a name derisively given to an administration comprising nine dukes and a grand coalition of all parties of weight and influence in the State, formed in November, 1744, and dissolved by the death of Mr. Pelham, March 6, 1755.

Broadbrim. (Pseud.) J. H. Warwick.

Broad Church. (Pseud.) Thomas Atcheson, Louisville correspondent of the "Spirit of the Times" (N. Y.).

Broadcloth Club of Boston. The gathering of clergymen, at Lundy's request, to protest against slavery, in 1828.

Broad-seal War. "A controversy which grew out of the Congressional election of 1838, when six members were to be chosen by a general ticket in New Jersey. In two of the counties the clerks had rejected some of the township returns for real or alleged irregularities, and thus five of the Whig candidates received majorities which they would not have obtained had all the votes been counted. The sixth, having run ahead of his ticket, was elected beyond dispute. The Governor and his council, in accordance with the law then in force, canvassed the votes, and to the six persons who had received the highest number issued commissions under the Great Seal of the State. Congress, on convening, found that the five votes from New Jersey must decide the speakership, and this gave rise to a stormy debate, which lasted several days, and finally ended in the choice of John Quincy Adams as temporary chairman. He decided that all members holding commissions could vote ; but the decision, being appealed from, was reversed, and a resolution adopted that only the names of members holding uncontested seats should be called. On the twelfth day of the session Robert M. T. Hunter was chosen Speaker, and on February 28 the five Democratic members were admitted to their seats. The subject was referred to a committee, which reported that the sitting members were elected." — APPLETON.

Broadway Lounger. (Pseud.) George Alfred Townsend in the "Tribune" (N. Y.). *See* GATH.

Brocolini, Signor. The professional name of John Clark, a well-known operatic singer.

Broke. "Flat broke," "Dead broke," and "Gone broke" are synonymous terms denoting a penniless or bankrupt condition. "Busted" is an equally inelegant, though fully as vigorous equivalent. The phrase sprang from the gambler's lingo, "breaking the bank."

Broncho John. Professional name of J. H. Sullivan.

Bronze John. Another name for Yellow Jack (*q. v.*).

Brooke. (Pseud.) Miss E. Nesbit in "Good Words" and "Saturday Night."

Brooklyn. (Pseud.) Thomas Kinsella in the "Brooklyn Daily Eagle."

Brooklyn of San Francisco. Oakland, Cal. It is, like its Eastern namesake, a city of homes.

Broomstraw. (Pseud.) Alfred Duke in the "State" of Richmond, Va.

Brother Abraham. (Pseud.) Rev. Richard King. *See* FATHER ABRAHAM.

Brother-german. A real brother. A uterine brother is a brother by the mother's side only.

Brother Jonathan. A collective personification of the people of the United States. When General Washington, after being appointed commander of the army of the Revolutionary War, came to Massachusetts to organize it and make preparations for the defence of the country, he found a great want of ammunition and other means necessary to meet the powerful foe he had to contend with, and great difficulty to obtain them. If attacked in such condition, the cause at once might be hopeless. On one occasion, at that anxious period, a consultation of the officers and others was had, when it seemed no way could be devised to make such preparation as was necessary. His Excellency Jonathan Trumbull the elder was then governor of the State of Connecticut, on whose judgment and aid the general placed the greatest reliance, and remarked: "We must consult 'Brother Jonathan' on the subject." The general did so, and the governor was successful in supplying many of the wants of the army. When difficulties afterwards arose, and the army was spread over the country, it became a byword, "We must consult Brother Jonathan." The term "Yankee" is still applied to a portion; but "Brother Jonathan" has now become a designation of the whole country, as "John Bull" has for England.

Brotherly Love, City of. *See* CITY OF BROTHERLY LOVE.

Brown. In England a colloquialism for a copper coin.

Brown Bess. A musket. *Bess* is a corruption of *buss*, the ancient name for the barrel of a fire-arm. We retain the original word in "arquebus" and "blunderbuss."

Brown Study. Dr. Brewer says that the expression comes from the French, *sombre rêverie. Sombre* and *brun* both mean "sad, gloomy, dull." Congreve uses the expression in his "An Impossible Thing." It has been thought to mean *brow* study. It is more probably one of the group of similar phrases in which colors are employed to designate characteristics or temper; as "black melancholy," "blue-devils," "green-eyed monster," "yellow-stockings," "blue-stockings," "white feather," etc.

Brudder Bones. (Pseud.) John F. Scott, an American humorous writer.

Brumaire Revolution. The popular uprising in Paris on the 9th of November (18th Brumaire, *i. e.*, the period from October 22 to November 20), 1799, which witnessed the overthrow of the Directory and the establishment of the Napoleonic sway.

Brummagem. Another name for Birmingham, England, common among the vulgar, and derived from Bromwichham = "Brummagem."

Brummagem Goods signify bogus articles of jewelry, or cheap and showy wares, for the manufacture of which the place is famous.

Brummagem Joe. A nickname be-stowed on Joseph Chamberlain, M. P. for Birmingham, by his political opponents.

Brunehilda. Daughter of the king of Issland, beloved by Günther, one of the two great chieftains of the Nibelungenlied. She was to be carried off by force, and Günther asked his friend Siegfried to help him. Siegfried contrived the matter by snatching from her the talisman which was her protector, but she never forgave him for his treachery.

Br. Univ. Brown University.

Brunswick. (Pseud.) Miss Jeannette L. Gilder, as New York correspondent of the Boston "Saturday Evening Gazette."

Brunswick's Fated Chieftain. The Duke of Brunswick, Frederick William, commander of the "Black Brunswickers," who fell at Quatre Bras, the day before Waterloo (1815).

Brutum fulmen. (Lat.) "A harmless thunderbolt." A loud but harmless threat; sound and fury, nothing else.

Brutus. (Pseud.) (1) Fisher Ames in his communications to the Boston press. (2) Stephen Simpson in the Philadelphia "Aurora." (3) One of the pen-names adopted by Junius (*q. v.*).

B. S. Bachelor in the Sciences.

Bubastis, a goddess of the Egyptians, was, in their mythology, the child of Isis and Osiris, and the sister of Horus. She was identified by the Greeks with Artemis (Diana), though upon what grounds is unknown, as the best information with regard to her is that she was the goddess who presided over pregnancy and childbirth. The chief temple erected to Bubastis was at Bubastis (*q. v.*). Bubastis is represented on monuments as having the head of a cat, an animal which was sacred to her.

Bubble Act. A popular name for an English law passed in 1719, which was designed to protect the public against the schemes of unprincipled promoters of "bubble" companies.

Bubbly Cuffs. The singular nickname conferred on the English Eighty-fourth Regiment.

Buccaneers. A celebrated association of piratical adventurers, who, from the commencement of the second quarter of the sixteenth century to the end of the seventeenth, maintained themselves in the Caribbean seas, at first by systematic reprisals on the Spaniards, afterward by less justifiable and indiscriminate piracy. The name is derived from the Caribbee *boucan*, a term for preserved meat, smoke-dried in a peculiar manner. From this the French adventurers formed the verb *boucaner* and the noun *boucanier*, which was adopted by the English; while, singularly enough, the French used, in preference, the word *flibustier*, a corruption of our "freebooter." The Buccaneers were also sometimes called "Brethren of the Coast." The arrogant assumption by the Spaniards of a divine right — sanctioned by the Pope's bull — to the whole New World, was not, of course, to be tolerated by the enterprising mariners of England and France; and the enormous cruelties practised by them upon all foreign interlopers, of which the history of that time is full, naturally led to an association for mutual defence among the adventurers of all other nations, but particularly among the English and French. The fundamental principles of their policy — for they, in course of time, formed distinct communities — were close mutual alliance, and mortal war with all that was Spanish. Their simple code of laws bound them to a common participation in the necessaries of life; locks and bars were proscribed as an insult to the general honor; and every man had his comrade, who stood by him when alive, and succeeded to his property after his death. The principal centre of their wild and predatory life was for some time the island of Tortuga, near St. Domingo. When they were not hunting Spaniards, or being hunted themselves, their chief occupation and means of subsistence was the chase. From the flesh of wild cattle they made their "boucan;" their skins and tallow they sold or bartered to Dutch and other traders. The history of these men embraces, as may be supposed, narratives of cruelty and bloodshed unsurpassed in the annals of crime. It has, however, not a few stories of high and romantic adventure, of chivalrous valor, and brilliant generalship. Among the "great captains" whose names figure most prominently in the records of buccaneering, were the Frenchman Montbars, surnamed by the terrible title of "The Exterminator;" his countrymen, Peter of Dieppe, surnamed "The Great," — as truly, perhaps, as others so distin-

guished, — and L'Olonnais, Michael de Busco, and Bartolommeo de Portuguez, Mansvelt, and Van Horn. Pre-eminent, however, among them all was the Welshman Henry Morgan, who organized fleets and armies, took strong fortresses and rich cities, and displayed throughout the bold genius of a born commander. He it was that led the way for the Buccaneers to the Southern Ocean, by his daring march in 1670 across the Isthmus of Panama to the city of that name, which he took and plundered after a desperate battle. This brilliant but most unscrupulous personage was knighted by Charles II., and became deputy-governor of Jamaica. A higher subordination of the love of gold to the passion for dominion in him might probably have made him Emperor of the West Indies, some dream of which seems at one time to have occupied his mind. In 1680 and 1689 extensive buccaneering expeditions were made to the Pacific, even as far as the coasts of China, of which the best record is preserved in the lively pages of "William Dampier," himself an important partner in these bold adventures. The war between France and Britain, after the accession of William III., dissolved the ancient alliance of the French and English buccaneers. After the peace of Ryswick, and the accession of the Bourbon Philip V. to the Spanish crown (1701), they finally disappeared, to make way for a race of mere cut-throats and vulgar desperadoes, not yet utterly extinct. The last great event in their history was the capture of Carthagena in 1697, where the booty was enormous. *See* KEEL-HAULING AND MAROONING.

Bucentaur. The name of a ship which acquired much celebrity in Venice at the time when that State was a flourishing republic. A bucentaur was known as early as the end of the twelfth century; and a vessel of the same name was burnt when the French took Venice more than six centuries afterwards; but it is not certain whether this was the same vessel, maintained by being repeatedly patched up with new ribs and planking. The "Bucentaur" is described as having been a galley, about one hundred feet long by twenty-one in extreme breadth; on a lower deck were thirty-two banks or rows of oars, manned by one hundred and sixty-eight rowers; and on an upper deck was accommodation for the illustrious visitors who occasionally came on board. The whole of the fittings were of the most gorgeous character. Although propelled mainly by oars, there were forty mariners employed in other ways to manage the galley. The "Bucentaur" was employed only once a year, when the doge "married the Adriatic." A splendid water-procession was formed, with the doge and the chief notables in the "Bucentaur," and other distinguished persons in gondolas.

Bucephalus. In classic mythology the name of the famed steed of Alexander the Great.

Buck and Breck. A popular nickname coupling the names of Buchanan and Breckinridge, the Democratic nominees for the Presidency in 1856.

Buckeye. (Pseud.) Samuel Sullivan Cox, in his "A Buckeye Abroad," etc.

Buckeye State. Ohio; so named after the Buckeye-tree (*Æsculus flava*), which flourishes extensively within its borders.

Buckmaster's Light Infantry. The Third West India Regiment was so nicknamed. Buckmaster, the military outfitter, used to furnish "Light Infantry uniforms" to the officers without authority of the commander-in-chief.

Buckra. Among his own race in the far South the negro still clings to the term *buckra*, imported from the west coast of Africa, and originally meaning a spirit or powerful being, and then by a natural transition, white man. In his new home he used it to designate anything specially good, as the *buckra yam*, which, to deserve the epithet, must be white and good at the same time.

Bucks County Rebellion. In the spring of 1799 the collection of what was known as the "window-tax" was forcibly resisted in Northampton, Bucks, and Montgomery counties, Penn., under the lead of John Fries (1764–1825). The United States officials were arrested or violently handled, and various excesses took place. Fries was sentenced to be hanged, but President Adams pardoned him.

Buckshot War. "In 1838 the defeated Democratic candidate of a congressional district in Pennsylvania claimed Whig frauds in the North Liberties district as the cause of his defeat. Thereupon the ten Democratic return judges threw out the vote of that district, thus electing their member.

The seven Whig judges met apart from the Democrats, and gave certificates to the Whig candidates for Congress, and also to the Whig candidates for the Legislature, although these latter had considered themselves fairly defeated. This proceeding was part of a scheme to elect a Whig senator. The Whig certificates reached the Secretary of State first, and he, also a Whig, declared his intention of recognizing them until discredited by investigation. The House met December 4 at Harrisburg; armed partisans of both sides were in town; two separate organizations of the House took place, side by side, amid great confusion. Governor Ritner, a Whig, declared the city in the hands of a mob, and sought the aid of United States troops from their commander, and then from President Van Buren. In both cases he met with refusal. After a time several Whigs seceded to the Democratic House, which had succeeded in keeping possession of the chamber and records, and the latter was recognized by the State Senate, when the other Whigs joined them; all but Thaddeus Stevens, who did not attempt to join until May, 1839. The House then declared his seat vacant, and he was obliged to be again elected before he was finally admitted. The remark of a Whig member that the mob should 'feel ball and buckshot before the day is over,' is said to have given rise to the name." — BROWN AND STRAUSS.

Buckskins. A term applied to the American troops during the Revolutionary War. The Marquis de Chastellux, in his "Travels in North America in 1780–1782," says: "The name of 'Buckskin' is given to the inhabitants of Virginia' because their ancestors were hunters, and sold buck or rather deer skins." As applied to certain American soldiers, we are inclined to believe that from their wearing garments made of dressed deerskins the term was applied to them.

Cornwallis fought as long 's he dought,
An' did the buckskins claw him.
BURNS.

Bucktails. (1) The name of a political party in the State of New York, which sprung up about the year 1815. Its origin is thus described by Mr. Hammond: "There was an order of the Tammany Society who wore in their hats, as an insignia, on certain occasions, a portion of the tail of the deer. They were a leading order, and from this circumstance the friends of DeWitt Clinton gave those who adopted the views of the members of the Tammany Society, in relation to him, the name of 'Bucktails;' which name was eventually applied to their friends and supporters in the country. Hence the party opposed to the administration of Mr. Clinton were for a long time called the 'Bucktail Party.'" — *Political History of New York.* (2) Under the call for troops to put down the Rebellion in April, 1861, the Second Pennsylvania Reserves were mustered into service. They rejoiced in the above sobriquet.

Buffalo Bill. The well-known sobriquet of William F. Cody (b. 1845), the famous Indian scout and hunter. The origin of this name was as follows : In 1867 he entered into a contract with the Kansas Pacific Railway, then building, at a monthly compensation of $500, to deliver all the buffalo meat that would be required for food for the army of laborers employed, and in eighteen months he killed 4,280 buffaloes, earning the title of "Buffalo Bill," by which he was subsequently known in both hemispheres.

Buffo, Buffa. (Ital.) An actor or singer who assumes light and humorous parts in opera. Likewise, an *Opera buffa* is a comic opera.

Buffs, Young Buffs. The Third Foot Regiment were so named because their coats were lined with buff, and they wore buff waistcoats, breeches, and stockings. The Thirty-first, raised in 1702, were dubbed "Young Buffs" for the same reason. In contradistinction the former were often named "Old Buffs;" they were also called "Resurrectionists."

Bug Bible. So called from its rendering of Psalm xci. 5 : "Afraid of bugs by night." It bears date 1551.

Buggy, in England a light one-horse chaise hardly known in our day, means in America the most popular of all vehicles, four-wheeled, but single-seated, and with or without a top.

Bull. A "bull" may be said to be a gross and often humorous contradiction or blunder in speech. The term was derived from one Obadiah Bull, a lawyer in the time of Henry VIII., who was celebrated, rather than famous, for the blunders which fell from his lips when he pleaded before the judges. A witty

Irishman, upon being asked for the definition of a bull, said : "If you see two cows lying down alone in the meadow, the one standing up is invariably a bull." Miss Edgeworth, in her essay on "Irish Bulls," gives the following : "When I first saw you I thought it was you, and now I see it is your brother." "I met you this morning and you did not come; I 'll meet you to-morrow morning whether you come or not." "Oh, if I had stayed in that climate until now I 'd have been dead two years." During the Irish rebellion an Irish paper published this item : "A man named McCarthy was run over by a passenger train and killed on Wednesday. He was injured in a similar way two years ago." In 1784 the Irish Commons issued an order to this effect: "Any member unable to write may get another member to frank his letter for him, but only on condition that he certifies with his own handwriting his inability on the back of it." A well-known English epitaph commences as follows : "Reader, if thou canst read." This is somewhat akin to the hand-board which read : "The ford is dangerous when this board is covered by the water." Sir Boyle Roche, a witty and well-known member of Parliament, was not only the parent of many blunders of this sort, but he had a number fathered on him. Here is his famous "letter": —

DEAR SIR, — Having now a little peace and quiet, I sit down to inform you of the bustle and confusion we are in from the blood-thirsty rebels, many of whom are now, thank God! killed and dispersed. We are in a pretty mess, — can get nothing to eat, and no wine to drink except whiskey. When we sit down to dinner we are obliged to keep both hands armed. While I write this I have my sword in one hand and my pistol in the other. I concluded from the beginning that this would be the end; and I am right, for it is not half over yet. At present there are such goings-on that everything is at a standstill. I should have answered your letter a fortnight ago, but I only received it this morning. Indeed, hardly a mail arrives safe without being robbed. No longer ago than yesterday, the mail-coach from Dublin was robbed near this town ; the bags had been very judiciously left behind, and by great good luck there was nobody in the coach but two outside passengers who had nothing for the thieves to take. Last Thursday an alarm was given that a gang of rebels in full retreat from Drogheda were advancing under the French standard, but they had no colors nor any drums except bagpipes. Immediately every man in the place, including women and children, ran out to meet them. We soon found our force a great deal too little, and were far too near to think of retreating. Death was in every face, and to it

we went. By the time half our party were killed we began to be all alive. Fortunately, the rebels had no guns except pistols, cutlasses, and pikes, and we had plenty of muskets and ammunition. We put them all to the sword; not a soul of them escaped, except some that were drowned in an adjoining bog. In fact, in a short time nothing was heard but silence. Their uniforms were all different, chiefly green. After the action was over, we went to rummage their camp. All we found was a few pikes without heads, a parcel of empty bottles filled with water, and a bundle of blank French commissions filled up with Irish names. Troops are now stationed round, which exactly squares with my ideas of security. Adieu! I have only time to add that I am yours in great haste,   B. R.
P. S. If you do not receive this, of course it must have miscarried; therefore I beg you to write and let me know.

Bull-dogs, in English University slang, are the two myrmidons of the proctor, who attend his heels like dogs, and are ready to spring on any offending undergraduate.

Bulldoze. A term growing out of the race antagonisms in the South subsequent to the civil war, where it was asserted that the blacks were intimidated by their former owners and forcibly prevented from voting the Republican ticket. The term is believed to have come from whipping a man with a bull-whip and giving him a "bull's dose."

Bullen-a-lah. *See* LILLIBURLERO.

Buller of Brazenose. John Hughes, an English author, was so called in Wilson's "Noctes Ambrosianæ." He was a fellow of Oriel College, Oxford.

Bulletin. (Pseud.) Mr. Guild, an American writer of the present day.

Bull-frogs. A nickname for the Rifle Brigade throughout the English service.

Bull-necked Forger. Cagliostro, the stalwart impostor (fl. 1743–1795), was so named.

Bulls. Stock-brokers or financiers who manipulate the market for a rise in values. *See* BEARS.

Bull's Eye. A small cloud suddenly appearing, seemingly in violent motion, soon covering the entire vault of heaven, producing a tumult of wind and rain.

Bull the Barrel, Bull the Teapot. "Bulling the barrel" is to pour water into an empty spirit-cask to prevent its leaking; the water becomes impregnated with the spirit, and is highly intoxicating. Sailor-men, when they make a second brew from tea leaves, call it "bulling the teapot."

Bully, or Bully-boy. This curious phrase often appears in American newspapers, and is thought to be indigenous. It is, however, an old English saying, as the following quotation from "Deuteromelia," etc., published in London (1609), will show: —

> "We be three poore mariners,
> Newly come from the seas,
> We spend oure liues in ieapordy
> Whiles others liue at ease;
> Shall we goe daunce the round, the round,
> And shall we goe daunce the round,
> And he that is a bully-boy,
> Come pledge me on the ground."

Ford. I'll give you a pottle of burned sack to give me recourse to him, and tell him my name is Brook, only for a jest.
Host. My hand, bully. Thou shalt have egress and regress, . . . and thy name shall be Brook.
— SHAKSPEARE, *Merry Wives of Windsor.*

Bully Brooks. Preston S. Brooks (1819–1857), an American politician elected to Congress in 1853 and in 1855. Mr. Sumner, having made a strong anti-slavery speech, in which he gave great offence to members from the South, "was, on May 22, 1856, violently assaulted in the Senate-chamber by Mr. Brooks, and beaten on the head with a cane. A committee of the House reported in favor of the expulsion of Mr. Brooks; but the report failed to receive the requisite majority of two thirds. He was indicted for assault, pleaded guilty, was sentenced to pay a fine of $300, and resigned his seat in Congress, but was re-elected without opposition."

Bully Dawson. A notorious London blackleg who roystered about town in the dissolute days of the Restoration.

Bully Waterman. This character was one of the most inhuman monsters who ever sailed the seas. He commanded a ship between New York and San Francisco. On one of his voyages he left New York with a crew of forty-two men, and when he reached the Golden Gate seventeen of them had been shot by Captain Waterman, most of them fatally, his excuse being that they would not obey orders. Upon the return of the vessel to New York Captain Waterman, knowing that trouble awaited him, had himself put ashore on the Jersey coast and remained in hiding until the vessel discharged her cargo, loaded and cleared in the name of the first officer, acting as captain. The sheriff, who had a warrant in his hands for the arrest of Waterman, refused to leave the vessel even when she got under way, believing that Waterman would regain his vessel when he thought danger was over. The manner in which the sheriff was outwitted and Waterman actually succeeded in regaining his vessel without jeopardizing the insurance regulations — which provided that the vessel shall enter no port except the port of destination — was as follows : " When Sandy Hook was reached the acting captain informed the sheriff that he was about taking departure and steering for Cape Horn, and unless he intended to accompany the ship to San Francisco he had better go back to New York in the pilot boat. The sheriff gave up the chase for Waterman and went back to the city. The ship now stood in shore a few miles and then brought her main-topsail to the mast in order to allow a small boat which had put off from a coasting schooner to run alongside. It contained the notorious Waterman, who had succeeded in escaping the penalties of his crimes and reaching his ship in safety. He never returned to New York, but died in California.

Bulwark, Lud's. *See* LUD'S BULWARK.

Bummer. Even students of language may be surprised to hear that the word "bummer" is not only not slang, but it is not even a pure Americanism, being found in the " English Market By-Laws " of two hundred years ago, and appears in several advertisements in the London " Publick Intelligencer " of the year 1660 under the form " bummaree." It originally meant a man who retails fish by peddling outside of the regular market. These persons being looked down upon and regarded as cheats by the established dealers, the name became one of contempt for a dishonest person of irregular habits. The word first appeared in the United States during the Fifties in California, and travelled eastward until, during the civil war, it came into general use.

Buncombe. A colloquial term in the United States, signifying " speechmaking for mere show." It is related that the word grew out of an incident in the Sixteenth Congress, when a member for a district in North Carolina which embraced Buncombe County insisted on delaying a vote on the famous " Missouri Question " by making a speech, saying, " he was bound to talk for Buncombe."

Bundschuh (a kind of large heavy shoe). The name given to the peasant-rising in Germany in the first half of the sixteenth century, because they carried as an insignia a shoe hoisted on a pole.

Bungtown Copper. "A spurious coin of base metal, a very clumsy counterfeit of the English halfpenny or copper. It derived its name from the place where it was first manufactured, then called Bungtown, now Barneysville, in the town of Rehoboth, Mass. The Bungtown copper never was a legal coin ; the British halfpenny or copper was. The term is used only in New England." — BARTLETT.

Bunker Hill. (Pseud.) Rev. Benjamin Franklin De Costa, correspondent of the " Boston Advertiser," in 1861–1862.

Burdon's Hotel. Whitecross Street debtor's prison, London. Mr. Burdon was once governor for a long term of years.

Bureaucracy. A system of government in which the business is carried on in bureaux, or departments. The French bureau means not only the office of a public functionary, but also the whole staff of officers attached to the department.

Burgundian Blow. Decapitation by the headsman. The Duc de Biron, who was put to death for treason by Henry IV., was told in his youth, by a fortune-teller, " to beware of a Burgundian blow." When going to execution, he asked who was to be his executioner, and was told he was a man from Burgundy.

Buri. In Scandinavian mythology the progenitor of all the gods.

Burial of an Ass. No burial at all

He shall be buried with the burial of an ass, drawn and cast forth beyond the gates of Jerusalem. — JER. xxii. 19.

Buridan's Ass. A man of indecision. " If a hungry ass were placed exactly between two hay-stacks in every respect equal, it would starve to death, because there would be no motive why it should go to one rather than to the other." — BURIDAN.

Burl. Burlesque.

Burleigh. (Pseud.) Rev. Matthew Hale Smith, American minister (1810–1879).

Burlesco. (Ital.) In a farcical or comic vein. (Mus.)

Burletta. (Ital.) A iight species of musical drama, analogous to the English farce. (Mus.)

Burlington. (Pseud.) Robert Saunders, English statistical writer (1727–1783).

Burlington Accident. The first great railroad disaster in the United States. It occurred in 1855, near Burlington, N. J., causing the death and injury of many passengers. So horror-stricken was the public, that new regulations in regard to the backing of trains, signalling, etc., were adopted on every railroad in the Union. The Rev. Dr. Boardman, a celebrated Philadelphia divine, preached a sermon; and the "Burlington accident" was remembered and talked of for years by those who were in the railway service.

Burly King Harry. *See* BLUFF KING HAL.

Burnbill. Henry de Londres, archbishop of Dublin in the reign of Henry III. He was said to have surreptitiously obtained and then burned all the title-deeds by which the tenants of the see held their lands.

Burned District. Localities in Boston, Mass., and Chicago, Ill., and referring in each case to the area burned over by the great fires of 1872 and 1871 respectively. In both cities the region is now covered with imposing and substantial structures.

Burning Mines. These are situated on what is known as Summit Hill, near Mauch Chunk, Penn.; they have been on fire since 1858. All that can be seen is a large hill from which, in innumerable places, steam and gas issue. In some places the rocks are so hot that the hand cannot touch them without scorching.

Burns of France. A name conferred on Pierre Jean de Béranger (fl. 1780–1857). *See* HORACE OF FRANCE.

Burns Riot. A disturbance in Boston, in 1854, caused by efforts to liberate Anthony Burns, an escaped slave.

Burr Conspiracy. "In consequence of Burr's duel with Hamilton, in which the latter met his death, Burr was indicted in New York and New Jersey for murder. He went West, and made an extensive tour, in the course of which he made preparations for a gigantic but mysterious scheme. The real object of this is unknown. It was either to separate the Mississippi Valley from the rest of the Union and erect it into a new nation, or to conquer Mexico. In 1806 he gathered a number of reckless persons about him, and started for the region of Texas, ostensibly on a colonizing expedition. President Jefferson issued a proclamation warning citizens against joining the expedition. Burr was arrested by Jefferson's orders, sent to Virginia, and indicted there by a United States grand jury for treason and for a misdemeanor, based on his course in levying war within this country on a friendly nation; but it was hoped that Burr could also be shown to have had treasonable designs against the unity of this country. He was acquitted of treason for want of jurisdiction, on the failure of the evidence required by article 3, section 3, clause 1 of the Constitution; he was also acquitted of misdemeanor. He was bound over to present himself for trial in Ohio, but the matter was pressed no further. One of Burr's dupes in this scheme was Harman Blennerhasset, who was also arrested, but was discharged after Burr's acquittal." — BROWN AND STRAUSS.

Burwell Fire. On Sept. 8, 1727, a number of persons assembled to witness a puppet-show in a barn at Burwell, near Newmarket. A lighted candle set fire to a heap of straw, and in the ensuing conflagration seventy-six persons perished. Many others died of their injuries.

Bury the Hatchet. Let by-gones be by-gones. The "Great Spirit" commanded the North American Indians, when they smoked the calumet or peace-pipe, to bury their hatchets, scalping-knives, and war-clubs in the ground, that all thought of hostility might be buried out of sight.

It is much to be regretted that the American Government, having brought the great war to a conclusion, did not bury the hatchet altogether. — *London Times.*

> Buried was the bloody hatchet;
> Buried was the dreadful war-club;
> Buried were all warlike weapons,
> And the war-cry was forgotten:
> Then was peace among the nations.
> LONGFELLOW, *Hiawatha.*

Bush. Bushel; bushels.

Bushrangers. Australian highwaymen, who range the "bush," lying in wait for travellers, whom they strip of all they have about them. Gold-finders are frequent objects of their attack.

Bushwhacker. The word "bush" has in some places, notably in Australia and South Africa, taken the Dutch meaning of a region abounding in trees and underwood (*bosch*). It is not likely that the term "bushwhacker" is a pure Americanism; though it is hardly known in England, it is heard in Australia and in South Africa. Originally used to designate the process of propelling a boat by pulling the bushes on the banks of the stream, it became afterward a name for lawless persons and fugitives from justice who took refuge in the bush.

Busiris. A king of Egypt, who used to immolate to the gods all strangers who set foot on his shores. Hercules was seized by him, and would have fallen a victim, but he broke his chain, and slew the inhospitable king.

Busted. *See* BROKE.

Butcher, The. (1) Achmed Pasha, famous for his defence of Acre against Napoleon I. (2) John, ninth Earl Clifford (d. 1461). *See* BLOODY BUTCHER and ROYALIST BUTCHER.

Butte. A term of French origin, and applied throughout the West to solitary peaks or mounds of earth of no great altitude. The word is also used as a verb, and denotes the hacking off of any substance with a dull weapon.

Buzzard called Hawk by Courtesy. A euphemism. A brevet rank; a complimentary title.

> Of small renown, 't is true ; for, not to lie,
> We call your buzzard "hawk" by courtesy.
> DRYDEN, *Hind and Panther.*

Buzz the Bottle. This is a common expression at wine parties when the bottle does not contain sufficient to fill all the glasses. It means "equally divide what is left." The word "buzz" meant anciently "to empty." Perhaps the word "booze" comes from the same root.

B. V. *Bene vale.* Farewell.

B. V. *Beata Virgo.* Blessed Virgin.

Bx., Bxs. Box, boxes.

Byblis. In classical mythology a daughter of Miletus, who wept herself into a fountain from hopeless love for her brother Caunus.

Bye Plot. A conspiracy of Lord Gray of Wilton, and others, to imprison James I. and extort from him freedom of worship to Romanists. It was suppressed in 1603. It was also named the "Surprise Plot."

By Hook or by Crook. In Marsh's Library, Dublin, is a manuscript entitled "Annales Hiberniæ," written in the seventeenth century by Dudley Loftus, a descendant of Adam Loftus, Archbishop of Armagh. The following extract gives a feasible account of the origin of this popular saying : —

"1172. King Henry the 2d landed in Ireland this year, on St. Luke's eve, at a place in the bay of Waterford, beyond the fort of Duncannon, on Munster syde, at a place called ye Crook over agt. the tower of ye Hook ; whence arose the proverbe to gayne a thing by Hook or by Crook ; it being safe to gayne land in one of those places when the winde drives from the other."

There is, however, another more probable origin. Anciently the poor of a manor were allowed to go into the woods to gather dead wood; they were allowed to cut off dead branches with a billhook, or to pull down by means of a crook any dead branches that otherwise would be above their reach. In the records of the town of Bodmin there is a document claiming for the burgesses of the town, under a concession of the Prior of Bodmin, "to bear and carry away on their backs, and in no other way, the lop, crop, hoop, crook, and bag wood in the prior's wood of Dunmeer." Another part of the record calls this right "a right with hook and crook to lop, crop, and carry away fuel, etc., in the same wood." The date of the document is 1525.

Byles. (Pseud.) Edmund Quincy, in the New York "Tribune."

By'r Lakin. "Lakin" is a contraction of "ladykin," which is a diminutive of endearment for "lady." Thus, " our Lakin" meant " our dear Lady," and was usually applied to the Virgin Mary. The contracted form " by 'r Lakin" was frequently used by the old dramatists as a kind of oath.

> By 'r Lakin ! I can go no further, sir. — *The Tempest.*
> By 'r Lakin ! a parlous fear. — *Midsummer Night's Dream.*

Byzantine Historians. Certain Greek historians who lived under the Eastern Empire between the sixth and fifteenth centuries.

C.

C. Carbon; cent; consul.

C., or **Cels.** Celsius's scale for the thermometer.

C., or **Cent.** *Centum.* A hundred.

C., **Ch.**, or **Chap.** Chapter.

C. A. Chartered Accountant; Chief Accountant; Commissioner of Accounts.

Ca. *Circa.* Year.

Ca. Cæsium; calcium.

Cabal. A term employed to denote a small, intriguing, factious party in the State, and also the union of several such, which for personal or political objects agree to sacrifice or modify their respective claims and principles. The word was coined to designate an English ministry in the reign of Charles II., the initials of whose names — viz., Clifford, Ashley, Buckingham, Arlington, and Lauderdale — composed the word in question.

Cabala. The oral law of the Jews delivered from father to son by word of mouth. Some of the rabbins say that the angel Raziel instructed Adam in it, the angel Japhiel instructed Shem, and the angel Zedekiel instructed Abraham; but the more usual belief is that God instructed Moses, and Moses his brother Aaron, and so on from age to age.

Cabalist. A Jewish doctor who professed the study of the Cabala. See *supra.* This science consisted mainly in understanding the combination of certain significant letters, words, and numbers.

Cachecope Bell. A bell rung at funerals when the pall was thrown over the coffin. From the French, *cache corps,* "over the body."

Cachet, Lettres de ("letters sealed"). Under the old French *régime, carte-blanche* warrants, sealed with the king's seal, might be obtained for a consideration, and the person who held them might fill in any name. Sometimes the warrant was to set a prisoner at large, but it was more frequently for detention in the Bastile. During the administration of Cardinal Fleury 80,000 of these *cachets* were issued, the larger number being against the Jansenists. In the reigns of Louis XV. and XVI. fifty-nine were obtained against the one family of Mirabeau. This scandal was abolished Jan. 15, 1790.

Cacoethes carpendi. (Lat.) A rage for finding fault.

Cacoethes loquendi. (Lat.) An incurable passion for speaking.

Cacoethes scribendi. (Lat.) An incurable passion for writing.

Cactus. (Pseud.) Mary F. Foster.

Cacus. In classic mythology an Italian shepherd, son of Vulcan, and of gigantic stature. He was slain by Hercules for stealing his oxen.

Cad. (Lat., *cadaver,* a dead body.) A non-member of the university. Men, in university slang, are sorted under two groups, — those who are members of the university, and those who are not. As the former are called men, the others must be no men; but as they bear the human form, they are human bodies (cads), though not human beings (men). Another authority derives "cad" from "cadet," a younger son. The younger sons of the nobility were no doubt looked upon with something like scorn by their elder and richer brothers. Hence the depreciatory remark, "Oh, he's only a cad!"—*i. e.*, he's only a cadet, having no property, and therefore not worth notice. When omnibuses were first introduced, the conductor was always known as the "cad." In Dickens's earlier works the word frequently appears in this sense.

Caddee League. *See* LEAGUE OF GOD'S HOUSE.

Caddice-garter. A nickname for a valet or servant. "Caddice" is the name formerly given to a worsted fabric. When garters were worn by men the gentry wore expensive ones, but menials were fain to be content with common worsted ones.

Cadenus. An anagrammatic name under which Swift alludes to himself in his poem of "Cadenus and Vanessa." It is formed by transposing the letters of the Latin word *decanus,* dean. *See* VANESSA.

Cadenza. (Ital.) (1) An ornamental passage introduced at the close of a vocal or instrumental composition. In modern music the *cadenza* is usually written in small notes. (2) The fall or modulation of the voice.

Cadger. One who carries poultry, butter, eggs, etc., to market; a packman or huckster. From "cadge," to carry. The frame on which hawks were carried was called a "cadge."

Cadit quæstio. (Lat.) "The question falls." The matter falls to the ground.

Cadmean Letters. *See* CADMUS.

Cadmean Victory. A triumph in which the victors suffer as much as their enemies. So named from the victory of the Thebans (then known as Cadmeans) over the famous Seven, which was shortly after terribly avenged by the Epigoni, the descendants of the vanquished.

Cadmus. In classic mythology the son of Agenor and brother of Europa. He was the reputed founder of Thebes in Bœotia, and was said to have invented the old Greek alphabet of sixteen letters,— $a \beta \gamma \delta \epsilon \iota \kappa \lambda \mu \nu o \pi \rho \sigma \tau \upsilon$. These were named Cadmean letters. The eight additional — $\varsigma \eta \theta \xi \phi \chi \psi \omega$ — were named Ionic letters.

Cadmus. (Pseud.) John C. Zachos.

Caduceus. In classic mythology the winged staff or rod with two serpents twined about it, — the emblem borne by Mercury.

Cadwallader. (Pseud.) William G. Hudson in the "Brooklyn Daily Eagle."

Cæca est invidia. (Lat.) Envy is blind.

Cæsarian Operation. The extraction of a child from the womb by an incision in the abdominal wall. Julius Cæsar is said to have been thus brought into the world; whence the term.

Cæsariensis. (Pseud.) James Waddell Alexander, contributor to the "Newark Daily Advertiser," the "Literary World," etc.

Cæsar's Wife must be above Suspicion. "This phrase, according to Suetonius and Plutarch, originated with Cæsar, under the following circumstances: His wife Pompeia had an intrigue with Publius Clodius, a member of one of the noblest families of Rome, and a brilliant and handsome profligate. As he could not easily gain access to her, he took the opportunity, while she was celebrating the mysteries of the Bona Dea (*q. v.*), 'Good Goddess,' a dryad with whom the god Faunus had an amour, to enter disguised in a woman's habit. These mysteries were celebrated annually by women with the most profound secrecy at the house of the consul or prætor. The presence of a man was a hideous pollution; even the pictures of male animals had to be veiled in the room where these ceremonies were performed. While Clodius was waiting in one of the apartments for Pompeia, he was discovered by a maidservant of Cæsar's mother, who gave the alarm. He was driven out of the assembly with indignation. The news spread a general horror throughout the city. Pompeia was divorced by Cæsar; but when Clodius came up for trial, Cæsar declared that he knew nothing of the affair, though his mother Aurelia and his sister Julia gave the court an exact account of all the circumstances. Being asked why, then, he had divorced Pompeia, 'Because,' answered Cæsar, 'my family should not only be free from guilt, but even from the suspicion of it.'"

Cætera desunt. (Lat.) The remainder is wanting.

Cæt. par. *Cæteris paribus.* "With other things equal." Other things being equal.

Cagliostro, Count de. The name assumed by Joseph Balsamo (1743–1795), "one of the most impudent and successful impostors of modern times." *See* BULL-NECKED FORGER.

Cahoot. A word used in the Western and Southern States to denote a companionship or partnership.

Cain-colored Beard. Yellow. In the ancient tapestries Cain and Judas are represented with yellow beards.

He hath but a little wee face, with a little yellow beard, a Cain-colored beard. — *Merry Wives of Windsor.*

Cainites. Disciples of Cain, a pseudo-Gnostic sect of the second century, who renounced the New Testament, and received instead the Gospel of Judas, which justified the false disciple and the crucifixion of Jesus. This sect maintained that heaven and earth were created by the evil principle, and that Cain, with his descendants, were the persecuted party.

Cain of America. An opprobrious nickname bestowed on Nicholas Durand Villegaignon (1510–1571), a French naval officer, for his supposed treachery toward a colony of French Protestants who landed on Coligny Island, in the Bay of Rio Janeiro, 1555–1557.

Ça ira! The refrain of a popular song during the French Revolution of 1791 :

> " Ah, ça ira, ça ira, ça ira,
> Les aristocrats à la lanterne ! "
> (" It will go on," etc.
> " Hang the aristocrats.")

" La lanterne " means the lamp-posts of Paris, whereon so many suspects were hung. *See* CARMAGNOLE.

Caius. (Pseud.) Donald Grant Mitchell, in his " Notes by the Road," in the " American Whig Review."

Caius Claudius Nero. A reportorial personification of the Earl of Winchelsea in the days when newspaper reports of Parliamentary proceedings were not legalized.

Caius Gracchus. (Pseud.) François Noel Babeuf (fl. 1764-1797) affixed this name to his political articles during the French Revolution. *See* BABEUF'S CONSPIRACY.

Cake. A fool, a poor thing. In University slang a clever man is called a good man, and the opposite is a bad one, or a " cake."

Cal. California; calends.

Calamity Weller. So Congressman Weller, of Iowa, was known in Congress, because he seemed to see in every measure of which he disapproved ruin and disaster.

Calash, a corruption of the French *calèche*, signifies (1) an old-fashioned gig, and (2) a feminine head-dress or enveloper known in England as an "ugly."

Calculate. *See* GUESS.

Caleb D'Anvers. (Pseud.) Nicholas Amherst, *circa* 1726, as editor of " The Craftsman."

Caleb Quotem. A parish clerk, or jack-of-all-trades, in Colman's play called " The Review."

> I resolved, like Caleb Quotem, to have a place at the review. — WASHINGTON IRVING.

Calecuegers. A tribe of giants in Indian mythology.

Caledon. A contraction of Caledonia (*q. v.*).

Caledonia. In modern poetry Scotland is often referred to by this its ancient name. It is a corruption of *Celyddon*, a Celtic word meaning " a dweller in woods and forests." The word *Celt* is from the same source, and means the same thing.

> Sees Caledonia in romantic view. — THOMSON.
> O Caledonia. stern and wild,
> Meet muse for a poetic child.
> SCOTT.

Caledonian Comet. Sir Walter Scott was so named.

Caliban. (Pseud.) (1) Robert Buchanan in the " Spectator," London, *circa* 1867. (2) Under this pseudonym Louis Jean Emmanuel Gonzales, the French journalist and feuilletonist (1815-1887), contributed to the Paris press. *See also* MELCHIOR GOMEZ and RAMON GONERIL.

Caliban of Science. Alexander Ramsay, the anatomist (1754-1824).

> He possessed much professional learning, but his vanity, arrogance, and pomp, combined with a grotesque person, interfered with his success as a teacher, and gained him his nickname. — APPLETON.

Calico Foster. A nickname given to Charles Foster, who was governor of Ohio, 1880-1884, in allusion to his having kept a dry-goods store in early life.

California. The name is derived from the Spanish *Caliente Fornalla* (hot furnace), in allusion to the climate of Lower California.

California Column. A body of troops raised in 1862 by James Henry Carleton (1814-1873), with whom he marched across the Yuma and Gila deserts to Mesilla on the Rio Grande.

Caligorant. " An Egyptian giant and cannibal, who used to entrap strangers with a hidden net. This net was made by Vulcan to catch Mars and Venus ; Mercury stole it for the purpose of catching Chloris, and left it in the temple of Anubis ; Caligorant stole it thence. At length Astolpho blew his magic horn, and the giant ran affrighted into his own net, which dragged him to the ground. Whereupon Astolpho made the giant his captive, and despoiled him of his net. This is an allegory. Caligorant was a great sophist and heretic in the days of Ariosto, who used to entangle people ; but being converted by Astolpho to the true faith, was, as it were, caught in his own net, and both his sophistry and heresy were taken from him."

Calixtins. (1) A sect springing from the followers of Huss in 1420, who demanded the cup (Greek, κάλυξ) in the Lord's Supper. They were also called Utraquists, as demanding both elements. (2) Followers of George Calixtus, a Lutheran, who died in 1656. He inveighed against the celibacy of the priesthood.

Call. The American minister who wishes to find a field of usefulness waits for a *call*, or invitation from a congregation to come and minister to their spiritual wants. When it is accepted he is *settled*, and receives a *stated salary*.

Call a Spade a Spade. Plain speech. "Brought up like a Macedon, and taught to call a spade a spade." — GOSSON, *Ephemerides of Phialo.*

Call-boy, The. (Pseud.) Charles J. Smith, in "Noah's Sunday Times."

Calliope. In classic mythology one of the Nine Muses. She presided over eloquence and epic poetry.

Callippic Period. The correction of the Metonic cycle by Callippos. In four cycles, or seventy-six years, the Metonic calculation was several hours in excess. Callippos proposed to quadruple the period of Meton, and deduct a day at the end of it. *See* METONIC CYCLE.

Callirrhoe. The lady-love of Chæreas, in Chariton's eighth-century Greek romance, "The Loves of Chæreas and Callirrhoe."

Callisto. In classic mythology an Arcadian nymph, beloved by Jupiter, who changed her into a she-bear that Juno might not discover the intrigue. Her son Arcas, having met her while hunting, was about to kill her; but Jupiter prevented the act by translating both to the heavens as the two constellations, the Great Bear and the Little Bear.

Callithumpians. "It was a common practice in New York, as well as in other parts of the country, on New Year's Eve, for persons to assemble with tin horns, bells, rattles, and similar euphonious instruments, and parade the streets, making all the noise and discord possible. This party was called the *Callithumpians*, or the *Callithumpian Band*, — an allusion to *Calliope* as well as to *thumping*. The custom has now fallen almost, if not entirely, into disuse. A gang of Baltimore rowdies once assumed the name. The present substitute for this is a procession of roughs at sunrise on the Fourth of July, in grotesque or worse attire, calling themselves 'Antiques and Horribles,' a corruption of the venerable *Ancient* and *Honorable* Artillery Company of Boston. Applied also to any burlesque serenade, particularly when given to unpopular persons on their marriage." — BARTLETT.

Calmar, Union of. The treaty whereby Denmark, Sweden, and Norway were united under one sovereign, 1397. It was dissolved by Gustavus Vasa, 1523.

Calore. (Ital.) With warmth and animation. (Mus.)

Caloyers. Monks in the Greek Church who follow the rule of Saint Basil. They are divided into cenobites, who recite the offices from midnight to sunrise; anchorites, who live in hermitages; and recluses, who shut themselves up in caverns and live on alms. The word means "good old men."

Calpe and Abyla. The two pillars of Hercules. According to one account, these two were originally only one mountain, which Hercules tore asunder; but some say he piled up each mountain separately, and poured the sea between them.

Calvert's Entire. A nickname for the Fourteenth Foot. Sir Harry Calvert, from 1806 to 1826, was their colonel; and three *entire* battalions were kept up to please Sir Harry when adjutant-general. Of course the pun is on Calvert's malt liquor.

For the benefit of American readers it should be explained that the walls of English public-houses are covered with gaudy signs of the various brewers, announcing that "Buxton & Co.'s Entire," "Calvert's Entire," "Bass's Entire," etc., are sold within. The word "entire" means beer or porter drawn from one tap or cask and unmixed with anything else.

Calves' Head Club. Instituted in London in ridicule of Charles I. An annual banquet was held on the 30th of January, and consisted of a cod's head, to represent the person of Charles Stuart; a pike with little ones in its mouth, an emblem of tyranny; a boar's head with an apple in its mouth, to represent the king preying on his subjects; and calves' heads dressed in sundry ways, to represent Charles in his regal capacity. After the banquet the king's book ("Icon Basilike") was burned, and the parting cup was "To those worthy patriots who killed the tyrant."

Calvin's Case, also called the "case of the *post-nati*," 1608, — an action turning on questions of allegiance and natural-born subjects. It was brought to recover lands by Robert Calvin against Richard and Nicholas Smith, to which defendants pleaded that the plaintiff was an alien, and incapable of bringing the action, because he was born in

Scotland, though after the crown of England descended to James I., who was also king of Scotland. It was argued by lawyers and judges of the greatest renown, including Lords Bacon, Coke, Ellesmere, Yelverton, and Warburton, and was decided in favor of the plaintiff.

Calypso, in Fénelon's "Télémaque," figures Madame de Montespan. In mythology she was queen of the island Ogygia, on which Ulysses was wrecked, and where he was detained for seven years.

Calypso's Isle. Gozo, near Malta. Called in mythology Ogygia. See *supra.*

Cam. (Pseud.) Waller Lewis, M.D., English medical writer (1711–1781).

Cam., Camb. Cambridge.

Camaldolites. A religious order of great rigidity of life, founded in the vale of Camaldoli, in the Tuscan Apennines, by Saint Romauld, a Benedictine, in the eleventh century.

Cam and Isis. A familiar couplet by which the sister universities of Cambridge and Oxford are often mentioned. The allusion is to the rivers on which they are situated.

> May you, my Cam and Isis, preach it long,
> The right divine of kings to govern wrong.
> > POPE, *The Dunciad.*

> The drooping Muses (Sir Industry),
> Brought to another Castalie,
> Where Isis many a famous nursling breeds,
> Or where old Cam soft passes o'er the lea,
> In pensive mood.
> > THOMSON, *Castle of Indolence.*

Camarilla. A clique; the confidants or private advisers of the sovereign. It literally means a small private chamber, and is in Spain applied to the room in which boys are flogged.

Cambria. The ancient Latin name of Wales, the home of the Cimbri.

> Cambria's fatal day. — GRAY.

Cambuscan. A prince of Cambaluc (Pekin), whose name is a corruption of Genghis Khan; while the description applies apparently to his grandson Kublai Khan. This was Milton's form of the Cambyuskan of Chaucer's fragment of a metrical romance, "The Squieres Tale."

> Or call him up that left half told
> The story of Cambuscan bold,
> Of Camball and of Algarsife,
> And who had Canace to wife,
> That owned the virtuous ring and glass,
> And of the wondrous horse of brass
> On which the Tartar king did ride.
> > *Il Penseroso.*

Camden of the Eighteenth Century. Richard Gough was so named.

Camdeo. In Hindu mythology the god of love.

Camel, Day of the. *See* DAY OF THE CAMEL.

Camenæ. Prophetic nymphs, of whom Egeria was the most renowned.

Camera. (Ital.) A chamber; as *camera di musica,* the music-chamber.

Camera obscura. A dark chamber.

Cameronian Regiment. The Twenty-sixth Regiment of Infantry in the English army. It originated in a body of Cameronians in the Revolution of 1688.

Cameroy. (Pseud.) James Woods Lane, S.T.D., in the "Observer," New York, *circa* 1858.

Camilla. Virgin queen of the Volscians. Virgil says that she was so swift that she could run over a field of corn without bending a single blade, or make her way over the sea without even wetting her feet.

Camille Lorrain. (Pseud.) Hippolyte Babou, in various Parisian journals.

Camillus. (Pseud.) Fisher Ames, in occasional contributions to Boston newspapers.

Camisard. A night attack. In French history the Camisards were the Protestant insurgents of the Cévennes, who resisted the violence of the Dragonnades after the Revocation of the Edict of Nantes. They were so called because they wore a *camise,* or peasant's smock, over their armor, to conceal it, and that they might the better recognize each other in the dark. Their leader was Cavalier, afterward governor of Jersey.

Campaign = CONTEST. The English "election contest" becomes in America a "political campaign."

Campania. The popular name of the plain surrounding Capua, in Italy, properly called the *Terra di Lavoro.*

> Disdainful of Campania's gentle plains.
> > THOMSON, *The Seasons.*

Campeador. The Cid (*q. v.*).

Camphene. A nickname in the Eastern States for whiskey. *See* POISON.

Camp-meeting. An open-air gathering. Common everywhere in the United States; usually held in summer-time in a grove, for religious purposes, notably preaching and prayer. It is a purely American institution.

Campo Santo of Dissenters. Bunhill Fields burying-ground, in London; so named by Southey, and with good reason. Among those who lie buried there are John Bunyan; George Fox, the founder of the Quakers; Dr. Thomas Goodwin, who attended Cromwell on his death-bed; Dr. John Owen, who preached the first sermon before Parliament after Charles I. was executed; Susannah Wesley, the mother of John Wesley; Dr. Isaac Watts; William Blake, the painter and poet; Daniel De Foe, and Horne Tooke. On a remnant of land in the neighborhood the Friends have built a coffee tavern and memorial hall.

Campus Martius. The field of Mars; a place for military exercises.

Can. Canon.

Canace. "A paragon of women, the daughter of King Cambuscan [*q. v.*], to whom the king of Arabia and India sent as a present a mirror and a ring. The mirror would tell the lady if any man on whom she set her heart would prove true or false; and the ring (which was to be worn on her thumb) would enable her to understand the language of birds, and converse with them. It would also give the wearer perfect knowledge of the medicinal properties of all roots." Canace was courted by a crowd of suitors; but her brother Cambalo gave out that any one who pretended to her hand must encounter him in single combat, and overthrow him. She ultimately married Triamond, son of the fairy Agape.

Canadian Rebellion. "In 1837 an insurrection took place in Canada, many of the inhabitants being dissatisfied with governmental methods. The rebellion was completely crushed in about a year. It is of interest in our history because it threatened to cause international complications between Great Britain and the United States. Many inhabitants of this country, largely those of Irish extraction, sympathized with the Canadians, and sought to aid them. In spite of the fact that our Government declared its strict neutrality, about seven hundred men, chiefly from New York State, under the lead of Mackenzie, one of the leaders of the Canadian revolt, seized and fortified Navy Island, situated in the Niagara River and within British jurisdiction. They made this a base of operations for raids on the Canadian shore, until they were forced to evacuate by a battery of guns on the Canadian side. The steamer 'Caroline,' which they had made use of, was seized by the Canadian militia at a wharf on the American side of the river, and sent, on fire, over Niagara Falls. Our Government sent General Scott with a force of soldiers to prevent infractions of our neutral position."— BROWN AND STRAUSS.

Canaille (dregs). A French term for the rabble, the mob, the "dangerous classes."

Canal Scrip Fraud. "In 1839 the Canal Trustees of the State of Illinois issued about $390,000 of canal scrip, payable in ninety days. This had practically all been presented for redemption before 1843, but, as subsequently appeared, the certificates had simply been laid away and not cancelled. In 1859 some of the scrip appeared in circulation, and a legislative inquiry revealed the fact that $223,182.66 of these redeemed but uncancelled certificates had been re-issued by Gov. Joel A. Matteson. As soon as his name was connected with the matter, Matteson offered to make good any loss to the State, while at the same time maintaining that he had acquired the scrip by investment. The legislative committee was not disposed to press the matter, and although the grand jury of Sangamon County had voted to indict him, the vote was reconsidered and the matter dropped. The State was reimbursed for all but a small part of its loss."— BROWN AND STRAUSS.

Candida pax (Lat.) White-robed peace.

Candide. (Pseud.) Jules Arnaud Arsène Claretie, a French feuilletonist in the Paris "Figaro," 1868.

Candidus. (Pseud.) Thomas White, English philosopher and priest (1582–1676).

Candlemas Day. The 2d of February, when, in the Romish Church, there is a candle procession, to consecrate all the candles which will be needed in the church during the year. The candles symbolize Christ, called "the light of the world," and "a light to lighten the Gentiles." It was the old Roman custom to burn candles to the goddess Februa, mother of Mars, to scare away evil spirits.

Candor. (Pseud.) Noah Webster in the "Connecticut Courant," 1793.

Canicular Period. Same as Dog-days (*q. v.*).

Canicular Year. The ancient solar year of the Egyptians, which began and ended with the rising of the Dog-star, and corresponded with the overflow of the Nile.

Canmore. *See* GREAT HEAD.

Canonical Hours. The times within which the sacred offices may be performed. In the Roman Catholic Church they are seven, — viz., matins, prime, tierce, sext, nones, vespers, and compline. Prime, tierce, sext, and nones are the first, third, sixth, and ninth hours of the day, counting from six in the morning. There are seven canonical hours, because David says, "Seven times a day do I praise thee."

Canonical Punishments are those which the Church is authorized to inflict.

Canopic Vases. Used by the Egyptian priests for the viscera of bodies embalmed, four vases being provided for each body. So called from Canopus, Egypt, where they were first used.

Canopus. "The Egyptian god of water. The Chaldeans worshipped fire, and sent all the other gods a challenge, which was accepted by a priest of Canopus. The Chaldeans lighted a vast fire round the god Canopus, when the Egyptian deity spouted out torrents of water and quenched the fire, thereby obtaining the triumph of water over fire."

Cant. Canticles.

Cantab. *Cantabrigiensis.* Of Cambridge.

Cantabile, or **Cantando.** (Ital.) In a graceful and singing style. (Mus.)

Cantabile, ornamenti ad libitum, ma più tosto pochi e buoni. (Ital.) In a singing style, with embellishments at will, but few and well chosen. (Mus.)

Cantabrigiensis. (Pseud.) Richard Porson, in the "Gentleman's Magazine," 1788–1790.

Cantante. (Ital.) A part to be executed by the voice. (Mus.)

Cantate Domino. (Lat.) Sing to the Lord.

Cantatrice. (Ital.) A female singer.

Cantell A. Bigly. (Pseud., "Can-tell-a-big-lie.") George W. Peck, American miscellaneous writer (1817–1859).

Canterbury of Russia. The Monastery of Troitsa, near Moscow, a shrine of much esteem among pious Russians.

Canterbury Tales. In writing these, Chaucer supposed that he was in company with a party of pilgrims going to Canterbury to pay their devotions at the shrine of Thomas à Becket. The party assembled at an inn in Southwark, called the Tabard, and there agreed to tell one tale each.

Cantianus. (Pseud.) Rev. Edmund Marshall, in the "Kentish Gazette."

Canto. (Ital.) The highest part in vocal music.

Cantons, Lake of the Four Forest. *See* LAKE OF THE FOUR FOREST CANTONS.

Cantons, The Four Forest. *See* FOUR FOREST CANTONS.

Cantuar. Of Canterbury.

Canty Carl. (Pseud.) Frederick William Sawyer, American legal writer (b. 1810).

Canucks. The nickname for the people of Canada in common use in the United States.

Cap. *Caput, capitulum.* Chapter.

Capability Brown. Lancelot Brown, an able English gardener of the eighteenth century. He was much ridiculed for his constant use of the word "capability," but was famous for his skill in making the most sterile tracts "blossom as the rose."

Capaneus. In classic mythology one of the seven who set out from Argos against Thebes. Jupiter killed him by a lightning-bolt for profanely declaring that not even fire from heaven should deter him from scaling the walls of the city.

Cap-a-pie. From head to foot.

Cape Cod Bard. Henry S. Ellenwood was so named.

Capel Court. The London Stock Exchange is in Capel Court, which took its name from Sir William Capel, lord mayor in 1504. "Capel Court" is often used as a synonym for the London financial world, just as "Wall Street" is for that of New York.

Cape of Storms. (Port., *Cabo Tormentoso.*) A name by which the Cape of Good Hope is often referred to. It was bestowed in 1486 by the navigator Bartholomew Diaz.

Capful of Wind. Olaus Magnus says that Eric, king of Sweden, was so familiar with evil spirits that what way soever he turned his cap the wind would blow, and for this he was called Windy Cap. *See* SALE OF WINDS.

Capias ad satisfaciendum. (Lat.) You may take to satisfy.

Capital City of the Empire State of the South. Atlanta, Ga.

Capital-mover. A name given to T. M. Reavis, who advocated shifting the capital of the United States from Washington to St. Louis, Mo.

Capitano del Popolo. (Ital.) "Captain of the People." Garibaldi (1807–1882).

Cap of Maintenance ("Maintenance" = "Defiance.") A cap of dignity anciently belonging to the rank of duke; the fur cap of the Lord Mayor of London, worn on days of state; also a cap carried before the British sovereigns at their coronation.

Capriccio. (Ital.) A fanciful and irregular composition. (Mus.)

Capriole. A leap without advancing.

Caps and Hats. *See* HATS AND CAPS.

Capt. Captain.

Captain. Gonzalvo di Cordova (1453–1515) and Manuel Comnenus (1120–1180) were each named "the Great Captain." *See* CAPITANO DEL POPOLO.

Captain Absolute. A bold, despotic man, determined to have his own way. The characterization is founded on the traits of Sir Anthony Absolute in Sheridan's play, "The Rivals."

Captain George North. (Pseud.) The name under which Robert Louis Stevenson published "The Outlaws of Tunstall Forest" in "Young Folks" in 1883.

Captain Jack. (Pseud.) Capt. J. W. Crawford, who published a volume of poems in New York (1886).

Captain Loys. Louise Labé (1526–1566), who received this sobriquet because in early life she became a soldier and evinced great courage.

Captain Rawdon Crawley. (Pseud.) George Frederick Pardon, English author and critic (b. 1829).

Captain Right, Captain Rock. Imaginary leaders of the Irish insurgents in their risings at various times during the last two centuries.

Captain Schreier. (Pseud.) Leopold Schenck, editor of the German reprint of "Puck."

Capt.-Gen. Captain-General.

Capulet. A noble house in Verona, the rival of that of Montague; Juliet is of the former, and Romeo of the latter. Lady Capulet is the beau-ideal of a proud Italian matron of the fifteenth century. The expression, "the tomb of all the Capulets," is from Burke.

Caput. (Lat.) "Head." Chapter of a book.

Caput mortuum. (Lat.) The dead body; the worthless remains; in alchemy an exhausted residue.

Caput scabere. (Lat.) To scratch one's head as a preliminary in commencing some important work.

Caqueteur. (Pseud.) Charles Hull Webb, in the "Boys' and Girls' Weekly," New York.

Car. Carat.

Caracalla. Aurelius Antoninus, who was born in Gaul, was so called because he adopted the Gaulish caracalla in preference to the Roman toga. It was a large, close-fitting, hooded mantle, reaching to the heels, and slit up before and behind to the waist.

Caracci. Founder of the Eclectic School in Italy. Luis and his two cousins, Augustin and Annibale, founded the school called Incamminati ("progressive"), which had for its chief principle the strict observance of Nature. They flourished 1554–1609.

Caracci of France. Jean Jouvinet, a famous artist (1647–1707), whose right side was paralyzed, so he painted entirely with his left hand.

Caracci of the Eclectic School. Bernardino Campi, the Italian (1522–1590), is so called by Lanzi.

Caractacus. (Pseud.) E. Sendall, in the "Live-Stock Journal."

Caradoc. One of the Knights of the Round Table, husband of the only lady in the queen's train who could wear "the mantle of matrimonial fidelity."

Caraites. A religious sect among the Jews, who rigidly adhered to the words and letters of Scripture, regardless of metaphor, etc. They rejected the rabbinical interpretations and the Cabala.

Carbonari ("charcoal-burners"). A name assumed by a secret revolutionary society in Italy in 1820. They adopted a code of signals consisting of words taken from the lingo of the charcoal-burners of the forests.

Card. Cardinal.

Cardinal Virtues. Justice, prudence, temperance, and fortitude, on which all the other virtues depend.

Ca. resp. *Capias ad respondendum.* A legal writ.

Caret initio et fine. (Lat.) It wants beginning and end.

Carinæ. Women hired by the Romans to weep at funerals. So called from Caria, whence most of them came.

Carisbrooke. (Pseud.) Miss E. Nesbit, in "Good Words," "Sunday Magazine," etc.

Carl. (Pseud.) (1) Frederick William Sawyer, American legal writer (b. 1810). (2) Rev. Charles Hanbury Williams.

Carl Benson. (Pseud.) Charles Astor Bristed, American author (1820-1874).

Carleton. (Pseud.) Walter Charlton, M. D., English philosophical writer (1619-1707).

Carlfried. (Pseud.) C. F. Wingate, *littérateur.*

Carling Sunday. The octave preceding Palm Sunday. So called because the special food of the day was carling, *i. e.*, peas fried in butter. The custom is a continuation of the pagan bean-feast.

Carlo Khan. A sobriquet conferred on Charles James Fox (fl. 1749-1806). He introduced a bill in Parliament in 1783 regulating the government of the East Indies. The nickname arose out of a supposition that he aimed to establish for himself a sort of dictatorship over those colonies.

Carlotta Patti. The professional and the maiden name of Madame De Münck.

Carludovica. A Panama hat, made from the *Carludovica palmata.* So called in compliment to Carlos IV. of Spain, whose second name was Ludovic.

Carlyle, Jupiter. *See* JUPITER CARLYLE.

Carmagnole. A red republican song and dance in the French Revolution. So called from Carmagnola in Piedmont, the great nest of the Savoyards, noted for street music and dancing. Besides the song, the word is applied to the dress worn by the Jacobins, consisting of a blouse, red cap, and tricolored girdle ; to the wearer of this dress, or any violent revolutionist ; and to the dance performed by the mob round the guillotine.

Carmelites. Monks of Mount Carmel, the monastery of which is named Elias, from Elijah the prophet, who on Mount Carmel told Ahab that rain was at hand.

Carmen Pisani. The stage-name of Madame Frapolli.

Carmen Silva. (Pseud.) Princess Elizabeth of Roumania, translator of Roumanian poems.

Carmilhan. The phantom ship on which the kobold of the Baltic sits when he appears to doomed vessels.

Caro. (Pseud.) Mrs. C. A. B. Mason, an American poet, in the Salem (Mass.) "Register."

Carolina Doctrine. Additional duties having been levied by order of Congress upon manufactured goods imported from abroad, South Carolina was greatly offended at this act, because "the manufacturing districts were favored at the expense of the agricultural States." It claimed that a State had a right to declare null and void a law passed by Congress which was injurious to its (the State's) interests.

Caroline Bell. The stage-name of Mrs. George Hearne.

Caroline Hill. The stage-name of Mrs. Herbert Kelcey.

Caroline Howard, Vernon Grove, N. Y. (Pseud.) Mrs. Caroline H. Glover, American writer for children (b. 1823).

Caroline Parker. The stage-name of Mrs. Charles Fenton.

Carp. (Pseud.) Frank Carpenter, sometime Washington correspondent of the "Cleveland Leader."

Carpathian Wizard. Proteus (*q. v.*).

Carpe diem. (Lat.) Enjoy the present day ; seize the present opportunity.

Carpet-baggers. Corrupt and often ignorant politicians — mostly from the North — who flocked to the South during the era of Reconstruction. They were uniformly "on the make," and were responsible for much of the venality and rascality that disgraced that period of the history of the South.

Some of them were the dregs of the Federal army, — the meanest of the camp followers ; many were fugitives from Northern justice ; the best of them were those who went down after the peace, ready for any deed of shame that was safe and profitable. These, combining with a few treacherous "scalawags," and some leading negroes to serve as decoys for the rest, and backed by the power of the General Government, beeame the strongest body of thieves that ever pillaged a people. Their moral grade was far lower. . . . They swarmed on all the States from the Potomac to the Gulf, and settled in hordes, not with the intent to remain there, but merely to feed on the substance of a prostrate and defenceless people. They took whatever came within their reach, intruded themselves into all private corporations, assumed the functions of all offices, including the courts of justice, and in many places they even "ran the churches." By force of fraud, they either controlled all elections, or else prevented elections from being held. — *North American Review*, for July, 1877.

Carpet Knight. One dubbed at court by favor, not having won his spurs by service in the field. Mayors, lawyers, and other civilians are knighted as they kneel on a carpet before the sovereign.

"Carpet knights are such as have studied law, physic, or other arts or sciences, whereby they have become famous, and seeing that they are not knighted as soldiers, they are not therefore to use the horseman's title or spurs ; they are only termed simply *miles* and *milites*, 'Knight,' or 'Knights of the Carpetry,' or 'Knights of the Green Cloth,' to distinguish them from those knights that are dubbed as soldiers in the field." — RANDLE HOLMES, *Academy of Armour*, iii. 57.

Carpocratians. The Gnostic sect, so called from Carpocrates, who flourished in the middle of the second century.

Carrie Andrews. The stage-name of Mrs. Leander Richardson.

Carrie Carlton. (Pseud.) Mrs. M. H. Chamberlain, an American poet.

Carrie Turner. The stage-name of Mrs. Albert His.

Carryall. A vehicle for freight and passengers. A corruption of the French *carriole*.

Cars = CARRIAGES. On American railroads the passenger vehicles are called "cars" or "coaches," while in England they are called "carriages." *See* HORSE-CAR.

Carte blanche. (Fr.) Unconditional terms.

Carte du pays. (Fr.) Map of the country.

Cartesian Devil, or Bottle Imp. An ingenious scientific toy named after Descartes. A tall glass vessel, as a preserve-jar, is nearly filled with water, and the mouth covered with an air-tight piece of bladder or india-rubber. In and on the water floats a small hollow figure, with a hole near the top, partly filled with air and partly with water. When the cover of the glass is pressed, the air beneath is compressed, and water enters the floating figure, so as to bring the air in it to the same degree of compression, and the figure sinks in the water, not rising again till the pressure is removed.

C. A. S. *Connecticutensis Academiæ Socius.* Fellow of the Connecticut Academy of Arts and Sciences.

Ca. sa. *Capias ad satisfaciendum.* A legal writ.

Casa de pupilos. (Span.) "A house of pupils." A boarding-house.

Case of the Impositions. *See* BATES'S CASE.

Case of the Post-nati. *See* CALVIN'S CASE.

Cash. Cashier.

Casket Homer. Alexander the Great's edition, with Aristotle's corrections. "After the battle of Arbela, a golden casket, studded with jewels, was found in the tent of Darius. Alexander being asked to what purpose it should be applied, made answer, 'There is but one production in the world worthy of so costly a depository ;' and placed therein his edition of Homer, which received from this circumstance the term of Casket Homer."

Caspar Hauser. Nearly a century ago the civilized world was shocked at the discovery of one of the cruelest crimes that ever disgraced humanity, the victim of which had been kept in a narrow and dimly lighted dungeon, separated from all communication with his kind from babyhood, robbed of his childhood and boyhood and of the care of his natural guardians, until, at the age of seventeen, he was cast adrift on the common highway, helpless as an infant, unable to talk or to walk, his mind a blank, his faculties undeveloped, and his body a torment. Scarcely had this youth been restored to the companionship of mankind, and partially taught and civilized, — the progress of his mental and moral education being watched with intense interest by the physician and the physiologist, by the minister and the moralist, — than an attack upon his life was made by persons unknown. He recovered from this assault, but a second attempt to murder him, made some three years later, was only too successful. All efforts to discover the authors of these villanies failed, and the youth bade farewell to the world as mysteriously and as tragically as he had entered it. Needless to say that these events aroused widespread wonder. Great pains were taken to rend the veil of darkness enshrouding the foul transaction, but without avail; and in all the capitals of Europe men asked one another, Who was he? The query has never yet been answered, and the crime has never yet been brought home to its perpetrators. In the city of Nuremberg, between four and five o'clock on the afternoon of Whit-Monday, May 26, 1828, a citizen who resided in the Unschlitt Place, near the lonely Haller Gate, was standing at his door enjoying the cool of the evening. A short distance away, just within the barrier, he noticed a youth, clad in peasant's clothes, who with a shambling and staggering gait was endeavoring to move forward, but who appeared to be unable to stand erect or to control the motions of his body. The citizen approached the stranger, who with an appealing look handed him a letter addressed "To his Honor the Captain of the Fourth Squadron of the Cavalry Regiment, Nuremberg." As the captain lived not far from the Haller Gate, the citizen undertook to lead the strange lad thither. The boy walked, or rather painfully stumbled along, when unsupported, with hands thrust out before him, swaying from side to side, and lifting his feet wholly from the ground like a toddling infant. On the way to the residence of Captain W——, who at that time commanded the fourth squadron of the Sixth Regiment of the Chevaux-legers, the citizen made several efforts to learn whence he came, his name, and how he came to be so helpless. But he soon found that his questions were entirely unintelligible to the lad. To all interrogatories he returned answer in a jargon of words: "Ae sechtene möcht ih waeh ne, wie mei waehn is;" or, "Woas nicht;" or Votta "Reuta wähn, wie mei Votta wähn is;" or, "Hoam wissa." These nearly unintelligible phrases comprised his sole vocabulary; and they were delivered in a groaning, guttural tone of voice, more like the whining of an animal than the speech of a human being. As he seemed to be suffering from hunger and thirst, a piece of meat was handed to him; but scarcely had it touched his lips when his face became convulsed with horror, and he violently spat it out. The same disgust was manifested at a glass of beer. A slice of bread and a goblet of fresh water he consumed eagerly and with every sign of relish. The children

stood around him in silent wonder. His language consisted of tears, moans, and meaningless sounds, while with gestures of pain he pointed to his feet. Being led to the stable, he fell into a sound sleep. A dozen hours after his arrival Captain W—— arrived home, and immediately went to the stable to look at the strange creature who had been so mysteriously directed to his house, and of whose antics the children told such strange tales. The boy was still sleeping, and all efforts to arouse him were for a long time fruitless. He was shaken, pinched, rolled over and over, stood on his feet, and shouted at, but still he slept on. At length, we are told, "after many troublesome and painful experiments upon the sleeper's capacity of feeling," he slowly opened his eyes, awoke, gazed intently at the gay colors and gold braid of the captain's uniform, and then groaned out, with tearful eyes: "Reuta wähn, wie mei Votta wähn is" ("I would be a rider, or trooper, as my father was"). Could anything be more puzzling or ridiculous? Recourse was next had to the letter which the boy had brought. It ran as follows: "From a place near the Bavarian frontier which shall be nameless, 1828. *High and Well-born Captain:* I send you a boy who wishes to serve his king. This boy was left in my house the seventh day of October, 1812; and I am myself a poor day-laborer, who have also ten children, and have enough to do to maintain my own family. The mother of the child only put him in my house for the sake of having him brought up. But I have never been able to discover who his mother is, nor have I ever given information to the provincial court that such a child was placed in my house. I thought I ought to receive him as my son. I have given him a Christian education, and since 1812 I have never suffered him to take a single step out of my house. So that no one knows where he was brought up. Nor does he know either the name of my house or where it is. You may ask him, but he cannot tell you. I have already taught him to read and write, and he writes my handwriting exactly as I do. And when we asked him what he would be he said he would be one of the Chevaux-legers, as his father was. If he had had parents different from what he has, he would have become a learned lad. If you show him anything, he learns it immediately. I have only showed him the way to Neumark, whence he was to go to you. I told him that when he had once become a soldier I should come to take him home or I should lose my head. Good Mr. Captain, you need not try him; he does not know the place where I am. I took him away in the middle of the night, and he knows not the way home. I am your most obedient servant. I do not sign my name, for I might be punished. He has not a kreutzer of money, because I have none myself. If you do not keep him you may get rid of him or let him be scrambled for." This remarkable "lying letter" was written in German characters, but the style and orthography were evidently disguised so as to pass for those of some ignorant peasant. But with it, in the same hand, but in Latin, was inclosed the following paper: "The child is already baptized. You must give him a surname yourself; you must educate the child. His father was one of the Chevaux-legers. When he is seventeen years old send him to Nuremberg to the Sixth Chevaux-leger Regiment, for there his father also was. I ask for his education till he is seventeen years old. He was born the 30th of April, 1812. I am a poor girl and cannot support him. His father is dead." These documents shed no light on the matter; on the contrary, they rather deepened the mystery. Captain W—— knew nothing of the stranger, nor could he gather any clew to his past history from the foregoing papers. The assertion that his father had been a member of the regiment it was impossible either to verify or disprove. As nothing could be ascertained by questioning the chief performer in this strange case but the interminable "Woas nicht," or "Reuta wähn," etc., he was turned over to the police, and to them was confided the task of discovering the stranger's identity. The police could make nothing of him. He appeared to possess no more intelligence than a dog or a horse. The objects and persons surrounding him appeared to arouse neither emotion nor confusion. He stared about him, but apparently the things he saw excited no thought, and, as a bystander said, "he evinced as much perception as a turnip." Some present even doubted whether he were not a clever impostor, so difficult did they find it to believe that so much vacuity could be contained in a single human being. This suspicion, unfounded as it afterward proved to be, received apparent confirmation from an unexpected source. As a last resort an officer handed the boy a pen and paper, motioning that he should write. An expression of placid pleasure spread over his face, and not at all awkwardly he took the pen between his fingers and wrote in a good plain hand the name "Caspar Hauser." Then he was told to add the name of the place whence he came, but laying down the pen he only groaned out the interminable "Reuta wähn " and " Woas nicht." Caspar Hauser was, when he appeared at Nuremberg, four feet nine inches in height, and from sixteen to seventeen years old. His chin and lips were very thinly covered with down; the so-called wisdom teeth were yet wanting, nor did they make their appearance before the year 1831. His light brown hair, which was very fine, and curled in ringlets, was cut according to the fashion of peasants. The structure of his body, which was stout and broad-shouldered, showed perfect symmetry without any visible defect. His skin was fine and very fair; his complexion was not florid, but neither was it of a sickly hue; his limbs were delicately built; his small hands were beautifully formed, and his feet, which showed no marks of ever before having been confined or pressed by a shoe, were equally so. The soles of his feet, which were without any horny skin, were as soft as the palms of his hands, and they were covered all over with blood blisters, the marks of which were some months later still visible. Both his arms showed the marks of inoculation, and on his right arm a wound, still covered with a fresh scab, was observable, which, as Caspar afterward related, was occasioned by a blow given him with a stick or a piece of wood by the man "with whom he had always been," because he had made too much noise. His face was at that time very vulgar; when in a state of tranquillity it was almost without any expression, and its lower features, being somewhat prominent, gave him a brutish appearance. The staring look of his blue but clear and bright eyes had also an expression of brutish obtuseness. The formation of his face altered in a few months almost entirely, his countenance gained expression and animation, the prominent lower features of his face receded more and more, and his earlier physiognomy could scarcely any longer be recognized. As time passed, the fruitless efforts of the police to discover a clew to the dark enigma gradually lessened, and public interest in the case died away for want of food to feed upon. But a number of scholarly and humane gentlemen had become interested in the phenomenon of a youth of seventeen with a normal body and the mind of an infant. Among these were Messrs. Daumer and Binder, the first a professor at the university, and who at once interested himself in the education of the lad. It was soon discovered that the boy was neither an idiot nor a madman. On the contrary, so mild, so obedient, so sunny-tempered was he, that no one could be tempted to believe that he came of brutish parents, or had grown up among such. When Caspar had been a little over a month at Nuremberg he came under the notice of Herr Anselm von Feuerbach, president of one of the Bavarian Courts of Appeal, to whom the world is indebted for a dispassionate and candid history of this remarkable youth, "An Account of an Individual Kept in a Dungeon." On July 11, 1828, this gentleman went to Nuremberg expressly to visit and to study Caspar Hauser. That the study of his unfolding mind and the development of his body yielded an interest surpassing for the time being the question of his identity can readily be credited. Such an opportunity for physiological and psychological investigations had never before been afforded men of science, and they embraced it with such ardor that before long the health of the subject of their studies began to suffer seriously under the strain to which he was subjected. This, together with the high-pressure efforts at educating him, and the varied influences brought to bear upon his immature brain by the interminable procession of visitors, resulted at length in an illness that for a time threatened serious results. On July 18, 1829, Caspar Hauser was removed from his abode in the police tower and transferred to the home-like care and superintendence of Professor Daumer, who assumed entire charge of his education, and in whose house he was shielded from the exciting influences that had come so near costing him his life. As may be imagined, the labor of instilling into such a mind ideas of God, relig-

ion, nature, humanity, and the thousand things which ordinary children learn by imitation, was a slow and tedious process. But, assisted both by his natural aptitude and by his intense desire to learn, his progress in the first year was phenomenally rapid, and, under the kind care of the Professor and his mother and sister, Caspar soon became a rational, well-informed being. By the careful attention of these same worthy people, too, the boy's health was vastly improved. Such was his mental progress, that in the summer of 1829, a little more than a year after his entry into Nuremberg, he was able to collect his recollections of his marvellous career into a well-written memoir. This production so delighted him that, like many another young author, he never wearied of telling of his performance; and it was soon announced in various European journals that the Foundling of Nuremberg was writing his life. It has been thought by his biographers that it was this announcement that precipitated an attack that was doubtless intended to terminate abruptly his short but sorrowful career. On Saturday, Oct. 15, 1829, Caspar happened to be left alone in the home of Professor Daumer. The house then stood in a thinly peopled quarter, surrounded by open fields, and far from any other structure. About eleven o'clock he had occasion to visit an outhouse, and on his return thence was stabbed or struck in the temple with some sharp instrument by a man whose features were probably masked, and who immediately fled. Caspar staggered toward the house, and either fell or stumbled down the cellar steps, at the foot of which he was found an hour later, insensible from loss of blood. A little after noon Miss Daumer was sweeping the hall-way, when she observed on the stairs several drops of blood, and bloody footsteps. These marks she traced along the passage-way to the closet, and there, to her horror, found a mass of clotted blood. In great alarm she summoned her mother, and together they tracked the boy to the cellar, whence he was carefully and tenderly removed to his room. The blow, said the physicians and other experts, was doubtless intended for the boy's throat; but he probably "ducked his head" in time, and thus escaped a fatal stroke. Beyond the shock and pain, confinement to his room for a few days was all the inconvenience

8

Caspar suffered. By order of the municipal authorities, the boy was attended by the medical officer of the city, and constantly guarded by two soldiers. Under the loving care of the Daumer family he soon recovered, and when strong enough the magistrates caused him to be examined concerning the attempt on his life, but no clew to the criminal was elicited. Among the privileged visitors while Caspar was under Professor Daumer's care was Lord Stanhope, an English nobleman of wealth and generosity, who had become interested in the boy, his story, and his career. This gentleman offered to assume the entire charge and expense of his education. The offer was accepted, and, as a first step, Caspar was sent to Anspach, and there placed under the care of an accomplished tutor. His career while at Anspach fulfilled every expectation; and in a few months he was deemed competent to assume the duties of an official appointment, and he was accordingly made clerk in the Registrar's Office of the Court of Appeal. It was Lord Stanhope's idea by this means to accustom Caspar to the duties of life, and in time to take him to England and adopt him as his foster-son. But the deep and diabolical mystery which hung over his young existence pursued him to his new abode, and the benevolent intentions of the philanthropist were frustrated. At midday on Dec. 17, 1833, while the youth was returning home from his official duties, he was accosted by a stranger, who said he was in possession of important information concerning the birth and origin of Caspar Hauser (though he informed him that this was not his rightful name), which he would divulge if he would meet him in the park attached to the Castle of Anspach late that afternoon. All on fire to possess the priceless secret, Caspar very imprudently kept the appointment without informing his protectors or his friends of his intention, secrecy having been enjoined by his unknown acquaintance. Arrived at the rendezvous, the stranger was at his post. Without a word he took Caspar by the arm, and led him aside until they were absolutely alone. Then, in silence, he plunged a dagger into his breast, and was gone! Caspar had only strength to totter to the public highway. He was speedily carried to the residence of his tutor, gasped out a few indistinct phrases telling of the attempt on his life, and fell fainting to the floor. The police were summoned, but ere a final deposition could be taken, or he could furnish any clew to the perpetrator of the outrage, Caspar Hauser was no more. All the resources of the police were set in motion to endeavor to apprehend the murderer, but without avail. The author of the dual crime (for doubtless the same coward hand dealt both blows) was never discovered, and the secret preserved at the expense of so much iniquity is still masked from the eyes of men. Professor Daumer considered him to have been a son of the Grand-Duke Charles of Baden and of his wife Stephanie, "pushed aside in some criminal way in order to secure the succession to the children of the Grand-Duke Charles Frederick and the Countess of Hochberg." But this theory, though substantiated by an array of corroborative incidents, is little more than a mere guess, although it is perhaps the most plausible, not to say probable, of all the theories offered in solution of the puzzle. After all, as has been well said, this part of the story has comparatively little interest in view of the many curious psychological problems presented in the course of the boy's education.

Caspian Gates (*Pylæ Caspiæ*). A name given to the Russian fortress of Dariel, situated in a narrow defile of the Caucasus, on the Terek, eighty miles north of Tiflis.

Cassander. (Pseud.) John Bruckner, French preacher in England (1726–1804).

Cassandra. In classic mythology a daughter of Priam and Hecuba. She possessed the gift of prophecy, but no one would believe her.

Cassi. Inhabitants of Cassio Hundred, Hertfordshire, referred to by Cæsar in his Commentaries.

Cassiope. Wife of Cepheus and mother of Andromeda, and renowned for her beauty. After her death she was relegated to the firmament, forming the constellation known as the "Lady in her Chair."

Cassius of Britain. Algernon Sidney is so named by Thomson in "The Seasons."

Castaly. A fountain of Parnassus sacred to the Muses. Its waters had the power of inspiring with the gift of poetry those who drank of them.

Castara. Under this fanciful name William Habington, the poet (fl. 1605-1654), sung the praises of Lucia, daughter of Lord Powis, — the lady who afterward became his wife.

Castles in Spain. (Fr., *châteaux en Espagne*.) Groundless or visionary projects. In the fifteenth century they said, in a similar sense, *Faire des châteaux en Asie*, — " To build castles in Asia."

Castor and Pollux. Twin sons of Leda and Tyndareus, king of Lacedæmon. On account of their mutual attachment Zeus placed them among the stars, where they form the two principal luminaries in the constellation Gemini.

Casus belli. (Lat.) An occasion of war ; a cause for going to war.

Casus fœderis. (Lat.) A case of conspiracy; the end of the league.

Casus in eventu est. (Lat.) The result is doubtful.

Casus necessitatis. (Lat.) A case of necessity.

Cat. or **Cata.** Catalogue.

Catacazy Affair. An episode in the diplomatic relations between the United States and Russia. M. Catacazy arrived in Washington as the accredited Russian ambassador in 1870, made a very agreeable impression, and gave promise of being a very acceptable envoy. It was soon found, however, that Catacazy began interfering in questions not appropriately connected with his Legation, and in those pending before Congress, importuning senators and members, and resorting to personal interviews and solicitations unusual on the part of representatives of other Powers accredited to this Government ; and he did not hesitate to use the press of this country to influence public opinion upon questions pending before the Government. This was borne with ; but the act which particularly outraged President Grant was an article published in the New York "World" of Nov. 29, 1870, purporting to be from its Washington correspondent, under the caption of " Russia and America," which bore evidence of inspiration from some one familiar with the instructions from his Government to the Russian minister, and of his confidential correspondence and conversation. Catacazy, when charged by Secretary Fish with having inspired this article, denied all knowledge of its authorship, but asserted that the information was furnished by his enemies to bring him into disrepute with our Government. He subsequently wrote a note to Mr. Fish, in which he denied " emphatically and categorically all connection, direct or indirect, with the ' World's ' false and absurd assertions," which he characterized from beginning to end as "a tissue of lies and absurdities." Nevertheless George W. Adams, the " World " correspondent, in reply to a note from Secretary Fish, informed that gentleman that the article in question was written from notes made in the course of an interview of Catacazy's own timing at his own house. It was written under the stipulation that Catacazy should revise the writer's manuscript, that it was so revised by Catacazy, and was sent to the " World " as revised, and printed as sent. Upon the receipt of this information, Secretary Fish at once sent a despatch to Minister Curtin at St. Petersburg saying that the President could no longer hold any official or social intercourse with Catacazy, and asking that he be recalled. Curtin was not as expeditious in securing the object desired as the President thought he should have been, and a subsequent despatch was sent saying that if Catacazy was not at once recalled by his own Government, his passports would be sent him. The Russian Government begged that the President would tolerate Catacazy until after the visit of the Grand Duke Alexis, and this request was acceded to, with the condition that the President would only receive Catacazy when he was in attendance upon the Grand Duke. After the reception of the Grand Duke in New York, Secretary Fish, under date of Nov. 24, 1871, informed Catacazy that intercourse with him as the diplomatic representative of the Russian Government would cease.

Catalogue raisonné. (Fr.) A catalogue of books arranged according to their subjects, with illustrations, proofs, etc.

Catch a Crab. This phrase originated with the Italians, who have several proverbial sayings of similar import. *Chiappar un granchio* is used exactly in the same sense as our " catch a crab." *Pigliare un granchio* means " to commit a blunder; " and *Pigliare un granchio a secco*, " to catch a crab on dry land," is used when a person pinches his finger.

Catch Club. A society of amateur musicians founded in London in 1761. A "catch" is a humorous canon or round, so contrived that the singers catch up each other's sentences.

Catching a Tartar. To be outdone or outwitted. An Irish soldier in a battle against the Turks shouted to his commanding officer that he had caught a "Tartar." "Bring him along, then," said the general. "But he won't come." "Then come along yourself." "Bedad, and so I would, but he won't let me," answered Pat.

Catch-penny. This well-known term for anything brought out for sale with a view to entrap unwary purchasers, originated in the year 1824, just after the execution of Thurtell for the murder of Weare. This murder had created a great sensation, and Catnach, the celebrated printer of Seven Dials, in London, made a very large sum by the sale of Thurtell's "last dying speech." When the sale of this speech began to fall off, Catnach brought out a second edition, with the heading "WE ARE alive again!" the words "we are" being printed with a very narrow space between them. These two words the people took for the name of the murdered man, reading it "WEARE alive again;" and a large edition was rapidly cleared off. Some one called it a "catchpenny," and the word rapidly spread, until Catnach's productions were usually so styled, and the word became adopted into the language.

Catchpole. A constable, whose business it was to apprehend criminals. Pole, or poll, means "head, person;" and the word means "one who catches persons by the poll or neck." This was formerly done by means of an instrument something like a shepherd's crook.

Cater-cousin. An intimate friend; a remote kinsman. It is a corruption of the French *quatre-cousin*, a fourth cousin.

Catharine Earnshaw. (Pseud.) Maria L. Pool, in the New York "Weekly."

Catharists. (Gr. καθαρός, pure.) The last surviving sect of the Gnostics, so called from their professed purity of faith. They maintained that matter is the source of all evil, that Christ had not a real body, that the human body is incapable of newness of life, and that the sacraments do not convey grace.

Cathay. In modern times the poetical sobriquet for the Far East, — China and Japan, — but in olden times the name for those countries. It is said to have been brought into Europe by Marco Polo, and is derived from the Tartar word *Khitai*, the land of the Khitans, a people who occupied a portion of China at the time of the great Mongol invasion.

Better fifty years of Europe than a cycle of Cathay.
TENNYSON, *Locksley Hall.*

Cathedral of Methodism. City Road Chapel, London. John Wesley's tomb is here.

Catherine Cole. (Pseud.) Mrs. M. R. Field, a writer on the staff of the New Orleans "Picayune."

Catherine Corcoran. The stage-name of Mrs. J. A. Herne.

Catherine Lewis. The stage-name of Mrs. Donald Robertson, formerly Mrs. Arfwedson.

Catholic, The. (1) Alfonso I., king of Asturias. (2) Ferdinand II., king of Aragon and (V.) of Castile. (3) Isabella, queen of Castile.

Catholic Majesty. A title bestowed by the Holy See on certain Spanish monarchs, because of their zeal for the faith. *See* CATHOLIC, THE.

Catiline's Conspiracy. Lucius Sergius Catiline, a dissolute Roman noble, having been refused the consulship, in 65 B.C. conspired to kill the Senate, plunder the treasury, and set Rome on fire. Catiline fled to Gaul, where he was slain by Petreius, 62 B.C.

Cato. (Pseud.) John Trenchard in the London "Times" and the "British Journal."

Cato Street Conspiracy. A gang of desperate politicians, formed by Arthur Thistlewood, which assembled in Cato Street, Edgeware Road, London, proposed the assassination of the ministers of the crown at a cabinet dinner, and the overthrow of the government. They were betrayed by one of their number, and arrested Feb. 23, 1820; and the principals were executed as traitors on the May 1 following.

Cat Raphael. Godfrey Mind, a famous painter of feline figures.

Cat's Paw. The tool of another; the medium who does another's dirty work. The allusion is to the fable of the monkey who wanted to get from the fire some roasted chestnuts, and used the paw of the cat.

Cattle, in England used promiscuously for all animals that serve for food or draught, designates in America only. the bovine genus.

Cattle-ranges. Those vast tracts of country in the West and Southwest given up to the pasturage of cattle. *See* RANCH.

Caucus. This is peculiarly an American institution. It consists of a secret conference of the members of the National or State legislature of the same political stripe. The conclusions arrived at are usually considered as binding on the members of the caucus during the succeeding public proceedings. Gordon (History of the American Revolution) speaks of this word as having been in use in 1724. Dr. Trumbull, of Hartford, Conn., says, "Its origin is the Indian *cau-cau-as'u*," which he defines or translates as "one who advises, urges, encourages, etc." (Am. Philol. Assoc. Trans. 1872). In "Webster's Dictionary" is a quotation from "The Political Passing-bell," a Parody on Gray's "Elegy," Boston, 1789: —

That mob of mobs, a *caucus*, to command,
Hurl wild dissension round a maddening land.

There is, however, another theory as to the origin of the term. About 1724 Henry Adams, father of Samuel Adams, in company with some friends, mostly sea-captains, shipwrights, and persons otherwise connected with the shipping interest, which was then very powerful, founded a political club in Boston, designed "to lay plans for introducing certain persons into places of trust and power." This institution was known as "the calkers' club," and the term "caucus " may have been derived therefrom.

Caudine Forks. (*Furculæ Caudinæ.*) Two high, narrow, and wooded mountain gorges near the town of Caudium, in ancient Samnium, on the boundary toward Campania. These gorges are celebrated on account of the defeat here suffered by the Romans in the second Samnite war (321 B. C.).

Cauliflowers, The. A nickname by which the Forty-seventh Regiment is known throughout the English service. It is also called " Lancashire Lads," in allusion to the place of recruitment.

Causa causans. (Lat.) " The cause causing." The great First Cause; the Supreme Being.

Causa sine quâ non. (Lat.) An indispensable cause.

Cause célèbre. (Fr.) A remarkable trial in a court of justice.

Causeur. (Pseud.) William Alfred Hovey, in the " Evening Transcript," Boston, *circa* 1880.

Cautionary Towns. Four towns in Holland — the Briel, Flushing, Rammekins, and Walcheren — were so named because they were given to Queen Elizabeth in 1585 as security for their repaying her for assistance in their struggle with Spain. They were restored to the Dutch Republic by James I. in 1616, although only a portion of the sum advanced was refunded.

Caution Money. A sum of fifteen pounds paid before entering Oxford or Cambridge Universities, by way of security. This money is deducted from the account of the last term, when only the balance has to be paid.

Cavalazzi, Madame. The stage-name of Mrs. Charles Mapleson, a famous danseuse.

Cavalier, The. (1) Eon de Beaumont, French soldier (fl.1728–1810). (2) Charles Breydel, the Flemish landscape painter (fl. 1677–1744). (3) Francesco Cairo, the historian (fl. 1598–1674). (4) Jean Le Clerc (fl. 1587–1633). (5) Jean Baptiste Marini, Italian poet (fl. 1569–1625). (6) Andrew Michael Ramsay (fl. 1686–1743).

Cavaliers. The royalist party during the civil war in England. The Parliamentarians were nicknamed Roundheads (*q. v.*).

Cavatina. (Ital.) An air having one movement or part only, generally preceded by a recitative.

Caveat actor. (Lat.) Let the doer beware.

Caveat creditor. (Lat.) Let the creditor beware, or be on his guard.

Caveat emptor. This is a Latin phrase, signifying " Let the purchaser beware, or take care of himself." It was formerly held that a buyer must be bound by a bargain under all circumstances. Chief-Justice Tindal, in giving judgment in the case Brown *v.* Edgington (2 Scott N. R. 504), modified this ancient rule. He said: " If a man purchases goods of a tradesman without in any way relying upon the skill and judgment of the vendor, the latter is not responsible for their turning out contrary to his expectation; but if the tradesman be informed, at the time the order is given, of the purpose for which the article is wanted, the buyer relying upon the seller's judgment, the latter impliedly warrants that the thing furnished shall be reasonably fit and proper for the purposes for which it is required."

Cavendish. (Pseud.) Henry Jones, M. R. C. S., Irish poet and dramatist (1720–1770).

Cavendo tutus. (Lat.) Safe through caution.

Cave of Adullam. *See* ADULLAMITES.

Caxa de consolidacion. (Span.) The sinking fund.

Caxton Memorial Bible. An edition printed in 1877, during the Caxton celebration in England, and which constituted one of the most remarkable mechanical feats of modern times. It was wholly printed and bound in twelve hours. Only a hundred copies were struck off.

C. B. Cape Breton; *Communis bancus*, Common Bench; Companion of the Bath.

C. C. Caius College; account current; County Commissioner; County Court; cubic centimetre.

C. C. A. Chief Clerk to the Admiralty.

C. C. C. Corpus Christi College.

C. C. P. Court of Common Pleas.

C. D. V. *Carte de visite.*

Cd. Cadmium.

C. E. Canada East; Civil Engineer.

Ce. Cerium.

Cecil. (Pseud.) William Hone, English writer (1779–1842).

Cecil Davenant. (Pseud.) Rev. Derwent Coleridge in "Knight's Quarterly Magazine."

Cecil Laker. (Pseud.) Mrs. Harriette Smith Bainbridge, an American contributor to periodical literature, and author of a volume of poems, "Irene Floss," 1878.

Cecil Power. (Pseud.) Grant Allen, naturalist and author (b. 1848). *See* J. ARBUTHNOT WILSON.

Cecrops. In classical mythology the first king of Attica, an autochthon; the upper part of his body being human, the lower part that of a dragon.

Cedant arma togæ. (Lat.) "Let arms yield to the gown." Let military authority yield to the civil power.

Cede Deo. (Lat.) Submit to Providence.

Cel., or **Celt.** Celtic.

Cela va sans dire. (Fr.) "That goes without saying." That requires no explanation; that is understood; of course.

Cela viendra. (Fr.) "That will come." All in good time.

Celeste. (Pseud.) Mrs. George C. [Bowlin Jenkins] Brown.

Celestial City. Heaven is so named by Bunyan in the "Pilgrim's Progress."

Celestial Empire. A popular designation of the Chinese Empire, derived from the words *Tien Chan* (heavenly dynasty), implying that the kingdom is swayed by rulers appointed by Heaven. But the right of the emperor to the throne as the *Tien Tze* (son of heaven) can only be established by good government.

Celestials. (1) The Chinese, because they call their country the Celestial Empire. (2) A nickname conferred on the Ninety-seventh English Regiment, and gained during its long service in China.

Celestial Talleyrand. Marquis Tseng, the Chinese ambassador to France during the Tonquin troubles in 1883–1884, was so named.

Celestians. Followers of Celestius, disciple of Pelagius. Saint Jerome calls him "a blockhead swollen with Scotch pottage."

Celestines. A religious order founded in 1254 by Pietro Morone, afterward Pope Celestine V., and suppressed in 1778.

Celia. (Pseud.) Mrs. C. M. Burleigh, in the Western press.

Celtic Homer. Ossian, son of Fingal, king of Morven.

Ce n'est que le premier pas qui coûte. (Fr.) It is only the first step which is painful, or costs an effort.

Cenobites. Monks, because they live in common. Hermits and anchorites are not cenobites, since they live alone.

Censor. (Pseud.) Oliver Bell Bunce, in "Don't: a Manual of Mistakes and Improprieties," New York, 1883.

Cent. Centigrade, a scale of one hundred degrees from freezing to boiling.

Centaur. (Pseud.) Charles Sass in the "Mail and Express," New York.

Centaurs. In classical mythology a fabulous people of Thessaly, half men and half horses.

Centennial State. Colorado; it was admitted to the Union in 1876, the one hundredth year of American independence.

Cento. (Pseud.) Philip Millington.

Century White. John White (fl. 1590–1645), the nonconformist jurist, so named from his great work, " The First Century of Scandalous and Malignant Priests made and admitted into Benefices by the Prelates."

Cerberus. In classical mythology a dog with three heads, a serpent's tail, and a snaky mane, who guarded the gates of Hades so effectually that none who entered could make their exit thence. Hercules overpowered him and brought him away.

Cerberus. (Pseud.) Nathan Haskell Dole, dramatic critic on the Philadelphia " Press."

Cerdonians. A sect of heretics, established by Cerdon of Syria, who lived in the time of Pope Hyginus, and maintained the errors of the Manichees.

Ceremonious, The. Peter IV. of Aragon (1319–1387).

Ceres. In classical mythology the daughter of Saturn and Ops, sister of Jupiter, Pluto, Neptune, Juno, and Vesta, mother of Proserpine, and the goddess of the harvest, corn, and flowers.

Cerinthians. Disciples of Cerinthus, a heresiarch of the first century. They denied the divinity of Christ, but held that a certain virtue descended into him at baptism, which filled him with the Holy Ghost.

Cert. Certify.

Certif. Certificate.

Certiorari. (Lat.) To be made more certain.

Cesarewitch. The name (pronounced *Zar'o-vitz*) of an English turf stake instituted and named in honor of the eldest son of the Emperor of Russia.

Cessio bonarum. (Lat.) Yielding up of goods.

C'est à dire. (Fr.) " That is to say." Namely.

C'est une autre chose. (Fr.) That is quite a different thing.

Cf., or **cf.** *Confer.* Compare.

C. G. Commissary-General ; Consul-General.

C. G. H. Cape of Good Hope.

C. H. Court-house.

Ch. Church ; chapter ; Charles.

Chacun à son goût. (Fr.) Every one to his taste.

Chad. (Pseud.) Henry Chadwick, an American writer on sport.

Chal. Chaldron.

Chald. Chaldea; Chaldean; Chaldaic.

Chalk for Cheese. In Nicholas Grinald's " Translation of Cicero," published in 1568, there is an address to the reader, in which the following words occur : " and wanting the right rule, they take chalke for cheese, as the sainge is."

Chalking the Door. In Scotland a landlord gives his tenant notice to quit by " chalking the door." The " chalking" is done by a " burgh officer," upon the verbal authority of the landlord. It is usual, though not necessary, for the officer to give notice to the tenant of the object of his visit.

Cham. (Pseud.) Amedée de Noe, a French caricaturist (1819–1879).

Cham. *See* GREAT CHAM.

Chambre Ardente. (Fr., " the fiery chamber.") The name in France for a peculiar court of justice, probably so called on account of the unusual severity of the punishments it meted out, death by fire being the most frequent sentence.

In the year 1535 Francis I. established an Inquisitorial Tribunal and a Chambre Ardente. Both were intended for the extirpation of heresy. The former, of which the pope was a corresponding member, searched out by means of spies cases of heresy, and instructed the processes ; while the latter both pronounced and executed the final judgment. Under Henry II. the activity of the Chambre Ardente received a new impulse, — the entrance of that monarch into Paris on the 4th of July, 1559. By and by, the Chambre Ardente relaxed its penalties, and a cry was got up among the more bigoted Roman Catholics that it was conniving at heresy. This seems to have roused the "lurking devil" in its members ; and in order to wipe away the reproach, they commenced a series of unheard-of cruelties, which, along with other events, contributed to originate the religious war of 1560. —CHAMBERS.

Chambre Introuvable. (Fr., "unfindable chamber," — *i.e.*, the chamber the like of which is not to be found again.) " The name sarcastically given to that Chamber of Deputies in France which met after the second return of Louis XVIII. (July, 1815), and which by its fanatical royalty began to throw the country and society anew into commotion. The former chamber, which had shown much moderation, had been dissolved under the influence of the court party, and the ministry, led by Talleyrand, had done everything to procure for the ruling party at least a manageable chamber adapted for business. The number of the deputies was arbitrarily raised from two hundred and fifty-nine to three hundred and ninety-two ; and to secure the victory of a complete restoration, all rushed forward who saw in the constitutional charter an encroachment on their privileges and pretensions. When it is considered, in addition, that the elections — at least in the departments of the south — took place under terror and the sanguinary outrages of a populace in a state of political and religious excitement, that the press was stifled, and the people deprived of all freedom of expression by the foreign armies, ultra-royalism could not fail to be completely triumphant. When the ministers saw this startling result they did not venture to open the session; they resigned, and gave place to the Richelieu ministry. Then broke out the most frightful excesses in the southern provinces. At the elections in Nîmes (August 22) more than one hundred persons were killed by the royalist bands. At last, on October 7, the king opened the chamber, on which he enjoined quietness and moderation; and it appeared as if it did take this advice to heart for an instant. But when, in one of the first sittings, Boyer d'Argenson asked for the intervention of the chamber in behalf of the Protestants, who were being slaughtered in the south by the ultra-royalist bands, the speaker was called to order, and the chamber from that time ceased to observe any bounds or moderation. The fanatical legislation of this chamber inspired the ministers, the king, and especially the Emperor Alexander, with so much aversion and apprehension, and also met so decidedly with the disapprobation of all peaceful and sincere friends of the throne, that the news of its dissolution, on April 5, 1816, was received with universal rejoicing. The electoral law of Feb. 5, 1817, prevented the return of a similar chamber; and it was not till by the modified electoral law of 1820 that ultra-royalism regained a predominating influence in Parliament. It is said that Louis XVIII. first used the epithet *Chambre*

Introuvable in an ironical sense, and that the majority of the chamber took it seriously as a compliment."

Champ. (Pseud.) The professional signature of J. W. Champney, the American artist.

Champion City. Springfield, Ohio, is so named.

Champion of England. A dignitary who rides up Westminster Hall, London, on coronation day, and challenges any one who disputes the right of succession. The office was established by William the Conqueror, and was given to Marmion and his male descendants, with the manor of "broad Scrivelsby." De Ludlow received the office and manor through the female line ; and in the reign of Richard II. Sir John Dymoke succeeded, and since then the office has continued in that family.

Champion of the Virgin. Saint Cyril of Alexandria. *See* DOCTOR OF THE INCARNATION.

Champion of the Whistle. A great toper. There is a story told of a gigantic Dane who came from Denmark in the retinue of the Princess Anne, when she married James VI. of Scotland. He had an ebony whistle, which at the beginning of a carouse he would lay on the table, and whoever was last able to blow it — *i. e.*, whoever was the last man to get "whistle drunk"—was considered the "champion of the whistle." Sir Robert Laurie, of Maxwellton, defeated the Dane, after a drinking-bout which lasted three days and three nights, and carried off the whistle as a prize. *See* WHISTLE DRUNK.

Chanc. Chancellor.

Changer de note. (Fr.) To turn over a new leaf.

Channel Archipelago. Another name for the Channel Islands, — Jersey, Guernsey, Alderney, and Sark, besides a multitude of rocky islets.

Chanson. (Fr.) A song.

Chansonette. (Fr.) A little song.

Chant du départ. After the "Marseillaise" this was the most celebrated song of the French Revolution. It was written by Chenier for a festival, held June 11, 1794, to commemorate the taking of the Bastile. The music is by Mehul. A mother, an old man, a child, a wife, a girl, and three warriors sing a verse in turn.

Chap. Chapter.

Chap. An abbreviation of the word "chapman," one who sells in a cheaping or market. Todd says : " If the phrase be ' a good chap,' it implies a dealer to whom credit may be given ; if simply ' a chap,' it designates a person of whom a contemptuous opinion is entertained." The general application of the word to a boy or youth of inferior position is of modern usage.

Chapeau. (Fr.) A hat.

Chapelle Ardente. (Fr.) The place where a dead person lies in state.

Chaperon. This word is frequently incorrectly spelled *chaperone*. The word is not feminine, although it is generally applied to a lady. It means a hood, and when used metaphorically signifies that the married lady shields her youthful *protégée* as the hood shields the face. The word " chaperoness " is used in the "Devil's Law Cure," a play written about the year 1620.

Chapter and Verse. "The proverbial expression of ' chapter and verse ' seems peculiar to ourselves, and I suspect originated in the Puritanic period, probably just before the civil wars under Charles I., from the frequent use of appealing to the Bible on the most frivolous occasions practised by those whom South calls ' those mighty men at chapter and verse.' " — DISRAELI, *Curiosities of Literature.*

Chapter of Mitton. The battle of Mitton was so called because so many priests took part therein. Hailes says that " three hundred ecclesiastics fell in this battle, which was fought Sept. 20, 1319."

Charbonnerie Démocratique. A new Carbonari society, founded in Paris on the principles of Babeuf. The object was to make Paris the centre of all political movements.

Chargé d'affaires. (Fr.) An ambassador of second rank.

Charles Ardesier-Macdonald. The pen-name of Andrew H. K. Boyd in his contributions *circa* 1860 in " Fraser's Magazine " entitled " Recreations of a Country Parson."

Charles Barron. The stage-name of Charles Brown.

Charles Broadbent. (Pseud.) Charles G. Halpine, as associate editor of the "Carpet-bag," about 1852.

Charles Burton. The stage-name of A. Burton Chadwick.

Charles Egbert Craddock. The pen-name of Miss Mary Noailles Murfree, a favorite contributor to the " Atlantic " for several years, and to which she contributed her sketches of Tennessee life, since gathered into book form with the title " In the Tennessee Mountains." She was born at Murfreesboro', Tenn.

Charles Holmes. (Pseud.) Charles Nordhoff, in " Harper's Magazine."

Charles M. Clay. The pen-name of Mrs. Charles Moon Clarke, an American author.

Charles Summerfield. (Pseud.) A.W. Arrington, *littérateur* and traveller (b. 1810).

Charles Wilford. The stage-name of Charles W. Dukes.

Charlies. An old name for the watchmen who preceded the present policemen of London. So named from Charles I., in whose reign they were reorganized.

Charlotte Dacre. (Pseud.) Mrs. Charlotte Dacre Byrne.

Charlotte Elizabeth. (Pseud.) Mrs. Charlotte E. [Brown] Tonna, novelist (1792–1846).

Charlotte Thompson. The stage-name of Mrs. Lorain Rogers.

Charon. In classical mythology son of Erebus and Nox, who ferried the souls of the dead across the river Styx. He is always depicted as an aged personage.

Charon's Toll. A coin placed in the mouth or hand or on the eyes of the dead, to pay Charon for ferrying the spirit across the Styx to the Elysian Fields.

Chartist Parson. Charles Kingsley was so named for his participation in the upward movement of the masses known in England as Chartism. He subsequently adopted the epithet as a pen-name to several magazine articles.

Charybdis. *See* SCYLLA AND CHARYBDIS.

Chasse. (Fr.) In the hunting style. (Mus.)

Chaste, The. Alfonso II., king of Asturias and Leon (758–842).

Chateaux en Espagne. Castles in the air ; something that exists only in the imagination. In Spain there are no chateaux.

Chat-Huant. (Pseud.) E. F. S. Pigott, in his paper, the " London Leader."

Chatty Brooks. (Pseud.) Miss Rosella Rice, in " Arthur's Magazine."

Chauvinisme, Chauviniste. (Fr.) Chauvin was the principal character in a French comedy which was played with immense success at the epoch of the Restoration. Since then a *chauviniste* has come to mean a man who has extravagant and narrow-minded ideas of patriotism accompanied with unreasoning enmity toward foreign peoples.

Che. (Ital.) Than ; as *poco più che andante*, rather slower than *andante*. (Mus.)

Cheddar Letter. A letter written by the contribution of several friends, each furnishing a paragraph. In Cheddar, Somersetshire, England, all the dairies contribute to make a cheese, which is thus sure to be made of quite fresh milk. The phrase " Cheddar letter " is used by Lord Bolingbroke in a letter to Swift.

Cheers but not inebriates. Cowper used this phrase in reference to tea, but it had been previously applied by Bishop Berkeley to tar-water. In the 217th paragraph of his work " Siris " he says that tar-water "is of a nature so mild and benign and proportioned to the human constitution, as to warm without heating, to cheer but not inebriate, and to produce a calm and steady joy, like the effect of good news."

Cheese. *See* QUITE THE CHEESE.

Cheese-paring. A word used to characterize the kind of national economy advocated by some public men who would effect a saving in places where justice and foresight demand liberality, while the amount so saved would be insignificant. Examples of this are opposition to steps for increasing the salaries of judges in cities, or reductions of the salaries of foreign ministers who must in their persons represent the Government.

Cheese-wring, The. A fanciful appellation given to a pile of eight stones, thirty-two feet high, in Cornwall, England. So named from their resemblance to a cheese-press. They are probably a freak of Nature.

Chef-de-bataillon. (Fr.) " Chief of batallion." A major.

Chef-de-cuisine. (Fr.) " Chief of kitchen." Head-cook.

Chef-de-mission. (Fr.) " Chief of mission." The head of an embassy.

Chef-de-police. (Fr.) " Chief of police." The head of the police.

Chef-d'œuvre. (Fr.) A masterpiece.

Chelsea. (Pseud.) Charles A. Nelson, Boston correspondent of the Chicago " Bookseller and Stationer," 1883–1884.

Chem. Chemistry.

Chère amie. (Fr., fem.) " Dear friend." A dear friend ; a mistress.

Cherokee Outlet, or **Cherokee Strip.** The " Cherokee Outlet " is a narrow strip of land, situated at the northwestern end of the Indian Territory, about 60 miles wide and 230 miles long. It embraces an area of 6,022,244 acres. Its surface is rolling, with no great elevations, and it is watered by the Cimarron River and the Salt Fork of the Arkansas River. Its luxurious and rich grasses furnish excellent food, and its broad prairies and plains extensive ranges for stock. With sufficient rainfall or proper irrigation, its naturally fertile lands for farming purposes will rival any elsewhere.

Cherokee War. Early in " the thirties " troubles arose with the Cherokees of Georgia, the most civilized and tractable of the native tribes. They possessed towns, schools, and a code of their own, and had adopted to a great extent the manners and customs of the whites. But their lands were desired, and the United States Government had pledged itself to Georgia to purchase their territory for the benefit of the State. This promise was not carried out. The authorities of the State grew tired of waiting, and so declared the Indian territory subject to the laws of the State, and their own code null and void. This act was declared unconstitutional by the United States Supreme Court. The Indians appealed to the President for help; but he refused to interfere, and recommended their removal west of the Mississippi, and for this purpose the Indian Territory was organized in 1834. Although more than five million dollars was paid them for their lands, the Indians yielded very reluctantly, and at last General Scott was detailed to remove them to the new territory, using force if needful, and in 1837–1838 the final transfer of the Indians was effected.

Cheronean Sage. Plutarch ; he was born at Cheronea in Bœotia.

Cherry Fairs. Meetings in "cherry orchards" for the young and gay on Sunday evenings, — not to buy and sell cherries, but to enjoy themselves. The "cherry orchards" did not necessarily grow cherries, but were similar to what the English call tea-gardens, where, by the way, little tea is ever sold.

> They prechen us in audience
> That no man schalle hys soule empeyre,
> For all is but a chery fayre.
> GOWER.

Cherry-pickers, or **Cherry-buns.** A nickname for the crack Eleventh Regiment of the English army, in allusion to the color of their trousers.

Cherry Valley Massacre. "On the 11th and 12th of November, 1778, a party of Tories under Walter N. Butler, accompanied by Indians under Brant, fell like lightning upon the settlement of Cherry Valley. Many of the people were killed, or carried into captivity; and for months no eye was closed in security at night within an area of a hundred miles and more around this desolate village. Tryon County, as that region of New York was then called, was a 'dark and bloody ground' for full four years, and the records of the woes of the people have filled volumes." — LOSSING.

Chersonese. *See* GOLDEN CHERSONESE.

Cherubims. The Eleventh Hussars of the British army are so called, by a bad pun, because their trousers are of a cherry color.

Ches. Chesapeake.

Che sarà, sarà. (Ital.) Whatever will be, will be.

Cheshire Cats. The nickname of the Twenty-second Regiment of the line (English).

Chester. (Pseud.) William Broome, English poet and divine (1694-1745).

Chevalier de Saint George. James Francis Edward Stuart, the "Pretender," or the "Old Pretender" (1688–1765).

Chevalier d'industrie. (Fr.) "Knight of industry." A swindler or sharper.

Chevaux-de-frise. "Horses of Friesland." Beams filled with spikes to keep off horses. So called from their use in the siege of Gröningen, Friesland, in 1594. Somewhat similar engines had been used before, but were not called by the same name. In German they are "Spanish horsemen."

Chi. China; Chinese.

Chibiabos. The musician; the harmony of Nature personified. He teaches the birds to sing and the brooks to warble as they flow. "All the many sounds of Nature borrow sweetness from his singing."

> Very dear to Hiawatha
> Was the gentle Chibiabos. . . .
> For his gentleness he loved him,
> And the magic of his singing.
> LONGFELLOW, *Hiawatha.*

Chic. Chicago.

Chicago of the South. Atlanta, Ga.

Child of Hale. John Middleton (b. 1578), the famous English giant, was thus humorously nicknamed. His height was nine feet three inches.

Chiliasts. Another word for Millenarians; those who believe that Christ will come again to this earth, and reign a thousand years in the midst of his saints.

Chiltern Hundreds. In former times the beech forests which covered the Chiltern Hills, in Buckinghamshire, England, were infested with robbers; and in order to restrain them, and protect the peaceable inhabitants of the neighborhood from their inroads, it was usual for the crown to appoint an officer, who was called the Steward of the Chiltern Hundreds. The office, which has long ceased to serve its primary, now serves a secondary purpose. A member of the House of Commons cannot resign his seat unless disqualified either by the acceptance of a place of honor or profit under the crown, or by some other cause. Now the stewardship of the Chiltern Hundreds is held to be such a place, and is consequently applied for by, and granted, in the general case as a matter of course, to any member who wishes to resign. As soon as it is obtained it is again resigned, and is thus generally vacant when required for the purpose in question. When the Chiltern Hundreds are not vacant, however, the same purpose is served by the stewardship of the manors of East Hendred, Northshead, and Hempholme. The practice of granting the Chiltern Hundreds for the above purpose began only about the year 1750.

Chimæra. In classic mythology a fire-breathing dragon or monster that ravaged Lycia, and was killed by Bellerophon.

Chimborazo of Suicide. At one period the kingdom of Saxony was so named by a compiler of social statistics, who stated that the number of those who took their own lives was higher in Saxony than in any other country of Europe.

Chimney-sweeps' Day. *See* MAY DAY.

China, Birmingham of. *See* BIRMINGHAM OF CHINA.

China of Europe, The. "Austria is the China of Europe: despotism, ferocity, and immobility." — MAZZINI.

China's Sorrow. The river Hoangho, or Yellow River, in China, has obtained this epithet from the fact that it not infrequently changes its course, causing great loss in property and much damage through inundations.

Chincapin. (Pseud.) W. R. Barber, in "Punchinello," New York.

Chinese Gordon. Maj.-Gen. Charles George Gordon, C. B., R. E., an English soldier (b. 1833). He visited China in 1860, where, by his bold and judicious conduct in supporting the Chinese Emperor against the Taeping rebels, he earned the thanks of both England and China, as well as the above sobriquet. He was killed in the Soudan, 1884.

Chink. Money; so called because it chinks or jingles in the purse. Thus, if a person is asked if he has money, he rattles that which he has in his purse or pocket.

Have chinks in thy purse. — TUSSER.

Chip. The signature of Frank P. W. Bellew, American author and artist.

Chiron. In classic mythology the wisest of all the Centaurs, skilled in music, medicine, and the chase. Jupiter placed him in the heavens as the constellation Sagittarius, "the Archer."

Chi tace confessa. (Ital.) Silence is confession.

Chloris. The Greek goddess of flowers, — the same as the Roman Flora.

Choke-pear. An argument to which there is no answer. Robbers in Holland at one time made use of a piece of iron in the shape of a pear, which they forced into the mouth of their victim. On turning a key, a number of springs thrust forth points of iron in all directions, so that the instrument of torture could never be taken out except by means of the key.

Chollet. (Pseud.) Louise E. Furniss, in "Harper's Magazine."

Chon. The Egyptian Hercules.

Chondaravali. In Hindu mythology the daughter of Vishnu.

Chop Logic. To bandy words; to altercate.

How now, how now, chop logic! What is this? "Proud," and "I thank you," and "I thank you not;" And yet "not proud."
　　　　　　　Romeo and Juliet.

Chopping and Changing. The word "chopping," in this familiar phrase, was probably originally "chapping," an old term for "dealing." The term "chapman" is not yet quite extinct as a legal phrase; and the words "cheap, chepe, chipping, cheaping," all refer to marketing, or buying and selling.

Chores. A pure Americanism, naming collectively the hundred and one odd jobs that need daily attendance about the house or farm.

Chose qui plaît est à demi vendue. (Fr.) A thing which pleases is already half sold.

Chowder. The name and the dish come to us from Canada, the name being a corruption of *chaudière* (kettle), in which utensil is made this Norman variety of the Provençal *bouillabaisse* immortalized by Thackeray.

Chr. Christ; Christian; Christopher.

Chrisom Child. A child that dies within a month of its birth. So called because it is buried in the white cloth, anointed with *chrism* (oil and balm), worn at its baptism.

He's in Arthur's [Abraham's] bosom, if ever man went to Arthur's bosom. 'A made a finer end, and went away, an it had been any christom [chrisom] child. 'A parted just . . . at turning o' the tide. (Quickly's description of the death of Falstaff.) — SHAKSPEARE, *Henry V.*

Why, Mike's a child to him . . a chrisom child.
　　JEAN INGELOW, *Brothers and a Sermon.*

Christabel. (Pseud.) Miss Mahony, *littérateur.*

Christendom. A term of wide application, in its modern meaning referring to all Christian countries. But Shakspeare uses it for Christian fellowship, or baptism: —

By my christendom,
So I were out of prison and kept sheep,
I should be as merry as the day is long.
　　　　　　　King John, act iv.

Christendom, Key of. *See* KEY OF CHRISTENDOM.

Christian Adam. (Pseud.) Carl Christian Thorvaldus Andersen, a Danish writer.

Christian Atticus. Reginald Heber, bishop of Calcutta, was so named (1783–1826).

Christian Cicero. Lucius Cœlius Lactantius, a Christian Father (d. 330).

Christianissimus Rex (Most Christian King). The title conferred by Pope Paul II. on Louis XI. of France.

Christian Seneca. Bishop Hall, of Norwich (fl. 1574–1656).

Christine McKenzie. (Pseud.) Miss Annie Duffell, author of "In the Meshes," 1877.

Christine Nilsson. The professional name of the Countess Casa Miranda, formerly Madame Rouzeaud, the famous prima donna.

Christinos. Supporters of the Queen Regent Christina against the Carlists in Spain during the war, 1833–1840.

Christmas. The name Christmas arose from the fact that in the primitive Church an especial Mass — the "Mass of Christ" — was celebrated on that day. The other term which designates this greatest of feasts of Christendom — "Christ-tide" — was coined by the Puritans, in order to avoid using the word "mass." The initial observance of the 25th of December is commonly ascribed to Julius, bishop of Rome, A. D. 337–352. Previous to his time the Eastern Church had kept the 6th of January in commemoration of both the birth and the baptism of our Lord. Singularly enough, before the end of the fourth century the East and the West had exchanged dates, the Western Church adopting January 6 as the anniversary of Christ's baptism, and the Eastern Church keeping holiday on December 25 in honor of the Saviour's nativity. In common with many other Church red-letter days, the cause that influenced the fixing of the festival at this period was the fact that most of the heathen nations of Europe regarded the winter solstice as the time when Nature took on renewed life and vigor. At this part of the year, too, the sun is nearest the earth, and then occurred those hoary rites common among our rude ancestors, which had their origin in a species of sun-worship. The Germans, when they were Christianized, had a festival at this time. Of course, December 25 is probably not the true date of Christ's birth, which cannot be ascertained from the New Testament nor from any other source. Nor for the first three centuries of our era was there any special observance of the festival of the Nativity. It was not till 220 A. D. that the Eastern Church commemorated the baptism of Jesus, and it is historically certain that the Christmas festival proper is of comparatively late institution. Not until the sixth century did the whole of Christendom unite in keeping Christmas on the same day. The comparative lateness of the founding of this feast may be accounted for in a variety of ways. Schaff says that, in the first place, "no corresponding festival was presented by the Old Testament, as in the case of Easter and Pentecost. In the second place, the day and month of the birth of Christ are nowhere stated in the Gospel history, and cannot be certainly determined. Again, the Church lingered at first about the death and resurrection of Christ, the completed fact of redemption, and made this the centre of the weekly worship and the Church year. Finally, the earlier feast of Epiphany afforded a substitute. The artistic religious impulses, however, which produced the whole Church year must, sooner or later, have called into existence a festival which forms the groundwork of all other annual festivals in honor of Christ." As we have seen, the heathen winter holidays — the Saturnalia, the Juvenalia, and the Brumalia — were transmuted into and sanctified by the establishment of the Christian cycle of Christmas observance, and along with them were brought over a number of harmless customs, such as the giving of presents, the lighting of tapers, and so forth. Similarly, what has been called the Christmas cycle of festivals gradually attached itself to the observance of the Nativity of Christ. Beginning with Christmas Eve and ending with January 8 (the Epiphany), it includes Saint Stephen's Day (December 26), Saint John's Day (December 27), Massacre of the Innocents (December 28), the New Year observances; and the Baptism of Christ (January 6) — the present English Twelfth-Night, or Little Christmas. What may be termed the adjuncts of Christmas — the boar's head, the mince-pie, the yule-log, the Christmas-tree, the mistletoe and the holly, the carol and the Christmas-box, — the last two especially cherished among our English kith and kin — are all, save the mince-pie, of heathen parentage. The boar's head was originally esteemed "a dainty dish" fit "to set before a king," and it was deemed most proper to serve it up at the Christmas feast, which honored the birth of the King of kings. The smoking head was brought into the dining-hall ornamented with flowers and ribbons, an apple or an orange stuck in its mouth; and when it appeared the company received the "monarch of dishes" standing, while a Latin ode was chanted in its honor. Mince-pies were probably of partial Christian origin, at least, though they too may have been a remnant of the cakes consumed in such large quantities at the Roman winter sports. In time they came to be made in oblong form, like the shape of a manger; and the eating of them was a test of orthodoxy, seeing that the Puritans considered them to be a relic of Popery, and would not touch them. The dressing of houses and churches with evergreens, holly, and mistletoe is a relic of customs as old as the Druidic worship. The last-named plant was regarded as sacred by those ancient worshippers of the groves. Although the custom of kissing under the mistletoe-bough is mentioned in the very oldest English and German annals, its origin is lost in the darkness of antiquity. The Christmas-tree is of German birth, and dates back to the practice of the early Christian missionaries to that people. In order to convert the barbarians, they invested Christmas-tide with all manner of merry-making and songs, and adopted bodily the German custom of placing a green bush over the door of each hut at the mid-winter festival. The "Christmas box," equivalent to the Scottish "hansel," a present of money to children or dependants, is another observance of this convivial season derived from the Roman custom of making presents at that time; while, of course, our own habit of making gifts to friends is a scion from the same root. The yule-log (from *huel*, a wheel) is a survival of the sun-worship of our ancestors. The luminary was termed "the fire-wheel;" and the burning of the yule, peculiar to the English Christmas from time immemorial, recalls the fact by which they sought to typify the coming return of the warmth of spring and summer. The Christmas carol, which grew out of the Nativity hymns of the early Christians, was at one time prohibited by the clergy, on account of the license to which it gave rise. Under the Saxon kings the singing of carols formed an important part of the day's observance; but in 1642 the Puritans abolished them, and substituted psalm tunes. It only remains to mention the patron saint of Christmas, — the good Saint Nicholas, — the Santa Claus of the Germans and the Kris Kringle of the Dutch. Saint Nicholas was a saint of the primitive Church, the especial friend of children; and his festival was kept in Germany about December 6 with joyful games and ceremonies. As time passed, the celebration of Saint Nicholas' Day and of Christ's Nativity became merged in each other. Christmas Day is a legal holiday in all the United States.

Christmas Box. A small gratuity given to English servants, etc., on Boxing Day (the day after Christmas Day). In the early days of Christianity boxes were placed in churches for promiscuous charities, and opened on Christmas Day. The contents were distributed next day by the priests, and called the "dole of the Christmas box," or the "box money." It was customary for heads of houses to give small sums of money to their subordinates "to put into the box" before mass on Christmas Day. Somewhat later, apprentices carried a box round to their masters' customers for small gratuities.

Christmas of the Gentiles. *See* EPIPHANY.

Christolytes. A sect of Christians which appeared in the sixth century. They maintained that when Christ descended into hell he left his soul and body there, and rose only with his heavenly nature.

Christopher Caustic. (Pseud.) Thomas Green Fessenden, American satirical poet (1771–1837).

Christopher Crowfield. (Pseud.) Mrs. Harriet Beecher Stowe, American authoress (b. 1812).

Christopher North. (Pseud.) John Wilson, Scottish critic and poet (1785–1854).

Chron. Chronicles.

Chronogram, The. One of the simplest devices of the word-juggler, and as old as the Romans. It consists in selecting certain letters indicating a date from a name or an inscription on a tomb, an arch, or a medal, printing them larger than the others, and obtaining thereby a date which is regarded as an augury. In some chronograms only the initial letters are counted as forming the solution of the puzzle, but in others all the characters used for Roman numerals are taken into account. History supplies many first-rate chronograms ; in fact, it was once the custom to strike medals with chronogramic sentences, in which the date of the occasion commemorated was set forth by the letters selected. Thus, on a medal struck by Gustavus Adolphus is the chronogram, "CHRISTVS DVX; ERGO TRIVMPHVS," — " Christ our Leader; therefore triumphant," — the numerals serving to indicate the date of the medal (1632), in which year occurred one of his famous victories. Another is made from the Latinized name of George Villiers, first Duke of Buckingham : "GEORGIVS. DVX. BVCKINGAMIæ." The date MDCXVVVIII (1628) is that of the year in which the duke was murdered by Felton at Portsmouth. Queen Elizabeth died in the year 1603, and the following chronogram relating to that event has come down to us : " MY DAY IS CLOSED IN IMMORTALITY." This is a "perfect" chronogram, because initials only are used to make up the date (1603).

Chrononhotonthologos. A nickname bestowed on General Burgoyne, because of a pompous speech made to the Indians during the Revolutionary War.

Chrysotome Dagobert. (Pseud.) Jean Baptiste Alphonse Led'huy, French writer.

Chrystal Croftangry (Pseud.) Sir Walter Scott, Scottish novelist (1771–1832).

Churches, Mother of all the. *See* MOTHER OF ALL THE CHURCHES.

Churches, Seven. *See* SEVEN CHURCHES OF ASIA.

Chute. A stream of water suddenly hemmed in between high and narrow banks, and thereby forced to reach a lower level with more or less velocity. In mining parlance the name is given to an artificial stream of water confined within narrow limits. *See* FLUME.

Cic. Cicero.

Cicerone. (Ital.) A guide.

Cicero of France. Jean Baptiste Massillon (1663–1742).

Cicero of Germany. (1) Johann III., Elector of Brandenburg (1455–1499). (2) Johann Sturm, printer and scholar (1507–1589).

Cicero of the British Senate. George Canning (1770–1827).

Cicero's Mouth. Philippe Pot (1428–1494), prime minister to Louis XI. of France, was thus nicknamed on account of his eloquence.

Cicisbeo. A dangler about women ; the professed gallant of a married woman. CICISBEISM, the practice of dangling about women.

Ciclenius. Mercury. So called from Mount Cyllene, in Peloponnesus, where he was born.

Cid. (Arabic for "lord.") Don Roderigo Laynez, Ruy Diaz (son of Diaz), count of Bivar. He was called " Mio cid el campeador," — " My lord the champion " (1025–1099).

Ci-devant. (Fr.) Former; formerly.

Cid of Portugal. Nuñez Alvarez Pereira, the famous diplomatist (1360–1431).

Ci-gît. (Fr.) Here lies.

Cimmerian Bosphorus. An ancient name for the Strait of Kaffa.

Cimmerian Darkness. Homer supposes the Cimmerians to dwell in a land " beyond the ocean-stream," where the sun never shone.

Cimmerians. In classic mythology a people, according to the Homeric legends, who dwell " beyond the ocean stream," in a land where the sun never shines and where the blackest darkness always prevails.

Cin. Cincinnati.

Cincinnatus. (Pseud.) William Plumer, a voluminous newspaper contributor.

Cincinnatus of the Americans. George Washington (1732–1799).

Cincinnatus of the West. William Henry Harrison.

" It is narrated by an ancient historian, though the story is discredited by modern ones, that on an occasion when Rome was in great danger, and Lucius Quintius Cincinnatus had been made dictator to deliver her from danger, the message of his appointment found him at the plough. It is in allusion to this that William Henry Harrison was spoken of as the ' Cincinnatus of the West ' when he was called to the presidency from his estate on the Ohio River."

Cinna. (Pseud.) Robert Baldwin Sullivan, contributor to various Canadian journals, *circa* 1833.

Cinquecento. The fifteenth century of Italian notables. They were Ariosto (1474–1533), Tasso (1544–1595), and Giovanni Rucellai (1475–1526), poets ; Raphael (1483–1520), Titian (1480–1576), and Michael Angelo (1474–1564), painters. These, with Macchiavelli, Luigi Alamanni, Bernardo Baldi, etc., make up what is termed the " Cinquecentesti." The word means the worthies of the '500 epoch, and they all flourished between 1500 and the close of that century.

Cipher Despatches. " The presidential election of 1876 was long doubtful ; the change of a single electoral vote would have turned the result. After the election a number of cipher despatches were discovered, which on translation proved to have been sent by persons closely identified with Samuel J. Tilden, relating to corrupt agreements for the purchase of electoral votes in Florida and Oregon for the Democratic party. The allegations were investigated by a congressional committee, which concluded that while at least one of the Florida Canvassing Board was purchasable, still that Tilden was not implicated in any attempts to purchase him, even if these were made. The minority report, being that of the Republican members of the investigating committee, concluded that the charges of corruptibility on the part of members of canvassing boards were 'but the slanders of foiled suborners of corruption.' They regarded the proofs of attempted corruption as conclusive, and did not hesitate to indicate their belief that Tilden had knowledge of the matter. In a card dated Oct. 16, 1878, Tilden denied in most emphatic terms all connection with the matter." — BROWN AND STRAUSS.

Circ. Circuit.

Circe. In classic mythology a daughter of Sol, and a famous sorceress, who attracted numbers of persons to her abode and then changed them into various animal shapes.

Circle of Ulloa. A white rainbow or luminous ring sometimes seen in Alpine regions opposite the sun in foggy weather.

Circumlocution Office. A popular synonym for governmental routine or bureaucratic red tape, or a dilatory, round-about way of doing business. Dickens coined the phrase in his " Little Dorrit."

Cistercians. A religious order, so called from the monastery of Cistercium, near Dijon, in France. The abbey of Cistercium or Citeaux was founded by Robert, abbot of Moleme, in Burgundy, at the close of the eleventh century.

Cit. Citation ; citizen.

Cities of the Plain. Another name for Sodom and Gomorrah, chief of those five cities which, according to the commonly received account, were destroyed by fire from heaven, and their sites overwhelmed by the waters of the Dead Sea.

Cities, Queen of. *See* QUEEN OF CITIES.

Citizen King. Louis Philippe of France (1773–1850). So named because he was elected king by the citizens of Paris.

Cito maturum, cito putridum. (Lat.) Soon ripe, soon rotten.

City by the Sea. Newport, R. I., a famous and fashionable summer resort.

City Golgotha, The. An old name for Temple Bar, London. So named because the heads of traitors were impaled thereon.

City of Beer and Bricks. Milwaukee, Wis.

City of Brotherly Love. Philadelphia, Penn. It is the meaning of the name (φιλαδελφία) in Greek.

City of Churches. Brooklyn, N.Y. So named because of the many churches it contains in proportion to its size and population ; but according to the census of 1880 it seems that Brooklyn has no primary right to the title on the grounds stated above. The following table shows the rank of eight of the leading cities of the Union as a "city of churches," and establishes the right of Cincinnati to the first place, while Brooklyn falls to the fifth.

CITIES.	Population.	No. of Churches.	Average Persons to a Church.	Rank of the Cities.
New York	1,206,577	489	2,468	Seventh
Philadelphia	1,000,000	593	1,427	Second
Brooklyn	566,663	285	1,983	Fifth
Chicago	503,185	255	1,973	Fourth
Boston	362,839	213	1,778	Third
Cincinnati	255,139	204	1,253	First
San Francisco	233,959	95	2,462	Sixth
New Orleans	216,090	50	4,323	Eighth

City of David. Jerusalem. So named by King David, who captured it from the Canaanites, 1049 B. C.

City of Elms. New Haven, Conn., whose streets are shaded by many of these noble trees.

City of Flour and Sawdust. Minneapolis, Minn.

City of Hills. Yonkers, N. Y.

City of Homes. Philadelphia, Penn. So named on account of the large number of private dwellings it contains, and the almost total absence of tenement-houses.

City of Intelligence. A name given by its inhabitants to the city of Berlin.

City of Magnificent Distances. Washington, D. C., the political capital of the United States, the plan of which, designed by an architect named L'Enfant, is conceived on an exceedingly broad and generous scale, showing an anticipation of a great metropolis. Its plot extends 4½ miles northwest and southeast, and 2½ miles northeast and southwest, an area of nearly eleven square miles; and the streets, cutting each other at right angles, are of noble width.

City of Masts. London, England. So named from the spectacle presented by its vast array of shipping.

City of Men and Ideas. Atlanta, Ga.

City of Mobs. Baltimore, Md. So named in allusion to the mobbing of the Massachusetts Sixth Regiment on its way to the front in 1861.

City of Notions. .Boston, Mass., the home of "notions," — *i. e.*, articles of all kinds, trifling in size and value, but for which there is a large sale.

City of Palaces. (1) Rome. Agrippa converted it from "a city of brick huts to one of marble palaces." (2) Modern Paris has been so named, and justly. (3) Calcutta, the capital of British India, from the large number of elegant European residences. Black Town, the native quarter, is poorly built. (4) Edinburgh is occasionally alluded to by this name, but it is only of late years, if at all, that the name has become an appropriate one.

City of Peace. Jerusalem. Its ancient name, Salem, signifies "peace."

City of Perspectives. St. Petersburg. Its streets and quays are famous for the long vistas they present.

City of Rocks. Nashville, Tenn. In the immediate vicinity quarries of fine limestone abound, which enters largely into the construction of its buildings.

City of Roses. (1) Lucknow, India. (2) Little Rock, Ark.

City of Smoke. London, England, has been so named. *See* SMOKY CITY, also IRON CITY.

City of Snow. St. Petersburg. For nine months in every year it is shrouded in a canopy of snow.

City of Spindles. Lowell, Mass. It contains more mills for the manufacture of cotton and woollen goods than any other city in the United States.

City of the Dead. A cemetery. *See* SILENT CITY.

City of the Great King. Jerusalem is so named in the Scriptures (Ps. xlviii. 21; Matt. v. 35).

City of the Holy Faith. Santa Fé, New Mexico.

City of the Kings. Before the English invasion of Ireland the town of Cashel was known by this name.

City of the Mines. Iglesias, Sardinia, on account of the magnitude of its mining operations.

City of the Plains. Denver, Col.

City of the Prophet. *See* PROPHET'S CITY.

City of the Reef. Pernambuco, Brazil. The harbor is protected by an extensive reef of rocks.

City of the Saints. (1) St. Paul, Minn. (2) Salt Lake City, Utah. Here is located the headquarters of the Mormon hierarchy, "the Church of Latter-Day Saints of Jesus Christ."

City of the Simple. The Belgian town of Gheel, to which lunatics are consigned for restraint and treatment.

City of the Straits. *See* STRAIT CITY.

City of the Sun. Baalbec, in Cœle-Syria, the Heliopolis of the Greeks, is often referred to by this title, which is a translation of its two names. It is celebrated for its superb ruins, yet extant, of an ancient temple dedicated to the sun.

City of the Three Kings. Cologne, on the Rhine, in reference to the old legend which makes Cologne the burial-place of Balthazar, Melchior, and Jasper, the "wise men of the East."

City of the Tribes. Galway, Ireland, because, in 1235, there settled here thirteen clans, named Athy, Blake, Browne, Budkin, Burke, D'Arcy, Ffont, Joyce, Kirwan, Lynch, Martin, Morris, and Skerrett.

City of the Violated Treaty. Limerick, Ireland, because of the frequent infractions of the treaty signed'Oct. 3, 1691.

City of the Violet Crown. A poetical designation of the city of Athens, the origin of which is now forgotten.

"He [Pitt] loved England as an Athenian loved the city of the Violet Crown." — MACAULAY.

City of the West. Glasgow, Scotland, situated on the Clyde, the greatest of western Scottish streams. It is the commercial and manufacturing metropolis of the country.

City of Victory. *See* VICTORIOUS CITY.

Civilation. A euphony for intoxication. A Cork orator at a debating society was speaking on the state of Ireland before it was added to England, and said, "Sir, the Irish had no civilation — cilivation, I mean — no civilation," and sat down, too far gone to pronounce the word "civilization."

Civiliter mortuus. (Lat.) "Civilly dead." Deprived of all civil rights. One was "civilly put to death" who formerly retired into a religious house; also one sentenced to penal servitude for life; and likewise an outlaw.

Civil Rights. By this phrase is meant equal social rights and privileges for negroes in hotels, public conveyances, theatres, schools, and the like, as are accorded to whites.

Civil-service Reform. A movement having for its object the abolishment of the "spoils" system (the bestowal of office as a reward for party service) and the substitution therefor of a system of selection on the ground of merit and fitness solely, no removals to be made except for cause. Laws embodying these ideas were passed by Congress, and a "Civil Service Commission" appointed.

C. J. Chief-Justice.

Cl. Chlorine.

Clabber Napper's Hole. A cavern near Gravesend, England. The odd name is by some thought to have been derived from a smuggler; but others derive it from the Celtic *Caer-ber-l'arber*, "Watertown lower camp."

Clapham Sect. A name bestowed by Rev. Sydney Smith upon the Evangelical party in the Church of England in the latter part of the eighteenth century. Many of its members resided at Clapham, a suburb of London; *vide* Thackeray's "The Newcomes."

Clap-trap. This phrase seems to have been derived from the *clap-net*, used for trapping larks and other birds. Bailey says that "*clap-trap* is a name given to the rant that dramatic authors, to please actors, let them go off with; as much as to say, to catch a clap of applause from the spectators at a play."

Clara. (Pseud.) Miss Carrie Bell Sinclair, author of poems in the "Georgia Gazette."

Clara Augusta. (Pseud.) (1) Mrs. S. Trask, of Framingham, Mass. (2) Winifred Winthorpe.

Clara Belden. The stage-name of Mrs. Henry Trippetts.

Clara Belle. (Pseud.) (1) Olive Logan, Junius Henri Browne, his wife, and others, in the Cincinnati "Enquirer." (2) Mrs. William Thompson, a writer on fashions in the Western press. (3) Mrs. Mary Hewins Fiske, a well-known newspaper correspondent. *See* GIDDY GUSHER.

Clara Belmont. The stage-name of Mrs. C. H. Calvert.

Clara Bernetta, Mlle. The stage-name of Clara Johnson.

Clara Byron. The stage-name of Mrs. W. P. Lake.

Clara Cushman. (Pseud.) Emily Bradley.

Clara Morris. The stage-name of Mrs. F. C. Harriott, *née* Morrison.

Clara Ormsby. The stage-name of Mrs. Alma Lewis.

Clarendon Constitutions. This is the name given to the concordat between Church and State in England, drawn up at a council of nobility and clergy held at the village of Clarendon, in Wiltshire, in 1164, in the reign of Henry II. These constitutions or laws were sixteen in number, and their main object was to restrict the power of the Church in England, and to give the Crown the right to interfere in the election to all vacant livings and offices in the Church. "Many of the clauses," says Mr. J. R. Green, "were simply a re-enactment of the system established by the Conqueror;" yet it is impossible to doubt "that the sharp separation between the civil and ecclesiastical jurisdictions introduced into England by William was the reason of the conflict between the two." The Primate, Thomas Becket, signed them, but they were rejected by Pope Alexander III., upon which Becket himself vehemently re-canted his consent, which led to his assassination and the penance done by Henry II. But in spite of these events the Clarendon Constitutions remained on the statute-book, and may be regarded as the germ of the ecclesiastical revolution accomplished in the reign of Henry VIII.

Clarendon Press. The university press of Oxford, England, now known as "the University Printing-House," or "University Press."

Claribel. (Pseud.) Mrs. Caroline Barnard, author of "Tales for Children."

Clarior e tenebris. (Lat.) Brighter from obscurity.

Claud Halcro. (Pseud.) John Breckinridge, a Canadian author, *circa* 1843.

Claudia. (Pseud.) Miss Clara V. Dargan, in the Charleston "Courant," 1859.

Claw-backs. Flatterers. Bishop Jewel speaks of "the pope's claw-backs."

Clay-eaters. "A miserable set of people inhabiting some of the Southern States, who subsist chiefly on turpentine whiskey, and appease their craving for more substantial food by filling their stomachs with a kind of aluminous earth which abounds everywhere. This gives them a yellowish, drab-colored complexion, with dull eyes, and faces whose idiotic expression is only varied by a dull despair or a devilish malignity. They are looked down upon by the negroes with a contempt which they return by a hearty hatred." — BARTLETT.

Clay's Compromise. Two episodes in American history are known by this name: (1) Henry Clay's tariff compromise, 1833; and (2) his measures providing for the admission of California as a free State, the organization of New Mexico and Utah into Territories, the settlement of the Texas boundary, the abolition of the slave-trade in the District of Columbia, and the rendition of fugitive slaves.

Clay Whigs. "The death of William Henry Harrison raised John Tyler to the presidency. Both were Whigs. Henry Clay was the leader of the Whig party. Tyler was one of those nullifiers that had remained with the Whig party when Calhoun and his followers withdrew about 1838. The contrast between him and the other leaders of his party

at once showed itself, and a bitter fight ensued between the followers of Clay and those of Tyler. Clay's adherents were known as Clay Whigs. The first quarrel was on the subject of a charter for a national bank. The President was opposed to its being chartered, and vetoed a bill for that purpose drawn by the Secretary of the Treasury, giving as his reason the presence of certain features which he considered objectionable. A bill was hastily drawn up embodying the President's suggestions, but this, too, received his veto. The conflict was continued on other measures. The House next elected was more strongly Democratic." — BROWN AND STRAUSS.

Cld. Cleared.

Cleanliness is next to Godliness. The author of this phrase, quoted by John Wesley, is not known. Something similar to it is found in the Talmud, and Plutarch tells us that among the ancient Egyptians "health was no less respected than devotion." A Jewish lecturer, on Dec. 3, 1878, reported in "The Jewish World," said, "This well-known English phrase had been taught by the Rabbins of the Talmud many centuries ago, both as a religious principle and a sanitary law."

Clean Sweep is a phrase used in American politics to indicate the removal by an official of all his subordinates not belonging to his political party.

Clean-the-Causeway Riot. A faction fight between the rival clans of Douglas and Hamilton in Edinburgh in 1515. The former were worsted and fled in great confusion, being, as was said, swept from the streets.

Clear Grit. *See* GRIT.

Cleophil. (Pseud.) William Congreve, English dramatic poet (1670–1729).

Clever is one of the most cruelly ill-treated Americanisms. It has assumed two very different meanings, designating in the North a good-natured, obliging person, while at the South it means "gifted and talented." The American pet word *smart* (*q. v.*) has, however, largely superseded it.

Climacteric Years. The seventh and ninth, with their multiples by the odd numbers 3, 5, 7, 9, — namely, 7, 9, 21, 27, 35, 45, 49, 63, and 81, — over which the astrologers thought Saturn, the malevolent planet, presided.

Climb. In England this word is always used in the sense "to mount, to rise, to ascend." In America, people climb *down*. Rev. H. W. Beecher, who may be considered a competent judge of correct English, in describing his visit to Oxford, says, "To *climb down* the wall was easy enough." And in the "Star Papers," p. 41, we find, "I partly *climbed down*, and wholly clambered back again."

Climbing Leaves. *See* WALKING LEAVES.

Clincher. Something that settles a point or argument. This application of the word is said to have arisen from two notorious liars being matched against each other. "I drove a nail through the moon once," said the first. "Yes," said the other, "I remember the circumstance; and I went round to the back and *clinched* it."

Clinton Bridge Case. An important litigation in the United States Supreme Court (1870), which established the doctrine by which railroad bridges may be said to have gained clear recognition of their rights of way in preference to the navigable waters crossed by them, through the power of Congress to regulate inter-State commerce.

Clinton's Big Ditch. The Erie Canal, connecting New York with the great lakes, has been jocularly so named. It was planned and carried to completion by DeWitt Clinton.

C. L. I. O. ("Clio"). (Pseud.) Joseph Addison, English essayist and humorist (1672–1719). It is said that this pen-name arose in the following manner: Addison would append various initials to his manuscript, according to the place where it was penned, "C." denoting the city, "L." denoting London, "I." denoting Islington, where he lived, while "O." indicated the office. The four combined made the word "Clio."

Clio. One of the Nine Muses. She presided over history.

Clionas. (Pseud.) Sir Nicholas Harris Nicolas in the "Gentleman's Magazine." It is an anagram on his surname.

Clipper. The origin of this name for a fast-sailing vessel has been much debated. The following, from "Alice Lorraine," vol. iii. p. 2, seems plausible: "The British corvette 'Cleopatra-cum-Antonio' was the nimblest little craft ever captured _from the French; and

her name had been reefed into 'Clipater' first, and then into 'Clipper,' which still holds sway."

Cliquot. A nickname for Frederick William IV. of Prussia, coined by the London "Punch," and containing an allusion to his fondness for champagne.

Clk. Clerk.

Clock of the King's Death. A clock in the palace at Versailles; it had no works but a dial and one hand, which latter was set at the minute of the death of the last monarch of France, and remained so all through the reign of his successor.

Clog Almanac. A primitive almanac or calendar, called in Scandinavia a Runic staff, from the Runic characters used in its numerical notation.

Clotha virumque cano. (Lat.) "Clothes and the man I sing." I sing of clothes and the man. Carlyle: a parody of the first words of the Æneid, "Arma virumque cano" (Arms and the man I sing).

Clothier of England. *See* JACK OF NEWBURY.

Clotho. In classic mythology one of the three Fates, who presided over birth, and spun the thread of life.

Cloth, The. A collective name for the clergy. In former times the priesthood wore a distinguishing costume of gray or black cloth by which they might be recognized.

Cloth of Gold, Field of the. *See* FIELD OF THE CLOTH OF GOLD.

Cloud City, The. Leadville, Col., has been so named. It is situated at an altitude of nine thousand feet above sea-level, and is surrounded by mountain peaks whose summits pierce the clouds.

Cluacina. A surname of Venus.

Club, The. (1) A group of Whig malcontents in Edinburgh in the time of William III. Their aim was to annoy the Government, and so obtain for themselves fat places. But they finally fell to pieces, the chiefs betraying each other. (2) A celebrated coterie of men of letters, and others, which flourished in London in the last century. The original members were Reynolds, Burke, Johnson, Goldsmith, Nugent, Beauclerk, Langton, and Sir John Hawkins. Many other eminent names in science, letters, and art were borne upon its roll.

Clubmen. Associations formed in the southern and western counties of England to restrain the excesses of the soldiery during the civil war, 1642–1649. They professed neutrality, but were believed to favor the king by his enemies.

Clytemnestra. In classic mythology the unfaithful wife of Agamemnon, slain by her son Orestes for her enormities.

Clytie. In classic mythology a water-nymph who became enamored of Apollo, the sun-god. Meeting with no encouragement, she changed herself into a sunflower, and keeps her face constantly turned toward him in his daily course.

C. M. Common metre.

C. M. G. Companion of the Order of Saint Michael and Saint George.

Cnæus Fulvius. A reportorial personification of Mr. Fox in the days before newspaper reports of the Parliamentary proceedings were legalized.

C. O. Crown Office; Colonial Office; Criminal Office.

Co. Company; county; cobalt.

Coal-oil Johnny. A nickname given to John Steele, a famous oil-operator in the Pennsylvania oil-fields, who amassed a great fortune and squandered it in riotous living.

Coal-oil Payne. A nickname conferred on Senator Payne, of Ohio.

Coat-of-arms, A Yorkshireman's. *See* YORKSHIREMAN'S COAT-OF-ARMS.

Cob. The name given to the spikes of the maize plant after the grains are "shucked" or removed. *See* EAR.

Cobden Club. The Cobden Club, of England, takes its name from the great free-trader Richard Cobden. It is the centre of the free-trade doctrine in British politics.

Cocagne. An imaginary land of idleness, luxury, and delight. The French *pays de cocagne*, and similar terms in other tongues, convey the idea of a Utopia. Particularly the term has been applied to London and its suburbs, famed for luxury and plenty from earliest times. The word "cockney," a denizen of London as distinct from a countryman, is, according to some, derived from *cocagne*. *See* COCKNEY.

Coch., or **Cochl.** *Cochleare.* A spoonful.

Cockade City. Petersburg, Va.

Cock-a-hoop. A crested cock (Old French *hupé*, crested, proud). The term is applied to vainglorious, conceited persons, who carry their heads thrown backward, as a peacock does.

Cock-and-Bull Story. The most probable explanation of this term as applied to preposterous tales related in private life, is that which refers it to the old fables in which cocks, bulls, and other animals are represented as endowed with speech. Matthew Prior's "Riddle on Beauty" closes with these lines : —

"Of cocks and bulls, and flutes and fiddles, Of idle tales and foolish riddles."

Another version says that the pope's bulls were named from the *bulla*, or seal, which was attached. The seal bore the impression of a figure of Saint Peter accompanied by the cock. Hence after the Reformation any tale or discourse that was unheeded was on a par with a pope's bull, which was a "cock-and-bull affair."

Cockatrice. A fabulous animal of the basilisk species. Its distinguishing peculiarity was a crest or comb like a cock's. Sometimes, indeed, the beak, head, and claws of the cock were added. It differed in no other respect from the ordinary basilisk, and by some authorities is looked upon not as a separate species, but as the same animal under another name. Sir Thomas Browne, however, in his book of "Vulgar Errors" (book iii. p. 7), draws a clear distinction between the two. Sir Thomas rather argues for the possibility of the existence of such an animal, and strives to give to its "death-darting eye" a rationalistic explanation : —

Say thou but "I,"
And that bare vowel, "I," shall poison more
Than the death-darting eye of cockatrice.
SHAKSPEARE, *Romeo and Juliet*, act iii. sc. 2.

Cocker, According to Cocker. Edward Cocker, a writing-master, engraver, and arithmetician, was born in 1632 and died about 1673. He is said to have published fourteen engraved copybooks. He published some time before 1664 the "Tutor to Writing and Arithmetic." His work was for a long time the standard authority on arithmetic; hence the phrase. In an edition of Cocker's "Pen's Triumphs," published in 1657, is his portrait, with the following lines : —

"Behold rare Cocker's life-resembling shade,
Whom envy's clouds have more illustrious made ;

Whose pen and graver have displayed his name
With virtuosos in the book of fame."

In Wing's "Ephemeris," 1669, is an advertisement as follows : " Cocker's Compleat Arithmetician, which hath been nine years his study and practice. The piece so long and so much expected." Cocker also published a dictionary, of which a posthumous edition (the third) appeared in 1724. *See* ACCORDING TO GUNTER.

Cockerel Church. The M. E. church on Hanover Street in Boston, between Prince and Richmond streets, was known as the "Cockerel" Church, from having a rooster on its spire. It was for the dedication of this church that N. P. Willis wrote the hymn which opened thus : —

" The perfect world by Adam trod,
Was the first temple, built by God ;
His fiat laid the corner-stone,
And heaved its pillars, one by one."

Cockeye. A by-name conferred upon Gen. B. F. Butler by the men in the ranks, for obvious reasons.

Cock Lane Ghost. " In the year 1762 London was thrown into a state of extraordinary excitement by the reported existence of a ghost in the house of a Mr. Parsons, in Cock Lane, Smithfield. Strange and unaccountable noises were heard in the house, and a luminous lady, bearing a strong resemblance to one who under the name of Mrs. Kemt had once resided in the house, but who had died two years before, was said to have been seen. Dark suspicions as to Mr. Kemt having poisoned the lady were immediately aroused, and were confirmed by the ghost, who on being interrogated answered after the fashion of the spirits of our own day, by knocking. Crowds, including Dr. Johnson, were attracted to the house to hear the ghost, and the great majority became believers. At length a plan was formed by a few sceptics to ascertain the real origin of the noises. The girl from whom the sounds were supposed to proceed was taken to another house, and threatened with the imprisonment of her father in Newgate if she did not renew the rappings that evening, the noises having for some time been discontinued. She was observed to take a board with her into bed ; and when the noises took place, no doubt was entertained that they had all along been produced by similar methods, and by the aid of ventriloquism, in which she was now found to be an adept. The entire affair was discovered to be a conspiracy on the part of the girl and her parents to extort money from Mr. Kemt, and two of the delinquents were pilloried and imprisoned July 10, 1762." — CHAMBERS.

Cockle-hat. A pilgrim's hat. Warburton says, as the chief places of devotion were beyond sea or on the coasts, pilgrims used to put cockleshells upon their hats to indicate that they were pilgrims. Cockles are symbols of Saint James, patron saint of Spain.

Cockney. A Londoner. Camden says the Thames was once called the Cockney, and therefore a Cockney means simply one who lives on the banks of the Thames. One born within the sound of Bow Bells, *i. e.*, the bells of the church of St. Mary-le-Bow, Cheapside.

Wedgwood suggests *cocker*, "to fondle," and says a Cockerney or Cockney is one pampered by city indulgence, in contradistinction to rustics hardened by out-door work.

"I am a Cockney because I was born within the sound of Bow Bells. My father used to tell me that a London boy went into the country to see some cousins, and heard a horse neigh; he asked what the noise was, and was told that it was a neigh. Soon afterward the boy heard a cock crow, and not knowing what to call the noise, exclaimed, 'Uncle, the cock neighs too.' From that Londoners were called 'cockneys.'"

Chambers, in his "Journal," derives the word from a French poem of the thirteenth century, called "The Land of Cocagne," where the houses were made of barley-sugar and cakes, the streets paved with pastry, and the shops supplied goods without requiring money in payment. The French, at a very early period, called the English *cocagne men*, i. e., *bons-vivants* (beef and pudding men).

Cockney School. Leigh Hunt, Hazlitt, Shelley, and Keats were so dubbed by Lockhart in 1817.

Cock of the North. The Duke of Gordon is so called on a monument erected in his honor at Fochabers in Aberdeenshire. He died in 1836.

Cock of the Walk. The dominant bully or master-spirit. The place where barndoor fowls are fed is called the walk ; and the cocks, if there is more than one, will fight for the supremacy of this domain.

Cockpit of Europe. Belgium is so called because it has been the site of more European battles than any other ; *e. g.*, Oudenarde, Ramillies, Fontenoy, Fleurus, Jemappes, Ligny, Quatre Bras, Waterloo, etc.

Cocktail. The national American "drink," said to have been invented by one Elizabeth Flanagan.

She was the widow of an Irish soldier who fell in the service of this country. She appears after his death to have been a sutler, and in that capacity to have followed a troop of Virginia horse who, under command of Colonel Burr, took up quarters in the winter of 1779 in a place called the "Four Corners," situated on the road between Tarrytown and White Plains, Westchester County, N. Y. Here Elizabeth Flanagan set up a hotel, which was largely patronized by the officers of the French and American forces quartered in the vicinity ; and here it is that the drink known as the "cocktail" was invented.

Cocytus. In classic mythology one of the streams that flowed by the shores of Hades, and prevented the dead from returning to earth. It was a branch of the Styx.

C. O. D. Cash (or collect) on delivery.

Coda. (Ital.) A few bars added at the close of a piece, beyond its natural termination. (Mus.)

Codfish. *See* HOOKS AND CODFISH.

Cœur de Lion. (1) Richard I. of England. (2) Louis VIII. of France. (3) Boleslaus I. of Poland.

Cogia Hassan's Stone. This phrase occurs in Thackeray's "Pendennis." Cogia Hassan was he of the "Arabian Nights," and his surname was Al Habbal (the ropemaker). Cogia (the merchant) was an addition made to the name after that of Al Habbal ; so the full name came to be Cogia Hassan Alhabbal. It is related that two friends, Saad and Saadi, tried an experiment upon him. Saadi gave him two hundred pieces of gold, in order to see if it would raise him from extreme poverty to affluence. Hassan took ten pieces for immediate use, and sewed the rest in his turban ; but a kite pounced on his turban and carried it away. The two friends, after a time, visited Hassan again, but found him in the same state of poverty ; and having heard his tale, Saadi gave him another two hundred pieces of gold. Again he took out ten pieces, and wrapping the rest in a linen rag, hid it in a jar of bran. While Hassan was at work, his wife exchanged this jar of bran for fuller's earth, and again the condition of the man was not bettered by the gift. Saad now gave the ropemaker a small piece of lead, and this made his fortune thus : A fisherman wanted a piece of lead for his nets, and promised to give Hassan for Saad's piece whatever he

caught in his first draught. This was a large fish, and in it the wife found a splendid diamond, which was sold for 100,000 pieces of gold. Hassan now became very rich, and when the two friends visited him again they found him a man of consequence. He asked them to stay with him, and took them to his country-house, when one of his sons showed him a curious nest made out of a turban. This was the very turban which the kite had carried off, and the money was found in the lining. As they returned to the city they stopped and purchased a jar of bran. This happened to be the very jar which the wife had given in exchange, and the money was discovered wrapped in linen at the bottom. Hassan was delighted, and gave the one hundred and eighty pieces to the poor. As to what is meant by Cogia Hassan's stone, in whatever sense used, may not be difficult to comprehend in the light of the foregoing.

Cogito, ergo sum. (Lat.) "I think, therefore I am."

Cognomen. A surname.

Cognoscenti. (Ital.) "Knowing ones." The scientific ; those who know how to look at things.

Cohesive Power of Public Plunder. "This phrase has grown out of words used by John C. Calhoun in a speech, May 27, 1836: 'A power has risen up in the government greater than the people themselves, consisting of many and various and powerful interests, combined into one mass, and held together by the cohesive power of the vast surplus in the banks.'" — BARTLETT.

Coila. (1) The Latin name of Kyle, County Ayr, Scotland, embalmed in the lyrics of Burns. (2) The word is also used as a fanciful designation for Scotland, —

Farewell, old Coila's hills and dales,
Her heathy moors and winding vales.
BURNS.

Col. Colorado ; Colonel ; Colossians.

Col, Coll', Colla. (Ital.) With ; as, *Col arco,* with the bow. (Mus.)

Cold-slaw. A dish peculiar to the United States, and derived, as is the name, from the early Dutch settlers, who called it *kool-slaa.*

Coldstream Guards are so named from the town of that name in Berwickshire, where, in 1660, General Monk raised the regiment known at first as

Monk's Regiment. When Parliament agreed to give Charles II. a brigade of guards, this corps, under the name of Coldstream Guards, was included in it. With the exception of the First Regiment of Foot, the Coldstream is the oldest corps in the British service.

Cold Tea. In the early part of the last century this was a cant term for brandy. In the " Spectator," " Tatler," and "Guardian," mention is often made of a "keg of cold tea," as an appropriate present for a lady. At the present day in American legislative assemblies "cold tea" is a jocose phrase, meaning something a good deal stronger.

Cold-water Ordeal. An ancient method of testing the guilt or innocence of the common sort of people. The accused, being tied under the arms, was thrown into a river. If he sank to the bottom, he was held to be guiltless, and drawn up by the cord; but if he floated, the water rejected him because of his guilt.

Colin Ballantyne, R. N. (Pseud.) William Dunlop, M.D., in his sketches of East Indian life and character published in " Blackwood."

Colin Clout. A name which Spenser assumes in "The Shepherd's Calendar," and in the pastoral entitled " Colin Clout's come Home again," which represents his return from a visit to Sir Walter Raleigh.

Colin Tampon. The nickname of a Swiss, as " John Bull " is of an Englishman, " Brother Jonathan " of a North American, " Monsieur Crapaud " of a Frenchman, etc.

Coll. Collector; colloquial; college; collection.

Colla parte. (Ital.) Signifies that the accompanist must follow the leading part in regard to time. (Mus.)

Colla pii forza e prestezza. (Ital.) As loudly and as quickly as possible. (Mus.)

Colleen Bawn. The pet name of Eily O'Connor, the heroine of Gerald Griffin's novel " The Collegians," and of Boucicault's play, " The Colleen Bawn," The story of both was founded on fact. " Eily O'Connor was the daughter of a ropemaker, who lived in Garryowen, a suburb of the city of Limerick, Ireland. Scanlon, a gentleman of fortune, lived on his estate, near Glin, in County Kerry, adjoining Limerick. On one of his frequent visits to the city he saw the ropemaker's beautiful daughter, and was smitten by her charms. It was a case of love at first sight, sudden and decisive. He sought an introduction to her, and cultivated the acquaintance assiduously. Her simple armor was of the 'wild, sweet-briery-fence' sort, — sweet, yet thorny ; so that while he was attracted, any rude advances were repulsed. Finding her firm, he entrapped her into a private marriage, enjoining the utmost secrecy. Not long after this secret marriage Scanlon won the affections of a lady of fortune in County Limerick, Miss Chute, of Castle Chute, and a day was appointed for their marriage. As that day approached, how to get rid of his lawful wife, Eily O'Connor, was a problem that worried him. He had her conveyed to a cottage in the mountains, and afterwards to a place near Glin, where he induced his hunchback servant and foster-brother, Danny Mann, or Sullivan, to take her out boating on the river Shannon and drown her. Danny's first attempt was a failure. He returned to shore, and said to his unrelenting master, ' When I looked at her innocent face I had n't the heart to do it.' A second attempt was made, Scanlon himself accompanying them in the boat. This time she was thrown into the water, one hand grasping the boat-rail, the fingers of which were promptly chopped off by a hatchet in the hands of Danny Mann. Thus her struggle for life ended. Before many days elapsed her body was washed ashore on the opposite bank of the river, near Kilrush, in the County Clare. It was identified. Scanlon was arrested, tried, and convicted. Though a man of large influence with the Dublin Castle authorities, a bitter denunciation of the crime by Daniel O'Connell made them unwilling to interfere in granting a reprieve. On the day of the execution a horse could not be procured for love or money from any of the citizens to convey him from the prison to ' Gallows Green,' the place of execution. When all hope of procuring one had vanished, two turf carts belonging to tenants on his estate were seen approaching on the street. The horses were immediately taken from the carts and harnessed to a carriage. Scanlon got in, and was driven to the foot of the bridge leading to Gallows Green, when the horses suddenly stopped, and neither whips, spurs, kicks, nor the bayonet thrusts of the soldiers could induce them to go a step farther. Scanlon got out, amid the execrations and hootings of the multitude, who thought the action of the dumb animals a manifestation of the abhorrence of Heaven at the crime. He walked to the place of execution between files of soldiers, and was hanged. Danny Mann was apprehended, tried, and convicted at the following assizes for the city and county of Limerick, when he made a full confession of the facts and of the guilt of Scanlon, who protested his innocence of the crime, even on the scaffold."

College Port. The worst species of red wine that can be manufactured and palmed off upon young men at college. It is chiefly made from potatoes, sloes, and logwood.

Colley Cibber. (Pseud.) James Rees in the "Sunday Mercury" of Philadelphia, *circa* 1874.

Collop Monday. The Monday before Shrove Tuesday (*q. v.*). The name refers to the dinner which in some parts of England is almost universal on that day. It is customary to have collops of bacon and eggs for dinner. Go into some districts in England at dinner-time on Collop Monday, and you will be sure to be saluted by the smell of fried slices of bacon and eggs.

Colloquy of Poissy. A famous meeting of Catholics and Calvinists which assembled at Poissy in 1561 to settle the bitter religious warfare which then agitated France. It was, however, productive of no good result, and devastating religious wars followed.

Collyridians. A sect of Arabian Christians, chiefly women, which first appeared in 373. They worshipped the Virgin Mary, and made offerings to her in a twisted cake called a collyris.

Col. Frederic Ingham. The pen-name under which Edward E. Hale published "Ten Times One is Ten."

Colonization. A form of political corruption peculiar to the cities of the United States, and by which bodies of voters from one district are domiciled in another just previous to election time for the purpose of influencing the result.

Colophon. The end clause of a book, containing the names of the printer and publisher, and the place where the book was printed; in former times the date and the edition were added also.

Colophon was a city of Iona, the inhabitants of which were such excellent horsemen that they could turn the scale of battle; hence the Greek proverb to " add a colophon " meant to " put a finishing stroke to an affair."

Colorado. The name is derived from a Spanish word meaning " red," in allusion to the prevailing color of the soil or rocks in many localities.

Colossus of Fairmount. The great wooden bridge across the Schuylkill at Philadelphia, erected in 1812 by Lewis Wernwag, a famous engineer (1769–1843). It consisted of a single arch with a span of three hundred and forty feet.

Colston Day. The anniversary of the birthday (November 13) of Edward Colston, a citizen of Bristol, England. He founded various charities in the city, and his memory is kept green by an annual celebration on the day above mentioned.

Colubram in sinu fovere. (Lat.) " To cherish a snake in one's bosom." To have an enemy in your confidence.

Columba (the Dove). A constellation of ten stars, only one of which is of the second magnitude; situated about sixteen degrees south of the Hare, and nearly on the same meridian with the three stars in Orion's belt. It was named after Noah's dove sent out from the ark to find dry land.

Columbia. The United States. Derived from Columbus, the discoverer of the New World, and applied to its greatest nation from a feeling of poetic justice to the memory of the great explorer.

Columella of New England. John Lowell, the political writer (b. in Newburyport, Mass., 1769; d. 1840). He inherited the love of his father (John Lowell, 1743–1802) for horticulture, and received the above appellation.

Com. Commerce; Committee; Commissioner; Commodore.

Com. & Nav. Commerce and Navigation.

Com. Arr. Committee of Arrangements.

Comdg. Commanding.

Come 'l primo tempo. (Ital.) In the same movement as at first. (Mus.)

Come-outers. " This name has been applied to a considerable number of persons in various parts of the Northern States, principally in New England, who have recently come out of the various religious denominations with which they have been connected; hence the name. They have not themselves assumed any distinctive organization. They have no creed, believing that every one should be left free to hold such opinions on religious subjects as he pleases, without being held accountable for the same to any human authority. They hold a diversity of opinions on many points, — some believing in the divine inspiration of the Scriptures, and others that they are but human compositions. They believe Jesus Christ to have been a divinely inspired teacher, and his religion a revelation of eternal truth; that, according to his teachings, true religion consists in purity of heart, holiness of life, and not in opinions; that Christianity, as it existed in Christ, is a life rather than a belief." — BARTLETT.

Come tempo del tema. (Ital.) Same movement as the theme. (Mus.)

Comet Wine. A term of praise to signify wine of superior quality. A notion prevails that the grapes in comet years are better in flavor than in other years, either because the weather is warmer and ripens them better, or because the comets themselves exercise some chemical influence on them. Thus wine of the years 1811, 1826, 1839, 1845, 1852, 1858, 1861, 1882, etc., has a repute.

Coming-out Sunday. The day on which a new-married couple made their first appearance at church, — usually the Sunday after the wedding. This custom continued more than a century after 1719 (when Mather mentioned it). It was termed "coming out groom and bride." It still remains in many places.

Coming to the Scratch. This was originally a phrase used by boxers. In the prize-ring it was usual to make a distinct mark or *scratch* in the turf, dividing the ring into two equal parts. "To come to the scratch" meant to walk to the boundary to meet the antagonist.

Comitas inter gentes. (Lat.) Courteousness between nations.

Comm. Commentary.

Commander of the Faithful. A title assumed by Omar I. (d. 644) and since retained by his successors in the Caliphate.

Comme il faut. (Fr.) As it should be.

Commencement. The contradictory title, in America, for the ceremonies at the close of a college year.

Originally "commencement" was held at the beginning of the new college year, in the fall. Those who had passed the graduating examinations received their diplomas and spoke their pieces then. But as this custom proved inconvenient, it gradually became the practice of colleges to unite the commencement with the final examinations. But the name of the function was retained.

Commencement de la fin. (Fr.) The beginning of the end.

Commendation Ninepence. A bent silver ninepence, supposed to be lucky, and commonly used in the seventeenth century as a love-token; the giver or sender using these words, "From my love to my love." Sometimes the coin was broken, and each kept a part.

Commissaire de police. (Fr.) A commissioner of police.

Commodity of Brown Paper. This phrase is very common among the old dramatists. It always has the meaning of a custom among young rakes of the period, when in want of money, of buying merchandise upon credit, which they sold for ready money at a loss. Thus in Green's "Quip for an Upstart Count," we find, "So that if he borrow an hundred pounds, he shall have forty in silver, and threescore in wares, as lutestrings, hobby-horses, or brown paper." So, in "Measure for Measure" (iv. 3), we have, "First here's young Master Rash, he's in for a commodity of brown paper and old ginger, ninescore and seventeen pounds;" that is, he is charged £197 for a lot of stuff not worth more, probably, than half the money. Nares, from whom this article is quoted, well says: "Such schemes have been heard of in later times."

Commodo, Commodamente. (Ital.) Quietly and with composure. (Mus.)

Commonwealth, Heart of the. *See* HEART OF THE COMMONWEALTH.

Commonwealth, Right Arm of the. *See* RIGHT ARM OF THE COMMONWEALTH.

Commune bonum. (Lat.) A common good.

Communia proprie dicere. (Lat.) To express common things with propriety.

Communibus annis. (Lat.) One year with another.

Communipaw. (Pseud.) Pliny Miles, foreign correspondent of several American newspapers.

Communists. An anarchical party in France who propose to divide France into about a thousand small thoroughly independent States, with councils elected by all the population, Paris to be the ruling head. They declare that capital and its holders must be adapted to nobler uses, or cease to exist. Their creed is stated to be atheism and materialism. They are intimately connected with the International Society of Workmen. A "communist" is often confounded with a "socialist," but the conjunction is very unjust to the latter. The communist is simply a destructionist, while the socialist is more or less of a reformer, proposing definite remedies for acknowledged political and social evils.

Comp. Compare; comparative; compound; compounded.

Compagnon de voyage. (Fr.) A travelling-companion.

Companions of Jehu. A nickname given to the Chouans from a supposed similarity between their self-imposed task and that assigned to Jehu. The latter was to cut off Ahab and all his house and the idolatrous priests of Baal; the Chouans aimed to annihilate all who bore any part in the assassination of Louis XVI., and to place his brother, the Comte de Provence, on the throne.

Competition Waller. (Pseud.) George Otto Trevelyan, M.P., English writer (b. 1831).

Complutensian Bible. Another name for the great Polyglot Bible printed at Complutum, the ancient name of Alcala de Henares, in Spain.

Compos mentis. (Lat.) "Sound of mind." One who is not insane or weak in mind.

Compromise of 1850. "For more than a year after the termination of the Mexican War, the territory acquired by that war had remained under military rule. But in 1850 California adopted a constitution prohibiting slavery, and then applied for admission. The slave States would not agree to admit her unless a new slave State were also formed. At the same time the organization of the newly acquired territory came up for discussion. Henry Clay then proposed a compromise, which, having been referred to a select committee of thirteen, of which he was chairman, was reported by them in sub-stantially the same shape as proposed. It provided for : (1) The postponement of the admission of new States to be formed out of Texas until demanded by such State. (2) The admission of California as a free State. (3) The organization, without the Wilmot Proviso, of all territory acquired from Mexico, and not included in California, as the Territories of New Mexico and Utah. (4) The combination of the last two measures in one bill. (5) The establishment of the boundaries of Texas, and the payment to her of $10,000,000 for the abandonment of her claim to New Mexico. (6) More effectual laws for the return of fugitive slaves. (7) Abolishing the slave trade in the District of Columbia, but leaving slavery there undisturbed. These measures all became laws, and together were commonly known as the Omnibus Bill. It is charged that the indemnity of $10,000,000, the payment of which raised the market value of Texas securities from twenty or thirty to nearly par, was not without influence in the passage of the bill. The Kansas-Nebraska Bill, passed in 1854, virtually repealed this compromise."—BROWN AND STRAUSS.

Compte rendu. (Fr.) Account rendered; a report.

Comus. In classic mythology the god of festivity and mirth.

Com. Ver. Common Version (of the Bible).

Con. *Contra.* Against; in opposition.

Con. (Ital.) With; as, *con espressione,* with expression; *con brio,* with brilliancy and spirit. (Mus.)

Con abbandono ed espressione. (Ital.) With self-abandon and expression. (Mus.)

Con amore. (Ital.) "With love." From a love to the work; with great and earnest zeal.

Con anima. (Ital.) With airiness and animation.

Con brio ed animato. (Ital.) Animated and brilliant. (Mus.)

Concerning Snakes in Ireland. This phrase is constantly cropping out as a genuine quotation. It, however, does not refer to Ireland in any way, but to Iceland. In a translation of Horrebow's work, "The Natural History of Iceland," London, 1758, chapter xlii. is headed "Concerning Owls," and is as follows: "There are no owls of any kind in the whole island." Chapter lxxii. is entitled "Concerning Snakes," and the entire chapter is as follows: "No snakes of any kind are to be met with throughout the whole of the island." The application of the phrase to Ireland probably at first arose from a printer's error.

Concetto, Concetti (plu.). (Ital.) A stroke of wit; a turn or point.

Conch. Conchology.

Concio ad clerum. A discourse to the clergy.

Con commodo. (Ital.) In a convenient degree of movement. (Mus.)

Concordia discors. (Lat.) Discordant harmony.

Concord Mob. In August, 1835, a time when the anti-slavery leaders were decried and insulted even in New England, John Greenleaf Whittier accompanied George Thompson, an English orator, to Concord, N. H., to make arrangements for an anti-slavery meeting. A mob of several hundred gathered, assailed Whittier with sticks and stones, injured him, and drove him into the house of an honorable man, though not an Abolitionist. Meanwhile the house which held Thompson was also attacked. Whittier managed to join him. A cannon was actually brought to bombard the house; but finally the rioters dispersed without doing serious damage, and Whittier and Thompson escaped from the town.

Concours comparatif. (Fr.) A competitive examination among selected candidates for government appointments.

Concours universel. (Fr.) "Competition universal." A competitive examination for all comers who aspire to government appointments.

Con. Cr. Contra credit.

Condé and Bartlett Line. The boundary between the United States and Mexico. Under the provisions of the treaty of Guadalupe-Hidalgo, signed Feb. 2, 1848, Mr. John Russell Bartlett was sent to New Mexico as commissioner to lay out, with Mexican commissioners, the boundary line. The Mexican commissioner was probably named Condé, though we do not find him mentioned in any history. Hence the line decided on was called for a time the "Condé and Bartlett Line;"

just as the famous "Mason and Dixon Line" was named after the surveyors who laid it out a hundred years ago and more. *See* MASON AND DIXON'S LINE.

Con diligenza. (Ital.) Diligently; in a studied manner. (Mus.)

Conditio sine qua non. (Lat.) "Condition without which not." An indispensable or necessary condition.

Con dolore. (Ital.) Mournfully; with grief and pathos. (Mus.)

Condottieri. Leaders of military adventurers in the fifteenth century. The most noted of these brigand leaders in Italy were Guarnieri, Lando, Francesco of Carmagnola, and Francesco Sforza.

Conductor = GUARD. The American and English terms, respectively, for the officer in charge of a passenger train.

C. O. Nevers. (Pseud.) Charles Crozet Converse, American *littérateur* (b. 1834).

Confed. Confederate.

Confederates. The Southerners during the late civil war were called "Confederates," from the fact that the eleven seceding States were known as "the Confederate States of America."

Confederate States. The eleven States which seceded from the American Union in 1861; namely, Georgia, North and South Carolina, Virginia, Tennessee, Alabama, Louisiana, Arkansas, Mississippi, Florida, and Texas. *See* SECESSIA.

Confession of Brandenburg. Formula of faith drawn up by order of the Elector of Brandenburg, with a view to harmonizing the views of Luther and Calvin, and healing the controversy caused by the Augsburg Confession.

Confidence Man. One who by plausible stories and falsehoods or by assurance obtains the confidence of kind-hearted people. This well-known phrase is said to have thus originated: A few years ago, a man in New York, well dressed and of exceedingly genteel manners, went about saying, in a very winning manner, to almost every gentleman he met, "Have you confidence enough in me, an entire stranger, to lend me five dollars for an hour or two?" In this way he got a good deal of money, and came to be generally known in the courts and elsewhere as "the confidence man."

Confrère. (Fr.) A brother of the same society; an associate or professional companion.

Cong. Congress.

Congé d'élire. (Fr.) "Leave to elect." A writ by the sovereign granting leave to elect a bishop.

Congl. Congregational; Conglomerate.

Congleton Bears. The men of Congleton. The story runs that a certain parish clerk of Congleton sold the church Bible to buy a bear.

Con grazia. (Ital.) With grace. (Mus.)

Con gusto. (Ital.) With taste. (Mus.)

Conj., or **conj.** Conjunction.

Con moto. (Ital.) In an agitated style; with spirit. (Mus.)

Conn., or **Ct.** Connecticut.

Connecticut. The name is derived from the Mohegan dialect; spelled phonetically *Quon-eh-ta-cut*, and signifying " a long river."

Connecticut Reserve. *See* WESTERN RESERVE.

Connoisseur. (Fr.) A good judge in matters of taste or the fine arts.

Con 8va ad libitum. (Ital.) With octaves at pleasure. (Mus.)

Conqueror, The. (1) Alfonso of Portugal (fl. 1094–1185). (2) Aurungzebe the Great, most powerful of the Mogul emperors (fl. 1618–1707). (3) James I. of Aragon (fl. 1206–1276). (4) Othman, the founder of the Turkish power (fl. 1259–1326). (5) Francisco Pizarro, who conquered Peru (fl. 1475–1541). (6) William, Duke of Normandy, who subjugated England (fl. 1027–1087).

Conqueror of the World. Alexander the Great.

Conscia mens recti famæ mendacia ridet. (Lat.) A mind which is conscious of rectitude treats with contempt lying rumors.

Conscience, Courts of. In England, courts for the recovery of small debts. They were also called " Courts of Requests." On the establishment of county courts, they were mostly abolished.

Conscience Whigs. " In 1850 the Whigs in Congress had taken the position that the slavery question, which they regarded as settled by the Compromise of 1850, should not be reopened. This policy was approved by President Fillmore. Their attitude led to dissensions in the party in many of the States. In Massachusetts those opposed to the stand thus taken by the leaders were known as Conscience Whigs; those that approved it, as Cotton Whigs. The reason of the name is obvious. In New York, Fillmore's State, the supporters of his view were known as Silver Grays, a name given to them because they were mostly the older members. They were also called Snuff-takers. Those opposing it, headed by William H. Seward, were called Woolly Heads, or Seward Whigs." — BROWN AND STRAUSS.

Con scienza. (Ital.) " With knowledge." With a complete knowledge of the subject.

Conscript Fathers (*Patres Conscriptii*). The designation given to the Roman senators because their names were inscribed in the registers of the Senate.

Con. Sec. Conic Sections.

Conseil de famille. (Fr.) A family consultation.

Conseil d'état. (Fr.) " Council of State." A privy council.

Conseiller d'état. (Fr.) A privy councillor.

Conseils de prud'hommes. (Fr.) " Councils of discreet men." A mixed council of masters and workmen for the settlement of trade disputes.

Consensus facit legem. (Lat.) Consent makes the law.

Consentes dii. The twelve chief Roman deities, — Jupiter, Apollo, Mars, Neptune, Mercury, Vulcan, Juno, Vesta, Minerva, Ceres, Diana, and Venus.

Consenting Stars. Stars forming certain configurations for good or evil. Thus, we read in the Book of Judges (v. 20), " The stars in their courses fought against Sisera; " *i. e.*, formed configurations which were unlucky or malignant.

> . . . scourge the bad revolving stars,
> That have consented unto Henry's death !
> King Henry the Fifth, too famous to live long !
> SHAKSPEARE, 1 *Henry VI.*

Conservatives. The name given in recent times, or since 1830, in English political affairs to a political party whose leading principle is the preservation of national institutions. *Conservative*, in popular language, is now opposed to *Liberal*. Sir Robert Peel acknowledged himself a Conservative when reproached by the Irish party in Parliament with being an Orangeman ; but the party that afterward separated from him called their principles conservative in contradistinction to his policy and measures. A great meeting of the National Union of Conservative Associations was held at the Crystal Palace, June 24, 1872. The party in the minority at the elections in 1868 obtained a majority at those in February, 1874, and came into office. They resigned April 22, 1880. The Marquis of Salisbury was elected leader of the party May 9, 1881, succeeding the Earl of Beaconsfield, who died April 19, previous.

Consistency, thou art a Jewel. "This is one of those popular sayings, like 'Be good, and you will be happy,' or 'Virtue is its own reward ;' that like Topsy 'never was born, only jist growed.' From the earliest times it has been the popular tendency to call this or that cardinal virtue or bright and shining excellence a jewel, by way of emphasis. For example, Iago says :
'Good name in man or woman, dear my lord,
Is the immediate jewel of their souls.'
Shakspeare elsewhere calls experience a jewel ; Miranda says her modesty is the jewel in her dower ; and in 'All's Well that Ends Well,' Diana terms her chastity the jewel of her house." — WIGHT.

Consistory. Any solemn assembly or council ; a religious court for the settlement of Church questions ; the College of Cardinals at Rome.

Consociation. A free-will confederacy of neighboring Congregational churches for mutual advice and co-operation in church matters, composed of lay members.

Conspicuous by his Absence. Lord John Russell, alluding to this expression used by him in his address to the electors of the city of London, said, "It is not an original expression of mine, but is taken from one of the greatest historians of antiquity."

Con spirito. (Ital.) With quickness and spirit. (Mus.)

Const. Constable ; constitution.

Constance. (Pseud.) Mrs. B. W. J. Williams, contributor to "Scott's Magazine " and the Mobile " Sunday Times."

Constance Murielle. The stage-name of Mrs. Clement Bennett, formerly Mrs. W. B. Price.

Constantia. (Pseud.) Mrs. Judith Sargent Murray, in various New England publications.

Constantia et virtute. (Lat.) By constancy and virtue.

Constantine Tolmen. A great oblong stone, 33 feet long, 18 wide, and 14 thick, poised on the points of two upright rocks in Cornwall, England. This uplifted mass weighs 750 tons, and is a freak of Nature.

Constitutional Union Party, The, consisted of moderate Southerners and some Webster Whigs. It claimed for its platform the Constitution of the United States and the enforcement of the laws. At its convention, held May, 1860, it nominated John Bell for President and Edward Everett for Vice-President.

Consubstantiation. A Lutheran doctrine that the actual, substantial presence of the body of Christ is with the bread and wine of the Lord's Supper.

Consuelo. The impersonation of moral purity in the midst of temptations. Consuelo is the heroine of a novel so-called by George Sand.

Cont. _Contra._ Against.

Continental System. A name given to Napoleon's plan for shutting out Great Britain from all commerce with the continent of Europe. He forbade, under pain of war, any nation of Europe to receive British exports or to send imports to any of the British dominions. The embargo began Nov. 21, 1806, but soon ended.

Continent, The Dark. _See_ DARK CONTINENT.

Continuator of Fordun. A title conferred on Robert Bower, or Bowmaker (b. 1385), because he completed the history of Scotland known as "Scotichronicon," which was begun by Fordun. Like the latter, he wrote in Latin.

Contraband of War, or **Contrabands.** Gen. B. F. Butler so dubbed the negroes during the civil war.

Contra bonos mores. (Lat.) Contrary to good manners.

Contrada dei nobili. (Ital.) "The street of the nobles." The part of an Italian town where the nobles reside.

Contra quoscunque. (Lat.) Against all persons whatever.

Contre fortune bon cœur. (Fr.) "Against fortune good heart." Keep up the spirits in every case of misfortune.

Contretemps. (Fr.) A mischance; a disappointment.

Con variazione. (Ital.) With variations. (Mus.)

Conversation Sharp. Richard Sharp, the critic (1759–1835).

Convicts. A by-name conferred on the Sixtieth Rifles in the English army, because of the dingy color of its uniform.

Convocation. A general assembly of clergymen of the Church of England to consult as to the affairs of the Church; any called assemblage.

Conway Cabal. In American history the name given to a faction which arose in 1777, with the avowed object of elevating General Gates to the command of the Continental troops.

Coodies. The name of a political sect in the State of New York, which originated in the year 1814. At that time a series of well-written articles appeared in a New York paper, signed Abimelech Coody. He professed to be a mechanic. "He was a Federalist, and addressed himself principally to the party to which he belonged. He endeavored to show the impropriety of opposing the war, and urged them to come forward in defence of their country. He also attacked De Witt Clinton with great severity." The writer was ascertained to be Mr. Gulian C. Verplanck, then, as now, distinguished for his talents. He was replied to by a writer under the signature of "A Traveller," said to be De Witt Clinton, who thus speaks of this party: "The political sect called the Coodies, of hybrid nature, is composed of the combined spawn of Federalism and Jacobinism, and generated in the venomous passions of disappointment and revenge, without any definite character; neither fish nor flesh nor bird nor beast, but a nondescript made up of 'all monstrous, all prodigious things.'" — HAMMOND, *Political History of New York.*

Cooked Accounts. Said of a ledger, cash-book, etc., that have been tampered with, in order to show a false balance.

The term was first used in reference to George Hudson, the railway king, under whose chairmanship the Eastern Counties Railway accounts were falsified. The allusion is to preparing meat for table.

Cooly. As generally used in this country, the word is applied to Chinese laborers of the lower classes who have come to this country. It obtained this broad meaning during the discussion of the Chinese question. Strictly, it includes only such laborers as have been imported under contract or by force or fraud.

Coon. (1) A nickname for a negro. (2) Henry Clay was sneered at by the Democrats as "that same old coon," in retaliation for the Whigs calling Martin Van Buren an "old fox."

Cop., or **Copt.** Coptic.

Cope. (Pseud.) William P. Copeland, a well-known American newspaper correspondent (1843–1883).

Copia. In classic mythology the goddess of plenty.

Copia fandi. (Lat.) Copiousness of speech.

Copia verborum. (Lat.) Abundance of words; copiousness of speech.

Copper-Farthing Dean. Jonathan Swift was thus named.

Copperheads. A popular nickname originating in the time of the great civil war in the United States, and applied to a faction in the North which was very generally considered to be in secret sympathy with the Rebellion, and to give it aid and comfort by attempting to thwart the measures of the Government. The name is derived from a poisonous serpent called the copperhead (*Trigonocephalus contortrix*), whose bite is considered as deadly as that of the rattlesnake, and whose geographical range extends from Florida to 45° north. The copperhead, unlike the rattlesnake, gives no warning of its attack, and is therefore the type of a concealed foe.

Coppernose. Henry VIII. was so called, because he mixed so much copper with the silver coin that it showed after a little wear in the parts most pronounced, as the nose; hence the sobriquets "Coppernosed Harry," "Old Coppernose," etc.

Coquina. (Pseud.) G. O. Shields, a sporting writer.

Cor. Corinthians.

Cora Ferris. The stage-name of Mrs. Herman Gruen.

Cora Macy. The stage-name of Mrs. Charles E. McGeachy.

Cora Neilson. The stage-name of Mrs. J. H. Carver.

Cora Tanner. The stage-name of Mrs. William E. Sinn.

Cora Van Tassell. The stage-name of Mrs. Edwin Young.

Cora Vaughn. The stage-name of Mrs. J. R. Oakley.

Cora Wilson. The stage-name of Mrs. J. W. Conner.

Coram domino rege. (Lat.) In the presence of our lord the king.

Coram nobis. (Lat.) "In the presence of us." In our presence, — i. e., before the court of law.

Coram non judice. (Lat.) Before one not the proper judge; before an improper tribunal.

Coram populo. (Lat.) Before the people.

Cor cordium ("heart of hearts"). A poetical name applied to Shelley by Trelawney, and which was engraved on Shelley's tombstone.

Cordelia Howard. The stage-name of Mrs. Edmond Macdonald.

Cordeliers (lit. "cord-wearers"). Franciscan friars who wore a knotted rope around the waist for a girdle. During the French Revolution a conspicuous party was so named because it held its meetings in the chapel of the Franciscan monastery. Danton, Hébert, Camille Desmoulins, Chaumette, and Marat were members of this club, which opposed the Jacobins.

Cordière, La Belle. *See* BEAUTIFUL ROPEMAKER.

Cordon bleu. (1) A knight of the ancient Order of the Holy Ghost. So called because the decoration is suspended on a blue ribbon. It was at one time the highest order in the kingdom. (2) A first-rate cook. The Commander de Souve, Comte d'Olonne, and some others, who were *cordons bleus*, met together as a sort of club, and were noted for their well-appointed dinners. Hence, when any one had dined well, he said, "Bien, c'est un vrai repas de cordon-bleu;" and a superior cook was one of the *cordon bleu* type, or, briefly, a *cordon bleu.*

Cordon rouge. A chevalier of the Order of Saint Louis, the decoration being suspended on a red ribbon. A "grand cordon" is a member of the Légion d'Honneur, whose cross is attached to a grand, or broad, ribbon.

Corinthian. A licentious fellow. The immorality of Corinth was proverbial in the ancient world.

Corinthian Brass. A mixture of gold, silver, and brass, which forms the best of all mixed metals. When Mummius set fire to Corinth, the heat of the conflagration was so great that it melted the metal, which ran down the streets in streams. The three mentioned above ran together, and obtained the name of "Corinthian brass."

> I think it may be of "Corinthian brass,"
> Which was a mixture of all metals, but
> The brazen uppermost.
> BYRON, *Don Juan.*

Corinthian War. Begun 395 B. C. It received this name from the fact that it raged mostly in the neighborhood of Corinth by a confederacy of Athenians, Thebans, Argives, and Corinthians against the Lacedæmonians. Its two most famous battles were at Coronea and Leuctra. The peace of Antalcidas, 387 B. C., closed the conflict.

Corinth's Pedagogue. Dionysius the Younger. At his second banishment from Syracuse, he went to Corinth and became a schoolmaster.

Corisande. (Pseud.) Mrs. Adolphe Jerrold Smith, in "The Graphic" (London) and the Liverpool "Courier."

Cor. Mem. Corresponding Member.

Corn. Cornwall; Cornish.

Corn = WHEAT. In the United States the term "corn" is applied exclusively to maize, or "Indian corn." In England "corn" means *wheat.*

Cornalba, Mlle. The stage-name of Mme. Morelli.

Corn City. Toledo, Ohio.

Corncrackers. A colloquial nickname for an inhabitant or a native of Kentucky.

Corncracker State. Kentucky. See *supra.*

Cornelie d'Anka. The stage-name of Mrs. Ingram.

Cornelius O'Dowd. (Pseud.) Charles James Lever, Irish novelist (1806–1872).

Cornish Hug. A hug to overthrow one. The Cornish men were famous wrestlers, and tried to throttle their antagonists with a particular lock, called the Cornish hug.

Cornish Wonder. John Opie, the painter (fl. 1761–1807). He was a native of Cornwall.

Corn-juice. The slang term current in the West for whiskey.

Corn-law Rhymer. Ebenezer Elliott (fl. 1781–1849), who wrote largely
against the corn-laws during the agitation for their repeal.

Corol. Corollary.

Corporal's Guard. A colloquial term
for an insignificant force. In American
political nomenclature the term denotes
the small body of Whigs in Congress
who stood by President Tyler after he
had vetoed the tariff bill of his party.

Corporealist. One who denies the
existence of spiritual beings.

Corps d'armée. (Fr.) A division of
a military force.

Corps diplomatique. (Fr.) " Body
diplomatic." All the ambassadors from
the several countries.

Corps d'observation. (Fr.) A body
of soldiers for watching the movements
of the enemy.

Corps dramatique. (Fr.) " Body
dramatic." The whole company of actors or of a theatre.

Corpse Candle. (1) The *ignis fatuus*
is so called by the Welsh, because it is
supposed to forbode death, and to show
the road that the corpse would take.
(2) A large candle used at wakes.

Corpus Christi. (Lat.) " The body
of Christ." The most splendid festival
of the Roman Catholic Church. It
was instituted in 1264 in honor of the
Consecrated Host, and with a view to
its adoration by Pope Urban IV., who
appointed for its celebration the Thursday after the festival of the Trinity, and
promised to all the penitent who took
part in it indulgence for a period of
from forty to one hundred days. The
festival is chiefly distinguished by magnificent processions. In France it is
known as the *Fête Dieu.*

Corpus delicti. (Lat.) " The body
of the crime." The substance or foundation of the defence.

Corpus exsangue. (Lat.) The lifeless body.

Corpus juris. (Lat.) " The body of
the law." The whole mass of the law.

Corpus sine pectore. (Lat.) The
body without a mind or soul.

Corrector of the People. *See* Al-
EXANDER THE CORRECTOR.

Correggio. One of the pen-names
usually attributed to Junius (*q. v.*).

Correggio of Sculptors. Jean Goujon (fl. 1510–1572). *See also* FRENCH
PHIDIAS.

Corrigenda. (Lat.) Corrections to
be made.

Corsair. (Pseud.) James Wood Davidson in Southern newspaper press.

Cor. Sec. Corresponding Secretary.

Corsica Paoli. Pasquale de Paoli
(fl. 1726–1807), a Corsican patriot, and
leader of his people in their struggle
against Genoa.

Cortez of Africa. Henry M. Stanley, the dauntless explorer of the Dark
Continent, has been so named.

Corvinus (" raven "). Janos Hunyady,
governor of Hungary, was so named on
account of the raven on his shield.

Coryphæus. A model man or leader.
From the κορυφαῖος, or leader of the
chorus in the Greek drama.

Coryphæus of German Literature.
Goethe.

The Polish poet called upon . . . the great
Coryphæus of German literature. — W. R. Mor-
FELL, *Notes and Queries.*

Coryphæus of Grammarians. Aristarchus of Samothrace, the most celebrated grammarian of antiquity.

Cos. Cosine.

Cosas de Espana. (Span.) " Things
of Spain." Spanish doings; strange or
unintelligible actions.

Coss. *Consules.* Consuls.

Cossack Marlinski. (Pseud.) Alexander Bestuschew, a Russian novelist
(1795-1837), author of " Marlinski's
Tales," St. Petersburg, 1840.

Coster's Friend, The. Anthony Ashley Cooper, Earl Shaftesbury, the English philanthropist (d. 1885), was so
named. Though his active benevolence
was extended to all classes, it was
among the London " barrow-men " that
he achieved the greatest good. He often
said it was the proudest moment of his
life, when the handsomest donkey in the
East End of London was publicly presented by a delegation from the class he
loved to befriend.

Costumier. (Fr.) A dealer in costumes or dresses, particularly of a theatrical character.

Cotillon. A lively dance.

Cotswold Lion. A sheep. The
Cotswold hills are famous for their
flocks of sheep; and there is a local
ironical saying, " Fierce as a Cotswold
lion."

Cottage orné. (Fr.) A cottage villa.

Cotton Famine, so called. A fearful
time of suffering in Great Britain in

1861 and following years, occasioned by the war of secession in the United States. The years 1859 and 1860, unparalleled for the magnitude of the cotton manufacture, had much to do with the collapse that followed. The fact that of 1,390,000,000 lbs. of cotton imported in 1860 no less a weight than 1,120,000,000 came from the United States, shows the tremendous effect to be expected from any stoppage in the American cotton-trade. Irrespective of this, however, there would have been stagnation in British manufacturing districts in 1861, even if raw cotton had been plentiful and cheap. The manufacturers had glutted all the markets by the wholly unprecedented extent of their operations in 1860. The English warehouses, as well as those elsewhere, were full, and time was needed to carry off the immense stock. There were cotton goods on hand in Great Britain at the end of the year valued at £20,000,000; while in India British merchants continued to pour in goods even when the consignments of 1860 exceeded £17,000,000. Fort Sumter was bombarded April, 1861. This was virtually the beginning of the war of secession and of the rise in the price of cotton. A blockade was early established by the Federal Government; and it was only by "running" this blockade that cotton-laden ships could clear from the Southern or Confederate ports. The price of Middling Orleans (the kind of cotton mostly used, and that which governs the price of all other kinds) rose fron 7¾ d. to 9d., 10d., and 12d., as the year advanced. There was thus a twofold motive for lessening the operations of the Lancashire mills, — the markets were so fully supplied with manufactured goods that no immediate augmentation was necessary; while the increase in the price of the raw material rendered manufacturing less profitable than before. The Liverpool dealers made colossal fortunes by the enormous rise in price of every bale of cotton which could reach the country from any quarter; while the manufacturers were also prosperous, because they could sell their accumulated stocks of calicoes and yarns at much higher prices than had been obtainable in 1860. It was the operatives who suffered. One by one the mills were put upon half-time, because the millowners had not much inducement to spin and weave under the extraordinary

double influence above adverted to. It was not until autumn, however, that these effects were heavily felt, when there was the enormous quantity of 1,000,000,000 lbs. of cotton, raw and manufactured, on hand in Great Britain. In November there were 49 mills stopped, throwing out 8,063 hands, while 119 were working half-time, placing something like 20,000 persons on half their usual wages. So singular was the state of things, and so unlike what would be called a "famine" under other circumstances, that the actual quantity of raw cotton in Great Britain at the end of the year (280,000,000 lbs.) was greater than ever before known in the history of the trade; but as the market price of yarns and piece goods at that time scarcely equalled that of raw cotton *plus* wages, the manufacturer could scarcely operate without a loss; and therefore he either closed his mill or placed his hands on half-time. It was not so much a famine of cotton as a famine of employment. The first relief was from the United States. During the autumn and early winter of 1862 the citizens of the United States, though with hearts and hands full with the agonies and necessities of war, contributed sufficient food and clothing to load three vessels, the "George Griswold," "Achilles," and "Hope," which hastened to the relief of their suffering cousins, and reached Liverpool in February, 1863. The year 1862 opened very gloomily. Relief committees began to be formed in Manchester, Wigan, Blackburn, Preston, and other towns, to distribute subscribed funds to such of the hands as were totally out of work. The streets were thronged with the unemployed; but there was no disturbance, and scarcely any begging. Sewing-schools were established by ladies in the several districts, to teach the factory girls useful domestic needle-work, of which they are generally very ignorant; to get them to make clothes for themselves and others; and to shield them from the vicious temptations which would beset them during a period of idleness. The ladies also won upon the affections of the girls by reading to them and sympathizing in many ways with their sorrows. Many of the manufacturers set apart large rooms as school-rooms and soup-kitchens for the boys and men, and abundant stores of soup were provided at 1d. per basin. In

April, Blackburn had only 18 mills on full-time out of 84, the rest being either on half-time or closed; and there were 9,000 of the inhabitants receiving parochial relief. Preston had 10,000 operatives out of work, and Blackburn had about half employment for 27,000. Middling Orleans rose in price to 15d., and manufacturers had more inducement to speculate in cotton than to spin it. Meanwhile great efforts were made to assist the distressed operatives. The letters of a " Lancashire Lad " in the " Times," with the text " Con yo help us a bit?" made a great impression. The " Daily Telegraph " raised a fund of £5,000 by its own exertions. The Lancashire landowners established a " cotton district relief fund " in London, to which they subscribed £11,000 in one day; the Lord Mayor established a " Mansion-House Committee," which received subscriptions from all parts of the world; Manchester established a "central relief committee," as a nucleus for various local funds; while a great county meeting brought in £130,000, of which £70,000 was subscribed in one day in one room. Notwithstanding all these sources of assistance, the workpeople became reduced to great distress. " The pawnbrokers' stores," said an eyewitness, " were glutted with the heirlooms of many an honest family. Little hoards were drained to meet the exigencies of the time. Rents were falling in arrears, and many a house which had held only one family was now occupied by three or four, in order to economize rent, fuel, and furniture." Nevertheless, none died of privation, and the average sickness was even less than usual. It was a gloomy winter, that of 1862–1863, for the mill hands. The imports of cotton fell to 524,000,000 lbs., against 1,257,000,000 in 1861, and 1,391,000,000 in 1860. In October the loss of wages was estimated at £136,000 per week. Vast sums were sent from various parts of the world to be spent in winter clothing only; and prodigious stores of second-hand clothing were contributed by private families. As the money relief seldom exceeded 2s. or 2s. 6d. per week per applicant, to purchase clothing out of this was of course impracticable. The small shopkeepers also suffered greatly; for there was only one third the amount of wages received by their customers per week that had been received two years before. Emi-

gration schemes were much discussed, but were not carried on very largely, because Lancashire men felt convinced that trade would revive after a time. Meanwhile the *rate* of wages was not lowered; few mill-owners proposed it, and the operatives were immovably against it; however small the quantity of work, it was paid for at the old rate. In 1863 the average number of persons out of work was 189,000, and that of those only partially employed, 129,000; in 1864 the figures were 134,000 and 97,000 respectively; and those for the first five months of 1865, 107,000 and 68,000. No date can be named for the actual cessation of the distress; it died out by degrees. When the manufacturers had sold off their old stocks, they recommenced buying more to spin and weave; because, though the price of raw cotton was enormously high, the selling price for calicoes and muslins was proportionably high, and therefore they could manufacture at a profit.

Cotton Lord. A wealthy Manchester cotton-spinner, rich in money, houses, lands, and dependants.

Cotton States. South Carolina, Georgia, Florida, Alabama, Mississippi, Louisiana, and Texas.

Cotton, To. " To cotton," meaning " to agree with, to take to," is now a common colloquial expression. As the poet says in the " Ingoldsby Legends : "
" For when once Madame Fortune deals out her hard raps,
    It 's amazing to think
    How one cottons to drink ! "

This use of the word, however, was common several centuries ago. It is found occasionally in the Elizabethan writers; but perhaps the earliest known example is the following, from Thomas Drant's translation of Horace, published in 1567 : —
" So feyneth he, things true and false
    So always mingleth he,
    That first with midst, and midst with laste,
    Maye cotten and agree."

The word is entered in Bartlett's " Dictionary of Americanisms ; " but, as this quotation shows, " to cotton," like so many other so-called Americanisms, is simply a survival, in vulgar use on both sides of the Atlantic, of a respectable old English word. It may be noted, by the way, as regards its etymology, that it has no connection with the plant cotton, but is derived from a Welsh verb meaning " to agree, to consent."

Cotylto. In classic mythology the goddess of licentiousness.

Couleur de rose. (Fr.) "Color of rose." Rose-color; an aspect of beauty and attractiveness; too highly colored; overdrawn with embellishments.

Council of the Vatican. The twenty-first General or Œcumenical Council. It commenced in 1869, Pius IX. being pope.

Counter-jumper. A nickname for a draper's assistant, "who jumps over the counter to go from one part of the establishment to another."

Counties Palatine. Certain counties in England where the earl exercised *jura regalia*, or independent jurisdiction, corresponding to the *Comes Palatii*. They were three in number, — Cheshire, Durham, and Lancashire, — all frontier counties. The Palatine jurisdiction of Chester was abolished in 1830, and of Durham in 1836. Lancaster alone retains the custom or right.

Counting Out. It sometimes happens that the political candidate who has received the largest number of votes is, by fraud in the canvass, deprived of the office to which he has been elected, the vote of his opponent being made to appear larger than his. He is then said to have been "counted out."

Country of Paradoxes. Holland, where houses are built on the sand, where the ocean is higher than the land, and where the keels of ships are often higher than the housetops.

A land that rides at anchor and is moored,
In which they do not live, but go aboard.
            BUTLER, *Hudibras.*

Country Parson. (Pseud.) Rev. A. K. H. Boyd, Scottish writer (b. 1825.)

Coup-d'état. (Fr.) "Stroke of State." A sudden and decisive blow; violent measures taken by the Government when the State is supposed to be in danger.

Coup-de-grace. (Fr.) "Stroke of mercy." The finishing stroke; the death-stroke which ended the sufferings of criminals broken on the wheel.

Coup-de-main. (Fr.) "Stroke of hand." A bold effort; a sudden or unexpected attack; a surprise.

Coup-de-pied. (Fr.) A kick.

Coup-de-plume. (Fr.) An attack in writing.

Coup-d'essai. (Fr.) First trial or essay.

Coup-de-soleil. (Fr.) "Stroke of the sun." Sunstroke; the disease produced by undue exposure of the head to the rays of the sun.

Coup-de-théâtre. (Fr.) An unforeseen event.

Coup-d'œil. (Fr.) "Stroke or glance of the eye." A rapid glance of the eye.

Courtney Melmoth. (Pseud.) Samuel Jackson Pratt, English poet and novelist (1749–1814).

Court of Cassation, in France, is the court which can *casser* (or quash) the judgment of other courts.

Court of Love. *See* PARLIAMENT OF LOVE.

Cousin Alice. (Pseud.) Mrs. Alice B. (Bradley) Haven, American writer (1825–1863).

Cousin Clara. (Pseud.) Rev. Daniel Wise, D.D., author of the "Lindendale Stories."

Cousin Kate. (Pseud.) (1) Maria J. McIntosh. (2) Mrs. Catherine M. Edwards. (3) Kate M. T. Cozans, an American writer. (4) Catherine D. Bell, an American *littérateur.*

Cousin May Carleton. (Pseud.) Mrs. May Agnes Fleming.

Cousin Michael. The Germans are so called, as the Americans are called "Brother Jonathan," and the English "John Bull." *Michel*, in Old German, means "gross." Cousin Michael means "Cousin Gourmand," or gross feeder; and indicates a slow, heavy, simple, unrefined, coarse-feeding people.

Cousin Virginia. (Pseud.) (1) Virginia W. Johnson, an American author; she wrote "The Calderwood Secret." (2) Virginia Frances Townsend.

Coûte que coûte, or **coûte qu'il coûte.** (Fr.) "Cost what it may." Come what may; at whatever cost.

Cove. Slang for "a man." This word has so bad a reputation that it is not admitted into modern dictionaries. It appears always to have been slang; for Bailey defines it thus: "a little harbor for boats; also a man (*cant*)." He also has it in the compound "Abram-cove, a naked or poor man (*cant*)."

Coventry Antiquary. (Pseud.) Thomas Sharp, English ecclesiastical writer (1693–1758).

Coventry Mysteries. Certain miracle plays acted at Coventry till 1591. They were published in 1841 for the

Shakspeare Society, under the care of J. O. Halliwell.

Covode Investigation. An inquiry made at the instance of John Covode, a Republican Congressman from Pennsylvania, in 1860, into the alleged corruption and unconstitutionality of the pro-slavery convention which met at Lecompton, Kan., and is known by that name.

Cowdray, Curse of. *See* CURSE OF COWDRAY.

Cowkiller, The. So Brant named the famous Indian chieftain, Red Jacket (1751–1830), in allusion to his lack of physical courage.

Cowper Law is trying a man after execution. Similar expressions are Jedwood, Jeddart, and Jedburgh Justice.

Coxcomb, The. (1) Richard II. of England. (2) Henry III. of France (*le Mignon*).

Coyote. *See* PRAIRIE WOLF.

C. P. Common Pleas; Court of Probate.

C. P. S. *Custos Privati Sigilli.* Keeper of the Privy Seal.

C. R. (1) *Custos Rotulorum.* Keeper of the Rolls. (2) *Carolus Rex.* King Charles.

Cr. Chromium; creditor; credit.

Cradle of Liberty. The familiar appellative bestowed on Faneuil Hall, Boston, Mass., erected in 1742 by Peter Faneuil (1700–1743), and presented by him to the town. In 1761 it was destroyed by fire, and was rebuilt. During the Revolutionary struggle the hall was so often used for political meetings that it became known as the "cradle of American liberty."

Cradle of Swiss Freedom. The town of Schuytz, in the canton of the same name.

Cradle of the Reformation. The Castle Church (Schlosskirche), in Wittenberg, erected in 1499, has been so named. Here Martin Luther preached, and here rest his ashes. *See* LUTHER TOWNS.

Crag, The King's. *See* KING'S CRAG.

Crank. A name first bestowed on Charles J. Guiteau, the assassin of President Garfield. It was felt that he was neither insane nor wholly sane, but that he was a monomaniac on one idea. Since then the word has passed into popular phraseology to denote one who is slightly unbalanced.

Cranmer's Bible. An edition of the Scriptures, a revision of the Great Bible (*q. v.*), which appeared in England in the year 1540.

Cream City. Milwaukee.

Credat Judæus. (Lat.) A Jew may believe it.

Crédit Mobilier. On the 18th of November, 1852, the French Government sanctioned the statutes of a new bank under the name of the "Société Général de Crédit Mobilier." The name was intended as a contrast to the Sociétés de Crédit Foncier, which are of the nature of land banks, and advance money on the security of real or immovable property; while the Crédit Mobilier proposed to give similar aid to the owners of movable property. The declared object of this bank is especially to promote industrial enterprises of all kinds, such as the construction of railways, sinking of mines, etc. The operations of the society were conducted upon a very extensive scale. In 1854 it subscribed largely to the Government loan on account of the Russian war, to the Grand Central Railway Company, to the General Omnibus Company of Paris, and to various other important undertakings. In 1855 it lent two sums to the Government, — the one of 250,000,000 and the other of 375,000,-000 francs. Its operations were vast during this year. The directors had not hitherto availed themselves of their privilege of issuing their own obligations, but this they now resolved on doing. They proposed to issue two kinds, the one at short dates, the other at long dates, and redeemable by instalments. The proposed issue was to amount to 240,000,000 francs ; but the public became alarmed at the prospect of so vast an issue of paper money, so that in March, 1856, the French Government deemed it necessary to prohibit the carrying out of the proposed scheme. This was a severe blow to the institution. In 1856 its dividends did not exceed twenty-two per cent; in 1857 they were only five per cent; in 1860 they were ten per cent. In 1867 stock fell greatly, and the company had to go into liquidation. The managers, however, retired with large fortunes. — "The Crédit Mobilier of America" was chartered in Pennsylvania in 1859 as a corporation for a general loan and contract business, and was reorganized in 1864 for enabling, as it would appear, the shareholders of the Union Pacific Railroad to build their line without incurring any pecuniary loss in case the enterprise failed. The honesty of the management having been impeached, the affairs of the organization were investigated by Congress in 1872–1873, when some of those connected with it were highly censured.

Credula res amor est. (Lat.) Love is a credulous thing.

Cremera, English. *See* ENGLISH CREMERA.

Creole. One born in the Southern States or the West Indies of European ancestors. It is from the Spanish *criollo*. In Louisiana alone an admixture of French blood makes the true Creole; and his patois, consisting of a mixture of English, French, and a few real African words, is called " Creole French."

Creole State. Louisiana. In this State the direct descendants of the original French and Spanish colonists form an important element in the social fabric.

Crepin. (Pseud.) Charles Wolcott Balestier, in the columns of the Rochester (N. Y.) " Post-Express."

Crescendo. (Ital.) A gradual increase of tone. (Mus.)

Crescent City. A name by which New Orleans is widely known, though at the present time it is no longer entirely appropriate. The older portion is built around a semicircular bend of the Mississippi; but in its recent growth the city has spread around another bend farther up stream, and is now nearly S-shaped.

Crescit amor nummi quantum ipsa pecunia crescit. (Lat.) The love of money increases as rapidly as the money itself increases.

Crescite et multiplicamini. (Lat.) Increase and multiply.

Crescit eundo. (Lat.) It increases by going.

Crevasse. A break in an embankment confining a river or canal. It is of French origin, and was originally applied by the *voyageurs* to a break in a levee (*q. v.*). *See also* WASH-OUT.

Cribro aquam haurire. (Lat.) " To draw water with a sieve." To lose one's time in vain labor.

Crim. con. Criminal conversation; adultery.

Crime against Kansas is the name by which the speech of Charles Sumner,

delivered in the Senate May 19 and 20, 1856, is known. It was directed against the acts of the slavery faction in the United States in its endeavors to secure the admission of Kansas as a slave State. Senator Butler had attacked Sumner in debate, and in this speech Sumner retorted. For this he was brutally assaulted by Butler's nephew, Preston S. Brooks. *See* BORDER WAR; JOHN BROWN; LECOMPTON CONSTITUTION.

Crimen falsi. (Lat.) Falsehood or perjury.

Crimen læsæ majestatis. (Lat.) The crime of high treason.

Crimps. *See* SPIRITS AND CRIMPS.

Crispin Catiline. An opprobrious nickname bestowed by Mirabeau on D'Espremesnil, in ridicule of his conspiracies.

Crispin's Day. The 25th of October, the day of the battle of Agincourt.

Crispin's Holiday. Every Monday. Shoemakers in some parts begin the working week on Tuesday. Saint Crispin was a shoemaker, and the patron saint of the craft.

Crispus. (Pseud.) Major C. C. Wheeler, a frequent contributor to the Brooklyn " Daily Eagle."

Criss-cross Row. The alphabet, either from the fact that in the old hornbooks the sign of the cross preceded the letter A, or because the letters were arranged in the form of a cross.

The assertion that the alphabet was written or printed in hornbooks in the form of a cross is one that may be moralized on to advantage by explainers of old stories and would-be etymologists. Christ's cross was cruciform, the alphabet was called Christ's cross, — the word "row" being of no consequence when it stops a theory, — therefore the alphabet was in a cruciform shape. Imagination further asks, "How could this be done?" The answer comes readily, even from one of the meanest capacity, — the consonants formed the perpendicular, the vowels the shorter transverse. Q. E. D. Yet all is imagination, and the fact that the cross commenced the alphabetic row is wholly ignored. I say "imagination," for I doubt extremely whether such an eccentric arrangement as a cruciform one can be found in any hornbook. Our ancestors had various faults, but they were practical, and not faddists; they seldom, too, moved out of a groove. In addition to the examples of hornbooks quoted, or representations that I have seen, I would give these: Minsheu (1617) has, " The Chrisse-cross (and Christ's cross) Row, or A B C;" Cotgrave, " Le croix de par Dieu, The Christ's-cross row, or the hornbook wherein a child learns it;" while Sherwood synonymizes the cross-row with " Le croix," etc., and with "l'Alphabet," this last work being omitted by Cotgrave. Again, Th. Cooper (1574) and Holyoke's " Rider," speak, under " Alphabetum " and " Abecedarius," not of the "cross-rows" nor of the "cross," but of "the cross " as synonymous with the alphabet; and Thomasius (1594) says, " The cross row, or A B C."— *Notes and Queries.*

Criticus. (Pseud.) Thomas Barnes, sometime editor of the London " Times."

Crito. (Pseud.) (1) One of the pseudonyms attributed to Junius (*q. v.*). (2) Rev. John Duncombe, a contributor to the " Gentleman's Magazine," 1765–1785.

Crittenden Compromise. " In 1860, when secession of the Southern States was threatening, John J. Crittenden, of Kentucky, offered a resolution that the Constitution be amended as follows : In all territory north of thirty-six degrees thirty minutes slavery was to be prohibited; in all territory south of that line it was to be protected. New States in either section were to determine for themselves. The resolution further declared that Congress had no power to abolish slavery in the District of Columbia as long as it existed in either Virginia or Maryland, nor without the consent of the inhabitants and compensation to non-assenting owners. Further provisions concerned slaves held by federal officers in the District, and damages for slaves freed by violence ; while still others prohibited Congress from abolishing the inter-State slave trade, and forbade future amendments to the Constitution changing any of these provisions, or Article 1, section 2, clause 3, and Article 4, section 2, clause 3, of the Constitution, or abolishing slavery in any State. Then followed resolutions which declared the fugitive slave laws to be constitutional, recommending some slight changes in them, and requesting the State legislatures to repeal or modify the 'personal-liberty laws,' and concluded by a denunciation of the African slave trade. It was not adopted." — BROWN AND STRAUSS.

Croaker. (Pseud.) Joseph Rodman Drake in the " Evening Post," New York (1819).

Crocodile's Tears. Hypocritical tears. The tale is, that crocodiles moan and sigh like a person in deep distress, to allure travellers to the spot, and even shed tears over their prey while in the act of devouring it.

Crocus. In classic mythology a youth who, suffering from unrequited affection for the nymph Smilax, was changed by the gods into a saffron plant.

Crœsus of English Abbeys. *See* RAMSAY THE RICH.

Cromwellian Board of Aldermen. A name given to a small body of men who in 1874–1875 claimed that they had been elected aldermen in New York. The newspapers dubbed them the Cromwellian Board, because they strove to get possession of the council-chamber.

Cronian Sea. The Frozen Ocean. The Cimbri called it " the dead sea."

As when two polar winds, blowing adverse,
Upon the Cronian Sea.
        MILTON, *Paradise Lost.*

Cronos. In classic mythology the youngest of the Titans.

Crook. A slang term for a sharper, —a *chevalier d' industrie.*

Croppies. An opprobrious name applied to Catholic Irishmen. Previous to and during the rebellion of 1798 in Ireland many brutal massacres and house-burnings were perpetrated by Orangemen. By the connivance of the English Government they were formed into yeomanry companies and battalions, whose privilege it was to ravage and destroy the lives, homes, and lands of all Irishmen suspected of the slightest hostility to English rule. The patriots formed themselves into an organization called the " United Irishmen." Theobald Wolfe Tone was the founder and director. He, though an Irishman, held a commission of high rank in the French army, and introduced into Ireland some of the customs of the French soldiery. One of these was cropping the hair closely. The United Irishmen adopted it, and they were dubbed Croppies. Hence the Orange tune, " Down, Croppies, lie down."

Croquis, Alfred. Daniel Maclise, R. A. This pseudonym was attached to a series of character-portraits in " Fraser's Magazine " between the years 1830 and 1838. Maclise was born 1811, and died 1870.

Crotona's Sage. Pythagoras.

Crow. From very early times — indeed, from the time of Noah — the crow has been looked upon as an unclean bird, not fit to serve as food for man. Hence the expression " to have to eat

crow" is synonymous with the performance of any distasteful gastronomic feat,
mental or physical, but is particularly applied to an enforced diet of metaphorical
carrion, such as eating one's words, and
the like.

The sentiment of the phrase "eating crow"
has been recognized in all ages; but the origin
of this particular form may have arisen from the
old tale of the poacher who compelled his captor
to finish the bird, or from the kindred story of
the officer and private. A soldier, having shot a
tame crow belonging to one of the officers, was
discovered by its owner with the dead bird in his
hand. Seizing the private's gun, the officer declared that, having killed the bird, he must eat
it; but no sooner had he returned the gun than
the soldier, pointing it at his companion's head,
vowed that he should finish the bird. The next
day the soldier was court-martialled; and when
asked by the examiners what had occurred the
day before to lead to his arrest, he coolly replied,
"Nothing, except that Captain Blank and I
dined together." Many anecdotes of the crow
have grown gray in the service of their country,
for one rarely hears or reads a political speech
that does not make use of the expression.

Crow, The. Mrs. Aitken (d. 1888), a
sister of Thomas Carlyle, was so known
among her family intimates and in correspondence on account of her swarthy
complexion.

Crown of the East. The city of Antioch, capital of Syria, which was composed of four distinct walled quarters,
the whole encompassed by a common
rampart, which "surrounded them like
a coronet."

Cruda viridisque senectus. (Lat.)
A vigorous and green old age.

Cruel, The. (1) Pedro, king of Castile (fl. 1334-1369). (2) Pedro I. of
Portugal (fl. 1320-1367).

Crux criticorum. (Lat.) The cross
or puzzle of critics.

Cry of Haro (*Clameur de Haro*). An
appeal for justice. It is said that Raoul,
or Rollo, of Normandy, administered
justice so impartially that injured persons cried "à Raoul !"

Cryptograms. Crypt or cipher writing is of very ancient origin, having
been used from time immemorial in
State or diplomatic correspondence
where secrecy was indispensable to
success or safety. Cryptograms or
private alphabets have been devised
which absolutely defy detection by
those not in possession of the key,
and to this class belong the modern
commercial and cable "codes," many
thousands of which are in use throughout the civilized and business world.

In recent years a series of novel contests raged in England which were based
on the selection of a given sentence and
the endeavor to make as many new
words therefrom as possible. Numerous prizes were offered to the persons
building up the largest list of names,
and the plan was also tried in the United
States to raise funds for a worthy public
object. In connection with these English
word-juggles a lady in London offered
thirty pounds for the translation of the
following ingenious cryptogram: "If the
B m t put : but if the B. putting : " The
answer is, "If the grate be empty, put
coal on ; but if the grate be full, stop
putting coal on."

A cryptogram once did good service in one
of the greatest astronomical discoveries of modern times, and the incident is thus related by
Mr. Langley in one of his "New Astronomy"
articles : " When Galileo first turned his glass
on Saturn he saw, as he thought, that it consisted of three spheres close together, the middle
one being the largest. He was not quite sure of
the fact, and was in a dilemma between his desire
to wait longer for further observation and his fear
that some other observer might announce the discovery if he hesitated. To combine these incom-
patibles — to announce it so as to secure the pri-
ority and yet not announce it till he was ready
— might seem to present as great a difficulty as
the discovery itself; but Galileo solved this by
writing it in the sentence, 'Altissimum planetam
tergeminum observavi' ('I have observed the
highest planet to be triple'), and then jumbling
the letters, which made the sentence into the
monstrous word,

SMAJSMRMJLMEPOETALEVNJBVNEMVGTTAJRAS,

and publishing this, which contained his discovery, but under lock and key. He had reason to
congratulate himself on his prudence, for within
two years two of the supposed bodies disappeared, leaving only one. This was in 1612, and
for nearly fifty years Saturn continued to all
astronomers the enigma which it was to Galileo,
till in 1656 it was finally made clear that it was
surrounded by a thin, flat ring which, when seen
fully, gave rise to the first appearance in Galileo's small telescope, and when seen edgewise
disappeared from its view altogether." This is
probably the only instance on record where crypt
writing became handmaid to science, though its
importance in the affairs of the present time can
scarcely be overrated.

Crystal Hills. (1) On the coast of
the Caspian, near Badku, is a mountain
which sparkles like diamonds, from the
sea-glass and crystals with which it
abounds. (2) An old poetical name for the
White Mountains in New Hampshire.

C. S. (1) Court of Sessions. (2) *Custos
Sigilli.* Keeper of the Seal.

Cs. Cases.

C. S. A. Confederate States of
America.

Csk. Cask.

C. S. N. Confederate States Navy.

C. T. Certificated Teacher.

Ct. Court.

C. Theod. *Codice Theodosiano.* In the Theodosian Code.

Ctl. Central.

Cts. Cents.

Cu. *Cuprum.* Copper.

Cub. Cubic.

Cubben Noach (" Old Noah "). The pen-name of the Swedish novelist, Carl Ekström (1836–1886).

Cub. ft. Cubic foot.

Cubittopolis. *See* MESOPOTAMIA.

Cuckold King. Mark of Cornwall. " His wife, Yseult, intrigued with Sir Tristram, one of the Knights of the Round Table."

Cuckold's Point. A very old name for a spot on the bank of the Thames near Deptford. It is traditionally related that here King John made successful love to a buxom farmer's wife.

Cucumber Time. The dull season in the tailoring trade. The Germans call it *Die saure Gurken Zeit* (pickled-gherkin time). Hence the expression : "Tailors are vegetarians, because they live on 'cucumber' when without work, and on 'cabbage' when in full employ."

Cuffey. Among spurious American-isms *cuffey* stands foremost. Constantly spoken of as a negro term, it is nothing more than a corruption of the slang term *covey.*

Cui bono? (Lat.) " For whose good?" For whose benefit is it? What good will it do?

Cuilibet in arte sua credendum est. (Lat.) Every man should be trusted in his own art or profession.

Cui malo? (Lat.) To whose harm?

Cul de sac. (Fr.) The bottom of the bag; a difficulty; a street or lane that has no outlet.

Cultivator Mary. Mrs. Mary Ase-nath Short, a well-known writer on agri-cultural and household topics in the "Ohio Cultivator."

Cumberland Poet. William Words-worth, who was born at Cockermouth.

Cum grano salis. (Lat.) " With a grain of salt." With some allowance or deduction.

Cum multis aliis. (Lat.) With many other things.

Cum notis variorum. (Lat.) With notes of various authors.

Cum privilegio. (Lat.) With privi-lege.

Cunning. A colloquial word signify-ing attractiveness, ingenuity, playful-ness; generally said of children.

Cunobelin's Gold Mines. Some caverns in the chalk cliffs of Little Thurrock, Essex, England, are so named on account of a legend that in them King Cunobelin hid his treasures. They are also called Dane Holes, from the fact that the Danish invaders used to lurk therein.

Cupboard Love. Love from inter-ested motives. The allusion is to the love of children for some indulgent per-son who gives them something nice from her cupboard.

Cupid. The son of Mars and Venus, and the god of love.

Cup-tosser. A juggler. The old symbol for a juggler was a goblet. The phrase and symbol are derived from the practice of jugglers, who toss in the air, twist on a stick, and play all sorts of tricks with goblets or cups.

Cur. Currency.

Curæ secundæ. (Lat.) Additional improvements, as in literary work.

Curate of Meudon. Rabelais (fl. 1483-1553). During the latter part of his life he was parish priest of Meudon.

Curator bonis. (Lat.) " One who cares for the goods." A guardian or trustee over property.

Curia advisari vult. The court wishes to be advised.

Curiosa felicitas. (Lat.) " Pains-taking felicity " (of expression). A lucky hit; a happy idea.

Currente calamo. (Lat.) " With a running pen." Off-hand; with great rapidity.

Currer Bell. (Pseud.) Charlotte Brontë (Mrs. Nichols), 1816-1855.

Currer Lyle. (Pseud.) Mrs. M. L. R. Crossley, in the " Literary Companion," Newnan, Ga.

Curry favor. To curry a horse was to rub him down, comb him, and dress him. *Favel* was a general name for a chestnut horse, derived from the French *faveau,* the color of fallow land or chest-nut. The phrase was originally " to curry

Favel," but it has been corrupted. The saying no doubt originated in the case of a favorite horse *Favel*, to curry whom well was a sure passport to the favor of his master.

Curse of Cowdray. Cowdray, near Midhurst, in England, was, until its destruction by fire on Sept. 24, 1793, one of the largest and finest of the great Tudor houses, of which Hatfield and Audley End are, though much later in date, perhaps the two best-known surviving examples. The "curse of fire and water" had been invoked on the family by the despoiled monks, and it required but little superstition to believe that such a frightful double disaster was the fulfilment of it. "The curse of Cowdray" has become a well-known phrase since the curse was apparently fulfilled in 1793. In that year, almost on the same day, the young owner, the eighth Lord Montague, was drowned in the Rhine, and the beautiful house was totally destroyed by fire.

Curse of Scotland. The nine of diamonds is so named. There are a number of explanations of the origin of this allusion. In the distracted state of the country during the reign of Mary, a man named George Campbell attempted to steal the crown out of Edinburgh Castle. He did not succeed in getting away with the crown itself, but did manage to abstract nine valuable diamonds, and to get off with them out of the country. To replace these a heavy tax was laid upon the people, which, being found burdensome and oppressive, was by them termed the Curse of Scotland; and until quite recently, in certain districts of Scotland, the card itself was called "George Campbell." Another explanation relates to the massacre of Glencoe, which is well remembered. The order for this cruel deed was signed by the eldest son of the Earl of Stair, who was at that time Secretary of State for Scotland. The coat-of-arms of this family bears nine diamonds on its shield; and the indignant people, not daring to stigmatize the Lord of Stair as the Curse of Scotland, applied the term to his shield. Still another solution, and equally good, relates to the battle of Culloden, the result of which extinguished the hopes of the Stuarts, and was at the time regarded as a national curse. The Duke of Cumberland, who was known to be very fond of cards,

and who always carried a pack in his pocket, when he had made his victory of Culloden complete, took a card from his pocket, and wrote thereon a despatch announcing his victory, and that card proved to be the nine of diamonds. Another authority says there are "two most plausible suggestions to account for the phrase: (1) The nine of diamonds in the game of 'Pope Joan' is called the Pope, the Antichrist of the Scotch Reformers. (2) In the game of 'Commette,' introduced by Queen Mary, it is the winning card; and the game was the curse of Scotland because it was the ruin of so many families.

Curt. Curtis's Supreme Court Reports.

Curtain Lecture. These words occur as a marginal reference in Sir R. Stapleton's "Translation of Juvenal's Sixth Satire," A. D. 1647, lines 267, 268, which he renders as follows: —

THE CURTAIN LECTURE.	Debates, alternate brawlings, ever were I' th' marriage bed; there is no sleeping there.

Curthose. Robert II., Duke of Normandy (fl. 1087–1134).

Curtius. (Pseud.) Dr. William Jackson in the Philadelphia "Ledger."

Curtmantle. The surname of Henry II. (1133–1189.) He introduced the Anjou mantle, which was shorter than the robe worn by his predecessors.

Cush. Cushing's Massachusetts Reports.

Custos rotulorum. (Lat.) "The keeper of the rolls." The officer in charge of the rolls or records of sessions of the peace, a county title usually borne by the Lord Lieutenant.

Cut Blocks with a Razor. Oliver Goldsmith said of Edmund Burke, the statesman,—

Too deep for his hearers, he went on refining,
And thought of convincing, while they thought
of dining;
Tho' equal to all things, to all things unfit:
Too nice for a statesman, too proud for a wit;
For a patriot too cool; for a drudge disobedient;
And too fond of the *right* to pursue the *expedient*.
In short, 't was his fate, unemployed or in place,
sir,
To eat mutton cold, and cut blocks with a razor.
Retaliation.

Cuthbert Bede. (Pseud.) Rev. Edmund Bradley, English poet (b. 1827).

Cute, Cuteness. This so-called Americanism appears to be older than

Goldsmith's "Good-Natured Man." In the "Percy Anecdotes: Benevolence" there is a story of an old woman who addressed Arbuthnot as "a cute doctor." No reference is given; but if it is a genuine contemporary anecdote, it brings "cute" up to the time of Queen Anne. Foote uses "cute" in "The Commissary" (1765), act iii.: "I did not know but they might be apter, more cuterer now in catching their larning." He has also the adverb in "The Orators" (1762), act i.: "I did speechify once at a vestry concerning new lettering the church buckets, and came off cutely enough." "Cute, a low word, used instead of acute," is given in B. Martin's "English Dictionary" (1754). — *Notes and Queries.*

Cut of his Jib. The foremost sail of a ship is called the jib; and its shape indicates, to some extent, the class of vessel bearing it. At sea, particularly in war-time, every vessel coming in sight is carefully scanned; and if the strange craft looks suspicious, the man on the lookout expresses his opinion by saying, "I don't like the cut of her jib." The expression is easily transferred by Jack to the personal appearance of any person to whom he may feel a dislike.

Cutting off with a Shilling. Blackstone says that "the Romans were wont to set aside testaments as being *inofficiosa*, deficient in natural duty, if they disinherited or totally passed by any of the children of the testator. But if the child had any legacy, however small, it was a proof that the testator had not lost his reason or his memory, which otherwise the law presumed. Hence, probably, has arisen that groundless error of the necessity of leaving the heir a shilling, or some express legacy, in order to disinherit him effectually. Whereas the law of England makes no such constrained suppositions of forgetfulness or insanity, and therefore, though the heir or next of kin be totally omitted, it admits no *querela inofficiosa* to set aside such a testament."

Cut your Stick. A writer in "Notes and Queries," who dates from Glasgow, says this phrase originated as follows: "About the year 1820 a song was sung in the Salt Market, Glasgow, beginning,

"Oh, I creished my brogues, and I cut my stick."

The song related the adventures of an Irishman; and of course the 'cutting of the stick' referred to the common practice in Ireland of procuring a sapling before going off. It afterwards became the practice, when any one ran off or absconded, to say, 'That chap has cut his stick too;' and thus the phrase originated and spread over the country. Americans claim the origin of this phrase. They say it arose from the fact that runaway slaves usually cut a great stick before starting, to help them on their way. Advertisements of runaway slaves were headed with woodcuts of a negro with a stick and bundle over his shoulder. Some have thought that the phrase may have originated in a printing-office, where a compositor who wanted a holiday, said "I shall cut the stick [composing-stick] for to day, and have a walk instead."

C. W. Canada West.

Cwt. Hundredweight.

Cybele. In classic mythology the daughter of Cœlus and Terra, and wife of Saturn. She was called the Mother of the Gods.

Cyc. Cyclopædia.

Cyclic Poets. "Inferior epic poets. On the death of Homer a host of minstrels caught the contagion of his poems, and wrote continuations, illustrations, or additions thereto. These poets were called *cyclic* because they confined themselves to the cycle of the Trojan war. The chief were Strasinos, Arctinos, Lesches, Agias, and Eugamon."

Cyclopean Masonry. Generally applied to the old Pelasgic ruins of Greece, such as the Gallery of Tiryns, the Gate of Lions, the Treasury of Athens, and the Tombs of Phoroneus and Danaos. They are said to have been the work of the Cyclops.

Cyclops. In classic mythology a giant race, having only one eye, who peopled the sea-coasts of Sicily.

Cynosure. In classic mythology a nymph of Idæa, the nurse of Jupiter, who placed her in the constellation Ursa Minor as the pole-star.

Cynthia. A surname of Diana, derived from Mount Cynthus, her birthplace.

Cynthius. A surname of Apollo, from Mount Cynthus, his birthplace.

Cyparissus. In classic mythology a beautiful youth, the favorite of Apollo, whose pet stag he accidentally killed.

Immoderate grief seized him on account of this mishap, and he was changed into a cypress.

Cyprian. A woman of easy virtue, so named from the island of Cyprus, where was one of the chief temples of Venus.

Cyrenaic School. Founded by Aristippos of Cyrene, in Africa. The chief dogma of this philosopher was that pleasure and pain are the criterions of what is good and bad.

Cyrenians. Philosophers of a school founded by Aristippos of Cyrene, a Grecian colony on the northern coast of Africa. They were an offshoot of the Epicureans.

Cyrus. (Pseud.) Another pen-name of George John Stevenson, M.A. *See* ALBION.

Cythera. In classic mythology a surname of Venus, derived from the town of the name in Crete, where the goddess was said to have first set foot on earth, and where she had a temple.

Czar of Pennsylvania Politics. Simon Cameron, the statesman (1799–1889), has been so named.

D.

D. (1) *Denarius* or *Denarii.* Penny or pence. (2) Died. (3) Five hundred.

Dabney, Isle de. *See* ISLE DE DABNEY.

Da capo, or **D. C.** (Ital.) "From the beginning." A musical expression often written at the end of a movement to indicate that the performer must return to the beginning and finish with the first strain.

Da capo senza repetitione, e poi la coda. (Ital.) Begin again, but with any repetition of the strain, and then proceed to the coda. (Mus.)

Da dextram misero. (Lat.) "Give the right hand to the unfortunate." Give a helping hand to the unfortunate.

Dædalus. In classic mythology an artist of Athens, who arranged the Cretan labyrinth, and who, by the aid of a pair of wings he constructed, fled from Crete across the Ægean Sea to escape the anger of Minerva.

D. A. G. Deputy Adjutant-General.

Dagger Scene in the House of Commons. It is well known that during the French Revolution Burke created a great sensation by suddenly throwing a dagger upon the floor of the House of Commons, vociferating, "There is French fraternity for you! Such is the poniard which French Jacobins would plunge in the heart of our Sovereign." It is said that Sheridan threw great ridicule upon this theatrical exhibition by saying, "The gentleman has brought his knife with him, but where's the fork?" At any rate, the matter created great amusement at Burke's expense.

Dago. A nickname for a Spaniard; a corruption of *hidalgo.*

Dagon. A Phœnician divinity, with the face and hands of a man and the tail of a fish.

Dagonet. (Pseud.) George Robert Sims, in the London "Referee" from 1877 on.

Dahak. The Satan of the Persian religion.

Daikoku. In Japanese mythology the god of artisans.

Dai-niz-no-Rai. In Japanese mythology the god of the sun.

Daisy Eyesbright. The pseudonym of Mrs. S. O. Johnson, a writer on women's topics of the present day.

Daisy Howard. (Pseud.) Myra Daisy McCrum.

Daisy Oakley. The stage-name of Mrs. Roger Harding.

Dak. Dakota.

Dakota. This is a Sioux word, meaning "many-headed," or many in one government, referring to a confederation of Sioux tribes under one chief.

Dal. (Ital.) By; as, *Dal segno,* from the sign; a mark of repetition. (Mus.)

Dall. Dallas's Pennsylvania Reports.

Da locum melioribus. (Lat.) Give way to your betters.

Dames quêteuses. (Fr.) "Lady collectors; money-gathering or collecting ladies." Ladies who collect privately for convents or to relieve certain poor under their care.

Damiens's Attempt. Louis XV. of France was stabbed in the right side with a knife by Damiens, a native of Arras, Jan. 5, 1757; the would-be assassin was broken on the wheel March 28 of the same year.

Damiens's Bed of Steel. An instrument of torture to inflict punishment on R. F. Damiens (see *supra*), consisting of a sort of bed or reclining chair in which the culprit was confined by chains. The phrase is used to denote hardship, terror, or pain.

Damnant quod non intelligunt. (Lat.) They condemn what they do not understand.

Damning with Faint Praise. This phrase is from Pope's epistle to Dr. Arbuthnot: —

" Damn with faint praise, assent with civil leer,
And, without sneering, teach the rest to sneer."

Damocles's Sword. *See* SWORD OF DAMOCLES.

Damon and Pythias. Two noble youths (Pythagoreans) of Syracuse, whose friendship has caused them to be quoted to posterity as models of faithful friendship.

Pythias, having been condemned to death by Dionysius the tyrant of Syracuse, begged to be allowed to go home, for the purpose of arranging his affairs ; Damon pledging his own life for the reappearance of his friend. Dionysius consented, and Pythias returned just in time to save Damon from death. Struck by so noble an example of mutual affection, the tyrant pardoned Pythias, and desired to be admitted to their sacred fellowship. — CHAMBERS.

Damsel of Brittany. Eleanora, daughter of Geoffrey, second son of Henry II. of England, and Duke of Brittany. She was confined by King John in Bristol Castle until her death in 1241.

Dan. Daniel; Danish.

Danae. In classic mythology the daughter of Acrisius and mother of Perseus by Jupiter, who visited her in the form of a golden shower when she was imprisoned by her father.

Danai. An ancient name for the Greeks, derived from Danaus, king of Argos, 1474 B. C.

Danaides. In classic mythology the fifty daughters of Danaus, king of Argos, betrothed to fifty sons of Ægyptus, all of whom save one, Lynceus, they killed on the first night after marriage. They were punished for their crime in Hades by being compelled everlastingly to draw water out of a well and pour it into a vessel full of holes.

Dance of Death. The name given to a species of allegorical exhibitions illustrating the universal sway of death, and originating in the fourteenth century.

When the introduction of Christianity first banished the ancient Germanic conception of a future state, a new description of death-mythology arose, partly out of Biblical sources, partly out of the popular character itself, wherein the Last Enemy was represented under simple and majestic images, such as that of the husbandman watering the ground with blood, ploughing it with swords, rooting out weeds, plucking up flowers, felling trees, or sowing it with corpses ; or of a monarch assembling his armies, making war, taking prisoners, inviting his subjects to a festival, or citing them to judgment. But with a gradual change in national manners came a change in the mode of treating the subject, and it was associated with every-day images, such as the confessional, chess-playing, and above all, with the adjuncts of a festival, namely, music and dancing. This tendency to familiarize the theme increased during the confusion and turmoil of the fourteenth century, when the national mind alternated between fits of devotion and license, or blent both elements in satire and humor. Such a mood as this naturally occupied itself with personifying death, and adopted by preference the most startling and grotesque images it could find: that of a musician playing to dancing-men, or a dancer leading them on ; and as the dance and the drama were then intimately connected, and employed on religious occasions, this particular idea soon assumed a dramatic form. — CHAMBERS.

Dancing Chancellor. Sir Christopher Hatton (d. 1591), who was bred a lawyer, but became a courtier, having attracted the notice of Queen Elizabeth by his graceful dancing at a court masque. She created him Lord Chancellor and a K. G.

Dan de le Dooley. (Pseud.) James Burke, who wrote " Pictures of New York Boy Life " (1883).

Dandeprat, or **Dandyprat.** A nickname for a small, inconsequential man. A *dandeprat* was a very small coin issued in the reign of Henry VII.

Dandy Wayne. A sobriquet applied to the famous Anthony Wayne (1745–1796), because of his fastidious attention to dress. *See* MAD ANTHONY.

Dane Holes. *See* CUNOBELIN'S GOLD MINES.

Daniel Shelby. The stage-name of Daniel J. Macher.

Daniel Stern. (Pseud.) Marie de Flavigny, Comtesse d'Agoult, French authoress (b. 1800).

Daphne. In classic mythology a lovely maiden adored by Apollo, changed into a laurel tree while trying to elude him.

Darby and Joan. A loving, old-fashioned, virtuous couple. The names belong to a ballad written by Henry Woodfall, and the characters are those of John Darby of Bartholomew Close, who died 1730, and his wife, "as chaste as a picture cut in alabaster. You might sooner move a Scythian rock than shoot fire into her bosom."

Darbyites. The Plymouth Brethren are so called after Mr. Darby, a barrister, who abandoned himself to the work, and was for years the "organ" of the sect.

Dark Ages. A term synonymous with "Middle Ages" — a period of about one thousand years, from the invasion of France by Clovis (486), to that of Naples by Charles VIII. — throughout which learning was at a very low ebb.

Dark and Bloody Ground. A name frequently applied to the State of Kentucky. It is said to be a translation of the Indian words "Kain-tuk-ee," though some authorities claim that they signify "at the head of the river." The epithet was originally bestowed because the region was the scene of many sanguinary conflicts between the red men of the Northern and Southern tribes. Later, the constant feuds between white settlers and the aborigines rendered the phrase peculiarly appropriate to this locality.

Dark Continent, The. Africa, in allusion to the almost total ignorance concerning the people and geography of its interior which until quite recently prevailed in Europe and America.

Dark Days. Occasions chronicled in history when the light of the sun has been so bedimmed as to cause serious inconvenience, if not terror, to mankind. The principal ones are given below. A dark day occurred in New England, May 19, 1780, during the session of the Connecticut Legislature at Hartford, which occasioned a proposition to adjourn. Remarkable dark days occurred B. C. 295, A. D. 252, 746, and 775; and the darkness which was "over all the earth" during the three hours of the Crucifixion is familiar to all. There was a dark day in England, January, 1807, and another Oct. 21, 1816. The 19th of October, 1762, was a dark day in Detroit; a remarkable instance of darkness of brief duration occurred in Canada, Oct. 16, 1863. London, for the greater part of the time enveloped in fog and smoke, has been greatly subject to dark days, among which may be mentioned May 10, 1812; Dec. 27, 28, and 29, 1813; and Nov. 27, 1816. "Several hypotheses have been suggested to account for these phenomena, the smoke of burning forests, volcanic smoke and ashes, vapors generated by internal heat, smoke from meteors, cosmical dust drifting from outer space into the atmosphere, terrestrial dust from deserts, and ordinary clouds reinforced by smoke from furnaces and factories, being among the suggestions."

Dark Horse. A frequent phrase in sporting and political parlance, and indicating one who, up to a certain time kept in the background, suddenly comes to the front, and snatches victory from the hands of others. The phrase, in its most recent sense, was used by Thackeray in his "Adventures of Philip." Said Philip, referring to some talk about a candidate for Parliament: "Well, bless my soul, he can't mean me. Who is the dark horse he has in his stable?" It also occurred in Lord Beaconsfield's "Young Duke." This brilliant novel had great vogue in this country fifty years ago; and May Dacre, the heroine, who gave her name to the "dark horse," had many namesakes in the racing calendars of that time. Here is the paragraph: —

"The first favorite was never heard of, the second favorite was never seen after the distance post, all the ten-to-ones were in the rear, and a dark horse which had never been thought of rushed past the grand stand in sweeping triumph."

Darley Arabians. A breed of English racers, from an Arab stallion introduced by a Mr. Darley. This stallion was the sire of "Flying Childers," and great-grandsire of "Eclipse."

Darnell's Case. A noted case in English constitutional law (1627), in which the imprisonment of Sir Thomas Darnell and four others, for refusing to subscribe to a forced loan, was sanctioned, the agitation resulting from which was followed by the granting of the Petition of Right.

Dartmoor Massacre. "During the war of 1812 many of the American prisoners captured by the British were confined in a prison at Dartmoor, Devonshire. At the close of the war there were several thousands of these, besides twenty-five hundred impressed sailors who claimed to be American seamen and refused to fight in the British navy against the United States. Some of these seamen had been imprisoned for years before the war broke out. The prisoners, not being released immediately on their hearing of the treaty of peace, grew impatient. Rigorous discipline and lack of satisfactory food further excited them, and there were signs of insubordination. On April 6, 1815, the guard fired on them, killing several and wounding more. This occurrence was, probably, the result of a mistake; but when the news of it reached this country it was called the ' Dartmoor Massacre,' and excited bitter feelings against England." — BROWN AND STRAUSS.

Dartmouth College Case. The leading American case (1819) on the vested rights of corporations, reported as Trustees of Dartmouth College v. Woodward (4 Wheaton, 518), deciding that a corporate charter, even though it be a British charter granted before the Revolution, cannot be materially altered by a State legislature, it being a contract within the meaning of the provision of the United States Constitution which deprives the States of the power to impair the obligation of a contract.

Dart of Abaris. Abaris, the Scythian, a priest of Apollo; the god gave him a golden arrow on which to ride through the air. This dart rendered him invisible; it also cured diseases, and gave oracles.

The dart of Abaris carried the philosopher wheresoever he desired it. — WILLMOTT.

Dat. Dative.

David Goodman. The name under which David G. Croly (d. 1889) edited "The Modern Thinker," published in New York, 1870–1873.

Davy Jones. The sailor-man's synonym for death. "Davy Jones's locker" is a euphony for the ocean grave which so often proves his last resting-place.

Day of Barricades. Several days in French history have been thus named: (1) May 12, 1588, when the populace rose against Henry III. (2) August 27,

1688, the beginning of the Fronde war. (3) June 27, 1830, the beginning of the uprising which drove Charles X. from the throne. (4) Feb. 24, 1848, when Louis Philippe was driven to abdicate. (5) June 23, 1848, when Abbé Affre, Archbishop of Paris, was shot in attempting to quell an uprising. (6) Dec. 2, 1851, the occasion of Louis Napoleon's *coup d'état*.

Day of Cornsacks. Jan. 3, 1591; so named on account of an attempt to surprise Paris made by Henry IV. on that date. Some of his adherents, disguised as corndealers, with meal-bags on their shoulders, tried to get possession of the St. Honoré Gate, but were detected and repulsed.

Day of Dupes. (1) Nov. 11, 1630, so named in reference to the defeat which overtook the opponents of Richelieu, headed by Marie de' Medici, and Anne of Austria, in an effort to effect his removal and disgrace. (2) August 4, 1789, received this name because it witnessed the renunciation by the French nobles and clergy of all their peculiar privileges.

Day of Gold Spurs. Another name for Battle of Spurs (2) (*q. v.*).

Day of New Clothes. Christmas Day; from an old French custom of giving those who belonged to the court new cloaks on that day.

On Christmas Eve, 1245, the king [Louis XI.] bade all his court be present at early morning Mass. At the chapel door each man received his new cloak, put it on, and went in. . . . As the day rose, each man saw on his neighbor's shoulder betokened " the crusading vow." — KITCHIN, *History of France.*

Day of the Annunciation. The 25th of March, also called Lady Day, on which the angel announced to the Virgin Mary that she would be the mother of the Messiah.

Day of the Camel. Nov. 4, 656 (or, according to some, 658 or 659), when Talha and Zobehr, rebellious Arab chieftains, were roasted to death by the Caliph Ali. Ayesha, the widow of Mohammed, viewed the conflict from the back of a camel, whence the name.

Day of the Sections. Oct. 4, 1793; so named because of an affray which occurred between the troops directed by the Convention and the National Guard acting for the sections of Paris. The soldiery of the Convention were successful.

Daysman. An old English word for an arbitrator or umpire. It is used in Job ix. 33, " Neither is there any daysman betwixt us." Also it is used in an old play quoted by Nares : —

If neighbours were at variance they ran not
     streight to law,
Daiesmen took up the matter and cost them
     not a straw.
                              Newe Custome.

Spenser has "dayes man " in the " Faerie Queene," viii. 28. It is also used by some of the old Puritan writers in reference to Christ, who is called the *Daysman* between God and man. The origin is not accurately known. Nares says, " from his fixing a day for decision ; " but this is hardly satisfactory.

Day, Saint Distaff's. See DISTAFF'S DAY, SAINT.

D. B., or Domesd. B. Domesday Book.

D. C. (1) *Da Capo.* Again. (2) District of Columbia.

D. C. L. Doctor of Civil Law.

D. C. S. Deputy Clerk of Session.

D. D. *Divinitatis doctor.* Doctor of Divinity.

D. D. S. Doctor of Dental Surgery.

Dea. Deacon.

Deacon. (Pseud.) Hiram Calkins, sometime Albany correspondent of the " Spectator," New York.

Deacon of a Trade. In Scotland, the president, for the time being, of an incorporated trade, formerly representing his trade or craft in the town council. In Edinburgh and Glasgow the deacon-convener of the trades is still a member of the town council. One of the duties of the office in former times was to essay, or try, the work of apprentices previous to their admission to the freedom of the trade.

Deacon off. " To give the cue. Derived from a custom, once universal but now extinct, in the New England Congregational churches. An important part of the office of deacon was to read aloud the hymns given out by the minister, one line at a time, the congregation singing each line as soon as read." — LOWELL.

" In some of the interior parts of New England the custom of ' deaconing off ' hymns is still continued. It used to be called ' lining out the psalm.' The custom is nearly as old as the Reformation, and long antedates early colonial days in New England. It was recommended to churches not supplied with books, by the Westminster Assembly, in 1664 ; and Dr. Watts complained of its prevalence in congregations and private families in England, — in the preface to an early edition of his psalms." — BARTLETT.

Dead as a Doornail. This seemingly odd simile is at least as old as the time of Shakspeare ; for Pistol remarks to Falstaff that the king is as dead " as the nail in a door." Doors of the sixteenth and seventeenth centuries were furnished with nails upon which the knockers fell ; hence the phrase is used to denote one irrecoverably dead, — death such as reiterated strokes on the head would naturally produce.

Dead as a Herring. It is a rare thing, even for fishermen, to see a really live herring. The fish dies the instant it is taken out of the water.

Dead as Chelsea. To get Chelsea ; to obtain the benefit of that hospital. " Dead as Chelsea, by G—d ! " — an exclamation uttered by a grenadier at Fontenoy, on having his leg carried away by a cannon-ball.

Dead Beat. (Pseud.) Joseph Howard, Jr., in Brooklyn " Eagle."

Dead-broke. *See* BROKE.

Dead Rabbit Riots. On Saturday, July 4, 1857, a fierce combat took place in Mulberry and Bayard and the Bowery, New York, between two desperate factions known as " Dead Rabbits " and " Bowery Boys." No particular cause was assigned for this outbreak except the disorganized condition of the police department of the city, following the change from the Municipal to the Metropolitan force, and the absence of the usual police restraint, which afforded a favorable opportunity for the denizens of the Sixth Ward and the neighboring districts to settle their old grudges and disputes by force of arms. Stones, clubs, and firearms were employed indiscriminately ; the police failed to restore order, and the fight ended by mutual consent or from physical exhaustion. On Sunday, July 5, the conflict was renewed with increased violence, the locality known as the Five Points being the scene of the riot. Firearms were freely and effectually used. At four o'clock in the afternoon orders were issued for the military to assemble, and at eight o'clock the Seventh Regiment marched to the City Arsenal in Elm Street. But the rioters had either completed the performances of the day to their mutual satisfaction, or had taken advantage of a timely notice to curtail their amusements; for when the troops reached their destination the "Dead Rabbits" had disappeared, and the streets assumed their usual quiet appearance.

Dead Sea. *See* CRONIAN SEA.

Dead-weight Loan. In 1823 the Bank of England loaned £11,000,000 to the English Government, to construct new ordnance, etc. It acquired its name from the locking up of the bank's capital which thus ensued.

Dean of St. Patrick's. A title by which Jonathan Swift (fl. 1667–1745), the famous satirist, is often alluded to. He was appointed to the post (in Dublin) in 1713, and filled it until his death.

"Dear Beaver: Don't Talk." This famous phrase originated in 1882 in this way: Col. William Rodearmel, the well-known Harrisburg newspaper correspondent, on the day that Beaver was nominated for Governor, remarked that he intended to get an interview out of him. The remark was heard by Quay, who had his reasons for keeping Beaver quiet. He asked Colonel Rodearmel if he would take a note to Beaver from him (Quay). The Colonel readily consented to bear the message, and Quay wrote it, sealed it, and the Colonel took it. Beaver opened the note, read it, and laid it on the table in his room, face upward, so that Colonel Rodearmel could not help seeing it. It contained only these words: "DEAR BEAVER: Don't talk. — QUAY." Dear Beaver did not talk, and Colonel Rodearmel is still waiting for his interview.

Death, Hour of. *See* HOUR OF DEATH.

Death-or-Glory Boys. A by-name for the Seventh Lancers (English), on account of the device of a death's head and cross-bones with the legend "Or Glory," which adorns their caps.

Death Ride. The charge of the Light Brigade at Balaklava, Oct. 25, 1854. In this action six hundred English horsemen, under the command of the Earl of Cardigan, charged a Russian force of five thousand cavalry and six battalions of infantry. They galloped through the battery of thirty guns, cutting down the artillerymen, and through the cavalry; but then discovered the battalions, and cut their way back again. Of the six hundred and seventy who advanced to this daring charge, not two hundred returned. This reckless exploit was the result of some misunderstanding in an order from the commander-in-chief. Tennyson has a poem on the subject, called "The Charge of the Light Brigade."

For chivalrous devotion and daring, "the Death Ride" of the Light Brigade will not easily be paralleled. — SIR EDWARD CREASY, *Fifteen Decisive Battles.*

Debatable Land, The. On the western frontier of England and Scotland, between the rivers Esk and Sark, there formerly existed a strip of territory jurisdiction over which was claimed by both countries. As a consequence, no settled authority could long make itself felt, and the locality became a haven of refuge for robbers and criminals, who preyed alike on English and Scots. In 1542 "it was divided by royal commissions appointed by the two crowns." By their award this land of contention was separated by a line drawn from east to west between the two rivers. The upper half was adjudged to Scotland, and the more eastern part to England. The Græmes, a troublesome clan of freebooters who inhabited the Debatable Land, were transported to Ireland at the beginning of the seventeenth century, and prohibited from returning on pain of death.

Debito justitiæ. (Lat.) By a debt of justice.

Debitum naturæ. (Lat.) "The debt of nature." Death.

De bonis non. (Lat.) Of the goods not yet administered on.

Débonnaire, Le. Louis I. of France (fl. 778–840). He was called by the English "The Meek."

De bonne grâce. (Fr.) "With good grace." Willingly.

Deborah Dunn. (Pseud.) Mrs. Frank R. Stockton, in various journals.

Debt of Nature. The origin of this phrase is probably the following from "Quarles's Emblems," 12, 13: —

"The slender debt to Nature's quickly paid, Discharged perchance with greater ease than made."

Debts of Honor, *i. e.*, losses at gambling, are so termed because the law cannot be relied on to enforce their liquidation, and the winner must trust to the "honor" of the loser for payment.

Début. (Fr.) First appearance; the beginning of an enterprise.

Dec. December; declination,

Deceptio visûs. (Lat.) An illusion of the sight.

Decius. (Pseud.) Samuel Jackson Gardner, sometime editor of the Newark "Daily Advertiser."

Dec. of Ind. Declaration of Independence.

Decoration Day. *See* MEMORIAL DAY.

De Courcy's Privilege. In 1203 John de Courcy, baron of Kingsale, was granted the privilege by King John of standing covered before royalty, and the right was also extended to his successors. The ancient privilege is still in force.

Decree of Fontainebleau. An edict dated Oct. 18, 1800, by which Napoleon directed that all English goods should be burned.

Decrescendo, or **Diminuendo.** (Ital.) Gradual diminution of tone (Mus.)

Decretals, False. A collection of Papal letters, etc., chiefly forgeries, ascribed to Isidorus Mercator, and dating from the first half of the ninth century. The object of the deception, which was first detected by German Protestant critics in the sixteenth century, was to exalt the ecclesiastical system above the civil; and upon it, as some Protestant historians assert, is based the claims to supremacy of the Catholic hierarchy.

Decus et tutamen. (Lat.) Honor and defence.

Decus summum virtus. (Lat.) Virtue the highest honor.

De die in diem. (Lat.) From day to day.

Dedimus potestatem. (Lat.) We have given power.

Deer-meat. Venison.

Def. Definition.

Def., or **Deft.** Defendant.

De facto. (Lat.) "From the fact." Actually; because it is so.

Defence Government. The name of the government established in France, Sept. 4, 1870, after Napoleon III. was deposed, and of which General Trochu was president. It resigned when Paris capitulated, Feb. 5 and 6, 1871. Gambetta and Simon were included in it.

Defender of the Faith. Henry VIII. of England received this title at the hands of Pope Leo X. in 1521, for a Latin treatise on the Seven Sacraments. *See* CATHOLIC MAJESTY AND MOST CHRISTIAN KING.

Defender of Thermopylæ. Leonidas.

Defenders. *See* PEEP-O'-DAY BOYS.

Defenders' Day. September 12 in Baltimore. In 1842 one thousand men formed the Old Defenders' Association of Baltimore, and on September 12 of each year celebrated the battle of North Point, fought in 1812.

Defend me from my Friends. The French assign to Maréchal Villars taking leave of Louis XIV., this aphorism: "Defend me from my friends; I can defend myself from my enemies."

But of all plagues, good Heaven, thy wrath can send,
Save, save, oh, save me from the candid friend!
CANNING, *The New Morality.*

Deficit. A want or deficiency.

De fumo in flammam. (Lat.) "From the smoke into the flame." Out of the frying-pan into the fire."

Deg. Degree; degrees.

De gaieté du cœur. (Fr.) "From gayety of heart." Sportively; without motive.

De Golyer Contract. A famous episode in American politics. In the forty-third Congress there was an investigation into the conduct of the government of the District of Columbia, which revealed startling frauds in the matter of paving streets. The facts would seem to be as follows:—

In May, 1872, Richard C. Parsons, a Cleveland attorney, then marshal of the Supreme Court in Washington, having the interests of the patents owned by De Golyer in charge, was called away. He brought all his material to James A. Garfield, and asked him to prepare the brief. This brief was to show the superiority of the pavement (the subject of patent) over forty other kinds, and did not otherwise concern the contract, or have anything to do with its terms. The fraud, as is generally understood, was in the contract, not in the quality of the pavement. Garfield prepared the brief, and delivered it to Parsons, but did not himself make an argument. Parsons sent Garfield subsequently $5,000, which was part of the fee Parsons had received for his own services. The matter was brought up against Garfield during the Presidential canvass of 1880, and corrupt motives alleged against him; but as thoughtful people reviewed the case there was no harsher criticism than that suggested by Garfield's own lofty standard of avoiding even the appearance of evil,—that he had not shown his usual prudence in avoiding connection with any matter that could possibly come up for Congressional review.—APPLETON.

De gustibus non est disputandum. (Lat.) About tastes there is no disputing.

De haute lutte. (Fr.) By main force.

Dei gratiâ. (Lat.) By the grace of God.

Deiphobus. One of the sons of Priam, and, next to Hector, the bravest and boldest of all the Trojans. On the death of his brother Paris, he married Helen ; but Helen betrayed him to her first husband, Menelaus, who slew him.

Dejanira. In classic mythology daughter of Œneus and wife of Hercules, whose death she unwittingly caused by sending him a poisoned shirt, which had been steeped in the blood of Nessus, who told her that the one to whom she presented it would love her with undying love. When she heard that Hercules had put an end to his life to escape the torture it inflicted, she killed herself in remorse and despair.

Déjeuner à la fourchette. (Fr.) A meat breakfast ; "a breakfast with forks."

Déjeuner dinatoire. (Fr.) A breakfast serving as a dinner.

De jure. (Lat.) "From the law." Legally.

De Kalb. (Pseud.) Mrs. Kate Cross in the " Canadian Press."

Del. Delaware ; delegate.

Del. *Delineavit.* He (or she) drew it.

Delafield. (Pseud.) Mrs. M. L. Child in " Arthur's Magazine."

Delaware. This State derives its name from Thomas West, Lord De la Ware, governor of Virginia in colonial times.

Delayer, The. (Lat., *Cunctator.*) An honorable surname given to the Roman general Quintus Fabius Maximus Verrucosus (d. 203 B. C.), "because of his cautious but salutory measures in opposing the progress of Hannibal."

Dele. Erase.

Delenda est Carthago. (Lat.) "Carthage must be destroyed." Used to signify a war of extermination.

Delian King. Apollo, or the Sun, is so called in the Orphic hymn.

Oft as the Delian king with Sirius holds
The central heavens.
AKENSIDE, *Hymn to the Naiads.*

Delicate Investigation, The. An inquiry into the conduct of the Princess of Wales (afterward queen of England as consort of George IV.) commenced by a Committee of the Privy Council May 29, 1806. The charges were disproved.

Delicatezza. (Ital.) Delicacy of expression. (Mus.)

Delicato. (Ital.) Delicately. (Mus.)

Delightful = DELICIOUS. This use of "delightful" for "delicious" in such a sentence as " The ice-cream is delightful," is very common in the Southern States.

Delight of Mankind. Titus, the Roman emperor (A. D. 40–81).

Titus indeed gave one short evening gleam,
More cordial felt, as in the midst it spread
Of storm and horror : " The Delight of Men."
THOMSON, *Liberty.*

Della Crusca. (Pseud.) Robert Merry, English poet and dramatist (1755–1798).

Della-Cruscan School. So called from Crusca, the Florentine academy. The name is applied to a school of poetry started by some young Englishmen at Florence in the latter part of the eighteenth century. Their silly, sentimental affectations, which appeared in the " World " and the " Oracle," created for a time quite a furor. The whole affair was mercilessly gibbeted in the " Baviad " and " Mæviad " of Mr. Gifford.

Delphi of New England. Concord, Mass., is so named. Ralph Waldo Emerson lived there from 1835 till his death, and through his wise sayings the village became famous as "the Delphi of New England."

Delphic Oracle. *See* ORACLE.

Delphin Classics. An edition of the Greek and Roman classics prepared by thirty of the leading scholars of the day, edited by Bossuet and Huet, tutors to the Dauphin, son of Louis XIV. The titlepages bear the words "In usum Serenissimi Delphini," whence the name. They are lightly regarded by scholars of the present day.

Delta. (Pseud.) (1) Edward Denham in " Good Literature," New York. (2) Henry W. Domett, sometime New York correspondent of the " Boston Transcript." (3) Rev. Moses Harvey, Canadian correspondent. (4) David MacBeth Moir, Scottish writer and physician (1778–1851).

Delta City. Alexandria in Egypt.

Dem. Democrat ; Democratic.

Demens Egomet. (Pseud.) Thomas Williams, a New England clergyman (1779–1876), published several sermons over this signature.

Demeter. One of the fabulous divinities of the Greeks, akin to the Ceres of the Romans.

Demijohn. (Pseud.) F. Alcott Pratt, an American *littérateur* of the present day.

Demi-monde. Women of easy virtue, as opposed to *le beau monde*, fashionable society.

Demi-rep. A woman whose reputation will not bear scrutiny.

Democratic Federals. An English political party proposed by Joseph Cowen, M. P. for Newcastle, and opposed to the policy of Mr. Gladstone, 1881.

Democrats. Advocates for government by the people themselves (δῆμος, "people," and κρατεῖν, "to govern "), a term adopted by the French republicans in 1790 (who termed their opponents "aristocrats," from ἄριστος, "bravest or best "). The name Democrat was adopted by one of the two great political parties of the United States before the present and recent questions entered into politics, and was at its prime during the Jacksonian ascendancy. The political features of Jackson's administration were the opposition to the United States Bank, the denial of the right of any State to nullify the laws of Congress, and the excitement over the tariff question. In 1836, through the influence of Jackson, Martin Van Buren was elected President, and during his administration the prestige of the Democratic party began to wane. In 1837 the country went through a severe commercial panic. Credit, speculation, and banking had been carried to extreme limits, and disaster followed. For this state of affairs the administration was held responsible. The election of 1840 was a revolution; and in the choice of General Harrison by the electoral vote of 234 to 60 the Democratic party, after forty years of power, was forced to retire. But the Whig triumph was short-lived. General Harrison died one month after his inauguration, and John Tyler, who had been nominated for Vice-President to conciliate Virginia, succeeded to the presidential chair. All his life he had held and advocated Democratic doctrines, especially the

opposition to the United States Bank, a protective tariff, and internal improvements by the General Government. On his accession he continued the cabinet of his predecessor, Daniel Webster being Secretary of State But after two successive vetoes of the "Fiscal Bank of the United States " bill his cabinet left him, Mr. Webster remaining only till the conclusion of the Webster-Ashburton treaty, and his administration became essentially Democratic. In 1844 James K. Polk was elected President, after a bitter and exciting contest, over Henry Clay. The annexation of Texas, which was urged by the Democratic party, was the great question in determining this election, and was accomplished March 1, 1845, three days before the inauguration of Mr. Polk. This led to a war with Mexico, which was declared May 13, 1846. At its successful conclusion, not only was the Rio Grande established as the boundary of Texas, but all New Mexico and Upper California were relinquished to the United States. In March, 1820, an act, known as the Missouri Compromise, had been passed, forbidding the introduction of slavery in any of the States formed from the Louisiana cession north of thirty-six degrees thirty minutes. On August 8, 1846, the rejection of the so-called Wilmot Proviso by the Senate — which provided "That, as an express and fundamental condition to the acquisition of any territory from the Republic of Mexico by the United States, . . . neither slavery nor involuntary servitude shall ever exist in any part of said territory " — became the starting-point of the Free Soil party in 1848. Mr. Wilmot, the mover, was a Democrat. The popularity of General Taylor caused the defeat of Lewis Cass in the election of 1848, and the Democratic party went out of power till 1853, when Franklin Pierce became President. In 1856 it elected James Buchanan President, and John C. Breckenridge Vice-President. At the convention held in Charleston, S. C., April, 1856, the slavery issue caused a disruption of the party, — the slave section nominating John C. Breckenridge, and the free-soilers Stephen A. Douglas, — and, on Mr. Lincoln's election, it lost the supremacy which it had held with little interruption for sixty years. It had, however, a vigorous life, and contested hotly every Presidential election, its unsuccessful candidates being George B. McClellan, in 1864; Horatio Seymour, in 1868; Horace Greeley, in 1872; Samuel J. Tilden, in 1876; and Winfield S. Hancock, in 1880. In 1884, however, with the help of independent Republican votes, the party elected its candidate for the Presidency, Grover Cleveland, who was in his turn defeated in an effort at re-election by Benjamin Harrison in 1888.

Democritus Junior. (Pseud.) Robert Burton, English philosopher and humorist (1576–1640).

Demogorgon. A terrible deity, whose name alone was capable of producing most horrible effects. Milton speaks of "the dreaded name of Demogorgon." This tyrant-king of the elves and fays lived on the Himalayas, and once in five years summoned all his subjects before him.

Demon of Matrimonial Unhappiness. Asmodeus. He slew the seven husbands of Sara, as recorded in the Book of Tobit.

Demophoon. In classic myth a son of Theseus and Phædra, who, in returning from the siege of Troy, was shipwrecked on the coast of Thrace, where then reigned the beautiful Phyllis. The young queen graciously received the prince, fell in love with him, and became his wife. When recalled to Athens by his father's death, Demophoon promised to return in a month, and fixed the day. The affectionate Phyllis counted the hours of his absence, and at last the appointed day arrived. Nine times she repaired to the shore, but losing all hope of his return, she dropped down dead with grief, and was turned into an almond-tree. Three months afterward Demophoon returned. Overwhelmed with sorrow, he offered a sacrifice at the seaside to appease the manes of his bride. She seemed to sympathize with his repentance, for the almond-tree into which she had been transformed instantly put forth its flowers, and proved by this last effort that true love, strong as death, is incapable of change.

De mortuis nil nisi bonum. (Lat.) Let nothing but good be said of the dead.

De nihilo, nihil fit. (Lat.) Out of nothing, nothing is made.

Denmark, Orchard of. *See* ORCHARD OF DENMARK.

Dénouement. (Fr.) An unravelling or winding up.

De novo. (Lat.) Anew; over again from the beginning.

Deo adjuvante, non timendum. (Lat.) God helping, nothing need be feared.

Deo favente. (Lat.) With God's favor.

Deo gratias. (Lat.) Thanks to God.

Deo juvante. (Lat.) God helping.

De omnibus rebus. (Lat.) "Concerning all things." About everything.

Deo, non fortunâ. (Lat.) From God, not from fortune.

Deo volente. (Lat.) "God being willing." By God's will. Abbreviated into D. V.

Dep. Deputy.

Depot = STATION. *See* RAILROAD.

De profundis. (Lat.) Out of the depths.

Dept. Department,

Derby Day is the second day of the great Spring Meeting, which takes place at Epsom, in Surrey, England, the week preceding Whitsunday. Upon this day the famous Derby stakes, instituted by the Earl of Derby in 1780, and which consist of fifty sovereigns each entry, are contended for. The Derby Day is a great English holiday. To be present at Epsom on that occasion London almost empties itself, and proceeds to the Downs by modes of locomotion the most heterogeneous. For hours a continuous stream of carriages, gigs, dog-carts, vans, and vehicles of every description move tumultuously along the road to Epsom. Shopkeepers on that day shut up their shops; the benches of Parliament are deserted; one half of the aristocracy appear on the ground; people of every condition come in countless numbers from all districts; and huge trains arrive every few minutes at the station, bringing their thousands, until the entire downs are covered with a vast moving mass. So great is the demand for conveyances on this day, that scarcely a horse can be had either in London or within forty miles of it. The occasion is by common custom made a holiday in London and its vicinity; royalty is usually present; and the greatest interest is manifested in the contest for the "blue ribbon of the English turf," as Benjamin Disraeli nicknamed the Derby Stakes.

Deritend Martyr. John Rogers (1500–1555), the editor of Matthew's Bible (*q. v.*), and coadjutor of Tyndale in translating the Scriptures into English. He was a leader of the noble army of martyrs in Mary's reign, and was burned at Smithfield, 1555.

Dernier ressort. (Fr.) The last resource.

Derrydown Triangle. A nickname given to Lord Castlereagh (fl. 1769–1822) by William Hone.

Désagrément. (Fr) Something disagreeable or unpleasant.

Descender, The. A title by which the Jordan is known, — indeed, it is a translation of its name. It is a swiftly flowing stream, very crooked in its course and very rapid in its descent, — "a river that has never been navigable, flowing into a sea that never had a port." It rises in the northern part of Palestine, passes through Lake Merom and the Sea of Galilee, and at last empties into the Dead Sea. Its mouth is 3,000 feet lower than its source, and it has a descent of about fifteen feet for every mile. It is thus truly "The Descender."

Deseret. The Mŏrmon name for Utah, signifying "virtue and industry."

Desert, Gem of the. *See* GEM OF THE DESERT.

Desideratum. (Lat.) Something desired or wanted.

Désiré Hazard. (Pseud.) Octave Feuillet, in "Le Nationale," Paris, 1844.

Despard's Conspiracy. Col. Edward Marcus Despard (an Irishman), Broughton, Francis, Graham, Macnamara, Wood, and Wratten conspired to kill the king and establish a republic Nov. 16, 1802. More than thirty persons were apprehended, and Despard and six others were executed, Feb. 21, 1803.

De Speciosa Villa. (Pseud.) Edmund Gayton, English humorous writer (1609–1666).

Destinies. *See* PARCÆ.

Destra. (Ital.) The right hand. (Mus.)

Desunt cætera. (Lat.) The remainder is wanting.

Detached Badger. (Pseud.) J. H. Walford, author of angling and flyfishing in the London "Field."

Detective's Daughter. (Pseud.) Mrs. Robert P. Porter, in the Philadelphia "Press."

Détenu. (Fr.) "Detained." A prisoner. *Détenus*, prisoners.

Detour. (Fr.) A circuitous march.

De trop. (Fr.) Out of place; one too many.

Detur digniori. (Lat.) Let it be given to the more worthy.

Deucalion. In classic mythology the son of Prometheus; with his wife, Pyrrha, he was preserved from a deluge sent by Jupiter, and became the founder of a new race of men by throwing stones behind him as directed by an oracle. From stones thrown by Pyrrha there sprung up women.

Deus ex machina. A god from the clouds; unexpected aid in an emergency. In ancient dramas, at the crisis in the play a god would be let down from the air by machinery. Hence the intervention of a god or some unlikely event, in order to extricate a clumsy author from the difficulties in which he has involved himself; any forced incident, such as the arrival of a rich uncle from the Indies to help a young couple in their pecuniary embarrassments.

Deut. Deuteronomy.

Deva's Vale. The valley of the Dee (or Deva) in Cheshire, England.

> He chose a farm in Deva's vale,
> Where his long alleys peeped upon the main.
> THOMSON, *Castle of Indolence.*

Devil, The. Oliver Ledain, the pander and tool of Louis XI. of France, who was equally feared and hated. He was hanged in 1484.

Devil among the Tailors. This phrase arose in connection with a riot at the Haymarket on an occasion when Dowton announced the performance for his benefit of a burlesque entitled "The Tailors: a Tragedy for Warm Weather." At night many thousands of journeymen tailors congregated in and around the theatre, and by riotous proceedings interrupted the performances. Thirty-three of the rioters were brought up at Bow Street the next day. A full account of the proceedings will be found in "Biographica Dramatica" under the heading "Tailors."

Devil's Advocate. A person who makes baseless accusations against another. It is the usage of the Roman

Catholic Church, when it is proposed to canonize any person, to appoint two champions or advocates, one to defend and one to oppose the motion. The former, the *Advocatus Dei*, praises the personage whom it is proposed to honor; the latter, the *Advocatus Diaboli*, does all he can to defame him.

Devil's Arrows. A fanciful name appended to three Druidical stone obelisks near Boroughbridge, Yorkshire, England. They were probably set up as landmarks.

Devil's Bones. Dice, which are made of bones, and lead to ruin.

Devil's Books. Playing-cards. A Presbyterian phrase, used in opposition to the term "King's Book," applied to a pack of cards; from the French *livre des quatre rois*, "the book of the four kings" (*q. v.*).

Devil's Bridge. Over the falls of the Reuss, in the canton of Uri.

Devil's Candle. So the Arabs call the mandrake, from its shining appearance at night.

Devil's Courts. Three huge stones near Kennel, in Wiltshire, England.

Devil's Den. A cromlech in a valley, near Marlborough, England. It now consists of two large uprights and an impost. The third upright has fallen. Some farm laborers a few years ago fastened a team of horses to the impost, and tried, but without effect, to drag it down.

Devil's Dust. The dust and sweepings of cloth, made into a fabric by gum and pressure. The subject was introduced to the attention of Parliament, March 4, 1842. The material is so called from the dishonesty and falsehood which it covers. About the same as the American shoddy.

Devil's Frying-pan. A Cornish mine worked by the ancient Romans. According to a very primitive notion, precious stones are produced from condensed dew hardened by the sun. This mine was the frying-pan where dew was thus converted and hardened.

Devil's Own. (1) The Eighty-eighth Foot Regiment, "Connaught Boys," who were so named by General Picton on account of their daring, devil-may-care behavior in the Peninsula War (1809-1814). (2) The nickname has been since applied to the English volunteers recruited among the members of the four Inns of Court, most of them being lawyers.

Devil's Parliament. The Parliament assembled by Henry VI. at Coventry, in 1459, because it passed attainders against the Duke of York and his supporters.

Devil's Royals. See DIRTY HALF-HUNDRED.

Devil's Throat. A name popularly bestowed on Cromer Bay, on the coast of Norfolk, England, owing to the dangerous and tortuous character of its navigation.

Devil's Wall. In superstitious times a name given to the Roman wall (Hadrian's) separating Scotland from England. The peasantry firmly believed that, on account of the firmness of the mortar and the imperishability of the stones, Satan had a hand in its construction. It is even related that, in order to impart to their own cottages a corresponding durability, they incorporated in their walls fragments of the old Roman barricades.

De vive voix. (Fr.) By word of mouth; orally; *viva voce.*

Devoir. (Fr.) Duty.

Devoirs of Calais. The customs due to the king of England for merchandise brought to or carried out of Calais while the English staple was there.

Merchants of the west may buy merchandises, so that they find sureties to carry them to the west or to Calais. — 2 Rich. II. st. 1, c. 3.

Devonshire Poet. O. Jones, a working wool-comber, who flourished in the latter half of the eighteenth century.

D. F. Dean of the Faculty; Defender of the Faith.

D. G. *Dei gratiâ.* By the grace of God.

D. G. *Deo gratias.* Thanks to God.

D. H. Dead-head.

Di. Didymium.

Diam. Diameter.

Diamond Duke. Duke Charles of Brunswick (d. 1874), the cellars of whose hotel in the Champs Élysées, Paris, were found at his death to be crammed with gold and precious stones.

Diamond Joe. On the front of each locomotive on the Hot Springs (Ark.) Railroad is the coat-of-arms of the owner, Joseph Reynolds. It is a large diamond, inside of which is the letter "J." To the Southwestern public, and over a large portion of the West, Mr. Reynolds is known as " Diamond Joe," on account of his coat-of-arms, or, as he calls it, his trade-mark.

Diamond Necklace Affair. A wonderful piece of jewelry was made by Boehmer, the court jeweller of Paris, intended for Madame du Barry, the favorite of Louis XV. On the death of the monarch, however, she was excluded from court, and the bawble was left on the jeweller's hands. Its immense value, 1,800,000 livres ($400,000), precluded any one from becoming its purchaser ; but in 1785 Boehmer offered it to Marie Antoinette for $320,000, a considerable reduction. The queen much desired the necklace, but was deterred from its purchase by the great expense. Learning this, the Comtesse de la Motte forged the queen's signature, and by pretending that her Majesty had an attachment for him, persuaded the queen's almoner, the Cardinal de Rohan, to conclude a bargain with the jeweller for $280,000. De la Motte thus obtained possession of the necklace, and made off with it. For this she was tried in 1786, and sentenced to be branded on both shoulders and imprisoned for life, but she subsequently escaped and fled to London. The cardinal was tried and acquitted the same year. The French public at that time believed that the queen was a party to the fraud, but no conclusive evidence was ever adduced to support the charge. Talleyrand wrote at that time : " I shall not be surprised if this miserable affair overturn the throne." His prediction was, to a great extent, fulfilled.

Diamond State. Delaware ; so named on account of its size and its central location.

Diana. Originally an Italian divinity; afterward regarded as identical with the Greek Artemis, the daughter of Jupiter and Latona, and the twin sister of Apollo. She was the goddess of hunting, chastity, marriage, and nocturnal incantations. She was also regarded as the goddess of the moon. Her temple at Ephesus was one of the Seven Wonders of the World (*q. v.*).

Diana. (Pseud.) Mrs. Abigail Smith Adams.

Dian's Worshippers. Nocturnal revellers, because they travel homeward by the light of the moon, — Diana, or Dian.

Diarist. (Pseud.) Alexander Wheelock Thayer, in " Dwight's Journal of Music."

Dick Distich. (Pseud.) Alexander Pope, in the " Guardian."

Dick Ditson. (Pseud.) M. L. Saley, of Rockford, Ill., correspondent of various journals.

Dick Tinto. (Pseud.) The pen-name of Frank B. Goodrich (b. in Boston, 1826), for some time Paris correspondent of the New York " Times."

Dickens's Dutchman. Charles Langheimer, a jail-bird immortalized by the novelist in his " American Notes." He died in Philadelphia in 1883, seventy-seven years old, fifty of which he had spent behind prison bars.

Dickey Lingard. (Pseud.) Harriet Sarah Dunning.

Dickie Lingard. The stage-name of Mrs. Dalziel.

Dicky Sam. A nickname for a native or resident of Liverpool, — a Liverpudlian.

Dict. Dictionary; Dictator.

Dictator of Letters. Voltaire was so named. *See also* GREAT PAN.

Dictum de dicta. (Lat.) Report upon hearsay.

Diedrich Knickerbocker. (Pseud.) Washington Irving, American author (1783–1859).

Die-hards. The Fifty-seventh English Foot Regiment; so nicknamed because of their bravery at Albuera in 1811.

Die in the Last Ditch. " To William of Orange may be ascribed this saying. When Buckingham urged the inevitable destruction which hung over the United Provinces, and asked him whether he did not see that the Commonwealth was ruined, 'There is one certain means,' replied the Prince, 'by which I can be sure never to see my country's ruin, — I will die in the last ditch.' " — HUME.

Die-no-mores. A nickname conferred on the Forty-eighth Regiment N. G. S. N. Y., during the late civil war.

Dies datus. (Lat.) " The day given." The day or time appointed.

Dies faustus. (Lat.) A lucky day.

Dies iræ. (Lat.) " Day of wrath ; " the name of a Latin hymn.

Dies non. (Lat.) " A day not." A day on which the judges do not sit, or on which business is not transacted.

Dietrich of Bern. The name under which the Ostrogoth king, Theodoric the Great, appears in the German heroic legends; in which by Bern, his capital, Verona is to be understood. As early as the seventh century, he would seem to have become the centre of a distinct cycle of legends. A little later, he was, with a not unusual disregard of all historical truth, brought into connection with the traditions of Attila, or Etzel. According to these legends, Dietrich is said to have fled from Italy before Ottacher (Odoacer), or Ermanarich; to have met, along with his attendant vassals, with a hospitable reception from Etzel; but after many years, to have again got possession of his kingdom. The extermination of the royal House of Burgundy by Attila, which is an historical event, was the cause that Dietrich, as well as Etzel himself, was woven into the Burgundian and Frankish Siegfriedssage; and thus he appears, in the second part of the "Nibelungen," at Etzel's court, and is handled by the poet with special predilection. There have been numerous poems, besides, of which Dietrich was the centre and principal hero.

Dieu défend le droit. (Fr.) God defend the right.

Dieu-donné ("Gift of God"). (1) The name given in infancy to Louis le Grand, king of France; the queen, his mother, having been barren for twenty-three years previously (1638). (2) The Comte de Chambord (1820–1884), son of the Duchesse de Berri, was also so named.

Dieu et mon droit. (Fr.) God and my right.

Dieu vous garde. (Fr.) God guard you.

Digby Chicken. A colloquial euphuism for red herring.

Diggings. The word "diggings" has become familiar to English ears from its use in the gold-mines of Australia. There it generally denotes only a place where precious metals are dug for, but as an Americanism it serves to designate any special locality.

Dignus vindice nodus. (Lat.) A knot worthy to be untied; a difficulty calling for the highest interposition for its unravelment.

Dii majores et minores. (Lat.) The gods greater and less.

Dii majorum gentium. (Lat.) The gods of the superior class; the twelve superior gods.

Dii penates. (Lat.) The household gods; objects of love or affection.

Dilettanti. (Ital.) Persons who devote themselves to science merely as a pastime.

Dill. Dillon's Reports.

Dim. Diminutive.

Dimanche, M. (lit., "Mr. Sunday"). A name given in France to a creditor or dun, in allusion to the fact that tradesmen and artisans have no other holiday, and usually take Sunday for collecting their debts.

Di molto. (Ital.) An expression which seems to increase the significance of the word to which it is attached; as, *Allegro di molto*, very quick. (Mus.)

Dine with Duke Humphrey. A correspondent of the "Gentleman's Magazine," March, 1794, p. ₋10, says: "This proverb originated from the accidental circumstance of a wit in the seventeenth century being shut up in the Abbey of St. Albans, where the remains of Humphrey, the good Duke regent, are yet to be seen, while a party of his friends who came down to that borough on an excursion were enjoying a convivial dinner at the White Hart Inn." The proverb, however, seems to have been known at an earlier period than this story refers to, and it meant "to have no dinner to eat." The phrase, perhaps, arose from the custom of making a part of Old St. Paul's Cathedral, which was called Duke Humphrey's Walk, a common place of meeting. People short of a dinner used to promenade this spot in the hope of meeting some one who would invite them.

Dîner à la carte. (Fr.) To dine by the bill-of-fare prices.

Dinna Kens. A nickname of the Seventy-first Regiment in the English army.

Dinner-bell. A nickname conferred on Edmund Burke because of his long speeches, which were often interrupted by the members of Parliament leaving for dinner.

Diocletian Era, or Era of Martyrs. From the proclamation of Diocletian as emperor, at Chalcedon, A. D. 284, until his abdication, in 305. His reign was notorious for a determined and sanguinary persecution of the Christians.

Diogenes. A surname conferred on Romanus IV., Emperor of the East, who reigned 1067–1071.

Diogenes. (Pseud.) John Trenchard in the "London Times" and the "British Journal."

Diomed. In classic mythology son of Tydæus, king of Ætolia. He was one of the most valiant of the Greeks at the siege of Troy. He and Ulysses carried off the Palladium, on which the safety of Troy depended.

Diomedean Swap. An exchange in which all the profit is on one side. The expression is founded on an incident related by Homer in the Iliad. Glaucus recognizes Diomed on the battle-field, and the friends change armor.

Dion. (Pseud.) Joseph Leonard Tillinghast, American jurist, in the Providence "Gazette" (1790–1840). He also used the signature "Carroll."

Dione. Venus, who sprang from the froth of the sea after the mutilated body of Uranus had been thrown there by Saturn.

Dionysius, Ear of. *See* EAR OF DIONYSIUS.

Diosc. Dioscorides.

Dioscuri. (Gr., "Sons of Zeus.") Another name for Castor and Pollux.

Dircæan Swan. The poet Pindar; so named after Dirce, a fountain near Thebes, his place of birth.

Dire des fleurettes. (Fr.) To say pretty things.

Dirigo. (Lat.) "I direct or guide." The motto of the State of Maine. *See infra.*

Dirigoes. A sobriquet for the inhabitants of Maine, in allusion to the motto *Dirigo*, "I direct," on its coat-of-arms.

Dirty Half-Acre. The upper castle-yard in Dublin Castle; so named from the jobs perpetrated within its enclosure during the traitorous times immediately preceding the Union.

Dirty Half-Hundred. The Fiftieth Foot Regiment in the English army. The story goes that on a certain sultry day the men wiped their sweaty faces with the black cuffs of their coats, and the dye came off.

Dirty Shirts. The English Coldstream Guards are thus nicknamed throughout the service.

Disastrous Peace. That which followed the battle of Gravelines, 1559, signed at Château-Cambrésis. By it Henry II. gave up Genoa, Milan, Naples, and Corsica.

Disc. Discount.

Disguised as a Gentleman. This phrase originated in a play of the poet Cowley, in 1661. In the comedy of "The Cutter of Coleman Street," act i., sc. 5, Colonel Jolly and Captain Worms are chaffing Cutter, who boasts that he, "like the king himself, and all the great ones, got away in a disguise;" to which Jolly replies, "Take one more disguise, and put thyself into the habit of a gentleman."

Dished, in the sense of "ruined or frustrated," is a contraction of the old English word "disherit" for "disinherit." A person is said to be *dished* when property he expected to inherit is left to some one else. Byron, in "Don Juan," asks, —

"Where's Brummel? Dished!"

Disjecta membra. (Lat.) "Disjointed members." Scattered limbs or remains.

Dismal Science. The name given by Carlyle to the science of political economy.

Dissenters. The modern name for the Puritans and Nonconformists in England.

Diss. Dissertation.

Dissenters, Campo Santo of. *See* CAMPO SANTO OF DISSENTERS.

Dist. District.

Distaff's Day. January 7. So called because the Christmas festival terminates on Twelfth Day, and on the following day women return to their distaffs or daily occupations.

Dist.-Atty. District-Attorney.

Distingué. (Fr.) "Distinguished." Eminent: gentlemanly,

Distrait. (Fr.) "Absent." Absent in thought. *Distraite* (fem.).

Distringas. (Lat.) A writ for distraining.

Dito. (Ital.) The finger. (Mus.)

Div. Division.

Divertimento. (Ital.) A short composition, written in a light and pleasing manner. (Mus.)

Divertissement. (Fr.) (1) Certain airs and dances introduced between the acts of Italian opera; also a piece light and airy in style. (2) Amusement; entertainment; diversion.

Divide. Long ridges, forming a watershed.

Divide et impera. (Lat.) Divide and govern.

Dividing Fence, The. *See* PICTS' WORK-DITCH.

Divine, The. (1) Ferdinand de Herrara, Spanish poet (fl. 1516-1595). (2) Raphael, the painter (fl. 1483-1520). (3) Luis Morales, Spanish painter (fl. 1509-1586).

Divine Doctor. Jean de Ruysbroek, the mystic (fl. 1294-1381).

Divine Speaker. Tyrtamos was so named by Aristotle, whereupon he assumed the name Theophrastos. He lived 370-287 B. C.

Divoto. (Ital.) Devoutly; in a solemn style. (Mus.)

Dixie. (1) The States and Territories south of Mason and Dixon's line, the former boundary of slavedom. (2) A fabulous realm of peace, plenty, and indolence, whose charms form the burden of many a negro melody. Brewer says that a Mr. Dixie was a slaveholder of Manhattan Island, compelled by public opinion to remove his human chattels to the South. In their new abode they had to toil ceaselessly, and often sighed for their old home at the North, which lapse of time and distance invested with a halo of paradisaic pleasures. Thus " Dixie Land " became to the entire colored race in the South a species of Utopia, similar to the Scottish " Land o' the Leal " or the Fortunate Islands of the ancients.

Dixie. (Pseud.) J. Dixie Doyle, Washington correspondent of the "Spirit of the Times," New York.

Dixon. (Pseud.) Mme. Clémence Harding Masson, author of " Stories and Sketches."

Dizzy. " Punch " thus nicknamed Benjamin Disraeli, Lord Beaconsfield (fl. 1805-1881).

D. L. O. Dead-Letter Office.

D. M. Doctor of Music.

Do. *Ditto.* The same.

Doc. Document.

Docendo dicimus. (Lat.) We learn by teaching.

Docetæ. (From the Greek δοκεῖν, to appear.) The name given to a set of ancient heretics who maintained that Christ acted and suffered in appearance only.

Doce ut discas. (Lat.) Teach that you may learn.

Doctor, The. A nickname for the first Lord Sidmouth (fl. 1757-1844), in allusion to the fact that he was the son of Dr. Anthony Addington of Reading.

Dr. Bonham's Case. An important decision upon English constitutional law, rendered in 1609, in the case of Thomas Bonham *v.* the College of Physicians for false imprisonment. It was held that an act of Parliament which is against common right and reason, or is impossible to be performed, is void by the common law; also that where the power to commit to prison is vested by patent or act of Parliament in parties not being a court, their proceedings ought to be of record, and the facts upon which such power is exercised are traversable.

Doctor Mirabilis. Roger Bacon (fl. 1214-1292).

Doctor My-Book. A nickname given to Dr. John Abernethy (fl. 1765-1830), because he used to advise his patients to " read *my* book," that on " Surgical Observations."

Doctor of the Incarnation. An honorable title bestowed on Saint Cyril of Alexandria, because of his championship of the Virgin.

Dr. Oldham of Greystones. (Pseud.) Caleb Sprague Henry, LL.D., American author (b. 1804).

Doctor Scholasticus. Anselm the schoolman (fl. 1050-1117).

Doctor Singularis. William of Accam (a Surrey hamlet), fl. 1270-1347. *See also* INVINCIBLE DOCTOR.

Doctor Slop. A nickname given to Sir John Stoddart, M.D. (fl. 1773-1856), a hot-tempered physician, who bitterly assailed Napoleon in the " Times," of which he was for a time editor.

Doctor Squintum. (1) George Whitefield (fl. 1714-1770) was so named by Foote in his farce " The Minor." (2) Edward Irving was also so nicknamed by Theodore Hook.

Doctor Syntax. A simple, unsophisticated, pious, henpecked clergyman, of excellent taste and scholarship, who left home in search of the picturesque. His adventures are told in eight-syllable verse in " The Tour of Dr. Syntax," by William Combe, English satirical writer (1741-1823).

Doctor with Good Foundations.
Giles, archbishop of Bourges.

Doctrinaires. A name given since 1814 to a class of politicians in France (Guizot, Molé, the Duc de Broglie, and others), who upheld constitutional principles, in opposition to arbitrary monarchical power. The party came into office in 1830 under Louis Philippe, and fell with him in 1848.

Dodona. A famous oracle in Dodona, in Epirus, and the most ancient of Greece. It was dedicated to Zeus.

Do don't. *See* TO GET TO GO.

Doeface. *See* DOUGHFACE.

Doeg, in Dryden and Tate's "Absalom and Achitophel," is meant for Elkanah Settle, a poet who wrote ineffective satires upon Dryden. Doeg was Saul's herdsman, who had charge of his mules and asses. He told Saul that the priests of Nob had provided David with food; whereupon Saul sent him to put them to death, and eighty-five were ruthlessly massacred.

Dog Days. From July 3 to August 11. Dog Days have a more classic name, — "Canicular Days." Canicula was the old name of Canus Minor, and so came to be used to denote Sirius, or the Dog Star, the largest and the brightest of the stars situated in the mouth of Canus Major. The ancients counted the Dies Canicular, or Dog Days, from the heliacal rising of Sirius, and made them forty in number, — twenty before and twenty after the rising of the star. The heliacal rising means the time when the star, after being practically in conjunction with the sun and invisible, emerges from the light so as to be visible in the morning before sunrise.

There was a superstition in old times that the rising of the Dog Star with the sun would produce pestilential heat. The Egyptians thought it produced either the rising of the Nile or destructive droughts. The date has been changing at the rate of about one day in seventy years, on account of the precession of the equinoxes; so at the present time Dog Days in general commence in the latter part of July, and end in the beginning of September. Practically, they do not in our time have any connection with the rising of any star. Many of the most curious ideas prevail on this subject. We have heard a man supposed to possess considerable general information announce gravely and in good faith that Dog Days were so called because during those days the atmosphere was in a peculiar condition of humidity, which, together with the heat, induced hydrophobia in dogs. We class him with the brother who said that vaccination was named after Dr. Vacca, the inventor! — REV. J. M. BUCKLEY, D.D.

Dog Derby. The name given in England to the coursing by greyhounds for the Waterloo Cup, every Ash-Wednesday, on Altcar Meadows, near Liverpool.

Dogget's Coat and Badge. Prize at a rowing-match on the Thames, from London Bridge to the Old Swan at Chelsea, yearly, August 1. Beside the original prize (the bequest of Thomas Dogget, actor at Drury Lane, 1715), other prizes are competed for. The competition is by six young watermen whose apprenticeships have expired the previous year, each in a boat by himself, with short oars or sculls; and the race is at the hour when the current of the Thames, by recession of the tide, is strongest against the rowers.

Dog-watch. A corruption of "dodge-watch." Two short turns of deck duty, or "watches," at sea, — one from four to six, and the other from six to eight in the evening. Time on shipboard is divided into periods of four hours' duration (*see* BELLS), the crew being divided into two portions, or watches, and being on duty alternately. But to prevent the same men from being on duty at the same hours every day, the dog-watches were introduced in order to change, or "dodge," the watch. But there is another theory as to the origin of the phrase: "In the Celtic language — spoken in the British Isles before the irruption of the Teutonic races, the Danes, the Saxons, the Dutch, and the Flemish — 'dog' signified 'common, inferior, imperfect,' etc. Many examples of its use in this sense are still existent in the vernacular. 'Dog bolt' is an inferior or blunt arrow; 'dog rose,' a wild, common, or hedge rose; 'doggerel' means common and inferior verse or rhyme; 'dog Latin,' the inferior and corrupt Latin spoken or written in the Middle Ages; and 'dog watch,' the short or inferior watch, only half the length of the ordinary watch kept on ship-board. In like manner, 'dog cheap' does not mean 'cheap as a dog,' for dogs are not invariably cheap; but 'cheap to commonness' or almost to worthlessness.' Many more examples of 'dog' as an adjective might be cited."

Dog Whip. (Pseud.) L. D. Smith.

Dolce. (Ital.) Sweet, soft, or agreeable.

Dolce, Dolcemente, or Dol. (Ital.) With sweetness.

Dolce e piacevolmente espressivo. (Ital.) Soft, and with pleasing expression. (Mus.)

Dolce far niente. (Ital.) "This is a clear translation from the Latin. It describes the 'summum bonum' of an Italian, and the idea was thrown into an expression at a very early period. In Cicero, De Oratore, ii., s. 24, is the following: 'Nihil agere delectat.' The same idea is in Pliny's Letters, viii. 9: 'Illud jucundum nil agere.' These express the same idea precisely, — the 'sweet to do nothing' of a life in a country where the climate would naturally produce a lassitude that would make labor a doubly hard task." — OLIVE OLDSCHOOL.

Doldrums. (A. S. *dol-drunc*, foolish — from *dol*, erring; *druncuian*, to have the mind submerged by drinking: Gael. *dol-dream*, a state of sulking; *doltrum*, grief, vexation.) A sailor's term for the tropical zones of calms and variable winds. "To be in the doldrums," to be in low spirits, dejected, or melancholy.

Dolente, Con dolore, or **Con duolo.** (Ital.) Sorrowfully; pathetically. (Mus.)

Doli incapax. (Lat.) Incapable of mischief.

Dolly Dawdle. (Pseud.) Mrs. Mary C. P. Lukens.

Dolly Mitchell. The stage-name of Mrs. William Melton.

Dolores. (Pseud.) Miss Dickson, composer of musical settings for various poems.

Doloroso. (Ital.) In a soft and pathetic style. (Mus.)

Dols. Dollars.

D. O. M. *Deo Optimo Maximo.* To God, the best, the greatest.

Domat omnia virtus. (Lat.) Valor subdues all things.

Dome of the Rock. A name conferred on the Mosque of Omar, Jerusalem. It stands on Mount Moriah, on the site once occupied by the Temple of Solomon. Immediately under its dome an irregular-shaped rock projects above the pavement. This rock was the scene of many Scriptural events, and has been greatly revered for ages.

Domestic Poet of England. William Cowper, author of "The Task."

Domestic Poultry, in Dryden's epic of the "Hind and Panther," means the Roman Catholic clergy.

Domestics. A term used to distinguish native from imported wares.

Domine, dirige nos. (Lat.) O Lord, direct us.

Dominick Murray. The stage-name of Dominick Morogh.

Dominie Sampson of Germany. Carlyle so named John Henry Stilling, the mystic (fl. 1740–1817), as being "awkward, honest, irascible, in old-fashioned clothes and bag-wig."

Dominion Day. A Canadian national holiday, occurring on July 1 in each year.

Dominus vobiscum. (Lat.) The Lord be with you.

Domitian. One of the signatures of Junius (*q. v.*).

Donald Campbell. (Pseud.) Stephen Cullen Carpenter, American journalist (1761–1820).

Donatello. (Pseud.) Francis Julius Le Moyne Burleigh, a well-known American journalist and editor.

Donation-party. A gathering of church-members who supplement the pastor's often inadequate salary by presents of goods in kind.

Don Carlos. (Pseud.) Henry T. Cheever, in the "Sunday Mercury."

Do-nothing Kings. *See* FAINÉANTS.

Don't care a Fig is properly "Don't care a *fico*." *Fico* means a contemptuous snapping of the fingers. Shakspeare has "A fico for the phrase."

Don't give up the Ship. The author of this historic phrase, which deserves to rank with Nelson's "England expects every man to do his duty," was Capt. James Lawrence, commanding the United States frigate "Chesapeake." He had accepted a challenge from Commander Brooke of the British frigate "Shannon," to a duel between the two vessels. The engagement took place just outside of Boston harbor, and lasted only a few minutes. Captain Lawrence was wounded, and, as he was carried below, exclaimed, "Don't give up the ship." The "Chesapeake" had to surrender, however. Lawrence died on the voyage to Halifax, and is buried there. He was not quite twenty-six years old.

Doomsday Sedgwick. William Sedgwick, a fanatic exhorter during the Commonwealth. He professed to have had a vision foretelling that the day of doom was at hand, and went about the country calling upon all to prepare for that event.

Door-opener. A nickname given to Crates, the Theban, by the people of Athens, because every morning he used to perambulate the city berating the late risers.

Doppel. (Ger.) Double.

Dora d' Istria. (Pseud.) Princess Koltzoff Massalsky, *née* Helen Ghika (b. 1829).

Dora Roberts. The stage-name of Mrs. Paige.

Dora Stuart. The stage-name of Mrs. J. O. Bradford, *née* Haines.

Dora Wiley. The stage-name of Mrs. Richard Golden.

Dorer la pilule. (Fr.) To gild the pill.

Doric Land. Greece; Doris being an important part of it.

> Through all the bounds
> Of Doric land.
> MILTON, *Paradise Lost.*

Doric Muse. Pastoral poetry. Everything Doric was very plain, but cheerful, chaste, and solid. The Dorians were the pastoral people of Greece, and their dialect was that of the country rustics.

Doris. In classic mythology daughter of Oceanus and Tethys, and mother of the Nereids.

Dorr's Rebellion. In 1843 a controversy arose in Rhode Island out of a desire to change the old Constitution, which dated from the time of Charles II. Rival factions were formed, named the "Suffrage" and the "Law and Order" parties. Each elected a set of State officers, and each was determined to secure control of the government. Thomas W. Dorr was chosen Governor by the "Suffrage" party, and attempted to seize the government, for which he was sentenced to imprisonment for life, but was subsequently pardoned.

Dorsetian Downs. The uplands of Dorsetshire, England.

> Spread the pure Dorsetian downs
> In boundless prospect.
> THOMSON, *The Seasons.*

Dositheans. A religious sect which sprang up in the first century; so called because they believed that Dositheus had a divine mission, superior to that of prophets and apostles.

Doson. A promise-maker and a promise-breaker. Antigonus, grandson of Demetrius the besieger, was so called.

Dot Harrison. The stage-name of Mrs. John M. Cook.

Dotted Bible. A folio edition of the Scriptures published in London in 1578; so named by bibliographers because it is a perfect fac-simile of that of 1574.

Dotti, Mlle. The stage-name of Mrs. Swift.

Douay Bible. A translation of the Scriptures made by English Romanists from the Latin Vulgate. It was given to the world in 1610. *See* ROSIN BIBLE.

Double Dutch. Nonsense, outlandish jargon, or a foreign tongue not understood by the hearer. "Double" is simply "excessive, in a twofold degree."

Double entendre. (Corrupt Fr.) "Double meaning." A play on words, in which the word or phrase is capable of more than one sense. The correct French form is *double entente*, of which the full expression is *mot à double entente*, "a word with a double meaning" — used generally in a bad sense.

Double X or XX. A corruption of "duplex." It is a frequent sign in front of liquor shops, both in the United States and England, and signifies that the ales and beers are of "double strength." So of course the triple X (XXX) and quadruple X (XXXX) indicate that the strength is proportionately increased.

Douceur. (Fr.) A present or bribe.

Doughface. In 1838 the Democratic Congressmen from the Northern States decided in caucus in favor of a resolution requiring all petitions relating to slavery to be laid upon the table without debate. This identified the party as it then existed with the slaveholding interest, and its Northern representatives were stigmatized as "Doughfaces." Says Mr. W. P. Garrison: "George Bradburn, of Massachusetts, in a political speech in Ohio said, of 'the baser sort of Northern demagogues,' that John Randolph, 'the caustic Virginian,' in his Congressional seat branded them as 'doughfaces.' I am not sure but we have dulled the point of that pungent epithet by changing its original orthography. Randolph spelled the word, 'D-O-E face,' in allusion to the timid, startled look of that animal, which is said to shrink from the reflection of its own face in the water."

Doughnuts. A name as distinctively American as the edible it stands for. It is the English corruption of the Dutch *donnets.*

Douglas Larder. In 1307, at the siege of Douglas Castle, the Good (!) Earl, James Douglas, on sacking the place, caused the barrels of flour, grain, wine, ale, etc., to be smashed, and allowed their contents to run out and mingle on the floor of the storeroom. Into this mess he caused to be flung the dead bodies of the slaughtered garrison. The whole, to signify their contempt for the English, his men called " The Douglas Larder."

Dow, Jr. (Pseud.) Eldridge Paige.

Down East, Down-Easter. The New England States and the New-Englander.

Downright. One of the signatures attributed to Junius (*q. v.*)

Doz. Dozen.

D. P. Doctor of Philosophy.

D. P. O. Distributing Post-Office.

Dpt. Department.

Dr. Debtor ; Doctor; dram; drachm.

Draconian Laws. In modern parlance, statutes of unusual severity. The laws of Draco, enacted by him when archon of Athens (B. C. 621), on account of their rigor were said to be written in blood. This code was set aside by Solon's, B. C. 594.

Draft Riots. A brutal and frantic protest in New York in the summer of 1863 against the conscriptions for the Union army. Four hundred lives were lost, and much property was destroyed.

Dragonnades. The name given to the fierce persecutions of the Protestants in the reign of Louis XIV. in France by dragoons at the instigation of Louvois. They culminated in the revocation of the Edict of Nantes (*q. v.*).

Dragon of Wantley. A monster slain by More of More Hill, Yorkshire, who " procured a suit of armor studded with spikes, and, proceeding to the well where the dragon had his lair, kicked it in the mouth, where alone it was vulnerable."

Dragon's Teeth. Sources of internecine strife. The allusion is to the dragon that guarded the well of Ares. Cadmus slew it, and sowed some of the teeth, from which sprang up the men called Spartans, who all killed each other except five, who were the ancestors of the Thebans.

Dramatis personæ. (Lat.) The characters or persons represented on the stage in a play.

Drapier's Letters. Famous epistles written by Dean Swift under the pseudonym of " M. B. Drapier," were published in 1724 against Wood's Halfpence (*q. v.*).

Drat 'em and **Od rot 'em.** " These colloquial terms, used so frequently by old playwriters and by modern scolds, are probably contractions of ' May the gods outroot them.' " — *Notes and Queries.*

Dred Scott Decision. This was a case brought for final decision before the Supreme Court of the United States in 1856, which excited much interest in this country and in Europe. The plaintiff was a negro named Dred Scott, who with his wife and two children had been held as slaves by a Dr. Emerson in the State of Missouri. After the death of Emerson, Dred Scott and his family claimed to be free, on the ground that they had resided for some time with their late proprietor in a free territory; so that having, as Scott alleged, been free in that territory, they could not now be held to slavery. The case was carried to the United States Supreme Court, and on March 6, 1857, Chief-Justice Roger Brooke Taney, of Maryland, announced the decision. " The court held that Scott had no right to sue, because, even if he were free, no colored person was regarded by the Constitution as a citizen. He says " they had for more than a century before been regarded as . . . so far inferior that they had no rights which the white man was bound to respect." After deciding this, the question at issue, the court went out of its way to declare the Missouri Compromise void, and to deny the right of Congress to exclude slavery from any territory. Of the associate justices, six supported the Chief-Justice, and two, McLean of Ohio and Curtis of Massachusetts, dissented. The opinion was for a time withheld from publication, in order not to increase the excitement of the Presidential election then pending."

Dress-improver. *See* NEW DRESS-IMPROVER.

Drink. Synonymous with the English "dram."

Drisheen City. Cork, Ireland. The name arises from a favorite dish, native to the place, composed of cows' milk and the blood serum of sheep in equal quantities, flavored with pepper, salt, and tansy, served hot, and eaten at breakfast.

Droit d'Aubaine. A peculiar right of the king of France, who by the old custom of the kingdom was entitled, on the death of a foreigner who had taken up his fixed residence there, to claim his movable estate, notwithstanding any testamentary settlement which he might have left. But when a foreigner went to France as a traveller, merchant, or foreign minister, without any intention of fixing his residence there, the *droit d'aubaine* was excluded. The Swiss, Savoyards, Scotch, and Portuguese were exempted. This antiquated piece of injustice was abolished in 1819.

Drop Shot. (Pseud.) George Washington Cable, the famous novelist (b. 1844), began writing for the New Orleans "Picayune" over the above signature.

Drown the Miller is to put too much water to the flour in making bread. It is doubtless an English expression. At all events, Wright says that *putting the miller's eye out* is a phrase used when too much liquid is put to any dry or powdery substance. The latter is also used in New England.

Druid. (Pseud.) (1) Henry M. Flint in the New York "World." (2) John Witherspoon.

Druid Money. A promise to pay on the Greek Kalends. Patricius says: "Druidæ pecuniam mutuo accipiebant in posteriore vita reddituri."

> Like money by the Druids borrowed,
> In th' other world to be restorèd.
> BUTLER, *Hudibras*, iii. 1.

Drum Ecclesiastic. The pulpit cushion, often vigorously thumped by what are termed "rousing preachers."

Drum-head Court-martial. A military tribunal convened in haste, as on the battle-field, to deal summarily with some culprit, when a big drum is used as a table.

Drummer. In America, a commercial traveller is called a "drummer,"

and travelling in search of business is called "drumming."

> The expenses of "drumming" amount to no small sum. Besides employing extra clerks, and paying the extra price for their board at the hotels, the merchant has to be very liberal with his money in paying for wine, oyster suppers, theatre tickets, and such other means of conciliating the favor of the country merchant as are usually resorted to by "drummers." — *Perils of Pearl Street*, ix.

Drummer-boy of Mission Ridge. John S. Kountz, a gallant soldier in the civil war (b. 1846). At the battle of Mission Ridge, Tenn., Nov. 25, 1863, when the drum-corps was ordered to the rear, he threw away his drum, seized a musket, and was severely wounded in the first assault, being left on the field. The episode is the subject of a poem by Kate B. Sherwood, which is widely known.

Drunk as Blazes. This vulgar expression is a corruption of "drunk as Blaizers." Bishop Blaize is the patron saint of wool-combers, who at Leicester and elsewhere celebrate his festival with marchings and great convivialities. In Sir Thomas Wyse's "Impressions of Greece," he mentions this custom, and says: "Those who took part in the procession were called 'Blaizers,' and the phrase 'as drunk as Blaizers' originated in the convivialities common on these occasions."

Drunk as Chloe. This saying probably refers to the lady of that name, notorious for her drinking habits, so often mentioned by Matthew Prior in his poems.

Drunken Parliament. That which assembled at Edinburgh, Jan. 1, 1661. Burnet says the members were "almost perpetually drunk."

Dryads. In classic myth nymphs who presided over the forests, and who were thought to perish with the trees in which they abode.

Dryasdust, Rev. Dr. A pseudonym employed by Sir Walter Scott in the prefatory matter of some of his novels.

Dry Bobs, Wet Bobs. Names applied to rival parties or sets at Eton College, — the former going in for land sports, as cricket and football; the latter for boating, swimming, fishing, etc.

Dry-goods. This word is universally used in the United States for the wares known in England as linen-drapery or haberdashery. Dry-goods for men's use are called "men's furnishings."

Dryope. In classic myth a daughter of King Dryops and wife of Andræmon; turned into a poplar or a lotus by the Hamadryads.

Drys. *See* WETS AND DRYS.

D. S. *Dal segno.* From the sign.

D. Sc. Doctor of Science.

D. S. P. *Decessit sine prole.* He died without issue.

D. T. *Doctor theologiæ.* Doctor of Theology; Doctor of Divinity.

Dualists. A name given in Hungary, in 1867, to the advocates of a separate form of government under the Emperor of Austria, which was carried in the year named.

Dub. Dublin.

Dubbs, Goose. *See* GOOSE DUBBS.

Duchesne. Jacques Réné Hébert (fl. 1755–1794), the chief of the Cordeliers (*q. v.*), was nicknamed "Père Duchesne" from the name of his scurrilous journal.

Ducit amor patriæ. (Lat.) The love of my country leads me on.

Ducks and Drakes. To "make ducks and drakes" with one's money is an allusion to a game played by boys, who take oyster-shells or flat stones, and throw them horizontally along the surface of a piece of water in such a manner that the missiles skim along the surface, touching it many times and again emerging. The first time the stone emerges it is a *duck*, the second a *drake;* and so on, according to the old doggerel —

> " A duck and a drake,
> And a halfpenny cake,
> And a penny to pay the baker," etc.

The meaning, in the case of money, is, that the spendthrift metaphorically uses coins, as boys use stones, to make "ducks and drakes."

Dudder. *See* DUFFER.

Dude. A languid, conceited, vapid dandy, dressed in the extreme of the prevailing fashion, distinguished alike for the inanity of his talk and an inordinate craving for the cheap notoriety to be gained by late hours and fast living. The remote origin of the word is probably to be found in the Scotch "duddies," or "duds," both meaning "clothes." The application of the idea in the form with which we are familiar is said to have originated with a prominent New-Yorker, who described one of the now familiar tailor's manikins as a "dude." So far back as 1870 we find in "Putnam's Magazine" the expression, "She is dressed like a dud," etc.

Duff. A sailor-man's name for pudding of any kind, but meaning especially a stiff flour pudding, with a few handfuls of raisins or currants or prunes thrown in, boiled in a bag, in the cook's coppers, in the same greasy water in which salt beef and pork have been cooked.

Duffer. A slang name for a pretended smuggler, — one who goes around selling cheap cigars, brass watches, common silks, etc., at ostensibly cheap prices, on the pretence that the same have been smuggled and have evaded the payment of the legal duty. "Dudder" means the same as "duffer."

Dugald Dalgetty. (Pseud.) Maj.-Gen. Sir A. M. Tulloch, K. C. B., in the Indian press.

Duke of Exeter's Daughter. A torture rack, erected by the Duke of Exeter in the reign of Henry VI., was so named. *See* RACK.

Dulce domum. (Lat.) Sweet home.

Dulce est desipere in loco. (Lat.) It is pleasant to jest at the proper time.

Dulce et decorum est pro patria mori. (Lat.) It is pleasant and honorable to die in behalf of one's country.

Dulce quod utile. (Lat.) What is useful is agreeable.

Dulcifluous Doctor. A name given to Antony Andreas (d. 1320), a Spanish minorite and a famous theologian.

Dulia. An inferior kind of worship.

Dumb Ox. Saint Thomas Aquinas, said to have been so dubbed by his fellow-pupils, at Cologne, "on account of his silence and apparent dulness." But it is said that his teacher penetrated the mask, and predicted his future greatness in the words, "That dumb ox will some day speak and shake the world!"

Dump. "To dump," in the sense of tilting a cart and thus unloading it, is an Americanism; and open lots where "rubbish may be shot," as is said in England, are in America called "dumping-grounds."

Dum spiro, spero. (Lat.) While I breathe, I hope.

Dum vita est, spes est. (Lat.) "While life is, hope is." While there is life, there is hope.

Dum vivimus, vivamus. (Lat.) "While we live, let us live." Let us enjoy life as long as we can.

Dunces' Parliament. A nickname given to a parliament convened by Henry IV. at Coventry in 1404, and so called because all lawyers were excluded therefrom.

Dun Cow of Warwick. Guy, Earl of Warwick, is said to have killed a monster cow of a dun color, which had ravaged the neighborhood. Some huge bones are shown to visitors at Warwick Castle as those of the veritable dun cow. Professor Owen pronounced the bones to be those of a mastodon; and Mr. Isaac Taylor says that the tradition is founded upon the conquest of the *Dena gau*, or Danish settlement in the neighborhood.

Dune Edin, Dunedin. The old Gaelic name for Edinburgh (Edwin's burgh). The term also embodies a description of the site, the words signifying literally "the face of a rock." The name is frequent in Scottish poesy as a synonym for Edinburgh.

Dunelm. Durham.

Dunheved. (Pseud.) Alfred Farthing Robbins, a writer in the English provincial press.

Dunmow Flitch. A prize instituted at Dunmow, in Essex, in 1244, by Robert de Fitzwalter, on the following conditions: "That whatever married couple will go to the priory, and kneeling on two sharp-pointed stones will swear that they have not quarrelled nor repented of their marriage within a year and a day after its celebration, shall receive a flitch of bacon." The prize was first claimed in 1445, two hundred years after it had been instituted. After 1751, up to which date only five presentations had taken place, the flitch was not claimed till 1855. The tenth occasion of awarding the flitch occurred in 1876.

Dunn Browne. (Pseud.) Rev. Samuel Fiske, Congregational divine and author (1828–1864).

Duo. Duodecimo, twelve folds.

Duo. (Ital.) For two voices or instruments. (Mus.)

Durante placito. (Lat.) During pleasure.

Durante vita. (Lat.) While life endures; during life.

Durga. In Hindu mythology the consort of Siva, depicted with ten arms.

Dusty Foot, Court of. *See* PIEPOWDER COURT.

Dutch. In New York especially, and in many other parts of the United States, the name "Dutch" is misapplied to Germans as well as to Hollanders. As Archbishop Trench tells us, "Till late in the seventeenth century 'Dutch' meant (in England) generally German, and a 'Dutchman' a native of Germany," it is evident that this arose, not from a tendency to underrate Germans, but from a courteous effort to call them by their own name, "Deutsch," which but too readily changed into "Dutch." The Americans, therefore, only follow the example of their forefathers, if they still continue to call all Germans "Dutchmen" and their language "Dutch."

Dutch Concert. A great uproar, like that supposed to be made by a party of Dutchmen in sundry stages of intoxication, some singing, others quarrelling, wrangling, and so on.

Dutch Courage. The courage excited by drink; pot valor.

Dutch School of painting is a sort of "pre-Raphaelite" exactness of detail without selection. It is, in fact, photographing exactly what appears before the artist, as faithfully as his art will allow. The subjects are generally the lower classes of social life, as pothouse scenes, drunken orgies, street groups, Dutch boors, etc., with landscapes and still-life.

Dutchy. A by-name conferred on General Sigel by the soldiers of his command in the late civil war.

Duthus. (Pseud.) Alexander Taylor Innes in "Good Words."

Dux femina facti. (Lat.) A woman was the spirit and soul of the enterprise.

D. V. *Deo volente.* God willing.

Dwarfie Stone. "This is one of the wonders of the Orkney Islands, though it has been rather undervalued by their historian, Mr. Barry. The island of Hoy rises abruptly, starting as it were out of the sea, which is contrary to the gentle and flat character of the other Isles of Orkney. It consists of a mountain having different eminences or peaks. It is very steep, furrowed with ravines, and placed so as to catch the mists of the Western Ocean; and has a noble and picturesque effect from all points of view. The highest peak is divided from another eminence, called the Ward Hill, by a long swampy valley full of peat-bogs. Upon the slope of this last hill, and just where the principal mountain of Hoy opens into a hollow swamp, or corrie, lies what is called the Dwarfie Stone. It is a great fragment of sandstone, composing one solid mass, which has long since been detached from a belt of the same materials cresting the eminence above the spot where it now lies, and which has slid down till it reached its present situation. The rock is about seven feet high, twenty-two feet long, and seventeen feet broad. The upper end of it is hollowed by iron tools, of which the marks are evident, into a sort of, apartment, containing two beds of stone, with a passage between them. The uppermost and largest bed is five feet eight inches long, by two feet broad, which was supposed to be used by the dwarf himself; the lower couch is shorter, and rounded off, instead of being squared at the corners. There is an entrance of about three feet and a half square, and a stone lies before it calculated to fit the opening. A sort of skylight window gives light to the apartment. We can only guess at the purpose of this monument, and different ideas have been suggested. Some have supposed it the work of some travelling mason; but the *cui bono* would remain to be accounted for." — SCOTT.

Dwt. Pennyweight.

Dyke, Grahame's. *See* GRAHAME'S DYKE.

Dyn. Dynamics.

E.

E. East.

Ea. Each.

Eagle of Brittany. Bertrand du Guesclin, Constable of France (fl. 1320–1380).

Eagle of Divines. Thomas Aquinas. *See* DUMB OX.

Eagle of France, or Eagle of the Doctors of France. Pierre d'Ailly, the French cardinal and astrologer (fl. 1350–1420). *See* HAMMER, THE.

Eagle of Meaux. Bossuet, bishop of Meaux, was so named. He was by all odds the greatest pulpit orator France ever possessed.

Eagle Orator of Tennessee. Gustavus Adolphus Henry (1804–1880), who achieved great reputation as a public speaker, and was known throughout the South by the above sobriquet.

E. & O. E. Errors and omissions excepted.

Ear. The spikes of the maize-plant are called "ears" only so long as the grains adhere thereto; after "shucking" the spike becomes a "corn-cob." *See* COB.

Earl of Mar's Gray Breeks. The Twenty-first Regiment of Foot in the English army; so named because they wore gray breeches when the Earl of Mar was their colonel, 1678–1686.

Earl of Pleasure Bay. A humorous nickname given to the late Hugh J. Hastings (1820–1883), the American journalist, by the New York "Herald." He possessed an estate at Pleasure Bay, Long Island, where he dispensed lavish hospitality to his friends.

Ear of Dionysius. A famous cavern near Neapolis, in which the slightest whisper was audible at a great distance.

Ears-to-Ear Bible. So named because of a misprint in Matthew xi. 15: "He that hath ears to ear," etc.

East, Crown of the. *See* CROWN OF THE EAST.

Easter Day. Next to Christmas, the Easter festival — the anniversary of the resurrection of our Lord — is the most significant of the several festivals of the Church, and is most commonly and zealously observed. The word "Easter" had, at first, no reference to this Christian event. It is a modified form of the Anglo-Saxon *Eastre*, the name of the goddess of spring, in whose honor a festival was annually celebrated in the month of April. In the only instance in which this word occurs in the New Testament it is a mistranslation of *pascha*, the passover. A movable feast, it occurs, by the authority of the Church, annually on the first Sunday after Good Friday, and corresponds as to time with the Passover of the Jews. Its observance, if not apostolic, dates back to the early post-apostolic times. And yet it is everywhere seen in the writings of the Christian Fathers of the first three centuries that the resurrection of Christ and the general resurrection of the dead are strongly and constantly defined and maintained, and doubtless the anniversary of our Lord's resurrection was observed from the beginning. The observance of Easter was instituted about 68. After much contention between the Eastern and Western churches, it was ordained by the Council of Nice, 325, to be observed on the same day throughout the whole Christian world. " Easter Day is the Sunday following that fourteenth day of the calendar moon which happens upon or next after the 21st of March; so that, if the said fourteenth day be a Sunday, Easter Day is not that Sunday, but the next." Easter-Day may be any day of the five weeks which commence with March 22 and end with April 25; that is to say, Easter Day cannot fall earlier than March 22, nor later than April 25. Some of the most superstitious ideas have been connected with the observance of Easter. It was once believed all over England that the sun dances in a peculiar way on Easter Day. The celebrated Sir Thomas Browne, in his book called "Vulgar Errors," devotes considerable space to upsetting that superstition. Sir John Suckling introduced this error in complimenting the dancing of a young woman, saying:

" No sun upon an Easter Day
Is half as fine a sight."

Easter Eggs. The following interesting account of the present custom of making gifts of eggs at Eastertide is from the pen of Mr. Frank Bellew: " In ancient Persia," he says, "many hundred years before the birth of Christ, the people were all worshippers of fire. According to their religion, as communicated to them by their prophet Zoroaster, there was first a great spirit who had existed from all eternity. From him came the first light; and from this light sprang two brothers, Ormuzd and Ahriman. Ahriman grew jealous of his elder brother, and was condemned by the Eternal One to pass three thousand years in utter darkness. On his release he created a number of bad spirits to oppose the good spirits cre-

ated by Ormuzd; and when the latter made an egg containing good genii, Ahriman produced another full of evil demons, and broke the two together, so that good and evil became mixed in the new creation. This is the legend of Ahriman and Ormuzd. In memory of it the Persians of the present day, on a certain festival in March, present each other with colored eggs; and it is, perhaps, from this that we get our similar Easter custom. But, independently of Persian history, eggs are as full of interest to us as they are proverbially full of meat. They have always been held as symbols of the springing forth of life, and are therefore very naturally associated with the rising of our Lord from the tomb. The festival of Easter, often called the Queen of Festivals, is held to commemorate the resurrection of Christ. Formerly the churches were ornamented with large wax candles, bonfires were lighted, and Christians saluted each other with a kiss and the words 'Christ is risen,' to which answer was made, 'He is risen indeed.' In the present time, as you well know, we celebrate the day by going to church and by making presents of painted eggs and Easter cards. In older times the festival of Easter was celebrated with many ceremonies, sports, and observances. Chief among them then as now was the giving of colored eggs, called 'pasch' or 'pace' eggs, which the boys and girls rolled down some grassy hillside until they broke, the one whose egg held out the longest being the victor, and claiming those of the other contestants. While they were doing this they would sing some ditty with the refrain ' Carland parland, paste egg day.' In a royal roll of the time of Edward I., preserved in the Tower, appears an entry of eighteen pence (thirty-six cents) for four hundred eggs to be used for Easter gifts. The game of ball was a favorite sport on this day, in which the town authorities engaged with due dignity and parade. At Bury St. Edmunds, in England, within a few years, the game was kept up with great spirit by twelve old women. In the northern part of England the men parade the streets on Easter Sunday, and claim the privilege of lifting every woman they meet three times from the ground, receiving in payment a kiss or a silver sixpence. The same is done by the women to the men on the next day. This custom had no doubt originally a religious significance, intended to typify the rising of our Lord on the third day. In Lancashire, England, they keep up the traditions of centuries on Easter Monday. In Preston the young folks of both sexes make a pilgrimage to a park outside the town, each with a colored egg, hard boiled, with an initial or distinguishing mark on it. Everybody makes for the summit of a hill, down which the great aim is to roll the egg without getting it smashed. To see crowds of well-dressed people rolling eggs against one another, is a most amusing spectacle."

Eastern Archipelago, Queen of the. *See* QUEEN OF THE EASTERN ARCHIPELAGO.

Eastern States. In popular parlance, in America, the six New England States, — Maine, New Hampshire, Vermont, Massachusetts, Rhode Island, and Connecticut.

East, Queen of the. *See* QUEEN OF THE EAST.

Easy Accession, The. A phrase at one time current in American politics. It had been the general practice of Presidents, from the first organization of the Government, to tender the post of Secretary of State to the man considered to be next in prominence to himself in the party to which both belonged. In the earlier history of the country the expected successor in the executive office was selected. This was, indeed, for so long a period so uniform that the appointment to the State Department came to be regarded as a designation to the Presidency. In political phrase this mode of reaching coveted place was known as the "easy accession." By its operation Madison succeeded Jefferson, Monroe succeeded Madison, John Quincy Adams succeeded Monroe. After successful application for a quarter of a century the custom fell into disfavor, and by bitter agitation into disuse. The cause of its overthrow was the appointment of Henry Clay to the State Department; and the baseless scandal of a bargain and sale was invented to deprive Mr. Clay of the "easy accession."

Eau de Cologne. (Fr.) "Water of Cologne." A perfume so called.

Eau-de-vie. (Fr.) "Water of life." Brandy.

Eau sucrée. (Fr.) Sugared or sweetened water.

E. B. English Bible.

Eben. Ebenezer.

Eblis. The ruler of the evil genii or fallen angels. Before his fall he was called Azazil. When Adam was created, God commanded all the angels to worship him; but Eblis replied, "Me thou hast created of smokeless fire; and shall I reverence a creature made of dust?" God was very angry at this insolent answer, and turned the disobedient fay into a devil; and he became the father of devils. *See* AZAZIL.

Ebony. A humorous nickname given to William Blackwood (fl. 1777–1834), the founder of "Blackwood's Magazine." "Ebony," of course, means *black-wood*.

Ebor. *Eboracum.* York.

Ebudæ. The Hebrides.

E. by S. East by South.

E. C. Eastern Central, a postal district of London.

Ecce Homo! (Lat.) "Behold the man!" The title of a picture representing the Lord Jesus as given up to the Jews by Pilate, or wearing a crown of thorns.

Ecce signum! (Lat.) "Behold the sign!" Here is the proof.

Eccl. Ecclesiastes.

Ecclus. Ecclesiasticus.

Echion. (Pseud.) Edward Chatfield, in "Blackwood."

Echo. In classic mythology a nymph who became enamored of Narcissus. Her love being unreciprocated, she pined away till there remained of her nothing but her voice.

Eclaircissement. (Fr.) The clearing up of an affair.

Eclat. (Fr.) Splendor; applause.

Eclat de rire. (Fr.) A burst of laughter.

Eclipse first, the Rest nowhere. "Declared by Captain O'Kelley at Epsom, May 3, 1769, when the horse Eclipse distanced the field." — *Annals of Sporting.*

Ecorcheurs. Freebooters of the twelfth century, in France; so called because they stripped their victims of everything, even their clothes.

Ecossais. (Fr.) An air in Scotch style. (Mus.)

E. C. Revons. (Pseud.) Charles Crozet Converse, American *littérateur* (b. 1834).

Ecstatic Doctor. Jean de Ruysbroek, the mystic (fl. 1294–1381).

E. D. Eastern District (of Brooklyn, N. Y.).

Ed. Editor; edition.

E. D. E. N. (Pseud.) Mrs. Emma D. E. (Nevitte) Southworth, American novelist (b. 1818).

Eden, Garden of. *See* GARDEN OF EDEN.

Eden of America. A name bestowed upon the island of Aquidneck, off the coast of Rhode Island, on account of its great fertility.

Edict of Milan. A proclamation by Constantine, after the conquest of Italy, 313, to "secure to Christians the restitution of their civil and religious rights."

Edict of Nantes. A state paper by which Henry IV. of France granted toleration to his Protestant subjects, April 13, 1598. It was confirmed by Louis XIII. in 1610, and by Louis XIV. in 1652. It was revoked by the latter Oct. 22, 1685. This unjust and impolitic act cost France fifty thousand Protestant families, and gave to England and Germany thousands of industrious artisans, who carried with them and established in those countries several valuable handicrafts. *See* REVOCATION.

Edict of Restitution. The decree issued by Frederick II., of Germany, in 1629, requiring the relinquishment of many Church lands.

Edin. Edinburgh.

Edina, or **Edin.** A synonym for Edinburgh, introduced by George Buchanan, and frequently met in Scottish poetry. *See* DUNE EDIN.

Edith Alston. (Pseud.) Mrs. Mary Green Goodale, of New Orleans, a poet of note.

Edith Bland. The stage-name of Mrs. Austin Brereton.

Edith Blande. The stage-name of Mrs. Edward Solomon.

Edith Elliot. (Pseud.) Mrs. A. H. C. Howard, in the "Household," of Brattleboro, Vt.

Edith Harding. The stage-name of Mrs. Charles T. Dazey.

Edith May. (Pseud.) Anna Drinker, American poetess (b. 1830).

Edith Murillo. The stage-name of Mme. Ignacio Martinetti.

Edith Sinclair. The stage-name of Mrs. Edward M. Favor.

Edition de luxe. (Fr.) A handsome edition of a book.

Editio princeps. (Lat.) The first edition.

Edm. Edmund.

Edmund Kirke. (Pseud.) James Roberts Gilmore, American *littérateur.*

Edna Lyall. (Pseud.) Ada Ellen Bayly, an English novelist, author of "Donovan," etc.

Edw. Edward.

Edward Bradwardine Waverly. (Pseud.) John Wilson Croker, English author and critic (1780–1857).

Edward Fitzball. (Pseud.) Edward Ball, English dramatic writer (b. 1814).

Edward Herbert. (Pseud.) John Hamilton Reynolds, English poet (1794–1842).

Edward Lee. The stage-name of Edward Seabrooke.

Edward Search. (Pseud.) (1) William Hazlitt, English critic and miscellaneous writer (1778–1830). (2) Abraham Tucker, English metaphysician (1705–1774).

Edward Sexby. (Pseud.) Josiah Quincy, American orator and patriot (1744–1775).

Edward Spencer. (Pseud.) Caroline Seymour in "Harper's Magazine."

Edward the Robber. Edward IV. was so named by the Scotch.

Edward William Sidney. (Pseud.) Beverly Tucker, American lawyer and novelist (1784–1851).

Edwin Arnott. The stage-name of Edwin Job.

E. E. Errors excepted.

E. E. T. S. Early English Text Society.

Eel-skin. A former name for a thin narrow slip of paper, with the name of a candidate on one side, and coated with mucilage on the other, so as to be quickly and secretly placed over the name of an opponent on a printed ballot. "Eel-skins," judiciously distributed, are the most efficient instruments for "splitting tickets," and securing the election of some favored nominee on a ticket otherwise in the minority. They are now called "pasters."

Effie Afton. (Pseud.) Mrs. Frances Ellen Watkins Harper.

Effie Ellsler. The stage-name of Mrs. Frank Weston.

Effie Weaver. The stage-name of Mrs. Horace McVicker.

Effigy Sargent. Aaron A. Sargent (1827–1887), an American legislator and diplomat.

E. Fl. Ells Flemish.

E. Fr. Ells French.

E. G. *Exempli gratiâ*, for example; *Ex grege*, among the rest.

Egalite. (Fr.) Equality.

Egalité. Philippe, Duc d'Orléans, the father of Louis Philippe, was so surnamed because he sided with the revolutionary party, whose motto was " Liberty, equality, fraternity." Nevertheless he met death on the guillotine in 1793.

Egeria. In classical mythology a nymph who was fabled to have transmitted to Numa Pompilius directions respecting the modes of public worship which he established in Rome.

Ego et rex meus. (Lat.) I and my king.

Ego hoc feci. (Lat.) I did this.

Egomet me ignosco. (Lat.) I overlook my own faults.

Egypt. A slang term, supposed to be descriptive of the people or of the soil of Southern Illinois. The inhabitants at one time possessed the reputation of being extremely ignorant; hence a figurative allusion to the " thick darkness " in which Egypt was involved at the command of Moses. The soil of the locality in question is of unsurpassed fertility, as was the case with that of the land of the Nile. Another writer says, controverting the above explanation: About the year 1835 there was throughout Northern and Central Illinois a great scarcity of corn, while all through Southern Illinois there was a very great abundance; as a consequence, the following fall and winter great numbers came down into " Egypt " (as in ancient times the people went down into ancient Egypt for a like purpose) to buy and carry back corn to supply the wants of the people in that part of the State where the corn crop for that year had been a total failure. The chief product of the State at that time was corn ; but little else was cultivated. It was the staple article of food, both for man and beast. And thus Southern Illinois came to be called " Egypt."

The " thick darkness " and the extreme ignorance never did exist there.

Egyptian Hercules. Sesostris (B. C. 1500).

Egyptus. (Pseud.) Rev. Joseph Parrish Thompson, D. D., American Congregational divine (1819–1879).

E. I. East Indies or East India.

E. I. C., or **E. I. Co.** East India Company.

E. I. C. S. East India Company's Service.

Eight Bells, Four Bells, etc. These shipboard terms have a peculiar meaning, not exactly equivalent to, but serving as a substitute for, " time " or " o'clock " in ordinary land life. The day, or rather the night, is divided into watches or periods, usually of four hours' duration each ; and each half-hour is marked by striking on a bell. The number of strokes depends, not on the hour, according to the ordinary reckoning, but on the number of half-hours which have elapsed in that particular watch. Thus, " three bells " is a phrase denoting that three half-hours have elapsed, but it does not in itself show to which particular watch it refers. *See* DOG-WATCH.

Eikon Basilike (" The Portraiture of His Sacred Majesty in his Solitudes and Sufferings "). A book of devotion formerly believed to have been written by Charles I. during his imprisonment, but now generally attributed to Bishop Gauden. It was published in 1648, and sold rapidly. *See* CALVES' HEAD CLUB.

Ejusdem generis. (Lat.) Of the same kind.

Elagabalus. The Syro-Phœnician sun-god. One of the Roman emperors was so called because he was a priest of Elagabalus. This madman invited the principal men of Rome to a banquet, and smothered them in a shower of roses.

Elan. (Fr.) Buoyancy; dash.

El Atchby. (Pseud.) Lyman Hotchkiss Bazy, in the " Graphic " and the " World," 1873–1878.

Elbe Florence. The city of Dresden; so called from the important part which the river Elbe plays in the city's life and topography.

El Dorado (" the golden," or, rather, " the gilded "). This name was first applied to a man, " el rey dorado," who existed originally in the visions of the Spanish conquerors of America, whose insatiable avarice loved to dream of richer rewards than those of Mexico and Peru. The Castilians found an imitator in Sir Walter Raleigh, who twice visited Guiana in quest of this fabulous region. The name has at last made for itself an abiding-place beyond the furthest limits of Spanish possession. It indicates a county in the northeast of California, of which the capital, Calloma, stands near the spot where the first discovery of gold was made in that State. The district in question is drained by some of the northern feeders of the Sacramento, which empties itself into the Bay of San Francisco.

Eldred Grayson. (Pseud.) Robert Hare, the American scientist (1781–1858), who contributed moral essays to the "Portfolio" under this name.

Eleanor Barry. The stage-name of Mrs. J. G. Chesley.

Eleanor Kirk. (Pseud.) Mrs. Ames, a well-known writer of Brooklyn, N. Y.

Eleanor Moretti. The stage-name of Eleanor Rogers.

Eleanor Putnam. (Pseud.) Mrs. Harriet L. Vose Bates, in the "Atlantic Monthly."

Election Bonfires. *See* GUY FAWKES DAY.

Election Day. The general election day throughout the United States for national officers. By act of Congress, March 1, 1792, amended Jan. 23, 1845, a uniform day of election for Electors of President and Vice-President was fixed for all the States, — being the Tuesday next after the first Monday in November, every fourth year after a President has been elected. Many of the State elections fall on the same day. This occasion is a legal holiday in the States of California, Maine, Missouri, New Jersey, New York, Oregon, South Carolina, and Wisconsin. By act of March 3, 1875, elections of Representatives in Congress are required to be held on the Tuesday next after the first Monday in November, every second year, in 1876 and following years. Subsequent special acts enable States whose Constitutions fix a different date to elect earlier, until they amend their Constitutions. Following is a list of the days upon which State elections fall in the United States : —

STATES.	Times for Election.	Elections. — State. Month and Day.	Elections. — Congressional and Presidential. Month and Day.
Alabama	Bien.	1st Mon. Aug.	Tu. aft. 1 Mon. Nov.
Arkansas	Bien.	1st Mon. Sept.	Tu. aft. 1 Mon. Nov.
California *a*	Bien.	Tu. aft. 1 Mon. Nov.	Tu. aft. 1 Mon. Nov.
Colorado	Bien.	Tu. aft. 1 Mon. Nov.	Tu. aft. 1 Mon. Nov.
Connecticut	Ann.	Tu. aft. 1 Mon. Nov.	Tu. aft. 1 Mon. Nov.
Dakotas	Bien.	Tu. aft. 1 Mon. Nov.	Tu. aft. 1 Mon. Nov.
Delaware	Bien.	Tu. aft. 1 Mon. Nov.	Tu. aft. 1 Mon. Nov.
Florida	Bien.	Tu. aft. 1 Mon. Nov.	Tu. aft. 1 Mon. Nov.
Georgia	Bien.	1st Wed. Oct.	Tu. aft. 1 Mon. Nov.
Illinois	Bien.	Tu. aft. 1 Mon. Nov.	Tu. aft. 1 Mon. Nov.
Indiana	Bien.	Tu. aft. 1 Mon. Nov.	Tu. aft. 1 Mon. Nov.
Iowa *b*	Ann.	Tu. aft. 2 Mon. Oct.	Tu. aft. 1 Mon. Nov.
Kansas	Bien.	Tu. aft. 1 Mon. Nov.	Tu. aft. 1 Mon. Nov.
Kentucky	Bien.	1st Mon. Aug.	Tu. aft. 1 Mon. Nov.
Louisiana *c*	Bien.	Tu. aft. 3 Mon. Apr.	Tu. aft. 1 Mon. Nov.
Maine	Bien.	2d Mon. Sept.	Tu. aft. 1 Mon. Nov.
Maryland	Bien.	Tu. aft. 1 Mon. Nov.	Tu. aft. 1 Mon. Nov.
Massachusetts	Ann.	Tu. aft. 1 Mon. Nov.	Tu. aft. 1 Mon. Nov.
Michigan	Bien.	Tu. aft. 1 Mon. Nov.	Tu. aft. 1 Mon. Nov.
Minnesota	Bien.	Tu. aft. 1 Mon. Nov.	Tu. aft. 1 Mon. Nov.
Mississippi *a*	Bien.	Tu. aft. 1 Mon. Nov.	Tu. aft. 1 Mon. Nov.
Missouri *a*	Bien.	Tu. aft. 1 Mon. Nov.	Tu. aft. 1 Mon. Nov.
Montana	Bien.	Tu. aft. 1 Mon. Nov.	Tu. aft. 1 Mon. Nov
Nebraska	Bien.	Tu. aft. 1 Mon. Nov.	Tu. aft. 1 Mon. Nov.
Nevada *a*	Bien.	Tu. aft. 1 Mon. Nov.	Tu. aft. 1 Mon. Nov.
N. Hampshire	Bien.	Tu. aft. 1 Mon. Nov.	Tu. aft. 1 Mon. Nov.
New Jersey	Ann.	Tu. aft. 1 Mon. Nov.	Tu. aft. 1 Mon. Nov.
New York *a*	Ann.	Tu. aft. 1 Mon. Nov.	Tu. aft. 1 Mon. Nov.
N. Carolina	Bien.	Tu. aft. 1 Mon. Nov.	Tu. aft. 1 Mon. Nov.
Ohio *d*	Ann.	2d Tu. Oct.	2d Tu. Oct.
Oregon *a*	Bien.	1st Mon. June	Tu. aft. 1 Mon. Nov.
Pennsylvania	Ann.	Tu. aft. 1 Mon. Nov.	Tu. aft. 1 Mon. Nov.
Rhode Island	Ann.	1st Wed. April	Tu. aft. 1 Mon. Nov.
S. Carolina	Bien.	Tu. aft. 1 Mon. Nov.	Tu. aft. 1 Mon. Nov.
Tennessee	Bien.	Tu. aft. 1 Mon. Nov.	Tu. aft. 1 Mon. Nov.
Texas	Bien.	1st Tu. Sept.	Tu. aft. 1 Mon. Nov.
Vermont	Bien.	Tu. aft. 1 Mon. Nov.	Tu. aft. 1 Mon. Nov.
Virginia	Bien.	Tu. aft. 1 Mon. Nov.	Tu. aft. 1 Mon. Nov.
Washington	Bien.	Tu. aft. 1 Mon. Nov.	Tu. aft. 1 Mon. Nov.
W. Virginia *a*	Bien.	2d Tu. Oct.	Tu. aft. 1 Mon. Nov.
Wisconsin	Bien.	Tu. aft. 1 Mon. Nov.	Tu. aft. 1 Mon. Nov.
Territories.			
Arizona	Bien.	Tu. aft. 1 Mon. Nov.	Tu. aft. 1 Mon. Nov.
Idaho	Bien.	Tu. aft. 1 Mon. Nov.	Tu. aft. 1 Mon. Nov.
New Mexico	Bien.	Tu. aft. 1 Mon. Nov.	Tu. aft. 1 Mon. Nov.
Utah	Ann.	1st Mon. Aug.	Tu. aft. 1 Mon. Nov.
Wyoming	Bien.	Tu. aft. 1 Mon. Nov.	Tu. aft. 1 Mon. Nov

a In these States the Governor and State officers are elected quadrennially, and the Legislature (or members of the Assembly) every two years.

b In Presidential election years Iowa's election day is the Tuesday after the first Monday in November.

c In Louisiana the Legislature and State officers are elected quadrennially ; members of Congress biennially.

d The Ohio election, for State ticket and Congress, is in October ; for Presidential electors, in November.

Electoral Commission. A temporary expedient to meet the crisis attending the Presidential election of 1876; four States — Louisiana, Oregon, South Carolina, and Florida — having given double, in one case threefold, returns. It was elected by a committee appointed by the two houses of Congress, January, 1877, and consisted of three Republicans and two Democrats from the Senate, and three Democrats and two Republicans from the House, four justices of the Supreme Court, and a fifth justice selected by these. It commenced its examination of the certificates February 1, and on the afternoon of March 2 announced that Hayes and Wheeler were legally elected.

Electra. In classic mythology daughter of Agamemnon and of Clytemnestra, and who conspired with Orestes to murder their mother.

Elegant Extracts. The Eighty-fifth Foot Regiment was so named on being re-organized in 1813, after a series of court-martials. A number of the officers were removed, and their places filled by transfers from other corps.

Elegit. (Lat.) "He hath elected." A writ of execution.

Eleusinian Mysteries. The name given to the sacred rites with which the annual festival of Ceres was celebrated at Eleusis. "Many traditions were afloat in ancient times as to the origin of this festival. Of these, the most generally accepted was to the effect that Ceres, wandering over the earth in quest of her daughter Proserpine, arrived at Eleusis, where she took rest on the 'sorrowful stone' beside the well Callichorus. In return for some small acts of kindness, and to commemorate her visit, she taught Triptolemus the use of corn on the Rharian plain near the city, and instituted the mystic rites peculiarly known as hers. The festival itself consisted of two parts, the greater and the lesser mysteries. The less important feast, serving as a sort of preparation for the greater, was held at Agræ, on the Ilissus. The celebration of the great mysteries began at Eleusis on the fifteenth day of Boëdromion, the third month of the Attic year, and lasted over nine days." — CHAMBERS.

Elève. (Fr.) A pupil.

Eleven Thousand Virgins. An interesting mediæval legend states that a certain Ursula was the daughter of Theonotus, or Diognetus, of Britain. " She was demanded in marriage by a heathen prince named Holofernes, and consented to his demand on condition that he should become a Christian and allow her three years before the marriage in which to make a pilgrimage. He conformed to her will, and with his religion changed his name into Ætherius; and she took ship with eleven thousand virgins. They went first to the port of Tila, in Gaul, and thence up the Rhine to Cologne and Basle, afterwards continuing the pilgrimage by land as far as Rome. When they returned, Pope Cyriacus, with a retinue of clergy, joined the immense procession ; and at Basle the Bishop Paul, or Pantulus, likewise. At Cologne the returning pilgrims were attacked, while disembarking, by hordes of wild Hunnish barbarians, and were all massacred, though the heathen king Attila (Etzel) admired the beauty of Ursula and desired to spare her, that she might become his wife. She fell pierced with an arrow, which has become her peculiar attribute in artistic representations of this saint. Immediately after the massacre heavenly hosts, equal in number to the murdered virgins, appeared and put the barbarians to flight. The delivered inhabitants of the city thereupon buried the fallen pilgrims, and erected to each one a stone bearing her name, — the names having been obtained from James, a bishop, who was in the train of the pilgrims, and who had found a refuge in a cave from the fate of his companions. Soon afterwards Clemantius, a pilgrim from Greece, having been urged in repeated dreams, erected a church among the graves in honor of Ursula and her eleven thousand cómpanions. The sanctity of this place of burial is apparent from the fact that no other interments, even though they be of the bodies of baptized children, can be performed in its hallowed soil." — McCLINTOCK AND STRONG.

Elia. (Pseud.) Charles Lamb, English essayist and humorist (1775–1834).

Eliab. Henry Bennet, Earl of Arlington, was meant by this character in Dryden's satire "Absalom and Achitophel."

Elias of Guatemala. Tomás Victoria, a Spanish missionary to Guatemala in the sixteenth century. He numbered his converts by thousands.

Eli Fant. (Pseud.) Edward Bean Underhill, in various publications in the United States.

Elinor Vey. (Pseud.) Mrs. Eliot Glover, in the " Independent," New York.

Eli Perkins. (Pseud.) Melville D. Landon, American humorous writer.

Elise Holt. The stage-name of Mrs. Henry Wall.

Elite. (Fr.) The best part.

Elivaga. In Scandinavian mythology the name of a mighty river rising in a fountain in Niflheim.

Elixir vitæ. (Lat.) The quintessence of life.

Eliz. Elizabeth.

Eliza. (Pseud.) Mrs. E. J. P. Nicholson, in the New Orleans "Times-Democrat."

Eliza Grace. (Pseud.) Mrs. Katherine Byerly Thompson.

Eliza Orchard. (Pseud.) Mrs. E. A. Connor, sometime literary editor of the New York "World," and later agricultural and scientific editor on the staff of the American Press Association, New York.

Eliza Weathersby. The stage-name of Mrs. Nat C. Goodwin.

Elizabeth Berger. (Pseud.) Elizabeth Sara Sheppard, English novelist (1830–1862).

Elizabeth Robins. The stage-name of Mrs. George R. Barks.

Elizabeth Wetherell. (Pseud.) Susan Warner, American novelist, author of "The Wide, Wide World" (1818–1885).

Ella Beebe. The stage-name of Mrs. M. J. Fitzpatrick.

Ella Bordeaux. The stage-name of Mrs. J. W. Ransome.

Ella Rodman. (Pseud.) Mrs. Eliza Rodman (M'Ilvaine) Church, American poetess (b. 1831).

Ella Sothern. The stage-name of Mrs. Charles Willard.

Ella Stokes. The professional name of Mrs. John B. Doris.

Ella Weaver. The stage-name of Mrs. John H. Whiteley.

Ellen. (Pseud.) Mrs. R. S. R. Nichols (b. 1820), author of poems in the Louisville "News-Letter." *See* KATE CLEAVELAND.

Ellen Allyn. (Pseud.) Christina Georgina Rossetti, an English poetess.

Ellen Louise. (Pseud.) Mrs. Ellen Louise Chandler Moulton, whose earliest writings, *circa* 1841, appeared over this signature.

Ellen Rand. The stage-name of Nellie Fleming.

Ellis Bell. (Pseud.) Emily Brontë, sister of Charlotte Brontë (1819–1848).

Ellis Dale. (Pseud.) G. A. Mackenzie, in the "Canadian Monthly Magazine."

Ellsworth. (Pseud.) Elmer E. Wadman, in various Boston papers.

Ellsworth Outrage. In 1854 the Roman Catholic church of Dorchester, Mass., was blown up by unknown persons, and the "Ellsworth Outrage" took place, in which a priest was inhumanly treated by his fellow-citizens.

Ellyllon. In Welsh mythology souls of the ancient Druids, which, being too good for hell and not good enough for heaven, are permitted to wander upon earth till the judgment day, when they will be admitted to a higher state of being.

Elma South. (Pseud.) Essie B. Cheeseborough.

Elm City, or **Elms, City of.** *See* CITY OF ELMS.

Elmo. The pseudonym of Thomas W. Handford, an American author.

Elocution Walker. A humorous nickname bestowed on John Walker, the English lexicographer (fl. 1732–1807). For many years he taught elocution among the gentry of England.

E. Lon. East longitude.

Eloquent Doctor. Peter Aureolus, Archbishop of Aix, one of the Schoolmen.

El Penseroso. (Pseud.) G. F. Lanigan, a Canadian author, in the "Western Journal."

Elsie Moore. The stage-name of Louise T. O'Loughlin.

Elsie Warwick. (Pseud.) Mrs. E J. Fullilove, in the "New York Weekly."

Elysium. In classic mythology the blissful abode of the good after death. Called also the Elysian Fields.

Elzevirs. Fine pocket editions of the classics, printed by the celebrated family of printers in Holland named Elzevir. Their first book bears date 1683.

E. M. Mining Engineer.

Emancipation Day. April 16. An annual commemorative holiday kept by the colored people in the United States, particularly in Washington, D. C., the day being the anniversary of the signing of the Emancipation Proclamation by President Lincoln in 1863.

Emancipation Proclamation. This was dated Jan. 1, 1863; and in it Lincoln declared all slaves within the Secession States free and untrammelled.

Embargo of 1807. *See* TERRAPIN POLICY.

Embarras de richesse. (Fr.) "Embarrassment of riches." An inexhaustible mine of wealth; difficulties arising from an over-abundance.

Ember Weeks. Four weeks after Quadragesima Sunday, Whit-Sunday, Holyrood Day (September), and St.

Lucia's Day (December). But the belief that persons sat in embers (or
ashes) on these days is without foundation.

Embonpoint. (Fr.) Roundness; good
condition.

Embro. A corrupted form of the
name Edinburgh. *See* DUNE EDIN.

Emerald Isle. A descriptive designation of Ireland, from the brilliant
green of its herbage and foliage in
many parts of the country. It was
coined by the poet Drennan (1754–
1820), in his poem "Erin," where he
also spoke of Ireland as "the Emerald
of Europe."

> An emerald set in the ring of the sea.
> *Cushlamachree.*

Emerald of Europe. *See* EMERALD
ISLE.

Emeritus. (Lat.) One retired from
active official duties.

Eme Roseau. The stage-name of
Mrs. Samuel Colville, formerly Mrs.
Reed.

Emeute. (Fr.) Insurrection; an
uproar.

Emigré. (Fr.) An emigrant; a
refugee.

Emilia. (Pseud.) Miss Pamelia S.
Vinning, a Canadian authoress, who
contributed to various periodicals in
Canada and the United States.

Emily Hare. (Pseud.) Laura Winthrop, an American authoress (b. 1825),
in "Little Blossom's Reward," a book
for children, 1854.

Emily Hermann. (Pseud.) Mrs.
Catherine Luders, American poetess
(b. about 1828).

Emily Jordan. The stage-name of
Mrs. John Chamberlain.

Emily Verdery. (Pseud.) Mrs. E. V.
Battey in the "Sun," New York, and the
"Woman's World" (about 1870).

Emily Vivian. The stage-name of
Mrs. John Kernell.

Emiro Kastos. (Pseud.) Fermin
Toro, Venezuelan statesman (1807–1865),
as editor of a volume of poems by
Manuel Cañete.

Emma Abbott. The professional
name of Mrs. Wetherell, the well-known
operatic singer.

Emma Hanley. The stage-name of
Mrs. Louise Allen.

Emma Lascelles. The stage-name of
Mrs. Frederick E. Queen.

Emma Leslie. (Pseud.) Mrs. Dixon,
authoress of Sunday-school fiction.

Emma Nevada. The professional
name of Mrs. Palmer, *née* Wixon, the
famous prima donna. "Nevada" is derived from the State in which she was
born.

Emma Pierce. The stage-name of
Mrs. Warren Schulz.

Emma Schutz. The stage-name of
Mrs. Louise Harrison.

Emma Sidnal. The stage-name of
Mrs. E. W. Freeman, *née* Landis.

Emma Skerrett. The stage-name
of Mrs. R. F. McClannin.

Emma Whittle. The stage-name of
Mrs. J. P. Clark.

Emp. Emperor; Empress.

Emperor of Believers. A title given
to Omar I., father-in-law of Mahomet
(fl. 581–644).

Emperor of the West. A sobriquet
of John Murray, the famous London
bookseller and publisher (fl. 1778–1843).
He removed from Fleet Street (City) to
Albemarle Street (West End).

Empire of Bees. Mount Hybla, in
Sicily, was so named on account of its
odorous flowers, thyme, and abundance
of honey.

Empire of the Seven Rivers. The
Punjab, India.

Empire State. New York State is
so named because of its predominant
wealth and commerce. The name
"Empire City" is also bestowed upon
its commercial metropolis for the same
reason.

Empire State of the South. Georgia
is so named.

Empressement. (Fr.) Alacrity; haste.

En ami. (Fr.) As a friend.

En arrière. (Fr.) "In the rear."
Behind.

En attendant. (Fr.) In the mean
time.

En avant. (Fr.) Forward.

En beau. (Fr.) In a favorable
light.

En bloc. (Fr.) In a lump.

En bon train. (Fr.) "In good
train." In a fair way.

En buste. (Fr.) "In bust." Half
length.

En cachette. (Fr.) Privately; secretly; by stealth.

En cavalier. (Fr.) As a gentleman.

Enceladus. In classic mythology son of Titan and Terra, and most powerful of the giants who rose against Jupiter and attempted to scale the heights of heaven. He was overwhelmed by Mount Etna.

En commandite. (Fr.) "In partnership." As in *société en commandite*, in France, a commercial company with unlimited responsibility as regards its acting partners only; a limited liability company.

Encratites. A sect of the second century, who condemned marriage, forbade eating flesh or drinking wine, and rejected all the luxuries and comforts of life as "things sinful." The sect was founded by Tatian, a disciple of Justin Martyr.

Encyc. Encyclopædia.

Encyc. Amer. Encyclopædia Americana.

Encyc. Brit. Encyclopædia Britannica.

Encyclopédists. A brilliant company of Frenchmen, of high literary and philosophical attainments, but whose opinions were tainted with the scepticism and impracticable revolutionary ideas of the last half of the eighteenth century. The names of the chief of them were: D'Alembert, Diderot, Rousseau, Grimm, Dumarsais, Voltaire, Baron d'Holbach, and Jancourt. Their "Encyclopédie" was founded on Chambers's Encyclopædia, published in Edinburgh. Speaking of the rise of the Encyclopédists and their influence in this "storm and stress" period of French history, Guizot says,—

Other influences, more sincere and at the same time more dangerous, were simultaneously undermining men's minds. The group of Encyclopédists, less prudent and less temperate than Voltaire, flaunted openly the flag of revolt. At the head marched Denis Diderot, born in 1715, the most daring of all, the most genuinely affected by his own ardor, without perhaps being the most sure of his ground in his negations. He was an original and exuberant nature, expansively open to all new impressions; it was in conjunction with his friends and in community of ideas that Diderot undertook the immense labor of the "Encyclopédie." Having, in the first instance, received a commission from a publisher to translate the English collection of Ephraim Chambers, Diderot was impressed with a desire to unite in one and the same collection all the efforts and all the talents of his epoch, so as to render joint homage to the rapid progress of science. Won over by his enthusiasm, D'Alembert consented to share the task; and he wrote the beautiful exposition in the introduction. Voltaire sent his articles from "Les Dé-

lices." The Jesuits had proposed to take upon themselves a certain number of questions, but their co-operation was declined : it was a monument to philosophy that the Encyclopédists aspired to raise; the clergy were in commotion at seeing the hostile army, till then uncertain and unbanded, rally organized and disciplined around this vast enterprise. An early veto, soon, however, taken off, compelled the philosophers to a certain moderation. Voltaire ceased writing for the "Encyclopédie;" it was not sufficiently free-going for him. New severities on the part of the Parliament and the Grand Council dealt a blow to the philosophers before long : the editors' privilege was revoked. Orders were given to seize Diderot's papers. Lamoignon de Malesherbes, who was at that time director of the press, and favorable to freedom without ever having abused it in thought or action, sent him secret warning. Diderot ran home in consternation. "What's to be done?" he cried; "how move all my manuscripts in twenty-four hours? I have n't time even to make a selection. And, above all, where find people who would and can take charge of them safely?" "Send them all to me," replied M. de Malesherbes, "nobody will come thither to look for them." — *History of France.*

En déshabille. (Fr.) In undress.

En Dieu est ma fiance. (Fr.) In God is my trust.

Endymion. In classical mythology a beauteous youth of Caria, whose life passed in perpetual sleep. Diana was said to visit him nightly, as he lay in a cave, that she might kiss him unobserved.

E. N. E. East Northeast.

En échelon. (Fr.) "In echelon;" applied to a body of troops formed in divisions appearing as the steps of a stair.

Energico, or **Con energia.** (Ital.) With energy. (Mus.)

E. Nesbit. The pen-name of an English poet named Mrs. Edith Bland, wife of Hubert Bland.

En famille. (Fr.) With one's family; alone; by themselves.

Enfants perdus. (Fr.) "Lost children." In an attack on a fortified place, "the forlorn hope."

Enfant terrible. (Fr.) "A terrible child." A child that causes annoyance by innocent but ill-timed remarks to others.

En flute. (Fr.) Carrying guns on the upper deck only.

Eng. England; English.

Eng. Dept. Department of Engineers.

Engineer = Engine-driver. The expert who handles the throttle of an English locomotive is called the "engine-driver," — a wise distinction as compared with our American use of the term "engineer," which confounds men of vastly different callings.

England, Achilles' Heel of. *See* ACHILLES' HEEL OF ENGLAND.

England, Garden of. *See* GARDEN OF ENGLAND.

England's Domestic Poet. William Cowper, author of " The Task" (1731–1800).

English Aristophanes. Samuel Foote, the comic dramatist (fl. 1772–1777). Sometimes altered to " Modern Aristophanes."

English Atticus. Joseph Addison was christened thus by Pope, because of the polish of his style and the refinement of his taste.

English Bastile. A name bestowed, in the early years of the present century, on Coldbath Fields Prison, London, from the number of prisoners of State immured there.

English Connemara. A name conferred by Charles Dickens on the district known as Agar-town in the parish of St. Pancras, London, because of the squalid and uncivilized condition of its population.

English Cremera. A name given to the disastrous battle of Isandula, in Zululand, Jan. 22, 1879. Five companies of the Twenty-fourth Regiment were annihilated. The allusion is to the slaying of all the grown-up males of the Fabii, to the number of three hundred and six, near Cremera, B. C. 447.

English Ennius. Layamon, who wrote a translation in Saxon of Wace's " Brute."

English Mersenne. John Collins, mathematician and physicist (1624–1683); so called from Marin Mersenne, the French philosopher.

English Opium-eater. Thomas De Quincey, author of the famous " Confessions " (fl. 1785–1850).

English Pale. *See* PALE, THE.

English Palestrina. Orlando Gibbons (1583–1625), an English composer of sacred music, the excellence of which gained him the above title.

English Petrarch. Sir Philip Sidney (fl. 1554–1586) was so named by Sir Walter Raleigh. *See* WARBLER OF POETIC PROSE.

English Solomon. (1) A satirical sobriquet given to James I. of England, called by Sully "the wisest fool in Christendom." (2) Henry VII. was so named on account of his wise policy in uniting the rival White and Red Rose factions.

English Thoreau. Richard Jefferies, an English author, because of his profound and sympathetic knowledge of wood lore.

En grand seigneur. (Fr.) In lordly style.

En grande tenue. (Fr.) In full dress.

En grande toilette. (Fr.) In full dress.

Enid Hart. The stage-name of Mrs. Frederick Fallen.

Enlightened Doctor. Raymond Lully, of Parma, one of the most learned philosophers and physicists of his day (fl. 1234–1315).

En masse. (Fr.) In a body.

En mauvaise odeur. (Fr.) "In bad odor." In bad repute.

Ennui. (Fr.) Weariness; lassitude.

En papillotes. (Fr.) In curl-papers.

En passant. (Fr.) By the way; in passing.

En pension. (Fr.) At a boarding-house; as a boarder.

En rapport. (Fr.) In communication; in harmony.

En règle. (Fr.) As it should be; according to regulations.

En résumé. (Fr.) To sum up; on the whole.

En revanche (Fr.) "In revenge." Another chance to make up for it.

En route. (Fr.) On one's way.

Ensanguined Garment. *See* BLOODY SHIRT.

Ense petit placidam sub libertate quietem. (Lat.) By his sword he seeks the calm repose of liberty.

Ensemble. (Fr.) The whole taken together.

En suite. (Fr.) In company.

Ent., Entom. Entomology.

Entente cordiale. (Fr.) A cordial understanding, as between two or more governments.

En titre. (Fr.) "In title." In name only; titular.

Entourage. (Fr.) "Surroundings." The immediate attendants of a prince; adjuncts; ornaments.

En tout. (Fr.) "In all." Wholly.

Entrée. (Fr.) Entrance.

Entremets. (Fr.) Small and dainty dishes set between the chief ones at table.

Entre nous. (Fr.) Between ourselves.

En vérité. (Fr.) "In truth." Verily.

Env. Ext. Envoy Extraordinary.

Eo nomine. (Lat.) "By that name." For this reason.

Eos. In classic myth the goddess of the dawn. The same as Aurora (*q. v.*).

e. o. w. Every other week.

Ep. Epistle.

Epaminondas. (Pseud.) Gideon Granger, American statesman (1767–1822), published several political essays under this signature.

Eph. Ephesians; Ephraim.

Ephesian Poet. Hipponax. He was born at Ephesus in the sixth century B. C.

Ephialtes. In classic myth one of the Titans who warred on the celestial gods. Apollo deprived him of his left eye, and Hercules put out his right eye.

Epicurus of China. Tao-tse, who flourished about 540 B. C. He sought to discover the elixir of life; and several Chinese emperors lost their lives by swallowing his "Potion of Immortality."

Epicurus Rotundus. (Pseud.) Shirley Brooks in London "Punch."

Epigoni. In classic myth the name given to the seven Greek heroes who besieged Thebes.

Epimenides. A philosopher of Crete, who fell asleep in a cave when a boy, and did not wake again for fifty-seven years, when he found himself endowed with miraculous wisdom.

Epiphany ("appearance" or "manifestation"). January 6, celebrating the manifestation of the Saviour by the appearance of the star which conducted the Magi to the place where he was to be found. Its observance as a church festival dates from 813. It was formerly named "Christmas of the Gentiles." *See* TWELFTH NIGHT.

Epis. Episcopal.

E pluribus unum. (Lat.) "One composed of many." The motto of the United States.

Epsilon. (Pseud.) Edward Denham, in the Boston "Transcript."

Equal-Rights Party. This was the name of the New York faction of the Democratic party that subsequently became known as the Loco-foco party. In the presidential contest of 1884 Mrs. Belva A. Lockwood was the candidate of an Equal-Rights party advocating woman suffrage. She had practically no following. Her vote in the United States was less than 2,500 out of a total of over 10,000,000.

E. R. East River.

Er. Erbium.

Era of Good Feeling. Monroe's administration (1817–1825); "the excitement and animosities aroused by the War of 1812 had subsided, and there was no sectionalism to disturb the repose and progress of the country." Benjamin Russell, editor of the Boston "Centinel" (1761–1845), originated the phrase in his paper on the occasion of President Monroe's visit in 1817.

Era of Martyrs. The reign of Diocletian. *See* DIOCLETIAN ERA.

Erasmus. (Pseud.) Miss Jeannette L. Gilder, New York literary correspondent of the Philadelphia "Press."

Erato. In classic myth one of the Nine Muses. She presided over amatory poetry.

Erceldoune. (Pseud.) Willis H. Bocock, in the "Central Presbyterian," Richmond, Va.

Erebus ("darkness"). In classic myth son of Chaos, and one of the gods of Hades.

Eretrian Bull. Menedemos of Eretria, in Eubœa; a Greek philosopher of the fourth century B. C., and founder of the Eretrian school, which was a branch of the Socratic. He was so called from the bull-like gravity of his face.

Ergo. (Lat.) Therefore.

Erigena. A surname of John Scotus the Schoolman (d. 886).

Erin. A very old name for Ireland, but now used only in poetry.

> There came to the beach a poor exile of Erin,
>   The dew on his thin coat was heavy and chill ;
> For his country he sighed when at twilight repairing
>   To wander alone by the wind-beaten hill.
>   CAMPBELL, *The Exile of Erin.*

Erinnys. In classic mythology an avenging deity, — one of the Furies (*q. v.*).

Eripitur persona, manet res. (Lat.) The person is snatched away, the goods remain.

Eripuit cœlo fulmen, sceptrumque tyrannis. (Lat.) He snatched the thunderbolt from heaven, and the sceptre from tyrants.

Eris. In classic mythology the goddess of discord; the same as the Roman Discordia.

Erminage Street. One of the four great roads constructed in England by the Romans. *See also* FOSSE, THE, IKENILD STREET, and WATLING STREET.

Fair weyes many on ther ben in Englond,
But four most of all ben zunderstond.
From the south into the north takit Erming strete.
ROBERT OF GLOUCESTER.

Ermite. (Pseud.) Patrick Eugene Moriarty, American Catholic clergyman (1804–1875), who published numerous essays in the Philadelphia press on Irish history and controversial subjects. *See* HIEROPHILOS.

Ernest Hoven. (Pseud.) Fanny Hooker.

Ernest Sutton. The stage-name of Ernest James Sorl.

Eros. In classic mythology the Greek name of the Roman Cupid.

Errare est humanum. (Lat.) To err is human.

Erratic Enrique. (Pseud.) Henry Clay Lukens, in the "Daily News" of New York, and author of "Jets and Flashes," New York (1883).

Erycina. In classic mythology another name for Venus (*q. v.*); derived from Mount Eryx in Sicily, where she had a temple.

Erysichthon. In classic mythology a thoughtless fellow who felled trees in a grove sacred to Ceres. The goddess, as a punishment, afflicted him with raging and never-satisfied hunger.

E. S. Ells Scotch.

Esd. Esdras.

E. S. E. East Southeast.

Eskdale Tam. (Pseud.) Thomas Telford, a Scottish poet, in "Ruddiman's Weekly Magazine."

Espièglerie. (Fr.) Waggish tricks.

Espressivo, or **Con espress.** (Ital.) With expression. (Mus.)

Espriella. (Pseud.) Robert Southey, English poet laureate (1774–1843).

Esprit de corps. (Fr.) The prevailing spirit of honor which guides the actions of individuals of any "collective body," such as the army and the bar, in the interests of that "body."

Esprit délicat. (Fr.) A person of refined or correct taste.

Esprit fort. (Fr.) A free-thinker: a rationalist.

Esq. Esquire.

Essay Kaigh. (Pseud.) S. A. Kenner in the "Salt Lake City Herald."

Esse quam videri. (Lat.) "To be [rather] than to seem." It is infinitely better to possess the actual thing than only to seem to have it.

Essex Junto, The. "In 1781 John Hancock applied this name to a number of public men from Essex County, Mass., and their followers. The commercial classes were naturally those that desired a strong Federal Government, and these men were the ablest representatives of that class and foremost among the advocates of the adoption of the Constitution. After the adoption they formed a part of the Federal party, and were more particularly adherents of Hamilton. They thus incurred the opposition of John Adams, who attempted to make them appear as a 'British faction' hostile to France. It was he, also, that revived the name that had fallen into disuse. Subsequently the name came to stand generally for the Federalist spirit of New England; and the troubles in that section during the War of 1812, as the Hartford Convention, etc., were attributed to the Essex Junto. Among its members were Pickering and Fisher Ames." — BROWN AND STRAUSS.

Essex Lions. Calves, for which the county is famous. Whence the ironical saying, "As brave as an Essex lion."

Essex Stile. A local nickname in Essex, England, for a ditch. As the country is very marshy and wet, it has many ditches which serve as fences, and hence there are few stiles.

Estates of the Realm. It is generally believed that the three estates of the realm are Queen, Lords, and Commons. Whatever may be meant by the phrase now, it was clear that this was not the original meaning. The Collect for the 5th of November in the old Prayer Books speaks of "the King, *and* the three estates of the realm of England assembled in Parliament." The meaning evidently was : (1) The Lords Spiritual ; (2) The Lords Temporal ; (3) The Commons. As the word "realm" means "a kingdom, a state, a region," it is clear that the king or queen cannot be a part of it. *See* FOURTH ESTATE.

Estelle. (Pseud.) (1) Miss Elizabeth Bogart, in the "Mirror," of New York. (2) Mrs. M. W. F. Brown, in the "Southern Literary Messenger."

Estelle Clayton. The stage-name of Mrs. S. E. Cooper, *née* Evesson.

Estelle Purcell. The stage-name of Mrs. Frank M. Fielders.

Esth. Esther.

Esther Chesney. (Pseud.) Miss Clara V. Durgan, author of stories and sketches in Southern papers.

Esther Sarah Kenneth. (Pseud.) Mrs. E. M. Babson.

Est-il-possible. A nickname conferred on Prince George of Denmark, by James II. It is said that when the startling events of the Revolution of 1688 succeeded one another with breathless rapidity, the emotions of Prince George found vent in the repeated exclamation, " Est-il-possible ? " King James, enumerating those who had forsaken him, said, " And *Est-il-possible* has gone too! "

Est modus in rebus. (Lat.) There is a middle way or medium in all things.

Esto perpetua. (Lat.) " Let it be perpetual." Let it endure forever.

Estotiland. A vast arctic country having no existence save in the fertile brains of the old geographers, and placed by them on the spot now occupied by portions of Newfoundland, Labrador, and that part of British America bordering on Hudson's Bay. It was said to have been discovered by two Friesland fishermen driven out of their course by a storm, two centuries before the time of Columbus ; but the story is nothing more than a legend. In 1497 the Cabots set sail from England for Estotiland, but discovered instead Newfoundland.

> The snow
> From cold Estotiland.
> MILTON, *Paradise Lost.*

E. T. Electric telegraph ; English translation.

Et al. *Et alii.* And others.

Etc., or **&c.** *Et cæteri, et cæteræ, et cætera.* And others ; and so forth.

The "ampersand," as the sign & is named, is simply a contracted form of *et*, which in old MSS. was written *&.* Modern type-founders have restored this shape to the ampersand. The latter word is thought to be a corruption of "and per se and."

Et cætera. (Lat.) "And the others." And other things ; etc.

Etelka Gerster. The professional name of Mrs. Gardini, the famous prima donna.

Etelka Wardell. The stage-name of Eva Heaton.

Eteocles. In classic mythology son of Œdipus, king of Thebes, and brother of Polynices. The brothers agreed to reign on alternate years, but Eteocles broke the compact. A duel ensued, in which both were slain.

Eternal City. Rome, the capital of Italy. Legend states that it was raised by or under the immediate supervision of the immortal gods. The term is frequently to be met in classic literature.

Eternal Table. A pearl, extending from east to west and from heaven to earth, on which, according to Mahomet, God records every event, past, present, and future.

Etesian Winds. The name given to breezes that blow in summer from the African Sahara over the south of Europe. They are dry and warm.

Eth. Ethiopic ; Ethiopian.

Ethan Spike. (Pseud.) Matthew F. Whittier, American *littérateur* (1812–1883).

Ethel Brandon. The stage-name of Mrs. L. R. Stockwell.

Ethel Deen. (Pseud.) Mrs. Augusta De Milley, a well-known contributor to various Southern periodicals.

Ethel Gale. (Pseud.) Helen E. Smith, in "The Independent," New York.

Ethel Hope. (Pseud.) Mrs. I M. P. Henry, contributor to various Southern magazines.

Ethelyn Hodgson. The stage-name of Mrs. U. E. McCoy.

Ethel Lynn. (Pseud.) Mrs. E. L. Beers (*née* Eliot, 1827–1879), an American author, whose earliest writings bore the above pen-name. She was christened " Ethelinda," but after her marriage wrote her Christian name " Ethel Lynn."

Ethnic Plot. The "Popish Plot" is so called in Dryden's satire of "Absalom and Achitophel." As Dryden calls the royalists "Jews," and calls Charles II. "David king of the Jews," the papists were " Gentiles " (or "Εθνη), whence the " Ethnic Plot " means the plot of the Ethnoi against the people of God.

Et hoc genus omne. (Lat.) And everything of the same kind.

Ethon. In classic myth the bird of prey that tore at the vitals of Prometheus.

Etincelle. (Pseud.) Vicomtesse de Peyronney, French novelist and writer (b. 1841).

Etre un melon. (Fr.) "To be a melon." To be without understanding.

Et seq. *Et sequentia.* And what follows.

Et sequentes. (Lat.) And those (persons) that follow. *Et sequentia,* and those (things) that follow.

Et sic de cæteris. (Lat.) And so of the rest.

Et sic de similibus. (Lat.) "And so concerning similar" (things). And the same may be said of everything similar.

Ettrick Shepherd. James Hogg, the Scottish poet (fl. 1772–1835), who was born in Ettrick Forest, Selkirkshire, where his father kept sheep.

Et tu, Brute. (Lat.) "And thou, too, O Brutus;" "and thou, also, Brutus;" said of one from whom the conduct of a friend and not of an enemy would have been expected. In this, reference is made to the exclamation which Cæsar uttered, on receiving the stab from his friend Brutus.

Etude. (Fr.) A study.

Etym. Etymology.

E. U. Evangelical Union.

Eudorchawg Chains, or "Gold Chains of the Welsh," were the distinguished marks of rank and valor among the numerous tribes of Celtic extraction. Manlius, the Roman champion, gained the name of Torquatus, or "He of the Chain," on account of an ornament of this kind won, in single combat, from a gigantic Gaul. Aneurin, the Welsh bard, mentions, in his poem on the battle of Catterath, that no less than three hundred of the British who fell there had their necks wreathed with the Eudorchawg. This seems to infer that the chain was a badge of distinction and valor, perhaps, but not of royalty; otherwise there would scarce have been so many kings present in one battle. This chain has been found in Ireland and Wales, and sometimes, though more rarely, in Scotland. Doubtless it was of too precious materials not to be usually converted into money by the enemy into whose hands it fell.

Eugene Pomeroy. (Pseud.) Thomas F. Donnelly, American *littérateur.*

Eugene Revillo. The stage-name of Eugene Oliver.

Eugenia Blair. The stage-name of Mrs. Forrest Robinson, *née* Wren.

Eumenides. In classic myth a pleasant-sounding name given by the Greeks to the Furies (*q. v.*), whose real name, Erinnyes, they were afraid to speak.

Euphrosyne. One of the Three Graces (*q. v.*).

Euphrosyne. (Pseud.) Richard Graves, English divine and author (1715–1804).

Eurasian Plain. A name given to the great central plateau of Europe and Asia by ethnologists.

Eureka. (Gr.) I have found it.

Euroclydon. The name given by the ancients to a tempestuous wind blowing from the east on the Mediterranean.

Eurolychus. In classic myth one of the comrades of Ulysses in his travels, and the only one who was not metamorphosed by Circe into a hog.

Europa. In classic myth the lovely daughter of Phœnix, carried off by Jupiter from Phœnicia to Crete in the form of a white bull.

Europe, Granary of. *See* GRANARY OF EUROPE.

European Saratoga, The. Baden-Baden, famous for its medicinal waters and as a resort of fashion. Similarly, Saratoga has been named the "American Baden-Baden."

Euryale. One of the Three Gorgons, in the mythology of the ancients.

Euryalus. In classic myth a youth of Troy eulogized by Virgil as the *fidus achates* of Nidus.

Eurydice. In classic myth wife of Orpheus, slain by a serpent on her bridal day.

Eurynome. In classic myth the mother of the Graces.

Eusebia. (Pseud.) Frances Thynne Somerset, Countess of Hertford (1699–1754).

Eusebius. (Pseud.) Rev. Edward Dorr Griffith Prime, American Presbyterian divine (b. 1814).

Euterpe. In classic myth the goddess of music.

Eutychians. Heretics of the fifth century, opposed to the Nestorians. They maintained that Jesus-Christ was entirely God previous to the incarnation, and entirely man during his sojourn on earth. The founder was Eutyches, an abbot of Constantinople, who was excommunicated in 448.

Eva Boucicault. The stage-name of Mrs. John Clayton.

Evacuation Day. The day on which the British army evacuated the city of New York, Nov. 25, 1783, the annual return of which has been celebrated in that city for over a century. Samuel Woodworth thus alludes to the day: —

> The British troops had gone away ;
> And every patriot true
> Then kept Evacuation Day,
> When this old house was new.
> *New York Post.*

Evadne. In classic myth the wife of Capaneus. Her husband having been slain at the siege of Troy, she threw herself on the funeral pile and was consumed with him.

Eva Fetrazzini. The stage-name of Signora Cleofonte Campanini.

Eva Florence Ross. The stage-name of Mrs. Victor Stevens, *née* Maryatt.

Evander. In classic myth a son of Mercury by a nymph of Arcadia, said to have headed a Pelasgian colony from Arcadia into Italy sixty years before the Trojan War.

Evangelic Doctor. John Wycliffe, "the morning star of the Reformation" (1324-1384).

Evangeline. (Pseud.) Miss Ellen A. Moriarty in the "Citizen" published by "Miles O'Reilly."

Everard Berkeley. (Pseud.) Tryon Edwards, D.D., American theologian (b. 1809).

Ever-Faithful Isle. Cuba, in reference to its attachment to Spain despite centuries of misgovernment.

Evergreen. The signature of Washington Irving in "Salmagundi."

Ever-Memorable. A title often given to John Hales, an able and scholarly divine of the Church of England (fl. 1584-1656).

Everybody's Business is Nobody's Business. In Izaak Walton's glorious "Compleat Angler" (part i., c. 2), he says, "I remember that a wise friend of mine did usually say, 'That which is everybody's business is nobody's business.'"

Evil Eye. It was anciently believed that the eyes of some persons darted noxious rays on objects which they looked at. The first morning glance of such eyes was certain destruction to man or beast. Virgil speaks of an evil eye making cattle lean.

> Who has bewitched my lambs, prithee say, if any the hag knows ? — *Eclogues.*

Shortly after his election Pius IX., who was then adored by the Romans and perhaps the best-loved man in Italy, was driving through the streets when he happened to glance upward at an open window at which a nurse was standing with a child. A few minutes afterward the nurse let the child drop and it was killed. No one thought the Pope had wished this, but the fancy that he had the evil eye became universal and lasted till his death. In Carniola if you tell a mother that her baby is strong and large for its age, a farmer that his crops are looking well, or a coachman that his team is good, all three will spit at your feet to avert the omen ; and if you understand the custom, you will do the same as an act of politeness. A person who wandered through upper Carniola, and praised everything he saw, would soon come to be considered the most malevolent of men. In Naples exactly the same feeling exists. This superstition, however, is by no means confined to Naples or Italy ; it is said to be common in China and Japan, and among negroes and red Indians. Even in England it is not unknown. — *Saturday Review.*

Evil May Day. May 1, 1517; so named because of the atrocities committed on that day by English apprentices against foreigners, especially the French.

Ex. Out of ; lately of, etc.

Ex. Example; Exodus.

Exactress of Gold. An old name for Babylon.

Ex adverso. (Lat.) In opposition; from the opposite side.

Ex animo. (Lat.) "From the soul." Heartily; with the whole heart.

Exc. Excellency; exception.

Ex capite. (Lat.) "From the head." From memory.

Ex cathedra. (Lat.) "From the chair." As a professor teaches; with official authority.

Excelsior. (Lat.) "Higher." More elevated ; onward ; upward.

Excelsior State. The State of New York, from the motto on its coat-of-arms.

Exceptio probat regulam. (Lat.) The exception proves the rule

Exception proves the Rule. This proverbial saying is very generally misunderstood. The word "prove" anciently meant "test," and is so used in this saying. An old use of the word "prove" occurs in the advice of Saint Paul, "Prove all things," etc.; which means that we should *test* all things, so as to know which good ones to "hold fast." An exception cannot prove a rule in the modern sense, it tends rather to render it invalid; but an exception may *test* a rule, and in some cases prove it to be wrong, while in others the test may show that the so-called exception may be explained. Another theory on the subject is that the very word "exception" implies that there is a rule; so that the word "prove" means "proves the existence of."

Exceptis excipiendis. (Lat.) The requisite exceptions being made.

Excerpta. (Lat.) Extracts.

Exch. Exchequer; exchange.

Ex commodo. (Lat.) Conveniently; at one's leisure.

Ex concesso. (Lat.) From what has been granted.

Ex confesso. (Lat.) Confessedly; from one's own confession.

Ex curia. (Lat.) Out of court.

Ex delicto. (Lat.) From the crime.

Ex. Doc. Executive Document.

Ex dono Dei. (Lat.) By the gift of God.

Exeat. (Lat.) "Let him go out." He may depart for a time.

Exec. Com. Executive Committee.

Execution Bell, that tolled from the steeple of the Church of St. Sepulchre, London, prior to the execution of criminals at Newgate.

Execx. Executrix.

Exempli gratia. (Lat.) For the sake of example. Abbreviated *e. g.*

Exeter Controversy. A pamphlet war between Episcopalians and Dissenters (1707–1715) anent a tract entitled " Plain Truth," by the Rev. John Agate, of Exeter, an Episcopalian.

Exeter Domesday. A record containing a description of the counties of Wilts, Dorset, Somerset, Devon, and Cornwall, England, kept among the muniments of the dean and chapter of Exeter.

Exeunt omnes. (Lat.) They all depart.

Ex facie. (Lat.) "On the surface." Manifestly; on the very face of it.

Ex fumo dare lucem. (Lat.) Out of smoke to bring light.

Ex. gr. *Exempli gratiâ.* For example.

Ex hypothesi. (Lat.) "From supposition." On a supposition; hypothetically.

Exit. (Lat.) "He goes out." He walks off or departs.

Ex mero motu. (Lat.) Of one's own free-will.

Ex necessitate. (Lat.) Out of necessity; necessarily.

Ex necessitate rei. (Lat.) "From the necessity of the thing." From the urgency of the case.

Ex nihilo nihil fit. (Lat.) "Out of nothing, nothing is made." Nothing can be produced out of nothing.

Ex occulto. (Lat.) Secretly; by way of surprise.

Exodus. (1) The "going out" of the Hebrews from Egypt under the leadership of Moses and Aaron. (2) A widespread movement in 1879 among the blacks of the South to Kansas and the West.

Ex officio. (Lat.) By virtue of his office; officially.

Exon. *Exonia.* Exeter.

Ex parte. (Lat.) From one side; one-sided.

Expect. The equivalent in the Middle States for the New England "guess."

Expectation Week. Between the Ascension and Whit-Sunday, when the Apostles continued praying "in earnest expectation of the Comforter."

Ex pede Herculem. (Lat.) "From the foot Hercules." We recognize a Hercules from the foot; we can judge the whole from the specimen.

Experientia docet. (Lat.) "Experience teaches." We are taught by experience.

Experimentum crucis. (Lat.) "The experiment of the cross." A crucial experiment; a most searching test.

Experto crede. (Lat.) Trust one who has had experience.

Exposé. An exposure; a recital.

Ex post facto. (Lat.) After the deed is done.

Expounder of the Constitution. Daniel Webster (fl. 1782–1852) was so named because of his masterly interpretations of the Constitution of the United States.

Expunging Resolution. In the Senate of the United States, Dec. 26, 1836,

Thomas Hart Benton, of Missouri, made a motion by which a resolution adopted by the Senate March 28, 1834, reflecting on President Jackson, was ordered to be expunged from the journal of the Senate by drawing black lines around it and writing across it the following words : " Expunged by order of the Senate this —— day of —— 1837." Benton's resolution was adopted March 16, 1837.

Exr., or Exec. Executor.

Ex tempore. Without premeditation.

Exterminator, The. An epithet bestowed by the Spaniards on Montbars, a cruel French buccaneer (b. 1645), who made his name notorious by the atrocities he committed in the Antilles and other colonies of Spain.

Extra Billy. William Smith, Governor of Virginia (1796–1887). In early manhood he established a line of postcoaches through Maryland, Virginia, and Georgia, on which he contracted to carry the United States mail. His sobriquet of " Extra Billy " Smith, which clung to him throughout his life, grew out of his demands for extra compensation for that service.

Extra muros. (Lat.) " Beyond the walls."

Ex uno, disce omnes. (Lat.) " From one, learn all." From one you can judge of the whole.

Ex vano. (Lat.) Without cause; foolishly.

Eye of Greece. The ancients so named the city of Athens, the most renowned of Greek cities.

> Athens the eye of Greece, mother of arts
> And eloquence, native to famous wits
> Or hospitable.
> MILTON, *Paradise Regained*, Book iv.

Eyes, Symbolism of the. Long almond-shaped eyes, with thick-skinned eyelids that cover half the pupil, are indicative of genius when they are found in conjunction with a brow which is full over the eyebrows, and which has one deep perpendicular line between the eyebrows. This combination may be frequently noticed in the faces of distinguished literary men and artists. The almond-shaped eye, however, even without this particular form of forehead, always means a susceptible, impressionable nature. Eyes which are large, open, and very transparent, and which sparkle with a rapid motion under well-defined eyelids, denote elegance in taste, a somewhat susceptible temper, and great interest in the opposite sex. Eyes with weakly marked eyebrows above them, and with thinly growing eyelashes which are completely without any upward curve, denote a feeble constitution and a melancholy disposition. Deep-sunken and small blue eyes, under a bony, almost perpendicular forehead, are indicative of selfish and cold-hearted natures. Eyes which show not only the whole of the iris, but also some of the white both above and below it, denote a restless, uncertain nature, incapable of repose or of concentrated thought on any subject. The eyes of a voluptuary move slowly under heavy lids. Round-shaped eyes are never seen in the face of a highly intellectual person, but they denote a kindly, truthful, and innocent nature. Eyes which, when seen in profile, are so protuberant as to run almost parallel with the profile of the nose, show a weak organization of the body and mind. Eyes rather close together show penetration, but eyes close together denote cunning and an untruthful disposition. Eyes rather far apart are indicative of frankness and simplicity of purpose, an honest and guileless nature. When, however, the eyes are not very far apart, they denote stupidity. Eyes with sharply defined angles sinking at the corners, show subtlety of mind; the sharper the angle and the more it sinks, the greater the delicacy of perception it denotes ; but when very much developed, it shows also craftiness amounting to deceit. Well-opened eyes, with smooth eyelids and a steady and somewhat fixed glance, denote sincerity. Lines running along the eyelids from side to side, and passing out upon the temples, denote habitual laughter, — a cheerful temperament, or, at any rate, one in which the sense of fun is strong.

Ezek Richards. (Pseud.) John Savage, in the Philadelphia " Press."

Ez. Ezra.

Ezek. Ezekiel.

F.

F. Fluorine.

F., or Fahr. Fahrenheit (thermometer).

Faber quisque suæ fortunæ. (Lat.) Every man is the architect of his own fortune.

Fac et Spera. (Pseud.) William Harding, in the New York "Clipper."

Facile est inventis addere. (Lat.) It is an easy thing to improve on things already invented.

Facile primus. (Lat.) By far the first.

Facile princeps. (Lat.) "Easily the first." Without dispute the first man; the admitted chief.

Facilis est descensus Averni. (Lat.) "The descent to the lower world is easy." The road to evil is an easy one.

Façon de parler. (Fr.) Manner of speaking; a form or mode of speech.

Fac simile. (Lat.) "Make it like." Hence, an exact copy.

Facta est lux. (Lat.) There was light.

Factory King. Richard Oastler, of Bradford, the successful champion of the "Ten Hours Bill" (fl. 1789-1861).

Factotum. (From the Latin *facio*, to do, and *totus*, all.) "Do-all;" a man of all work. The phrase is an old one. Ben Jonson in one of his plays makes Tip ask, "Art thou the Dominus?" to which the host replies, "Factotum here, sir." And Foulis, in his "History of the Plots of our Pretended Saints," 1674, says, "He was so farre the *dominus factotum* in this *juncto* that his words were laws."

Fadette. (Pseud.) Mrs. M. C. L. Reeves.

Fæx populi. (Lat.) "The dregs of the people." The very lowest classes of the people.

Fagerman. (Pseud.) Annie E. Bartholomew.

Fagot Votes. Votes given by electors expressly qualified for party purposes. Bailey says, "Ineffective persons, who receive no regular pay, but are hired to appear at muster and fill up the companies," are called fagots.

Fainéants. "Les Rois Fainéants," or Do-nothing Kings, in the annals of France, were Clovis II. and his ten successors. Their affairs were managed by the mayors of the palace. Louis V., the last of the Carlovingians, received the same name.

Faint Heart never won Fair Lady. This is a very old proverb. In "A Proper New Balad in Praise of my Lady Marques," printed in 1569, are these lines : —

> Then have amongst ye once again,
> Faint harts faire ladies neuer win.
> *Reprint, Philobiblion So.*, 1867, p. 22.

"The Rocke of Regard," 1576, concludes as follows : —

> The silente man still suffers wrong, the proverbe olde doth say,
> And where adventure wants, the wishing man ne'er thrives;
> Faint heart, hath been a common phrase, faire ladie never wives.
> *J. P. Collier's Reprint*, p. 122.

And in "Britain's Ida," by Spenser, canto v. stanza 1, the second line is, —

> "Ah, fool! faint heart fair lady ne'er could win."

Fair, The. (1) Charles IV. of France (1294-1328). (2) Philippe IV. of France (1268-1314). (3) Albert, Margrave of Brandenburg (1106-1170). *See* BEAR, THE.

Fair City, The. Perth in Scotland. It is elegantly built and picturesquely situated.

Faire de l'esprit. (Fr.) To be witty.

Faire sans dire. (Fr.) To act without parade.

Fairies, Wife of the. *See* BANSHEE.

Fairlop Oak. A giant oak-tree in Hainault Forest, Essex, whose girth was forty-eight feet, and beneath whose widely spreading branches an annual fair was held on the first Friday in July. The tree was blown down in February, 1820.

Fair Maid of Anjou. Lady Edith Plantagenet, who married David, Prince Royal of Scotland.

Fair Maid of February. The snowdrop, which blossoms in February.

Fair Maid of Galloway. Margaret, only daughter of Archibald V., Earl of Douglas.

Fair Maid of Kent. Joan, Countess of Salisbury, wife of the Black Prince, and only daughter of Edmund Plantagenet, Earl of Kent. She had been twice married ere she gave her hand to the prince.

Fair Maid of Norway. Margaret, daughter of Eric II. of Norway, and granddaughter of Alexander III. of Scotland. Being recognized by the States of Scotland as successor to the throne, she set out for her new kingdom, but died on her passage from sea-sickness, 1290.

Fair Maid of Perth. Katie Glover, the loveliest girl in Perth, Scotland. She is the heroine of Scott's novel of the name.

Fair Rosamond. The name by which Rosamond, daughter of Lord Clifford, is known in English history. She was the mistress of Henry II., who kept her secluded in a "bower" at Woodstock. The approaches to this retreat were through an intricate labyrinth, and his jealous queen tracked him thither by means of a silken thread which he had used for a clew.

Fait accompli. (Fr.) "Deed accomplished." A thing already completed.

Faithful Monitor. One of the pen-names attributed to Junius (*q. v.*).

Fake, Fakir. The word "fake" has been used for fifty years at least in the theatrical profession to express the idea of a makeshift. Thus, to "fake a dress" is to get up a costume which is not correct, but which can be made to serve its purpose on a pinch. Costumes of this kind are called "fakements." To "fake a part" is to play it imperfectly, without proper knowledge of its lines. Men much given to this sort of thing were known in the profession as "fakirs."

Fakir of Lahore. The hero of one of the best authenticated cases of "suspended animation" on record. "It is quite certain that an apparent cessation of all the vital functions may take place without that entire loss of vitality which would leave the organism in the condition of a dead body, liable to be speedily disintegrated by the operation of chemical and physical agencies." (Dr. W. B. Carpenter's Physiology.) It is also probably a fact that such "apparent cessation of all the vital functions" may continue for an indefinite period when the right conditions exist. The best known illustration of this, says a recent writer, is the case of the Fakir of

Lahore, who was buried for six weeks, at the instance of Runjeet Singh, as attested by Sir Claude Wade, the British Resident at the Court of Loodhiana, in 1837. In this thoroughly authenticated case — which, however, is but one of a class of similar facts known to Anglo-Indians and travellers — the Fakir was first put into a linen bag, the bag was placed in a wooden box, fastened with a padlock, the wooden box was deposited in a cell in the middle of a square brick vault, every aperture of which but one was bricked up, while the remaining door was built up with mud above the lock, and fastened with the rajah's seal. As a final precaution, a company of soldiers was detailed to guard the vault day and night, four sentries constantly patrolling its four sides during the whole period. When, at the expiration of six weeks, the vault and the box were successively opened, and Sir Claude Wade and Runjeet Singh had entered the building and taken their places close to the body, so as to see everything, this is what appeared before them : —

"The servant then began pouring warm water over the figure; but as my object was to see if any fraudulent practices could be detected, I proposed to Runjeet Singh to tear open the bag and have a perfect view of the body before any means of resuscitation were employed. I accordingly did so; and may here remark that the bag when first seen by us appeared mildewed, as if it had been buried some time. The legs and arms of the body were shrivelled and stiff, the face full, the head reclining on the shoulder like that of a corpse. I then called to the medical gentleman who was attending me to come down and inspect the body, which he did, but could discover no pulsation in the heart, the temples, or the arm. There was, however, a heat about the region of the brain, which no other part of the body exhibited. The servant then recommended bathing him with hot water, and gradually relaxing his arms and legs from the rigid state in which they were contracted, Runjeet Singh taking his right and I his left leg, to aid by friction in restoring them to their proper action ; during which time the servant placed a hot wheaten cake, about an inch thick, on the top of the head, — a process which he twice or thrice renewed. He then pulled out of his nostrils and ears the wax and cotton with which they were stopped ; and after great exertion opened his mouth by inserting the point of a knife between his teeth, and while holding his jaws open with his left hand, drew the tongue forward with his right, — in the course of which the tongue flew back several times to its curved position upward, in which it had originally been, so as to close the gullet. He then rubbed his eyelids with ghee (or clarified butter) for some seconds, until he succeeded in opening them, when the eyes appeared quite motionless and glazed. After the cake had been applied for the third time to the top of his head, his body was violently convulsed, the nostrils became inflated, respiration ensued, and the limbs began to assume a natural fulness; but the pulsation was still faintly perceptible. The servant then put some of the ghee on his tongue, and made him swallow it. A few minutes afterward the eyeballs became dilated, and recovered their natural color, when the Fakir, recognizing Runjeet Singh sitting close to him, articulated, in a low, sepulchral tone, scarcely audible, " Do you believe me now? " Runjeet Singh replied in the affirmative, and invested the Fakir with a pearl necklace and superb pair of gold bracelets, and pieces of muslin and silk, and shawls forming what is called a khelat, such as is usually conferred by the princes of India on persons of distinction. From the time of the box being opened to the recovery of the voice, not more than half an hour could have elapsed; and in another half-hour the Fakir talked with myself and those about him freely, though feebly, like a sick person; and we then left him, convinced that there had been no fraud or collusion in the exhibition we had witnessed."

Falcon. (Pseud.) Soulé Smith, a miscellaneous American writer of the present day.

Falconbridge. (Pseud.) Jonathan F. Kelly, American writer (b. 1820).

Falkland. (Pseud.) Nathaniel Chapman, M.D., in the " Philadelphia Portfolio."

Falls City, The. Louisville, Ky. So named from its situation on the falls of the Ohio River.

False Decretals. *See* DECRETALS, FALSE.

False Reynard. Under this name Dryden satirizes the Unitarians, in his " Hind and Panther."

Falsum in uno, falsum in omnibus. (Lat.) " False in one, false in all." One who has given false evidence on one point may be doubted on all points.

Fama. (Lat.) A rumor; a report.

Fama clamosa. (Lat.) A public or current rumor, generally of a scandalous nature, concerning a person or persons.

Familists, The. Originally founded by George of Delft, an enthusiast, who believed himself the Messiah. They branched off into various sects of Grindletonians, Familists of Cape Order, of the Scattered Flock, etc. Among doctrines too wild and foul to be quoted they held the lawfulness of occasional conformity with any predominant sect when it suited their convenience, of complying with the order of any magistrate, or superior power, however sinful. They disowned the principal doctrines of Christianity, as a law which had been superseded by the advent of David George, — nay, obeyed the wildest and loosest dictates of evil passions, and are said to have practised among themselves the grossest libertinism. See Edward's " Gangræna," Pagitt's " Heresiographia," and a very curious work written by Ludovic Claxton, one of the leaders of the sect, called the " Lost Sheep Found," London, 1660.

Family Compact. A defensive alliance between the Bourbon rulers of France, Spain, and the Two Sicilies, concluded by M. Choiseul, August 15, 1761.

Fanchon. (Pseud.) (1) Mrs. Laura B. Starr, correspondent of the " Cleveland Leader." (2) Mrs. Laura G. Sandford, American historical writer (b. 1835).

F. and A. M. Free and Accepted Masons.

Fannie Addison. The stage-name of Mrs. H. M. Pitt.

Fannie Beane. The stage-name of Mrs. Charles Gilday.

Fannie Dillon. The stage-name of Mrs. Richard E. Parker.

Fannie Meserole. The stage-name of Mrs. Samuel Lynch.

Fannie Reeves. The professional name of Mrs. E. A. McDowell, daughter of Sims Reeves, the famous English tenor.

Fanny Davenport. The stage-name of Mrs. E. H. Price.

Fanny Fairie. (Pseud.) Mrs. Mary T. Waggamon, in the New York " Weekly."

Fanny Fales. (Pseud.) Mrs. Frances Elizabeth Smith, American poet (b. 1832?).

Fanny Fern. (Pseud.) Sarah Payson Willis Parton, American author (1811–1872).

Fanny Fielding. (Pseud.) Mary J. S. Upshur, a favorite contributor to the Southern press.

Fanny Forester. (Pseud.) Emily (Chubbuck) Judson, American author (1817–1854).

Fanny Louise Buckingham. The stage-name of Mrs. Pettitt, *née* Ward.

Fanny Mountcastle. The stage-name of Mrs. Charles R. Thorp.

Fanny True. (Pseud.) Mrs. Mary Asenath Short, an American poet, who contributed to " Arthur's Home Magazine " and " Beadle's Home Monthly."

Fanny Vernon. The stage-name of Mrs. Harry Sinclair.

Fanny Wheeler. The stage-name of Mrs. Martin Stell.

Fan, Queen Anne's. *See* QUEEN ANNE'S FAN.

Fanshawe Brook. (Pseud.) Fanny Susan Wyvill, an American poet.

F. Anstey. Pen-name of F. Anstey Guthrie, the English novelist.

Fantaisie. (Fr.) A species of musical composition in which the author gives free scope to his ideas, without regard to those rules and forms which regulate other compositions.

Fantasia. (Ital.) The same as the French *fantaisie.*

Far. Farthing.

Farceur, The. Angelo Beolco, the Italian humorous dramatist (fl. 1502–1542).

Farmer George. George III. of England; so named because of his bucolic manners, dress, and pastimes.

Farrago libelli. (Lat.) "A medley of a little book." A hotchpotch or jumble of a book.

Farthing Poet. Richard Hengist Horne, *circa* 1843.

F. A. S. Fellow of the Antiquarian Society.

F. A. S. E. Fellow of the Antiquarian Society of Edinburgh.

Fas est ab hoste doceri. (Lat.) It is allowable to learn, even from an enemy.

Fashionable Salad-maker. The Marquis d'Abegnac, one of the French refugees in England during the Reign of Terror, used to be in great request at fashionable houses because of his skill in concocting a salad. It is said that he received a handsome fee in every case, and eventually amassed a fortune in this manner.

Fast-Day. This is peculiarly a New England institution, dating from a very early period in the annals of the country. It is — or rather was, for it is falling into desuetude — an annual observance, and in later years was usually appointed to be kept on Good Friday, when the people were admonished to abstain from all secular business and to mortify the flesh by abstention from food between sunrise and sunset. From time to time, however, Fast-days have been appointed during seasons of national calamity; and such Fast-days, whenever appointed, are legal holidays in all the States.

Fasten-e'en. *See* SHROVE TUESDAY.

Fat, The. In the days of the Italian Republics the city of Bologna was so named. *See* BEAUTIFUL, THE.

Fat, The. (1) Alonzo II. of Portugal (fl. 1212–1223). (2) Charles II. of France (fl. 832–888). (3) Louis VI. of France (fl. 1078–1137).

Fatal Saturday. The following record shows that for one hundred and seventy-six years Saturday was a very fatal day to the royal family in England : William III. died Saturday, March 18, 1702; Queen Anne died Saturday, August 1, 1714; George I. died Saturday, June 10, 1727; George II. died Saturday, Oct. 25, 1769; George III. died Saturday, Jan. 29, 1820; George IV. died Saturday, June 26, 1830; the Duchess of Kent died Saturday, March 16, 1861; the prince consort died Saturday, Dec. 14, 1861; Princess Alice died Saturday, Dec. 14, 1878.

Fatal Stone. The facts in relation to the stone called the "Lia Fail," or Fatal Stone, are as follows : On this stone it appears that the kings of Munster were crowned. It was originally deposited in the Cathedral of Cashel, their metropolis. In the year 1213 Fergus, a prince of the royal line, having obtained the Scottish throne, procured this stone for his coronation at Dunstaffnage, where it continued until the time of Kenneth II., who removed it to Scone; and in 1226 it was removed by Edward I. from Scone to London, where it was deposited in Westminster Abbey.

Fata obstant. (Lat.) "The Fates oppose." The Fates order that the matter should be otherwise settled.

Fat Contributor. (Pseud.) A. M. Griswold, American writer (1805–1866).

Fates, The. *See* PARCÆ.

Father Abraham. (Pseud.) Benjamin Franklin. *See* BROTHER ABRAHAM.

Father Ambrose. (Pseud.) Matthew Henry Barker.

Fatherland, The. The term of endearment among Teutons for their native land.

Father Neptune. The ocean.

Father Norbert. Pierre Parisot, the French evangelist (fl. 1697–1769).

Father of American Anthropology. Lewis Henry Morgan, scientist (1818–1881).

Father of American Geography. Jedediah Morse, clergyman and author (1761–1826).

Father of American Geology. William Maclure (1763–1840).

Father of American Shipbuilding. John Roach (1813–1887), founder and owner of great shipbuilding yards at Chester, Penn.

Father of American Surgery. Philip Tyng Physick (1768–1837).

Father of Angling. A nickname often given to Izaak Walton, the famous author of "The Compleat Angler" (fl. 1593–1683).

Father of Biblical Criticism. Origen was so named.

Father of British Inland Navigation. A nickname bestowed on Francis Egerton, Duke of Bridgewater (fl. 1736–1803), the projector of the first navigable canal constructed in Great Britain in modern times.

Father of Chautauqua County. Elial Todd Foote, physician (1796–1877).

Father of Choral Epode. Stesichorus of Sicily (fl. 632–552 B. C.).

Father of Colonization in America. Sir Ferdinando Gorges, proprietor of Maine (1565–1647).

Father of Comedy. Aristophanes (fl. 444–380 B. C.), a celebrated early Greek dramatist. He is the only writer of ancient Greek comedy of whom any complete works have been preserved to posterity.

Father of Dutch Poetry. Jacob Maerlant (fl. 1235–1300). Named also "Father of Flemish Poets."

Father of Ecclesiastical History. Eusebius of Cæsarea (fl. 264–340).

Father of English Geology. A nickname given to William Smith (fl. 1769–1840), who compiled the first geological map of Great Britain.

Father of English Poetry. A title given by Dryden to Chaucer, who was the first great English poet.

Father of English Printing. William Caxton.

Father of English Prose. (1) Roger Ascham, one of the earliest English writers on general topics (fl. 1515–1568). (2) Wycliffe.

Father of Epic Poetry. Homer, author of the Iliad and the Odyssey. The title was conferred by Sir Walter Scott.

Father of Equity. A title conferred on Heneage Finch, Earl of Nottingham (fl. 1621–1682). He is the Amri of Dryden's "Absalom and Achitophel," and filled the high post of Lord Chancellor at the Restoration.

Father of Flemish Poets. *See* FATHER OF DUTCH POETRY.

Father of Foreign Mission Work. Samuel John Mills, American clergyman (1783–1818).

Father of French History. A sobriquet of André Duchesne (fl. 1584–1640), an able and learned French writer and student of history.

Father of French Prose. Villehardouin.

Father of French Satire. Mathurin Regnier (fl. 1573–1613).

Father of French Sculpture. (1) Jean Goujon (fl. 1510–1572). (2) Germain Pilon (fl. 1515–1590).

Father of French Tragedy. Garnier (fl. 1534–1590).

Father of German Literature. A title conferred on Gotthold Ephraim Lessing (fl. 1729–1781). He has also been named "the Frederick the Great of Thought."

Father of Grace and Eloquence. Du Bellay (fl. 1524–1560), one of the "Pleiad" poets. *See* OVID OF FRANCE.

Father of Grain Inspection. Julian Sidney Rumsey, American merchant (1823–1886).

Father of Greek Music. Terpander of Lesbos (fl. about 676 B. C.). He was the first to reduce to a connected system the various rules of singing then in vogue; and he gave to Greek music a character that it never lost.

Father of Greek Prose. Herodotus, the historian.

Father of Greenbacks. Elbridge Gerry Spaulding, American banker (b. 1809).

Father of his Country. (1) Cicero was so named by the Roman Senate, as were several of the Cæsars, notably Julius and Augustus. (2) Cosmo de' Medici (fl. 1389–1464). (3) George Washington. (4) Andrea Doria, the Genoese patriot (fl. 1468–1560). (5) Andronicus Palæologus II., who assumed the title.

Father of Historical Societies. Lewis Pintard, American merchant (1732–1818).

Father of Historic Painting. Polygnotus of Thasos (fl. 463–435 B. C.).

Father of History. Herodotus. Though he was perhaps not the first historian, yet he was the first who reduced the art of writing history to a system.

Father of Iambic Verse. Archilochus of Paros was so named (fl. 714–676 B. C.).

Father of Iron Bridges. Squire Whipple, American engineer (1804–1888).

Father of Jests. A nickname given to Joseph Miller (fl. 1684–1738), an English comic actor, many of whose witticisms were after his death gathered into a book.

Father of Landscape Gardening. A. Lenotre (fl. 1613–1700).

Father of Letters. (1) A title conferred on Francis I. of France (fl. 1494–1547), a patron of letters and a friend to scholars. (2) Lorenzo de' Medici, the Florentine (d. 1492), who was likewise a generous friend to learning.

Father of Lies. (1) A colloquial nickname for the Evil One. (2) An epithet sometimes conferred on Herodotus (see *supra*) by those who doubted his narrative. But the name is not at all deserved.

Father of Medicine. Hippocrates, the most learned of the Greek physicians (fl. 460 B. C.) He was the first to attempt the treatment of medicine on a scientific basis.

Father of Modern French Song. Panard (fl. 1691–1765). *See also* LA FONTAINE OF THE VAUDEVILLE.

Father of Modern Music. Palestrina (fl. 1529–1594). He did much for church music, and brought it to a pitch of perfection until his day unattained.

Father of Modern Pantheism. Johannes Eckhart (1260–1329), the greatest of the mediæval mystical writers, and one of the greatest minds of the German race.

Father of Monks. Ethelwold of Winchester, who d. 984. He effected many needed changes in the English monastic orders.

Father of Moral Philosophy. Thomas Aquinas, the Schoolman, was so named.

Father of Musicians. Jubal. See Genesis iv. 21.

Father of Navigation. Don Henrique, Duke of Vasco (fl. 1394–1460), — perhaps the greatest man that Portugal ever produced.

Father of New Spain. Luis de Velasco, Viceroy of Mexico (1500–1564).

Father of Ornithologists. A name conferred on George Edwards (fl. 1693–1773), the English naturalist.

Father of Orthodoxy. Athanasius, Archbishop of Alexandria (fl. 296–373), the illustrious defender of the Church against the Arians and all forms of heresy.

Father of Paper Currency. Abraham Clark, signer of the Declaration of Independence (1726–1794).

Father of Parody. Hipponax of Ephesus.

Father of Peace. The Genoese so named Andrea Doria (fl. 1468–1560), the intrepid doge and admiral.

Father of Physiology. Albrecht von Haller, of Berne (fl. 1708–1777).

Father of Poetry. A name given alike to Orpheus and Homer. The latter is also named Father of Epic Poetry (*q. v.*).

Father of Presbyterianism in New York. George McNish, clergyman (1660–1722).

Father of Presbyterianism in Virginia. Samuel Morris, lay preacher (1700–1770?).

Father of Rhode Island and of American Baptists. John Clarke, physician (1609–1676).

Father of Riddles. A self-assumed title of the Abbé Cotin, which has not, however, been confirmed to him by critics. He flourished 1604–1682.

Father of Ridicule. François Rabelais (fl. 1483–1553), perhaps the greatest humorist and "comic romancer" of modern times.

Father of Rifle Practice. George Wood Wingate, American lawyer (b. 1840).

Father of Roman Satire. Lucilius (fl. 148–103 B. C.).

Father of Satire. Archilochus of Paros (fl. seventh century B. C.).

Father of Song. Homer, to whom are attributed the earliest of the Greek heroic epics.

Father of the American Navy. Joshua Humphries, shipbuilder (1751–1838).

Father of the Connecticut School Fund. Gideon Granger, statesman (1767–1822).

Father of the Drama. (1) Etienne Jodelle of the French. (2) Thespis of the Greek. (3) Lope de Vega of the Spanish.

Father of the Dutch Reformed Church in America. John Henry Livingston, clergyman (1746–1825).

Father of the Faithful. A name often given to Abraham, the Jewish patriarch. He was the recipient of the divine promises, and the progenitor of the Jewish race.

Father of the Hotel System of the United States. Simeon Boyden, the owner of the City Tavern, on Brattle Street, Boston, a famous hostelry in stage-coaching days.

Father of the House of Lords. The Earl of Mount-Cashel, an Irish hereditary peer, who died in 1883 at the great age of ninety-two years.

Father of the Jurisprudence of Louisiana. François Xavier Martin, American jurist (1764–1846).

Father of the Monitors. Rear-Admiral Joseph Smith, U. S. N.

Father of the New York Bar. (1) Samuel Jones (1734–1819). (2) Abraham van Vechten (1762–1823).

Father of the North Carolina Bar. Bartholomew Figures Moore (1801–1878).

Father of the People. (1) Louis XII. of France (fl. 1462–1515). (2) Henri IV. (fl. 1553–1610). (3) Christian III. of Denmark (fl. 1502–1559). (4) Gabriel du Pineau, the French advocate (fl. 1573–1644).

Father of the Poor. A sobriquet bestowed on Bernard Gilpin (fl. 1517–1583), the English reformer. He was noted for his philanthropic labors among the poor and distressed.

Father of the Public School System of Pennsylvania. George Wolf, Governor of Pennsylvania (1777–1840).

Father of the Rondo. J. B. Davaux, who excelled in that species of musical composition (d. 1822).

Father of the Telegraph. Samuel Finley Breese Morse.

Father of the Vaudeville. A nickname given to Oliver Basselin, the Norman peasant poet, who composed and gave to the world at large many of the lyrics of his native valleys, called in Old French *vau-de-vire*, since corrupted into *vaudeville*. He flourished in the fifteenth century.

Father of Tragedy. Æschylus was so named by the Athenians.

Father of Universalism in America. John Murray, clergyman (1741–1815).

Father of Waters. (1) The Mississippi River is popularly so named in allusion to its great length and the number of its affluents. (2) The Irrawaddy River, in India, whose name is said to include this meaning.

Father Paul. Pietro Sarpi, of the Order of Servites in Venice (fl. 1552–1623). He changed his Christian name when he became a monk.

Father Prout. (Pseud.) Francis Mahony, Irish author and wit (1805–1866).

Fathers of the Church. The early exponents of the Christian faith. They may be divided as follows : Five Apostolic Fathers, — Clement of Rome, Barnabas, Hermas, Ignatius, and Polycarp. The Primitive Fathers, — the foregoing and Justin, Theophilus of Antioch, Irenæus, Clement of Alexandria, Cyprian, Origen, Gregory Thaumaturgus, Dionysius, and Tertullian. *See* FATHERS OF THE GREEK AND LATIN CHURCHES.

Fathers of the Greek Church. Athanasius, Eusebius, Basil, Gregory Nazianzen, Gregory of Nyssa, Cyril of Jerusalem, Chrysostom, Epiphanius, Cyril of Alexandria, and Ephraim of Edessa.

Fathers of the Latin Church. Lactantius, Hilary, Ambrose, Jerome, Augustine of Hippo, and Saint Bernard.

Father Thames, Father Tiber, etc. Epithets not uncommonly applied to great rivers. The river may be regarded as the father of the city, or the cause of that site being chosen by its founders.

> Say, Father Thames, for thou hast seen
> Full many a sprightly race
> Disporting on thy margined green
> The paths of pleasure trace.
> GRAY, *Distant Prospect of Eton College.*

> O Tiber, Father Tiber, to whom the Romans pray.
> MACAULAY.

Father Thoughtful. Nickname given to Nicholas Catinat, Marshal of France, by his soldiery, on account of his deliberate and careful movements (d. 1712).

Father Violet. A sobriquet conferred by the rabble of Paris on Napoleon I. *See* CORPORAL VIOLET.

Faugh-a-Ballaghs. *See* OLD FOGS.

Faun, or **Faunus.** In classic myth a king of Italy, and teacher of agriculture to his people and founder of their religion, fabled to have lived 1300 B. C. After his death he was worshipped as a sylvan deity; and hence arose the fauns, corresponding to the Greek satyrs (*q.v.*).

Fauna. The sister of Faun. See *supra.*

Fauteuil. (Fr.) An easy-chair.

Faux pas. (Fr.) "A false step." A mistake.

Favonius. In classic myth the personification of the west wind, the same as Zephyrus, and the harbinger of spring.

Fay Templeton. The stage-name of Mrs. William West.

F. B. S. Fellow of the Botanical Society.

F. B. S. E. Fellow of the Botanical Society of Edinburgh.

F. C. Free Church of Scotland.

Fcap, or **Fcp.** Foolscap.

F. C. P. S. Fellow of the Cambridge Philological Society.

F. C. S. Fellow of the Chemical Society.

F. D. *Fidei Defensor* or *Defensatrix.* Defender of the Faith.

F. E., or **Fl. E.** Flemish ells.

Fe. *Ferrum.* Iron.

Fearless, The. Jean, Duke of Burgundy (fl. 1371-1419).

Feast of Fools. "A kind of Saturnalia, popular in the Middle Ages. Its chief object was to honor the ass on which our Lord made his triumphal entry into Jerusalem. This ridiculous mummery was held on the day of circumcision (January 1). The office of the day was first chanted in travesty; then, a procession being formed, all sorts of absurdities of dress, manner, and instrumentation were indulged in. An ass formed an essential feature, and from time to time the whole procession imitated the braying of this animal." — BREWER. Similar festivals were held in Paris on January 1, from 1198 to 1348, where various absurdities were committed.

Feather-heads. Another name for the Half-breeds (*q. v.*).

Feb. February.

Fec. *Fecit.* He did it.

Fecit. (Lat.) He or she made it. On a painting, put after the artist's name.

Federalists, The, were the advocates of a strong government. Under the leadership of Alexander Hamilton, who, with the aid of James Madison and John Jay, published eighty-six essays known as "The Federalist," in which these views were urged, aided, too, by the known opinions of Washington, their efforts for the adoption of the Constitution were successful. The wealthy and commercial classes were generally in accord with them, and the party came into power on the accession of Washington to the Presidency, April 30, 1789. On September 11 Hamilton was appointed Secretary of the Treasury, and his genius had much to do with the success of the administration. He proposed that the indebtedness of the United States and Revolutionary expenses of the States, in all nearly $80,000,000, should be assumed by the General Government, and fully paid by revenue derived from customs and a duty on ships. This met with a sharp opposition, but was finally adopted, and the credit of the country set on a firm basis. In 1791 the Bank of the United States, with a capital of $10,000,000, was established, three fourths to be paid in United States stock at six per cent, thus furnishing a market for the bonds of the Government. There was no opposition to the re-election of Washington in 1792, but during his second term the diverse elements of his Cabinet caused an explosion. Alexander Hamilton and Henry Knox were earnest Federalists, while Thomas Jefferson and Edmund Randolph were opposed to that party. This led, at the retirement of Washington, to a party strife on the election of a President. The Federalists were successful, and John Adams became President, March 4, 1797, and, as the electoral law then stood, his competitor, Thomas Jefferson, having the next highest number of votes, became Vice-President. His administration was unfortunate, and some of his acts gave offence to his own followers, especially in his dealing with France. The Alien and Sedition laws, for which the Federalists were responsible, had made the party unpopular, and Mr. Adams was defeated as a candidate for a second term by Thomas Jefferson, which virtually destroyed the power of the Federalists. During the administration of James Madison, who had long before left the Federalists, June 4, 1812, war was declared against Great Britain; and the measures adopted pressed hardly upon New England, where many had opposed it from the beginning. The Hartford Convention met Dec. 15, 1814. Its President, George Cabot, of Massachusetts, and all its members were Federalists. It sat with closed doors, and its proceedings were hostile to the government; and this, coupled with a suspicion of disloyalty, wrought the complete ruin of the party, and it disappeared on the election of James Monroe in 1816.

Federals. The Northern troops during the American civil war. Their opponents, the Southerners, were called Confederates.

F. E. I. S. Fellow of the Educational Institute of Scotland.

Feliciter. (Lat.) "Happily." Successfully.

Felix Ago. (Pseud.) Samuel Stehman Haldeman (1812–1880), in his "Rhymes of the Poets."

Felix and Urner. Under this double pseudonym appeared in 1830 a historical romance entitled "Walfthrum," written in collaboration by Louis Henri Martin the French historian (1810–1833), and Felix Davin.

Felix Merry. (Pseud.) Evert Augustus Duyckinck, American essayist and critic (1816–1878).

Felix Oldboy. (Pseud.) John F. Mines, author of some charming sketches of old New York in the "Evening Post" from time to time.

Felix Summerly. (Pseud.) Sir Henry Cole, K. C. B., English art critic (b. 1808).

Felo de se. A self-murderer; a suicide.

Fem. Feminine.

Female Howard. A title conferred on Mrs. Elizabeth Fry (fl. 1780–1844), a philanthropic Englishwoman, who did much to ameliorate the condition of prisoners, lunatics, and the poor.

Femme couverte. (Fr.) A married woman.

Femme de chambre. (Fr.) Lady's-maid; tiring-woman.

Femme sole. (Fr.) "A woman alone." An unmarried woman; a spinster.

Fence Month, or Defence Month. "A time during which deer in forests do fawn, and their hunting is unlawful. It begins fifteen days before Old Mid-summer, and ends fifteen days after it." — MANWOOD's *Forest Laws*, part ii. c. 13. By recent legislation "fence" times have been established in the case of birds and fishes, during which their capture or injury is unlawful.

Fen Nightingale. A humorous name for a frog, who sings in the swamps and fens as the nightingale does in the groves.

Fenrir. In Scandinavian myth a hideous demon, son of Loki, bound in chains by the gods, and cast down into Niflheim, where he is to remain till Ragnarok.

Feræ naturæ. (Lat.) Of a wild or savage nature.

Fernan Caballero. (Pseud.) Dona Cecelia (Bohl de Faber) Arrom, Spanish novelist (b. 1797).

Feronia. An ancient Roman deity, the patroness of plants and of freedmen.

Ferrars's Arrest. In March, 1542, Mr. George Ferrars, while attending the sessions of the House of Commons, was arrested by the sheriff for debt, and lodged in the Conyster Prison. The House demanded his release, and, it being refused, repaired to the Lords, and that body adjudged the civil officers in contempt, and they in turn were committed to jail. The occurrence became the basis of that rule which exempted members of Parliament from arrest while in attendance on the session.

Fervet opus. (Lat.) The work prospers greatly.

F. E. S. Fellow of the Entomological Society; Fellow of the Ethnographical Society.

Festina lente. (Lat.) Hasten slowly.

Festinatio tardo est. (Lat.) Too much haste does not accomplish its object well; much haste, little speed.

Fête. (Fr.) A feast or celebration.

Fête champêtre. (Fr.) A rural festivity.

Fête-Dieu. (Fr.) The Corpus Christi festival of the Roman Catholic Church.

Feu de joie. (Fr.) A bonfire; a discharge of musketry on days of rejoicing.

Feuilleton. (Fr.) A small leaf; a supplement to a newspaper; a pamphlet.

Ff. Following; the pandects.

F. F. A. Fellow of the Faculty of Actuaries.

F. F. V.'s. An abbreviation of the sentence "First Families of Virginia," often humorously used to denote a respectable lineage in the Old Dominion.

F. G. S. Fellow of the Geological Society.

F. H. S. Fellow of the Horticultural Society.

F. I. A. Fellow of the Institute of Actuaries.

Fiat. (Lat.) Let it be done.

Fiat confirmatio. (Lat.) Let the confirmation take place.

Fiatist. One who believes in "fiat," or paper, money; a term current in the United States during the greenback agitation.

Fiat justitia, ruat cœlum. (Lat.) "Though the heavens should fall, let justice be done." Though even ruin should follow, let justice be administered.

Fiat lux. (Lat.) Let there be light.

Fid. Def. Defender of the Faith.

Fiddler Josh. Mr. Joseph Poole, a reformed drunkard, who subsequently turned preacher in London, but retained his former sobriquet.

Fiddler's Green. The Elysium of sailors; a land flowing with rum and lime-juice; a land of perpetual music, mirth, dancing, drinking, and tobacco; a sort of Dixey's land, or land of the leal.

Fidei defensor. (Lat.) Defender of the faith, as applied to an English sovereign.

Fide, non armis. (Lat.) By faith, not by arms.

Fide, sed cui vide. (Lat.) Trust, but see whom.

Fides et justitia. (Lat.) Fidelity and justice.

Fides Punica. (Lat.) "Punic faith." Treachery. A phrase originating among the Romans, from the treachery which, as they alleged, characterized the actions of the Pœni, or Carthaginians.

Fidus Achates. (Lat.) "Faithful Achates." A true friend. Achates was the faithful attendant on Æneas in his flight from Troy.

Fielding of the Drama. George Farquhar (fl. 1678–1707). He wrote "The Beaux Stratagem," etc.

Field of Blood. (1) The meaning of the Hebrew word *Aceldama*, the descriptive designation of the plot of land purchased by Judas with the thirty pieces of silver, the price of his treachery. (Matt. xxvii. 5). (2) "The battlefield of Cannæ (Apulia) has been so named. Here, August 2, 216 B. C., Hannibal, with 50,000 Africans, Gauls, and Spaniards, defeated Paulus Æmilius and Terentius Varro, with 80,000 Romans, 40,000 of whom were slain. The victor sent to Carthage three bushels of rings taken from the Roman knights." — HAYDN.

Field of March and May. A name by which the Champ de Mars, Paris, is sometimes alluded to. On this spot, now given over to reviews, etc., were formerly held annually in March the ancient assemblies of the Frankish people. the germ of the French parliaments. In 747 King Pepin changed the date to May.

Field of Mourning. The name bestowed on a famous battle-field near the city of Aragon, memorable as the scéne of a sanguinary conflict between Christians and Moors, July 17, 1134.

Field of Peterloo. A popular nickname given to the famous Manchester Reform Meeting, August 16, 1819. The assembly consisted of from 60,000 to 100,000 persons, — men, women, and children. Mr. Hunt, who had taken the chair, had spoken a few words, when the meeting was suddenly assailed by a charge of the Manchester cavalry, assisted by a Cheshire regiment of yeomanry and a regiment of hussars, the outlets being guarded by other military detachments. The unarmed multitude were consequently driven upon one another (by which alone many were killed), ridden down by the horses, or sabred by their riders. The deaths were 11 men, women, and children, and the wounded numbered over 600. The word "Peterloo" was of course coined in burlesque allusion to the then recent battle of Waterloo, the gathering being held in St. Peter's Field, near Manchester.

Field of the Cloth of Gold. A meeting between Henry VIII. of England and Francis I. of France, June 7–25, 1520, midway between Ardres and Guisnes, within the English Pale, conducted with such magnificence as to gain for it this title. Paintings of the embarkation and of the interview are preserved at Windsor. Many of the nobility in attendance seriously embarrassed themselves by their senseless prodigality.

Field of the Forty Footsteps. A meadow that formerly existed near where the British Museum now stands, later known as Southampton Fields. The story goes that two brothers at the time of Monmouth's rebellion espoused opposite sides, and fought a duel in this place. Both were slain, and for many years forty footprints were visible, because no grass would grow there.

Fieri facias. (Lat.) "Cause it to be done." A kind of writ.

Fi. fa. *Fieri facias.* Cause it to be done.

Fifth Doctor of the Church. Thomas Aquinas, the Schoolman.

Fifth Monarchy. About 1645 a strange sect appeared in England, who maintained that the millennium was at hand, when Jesus would descend from heaven, and erect the fifth universal monarchy or world-kingdom. They proceeded so far as to elect Christ king at London. Cromwell dispersed them, 1653; but another rising occurred in 1661, which was only suppressed after the loss of several lives. In politics they were republicans of the most radical type. They conspired to murder the Protector and usurp the government.

Fifty-five, The. Abijah Willard, an American royalist soldier (1722–1789), and fifty-four associates, who in 1783 petitioned Sir Guy Carleton for extensive grants of land in Nova Scotia.

Fifty-four Forty or Fight. A famous campaign battle-cry in the canvass resulting in the election of James K. Polk to the Presidency. It grew out of the dispute concerning the boundary between the United States and British America in the Northwest. It was claimed by America that her limits extended to the parallel of fifty-four degrees forty minutes north latitude. The arbitrator, the Emperor of Germany, eventually decided in favor of the American claim.

Fig. Figure.

Figaro. (Pseud.) (1) Henry Clapp, Jr., in various periodicals. (2) Mariano Jose de Larra, Spanish poet (1809–1837).

Fighting Chasseurs. The Sixty-Fifth New York Regiment in the civil war.

Fighting Dick. Israel Bush Richardson (1815–1862), a soldier in the civil war, was so named on account of his coolness in action.

Fighting Fifth. (1) A nickname earned by the Fifth Foot Regiment in the English army during the Crimean War. (2) The Fifth New Hampshire Regiment during the civil war, under the command of Edward Ephraim Cross.

Fighting Joe. A sobriquet conferred on Gen. Joseph Hooker. It is said that he never relished the appellation, though he always justified it in the field, especially at the battle of Manassas, 1862.

Fighting Nat. Nathaniel Fitz Randolph, a soldier in the Revolutionary War.

Fighting Parson. Rev. Granville Moody, a Methodist itinerant (1812–1887), who left the ministry to take up arms for the North in the civil war, He won the above title by his gallantry at the battle of Stone River, for which he was brevetted brigadier-general.

Fighting Quakers. Another name for the "Free Quakers," who in the eighteenth century in Pennsylvania seceded from the Society of Friends.

Fighting like Devils, etc. In Lady Morgan's "Memoirs," vol. ii. p. 232, the writer, in an extract from her diary, Oct. 30, 1826, in which she describes a compliment paid to her by a Dublin street-ballad singer, gives the following as a stanza from his carol : —

"Och, Dublin City, there's no doubtin',
 Bates every city upon the say ;
'T is there you'll see O'Connell spoutin',
 An' Lady Morgan makin' tay ;
For 't is the capital of the finest nation,
 Wid charmin' pisantry on a fruitful sod
Fightin' like divils for conciliation,
 An' hatin' each other for the love of God."

Fighting McCook. General McCook was so named throughout the army.

Fighting Prelate. Henry Spencer, Bishop of Norwich, who played a prominent part in quelling the rebellion of Wat Tyler. It is said that he met the rebels sword in hand ; next absolved them, and then consigned them to the gibbet.

Fig Sunday (Palm Sunday). So called from the custom of eating figs on this day, as snapdragons on Christmas Eve, plum-pudding on Christmas Day, oranges and barley sugar on St. Valentine's Eve, pancakes on Shrove Tuesday, salt cod-fish on Ash Wednesday, frumenty on Mothering Sunday (Mid-lent), cross-buns on Good Friday, gooseberry tart on Whit-Sunday, goose on Michaelmas Day, nuts on All-Hallows, and so on.

Filia Dolorosa. A name given to the Duchesse d'Angoulême, daughter of Louis XVI. of France. *See also* MODERN ANTIGONE.

Filia Ecclesiæ. (Pseud.) Sarah Anne Dorsey (1829–1879). She began her literary career by writing for the New York "Churchman," and received from that journal her pen-name.

Filibusters, Filibustering. "A filibuster is defined as a 'lawless adventurer, especially one in quest of plunder.'"— WEBSTER.

"The original *filibusteros* were West Indian pirates. Their name was derived from a small fast-sailing vessel which they employed, called a 'filibote' (originally fly-boat), and said to have been so styled from the river Vly in Holland. The term 'filibusters' came to be applied to all military adventurers. In the United States it has two meanings. First, it is given to the members of the minority of a legislative body who seek to delay or defeat the adoption of measures obnoxious to them by obstruction and dilatory tactics, such as constant motions to adjourn, or calls for yeas and nays. Secondly, the name 'filibusters' is applied to the adventurers who organized expeditions in the United States to gain control of West India and Central American regions with the hope of having them annexed to the United States, and thus extending the slave territory of the nation. The first of these expeditions was organized by a Cuban, Narcisco Lopez. After making two attempts in 1849 and 1850, which proved failures, he sailed from New Orleans with about five hundred men and landed in Cuba in August, 1851. His force was overpowered by the authorities, and he and several other leaders were executed. The next filibustering expeditions were undertaken by Gen. William Walker. In 1853 and 1854 he attempted to conquer Lower California and the State of Sonora, Mexico, but failed. In 1855 he went to Nicaragua with a few followers. Profiting by internal dissensions in that country, he gained several victories and had himself elected President. He re-established slavery and seized the property of the Vanderbilt Steamship Company. But his arbitrary acts created a revolution, and early in 1857 he surrendered himself to Commander Davis, of the United States Navy, who took him to New Orleans. He was released under bonds to keep the peace, but in November he was found once more in Nicaragua. In December, however, he surrendered again, this time to Commodore Paulding of our Navy, who carried him to New York. Finding himself again at liberty, he attempted to start with a new expedition from New Orleans, but was prevented by the national authorities. His last expedition was directed against Honduras in 1860. In June of that year he landed with a small force at Trujillo, but was captured, court-martialled, and, on September 12, shot. Since then no filibustering expeditions from this country have been known."— BROWN AND STRAUSS.

Filius nullius. (Lat.) "The son of nobody." A bastard.

Filius populi. (Lat.) A son of the people.

Fille de chambre. (Fr.) "Girl of the chamber." A chambermaid.

Filomena, Saint. The sobriquet bestowed on Florence Nightingale by the poet Longfellow. The saint of the name is depicted, in Sabatelli's painting, as bending over a group of maimed and wounded, healed by her ministrations.

Fin. Finland.

Finale. (Fr.) The close, or end. In music, the last piece of an opera or concert, or the last movement of a sonata or symphony.

Finality John. Lord John Russell, who stoutly maintained that the Reform Bill of 1832 was a finality. Yet several others have been passed, some of which he lived to see.

Fin-Bec. (Pseud.) William Blanchard Jerrold.

Fine (Ital.), or **Fin.** (Fr.). The end; a term used to denote the close of a musical or other composition.

Finem respice. (Lat.) Look to the end.

Finger Benediction. In the Greek and Roman Churches the thumb and first two fingers represent the Trinity. The thumb, being strong, represents the Father; the long or second finger, Jesus Christ; and the first finger, the Holy Ghost.

Finis. (Lat.) The end.

Finis coronat opus. (Lat.) "The end crowns the work." No one can determine justly the merits of a thing till its completion or termination.

Finn. Finnish.

Finn. (Pseud.) Peter Auguste Godecke, Swedish author and editor.

Finnan Haddie. Another name for Findon Haddock, which derives its name from the Scotch village of that name, which lies on the sea-coast and is six miles by rail south of Aberdeen. The village is famous for its smoked haddocks.

Fir. Firkin.

Firbolgs. The name given in the fabulous early history of Ireland to a tribe said to have descended from the Nemedians, who under their leader Nemedius landed in the island about 2260 B. C.; and after two hundred and seventeen years left it, on account of the oppression to which they were subjected by pirates called the Fomorians. The emigrating Nemedians formed three bands, — one went to Thrace, and from them descended the Firbolgs; a second to the north of Europe, or Lochlan, from whom descended the Tuatha de Danann; and the third to Alban, or Scotland, from whom sprung the Britons. The Firbolgs returned to Ireland in three tribes, one of which more especially bore the name Firbolg; the others were called Firdomnan, and Firgailian. The three tribes, however, were under five leaders, by whom Ireland was divided into five provinces. With Slainge, the first Firbolg king, who began to reign 1934 B. C., and reigned only one year, the Irish historians begin their account of the Irish monarchy and list of kings. The Firbolgs were driven out, after they had been thirty-six years in Ireland, by their kinsmen, the Tuatha de Danann, from Scotland, they having previously passed over to that country from Lochlan; and these, in their turn, were expelled or conquered by the Milesians. The most recent investigators of the early history of Ireland regard the story of the Firbolgs as having some basis of truth, but no chronological accuracy; the different tribes having long subsisted in the country together, and with varying fortunes as to temporary superiority.

Fire and Water. "I would go through fire and water to serve you." This saying is a relic of the old trials by ordeal. In the old times when trial by ordeal of fire or water was recognized by English law, both ordeals could be performed by deputy. This was sometimes done for hire and sometimes out of friendship.

The ordeal of fire was passing blindfolded and barefooted through a place where nine red-hot ploughshares were arranged at irregular intervals. In the trial by water the person to be tried was bound hand and foot and thrown into a pond or river. If he swam, he saved his life and redeemed his character. If drowned, he was considered to have met with a just retribution for the crime of which his drowning was held to be proof that he was guilty. The saying "I would go through fire and water," etc., was, therefore, equivalent to saying that the person using it was ready to sacrifice life or limb to serve his friend."

Firebrand of the Universe. Tamerlane (fl. 1336-1405), the famous Asiatic conqueror. Though one of the greatest of warriors, he was one of the worst of monarchs.

Fire-eater. "A truculent, unreconstructed Southerner." A second Sir Lucius O'Trigger.

Fireman = STOKER. The "fireman" of American locomotives and steamships becomes the "stoker" on similar English conveyances.

Firemen's Anniversary. This occurs on March 4, and is a legal holiday in Louisiana.

Fire, Mountain of. *See* MOUNTAIN OF FIRE.

Fire, St. Anthony's. *See* ANTHONY'S FIRE.

First catch your Hare. This saying is, perhaps, a play upon an ancient word still in use in Norfolk and Suffolk, England. In those counties, where the word "skatch" means to skin and dress an animal for cooking, the direction "first *skatch* your hare" might be easily mistaken for the mythical phrase "first *catch* your hare," a saying which has been productive of so much merriment that it seems a pity to disturb it. There is, however, another theory, which is that the word used was "case," one meaning of which was formerly, according to Johnson, "to strip off the covering; to take off the skin." Shakspeare also uses the word in this sense in "All's Well that Ends Well," where he says, —

"We'll make you some sport with the fox ere we case him."

First-chop. This phrase was once used all through the United States as a synonym for "first-rate." The word "chop" is Chinese for "quality."

He looks like a first-chop article.
Sam Slick in England, ch. ii.

First Gentleman of Europe. (1) A nickname given to George IV. of England. First in *rank* he may have been, but he was certainly devoid of pre-eminence either in manners, feeling, or deportment. (2) The name was also bestowed on Louis d'Artois.

First Grenadier of France. A sobriquet given by Napoleon I. to Latour d'Auvergne (fl. 1743-1800).

First in a Village than Second in Rome. " Cæsar said, ' For my part, I had rather to be the first man among these fellows than the second man in Rome.' " — PLUTARCH, *Life of Cæsar.*

First in War, First in Peace, First in the Hearts of his Countrymen. This phrase, in the form in which we have it now, was said of George Washington by Gen. Henry Lee in his famous funeral oration. The apostrophe was also contained in the resolutions prepared by Richard Henry Lee and offered in the House of Representatives by John Marshall on announcing the death of Washington, but with a slight variation : " First in war, first in peace, and first in the hearts of his fellow-citizens."

First Scottish Reformer. Patrick Hamilton (fl. 1503–1527), who was sent to the stake for preaching the doctrines of Luther.

Fitche's Grenadiers. A nickname of the Eighty-third English Regiment, after a former colonel.

Fits to a T. The expression " It suits (or fits) to a T " means " It suits (or fits) exactly," and comes from the Tee-square, or T-rule, an instrument (so called from its resemblance to a capital T) used by mechanics and draughtsmen, especially valuable in making angles true, and in obtaining perpendiculars on paper or wood. The phrase is one in common use. Boswell quotes Johnson as saying, " You see they 'd have fitted him [Warburton] to a T."

Fitzroy Clarence. (Pseud.) William M. Thackeray in " Punch."

Five-and-Threepennies. *See* BRICK-DUSTS.

Five Articles of Perth. A code passed in 1618 by order of James VI., enforcing kneeling at the Sacrament, the keeping of Christmas, Good Friday, Easter, and Pentecost, the observance of the rite of confirmation, etc. They were ratified on Black Saturday (*q. v.*), and condemned by the General Assembly of Glasgow in 1638.

Five-mile Act. An act of Parliament (17 Charles II. chap. ii., October, 1665), was so named because it forbade Nonconformist preachers who refused to take the non-resistance oath to come within five miles of any corporation where they had preached since the Act of Oblivion (unless they were on a journey), under penalty of a fine of £40.

The act was repealed under William III. in 1689.

Five Nations. The Indian tribes grouped under this name are the Cherokees, the Chickasaws, the Choctaws, the Creeks, and the Seminoles — all now domiciled in the Indian Territory. *See* IROQUOIS.

Five of Clubs. A famous coterie of Harvard graduates, consisting of H. R. Cleveland, Charles Sumner, H. W. Longfellow, C. C. Felton, and G. C. Hillard.

Five of Clubs. (Pseud.) Richard A. Proctor in his " How to Play Whist."

Five per Cent. Cases. A decision of the United States Supreme Court in 1884, holding that an act of Congress by which a percentage of the proceeds of land " sold by Congress " is reserved to certain public uses of a State does not include lands disposed of by the United States in satisfaction of military land-warrants.

Five P's. A nickname given to William Oxberry (fl. 1784–1824), an English *P*oet, *P*rinter, *P*ublisher, *P*ublican, and *P*layer.

Fix. " To *fix*," says a writer, " may be said to be the American word of words, since there is probably no action of mind or body which is not at some time or other represented by this word. Whatever is to be made, whatever needs repair, whatever requires arrangement, — all is *fixed.* The President *fixes* his cabinet, the mechanic his work-bench, and the seamstress her sewing-machine. And yet *fix* may mean trouble and embarrassment. The New York ' Herald ' speaks of President Arthur ' being in a *fix ;*' and a young lady hesitating between two suitors is in a ' painful *fix.*' *Fixings* naturally abound also, and denote well-nigh everything, from the *railway fixings* of a new branch to the *chicken fixings* of the West and the South."

Fizzle. The meaning given to this word in the United States constitutes an Americanism. The old-fashioned musket would frequently refuse to explode, the priming in the pan going off with a fizzling sound. Hence the word " fizzle " signifies any ridiculous failure after great expectations had been aroused.

F. K. Q. C. P. I. Fellow of King's and Queen's College of Physicians, Ireland.

Fla. Florida.

Flagrante bello. (Lat.) While war is raging; during hostilities.

Flagrante delicto. (Lat.) In the act of committing the crime.

Flags, Ford of. *See* FORD OF FLAGS.

Flambeau. (Pseud.) Floyd Vail, in the New York " Mail and Express."

Flaminian Way. The great northern road of ancient Italy, constructed by C. Flaminius. It commenced at the Flaminian Gate of Rome.

Flâneur. (Fr.) A lounger.

Flaneur. (Pseud.) (1) Col. Charles G. Greene, in the Boston " Post." (2) Blakely Hall, in the San Francisco " Argonaut." (3) Kenward Philp, in the Brooklyn " Daily Eagle." (4) Edmund Hodgson Yates, the English journalist, in the London " Star " and " Tinsley's Magazine."

Flat Broke. *See* BROKE.

Flath-Innis (" Isle of the Brave "). In Celtic mythology the paradise of warriors and heroes.

Flats. In the far West the alluvial lands on the bank of a river liable to inundation by overflow, and also large sandy shoals in the bed of the stream.

Flebile. (Ital.) In a mournful style. (Mus.)

Flecti, non frangi. (Lat.) To be bent, not to be broken.

Fleet Marriages. The custom of contracting clandestine marriages was very prevalent in England before the passing of the first Marriage Act in 1753 put a check to the glaring abuse. No other place was equal in notoriety for this infamous traffic to the Fleet Prison. Between Oct. 19, 1704, and Feb. 12, 1705, there were celebrated 2,954 marriages in the Fleet without license or banns. Twenty or thirty couples were often united in one day, their names concealed by private marks if they chose to pay an extra fee. Painted signs with the legend " Marriages performed within " were openly displayed.

Fleet of the Desert. A caravan is so styled by Washington Irving. The camel is also called " the ship of the desert."

Fleshly School. A name given to a number of poets, among whom were Morris, Swinburne, and Rossetti; they were preceded by the Spasmodic School (*q. v.*).

Fleta. A poetical allusion to the Fleet Prison in London, of which name it is the Latinized form. It is also the title of a legal commentary composed by John Selden (1584–1654), which is based on the labors of two English judges, Glanvil and Bracton, who during the reign of Edward I. were confined in the Fleet Prison, and who occupied their enforced leisure in the production of an excellent legal treatise.

Fleta. (Pseud.) Kate W. Hamilton, an American writer.

Fleur-de-lis. The fleur-de-lis has been the emblem of the kings of France from Clovis downward. It is not certain whether it is derived from the common white lily of our gardens or from the flag, or iris, the other name of which, " flower-de-luce," is a corruption of the French *fleur - de - lis*. Some say that what is now a lily was originally intended to represent the head of a spear or javelin. At first the kings of France bore as their arms an indefinite number of golden lilies on a blue field; but eventually, either out of respect to the Trinity or to symbolize the three different races — the Merovingians, the Carlovingians, and the Capets — from which the royal line was descended, Charles VI. reduced the number to three golden fleurs-de-lis emblazoned on an azure field. There is an ancient legend to the effect that the original blue banner embroidered with golden lilies was given to King Clovis by an angel from heaven in the year 496, he having vowed to embrace Christianity if he should be victorious in an impending battle with the Alemanni (the ancestors of the Germans) near Cologne. During the Revolution of 1789 the fleur-de-lis was discarded as the banner of France in favor of the tricolor.

Flint Jack. Edward Simpson, sometime servant to Dr. Young, of Whitby, and so named because he peddled ancient (?) flint weapons up and down the country. In 1867 Professor Tennant charged him with forging these relics; and in the same year he was sent to prison for vagrancy.

Float Day. During Commencement at Wellesley College, Mass., the fair students engage in contests at the oar, the occasion being known as " Float Day."

Floaters. Under the Ohio Constitution of 1851, a district or county having a fraction of population over and above the number of inhabitants necessary to the senators or representatives apportioned to it, is treated as follows: If by multiplying the surplus inhabitants by five the result is equal to or exceeds the number of inhabitants required for one member, the county receives a member for the fifth of the five terms of two years into which the period between reapportionments is divided. If equal to the number necessary to more than one member, then for the fifth and fourth terms, or for as many as required. These members are called "floaters."

Flora. In classic myth the goddess of flowers and of the spring.

Flora Irwin. The stage-name of Mrs. (Senator) Grady.

Flora McFlimsey. (Pseud.) Miss Evelyn Kimball Johnson, associate editor of the "Bar Harbor (Me.) Tourist," 1885 *et seq.*

Flora Neale. (Pseud.) Mrs. G. A. H. McLeod, a well-known magazine writer of the present day.

Flora Walsh. The stage-name of Mrs. Charles H. Hoyt.

Florence. (Pseud.) (1) Mrs. Frances Sargent Osgood, in the "Juvenile Miscellany." (2) Miss Florence Tyng, contributor to various periodicals.

Florence Baldwin. The stage-name of Mrs. George Robinson.

Florence Girard. The stage-name of Mrs. Henry E. Abbey.

Florence Kennedy. The stage-name of Mrs. J. H. Huntley.

Florence Leigh. (Pseud.) Mrs. A. T. W. Wood, a miscellaneous American writer.

Florence Marryatt. (1) The stage-name of Mrs. Francis Lean. (2) (Pseud.) Mrs. Florence M. Ross-Church, a well-known contemporary novelist.

Florence Percy. The pen-name of Mrs. Elizabeth Akers Allen, well known as the writer of the song, "Rock me to sleep, mother."

Florence St. John. The stage-name of Madame Marius.

Florence, The German. *See* GERMAN FLORENCE.

Florence Thropp. The stage-name of Mrs. Edward A. Bulkley.

Florence Warden. The stage-name of Mrs. George E. James, *née* Price.

Florence Warden. (Pseud.) Mrs.

Florence Alice [Price] James, a noted novelist of the present day, author of "The House on the Marsh," "The Fog Princes," "A Prince of Darkness," etc.

Florida. The name of this State is derived from Pasqua de Flores, or "Feast of Flowers," upon which day it was discovered.

Florine Arnold. The stage-name of Mrs. Charles A. Andrews.

Florio. (Pseud.) James Gordon Brooks, in various periodicals.

Florizel. George IV., when prince, corresponded, under this name, with Mrs. Robinson, actress and poet, generally known as Perdita.

Florry. (Pseud.) J. Frank Kernan, an American writer.

Flossie Edwards. The stage-name of Mrs. J. H. W. Byrnes.

Flour City, The. Rochester, N. Y. The place is noted for its flour-mills.

Flower City, The. Springfield, Ill., famed for the beauty of its suburbs.

Flower of Chivalry. (1) William Douglas, Earl of Liddesdale. (2) Sir Philip Sidney (fl. 1554–1586). (3) Chevalier Bayard (fl. 1476–1524).

Flower of Islands. Another of the many poetical names conferred on Cuba.

Flower of Kings. Arthur of England is so styled by John of Exeter.

Flower of Poets. Geoffrey Chaucer (1328–1400).

Flower of Strathearn. Lady Carolina Oliphant Nairn, author of "The Land o' the Leal," was so named.

Flower of the Levant. Zante is so called from its great beauty and fertility.

"Zante! Zante! flor di Levanti."

Flower Sermon. A sermon preached on Whit-Sunday in St. Catherine Cree, London, when all the congregation wear flowers.

Flowers, Symbolism of. Lady Mary Wortley Montagu, in speaking of this flower language, says, "There is no color, no flower, no weed, no fruit, herb, pebble, or feather that has not a verse belonging to it; and you may quarrel, reproach, or send letters of passion, friendship, or civility, or even of news, without even inking your fingers."

Abatina	. . . . .	Fickleness.
Abecedary	. . . .	Volubility.
Acacia	. . . . . .	Friendship.
Acacia, rose or white	.	Elegance.
Acacia, yellow	. . .	Secret love.
Acalia	. . . . . .	Temperance.
Acanthus	. . . . .	The fine arts, artifice.
Achillea Millefolia	. .	War.

Achimenes Cupreata .	Such worth is rare.
Aconite (Wolfsbane) .	Misanthropy.
Aconite (Crowfoot) .	Lustre.
Adonis, Flos	Sad memories.
African Marigold . .	Vulgar minds.
Agnus Castus . . .	Coldness, indifference.
Agrimony	Thankfulness, gratitude
Allspice	Compassion.
Almond (common) . .	Stupidity, indiscretion.
Almond (flowering) .	Hope.
Almond, Laurel . .	Perfidy.
Aloe	Grief, religious superstition.
Althæa Frutex (Syrian Mallow).	Persuasion.
Alyssum (sweet). . .	Worth beyond beauty.
Amaranth (globe) . .	Immortality, unfading love.
Amaranth (Cockscomb)	Foppery, affectation.
Amaryllis	Pride, timidity, splendid beauty.
Ambrosia	Love returned.
American Cowslip . .	Divine beauty.
American Elm . . .	Patriotism.
American Linden . .	Matrimony.
American Scarwort .	Welcome to a stranger, cheerfulness in old age.
Amethyst	Admiration.
Andromeda	Self-sacrifice.
Anemone (Zephyr flower)	Sickness, expectation.
Anemone (garden) . .	Forsaken.
Angelica	Inspiration, or magic.
Angree	Royalty.
Apple	Temptation.
Apple (blossom) . .	Preference, fame speaks him great and good.
Apple, Thorn . . .	Deceitful charms.
Apocynum (Dogsbane)	Deceit.
Apricot (blossom) . .	Doubt.
Arbor Vitæ	Unchanging friendship, live for me.
Arum (Wake Robin) .	Ardor, zeal.
Ash-leaved Trumpet-flower	Separation.
Ash, Mountain . . .	Prudence, or With me you are safe.
Ash Tree	Grandeur.
Aspen Tree	Lamentation, or fear.
Asphodel	My regrets follow you to the grave.
Aster (China) . . .	Variety, afterthought.
Auricula	Painting.
Auricula, scarlet . .	Avarice.
Austurtium	Splendor.
Azalea	Temperance.
Bachelor's Buttons .	Celibacy.
Balm	Sympathy.
Balm, gentle	Pleasantry.
Balm of Gilead . . .	Cure, relief.
Balsam, red	Touch me not, impatient resolves.
Balsam, yellow . . .	Impatience.
Barberry	Sharpness of temper.
Basil	Hatred.
Bay leaf	I change but in death.
Bay (rose) Rhododendron	Danger beware.
Bay-tree	Glory.
Bay Wreath	Reward of merit.
Bearded Crepis . . .	Protection.
Beech Tree	Prosperity.
Bee Ophrys	Error.
Bee Orchis	Industry.
Begonia	Deformity.
Belladonna	Silence, hush !
Bell Flower, Pyramidal	Constancy.
Bell Flower (small white)	Gratitude.
Belvedere	I declare against you.
Betony	Surprise.
Bilberry	Treachery.
Bindweed, great . .	Insinuation, importunity.
Bindweed, small . .	Humility.
Birch	Meekness.
Birdsfoot, Trefoil . .	Revenge.

Bittersweet, Nightshade	Truth.
Black Poplar . . .	Courage.
Blackthorn	Difficulty.
Bladder Nut Tree . .	Frivolity, amusement.
Bluebell	Constancy, sorrowful regret.
Bluebottle	Delicacy.
Blue-flowered Greek Valerian	Rupture.
Bonus Henricus . .	Goodness.
Borage	Bluntness.
Box Tree	Stoicism.
Bramble	Lowliness, envy, remorse.
Branch of Currants .	You please all.
Branch of Thorns . .	Severity, rigor.
Bridal Rose	Happy love.
Broom	Humility, neatness.
Browallia Jamisonii .	Could you bear poverty ?
Buckbean	Calm repose.
Bud of White Rose .	Heart ignorance of love.
Buglos	Falsehood.
Bulrush	Indiscretion, docility.
Bundle of Reeds, with their Panicles . . .	Music.
Burdock	Importunity, touch me not.
Burr	Rudeness, you weary me.
Buttercup	Ingratitude, childishness.
Butterfly Orchis . .	Gayety.
Butterfly Weed . . .	Let me go.
Cabbage	Profit.
Cacalia	Adulation.
Cactus	Warmth.
Calceolaria	I offer you pecuniary assistance, or I offer you my fortune.
Calla Æthiopica . .	Magnificent beauty.
Calycanthus	Benevolence.
Camelia Japonica, red	Unpretending excellence.
Camelia Japonica, white	Perfected loveliness.
Camomile	Energy in adversity.
Campanula Pyramida .	Aspiring.
Canary Grass . . .	Perseverance.
Candytuft	Indifference.
Canterbury Bell . .	Acknowledgment.
Cape Jasmine . . .	I am too happy.
Cardamine	Paternal error.
Cardinal Flower . .	Distinction.
Carnation, deep red .	Alas ! for my poor heart.
Carnation, striped . .	Refusal.
Carnation, yellow . .	Disdain.
Catchfly	Snare.
Catchfly, red	Youthful love.
Catchfly, white . . .	Betrayed.
Cattleya	Mature charms.
Cattleya Pineli . . .	Matronly grace.
Cedar	Strength.
Cedar Leaf	I live for thee.
Cedar of Lebanon . .	Incorruptible.
Celandine, lesser . .	Joys to come.
Centaury	Delicacy.
Cereus, creeping . .	Modest genius.
Champignon	Suspicion.
Chequered Fritillary .	Persecution.
Cherry-tree, black . .	Deception.
Cherry-tree, white . .	Good education.
Chestnut Tree . . .	Do me justice.
Chiccory	Frugality.
Chickweed	Rendezvous.
China Aster	Variety.
China Aster, double .	I partake your sentiments.
China Aster, single .	I will think of it.
China or Indian Pink .	Aversion.
China Rose	Beauty always new.
Chinese Chrysanthemum	Cheerfulness under adversity.
Chinese Primrose . .	Lasting love.
Chorozema Varium .	You have many lovers.
Christmas Rose . . .	Relieve my anxiety.
Chrysanthemum, red .	I love.
Chrysanthemum, white	Truth.
Chrysanthemum, yellow	Slighted love.
Cineraria	Always delightful.

Cinquefoil . . . . Maternal affection.
Circæa . . . . . . Spell.
Cistus, or Rock Rose . Popular favor.
Cistus, gum . . . . I shall die to-morrow.
Citron . . . . . . Ill-natured beauty.
Clarkia . . . . . . The variety of your conversa-
                     tion delights me.
Clematis . . . . . Mental beauty.
Clematis, evergreen . Poverty.
Clianthus . . . . . Worldliness, self-seeking
Clotbur . . . . . Rudeness, pertinacity.
Clover, four-leaved . Be mine.
Clover, red . . . . Industry.
Clover, white . . . . Think of me.
Cloves . . . . . . Dignity.
Cobæa . . . . . . Gossip.
Cockscomb, Amaranth Foppery, affectation, singu-
                     larity.
Colchicum, or Meadow
  Saffron . . . . . My best days are past.
Coltsfoot . . . . . Justice shall be done.
Columbine . . . . Folly.
Columbine, purple . . Resolved to win.
Columbine, red . . . Anxious and trembling.
Convolvulus . . . . Bonds.
Convolvulus, blue (mi-
  nor) . . . . . . Repose, night.
Convolvulus, major . Extinguished hopes.
Convolvulus, pink . . Worth sustained by judicious
                     and tender affection.
Corchorus . . . . Impatient of absence.
Coreopsis . . . . . Always cheerful.
Coreopsis Arkansa . . Love at first sight.
Coriander . . . . . Hidden worth.
Corn . . . . . . Riches.
Corn, broken . . . Quarrel.
Corn Bottle . . . . Delicacy.
Corn Cockle . . . . Gentility.
Corn Straw . . . . Agreement.
Cornel Tree . . . . Duration.
Coronella . . . . . Success crown your wishes.
Cosmelia Subra . . . The charm of a blush.
Cowslip . . . . . . Pensiveness, winning grace.
Cowslip, American . . Divine beauty.
Crab, blossom . . . Ill nature.
Cranberry . . . . Cure for heartache.
Creeping Cereus . . Horror.
Cress . . . . . . Stability, power.
Crocus . . . . . . Abuse not.
Crocus, Saffron . . Mirth.
Crocus, Spring . . . Youthful gladness.
Crowfoot . . . . . Ingratitude.
Crown, Imperial . . Majesty, power.
Crowsbill . . . . . Envy.
Crowfoot, Aconite-
  leaved . . . . . Lustre.
Cuckoo Plant . . . Ardor.
Cudweed, American . Unceasing remembrance.
Currant . . . . . . Thy frown will kill me.
Cuscuta . . . . . . Meanness.
Cyclamen . . . . . Diffidence.
Cypress . . . . . . Death, mourning.

Daffodil . . . . . Regard.
Dahlia . . . . . . Instability.
Daisy . . . . . . Innocence.
Daisy, garden . . . I share your sentiments.
Daisy, Michaelmas . . Farewell, or afterthought.
Daisy, party-colored . Beauty.
Daisy, wild . . . . I will think of it.
Damask Rose . . . Brilliant complexion.
Dandelion . . . . Rustic oracle.
Daphne . . . . . . Glory, immortality.
Daphne Odora . . . Painting the lily.
Darnel . . . . . . Vice.
Dead Leaves . . . . Sadness.
Deadly Nightshade . Falsehood.
Dew Plant . . . . A serenade.
Dianthus . . . . . Make haste.
Diosma . . . . . . Your simple elegance charms
                     me.
Diplademia Crassinoda You are too bold.
Dipteracanthus Spec-
  tabilis . . . . . Fortitude.
Dittany of Crete . . Birth.
Dittany of Crete, white Passion.

Dock . . . . . . Patience.
Dodder of Thyme . . Baseness.
Dogsbane . . . . . Deceit, falsehood.
Dogwood . . . . . Durability.
Dragon Plant . . . Snare.
Dragonwort . . . . Horror.
Dried Flax . . . . Utility.

Ebony Tree . . . . Blackness.
Echites Atropurpurea . Be warned in time.
Eglantine (Sweet-brier) Poetry, I wound to heal.
Elder . . . . . . Zealousness.
Elm . . . . Dignity.
Enchanters' Night-
  shade . . . . . Witchcraft, sorcery.
Endive . . . . . . Frugality.
Eschscholtzia . . . Do not refuse me.
Eupatorium . . . . Delay.
Everflowering Candy-
  tuft . . . . . . Indifference.
Evergreen Clematis . Poverty.
Evergreen Thorn . . Solace in adversity.
Everlasting . . . . Never-ceasing remembrance.
Everlasting Pea . . . Lasting pleasure.

Fennel . . . . . . Worthy all praise, strength.
Fern . . . . . . Fascination, magic, since.ity.
Ficoides, Ice Plant . Your looks freeze me.
Fig . . . . Argument.
Fig Marigold . . . Idleness.
Fig Tree . . . . . Prolific.
Filbert . . . . . . Reconciliation.
Fir . . . . Time.
Fir Tree . . . . . Elevation.
Flax . . . . . . Domestic industry, fate, I
                     feel your kindness.
Flax-leaved Golden-
  locks . . . . . Tardiness.
Fleur-de-lis . . . . Flame, I burn.
Flower-de-Luce . . Fire.
Flowering Fern . . Reverie.
Flowering Reed . . Confidence in heaven.
Flower-of-an-Hour . Delicate beauty.
Fly Orchis . . . . Error.
Flytrap . . . . . . Deceit.
Fool's Parsley . . Silliness.
Forget-me-not . . . True love.
Foxglove . . . . . Insincerity.
Foxtail Grass . . . Sporting.
Francisca Latifolia . Beware of false friends.
French Honeysuckle . Rustic beauty.
French Marigold . . Jealousy.
French Willow . . . Bravery and humanity.
Frog Ophrys . . . Disgust.
Fuchsia, scarlet . . Taste.
Fuller's Teasel . . Misanthropy.
Fumitory . . . . . Spleen.
Furze, or Gorse . . Love for all seasons.

Garden Anemone . . Forsaken.
Garden Chervil . . Sincerity.
Garden Daisy . . . I partake your sentiments.
Garden Marigold . . Uneasiness.
Garden Ranunculus . You are rich in attractions.
Garden Sage . . . . Esteem.
Gardenia . . . . . Refinement.
Garland of Roses . . Reward of virtue.
Geranium, dark . . . Melancholy.
Geranium, Horseshoe-
  leaved . . . . . Stupidity.
Geranium, Ivy . . . Bridal favor.
Geranium, Lemon . . Unexpected meeting.
Geranium, Nutmeg . Expected meeting.
Geranium, Oak-leaved True friendship.
Geranium, Pencilled . Ingenuity.
Geranium, Rose-
  scented . . . . Preference.
Geranium, scarlet . . Comforting.
Geranium, Silver-
  leaved . . . . . Recall.
Geranium, wild . . Steadfast piety.
Germander Speedwell . Facility.
Gillvflower . . . . Bonds of affection.
Gladioli . . . . . Ready armed.
Glory Flower . . . Glorious beauty.
Goat's Rue . . . . Reason.

Goldenrod	Precaution.
Gooseberry	Anticipation.
Gourd	Extent, bulk.
Grammanthus Chlora-flora	Your temper is too hasty.
Grape, wild	Charity.
Grass	Submission, utility.
Guelder Rose . . .	Winter, age.
Hand Flower Tree .	Warning.
Harebell	Submission, grief.
Hawkweed	Quick-sightedness.
Hawthorn	Hope.
Hazel	Reconciliation.
Heartsease, or Pansy .	Thoughts.
Heath	Solitude.
Helenium	Tears.
Heliotrope	Devotion, or I turn to thee.
Hellebore	Scandal, calumny.
Helmet Flower (Monkshood) . . .	Knight-errantry.
Hemlock	You will be my death.
Hemp	Fate.
Henbane	Imperfection.
Hepatica	Confidence.
Hibiscus	Delicate beauty.
Holly	Foresight.
Holly Herb	Enchantment.
Hollyhock	Ambition, fecundity.
Honesty	Honesty, fascination.
Honey Flower . . .	Love sweet and secret.
Honeysuckle	Generous and devoted affection.
Honeysuckle (Coral) .	The color of my fate.
Honeysuckle (French)	Rustic beauty.
Hop	Injustice.
Hornbeam	Ornament.
Horsechestnut . . .	Luxury.
Hortensia	You are cold.
Houseleek	Vivacity, domestic industry.
Houstonia	Content.
Hoya	Sculpture.
Hoyabella	Contentment.
Humble Plant . . .	Despondency.
Hundred-leaved Rose .	Dignity of mind.
Hyacinth	Sport, game, play.
Hyacinth, purple . .	Sorrowful.
Hyacinth, white . .	Unobtrusive loveliness.
Hydrangea	A boaster.
Hyssop	Cleanliness.
Iceland Moss . . .	Health.
Ice Plant	Your looks freeze me.
Imbricata	Uprightness, sentiments of honor.
Imperial Montague. .	Power.
Indian Cress . . .	Warlike trophy.
Indian Jasmine (Ipomœa)	Attachment.
Indian Pink, double .	Always lovely.
Indian Plum	Privation.
Iris	Message.
Iris, German	Flame.
Ivy	Friendship, fidelity, marriage.
Ivy, sprig of, with tendrils	Assiduous to please.
Jacob's Ladder . . .	Come down.
Japan Rose	Beauty is your only attraction.
Jasmine	Amiability.
Jasmine, Cape . . .	Transport of joy.
Jasmine, Carolina . .	Separation.
Jasmine, Indian . .	I attach myself to you.
Jasmine, Spanish . .	Sensuality.
Jasmine, yellow . . .	Grace and elegance.
Jonquil	I desire a return of affection.
Judas Tree	Unbelief, betrayal.
Juniper	Succor, protection.
Justicia	The perfection of female loveliness.
Kennedia	Mental beauty.
King-cups	Desire of riches.

Laburnum	Forsaken, pensive beauty.
Lady's Slipper . . .	Capricious beauty, win me and wear me.
Lagerstræmia, Indian.	Eloquence.
Lantana	Rigor.
Lapageria Rosea . .	There is no unalloyed good.
Larch	Audacity, boldness.
Larkspur	Lightness, levity.
Larkspur, pink . . .	Fickleness.
Larkspur, purple . .	Haughtiness.
Laurel	Glory.
Laurel, common, in flower	Perfidy.
Laurel, Ground . . .	Perseverance.
Laurel, Mountain . .	Ambition.
Laurel-leaved Magnolia	Dignity.
Laurestina	A token.
Lavender	Distrust.
Leaves (dead) . . .	Melancholy.
Lemon	Zest.
Lemon Blossoms . .	Fidelity in love.
Leschenaultia Splendens	You are charming.
Lettuce	Cold-heartedness.
Lichen	Dejection, solitude.
Lilac, field	Humility.
Lilac, purple	First emotions of love.
Lilac, white	Youthful innocence.
Lily, Day	Coquetry.
Lily, Imperial . . .	Majesty.
Lily of the Valley . .	Return of happiness, unconscious sweetness.
Lily, white	Purity, sweetness.
Lily, yellow	Falsehood, gayety.
Linden or Lime Trees .	Conjugal love.
Lint	I feel my obligations.
Liquorice, wild . . .	I declare against you.
Live Oak	Liberty.
Liverwort	Confidence.
Lobelia	Malevolence.
Locust Tree	Elegance.
Locust Tree, green .	Affection beyond the grave.
London Pride . . .	Frivolity.
Lote Tree	Concord.
Lotus	Eloquence.
Lotus Flower . . .	Estranged love.
Lotus Leaf	Recantation.
Love in a Mist . . .	Perplexity.
Love lies Bleeding . .	Hopeless, not heartless.
Lucern	Life.
Lupine	Voraciousness.
Madder	Calumny.
Magnolia	Love of Nature.
Magnolia, Swamp . .	Perseverance.
Mallon Creeana . .	Will you share my fortunes?
Mallow	Mildness.
Mallow, Marsh . . .	Beneficence.
Mallow, Syrian . . .	Consumed by love.
Mallow, Venetian . .	Delicate beauty.
Manchineal Tree . .	Falsehood.
Mandrake	Horror.
Maple	Reserve.
Marianthus	Hope for better days.
Marigold	Grief.
Marigold, African . .	Vulgar minds.
Marigold, French . .	Jealousy.
Marigold, Prophetic .	Prediction.
Marigold and Cypress .	Despair.
Marjoram	Blushes.
Marvel of Peru . . .	Timidity.
Meadow Lychnis . .	Wit.
Meadow Saffron . .	My best days are past.
Meadowsweet . . .	Uselessness.
Mercury	Goodness.
Mesembryanthemum .	Idleness.
Mezereon	Desire to please.
Michaelmas Daisy . .	After-thought.
Mignonette	Your qualities surpass your charms.
Milfoil	War.
Milkvetch	Your presence softens my pains.
Milkwort	Hermitage.

Mimosa, Sensitive
  Plant . . . . . Sensitiveness.
Mint . . . . . . Virtue.
Mistletoe . . . . I surmount difficulties.
Mitraria Coccinea . . Indolence, dulness.
Mock Orange . . . Counterfeit.
Monarda Amplexicau-
  lis . . . . . . Your whims are quite un-
    bearable.
Monkshood . . . . A deadly foe is near.
Monkshood, Helmet-
  flower . . . . . Chivalry, knight-errantry.
Moonwort . . . . Forgetfulness.
Morning Glory . . . Affectation.
Moschatel . . . . Weakness.
Moss . . . . . . Maternal love.
Mosses. . . . . . Ennui.
Mossy Saxifrage . . Affection.
Motherwort . . . . Concealed love.
Mountain Ash . . . Prudence.
Mourning Bride . . Unfortunate attachment, I
    have lost all.
Mouse-eared Chick-
  weed . . . . . Ingenuous simplicity.
Mouse-eared Scorpion
  Grass . . . . . Forget me not.
Moving Plant . . . Agitation.
Mudwort . . . . . Happiness, tranquillity.
Mulberry Tree, black . I shall not survive you.
Mulberry Tree, white . Wisdom.
Mushroom . . . . Suspicion, or I can't entirely
    trust you.
Musk Plant . . . . Weakness.
Mustard Seed . . . Indifference.
Myrobalan . . . . Privation.
Myrrh . . . . . . Gladness.
Myrtle . . . . . . Love.

Narcissus . . . . . Egotism.
Nasturtium . . . . Patriotism.
Nemophila . . . . Success everywhere.
Nettle, common sting-
  ing . . . . . . You are spiteful.
Nettle, burning . . . Slander.
Nettle Tree . . . . Conceit.
Night-blooming Ce-
  reus . . . . . Transient beauty.
Night Convolvulus . Night.
Nightshade . . . . Falsehood.

Oak Leaves . . . . Bravery.
Oak Tree . . . . . Hospitality.
Oak, white . . . . Independence.
Oats. . . . . . . The witching soul of music.
Oleander . . . . . Beware.
Olive . . . . . . Peace.
Orange Blossoms . . Your purity equals your love-
    liness.
Orange Flowers . . . Chastity, bridal festivities.
Orange Tree . . . . Generosity.
Orchis . . . . . . A belle.
Osier . . . . . . Frankness.
Osmunda . . . . . Dreams.
Ox Eye . . . . . Patience.

Palm . . . . . . Victory.
Pansy . . . . . . Thoughts.
Parsley . . . . . . Festivity.
Pasque Flower . . . You have no claims.
Passion Flower . . . Religious superstition, when
    the flower is reversed, or
    Faith, if erect.
Patience Dock . . . Patience.
Pea, Everlasting . . An appointed meeting, last-
    ing pleasure.
Pea, Sweet . . . . Departure.
Peach . . . . . . Your qualities, like your
    charms, are unequalled.
Peach Blossom . . . I am your captive.
Pear . . . . Affection.
Pear Tree . . . . . Comfort.
Pennyroyal . . . . Flee away.
Penstemon Azureum High-bred.
Peony . . . . . . Shame, bashfulness.
Peppermint . . . . Warmth of feeling
Periwinkle, blue . . Early friendship
Periwinkle, white . . Pleasures of memory.

Persicaria . . . . . Restoration.
Persimmon . . . . Bury me amid Nature's beau-
    ties.
Peruvian Heliotrope . Devotion.
Petunia . . . . . Your presence soothes me.
Pheasant's Eye . . . Remembrance.
Phlox . . . . . . Unanimity.
Pigeon Berry . . . Indifference.
Pimpernel . . . . Change, assignation.
Pine. . . . . . . Pity.
Pine-apple . . . . You are perfect.
Pine, Pitch . . . . Philosophy.
Pine, Spruce . . . . Hope in adversity.
Pink . . . . . . Boldness.
Pink, Carnation . . Woman's love.
Pink, Indian, double . Always lovely.
Pink, Indian, single . Aversion.
Pink, Mountain . . Aspiring.
Pink, red, double . . Pure and ardent love.
Pink, single . . . . Pure love.
Pink, variegated . . Refusal.
Pink, white . . . . Ingeniousness, talent.
Plaintain . . . . . White man's footsteps.
Plane Tree . . . . Genius.
Plum, Indian . . . Privation.
Plum Tree . . . . Fidelity.
Plum, wild . . . . Independence.
Plumbago Larpenta . Holy wishes.
Polyanthus . . . . Pride of riches.
Polyanthus, crimson . The heart's mystery.
Polyanthus, lilac . . Confidence.
Pomegranate . . . Foolishness.
Pomegranate Flower . Mature elegance.
Poor Robin . . . . Compensation, or an equiva-
    lent.
Poplar, black . . . Courage.
Poplar, white . . . Time.
Poppy, red . . . . Consolation.
Poppy, scarlet . . . Fantastic extravagance.
Poppy, white . . . Sleep, my bane.
Potato . . . . . . Benevolence.
Potentilla . . . . . I claim, at least, your esteem.
Prickly Pear . . . . Satire.
Pride of China . . . Dissension.
Primrose . . . . . Early youth and sadness.
Primrose, Evening. . Inconstancy.
Primrose, red . . . Unpatronized merit.
Privet . . . . . . Prohibition.
Purple Clover . . . Provident.
Pyrus Japonica . . . Fairies' fire.

Quaking-grass . . . Agitation.
Quamoclit . . . . Busybody.
Queen's Rocket . . You are the queen of co-
    quettes, fashion.
Quince . . . . . . Temptation.

Ragged Robin . . . Wit.
Ranunculus . . . . You are radiant with charms.
Ranunculus, garden . You are rich in attractions.
Ranunculus, wild . . Ingratitude.
Raspberry . . . . Remorse.
Ray Grass . . . . Vice.
Red Catchfly . . . Youthful love.
Reed . . . . . . Complaisance, music.
Reed, split . . . . Indiscretion.
Rhododendron (Rose
  bay) . . . . . Danger, beware.
Rhubarb . . . . . Advice.
Rocket . . . . . . Rivalry.
Rose . . . . Love.
Rose, Austrian . . . Thou art all that is lovely.
Rose, Bridal . . . . Happy love.
Rose, Burgundy . . Unconscious beauty.
Rose, Cabbage . . . Embassador of love.
Rose, Campion . . . Only deserve my love.
Rose, Carolina . . . Love is dangerous.
Rose, China . . . . Beauty always done.
Rose, Christmas . . Tranquillize my anxiety.
Rose, Daily . . . . Thy smile I aspire to.
Rose, Damask . . . Brilliant complexion.
Rose, deep red . . . Bashful shame.
Rose, Dog . . . . Pleasure and pain.
Rose, full-blown,
  placed over two buds. Secrecy.
Rose, Guelder . . . Winter, age.

Rose, Hundred-leaved	Pride.
Rose, Japan	Beauty is your only attraction.
Rose, Maiden-blush .	If you love me, you will find it out.
Rose, Montiflora . .	Grace.
Rose, Mundi	Variety.
Rose, Musk	Capricious beauty.
Rose, Musk, cluster .	Charming.
Rose, single	Simplicity.
Rose, thornless . . .	Early attachment.
Rose, Unique . . .	Call me not beautiful.
Rose, white	I am worthy of you.
Rose, white and red together	Unity.
Rose, white, withered .	Transient impressions.
Rose, yellow . . .	Decrease of love, jealousy.
Rose, York and Lancaster	War.
Rosebud, Moss . . .	Confusion of love.
Rosebud, red . . .	Pure and lovely.
Rosebud (Rhododendron)	Beware, danger.
Rosebud, white . . .	Girlhood.
Rosemary	Remembrance.
Roses, crown of. . .	Reward of virtue.
Rudbeckia	Justice
Rue	Disdain.
Rush	Docility.
Rye Grass	Changeable disposition.
Saffron	Beware of excess.
Saffron Crocus . . .	Mirth.
Saffron, Meadow . .	My happiest days are past.
Sage	Domestic virtue.
Sage, garden	Esteem.
Sainfoin	Agitation.
Saint John's Wort . .	Animosity.
Salvia, blue	Wisdom.
Salvia, red	Energy.
Saxifrage, mossy . .	Affection.
Scabious	Unfortunate love.
Scabious, sweet . . .	Widowhood.
Scarlet Lychnis . . .	Sun-beaming eyes.
Schinus	Religious enthusiasm.
Scotch Fir	Elevation.
Sensitive Plant . . .	Sensibility.
Senvy	Indifference.
Shamrock	Light-heartedness.
Shepherd's Purse . .	I offer you my all.
Siphocampylos . . .	Resolved to be noticed.
Snakesfoot	Horror.
Snapdragon	Presumption, also No.
Snowball	Bound.
Snowdrop	Hope.
Sorrel	Affection.
Sorrel, wild	Wit ill-timed.
Sorrel, wood	Joy.
Southernwood . . .	Jest, bantering.
Spanish Jasmine . .	Sensuality.
Spearmint	Warmth of sentiment.
Speedwell	Female fidelity.
Speedwell, Germander	Facility.
Speedwell, Spiked . .	Semblance.
Spider Ophrys . . .	Adroitness.
Spiderwort	Esteem, not love.
Spiked Willow Herb .	Pretension.
Spindle Tree	Your charms are engraven on my heart.
Star of Bethlehem . .	Purity.
Starwort	After-thought.
Starwort, American .	Cheerfulness in old age.
Stephanotis	Will you accompany me to the East?
Stock	Lasting beauty.
Stock, Ten-Weeks . .	Promptness.
Stonecrop	Tranquillity.
Straw, broken . . .	Rupture of a contract.
Straw, whole . . .	Union.
Strawberry blossoms .	Foresight.
Strawberry Tree . .	Esteem, not love.
Sultan, lilac	I forgive you.
Sultan, white . . .	Sweetness.
Sultan, yellow . . .	Contempt.
Sumach, Venice . .	Splendor.
Sunflower, dwarf . .	Adoration.
Sunflower, tall . . .	Haughtiness.

Swallow-wort . . .	Cure for heartache.
Sweet Basil	Good wishes.
Sweet-brier, American	Simplicity.
Sweet-brier, European	I wound to heal.
Sweet-brier, yellow .	Decrease of love.
Sweet Pea	Delicate pleasures.
Sweet Sultan	Felicity.
Sweet William . . .	Gallantry.
Sycamore	Curiosity.
Syringa	Memory.
Syringa, Carolina . .	Disappointment.
Tamarisk	Crime.
Tansy, wild	I declare war against you.
Teasel	Misanthropy.
Tendrils of climbing plants	Ties.
Thistle, common . .	Austerity.
Thistle, Fuller's . .	Misanthropy.
Thistle, Scotch . . .	Retaliation.
Thorn, apple	Deceitful charms.
Thorn, branch of . .	Severity.
Thrift	Sympathy.
Throatwort	Neglected beauty
Thyme	Activity or courage.
Tiger Flower . . .	For once may pride befriend me.
Traveller's Joy . . .	Safety.
Tree of Life	Old age.
Trefoil	Revenge.
Tremella Nestoc . .	Resistance.
Trillium Pictum . .	Modest beauty.
Triptilion Spinosum .	Be prudent.
Truffle	Surprise.
Trumpet Flower . .	Fame.
Tuberose	Dangerous pleasures.
Tulip, red	Declaration of love.
Tulip, variegated . .	Beautiful eyes.
Tulip, yellow . . .	Hopeless love.
Turnip	Charity.
Tussilage (sweetscented)	Justice shall be done you.
Valerian	An accommodating disposition.
Valerian, Greek . . .	Rupture.
Venice, Sumach . .	Intellectual excellence, splendor.
Venus's Car	Fly with me.
Venus's Looking-glass	Flattery.
Venus's Trap . . .	Deceit.
Verbena, pink . . .	Family union.
Verbena, scarlet . .	Unite against evil, or Church unity.
Verbena, white . . .	Pray for me.
Vernal Grass . . .	Poor, but happy.
Veronica	Fidelity.
Veronica Speciosa . .	Keep this for my sake.
Vervain	Enchantment.
Vine	Intoxication.
Violet, blue	Faithfulness.
Violet, dame	Watchfulness.
Violet, sweet	Modesty.
Violet, yellow . . .	Rural happiness.
Virginia Creeper . .	I cling to you both in sunshine and shade.
Virgin's Bower . . .	Filial love.
Viscaria Oculata . .	Will you dance with me?
Volkamenia	May you be happy!
Wallflower	Fidelity in adversity.
Walnut	Intellect, stratagem.
Watcher by the Wayside	Never despair.
Water Lily	Purity of heart.
Watermelon	Bulkiness.
Wax Plant	Susceptibility.
Wheat Stalk	Riches.
Whin	Anger.
White Jasmine . . .	Amiability.
White Lily	Purity and modesty.
White Mullein . . .	Good nature.
White Oak	Independence.
White Pink	Talent.
White Poplar . . .	Time.

White Rose (dried) .	Death preferable to loss of innocence.
Whortleberry . . .	Treason.
Willow, Creeping . .	Love forsaken.
Willow, French . . .	Bravery and humanity.
Willow Herb . . .	Pretension.
Willow, Water . . .	Freedom.
Willow, Weeping . .	Mourning.
Winter Cherry . . .	Deception.
Wistaria	Welcome, fair stranger !
Witch Hazel	A spell.
Woodbine	Fraternal love.
Wood Sorrel	Joy, maternal tenderness.
Wormwood	Absence.
Xanthium	Rudeness, pertinacity.
Xeranthemum . . .	Cheerfulness under adversity.
Yew	Sorrow.
Zephyr Flower . . .	Expectation.
Zinnia	Thoughts of absent friends.

Flowery Land, The. This is the meaning of the words *Hwa Kwoh*, a name often given to China by its people. They deem themselves the most cultured and civilized among the nations.

Floyd Valentine. (Pseud.) Floyd Vail, in the "Freeman's Journal," New York, 1884 *et seq.*

F. L. S. Fellow of the Linnæan Society.

Flume. This word, though of good old Saxon origin, meaning originally a mill-race, has come to signify, in Western mining terms, a stream of water, often conveyed in trough-like boxes for many miles from the source of supply to the scene of action.

Flying Dutchman. (1) A spectral ship, seen in stormy weather off the Cape of Good Hope, and considered ominous of ill-luck. Sir Walter Scott says she was originally a vessel laden with precious metal; but a horrible murder having been committed on board, the plague broke out among the crew, and no port would allow the vessel to enter. The more popular form of the legend makes her cursed to beat forever against head-winds, because her captain impiously swore he would round the Cape in spite of God or devil. The ill-fated ship still wanders about like a ghost, doomed to be sea-tossed, and nevermore to enjoy rest. (2) A train which traverses the Great Western Railway from London to Bristol daily, a distance of 118¼ miles, in two hours thirty-six minutes. Allowing for stoppages, the speed is forty-nine miles an hour. See *infra.*

Flying Highwayman. A nickname of William Harrow, a notorious footpad or highway robber, executed at Hertford, England, March 28, 1763. For a long time he escaped pursuit, owing to his custom of compelling his horse to take flying leaps over the turnpike gates.

Flying Money. Bank-notes are so named by the Chinese.

Flying Scotchman. The fast mail trains running daily between London and Edinburgh. The distance is over four hundred miles, and in 1888 the time was reduced to eight hours on both the eastern and western routes. These trains are the fastest in the world. See *supra.*

Flying Scotch Squadron (*Squadrone Volante*) is the name of a party of Scotch politicians formed about 1705. It was borrowed from the famous "Flying Squadron" of independent cardinals during the previous generation at the Papal Court. Lord Tweeddale was the leader of this "New Party," which, by keeping close together and joining first one side and then the other in the Union debates, had for some time a good deal of power. It had the fate of the Union question in its own hands, and its adhesion to the cause of the Government in 1706 secured the triumph of that measure. This reference to the "Union" means the union of England and Scotland in one kingdom, bearing the name of Great Britain; that the succession to the crown of Scotland should be in all points the same as had been settled for England; that the United Kingdom should be represented by one Parliament; that thenceforward there should be community of rights and privileges between the two kingdoms, except where otherwise agreed upon by the Parliament; that all standards of coin, weights, and measures in Scotland should be assimilated to those of England; that the laws of trade, customs, and excise should be the same in both countries; that all other laws of Scotland should remain unchanged, but with the provision that they might be altered in time to come at the discretion of the United Parliament. To these articles was added an Act of Security for the maintenance of the Scottish Church and the four universities. This act required each sovereign, on his or her accession, to take an oath to protect the Presbyterian Church as the established Church of Scotland. The whole judicial machinery for the administration of the

Scottish law system remained untouched; but henceforward there would be a possibility of appeal from the decisions of the Court of Sessions to the House of Lords. In the Parliament of Great Britain Scotland was to be represented by forty-five members sent up by the Commons, and sixteen peers elected by their fellows as representatives of the peerage of Scotland. The articles of Union received the royal assent, and the first Parliament of Great Britain met Oct. 23, 1707. A standard on which was blended the flags of both nations, the crosses of St. Andrew and St. George, which had been first projected by James VI. under the name of the Union Jack, was adopted as the national flag of the United Kingdom.

F.-M. Field-Marshal.

F.-O. Field-Officer.

F. O. B. These letters, which are often met with in quotations of prices of merchandise, mean "free on board;" that is, the price includes carriage and all charges upon the goods until they are actually in the conveyance which is to carry them to their destination.

F. o. b. Free on board.

Fol. Folio.

Folk. See PEOPLE.

Fonda. (Span.) A hotel.

Fons et origo. (Lat.) "The fountain and source." The chief cause.

Fontarabia. The ancient, now the poetical, form of the name of a town in Gascony, at present called Fuenterabia. Here Charlemagne defeated the Saracens, though with immense loss to himself.

> When Charlemagne with all his peerage fell
> By Fontarabia.
> MILTON, *Paradise Lost.*

Fool Bible. Shortly after the invention of printing, the wife of a printer in Germany, while an edition of the Bible was in the press, on one occasion made a small but important change in the types. The sentence in Genesis in which it is declared that Eve shall be subject to her husband runs thus: "He shall be thy lord" (*Herr*). This was altered to "He shall be thy fool" (*Narr*). Many copies of the book got into circulation before the substitution of the one word for the other was discovered; for in black letter *Herr* and *Narr* much resemble each other. It is said that the practical joke cost the unfortunate woman her life, she hav-

ing been condemned to the stake by the ecclesiastical authorities.

Fool or Physician at Forty. Plutarch, in his "Treatise on the Preservation of Health," tells us that Tiberius said a man was either his own physician or a fool by the time he was forty.

Foot's Resolution. A resolution introduced in the Senate in December, 1829, by S. A. Foot, of Connecticut, designed to limit the sale of Western lands. Its importance lies in the fact of its having been seized on by the Southern members as the text for an attack on the North and the "centralization" theory.

Fop's Alley. Many years ago there existed in Her Majesty's Opera House, London, a gangway or promenade down the centre of the pit and between the latter and the boxes. Here the beaux of the day were wont to stroll between the acts, exchanging criticisms on the music and the singers, and ogling the belles in the boxes.

For. Foreign.

Force Bill. A measure famous in American political annals. Its full title was "An Act to enforce the provisions of the Fourteenth Amendment to the Constitution of the United States, and for other purposes." It was introduced in the House by Mr. Shellabarger, of Ohio, from the select committee appointed to consider the President's message calling attention to the necessity of such a measure, on March 28, 1871. It was debated at length in the House, passed April 4, debated in the Senate April 11, and passed with amendments; two conference committees considered it, and with certain amendments it was signed by the President on April 20, 1871. Mr. Blaine, we presume, was opposed to it as being unconstitutional and unnecessary. He was Speaker at the time, and did not take part in the debate. The Force Act gave to persons deprived by anybody of any constitutional right the power to sue their aggressors in the United States courts; it punished conspiracies to deprive persons of any rights by fine and imprisonment, besides allowing the injured parties to sue for damages; it gave the President power to use the army and the navy to put down such conspiracies and insurrections, and to suspend the writ of habeas corpus when he deemed it necessary, after proclamation; it instituted an "iron-clad" oath to be taken by jurors in cases arising under the act, that they were in no way implicated in the aggressive acts; and it provided that persons who did not oppose conspiracies of which they were aware should be liable in damages to persons injured by such conspiracies. There were other provisions of the same nature.

Ford of Flags. A translation of *Balleek*, the former name of the town of Ballina, Ireland, by which appellation it is often referred to.

Forefathers' Day. This is the anniversary of the landing of the Pilgrims at Plymouth Rock, which event took place on Dec. 11, 1620, according to the Old Style, or December 22, New Style, which of course is the date now observed. Throughout New England and in the chief cities of the Middle States the day is kept by various societies who seek to keep alive and commemorate the sturdy virtues of the Pilgrims, — the "Forefathers." In other places there are literary and festive gatherings in honor of the great event and the principles it illustrated. On such occasions Mrs. Hemans's immortal lyric, "The Landing of the Pilgrim Fathers in New England," is recited or sung: —

"The breaking waves dashed high
    On a stern and rock-bound coast,
And the woods against a stormy sky
    Their giant branches tossed;

"And the heavy night hung dark
    The hills and waters o'er,
When a band of exiles moored their bark
    On the wild New England shore.

"Not as the conqueror comes,
    They, the true-hearted, came;
Not with the roll of the stirring drums,
    And the trumpet that sings of fame;

"Not as the flying come,
    In silence and in fear; —
They shook the depths of the desert gloom
    With their hymns of lofty cheer.

"Amidst the storm they sang,
    And the stars heard, and the sea;
And the sounding aisles of the dim woods rang
    To the anthem of the free!

"The ocean eagle soared
    From his nest by the white wave's foam;
And the rocking pines of the forest roared:
    This was their welcome home!

"There were men with hoary hair
    Amidst that pilgrim band:
Why had they come to wither there,
    Away from their childhood's land?

"There was woman's fearless eye,
    Lit by her deep love's truth;
There was manhood's brow serenely high,
    And the fiery heart of youth.

"What sought they thus afar?
    Bright jewels of the mine?
The wealth of seas, the spoils of war? —
    They sought a faith's pure shrine!

"Ay, call it holy ground,
    The soil where first they trod;
They have left unstained 'what there they found, —
    Freedom to worship God."

Forest City. Three cities in the United States are known by this descriptive designation, owing to the profusion of shade-trees that adorn their streets: Cleveland, Ohio, Portland, Me., and Savannah, Ga.

Forks, The Caudine. *See* CAUDINE FORKS.

Forlorn Hope. (Pseud.) Mrs. Matilda A. Bailey, a contributor to the New Orleans "Times."

Fornax. In classic myth the goddess of corn and the patroness of bakers.

Forseti. In Scandinavian mythology a son of Baldur and god of justice.

Forte. (Ital.) Loud.

Fortes fortuna adjuvat. (Lat.) "Fortune assists the brave." Fortune favors brave men.

Fortissimo. (Lat.) Very loud.

Fortiter in re. (Lat.) Vigorous in action. *See* SUAVITER IN MODO.

Fortuna. In classic myth the goddess of chance, good luck, success, or prosperity. She is depicted as being blind.

Fortunæ filius. (Lat.) "The son of fortune." A favorite of fortune.

Fortuna favet fatuis. (Lat.) Fortune favors fools.

Fortunate City. Dowletabad, an inland town and fortress of India.

Fortunate Islands. The Canaries. *See* HAPPY ISLANDS.

Fortune Bay Outrages. "In January, 1878, the rights of our fishermen under the Treaty of Washington (1871) were infringed by the inhabitants of Fortune Bay, Newfoundland, who attacked several Gloucester vessels that were taking in cargoes of frozen herring, cut their nets and drove away the crews. A claim was made that local laws had been violated, but the British Government took a correct view of the matter by deciding that these could not stand in conflict with the treaty. The claims of the injured fishermen amounted to $105,305; Great Britain paid £15,000 (nearly $73,000), to be divided among them as compensation for the damages inflicted." — *American Political Dictionary.*

Fortune des armes. (Fr.) Fortune of war.

Forty Footsteps, Field of the. *See* FIELD OF THE FORTY FOOTSTEPS.

Forty Stripes save One. The Jews were forbidden by the Law of Moses to inflict more than forty stripes; and lest they should exceed that number, they generally gave fewer. It is thought that they used a whip with three thongs, and therefore could not strike more than thirteen times without exceeding the lawful number. This phrase is applied by a section of the Anglican Church to the Thirty-nine Articles.

Forza. (Ital.) Force; as, *Con forza,* with force. (Mus.)

Forzando, or **Forz,** or **Fz.** (Ital.) Implies that the note is to be marked with force and emphasis. (Mus.)

Fosse, The. One of the four great Roman thoroughfares that traversed England. A fosse or ditch ran along each side of it. *See* ERMINAGE STREET, IKENILD STREET, WATLING STREET.

The fourth is most of all that tills from Tote-
  neys
From the ene end of Cornwall anon to Cate-
  nays —
From the south to north-east into Englonde's
  end
Fosse men callith thisk voix.
              ROBERT OF GLOUCESTER.

Foul-weather Jack. (1) A nickname given to Commodore John Byron by the crews who sailed with him, because of the uniformly bad weather that attended his cruises. (2) Admiral Sir John Norris, who died 1746.

Founder of Christian Eloquence. Louis Bourdaloue, the French preacher (1632–1704).

Founder of Rome. (1) Romulus, the legendary founder, B. C. 752. (2) Camillus, because he saved the city from the Gauls, B. C. 365. (3) Caius Marius, who saved the city from the Teutones and Cimbri, B. C. 101.

Founder of the Fathers of Christian Doctrine. Cæsar de Bus (1544–1607).

Foundling of Nuremberg. *See* CASPAR HAUSER.

Fountain of Life. A complimentary title conferred on Alexander Hales, a thirteenth-century English friar. *See* IRREFRAGABLE DOCTOR.

Four-eyed George. A by-name conferred on General Meade by his soldiery, and containing a jocular allusion to the fact that he wore spectacles.

Four Forest Cantons, The. A name sometimes given to the four Swiss cantons, Uri, Schwytz, Unterwalden, and Lucerne, probably from the extensive forests with which they were once covered. *See* LAKE OF THE FOUR FOREST CANTONS.

Four Hundred. The "upper ten" of New York society. During the preparations for the centennial celebrations of 1889 a Mr. McAllister said there were only about four hundred people actually in "society" in New York. *See* UPPER TEN THOUSAND.

Four Masters. A name conferred on Michael, Conary, O'Clery, and O'Mulconry, four Celts who flourished in the first half of the seventeenth century, and who compiled from original documents the Annals of Ireland from 2242 B. C. to 1616 A. D.

Fourth Estate of the Realm. There is reason for believing that Carlyle originated this phrase. In "Hero Worship," Lecture V., he says, "Burke said there were three estates in Parliament, but in the Reporters' Gallery yonder there sat a fourth estate, more important far than they all."

Fourth of July. *See* INDEPENDENCE DAY.

Fourth Party. A small knot or clique of Conservatives in the English House of Commons, headed by Lord Randolph Churchill, who made themselves specially obnoxious to Mr. Gladstone, 1883–1884.

F. P. S. Fellow of the Philological Society.

Fr. Franc; France; French; Francis; from; fragment (*fragmentum*).

Fra Angelico of Ecuador. Peter Bedon, a South American clergyman who died in 1561. In early life he cultivated painting, and several of his works adorn the altars of churches in Santa Fé and Quito.

Fracas. Bustle; a slight quarrel; more ado about a thing than it is worth.

Fra Diavolo. Michael Pozza, a famous insurgent of Calabria (fl. 1760–1806). His story forms the libretto of Auber's opera of the name.

France, Garden of. *See* GARDEN OF FRANCE.

France, Iron Gate of. *See* IRON GATE OF FRANCE.

Frances Bishop. The stage-name of Mrs. John T. McKeever, Jr.

Francesco Abati. (Pseud.) William Winwood Reade.

Francis Fitznoodle. (Pseud.) B. B. Valentine, in "Puck," New York.

Francis Forrester, Esq. (Pseud.) Daniel Wise, D. D., American *littérateur* and divine (b. 1813).

Francis Oldys. (Pseud.) George Chalmers, Scottish writer and lawyer (1742–1825).

Francis Phiz. (Pseud.) Edward Smedley, English divine and miscellaneous writer (1814–1864).

Francis Troloppe. The literary signature of Paul Henri Féval, a famous French novelist (1817–1887), under which he published his "Mysteries of London."

Franck Careless. (Pseud.) Richard Head, Irish dramatist (d. 1678).

Frank Cooper. (Pseud.) William Gilmore Simms, American novelist and poet (1806–1870).

Frank Dashmore. (Pseud.) Fanny Murdaugh Downing, American poet (b. about 1835). Her novels include "Nameless," "Perfect through Suffering," and "Florida." She has written over the above pseudomyn, and also over that of "Viola."

Frank Douglas. (Pseud.) F. E. Langley.

Frank Fairleigh. (Pseud.) Edward Smedley, English divine and miscellaneous writer (1814–1864).

Frank Falconer. (Pseud.) E. N. Carvalho, in "Turf, Field, and Farm."

Frank Forester. (Pseud.) Henry William Herbert, English novelist and humorist (1807–1858).

Frank Lin. (Pseud.) Mrs. Gertrude Atherton, author of "Hermia Suydam," "What Dreams may Come," etc. She is a Californian author and newspaper correspondent.

Frank Mayo. The stage-name of Francis Maguire.

Frankenstein. The central character of Mary Wollstonecraft's tale, in which a young student makes a soulless monster out of fragments of men picked up from churchyards and dissecting-rooms, and endues it with life by galvanism. The creature longs for sympathy, but is shunned by every one. It is a parody on the creature man, powerful for evil, and the instrument of dreadful retribution on the student who usurped the prerogative of the Creator.

Frankie Kemble. The stage-name of the second Mrs. (Isabella) Clayburgh.

Franklin. The English freeholder in the Middle Ages. "Franklin" means "freeman."

Franklin of Poland. Thaddeus Czacki (fl. 1765–1813).

Franklin, State of. *See* STATE OF FRANKLIN.

F. R. A. S. Fellow of the Royal Astronomical Society.

F. R. C. P. Fellow of the Royal College of Physicians.

F. R. C. P. E. Fellow of the Royal College of Physicians, Edinburgh.

F. R. C. S. E. Fellow of the Royal College of Surgeons, Edinburgh.

F. R. C. S. I. Fellow of the Royal College of Surgeons, Ireland.

F. R. C. S. L. Fellow of the Royal College of Surgeons, London.

Fr. E. French ells.

Fred. Frederic.

Frederick Paulding. The stage-name of Frederick Dodge.

Freeborn John. A sobriquet given to John Lilburne (fl. 1613–1657), a noted Englishman who made a memorable defence of his republican principles and of his rights as a free-born Englishman before the Star-chamber.

Freedmen. The negroes were so named subsequently to the Proclamation of Emancipation, Jan. 1, 1863.

Free Lance. (Pseud.) J. T. Denny, in various English publications.

Free Lances. Another name for the Fourth Party (*q. v.*). in the English House of Commons.

Freeman, Mrs. A name assumed by the Duchess of Marlborough in her correspondence with Queen Anne. *See* MORLEY, MRS.

Free-soil Party, or **Free-soilers,** were organized at Buffalo, N. Y., in 1848, and comprised the Liberty party, the Barnburners (anti-slavery Democrats of New York), and anti-slavery Whigs. Their first candidate was Martin Van Buren, but he received no electoral votes. In 1852 it nominated John P. Hale, who met with no better success; and in 1856 it became part of the Republican party.

Free State of Patrick. Patrick County, Va., situated in a secluded corner of the State, and noteworthy because of the slight communication maintained between its people and the rest of the inhabitants of the Commonwealth.

Freestone State, The. Connecticut; so named in allusion to the extensive quarries of freestone found within its borders.

Free Trade. The principles embodied in this phrase triumphed in England when the Corn Laws were abolished in 1846, and the commercial treaty with France was adopted in 1860. Richard Cobden, who was very instrumental in passing these measures, named the "Apostle of Free Trade," died April 2, 1865. A new free-trade league was inaugurated in London in December, 1873; and one at Melbourne, Australia, September, 1876. Free trade was warmly advocated in New South Wales and New Zealand, but opposed in Canada and Victoria, 1877–1880. It was an "issue" in the Presidential campaign of 1888 in the United States.

Freight = GOODS. Articles shipped by railway are called "freight" in America and "goods" in England. Thus we have the American "freight-train" and the English "goods-train" or "luggage-train." The English never speak of matter sent by ship as "freight," but use the term "cargo" or "lading."

Freight-cars = TRUCKS. *See* RAILROAD.

French Anacreon. Pierre Lanjou (1727–1811), a famous poet, president of the Caveau Moderne, a club of *bons-vivants.* The knack of rhyming was an indispensable requisite to membership.

French and Indian War. In America, that during which Canada was conquered by the British (1759–1760), and in which the French and Indians were allied against the English.

French Aristophanes. Jean Baptiste Poquelin de Molière (fl. 1622–1673) was so named.

French Devil. An epithet conferred on Jean Bart, the intrepid French sailor, (fl. 1650–1702).

French Ennius. Guillaume di Lovris (fl. 1235–1265).

French Fabius. The Duc de Montmorency (fl. 1493-1567). *See* AMERICAN FABIUS.

French Fury. The descriptive name given to the attempt of the Duc d'Anjou to capture Antwerp by storm, Jan. 17, 1503. The entire attacking party were either killed or captured in less than an hour.

French Leave. This proverbial expression appears to have arisen from the ancient custom of French armies on their marches taking whatever they wished for or required without payment or any other consideration.

French Phidias. (1) Jean Goujon (fl. 1510–1572). (2) Jean Baptiste Pigalle (fl. 1714–1785).

French Politician. (Pseud.) Edmond Scherer, editor of the Paris "Temps," a French senator, and Paris correspondent of the London "Daily News," 1877–1878.

French Titian. Jacques Blanchard, the painter (fl. 1600–1638).

Frères d'armes. (Fr.) Brothers in arms.

Fresco. (Ital.) Quick and lively. (Mus.)

Frey. In Scandinavian mythology the god of the sun and rain, and hence of fertility and peace.

Freyja. In Scandinavian mythology wife of Odur, and the goddess of love, pleasure, beauty, and fecundity. Her husband abandoned her on her loss of youth and beauty, and was changed by Odin into a statue as a punishment.

F. R. G. S. Fellow of the Royal Geographical Society.

F. R. Hist. Soc. Fellow of the Royal Historical Society.

Fri. Friday.

Friar, The. (Pseud.) Phanuel Bacon, D.D., an English poet, author of the "Snipe."

Friar's Heel. The "Friar's Heel" is the name given to the outstanding upright stone at Stonehenge. It is related that Godfrey of Monmouth says the devil bought the stones of an old woman in Ireland, wrapped them up in a withe, and took them to Salisbury Plain. Just before he got to Mount Ambre the withe broke, and one of the stones fell into the Avon, the rest having been carried to the plain. After the fiend had fixed them in the ground he cried out: "No man will ever find out how these stones came here." A friar replied, "That's more than thee canst tell;" whereupon the foul fiend threw one of the stones at him and struck him on the heel. The stone stuck in the ground, and remains so to the present hour.

Friday, Black. *See* BLACK FRIDAY.

Friend of Man. The Marquis de Mirabeau (fl. 1715-1789), father of the great Mirabeau; so named from one of his works, "L'ami des hommes." *See* SHAKSPEARE OF ELOQUENCE.

Friends of the People. An association formed in London, 1792, to obtain Parliamentary reform.

Friends of Virtue. A Revolutionary society founded by Saint Amand Bazard, a French socialist (1791-1832).

Frigga. In Scandinavian mythology wife of Odin, and queen of the gods, mother of Baldur, Thor, etc. She typified the earth, as Odin did the heaven.

Frithiof ("peacemaker"). In the Icelandic myths he married Ingeborg, daughter of a king of Norway, to whose dominions he succeeded. His adventures are recorded in the Saga which bears his name, and which was written at the close of the thirteenth century.

Frogs = POINTS. The pointed iron plates placed where two lines of railroad part are called "points" in England; in the United States they are called "frogs," resembling the marks on a horse's hoof. *See* SWITCHMAN.

From the Sublime to the Ridiculous. The great Napoleon is generally credited with having originated this *mot*. It occurs, however, in Paine's "Age of Reason." The passage is as follows: "The sublime and the ridiculous are often so nearly related, that it is difficult to class them separately. One step above the sublime makes the ridiculous, and one step above the ridiculous makes the sublime again."

Fronde, The. The popular party in France, made up of the Parliament and the citizens, who were opposed to the court and the nobility, during the government of Queen Anne and Cardinal Mazarin at the period of the minority of Louis XVI. They were originally called "Frondeurs," "slingers," from a stone-throwing incident in a street fight. The civil wars of the Fronde lasted from 1648 to 1653.

Fronti nulla fides. (Lat.) There is no trusting to appearances.

Frozen Music. Schelling was the author of the phrase "Architecture is frozen music."

F. R. S. Fellow of the Royal Society.

Frs. Francs; Frisian.

F. R. S. E. Fellow of the Royal Society, Edinburgh.

F. R. S. L. Fellow of the Royal Society, London; Fellow of the Royal Society of Literature.

F. R. S. S. A. Fellow of the Royal Scottish Society of Arts.

Fruges consumere nati. (Lat.) Born merely to consume the fruits of the earth.

Frump. The modern dictionaries define this as a cross-tempered, old-fashioned woman. This is just the reverse of its original signification, which, according to Bailey, was "plump, fat, jolly."

Frying-pan of Andalusia. The town of Ecija, in Spain. The reference is to its torrid climate.

F's, The Three. *See* THREE F'S.

F. S. A. Fellow of the Society of Arts, or of Antiquaries.

F. S. A. E. Fellow of the Society of Antiquaries, Edinburgh.

F. S. A. Scot. Fellow of the Society of Antiquaries of Scotland.

F. S. S. Fellow of the Statistical Society.

Ft. Foot; feet; fort.

F. T. C. D. Fellow of Trinity College, Dublin.

Fth. Fathom.

Fudge Family, The. (Pseud.) Thomas Moore, Irish poet (1779-1852).

Fugam fecit. (Lat.) He has taken to flight.

Fugitive Slave Law. An act passed by the United States Congress in 1850. It imposed a fine of $1,000 and six months' imprisonment on any person harboring slaves or aiding in their escape. It was declared unconstitutional by the Supreme Court, Feb. 3, 1855, and was repealed June 13, 1864; it was never fully carried into effect, Massachusetts refusing to recognize it.

Fuit Ilium. (Lat.) "Troy has been." The object or source of strife has no longer an existence.

Fulmen brutum. (Lat.) A harmless thunderbolt; a blow that strikes blindly.

Functus officio. (Lat.) Out of office.

Funny Man of the "Times." William L. Alden (b. 1837), whose humorous editorials in the "sixth column of the New York 'Times'" gave him a national reputation.

Fuoco, or **Con fuoco.** (Ital.) With fire and intense animation. (Mus.)

Fur. Furlong.

Furies. In classic myth Alecto, Megæra, and Tisiphone, the three goddesses of vengeance. They were armed with smoking torches, snakes wreathed themselves about their heads, and their *toute ensemble* was hideous and appalling.

Furioso, or **Con furia.** (Ital.) With fire. (Mus.)

Furor arma ministrat. (Lat.) Fury supplies with weapons.

Furore. (Ital.) "Fury." Excitement.

Furor loquendi. (Lat.) A rage for speaking.

Furor poeticus. (Lat.) The poetic fire.

Furor scribendi. (Lat.) A rage for writing.

Fursch-Madi, Mme. The stage-name of Madame Emy Verle.

Fury of Antwerp. *See* SPANISH FURY.

Future Great City of the World. The people of St. Louis, Mo., used frequently to refer to their city by this name; it came to be humorously shortened to "Future Great."

Fuzzy Guzzy. (Pseud.) William Henry Burleigh.

F. Z. S. Fellow of the Zoölogical Society.

G.

G. Glucinum.

G., or **g.** Guineas.

Ga. Georgia.

G. A. General Assembly.

Gage d'amour. (Fr.) "A pledge or token of love." A keepsake.

Gagging Bill. A measure enacted in England Dec. 8, 1795, and aiming to protect the king and the government from the addresses of seditious persons or meetings. Again, in December, 1819, soon after the Manchester affray (*see* FIELD OF PETERLOO), an act was passed to restrain tumultuous public meetings and cheap periodicals; it was popularly called "the Gagging Bill."

Gaieté du cœur. (Fr.) "Gayety of heart." Animal spirits.

Gail Forrest. The stage-name of Mrs. Charles Barton.

Gail Hamilton. (Pseud.) Miss Mary Abigail Dodge, American *littérateur* (b. 1830).

Gal. Galatians; gallon.

Galantuomo. (Ital.) An honest man.

Gallant King. Victor Emmanuel of Italy was so named (fl. 1820–1878).

Gallic Bird. The game-cock, or the barnyard rooster, from a fancied resemblance of its boastful, strutting, overbearing manners to corresponding traits in the French nation.

Gallicè. (Lat.) In French.

Galloping Dick. Richard Ferguson, a notorious English highwayman, executed April 4, 1800; so named because of his reckless riding when pursued.

Galloping Head. Sir F. B. Head, the British traveller and author (1793–1875), on account of the breezy manner in which he penned his "Rough Notes" of South American experiences.

Gallows, The Walking. *See* WALKING GALLOWS.

Gallura's Bird. The cock, which was the cognizance of Gallura.

> For her so fair a burial will not make
> The viper . . .
> As had been made by shrill Gallura's bird.
> Dante, *Purgatory.*

Galv. Galvanism; Galveston.

Galway Jury. An enlightened or independent jury. The allusion is to certain state-trials held in Ireland in 1635 to decide the right of the English crown to Mayo, Sligo, Leitrim, Roscommon, etc. These four decided in favor of the king, but Galway voted the other way; in consequence, the sheriff was fined £1,000, and each of the jurors £4,000.

Gamaliel Smith. (Pseud.) Jeremy Bentham, English jurist (1748–1832).

Game-cock Brigade. The brigade commanded by George Edward Pickett (1825–1875), the Southern general, in the civil war.

Gamma. (Pseud.) Dr. John D. Osborne, in the New Orleans "Picayune."

Gamps and Harrises. A sobriquet for poorhouse nurses. The allusion is to the characters of the name in Dickens's "Martin Chuzzlewit."

Gander-Cleugh ("folly hill or cliff"). A species of No-Man's-Land where any one who makes a goose of himself takes up his abode. The pseudonymous Jedediah Cleishbotham of Scott's novels resided there.

Gar. (Pseud.) J. Garczynski, in the New York "Times."

Garçon de bureau. (Fr.) An office-boy.

Garçon d'esprit. (Fr.) A clever fellow.

Garde à vous. (Fr.) The military order of "Attention!"

Garde-chasse. (Fr.) A gamekeeper.

Garde du corps. (Fr.) A body-guard.

Garde mobile. (Fr.) A force liable for general service.

Garden City. Chicago, Ill., owing to the fertile stretch of country in which it is situated.

Gardener. Adam is named "the Grand Old Gardener" by Tennyson.

Garden of Eden. A name often applied to Eden Park, Cincinnati, O.

Garden of England. The Isle of Wight, and the counties of Worcestershire and Kent have all been so named.

Garden of Europe. Italy; an appellation well deserved on account of its healthful climate, picturesque scenery, astonishing fertility, and the great variety of its agricultural products.

Garden of France. The Department of Indre-et-Loire, a district noted for its rich soil and lovely landscapes.

Garden of Italy. The Island of Sicily, which bears the same relation to Italy, in respect of beauty and fertility, that Italy bears to the rest of Europe. *See* GARDEN OF EUROPE.

Garden of Kentucky. Bourbon County, in that State.

Garden of Scotland. Morayshire has been so named.

Garden of Spain. Andalusia. It is fertile to the highest degree.

Garden of the Hesperides. *See* HESPERIDES.

Garden of the West. A name sometimes applied to the whole of that vast arable district west of the Mississippi, on account of its generous yield of grain, but more particularly applied to Kansas. See *infra.*

Garden of the World. An appellation often bestowed on that vast expanse of country watered by the Mississippi and its tributaries, — a region whose soil is of unsurpassed productiveness.

Garden Sass. *See* SASS.

Garden Sect. The disciples of Epicurus. He discoursed to them in his own garden.

Gardez bien. (Fr.) Take good care.

Gardez la foi. (Fr.) Keep the faith.

Garrisonians. A name applied to those Abolitionists who adhered to William Lloyd Garrison.

Gasconnade. (Fr.) Boasting like that of the Gascons; bragging.

Gashed, The. Henry, Duke of Guise (fl. 1550–1588). In the battle of Dormans he received a frightful sword-cut which marked his face for life.

Gate City, The. (1) Keokuk, Iowa, situated at the foot of the lower rapids on the Mississippi. (2) Atlanta, Ga., a great railroad centre, so named by Jefferson Davis during the civil war; it being, in his estimation, the most important inland position, from a military point of view, in the South.

Gate of Asia. Kazan, a fortified city of Russia, has been so named. It is the *entrepôt* of commerce between Siberia, Bokhara, and Russia.

Gate of Italy. The gorge in the valley of the Adige, near the city of Trent.

Gate of Tears. The Straits of Bab-el-Mandeb are often referred to by this appellation; the term is an exact translation of the words *Bab-el-Mandeb*, which have reference to the many shipwrecks that anciently occurred thereabouts.

> Like some ill-destined bark that steers
> In silence through the Gate of Tears.
>   MOORE, *The Fire-Worshippers*

Gate of the Talisman. A famous portal in the city of Bagdad.

Gates of the Reformation. The historical doors of the church at Wittenberg upon which Luther nailed his ninety-five theses in 1517. They were known by this name throughout Germany. *See* CRADLE OF THE REFORMATION.

Gateway of Kansas. Kansas City, Mo., is so named. It is situated on the boundary between Kansas and Missouri, on the Kansas River, and is the point of transfer and departure for all business with Kansas, and the *entrepôt* for much of its trade.

Gath, in Dryden's satire of "Absalom and Achitophel," stands for Brussels, where Charles II. took refuge when in exile.

Gath. (Pseud.) George Alfred Townsend, American journalist.

Gath Brittle. (Pseud.) Robert W. McAlpine.

Gauche. (Fr.) "Left." As opposed to "right;" clumsy; awkward.

Gaucherie. (Fr.) Awkwardness; clumsiness.

Gaudeamus igitur. (Lat.) So let us be joyful.

Gauntlet. "To run the gauntlet." The word "gauntlet" in this phrase is improperly used. The word should be "gauntelope." Phillips, in his "World of Words," tells us that "to run the *gauntelope*" is a punishment among soldiers; the offender having to run, with his back naked, through the whole regiment, and to receive a lash from a switch from every soldier. It is derived from *Gant* (Ghent), a town of Flanders, where the punishment was invented, and the Dutch word *lope*, running.

Mr. Ingram, one of the survivors of the wreck of the "Royal George," who died a few years ago at Woodford in Gloucestershire, used to say that he had seen sailors run the gauntelope on board the king's ships, and that to prevent the runner from going too fast, the ship's corporal walked before him with his drawn cutlass under his arm, with the point backwards, and that he had seen a man get a scratch from the cutlass in trying to escape from the switches.

Gautier et Garguille. The French equivalent for "All the world and his wife."

Gay Lothario. A gay libertine; a seducer of female modesty; a debauchee.

G. B. Great Britain.

G. B. & I. Great Britain and Ireland.

G. C. Grand Chapter; Grand Conductor.

G. C. B. Grand Cross of the Bath.

G. C. H. Grand Cross of Hanover.

G. C. K. P. Grand Commander of the Knights of Saint Patrick.

G. C. L. H. Grand Cross of the Legion of Honor.

G. C. M. G. Grand Cross of Saint Michael and Saint George.

G. C. S. I. Grand Commander of the Star of India.

G. D. Grand Duke; Grand Duchess.

G. E. Grand Encampment.

Gefion. In Scandinavian mythology the goddess of virginity, to whom all maidens repair after death.

Gem Alphabet.

Transparent.	Opaque.
Amethyst	Agate
Beryl	Basalt
Chrysoberyl	Cacholong
Diamond	Diaspore
Emerald	Egyptian pebble
Felspar	Fire-stone
Garnet	Granite
Hyacinth	Heliotrope
Idocrase	Jasper
Kyanite	Krokidolite
Lynx-sapphire	Lapis-lazuli
Milk-opal	Malachite
Natrolite	Nephrite
Opal	Onyx
Pyrope	Porphyry
Quartz	Quartz-agate
Ruby	Rose-quartz
Sapphire	Sardonyx
Topaz	Turquoise
Unanite	Ultramarine
Vesuvianite	Verd-antique
Water-sapphire	Wood-opal
Xanthite	Xylotile
Zircon	Zurlite

Gem City. (1) Dayton, Ohio, is so named. (2) Quincy, Ill. (3) St. Paul, Minn.

Gemini ("the Twins"). The fourth constellation and the third sign in the order of the zodiac, between Cancer on the east and Taurus on the west, and south of the Lynx, the orbit of the earth passing through the centre of the constellation, which contains eighty-five stars; one of these, Castor, is of the first magnitude, and Pollux of the second, both appearing in the head of the Twins, not far apart.

Gem of Normandy. Emma, daughter of Richard I., Duke of Normandy, and married to Ethelred II., King of England. She died 1052.

Gem of the Desert, The. The town of Graaf-Reynet, in Cape Colony, Africa. It is most picturesquely situated in a hilly and wooded country.

Gem of the Mountains. The Territory of Idaho is so termed by her people.

Gen. Genesis; General; genus; genera; genealogy.

General Observer. (Pseud.) Nathan Fiske, S. T. D., in the "Massachusetts Magazine."

General Undertaker. A nickname given by the Parisian populace to Napoleon I. because of the vast improvements he planned for the capital but did not always carry to completion.

Genesee. (Pseud.) Prof. J. H. Gilmore, in the New York "Examiner."

Geneva Bible. A translation of the Scriptures printed in 1560. It was the work of English Protestant refugees domiciled in Geneva, whence its name. It is also known as the Breeches Bible (*q. v.*). A second edition, because of a curious misprint, became known also as the Place-maker's Bible (*q. v.*).

Geneva Bull. A nickname for Stephen Marshall, a Calvinistic preacher, who fairly bellowed in the pulpit.

Genevese Traveller. (Pseud.) Matthew L. Davis (1766–1850), an American author and correspondent in the London "Times." He was the "Spy in Washington" of the New York "Courier" and "Enquirer."

Genevieve Rogers. The stage-name of Mrs. Frank E. Aiken.

Gendarme. (Fr.) An armed policeman.

Gendarmerie. (Fr.) The armed police force.

Genii. In classic myth protecting spirits, similar to the guardian angels of the Christians.

Genius loci. (Lat.) "The genius of the place." The tutelary deity of a place.

Gens-d'armes. Armed policemen; in France, a military police.

Gens de condition. (Fr.) Persons of rank.

Gens de guerre. (Fr.) "Men of war." Military men.

Gens de lettres. (Fr.) "Men of letters." Literary people.

Gens de peu. (Fr.) The lower classes.

Gens du monde. (Fr). "People of the world." Persons employed in active life.

Gent. Gentleman.

Gentil Bernard, Le. Pierre Joseph Bernard, the French poet (1710–1775).

Gentilhomme. (Fr.) A gentleman.

Gentle, The. In the palmy days of the Italian republics Florence was so named. "In the mouth of an Italian this adjective includes all the amenities and agreeableness resulting from a high state of civilization." *See* BEAUTIFUL, THE.

Gentle Art. Angling has been so designated.

Gentle Craft. The trade of shoemaking. According to Brady, this designation arose from the fact that in an old romance a prince named Crispin is made to exercise, in honor of his namesake, Saint Crispin, the trade of making shoes. There is also a tradition that King Edward IV. once made merry with a party of cobblers; and the story is alluded to in an old play, "George-A-Greene," 1599: —

"Marry, because you have drank with the king,
And the king hath so graciously pledged you,
You shall no more be called shoemakers;
But you and yours, to the world's end,
Shall be called the trade of the gentle craft."

Gentle Lochiel. *See* LOCHIEL.

Gentleman George. (1) A nickname bestowed some twenty years ago on Senator Pendleton, the Ohio statesman, because of his courtly manners. (2) George Hooker Barrett, comedian (1794–1860), was so named on account of his elegance and stateliness.

Gentleman of the Four Outs. The nickname for a man with-*out* wit, with-*out* manners, with-*out* money, and with-*out* credit.

Gentle Shepherd. George Grenville, the statesman; a nickname derived from a line applied to him by Pitt, afterward Earl of Chatham. Grenville, in the course of one of his speeches, addressed the House interrogatively, "Tell me where? tell me where?" Pitt hummed a line of a song then very popular, "Gentle shepherd, tell me where?" and the House burst into laughter.

Gent. Mag. Gentlemen's Magazine.

Genus homo. (Lat.) The human race.

Genus irritabile vatum. (Lat.) Irritable tribe of poets.

Geo. George.

Geoffrey Crayon. (Pseud.) Washington Irving, American author (1783–1859).

Geog. Geography.

Geol. Geology.

Geom. Geometry.

George Alexander. The stage-name of George A. Sampson.

George Eliot. (Pseud.) Mrs. Marian (Evans) Lewes Cross, English novelist (1820–1880).

George Fitzdoodle. (Pseud.) William Makepeace Thackeray, English novelist and humorist (1811–1863).

George Fleming. The pen-name of Julia Fletcher, an American writer, and author of "Kismet," "Mirage," and "Vestigia."

George F. Moore. The professional name of George Fox.

George Garrulous. (Pseud.) George Arnold, writer of comic poetry.

George Howard, Esq. (Pseud.) Francis C. Laird, R. N., English historical writer (b. 1794).

George Sand. (Pseud.) Madame Amantine Lucille Aurore Dudevant, French novelist (1804–1876).

George S. Knight. The stage-name of George Sloan.

George Washington. A nickname conferred on Gen. George H. Thomas (1816–1870) by his associates at West Point, from a fancied resemblance in appearance and character to the great patriot."

George Wilson. The stage-name of Walter McNally.

Georges' Conspiracy. A plot in France to assassinate Bonaparte and restore Louis XVIII., discovered February, 1804. The prime movers were General Moreau, General Pichegru, and Georges Cadoudal (who was commonly known by the name of Georges). Pichegru was discovered strangled in prison, April 6, 1804; twelve others were executed on June 25; others were imprisoned, and Moreau was exiled and went to America.

Georges Letorière. (Pseud.) Vicomtesse de Peyronney, French novelist (b. 1841).

Georgia. The name of this State was given in honor of George II. of England.

Georgie Drew. The stage-name of Mrs. Maurice Barrymore.

Georgie Woodthorpe. The stage-name of Mrs. Fred Cooper.

Georgius Dounamus. (Pseud.) George Downame, D.D., English theologian (d. 1634).

Ger. German; Germany.

Gerald Eyre. The stage-name of Gerald Ryan.

Gerald Maxwell. The stage-name of Gerald Braddon, son of "Miss" Braddon, the novelist.

Gerald Montgomery. (Pseud.) Rev. John Moultrie, English poet (b. 1804).

Geraldine Stewart. The stage-name of Mrs. Shiel Barry.

German Barber. (Pseud.) Julian E. Ralph, in the New York "Sun," and other papers.

German Comb. A colloquialism meaning the four fingers and the thumb. The periwig never found much favor in Germany; and while the French constantly had a comb in hand to adjust their wigs, the Germans wore their own hair, and were content to smooth it by running their fingers through it.

German Florence, The. The city of Dresden, so named for its wealth in works of art and scientific treasures.

German Jerusalem. The town of Brody, in Galicia, Austria, is so named because its trade is well-nigh entirely in the hands of Jews.

German Milton. Friedrich Gottlieb Klopstock (1724–1803). He was the author of an epic poem entitled "The Messiah."

German Peabody. Baron John Henry Schröder (1784–1883) was so named on account of his great benevolence. He was a well-known banker and financier.

German Princess. *See* KENTISH MOLL.

Germinal Insurrection. A popular uprising in the Parisian faubourgs in 1795, suppressed, according to the Revolutionary calendar, on 12th Germinal, year III. (April 1, 1795).

Gerrymander. An attempt to divide a State into districts so that one of the parties shall obtain thereby more than its just share of the representatives. Elbridge Gerry, of Massachusetts, was once accused of attempting this, whence the origin of the term.

"In 1814 the Senate districts of Massachusetts were laid out with the aim of electing to that body a majority of Democrats. The result was great irregularity in the shape of many of the districts. One in particular was so distorted that the Boston "Centinel" published a colored map of it, to which a few artistic touches were added for the purpose of giving it resemblance to some monstrous animal. This mythical animal they named 'gerrymander.'"

Gertie Maddigan. The stage-name of Mrs. Benjamin Lodge.

Gertrude. (Pseud.) Mrs. Jane (Cross) Simpson, English poetess (b. 1804).

Gertrude Glenn. (Pseud.) Mrs. Mary Harris Ware, in "Godey's Lady's Book," etc.

Gertrude Toussaint. The stage-name of Mrs. W. H. Clark.

Geryon. In classic myth a being with three bodies and three heads. He fed his magnificent oxen with human flesh, for which he was killed by Hercules.

Getting into a Hole. This proverbial saying is said to arise from an accident which sometimes occurs in playing at golf, where, if a ball "gets into a hole," it is almost certain that the owner must lose the game.

Getting into a Scrape. "The deer are addicted, at certain seasons, to dig up the land with their forefeet, in holes, to the depth of a foot, or even of half a yard. These are called 'scrapes.' To tumble into one of these is sometimes done at the cost of a broken leg; hence a man who finds himself in an unpleasant position, from which extrication is difficult, is said to have 'got into a scrape.'" The Rev. H. T. Ellacombe, M.A., in "Notes and Queries," Feb. 14, 1880, says that in 1803 a woman was killed by a stag in Powderham Park, Devon. "It was said that, when walking across the park, she attempted to cross the stag's 'scrape,'" which he says is "a ring which stags make in rutting season, and woe be to any who get within it." He confirms his story by a copy of the parish register, which records that "Frances Tucker (killed by a stag) was buried December 14th, 1803."

Ghibellines. See GUELPHS and GHIBELLINES.

Ghost Walks. A colloquial phrase in vogue among theatrical people and others, and signifying that pay-day has come, or that the treasurer is around.

" In one of the itinerant companies of England, the manager, himself an actor, was very fond of playing ' The Ghost' in ' Hamlet,' which was one of the stock pieces of these unpaid nomads. Salary day came and went; but as the manager had no bank account, and the box-office receipts were too meagre to warrant the alleged treasurer in posting over the box-office door those letters so cheering to the actor's heart, 'S. P. Q. R.,' the stomachs and wardrobes of the players began to suffer. At last patience ceased to be a virtue. The company grew clam-

orous for their arrears. A strike was organized, and at one of the 'Hamlet' rehearsals, when Hamlet, speaking of 'The Ghost,' exclaimed, 'Perchance 't will walk again,' the leader of the revolt, who happened then to be 'The Ghost,' ignored Shakspeare, and shouted emphatically, 'No! I'm d——d if "The Ghost" walks any more until our salaries are paid.' All actors will easily concede that an incident like this would quickly become common sport, and soon furnish the material for a new bit of stage slang."

Giant, The. The river Nile is so named by the Egyptians.

Giant, The Northern. See NORTHERN GIANT.

Giant of Literature. Samuel Johnson (1709–1783). See CHAM and GREAT MORALIST.

Giants. In classic myth the sons of Tartarus and Terra, of enormous stature, with dragons' tails and hideous faces. They attempted to storm heaven, but were killed by the gods, assisted by Hercules, and buried under the volcanoes of Mount Etna.

Giants' Causeway between the East and West. The Aleutian Archipelago has been so named, from the belief that many races have migrated by this route from one continent to the other.

Giant's Grave. A height on the Adriatic shore of the Bosphorus, much frequented by holiday parties.

'T is a grand sight from off the "Giant's Grave"
To watch the progress of those rolling seas
Between the Bosphorus, as they lash and lave
Europe and Asia.
                                        BYRON, Don Juan.

Giaour (pronounced jour). The Turkish word for "infidel," a term applied in the Orient to all who do not believe in Mohammedanism.

Gibraltar of America. Quebec, Canada. Both on account of its commanding situation and its well-nigh impregnable defences, both natural and artificial, it is the most securely fortified city in America.

Gibraltar of the East. Aden, a town and seaport of Arabia. Since 1839 it has belonged to the British, and its fortifications have been greatly strengthened and improved. The citadel is built on a rocky eminence, and is of great strategic importance, having a position between Asia and Africa like that of Gibraltar between Europe and Africa.

Gibraltar of the New World. Cape Diamond, in the province of Quebec.

Gibson's Lambs. In the Revolutionary War the soldiers commanded by George Gibson (1747–1791) were so named for their good conduct and bravery.

Giddy Gusher. The pen-name of Mrs. Mary Hewins Fiske, a correspondent of the "Mirror." *See* CLARA BELLE.

Gilbert. (Pseud.) William Stevens Robinson, in the New York "Tribune," *circa* 1857–1860.

Gilbert Forrester. (Pseud.) Henry Braddon, in the old "Sporting Magazine."

Gimel. (Pseud.) Rev. Elisha Andrews, in the "Christian Watchman," Boston, Mass.

Gimli. In Scandinavian mythology the choicest of the Elysian abodes.

Ginnunga-gap. In Scandinavian myth the abyss which existed before the present world was formed.

Gipsy, The. Antonio da Solario, the Spanish artist (1382–1455).

Girdle of China. The great Yang-tse-Kiang River is so named by the Celestials. It forms a majestic waterway, connecting all the central provinces of the empire.

Girondists. An important party during the French Revolution, principally composed of deputies from the Gironde. They were ardent republicans, but after the excesses of August and September, 1792, labored in vain to restrain the cruelties of Robespierre and the Mountain party; their leaders, Brissot, Verguland, and many others, were guillotined Oct. 31, 1793. Lamartine's "Histoire des Girondins," published in 1847, tended to hasten the revolution in 1848.

Git thar, Eli. A common Western Americanism. The story goes that at a country fair in Ohio there was a greased pole for climbing, on which was perched a prize. Among the competitors was a lad named Eli, who secured the prize, being cheered on by his companions yelling, "Git thar, Eli."

Giulia Grisi. The professional name of Madame Augusta De Meley.

Giulia Valda, Mme. The professional name of Mrs. Julia Cameron, a well-known operatic singer.

Giusto. (Ital.) In just and exact time. (Mus.)

Give me Liberty or give me Death! Patrick Henry was the author of this famous exclamation, in a speech before the Virginia Legislature while pleading for the organization of the militia.

Given Name. This is merely a colloquial substitute for "Christian name," which, according to the Catechism, is "given" in baptism.

Gjallar. In Scandinavian myth the horn of Heimdall, which he sounds to warn the gods of the arrival of any one at the bridge Bifrost (*q. v.*).

G. L. Grand Lodge.

Gl. *Glossa.* A gloss.

Gladstone of America. (1) James G. Blaine was so named by Levi P. Morton in a speech in Madison Square, New York, on the night of August 10, 1888. (2) Allen Granbery Thurman was also so named by his admirers.

Gladstone's Umbrella. A phrase which became current in the political nomenclature of England in 1885, personifying the almost magical influence wielded by the ex-Premier, by which the conflicting elements composing the Liberal Party were harmonized in view of the impending election —

Is Mr. Gladstone's umbrella worn out beyond repair? Will it no longer protect the various wings of the Liberal party from the downpour of disintegration which must inevitably fall on a collection of such incongruous elements as whigs, radicals, and semi-socialists? — *Daily Paper.*

Gladys Wayne. (Pseud.) Julia Van Valkenburg, in the "Household," Brattleboro, Vt.

Glasgow Keelie. A nickname for a native of Glasgow.

Glaucus. In classic myth a son of Sisyphus, rent in pieces by his own steeds. Also, a son of Minos, king of Crete; he was drowned in a keg of honey, but was miraculously restored to life.

Gleaner. (Pseud.) Nathaniel Ingersoll Bowditch, in the "Transcript," Boston, *circa* 1855.

Glencoe Massacre. A wholesale slaughter of the Macdonald clan in Scotland, merely for not surrendering before the time stated in the proclamation of King William, Dec. 31, 1691: —

Sir John Dalrymple, the Master, afterward Earl, of Stair, their inveterate enemy, obtained a decree "to extirpate that pack of thieves," which the king is said to have signed without perusing. Every man under seventy was to be slain, and the mandate was executed with the blackest treachery. The one hundred and twenty soldiers, forming a part of the Earl of Argyle's regiment, were hospitably received by the High-landers. On Feb. 13, 1692, the massacre began. About sixty men were brutally slain, and many women and children, their wives and offspring, were turned out naked on a dark and freezing night, and perished by cold and hunger. This black deed excited great indignation in England, and an inquiry was set on foot in 1695, but no punishment followed. — CHAMBERS.

Glissando. (Ital.) In a gliding manner. (Mus.)

Gloria in excelsis. (Lat.) Glory to God in the highest.

Gloria Patri. (Lat.) Glory to the Father.

Glorious First of June. June 1, 1794, Lord Howe, with twenty-five ships, signally defeated the French fleet with twenty-six ships, off Brest harbor. The French loss was very great, and the day was long termed in England "the Glorious First of June."

Glorious John. John Dryden, the poet laureate (fl. 1631–1701).

Glorious Preacher. Saint Chrysostom. *See* GOLDEN MOUTH.

Glorious Uncertainty of the Law. In 1756, soon after Lord Mansfield had overruled several ancient legal decisions, and introduced many innovations in the practice, Mr. Wilbraham, at a dinner of judges and counsel in Serjeants' Hall, gave as a toast, " The glorious uncertainty of law." This was the origin of the phrase.

Glory Hole. A cupboard, ottoman, box, or other receptacle where anything may be thrown for the nonce to get it out of sight rapidly. A cupboard at the head of a staircase, for brooms, etc., is so called.

Glory of the East. The ancient Persepolis. No other city could be compared to it for wealth or magnificence.

Glückists and Piccinists. Names of rival parties in Paris, 1774–1780, during the musical controversy between the admirers of Glück and those of Piccini. It is said that all Paris was arrayed on one side or the other, though but few could have understood the principles at stake.

Glyn, Miss. The stage-name of Isabelle Gearns Dallas, a famous English actress (1823–1889).

G. M. Grand Master.

G. M. K. P. Grand Master of the Knights of Saint Patrick.

G. M. S. I. Grand Master of the Star of India.

G. O. General Order.

Gobe-mouches. (Fr.) "Fly-catchers." Persons having no opinions of their own.

Godam. The French nickname for an Englishman, from a familiar oath once common and still too frequently used.

God always favors the Heaviest Battalions. Napoleon said, " Providence is always on the side of the last reserve."

Le nombre des sages sera toujours petit. Il est vrai qu'il est augmente; mais ce n'est rien en comparison des sots, et par malheur on dit que Dieu est toujours pour les gros bataillons. — VOLTAIRE *to M. le Riche.*

La fortune est toujours pour les gros bataillons. — SÉVIGNÉ, *Lettre à sa Fille.*

God bless You. In the time of Pope Pelagius II. a plague raged at Rome, the victims of which died sneezing and gaping. Hence arose the custom of saying " God bless you !" when a person sneezes, and the habit among devout Roman Catholics of making the sign of the cross upon the mouth when a person gapes.

Goddess of Reason. Reason, considered as an impersonation of all those mental powers which distinguish mankind from the brute creation, was decreed to be worshipped as a goddess by the French Republicans, Nov. 10, 1793, when a festival was held in honor of the new faith. The Church of Notre Dâme was converted into a Temple of Reason, and every tenth day was appointed to supersede the Christian Sabbath.

God's Acre. A burying-ground attached to a church or place of worship.

God save the Mark. These words are connected with an old Irish superstition. If a person, on telling the story of some hurt or injury which another has received, should illustrate his narrative by touching the corresponding part of his own or his hearer's body, he averts the omen of similar injury by using as a sort of charm the words, " God save the mark."

God's Image done in Ebony. The negroes were so named by Thomas Fuller.

God's Truce. One of the most singular among the institutions of the Middle Ages, which was in vogue in France, the German Empire, and other nations of Europe. It consisted of the suspension, for a stated time and at stated seasons and festivals, of that right of private feud for the redress of wrongs which was recognized by the mediæval code.

God tempers the Wind to the Shorn Lamb. Sterne first used this phrase in English, by putting it into the mouth of Maria in the "Sentimental Journey." It is an adaptation of the French proverb, "A brebis tondue Dieu mesure le vent."

Godwin's Oath. Godwin, Earl of Kent, was charged with killing Alfred, brother of Edward Confessor, but died at the king's table while protesting with an oath his innocence of the crime. He was choked with a piece of bread while beseeching Heaven that it might stick in his throat if he were guilty of the murder. Hence the caution to a person taking a voluntary and intemperate oath: "Beware lest you are swearing Godwin's oath."

Gog and Magog. The names given to the pair of famous images of giants in Guildhall, London, and also frequently met in Scripture. "Magog is spoken of by the writer of Genesis as a son of Japheth; Ezekiel speaks of Gog, prince of Magog; Gog and Magog are spoken of in the Revelation. The figures in London, above referred to, are the legendary survivors of a race of giants who formerly inhabited the country; but there are various other tales told about them. They are of wood, hollow, and about fourteen feet high.

Going out to see a Man. The origin of this phrase was as follows: Lincoln Hall, Washington, D. C., was the scene of many lectures and "shows" of various kinds. Adjoining it was a restaurant, the name of the proprietor being Aman. One night in the winter of 1865 Artemus Ward lectured in the hall; and when the great humorist was about half through his discourse he surprised his audience with the announcement that they would have to take a recess of fifteen minutes so as to enable him to go across the street to see a man. H. R. Tracy, then editor of the "Washington Republican," was in the audience, and seeing an opportunity to improve upon the joke, pencilled the following lines and sent them to the platform: "Dear Artemus, — If you will place yourself under my guidance I'll take you to see a man without crossing the street." Artemus accepted the invitation; and while the audience impatiently but with much

amusement awaited the reappearance of the humorist, the latter was making the acquaintance of Aman and luxuriating at a well-laden refreshment board. Of course everybody "caught on to" the phrase, and men became fond of getting up between acts and "going out to see a man."

Go it Blind. An Americanism, meaning "to act without due information or deliberation." It is derived from the game of Poker, where a player may, if he chooses, "go it blind" by doubling the "ante" before looking at his cards, and if the other players refuse to see his "blind," he wins the "ante."

Gold Coast. *See* GUINEA COAST.

Golden Age. "In the mythologies of most peoples and religions there exists a tradition of a better time, when the earth was the common property of man, and produced spontaneously all things necessary for an enjoyable existence. The land flowed with milk and honey, beasts of prey lived peaceably with other animals, and man had not yet, by selfishness, pride, and other vices and passions, fallen from a state of innocence. The Greeks and Romans placed this golden age under the rule of Saturn; and many of their poets have turned this poetic *matériel* to admirable account, and defined the gradual decadence of the world as the Silver, the Brass, and the Iron Ages, holding out at the same time the consolatory hope that the pristine state of things will one day return." — CHAMBERS. The Golden Ages of other ancient nations were as follows: (1) New Assyrian Empire, B. C. 691–606. (2) Chaldeo-Babylonian Empire, B. C. 606–538. (3) China, the T'ang dynasty, 626–684; the reign of Taetsong, 618–626. (4) Egypt, B. C. 1336–1224. (5) Media, B. C. 634–594. (6) Persia, B. C. 628–531. *See* SILVER, BRASS, and IRON AGES, respectively.

Golden Age of Israel. The eighty years from the accession of David to the death of Solomon.

Golden Bay. The Bay of Rieselarke; so named because its sands glitter like gold.

Golden Bull. (1) An edict of the Emperor Charles IV., so called from its golden seal, was made the fundamental law of the German Empire at the Diet of Nuremberg, 1356. (2) A constitutional edict promulgated by

Andrew II. of Hungary in the thirteenth century. It remained in force till the dissolution of the German Empire in 1806.

Golden Chersonese. The Malay Peninsula is so alluded to by Ptolemy and Milton.

Golden Fleece. In Greek myth the fleece of the ram Chrysomallus, the recovery of which was the cause of the Argonautic Expedition. In more modern days the Golden Fleece "has given its name to a celebrated order of knighthood in Austria and Spain founded by Philip III., Duke of Burgundy and the Netherlands, at Bruges, on Jan. 10, 1429, on the occasion of his marriage with Isabella, daughter of King John I. of Portugal. This order was instituted for the protection of the Church; and the fleece was probably assumed for its emblem as much from being the material of the staple manufacture of the Low Countries as from its connection with heroic times."

Golden Horde. Tartars who invaded Russia in 1245, and did much damage, ravaging the country from Moscow to Hungary, under Batou, a grandson of Genghis Khan.

Golden Horn. The inlet of the Bosphorus on which the city of Constantinople is situated; so named from its crescent shape and the surpassing loveliness of its scenery.

Golden House of Nero. A palace erected by Nero in Rome. It was roofed with gilded tiles, and the inside walls and ceilings were inlaid with gold, ivory, and precious stones. The Farnese princes subsequently used the materials of this costly structure to embellish their own palaces.

Golden Legend. A celebrated collection of hagiology, which for a time enjoyed almost unexampled popularity, having passed through more than a hundred editions and being translated into almost all the European tongues. It is the work of James de Voragine (also written Vragine and Varagine), who was born about 1230.

Golden-mouthed. Saint Chrysostom was so named because of his surpassing eloquence.

Golden Palace. *See* GOLDEN HOUSE OF NERO.

Golden State. California; so named on account of its rich auriferous deposits.

Golden Stream. A title given to Johannes Damascenus (d. 756), who wrote a work entitled "Dogmatic Theology."

Golden-tongued. A title conferred on Saint Peter, bishop of Ravenna (fl. fifth century).

Golden Vale. The eastern part of the vale of Limerick, Ireland. The soil is remarkably fertile.

Goldlace. (Pseud.) Lieut. E. P. Banning, U. S. N., in various periodicals.

Gold Purse of Spain. The ancient province of Andalusia; so called because it is from thence that Spain derives much of its auriferous wealth.

Goldsmith of America. Benjamin Franklin Taylor (1819–1887), the American author, was so named by the London "Times."

Goldy. The diminutive nickname given by Dr. Johnson to Oliver Goldsmith. His intimates also dubbed him "Noll."

Gold Years. There is a superstition among miners on the Pacific Coast that years of the century ending with the figure 9 are sure to witness the discovery of rich deposits of the precious metals. In proof, they adduce California, 1849; Pike's Peak, 1859; Nevada, 1869; and Leadville, 1879.

Golgotha, The City. *See* CITY GOLGOTHA.

G. O. M. *See* GRAND OLD MAN.

Gondolas of the London Streets. Hansom cabs were so nicknamed by Lord Beaconsfield. The phrase also occurs in Balzac's writings applied to the Parisian *fiacres*, from whom Beaconsfield probably borrowed it.

Gone Broke. *See* BROKE.

Gone to the Devil. There was formerly a tavern next door to Child's Banking House in Fleet Street, near Temple Bar, known by the sign of the "Devil and Saint Dunstan." It was much frequented by lawyers as a place for dining, etc., and was noted for the excellence of its liquors. It was familiarly called the "Devil." When a lawyer from the Temple went to dinner there, he usually put a notice on his door, "Gone to the Devil." Some who neglected their business frequently had this notice exhibited, until at length "Gone to the Devil" became synonymous with "gone, or going, to ruin."

Gone Up, Gone Under. These apparently contrary expressions stand for one and the same thing in Western parlance; *i. e.*, to fail, to "go to smash," or even to die. The first may be supposed to be drawn from the sudden elevation attending an explosion; the second probably arose from the fate of some luckless pioneer who was drawn under the rapids of a river. "Of the facility with which the slang of England rises to the rank of unobjectionable words in the mouths of Americans, the term 'going up' is an instance. It arose from the spout or tube through which the pawnbroker sends the goods he has advanced upon to an upper story. Hence at first the phrase ran 'to go up the spout,' and meant simply disappearance or destruction. Then the 'spout' was deemed superfluous; and when the city of Richmond fell at the close of the civil war, the newspapers reported gravely that it had *gone up.*"

Good, The. (1) Alfonso VIII. of Leon (fl. 1158–1214). (2) Sir James Douglas, a friend of Robert Bruce (d. 1330). (3) Jean II. of France (fl. 1319–1364). (4) Jean III., Duc de Bourgogne (fl. 1286–1341). (5) Jean of Brittany (fl. 1389–1442). (6) Philippe III., Duc de Bourgogne (fl. 1396–1467). (7) Réné, titular King of Naples (fl. 1409–1452). (8) Richard II., Duc de Normandie (fl. 996–1026). (9) Richard de Beauchamp (d. 1439). (10) Prince Albert of England (d. 1861).

Good as a Play. "An exclamation of Charles II. when in Parliament attending the discussion of Lord Ross's Divorce Bill. The king remained in the House of Peers while his speech was taken into consideration, — a common practice with him; for the debates amused his sated mind, and were sometimes, he used to say, as good as a comedy." — MACAULAY.

Good Earl. Archibald, eighth Earl of Angus (d. 1588).

Good enough Morgan till after Election. "Thurlow Weed was one of the foremost of the anti-Masonic agitators in New York State. The disappearance of Morgan, and the discovery of what was supposed to be his dead body, created intense excitement. Weed took full advantage of this feeling; and when doubt was cast on the identity of the body thus found, he is said to have remarked in private that it was a 'good enough Morgan till after election.'" — *American Political Dictionary*.

Good Friday. This is probably a corruption of "God's Friday," the Friday before Easter Day, on which a solemn fast has long been observed by Christendom in remembrance of the crucifixion of Christ on Friday, April 3, 33 (or Friday, April 15, 29). Its appellation of "Good" appears to be peculiar to the English Church and its branches; the Saxons denominated it "Long Friday," because of the length of the offices and fasting enjoined on that day. It may be news to some that the religious observance of Good Friday, now so general, is not the continuation of an ancient custom so much as a revival of modern times. In the earlier part of the reign of George III. many church-going folk took no notice of the day; and in his "Restituta" Sir Egerton Brydges speaks of the "clamor, uproar, and rage" with which an order of Archbishop Cornwallis "to observe decently Good Friday" was received by persons of a different way of thinking from his Grace. But the animosity of what Sir Egerton Brydges calls "the Presbyterian newspapers" seems to have been chiefly directed against Porteus, afterward Bishop of London, who was supposed to have been the Primate's adviser in this matter. Good Friday is a legal holiday in Florida, Louisiana, Minnesota, and Pennsylvania.

Good Gray Poet. Walt Whitman, the American poet.

Good Hater. This phrase was first used by Dr. Johnson, who said of Bathurst, a physician: "He was a man to my very heart's content. He hated a fool, and he hated a rogue, and he hated a Whig; he was a *very good hater.*"

Good Lord Cobham. A nickname of Sir John Oldcastle, who was the first among the English nobility to suffer martyrdom, Dec. 14, 1417.

Goodman of Ballengeich. A name assumed by James VI. of Scotland during his peregrinations through the countryside around Edinburgh and Stirling, in which he imitated Louis XI. and Haroun-al-Raschid.

Goodman Palsgrave, Goody Palsgrave. Satirical nicknames bestowed on Frederick V., Elector Palatine, and his wife Elizabeth, daughter of James I. of England.

Good Old Men. *See* CALOYERS.

Good Parliament. Held in the time of Edward III., and so named from the rigor which it meted out to the hated Lancastrians.

Good Queen Bess. Elizabeth of England (fl. 1533–1603).

Good Regent. James Stewart, Earl of Murray, who was made Regent of Scotland after the arrest of Queen Mary.

Good Samaritan of London. Silas Todd, one of John Wesley's assistants.

Good Wine needs no Bush. The bush formerly hung out at the doors of taverns was always of ivy, probably in allusion to Bacchus, to whom the ivy-bush was sacred. The old poets and dramatists have many allusions to the custom of hanging out a bush. In Lily's "Euphues," A. 3, we have, "Things of greatest profit are set forth with least price. Where the wine is neat, there needeth no ivie-bush." Allot also, in his " English Parnassus," in a sonnet to the reader, says : —

" I hang no ivie out to sell my wine;
The nectar of good wits will sell itselfe."

The proverb means that where the wine sold was good no bush or other sign was necessary; customers would find their way to the place without. In the reign of Edward III. all the "taverners " in the city of London were summoned to the Guildhall, and warned that no sign or bush would henceforward be allowed to "extend over the king's highway beyond the length of seven feet." A new explanation of the proverb " Good wine needs no bush " is proposed by R. R. Sharpe, who presides over the manuscripts in the Guildhall of London. " Bush " appears to have been a term for a spray of rosemary or other herb which was laid in the bottom of a drinking-cup, by publicans, " either to give a particular flavor to the beverage, or, as was probably more often the case, in order to disguise the inferior quality of the wine." He cites a confession by Alice de Caustone to Mayor Adam de Bury, in the reign of Edward III., in which she acknowledges that she was in the habit of filling the bottom of her quart measure with one and a half inches of picche, and laying thereon rosemaryn, *in similitudinem arboris*, "so as to look like a bush in the sight of the common people."

Goose Dubbs. A locality in Glasgow, the counterpart of the London Alsatia (*q. v.*). *Dubbs* is colloquial Scottish for a filthy puddle.

Goosey Goderich. A nickname fastened by Cobbett on Viscount Goderich, afterward Earl of Ripon, because of his incapacity as a statesman. He was Premier in 1827–1828.

Gopher. This curious Americanism, from the French *gaufre*, honeycomb, was originally given by French *voyageurs* to many burrowing animals from their habit of honeycombing the earth. At the present day the name is appended in Canada and Illinois to a gray burrowing squirrel, in Wisconsin to a striped squirrel, in Missouri to a brown pouched rat, in Georgia to a snake, and in Florida to a turtle. Minnesota is called the Gopher State from the fact that the striped squirrel formerly there abounded.

Gopher State. See *supra*.

Gordian Knot. The subject of one of the most interesting fables of antiquity. The story runs that "Gordius, a Phrygian peasant, was once ploughing in his fields, when an eagle settled on his yoke of oxen, and remained till the labor of the day was over. Surprised at so wonderful a phenomenon, he sought an explanation of it, and was informed by a prophetess of Telmissus that he should offer sacrifice to Zeus. He did so, and out of gratitude for the kindness shown him, married the prophetess, by whom he had a son, the famous Midas. When Midas grew up, disturbances broke out in Phrygia, and the people sent messengers to the oracle at Delphi, to ask about choosing a new king. The messengers were informed that a king would come to them riding on a car, and that he would restore peace. Returning to Phrygia, they announced these things, and while the people were talking about them, Gordius, with his son, very opportunely arrived in the requisite manner. He was immediately elected king, whereupon he dedicated his car and yoke to Zeus, in the Acropolis of Gordium (a city named after himself), the knot of the yoke being tied in so skilful a manner that an oracle declared whoever should unloose it would be ruler of all Asia. When Alexander the Great came to Gordium he cut the knot in two with his sword, and applied the prophecy to himself."

Gordon Riots. *See* No-Popery Riots.

Gorgons. In classic myth Stheno, Euryale, and Medusa, daughters of Phorcus and Ceto. They had wings, brazen claws, and long teeth; their bodies were covered with scales, and their hair was entwined with hissing serpents. Medusa was killed by Perseus, and from her blood sprung the winged horse Pegasus.

Gorham Controversy. A dispute arising out of the refusal of the Bishop of Exeter to induct the Rev. Cornelius Gorham in the vicarage of Brampford Speke, "because he held unsound views on the doctrine of baptism," maintaining that spiritual regeneration is not conferred on children at baptism. In 1851 the Privy Council decided in favor of Mr. Gorham.

Gospellers. Adherents of Wycliffe, who was named "the Gospel Doctor."

Gossamer Days. A maiden was accustomed to spin late on Saturday in the moonlight. At one time the new moon on the eve of Sunday drew her up to itself, and now she sits in the moon and spins and spins. And now, when the "gossamer days" set in late in the summer, the white threads float around in the air. These threads are the spinning of the lunar spinner.

Gossypia. A personification of the cotton-plant.

Goth. Gothic.

Gotham. (Pseud.) Richard Wheatley, D.D., in "Zion's Herald," 1888.

Gotham. (1) A parish of Nottinghamshire, England. The people here were famed for their crass stupidity and simplicity, which obtained for them the satirical appellation of the "wise men of Gotham." Many nations have designated some particular locality as the paradise of fools; for example, Phrygia was the fools' home in Asia, Abdera of the Thracians, Bœotia of the Greeks, Swabia of the modern Germans, etc. (2) A colloquial term for the city of New York. Thus applied, it first appeared in "Salmagundi," by Washington Irving and James K. Paulding, and is supposed to hint sarcastically at the worldly wisdom of its inhabitants.

Go to Bath and get your Head shaved. Formerly persons who showed symptoms of insanity were sent to drink the mineral waters at Bath. Shaving the head was always performed where insanity was suspected. The obvious meaning of the proverbial saying is, therefore, satirically, "You are going mad; you had better 'go to Bath and get your head shaved.'"

Go to Grass. This is a common expression in America. It is equivalent to the English "Be off!" or "Get out!"

Got the Mitten. This is an American phrase, used when a young man is discarded by a lady to whom he has been paying his addresses. Sam Slick ("Human Nature," p. 90) says, "There is a young lady I have set my heart on; though whether she is a-goin' to give me hern, or give me the mitten, I ain't quite satisfied." This seems to be the only remaining use of the old English word "mittent" (Latin *mittens*, sending), which Johnson defines "sending forth, emitting." "Mittent" itself is obsolete, but it survives in the compound "intermittent."

Gottlieb Ackermann. (Pseud.) Franz Xaver Mayer.

Gourmet. (Fr.) "A wine-taster." A judge of wine.

Gourre. A nickname bestowed by the Parisians on Isabella of Bavaria. The term indicates a debauched woman.

Gov. Governor.

Gov.-Gen. Governor-General.

Govt. Government.

Gowrie Conspiracy. A plot formed by the Earl of Gowrie in 1600 to dethrone James VI. of Scotland, and usurp the government. For this end the king was decoyed into Gowrie's house in Perth, August 5, 1600. The plot was foiled, and the earl and his brother Alexander were slain on the spot.

G. P. *Gloria Patri.* "Glory be to the Father."

G. P. O. General Post-Office.

G. R. King George (*Georgius Rex*); Grand Recorder.

Gr. Greek; gross.

Gr., Grs. Grain; grains.

Grace Card. The six of hearts. The story goes that in 1688 one of the family of Grace, of Courtstown, Ireland, equipped at his own charge a body of soldiery to assist King James. William III. offered him weighty rewards if he would join the new party, but the indignant Jacobite hastily wrote on the back of a card: "Tell your master I despise his offer." The card was the six of hearts.

Grace Darling of America. Ida Lewis, the keeper of a lighthouse near Newport, R. I. Like her English namesake, she has been directly instrumental in saving a number of lives from shipwreck.

Grace Greenwood. (Pseud.) Mrs. Sara J. Lippincott, American *littérateur* (b. 1825).

Grace Hawthorne. The stage-name of Mrs. John Murray, *née* Cartland.

Graceless Florin. The earliest issue of the English two-shilling piece; so named because the letters " F. D." (" Fidei Defensor," " defender of the faith ") were omitted. There was no room for the letters, it was said; so the omission was not through inadvertence or carelessness.

Graces. In classic myth Aglaia, Euphrosyne, and Thalia, daughters of Jupiter and Euronyme. They were the sources of all grace, beauty, and favor. They attended on Venus.

Grace Thorne. The stage-name of Mrs. Frazer Coulter.

Grace Wharton. (Pseud.) Mrs. A. T. Thompson (Katherine Byerley), (1810-1862).

Grad. Graduated.

Gradual Psalms, Psalms of the Steps, or Songs of Degrees. A name given, both by Hebrews and in the Christian service-books, to the fifteen psalms, cxx.–cxxxiv. (cxix.–cxxxiii. in the Vulgate). The origin of the name is uncertain.

Gradus ad Parnassum. (Lat.) " A step to Parnassus." A well-known book containing aids to writing Greek and Latin verses. Parnassus, a mountain in central Greece, sacred to Apollo and the Muses; on a steep declivity on its southern slope were situated the town of Delphi and the famous temple containing the oracle of Apollo.

Grahame's Dike. The Roman wall between the Clyde and the Forth was so named by the peasantry from the fact that a chief named Grahame was the first to scale it after the Romans left Britain.

Grain Coast. A former name for Liberia, Africa. *See* GUINEA COAST.

Gram. Grammar.

Granary of Europe. The island of Sicily was so named by the ancients on account of its productiveness.

Grand, Le. Corneille, the French dramatist (fl. 1606-1684).

Grand Alliance. A treaty between England, the Emperor, and the States-General, principally to prevent the union of the French and Spanish monarchies in one person, which was signed in Vienna, May 12, 1689, and to which Spain and Savoy afterward acceded.

Grand bien vous fasse. (Fr.) Much good may it do you.

Grand cordon. (Fr.) The broad ribbon of the Legion of Honor.

Grand Corneille. The French dramatist (1606-1684).

Grand Corrupter. Sir Robert Walpole (fl. 1676-1745) was so named in the lampoons of his time and by his enemies.

Grand Dauphin. Louis, Duc de Bourgogne, eldest son of Louis XIV., was so named. *See* DELPHIN CLASSICS. His son was named the " Little Dauphin."

Grande Mademoiselle. The Duchesse de Montpensier, daughter of Gaston, Duc d'Orléans, and cousin of Louis XIV.

Grande parure. (Fr.) Full dress.

Grand gourmand. (Fr.) A great glutton.

Grand homme. (Fr.) A great man.

Grandison Cromwell. The witty nickname given by Mirabeau to Lafayette, meaning that he had the ambition of a Cromwell while wishing to appear as the careless Sir Charles Grandison, the worldling.

Grand Monarque. Louis XIV. (fl. 1638-1715). *See* BABOON.

Grandmother's Review, My. The " British Review;" so named jocosely by Byron.

I bribed my grandmamma's Review, the British.
                                Don Juan.

The editor, a Mr. Roberts, interpreted the foregoing line seriously, declared the charge to be a falsehood, and challenged its author to name when and where the bribe was given. Byron replied in a humorous letter which completely turned the laugh against the editor.

Grand Old Man. William Ewart Gladstone, the English statesman, was so named by his admirers. It was frequently abbreviated G. O. M. As an offset to this he was dubbed by those who differed from him " Grand Old Muddler," similarly abbreviated, and " Heartless Old Man," shortened to H. O. M.

Grand Old Muddler. A nickname bestowed on Mr. Gladstone during the Parliamentary session of 1884. *See* GRAND OLD MAN.

Grand Pan. *See* GREAT PAN.

Grand Panjandrum. A fictitious personage mentioned in a dozen lines of nonsense, written by the dramatist Foote on a wager to test the memory of a person who boasted of his wonderful powers in this direction. Foote won. The couplet is now used to denote in derision any high and mighty ruler or official.

Grand Remonstrance. *See* REMONSTRANCE.

Grand siècle. (Fr.) "Great century." A distinguished age.

Grangers, Granger Movement. A "grange" was originally a barn or storehouse, afterward a farmhouse of the better sort, and since 1867 used to designate the various organizations of the Patrons of Husbandry, as in a similar manner "lodge" is used for Odd Fellows. Every properly organized grange has thirteen officers. Meetings are held periodically, devoted to music, literature, etc., and each grange-room is generally provided with a library. There were 25,000 granges, with 2,000,000 members, in the United States in 1880. They have now practically ceased to be a factor in politics.

Granite Redoubt. The Grenadiers of the Consular Guard won this name by their bravery at the battle of Marengo, in 1800. When the French line had been broken they formed a solid square and repulsed every charge of the Austrians.

Granite State. New Hampshire. Fine building granite is quarried at many points, notably at Plymouth, Concord, Milford, Pelham, etc. Philip Carrigain (1772–1842), who surveyed a great part of the State about 1815, was the first to apply the name.

Grass Mail. *See* BLACK MAIL.

Grass Widow was originally "grace widow," — that is, a widow by grace or courtesy, not in fact. In England the term is bestowed on an unmarried mother or discarded mistress. In this country it means either a divorced wife or one separated from her husband. It appears to have first come into general use in the days of the California gold-fever, in 1849, and did not then carry any reproach with it, but

designated the adventurer's wife left at home for an indefinite period. Probably the fact that she often had "to pick up her own living," as the grazing phrase hath it, may have assisted in the not unnatural corruption from "grace" to "grass."

Gratia gratiam parit. (Lat.) "Kindness begets kindness." One good turn deserves another.

Gratis. (Lat.) Free of cost.

Gratis dictum. (Lat.) A gratuitous assertion.

Gravamen. (Lat.) The thing complained of.

Grave delictum. (Lat.) "A heavy offence." A grave crime.

Grave of France. The field of Waterloo.

Graveyard Walker. A nickname given to Dr. George Alfred Walker (1807–1884), a physician dwelling in North Wales. For many years he waged a successful warfare against intramural burials, which finally led to the location of cemeteries beyond city boundaries.

Gray Eagle. (Pseud.) Frederick J. Englehardt, in "Turf, Field, and Farm."

Gray League. A league of the Grisons, in 1424, similar in object to the Caddee League (*q. v.*).

Gray Man's Path. A strange cleft in a greenstone precipice in the vicinity of Ballycastle, Ireland.

Grazioso. (Ital.) Gracefully. (Mus.)

Great, The. This title has been borne by the following historical characters : —

Abbas I., Shah of Persia (1557–1628).
Albertus "Magnus," mediæval Schoolman (1193–1280).
Alexander of Macedon (356–323 B. C.).
Alfonso III., King of Asturias and Leon (848–912).
Alfred, King of England (849–901).
Basil, Saint, Bishop of Cæsarea (329–379).
Canute, King of Denmark (995–1036).
Casimir III. of Poland (1309–1370).
Charles I., Emperor of Germany (724–814) ; "Charlemagne," or "Carolus Magnus."
Charles III., Duke of Lorraine (1543–1608).
Charles Emmanuel I., Duke of Savoy (1562–1630).
Lewis I. of Hungary (1326–1381).
Louis II., Prince of Condé, Duc d'Enghien (1621–1686).
Ferdinand I. of Castile (d. 1065).
Frederick William, Elector of Brandenburg, (1620–1688) ; "the Great Elector."
Frederick II. of Prussia (1712–1786).
Gregory I., Pope (544–604).
Henri IV. of France (1553–1610).

Herod Agrippa I., Tetrarch (d. 44 A. D.).
Hiao-wen-tee, Emperor of China (206–157 B. C.).
John II. of Portugal (1455–1495).
Justinian I. (483–565).
Mahomet II., Sultan of the Turks (1430–1481).
Maximilian, Duke of Bavaria (1573–1651).
Cosmo de' Medici, Grand Duke of Tuscany (1519–1574).
Gonzales Pedro de Mendoza, of Spain (1503–1575); "the Great Cardinal."
Nicholas I., Pope (d. 867).
Otho I., Emperor of Germany (913–973).
Pierre III. of Aragon (1239–1285).
Sapor, Ninth Sassanide King (240–379).
James Sforza, Italian general (1369–1424).
Sigismund, King of Poland (1466–1548).
Theodoric, King of the Ostrogoths (454–526).
Theodosius I., Emperor (346–395).

Great American Condenser. John B. Wood, an American journalist (d. 1883), was so named by his intimates for his skill in eliminating superfluous words and sentences from news reports. He was born in New Hampshire, and served editorially on the New York "Tribune," "Sun," and "Herald," and on the St. Louis "Chronicle."

Great American Doctor. Philippe Ricord (b. 1800), long resident in Paris, is so named.

Great American Traveller. Daniel Pratt (1809–1887). He was a carpenter by trade; but, his mind becoming affected, he did little work, and spent the time roaming over the United States, subsisting on charity. His annual addresses to the New England colleges at Commencement came to be regarded as a feature of college life, and were a curious farrago of bombast and nonsense.

Great Awakening. The name given to the religious revival which swept over New England, 1740–1741, in consequence of the preaching of Jonathan Edwards and George Whitefield.

Great Bear. The great Dr. Samuel Johnson was so named by Boswell's father.

Great Bible. A version of the Scriptures published in 1539, under the supervision of Grafton.

Great Bullet-head. Georges Cadoudal, leader of the Chouans (fl. 1769–1804).

Great Captain. (1) Gonzalvo di Cordova (1453–1515). (2) Manuel Comnenus of Trebizond (1120–1180).

Great Cham of Literature. Dr. Samuel Johnson was so named by Smollett.

Great Charter. The document by which the Virginia Company of London

in 1618 granted the people of Virginia the right to make their own laws.

Great Commoner. (1) William Pitt, Earl of Chatham (fl. 1759–1806), for upward of a quarter of a century leader of the House of Commons. (2) Thaddeus Stevens. (3) Henry Clay.

Great Crooked River State. A name proposed for Tennessee by Andrew Jackson, 1796; since passed into a nickname.

Great Croysado. Gen. Lord Fairfax is so named in "Hudibras."

Great Cry and Little Wool. There are many variations of this proverbial saying, but the true one appears to be the Scottish one, "Great cry and little woo, as the Soutar said when he clippit the sow." *Soutar* is shoemaker; and the phrase doubtless arose in times when shoemakers were indebted, for the bristles which form the flexible needles of their thread, to native swine. In modern times shoemakers' bristles come principally from Russia.

Great Duke. The Duke of Wellington. *See* IRON DUKE.

Great Earl of Cork. Richard Boyle, Earl of Cork (fl. 1566–1643), who possessed the largest estate of any English subject. He devoted a large part of the income therefrom to making public improvements.

Great Elector. Frederick William, Elector of Brandenburg (fl. 1620–1688).

Greater Britain. The colonial dependencies of the British Empire. In area they many times surpass the mother country.

Greatest Happiness of the Greatest Number. "That action is best which procures the greatest happiness for the greatest numbers."— HUTCHESON'S *Inquiry: Concerning Moral Good and Evil.* "Priestley was the first (unless it was Beccaria) who taught my lips to pronounce this sacred truth,— that the greatest happiness of the greatest number is the foundation of morals and legislation."— BENTHAM. The expression is used by Beccaria in the introduction to his "Essay on Crimes and Punishments."

Great Head. Malcolm III. of Scotland; also called "Canmore," which has substantially the same meaning.

Great Jesuit of the West. The English so named François Picquet, the missionary (1708–1781), though he never belonged to that order.

Great King, City of the. *See* CITY OF THE GREAT KING.

Great Magician. Sir Walter Scott· was thus nicknamed by Prof. John Wilson ("Christopher North").

Great Marquis. James Graham, Marquis of Montrose (fl. 1612–1650), who fought valiantly for Charles I. in the civil war.

Great Moralist of Fleet Street. Dr. Samuel Johnson.

Great Mother. The earth. Junius Brutus and the sons of Tarquin consulted the oracle of Delphi in order to learn who should succeed Superbus on the throne of Rome. They received as answer : " He who shall first kiss his mother." The Tarquins hastened home to fulfil the apparent meaning, but Brutus fell to the ground, exclaiming, "Thus I kiss thee, O earth, the great mother of us all ! "

Great ·Objector. William Steele Holman, an American congressman (b. 1822); so named because in his legislative career he was the uncompromising enemy of all trickery and jobbery.

Great Pacificator. (1) Henry Clay was so named because of his facility in devising modes of settling party disputes. (2) Clark B. Cochrane, the American lawyer (1817–1867), was so named. He was a member of the Legislature of New York, and his tact in quieting angry debate earned him the sobriquet.

Great Pan. François Marie Arouet de Voltaire (fl. 1694–1778). *See* DICTATOR OF LETTERS and BABOON.

Great Prophets. Isaiah, Jeremiah, Ezekiel, and Daniel, — their writings being very extensive and weighty. *See* MINOR PROPHETS.

Great Puritan Epic. Milton's "Paradise Lost."

Great Rebellion. The revolt of the Long Parliament against Charles I.

Great Rock of Italy (Ital., *Gran Sasso d' Italia*), also called Monte Corno, from the resemblance to a horn which it presents on the east, is the highest summit of the Apennines, having an elevation of 10,206 feet. It is situated on the border of the Abruzzi, between Teramo and Aquila. It owes its name partly to its height, and partly to its being formed of a single mass of calcareous earth from its middle to its summit. The summit is covered with perpetual snow. Wolves, bears, and chamois abound on the mountain, the last of these animals being found in no other part of the Apennines.

Great Thirst Land, The. South Africa ; so named by travellers because of its liability to frequent and lengthy droughts, no rain falling sometimes for twelve months.

Great Unknown, The. Sir Walter Scott was so named because his works were at first published anonymously.

Great Unwashed. Artisans ; workingmen. A phrase coined by Edmund Burke.

Greece, Eye of. *See* EYE OF GREECE.

Greek. One who cheats at cards. The origin of the term is French, the story being that in the reign of Louis XIV. a Grecian nobleman was caught cheating at play. He was sent to the galleys.

Greek, The. Manuel Alvarez, the Spanish sculptor (fl. 1727–1797).

Greek Commentator. Fernando Nuñez de Guzman (fl. 1470–1553), who did much to promote the study of the Greek classics in Spain.

Greenbackers. The name given in the United States in 1876 *et seq.*, to a party who contended for the unlimited issue of " soft money," *i. e.* greenbacks or paper currency, and for the payment of the national debt in paper instead of coin. It was called by its members the " Independent National," was organized in 1876, and was the outgrowth of the Granger and Labor Reform movements. Its convention at Indianapolis in May, 1876, " demanded the unconditional repeal of the Specie Resumption Act of Jan. 14, 1875 ; " urged the issue of United States notes as a circulating medium and the suppression of bank paper ; and protested against the further issue of gold bonds, and the purchase of silver to replace the fractional currency. Peter Cooper was nominated for President, and received 81,740 votes. In 1880 its candidate was James B. Weaver, who received 306,305. It has never gained any electoral votes. In 1884 the party indorsed the nomination of Benjamin F. Butler by the so-called People's Party, which polled 175,370 votes.

Greenbacks. During the late civil war in the United States the immense expenditure of the United States Government led to the issue of paper money, bank-notes and currency of various denominations. These documents, from their prevailing color, obtained the nickname of "greenbacks," a term that became firmly fixed in the nomenclature of the country. "Shinplaster" was a name for the fractional paper currency.

Green Bag Inquiry. The name given to the investigation of the nature of the contents of a green bag full of Reports on the state of the country (thought by some to be seditious documents), which was presented to Parliament by the Prince Regent Feb. 3, 1817. These Reports led to the suspension of the Habeas Corpus Act and other coercive measures.

Green Horse, The. The Fifth Dragoon Guards.

Green Howards. The English Nineteenth Regiment is so dubbed after the color of their facings and the name of a favorite colonel.

Green Isle. The same as Emerald Isle (*q. v.*).

Green Linnets. *See* SANKEY'S HORSE.

Green Melons. A nickname conferred on the natives of Sydney, Australia.

Green Mountain State. A popular name for the State of Vermont, from the range of hills that crosses it from north to south, and from the signification of its name, which is derived from the French *verts monts*, green mountains.

Greens. This is a collective term for vegetables in general, though in England the same word is current to denote a species of kale.

Green Sea. The Persian Gulf; so named from a remarkable strip of water of a bright green color along the coast of Arabia.

Green Thursday. Maundy Thursday (*q. v.*) The great day of absolution in the Lutheran Church.

Greenwich Barbers. A local nickname for hawkers of sand, it being currently said that the people of Greenwich "shave the sand-pits" of the vicinity to supply London with sand.

Gregorian Tree. Another name for the gallows. Three successive hangmen bore the name of Gregory in England: Gregory, Sr.; his son, Gregory, Jr., and Gregory Brandon.

Gresham. The character of "Mr. Gresham" in Trollope's "Prime Minister" is a skit on Mr. Gladstone.

Gretna Green Marriages. "The name given to marriages of English persons contracted at Gretna Green. This spot, being the most convenient halting-place for runaway couples from England, gave the name to this kind of marriage, originally an easy mode of evading the English Marriage Act, which required the consent of parents and guardians, publication of banns, and the presence of a priest, — all of which involved considerable publicity and an inconvenient delay, but which were got rid of by the parties passing the English border into Scottish ground. The rule being that a marriage is valid if contracted according to the law of the place where the parties enter into the contract, it was easy for English couples to avail themselves of the mode of contracting marriage allowed by the law of Scotland, which required nothing but a mutual declaration of marriage to be exchanged in presence of witnesses, — a ceremony which could be performed instantly, — and it was immaterial whether the parties were minors or not. This declaration generally took place in the presence of a blacksmith, who in reality was no more necessary than any other witness. The declaration of marriage being exchanged, the parties could at once return to England, and their marriage was held ever after to be valid there and all the world over." — CHAMBERS.

Gretna Green of Ireland. Port Patrick, a seaport town of Scotland, the nearest port to Ireland. Runaway couples from the Emerald Isle bent on matrimony used frequently to fly thither.

Greyhound of the Atlantic. The steamer "Alaska" was so named because of the extremely short passages she accomplished between Europe and the United States.

Greyhounds. A modern constellation made by Hevelius out of the unformed stars of the ancients, which were scattered between Boötes on the east, and the Great Bear on the west, and between the handle of the Dipper on the north, and 'Berenice's Hair on the south; the northern hound is called Asterion and the southern one Chara; and the largest star is of the third magnitude, in the neck of Chara.

Gridiron Gabble. (Pseud.) Joseph Haslewood, English bibliographer (1769-1833).

Griffin (from Fr. *griffon*). A mulatto. A term often applied in Louisiana to the female creole.

Griffin Lee. (Pseud.) Paschal Beverly Randolph, M. D. (b. 1825).

Griffith's Valuation. The name given to that calculation of the rent value of land in Ireland made by Mr. (afterward Sir) Richard Griffith, and published in 1850. The phrase was much used during the " No Rent " agitation of 1880-1881.

Grin. (Pseud.) Leo C. Evans in the " Metropolis."

Grinder. (Pseud.) Harry H. Marks, in the New York " Sunday Times."

Gringo. The Mexican nickname for an American. When the American army invaded Mexico a favorite song in the camps was Burns's " Green grow the rushes, O." The Mexicans heard it repeated over and over, and finally began to call the Americans by the first two words, which they pronounced " grin go." Hence, " Gringo."

Grip Fast. (Pseud.) Frank Leslie Baker in the " Morning Mail," Lowell, Mass.

Gris. Grisons.

Grisette. Dressed in gray. A term applied to French shop-girls, etc.

Grit, Clear Grit. A pure Americanism, standing for pluck, or energy, or industry, or all three. Reference is probably had to the sandstones used for grindstones, — the more grit they contain the better they wear.

Gro. Gross.

Grot. Grotius.

Grub Street. A street near Moorfields, London (now Milton Street), much frequented by penny-a-liners, scribblers, and cheap newspaper-writers, though at various times not a few authors of ability resided there. Hence the term " Grub Street " passed into colloquial usage to designate a literary hack or a worthless production.

G. S. Grand Secretary; Grand Sentinel; Grand Scribe.

G. T. Good Templars; Grand Tyler.

Gtt. *Gutta* or *guttæ*. Drop; drops.

Guards of the Pole. The two stars β and γ of the *Great Bear*, and not the star Arctophylax, which Steevens says,

"literally signifies the guard of the Bear," *i. e.* Boötes (not the Polar Guards). Shakspeare refers to these two "guards" in " Othello," act ii. sc. 1, where he says the surge seems to "quench the guards of the ever-fixèd pole." Hood says they are so called "from the Spanish word *guardare*, which is 'to behold,' because they are diligently to be looked unto in regard of the singular use which they have in navigation."

Guelphs and Ghibellines. "The names of two great parties, the conflicts of which may almost be said to make up the history of Italy and Germany from the eleventh till the fourteenth century. The origin of these names was formerly the subject of much speculation; but antiquarians are now agreed in tracing them respectively to the two families, Waiblingen and Welf, which in the twelfth century were at the head of two rival parties in the German Empire, and whose feuds came to be identified historically with the respective principles for which these parties contended. The actual origin of the assumption of the names is commonly fixed at the great battle of Weinsberg, in Suabia, 1140 A. D., in which the two rival claimants for the empire, Conrad of Hohenstaufen, Duke of Franconia, and Henry the Lion, of the House of Welf, Duke of Saxony, rallied their followers by the respective war-cries, ' Hie Waiblingen!' ' Hie Welf!' but it is certain that the names were in use from an earlier date, although, probably, rather as representing the family feud than the political principles which the two families afterward severally supported. As the chief theatre of the conflict of these parties was Italy, the original names took the Italian form of Ghibellini and Guelfi." — CHAMBERS.

Guerre à mort. (Fr.) War to death.

Guerre à outrance. (Fr.) War to the uttermost.

Guess. " Guess," says a recent authority, is probably, of all words in the dictionary, the most thoroughly abused and the most passionately discussed. Quoted by almost every writer on America as one of the most obtrusive Americanisms, there is ample evidence that the word has been used in England from time immemorial in the precise sense in which the Yankee uses it now. The only difference in our day is perhaps that the English "guess" is a fair, candid supposition, while the American who "guesses" is apt to be quite sure of what he professes to doubt. As he only "calculates" when he has already solved his problem, so he "guesses" after having made sure of his fact. "I guess I can" means, from his lips, "I am sure I can." Like many so-called Americanisms, it is simply the survival of an old English use of the word, which was formerly in excellent repute, as may appear from the following extracts : —

> Amylia will be lov'd as I mote gheese.
> SPENSER.

> Her yellow hair was braided in a tress
> Behind her back, a yarde long, I guess.
> CHAUCER.

> Already by thy reasoning this I guess.
> MILTON.

> If thou canst the harder reason guess.
> POPE.

> A poet must confess
> His art, like physic, but a happy guess.
> DRYDEN.

She, guessing that he was a gardener. — JOHN xx. 15, *Wycliffe's Translation.*

Nobody, I guess, will think it too much. — LOCKE.

Guess rightly of things to come. — RALEIGH.

Richard Grant White, writing on the following passage from Richard III., act iv. sc. 4, —

> *Stanley.*   Richmond is on the seas.
> *K. Rich.* There let him sink, and be the seas on him!
> White-livered runagate, what doth he there?
> *Stanley.* I know not, mighty sovereign, but by guess.
> *K. Rich.* Well, sir, as you guess? —

says: "If there be two words for the use of which, more than any others, our English cousins twit us, they are 'well' as an interrogative exclamation, and 'guess.' Milton uses both, as Shakspeare also frequently does, and here we have them both in half a line. Like most of those words and phrases which it pleases John Bull to call 'Americanisms,' they are English of the purest and best, which have lived here, while they have died out in the mother country." Well may the Rev. A. C. Geikie retort: "To such 'English of the purest and best' are we fast hastening, if some check is not put on the present tendencies of our colloquial speech, and the style adopted in our periodical literature." — *Canadian Journal.* Chaucer uses "guess," —

> "This woful hande quod she
> Ys strong ynogh in swich a werke to me,
> For love shal me geve strengthe and hardyknesse,
> To make my wounde large ynogh I gesse."

Gueux ("the Beggars"). The name assumed by the confederated nobles and other malcontents who opposed the tyrannical policy of Philip II. of Spain in the Low Countries. Philip having sent nine inquisitors to that country to put into execution the decrees of the Council of Trent, provoked by this act the bitter resentment of the Protestants, as well as of the Catholics and nobility, who saw in it an attempt to curtail their ancient liberties. A party of opposition was thus formed, and, headed by Counts Louis of Nassau and Henry de Brederode, declared in an act called the "Compromise," which was remitted (April 5, 1566) to the Regent Margaret, their fixed determination to ignore utterly the authority of the inquisitors. On the admission of a deputation from them to an audience, the regent seemed somewhat unnerved by their bold front, and inclined to yield to their demands ; when one of her council approached her, and whispered that she "need not be afraid of these gatherings of beggars." The remark having been overheard by some of the deputation, the abusive epithet was assumed as the title of their association. As a sign of fraternity, each of the "beggars" wore a medal called the "beggar's denier," made of gold or silver, and stamped on the obverse with the image of Philip II., and the inscription, "In everything faithful to the king;" and on the reverse with a wallet, such as the mendicant monks carried, held in two hands, with the words, "even to the carrying of the wallet." The "beggars" maintained a long and vigorous contest against the despotic proceedings of Philip and his advisers, but were ultimately compelled to succumb to superior force. A branch of them, "the Beggars of the Sea," under the bold leadership of the savage Count de la Marck, were almost uniformly successful in their enterprises ; they several times defeated the Spanish fleet, captured transports with supplies for Alva's army, captured several fortresses, and succored besieged places along the coast.

Guinea. In New York a slang name for Italians, alluding to their sallow or yellow complexion.

Guinea Coast. The former name of the West African country now known as Guinea. It designates no political division, but was once much used in commerce. The seaboard from north to south is divided into Liberia (formerly the Grain Coast), Ivory Coast, Gold Coast (a British colony), Slave Coast (because of the cargoes of Negroes formerly shipped thence), and the Calabar Coast. An English coin, having first been made of gold brought from the Guinea Coast, thus obtained the name of guinea.

Guinea-dropper. A cheat. It was formerly the custom for swindlers to drop a counterfeit guinea in the street, at the feet of some innocent-looking person, and then, convincing him that it was his, induce him to give his informant half of it for a reward in good money. A variety of this game, known as Ring-dropping, was at one time very common in the cities of the United States.

Guinea-hen. A courtesan who is won by money is so termed in " Othello."

Guinea-pig. A term current on the London stock exchange to denote those persons who allow the use of their names on a list of Directors for the sake of the *guinea* and the *dinner* given to each at the board meetings.

Gulch. This is really a resurrected old English word, meaning a dry watercourse or gully, and, contrary to general belief, has no connection with the Spanish.

Gulf, Key of the. *See* KEY OF THE GULF.

Gulielmo Bellendenus. (Pseud.) William Bellenden, Scottish writer (d. 1633).

Gumsuckers. A nickname conferred on the natives of Tasmania.

Gunpowder Plot. A memorable conspiracy for springing a mine under the Houses of Parliament, and destroying at one *coup* the three estates of the realm,— king, lords, and commons,— discovered Nov. 4, 1605. It was projected by Robert Catesby, and several Roman Catholic persons of rank were drawn into the base scheme. Guy Faux, or Fawkes, an unprincipled adventurer, was detected in a vault preparing the train for firing the next day. Several of the ringleaders were executed Jan. 30, 31, 1606. *See* GUY FAWKES' DAY, *infra.*

Gure's Geese. A by-name for the English Sixth Regiment of Foot. *See* SHORT SIXES.

Gusto, Gustoso, or **Con gusto.** (Ital.) With taste; elegantly. (Mus.)

Gutenberg Bible. The earliest book known to have been printed from movable metal types. It was in the Latin tongue, and was issued by Gutenberg at Mentz in 1450.

Guy Fawkes' Day. This is the anniversary, on November 5, of the discovery of the Gunpowder Plot in England, 1605. It is peculiarly an English observance. In memory of the providential deliverance of the king and Parliament " Te Deums " were sung in the churches, and the anniversary became a red-letter day in English annals. It was and is still observed in a peculiar manner. During the day straw-stuffed effigies of Guy Fawkes are carried by boys and men about the streets on chairs or trestles supported by two poles, like a sedan-chair. Some of' these effigies are life-size, and are gotten up in tawdry finery, with a mask or " false-face " topped by a three-cornered cocked hat. They go from house to house, attended by troops of admiring urchins, stopping from time to time to sing or chant : —

" Please to remember the fifth of November,
  The Gunpowder treason and plot,
I see no reason why Gunpowder treason
  Should ever be forgot.
        Hip, Hip, Hurrah ! "

Another form of the doggerel sung is : —

" The fifth of November, since I can remember,
    Gunpowder treason and plot,
  This is the day that God did prevent
    To blow up his king and Parliament !
" A stick and a stake for Victoria's sake.
    If you won't give me one,
  Then I 'll take two, — the better for me
    And the worse for you."

The boys always close with the appeal, " Please to remember the guy ! " or " Please remember the fire ! " soliciting gifts of pennies or firewood. In this way they collect a good many shillings. The money goes to buy fireworks, and the fagots go to the fire; for at night the "guy," as the effigy of Fawkes is called (whence our word meaning a grotesque figure of any sort), is burned in an immense bonfire, the bigger the better, to the accompaniment of a fusillade of fireworks. Our Election Day often falls on the 5th of November, or thereabouts. So, about the time that American boys are dancing round the Election-night bonfire, English boys are burning the guy. In fact, the two observances are really one and the same thing. From the earliest colonial times in New England, the custom having been brought over by the first settlers, the 5th of November was celebrated by burning an effigy of Guy Fawkes and by letting off fireworks, or by carrying about the village street at night a pair of hideous "pumpkin faces" with candle-ends stuck inside. These were supposed to represent the Pope and the Devil, and they were burned together in a fire on the common. Gradually, however, the significance of the day faded from sight. At the present time, though the memory of the Gunpowder Plot and of the "pumpkin faces" has long disappeared, the boys in some of the New England towns annually build fires on the night of the 5th of November, though they cannot tell why they do so, any more than they can tell why tops, marbles, and kites are "in" or "out" of season. But in New York and its sister cities the custom, though still blindly kept up, has been shifted to the night of the annual Election Day; and both Protestant and Catholic boys, who know or care nothing about the Gunpowder Plot or Guy Fawkes' Day, unconsciously join in commemorating the old English custom that sprang from intense loyalty to the Protestant faith and to the Protestant king and Parliament of England.

Guy Pollock. (Pseud.) Robert Douglas Hamilton, M. D., a well-known Canadian miscellaneous writer.

Gyges. In classic myth a son of Cœlus and Terra, a hundred-handed giant, one of those who made war on the gods. He was slain by Hercules, and eternally punished in Tartarus.

Gyges' Ring rendered the wearer invisible. According to Plato, Gyges descended into a chasm of the earth, where he found a brazen horse; opening the sides of the animal, he found the carcass of a man, from whose finger he drew off a brazen ring, which rendered him invisible, and by means of this ring he entered the chamber of Candaules, and murdered him.

Gyp. A servant waiting on two or more collegians in the University of Cambridge. He runs on errands, waits at table, wakes men for morning chapel, brushes their clothes, and so on. His perquisites are innumerable, and he is called a "gyp" because he preys upon his employer like a vulture. *See* SCOUT.

Gyp. The pen-name of Madame de Martel, a French author of the present day. She wrote sketches for the "Vie Parisienne," which were afterward collected into a book entitled "Autour du Mariage."

H.

H. Hydrogen.

H. A. *Hoc anno.* This year.

Hab. Habakkuk.

Hab. corp. *Habeas corpus.* You may have the body.

Habeas corpus. (Lat.) "You are to have the body." A writ of right, by virtue of which every citizen can, when imprisoned, demand to be put on his trial.

Hab. fa. poss. *Habere facias possessionem.*

Hab. fa. seis. *Habere facias seisinam.*

Hackell's Quoit. A vast stone near Stantian Drew, in Somersetshire, England; so called from a tradition that it was thrown by Sir John Hautville.

Hackerston's Cow. A Scotch proverb, the origin of which is accounted for by the following story: "A tenant of Lord Hackerston, who was one of the judges of the court of sessions, one day waited on his lordship with a woful countenance. 'My lord,' said he, 'I am come to inform your lordship of a sad misfortune. My cow has gored one of your lordship's cows, so that I fear it cannot live.' 'Well, then, you must pay for it.' 'Indeed, my lord, it was not my fault, and you know I am a very poor man.' 'I can't help that. I say you must pay for it. I am not to lose my cow.' 'Well, my lord, if it must be so, I cannot say against your lordship; but stop, my lord, I believe I have made a mistake, — it was your lordship's cow that gored mine.' 'Oh, that is quite a different matter. Go along and don't trouble me! I am busy, — go along, I say!'"

Hades. In classic myth the abode of departed spirits; also the name of the deity of the nether world, — the same as Pluto.

Hæc olim meminisse juvabit. (Lat.) It will be pleasant hereafter to remember these things.

Hag. Haggai.

Hair of the Dog. "When a man is debilitated from the effects of the previous night's debauch, he is frequently counselled to take 'a hair of the dog that bit him,' the meaning being that he should take a little of the same kind of liquor that had upset him. The saying is a remnant of an old superstitious belief that the burnt hair of a dog was an antidote against the ill effects of intoxication." — TIMBS. In a song of the date 1650 the following verse occurs : —

"If any so wise is, that sack he despises,
Let him drink his small beer and be sober ;
And while we drink and sing, as if it were
    spring,
He shall droop like the trees in October.
But be sure overnight, if this dog do you bite,
You may take it henceforth for a warning,
Soon as out of your bed, to settle your head,
Take a hair of his tail in the morning."

Halcyon. (Pseud.) Miss Maud Howe, in her correspondence to Boston papers from New Orleans.

Halcyon Days. A name given by the ancients to the seven days which precede and the seven days which follow the shortest day, on account of a fable that during this time, while the halcyon bird, or kingfisher, was breeding, there always prevailed calms at sea. From this the phrase " halcyon days " has come to signify times of tranquillity or prosperity.

Half-breeds. A faction in Republican political circles in New York State, — the partisans of James G. Blaine, as distinguished from the Stalwarts. *See* FEATHER-HEADS.

Half-seas-over. Partially drunk. A probable corruption of the Dutch *ob-zee-zober*, " over-sea beer," a strong beverage introduced from England into Holland.

I am half-seas-over to death.
                    DRYDEN.

I do not like the dulness of your eye ;
It hath a heavy cast ; 't is upsee Dutch.
                    BEN JONSON.

Half-way Covenant. This was the familiar name given to a compromise in the early Congregational churches in New England. They recognized baptism as the first condition only of membership, and held that as each person came to years of discretion proof should be given of repentance from sin and faith in Christ. But as membership involved a large measure of civil rights and political privileges, there were those who called for relaxation as to such qualifications. In the disputes to which this demand gave rise, two councils were held in Boston, Mass. At the first the stricter rule was agreed upon, but at the second it was relaxed thus far, that all baptized persons were to be looked on as members of the Church, and to be admitted to all privileges of membership, except Holy Communion, provided they were not openly of bad life. This was the compromise known as the " Half-way Covenant." But there were those who regarded this compromise as opening the way to license in thought and deed, and certain Congregational writers attribute to it largely the undoubted fact that many of the Congregationalists of Eastern Massachusetts became Unitarians. The preaching of Whitefield was largely instrumental in kindling a warmer enthusiasm, and in consequence of it the " Half-way Covenant " was in course of time tacitly abandoned.

Halie Archmere. The stage-name of Mrs. Frederick Lucier.

Hallelujah Victory. That gained by newly converted Bretons, led by Germanus, Bishop of Auxerre, in 429. They went into battle shouting " Hallelujah!"

Hall-mark. The official stamp of the Goldsmith's Company in England, affixed to articles of gold and silver to attest their purity. Hence, in current phrase, " to bear the hall-mark " is to be above suspicion.

Hall of Odin. Among the Scandinavian peoples, those rocks from which the Berserkers, when tired of life, flung themselves into the sea; so named because they were regarded as the portals of the Scandinavian Valhalla.

Halloween, or All-Hallow-Eve, falls on the last day of October, the day following being All-Saints' Day (*q. v.*), or All-Hallows. This feast was kept in the Greek Church so early as the fourth century of our era, though it did not become common in the West till the beginning of the seventh century. The setting apart of one day sacred to the memory of saintly departed ones arose from the fact that the number of such became greatly multiplied as the Church grew and prospered, and it was found too burdensome to devote a feast-day to each. Indeed, so great was the number of the canonized, that there were not " sacred hours enough in the year to distribute among them all." So it was decided to commemorate on one special day those who had no particular days of their own. In the English Church the day is sometimes called All-Hallowmas. But it is with the eve of the festival that we have to do. In the seventh century the Roman temple dedicated to all the pagan gods, and hence called the Pan-theon, was freshly consecrated to the worship of the Virgin and the Martyrs. The new festival was held at first on May 14 in each year, but later it was shifted to November 1. Halloween was thereby made to fall on the same day as did an ancient festival among the Druids, those strange priests of a stranger religion who were scattered over many portions of Northern Europe before Christianity became its creed. They had many strange cere-monies. For instance, three times in each year — on May 1, at the time of sowing ; at the summer solstice, June 21, for the ripening of the crops ; and on October 31, at the harvest season — these priests built fires on the hill-tops in Britain, Ireland, and in France, in honor of the sun-god. At the latter festival the Druids for leagues round gathered in snow-white robes at the altar of stones on some hill. Here rested an emblem of the luminary they worshipped, and on the altar was the sacred fire which had been carefully kept alive during the past year. The Druids grouped themselves around it, and at a given signal quenched it, amid absolute silence on the part of the as-sembled people. Then a new fire was kindled on the cairn, the multitude raised a mighty shout, and from every eminence for miles around other fires blazed into view. The same night the fire was put out in every cabin and farm-house, only to be rekindled with embers from the sacred fire of the priests, which was believed to protect each homestead from peril so long as it remained burning. In those days

faith in the existence of fairies and gob-lins, witches and spirits, was very strong ; and as the Druidic faith faded before the advance of Christianity the heathen festivals lost much of their old grandeur and former significance, and took on a lower character. So, on the night of October 31, the simple country-folk believed the fairies came out of their grottos, witches and goblins gath-ered in forest glades, or plotted against mankind in the shadows of ruinous castles and keeps. By a very natural transition the Halloween fire came to be looked on as a charm against these sprites. So late as the seventeenth cen-tury it was customary for farmers to make the circuit of their fields with a lighted torch in hand, to protect them from harm during the year, chanting or singing a doggerel rhyme the while. For the reason, also, that these unseen magic powers were deemed to be so near at this season, Halloween was thought to be the night of all nights on which to pry into the secrets of the future, and thus arose all those simple ceremonies by which it was claimed that one's fate might be learned. Of course, no sensible person now believes that by cracking nuts, ducking one's head in a tub of water for apples, drop-ping melted lead in a goblet, pulling kale, or eating an apple before a mirror, anything supernatural or ghostly will be seen or heard. But the pleasant fireside revelries survive, though they have lost their superstitious significance. In Eng-land, in Scotland, in America, even in far-off Australia, — wherever, in fact, the Saxon tongue is spoken, — these Hal-loween festivities are kept up by young and old. But it is in the two first-named countries that Halloween frolics are seen at their best. Great bonfires are still kindled in many places, around which the villagers join hands in a merry dance. Then, as the flames sub-side into a pile of glowing embers, the real fun begins. The first ceremony in Scotland consists in " pulling the kale." Kale is a sort of cabbage. Lads and lasses go out in couples, hand in hand, with eyes shut, and pull the first head of kale they touch. The fact of its be-ing crooked or straight, large or small, is said to be emblematic of the height and figure of the coming husband or wife. If any earth clings to the roots, that means money ; while the sweet or bitter taste of the heart of the kale denotes the disposition of the prospective life-partner. Burning the nuts is another equally famous charm. Two hazel-nuts are placed in the fire, having been previously named for the particular lad and lass about to try their fortune. Accordingly, as they burn quietly side by side, or crack and sputter and break apart, will be the result of the wooing. Says Burns : —

> "The auld gudewife's weel hoarded nits
> Are round and round divided,
> And monie lads' and lasses' fates
> Are there that night decided.
> Some kindle, couthie, side by side,
> And burn thegither trimly ;
> Some start awa' with saucy pride,
> And jump out owre the chimlie."

In England the following charm is frequently tried : Three dishes are taken ; one is empty, one is filled with clear water, and the third with dirty water. A boy is blindfolded and led to the hearth where the dishes are set in a row. Then he dips the left hand in one of the dishes, — if in the clean water, she will be a widow; if in the empty dish, he will remain "a horrid old bachelor." The trial should be made three times, the dishes being shifted about meanwhile. In the country districts of Scotland much faith is reposed in this formula : Go to a south-running stream, and dip your sleeve in it at a spot where the lands of three lairds come together. Then go home, hang the wet garment before the fire, and go to bed in full view of it. Keep awake, and some time near midnight you will be rewarded by seeing an apparition, bearing an exact likeness to the future husband or wife, come and turn the sleeve "as if to dry the other side of it." Doubtless many an American girl of English or Scotch ancestry has heard of or tried the "looking-glass spell." The curious one must go, candle in hand, to a mirror, eat an apple while standing before it, and in due time the face of her destined husband will be seen reflected in the glass across her shoulder. There is a mirth-provoking game played in England on Halloween, — perhaps in this country, too, for aught the writer knows to the contrary. A hoop from a flour-barrel is taken, and around it are fastened alternately, at regular intervals, apples, cakes, candies, and candle-ends. The hoop is then suspended from the ceiling and set to revolving. The players gather in a circle round it, and each in turn tries to bite one of the

edibles. The boy or girl who is so unfortunate as to seize one of the candles pays forfeit. But in England and in America Halloween frolics are nowadays mere harmless sports, and though in Scotland they still retain a more or less superstitious character, yet it is clear that, in being repeated from year to year as simple holiday merrymakings, the mysteries of Halloween have arrived at their final stage, and ere many more years have flown they will perhaps be forgotten. The following accounts of Halloween sports and frolics are redolent of the soil of bonny Scotland, — essentially the home of Halloween observances. There was a very popular way of trying one's luck on Halloween, by putting in a pot of mashed potatoes a ring, a thimble, and a sixpence. All got a spoon and supped the potatoes out of the pot. Whoever got the ring was sure to be married within the year ; the thimble signified an old maid, and the sixpence a legacy. When the ring was found some laid down their spoons, afraid the thimble would come their way. One smart young lass on one occasion got the ring in the first mouthful, but never told, and kept it in her cheek till all the potatoes were eaten. "Ah, but ye are a sly customer," says one, "and whoever gets you will need to keep his eyes about him." The "dookin'" for apples was grand fun. The best place for it was a kitchen with paved or flagged floor. A large tub was half filled with water and set in the middle of the floor. A "deil's dozen" of well-rounded apples were put into the water in the tub. Those who were to take part in the sport took off their upper garments, — boys their jackets and the lasses their short gowns. Then, turning about, with their hands tied behind their backs, they tried to catch an apple with their teeth as it floated in the water in the tub. It was rather a difficult task, and often both boys and girls got thoroughly drenched during the fun. "Then came the candle and the apple. There was a small stick about two feet long suspended from the centre by a string from the ceiling. At one end was a lighted candle, and at the other an apple. It was hung about the height of your mouth, and spun quickly around. Then with your hands tied behind your back you had to take a bite of the apple in passing. Then it was the fun came in, in trying to catch the apple with your teeth. Ten chances to one you got the candle in your mouth instead. Another amusement at Halloween among the young people was turnip bogles. The country lads selected the largest turnip they could find, and laid it past till Halloween. Then the inside was scooped out clean to the skin; holes cut for eyes and mouth, with part left for the teeth, which were blackened, as well as the brow. A small candle, lighted, was put inside. The light shone through the holes in mouth and eyes. By small boys this was considered to be a most awful, frightful thing, and they held it up to the window to scare the inmates. Sometimes it was taken to dark places in the hope that somebody would see it and squeal with fright. When they did so the small boy was happy, yet all the time keeping a sharp lookout lest some real bogle rnn away with himself." Halloween was called the "Witches' Night," the "Devil's Sunday," when his Satanic Majesty was supposed to have full charge of all mundane things. He assembled all the witches together. To these assemblies he rode on a goat, with black human countenance. Before going to this place the witches anointed themselves with a preparation of the fat of murdered unbaptized infants. Then riding on a cat or broomstick, they flew up the chimney and rode to the place of meeting. At the feast they ate no bread nor salt, drank out of horses' skulls, and danced back to back. The devil supplied the music from a bag-pipe, — the bag a hen's skull, and cats' tails for a chanter. After indescribable orgies they returned home as they came. To keep their husbands in ignorance of their absence a stick was laid on the bed, which the husband mistook for his wife. The banquet-hall was lighted with torches. Their light was taken from the fire which burned between the horns of the goat. At the close the goat burned itself out. The ashes were divided among the witches to use in their incantations. All Scotch boys will remember how tired the cats were the day after Halloween. Some pitied their miserable appearance; others were mad at them for carrying the witches.

Hall Sunday. The Sunday preceding Shrove Tuesday; the next day is called Hall Monday, and Shrove Tues-

day eve is called Hall Night. "Hall" or "Halle" is a contraction of "Hallow," meaning "holy."

Hamadryads. In classic mythology wood-nymphs; their existence was supposed to be contemporaneous with that of certain trees.

Ham. Coll. Hamilton College.

Hameh. In Arabian mythology a bird formed from the blood near the brains of a murdered man. This bird cries "Iskoonee!" ("Give me drink!" meaning drink of the murderer's blood) incessantly till the crime is avenged, when it flies away.

Hamilton. (Pseud.) William Robinson Watson, the American politician (1799–1864), wrote State papers in the Providence "Journal" under this signature.

Hamilton Outrage. In 1829 an effigy of Sir John Colborne was carried through the streets of Hamilton, Ont., the event being known by the above name.

Hamilton Runaways. The English Fourteenth Regiment are thus dubbed in allusion to an event in the Peninsula, when the regiment, then under command of Colonel Hamilton, ran away without any perceivable cause.

Hammer, The. (1) Pierre d'Ailly (fl. 1350–1425), president of the council that sent John Huss to the stake. (2) Judas Asmonæus, the Jewish patriot, whose surname "Maccabæus" means "the Hammer." (3) Saint Augustine, "Hammer of Heresies." (4) John Faber (fl. 1470–1541), "Hammer of Heretics." (5) Saint Hilary, "Hammer of the Arians." (6) Charles Martel (fl. 689–741). (7) Thomas Cromwell, "Hammer of Monasteries." (8) Oliver Cromwell, "Hammer of Kings and Thrones." (9) Edward I., "Hammer of the Scotch."

Hampden. (Pseud.) (1) Isaac Orr, American clergyman (1793–1844), in the New York "Commercial Advertiser." (2) William Hooper (1742–1790), one of the signers of the Declaration of Independence, in some successful essays opposing the acts of the British Government.

Hampton Court Conferences. Efforts for accommodation between the English prelates and the Puritans, 1604.

Hampton Roads Conference. A meeting held on board a vessel in Hampton Roads, Feb. 3, 1865, between

Lincoln and Seward on the one side, and A. H. Stephens, Hunter, and Campbell, on the other. It was brought about by F. P. Blair, who thought that the North and the South might cease hostilities and join hands to enforce the Monroe Doctrine against the French in Mexico. But the Conference came to naught. *See* MONROE DOCTRINE.

Hampton's Legion. A command of infantry, cavalry, and artillery, raised by Wade Hampton (b. 1818) in the civil war.

Handle. "To fly off the handle" is to lose one's temper, or, in the case of a lady, to jilt her lover. The phrase has a backwoods flavor, and probably arose from the great value of the trusty axe to the hardy pioneer; when the head flew off the handle, the tool was useless.

Handsome Beard. Baldwin IV., Earl of Flanders (fl. 1160–1186).

Handsome Englishman. A nickname current among the Continental soldiery under Turenne for John Churchill, Duke of Marlborough (fl. 1650–1722).

Handsome Swordsman. A nickname given to Joachim Murat (fl. 1767–1815), who was alike distinguished for his beauty of person and his dashing bravery as a cavalry officer.

Hanged, Drawn, and Quartered. The description of the capital sentence on a traitor, which consisted of drawing him on a hurdle to the place of execution, and after hanging him, dividing the body into quarters.

Hanging Judge. A name of reproach bestowed on the Earl of Norbury (d. 1831), Chief-Justice of Common Pleas in Ireland from 1820–1827.

Hangman of Lithuania. General Mouravieff, a Russian soldier. He was governor of Lithuania during the insurrection of 1863–1864, and the cruelties which were perpetrated under his rule gained him his nickname.

Hangman's Day. Friday, from the fact that executions usually occur on that day. Friday is superstitiously thought to be an unlucky day upon which to commence any enterprise, from the fact that our Lord was crucified on a Friday.

Hang up One's Fiddle. "To hang up one's fiddle" is an American proverb, meaning "to desist, to give it up." Sam Slick says, "When a man loses his temper, and ain't cool, he might as well hang up his fiddle;" and in "Dow's Sermons," p. 78, we find : "If a man at forty-two is not in a fair way to get his share of the world's spoils, he might as well hang up his fiddle, and be content to dig his way through life as best he may." In English literature the phrase is used in a totally different sense. "To hang up one's fiddle with one's hat" is said of a man who, while pleasant abroad, is churlish or stupid at home; *e.g.,* —

"'May be so,' retorted the lady. 'Mr. N—— can be very agreeable when I am absent, and anywhere but at home; I always say he hangs his fiddle up with his hat. Did you ever hear the saying before, Mr. Gurney?' 'Once, I think, ma'am,' said I, with becoming gravity. 'Once!' said Nubley; 'a thousand times; it is in all the jest-books.'" — THEODORE HOOK, *Gilbert Gurney.*

Hank Messell. The stage-name of Henry Everts.

Hank Wagoner. (Pseud.) L. E. Mosher, in the "Graphic," New York.

Hannah Bailey. The stage-name of Mrs. H. J. Sargent.

Hannibal ante portas. (Lat.) "Hannibal before the gates." An enemy at the gates.

Hanover Rat. The Jacobites used to affirm that the rat was brought over by the Hanoverians when they succeeded to the crown.

Curse me the British vermin, the rat ;
I know not whether he came in the Hanover ship.
TENNYSON, *Maud.*

Hans Breitman. (Pseud.) Charles Godfrey Leland, American humorous writer (b. 1824).

Hansel Monday. The first Monday of the New Year. *Hansel* means "gift" or "bribe."

Hans Hammergafferstein. (Pseud.) Henry Wadsworth Longfellow.

Hans von Rippach. Jack of Rippach, a Monsieur Tonson, or Mr. Nobody; some one summoned who does not exist. A gay German spark calls at a house and asks for Herr Hans von Rippach. An English joker asks for Monsieur Tonson.

Hans Yorkel. (Pseud.) A. Oakey Hall, ex-Mayor of New York.

Hants. Hampshire.

Happy Arabia. A wrong rendering of the Latin *Arabia Felix ;* i. e., Arabia on the right hand of Mecca, the holy city of the Mohammedans.

Happy Islands. The Canaries were anciently so called (*Fortunatæ Insulæ*).

Hara-kiri. The official suicide of Japan. Certain criminals in Japan are bound to kill themselves when commanded by the Government. This they do by ripping themselves up with two gashes crosswise, called *hara-kiri*, meaning " happy despatch." Often incorrectly written *hari-kari*.

Hard-Cider and Log-Cabin Campaign. In the campaign of 1840 the party cry was raised that General Harrison was a plain farmer, content to live in a log-cabin and drink hard cider. As there were no great issues before the people, the canvas degenerated into a great frolic, in which the cry of " Hard Cider and Log-Cabin " was oftenest heard.

Hard Money. Specie; as distinguished from "soft money," or paper currency. Both terms were current in the United States from 1878 to 1880. *See* GREENBACKERS.

Hard Shell. From 1848–1854 one of the two factions into which the Democratic party in New York was divided, the rival faction being the Soft Shells. The Hards were pro-slavery; the Softs were anti-slavery.

Hardy, The. (1) William Douglas (d. 1302), the famous defender of Berwick. (2) Philippe III. of France (fl. 1245–1285). (3) Philippe II., Duc de Bourgogne (fl. 1342–1382).

Hari-Kari. (Pseud.) Elias F. Carr.

Harlequin. (1) A punning nickname given to Robert Harley, Earl of Oxford, an English statesman (fl. 1661–1724), notorious for his intrigues. (2) Charles V. was so named by Francis I. of France.

Harmonia's Necklace. An unlucky gift that brings evil to all who possess it. Harmonia was the daughter of Mars and Venus. On the day of her marriage with King Cadmus she received a necklace, which proved fatal to all who possessed it.

Harmonia's Robe. On the marriage of Harmonia, Vulcan, to avenge the infidelity of her mother, made the bride a present of a robe dyed in all sorts of crimes, which infused wickedness and impiety into all her offspring. Both Harmonia and Cadmus, after having suffered many griefs and misfortunes, were changed into serpents.

Harness-cask. A conical cask bound with iron hoops, from which salt meat is served out at sea. The cask is usually painted green, and the hoops black. The resemblance of the latter to the black leathern straps of harness, or the way by which the cask is fastened to the deck, has probably given rise to the name.

Haro, Cry of. *See* CRY OF HARO.

Harold Klett. (Anagrammatic Pseud.) Halkett Lord, in " The Bookmart."

Harold's Stones. At Trelech, Monmouthshire, are three stones, one of which is fourteen feet above the ground, and probably boundary stones.

Harpies. In classic myth Aello, Celæno, and Ocypete, daughters of Neptune and Terra, and ministers of the vengeance of the gods.

Harpocrates. The Greek name of Horus, the Egyptian god of the sun and of silence. He was depicted with his finger in his mouth.

Harriet Annie. (Pseud.) Miss H. A. Wilkins, a well-known Canadian poet (fl. 1860).

Harriet Myrtle. (Pseud.) Mrs. Lydia F. F. Miller, wife of Hugh Miller (b. 1805).

Harrington. A nickname for a farthing. So called from Lord Harrington, to whom James I. granted a patent for making them of brass.

Harry Birch. Charles Albert White, author of some comic songs.

Harry Bluff. (Pseud.) Matthew Fontaine Maury (1806–1873), the American scientist in the "Southern Literary Messenger."

Harry Flash. (Pseud.) Henry Lyden Flash (b. 1835,), an American poet. *See* LYDEN ECLAIR.

Harry Franco. (Pseud.) Charles F. Briggs, American writer (b. 1813).

Harry Gringo. (Pseud.) Henry Augustus Wise, American naval officer (1819–1869).

Harry Hazell. (Pseud.) Justin Jones, *littérateur.*

Harry Montague. The stage-name of Henry J. Mann, the famous English comedian.

Harry Richmond. The stage-name of Henry Boyle.

Harry Scratchley. (Pseud.) John D. Sherwood, American writer (b. 1840).

Harry Soph. A cant name for a student at Cambridge who is studying law or medicine, and who wears a full-sleeved gown. The term is a corruption of *Heri-sophos*, more than a sophomore, or student of the second year.

Harry Twitcher. (1) Lord Henry Brougham (fl. 1778–1868) was so dubbed on account of an affection of his facial muscles. (2) Lord John Sandwich (fl. 1718–1792) was also thus named in the political squibs of his time.

Harry Vokes. The stage-name of Henry Langlin.

Hartford Convention. In December, 1814, several of the New England States were politically opposed to the administration of Madison, and particularly to the then existing war with England. Delegates assembled in convention at Hartford to discuss the situation. Peace was soon proclaimed; so nothing resulted from their deliberations. It has been charged, probably unjustly, that secession on the part of the New England States was mooted.

Hartford Wits. A coterie of bright and genial spirits, comprising Richard Alsop, Joel Barlow, Theodore Dwight, D. Humphreys, Lemuel Hopkins, and John Trumbull.

Hart Leigh. (Pseud.) John Thomas Denny, in "Wide Awake," etc.

Harût and Marût. "Two angels sent by Allah to adminster justice upon earth, because there was no righteous judgment among men. They acted well till Zohara, a beautiful woman, applied to them, and then they both fell in love with her. She asked them to tell her the secret name of God, and immediately she uttered it she was borne upward into heaven, where she became the planet Venus. As for the two angels, they were imprisoned in a cave near Babylon." — SALE'S *Koran*, ii.

"Allah bade
That two untempted spirits should descend,
Judges on earth. Harûth and Marûth went,
The chosen sentencers."

Harvest Moon. The "Harvest Moon" is described in Webster as the moon near the full at the time of harvest in England, or about the time of the autumnal equinox, when, by reason of a small angle of the ecliptic and the moon's orbit with the horizon, it rises nearly at the same time for several days. Commonly speaking, it is called the "Harvest Moon," because its visit is made at the time of harvest, enabling the busy farmer to continue his labors by its light.

Hatfield's Attempt. On May 11, 1800, during a review in Hyde Park, London, a pistol-shot was fired by a person unknown, which wounded a young gentleman standing near King George III. In the evening of the same day, when the king was at Drury Lane Theatre, Hatfield fired a pistol at him. He was arrested and confined as a lunatic till his death in 1841, aged sixty-nine.

Hats and Caps. Nicknames for two political parties in Sweden in the eighteenth century, — the former favorable to France, and wearing a French cocked hat as their badge, and the latter friendly to Russia, and wearing a Russian peaked cap.

Hattie Bernard. The stage-name of Mrs. C. W. Chase.

Hattie L. Richmond. The stage-name of Mrs. Eugene Canfield.

Hattie O'Neill. The stage-name of Mrs. R. F. Russell, *née* Crehan.

Hattie Richard. The stage-name of Mrs. G. D. Hart.

Hattie Richardson. The stage-name of Mrs. G. Drury Hart.

Hattie Russell. The stage-name of Mrs. Francis Labadie.

Haud passibus æquis. (Lat.) Not with equal steps.

Hauteur. (Fr.) Haughtiness.

Haut goût. (Fr.) High flavor.

Havercake Lads. The Thirty-third Regiment in the English service, "the Duke of Wellington's Own," is so nick-named.

Havoc. A war-cry inciting general massacre without quarter. It was forbidden in the ninth year of Richard II. on pain of death. Shakspeare in his "Julius Cæsar," says, —

"Cry ' Havoc,' and let slip the dogs of war!"

Haw-eater. In the political parlance of Ohio and the Western Reserve, a haw-eater "is a Democrat who never uses a pencil at an election, who sells all of his blackberries because he can get money for them, and who eats haws because he can't sell them."

Hawkeye State. Iowa; so named in memory of the famous Indian warrior.

Haymarket Riot, otherwise known as the "May Riot," occurred on the West Side, in Chicago, May 4, 1886, in which there was serious fighting between anarchists and police. Dynamite bombs were thrown by some of the former, five policemen were killed, and twenty of the mob shot down by the police. *See* BOMB CITY.

Hazard Désiré. (Pseud.) Octave Feuillet, in "Le National," Paris, 1845.

H. B. C. Hudson's Bay Company.

H. B. M. His or Her Britannic Majesty.

H. C. House of Commons; Herald's College.

H. C. M. His or Her Catholic Majesty.

Hdkf. Handkerchief.

H. E. *Hoc est.* That is, or this is.

Head Act. A sanguinary law passed at Trim, in Ireland, in 1465, by the Earl of Desmond, Deputy. It empowered citizens to cut off the head of any thief or marauder caught red-handed, and put it on a stake on the castle of Trim, and to levy for every head so cut off a small tax upon landowners. Much slaughter is said to have ensued.

Head of Africa. The name by which the Cape of Good Hope is sometimes referred to.

Head of Iron. A sobriquet conferred on John Forbes, the British general (1710–1759), because of his obstinacy.

He-and-She Bibles. Editions of the Scriptures issued in 1611; so named from the variant readings of Ruth iii. 15, — one reading "He went into the city," the other "She went," etc.

Heartless Old Man. *See* GRAND OLD MAN.

Heart of Ireland. The town of Athlone. It is situated at almost the exact geographical centre of the island.

Heart of Midlothian. The old jail in Edinburgh was, for many years, known by this poetical sobriquet. Edinburgh is the capital of the county of Midlothian. The jail was torn down in 1817. A novel, by Sir Walter Scott, has this name for its title.

Heart of the Commonwealth. Worcester, Mass. It is situated nearly at the centre of the State, and wields great political and social influence. *See also* ACADEMIC CITY.

Heart of the Empire. The Russian nickname for Moscow.

Heatherbell. (Pseud.) Eleanor Smith, in "Good Words."

Heaven-sent Minister. William Pitt (1759–1806).

Heb. Hebrew; Hebrews.

Hebe. In classic myth daughter of Jupiter and Juno, and goddess of youth. She was constituted cup-bearer to the gods.

Hébertistes. Partisans of the demagogue, Jaques Réné Hébert, chief of the Cordeliers, in the French Revolution. *See* FATHER HÉBERT.

Hecate. In classic myth a cruel goddess, of hideous aspect, who sends on the earth all kinds of evil spirits and terrible appearances. She had all the forces of the universe at her command.

Hecatomb of Vera Cruz. In the night of June 24, 1879, Teran, then governor of Vera Cruz, executed nine citizens without any trial whatever; and this act is known in Mexican annals by the above name.

Hector. In classic myth son of Priam and of Hecuba, and the bravest and noblest of all the Trojans who fought against the Greeks.

Hector Bull-us. (Pseud.) James Kirke Paulding.

Hector of Germany. Joachim II., Elector of Brandenburg (fl. 1514–1571).

Hecuba. Second wife of Priam, and mother of nineteen children. When Troy was taken by the Greeks, she fell to the lot of Ulysses. She was afterward metamorphosed into a dog, and threw herself into the sea.

Hedge-priest. A poor or vagabond parson. Shakspeare uses the phrase, "hedge-born swain" as the very opposite of one gentle-born.

Heeler. In American political parlance one who, following at the heels of some local leader, obeys his behests and is, for the time being, his tool.

H. E. I. C. Honorable East India Company.

H. E. I. C. S. Honorable East India Company's Service.

Heimdall. In Norse mythology son of the nine virgins, all sisters, said to live at the further extremity of the bridge Bifrost and to keep the keys of heaven. He is watchman or sentinel of Asgard, sleeps less than a bird, sees even in sleep, can hear the grass grow and the wool on a lamb's back. Heimdall, at the end of the world, will wake the gods with his trumpet.

Heir of the Republic. A name given to Napoleon I. In 1799 he overthrew the Directory and made himself First

Consul of France, with regal powers and prerogatives.

Hel. In Scandinavian mythology the goddess of the dead, who dwelt beneath one of the three roots of the sacred ash, Yggdrasil, and daughter of the fire-god Loki, and of Angurboda. She was cast into Niflheim by Odin, where she was given especial charge of all who died of sickness or old age.

Helderberg War. *See* ANTI-RENT MOVEMENT.

Helen. In classic myth daughter of Jupiter and of Leda, wife of Menelaus, king of Sparta, and the most beautiful woman of her time. In the absence of her husband, Paris carried her off to Troy, which was the cause of the war against that city.

Helen. (Pseud.) Mrs. Sarah Helen Power Whitman.

Helena Dixon. (Pseud.) Adeline E. Story, in the New York "Weekly."

Helena Secor. The stage-name of Mrs. Helen Tons.

Helen Barry. The stage-name of Mrs. H. S. Holman.

Helen Campbell. (Pseud.) Mrs. Helen C. Weeks.

Hélène Maigille, Mme. The stage-name of Mrs. Helen Magill.

Helen Fawcitt. The stage-name of Lady Theodore Martin, the English actress.

Helen Forsythe. The stage-name of Mrs. Henry Bagge.

Helen Mar. (Pseud.) Mrs. D. M. F. Walker, *littérateur*.

Helen Mathers. The pen-name of Mrs. Reeve.

Helen Ottolengui. The stage-name of Mrs. George Monserrat.

Helen Sedgewick. The stage-name of Helen Brady, *née* Helen Perry.

Helen's Fire. A comazant, called "Saint Helme's" or "Saint Elmo's fire" by the Spaniards; the "fires of Saint Peter and Saint Nicholas" by the Italians; and "Castor and Pollux" by the ancient Romans. This electric light will sometimes play about the masts of ships. If only one appears, foul weather may be looked for; but if two or more flames appear, the worst of the storm is over.

Helios. In classic myth the sun-god; the same as Apollo or Phœbus.

Hell and Tommy. In some parts of England it is very common for an angry man to threaten another that he will "play hell and tommy" with him. It is thought that this is a corruption of "Hal and Tommy," and that the allusion is to Henry VIII. and his unscrupulous minister, Thomas Cromwell, who seized and rifled the religious houses, and turned out their occupants to starve.

Helle. In classic myth daughter of Athamas and Nephele. She was drowned in the strait called, after her, the Hellespont.

Hell is paved with Good Intentions. This is a Portuguese proverb.

> . . . saying "they *meant well*."
> 'T is pity "that such meanings should pave hell."
> BYRON, *Don Juan*.

Hell Kettles. Certain cavities three miles long at Oxen-le-Field, in Durham, England.

Hell's Half-Acre. The fanciful name given to a locality in the Yellowstone National Park, from the excessively weird and terrible appearance of the scenery.

Hell Shoe. In Norse mythology as indispensable for the journey to Valhalla as the obolus for crossing the Styx.

Helluo librorum. (Lat.) A bookworm.

Helmet of Invisibility. The helmet of Perseus rendered the wearer invisible. This was in reality the helmet of Hades; and after Perseus had slain Medusa he restored it, together with the winged sandals and magic wallet. The gorgon's head he presented to Minerva, who placed it in the middle of her ægis. Mambrino's helmet had the same magical power, though Don Quixote, even in his midsummer madness, never thought himself invisible when he donned the barber's basin.

Help = SERVANT. The word "help" was probably coined to avoid the use of the word "servant" in this "land of the free."

Helvetia. The old Latin name of Switzerland; often used as a poetical appellation in modern literature. The country is often mentioned as the "Helvetian Republic."

> See, from the ashes of Helvetia's pile,
> The whitened skull of old Servetus smile.
> HOLMES.

Helvetian Mountains. The Swiss Alps.

'T was sunset, and the *ranz-dez-vaches* was sung;
And lights were o'er th' Helvetian Mountains
  flung,
That tinged the lakes like molten gold below.
CAMPBELL, *Theodoric.*

Henricians. A religious sect, so called after its founder, Henricus, an Italian monk, who in the twelfth century undertook to reform certain vices of the clergy. They rejected infant baptism, festivals, and ceremonies.

Henrietta Beebe. The professional name of Mrs. W. H. Lawton, the famous singer.

Henrietta Crossman. The stage-name of Mrs. Sedley Brown.

Henry Ellen. (Pseud.) James Barron Hope, an American poet (b. 1827). He first won literary distinction from a series of poems published in a Baltimore periodical under the pen-name of "The late Henry Ellen, Esq."

Henry Gréville. (Pseud.) Alice Marie Celeste Fleury Durand, the French novelist and feuilletonist.

Henry Hayes. (Pseud.) Mrs. Ellen Olney Kirk, author of "The Story of Margaret Kent," 1885.

Henry Irving. The stage-name of Henry Brodribb, the English actor.

Henry J. Thurston. (Pseud.) Francis Turner Palgrave, English poet and art-writer (b. 1824).

Henry Karlsten. (Pseud.) Charles Henry Lüders, in the Philadelphia "Evening Bulletin."

Henry Richards. (Pseud.) Richard Henry Stoddard, in his contributions to the "Aldine," New York.

Henry Villard. (Pseud.) Heinrich Hilgard, a famous correspondent of the New York "Tribune" during the American civil war.

Hephæstus. The Greek name of the god called Vulcan by the Romans. *See* VULCAN.

Her. Heraldry.

Hera. The same as Juno (*q. v.*).

Heracleidæ. In classic myth the descendants of Hercules.

Hercules. In classic myth the son of Zeus and Alcmene, and the most celebrated hero of the Greek legends. He was the ideal of human perfection as conceived in the heroic ages; *i. e.,* the greatest physical strength, connected with every high quality of mind and

character which those ages recognized. He had a bitter enemy in Hera, who, knowing that the child who should be born that day was fated to rule over all the descendants of Perseus, contrived to prolong the travail of Alcmene, who was the daughter of Alcæus, son of Perseus, and hasten that of the wife of Sthenelus, another son of Perseus, who after a pregnancy of seven months gave birth to a son, named Eurystheus. Eurystheus thus, by decree of Fate, became chief of the Perseidæ. He was also called Alcides, after his grandfather Alcæus. *See* TWELVE LABORS OF HERCULES.

Hercules of Attica. Theseus. His career, according to classic legends, resembles greatly that of his illustrious namesake.

Hercules of Egypt. Sesostris (fl. 1500 B. C.).

Hercules of Music. Christopher Glück (fl. 1714-1787).

Hercules of the Jews. Samson (d. 1113 B. C.).

Hercules, Pillars of. The fanciful name given by the ancients to the two rocks forming the entrance of the Mediterranean at the Strait of Gibraltar. Their erection was ascribed by the Greeks to Hercules, on the occasion of his journey to the kingdom of Geryon. The pillars are not mentioned in Homer, though he speaks of Ulysses' passage out of the Mediterranean into the ocean and back, showing an apparent knowledge of the existence of the strait. The first author who mentions them is Pindar, who places them at Gades (Cadiz), and his opinion had many followers in later times. The most general opinion, however, identified them with Calpe (now Gibraltar) and Abyla (now Ceuta).

Hercules Secundus. A title assumed by Commodus, the Roman Emperor (fl. 161-192). He delighted in personally appearing in the gladiatorial arena, where he performed great feats.

Hermaphrodite. Son of Venus and Mercury. At the age of fifteen, he bathed in a fountain of Caria, when Salmacis, the fountain nymph, fell in love with him, and prayed the gods to make the two one body. Her prayers being heard, the two became united into one, but still preserved the double sex.

Not that bright spring where fair Hermaphrodite
Grew into one with wanton Salmacis . . .
. . . may dare compare with this.
PHIN. FLETCHER, *The Purple Island.*

Hermes. The Greek name of the Roman Mercury.

Hermes. (Pseud.) William Torrey Harris.

Hermetic Art. The science of alchemy, so named from Hermes Trismegistus, its reputed founder.

Hermine. (Pseud.) Susan Blanchard Elder, daughter of the late Gen. Albert Blanchard, U. S. A. She was born in Louisiana in 1835, and has written much, especially for Roman Catholic periodicals.

Hermione. In classic myth the only daughter of Menelaus and Helen, and famed for her beauty.

Hermit Nation, The. Japan, in allusion to the exclusive policy of its people that for so many years closed it to the influences of Western civilization. Corea has also received the same title.

Hermit of Newfane. David Brown, of Newfane, Vt., a noted book-collector (d. 1873).

Hermit of New York. (Pseud.) Washington Frothingham, American clergyman (b. 1832), correspondent of various journals in inland cities. Other signatures of his are " Martel," " Macaulay," and " Rosicrucian."

Hero. In classic myth a priestess of Venus, at Sestos, in Thrace, adored by Leander, who used to swim across the Hellespont to visit her. In one of these passages he was drowned, and Hero in despair threw herself into the sea.

Herodotus of Old London. J. Stow (1525–1605).

Heroic Age. The period when the heroes, or those called the children of the gods, are supposed to have lived.

Hero of a Hundred Fights. (1) Horatio Nelson (fl. 1758–1805). (2) The Duke of Wellington.

Hero of Austerlitz. Napoleon I.

Hero of Debt. The elder Sheridan was so named. Never was sobriquet more aptly applied.

Hero of Fable. The Duc de Guise, Called by the French " L'Héro de la Fable " (1614–1664).

Hero of History. (1) The Duc d'Enghien; called by the French " L'Héro de l'Histoire." (2) The great Condé (1621–1687).

Hero of Modern Italy. Garibaldi (1807–1882).

Hero of the Crater. William Mahone, senator (b. 1826), was so named for his heroic conduct in the fighting around Petersburg, Va., during the civil war.

Hero of the Nile. Horatio Nelson (fl. 1758–1805); so named in memory of his great victory over the French fleet in Aboukir Bay.

Herp. Herpetology.

Hesba Stretton. (Pseud.) Miss Hannah Smith, English novelist (b. 1841).

Hesperides. In classic myth three daughters of Hesperus, and guardians of the golden apples which Juno, on her nuptials with Jupiter, received from Terra. They were kept in a garden on an island beyond Mount Atlas in Africa.

Hesychasts. The " Quietists " of the East in the fourteenth century. They placed perfection in contemplation.

He that Runs may Read. Habakkuk ii. 2 reads, " That he may run that readeth it ; " but this is not the passage from which the common phrase " He that runs may read " is derived. That phrase is William Cowper's, not Habakkuk's ; and it occurs in the " Tirocinium," a poem directed against the want of discipline and inattention to morals that in Cowper's opinion prevailed in the English public schools :

" But truths on which depend our main concern,
That 't is our shame and misery to learn,
Shine by the side of every path we tread
With such a lustre, he that runs may read."

Hetty Tracy. The stage-name of Mrs. Jesse Williams.

Heu pietas! heu prisca fides! (Lat.) Alas for our piety ! Alas for our ancient faith !

Heureux hasard. (Fr.) " Happy chance." A fortunate chance.

He who Steals my Purse, etc. Shakspeare probably got the idea upon which he founded these words from the " Homily against Contention," set forth in the time of Edward VI., from which the following is an extract : —

" And many times there cometh less hurt of a thing than of a railing tongue ; for the one taketh away a man's good name, the other taketh away his riches, which is of much less value and estimation than is his good name."

Hewson the Cobbler. Col. John Hewson, who " rose from the profession of a cobbler to a high rank in Cromwell's army."

Hf.-bd. Half-bound.

H.-G. Horse-Guards.

Hg. *Hydrargyrum.* Mercury.

H. H. His or Her Highness ; His Holiness (the Pope).

Hhd. Hogshead.

Hibernia. The old Latin name for Ireland, often found in modern poetry.

Hibernian Homburg. The town of Lisdoomarna, a popular watering-place on the west coast of Ireland.

Hibernian St. Bartholomew. A name given to a massacre of Protestants by Catholics in Ireland shortly after the outbreak of the rebellion in 1640. According to various accounts, from 50,000 to 200,000 men, women, and children fell victims to the fury of the Irish.

Hibernicus. (Pseud.) De Witt Clinton, American statesman (1769–1828).

Hic et ubique. (Lat.) "Here and everywhere." Perpetually changing; here and there and everywhere.

Hic jacet. (Lat.) Here he (or she) lies.

Hickory. (Pseud.) Thomas W. Jackson, in "Truth," New York.

Hic labor, hoc opus est. (Lat.) "This is labor, this is work." It is a very difficult affair.

Hic sepultus. (Lat.) Here is buried.

Hid-Allan. (Pseud.) Allan Cunningham, in the London "Star," etc.

Hidden Island. *See* LOST ISLAND.

Hier. *Hierosolyma.* Jerusalem.

Hieroclean Legacy. The legacy of jokes. Hierocles, in the fifth century, was the first person who compiled witticisms ; after long labor he mustered twenty-eight, which he left to the world as his legacy.

Hierophilos. (Pseud.) Patrick Eugene Moriarty. *See* ERMITE.

Higher than Gilderoy's Kite. The origin of this expression is obscure. Gilderoy was a famous Scotch robber, who lived in the time of Queen Mary ; he was finally hanged. So, too, was a second Gilderoy, who robbed Cardinal Richelieu and Oliver Cromwell.

Highfaluten. Probably a corruption of "high flighting," though it may be from the Dutch *verlooten*, a term originating in the Western States of America to signify high-flown, stilted, or bombastic language. The word is be-

coming domesticated in England, and has even crept into a "Times" leader.

High License, Low License. Terms latterly in use in the United States, and denoting two phases of the temperance agitation, — one wherein a high license fee is imposed as a repressive measure, the other where the license fee is moderate or merely nominal. The opposite term is "No License" (*q. v.*).

High-minded Federalists. The defeat of the coalition of Clintonians and Federalists in New York State in 1815 practically killed the latter party in that State. What remained of it usually supported the Clintonians. A small section, however, opposed the Clintonians, which they called a personal party, and supported the Bucktails. Their reference to themselves as "high-minded" men led to the above nickname.

H. I. H. His or Her Imperial Highness.

Hil. Hilary.

Hilarius. (Pseud.) W. Feistkorn, in the German edition of "Puck."

Hilda. (Pseud.) (1) Miss Hilda Siller, of Milwaukee, a well-known writer of short stories and sketches. (2) Mrs. Peter E. Abel.

Hildegarde. (Pseud.) Mrs. Josephine R. Hoskins, in various Southern periodicals.

Hill City. Lynchburg, Va., and Rome, Ga., are so named. *See* CITY OF HILLS.

Hill of Scandal, The. The Mount of Olives is so called by Milton.

Hill of Tarik. The Rock of Gibraltar, named after the Berber leader, Tarik, who conquered the fort in 711.

Hil. T. Hilary Term.

Hinc illæ lacrimæ. (Lat.) Hence those tears.

Hind. Hindu; Hindustan; Hindustanee.

Hindus. A name given to the Know-Nothing party, in consequence of their candidate for the presidency, Daniel Ullman, having been charged with being a native of Calcutta.

Hindustan Regiment. The Seventy-sixth Regiment in the English Army ; so named because it first distinguished itself in India. *See* SEVEN-AND-SIX-PENNIES.

Hindustan, Rome of. *See* ROME OF HINDUSTAN.

Hipp. Hippocrates.

Hippocratic Oath. A solemn engagement entered into in ancient times by young men about to commence the practice of medicine. The formula, which is ascribed to Hippocrates himself, is at once comprehensive and binding. It ties the asseverator down, in the most rigorous manner, to the practice of his profession on the highest principles of humanity and honor, and pledges him to the most disinterested and exalted brotherhood with all those who are connected legitimately with the healing art, and to acts of kindness toward their offspring. In addition, it deals with the whole tenor of his morals, and essays to secure the utmost purity in this relation.

Hippolytus. In classic myth a son of Theseus, king of Athens, by Antiope. His stepmother, Phædra, fell in love with him, but Hippolytus not responding to her passion, she accused him to her husband of insulting her. The king cursed his son, and implored the gods to destroy him, whereupon Hippolytus was thrown out of his chariot and trampled to death by his steeds. Æsculapius, however, restored him to life.

Hippomenes. In classic myth the youth who captured Atalanta in a foot-race, and thus obtained her for his bride. *See* ATALANTA.

Hired Man, Hired Girl. Two terms coined in the United States to avoid the use of the word "servant."

Hi-Ski-Hi. (Pseud.) Mrs. Caroline E. S. Norton in her letters to Hayward.

His Superfluous Excellency. A title humorously suggested by the Democrats in 1791 for the Vice-President, in mockery of the title desired by some of the Federalists for the President; namely, "His Highness the President of the United States, and protector of their liberties."

Hist. History.

Historian of the Long Parliament. Thomas May (fl. 1595–1650).

Historicus. (Pseud.) William George Vernon Harcourt, English writer on international law (b. 1800).

H. J. S. *Hic jacet sepultus.* Here lies buried.

H. L. House of Lords.

H. M. His Majesty.

H. M. P. *Hoc monumentum posuit.* Erected this monument.

H. M. S. His or Her Majesty's Ship.

Hobbima of England. John Crome, the English landscape-painter.

Hobbima of Scotland. P. Nasmyth, a Scottish landscape-painter (b. 1831).

Hobson's Choice. One Tobias Hobson was the first man in England to hire out hack-horses. When a customer appeared he was led into the stable, where there was a goodly array of beasts, but was obliged to take the one standing nearest the door, so that every customer was alike well served, according to his chance. So it became a byword, when what ought to have been one's election was forced upon one to say, "Hobson's Choice."

Hoc age. (Lat.) "Do this." Attend to what you are doing.

Hock Day, or Hock Tuesday. The second Tuesday after Easter Day, long celebrated in England as the anniversary of the day on which the English slew and expelled the Danes who had ravaged the coasts for two hundred and fifty years.

Hodie mihi, cras tibi. (Lat.) It belongs to me to-day, and to you to-morrow.

Hodie nihil, cras credo. (Lat.) To-morrow I shall trust, not to-day.

Hodur. In Scandinavian mythology the blind god who killed his brother Baldur (*q. v.*). Hodur typifies darkness and night, as Baldur does light and day.

Hogarth of Scotland. David Allan (fl. 1744–1796).

Hogen-Mogen. A sobriquet for Holland, a corruption of *Hoogë en Mogendé* ("High and Mighty"), the Dutch term of address to their States-General.

> But I have sent him for a token
> To your Low-Country Hogen-Mogen.
> BUTLER, *Hudibras.*

Hog-wallows. Alternate hollows and hillocks caused by denudation. A Western term.

Hoi polloi. (Gr.) "The many." The people; the multitude; the name applied at Cambridge to those who do not graduate in honors, — abbreviated "the poll."

Hole-in-the-Wall, The. (1) A landmark, well known to seamen by this name, consisting of a natural perforation of the rock, at the southeast extremity of the island of Abaco, one of the Bahamas. (2) A famous resort of lobbyists and legislators in Washington, D. C., where refreshments were served.

"One of the Senators suggested to John Beall, who was sergeant-at-arms away back in the thirties, that it would be a good thing to have a little luncheon set near the hall, where Senators could run out and get a bite. So Beall's wife boiled hams and made bread, and Beall brought them down and set them up in a little circular room just north of the rotunda and on the east side of the corridor. Soon he added pickles, nuts, salads, and delicacies, and the place became very popular. In a little while the place became a regular saloon. There was no bar, not even a sideboard, the bottles and demijohns being set in rows on the shelves. For a long time the Senators used to go in there and help themselves to whatever they wanted, and the expense was run in under the contingent account. After a time the stock got so large and popular that it was no uncommon thing to see a dozen Senators and their friends in there drinking and having good times. The little room, not more than twelve or fifteen feet in diameter, and taking its name from the fact that it was simply a hole in the wall, lighted only by one window, was often badly crowded, and a good deal of confusion resulted in the arrangement of the stock, so that the Senator who had a favorite brand of liquor had much trouble in finding it. Thus it became necessary to put a man in charge; and after a time the expense became so great that it was not easy to work it off in the contingent account. Then the Senators were required to pay for what they got, and after this was done the popularity of the 'Hole in the Wall' fell off very rapidly. But it was kept up until some years after the Senate moved into its present chamber."

Holiday Phrases. Set speeches, high-flown phrases. So holiday "manners," holiday "clothes," meaning the "best" or those put on to make the best appearance. Hotspur, speaking of a fop sent to demand his prisoners, says to the king:

In many holiday and lady terms
He questioned me.
1 *Henry IV.* act i. sc. 3.

Holl. Holland.

Holme Lee. (Pseud.) Miss Harriett Parr, English writer (b. 1837).

Holy Alliance. A name given to the compact formed between the sovereigns of Russia, Austria, and Prussia, in 1815, ostensibly for the humane and liberal administration of their respective governments, but really to preserve the power and influence of the existing dynasties. Most of the other European rulers acceded to it, and the treaty was formally made public in the "Frankfort Journal," Feb. 2, 1816. It was in virtue of this league that Austria, in 1821,

crushed the revolutions in Naples and Piedmont, and that France, in 1823, restored absolutism in Spain. Subsequently both France and England seceded, after which it became a mere *nominis umbra.* A special article of the treaty excluded forever the members of the Bonaparte family from any European throne.

Holy Birds. *See* PILLAR SAINTS.

Holy City. An appellation given by different peoples to that particular city whence proceed all their religious traditions and worship. By Jew and Christian Jerusalem is so named ; by Catholics, Rome; by Mohammedans, Damascus, Mecca, and Medina; by the Hindus, Benares ; by the Mohammedans of India, Allahabad; by the ancient Incas, Cuzco.

Holy Coat. A relic carefully and reverently preserved in the cathedral of Treves. It is alleged to be the seamless coat of our Saviour, and to have been discovered in the fourth century by the Empress Helena in her memorable visit to Palestine. The Treves relics were concealed from the Normans, in the ninth century, in crypts; but the holy coat was rediscovered in 1196, and then solemnly exhibited to the public gaze, which did not take place again till 1512, when, multitudes flocking to see and venerate it, Leo X. appointed it to be exhibited every seven years.

Holy Faith, City of the. *See* CITY OF THE HOLY FAITH.

Holy Fridays. The Fridays in Ember Weeks.

Holy Handkerchief. The napkin or handkerchief which Saint Veronica lent to the Saviour on the way to the cross, to wipe the sweat and blood from his brow, and upon which, says the legend, was miraculously imprinted an exact likeness of his features.

Holy Innocents. *See* INNOCENTS.

Holy Island. (1) Ireland has been so named from the number of saints in its calendar. (2) Guernsey, one of the Channel Islands, because of the monks that formerly flocked thither. (3) The island of Rügen, so named by Varini. (4) A name now generally given to Lindisfarne, on the coast of Northumberland, where the famous Saint Cuthbert ruled over a Saxon abbey, founded 635. It is a peninsula, insulated at high tide.

Holy Land, The. (1) A name generally given among modern peoples to Palestine, the scene of Christ's birth, ministry, and death ; *e. g.*, Latin, *Terra Sancta;* French, *Terre Sainte;* Spanish, *Tierra Santa;* Italian, *Terra Santa*. It is first applied in Zech. ii. 12. (2) Elis, a kingdom of ancient Greece, was so named. Here was the temple of the Olympian Zeus, and sacred games were held every four years. (3) Arabia is so named by Mohammedans, because Mohammed was born there. (4) The Buddhists of China call India the Holy Land, because it was the country of Sakya Muni.

Holy League. (1) A coalition of the Pope, Venice, etc., against Louis XII. of France, 1510. (2) A politico-religious association in France to prevent the accession of Henry of Navarre (who was then of the reformed religion), was commenced at Peronne in 1576, and lasted till 1593, when Henry embraced Romanism, called "The League" by way of pre-eminence.

Holy Maid of Kent. Elizabeth Barton, a woman popularly endowed with miraculous powers, who was beheaded April 21, 1534, for high treason, in that she predicted various calamities for the English nation and people.

Holy Mountain, The. A name given by modern Greeks to Mount Athos. The flanks of this eminence are dotted with twenty-two convents, besides a number of chapels, cells, grottos, caves, etc., the abodes of over three thousand monks and hermits. It was the convents of Mount Athos that yielded to the libraries of Europe so many priceless MSS., the masterpieces of ancient literature.

Holy Places. Those localities intimately associated with leading events in the life of Christ ; *e. g.*, Gethsemane, the Mount of Olives, the Supper-Room, the Church of the Ascension, the Sepulchre, the Tomb of the Virgin, etc.

Holy Rood (*Rode* or *Rod*). An old name for the cross so often erected in churches.

Holy Saturday. The Saturday before Easter.

Holy Thursday. Ascension Day, forty days after Easter, and ten before Whitsuntide. *See* MAUNDY-THURSDAY.

Holy Union. *See* HOLY LEAGUE.

Holy Wars. Another name for the Crusades.

Holy-Water Sprinkle. A military club set with spikes. So called derisively, because it makes the blood to flow as water sprinkled by an aspergillum.

Holy Week. *See* WEEK OF INDULGENCES.

H. O. M. *See* GRAND OLD MAN.

Hombre de un libro. (Span.) A man of one book.

Homely = PLAIN. Americans say a girl is "homely" when they mean she possesses plain features, and thus a word denoting a woman's most lovable quality is perverted into a term of reproach.

Homer of Britain. John Milton.

Homer of Ferrara. Ariosto (fl. 1474–1533) is so named by Tasso.

Homer of Scotland. William Wilkie (fl. 1721–1772), author of the "Epigoniad."

Homer of the Celts. Ossian.

Homer of the Franks. Angilbert (d. 814) was so named by Charlemagne.

Home Rulers. An Irish parliamentary party, under the leadership of Charles Stewart Parnell, having for its object the granting of legislative control of Irish affairs to an Irish Parliament. Below will be found a chronology of the movement : —

Mr. Isaac Butt, a leader of the movement, elected M. P. for Limerick, 1871.
Home Rule advocated by Archbishop McHale and others of the Romanist clergy in Ireland, 1873.
The programme of the party, requiring an Irish Parliament of Queen, Lords, and Commons, and other powers, published Oct. 25, 1873.
A conference at the Rotunda, Dublin, reported a failure, Nov. 18–21, 1873.
A motion in the Commons in favor of Home Rule defeated (314 to 52), March 20, 1874.
Mr. I. Butt's motion for a committee on the subject, June 30 ; was negatived (458 to 61), July 2, 3, 1875 ; again (291 to 61), June 30, July 1, 1876 ; again (417 to 67), April 24, 1877.
Stormy convention at Dublin, Mr. Butt chairman, August 21, 22, 1877.
Meeting of Home Rule M. P.'s at Dublin, Oct. 9, 1877.
Mr. Butt yields to the obstructionists, January ; resigns, April, 1878.
Meeting at Dublin, October 14 ; continued dissensions between moderate party (Mr. Butt and others) and obstructives (Mr. Charles Stewart Parnell and others), October, November, 1878.
Death of Mr. Butt, May 5 ; succeeded by Mr. William Shaw, 1879.
Mr. Parnell proposes election of a convention to meet at Dublin, September 11 ; this is opposed by Mr. Shaw, Mitchell Henry, and others, September, 1879.
Meeting at Dublin ; pronounced opposition to British Government, Jan. 20, 21, 1880.

About sixty-five Home Rulers in the new Parliament, under Mr. Shaw and Mr. Parnell, April, 1880.

Mr. Parnell chosen by forty-five as parliamentary chairman, May 17, 1880.

Thirty-one Home Rulers voted with the Government, sixteen with Parnell, July 13, 1880.

Home Rule convention at Newcastle-on-Tyne, August 9, 1880.

Meeting at Dublin, Mr. Justin McCarthy appointed vice-president; resolution to resist coercion in Ireland adopted, Dec. 27, 1880.

Trial of Mr. Parnell and others at Dublin, Dec. 28, 1880, to Jan. 25, 1881.

Strong manifesto of Mr. Parnell; a counter one by Mr. Shaw, February, 1881.

From 1881–1885 the party met with varied success, until in the new Parliament of 1886 Mr. Parnell held the balance of power, and Mr. Gladstone committed himself and the Liberal Government to Home Rule. But it is doubtful if the "Grand Old Man," even had he continued in power, would have proved strong enough to carry out the proposed innovation, and the accession of a Conservative ministry in 1886 proved a decided set-back to the cause. There is at this writing no immediate prospect of its introduction.

Homme d'esprit. (Fr.) A witty man.

Homme d'état. (Fr.) A statesman.

Homme médiocre. (Fr.) A man with mediocrity of talent.

Homo. (Pseud.) Charles S. Westcott.

Homo multarum literarum. (Lat.) A man of great learning.

Homo nullorum hominum. (Lat.) "A man of no men." A man fit for nobody's society.

Homo perpaucorum hominum. (Lat.) "A man of very few men." A man who associates with a select few.

Homunculi quanti sunt. (Lat.) How many little-minded men there are.

Hon. Honorable.

Honest John. A nickname conferred on John Sherman, the American statesman.

Honey = FLATTER. "To honey" means "to cajole or to flatter."

Honey-fugling. A genuine Americanism, meaning "cheating or defrauding one's creditors."

Honey Madness. There is a rhododendron about Trebizond, the flowers of which the bees are fond of; but if any one eats the honey he becomes mad.

Hong Merchants. Those merchants who were alone permitted by the Government of China to trade with China, till the restriction was abolished in 1842. The Chinese applied the word "hong" to foreign factories situated at Canton.

Honi soit qui mal y pense. (Old Fr.) Evil be to him that evil thinks.

Honor and Glory Griffiths. Captain Griffiths, in the reign of William IV., was so called, because he used to address his letters to the Admiralty, to "Their Honors and Glories at the Admiralty."

Honores mutant mores. (Lat.) Honors change manners.

Honor of the Spear. A tournament.

He came to Runa's echoing halls, and sought the honor of the spear. — OSSIAN, *The War of Inis-Thona.*

Honos habet onus. (Lat.) Honor has its load or responsibility.

Hookanit Bee, Esq. (Pseud.) S. R. Wigram, an American writer of the present day.

Hookey Walker. "Notes and Queries" says that the original Hookey Walker was John Walker, who was a clerk in the employ of Longman, Clementi & Co., Cheapside, London. He had a crooked or hooked nose, from which his nickname was derived. He was employed by the firm as a kind of spy upon his fellow-servants. Jack's reports of the malpractices going on were always met by so many preconcerted denials that at last his reports were discredited and he was dismissed. In course of time any dubious statement in the city was received with the remark "Oh, that 's Hookey Walker!" and in that way the name of the old clerk has passed into a proverb. Another authority says the term is derived from the name of a London police magistrate of great acuteness and incredulity, who had a remarkably hooked nose. This peculiarity, it is said, also gave rise to the term "beak," as applied to magistrates generally.

Hooks and Codfish. The names of two rival factions in Holland. The Hooks were the followers of Margaret, Countess of Holland; the Codfish were the adherents of her son William, who endeavored to supplant her. Their bickerings caused a civil war in 1347, which continued many years.

Hoosier. (Pseud.) Samuel V. Morris, in various Western papers.

Hoosier Poet. A sobriquet bestowed on James Whitcomb Riley.

Hoosier State. Indiana. The people of the State are called "Hoosiers," a word said to be a corruption of *hussar*, or *husher*, formerly a colloquial name for a fighter or a bully throughout the West.

Horace Hornem. (Pseud.) George Gordon, Lord Byron, English poet (1788–1824).

Horace of England. Cowley, the poet (fl. 1618–1667), was effusively declared by the Duke of Buckingham to be the "Pindar, Horace, and Virgil of England."

Horace of France. Jean Macrinus (fl. 1490–1557). Pierre Jean de Béranger, otherwise named "the French Burns," is also known by this title.

Horaces of Spain. The brothers Lupercio and Bartolomé Argensola.

Horæ. In classic myth Eunonia, Dice, and Irene, daughters of Jupiter and of Themis, who kept watch over the changes of the seasons.

Hora fugit. (Lat.) The hour or time flies.

Horicon. A name applied to Lake George by the novelist Cooper. It is popularly believed that *Horicon* is a word of Indian origin, but the red men called the lake *Andialarocte* ("there the lake shuts itself"). Father Jogues, the French missionary pioneer, named it St. Sacramente, because he discovered it the day before that festival.

Horn. Another name for a dram or "drink" of liquor.

Hornes. (Pseud.) G. C. Fisher, *littérateur*.

Horn-mad. Quite mad. Madness in cattle was supposed to arise from a distemper in the internal substance of their horns, and furious or mad cattle had their horns bound with straw.

Horn of Africa. Somali Land, that part of Africa which lies east of a line drawn south from the head of the Gulf of Aden to the Indian Ocean.

Horn of Fontarabia. Roland, one of the greatest heroes of chivalry, was a nephew and the favorite captain of Charlemagne. He was killed while fighting gallantly at the battle of Roncesvalles in 778. He was of gigantic stature, and so strong that he could pull up the tallest pine by the roots and wield it as a club. His sword Durandal split a block of marble without dulling its edge. Among other wonderful achievements it is related that at the battle of Roncesvalles, when fatally wounded, he sounded his marvellous horn, called Olivant, which was to give Charlemagne notice

of his peril, and with such force that at the third blast it broke in two. Over all the din of the battle the blast was heard as if it had been a voice from the other world. Birds fell dead at the sound, and the whole Saracen army drew back in terror; while Charlemagne heard it at St. Jean Pied de Port, many miles distant. This horn was of ivory and gold, and of massive size, — larger than a massive beam, says Cervantes, — and endowed with such marvellous power that its notes could be heard for twenty miles. *See* ROLAND FOR AN OLIVER and SHOUT OF STENTOR.

> Oh for a blast of that dread horn,
> On Fontarabia's echoes borne,
> Which to King Charles did come,
> When Roland brave and Olivier,
> And every paladin and peer,
> On Roncesvalles died.
> SIR WALTER SCOTT.

The eloquence of the ancient Greeks can no more be heard again than the shout of Stentor or the blast of the dread horn of Fontarabia. — *Digest of Ancient and Modern History.*

Horn of Plenty. *See* AMALTHEA.

Horns of a Dilemma. A dilemma is technically defined as "a conditional syllogism with two or more antecedents in the major, and a disjunctive minor." The following dilemma, of the kind called "destructive," will perhaps convey a clearer notion than any definition. "If this man were wise, he would not speak irreverently of Scripture in jest; and if he were good, he would not do so in earnest; but he does it, either in jest or earnest; therefore he is either not wise or not good." There being two conclusions, one or other of which your opponent must admit, he is caught between them; hence we speak of the "horns of a dilemma."

Horresco referens. (Lat.) I shudder to relate.

Horribile dictu. (Lat.) "Terrible to be said." Horrible to tell.

Hors de combat. (Fr.) Out of condition for fighting, as by wounds, death, or from being demoralized by defeat.

Hors de la loi. (Fr.) Out of the pale of the law; outlawed.

Hors de propos. (Fr.) Unseasonably; out of place.

Horse-car = TRAM-CAR. The terms current in the United States and in England, respectively, for the vehicles in use on street railways.

Horse-latitudes. This is a phrase by which sailor-men designate a region in the North Atlantic bounded by the parallels of 30° and 35° north latitude, much subject to baffling calms and light airs. The name arose, so runs the legend, from the fact that ships formerly sailing from New England to the West Indies freighted with a load of horses were, from their detention in this vicinity, and the consequent exhaustion of their supply of fresh water, compelled to heave the live-stock overboard.

Horse-milliner. A horse-soldier, more fit for the toilet than the battle-field.

Hort. Horticulture.

Hortense Schneider, Mlle. The stage-name of Mrs. Edward Solomons.

Hortus siccus. (Lat.) "A dry garden." A collection of specimens of plants dried and arranged; a herbarium.

Horus. The Egyptian god of the sun; the same as the Greek Apollo.

Hos. Hosea.

Hosea Biglow. (Pseud.) James Russell Lowell, American poet and critic (b. 1819).

Hostis humani generis. (Lat.) An enemy of the human race.

Hôtel des Invalides. (Fr.) Mansion of the invalids. The military hospital in Paris.

Hôtel de ville. (Fr.) A town hall.

Hôtel-Dieu. (Fr.) The chief hospital in French cities.

Hotel Disease. A disease which broke out among the guests at the National Hotel in Washington in the year 1856, somewhat resembling cholera, attended with vomiting, diarrhœa, and rapid general prostration. Similar symptoms have since shown themselves at some other hotels, though not with the same virulence.

Hot Gospellers. A nickname applied to the Puritans after the Restoration.

Hotspur. (Pseud.) (1) Henry Mort Feist, in the "Daily Telegraph" and "Sporting Life" (London). (2) Henry Buck, in the "Morning Advertiser" and the "Daily Telegraph" (London).

Hotspur of Debate. Lord Derby. *See* RUPERT OF DEBATE.

Hot Water War. "Soon after the Whiskey Rebellion had been overcome, a fresh trouble arose from a tax laid by the Federal Government on houses, which were classified according to their dimensions, the size and number of the windows, and so forth. The people objected to these direct taxes, though they bore more lightly on the poor than on the rich, and Pennsylvania was again the scene of the chief resistance. When the officers went to make the necessary measurements, the women deluged them with hot water, and hence the disturbance was known as the Hot Water War. But further violence was offered, and when the United States Marshal, in March, 1799, arrested some offenders, they were rescued in the town of Bethlehem by an armed band led by one John Fries. The militia were called out, and they succeeded in restoring order. Fries was convicted of treason and sentenced to death, and a number of his followers were condemned to imprisonment. President Adams, however, soon pardoned them all; and two or three years later, under Jefferson, the house tax was abolished."— *American Political Dictionary.*

Hour of Death. There have been many speculations and controversies as to this theme. Charles Dickens said of Peggotty, "He went out with the tide." A writer in the "Quarterly Review" (British), several years ago, undertook to investigate the popular notion that there are certain hours during the twenty-four more fatal to life than others. He ascertained the hour of death in 2,880 cases, of all ages, and arrived at very interesting conclusions. The data were derived from a mixed population in every respect, and the deaths occurred during a period of several years. The maximum hour of death is from 5 to 6 o'clock A.M., when it is 40 per cent. above the average; and the minimum during the hours from 9 to 11 o'clock in the evening, when it is 6½ per cent. below the average. Thus the least mortality is during mid-day hours, namely, from 10 till 3 o'clock; the greatest, during early morning hours, from 3 till 6 o'clock. Fishermen say that times of the ebb and flow of the tides are always critical hours with invalids.

Household Troops. Those troops whose special duty it is to attend the English sovereign and guard the metropolis. They consist of the First and Second Life-guards, the Royal Horse-guards and the three regiments of Foot-guards, called the Grenadier, Coldstream, and Scots Fusilier Guards.

How. Howard's U. S. Supreme Court Reports.

Howard. (Pseud.) (1) Mordecai Manuel Noah, American journalist and politician (1785–1851). (2) Capt. Roland F. Coffin, an American writer of sea stories (1826–1888).

Howard Glyndon. (Pseud.) Laura C. R. Searing, American poetess (b. 1840).

Howard's Greens. The Twenty-fourth Regiment (English).

Howling Dervishes. The Howling Dervishes, as travellers style them, have a convent at St. Dimitry, a suburb of Constantinople. Their peculiar religious exercises consist in the recitation of the power and attributes of Allah to the accompaniment of a rocking motion of their bodies, which they say is an imitation of the tossing of vessels upon the ocean, an illustration of their relation to God, — Allah being the great deep, and they the ships. During their prayers and chants they put an energetic emphasis on the word "Allah" whenever it occurs, yelling it out at the highest pitch of their vocal organs. This is kept up with an intensity that culminates in a perfect frenzy or in utter exhaustion, when they fall, panting and foaming, to the ground. In the height of their transports they not infrequently wound themselves with knives and sharp stones, but it is remarked that there is sufficient method in their madness to preserve them from inflicting serious wounds.

H.-P. High-priest; horse-power; half-pay.

H. R. House of Representatives.

H. R. E. Holy Roman Emperor.

H. R. H. His Royal Highness.

H. R. I. P. *Hic requiescat in pace.* Here rests in peace.

H. S. *Hic situs.* Here lies.

H. S. H. His Serene Highness.

H. S. S. Fellow of the Historical Society (*Historiæ Societatis Socius*).

H. T. *Hoc titulum*, this title. *Hoc tituli*, in or under this title.

Hub of the Universe. A humorous appellation popularly applied to the city of Boston, Mass. It originated with Dr. O. W. Holmes.

Boston State-house is the hub of the solar system. You could n't pry that out of a Boston man if you had the tire of all creation straightened out for a crowbar.—*The Autocrat of the Breakfast-table.*

Hudson River of the West. The Mississippi, from St. Louis to St. Paul.

Hudson River School of Painters. Those artists, headed by Bierstadt, Inness, and others, who depicted the beauties of the Hudson River valley, or who resided upon the banks of that stream.

Hue and Cry. A gazette, established in England in 1710, for the purpose of advertising felons.

Huge Paws. A nickname given to the working-men of the Democratic party in New York City, about 1846, by J. T. Buckingham, in the "Boston Courier." He said: "The Huge Paws ought to have another meeting in Tammany Hall before they make their nominations."

Hugh Conway. Francis J. Fargus (d. 1885), an English novelist of much promise. He wrote "Called Back," "A Family Affair," "Dark Days," etc.

Hugh Littlejohn. The name conferred on John Hugh Lockhart by Sir Walter Scott, who dedicated to him the "Tales of a Grandfather."

Hugh Lloyd's Pulpit. A natural production of stone in Merionethshire, Wales. One pile resembles the Kilmarth rocks. There is a platform stone with a back.

Huguenot Pope. Philippe de Mornay (fl. 1549–1623), the stanch supporter of the French Protestants.

Huissier. (Fr.) "Doorkeeper." A bailiff.

Hulsean Lectures. Instituted by the Rev. John Hulse, of Cheshire, in 1777. Every year some four or six sermons are preached at Great St. Mary's, Cambridge, England, by what is now called the Hulsean Lecturer, who, till 1860, was entitled "Christian Advocate."

Humanum est errare. (Lat.) To err is human.

Hummock. The name given in the South to gently rounded hills clothed with timber. The name for such in the Northwest is "knobs," and such a district is called a "knobby country."

Humpback, The. (1) Geronimo Amelunghi (fl. sixteenth century). (2) Andrea Solari, the Italian painter (fl. 1470–1527).

Humphrey Hocus. The Duke of Marlborough is alluded to under this name in Arbuthnot's "History of John Bull."

Hunc tu caveto. (Lat.) Beware of him.

Hund. Hundred.

Hundred Days. The period between the entrance of Napoleon into Paris, March 20, 1815, after his escape from Elba, and the date of his abdication in favor of his son, after the battle of Waterloo.

Hundred Thousand Islands. A native nickname for the Laccadive Islands, a coral group in the Indian Ocean.

Hundred Years' War. The "Hundred Years War" is an accepted term in English history, and refers to conflicts which occurred from 1338 to 1453. During that long period hostility between England and France was almost constant. Of course there were intervals of peace, and the warfare more than once changed its character and objects. The conflict began with Edward III.'s asserting, by arms, his claims to the French throne, and it did not fully end until the expulsion of the English from France during the reign of Henry VI. As roughly and vaguely indicating, at least, the culminating century of the long mediæval struggle between the two nations, the term "The Hundred Years' War" is useful as well as convenient. It must not, however, be taken to indicate any definite war in the way that the "Thirty Years' War" or the "Seven Years' War" does. T. F. Tout, in Cassell's "Dictionary of English History," observes that "the outbreak of the Wars of the Roses finally prevented any prolongation of the long struggle which had caused so much misery and had been so barren of results, and which, if resulting in bracing up the national life of France, brought little to England but barren glory, checkered with disgrace, and a factious and unruly spirit that found its outcome in the civil wars that now fell upon the land."

Hung. Hungarian.

Hunkers. A faction of the Democratic party; so named because they were in possession of the "hunks" or "chunks" of office spoils.

Hunter Preacher. Benjamin Lynn, a Kentucky pioneer who lived in the eighteenth century. He was also called "The Daniel Boone of Southern Kentucky."

Hunter's Moon. The lunation after the harvest moon is often called the "hunter's moon." Sportsmen do not hunt by moonlight. The obvious meaning, therefore, is "hunter's *month;*" the crops being harvested, there is nothing to interfere with the sport of the hunter. "Honeymoon" is another example of the word "moon" being used to express "month."

Hurrah, Huzzah. This is probably the oldest and most common of exclamations. It has been observed that "Hurrah!" is one of those interjections in which sound so echoes sense, that men seem to have adopted it almost instinctively. In India and Ceylon the mahouts and attendants of baggage elephants cheer them on by perpetual repetitions of "Ur-re-re!" The Arabs and camel-drivers in Turkey, Palestine, and Egypt encourage their animals to speed by shouting, "Ar-re, ar-re!" The Moors in Spain drive their mules and horses with cries of "Arre!" In France the sportsman excites the hounds by his shouts of "Hare, hare!" and wagoners turn their horses by crying "Harhaut!" The herdsmen of Ireland and Scotland shout "Hurrish! hurrish!" to the cattle they are driving. It is said by the author of the "Queen's English" that the people of Charnwood Forest, Leicestershire, when they desire to hail a person at a distance, call out not "Halloo!" but "Halloup!" This he imagines is a survival of the times when one cried to another, "A loup! a loup!" or, as we would now say, "Wolf! wolf!" "Hurrah!" again, according to M. Littré, is derived from the Slavonic *huraj*, "to Paradise," which signifies that all soldiers who fell fighting valiantly went straight to heaven. It is evidently an exclamation common to many nations, and is probably a corruption of "Tur aie" (Thor, aid), a battle-cry of the ancient Norsemen, though some authorities derive it from the Jewish "Hosannah!" The word is very often, and was formerly invariably, spelled "Huzza!" and its pronunciation was "Hurray!" The following couplet shows that in Pope's time it was pronounced in this way:

"One self-approving hour whole years out-
          weighs
Of stupid starers and of loud huzzas."

Husk. *See* SHUCK.

Hustle. An Americanism, signifying "to bustle about," and is said to have originated with Mr. A. J. Wagner during the war, and has been commonly used along the Mohawk Valley ever since.

When Wagner was running for sheriff in 1870, he said to his friend and opponent, James Halligan, " If I don't get there, I 'll make you hustle, at all events." Since then, Wagner has been known as the " hustling Sheriff."

H. V. *Hoc verbum*, this word. *His verbis*, in these words.

Hvidsaerk Inscription. A clever hoax perpetrated by Frank Cowan, the American author (b. 1844), in a magazine article, 1866. The full title was " The Hvidsaerk Inscription of the Falls of the Potomac; " and although immediately explained by its author, it has found its way into European reference books.

Hyacinthus. In classic myth a youth of Sparta, of surpassing beauty, whom Apollo accidentally killed in a game of quoits. His blood was changed into the flower hyacinth, on the leaves of which appeared the exclamation of grief AI (" Alas ! "), or the letter Y, the initial of 'Yάκινθος.

Hyades. In classic myth seven nymphs, — Ambrosia, Eudora, Pedile, Coronis, Polyxo, Phyto, and Thyene. Being placed among the stars, in the constellation Taurus, they were thought to portend rain when they rose before the sun.

Hyd. Hydrostatics.

Hydra. In classic myth a poly-headed sea-serpent of Argolis. As fast as one of its heads was cut off, two grew in its place. Hercules killed it.

Hydrant Chuck. (Pseud.) J. F. Martin in the " Fireman's Journal," New York.

Hydrophilus. (Pseud.) Rev. Thomas Fenwick, a Canadian clergyman and author.

Hygeia. In classic myth a daughter of Æsculapius, and goddess of health.

Hygiene, Poet of. *See* POET OF HYGIENE.

Hymen. In classic myth the son of Bacchus and Venus, and god of marriage. He is represented as a winged boy, covered with flowers.

Hyperboreans. In classic myth a fabulous race, whose home was placed in the far north, where they were supposed to revel in the enjoyment of a terrestrial paradise and perpetual youth.

Hyperion. In classic myth son of Cœlus and Terra, one of the Titans, and father of Sol, Luna, and Aurora.

Hyperion. (Pseud.) Josiah Quincy, American orator and patriot (1744–1775).

Hypocrites, The. An epithet conferred by Mohammed on Abdallah Ibu Obba and his friends, because while they feigned to be his partisans they were in reality his foes.

Hypoth. Hypothesis ; hypothetical.

Hysterica passio. (Lat.) " Hysteric passion." Hysterics.

I.

I. Iodine.

Ia. Iowa.

Ianthe. (Pseud.) Mrs. Emma Catherine Embury, American writer (1805–1863).

Iapetus. In classic myth a giant, father of Atlas, Prometheus, and Epimetheus, and by the ancients regarded as the progenitor of the human race.

Ib., or **ibid.** *Ibidem.* In the same place.

Iberia. The ancient Greek, but now the modern poetical, name for Spain.

Iberia's Pilot. Christopher Columbus. Spain is called " Iberia," and the Spaniards the " Iberi." *Ebro*, the name of the river, is a corrupt form of the Latin word *Iberus*.

Launched with Iberia's pilot from the steep,
To worlds unknown and isles beyond the deep.
CAMPBELL, *The Pleasures of Hope.*

Ibidem (contracted **ibid.** or **id.**). (Lat.) In the same place.

I came, I saw, I conquered ! (Lat., *Veni, Vidi, Vici.*) The laconic despatch in which Julius Cæsar announced to the Senate his victory over Pharnaces. *See* VENI, VIDI, VICI.

Icarus. In classic myth a son of Dædalus, who, escaping with his father out of Crete, flew so near the sun that the heat thereof melted his wings, and he dropped into the sea, thence named the Icarian Sea.

Icel. Iceland; Icelandic.

Ich. Ichthyology.

Ichabod. According to some, Daniel Webster, and according to others, Robert Rantoul, was alluded to under this name in Whittier's poem entitled "Ichabod," as a rebuke for betraying the anti-slavery cause by his services to the South.

Ich dien. (Prov. Ger.) I serve.

I. Ch. Th. U. S. (Ιχθύς.) Jesus Christ, the Son of God, the Saviour. (*Iesous Christos Theon Huios Sotor.*)

Ici on parle Français. (Fr.) "Here one speaks French." Here French is spoken.

Icon. Encyc. Iconographic Encyclopædia.

Ictus. *Jurisconsultus.*

Id. Idaho; the same (*idem*); the Ides (*Idus*).

Ida Bell. The stage-name of Mrs. Frederick J. Eustis.

Ida Clare. (Pseud.) Mrs. L. J. R. Chute, correspondent of various papers in the Southwest.

Idæan Mother. Another name for the goddess Cybele, who had a temple on Mount Ida in Asia Minor.

Ida Freeman. The stage-name of Mrs. Castel Brydges.

Ida Glenn. The stage-name of Mrs. Frank Perley.

Ida Glover. The stage-name of Mrs. Henry E. Dixey.

Idaho. An Indian name, meaning "The Gem of the Mountains."

Ida Lewis. The stage-name of Mrs. W. H. Cooper.

Ida Mason. (Pseud.) Eliza M. A. Fisher, in "Peterson's Magazine," Philadelphia, *circa* 1860.

Ida May. (Pseud.) Mrs. Mary H. G. Pike.

Ida Quick. The stage-name of Mrs. George W. Maurer.

Ida Van Cortlandt. The stage-name of Mrs. Albert Tavernier.

Ida Vernon. The stage-name of Bridget McGowan.

Ide Delmer. (Pseud.) Miss Essie B. Cheesborough, in the "Southern Literary Gazette."

Idée fixe. (Fr.) A fixed idea.

Idem (contracted *Id.*). (Lat.) The same.

Idem sonans. (Lat.) Sounding alike; of the same sound, as a word.

Id est (usually contracted *i. e.*). (Lat.) That is.

Id genus omne. (Lat.) All of that sort.

Id. ib. The same author; in the same place.

Idoneus homo. (Lat.) "A fit man." A man of recognized ability.

Iduna. In Scandinavian mythology the goddess of youth, wife of Bragi.

i. e. *Id est.* That is.

I. G. Inside Guardian.

Ignobile vulgus. (Lat.) "The ignoble vulgar." The rude multitude.

Ignoramus Jury. This was formerly the title of the body now known as a grand jury, from the custom of their writing the Latin word *Ignoramus* — meaning "We do not know," "The evidence does not inform us" — on the back of a bill of indictment when they "ignored" it. The words now used are "No true bill." In "Collectanea Curiosa," Oxford, 1781, p. 393, is a copy of a charge by Judge Allibon, at the Croydon Assizes, in 1688, in which the judge directs the jury thus : —

"If you find that anything proceeds from envy and malice, and not of due prosecution, you may acquit the person that is so wrongfully prosecuted, and so justice is done between party and party, so an ignoramus jury may not be of no use."

Ignorantia legis neminem excusat. (Lat.) Ignorance of the law excuses no one.

Ignorantines. A religious association founded by the Abbé de la Salle in 1724 for educating gratuitously the children of the poor.

Ignotus. (Pseud.) Baron Platel, a brilliant writer in the Paris "Figaro" (d. 1888).

I. H. S. (*Jesus Hominum Salvator*). Jesus the Saviour of Men. In the German these letters stand for I[esus], H[eiland], S[eligmacher]; *i. e.*, "Jesus, Saviour, Sanctifier." In Greek, I[esous], H[emeteros], S[oter]; *i. e.*, "Jesus, Our Saviour." In Latin, I[esus] H[ominum] S[alvator]; *i. e.*, "Jesus, Men's Saviour." Brewer suggests that those who would like an English equivalent may adopt J[esus], H[eavenly] S[aviour].

A curious instance of ignorance as to the signification of the symbolic use of these letters occurred in 1860, when some thief managed to cut out the gold embroidered letters from the altar-cloth of Mary-le-bone Church. The vestry were in full conclave on the question of the sacrilege, when a sage churchwarden observed that he did not approve of the Vicar (John Henry Spry) putting his initials on the cloth.

Ikenild Street. One of the ancient Roman roads that intersected England. *See* ERMINAGE STREET, FOSSE, THE, and WATLING STREET.

From the east into the west goeth Ikenild Strete.
ROBERT OF GLOUCESTER.

Ike Reid. (Pseud.) Ike Reid Cauldwell, who wrote " Harry Hill's Reminiscences," in the New York " Sunday Mercury," 1885–1886.

Ikey Solomons, Esq. W. M. Thackeray wrote several stories under this pseudonym.

Ik Marvel. (Pseud.) Donald Grant Mitchell, American miscellaneous writer (b. 1822).

Il. (Ital.) The.

Il a le diable au corps. (Fr.) The devil is in him.

Iliad of France. The " Romance of the Rose," which was begun by Guillaume di Lorris in the latter end of the thirteenth century, and continued by Jean de Meung in the beginning of the fourteenth, who added 18,000 lines as a sequel.

Iliad of Germany. The Nibelungenlied.

Iliad of India. The epic poem, " The Light of Asia," by Edwin Arnold, has been so named.

Iliad of Portugal. The " Lusiad," by Camoens.

Iliad of Scotland. The " Epigoniad," by William Wilkie. *See* HOMER OF SCOTLAND.

Ilithyia. In classic myth the goddess who watched over women during the pains of maternity ; the same as the Roman Lucina.

Ilium, or Ilion. Troy, in Greece, which was founded by Ilus.

Was this the face that launched a thousand ships
And burnt the topmost towers of Ilium?
MARLOWE, *Faustus.*

Ill. Illinois.

Ill-grounded Peace. *See* LAME AND UNSTABLE PEACE.

Illinois. This name comes to us from the Indian word *illini*, " men," and the French affix *ois ;* making " tribe of men."

Illuminated Doctor. (1) Raymond Sully (fl. 1235–1315). (2) John Tauler, the German mystic (fl. 1294–1361).

Illuminator, The. A title of honor given to Saint Gregory of Armenia, a celebrated bishop of the early Church.

Illustrious, The. (1) Albert V., Duke and second Emperor of Austria (fl. 1398–1439). (2) Nicomedes II. (fl. 149–191). (3) Ptolemy V. (fl. 210–181 B. C.). (4) Jam-Sheid, King of Persia (fl. 840–800 B. C.). (5) Kien-Long, the fourth of the Manchoo rulers of China (fl. 1736–1796).

Ilma di Murska. The professional name of Mrs. Hill, a famous primadonna.

Il terzo dite a tutte le notte di basso. (Ital.) The third finger on all the notes in the bass. (Mus.)

Il va du blanc au noir. (Fr.) "He goes from the white to the black." He runs into extremes.

Imitatores servum pecus. (Lat.) Imitators are a servile herd.

Immortal Dreamer. John Bunyan (fl. 1628–1688). His " Pilgrim's Progress " is supposed to be an allegory in the form of a dream.

Immortal Tinker. John Bunyan (fl. 1628–1688), author of " The Pilgrim's Progress," who was a tinker by trade.

Imp. Imperative ; imperfect. Imperial ; Emperor (*Imperator*).

Impeachment. A state-trial of an official for "high crimes and misdemeanors." In English history the impeachment of Warren Hastings and of Lord Melville are famous. In United States political annals the impeachment of President Johnson for the removal of E. M. Stanton from office as Secretary of War, contrary, as was alleged, to the Tenure of Office Act, took place February to May, 1868. He was acquitted.

Imperial City. Rome ; for ages the mistress of the world.

Imperial Machiavelli. Tiberius, the Roman emperor (42 B. C.–37 A. D.).

Imperium in imperio. (Lat.) "An empire in an empire." A supreme power within a supreme power.

Impetuoso, or Con impetuosita. (Ital.) With impetuosity. (Mus.)

Impransus. (Lat.) One who has dined.

Imprimatur. (Lat.) Let it be printed.

Imprimis. (Lat.) In the first place.

Impromptu. (Lat.) A prompt remark ; without study.

In. Inch ; inches ; indium.

In. (Ital.) In; as *In tempo*, in time. (Mus.)

In absolutissima forma. (Lat.) In the most absolute form.

In actu. (Lat.) In reality.

In æternum. (Lat.) "To eternity." Forever.

In ambiguo. (Lat.) In uncertainty.

In armis. (Lat.) "In arms." Under arms.

In articulo mortis. (Lat.) At the point of death.

Inauguration Day. March 4, in the United States. Washington's first inauguration took place on April 30, 1789. March 4 was chosen for this purpose rather by accident than design. A committee appointed by the Constitutional Convention chose the first Wednesday in March, 1789, as the date for the first Congress under the Constitution to meet. This date happened to be March 4, which has since then been used as the date of presidential inauguration. Eighteen presidents have been inaugurated on March 4; viz., George Washington in 1793, John Adams in 1797, Thomas Jefferson in 1801 and 1805, James Madison in 1809 and 1813, James Monroe in 1817 and 1821, John Quincy Adams in 1825, Andrew Jackson in 1829 and 1833, Martin Van Buren in 1837, William Henry Harrison in 1841, James K. Polk in 1845, Zachary Taylor in 1849, Franklin Pierce in 1853, James Buchanan in 1857, Abraham Lincoln in 1861 and 1865, Ulysses S. Grant in 1869 and 1873, Rutherford B. Hayes in 1877, James A. Garfield in 1881, Grover Cleveland in 1885, and Benjamin Harrison in 1889. George Washington was inaugurated on April 30, 1789, because the bad weather had prevented Congress from assembling and organizing. James Monroe and Zachary Taylor were inaugurated on March 5, 1821 and 1849, respectively, because March 4 in those years fell on Sunday. John Tyler was inaugurated April 6, 1841; President Harrison died on April 4, and Tyler could not reach Washington sooner. Millard Fillmore took the oath on July 9, 1850, the same day that General Taylor died. Andrew Johnson was sworn in on April 15, 1865, a few hours after Lincoln expired. Chester A. Arthur took the oath late on Monday night, Sept. 19, 1881, about an hour after Garfield died.

In capite. (Lat.) In chief.

Incidit in Scyllam cupiens vitare Charybdin. (Lat.) He falls into Scylla while seeking to avoid Charybdis.

In cœlo quies. (Lat.) "In heaven rest." There is rest in heaven.

Incog. *Incognito.* Unknown.

Incognita. A woman of doubtful reputation, or with a name unknown or unrecognized by polite society.

Incognito. Unknown; in privacy.

In commendam. (Lat.) "In trust." A vacant church-living as intrusted to the charge of another person till it can be supplied with an incumbent.

Incomparable Orinda. Under this name the poets Cowley and Dryden sung the praises of Mrs. Katharine Phillips, a beauty of the reign of Charles II.

In conspectu fori. (Lat.) In the eye of the law; in the sight of the court.

Incor. Incorporated.

In cumulo. (Lat.) "In a heap." In a mass; at once.

In curia. (Lat.) In the court.

I. N. D. *In nomine Dei.* In the name of God.

Ind. Indiana; index.

Ind. A poetic diminutive for the land of India.

> High on a throne of royal state which far
> Outshone the wealth of Ormuz and of Ind.
> MILTON, *Paradise Lost*, book ii.

Indef. Indefinite.

Independence Day. This, one of the three peculiarly American national holidays, is better known as "Fourth of July," or "The Fourth," on which day of the month it falls, and, as the reader is well aware, is kept in commemoration of the signing of the Declaration of Independence at Philadelphia in 1776. It is a legal holiday in all the States.

Independent, An. (Pseud.) Josiah Quincy, American author and patriot (1744–1775).

Independents. In the presidential election of 1884 a faction of the Republican party were known by this name. They were virtually the successors of the Liberal Republicans of 1872, their party shibboleth being "Civil Service Reform." They claimed through their press organs to have elected Mr. Cleveland, though the claim was disputed.

Index expurgatorius. (Lat.) A list of passages of books which are to be expunged or altered; a list of books strictly prohibited to be read.

Indiana. The name of this State is derived from the word "Indian."

Indian Fighter. John Talcott, colonist (1630–1688). He commanded the white troops in the Indian War of 1676.

Indian Summer. In North America a period of mild, balmy weather which regularly recurs during the month of November or the early part of December. It has been jocularly described as "every warm day between Michaelmas and Christmas."

In diem vivere. (Lat.) To live from hand to mouth.

Indra. In Hindu mythology the god of the heavens, the all-powerful ruler of the elements. He was supposed to be endowed with perpetual youth and beauty.

Ind. Ter. Indian Territory.

In dubiis. (Lat.) In doubtful matters.

In duplo. (Lat.) Twice as much.

Industrious, The. In mediæval days Lucca, in Italy, was so named. *See* BEAUTIFUL, THE.

In eadem conditione. (Lat.) In the same condition.

In equilibrio. (Lat.) Equally balanced.

In esse. (Lat.) In being.

In esse et in posse. (Lat.) Actual and possible.

Inexorable Logic of Facts. This phrase, which is supposed to have originated in Napoleon's proclamation from Milan, before the battle of Solferino, is really Mazzini's. It occurred in a leading article, published in 1849, which commences thus: "Nella genesi dei fatti la logica è inesorabile."

In extenso. (Lat.) In the extended form; at full length.

In extremis. (Lat.) At the point of death; on its last legs.

Inez Periere. The stage-name of Mrs. Wright Huntington.

Inf. *Infra.* Beneath, or below.

In f. *In fine.* At the end of the title, law, or paragraph quoted.

Infamous, The. *See* NORTHERN HARLOT.

Infant of Lubeck. Christian Henry Heinecken (fl. 1721–1725). His precep-

tor, Schöneich, says that "at one year old he knew the chief events of the Pentateuch; at thirteen months he knew the history of the Old Testament; at fourteen months he knew the events of the New Testament; at two and a half years he could answer any ordinary question of history or geography; at three he knew well both French and Latin."

Infernal Column. A body of 8,000 French grenadiers, led by La Tour d'Auvergne (*see* FIRST GRENADIER OF THE REPUBLIC). It formed the vanguard of the Army of the Pyrenees, and was renowned for the rapidity of its movements and the fury of its onsets.

In flagrante crimine. (Lat.) In the very commission of the crime.

In flagrante delicto. (Lat.) The same in meaning as the preceding.

In forma pauperis. (Lat.) To plead as a man without means in a court of law, in which case fees are not charged.

In foro conscientiæ. (Lat.) "At the forum of conscience." Before the judgment-seat of conscience.

In foro divino. (Lat.) Before the divine tribunal; in God's sight.

In foro humano. (Lat.) Before a human tribunal.

Infra dignitatem. (Lat.) "Beneath dignity." Derogatory to one's dignity; contracted into *infra dig.*

In futuro. (Lat.) In the future.

In futurum. (Lat.) For the future.

Ingathering, Feast of. *See* TABERNACLES, FEAST OF.

Ingens telum necessitas. (Lat.) Necessity is a most powerful incitement to exertion.

Inhab. Inhabitant.

In hoc signo vinces. (Lat.) "Under this standard (the cross) thou shalt conquer." The motto assumed by the Roman Emperor Constantine, after having seen, it is said, in the air a miraculous cross with those words on it.

In hoc statu. (Lat.) In this state or condition.

In horas. (Lat.) Every hour.

Inhospitable Sea. A name sometimes applied to the Black Sea. It is a translation of its most ancient name, Axenus, and was considered to describe accurately the manners of the inhabitants of its coasts.

In initio. (Lat.) "In the beginning." At the outset.

Initium sapientiæ timor Domini. (Lat.) The fear of the Lord is the beginning of wisdom.

In lim. *In limine.* At the outset.

In limine. (Lat.) "In the entrance." On the threshold, as of an enterprise.

In literis humanioribus. (Lat.) In Latin or Greek literature.

In loc. *In loco.* In the place; on the passage.

In loco. (Lat.) "In the place." On the spot.

In loco parentis. (Lat.) In the place of a parent.

In medias res. (Lat.) Into the midst of a subject.

In medio tutissimus ibis. (Lat.) You will go most safely in the middle; a middle course is the safest.

In memoriam. (Lat.) "To memory." To the memory of.

Innisfail ("Isle of Destiny"). An old name for Ireland.

Innocents. The name given to the babes whom Herod massacred at Bethlehem. It dates from very early times, and the Church has always honored and revered these harmless ones. Holy Innocents' Day (the third day after Christmas) is specially observed by the young in Catholic countries, to the accompaniment of many quaint and curious customs.

Inn of the Kings ("Cabaret du Rois"). A name given to Paris on account of the number of exiled or dethroned monarchs who have at various times sought refuge there.

In nomine. (Lat.) In the name of.

In nomine Domini. (Lat.) In the name of the Lord.

In nubibus. (Lat.) "In the clouds." In the region of theory.

Ino. In classic myth wife of Cadmus, king of Thebes. Being pursued by her mad husband, she threw herself and her son, Melicertes, into the sea, when they were both metamorphosed into sea deities.

In obscuro. (Lat.) In obscurity.

In oculis civium. (Lat.) "In the eyes of the public." Before the public.

Inops consilii. (Lat.) Without counsel.

In pace. (Lat.) In peace.

In pari materia. (Lat.) Of a similar nature.

In partibus infidelium. (Lat.) "In the parts of the unfaithful." In the countries that are not obedient to the faith. A phrase employed by the Roman Catholic Church to designate those countries that are not of their faith; as "a bishop *in partibus infidelium.*"

In perpetuam. (Lat.) "To perpetuity." Without intermission; perpetually; forever.

In perpetuam rei memoriam. (Lat.) As a perpetual memorial of a thing.

In petto. (Ital.) "In the breast." Held in reserve.

In pleno. (Lat.) In full.

In pontificalibus. (Lat.) "In pontificals." In pontifical robes.

In posse. (Lat.) In possible existence; that may be possible.

In posterum. (Lat.) For the time to come.

In pr. *In principio.* In the beginning and before the first paragraph of a law.

In præsenti. (Lat.) At the present time.

In propria persona. (Lat.) "In one's own person." A personal attendance.

In prospectu. (Lat.) "In prospect." In view.

In puris naturalibus. (Lat.) In a purely natural state; completely naked.

In re. (Lat.) In the matter of.

In rerum natura. (Lat.) In the nature of things.

I. N. R. I. *Jesus Nazarenus, Rex Judæorum.* Jesus of Nazareth, King of the Jews.

In sacris. (Lat.) In sacred things.

In secula seculorum. (Lat.) To the end of time; for ever and ever.

In situ. (Lat.) "In position." In its natural position or condition.

Insouciance. (Fr.) Carelessness; indifference.

Inspired Idiot. A nickname bestowed by Horace Walpole on Oliver Goldsmith, because of the strange medley of wit and foolishness, genius and stupidity, which entered into his mental make-up.

Inspired Tinker. John Bunyan.

In spiritualibus. (Lat.) In spiritual matters.

Inst. Instant, of this month; Institutes; institute; institution.

Instanter. (Lat.) Instantly; at once.

Instar omnium. (Lat.) One will suffice for all; an example to others.

In statu esse. (Lat.) To be upon one's guard.

In statu quo. (Lat.) "In the position in which." In the position in which it was.

In statu quo ante bellum. (Lat.) In the same condition as before the war.

Insubri. A district of Lombardy, containing Milan, Como, Pavia, Lodi, Novara, and Vercelli.

Insula Sanctorum. *See* HOLY ISLAND.

In sum. *In summa.* In the summary.

In suo proprio loco. (Lat.) In its own proper place.

Int. Interest.

Int. Dept. Department of the Interior.

In te, Domine, speravi. (Lat.) In thee, Lord, have I put my trust.

Intellectus communis. (Lat.) Common-sense.

Inter alia. (Lat.) Among other things.

Inter arma leges silent. (Lat.) In the midst of arms the laws are silent.

Interim of Augsburg. The name given to a decree issued by Charles V. in 1548, having for its object the reconciliation of the Catholics and Protestants. It utterly failed, however.

Interj. Interjection.

Inter nos. (Lat.) Between ourselves.

Inter pocula. (Lat.) "In the midst of the cups." Engaged in drinking.

In terrorem. (Lat.) "In terror." As a warning; as a bugbear.

Inter se. (Lat.) Among themselves.

Inter spem et metum. (Lat.) Between hope and fear.

In the Soup. A phrase which obtained wide currency during the political campaign of 1888. The phrase indicates embarrassment, disappointment, demoralization, discomfiture, or defeat, moral, material, or political. Like many other slang phrases, it may mean almost anything, because it means

nothing. A defeated candidate for President is "in the soup;" so are the men who bet and lost thousands on him, the defaulting banker, the embarrassed merchant, the jilted lover, the young lady surprised in her curl-papers, the truckster whose stand is upset, the market-woman who drops her basket, the watchman who is caught asleep on his post, the newsboy who gets "stuck" on papers, the boot-black whose loose change runs out through a hole in his pocket. In short, everybody who "gets left" is "in the soup." It is a very ridiculous phrase, and not a very nice one, but slang knows no law. One account of its origin is that it first achieved popularity June 8, 1888, in New York, at the polo grounds during a game of ball between New York and Chicago. The members of the Chicago club made their appearance in full-dress suits, and were dubbed waiters by the crowd. Chicago suffered an ignominious defeat, by the score of 19 to 2, whereupon somebody remarked that "the waiters were in the soup." The phrase spread through the crowd like wildfire. Still later, in the autumn of the same year, a certain pugilist arrived at New York from Europe. The Cunarder "Etruria," with the pugilist aboard, lay in the darkness off Quarantine, waiting for morning; and a tug with Kilrain's friends aboard was hovering about, anxious to get the fighter off and bring him up to the city. The captain of the "Etruria" had announced that no such drunken crew should come anywhere near his vessel. The disconsolate but not unhappy crowd on the tug had to content itself with howling greetings to Kilrain across a watery gulf that separated the two vessels. One of the men on the tug was so anxious to get as near the fighter as possible that he tumbled overboard. One of his companions, witnessing this act, balanced himself against the rail and called out, "Ho! Johnston's fell in de soup!" There is yet another possible origin, which antedates the two foregoing. In 1866 James Greenwood, a London journalist, wanted to learn the treatment men received in the casual wards; so he dressed himself one night as a tramp and went to St. Giles's casual. When he wrote about it he spoke of the men having to take a bath; when it came to his turn he said the water looked like soup, it was so thick. From this it got to be a byword in London; boys going bathing would say they were going "into the soup." But the New York "Sun" says the phrase is much older than 1866, and comes to us from the German.

In the Straw. "This expression, commonly used to signify that a lady of whom it is spoken has recently been delivered of a child, is derived from the fact that formerly all beds were stuffed with straw. In old books are frequent allusions to straw for beds. Even the luxurious Henry VIII. lay upon straw, for we read that 'there were directions for certain persons to examine every night the straw of the king's bed, that no daggers might be concealed therein.'" — BRAND.

In the Wrong Box. (1) George Lord Lyttelton was of rather a moody disposition and of restless habits. He used to go to Vauxhall, and frequently said that he always "got in the wrong box," for the folks in those next to which he sat were always merry enough, but he felt dull and melancholy. (2) In a printing-office, when a letter is found in the compartment appointed for some other letter, it is said to be "in the wrong box."

Intima præcordia. (Lat.) "The inmost entrails." The very dearest affections.

In totidem verbis. (Lat.) "In just so many words." In terms that scarcely could be mistaken.

In toto. (Lat.) Wholly; entirely.

Intra ecclesiam Anglicanam. (Lat.) Within the pale of the Church of England.

Intra muros. (Lat.) Within the walls.

In trans. *In transitu.* On the passage.

Intransigentes, or Irreconcilables. A party of Spanish republicans of extreme opinions, who withdrew from the Cortes and became very troublesome, July 1, 1873. Since then the word has become current to denote any body holding impracticable or revolutionary doctrines.

In transitu. (Lat.) "In the passage." During the conveyance; in the passing.

Int. Rev. Internal Revenue.

Introd. Introduction.

In usum vulgi. (Lat.) "For the use of the multitude." For the general use of the public.

In utrumque paratus. (Lat.) Prepared for either event.

In vacuo. (Lat.) "In empty space." In a space free, or nearly free, from air.

Invalide. A nickname for a four-sou piece; so called because it was debased to the value of three sous and a half.

Invalids. A nickname for the Forty-first Regiment in the English army. It is also known as "Wardrow's Regiment."

Invention of the Cross. A festival held on May 3, in commemoration of the discovery of the true cross by Saint Helena, mother of Constantine the Emperor in 316 A.D. "Invention" here means "discovery."

Invincible Doctor. William of Occam, a hamlet in Surrey (fl. 1270–1347). He was also named "Doctor Singularis."

In vino veritas. (Lat.) "There is truth in wine;" from the fact that an intoxicated man is off his guard, and likely to speak the truth.

Invisible Prince. A name given to the Duke of Portland (d. 1883). His love of privacy was such that he constructed at his country-seat, Welbeck, a series of underground rooms and passages, from which the light of day and strangers were rigidly excluded.

Invita Minerva. (Lat.) "Against the will of Minerva." Against the grain, or one's inclination; destitute of genius. Minerva was the Goddess of Wisdom among the ancient Romans, and according to them the intellect could accomplish nothing without her aid.

Io. In classic myth daughter of Inachus, king of Argos. Jupiter loved her, and changed her into a cow, fearing the jealousy of Juno. But Juno persuaded Argus to watch her, so Jupiter had him killed by Mercury. Io was smitten with madness by Juno, and wandering about the earth, came to Egypt, married King Osiris, and after death was worshipped by the Egyptians under the name of Isis.

I. of M. Instructor of musketry.

Iola Pomeroy. The stage-name of Mrs. Dr. L. Howard.

Ion. Ionic.

Ione. (Pseud.) Mrs. Mary Elizabeth (Moore) Hewitt, American poetess, (b. 1808).

Ionic Letters. *See* CADMUS.

I. O. O. F. Independent Order of Odd Fellows.

I. O. S. M. Independent Order of the Sons of Malta.

I. O. U. I owe you.

Iowa. This is an Indian word, meaning "drowsy ones."

I. P. D. *In præsentiâ Dominorum.* In presence of the Lords of Session.

Ipecac. Ipecacuanha.

Iphigenia. In classic myth daughter of Agamemnon and Clytemnestra. She was carried to Tauris by Diana, and made a priestess in her temple, to prevent her being sacrificed.

Iphis. In classic myth a young man of Cyprus, who, his love for Anaxarete being unrequited, hanged himself. The gods, to avenge his death, turned Anaxarete into stone.

Ipse dixit. (Lat.) "He himself said it." On his sole assertion, — a piece of dogmatism.

Ipsissima verba. (Lat.) The very words.

Ipsissimis verbis. (Lat.) In the very same words.

Ipso facto. (Lat.) By the fact itself; by the very act.

Ipso jure. (Lat.) By the law itself.

I. Q. *Idem quod.* The same as.

Ir. Iridium.

Ira furor brevis est. (Lat.) Anger is a short madness.

Ire. Ireland.

Ireland Forgeries. In the year 1786 W. H. Ireland gave to the public several Shakspearean manuscripts which he claimed to have discovered, but which he had really forged. One of these, a play entitled "Vortigern," was performed at Drury Lane Theatre April 2, 1796. In 1805 he acknowledged the imposture, and published his "Confessions." He died 1835.

Irenæus. (Pseud.) Rev. S. Irenæus Prime, D.D., American Presbyterian divine (1812–1885).

Irene. In classic myth the goddess of peace.

Irene Lunt. (Pseud.) Irene Bradbury, in the "Cottage Hearth."

Irene Perry. (1) The stage-name of Irene Brady. (2) The professional name of Mrs. Albert Weber.

Iris. In classic myth one of the Oceanides, and messenger of the gods.

She is generally regarded as the personification of the rainbow. The legend says that the rainbow was the path on which the goddess walked between earth and heaven; that it appeared whenever she needed it, and vanished when her journey was done.

Irish Agitator. A nickname given to Daniel O'Connell (1775–1847).

Irish Atticus. George Faulkner (fl. 1700–1775) was so named by Lord Chesterfield.

Irish Night. A report, shortly after the flight of James II., that the Irish Catholics of Feversham's army had been let loose to murder the Protestant population of London, occasioned a night of terror and agitation known to history by the above appellation.

Irish Nightingale. Catherine Hayes (Mrs. Bushnell), a famous vocalist. She closed her professional career in London in 1856, and died in Sydenham, England, 1861.

Iron Age. The last of the four periods into which the ancients divided human history. It was the "age of Pluto," and was distinguished by the frequency of crime and the prevalence of cunning, fraud, and avarice, and the consequent absence of honor and truth, probity and piety.

Iron Arm. François de Lanone, the Huguenot captain (fl. 1531–1591).

Iron Chancellor. Prince Otto von Bismarck.

Iron City. Pittsburg, Penn., noted for its furnaces, rolling-mills, and foundries. It is also called "the Smoky City." Bituminous coal was, before the introduction of natural gas as fuel, largely used, causing a dense canopy of smoke to hover over the place, often obscuring the sun's light.

Ironclad Oath. The oath of office prescribed by Congress after the close of the civil war as a safeguard against future disloyalty on the part of citizens of the reconstructed States. *See* RECONSTRUCTION.

Ironclad Regiment. The One Hundred and Seventy-first New York Volunteers was so nicknamed. Under its colonel, A. J. H. Duganne, it achieved so many victories that the name clung to it throughout the civil war.

Iron Crown of Lombardy. Is so called from a narrow band of iron within it, said to be beaten out of one of the nails used at the Crucifixion. According to tradition, the nail was first given to Constantine by his mother, who discovered the cross. The crown is preserved at Monza, near Milan. After the war between Austria and Italy the Iron Crown was delivered by the former power to Victor Emmanuel.

Irondequoit. (Pseud.) Francis Trevelyan Buckland, in the New York "Examiner."

Iron Duke. A familiar appellation by which the Duke of Wellington is often referred to.

Iron Gate of France. The town of Longwy, a fortress of France on the Belgian frontier. Louis XIV. gave it the name.

Iron Gate of the Danube. A dangerous barrier of rocks between Alt-Orsova, in Hungary, and Gladova, in Servia. It once formed an effectual bar to navigation, but modern science has largely overcome the obstacle.

Iron Gates. The city of Derbend, in the province of Shirwan.

> Beyond the Caspian's iron gates.
> MOORE, *The Fire-Worshippers.*

Iron Hand. Goetz von Berlichingen (fl. 1480–1562), who lost his right hand at the siege of Landshut, and had one made of iron to supply its place.

Iron Mask, The. One of the most perplexing and at the same time one of the most romantic of the enigmas of history is the mystery concerning the identity of the personage known in French State annals as *L'Homme au Masque de Fer,* "the Man of the Iron Mask." "No certain clew," says Voltaire, writing in 1752, "has ever been obtained as to the history of the mysterious stranger. The closest scrutiny has been baffled, the most diligent search foiled, in the attempt to fathom the most singular historical mystery that has ever presented itself." Briefly, the commonly received story of the Iron Mask runs as follows: In 1662, shortly after the death of Cardinal Mazarin in 1661 and the accession of Louis XIV., there was sent to the fortress of the Isle de Ste. Marguerite, in the Mediterranean, an unknown prisoner. He was young, in stature above the average height, and of a handsome, noble figure. On the journey thither he wore a mask of black velvet, strengthened by steel bands (popularly called an iron mask), the lower part of which was provided with a hinged

attachment that permitted of his eating without ever removing the mask. His guards were told to kill him if he ever told who he was or removed his disguise. He remained at Ste. Marguerite and Pignerol for twenty-nine years, all the time closely guarded, and was then removed to the Bastile in Paris. The physician who prescribed for the Mask during his detention at the Bastile said that, though he had long attended him, he had never seen his face, only his tongue, and that he was admirably formed. The mysterious prisoner never complained of his condition, nor did he ever drop a chance word that might afford an insight into his identity. It was, however, clear to all who came in contact with him, that he was a personage of rank and social importance. "His rooms," we are told, "were handsomely furnished; he was served with the greatest respect possible; the governor of his prison himself waited upon him at meals, and never remained covered or seated in his presence without permission. The prisoner's taste for fine linen and lace was gratified to the utmost, and many diversions were allowed with a view to making his rigorous confinement as light as possible, and he amused himself frequently with a guitar." In 1703 the Masque de Fer died suddenly in the Bastile. His funeral was conducted with the greatest secrecy, the body being interred at night in the churchyard of St. Paul, with the facial lineaments hidden from mortal ken. After his death his effects were burned, and the walls of his chamber were scraped and freshly painted, so as to obliterate completely all trace of any telltale inscriptions. The array of names put forward by various writers and theorizers on this alluring topic is sufficient evidence of the magnificent conjectures of former days. The "claims" of Arwediks, an Armenian patriarch, forcibly carried off from Constantinople; of the Duc de Vermandois, son of Louis XIV., who was reported to have perished in the French camp before Dixmude; of the Duc de Beaufort, whose head was said to have been taken off before Candia; of James, Duke of Monmouth, executed on Tower Hill after the fatal battle of Sedgemoor, but whom many believed to have escaped; of a natural son of Anne of Austria, wife of Louis XIII., by Cardinal Mazarin or by the Duke of Buckingham; of the twin brother of

Louis XIV.; of a Chevalier de Kiffenbach, accused of plotting against the life of Louis; of Foucquet, an eminent and accomplished statesman of the time of Louis XIV.; and of Count Matthioli, secretary of state to Charles III., Duke of Mantua, have been presented by such writers as Voltaire, Dutens, Saint-Foix, La Grange Chancel, Gibbon, Père Papon, Père Griffet, the Chevalier de Tantes, Mr. Quintin Crawford, the Hon. G. Agar-Ellis, M. Delort, M. Iung, Paul Lacroix, M. Letournier, and M. Roux-Fazillac. But most of the foregoing can be readily disposed of. (1) Arwediks, the Armenian patriarch, is known to have died at least ten years before the Mask. (2) The Comte de Vermandois, son of Louis XIV. and Madame de Vallière, died in the camp before Dixmude in 1683, and his body was interred at Arras. (3) The Duc de Beaufort was a grandson of Henry IV. Being sent to assist the Venetians against the Turks, he was slain and beheaded by the latter at the siege of Candia in 1669. (4) The belief that James, Duke of Monmouth, the darling of the people, who was executed on Tower Hill by order of James II., was the Mask, has no other basis than the reluctance of the masses, peculiar to all climes and to all peoples, to believe in the death of a popular idol. (5) The hypothesis that makes the Mask a natural and elder son of Anne of Austria, mother of Louis XIV., is the one that finds favor with Voltaire. Dujonca, Lieutenant of the Bastile, kept a journal, which subsequently came to light, the editor of which states that the Mask was an elder brother of Louis XIV.; that Anne of Austria had this son by a court favorite, and being thus undeceived as to her supposed barrenness, brought about a reconciliation with her husband, and bore Louis XIV. The latter is supposed to have first heard of this brother when he came of age, and immediately put him in confinement. Such a child might have disputed the succession; hence the motive for his suppression by a life-long imprisonment. The historian Gibbon arrives at much the same conclusion. The prisoner's love of fine linen was adduced as corroborative evidence, as Anne's aversion to coarse drapery amounted to almost a mania. (6) That the Mask was a twin brother of Louis XIV. is believed by many, — that he was the latest born, — and for reasons of State policy was sup-

pressed, and his existence kept a secret. The story that he was imprisoned for boxing the dauphin's ears is probably only another of the many wild conjectures drawn forth by this thrilling tale. Foucquet and Kiffenbach are now admitted to have had no proper place in the controversy. These, then, are some of the leading theories put forward by those who have essayed to clear up what has been termed the most singular and astounding of all historical mysteries. Of them all, Nos. 5 and 6 least violate the laws of probability. But amid these romantic, conflicting, and highly spiced conjectures, the assertion was made that the Iron Mask was really a personage of no great importance in the social scale; that no noble blood coursed through his veins, and that political treachery, and not the exigencies of royalty, was the cause of his merciless and life-long detention. Thus we come to the consideration of the last name on the list, that of the Count Matthioli. To M. Roux belongs the honor of first naming the count, for in a pamphlet issued in 1801 he published abstracts of several of the State documents subsequently seen by M. Delort. In 1827 the Hon. G. Agar-Ellis, afterward Lord Dover, gave to the world a work in English, "History of the State Prisoner called the Iron Mask," containing, besides his own narrative, translations of the whole series of State papers collated by Delort. These documents consisted chiefly of correspondence between Louvois and other French ministers and generals, and M. de Saint-Mars, the custodian of the Mask, and relate largely to the keeping and treating of the mysterious prisoner, who in these documents is often referred to as "the Sieur de Lestang." There is, however, one link missing in the case presented in favor of the count, to which we shall refer later. Hercules Anthony Matthioli was a native of Bologna. He came of an ancient and honorable family, distinguished in the legal profession. His parents were Valerian Matthioli and Girolama Maggi, and he first saw the light Dec. 1, 1640. He married, Jan. 13, 1661, Camilla Piatesi, a widow, by whom he had two sons; but his posterity ultimately sank into obscurity. About the time of his marriage he filled the post of public reader in the famous University of Bologna, but eventually quitted his native city to enter the service of

Charles III., Duke of Mantua. So greatly pleased was the duke with his services that he promoted Matthioli to be secretary of state. The successor of Charles III., Ferdinand Charles IV., the last ruler of the house of Gonzaga, created Matthioli supernumerary senator of Mantua, a post that had been hereditary in his family, and gave him the title of Count. Precisely when Matthioli ceased to be secretary of state does not appear. It is certain that he was not in that office when he became involved in an intrigue which, as is believed by many, cost him liberty and life. Ferdinand was a weak and unfortunate prince. Himself and his court were ruled by his mother. At this time France and Spain were bitter rivals in the Italian States bordering on the Mediterranean. About the end of 1677 the Abbé d'Estrades was ambassador from the Court of Louis XIV. to the Republic of Venice. He "conceived the idea, which he was well aware would be highly acceptable to the insatiable ambition of his master, of inducing the Duke of Mantua to permit the introduction of a French garrison into Casale, a strongly fortified town, the capital of the Montferrat," and then considered the key of Italy. In 1632 the French had become possessed of the fortress of Pignerol, which gave them control of Piedmont; could they but gain Casale, the Milanese would also be at their mercy. There was one great barrier to the success of this crafty scheme. Isabella Clara, the mother of the young duke, was a stanch partisan of the Court of Spain, and would be certain to oppose bitterly the project. It must be kept from her at any cost. So it was resolved to approach privately the duke himself, who was known to feel somewhat chagrined at the subjection in which he was kept by his mother. It was also believed that he was none too friendly to the Spaniards, whom he suspected of casting an equally longing eye on Casale and the Montferrat. A trusty emissary between D'Estrades and the duke was needed, and the Abbé thought he had found such in the Count Matthioli, who was an adept in the wiles of Italian politics, who was in the duke's confidence, and who shared his antipathies to the Spaniards. But the cautious D'Estrades would not trust his man till he had sent some one to spy on him and find out his inclinations. These being found favorable, one Giuliani was sent to Matthioli with proposals that he represent to the duke the advantages to be derived from placing himself under the protection of France. Matthioli apparently entered into the intrigue, and promised to see his prince. This he did, and reported to D'Estrades, through Giuliani, that the duke was entirely favorable to the alliance with France and to the cession of Casale, on condition that he receive a grant of money, and be made generalissimo of any French army that might be sent into Italy. When the matter was thus far advanced, the Abbé d'Estrades sent an account of the plot to Louis XIV., who, as might be expected, thought well of the scheme. The negotiations continued to progress favorably, and at length, on the 13th of March, 1678, during the carnival at Venice, the Duke of Mantua and the Abbé d'Estrades held a secret interview in one of the open squares of the city. On this occasion the duke expressed himself as very anxious for the settlement of the matter. In November, 1678, Matthioli set out for Paris, ostensibly to conduct the final negotiations, and obtained an interview with Louis XIV., who presented him with a valuable ring. But suddenly Matthioli's ardor cooled. By one pretext and another he delayed the conclusion of the affair. "At one moment his own ill-health detained him at Mantua; at another, the Duke of Mantua could not raise a sufficient sum of money to enable him to transport his court to Casale; and again, the duke was obliged to stay at Venice, having promised to hold a carnival there." The truth of the matter seems to be that Matthioli had been playing a double game with the French diplomat. Whether he at first really favored the scheme to sell Casale does not appear; it is certain, however, that at a later stage of the proceedings, while pretending to the French to forward their interests, he used all his influence with his master to dissuade him from the design. If he imagined that his movements were unknown to the agents of Louis XIV., he was mistaken. The ministers of the French court, by means of their spies, had been kept apprised of all his movements. The various excuses made by Matthioli for the non-execution of his pledges, all more or less frivolous, appear first to have awakened in the French Government a suspicion of his fidelity. But so secure did Matthioli feel, that he often visited the Marquis d'Arcy, the French ambassador at the Court of Savoy, though that minister was all the time kept fully informed of the doubts current about the integrity of his guest. "He paid him many civilities, asked him very often to dinner, and finally invited him to come and hunt with him at some distance from Turin." Matthioli endeavored to excuse himself on the plea of having no horses, but the ambassador disposed of that difficulty by offering to lend him some. The secretary dared not refuse, lest thereby he should invite suspicion. "The day for the hunt being arrived, they set off together; but they were hardly at the distance of a league from the town when Matthioli was surrounded by ten or twelve horsemen, who seized him, disguised him, masked him, and conducted him to the fortress of Pignerol." From this time Matthioli was lost to the haunts of men. Such is the narrative pieced together by Messrs. Delort and Ellis. It is undoubtedly historically correct up to the seizure of Matthioli and his incarceration in Pignerol. The identifying him with the Mask is not so certain a matter. The fortress of Pignerol was the citadel of the town of the same name in Italy, at the foot of the Alps, about twenty miles southwest of Turin. In the correspondence between Louvois and M. de Saint-Mars, respecting the treatment of the prisoner at Pignerol, the name of Matthioli frequently occurs until July 9, 1681, when all mention of him by name ceases, and thenceforward the difficulty of identifying Matthioli with the Mask is enhanced. That at this period his release was deemed possible is proved by a letter of Louvois on the eve of the removal of Saint-Mars to Exilles. The question arises, whether Matthioli was of sufficient importance, either socially or politically, to warrant such stringent precautions as we have seen were taken to insure his remaining incognito. On the other hand, had he been of royal blood and occupying the relation toward the throne of France of a possible claimant, is it conceivable that his release would ever have been deemed remotely possible? These are difficult questions for the advocates of the Matthioli theory to answer; they have never been answered. Louvois made no secret of the name of Matthioli

in his early correspondence with M. de Saint-Mars; why, then, if the Mask and Matthioli were identical, were the custodians of the former ordered to kill him if he uncovered or divulged his identity? Further, Matthioli having been kidnapped by a party of soldiers, there must have been for several years a number of witnesses living who were acquainted with the facts, and who, in the eager quest for the solution of the mystery surrounding the Iron Mask, could have easily been reached. Yet none of them ever spoke. Do not all the known facts point irresistibly to the conclusion that Matthioli could not have been the Mask? When this carefully guarded culprit enters France proper, his features are shrouded. Now, if Matthioli were the Mask, one would suppose that the time for disguise would be while he remained on foreign soil, where the risk of escape, discovery, or recapture would be greater, and that, once his captors had him safe on French soil, all necessity for concealment would be at an end. On the other hand, were the Mask of French royal lineage, the necessity of this precaution would be apparent. To the question so often propounded during this century, Who else but Matthioli could the Iron Mask be? the answer is that Saint-Mars, in all likelihood, had the custody of both Matthioli and the mysterious Mask; that the former died or was quietly released long prior to the removal of the latter to the Bastile, and that the personage so jealously guarded from discovery was probably of far greater importance than the secretary of the ruler of a petty Italian state. The testimony in favor of the supposition that Matthioli was the Iron Mask is in the main purely circumstantial. Yet the cumulative effect of this evidence, much of it fragmentary and gleaned from widely divergent sources, is very strong, and would be well-nigh conclusive but for a few serious flaws. Some of these we have already noted. Attention has been called by various writers to the undoubted fact that at the time of the seizure of Matthioli, and his subsequent disappearance from the scene of the world's activities, no second person of eminence in the whole of Europe was known to be missing. It has been claimed that all the clews connected with other names end abruptly, and that there is absolutely no other personage around whom the facts can be made to group themselves. But if we suppose that the Mask was in truth a brother of Louis XIV., and that, to avoid all chance of a war of succession, he had been immured in various prisons from infancy, this objection falls to the ground. The existence of such a child could have been known to but few, and the lips of that limited circle were resolutely silent concerning the mystery. Again, we are confronted with the fact that while the first record of the imprisonment of the Mask dates from 1662 (Louis XIV. having suddenly assumed control of the throne in 1661), the Count Matthioli was not arrested until 1678, sixteen years later. It is clear, then, that some other personage was confined during those sixteen years who was guarded with great secrecy, and who, at the time of the first public mention of his incarceration, in 1662, was young and handsome and of noble birth. Unless this discrepancy can be explained, it would seem that the elaborate case· of Messrs. Delort and Ellis must fall to the ground. Certain it is that Voltaire and others name the year 1662 as the beginning of the imprisonment of the person who afterward became celebrated as the Iron Mask, while it is equally unquestionable that the arrest of Matthioli did not occur until 1678. With regard to the treatment of the Mask during his long captivity authorities differ, as we have seen. Some represent that everything short of absolute cruelty or torture was done to render life intolerable to the prisoner; and Matthioli's confinement in the dungeon at Pignerol, and the placing of a crazy monk in his cell, are adduced to support this view. On the other hand, equally trustworthy authorities say that the Mask was treated with profound respect and "distinguished consideration;" that Saint-Mars waited on him in person, and always remained standing and bareheaded in his presence; and that his slightest wishes or caprices, within certain limits, were gratified. Does not the existence of these two sets of equally credible details point conclusively to the fact that there were two prisoners, — a disgraced ambassador and an unfortunate but personally blameless scion of the royal family of France? In the one case no punishment could be too severe for the outraged majesty of the foremost nation of Europe to inflict on him who had betrayed her; in the other, every effort was made to ameliorate the cruel condition of him who was perforce sacrificed to the welfare of the State. As bearing on the supposed identity of Matthioli with the Iron Mask, the two following extracts are not without interest. M. Dutens, in "La Correspondance Interceptée, 1789," says: "In order to treat this subject methodically, I will begin with what the Duc de Choiseul has often related to me. Louis XV. one day told him that he was acquainted with the history of the prisoner with the Mask. The duke begged the king to tell him who he was, but he could get no other answer from him except that all the conjectures which had been hitherto made with regard to the prisoner were false. Some time afterward Madame de Pompadour, at the request of the duke, pressed the king to explain himself upon this subject. Louis XV. upon this told her that he believed he was the minister of an Italian prince." The same testimony, in slightly different garb, is produced by Mr. Quintin Crawford, in his "Mélanges d'Histoire et de Littérateur": "I had heard it said that M. de Choiseul had spoken to Louis XV. on the subject of the masked prisoner, but that he had not been able to obtain any satisfactory answer. I addressed myself to the Abbé Barthélemy and to the Abbé Beliardi, who had both lived in intimacy with M. de Choiseul; they acquainted me that it was at their request the Duc de Choiseul had spoken upon this subject to Louis XV.; that the king had answered him that he believed the prisoner was a minister of one of the courts of Italy, but that the duke observed that this conversation appeared to embarrass him. The Abbé Beliardi told me in proper terms that the king wished to evade the subject. They then begged M. de Choiseul to engage Madame de Pompadour to speak to the king. She did so; but the answer of Louis XV. to his mistress was not more instructive than that which he had given to his minister. Up to 1869 the public had apparently come to the conclusion, mainly through the labors of M. Marius Topin, in his "Man with the Iron Mask," that Matthioli was the mysterious prisoner. But a still more recent work by a French officer, M. Iung, published at Paris in 1873, shows almost conclusively that Matthioli could *not* have been the man, and presents important evidence going to prove that the Mask was the unknown noble chief of a vast conspiracy working for the overthrow of Louis XIV. and his ministers. It is understood that M. Iung examined in the course of his labors upward of seventeen hundred volumes of State papers and despatches.

Ironside. Edmund II., king of the Anglo-Saxons (fl. 989–1017), was so named from his iron armor.

Ironsides. The Cromwellian soldiers were so named on account of the iron resolution they displayed at the battle of Marston Moor.

Iron Tooth. Frederick II., Elector of Brandenburg (fl. 1657–1713).

Iroquois. The name of a confederation of Indian tribes which formerly inhabited the central and western part of New York. Originally, the league consisted of only " five nations," — the Mohawks, Oneidas, Onondagas, Cayugas, and Senecas ; but about 1712 the Tuscaroras were admitted, and the confederation adopted the name " Six Nations." The total number was about 15,000, and the people lived in villages and followed agriculture. They were the most powerful and advanced of all the Indian tribes of North America.

Irrefragable Doctor. Alexander Hales, an English friar (fl. thirteenth century), and founder of the scholastic theology.

Irrepressible Conflict. A term used by William H. Seward, in a speech at Rochester, N. Y., in 1860, to denote the inevitableness of the struggle between freedom and slavery then darkening the political horizon.

Irrevocabile verbum. (Lat.) " Irrevocable word." A word that cannot be recalled.

I. S. Inside Sentinel; Irish Society.

Isa. Isaiah.

Isaac Bickerstaff, Esq. (Pseud.) (1) Jonathan Swift, English divine and satirist (1667-1745.) (2) Sir Richard Steele, English essayist and dramatist (1671–1729).

Isabel. (Pseud.) William Gilmore Simms, American novelist (1806–1870).

Isiac Table. A spurious Egyptian monument sold by a soldier to Cardinal Bembo in 1527, and preserved at Turin. It is of copper, and on it are represented most of the Egyptian deities in the mysteries of Isis. It was said to have been found at the siege of Rome in 1525.

Isidora Martinez. The stage-name of Mrs. John J. King.

Isis. In classic myth an Egyptian divinity, the goddess of the moon. *See* Io ; CAM AND ISIS.

Isl. Island.

Island. An isolated grove of trees in a wide expanse of prairie land.

Island City, The. Montreal, Canada. It is built on an island of the same name.

Island of the Seven Cities. A kind of Dixie's land, where seven bishops who quitted Spain during the dominion of the Moors founded seven cities. The legend says that many have visited the island, but no one has ever quitted it.

Island Sea, The (" Aral Tengheez "). A name given to the Sea of Aral by the Kirgheez, from the multitude of islets it contains.

Islands of the Blest. In classic myth an imaginary cluster of islands in the West, the happy abode of the favorites of the gods after death, and overflowing with the richest and rarest products of Nature.

Isle de Dabney. A sailor's name for the island of Madeira. " 'Cause ever since the world was created the American consul there has been named Dabney, and has kind o' been the king pin there, ownin' pretty nearly all the water-front and bein' consul and shipchandler and merchant all combined together." — COFFIN.

Isle of Peace. A name often given to Aquidneck Island in Narragansett Bay. It is said to be a translation of the Indian name.

Isle of Saints. (Lat. *Insula Sanctorum.*) A mediæval name for Ireland. Christianity there gained many adherents in a remarkably short time, and the country was for ages renowned for the number of erudite and pious clergy it brought forth. *See* HOLY ISLAND (1).

Isocrates of France. Fléchier, Bishop of Nîmes (fl. 1632–1710).

Israfeel. In Mohammedan mythology the name of the angel who is to sound the resurrection trumpet.

Issachar, in Dryden's satire of " Absalom and Achitophel," means

Thomas Thynne, of Longleate Hall, a friend of the Duke of Monmouth. He was assassinated in his carriage, in Pall Mall, by ruffians hired by Count Koningsmark. The cause of this murder was jealousy; both Mr. Thynne and the Count were in love with Lady Elizabeth Percy, the widow of the Earl of Ogle. Her friends contracted her to the rich commoner, but before the marriage was consummated Mr. Thynne was murdered. Within three months the lady married the Duke of Somerset.

Ista colluvies vitiorum. (Lat.) That sink of vices.

Istesso valore, ma un poco più tento. (Ital.) The same time, but rather slower. (Mus.)

Isthmian Games of England. The Epsom Races were so named by Mr. Gladstone. His reputation as a classical scholar is international, and it was therefore quite in keeping with the character of the English Premier to move, as he did on a certain occasion, " that the House do adjourn over Wednesday [the Derby Day], to allow honorable members to be present at our Isthmian Games." *See* BLUE RIBBON OF THE TURF.

I. T. Inner Temple.

It. Italy.

Ita est. (Lat.) It is so.

Ital. Italic; Italian.

Ita lex scripta est. (Lat.) Thus the law is written.

Italic School of Philosophy. The Pythagorean; so called because Pythagoras taught in Italy.

Italic Version. A version of the Bible from the Septuagint, which preceded the Vulgate, or the version by Saint Jerome.

Italy, Garden of. *See* GARDEN OF ITALY.

Italy of the United States. Florida.

Iterum. (Lat.) Further; besides; again.

Itinerant Dey of New Jersey. Gov. William Livingstone, of New Jersey (1723–1790), was so dubbed from his success in eluding capture by the British during the Revolutionary War. Because he was so tall and thin, he was called "The Don Quixote of New Jersey," and a female wit named him "The Whipping-post."

It is easier for a Camel, etc. Lady Duff Gordon, writing from Cairo, says, "Yesterday I saw a camel go through the *eye of a needle;* i. e., the low arched door of an enclosure. He must kneel and bow his head to go through, and thus the rich man must humble himself." Lord Nugent, in his " Travels," tells us that when at Hebron, he was directed to "go out by the needle's eye; that is, by the small side gate of the city."

Ivan Belkine. (Pseud.) Alexander Sergeivitch Pushkin, the Russian novelist and dramatist.

Ivan Ivanovitch. A popular personification of the Russian people, similar to the "John Bull" of the English and the "Jean Crapaud" of the French.

Ivan the Terrible. Ivan IV. of Russia (1529–1584), infamous for his cruelties, but a man of great energy. He first adopted the title of czar.

Ivory Coast. *See* GUINEA COAST.

Ivory Gate of Dreams. Dreams which delude pass through the *ivory* gate, but those which come true through the *horn* gate. This whim depends upon two puns: Ivory, in Greek, is ἐλέφας, and the verb ἐλεφαίρω means "to cheat;" horn, in Greek, is κέρας, and the verb καρανόω means "to accomplish."

Sunt geminæ somni portæ, quarum altera fertur
Cornea, qua veris facilis datur exitus umbris;
Altera candenti perfecta nitens elephanto,
Sed falsa ad cælum mittunt insomnia Manes.
    VIRGIL, *Æneid,* vi. 893–896.
" From gate of horn or ivory, dreams are sent:
These to deceive, and those for warning meant."

Ivory Shoulder. Demeter ate the shoulder of Pelops, served up by Tantalos; so when the gods restored the body to life, Demeter supplied the lacking shoulder by one made of ivory.

Not Pelops' shoulder whiter than her hands,
Nor snowy swans that jet on Isca's sands.
    WM. BROWNE, *Britannia's Pastorals.*

I. W. Isle of Wight.

Ixion. In classic myth king of the Lapithæ, in Thessaly, and father to the Centaurs. He was committed to Hades for gross impiety, and there bound to a swiftly revolving burning wheel.

Ixion. Llewellyn H. Johnson, the earliest champion amateur bicyclist in the United States.

J.

J. Justice, or Judge.

J. A. Judge-Advocate.

Jac. Jacob.

Jack. The anglicized form of the exceedingly frequent French name Jacques, and so adopted as a nickname or diminutive of John, the commonest of English Christian names. Also, as a prefix to terms of reproach or contempt; as Jack-a-napes, Jack-of-all-trades, Jack-a-dandy, Jack Sauce, etc.

Jack-a-Dan and **Kick-'em-Jenny.** "Two islands in the Windward group of islands which belong to the Caribbean division of the West Indies. They are very small; indeed, they are little more than mere islets, which, while they are not sufficiently large and important to appear on any but the most elaborate charts, must be known and recognized by pilots cruising in those waters, in order that they may be avoided. Jack-a-Dan is only thirty-three feet above the sea, and lies in Hillsborough Bay, on the westward coast of the English island of Barbadoes, off what is known as the Hope estate, a large tract of land originally occupied by Sir Edward Hope and still in the possession of the Hope family. Diamond Islet (probably so called from its shape), or Kick-'em-Jenny, lies in the near vicinity. East of the west embankment of Hillsborough Bay is a strip of land, usually covered by twenty-one feet of water, which breaks in a strong breeze."—"DAVUS," in *Lippincott's Magazine.*

Jack-a-Lent. A stuffed image, dressed in tawdry finery, formerly pelted in Lent.

Jack Brag. A vulgar, pretentious braggart, who gets into aristocratic society. The character is in Theodore Hook's novel of the name.

> He was a sort of literary Jack Brag.
> T. H. BURTON.

Jackdaw. A popular name for the daw, a common English bird.

Jack Frost. The popular nursery name by which nipping cold is personified. Frost is a dwarf in the Scandinavian mythology, from whom it is probable our nursery hero is derived.

Jack Harkaway. (Pseud.) Bracebridge Hemynge, a famous writer for boys.

Jack Humphries. (Pseud.) Jonathan F. Kelly, American writer (b. 1820).

Jack Ketch. A sobriquet for the common hangman in England. Jack Ketch is first mentioned in 1678. It was he who beheaded Lord William Russell and later the Duke of Monmouth; and his successors in office have been popularly clothed with his name as well as with his functions.

Jackknife = POCKET-KNIFE. The term "jackknife" has been supposed to be derived from "jack-a-legs," which as a name for a clasp-knife has a queer history. In New England we call to-day a particular kind of cutting implement a jackknife. In the fifteenth and sixteenth centuries communication between Scotland and France of a social and mercantile character was constant. There was a famous French cutler, whose name was Jacque le Coultre. To this day there are fine razors made in France having this name stamped on them. The knives of this Jack le Coultre were sent to Scotland; and so, beyond a doubt, the name jackknife, or jack-a-legs, derived its origin.

Jack Manley. (Pseud.) Entertaining tales in the "Boys and Girls' Weekly," New York, were collaborated by Alfred Trimble and Charles Hull Webb.

Jack of both Sides. One who is, or tries to be, neutral. An English colloquialism.

Jack of Dover. The sole. A very plentiful fish in English waters.

Jack of Newbury. John Winchcomb, "the greatest clothier of the world in the reign of Henry VIII." He kept over a hundred looms at work in his house at Newbury, and raised and armed a hundred men to aid the king against the Scotch at Flodden Field.

Jack of the Feather. An Indian brave who was prominent in the struggles between the settlers and the aborigines of Virginia in 1619.

Jack Robinson. "Before you could say Jack Robinson." This current phrase is said to be derived from a humorous song by Hudson, a tobacconist in Shoe Lane, London. He was a professional song-writer and vocalist, who used to be engaged to sing at supper-rooms and theatrical houses.

> A warke it ys as easie to be done
> As tys to save Jacke! robys on.
>
> HALLIWELL, *Arch. Dictionary.*

During the last half of the eighteenth century in England the governments of the day frequently kept themselves in power by bribing and corrupting members of Parliament; and this was the case during the debates on the India bill, when the opposition, led by Fox, found its majorities steadily decreasing, This, it was known, was the work of the secretary of the treasury, John Robinson, who used both places and money to carry out the ministerial policy. One evening Sheridan, speaking of the decrease, said: "This is not to be wondered at, Mr. Speaker, when a member is employed to corrupt everybody to obtain votes." "Who is it? Name him or withdraw!" rose fiercely from all parts of the house. Sheridan saw that he was in a predicament, but he was equal to the emergency. "Sir," he said, "it would be an unpleasant and an invidious thing to name the person, and therefore I shall not do it. But don't suppose, sir, that I refrain because there is any difficulty in naming him; I could do that, sir, as soon as you could say 'Jack Robinson.'"

Jack the Giant-killer. John Randolph of Roanoke was so named because in a debate he compared himself to David, and his opponent to Goliath.

Jacob Omnium. (Pseud.) Matthew James Higgins, English novelist (1815–1868).

Jacob's Ladder. A stairway or ladder seen in a vision by Jacob (Gen. xxxiii. 12).

Jacquerie. A term applied to bands of revolted peasants, headed by one Caillot, nicknamed "Jacques Bonhomme," who ravaged France during the confinement of King John, in 1358. They were quelled with much bloodshed.

Jacques. (Pseud.) Samuel Ewing, in the "Portfolio."

Jacques Bonhomme (lit., "John Goodman," a homely honest fellow). A sobriquet for the French tradesman.

Jacques Vincent. (Pseud.) Madame Dussaud, French novelist.

Jacta est alea. (Lat.) The die is cast.

J. A. G. Judge Advocate-General.

Jam. Jamaica.

Jamais arrière. (Fr.) Never behind.

James Adair. (Pseud.) Sir Richard Phillips.

James Hasolle. (Anagrammatic Pseud.) Elias Ashmole, English antiquary and alchemist (1617–1692).

James Jessamine. (Pseud.) Bryan Waller Procter ("Barry Cornwall"), in the "Literary Gazette," London.

James Otis. (Pseud.) James Otis Kaler, in "Harper's Young People."

James Russell. The stage-name of James Craythorne.

Jan. January.

Janauschek, Mme. The stage-name of Mrs. Frederick Pillot.

Jane Brown. (Pseud.) Mlle. Blase de Bury, who published in Paris in 1885 a collection of Shakspearian studies.

Jane Hading. The stage-name of Madame Victor König.

Jansenists. A sect who followed the opinions of Jansenius, Bishop of Ypres, in France. They entertained Calvinistic views, and antagonized the Jesuits; but Louis XIV. took part against them, and they were put down by Clement XI. in 1705, in the famous bull called "Unigenitus."

Januæ mentis. (Lat.) "The gates of the mind." The sources of knowledge, — which are the five senses, or, according to Locke, "sensation" and "reflection."

January Searle. (Pseud.) George Searle Phillips, American journalist and author (b. 1817).

Januis clausis. (Lat.) "The doors being closed." With closed doors.

Janus. In classic myth a Roman deity who presided over the beginning of each year, and also over the commencement of all ventures. He is depicted with two faces, — one in front, the other in the back of his head; one youthful, the other venerable. The temple of Janus at Rome was erected by Romulus. It was kept open in wartime, and closed when peace reigned throughout the empire. In seven centuries it was shut only five times, — under Numa, 714 B. C.; at the close of the first Punic War, 235 B. C.; and in the time of Augustus, 29, 25, and 5 B. C.

Janvier. (Pseud.) Joseph J. Woodward.

Japheth's Stone. According to tradition, Noah gave Japheth a stone, and whoever possesses this stone has the power of bringing rain from heaven at will. It was for a long time preserved by the Moguls.

Jaques. (Pseud.) J. Hain Friswell, *littérateur.*

J. Arbuthnot Wilson. (Pseud.) Grant Allen (b. 1848), naturalist and author. *See also* CECIL POWER.

Jardin des plantes. (Fr.) "Garden of plants." A botanical garden.

Jas. James.

Jason. In classic myth a renowned hero, king of Thessaly, and leader of the Argonauts. He espoused Medea and Creusa.

Jay Carlton. (Pseud.) Jay Carlton Goldsmith.

Jayhawker. A nickname for the male inhabitants of Kansas. According to Bartlett's "Dictionary of Americanisms," "Jayhawker" is a cant name in the Western States for a freebooter. Colonel Jennison of New York was a "festive cuss, and his comrades always spoke of him as the 'Gay Yorker.' The expression was afterward used to designate his men, and in its various travels underwent many changes, until at last it crystallized into 'Jayhawker.'" The derivation is far fetched, but it is the only one we find.

Jayhawker. (Pseud.) Col. J. H. Woodard, in the Cincinnati "Enquirer."

Jay's Treaty. The treaty with England, made by John Jay (1794), and which averted war.

J. C. *Juris Consultus.* Jurisconsult.

J. C. D. *Juris Civilis Doctor.* Doctor of Civil Law.

J. Cypress, Jr. (Pseud.) William Post Hawes, American miscellaneous writer (1821–1842).

J. D. Doctor of Laws (*Jurum Doctor*); Junior Deacon.

Jeames. A flunkey, or footman. This was formerly the polite pronunciation of the name James in the best London society, but about the end of the last century it became obsolete and was relegated to the lower classes. Thackeray's "Diary of Jeames Yellowplush" gave the name a proverbial currency in the above sense.

Jean Burnside. The stage-name of Jean B. Carr.

Jean Crapaud (lit., "Johnny Frogs"). A humorous nickname for the French, in allusion to the three frogs which originally formed the armorial bearings of the French kings. *See* LILY OF FRANCE.

Jean Davenport. The stage-name of Mrs. (General) Davenport.

Jean d'Épée ("John with the Sword"). A nickname given to Napoleon I. by his adherents in France who conspired to effect his restoration to power during the Hundred Days.

Jean Froissart. (Pseud.) Alphonse Daudet, in the Parisian newspapers.

Jeanie Yeamans. The stage-name of Mrs. Hyde, *née* Griffiths.

Jean Paul. (Pseud.) Jean Paul Friedrich Richter, German author (1763–1825).

Jebis. The Neptune of Japanese mythology, especially revered by fishermen.

Jebusites, in Dryden's satire of "Absalom and Achitophel," stands for the Roman Catholics; so called because England was Roman Catholic before the Reformation, and Jerusalem was called Jebus before the time of David.

Jedburgh Justice. *See* COWPER LAW.

Jeddart Justice. *See* COWPER LAW.

Jedediah Cleishbotham. (Pseud.) Sir Walter Scott, Scottish novelist (1771–1832).

Jedge Waxem of Wayback. W. J. Lampton, of the Washington "Critic."

Jedwood Justice. *See* COWPER LAW.

Jeems Pipes of Pipesville. (Pseud.) Stephen Massett, the composer and author.

Jefferson Brick. (Pseud.) Alexander Black, in the Brooklyn "Times."

Jeffersonian Simplicity. Thomas Jefferson intensely disliked all display. He objected even to the title of *Mister;* he refused to wear knee-breeches, and wore pantaloons; he abolished the presidential levees, and in going to the Capitol to his inauguration he rode on horseback alone. The Democratic party, deriving as it does, many of its principles from Jefferson, has always affected to follow him in the matter of simplicity.

Jefferson's Embargo. *See* TERRAPIN POLICY.

Jeff Josslyn. (Pseud.) J. E. Ferguson, Washington correspondent of "Texas Siftings."

Jeffreys' Campaign. The name by which James II. designated the judicial tour of Lord Chief-Justice Jeffreys through the west of England in 1685. *See* BLOODY ASSIZE.

Jeffreys Lewis. The stage-name of Mrs. Henry Mainhall, formerly Mrs. J. A. Maitland.

Jehu O'Cataract. (Pseud.) John Neal, American poet and *littérateur* (1793–1876).

Jelly Pardons. When Thomas Cromwell was a clerk in the English factory at Antwerp, two of his fellow-countrymen consulted with him as to the best means of getting the "pardons" renewed for the repair of Boston harbor. Cromwell, knowing that Pope Julius was very fond of dainties, provided for him some exquisite jelly, and told his Holiness that only royalty ever ate it in England. The pope was so pleased with the delicacy that he signed the pardons, on condition of having the receipt of the jelly.

Jemima Compton. (Pseud.) Mrs. Jemima Compton Gladstone.

Jemmy. The signature of James Woesdale, an eighteenth-century painter and dramatic critic.

Je ne sais quoi. (Fr.) "I know not what." Something indefinite.

Jenkins. The colloquial or cant name for a snobbish or servile penny-a-liner. The London "Punch" applied the term to a vulgar reporter of fashionable events for the "Morning Post" who was said to have been originally a footman.

Jennie Bartine. The stage-name of Mrs. Frank David.

Jennie Benson. The stage-name of Mrs. M. J. Fish.

Jennie Cluzette. The stage-name of Mrs. Henry H. Cooke.

Jennie Deans. (Pseud.) Mrs. Jane Grey Swisshelm, in the Philadelphia "Saturday Gazette" and other papers.

Jennie June. (Pseud.) Mrs. Jenny Cunningham Croly, American editress and *littérateur* (b. 1840).

Jennie Wallace. The stage-name of Mrs. Frank Dobson.

Jennie Ward. The stage-name of Mrs. Odell Williams.

Jennie Worrell. The stage-name of Mrs. Hatfield.

Jennison's Jayhawkers. A famous body of raiders during the political troubles of the free-soil war in Kansas.

Jenny l'Ouvrière. A sobriquet for a hard-working and indigent but contented needlewoman. It was coined by Emile Barateau.

Jer. Jeremiah.

Jeremiah. Gibbon called Gildas (fl. 516–570), author of "Lamentations over the Destruction of Britain," the "British Jeremiah."

Jeremiah Ringletub. (Pseud.) John Styles, English Methodist divine (1770–1860).

Jeremias Gotthelf. Albert Bitzius, Swiss author (1797–1854), who wrote "The Mirror of Peasants," "The Clergyman's Wife," "Kate the Grandmother," etc.

Jeremy Diddler. An artful, scheming fellow who lives by his wits. The original of the character is in Kenny's farce, "Raising the Wind." *See* CHEVALIER D'INDUSTRIE.

Jeremy Jaunt. (Pseud.) George Mogridge, an English writer in the Birmingham "Chronicle."

Jericho. "Gone to Jericho." In the manor of Blackmore, about seven miles from Chelmsford, King Henry VIII. had a house which had been a priory, to which he frequently retired when he desired to be free from disturbance. To this place the name Jericho was given as a disguise, so that when any one inquired for the king when he was indulging himself in animal pleasures in Essex, it was customary to say he had "gone to Jericho." In a letter from the Rev. W. Callandar, vicar of Blackmore, dated Oct. 21, 1880, we learn that the place still goes by the name of the 'Jericho estate,' or the 'Blackmore Priory.'" There is a brooklet running through the village, which, Mr. Callandar says, "I have heard called 'the Jordan.'" There seems evidence that the phrase was used in the time of Henry VIII., but it is not quite clear that it originated in the circumstances stated. It may have been originally a rebuke to young upstarts, in allusion to the verse (2 Samuel x. 5), "Tarry at Jericho until your beards be grown."

Jeroboam of Claret. In the works of Walter Scott this phrase frequently occurs. It is understood to mean a large bottle, but the exact contents are not known. Mr. John Hall, writing to "Notes and Queries," Jan. 17, 1880, says, "A *magnum* [of claret] was [contained?] two bottles; a *tappit hen*, four bottles; a *jeroboam*, six bottles."

Jerry Rescue. In October, 1851, while a convention of the Liberty Party was being held in Syracuse, N. Y., Gerrit Smith presiding, Jerry Henry, a slave escaped from Missouri, was seized by a United States marshal in the name of his master. The bell in the Congregational meeting-house was rung, and news of the attempt being communicated to the convention, it broke up, and, assisted by citizens, rescued Jerry from the officers of the law and sent him on his way to Canada.

Jerry Sneak. A henpecked husband. The original of the character is in Foote's farce, "The Mayor of Garratt."

Jersey Lightning. A colloquial term for the apple-jack sold in the State of New Jersey. It is popularly supposed to be extraordinarily rapid in its intoxicating effects.

Jerusalem Pony. Another name for the insects euphoniously named B-Flats and Norfolk Howards (*q. v.*).

Jerusalem Whalley. A famous English traveller and antiquary. It was in 1788 that "Jerusalem" Whalley made the journey which earned him his name. Being asked on one occasion where he was going, he answered in jest to Jerusalem. The company present offered to wager any sum that he would not go there, and he took bets to the amount of between £15,000 and £20,000. The journey was to be performed on foot, except so far as it was necessary to cross the sea, and the exploit was to be finished by playing ball against the walls of that celebrated city. In the "Annual Register" for 1789 it is stated that "Mr. Whalley arrived about June in Dublin from his journey to the Holy Land, considerably within the limited time of twelve months."

Jessie Bartlett Davis. The stage-name of Mrs. C. J. Davis.

Jessie Warner. The stage-name of Mrs. Edward Clarance.

Je suis prêt. (Fr.) I am ready.

Jesuits' Bark. Another name for quinine, the product of the cinchona tree, discovered by a Jesuit, it is said, about 1535, and first used by the Order.

Jet d'eau. (Fr.) A jet of water; a fountain.

Jeu de mots. (Fr.) A play upon words; a pun; a quirk.

Jeu d'esprit. (Fr.) "A play of wit." A witticism.

Jeu de théâtre. (Fr.) A dumb show; gesture.

Jeune Cupidon. *See* BEAU D'ORSAY.

Jewish Hercules. Samson (d. B. C. 1113).

Jewish Plato. A name given to Philo Judæus, an Alexandrian Jew and member of the Platonic sect in the first century A. D.

J. G. W. Junior Grand Warden.

Jim-jams. A miner's term for *delirium tremens.*

Jimmy Brown. (Pseud.) William L. Alden, in "Harper's Young People." *See* FUNNY MAN OF THE "TIMES."

Jingoes, Jingo Party. Nicknames given to the war party in England during the disputes that have embroiled that country in various petty wars since 1876. It arose from the refrain of a music-hall song, once intensely popular, which ran, —

"We don't want to fight, but by jingo, if we do,
We've got the ships, we've got the men, we've got the money too!"

Jinn. In Arabian mythology a fairy, the offspring of fire. They propagate their species like human beings, and are governed by a race of kings named Suleiman. Their chief abode is the mountain Kaf, and they appear to men under the forms of serpents, dogs, cats, monsters, or even human beings, and become invisible at pleasure. The evil jinns are hideously ugly, but the good jinns are exquisitely beautiful.

JJ. Justices.

Jno. John.

Joaquin Miller. (Pseud.) Cincinnatus Heine Miller, famous American poet and novelist.

Job Sass. (Pseud.) George A. Foxcroft, in the Boston "Herald," *circa* 1850.

Job's Comforter. One who pretends to sympathize with your grief, but says that you brought it on yourself; thus in reality adding weight to sorrow.

Jocasta. In classic myth the mother of Œdipus, whom fate decreed that she should marry unknowingly, and by whom she bore Eteocles and Polynices.

Jockey of Norfolk. Sir John Howard, a stanch adherent of Richard III. The night preceding the battle of Bosworth he received a warning as follows: —

"Jockey of Norfolk, be not too bold,
For Dickon, thy master, is bought and sold."

Jo Daviess. (Pseud.) Joseph Hamilton Daviess.

Joe Tukesbury. (Pseud.) Joseph X. Wright, in the St. Louis "Republican."

Johann Abricht. (Pseud.) Jonathan Birch.

Johann Saville Stein. (Pseud.) John Saville Stone, *littérateur.*

John. (Pseud.) John Wesley Beach, in the New York "Sun."

John Ackerlos. (Pseud.) John Stores Smith.

John Bull. A collective nickname for the English people, first used in Arbuthnot's ludicrous "History of Europe." *See* BABOON, NICHOLAS FROG, etc.

John Bull's Mother. The Church of England; so called by Dr. Arbuthnot.

"John had a mother, whom he loved and honored extremely; a discreet, grave, sober, good-conditioned,cleanly old gentlewoman as ever lived. She was none of your cross-grained, termagant, scolding jades . . . always censuring your conduct . . . on the contrary, she was of a meek spirit . . . and put the best construction upon the words and actions of her neighbors. . . . She neither wore a ruff, forehead cloth, nor high-crowned hat. . . . She scorned to patch and paint, yet she loved cleanliness. . . . She was no less genteel in her behavior . . . in the due mean between one of your affected courtesying pieces of formality, and your ill-mannered creatures which have no regard to the common rules of civility."

John Bull's Sister Peg. The Scotch are called "John Bull's Sister Peg," — a poor girl raised on oatmeal and water and lodged in a garret exposed to the north wind, — in Arbuthnot's satirical "History of Europe." She is represented as being very much in love with Jack, who represents John Calvin. *See* JOHN BULL, LOUIS BABOON, NICHOLAS FROG, etc.

John Chalkhill. (Pseud.) Izaak Walton, English writer, author of "The Compleat Angler" (1593–1683).

John Chinaman. A cant nickname for the Chinese among English-speaking people. *See* WASHEE-WASHEE.

John Company. A wide-spread nickname among East Indian peoples for the East India Company. *See* MOTHER COMPANY.

John Dangerfield. The pen-name of Oswald Crawfurd.

John Davids. The name assumed by John Dixwell, the regicide (1607–

1689), on his coming to America after being condemned to death for his participation in the trial and execution of Charles I.

John Doe, Richard Roe. In actions for ejectment at common law John Doe is the nominal plaintiff, who alleges, by a legal fiction, that he has been ousted by an equally sham defendant, Richard Roe. This mode of pleading, which was only resorted to in order to make the trial of the lessor's title the direct and main object of the action, has been abolished in England and in many of the United States.

John Dralloc. (Anagrammatic Pseud.) John Collard, English author (1769–1810.)

John Drum's Entertainment. A colloquialism, denoting the expulsion of an unwelcome guest; derived from the custom of drumming a disgraced soldier out of a regiment.

John Gifford. (Pseud.) (1) Edward Foss, English lawyer and biographer (1788–1866). (2) John Richard Greene, English journalist (1758–1818).

John Green. (Pseud.) George Alfred Townsend (b. 1833). *See* GATH.

John Howlett. (Pseud.) Robert Parsons, English Jesuit (1546–1610).

John H. Selywn. The stage-name of John Josephs.

John Iredale. (Pseud.) B. B. Valentine, a contributor to " Puck."

Johnness. A nickname conferred on Dominique You, one of the Lafitte crew of pirates (1775–1830), by the Americans.

Johnny Bouquet. (Pseud.) George Alfred Townsend, in his letters to the "Tribune," New York. See *supra.*

Johnny Crapaud. A nickname for a Frenchman, taken from the ancient device of the monarchs of France: "Three toads [or frogs] erect, saltant." *See* NICHOLAS FROG.

Johnny Rebs. A sobriquet current among the Union armies during the civil war to denote the soldiers of the Confederacy.

John of Bruges. Jan van Eyck, the Flemish painter (fl. 1370–1441).

John O'Groat's House. The name of an ancient building, once situated on Duncansby Head, the most northerly point in Great Britain. The common phrase "from Land's End to John

O'Groat's " signifies from one extremity of England to the other.

The name Groat or Groot is constantly cropping up in deeds dated from 1488 to 1741, when Malcolm Groat sold his " lands in Dungansby, with the ferry house," to William Sinclair of Freswick. There are still persons of the name of Grot or Groat in the neighborhood ; " but a small green knoll is now all that remains of John O'Groat's house."

John Oldcastle. The pen-name of Wilfrid Meynell, the English writer.

John O'Noakes. A fictitious name made use of by lawyers in actions for ejectment. *See* JOHN DOE and TOM STYLES. It is commonly coupled with " Tom Styles," as is the case with " John Doe " and " Richard Roe."

John Paul. (Pseud.) Charles Henry Webb, a well-known American poet (b. 1834 ?).

John Phœnix, Gentleman. (Pseud.) George H. Derby, U.S.N., American actor and writer (1823–1861).

John Quod. (Pseud.) John Treat Irving, American writer, brother of Washington Irving (b. 1804).

John Sands. (Pseud.) William Hutchinson, in the Newark " Journal."

John Search. (Pseud.) Archbishop Richard Whately, English thinker and writer (1787–1863).

John Shadow. (Pseud). John Byrom, English poet (1691–1763).

Johnson the Terror. Daniel Johnson, the English buccaneer (1629–1675). Having been captured and imprisoned by the Spaniards, he vowed revenge, and on his escape kept his word so effectually that to the Spaniards he was known by the above sobriquet.

John Sterling. (Pseud.) Mrs. Mary Neal Sherwood, translator of the works of Émile Zola into English.

John Strange Winter. (Pseud.) Mrs. Stannard, an English writer, author of several stories of army life, such as " Pluck," " Driver Dallas," etc.

John Surrebutter, Esq. (Pseud.) John Anstey, Irish poet (1796–1867).

John the Almoner. Saint Chrysostom was so named because of the vast sums he gave away in charity.

John the Bearded. Johann Mayo, the German painter, whose beard touched the ground when he stood upright.

John Timon. (Pseud.) Donald G. Mitchell, American miscellaneous writer (b. 1822).

John T. Raymond. The stage-name of John O'Brien, the celebrated comedian (1836–1887).

John Waters. (Pseud.) Henry Carey, English poet and musician (d. 1743).

John with the Leaden Sword. A nickname conferred by Earl Douglas on the Duke of Bedford, Regent for Henry VI. in France.

Jon. (Pseud.) E. Kingman, in the Baltimore " Sun."

Jona. Jonathan.

Jonathan B. Wise. (Pseud.) Stephen Colwell, American writer on finance (1800–1871).

Jonathan Farbrick. (Pseud.) Silas Pinckney Holbrook, American author (1796–1835), in the Boston " Courier."

Jonathan Freke Slingsby. (Pseud.) John Francis Waller, English *littérateur* (b. 1810).

Jonathan Oldbug. (Pseud.) Leonard Withington, D.D., American writer (b. 1789).

Jonathan Oldstyle. (Pseud.) Washington Irving, American author and humorist (1783–1859).

Jonathan Wild the Second. A nickname conferred by the Duke of Wellington on Napoleon I., in allusion to the duplicity, meanness, and treachery displayed by the Corsican on more than one occasion. Jonathan Wild was a noted English thief-taker, whose methods were only less reprehensible than the crimes of those whom he caught.

Jones County Calf Case. A *cause célèbre* in Jones County, Iowa, which was tried no less than six times between 1877 and 1889. The original action arose out of the depredations of a calf, and was for malicious prosecution ; and at each trial, with one exception, the plaintiff secured a verdict ranging from $1,000 to $7,500. The value of the calves out of which the suit grew was $45. The court costs amounted to about $3,500.

Jormungand. In Scandinavian mythology a terrible serpent, offspring of Loki, and whom the gods consigned to the ocean surrounding Midgard, in the depths of which he is to remain till Ragnarok.

Jos. Joseph.

Joseph Arthur. The stage-name of Arthur F. Smith.

Joseph Gay. (Pseud.) Capt. John Durant de Bréval, English soldier and author (1661?–1789).

Josephine Bailey. The stage-name of Mrs. Walter Eytinge.

Josephine Baker. The stage-name of Mrs. John Drew, Jr.

Josephine Cushman. The stage-name of Mrs. William Tetley.

Joseph W. Shannon. The stage-name of J. W. Sendelbach.

Josh. Joshua.

Josh Billings. (Pseud.) Henry W. Shaw, American humorous writer (1815–1885).

Josiah Allen's Wife. Marietta Holley, an American writer.

Josie Hanley. The stage-name of Mrs. John F. Donnelly.

Josie Lee Randolph. The stage-name of Mrs. J. Newton Beers.

Josie Robinson. The stage-name of Mrs. Louis Hayward.

Josie Sutherland. The stage-name of Mrs. William H. Mayo.

Jotunheim. In Scandinavian mythology the abode of the Jotun, or giants.

Jour de fête. (Fr.) "Day of festivity." A saint's day; a festival.

Jove. *See* JUPITER.

Jovial Toper. *See* ANACREON OF THE TWELFTH CENTURY.

Joy City. The national capital, Washington, D. C.

J. P. Justice of the Peace.

J. Prob. Judge of Probate.

J. R. *Jacobus Rex.* King James.

Jr., or **Jun.** Junior.

J. S. of Dale. The pen-name of J. F. Stimson, a Bostonian *littérateur* and novelist of the present day.

Jubilate Deo. (Lat.) Be joyful in God.

Jucundi acti labores. (Lat.) Labors past are pleasant.

J. U. D., or **J. V. D.** *Juris utriusque Doctor.* Doctor of both laws (of the Canon and the Civil Law).

Jud. Judicial; Judith.

Judas-colored Hair. It has long been a current belief that Judas Iscariot had red hair and beard, though there was probably nothing but the popular dislike of the color to justify the opinion. The old dramatists and poets have frequent allusions to the subject. Shakspeare, in "As You Like It," makes Rosalind

say, "His hair is of the dissembling color," to which Celia replies, "Something browner than Judas's" (act iii. sc. 4). Middleton, in the "Chaste Maid of Cheapside," 1620, makes one of his characters, speaking of a gilt Apostle spoon, say, "Sure that was Judas with the red beard." Dryden, in "Amboyna," has, "There's treachery in that Judas-colored beard," and in his celebrated epigram on Jacob Tonson describes him as having "two left legs and Judas-colored hair." The national dislike to red hair has been conjectured to have originated in the aversion English people felt to the red-haired Danes. It is curious that Cain is also credited with having had a red beard.

Judas Tree. A corruption of Kuamos tree; *i. e.*, the leguminous or bean tree. The corrupt name has given rise to the tradition that it was upon one of these trees that Judas Iscariot hanged himself.

Judenhasse and Judenhetze ("hatred of the Jews"). Terms given to the uprisings against that people in Germany, Austria, and Russia, in 1880 and subsequent years, occasioned by jealousy of their prosperity and exclusiveness.

Judg. Judges.

Judge-Adv. Judge-Advocate.

Judge Lynch. A personification of turbulent or lawless justice or of mob law. "Lynch law" is the name given to the trial and punishment of offenders in popular assemblies without reference to the ordinary laws and institutions of the country. This barbarous mode of administering justice has always more or less prevailed in every country in times of great popular excitement, and has been necessarily resorted to in countries newly settled, where the power of the civil government is not yet established. "Judge" Lynch was a resident on the Virginia frontier, to whom, in the absence of a legal tribunal, it was usual to refer local disputes for settlement, and whose wisdom and impartiality caused his name to become a byword.

Judge Vernon. (Pseud.) E. C. Tuttle, in the Western press.

Judicious Hooker. Richard Hooker (fl. 1553–1600), an eminent English divine, was so named because of his candor and moderation.

Judicium Dei. (Lat.) The judgment of God.

Jugulare mortuos. (Lat.) "To stab the dead." To be guilty of superfluous cruelty.

Julep. In its original significance this term indicates a decoction compounded of brandy, mint leaves, and chopped ice; yet in Virginia "julep" takes the place of the word "drink" current elsewhere.

Jules Levy. The professional name of Isaac Levi, the famous cornet-player.

Julia Melrose. The stage-name of Mrs. Henry W. Lemon.

Julia Wilson. The stage-name of Mrs. Charles F. Fox.

Julius Florus. A reportorial personification of Mr. Pitt in the days when newspaper reports of Parliamentary proceedings were not legalized.

Jul. Per. Julian Period.

June Winter. (Pseud.) Emily Frances Wheeler.

Juniores ad labores. (Lat.) Young men for labors.

Juniper. One of the signatures commonly attributed to Junius (*q. v.*).

Junius. The years 1767–68 are memorable as the first of a period of storm and stress in English political affairs. George III. was in the twenty-ninth year of his extended and eventful reign. The clever and courageous but utterly unscrupulous John Wilkes was at the zenith of his dearly bought popularity with the people, and his no less well-deserved disfavor with the king and court. In October, 1768, Lord Chatham retired from the ministry which he had formed out of very discordant materials two years before, to be succeeded for a brief term by the Duke of Grafton, a well-meaning but unwise and incompetent statesman. Almost the first event of the new régime was the arrival of a military force in Boston, the initial act in a drama out of the throes of which, fifteen years later, a nation was to be born. In the same year Captain Cook sailed on his first voyage round the world, and James Bruce set out on his memorable travels for the discovery of the sources of the Egyptian Father of Waters. On the continent of Europe there were "wars and rumors of wars," in which England could scarcely escape embroilment. At the threshold of this season of ferment, about the middle of the year 1767, a new political writer arose sun-like above the stormy horizon, whose effulgence marks an epoch in the affairs of England. He wielded a trenchant and truculent pen, and possessed an evident familiarity with public affairs, coupled with brilliant sarcasm, pungent invective, and incisive wit. These qualities took men of all parties by storm. No former English writer, it was said, succeeded in at once so completely exasperating and delighting the English nation. The "Public Advertiser" newspaper was made the vehicle for the dissemination of these political epistles, which were addressed to various persons. The identity of their author was concealed under a variety of pseudonyms, — "Poplicola," "Memnon," "Lucius," "Junius," "Philo-Junius," "Brutus," "Nemesis," and others; but the celebrity attaching to the entire series centres around the pseudonym of "Junius," which was appended to the greater number and the more pungent and powerful of the letters. The same hand is now known to have indited many of the others, so that the question of the authorship of most of these may be considered as substantially settled. As a "Grenville" or "Rockingham" Whig, the polyonomous critic mercilessly assailed the new prime minister, Grafton, and his foreign and domestic policy, and similarly antagonized many features of the ministerial programme during the two years immediately following the accession of Lord North to power. Nor was royalty itself sacred from attack. The "divinity that doth hedge a king" offered no protection from the well-feathered bolts that flew thick and fast from the pen of this incomparable literary archer. John Wilkes, in his famous "Number 45," five or six years earlier, had the temerity to accuse the monarch of uttering falsehood in a speech from the throne. While "Junius" did not proceed to such coarse extremes, his utterances were sufficiently caustic and rancorous to arouse feelings of bitterest hatred in the hearts of the king and the Tories. Could his identity have been unmasked, there is little doubt that a worse fate than that of Wilkes would have been his. On the other hand, "Junius" became the idol of the popular and thinking heart of England. No efforts were spared to discover the personality veiled behind the pen-name of "Junius." Said Edmund Burke, in a famous speech in the House of Commons : "How comes this 'Junius' to have broken through the cobwebs of the law, and to rage uncontrolled, unpunished, through the land? The myrmidons of the court have been long, and are still, pursuing him in vain. They will not spend their time upon me or you. No; they disdain such vermin when the mighty boar of the forest, that has broken through all their toils, is before them. But what will all their efforts avail? No sooner has he wounded one than he lays another dead at his feet. For my part, when I saw his attack upon the king, I own my blood ran cold. King, Lords, and Commons are but the sport of his fury. Were he a member of this House, what might not be expected from his knowledge, his firmness, his integrity! He would be easily known by his contempt of all danger, by his penetration, by his vigor. Nothing would escape his vigilance and activity. Bad ministers could conceal nothing from his sagacity, nor could promises nor threats cajole him to conceal anything from the public." The theme of the "Letters of Junius" has been briefly described as the vindication of popular liberty. The key-note of the whole series is pitched in the following passage : " The submission of a free people to the executive authority of government is no more than a compliance with laws which they themselves have enacted." The period covered by the "Letters" extends from the communication signed "Poplicola," dated April 28, 1767, down to the epistle of "Nemesis," dated May 12, 1772. The "Letters of Junius," properly so named, and fathered by him, number in all fifty-nine, from Jan. 21, 1769, to Jan. 21, 1772, a period of exactly three years. Forty-four bear the signature of "Junius," and fifteen that of "Philo-Junius" (acknowledged by "Junius" as his). The titles of these are : Written by "Junius" : To the Duke of Grafton, eleven; to the printer of the "Public Advertiser," ten; to Sir William Draper, five; to Chief-Justice Mansfield, three; to Edward Weston, to Dr. William Blackstone, on Walpole's Case, to the Duke of Bedford, on the Rescue of General Gansel, on Modestus, Address to the King, Retrospect of the Parliamentary Session, to Lord North, on the Falkland Islands, on Privileges of Parliament, on Parliamentary Resolutions, to the Rev. Mr. Home, to the Livery of London, to Lord Camden, one each, — forty-four in all. Written by "Philo-Junius:" To the printer of the "Public Advertiser," ten; on Walpole's Case, one; on the Spanish Convention, one; to Modestus, one; to Zeno, one; to an Advocate of the Cause of the People, one, — fifteen in all. Almost sphinx-like was the air of cold, haughty, and impenetrable secrecy with which "Junius" enveloped himself. The only being whom he admitted to anything approaching confidential relations was Woodfall. To him "Junius" wrote frequently, and his communications are couched in friendly and amiable terms, but always in the feigned "Junian" handwriting, of which more anon. Perhaps Woodfall may have made a shrewd guess at the secret of his unknown contributor; it almost certainly was not confided to him. There is a story to the effect that the identity of "Junius" eventually became known to the Government, and that immediately the "Letters" ceased. George III. is reported to have said, "We know who 'Junius' is. He will write no more." The anecdote is probably an apocryphal one, yet it is at least a curious coincidence that almost immediately after the sudden cessation of the "Letters" one of the very few men in opposition to the Government capable of penning such able philippics should have been appointed by the ministry to a lucrative and magnificent post in India. "I am the sole depository of my own secret, and it shall perish with me," wrote "Junius" to Woodfall. It is safe to assert that he was in truth, as he said, the depository of his own secret. He made no confidants, and no one survived him who could throw a gleam of radiance in the shape of direct evidence on the darkness of the mystery. The testimony, however cumulative and conclusive, is purely circumstantial. Doubtless much of the interest excited in the popular mind was owing to the success with which the identity of the writer was concealed. Public curiosity was whetted to the utmost, and they read who never read before. Says Dr. Samuel Johnson, in his sonorous style, alluding to this feature : "'Junius' burst into notice with a blaze of impudence which has rarely glared upon the world before, and drew the rabble after him as a monster makes a show. When he had once provided for his safety by impenetrable secrecy, he had nothing to combat but truth and justice, — enemies whom he knows to be feeble in the dark. Being then at liberty to indulge himself in all the immunities of invisibility, out of the reach of danger he has been bold, out of the reach of shame he has been confident. As a rhetorician he has the art of persuading when he seconded desire; as a reasoner, he has convinced those who had no doubt before; as a moralist, he has taught that virtue may disgrace; and as a patriot he has gratified the mean by insults on the high. It is not by his liveliness of imagery, his pungency of periods, or his fertility of allusion, that he detains the cits of London or the boors of Middlesex. Of style and sentiment they take no cognizance." Clearly the "Great Cham" was not among those who were dazzled by the Junian "blaze of impudence." It may be of interest if we reproduce here the names of the more prominent persons to whom has been ascribed the authorship of the "Letters of Junius." Wellnigh every Englishman of note then on the stage of human action has been mentioned in connection with them, and his "claims" advocated, at some time or other during the past eighty years. The list embraces Mr. Sergeant Adair, Col. Isaac Barré, Hugh Macaulay Boyd, Edmund Burke, Bishop Butler, Lord Camden, Lord Chatham, Lord Chesterfield, M. de Lolme, Lord Ashburton, Samuel Dyer, Henry Flood, Philip Francis, D.D. (father of the following), Sir Philip Francis, Edward Gibbon, Richard Glover, Henry Grattan, William Greatrakes, George Grenville, James Grenville, William Gerard ("Single-Speech") Hamilton, James Hollis, Sir William Jones, John Kent, Gen. Charles Lee, Charles Lloyd, Lord Thomas Lyttleton, Laughlin Mac-Leary, the Duke of Portland, Gov. Thomas Pownall, Sir Robert Rich, John Roberts, Rev. Philip Rosenhagen, Lord George Sackville, Earl Shelburne, Earl Temple, John Horne Tooke, Horace Walpole, John Wilkes, Alexander Wedderburn, James Wilmot, and Daniel Wray, — no less than forty-two, — and we have only named the more prominent names. But out of this lengthy list there are very few who really possessed the intellect, the statesmanship, and the knowledge of affairs manifested

in the "Letters." The suggestion of so many names, however, all more or less probable, shows how difficult was the task of discovering the real name of the hidden writer, and how completely nonplussed were the critics. The "claims" of Boyd, Burke, Butler, Dunning, Dyer, Flood, Roberts, Rosenhagen, and Sackville were laboriously considered and sifted by Dr. Good, and for wise and weighty reasons all were declared out of the question. Macaulay disposed of five of the greatest names in as many lines. He says: "Lord Lyttleton's claims to the authorship of 'Junius' are better than those of Burke and Barré, and quite as good as those of Lord George Sackville or 'Single-Speech' Hamilton." His opinion as to the true identity of "Junius" will appear later. The evidence "of places and circumstances, of sentiments and opinions, of political connections and of handwriting seems decisive" against nearly all of those just enumerated. After the lapse of years there remain but four or five names to whom the authorship of the "Letters" can be attributed with the faintest show of probability. These names are those of Colonel Barré, Lord George Sackville, the Grenvilles, and Sir Philip Francis. But the field of inquiry has been still further circumscribed, and the first member of this quintet may be declared out of the race. It is now believed by many critics that "either the authorship remains an impenetrable enigma, or that it belongs to one whose name was not mentioned in connection with it for many years subsequently" to the cessation of the "Letters," — Sir Philip Francis. As might be expected, the Junian controversy gave birth to a vast literature, a perusal of the bibliography of which would only afford evidence of the follies and foibles which have dominated many otherwise well-balanced and estimable persons. Suffice it to say that although the judicious Allibone has expressed the opinion that men are hanged every year on less evidence than has been adduced in favor of more than one of these claimants, the majority of the publications on the subject are devoted to the support of theories so wild and visionary that the wonder is that men capable of wielding a pen should lend themselves to their advocacy. We shall content ourselves, therefore, with glancing only at those works whose authors devote themselves to considering or pushing the claims of the candidates for honors already named, — the Grenvilles, Colonel Barré, Lord Sackville, and Sir Philip Francis; seeing that all other clews land the investigator, sooner or later, in a blind alley. A number of books, essays, etc., were written to prove that Col. Isaac Barré was "Junius," chief among which is the work of Mr. John Britton, who contends that Barré was aided by Lord Shelburne and Mr. Dunning. Conversely, in an article published in the London "Morning Herald" in 1813, the men composing this talented trio were shifted about, and the assertion made that Lord Shelburne was "Junius," and that he was assisted by Barré and Dunning. Col. Isaac Barré was an officer in the English army, and was born in Dublin in 1726. He served in Canada under Wolfe, and was returned to Parliament in 1761. In 1765 he won the applause of the North American colonists by a spirited speech against the iniquitous Stamp Act. This latter event, and his subsequent course of action during Lord North's administration, would seem to be among the chief grounds on which his claims are based. But "one swallow does not make a summer." Britton's work has been summarized as " a curious instance of the delusion to which ingenious men may resign themselves when they have a favorite opinion to uphold." Lord George Sackville, who afterward became Lord Germain, is the second of the quintet whose claims have alone been thought worthy of serious consideration. In a work by George Coventry, published in 1825, and entitled "A Critical Inquiry regarding the Real Author of the ' Letters of Junius,' " they are proved (?) to have been written by Lord Sackville. This theory was amplified and improved on in an American publication emanating from Boston in 1828. Charles Butler, in his " Reminiscences," also thinks that Lord Sackville was the author of the " Junian Letters," and that Sir Philip Francis was his amanuensis and secretary. Still another change has been rung on this pretty combination. Mr. Jaques adopts the theory that D'Oyly was a fellow-clerk with Francis in the War Office, and the confidential agent between Sackville and Francis. Dr. Good decidedly

rejects the Sackvillian theory. Come we now to the most important of the coterie above named, and the only one whose " claims " to the authorship of the " Letters of Junius " have stood the test of time and controversy, — Sir Philip Francis. To the consideration of the evidence pointing to this personage many voluminous works have been devoted, to say nothing of a vast number of essays, reviews, and magazine articles. Incidentally, also, the advocates of the claims of others give more or less space to the case against Francis. But among all the Junian literature the palm for scholarship, critical acumen, and painstaking investigation must be awarded to " The Identity of Junius with a Distinguished Living Character Established," by Mr. John Taylor, published in London in 1816, during the lifetime of Sir Philip Francis, and never contradicted, noticed, or refuted by him. Concerning this work and the evidence presented therein, Lord Brougham wrote: " That it proves Sir Philip to be ' Junius ' we will not affirm, but this we can safely assert, that it accumulates such a mass of circumstantial evidence as renders it extremely difficult to believe he is not; and that if so many coincidences shall be found to have misled in this case, our faith in all conclusions drawn from proofs of a similar kind may henceforth be shaken." Sir Philip Francis first saw the light in 1740, in Dublin, which was likewise the place of nativity of Col. Isaac Barré, who was, as we have seen, another fetich of the "Junius " seekers. His father was the Rev. Philip Francis, chaplain to Lord Holland, and preceptor to Charles James Fox. Dr. Johnson considered his translation of Horace the best then extant. Young Francis removed to London when about ten years of age. He was a clerk in the War Office from 1763 to 1772, and in 1773 was appointed a member of the Supreme Council of Bengal, of which Warren Hastings was president. The outcome of Francis's official residence in India was a duel between him and Hastings, who asserted that the former was destitute of feelings of truth and honor, in which Francis was seriously wounded. He returned to England in 1780, entered Parliament in 1784, and took a leading part in the impeachment and trial of his former enemy, Warren Hastings. He voted with Fox, and strenuously advocated the abolition of the slave-trade. In 1806 he was made a Knight of the Bath, and shortly thereafter retired from public life. He died in London in 1818. When the publication of the " Junian Letters " was begun Francis had for some years been a clerk in the War Office, and this circumstance furnished the basis of the argument advanced by Mr. Taylor. Many of the letters were penned on War Office paper. " So accurate is the knowledge of the business of that bureau betrayed by the writer, that the conviction of his having been concerned in that department is irresistible, nor can any other person in a similar position capable of having penned the 'Letters' be pointed out." This may be; yet the reader is immediately prompted to inquire whether it was not an extremely daring step for the writer of the famous philippics, supposing him to have been on the staff at the War Office, to have used the official paper of that branch of the service, seeing that such a course must inevitably direct attention to the employes thereof? The handwriting, of course, was feigned, and before the case against Sir Philip could be advanced beyond conjecture, it was necessary to settle the question whether the feigned Junian hand could be identified with his. An old love-letter was the means of starting this pregnant inquiry. Just here the following anecdote may not be out of place. It was related to Mr. Twistleton by Mr. W. J. Blake of Danesbury, to whom it was told by his father, Mr. William Blake, and deals with the Junian signature: " After the publication of ' Junius Identified,' Mr. William Blake was in a country-house with Sir Philip Francis, and happened to converse with him on the poetry of Lord Byron, to which Sir Philip expressed his aversion. This induced Mr. Blake to single out for his perusal the well-known lines in the ' Giaour,' beginning with ' He who hath bent him o'er the dead.' Francis read them, went to a writing-table, seized a piece of paper, wrote down on it a string of words which he extracted from those lines, ending with ' nothingness ' and ' changeless," added below them the word ' senseless,' and then rapidly subscribed his initials between two dashes. On observing the signature, Mr. Blake said to him, ' Pray, will you allow me to ask you, Sir Philip,

do you always sign your initials in that manner?' Sir Philip merely answered gruffly, ' I know what you mean, sir,' and walked away." This took place in or about the year 1817, forty-eight years after May 3, 1769, the date of the " Letter " in which the signature of his initials between two dashes first occurs. It occurred to Mr. Twistleton that if sufficient documentary materials were placed at the disposal of Mr. Chabot, the expert, he would be able to give a valuable and trustworthy opinion as to whether Sir Philip Francis did or did not write the " Letters of Junius." Mr. Twistleton therefore procured from a granddaughter of Francis a letter-book containing forty-two original private letters written and sent by Francis to his brother-in-law and to his wife during the years 1767–1771 inclusive, very nearly the period covered by the whole Junian correspondence. From the trustees of the British Museum access was gained to all the original manuscripts of the writings of " Junius," while Mr. Murray allowed Mr. Grenville the use of the autograph manuscripts of the " Letters of Junius " which were in his possession. Mr. Twistleton's instructions to Mr. Chabot were, " that he should submit the handwriting of ' Junius ' to a searching comparison with the letters of Sir Philip Francis, and should state professionally his opinion in writing whether the letters of Francis and the letters of ' Junius ' were or were not written by the same hand." The results of this inquiry were published by Mr. Twistleton in a volume of 197 pages quarto, with a large number of fac-simile plates of specimens from Sir Philip's handwriting, that of " Junius," and that of Lord George Sackville, and must convince the unbiassed reader that, so far as the matter of penmanship is concerned, the evidence which proves Francis and " Junius " to have been one is circumstantially complete. One of the most interesting and romantic episodes of this inquiry into the Junian and Francisan handwriting remains to be narrated. Who would imagine that a love-letter could supply an important clew in determining the author of epistles breathing biting sarcasm and bitter invective? Says Twistleton: " In the Christmas season of 1770 or 1771, when Mr. Francis was on a visit to his father at Bath, he danced at the Assembly

Rooms more than one evening with a young lady named Miss Giles. This lady, born in 1751, was a daughter of Daniel Giles, Esq., afterward Governor of the Bank of England; and in January, 1772, she became Mrs. King by marrying Joseph King, Esq., of Taplow. It was the custom at balls, a hundred years ago, for a lady to retain the same partner during the whole of the evening; so that the fact of Miss Giles having thus danced with Mr. Francis would imply more of an acquaintance than would necessarily be involved in a young lady's dancing with a gentleman at the present day." One result of this acquaintance was that a set of verses, accompanied by an anonymous note, was sent to Miss Giles. The writer of the note declared that he had found the verses, which were unaddressed, and that he could not conceive for whom they were meant unless for her. The anonymous note ran as follows: "The inclosed paper of Verses was found this morning by Accident. The person who found them, not knowing to whom they belong, is obliged to trust to his own Judgment, and takes for granted that they could only be meant for Miss Giles." The verses were: —

"When Nature has, happily, finished her Part,
    There is Work enough left for the Graces;
'T is harder to keep than to conquer the Heart;
    We admire and forget pretty Faces.

"In the School of the Graces, by Venus attended,
    Belinda improves ev'ry hour;
They tell her that Beauty itself may be mended,
    And shew her the use of her Pow'r.

"They alone have instructed the fortunate Maid
    In Motion, in Speech, and Address;
They gave her that wonderful Smile to persuade,
    And the Language of Looks to express.

"They directed her Eye, they pointed the Dart,
    And have taught her a dangerous Skill;
For whether she aims at the Head or the Heart,
    She can wound, if she pleases, or kill."

At the time their fair recipient suspected that Francis was the author, but of course said nothing. Though she subsequently became the wife of another gentleman she preserved the verses and the anonymous note. Many years afterward it fell out that a scrap of Junius's handwriting was being handed round in the circle in which she happened to be. "Why," exclaimed Mrs. King, "I know that writing. The person who wrote that wrote me some verses and a letter." The verses and the note in question " were written each on a separate sheet of common letter-paper, and the handwriting of the two is different. The reason of this is obvious. The humor of the compliment required such a difference. The two documents, though wholly unconnected with St. Valentine's Day, must be regarded in the light of a valentine; the essential idea of which is, that whereas certain verses in praise of a young lady had been found by accident, Miss Giles alone merited such praise, and the verses were therefore sent to her as the person for whom they were intended. Hence it would have been out of keeping with the plan of the valentine if the verses and the note had been in the same handwriting. Now for the linking of these twin documents with the solution of the query, Who wrote the " Letters of Junius "? The anonymous note is in the handwriting of " Junius; " the verses are in the handwriting of Francis's cousin, Tilghman. But at first it was thought that the verses were in the natural handwriting of Francis. Mr. Twistleton and a number of experts and others were of this opinion. But here the plot thickened. To establish clearly this hypothesis, Twistleton applied to Netherclift, the famous expert, who had previously examined the handwriting of the anonymous note, for an opinion. But that gentleman, in consequence of illness, could not undertake the labor of an investigation, so the case was placed in the hands of Chabot. But Chabot, after comparing the verses with the letters of Francis, pronounced an opinion directly contrary to what was expected. He maintained that "he should not be justified in stating that the verses were in the handwriting of Francis, for he thought he could prove the negative, — that Francis had not and could not have written the verses," and in corroboration of his opinion he pointed out numerous peculiarities of writing in the verses which were not in the letters, and *vice versa.* Mr. Twistleton, we are told, at once acquiesced in the professional opinion of Mr. Chabot; but recollecting, from the recently published " Life of Francis," that his cousin and familiar friend, Mr. Richard Tilghman, was with Francis at Bath when the verses were sent to Miss Giles, it struck Mr. Twistleton that Francis might possibly have availed himself of the services of Tilghman as an amanuensis. Fortunately, in the letter-book of Francis, which was in Mr. Twistleton's possession, there were six letters written to Francis by Tilghman. These were now submitted, together with the verses, to Mr. Chabot, who expressed his unhesitating conviction that the verses were in the handwriting of Tilghman. From which it would seem that "Francis, with his usual caution, was unwilling to bring his own handwriting into any connection with that of 'Junius,' and accordingly wrote the anonymous note himself in the Junian hand, employing Tilghman to copy the verses, who probably never saw the note." The latter, as we have seen, is in the disguised upright hand of Sir Philip Francis, identical with that in which the "Junian Letters" were penned. That the two documents were really sent by Francis to Miss Giles there is no reasonable doubt. Out of the foregoing inquiry as to who wrote the love-letter and the accompanying verses, grew the greater investigation undertaken by Chabot into the whole of the Junian correspondence, the results of which we have already seen. That Sir Philip publicly and in the strongest terms denied the authorship of the "Letters" is very well known; but by that denial one is only reminded of the reply said to have been made under similar circumstances by the famous author of "Ecce Homo": "Why, if I had written it, you know, I should certainly say I had n't." The following passage occurs in Lord Malmesbury's "Memoirs of an ex-Minister." According to Lord Tankerville, "it was supposed that Francis intended his name to be disclosed after his death, and had left papers establishing his identity with 'Junius,' but they were destroyed by his son-in-law. He determined not to acknowledge himself as the author of those 'Letters' during his lifetime, and disliked to be asked questions on the subject. One evening, at Brooks's, the conversation having fallen on a book just published which proved Francis to be 'Junius,' Rogers the poet went up to him and said, 'Sir Philip, will you allow me to ask you a question?' To which the other replied very fiercely, 'Yes, sir, at your peril.' Upon which Rogers turned round to some one near him, and said, 'If he is not "Junius," he is Junius Brutus.'" The following concise and able sum-

mary of the whole subject is from the pen of Mr. R. Garnett, who evinces an intimate acquaintance with the mazes of the Junius Quest: "The external evidence for the Francisan authorship of 'Junius,' then, appears as strong as could be reasonably expected. The impression left by the whole investigation cannot be better summed up than in the words of Mr. Merivale: 'All the lines of investigation which have been followed in order to trace the authorship of this or that known individual, except Francis, fail at a certain point. They end in impossibilities. The remaining path, to which one clew only leads us, becomes plainer and plainer the further the investigation is conducted. The ingenuity of most formidable opponents has been exerted to discover some demonstrable incompatibility between the circumstances attending the production of the "Letters" and the authorship of Francis. None such has been adduced. Francis, as was said of Godolphin, is never in the way and never out of the way. The one argument against him is derived from the evidence of style. But the distinction established is rather one of degree than of kind. There is no such incompatibility between the style of his acknowledged writings and that of the "Letters" as to render it morally impossible to attribute them to the same writer. It is not as though a pamphlet attributed to Swift should bear the impress of Bolingbroke. The admitted productions of Francis might pass for the work of a disciple of "Junius." The real difficulty is that Francis should never have equalled himself. This, certainly, is a difficulty, and is hardly obviated by Lord Macaulay's sensible but somewhat superficial reply, that every work of the same author cannot be the best. It can hardly, however, be held to count for much against the weight of external testimony, especially when the extraordinary moral resemblance between Francis and "Junius" is taken into account. Whoever "Junius" was, he must have been in temperament very much such a man as Francis is known to have been,—vehement, combative, opinionated, disdainful, sarcastic, enthusiastically and disinterestedly devoted to the public good as he conceived it, but capable of the most unrelenting and unscrupulous animosity to all who crossed his path.

When, in his extreme old age, the authorship was first publicly imputed to him, he neither denied nor admitted it, but his demeanor showed that he wished it to be believed.'" Says Macaulay, in answer to the query, Was Philip Francis the author of the "Letters of Junius"?—"Our own firm belief is that he was. The evidence is, we think, such as would support a verdict in a civil, nay, in a criminal proceeding. The handwriting of 'Junius' is the very peculiar handwriting of Francis, slightly disguised. As to the position, pursuits, and connections of 'Junius,' the following are the most important facts which can be considered as clearly proved: (1) That he was acquainted with the technical forms of the Secretary of State's office; (2) That he was intimately acquainted with the business of the War Office; (3) That he, during the year 1770, attended debates in the House of Lords, and took notes of speeches, particularly of the speeches of Lord Chatham; (4) That he bitterly resented the appointment of Mr. Chamier to the place of Deputy Secretary at War; (5) That he was bound by some strong tie to the first Lord Holland. Now, Francis passed some years in the Secretary of State's office. He was subsequently chief clerk of the War Office. He repeatedly mentioned that he had himself, in 1770, heard speeches of Lord Chatham, and some of these speeches were actually printed from his notes. He resigned his clerkship at the War Office from resentment at the appointment of Mr. Chamier. It was by Lord Holland that he was first introduced into the public service. Now, here are five marks, all of which ought to be found in 'Junius.' They are all five found in Francis. We do not believe that more than two of them can be found in any other person whatever. If this argument does not settle the question, there is an end of all reasoning on circumstantial evidence. The internal evidence seems to us to point the same way. The style of Francis bears a strong resemblance to that of 'Junius;' nor are we disposed to admit, what is generally taken for granted, that the acknowledged compositions of Francis are very decidedly inferior to the anonymous letters. The argument from inferiority, at all events, is one which may be urged with at least equal force against every claimant

that has ever been mentioned, with the single exception of Burke; and it would be a waste of time to prove that Burke was not 'Junius.' And what conclusion, after all, can be drawn from mere inferiority? Every writer must produce his best work; and the interval between his best work and his second best work may be very wide indeed. Nobody will say that the best letters of 'Junius' are more decidedly superior to the acknowledged works of Francis than three or four of Corneille's tragedies to the rest, than the 'Pilgrim's Progress' to the other works of Bunyan, than 'Don Quixote' to the other works of Cervantes. Nay, it is certain that 'Junius,' whoever he may have been, was a most unequal writer. To go no further than the letters which bear the signature of 'Junius,' the 'Letter to the King' and the 'Letters to Horne Tooke' have little in common except the asperity; and asperity was an ingredient seldom wanting either in the writings or in the speeches of Francis. Indeed, one of the strongest reasons for believing that Francis was 'Junius' is the moral resemblance between the two men. It is not difficult, from the letters which under various signatures are known to have been written by 'Junius,' and from his dealings with Woodfall and others, to form a tolerably correct notion of his character. He was clearly a man not destitute of real patriotism and magnanimity, a man whose vices were not of the sordid kind. But he must also have been a man in the highest degree arrogant and insolent, a man prone to malevolence, and prone to the error of mistaking his private malevolence for public virtue. 'Doest thou well to be angry?' was the question asked in old time of the Hebrew prophet. And he answered: 'I do well.' This was evidently the temper of 'Junius,' and to this cause we attribute the savage cruelty which disgraces several of his 'Letters.' No man is so merciless as he who under a strong self-delusion confounds his antipathies with his duties. It may be added that 'Junius,' though allied with the democratic party by common enmities, was the very opposite of a democratic politician. While attacking individuals with a ferocity which perpetually violated all the laws of literary warfare, he regarded the most defective parts of old institutions with a respect amounting to pedantry, pleaded the cause of Old Sarum with fervor, and contemptuously told the capitalists of Manchester and Leeds that if they wanted votes they might buy land and become freeholders of Lancashire and Yorkshire. All this, we believe, might stand, with scarcely any change, for a character of Philip Francis." In the face of this judgment from so high an authority it would be rash to affirm with certainty that the quest of the "Junius" seekers has been unrewarded. On the other hand, Mr. Pitt told Lord Aberdeen that he knew who wrote the "Junius Letters," and that it was not Francis! Lady Grenville sent a letter to the editor of the "Diaries of a Lady of Quality" to the same effect. The late Abraham Hayward, critic and essayist, wrote a pamphlet on the "Junius" mystery, in 1868, in order to disprove the claims of Sir Philip Francis. In the judgment of Sir Alexander Cockburn he successfully demolished the case for the defendant. And in an article in the "London Quarterly Review" Mr. Hayward leaned toward Lord George Sackville, for whom, he told a correspondent, he "could make out a capital case if he thought it worth while." But afterward he "settled down in the belief that the famous ' Letters ' were supplied by the Grenvilles, but did not come to a conclusion as to which of them, if either, was the actual writer of them. He did not doubt that Pitt knew who the writer was. No doubt Sir Philip Francis desired it to be believed that he was the author, and tried to leave proofs of his claim." But, as one of Mr. Hayward's correspondents points out, the real "Junius" had three sets of the "Letters" bound in a specific fashion, and had Francis been the author he could have produced or accounted for these books.

Junius. (Pseud.) Cornelius Walford, a writer in the "Insurance Times."

Junius Americanus. (Pseud.) (1) Dr. Charles Lee, a constant contributor to the "Gazetteer" and the "Public Advertiser" from 1769 to 1771. (2) David Everett, who wrote political articles in the Boston "Gazette."

Junker Party. The nickname given to the aristocratic party in Prussia which came into ascendency with the appointment of Bismarck as chancellor,

Oct. 9, 1862. *Junker* means "young noble."

Juno. In classic myth the queen of heaven, wife of Jupiter, and the guardian deity of women.

Junto, The. A little group of great men who, in the reign of William III. (*circa* 1690 *et seq.*), dictated the policy of the Whig party. Its leading members were Russell, Somers, and Charles Montagu.

Jupiter. In classic myth the father and king of gods and men, and supreme ruler of the universe. He is also called Jove and Zeus (*q. v.*).

Jupiter Carlyle. A nickname bestowed on the Rev. Alexander Carlyle (fl. 1722–1805), a minister of Inveresk, Scotland, who was famed for his magnificent torso.

Jupiter of the Press. The London "Times" has been so named.

Jupiter Scapin. A nickname conferred on Napoleon I. by the Abbé Pradt, in allusion to the strange compound of nobility and meanness which entered into his character. Scapin is a knavish and thievish servant in Molière's comedy, "Les Fourberies de Scapin."

Jupiter tonans. (Lat.) Jupiter the thunderer.

Jure devoluto. (Lat.) By the right lapsing.

Jure divino. (Lat.) By divine law.

Jure humano. (Lat.) By human law.

Jure matrimonii. (Lat.) By right of marriage.

Juris Consultus. (Pseud.) Rev. Alonzo Bowen Chapin, a writer in the "Knickerbocker."

Jus canonicum. (Lat.) Canonical law.

Jus civile. (Lat.) The civil law.

Jus devolutum. (Lat.) The right devolved; said when a right lapses from failing to exercise it.

Jus gentium. (Lat.) The law of nations.

Jus gladii. (Lat.) Right of the sword.

Jus. P. Justice of the Peace.

Jusqu'au revoir. (Fr.) Good-by.

Just. Justinian.

Just, The. (1) Aristides, the Athenian (d. 468 B. C.). (2) Baharam, fifth monarch of the Sassanides (fl. about

220–296). (3) Casimir II., king of Poland (fl. 1117–1194). (4) Ferdinand I. of Aragon (fl. 1373–1416). (5) Haroun-al-Raschid (fl. 765–808). (6) James II. of Aragon (fl. 1261–1327). (7) Chosroes. (8) Pedro I. of Portugal (fl. 1320–1367).

Juste milieu. (Fr.) The golden mean.

Justice of Trajan. While starting on a campaign, the Emperor Trajan, it was said, was stopped by a poor widow, who flung herself on her knees and begged for justice. He expostulated, but finally yielded, and did her justice before resuming his march. This is the first half of the story; the second followed at a later date. Gregory the Great (so the addendum ran) passed through the Forum of Trajan one day, musing on that emperor's many merits, and especially on his charity to the friendless widow; and a great sorrow came over him that a pagan with so many virtues should be lost eternally. Whereupon he prayed loud and long for Trajan's salvation, till at last a voice from on high announced that his prayer was granted, but that henceforth he must pray only for Christian souls; and a later addition to the legend caused Gregory to be punished for his indiscreet though successful intervention by the infliction of certain maladies. The question as to whether Gregory's conduct were justifiable exercised the minds of many mediæval casuists. One affirmative voice thus escaped from the theological difficulties involved: No one can be saved unless he be baptized; now, at the Pope's prayer Trajan's soul returned to his body, Gregory baptized it, "and the soul, again quitting its earthly case, went straight up to heaven."

Justinian of England. Edward I. (fl. 1239–1307) was so named.

Justitiæ propositique tenax. (Lat.) Tenacious of justice and of purpose.

Justitiæ soror fides. (Lat.) Faith is the sister of justice.

Juvenal of England. John Oldham (fl. 1653–1683).

Juvenal of Painters. William Hogarth (fl. 1697–1764).

J. W. Junior Warden.

K.

K. Kalium, or Potassium; King.

K. A. Knight of Saint Andrew, in Russia.

Kal. *Kalendæ.* The Kalends.

Kalula. (Pseud.) F. E. Ramsden, in the New York "Dramatic News."

K. A. N. Knight of Alexander Nevskoi, in Russia.

Kan. Kansas.

Kansas. This is an Indian word, meaning "smoky water."

Kansas and Nebraska Bill. In a proposition presented to Congress in 1854 to organize Kansas and Nebraska into territorial governments, a clause was inserted providing "that the people of the Territories, in forming their constitutions, *should decide for themselves* whether the new States should be free or slaveholding." This was in direct contradiction to the Missouri Compromise (*q. v.*).

Kansas, Bleeding or **Bloody.** *See* BLEEDING KANSAS.

Kansas Hero. James Montgomery (1814–1871), a prominent character in the anti-slavery troubles in Kansas and Missouri.

Karl Reden. (Pseud.) Charles Crozet Converse, American *littérateur* and musician (b. 1834).

Karl Sterne. The pen-name of Madame Alphonse Daudet.

Karl Stille. (Pseud.) Hermann Christoph Gottfried Demme, German moralist and novelist (1760–1822).

Kate. (Pseud.) Mrs. Katherine R. Barmby in the "Moral World."

Kate Cameron. (Pseud.) Kate D. W. Barnes.

Kate Campbell. (Pseud.) Jane Elizabeth (Larcombe) Lincoln, American religious writer (b. 1829).

Kate Castleton. The stage-name of Mrs. Henry Phillips, *née* Freeman.

Kate Claxton. The stage-name of Mrs. Charles Stevenson, *née* Cone.

Kate Cleaveland. (Pseud.) Rebecca S. Reed Nichols, an American author (b. 1820), in a series of letters to the Cincinnati "Herald." *See* ELLEN.

Kate Clyde. (Pseud.) Miss C. G. Thanie, in the New York "Weekly."

Kate Conynghame. (Pseud.) Rev. Joseph Holt Ingraham.

Kate De Courcy. (Pseud.) Miss Catherine Armstrong.

Kate Glassford. The stage-name of Mrs. John Burnett.

Kate Hawthorne. The stage-name of Mrs. Henry Lacey, *née* Cartland.

Kate Montrose. The stage-name of Mrs. A. J. Faust.

Kate Reignolds. The stage-name of Mrs. Irving Winslow.

Kate Ryan. The stage-name of Mrs. James Nolan.

Kate Sanborn. (Pseud.) Katherine Abbott Sanborn, an American educator and author.

Kate Toucey. The stage-name of Mrs. Austin W. Morris.

Kate True. (Pseud.) Mrs. Kate Tannant Woods, in "Ehrich's Magazine."

Kate Vaughn. (Pseud.) Mrs. Helen Kestin, in the New York "Weekly."

Katherine de' Medici of China. Voochee, the widow of King Tae-tsong.

Katie Baker. The stage-name of Mrs. Clarence Handysides.

Katie Mayhew. The stage-name of Mrs. Harry Widmer.

Katie Stokes. The professional name of Mrs. John Stetson, formerly Mrs. Carl Anthony.

K. B. King's Bench; Knight of the Bath.

K. B. A. Knight of Saint Bento d'Avis, in Portugal.

K. B. E. Knight of the Black Eagle, in Russia.

K. C. King's Counsel; Knight of the Crescent, in Turkey.

K. C. B. Knight Commander of the Bath.

K. C. H. Knight Commander of Hanover.

K. C. S. Knight of Charles III. of Spain.

K. E. Knight of the Elephant, in Denmark.

Keewaydin. An Indian name for the northwest wind, but now adopted for the territory lying to the north and east of Manitoba and extending to Ontario.

Kempferhausen. In the "Noctes Ambrosianæ" this was the pseudonym of Robert Peace Gillies.

Kendall's Case. A decision of the United States Supreme Court (1838), noted in American constitutional law, that the court may compel a cabinet officer to perform a ministerial duty.

Kendals, The. "W. H. Kendal" and "Mrs. W. H. Kendal" are the stage-names of Mr. and Mrs. William Hunter Grimstone, two famous London actors.

Kennaquhair. (Scottish for "Don't know where," equivalent to the German *Weissnichtwo*.) Nowhere; a fabulous place. *See* WEISSNICHTWO.

Kenner Deane. (Pseud.) Miss Charlotte Smith, English novelist (1749–1806).

Kent. (Pseud.) Sidney George Fisher, an American writer on political themes.

Kentish Fire. Rapturous applause; "three times three and one more." The expression originated with Lord Winchelsea, who proposed the health of the Earl of Roden, on August 15, 1834, and added, "Let it be given with Kentish Fire." In proposing another toast he asked permission to bring his "Kentish Artillery" again into action.

Kentish Moll. A nickname of Mary Carlton, a notorious woman of the town. She was transported to Jamaica in 1671. but returning without leave was hanged at Tyburn in 1673. She was also dubbed "The German Princess."

Kentish Petition. A paper addressed to the House of Commons censuring its proceedings, was drawn up and signed at Maidstone, April 29, 1701.

Kent's Cavern, or Kent's Hole. A celebrated bone-cave situated in a small, wooded limestone hill, at the junction of two valleys, about a mile eastward from Torquay Harbor, and half a mile from the northern shore of Torbay. It consists of two parallel series of chambers and galleries, having an approximately north and south direction. The aggregate length of the eastern series is upwards of two hundred and fifty feet, and the western is probably longer. It has two narrow external openings or entrances, in the face of one and the same low natural cliff, on the eastern side of the hill, and both opening into the eastern suite of apartments. They are nearly on the same level, about fifty feet apart, seventy feet above the bottom of the valley immediately beneath, and from one hundred and eighty to one hundred and ninety feet above the level of mean tide. Nothing is known respecting the origin of its name. The earliest known mention of the cave is in 1778; but it did not attract the attention of scientific inquirers until September, 1824, when Mr. Northmore visited it with the "double object of discovering organic remains, and of ascertaining the existence of a temple of Mithras." In 1825 the Rev. J. M'Enery commenced researches, which extended at intervals over fully four years. The MS. account of his labors, long supposed to have been lost, was published in 1869 in the "Transactions" of the Devonshire Association. In the cave-earth, beneath a thick floor of stalagmite, Mr. M'Enery discovered remains of upwards of twenty species of extinct and recent animals commingled. Among them were a few teeth of Machairodus latidens; a species not met with elsewhere in Britain, and which many palæontologists hesitated to place in the cave fauna. Mixed up with those remains, he found a number of human flint "implements."

Kent's Lucky Devils. The Seventh Foot Regiment in the English army won this title by its "wonderful good fortune in losing fewer men and in doing more hard fighting than any other regiment in the service."

Kent Street Ejectment. An ingenious mode of ejectment, consisting of taking away the front door of a house, resorted to by the landlords of Kent Street, Southwark, when the tenants of that choice neighborhood were in arrears with their rent.

Kentucky. This is an Indian word, signifying "at the head of the river."

Kentucky Colonel. (Pseud.) Colonel Maynard, in the Indianapolis "Sentinel."

Kentucky, Garden of. *See* GARDEN OF KENTUCKY.

Kentucs. A nickname applied to the boatmen of the Kentucky River about the year 1800. They were said to be "half horse, half alligator, tipped with snapping-turtle;" lawless, and a terror to quiet folk.

Kettle of Fish. In a note appended to "St. Ronan's Well," Sir Walter Scott says that a "kettle of fish is a *fête-champêtre* of a particular kind, which is to other *fêtes-champêtres* what the piscatory eclogues of Brown or Sannazario are to pastoral poetry. A large caldron is boiled by the side of a salmon river, containing a quantity of water, thickened with salt to the consistence of brine. In this the fish is plunged when taken, and eaten by the company *fronde super viridi*. This is accounted the best way of eating salmon by those who desire to taste the fish in a state of extreme freshness. Others prefer it after being kept a day or two, when the curd melts into oil, and the fish becomes richer and more luscious. The more judicious gastronomes eat no other sauce than a spoonful of the water in which the salmon is boiled, together with a little pepper and vinegar." Hence the proverbial expression "a pretty kettle of fish" signifies a mixture of any kind, a hodge-podge. In a "Report of the Inspectors of Salmon Fisheries" Mr. Inspector Walpole, in reporting on the fisheries on the coast of Sussex, says: "The kettle-nets, it may be interesting to note, probably derive their name from the old fishing-weir, the *kidellus*, or kiddle, which is mentioned in Magna Charta and many early fishery statutes. In their turn the kettle-nets are, I conceive, responsible for the old proverb 'a pretty kettle of fish.'"

Key and Bible. Used for the detection of thieves. A key is placed over an open Bible at the words, "Whither thou goest, I will go" (Ruth i. 16); and, the fingers of the person being held so as to form a cross, the text is repeated. The names of suspected persons are then pronounced in succession; and when the name of the thief is uttered, the key jumps and dances about. An instance of this method of thief-finding was brought before the magistrates at the borough petty sessions at Ludlow, in January, 1879.

A married woman, named Mary Ann Collier, was charged with using abusive and insulting language to her neighbor, Eliza Oliver; and the complainant, in her statement to the magistrates, said that on December 27 she was engaged in carrying water, when Mrs. Collier stopped her, and stated that another neighbor had had a sheet stolen, and had "turned the key on the Bible near several houses; that when it came to her (Oliver's) house, the key moved of itself, and that when complainant's name was mentioned the key and the Book turned completely round, and fell out of their hands." She also stated that the owner of the sheet then inquired from the key and the Book whether the theft was committed at dark or daylight, and the reply was "Daylight." Defendant then called complainant "a —— daylight thief," and charged her with stealing the sheet. — *Newspaper paragraph* (January, 1879).

Key of Christendom. Buda, the capital of Hungary, was formerly so named. Its location on the Danube and its nearness to Turkey rendered it of great importance from a strategic point of view. The Turks captured it on two occasions in the sixteenth century, but in 1686 they were finally driven out.

Key of Death. About 1600 a stranger named Tebaldo established himself as a merchant in Venice. He became enamoured of the daughter of an ancient house, and asking her hand was rejected, the young lady being already affianced. Enraged, he set himself to plan revenge, and being a skilful mechanician invented a formidable weapon. This was a large key, the handle of which could be turned easily. Being turned, it discovered a spring, which, when pressed, sent out from the other end of the key a poisoned needle of such fineness that it entered the flesh and buried itself there, leaving no external trace. With this weapon Tebaldo waited at the church door till the maiden he loved passed in to her marriage. Then, unperceived, he sent the slender needle into the breast of the bridegroom, who, seized with a sharp pain from an unknown cause, fainted, was carried home, and soon died, his strange illness baffling the skill of the physicians. Again Tebaldo demanded the maiden's hand, and was again refused. In a few days both her parents died in a like manner. Suspicion was excited, and on examination of the bodies the small steel instrument was found in the flesh. There was universal terror; no one felt that his own life was secure. The young lady went into a convent during her mourning; and after a few months Tebaldo begged to see and speak with her, hoping now to bend her to his will. She, with instinctive horror of this man,

who had from the first been displeasing to her, returned a decisive negative; whereupon Tebaldo contrived to wound her through the gate. On returning to her room she felt a pain in her breast, and discovered a single drop of blood. Surgeons were hastily summoned. Taught by the past, they cut into the wounded part, extracted the needle, and saved her life. Tebaldo was suspected; his house was searched, the key discovered, and he perished on the gallows.

Key of India. The city of Herat, in Afghanistan. The citadel is a well-nigh impregnable fortress.

Key of Russia. Smolensk, a strongly fortified town on the Dnieper, two hundred and fifty miles west-southwest of Moscow. It is famous for its spirited resistance to the French in 1812.

Key of the Dutch Seas. In the fifteenth and sixteenth centuries the fame of Middelburg and Flushing, in Holland, extended all over Europe. The latter especially was so important that it was called "the key of the Dutch Seas." The Emperor Charles V. visited the city, and spent some days in the small adjoining town of Zuytburg. It was there that in September, 1556, he dated his act of abdication, before sailing from Flushing to Spain and retiring to the monastery of St. Juste.

Key of the Gulf. The island of Cuba; so named in allusion to its location, commanding the entrance to the Gulf of Mexico.

Key of the Mediterranean. The impregnable fortress of Gibraltar has been so named. It may be said to control the entrance to the Mediterranean from the Atlantic.

Keystone State. An appellation bestowed on Pennsylvania because it was the seventh, or central, one of the original thirteen States.

K. F. Knight of Ferdinand of Spain.

K. F. M. Knight of Saint Ferdinand and Merit, in Sicily.

K. G. Knight of the Garter.

Kg., Kgs. Keg; kegs.

K. G. C. Knight of the Grand Cross.

K. G. C. B. Knight of the Grand Cross of the Bath.

K. G. F. Knight of the Golden Fleece, in Spain.

K. G. H. Knight of the Guelphs of Hanover.

K. G. V. Knight of Gustavus Vasa of Sweden.

K. H. Knight of Hanover.

Ki. Kings.

Kick the Bucket. A vulgarism for the act of dying. When pigs are killed they are hung up by their hind legs on a pulley called a "bucket."

Kidderminster Poetry. A name coined by Shenstone, and applied to rough doggerel verses, coarse as the woollen fabrics for which the town of Kidderminster is famed.

Kil. Kilometre.

Kilkenny Cats. Everybody has heard of the two cats of Kilkenny that fought till nothing was left but their tails. Strange as the tale seems, there is a substratum of fact upon which it is founded. During the Rebellion in Ireland in 1803 Kilkenny was garrisoned by a troop of Hessian soldiers, who amused themselves in barracks by tying two cats together by their tails and throwing them across a clothes-line to fight. The officers, hearing of the cruel practice, resolved to stop it, and deputed one of their number to watch. The soldiers, on their part, set a man to watch for the coming officer. One day the sentinel neglected his duty, and the heavy tramp of the officer was heard ascending the stairs. One of the troopers, seizing a sword, cut the tails in two as the animals hung across the line. The two cats escaped, minus their tails, through the open window; and when the officer inquired the meaning of the two bleeding tails being left in the room, he was coolly told that two cats had been fighting, and had devoured each other all but the tails.

Kill. The nickname by which his soldiers always alluded to Gen. Judson Kilpatrick.

Kilmainham Treaty. During the Irish agrarian troubles of 1880-1882 several Irish members of Parliament were imprisoned in Kilmainham jail for seditious utterances. After brief incarceration they were released, having, it was currently stated, agreed to support Mr. Gladstone in return for certain concessions to be made by him to Ireland. This compact aroused much ire among the Conservatives, and became known by the above name, the details having been arranged inside the prison.

Kilo. Kilogramme.

Kinderhook Roarer. Aaron Vanderpoel, congressman from New York (1799-1871), was so named on account of the power of his voice and his florid oratorical flights.

King Caucus. Silas Moore Stilwell, an American lawyer (1800-1881). He was elected alderman in New York in 1835, and made chairman of the board; the political parties being equally divided, he had the casting vote, and on this account was dubbed "King Caucus."

King Cotton. An impersonation of the great staple commodity of the southern States of the Union.

Kingd. Kingdom.

Kingdom of Snow. Norway. Sweden also is so called. When these kingdoms had each a separate king, either of them was called "The Snow King."

Let no vessel of the kingdom of snow bound on the dark-rolling waves of Inistore [the Orkneys]. — OSSIAN, *Fingal*, i.

King Franconi. A nickname conferred on Joachim Murat (fl. 1767-1815), because in his love of finery he resembled Franconi, the mountebank.

King George's War. A colonial struggle between England and France, begun 1744. The colonists were victorious.

King-maker. Richard Neville, Earl of Warwick (fl. 1420-1471); so named because, when he espoused the cause of Henry VI., Henry was king; but when he transferred his allegiance to Edward IV., Henry was deposed and Edward became king. Warwick was slain at the battle of Barnet. His career is delineated in Bulwer's "Last of the Barons."

King of Bark. Christopher III., a Scandinavian ruler of the fifteenth century, was thus named, because in time of scarcity he had the powdered bark of birchwood mixed with flour for food.

King of Bath. Richard Nash ("Beau Nash"), who was master of ceremonies at that resort of fashion for some fifty-six years (fl. 1674-1761).

King of Brave Men. A surname bestowed on Henry IV. of France (fl. 1553-1610), an intrepid and dashing commander.

King of Cotswold. A nickname given to Grey Brydges, Lord Chandos (d. 1621), on account of the princely style of living and the large retinue he maintained. The Cotswold Hills are in Gloucestershire, in full view from Sudley Castle, the chief residence of Lord Chandos.

King of Dance. The elder Vestris so styled himself. He once scolded his son for refusing to dance on an off night, although the Queen of France went to the opera purposely to see him, by saying, " Go, my son, and dance your very best. A coolness shall never be allowed to exist between the house of Vestris and the house of Bourbon."

King of Day. The sun.

But yonder comes the powerful king of day,
Rejoicing in the east.
THOMSON, *The Seasons.*

Similarly the moon is called the Queen of Night.

King of Dulness. Colley Cibber, Poet Laureate of England after Eusden, was so dubbed by Pope, in the " Dunciad."

King of England's Viceroy. A jeering nickname given to Louis XVIII. of France (fl. 1755–1824), because of his almost slavish gratitude to England for the assistance rendered in reclaiming the throne of the House of Capet.

King of Feuilletons. Jules Gabriel Janin (fl. 1804–1874), a talented and popular French journalist, received this sobriquet. For many years he was on the staff of the " Journal des Débats," and wrote for that part of the paper known as the *feuilleton,* devoted to current literature and musical and dramatic criticism.

King of Khorassan. A title given to Anvari, a Persian poet of the twelfth century.

King of Kings. (1) A title given to the Christ (Rev. xvii. 14). (2) The name was bestowed on Artaxerxes (d. 241), the first of the Sassanide rulers of Persia.

King of Misrule. *See* ABBOT OF MISRULE.

King of Painters. A self-assumed title of Parrhasius (fl. about 400 B. C.), the Athenian artist.

King of Preachers. Louis Bourdaloue (fl. 1632–1704), the French pulpit orator and divine.

King of Reptiles. A sobriquet bestowed on Bernard Germain Etienne de la Ville, Count Lacépède (fl. 1758–1825), the great French naturalist. His specialty was the Reptilia.

King of Slops (*Roi Panade*). Louis XVIII. was so nicknamed.

King of Snowdonia. Moel-y-Wyddfa, " the conspicuous peak," 3,571 feet above the sea, the highest summit in South Britain.

King of the Beggars. Bamfylde Moore Carew (fl. 1693–1770), who led a wild life and associated much with gypsies and mendicants.

King of the Border. Adam Scott, of Tushielaw, a noted marauder of the Scottish border.

King of the Courts. Cicero thus named Quintus Hortensius (d. 50 B. C.), the famous Roman tribune.

King of the Feds. Alexander Hamilton, the leader of the Federalists.

King of the Gypsies. *See* KING OF THE BEGGARS.

King of the Lobby. Samuel Ward, American author and raconteur, familiarly known as " Sam Ward " and " Uncle Sam Ward " (1814–1884). " His powers of conversation, persuasive manners, and skill in entertaining his friends in Washington enabled him to exercise such an influence over legislators that he was named "the king of the lobby."

King of the Markets. A nickname given to François de Vendôme Beaufort (fl. 1616–1669), a grandson of Henry IV., because of his popularity with the rabble of Paris.

King of the Quakers. Israel Pemberton (1715–1779), a famous character in the early history of Pennsylvania. *See* KING WAMPUM.

King of the World (" Shah Jehan "). The title adopted by Khovrum Shah (d. 1666), the third of the Mogul emperors of Delhi.

King of Waters. The river Amazon.

King of Yvetot. Yvetot is a town in Normandy, and the king referred to is the lord of the town, called " Roi d'Yvetot " in old chronicles. The tradition is that Clotaire, son of Clovis, having slain Gaulthier, lord of Yvetot, before the high altar of Soissons, made atonement by conferring the title of king on the heirs of the murdered man.

King Philip's War. In 1652 Massasoit, chief of the Wampanoags, died. For forty-one years the treaty between himself and the Plymouth colony had been kept faithfully. His eldest son, Alexander, now became chief of the nation; but he dying within a year, the chieftainship descended to the younger brother, Philip of Mount Hope. Both by real and imaginary wrongs the young chief was induced to declare war upon the handful of Europeans, in the hope of exterminating them. This gave rise to what is known in history as King Philip's War. He struck his first blow at Swanzey, R. I., on June 24, 1675. The whites sprang to arms. Philip induced other tribes to join him, and during that year and the spring of 1676 there were alarm and bloodshed in all the New England colonies. But the Indians were finally subdued, and Philip was compelled to fly for his life to the country of the Nipmucks in central Massachusetts. Here the fugitives became the nucleus around which all the dissatisfied natives, who only desired a chance to declare war, rallied. The war was next transferred to the Connecticut valley. Slaughter and rapine were rife all through the colonies of the valley; and the whites, terribly overmatched, suffered greatly. On the whole, however, the Indians got the worst of the many fights, and at length, finding he could accomplish nothing more, Philip took refuge among the Narragansetts, who were supposed to be on terms of peace with the English; and, by receiving the fugitive, Canonchet, their chief, openly violated a treaty. War was immediately declared against the Narragansetts, and Rhode Island was invaded by a force of a thousand men under Capt. Josiah Winslow. The combined tribes of the Narragansetts and the Wampanoags took refuge in a swamp a short distance southwest of Kingston, which they fortified, and thought themselves secure. But the English carried the place by storm, set fire to the wigwams, and shot down the natives as they attempted to escape from the blazing morass. The power of the Narragansetts was broken forever. A few, however, led by Philip, escaped, repaired again to the Nipmucks, and carried on the war with more violence than ever. In April, 1676, Canonchet was captured and was put to death. Philip was still at large, but his hiding-place was betrayed to the English. A company of soldiers was detailed to capture him, but in the *mêlée* Philip was shot through the heart. The expenses of this war amounted to $500,000; thirteen towns and six hundred dwellings were laid in ruins, and the whole country suffered terribly. But the Indians were completely crushed and incapable of mischief for many a day.

King Pym. A title given to John Pym (fl. 1584–1643), the English Parliamentarian and leader of the House of Commons during its memorable struggle with Charles I.

King's Book. Another name for the *Valor Ecclesiasticus temp. Henrici VIII.*, the return of the commission charged in 1534 with the duty of appraising the first-fruits and tenths granted to the king. It was reprinted in 1780 and 1810–1825.

King's Chair. A seat made by two bearers crossing their hands. On Candlemas Day the children of Scotland used to bring their schoolmaster a present in money, and the boy who brought the largest sum was king for the nonce. When school was dismissed, the "king" was carried on a seat of hands in procession, and the seat was called the "king's chair."

King's Crag. Fife, in Scotland; so named because Alexander III. of Scotland was killed there by his horse falling over the precipice in the dusk of evening.

King's Evil. Scrofula; so called from a notion which prevailed from the reign of Edward the Confessor to that of Queen Anne, that it could be cured by the royal touch. The last person touched in England was Dr. Johnson, in 1712, when only thirty months old, by Queen Anne. The French kings laid claim to the same divine power even from the time of Anne of Clovis, A. D. 481; and on Easter Sunday, 1686, Louis XIV. touched 1,600 persons. Henry VII. introduced the practice of presenting the person "touched" with a small gold or silver coin, called a touchpiece.

King's Friends. Successive administrations in the reign of George III. were known by this name. They were: 1762, under Bute and Henley; 1763, mainly Whigs, under Grenville, Bedford, and Sandwich; 1767, under Grafton and North; 1770, mainly Tories, under North.

Kingsley's Stand. *See* MINDEN BOYS.

King's Men. The Seventy-eighth Foot Regiment; so named from its Gaelic motto, *Cuidich'r Rhi*, "Help the king."

Kingswood Lions. Donkeys. Kingswood was at one time famous for the number of these patient beasts kept by the colliers there.

King Wampum. Israel Pemberton (1715–1779), a Philadelphia Quaker, was so named by his friends on account of his friendship for the Indians.

King William's War. A colonial struggle with the French (1689–1697); so named from William III. of England.

Kinless Loons. When Cromwell despatched judges into Scotland to try numerous civil and criminal cases, justice was administered right and left with impartial hand; the accused was tried and dealt with strictly on the merits of his case, irrespective of his family connections or influence. Hence the judges were dubbed by the astonished people, who were used to a far different order under the Stuarts, "Kinless Loons."

Kirke's Lambs. The Second Foot Regiment, Col. Percy Kirke. The corps was appointed a guard of honor to Henrietta, queen of Charles II., on her journey to London. In consideration of this service they were allowed to carry a figure of the Paschal Lamb emblazoned on their colors.

Kirkland. (Pseud.) Miss Amanda Bartlett Harris, in the "Christian Union."

Kirk of Skulls. Gowrie Church in Baffshire, Scotland; so called because the skulls and bones of the Norsemen who fell in the battle called the Bloody Pots were built into its walls.

Kirwan. (Pseud.) Rev. Nicholas Murray, Presbyterian divine and theologian (1803–1861).

Kissing the Blarney Stone. *See* BLARNEY STONE.

Kiss the Scavenger's Daughter. *See* SCAVENGER'S DAUGHTER.

Kit. (Pseud.) J. B. Adams, in the Denver "Tribune."

Kit-Cat Club. An organization formed in 1688 in London, in the house of a pastry-cook named Christopher Cat, in Shire Lane, who supplied the mutton pies, and after whom the club was named. Sir Godfrey Kneller painted a set of portraits of the members for Jacob Tonson, the secretary, at whose house at Barn Elms the meetings were afterward held. But in order that the room might contain them all, Sir Godfrey was forced to paint them in three-quarter lengths. To this day a *kit-kat portrait* is a picture of this size.

Kit-Cats. Mutton pies are so called in London. See *supra*.

Kitchen Cabinet. "A name sportively given in the United States to Francis P. Blair and Amos Kendall, by the opponents of President Jackson's administration. Blair was the editor of the 'Globe,' the organ of the President, and Kendall was one of the principal contributors to the paper. As it was necessary for Jackson to consult frequently with these gentlemen, and as, to avoid observation, they were accustomed, when they called upon him, to go in by a back door, the Whig party styled them, in derision, the 'Kitchen Cabinet,' alleging that it was by their advice that the President removed so many Whigs from office and put Democrats in their places."—WHEELER.

Kitchen-maid in Ireland. A nickname used by Queen Elizabeth for Earl Mountjoy.

Kite-flying. "An expression well known to mercantile men of limited means, or who are short of cash. It is a combination between two persons, neither of whom has any funds in bank, to exchange each other's checks, which may be deposited in lieu of money, taking good care to make their bank accounts good before their checks are presented for payment. *Kite-flying* is also practised by mercantile houses or persons in different cities. A house in Boston draws on a house in New York at sixty days or more, and gets its bill discounted. The New York house, in return, meets its acceptance by re-drawing on the Boston house."—BARTLETT.

Kittie Blanchard. The stage-name of Mrs. McKee Rankin.

Kittie O'Shea. The stage-name of Kate Scanlan.

Kittie Woodson. The stage-name of Mrs. Will H. Mack.

Kitty Allyne. The stage-name of Mrs. Fred J. Huber.

Kitty Bell. The stage-name of Mrs. Lewis Bloom.

Kitty Coleman. (1) The stage-name of Mrs. John Walsh. (2) The stage-name of Mrs. Daniel McCarthy.

Kitty Quinn. The stage-name of Mrs. R. O. Wilkinson.

K. J. Knight of Saint Joachim.

K. K. Kind. (Pseud.) Katherine C. Walker, in "Harper's Magazine."

K. L., or **K. L. A.** Knight of Leopold of Austria.

K. L. H. Knight of the Legion of Honor.

K. M. Knight of Malta.

K. Mess. King's Messenger.

K. M. H. Knight of Merit, in Holstein.

K. M. J. Knight of Maximilian Joseph of Bavaria.

K. M. T. Knight of Maria Theresa of Austria.

Knave Bible. A Bible in which Paul is said to call himself "a knave of Jesus Christ" (Rom. i. 1), meaning thereby a *servant*, as in all other versions. There is, however, no evidence of the existence of any such copy.

Knick. Knickerbocker.

Knickerbocker. Originally the name of an old Dutch burgher family of New York, the name has come to be bestowed as an honorary epithet on all worthy descendants of Dutch stock. *See* DUTCH.

Knife of Academic Knots. A nickname of Chrysippus (fl. 280–207 B.C.), and so called "because he was the keenest disputant of his age."

Knifing "is a form of political treachery practised by political organizations against candidates of their own party distasteful to the organization. Although openly pretending to support and aid the candidate of the party, the organization secretly uses its influence against him, and on election day either fails to furnish ballots bearing the candidate's name, or distributes those bearing the name of his opponent. This form of treachery is allied to trading, but differs from it in motive. The motive in trading is not directly a desire to defeat this particular candidate of its own party, but the desire either to elect some other member of the party or to gain the pecuniary reward offered, the defeat of the candidate traded off being merely incidental. In knifing the motive is revenge or hate of the candidate knifed, the trading necessary to accomplish this end being merely incidental. Both of these forms of treachery may usually be discovered by comparison, district by district, of the votes for the particular candidate with the vote for other candidates of the party, and with the vote of previous years."— BROWN AND STRAUSS.

Knight of Innishowen. John Sheehan, Irish poet and humorous writer (b. 1831).

Knight of the Pestle. An apothecary or druggist, whose trade-sign consists of a pestle and mortar.

Knight Russ Ockside. (Pseud.) Mortimer Thompson, American humorist (1832–1875). *See* Q. K. PHILANDER DOESTICKS, P. B.

Knipperdollings. A set of German heretics about the time of the Reformation, disciples of a man named Bernard Knipperdolling.

Knob. *See* HUMMOCK.

Knowledge is Power. Lord Lytton, in "My Novel," says that no such sentence or thought as this is to be found in Lord Bacon's works. The great novelist was wrong. It occurs in Bacon's treatise "De Hæresibus," and is in Latin, "Nam et ipsa scientia potestas est." The sentence means, not that knowledge confers power, but that the capacity to know may be termed a power. The expression is perhaps founded on the passage, "A wise man is strong" (Prov. xxiv. 5).

Know-Nothings. Another name for the "American Party," which arose in the United States in 1853, and which proposed to keep foreigners out of office and to make them wait longer before becoming citizens. Its members were organized in secret lodges, and to all questions about its doings answered, "I don't know," whence the nickname of "Know-Nothings." *See* AMERICAN PARTY.

K. N. Pepper. (Pseud.) James M. Morris, American *littérateur*.

K. N. S. Knight of the Royal North Star, in Sweden.

Knt., or **Kt.** Knight.

Kolis. An acrostical nickname of the Fifty-first King's Own Light Infantry in the English army.

Konx Ompax. The pen-name used by Richard Whately in his famous "Historic Doubts relative to Napoleon Bonaparte," published 1832.

Kosak Luganski. (Pseud.) Vladimir Ivanovitch Dahl, Russian novelist (1802–1872).

Kossuth Hat. A low, soft felt hat, once very popular in the United States. The story of its introduction by John Nicholas Genin, the New York merchant and hat-maker (1819–1878), is as follows : —

"In the autumn of 1851 it was advertised that Louis Kossuth, the Hungarian patriot, was on his way to this country ; and Mr. Genin proposed that one hundred wealthy citizens should contribute one thousand dollars each for his use, and gave that amount himself. He was also an active promoter of the public reception, which included a military parade. Having on hand a lot of "dead stock" in the shape of low-crowned felt hats, he fastened the left side of the brim to the crown, ornamented it with a black feather, and boarding the vessel at Sandy Hook presented all of the refugees, many of whom were ragged and shoeless, with "Kossuth" hats, which they wore on the march up Broadway. Low-crowned soft felt hats at once became popular, and the manufacturers subsequently recognized Mr. Genin's services in their behalf by presenting him with a silver service valued at twelve hundred dollars."

Koszta's Çase. The facts and resulting diplomatic correspondence (1853) by which the United States Government maintained the claim that Martin Koszta, a native of Hungary, was entitled to protection as an American citizen from seizure by the Austrian Government while in Turkish jurisdiction, he having previously legally declared his intention to become an American citizen.

K. P. Knight of Saint Patrick.

K. R. C. Knight of the Red Cross.

K. R. E. Knight of the Red Eagle, in Prussia.

Kremlin. (Pseud.) William Stevens Robinson, in the Hartford "Press," about 1865.

Krik. (Pseud.) Henry G. Crickmore, sporting editor of the New York "World."

K's, The Three. *See* THREE K'S.

K. S. Knight of the Sword, in Sweden.

K. S. A. Knight of Saint Anne of Russia.

K. S. E. Knight of Saint Esprit, in France.

K. S. F. Knight of Saint Fernando of Spain.

K. S. F. M. Knight of Saint Ferdinand and Merit, in Naples.

K. S. G. Knight of Saint George of Russia.

K. S. H. Knight of Saint Hubert of Bavaria.

K. S. J. Knight of Saint Januarius of Naples.

K. S. L. Knight of the Sun and Lion, in Persia.

K. S. M. & S. G. Knight of Saint Michael and Saint George of the Ionian Islands.

K. S. P. Knight of Saint Stanislaus of Poland.

K. S. S. Knight of the Southern Star of the Brazils; Knight of the Sword, in Sweden.

K. S. W. Knight of Saint Wladimir of Russia.

K. T. Knight of the Thistle; Knight Templar.

Kt. Knight.

K. τ. λ. (Καὶ τὰ λειπόμερα). The same as "etc."

K. T. S. Knight of the Tower and Sword, in Portugal.

Ku-Klux-Klan. "The name of a secret society in the Southern States of the United States, bitterly opposed to the exercise of the electoral franchise by the negroes. Early in 1868 this society issued lists of proscribed persons, who, if they did not quit the country after warning, became liable to assassination. General Grant endeavored to suppress this society. Its repression by the militia in Arkansas was ordered November, 1868, and it became the subject of legislation at Washington, June, 1871, under which many persons were tried and convicted for lawless outrages and murders. The Ku-Klux outrages were generally committed at night, the men being masked and even their horses being disguised. The vigorous prosecution of Ku-Klux offenders speedily destroyed the organization." — HAYDN.

Kulturkampf. The name given to the conflict in Prussia respecting public worship in 1873 and succeeding years.

Kuvera. In Hindu mythology the god of riches, depicted as hideously deformed.

K. W. Knight of William of the Netherlands.

K. W. E. Knight of the White Eagle, in Poland.

Ky. Kentucky.

L.

L. Fifty, or fiftieth; book (*liber*); lake; lanthanum.

L., £, or **l.** *Libra* or *libræ.* Pound or pounds sterling.

La. Louisiana.

Labadists. A religious sect of the seventeenth century, so called from Jean Labadie, of Bourg in Guyenne. They were Protestant ascetics, who sought reform of morals rather than reform of doctrine. They rejected the observance of all holy days, and held certain mystic notions. The sect fell to pieces early in the eighteenth century.

Labby. Henry Labouchere. *See* BESIEGED RESIDENT.

Labor Day. Of late years, especially since the prominence of the Knights of Labor in the United States, public parades of various craftsmen have been held in the larger American cities on some designated day in September — usually the first Monday. In 1886 it was proposed to add another day to our scanty American holiday calendar, to be denominated "Labor Day," and which, falling on the first Monday in September, coming midway between Independence Day and Thanksgiving, should afford to the artisan class a brief respite from toil. The observance of this holiday was provided for by legislative enactment in New York, Ohio, Illinois, etc., and the day is usually the occasion of parades and merrymaking.

Labore et honore. (Lat.) By labor and honor.

Labor ipse voluptas. (Lat.) "Labor itself a pleasure." Labor itself is a pleasure.

Labor omnia vincit. (Lat.) Labor conquers everything.

L. A. C. Licentiate of the Apothecaries' Company.

La carrière des armes. (Fr.) The career of arms.

La chasse. (Fr.) A piece of music in the hunting style.

Lachesis. In classic myth one of the Three Fates, or Parcæ (*q. v.*). She who spun the thread of life.

Laconia. A former name for a tract of country granted by royal patent to Ferdinando Gorges and John Mason. It was bounded by the Merrimac and Kennebec rivers, the ocean, and the so-called River of Canada. The present State of New Hampshire formed a considerable portion of Laconia. The colony was of short duration.

Lacordaire of America. Mamertus Esquin, a South American bishop (1826-1883), was so named by his countrymen on account of his learning.

La critique est aisée, et l'art est difficile. (Fr.) Criticism is easy, but art is difficult.

Lacunæ. (Lat.) "Gaps." Gaps in a manuscript; gaps left where anything may be wanting in the writings of an author.

Ladies' Mile, The. A portion of the famous driveway and promenade in Hyde Park, London, known as Rotten Row.

Ladies of the Meuse. (Fr., *Dames de la Meuse.*) Two wood-crowned heights overhanging the river Meuse in the vicinity of the town of Furnay in Ardennes.

Ladies of the Vale. The two beautiful spires of Lichfield Cathedral, England, are locally known by this name.

Ladies' Peace. The treaty of peace agreed on at Cambrai (1529), between Francis I. of France and Charles V. of Germany; so named from the fact that its terms were mainly arranged by Louise of Savoy and Margaret of Savoy.

Ladies' Rock. Stirling, Scotland.

In the castle hill is a hollow called "The Valley," comprehending about an acre . . . for joustings and tournaments. . . . Closely adjoining . . . is a small rocky . . . mount called "The Ladies' Hill," where the fair ones of the court took their station to behold these feats. — NIMMO, *History of Stirlingshire*, p. 282.

Ladies' Street. A familiar name given to Winter Street, Boston, because the stores upon it are exclusively for ladies' trade, and crowds of fair shoppers throng it on pleasant days.

Lad o' Wax. A little boy, a doll of a man. In "Romeo and Juliet," the nurse calls Paris "a man of wax," meaning "a very proper man." Horace speaks of the "waxen arms of Telephus," meaning "well modelled."

Lady Day. March 25; one of the four quarter-days for the payment of rent in England. *See* ANNUNCIATION DAY.

Lady Freemason. Hon. Miss Elizabeth St. Leger, daughter of Lord Doneraile. The story runs that she hid herself in an old clock-case in a room where the lodge was being held, but being discovered, was compelled to submit to initiation as a member of the craft.

Lady in her Chair, The. See CASSIOPE.

Lady Magistrate. Lady Berkley, made justice of the peace for Gloucestershire by Queen Mary. She sat on the bench at assizes and sessions, girt with a sword.

Lady Margaret's Professor. A professor of divinity in the University of Cambridge, England. This professorship was founded in 1502 by Lady Margaret, mother of Henry VII.

Lady Margaret's Preacher. A preacher who has to preach a sermon before Cambridge University on the day preceding Easter term. This preachership was founded in 1503 by Lady Margaret, mother of Henry VII.

Lady of England. Maud, daughter of Henry I., the title "Domina Anglorum" having been conferred on her by the Council of Winchester, 1141.

Lady of the Haystack. A mysterious woman who made her appearance in 1776 at Bourton, near Bristol. She was young, beautiful, graceful, and accustomed to good society. She lived for four years in a haystack; but was ultimately kept by Mrs. Hannah More in an asylum, and died suddenly in December, 1801. She was probably a Mademoiselle La Frülen, natural daughter of Francis Joseph I., Emperor of Austria.

Lady of the Sun. A complimentary title given to Alice Perrers, a mistress of Edward III. of England. Her beauty was of a remarkable order, and she was loaded with favors; yet she did not scruple to purloin the king's jewels at his death, even taking the rings from his fingers.

Lady with a Lamp. Florence Nightingale (b. 1820).

> On England's annals . . .
> A Lady with a Lamp shall stand . . .
> A noble type of good,
> Heroic womanhood.
> LONGFELLOW, *Santa Filomena.*

Laertes. (Pseud.) George Alfred Townsend, American journalist.

Læsio majestatis. (Lat.) High treason.

Laetare Sunday. The fourth Sunday in Lent (Mid-Lent Sunday), on which day the pope blesses the Golden Rose. On this day only is the organ permitted to be played in Lent in Catholic churches.

La fleur des pois. (Fr.) "The flower of the peas." The very pink of fashion.

La fleur des troupes. (Fr.) "The flower of the troops." Picked men.

La Fontaine of the Vaudeville. Panard, the French poet (fl. 1691–1765). *See also* FATHER OF MODERN FRENCH SONG.

La grande nation. (Fr.) The great nation, — as applied by Frenchmen to France.

Laicus. (Pseud.) Rev. Lyman Abbott, American divine (b. 1835).

Laïs. A courtesan or Greek Hetaira. There were two of the name; the elder was the most beautiful woman of Corinth, and lived at the time of the Peloponnesian war. The beauty of the latter excited the jealousy of the Thessalonian women, who stoned her to death. She was contemporary with Phryne, her rival, and sat to Apelles as a model.

Laisser aller. (Fr.) "To allow to go." To let matters go on as they will.

Laissez nous faire. (Fr.) Let us alone.

Laissez faire, Laissez passer. Lord John Russell said: "Colbert, with the intention of fostering the manufactures of France, established regulations which limited the webs woven in looms to a particular size. He also prohibited the introduction of foreign manufactures. The French vine-growers, finding they could no longer get rid of their wine, began to grumble. Then Colbert asked a merchant what relief he could give, and received for answer, 'Laissez faire, laissez passer,' — Don't interfere with our mode of manufactures, and don't stop the introduction of foreign imports." Hence the *laissez-faire system* is the "let-alone system."

Laius. In classic myth king of Thebes and father of Œdipus, by whom he was killed in ignorance of his identity.

Lajos Abafi. (Pseud.) Lajos Aigner, a Hungarian author.

Lake City. Madison, Wis.

Lake George of New Jersey. Lake Hopatcong, Sussex County.

Lake of Lot. The Arabic name for the Dead Sea.

Lake of the Four Forest Cantons. (Ger., *Vierwaldstäter See.*) Another name for the Lake of Lucerne. The city of Lucerne, and the towns of Küsnacht, Brunnen, and Flüelen are on its shores.

Lake Poets. See *infra.*

Lake School. A school of poetry introduced by the Lake Poets, — Wordsworth, Coleridge, and Southey, — who resided in the Lake District of England. The term was first used in the "Edinburgh Review," and the distinguishing characteristics of the poetry of this school are simplicity and truth to Nature.

Lakes, Queen City of the. *See* QUEEN CITY OF THE LAKES.

Lake State, The. Michigan is so named. Its shores are watered by Lakes Superior, Michigan, Huron, and Erie. The Indian word "Michigan" signifies "great lake."

Laksmi. In Hindu mythology the consort of Vishnu, and goddess of beauty, grace, riches, and pleasure.

Lam. Lamentations.

La maladie sans maladie. (Fr.) "The disease without disease." Hypochondria.

Lame and Unstable Peace. The treaty of peace between the Calvinists and Charles IX. in 1568. Called also the "Ill-grounded Peace" and "Patched-up Peace." It was of short duration; and its details were arranged by Biron, who was afflicted with lameness.

Lame Duck is a Stock Exchange term for a member who has made default on settlement day. The names of defaulters are posted on a blackboard in the room where the members transact their buying and selling.

Lame Vicegerent, The, in "Hudibras," stands for Richard Cromwell.

Lamia. In classic myth the name of a queen of Libya who was despoiled of her children by Juno, and who, in revenge, went up and down the earth robbing others of their offspring. Her name was used as a bugbear to frighten children.

Lammas-Day ("loaf-mass day"). August 1 means the day of first-fruit offerings, when a loaf was given to the priests in lieu of the first-fruits.

Lammer Beads. Amber beads, once used as charms.

Lamourette's Kiss. The title given in ridicule to a sudden cessation of hostilities between the various factions in the French National Assembly, July 7, 1792. It was brought about by an eloquent appeal of the Abbé Lamourette (whose name signifies "the sweetheart"), but was of brief duration. It is also known as "The Norman Reconciliation."

Lamp of the Law. Irnerius the German was so called, who first lectured on the Pandects of Justinian, after their discovery at Amalfi in 1137.

Lancashire Lads. *See* CAULIFLOWERS.

Landaulet Williams. George H. Williams (b. 1823), Attorney-General in the Grant Cabinet. It was then the fashion for officers of the Government to maintain horses and carriages at public expense for the use of themselves and their families. Mr. Williams gained his sobriquet because of his maintaining a landaulet in this manner.

Landlords of New York. The Astor family, on account of their large ownership of real estate in that city.

Land of Bondage. A Scripture name for Egypt, in allusion to the harsh treatment received by the Israelites during the latter part of their sojourn in that country.

Land o' Cakes. Scotland. Oatmeal cakes are a common article of food among all classes.

Land of Fetich. Africa has been so named. Among its natives many hideous and repulsive or foolish objects are made the subject of superstitious worship.

Land of Green Ginger. This is the strange name of a street in the town of Hull, and has given rise to many conjectures. Some manuscripts discovered a few years ago mention that, in the year 1685, Sir Willoughby Hickman was a candidate for the representation of the borough in Parliament. He came to Hull by way of the Humber, and on arriving "one of Jonas Gould's coaches was taken to the waterside to meet him, and in he got, and the men pulled it right away to the George Inn, at the corner of the land of Moses Greenhinger, the boat-builder in Whitefriars Gate." The boat-builder's name has been strangely metamorphosed.

Land of Health. The Moors so designated the ancient province of Badajos in Spain.

Land of Kings and Prophets. Palestine has been so named.

Land of Knives and Forks. A sailor-man's phrase to designate the cabin as distinguished from the forecastle of a ship.

Land of Myrrh. Azab, or Saba.

Land of Nod. Dreamland; the realm of slumber.

Land of Song. Italy.

Land of Steady Habits. Connecticut has been called by this name. The term contains an allusion to the gravity of its people and the uniformity of its customs.

Land of the Bee. Utah; in allusion to the busy industry of its population.

Land of the Boar. Germany was so named in classic days.

Land of the Chaldees. Babylonia.

Land of the Hyacinth and Ruby. A poetic name given to the island of Ceylon by the Chinese writers.

Land of the Leek. Wales.

Land of the Midnight Sun. Scandinavia, — Norway, Lapland, Sweden, Iceland, etc.; so called by the traveller Du Chaillu, who published a book bearing the title.

Land of the Morning Calm. A poetical name given by the Coreans to their country.

Land of the Rose. England. The rose is the national emblem, like the thistle of Scotland and the shamrock of Ireland.

Land of the Shamrock. Ireland. The shamrock was chosen by Saint Patrick to convey to the Irish the idea of the Trinity.

Land of the Stars and Stripes. The United States, in allusion to the national ensign.

Land of the Sun. The peninsula of Hindustan.

Land of the Thistle. Scotland. The thistle is the national emblem, as the rose is of England and the shamrock of Ireland.

Land of the Veda. India. "Veda" (from a Sanscrit word meaning "to know," literally signifying "knowledge ") is the name commonly applied to "those Sanscrit writings on which the Hindu religion was based."

Land of Wisdom. Normandy, a district of France; so named in allusion to its sensible social and civil customs.

Land o' the Leal. (1) Scotland. The Scotch have always been famed for a loving devotion to the land of their birth. (2) Heaven, the home of the faithful.

> I 'm wearing awa, Jean,
> To the Land o' the Leal.
> BURNS.

In Lady Nairn's beautiful song, "The Land o' the Leal," heaven is clearly meant; but the term also signifies a species of Scottish Utopia, where all the men are brave and honorable and all the women beautiful and virtuous. *See* DIXIE.

Landseer of the Present. Richard Ansdell, R. A., a famous English animal painter (fl. 1815–1885), was so named during his lifetime by his friends and admirers.

Lang. Language.

Langage des halles. (Fr.) "Language of the markets." Profane language; Billingsgate.

Langel. (Pseud.) The Comte de Paris, who furnished a series of papers on the United States to the "Revue des Deux Mondes," Paris, 1865.

Language of Flowers. *See* FLOWERS, SYMBOLISM OF.

Language of Hell. The name given by Mohammed to the Puchtoo tongue, spoken by the Afghans, because of its harshness.

Language of Horses. So Charles V. nicknamed the German tongue.

Languente, or **Languido.** (Ital.) With languor. (Mus.)

Laocoön. In classic myth a son of Priam and Hecuba, and a priest in the temple of Apollo, in Troy, who in vain warned his countrymen of the deceit practised by the Greeks in their pretended offering of the wooden horse to Minerva, and was destroyed along with his two sons by two enormous serpents which came from the sea. They first fastened on his children; and when he attempted to rescue them, he was involved in their coils. This legend is not Homeric, but of later origin. This myth has found expression in marble in the celebrated group of the Laocoön, exhumed on the Esquiline Hill, Rome, in 1506, and now in the Vatican. It is from the chisel of some artist whose name has not been clearly ascertained, and is regarded as one of the most magnificent pieces of ancient sculpture.

Laodamia. Wife of Protesilaus, who was slain before Troy. She begged to be allowed to converse with her dead husband for only three hours, and her request was granted; when the respite was over, she accompanied the dead hero to the shades of death.

Laodicean. One indifferent to religion, caring little or nothing about the matter, like the Christians of that Church mentioned in the Book of Revelation.

Lapp. Lappish.

Lapsus calami. (Lat.) A slip of the pen.

Lapsus linguæ. (Lat.) A slip of the tongue.

Lapsus memoriæ. (Lat.) A slip of the memory.

Lares. In classic myth the deities of special localities, either domestic or public.

Lares et penates. (Lat.) The domestic and household gods of ancient Rome; all our household gods; our loved homes and home treasures.

Largamente, or **Larghissimo.** (Ital.) Extremely slow. (Mus.)

L'argent. Silver; money.

Larghetto. (Ital.) A tune slow and measured in speed, but less so than *largo.*

Largo. (Ital.) A very slow and solemn movement. (Mus.)

La Roque. (Pseud.) Louis Boyer, a French vaudevillist.

Larry Dugan's Eyewater. Shoeblacking; so called because a certain bootblack of Dublin, named Larry Dugan, always had a smutty face.

L. A. S. Lord Advocate of Scotland.

Last Man. Charles I. of England was so named by the Parliamentarians, they meaning that he would be the last monarch to sit on the throne of England. His son, Charles II., was illogically called "the Son of the Last Man."

Last of the Cocked Hats. John Mease, American Revolutionary soldier (1746–1826). Down to his death he persisted in wearing the cocked hat, long after it had gone out of fashion.

Last of the Fathers. Saint Bernard, Abbot of Clairvaux (fl. 1091–1153).

Last of the Goths. Roderick, the thirty-fourth of the Visigothic line of kings (414–711).

Last of the Greeks. Philopœmen (fl. 252–183 B. C.). He aimed to make of the Achaians a martial people and establish their independence.

Last of the Knights. A title given to the Emperor Maximilian I. of Germany (fl. 1459–1519).

Last of the Mohicans. The Indian chieftain Uncas; so named by James Fenimore Cooper in his novel of the name.

Last of the Romans. (1) Marcus Junius Brutus (fl. 85–42 B. C.), one of the assassins of Cæsar. (2) Caius Cassius Longinus (d. 42 B. C.) was so named by Brutus. (3) The general Ætius, who defeated Attila in 451, was so named by Procopius. (4) François Joseph Terrasse Desbillons (fl. 1751–1789), in allusion to his great attainments as a Latin scholar. (5) Congreve was so named by Pope. (6) Rienzi the Reformer. (7) Charles James Fox. (8) Horace Walpole.

Last of the Schoolmen. François Suarez (fl. 1548–1617).

Last of the Tribunes. Cola di Rienzi, who assumed the title "tribune of liberty, peace, and justice." He flourished 1313–1354, and is the hero of Lord Lytton's novel of the name.

Last of the Troubadours. Jacques Jasmin, of Gascony (fl. 1798–1864).

Last Sigh of the Moor, The. (Span., *El ultimo sospiro del Moro.*) A rocky eminence in the outskirts of the city of Granada, Spain, is known by this poetical title. It is noted as the spot where Boabdil, the last Moorish monarch, took his farewell of the land of his birth.

Lat. Latitude; Latin.

Lateat scintillula forsan. (Lat.) "A small spark may perchance lie hid," — the motto of the Humane Society.

Latet anguis in herba. (Lat.) "A snake lies hid in the grass." There is a lurking danger in the way.

Late Unpleasantness. A euphemism for the civil war in the United States, 1861–1865. It was coined by "Petroleum V. Nasby" (*q. v.*), in a volume entitled "Swingin' round the Circle," and appears in a variety of forms; as "the late onpleasantness," "a season ov onpleasantness," "serious onpleasantness," and "the late onpleasantnesses." It obtained wide currency.

Latin Union. A compact between France, Italy, Belgium, and Switzerland to maintain the use of the same coinage from 1865 to 1880.

Latin War. An insurrection of the peasants in Salzburg, 1523. It arose through the unpopularity of a dignitary of the Church, but was speedily suppressed.

Latitudes, The Horse. *See* HORSE LATITUDES.

Latitudinarians. A name applied by contemporaries to a school of theologians within the English Church in the latter half of the seventeenth century. It grew out of the earlier movement in favor of a more liberal constitution for the Church, represented by the names of Falkland, Hales, Jeremy Taylor, and Chillingworth. This earlier movement was mainly ecclesiastical, aiming at a wider extension of the Anglican Church system ; the later was mainly philosophical, and had still more directly in view the interests of rational religion. The school was represented by a succession of well-known Cambridge divines, of whom the chief were Whichcote, Smith, Cudworth, and More. Starting from the same ground as Hales and Chillingworth, in the disregard for authority and tradition in matters of faith, and the assertion of the supremacy of reason as the test of truth, their liberalism takes a higher flight, and brings us to the discussion of larger questions and principles of a more fundamental and far-reaching character. The Cambridge divines, nurtured on Plato and the later Platonists, sought to wed philosophy to religion, and to confirm the union on an indestructible basis of reason. Theirs was the first attempt to link together philosophy and Christianity ever made by any Protestant school ; and, indeed, the first true attempt since the days of the great Alexandrine teachers, to construct a philosophy of religion at once free and conservative, in which the rights of faith and the claims of the speculative intellect should each have free scope, and blend together for mutual elevation and strength.

Latona. In classic myth daughter of Cœus and Phœbe, and the mother of Apollo and Diana.

La Trenella. (Pseud.) Mrs. Mary B. D. Clarke, popular contributor to the Southern press.

Latter-Day Saints. Another name for the Mormon hierarchy, they calling themselves "The Church of Jesus Christ of Latter-Day Saints."

Laudator temporis acti. (Lat.) One who praises times gone by.

Laughing Philosopher. Democritus of Abdera (fl. 460–357 B. C.), who was perpetually railing at the weaknesses of mankind. A better name would be "The Scolding Philosopher."

Laugh, Sardonic. *See* SARDONIC SMILE.

Launcelot Langstaff. (Pseud.) (1) Washington Irving, American humorous writer (1783–1859). (2) William Irving, merchant and poet, brother of above (1766–1821). (3) James Kirke Paulding, American novelist and writer (1779–1860).

Launcelot Temple. (Pseud.) John Armstrong, British poet and physician (1709–1779).

Laura Bellini. The stage-name of Mrs. Laura Woolwine, *née* Nobles.

Laura Clairon. The stage-name of Laura Lehnhoff.

Laura Dean. The stage-name of Mrs. William Fredericks.

Laura Don. The stage-name of Mrs. Fox.

Laura Francis. The stage-name of Mrs. Edward Conly.

Laura Joyce. The stage-name of Mrs. Digby Bell, *née* Maskell.

Laura Lorrimer. (Pseud.) Mrs. Julia Finley Shelton, contributor to "Godey's Lady's Book" and many Southern publications.

Laura Seymour. The stage-name of Mrs. Samo.

Laura Virgil. The stage-name of Mrs. Henry Mainhall.

Laura Wallace. The stage-name of Mrs. Frank Mordaunt.

Laureate of the Gentle Craft. Hans Sachs, the cobbler-poet of Nuremberg.

Laureate of the South. Paul Hamilton Hayne, the American poet.

Laurie Todd. The pen-name of Grant Thorburn (fl. 1775–1863), a Scottish American, and author of several books.

Laus Deo. (Lat.) Praise to God.

Laus propria sordet. (Lat.) Praise of one's self defiles.

La Vendée. A powerful party of French royalists, who in 1793, in the west of France, resisted the Republicans, and were victorious in several battles between July 12, 1793, and Jan. 1,

1794, when they met with a severe reverse. Their leader, Henri Comte de la Rochejaquelein, was killed March 4, 1794.

L'Avenir. (Fr.) The future.

Lavinia. An old name for Italy, derived from Lavinia, daughter of Latinus and wife of Æneas.

Lavinia Bennett. The stage-name of Mrs. John A. Mackay.

Lavinian Shore. Italy. Lavinium was a town of Latium, founded by Æneas in honor of his wife Lavinia.

> From the rich Lavinian shore,
> I your market come to store.
> SHAKSPEARE.

Law of Athens. By Athenian law, a father could dispose of his daughter in marriage as he liked. Egeus pleaded this law, and demanded that his daughter Hermia should marry Demetrius or suffer the penalty of the law; if she would not

> Consent to marry with Demetrius,
> I beg the ancient privilege of Athens;
> As she is mine, I may dispose of her:
> Which shall be either to this gentleman
> Or to her death, according to our law.
> *Midsummer Night's Dream,* act i. sc. i.

Law of Clan Macduff. This was a barbarous privilege which formerly belonged to those related within the ninth degree to Macduff, Earl of Fife. If one having the privilege was found guilty of homicide, he was absolved by coming to Macduff's Cross, between Fife and Strathearn, and giving nine *kye* (cows) and a *colpindash* (a young cow).

Law of Flanders. Charles "the Good," Earl of Flanders, made a law that a serf, unless legally emancipated, was always a serf, and that whoever married a serf became a serf. Sheridan Knowles founded his tragedy, called "The Provost of Bruges," on this law.

Law of Lombardy.

> " We have a law, peculiar to this realm,
> That subjects to a mortal penalty
> All women nobly born . . . who, to the shame
> Of chastity, o'erleap its thorny bounds,
> To wanton in the flowery path of pleasure."

On this law Robert Jephson founded the following tragedy: The Duke Bireno, heir to the crown, falsely charges the Princess Sophia of incontinence. The villany of the duke being discovered, he is slain in combat by a Briton named Paladore, and the victor marries the princess.

Lawrence Barrett. The stage-name of Larry Brannigan, a famous tragedian of the present day.

Lawrence Templeton. (Pseud.) Sir Walter Scott, Scottish novelist (1771–1832).

Law's Bubble. The gigantic commercial scheme known by this name was projected in France by the celebrated John Law (1671–1729), of Lauriston, in 1717, and collapsed in 1720. Its primary object was to develop the resources of Louisiana and the country bordering on the Mississippi, a tract of land then believed to abound in the precious metals. Law established a bank in France composed of twelve hundred shares of three thousand livres' value each; and by 1718 these shares had risen to twenty times their original value. Law was then at the zenith of his fame and popularity. But in 1720 the bubble burst; the shares sunk as rapidly as they had risen, occasioning much misery and financial distress.

Layer's Conspiracy. A plot of Christopher Layer, a barrister, and others, to seize the persons of George I., the Prince of Wales, Lord Cadogan, the Tower, and the Bank of England, and bring in the Pretender. Layer was hanged May 17, 1723.

Lazarus Piot. (Pseud.) Alexander Silvayn, English satirical writer (fl. 1596).

Lazy Man's Load. One too heavy to be carried; so called because lazy people, to save themselves the trouble of coming a second time, are apt to overload themselves.

Lb., or lb. *Libra* or *libræ.* Pound or pounds in weight.

L. C. Lower Canada; Lord Chamberlain; Lord Chancellor.

L. C. B. Lord Chief Baron.

L. C. J. Lord Chief-Justice.

L. D. Lady Day (March 25).

Ld. Lord.

Ldp. Lordship.

L. D. S. Licentiate of Dental Surgery.

Leader Scott. (Pseud.) Mrs. Lucy E. Baxter, Italian correspondent of Cassell's " Magazine of Art."

Leading Question. A question so worded as to suggest an answer. " Was he dressed in a black coat?" leads to the answer " Yes." In cross-examining a witness, leading questions are permitted, because the chief object of a cross-examination is to obtain contradictions.

League. The term employed in the sixteenth and seventeenth centuries to designate a political alliance or coalition. The most famous leagues were those of Cambray, Schmalkald, Nurnberg, etc. But the name has a peculiar importance in the history of France as applied to the opposition, organized by the Duke of Guise, to the granting of freedom of worship and political rights to the Huguenots in 1571. *See* HOLY LEAGUE, CADDEE LEAGUE, GRAY LEAGUE, etc., and *infra*.

League of Cambray, against the Republic of Venice, composed of Pope Julian II., the Emperor Maximilian, Louis XII. of France, and Ferdinand of Spain, was entered into, Dec. 10, 1508.

League of God's House. A famous coalition of the Grisons in 1400, with the object of resisting domestic tyranny.

League of Poor Conrad. *See* PEASANT WAR.

League of Public Good. The alliance which took place in 1464 between the Dukes of Burgundy, Brittany, and Bourgogne against Louis XI.

League of Schmalkald. *See* SCHMALKALD LEAGUE.

Leander. In classic myth the youth of Abydos who became enamored of Hero and nightly swam across the Hellespont. *See* HERO.

Lean Jimmy. James Chamberlain Jones (1809-1859), the Tennessee senator, who was often called "Lean Jimmy Jones," or "Bean Pole."

Leap in the Dark. In the debates on the Reform Bill in 1868, the late Lord Derby applied this phrase to the proposed legislation. It was, however, not original; it has been traced to a song in the "British Museum Collection" (H. 1601, p. 62), where it occurs in the line, —

"All you that must take a leap in the dark."

Thomas Hobbes on his death-bed (1679) is reported to have said, "I am taking a frightful leap into the dark," which is not unlike the exclamation of Rabelais in his last illness, "I am going to the Great Perhaps."

Leap, Sappho's. *See* SAPPHO'S LEAP.

Leap-year. A year containing 366 days, which thus "leaps over" a day more than an ordinary year, giving to February twenty-nine days.

Leap-year Day. February 29. This is a day which, occurring but once every four years, cannot be replete with interesting events. It was originally, in the Roman year, placed before the 24th of February, which was reckoned *twice*, and hence called *bissextile*, or *twice sixth*. In the Julian calendar the length of the year was reckoned at 365 days and 6 hours. This was eleven minutes more than the true length, the error amounting to ten entire days in the sixteenth century. To obviate this error, Pope Gregory XIII. ordained in 1582 that that year should consist of 355 days only (October 5 becoming October 15), and that the year ending a century should not be bissextile unless its figures, omitting the ciphers, were divisible by four. Thus, 1700, 1800, and 1900 are not counted as leap-years, but 2000 will be. This arrangement makes a very close approximation to the true time. The "New Style" calendar was quickly adopted by most of the countries of Europe, but by England not till 1752, in which year eleven days had to be dropped, September 3 becoming September 14. In Russia it has not yet been adopted, and that country is now twelve days behind the rest of Europe in its reckoning.

Learned, The. (1) In the days of the Italian Republics, Padua was so named. *See* BEAUTIFUL, THE. (2) Coloman, King of Hungary (fl. 1095–1114).

Learned Blacksmith. Elihu Burritt (fl. 1811–1879), the American linguist. He was in early life a blacksmith.

Learned Painter. Charles Lebrun (fl. 1619–1690); so named on account of the great accuracy displayed in the costuming of his characters.

Learned Tailor. Henry Wild, of Norwich (fl. 1684-1734). While on his bench he mastered Arabic, Persian, Syriac, Chaldaic, Hebrew, Latin, and Greek.

Learned Weaver. Joseph Young, a native of Allentown, Penn. (d. 1888), who spent almost all of his long life in mastering various trades and professions, having been a weaver, a blacksmith, a printer, a coachmaker, a painter, a carpenter, a druggist, an editor, a lawyer, a preacher, a doctor, and a wholesale hardware dealer. He was the oldest practical cotton and flannel weaver in the country.

Leave no Stone unturned. This may be traced to a response of the Delphic Oracle given to Polycrates, as the best means of finding a treasure buried by Xerxes' general, Mardonius, on the field of Platæa. The oracle replied, "Turn every stone."

Le beau monde. (Fr.) The gay world; the fashionable world.

Le bon temps viendra. (Fr.) The good time will come.

Le Bon Vieux Temps. (Pseud.) Either M. Viger or M. Quesnel, in the Montreal "Gazette," about 1815.

Le Clerc. (Pseud.) Mrs. Samuella Mardis Cowen, a well-known contributor to the Southern press.

Lecompton Constitution. In United States history a constitution drawn up by a pro-slavery convention in 1857. *See* COVODE INVESTIGATION.

Leda. In classic myth daughter of Thestius, and wife of Tyndareus. Jupiter fell in love with her, visited her in the form of a swan, and she bore two eggs, from one of which came forth Pollux and Hela, and from the other Castor and Clytemnestra.

Leek of the Welsh. The lowly leek, the Welsh emblem, seems just as unsuited for a national symbol as the rugged thistle. A more homely plant it would be hard to find. There are two stories told as to the reason of its selection. The first is to the effect that at each annual harvest time in Wales the product of the preceding year was usually so far exhausted that the Welshmen were reduced to a diet of leeks, and used to come to the field with two or three of them stuck in their caps for lack of pockets. But the more plausible legend has it that it was adopted in consequence of a command from the Archbishop of St. David's in 519. In that year Arthur won a great victory over the Saxons, and in honor of the event the prelate ordered the soldiery to wear a leek in their caps.

Leeward Isles. Another name for Antigua, Barbuda, Montserrat, St. Christopher's, Nevis, Anguilla, Virgin Isles, and Dominica, West Indies. They are so named with reference to their position in relation to the Trade-wind. *See* WINDWARD ISLES.

Left in the Lurch. This is a metaphor derived from the gaming-table. A *lurch* is where one player makes every point, before his opponent makes one.

The word in French is *lourche*, in German *lurtsch*, and in Italian *lurcio*.

Leg. Legate.

Legato. (Ital.) Smooth and connected. (Mus.)

Lege. (Lat.) Read.

Legem pone. (Lat.) A proverbial expression for ready money, often met with in old writers. In Ozell's "Rebelais," we find, "They were all at our service for the *legem pone;*" and in Minshull's "Essayes in Prison," p. 26, we have: "But in this there is nothing to be abated; all their speech is *legem pone.*" The origin is curious. The portion of Psalm cxix. appointed for the twenty-fifth day of the month has the title "Legem pone," being the first words in the Latin version. These words occurring in the service on the great pay-day, March 25, were associated with payment, and became a general synonym for prompt cash. From this use of the words also arose another proverbial expression, "Post the pony," meaning "Put down the money." "Pony up," for "pay up," comes from the same root.

Leges legum. (Lat.) The law of laws.

Leggiere. (Ital.) With lightness. (Mus.)

Legis. Legislature.

Legislator of Parnassus. Boileau (1636-1711) was so called by Voltaire, because of his "Art of Poetry," a production unequalled in the whole range of didactic poetry.

Legislature of a Thousand Drinks. This was the first legislature of the State of California, convened at San José in 1850. In regard to the sobriquet, it has always been alleged that the American-Californian of early days drank freely, and the United States senatorial candidates during this legislature kept "ranchos," as they were termed, or open house, where all might enter, drink freely, and wish their entertainers success. But the legislature did not so much receive its name from this custom, as from a man named Green, who kept a drinking-house near the State Hall in San José, for lobbying purposes. When the legislature would adjourn he would call to the members, "Come, boys, let's take a thousand drinks!"

Legitimists. A term applied (since 1814) to those who support the claims of the elder branch of the Bourbon family to the throne of France, whose present representative is Henry, Duc de Bordeaux, called Comte de Chambord (b. Sept. 29, 1820). They held a congress at Luzerne on June 24–29, 1862, and agreed to continue a pacific policy. The party was active in February, 1871–1875. Their efforts to recover power have proved ineffectual thus far.

Leg-of-Mutton School. A nickname given to a class of needy authors who in return for past or expected favors hang at the skirts of wealthy patrons and indulge in servile flattery.

Le grand monarque. (Fr.) "The great monarch." Louis XIV. of France.

Le grand œuvre. (Fr.) "The great work." The philosopher's stone.

Leighton. (Pseud.) Jesse Appleton, S. T. D., in the Boston "Panoplist" and the Piscataqua "Evangelical Magazine."

Leila. (Pseud.) (1) Mrs. Emma Barlow, a contributor to Harper's, Scribner's, and other magazines. (2) Miss Ella Caldwell, contributor of poems to the Louisville "Democrat."

Leila Cameron. (Pseud.) Mrs. Catherine A. (Richards) DuBose.

Leip. Leipsic.

L. E. L. (Pseud.) Letitia Elizabeth Landon, English poet (1802–1839).

Lemnian Act. One of unusual barbarity and cruelty. The phrase arose from two horrible massacres perpetrated by the Lemnians. The first was the murder of all the men and male children on the island by the women; and the other was the murder by the men of all the children in the island born of Athenian parents.

Le monde savant. (Fr.) The learned world.

Le mot d'énigme. (Fr.) The key of the riddle.

L'empire des lettres. (Fr.) "The empire of letters." The republic of letters; the learned.

Lemures. In classic myth spirits of the dead, believed to wander at night to affright the living.

Lena. (Pseud.) Mrs. Mary Torrans Lathrop.

Lene tormentum. (Lat.) "Gentle torture." Mild violence.

Lentando. (Ital.) With increasing slowness. (Mus.)

Lento. (Ital.) In slow time. (Mus.)

Leola. (Pseud.) Mrs. Loula K. Rogers.

Leoline. (Pseud.) Mrs. E. B. S. Dunham. in the Boston "Christian Leader."

Leon Edwards. (Pseud.) Alfred R. Calhoun, in the New York "Weekly."

Leone Leoni. (Pseud.) Dr. John D. Osborne, Paris correspondent of the New York "World."

Leonidas of Modern Greece. Marco Bozzaris. With 1,200 men he routed 4,000 Turko-Albanians at Kerpenisi, but himself was killed in the battle, 1823.

Leonidas Wedell. Frederick the Great so named Gen. C. H. Wedell, an officer in the Prussian service (fl. 1712–1782), in memory of his spirited defence of the crossing of the Elbe at Teinitz on the 19th of November, 1744.

Leonine Contract. A one-sided agreement; so called in allusion to the fable of "The Lion and his Fellow-Hunters."

Leonine Verses. Verses in which the middle word rhymes with the end one; so called from the inventor Leoninus, a canon of the Church of St. Victor, in Paris, in the twelfth century.

Leonora Braham. The stage-name of Mrs. Duncan Young.

Leono's Head. Porto Leono, the ancient Piræus; so called from a huge lion of white marble, removed by the Venetians to their arsenal.

The wandering stranger near the port descries
A milk-white lion of stupendous size,
Of antique marble, — hence the haven's name;
Unknown to modern natives whence it came.
   FALCONER, *The Shipwreck*, iii. 3.

Le pas. (Fr.) "The step." Precedence in place or rank.

Le petit caporal. (Fr.) The little corporal, — a name applied by the French soldiers to Napoleon I.

Le petit monde. (Fr.) "The little world." The lower classes.

Le roi s'en avisera. (Fr.) The king will consider or think of it.

Leroy. (Pseud.) Miss Annie M. Barnwell, a frequent contributor to the press of the South.

Le roy le veult. (Old Fr.) The king wills it.

Les absents ont toujours tort. (Fr.) The absent are always wrong.

Le savoir faire. (Fr.) The knowledge how to act; industry.

Le savoir vivre. (Fr.) The knowledge how to live; good breeding.

Lesbian Kiss. An immodest kiss. The ancient Lesbians were noted for their licentiousness, and hence to "Lesbianize" became synonymous with licentious indulgence, and "Lesbia" meant a harlot.

Lesbian Poets. Terpander, Alcæus, Arion, and the poetess Sappho. They were all natives of Lesbos.

Lèse majesté. (Fr.) High treason.

Lesser Ajax. *See* AJAX.

Lesser Britain (*Britannia Secunda*). Wales was formerly so called in distinction from *Britannia Prima* (England) and *North Britain* (Scotland). *See* GREATER BRITAIN.

Lesser Prophets. Hosea, Joel, Amos, Obadiah, Micah, Jonah, Nahum, Habakkuk, Zephaniah, Haggai, Zechariah, and Malachi. *See* GREAT PROPHETS.

Lester Lisle. (Pseud.) Miss Emmeline Lisle Walker.

Lethe. One of the five rivers of hell. The word means "forgetfulness." The other rivers are Styx, Acheron, Cocytus, and Phlegethon. Dante makes Lethe the boundary between purgatory and paradise.

Far off from these [*four*] a slow and silent
    stream,
Lethe, the river of oblivion, rolls
Her watery labyrinth, whereof who drinks
Forthwith his former state and being forgets,—
Forgets both joy and grief, pleasure and pain.
                    MILTON, *Paradise Lost.*

Let her go, Gallagher. This phrase, at one time heard all over the United States, had its origin with Judge Beaver, of Morgan County, Ky. He had a trotting mare, which was ridden by one Gallagher, City Marshal of Harrodsburg. On one occasion the judge entered the mare at a trotting meeting in Tipton County. Some sports there thought of catching the judge for once, so they entered a noted fast trotter against his mare. At the end of the first half-mile the two trotters passed under the wire neck and neck at a 2.40 pace. The judge shouted, "Let her go, Gallagher;" and Gallagher, catching the word, let loose the lines, when the mare picked up her feet and walked away from her opponent most beautifully, coming in at the pole more than a dozen lengths ahead.

L'étoile du nord. (Fr.) The north star.

Le tout ensemble. (Fr.) "All together." General effect.

Letters of the Sepulchre. The laws made by Godfrey and the patriarchs of the court of Jerusalem. There were two codes, — one respecting the privileges of the nobles, and the other respecting the rights and duties of burghers. These codes were laid up in a coffer with the treasures of the Church of the Holy Sepulchre.

Lett. Lettish.

Lettre de cachet. (Fr.) An arbitary warrant of imprisonment or banishment, formerly issued, in the form of a letter, by the kings of France.

Lettre de marque. (Fr.) A letter of marque.

Leucadia's Rock. A promontory, the south extremity of the island Leucas, or Leucadia, in the Ionian Sea. Sappho leaped from this rock when she found her love for Phaon unrequited. At the annual festival of Apollo a criminal was hurled from Leucadia's Rock into the sea; but birds of various sorts were attached to him, in order to break his fall, and if he was not killed he was set free. The leap from this rock is called "The Lover's Leap."

All those may leap who rather would be neuter
(Leucadia's Rock still overlooks the wave).
                    BYRON, *Don Juan.*

Lev. Leviticus.

Levana. In classic myth the name of the goddess who watched over newborn infants.

Levee. The name given to the vast earthworks necessary to keep the turbulent Mississippi within bounds, and to prevent inundation of the rich lowlands. It is from the French *lever*, to raise, and was coined by the French settlers of Louisiana.

Levée. (Fr.) A morning reception.

Levellers. The name of a fanatical party in Germany in the sixteenth century. They were headed by Münzer and Storck, and taught that all rank distinctions were usurpations on the rights of humanity. At the head of 40,000 followers Münzer called on princes and magistrates to step down from their posts, and ravaged the country. The rabble was defeated by the Landgrave of Hesse, May 15, 1525, and 7,000 were slain.

Leviathan of Literature. Dr. Samuel Johnson was so named.

Levi Blodgett. A pen-name sometimes used by Theodore Parker.

Levy. Elevenpence. In the States of Pennsylvania, Maryland, and Virginia the Spanish real, or eighth part of a dollar, or twelve and a half cents. Sometimes called an *elevenpenny bit.*

Lewis Baboon. The nickname under which Louis XIV. of France figures in Arbuthnot's "History of John Bull."

Lex. Lexicon.

Lex dubia non obligat. (Lat.) A dubious law has no binding force.

Lex et consuetudo Parliamenti. (Lat.) The law and usage of Parliament.

Lex loci. (Lat.) The law of the place.

Lex magna est, et prævelibet. (Lat.) The law is great, and will prevail.

Lex non scripta. (Lat.) The unwritten law; the common law.

Lex scripta. (Lat.) The written law; the statute law.

Lex talionis. (Lat.) Law of retaliation.

Lex terræ. (Lat.) Law of the land.

Lex terræ, lex patriæ. (Lat.) The law of the land.

L. G. Life-Guards.

L. H. A. Lord High Admiral.

L. H. C. Lord High Chancellor.

L. H. D. Doctor of Literature.

L'homme propose, et Dieu dispose. (Fr.) Man proposes, and God disposes.

L. H. T. Lord High Treasurer.

L. I. Long Island.

Li. Lithium.

Lib. *Liber.* Book.

Liberal Arts. Book-learning; viz., Grammar, Rhetoric, Philosophy, Arithmetic, Geometry, Astronomy, and Music.

Liberals. (1) A name given in England to the more advanced Whigs and reformers since 1828. The party held office under Earl Grey, Viscount Melbourne, Earl Russell, Viscount Palmerston, and Mr. Gladstone. (2) In the United States in 1872 the opponents of General Grant in the Republican Party met in convention at Cincinnati, and nominated Horace Greeley for President. He was defeated. *See* INDEPENDENTS.

This word, as applied to a political party, is said to be derived from the name of "The Liberal," a periodical of advanced views on politics and religion, which Lord Byron and some of his friends established about the year 1815.

Liberator, The. (1) Simon Bolivar (fl. 1785–1831), who established the independence of Mexico. (2) Daniel O'Connell (fl. 1775–1847), the famous Irish agitator, was so named because of his heroic efforts to effect a repeal of the Union between England and Ireland.

Liberator of the World. So Dr. Franklin has been called (1706–1790).

Libertines. A sect of heretics in Holland, led by Quinton, a factor, and Copin. They maintained that nothing is sinful but to those who think it sinful, and that perfect innocence is to live without doubt.

Liberty Cap. A peaked cap placed on the head of the goddess of Liberty or on liberty poles. The *pileus*, a half-egg-shaped cap, became the badge of liberty, because it was given to a Roman slave at his manumission, and was not permitted to be worn except by freedmen. Livy has the phrase "*servos ad pileum vocare*," "to summon slaves to freedom," *i.e.* to call them to assume the cap. The *pileus* was borne aloft on a staff or pike, as a banner or standard, by commanders who sought the aid of the slaves by the promise of freedom. Hence the liberty *pole* and *cap.*

Yes, France is free! O glorious France, that has burst out so : into universal sound and smoke; and attained — the Phrygian Cap of Liberty! — CARLYLE.

Liberty, Cradle of. *See* CRADLE OF LIBERTY.

Liberty Party grew out of the Anti-Slavery Society, and was more widely known for the persistent agitation of its adherents than its numbers. In 1840 it nominated James G. Birney, Secretary of the Anti-Slavery Society, for President, casting 7,059 votes; and again in 1844, when he received 62,300 votes. It contained such men as William Lloyd Garrison, Wendell Phillips, Lewis Tappan, Gerrit Smith, Samuel Lewis, and Salmon P. Chase. It merged into the Free Soil Party in 1848.

Liberty Pole. A tall pole, like a ship's mast, and surmounted by a "liberty cap."

Liberty Tree. An allusion very frequent in the history of New England.

In 1765 the "Sons of Liberty" were organized under the "Liberty Tree," — a wide-spreading, beautiful elm, which stood in front of a grocery, near what is now the corner of Essex and Washington Streets, Boston, a tablet on the present building marking the spot; and here were exposed the effigies of those men who had favored the passage of the odious Stamp Act. During the exciting period which followed, nearly all the great political meetings of the "Sons of Liberty," called together by the hoisting of a flag on the staff extending through the branches of the tree, were held under its waving boughs and in the square about it. During the siege of Boston, about the last of August, 1775, this tree was cut down by a gang in the pay of the British soldiers and the Tories, after standing one hundred and nineteen years. — KING.

Liberum arbitrium. (Lat.) "Free judgment." Free will; free choice.

Libretto. (Ital.) A little book or pamphlet.

Licentia vatum. (Lat.) A poetical license.

Lich-way. The path by which a funeral is conveyed to the church, which not unfrequently deviates from the ordinary road. It was long supposed that wherever a dead body passed became a public thoroughfare. *Lich* = Anglo-Saxon for a corpse.

Licked into Shape. According to legend, the young bear is born a shapeless mass, and the dam licks her cub into its proper shape.

> The she-bear licks her cubs into a sort
> Of shape.
> BYRON, *The Deformed Transformed.*

Lie in Lavender. "To lie in lavender" was anciently "to lie in pawn." The following quotations show the former use of the phrase : —

> But the poore gentleman paies so deere for the lavender it is laid up in, that if it lies long at a broker's house, he seemes to buy his apparel twice. — GREENE, *Imp. Harl. Misc.*
> And a black satten of his own to go before her in ; which suit, for the more sweet'ning, now lies in lavender. — BEN JONSON, *Every Man out of his Humor.*

Lieut. Lieutenant.

Lieut.-Col. Lieutenant-Colonel.

Lieut.-Gen. Lieutenant-General.

Lieut.-Gov. Lieutenant-Governor.

Light-horse Harry. The sobriquet conferred on Gen Henry Lee (fl. 1756-1818), a dashing cavalry officer on the patriot side during the Revolutionary War.

Lightning Story-writer. F. Marion Crawford, a novelist of the present day, in allusion to the rapidity with which he produces works of fiction.

Light of Greece. Corinth was so named by Cicero.

Light of the Age. Rabbi Moses ben Maimon, of Cordova (fl. 1135–1204), was so named by his admirers.

Ligurian Republic. Venetia, Genoa, and a part of Sardinia, tied up in one bundle by Napoleon I. in 1797, and bound with a constitution similar to that of the French " Directory ; " so called from the ancient Liguria, pretty well commensurate with these districts.

Ligurian Sage. Aulus Persius Flaccus (fl. 34–62).

Like Angels' Visits, etc. *See* ANGELS' VISITS.

Like as if. A common Southernism is the use of "like as if" or "like" for the words "as if." "She looked like she knew me " is a common expression, or, "She looked like as if she'd die." This is very common in Washington, and in all the States south of Mason and Dixon's Line.

Lil. (Pseud.) Waterman L. Ormsby, Jr., in the New York "Sun."

Lilis, or Lilith. There was a popular belief among the Hebrews that Adam had a wife named Lilis, or Lilith, before he married Eve. In revenge for his desertion of her, Lilith was believed to wander near the abodes of men, on the alert to kill their infant children. To frustrate this cruel purpose the mother would suspend an amulet around her child's neck, on which was inscribed the exclamation "Lilla, abi !" (Begone, Lilith !) ; and it is affirmed that our English word *lullaby*, which means "a song to quiet babes," is derived from this talismanic phrase.

Lillian Conway. The stage-name (and the maiden name) of Mrs. Charles S. Camblos.

Lillian Howard. The stage-name of Mrs. Charles O. White.

Lillian Richards. The stage-name of Mrs. Leander Richardson.

Lillian Russell. The stage-name of Mrs. Harry Braham, formerly Mrs. Edward Solomon, *née* Leonard.

Lillian Spencer. The stage-name of Mrs. Edward Clayburgh.

Lillian Wood. The stage-name of Mrs. W. S. Ross.

Lilli-burlero and **Bullen-a-la.** Party cries peculiar to the Irish Papists in their massacres of the Protestants in 1641. A song with the refrain of " Lilliburlero, bullen-a-la," was written by Lord Wharton, which contributed not a little to the great revolution of 1688.

Lillie Grubb. The stage-name of Mrs. David Hayman.

Lillie Pease. The stage-name of Mrs. Edward Chrissie.

Lillie West. The stage-name of Mrs. Henry Brown.

Lilliput. A jocose name given to Rhode Island, the smallest State in the Union.

Lily Bate. The stage-name of Mrs Charles Atkinson.

Lily of France. Although the royal French emblem is conventionally regarded as a lily, the heraldic painters have so effectually disguised it that it is now a mere matter of choice to say what it is. As early as the year 1611, Givillim (who was in those days considered a cunning finder out of hidden things) regarded the device on the Bourbon flag as "three toads," and it is affirmed that it was in allusion to these supposed symbols of their country that the popular nickname of "Jean Crapauds" was bestowed on the French people. Still more recently, owing to certain ornaments resembling bees having been found in the tomb of Childeric, father of Clovis, it has been thought that perhaps these insects, and not lilies or toads, are represented on the white flag.

Lilywhites. A nickname given to the Fifty-ninth Regiment of the English army.

Limæ labor et mora. (Lat.) The slow process of improving a literary production.

Limbo. (Lat. *limbus*, an edge.) A sort of neutral land on the confines of paradise for those who are not good enough for heaven and not bad enough for hell, or rather for those who cannot (according to the Church) be admitted into paradise, either because they have never heard the gospel or else have never been baptized.

> These of sin
> Were blameless; and if aught they merited,
> It profits not, since baptism was not theirs.
> . . . If they before
> The gospel lived, they served not God aright.
> . . . For these defects
> And for no other evil, we are lost.
> DANTE, *Inferno.*

Limbo Fatuorum, or the "Fool's Paradise," for idiots, madmen, and others who are not responsible for their sins, but yet have done nothing worthy of salvation. Milton says, from the earth fly to the Paradise of Fools, —

> All things transitory and vain . . . the fruits
> Of painful superstition and blind zeal . . .
> All the unaccomplished works of Nature's hand,
> Abortive, monstrous, or unkindly mixed . . .
> The builders here of Babel . . .
> Others come single. He who, to be deemed
> A god, leaped fondly into Etna's flames,
> Empedocles; and he who, to enjoy
> Plato's elysium, leaped into the sea . . .
> Embryos and idiots, eremites and friars.
> *Paradise Lost.*

Limbo of the Moon. Ariosto, in his "Orlando Furioso," says, in the moon are treasured up the precious time misspent in play, all vain efforts, all vows never paid, all counsel thrown away, all desires that lead to nothing, the vanity of titles, flattery, great men's promises, court services, and death-bed alms. Pope says : —

> There heroes' wits are kept in ponderous vases,
> And beaux' in snuff-boxes and tweezer-cases ;
> There broken vows and death-bed alms are found,
> And lovers' hearts with ends of ribbon bound ;
> The courtier's promises, and sick man's prayers,
> The smiles of harlots, and the tears of heirs ;
> Cages for gnats, and chains to yoke a flea,
> Dried butterflies, and tomes of casuistry.
> *Rape of the Lock.*

Limbo Patrum. That half-way house between purgatory and paradise, where patriarchs and prophets, saints, martyrs, and confessors, await the "second coming."

Lime-juicers. A nickname current among seafaring men for the sailors of the British mercantile marine. English ships are compelled to carry a supply of lime-juice among their stores to prevent scurvy.

Lin. Lineal.

Lincoln Brotherhood. Political associations established by the negroes at the South at the close of the civil war to protect their right of suffrage.

Lincoln's Birthday. This falls on February 12, and is a legal holiday in Louisiana.

Lincolnshire Bagpipes. In the "First Part of Henry IV.," act i. sc. 2, Shakspeare makes Falstaff speak of "the drone of a Lincolnshire bagpipe." Some commentators on Shakspeare have endeavored to prove from this passage that Lincolnshire was colonized by immigrants from Scotland. They are wrong; the phrase has no reference to the musical instruments known as bagpipes, but applies to the croaking of the innumerable frogs which flourish in the fenny portions of that country.

L'Inconnue. (Pseud.) Mrs. L. Virginia French, American authoress (1830–1881).

Linda Brent. (Pseud.) Mrs. Harriet Jacobs, an American writer.

Lingua Franca. (Ital.) "The Frank tongue." The mixed language spoken by Europeans in the East.

Lingua volgare. (Ital.) The vulgar or common tongue.

Linn. Linnæus ; Linnæan.

Lion, The. (1) Damelowicz, Prince of Halicz; he founded Lemberg in 1259, which was in turn called "the Lion City." (2) Henry, Duke of Bavaria and Saxony (fl. 1129–1195). (3) Louis VIII. of France (fl. 1187–1226), was so named because he was born under the constellation Leo. (4) William of Scotland (d. 1214) was so named from his cognizance, a lion rampant.

Lion-killer. Jules Gerard (fl. 1817–1864).

Lion King of Assyria. Arioch the Assyrian (fl. 1827–1897 B. C.).

Lion of God. Ali (fl. 602–661) was so named on account of his religious fervor and martial zeal.

Lion of Janina. Ali Pasha (fl. 1741–1822). He was deposed in the latter year by Ibrahim Pasha.

Lion of the North. Gustavus Adolphus (fl. 1594–1632).

Lion of the Sea. An old name for the Cape of Good Hope.

Lion of the Tribe of Judah. The Messiah (Rev. v. 5).

Lion's Provider. "A jackal; a foil to another man's wit; a humble friend who plays into your hand to show you to best advantage. The jackal feeds on the lion's leavings, and is supposed to serve the lion in much the same way as a dog serves a sportsman. The dog lifts up its foot to indicate that game is at hand, and the jackal yells to advertise the lion that prey is close by."

Liq. Liquor ; liquid.

Liqueur. (Fr.) A cordial.

Lisa Weber. The stage-name of Mrs. W. S. Mullaly.

Lis litem generat. (Lat.) Strife begets strife.

Lis sub judice. (Lat.) "A lawsuit before the judge." A case not yet decided.

Listener, The. (Pseud.) Nathan Henry Chamberlin, in the Boston "Transcript."

Lit. Literally; literature.

Litchfield House Compact. A bargain said to have been made between the Whig Government and Daniel O'Connell, in 1835, at Litchfield House, London.

Lite pendente. (Lat.) During the trial.

Literary Baker, The. Caleb Jeacocke, the celebrated baker, president of the Robin Hood Society (*circa* 1765).

Literary Leather-Dresser. Thomas Dowse, a famous American book-collector (1772–1856). He resided in Cambridgeport, Mass., and while following his trade of leather-dresser devoted a large part of his income to the purchase of books. Harvard gave him the degree of LL.D., which Edward Everett translated into "Literary Leather-Dresser."

Litera scripta manet. (Lat.) The written letter remains.

Literati. (Lat.) Men of letters.

Lith. Lithuanian.

Little Ben. The nickname by which Benjamin Harrison, twenty-third President of the United States, was known to his men during the civil war.

Little Britain. An English designation of the French province of Bretagne, or Brittany.

Little Church around the Corner. The Church of the Transfiguration (P. E.) in Twenty-ninth Street, New York. The occurrence which gave rise to the nickname is thus related by Dr. Houghton, the rector. George Holland, a popular comedian, died Dec. 20, 1870, and the clergyman to whom Holland's family first applied declined to bury him because the deceased was an actor. He directed the applicant to "the little church around the corner." Dr. Houghton readily consented, and the service was conducted at his church on December 22. Touching the incident of George Holland's funeral, Dr. Houghton said : —

"It drew toward the Church, to which my life had been given, a world of kindly, tender feelings, and it opened wide for personal ministration and usefulness such a door as few of you may imagine. It convinced many a one who had known nothing of the Church — not this Church of the Transfiguration in particular, but the Church in general — and her clergy, many a most wretched outcast, that hither he or she should come and find a heart, a hand, and an ear ever open, and a priest's lips that could keep knowledge, — could keep to themselves, as in honor and duty bound, the knowledge confided to him. From the prison and the gambling-house and the house of ill-repute, the message or the messenger has hither come that might not have elsewhere gone. God's blessing has rested upon this our parish and church by reason of the effort made to make the most of the greater opportunity thus offered for ministering to those who had need."

Little Comedy. A nickname given by Goldsmith to his friend Miss Kate Horneck, afterward Mrs. Bunbury, on account of her lively and intelligent disposition.

Little Constantinople. Kertch was so called by the Genoese from its extent and prosperity. Demosthenes calls it "the granary of Athens."

Little Corporal. Napoleon Bonaparte was so nicknamed by his troops because of his diminutive stature and indomitable courage.

Little Dauphin. A nickname given to the eldest son of the Great Dauphin, *i. e.*, the Duke of Bourgogne, grandson of Louis XIV.

Little End of the Horn. "To come out at the little end of the horn" is said when a ridiculously small effect has been produced after great effort and much boasting, and when a person or thing makes a failure.

Little England. The island of Barbadoes is often so named by its people, most of whom are of English blood.

Little Gentleman in Velvet. A favorite Jacobite toast in the reign of Queen Anne. The reference is to the mole that raised the hill against which the horse of William III. stumbled while riding in the park of Hampton Court. By this accident the king broke his collar-bone; a severe illness ensued, and he died early in 1702.

Little Giant. A sobriquet popularly conferred on Stephen A. Douglas (fl. 1813–1861), the American statesman, because of his small stature and gigantic intellect.

Little-Go. The examination held in the Cambridge University in the second year of residence, because it precedes by a year the examination for a degree. In Oxford the corresponding examination is called "Smalls."

Littlejohn. (Pseud.) Frederick Guest Tomlins, English journalist (1804–1867).

Little Legislature. The delegates from Hamilton County to the Ohio Legislature were at one time so nicknamed because of their controlling influence in State politics.

Little Mac. A name by which Gen. George B. McClellan was endeared to his command.

Little Magician. The sobriquet given by his admirers to Martin Van Buren (fl. 1782–1862), President of the United States 1837–1841, on account of his statesmanlike abilities and political foresight.

Little Marlborough. Count von Schwerin, a Prussian field-marshal, and a companion of the Duke of Marlborough (1684–1757).

Little Masters. The most famous of these were Jost Amman, Hans Burgkmair, Hans Sebald Beham, Albert Altdorfer, Heinrich Aldegrever, Albrecht Dürer, and Lucas von Leyden. They were thus named because of the minuteness and fineness of their work, fit for copper or wood engravings.

Little Paris. Milan, in Italy, has been so named, in allusion to its similarity to the Gallic capital in point of gayety and dissipation.

Little Parliament. Another name for Barebone's Parliament (*q. v.*).

Little Phil. An endearing nickname for Gen. Philip Sheridan, the noted cavalry leader, during the American civil war.

Little Preacher. Samuel de Marets, the reformed Controversialist (fl. 1599–1663).

Little Queen. Isabella of Valois (fl. 1387–1410) was thus nicknamed. She married Richard II. of England when she was but eight years old, and at thirteen was a widow.

Little Rhody. The State of Rhode Island has been jocularly so named.

Little Tennessee. A very picturesque and fertile portion of Virginia, in the southwest part of the State.

Little Thomas. (Pseud.) Thomas Moore, Irish poet (1779-1852).

Little Venice. (1) A small island in the river Moldau, within the limits of the city of Prague. (2) Amiens, a town of France, which is so intersected by different branches of the Somme and the numerous bridges over them, as to have moved Louis XI. to bestow on it the above name.

Little Whig. A nickname conferred on Anne, Countess of Sunderland (d. 1716), second daughter of the great Marlborough. She was "rather *petite* in person," and rather gloried in the appellation.

Live Forever. "The name of a fanatical sect in Kentucky whose principal article of faith was that those who had 'faith' would never die. Whenever a member died, the answer to this very striking *argumentum ad hominem* was that he had not the 'faith.' The number, never very large, was reduced in 1850 to two, and one of these had left the sect, leaving but one 'Live forever.'" —BARTLETT.

Live-oak George. George Law, the famous American ship-builder (1806–1881). The origin of the nickname was as follows: "In 1852 he had a contest with the Cuban captain-general, which brought him prominently into public notice. The Spanish official was incensed because the purser of one of his vessels had published an offensive statement in a New York newspaper, and refused entrance to any vessel having him on board. The American Government refused to sustain Mr. Law in his determination to send the 'Crescent City' to Havana with the purser on board, and withdrew the mail when he persisted. He nevertheless despatched the steamship, and the captain-general failed to carry out his threat to fire on her. Mr. Law after this was called 'Live-oak George,' from a nickname bestowed on him by the workmen in his shipyard."

Living Cyclopædia. Longinus (fl. 213–273); so named for his almost endless erudition.

Livy of Portugal. João de Barros, the leading Portuguese historian (fl. 1496–1570).

Lizzie Aaron. The stage-name of Mrs. Edward Aaron.

Lizzie Burton. The stage-name of Mrs. Herndon Morsell.

Lizzie Campbell. The stage-name of Mrs. J. Z. Little.

Lizzie Harold. The stage-name of Mrs. Comley.

Lizzie May Ulmer. The stage-name of Mrs. George T. Ulmer.

Lizzie McCall. The stage-name of Mrs. Nestor Lennon, formerly Mrs. Wall.

Lizzie Paine. The stage-name of Mrs. George Millbank.

Lizzie Webster. The stage-name of Mrs. Jacob Nunnemacher.

l. l. *Loco laudato*, in the place quoted.

L. L. A. Lady Literate of Arts, a Scottish academic degree conferred on women.

L. Lat. Low Latin; Law Latin.

LL. B. *Legum Baccalaureus.* Bachelor of Laws.

LL. D. *Legum Doctor.* Doctor of Laws.

Llewellin Acton. (Pseud.) Wynne Edwin Baxter.

Llewellyn. (Pseud.) Robert Saunders, English statistician (1727–1783).

L. L. I. Lord Lieutenant of Ireland.

LL. M. Master of Laws.

Lloyd's Books. Two enormous ledger-looking volumes, raised on desks at right and left of the entrance to Lloyd's Rooms. These books give the principal arrivals, and all losses by wreck, fire, or other accident at sea. The entries are written in a fine, bold, Roman hand legible to all readers. "Lloyd's List" is a London periodical, in which the shipping news received at Lloyd's Rooms is regularly published.

L. L. Whiskey. "Lord-Lieutenant Whiskey." Mr. Kinahan, being requested to preserve a certain cask of whiskey highly approved of by his Excellency, marked it with the initials L. L., and ever after called this particular quality L. L. Whiskey.

L. M. S. London Missionary Society.

L. N. R. Initialism of Mrs. Ranyard, authoress of "The Book and its Story," "The Missing Link," etc. (d. 1879).

Loafer. "An old Dutchman settled at New York and acquired a large fortune. He had an only daughter, and a young American fell in love with her. The father forbade him the house, but the daughter encouraged him. Whenever the old merchant saw the lover about the premises, he used to say to his daughter, 'There is that "lofer" of yours, the idle, good for nothing,' etc.; and so an idle man, hanging about, came to be called a 'lofer.' How the letter *a* got into the word is not known." This originally appeared in "Notes and Queries," but has been adopted by Bartlett in his "Dictionary of Americanisms."

Lobby. A name given in the United States to those who attend the national and State capitals during legislative sessions and frequent the lobbies or halls of the capitols for the purpose of influencing legislation. The term "lobbyist" is generally one of reproach, from a popular belief that the methods in use are often venal and corrupt.

Lobster. The word "lobster" as applied to English soldiers is of very old date. In Clarendon's "History of the Rebellion," vol. iii. p. 91, ed. 1849, it is stated that in 1643 "Sir William Waller received from London a fresh regiment of 500 horse under the command of Sir Arthur Haslerig, which were so prodigiously armed that they were called by the King's party 'the regiment of lobsters,' because of their bright iron shells with which they were covered, being perfect cuirassiers, and were the first seen so armed, on either side."

Local Option. In the temperance agitation in the United States in recent years this term signifies the power accorded to towns, villages, or counties, of signifying at the polls whether or not the sale of intoxicating liquor shall be permitted within their bounds.

Locate. This verb, in the sense of selecting public lands for allotment to settlers in a new country, is generally thought to be a pure Americanism. The earliest known use of the word is, however, English. It occurs in a speech made by Burke in the House of Commons, in 1774, part of which runs thus: "A peer, who, I think, does not always vote in the majority, made a sort of proposition for an address to the king, that no more lands be *located* in America."

loc. cit. *Loco citato.* In the place cited.

Lochiel. A surname of Sir Evan Cameron (d. 1719), of Lochiel, chief of the Cameron clan. He was also nicknamed "the Black." His grandson, Donald Cameron (d. 1748), was oftentimes called "the Gentle Lochiel."

Loci communes. (Lat.) Common places.

Loco. (Lat.) This term denotes that a musical passage is to be played just as written in regard to pitch; it generally occurs after *8va alta* or *8va bassa*.

Loco citato. (Lat.) In the place quoted.

Locofoco. (1) Lucifer matches were called in America "locofocoes." The origin of the term is thus given by Mr. Bartlett, in his "Glossary": In 1834 John Marck opened a store in Park Row, New York, and drew public attention to two novelties. One was champagne wine drawn like soda-water from a "fountain;" the other was a self-lighting cigar, with a match composition on the end. These he called "Locofoco cigars." The mode of getting at the name is obvious. The word "locomotive" was then rather new as applied to an engine on a railroad, and the common notion was that it meant self-moving; hence, as these cigars were self-firing, this queer name was coined. His patent for "self-igniting cigars" bears date April 16, 1834. (2) The name as applied to a political party in America originated in 1835, at a stormy political meeting at Tammany Hall. During the confusion the gaslights were suddenly turned out. The "Equal Rights" party, having received information that such would be the course of their opponents, had provided themselves with *locofoco* matches and candles, and the hall was re-lighted in a moment. The "Courier and Enquirer" newspaper dubbed the anti-monopolists who used the matches with the name of "Locofoco," which long clung to the Democratic party. — HAMMOND, *Political History of New York.*

Locomotive Chase. One of the most exciting episodes in the civil war, an incident of the Andrews Railroad Raid into Georgia, 1862, participated in by Gen. O. M. Mitchel.

Locum tenens. (Lat.) One holding the place; a deputy or substitute.

Locus in quo. (Lat.) The place in which.

Locus poenitentiæ. (Lat.) "Place for repentance." An institution for reformation; an opportunity for amending.

Locus sigilli. (Lat.) The place of the seal, — contracted into L. S.

Locus standi. (Lat.) Right to interfere or take a part.

Logan Act. An act of Congress, promoted by the Federalists, making it a high misdemeanor for an individual person to take part in a controversy between the United States and a foreign power. It was aimed at George Logan, Senator (1753–1821), who in 1798 went to France on his own responsibility for the purpose of averting war between that country and the United States.

Log College. In 1728 William Tennent, educator (1673–1746), built at Neshaminy, Penn., a small building where he trained candidates for the ministry. It was a log-house, twenty feet long and eighteen broad.

Logging. A pure Americanism, denoting the hauling of felled trunks to tide-water or to a saw-mill. A colony of lumbermen are called "loggers." This word has given rise to a political Americanism, "log-rolling."

Logria. A name given to England by mediæval romancers.

Log-rolling. A term of frequent occurrence in United States political nomenclature, whereby is signified an arrangement, made between legislators having diverse interests at stake, to vote for the measures of each, thereby securing their passage. Though the term, as commonly used, is one of reproach, there is nothing intrinsically wrong about log-rolling provided the object is a worthy one.

Loki. In Scandinavian mythology the Satan of the Eddas ; the companion and associate of the gods, yet the frequent source of disaster to them. He contrived the death of Baldur. In appearance he was very beautiful.

Lombard Fever. Laziness. Pawnbrokers are called Lombard brokers, because they retain the three golden balls of the Lombard money-changers ; and lazy folk will pawn anything rather than settle down to steady work.

Lon. Longitude.

Lond. London.

London Bridge built on Woolpacks. In the reign of Henry II., Pious Peter, a chaplain of St. Mary Colechurch, in the Poultry, built a stone bridge in lieu of the wooden one which had been destroyed by fire. The king helped him by a *tax on wool*, and hence the saying referred to above.

London, Lungs of. *See* LUNGS OF LONDON.

London Stone. A stone believed to have been placed by the Romans (15 B. C.) in Cannon Street, to mark the then centre of the city. In 1798 it was finally set into the wall of St. Swithin's Church. " It was on this stone that Jack Cade struck his sword, exclaiming ' Now is Mortimer lord of the city ! ' " in 1450.

Lone Star State, The. Texas ; the name is derived from the device on its coat-of-arms.

Long-bow. The long-bow was a powerful bow used by soldiers before the introduction of gunpowder. " To draw the long-bow " was formerly a term applied when one boasted of his skill or strength as an archer, not always truthfully, but as a vainglorious soldier might after the wars. It is now applied, in general terms, to notorious liars, who are said to " draw the long bow."

Long Branch of Boston. Swampscott, a seaside resort one mile from Lynn, thirteen miles northeast of Boston. There are three good beaches, and no undertow. Nahant, a bold promontory to the south, has a beach as hard as a floor. The Chelsea, or Revere Beach, nearer Boston, is a favorite resort of the working-classes. To the north are Salem, Marblehead, Beverly, Lowell Island, and the famous Singing Beach of Manchester. Farther north are Gloucester, Rockport, Pigeon Cove, Cape Ann, Newburyport, and Salisbury Beach.

Long Branch of Honolulu. The town of Waikiki, near Honolulu, is so nicknamed. It is famed for its surf-bathing.

Long Branch of Philadelphia. Cape May, N. J. It is near the entrance of Delaware Bay, and its fine surf and splendid beach drive are noteworthy.

Longfellow of the South. A name given to Paul H. Hayne, the poet.

Long Friday. *See* GOOD FRIDAY.

Long John. A nickname conferred on John Wentworth, the Illinois politician (d. 1888). He once related that he got the appellation in the following manner. " When," he said, " I was going to school down in Connecticut, I was the longest, skinniest boy you ever saw. I was fourteen years old. I used to have a habit in those days of getting my heels up on the seat, so that my knees towered above my head. I was sitting that way one day in school, when one of the examiners came around. He said to the teacher, ' What 's that boy doing standing up on the bench ? Why don't you make him sit down ? ' The teacher said I was sitting down. ' That 's the way he sits,' said the teacher. ' Who is he ? ' asked the examiner. ' John Wentworth,' said the teacher. ' He 's a pretty long John,' said the examiner ; and ever since then it 's stuck to me."

Long Man of Wilmington. An ancient landmark in Essex, England. It is one of the most primitive of English monuments, having been built by a people wholly impossible to determine. It consists of a trench cut in the turf in the form of a man 240 feet long and with a staff in either hand. It has been so overgrown with trees as to be hardly discernible. There are two other figures like this near Plymouth known as Gog and Magog, another on the Cambridgeshire hills, and another in Dorsetshire, all nearly of the same gigantic size. The White Horse of Berkshire, which is annually "scoured," as described by Thomas Hughes, is of the same sort.

Long Meg and her Daughters. At Little Salkeld (Cumberland) is a circle of sixty-seven stones, some of them ten feet high, ranged in a circle. Some seventeen paces off, on the south side, is a single stone, fifteen feet high, called Long Meg, the shorter ones being called her daughters.

Longo intervallo. (Lat.) By a long interval; at a great distance.

Long Parliament. Sat from Nov. 3, 1640, until April 20, 1658, when it was dissolved by Cromwell. Also named the Pensioner Parliament (*q. v.*).

Long Peter. Peter Aartsen, the Flemish painter (fl. 1507–1573), was so named on account of his extraordinary height.

Long Scribe. A nickname given to Vincent Dowling (d. 1852), an eminent sportsman and sporting authority of England, who was famed for his tall stature.

Long Sword. William I., Duke of Normandy (d. 943).

Long Time between Drinks. A famous phrase commemorating a traditional interchange of courtesies between the Governors of North and South Carolina, in the course of which one remarked to the other that it was "a long time between drinks." Various settings have been given to the tale, but George Cary Eggleston says : —

"Historically, I believe the origin of the story is lost in remote antiquity. Speculatively, I should say that the story is a native myth, a statement as of a particular fact, which conveys instead a universal truth. There is nowhere any record of any meeting between the Governors of any two Southern States in which one or the other did not in fact make a suggestion to the effect that the time for giving a helping hand to conversation by resort to alcoholic stimulation was rapidly approaching. The reduction of a general or universal truth of that character to particular statement, as of a single and actual incident, is a well-known process, familiar to all students of mythology."

Long Vacation. The Long Vacation is a relic of Norman usages in the English courts. The time of the long

vacation in Normandy was adapted to the season of the vintage ; and the same period was fixed in England by the Normans, and has remained unaltered to the present day.

Lonsdale's Ninepins. The late Earl of Lonsdale was so extensive a proprietor and patron of boroughs that he returned nine members to every English Parliament, who were facetiously called "Lord Lonsdale's Ninepins."

Loose-Coat Field. The battle of Stamford (1470) was so called because the men, led by Lord Wells, being attacked by the Yorkists, threw off their coats, that they might flee the faster.

Cast off their country's coats, to haste their speed
    away ;
Which "Loose-Coat Field" is called e'en to this
    day.
                                DRAYTON, *Polyolbion.*

Lord Fanny. A nickname given to Lord Hervey on account of his womanish manners and effeminate features. He painted his face, and wore corsets. He flourished in the reign of George II.

Lord Gawkey. A sobriquet conferred on Richard Grenville, Lord Temple (fl. 1711–1770), by the wits of his day.

Lord Mayor's Day. November 9, upon which occasion the newly elected Lord-Mayor of London is carried through the city streets in a gorgeous coach, attended by a brilliant pageant, on his way to be sworn at Westminster.

Lord of Crazy Castle. A nickname for John Hall Stevenson (fl. 1718–1785), who wrote some clever but rather lewd poems called "Crazy Tales." He lived at Skelton Castle, near Guisborough, dubbed by his intimates "Crazy Castle."

Lord of Misrule. *See* ABBOT OF UNREASON.

Lord of the Isles. A title assumed by Donald, a chief of Islay, who in 1346 reduced the whole of the Hebrides to subjection.

Lord Peter. The Pope is so named in Arbuthnot's "History of John Bull."

Loretto of Austria. Mariazel ("Mary in the cell"), in Styria; so called from the miracle-working image of the Virgin. The image is old and very ugly. Two pilgrimages are made to it yearly.

Loretto of Central Spain. A famous monastery, around which clusters the town of Guadalupe, Spain. Loretto, in Italy, is the site of the famous sanctuary of the Virgin called the "Sancta Casa" (Holy House), which is reputed to be the house, or a part of the house, in which the Virgin lived at Nazareth.

Loretto of Switzerland. Einsiedlen, a village containing a shrine of the "Black Lady of Switzerland." The church is of black marble, and the image of ebony.

Losing a Ship for a Hap'orth of Tar. This phrase does not apply to a ship at all. It refers to *sheep*, which word is generally pronounced 'ship' by rustics. The reference is to marking a sheep with its owner's initials in hot tar. To lose a sheep through its not being marked is losing it for the want of a hap'orth of tar.

Lost Atlantis. *See* ATLANTIS.

Lost Island. An appellation given to Cephalonia, because, on account of its diminutive size, ancient navigators were often unable to find it. The same as "Hidden Island."

Lot = PLOT or FIELD. "Lot" is a word which, in its application to land, is unknown to England and universal in the United States. It has its rise in an old Puritan custom. The first settlers in the seaboard plantations of New England owned the extensive salt-marshes, which produce such excellent salt-hay, in common, and every man cut and cocked, saved and salted, as much of the latter as he wanted. When, however, the population increased, and the first simplicity and harmony were no longer maintained, it was agreed to divide out these commons in equal parts to all the families. This was done, after the Biblical precedent in the election of a twelfth apostle, by *lot*; and the choice of every man, as his name was drawn and he became entitled to select his piece of land, was known as *his lot*. The firm belief of the Puritans in a special providence watching over them and their interests made them continually resort to this manner of distributing lands or other articles of value, held heretofore in common; and thus the term "lots" soon came to designate any great quantity.

Lotta. The stage-name of Charlotte Crabtree.

Lottie Beaumont. The stage-name of Mrs. Charles Chapelle.

Lottie Blair. The stage-name of Mrs. Harry D. Parker.

Lottie Delmaine. The stage-name of Mrs. George W. Allen.

Lottie Fay. The stage-name of Mrs. W. L. Woodson.

Lottie Mortimer. The stage-name of Mrs. Charles Paff.

Lottie Sinclair. The stage-name of Mrs. Frank Kennedy.

Louisa. Gen. Lew Wallace had his name shortened thus by the men of his command in the war for the Union.

Louis Aldrich. The stage-name of Louis Moses, a well-known American actor and dramatist.

Louis de Montait. (Pseud.) Blaise Pascal, French philosopher (1623–1662).

Louise Balfe. The stage-name of Mrs. William Harcourt, *née* Homcastle.

Louise Bliss. The stage-name of Mrs. Bonny Hedges.

Louise Davenport. The stage-name of Mrs. W. H. Sheridan.

Louise Ellen. (Pseud.) Louise Chandler Moulton, an American author (b. 1835). She began to contribute to periodicals under the above name at the early age of fifteen.

Louise Gerald. (Pseud.) Mlle. Mathilde de Lacoste, a French novelist.

Louise Lester. The stage-name of Mrs. Nathal, *née* Barnes.

Louise Parker. The professional name of Mrs. Eugene Oudin.

Louise Pomeroy. The stage-name of Mrs. Elliot, formerly Mrs. "Brick" Pomeroy.

Louise Raymond. The stage-name of Mrs. Daniels.

Louise Searle. The stage-name of Mrs. Henry Hunter.

Louise Sylvester. The stage-name of Mrs. F. A. Mackey.

Louise Thorndyke. The stage-name of Mrs. Dion Boucicault.

Louis Harrison. The stage-name of Louis Metz.

Louisiana. This State received its name in honor of Louis XIV. of France.

Louis Monrose. The professional pseudonym of Louis Martial Barizan (1800–1883), a famous French actor.

Lounger, The. (Pseud.) Joseph B. Gilder, in his contributions to the "Critic," New York.

Lounger at the Clubs. (Pseud.) Edmund Yates, in the London "Illustrated Times."

Lounger in the Lobby. (Pseud.) Royal W. Merrill, in the Philadelphia "Press."

Lovely Isle. Corfu, one of the Ionian Islands of Greece, in the Mediterranean.

O lovely isle, that, like a child,
Art sleeping on the sea!
LETITIA ELIZABETH LANDON, *Corfu.*

Lover of the Fine Arts. Maria Gowen Brooks; under which pen-name she published her "Judith," "Esther," and other poems.

Lover's Leap. *See* SAPPHO'S LEAP.

Lovers' War. The civil war that raged in France in 1580, during the reign of Henry V., was so named.

Love's White Star. The planet Venus, which is silvery white.

Till every daisy slept, and Love's white star
Beamed thro' the thickened cedar in the dusk.
TENNYSON, *The Gardener's Daughter.*

Low Sunday. The Sunday after Easter, and the octave of that festival. The name is said to be derived from the inferiority of its solemnities to those of Easter Sunday.

Loyalty Loans. Names given to loans raised during the Revolutionary War in England. Later, in 1798, the name was revived and applied to one opened in London on December 5. In fifteen hours and twenty minutes the sum of £18,000,000 was subscribed.

L. P. Lord Provost; Long Provost; large paper.

L. P. S. Lord Privy Seal.

L. Pylodet. (Anagrammatic Pseud.) Frederick Leypoldt, bibliographer(1837–1884).

L. R. C. P. Licentiate of the Royal College of Physicians.

L. R. C. S. Licentiate of the Royal College of Surgeons.

L. S. *Locus sigilli.* Place of the seal.

L. S. D. Pounds, shillings, and pence.

Lt. Lieutenant.

Lubberland. A slang term anciently applied to London, — substituted for "Cocaigne" (*q. v.*) by the poets and wits of the sixteenth century.

Lubbock's Day, St. *See* SAINT LUBBOCK.

Lucas Malet. (Pseud.) Miss Kingsley, a daughter of Charles Kingsley, an English authoress, and author of the novels "Colonel Enderby's Wife,"

"Mrs. Lorrimer," and "A Counsel of Perfection."

Lucasta. Under this poetic title Richard Lovelace (fl. 1618–1658) chanted the fame of his *inamorata*, whom he elsewhere calls "Lux Casta." She was probably Lucy Sacheverell, a girl of much beauty and wealth.

Lucidus ordo. (Lat.) "Lucid order." Clear arrangement.

Lucille Meredith. The stage-name of Lizzie Couch.

Lucina. In classic myth the Roman goddess who presided at childbirth. She was a daughter of Jupiter and Juno.

Lucullus. A nickname given to Samuel Bernard, the capitalist (fl. 1651–1739).

Lucus a non lucendo. (Lat.) "A grove from not shining." A grove is so called from its not shining. According to Servius, an ancient grammarian, *lucus*, "a grove," is derived from *lucere*, "to shine," from the fact that a grove is gloomy and does not shine. The derivation was ridiculed; one critic suggested that *ludus*, "a school," came from *non ludere*, "not to play." Hence the phrase *lucus a non lucendo* is applied to any absurd *non sequitur* or far-fetched etymology.

Lucy Ellice. (Pseud.) Mrs. Ellen Moriarty, in the "Citizen," published by "Miles O'Reilly."

Lucy Fountain. (Pseud.) Kate Hilliard, poetess and author.

Luddites. Riotous workmen who went about the manufacturing districts of England, 1811–1816, breaking machines, under the notion that machinery threw men out of employ. The term arose from Ned Lud, of Leicestershire, an imbecile who was much hounded by boys. One day he chased a set of tormentors into a house, and broke two stocking-frames; whence the leader of these rioters was called "General Lud," his chief abettors "Lud's Wives," and his followers "Luddites."

Ludere cum sacris. (Lat.) To trifle with sacred things.

Lud's Bulwark. An old name for Ludgate Prison in London.

Lud's Town. A name sometimes anciently given to London; so called after Lud, a mythical king of Britain.

And on the gates of Lud's town set your heads.
SHAKSPEARE, *Cymbeline.*

Luise Muhlbach. (Pseud.) Madame Clara Mundt, German novelist (1814–1873).

Luke Limmer, Esq. (Pseud.) Frederick Leighton, F. R. S. A., English painter (b. 1830).

Luke Sharp. (Pseud.) Robert Bare, sometime London correspondent of the Detroit " Free Press."

Luke's Summer. A few weeks of fine summerly weather which occur between St. Luke's Day (October 18) and St. Martin's Day (November 11).

In such St. Luke's short summer lived these men,
Nearing the goal of threescore years and ten.
W. MORRIS, *The Earthly Paradise.*

Lulu Blankenhorn. The stage-name of Mrs. Louis J. Cornu.

Lulu Hurst. The stage-name of Mrs. Paul Atkinson.

Lulu Prior. The stage-name of Mrs. Edward De Nyse.

Lumber = TIMBER. In the United States " lumber" means manufactured timber; hence we have the terms " lumber-yard " for the English " timber-yard," and " lumber-camp " for a colony of tree-fellers, who are said to be engaged in "lumbering," and are called " lumber-men." *See* LOGGING.

Lumber State. Maine. The felling of trees, and the preparation of their timber for market, affords employment to a large number of its people.

Lunatico de Cranki. (Pseud.) Edward Harris.

Lungs of London. Its public parks. The expression occurred in the course of a parliamentary debate, June 30, 1808, on a proposition to curtail Hyde Park.

Luola. (Pseud.) Mrs. Mary Ager Niller, author of many poems and of books for the young, the latter published by the Presbyterian Board.

Lupercus. In classic myth an old Roman deity, worshipped by shepherds as the guardian of their flocks against wolves.

Lusitania. The mediæval name for Portugal, so called after Lusus, the mythical companion of Bacchus, who settled in the land.

Lusus naturæ. (Lat.) A sport or freak of Nature.

Lutetia. A name by which the city of Paris was often anciently referred to. The word means " mud hovels." The Romans named the collection of huts

they found here *Lutetia Parisiorum*, " the mud-town of the Parisii." The first name being dropped left the present title, Paris.

Luther Towns. The cities of Eisleben, Erfurt, Magdeburg, Eisenach, Coburg, and Wittenberg have been grouped under the above name. They were all more or less intimately connected with the Great Reformer's life and deeds. *See* CRADLE OF THE REFORMATION.

Lutie Page. The stage-name of Mrs. Fred Mower.

Lux Dux. (Pseud.) Mrs. Anna H. C. Howard in the " Household," Brattleboro, Vt.

Lux lucet in tenebris. (Lat.) Light shines in darkness.

LX. Sixty, or sixtieth.

LXX. Seventy, or seventieth; the Septuagint (Version of the Old Testament).

LXXX. Eighty, or eightieth.

Lycaon. In classic myth a king of Arcadia, whom Juno turned into a wolf because he sacrificed human victims on his altars.

Lyden Eclair. (Pseud.) Henry Lyden Flash, an American poet (b. 1835). *See* HARRY FLASH.

Lydford Law. This was, " Punish first and try afterwards." Lydford, in the County of Devon, was a fortified town, in which was an ancient castle, where were held the courts of the duchy of Cornwall. Offenders against the stannary laws were confined before trial in a dungeon so loathsome and dreary that it gave rise to the proverb referred to. The castle was destroyed by the Danes. *See* COWPER'S LAW.

Lydia Thompson. The stage-name of Mrs. Alexander Henderson.

Lydian Poet. Alcman of Lydia (fl. 670 B. C.).

Lying Dick Talbot. A nickname given to the notorious Irish Jacobin Tyrconnel, who was a venal placeman during the latter years of the reign of James II. and the early years of William of Orange.

Lying Gazette. The opprobrious epithet popularly applied to Rivington's " New York Gazette and Commercial Advertiser," during the Revolution, on account of its utter disregard of truth.

Lying Traveller. An unjust epithet applied to Sir John Mandeville (fl. 1300–1372).

Lynceus. In classic myth one of the Argonauts, famed for the acuteness of his vision.

Lynch Law. Summary punishment without form of law; mob law; or, as in the case of the Vigilance Committee of the Far West, the mode of ridding an outraged community of its incorrigible offenders. There are various accounts of the origin of the term. One, which is perhaps as probable as any, is to the effect that the name of "Lynch Law" was derived from a native of Campbell Co., Va., old Colonel Lynch, who was in the habit of administering summary punishment to marauders and miscreants of every description without paying any attention to the ordinary processes of law. Hence he was called "Judge Lynch;" and this, it is said, is the true origin of the terms "lynching" and "lynch law." *See* VIGILANCE COMMITTEE and JUDGE LYNCH.

Lynde Palmer. (Pseud.) Mrs. Mary Peebles, American juvenile writer (b. 1839).

Lyric Muse. Corinna, a poetess of Tanagra, in Bœotia, was so named. She was contemporary with Pindar, whom she conquered in five separate musical contests.

M.

M. Married; mile; noon (*meridies*); a thousand (*mille*).

M., or **Mons.** Monsieur.

M. A. Master of Arts; military academy.

Ma. (Ital.) But; as, *Allegro ma non troppo*, quick, but not too much so. (Mus.)

Mabel Bert. The stage-name of Mabel Johnston.

Mabel Fenton. The stage-name of Mrs. Charles J. Ross, *née* Thorn.

Mabel Moulton. The stage-name of Mrs. A. C. Noyes.

Mabel St. Clair. (Pseud.) Miss Carrie S. Hibbard, in several Ohio journals.

Mabel Worthington. The stage-name of Mrs. O. W. Blake.

Macarone. (Pseud.) George Arnold, *littérateur*.

Macaroni. (1) A dandy. The word is derived from the Macaroni Club, instituted by a set of flashy men who had travelled in Italy, and introduced Italian macaroni at Almack's subscription table. The Macaronis were the most effeminate fops that ever disgraced the name of man. (2) A term current in England during the latter part of the eighteenth century, and applied to everything ridiculous in dress and manners. It was preceded by the formation of Macaroni Clubs (1772). The name "Macaroni" was first applied to trifling literary performances or punning poems, after an Italian cake of the same name, very pleasing to the taste but possessing little real nourishment.

Macaronic Verse. Verses in which foreign words are ludicrously distorted and jumbled together, as in Porson's lines on the threatened invasion of England by Napoleon. So called by Teofilo Folengo, a Mantuan monk of noble family, who published a book in 1520 entitled "Liber Macaronicorum," a poetical rhapsody made up of words of different languages, and treating of "pleasant matters" in a comical style.

Macaulay's New Zealander. Perhaps no passage of Macaulay's writings has been so frequently quoted or alluded to as that in which he pictures some future traveller from New Zealand sitting on a broken arch of London Bridge sketching the ruins of St. Paul's. Consciously or unconsciously, the sentence is a reproduction of similar passages by two previous writers, Walpole and Mrs. Barbauld. In a letter written by Horace Walpole to Sir Horace Mann, Nov. 24, 1774, is the following passage: —

"The next Augustan Age will dawn on the other side of the Atlantic. There will perhaps be a Thucydides at Boston, a Xenophon at New York, and, in time, a Virgil in Mexico, and a Newton in Peru. At last some curious traveller from Lima will visit England, and give a description of the ruins of St. Paul's."

Mrs. Barbauld wrote a poem in heroic rhyme, which she entitled "1811." In it she prophesies that at some future day a traveller from the antipodes will, from a broken arch on Blackfriars Bridge, contemplate the ruins of St. Paul's.

Macc. Maccabees.

MacDonald's Breed. Vermin or human parasites. Lord MacDonald, son of the "Lord of the Isles" once made a raid on the mainland. He and his followers dressed themselves in the clothes of the plundered party, but their own rags were so full of vermin that no one was poor enough to covet them.

Macduff, Law of. *See* LAW OF CLAN MACDUFF.

Maced. Macedonian.

Macedonian, The. Julius Polyamus (fl. second century), author of "Stratagemata."

Macedonian Cry. Any appeal for help. An allusion to the request of the man of Macedonia who appeared to Paul in a vision, saying, "Come over into Macedonia and help us" (Acts xvi. 9).

Macedonians. A religious sect. So named from Macedonius, patriarch of Constantinople, in the fourth century. They denied the divinity of the Holy Ghost, and that the essence of the Son is the same in kind with that of the Father.

Macedonia's Madman. Alexander the Great.

Macedoaicus. A surname conferred on Æmilius Paulus, the conqueror of Perseus (fl. 230–160 B. C.).

MacFarlane's Geese. The proverb is that "MacFarlane's geese like their play better than their meat." The wild geese of Loch Lomond used to be called "MacFarlane's geese" because the Mac-Farlanes had a house and garden on the island. It is said that these geese never returned after the extinction of that house. One day James VI. visited the chieftain, and was highly amused by the gambols of the geese, but the one served at table was so tough that the king exclaimed, "MacFarlane's geese like their play better than their meat."

MacFlecknoe. Under this name, in his famous satire, Dryden pokes fun at Thomas Shadwell, poet laureate (fl. 1640–1692).

Ma chère. (Fr. fem.) My dear.

Machine. A coterie of politicians, or an entire party, receives this name when the wishes of individual members succumb to the crack of the party whip, and the voters move unitedly in obedience to the behests of the leader or leaders. "Machine politics" has come to be a term of reproach, but it is doubtful if any system of popular government can be carried on without party organization and discipline of some sort.

Mack. (Pseud.) Joseph B. McCullough, editor at different times of the "Globe-Democrat," St. Louis, and of the Cincinnati "Commercial."

Mackerel Gale. A breeze just sufficient to ripple the surface of the water. Mackerel are caught with the bait in motion.

Mackerel Sky. A sky in which the clouds have the form denoted *cirrocumulus;* that is, broken into small, fleecy masses, popularly supposed to foretell rain or wind.

Macklin. A stage-name. The real name of this great actor was Charles M'Laughlin, but he changed it on going to England.

Macmillanites. A religious sect of Scotland, who succeeded the Covenanters; so named from John Macmillan, their leader.

Macon. A poetical or romantic mediæval name for Mecca, the birthplace of Mahomet.

Macswell. (Pseud.) W. L. Russ, in the Buffalo "Courier."

Macte virtute. (Lat.) Be strong in virtue; go on in virtue.

Mad = WILD, ANGRY. "Mad," in the sense of angry, and as a substitute for the English "wild," has been recognized as excellent old English. Captain John Smith says, "This made him halfe madde." Even the familiar phrase, "like mad," has old and high authority.

Mad. Madam.

Madame Bishop. The convivial name for a mixture of port-wine, sugar, and nutmeg.

Madame Deficit. Marie Antoinette was so named by the Parisian mob in 1787.

The cries heretofore raised against the queen under the name of "Austrian" were now uttered against "Madame Deficit," pending the time when the fearful title of "Madame Veto" would give place in its turn to the sad name of "the woman Capet" given to the victim of Oct. 16, 1793. — GUIZOT.

Madame Etiquette. The Duchesse de Noailles, grand-mistress of the ceremonies in the Court of Marie Antoinette; so called from her rigid enforcement of all the formalities and ceremonies of the *ancien régime.*

Madame Kinkel. (Pseud.) Elizabeth Sarah Sheppard, English novelist (1830–1862).

Madame Veto. *See* MADAME DEFICIT.

Mad Anthony. A nickname of Maj.-Gen. Anthony Wayne (fl. 1745–1796), a soldier of the American Revolution famed for his impetuous bravery.

Mad as a Hatter. In the Anglo-Saxon the word "mad" was used as a synonym for violent, furious, angry, or venomous. In some parts of England, and in the United States particularly, it is still used in this sense. *Atter* was the Anglo-Saxon name for an adder or viper. The proverbial saying has therefore probably no reference to hat-makers, but merely means "as venomous as an adder." The Germans call the viper *Natter*.

Mad as a March Hare. "'March' hare is 'marsh' hare. Hares are wilder in marshes than elsewhere, because of their greater flatness and the absence of hedges and cover."

Mad Bell. This was Isabel Lauchlan, the sister of "one of the ablest and most accomplished ministers of the North [of Scotland]." It appears that she was demented, and was not always the subject of humane treatment. Hugh Miller, while a mason, had spent the earlier part of the night in merriment in "the Bothy," or barrack, and subsequently repaired to a hayloft, the only place of shelter he could find, and flinging himself down in his clothes on a heap of straw was soon fast asleep; but unaccustomed to so rough a couch, he awoke about midnight, and took his station at a small window that looked out upon a dreary moor, a ruinous chapel, and solitary burying-ground. The evening was calm and still, but dark for the season, when, to the great astonishment of the solitary tenant of the loft, a light flickered among the grave-stones and ruins, — now seen, now hid, like the revolving lantern of a light-house; and what seemed a continuous screaming was distinctly heard. The light, quitting the churchyard, came downward across the moor in a straight line, though tossed with many a wave and flourish. In a moment one of the servant-girls of the mansion-house came rushing out half-dressed, and awakening the workmen summoned them immediately to rise, — "Mad Bell has broken

out again." The men instantly arose, and as they appeared at the door were joined by the solitary watcher from above; but on striking out a few paces into the moor the maniac was found in the custody of a couple of men dragging her to her own cottage, about half a mile away. On entering her hut they proceeded to bind her down to the damp floor. Hugh Miller and a comrade simultaneously and successfully interfered. The maniac was not bound. Her song ceased for a moment, and turning round, presenting full to the light the strongly marked features of a woman about fifty-five, surveying the youths who had spoken good for her with a keen, scrutinizing glance, she emphatically repeated the sacred text, "Blessed are the merciful, for they shall obtain mercy." The foregoing story, with a sequel, may be found in a book entitled "The Life and Times of Hugh Miller," by Thomas N. Brown, published in 1858.

Mad Cavalier. Prince Rupert (fl. 1619–1682), noted among the cavaliers for his dashing bravery and independence of control.

Mademoiselle. A young unmarried lady.

Madge Elliot. (Pseud.) Mrs. Sol. Eytinge, in "Harper's Magazine" and "Harper's Young People."

Madiana. (Pseud.) J. B. Ricord.

Mad Jack. John Percival, American naval commander (1779–1862), was so named on account of his rough and eccentric manners.

Madman of Macedonia. A name often given to Alexander the Great (fl. 356–323 B. C.), on account of his insatiable lust for conquest.

Madman of the North. Charles XII. of Sweden.

Mad Parliament. The body which sat in 1258, during the reign of Henry III., and noted for its antagonism to the king. It compelled him to confirm Magna Charta, and furthermore delegated twenty-four of its own members, with Simon de Montfort at their head, to administer the government.

Mad Poet. (1) Nathaniel Lee (fl. 1657–1690); he was immured in Bedlam for four years. (2) McDonald Clark (fl. 1798–1842), author of a number of scattered poems; he died in Bloomingdale Asylum, N. Y.

Mad. Univ. Madison University.

Mæcenas of England. Samuel Rogers (fl. 1763-1855), the "banker-poet."

Mæonides. Homer; either because he was the son of Mæon, or because he was born in Mæonia, Asia Minor.

Maestoso. (Ital.) With majestic and dignified expression. (Mus.)

Mae Wentworth. The stage-name of Mrs. Clarence Ostrander.

Ma foi. (Fr.) "My faith." Upon my word.

Mag. Magazine.

Maga means the Edinburgh "Review."

Magazin de nouveautés. (Fr.) "A magazine of novelties." A repository for the sale of fancy goods.

Maggie Dean. The stage-name of Mrs. Lionel E. Bland.

Maggie Harold. The stage-name of Mrs. William Davidge, Jr.

Maggie Holloway. The stage-name of Mrs. Frederick Fisher.

Maggie Mitchell. The stage-name of Mrs. Paddock.

Maggie Moore. The stage-name of Mrs. J. C. Williamson.

Maggie Morgan. The stage-name of Mrs. Cone.

Maggots of the Brain. Swift says it was the opinion of certain *virtuosi* that the brain is filled with little maggots, and that thought is produced by their biting the nerves.

To tickle the maggot born in an empty head.
TENNYSON, *Maud.*

Magic Carpet of Tangu. In the "Arabian Nights" a carpet to all appearances worthless, but if any one sat thereon it would transport him instantaneously to the place he wished to go. So called because it came from Tangu, in Persia.

Magic City. (1) Birmingham, Ala.; so named on account of its rapid rise into size and prominence. (2) Paisley, N. J., for similar reasons.

Magician of the North. (Pseud.) Johann Georg Hamann, German thinker and writer (1730-1788).

Magic Mirror of Japan. The mirror is one of the most conspicuous and universally diffused artificial objects in Japan. It is seen in the temples, in the hands of the street-conjurers, in all private houses, — even in those destitute, or nearly destitute of all other furniture, — in pictures, in the royal regalia. It is

the most precious possession of the woman, constituting the most important part of her trousseau. "The two Great Divine Palaces" at Isé, which harbor the first-made mirror, command the same reverence from the Japanese that the Holy Sepulchre commands from the Greeks and Armenians. The sun-goddess in a rage — so runs the Japanese myth — shut herself up in a cave, out of which she was enticed only by a mirror, then, in such sore extremity, first devised and made. It is usually circular, from three to twelve inches in diameter, of bronze, with bronze handle encased in bamboo; the reflecting surface, polished by a mercurial amalgam, is more or less convex; the back displays a finely executed raised design of birds, flowers, dragons, some scene of Japanese mythology, and occasionally also a few Chinese characters signifying long life, happiness, etc. The magic 'property, possessed, however, by but a few, — by two or three per cent., selling ten or twenty times dearer than the rest, — consists in the fact that, when looked at directly, the mirror reflects the objects in front of it like ordinary mirrors; but when a bright light is reflected from its polished face on to a screen, a bright-lined image on a dark ground, representing more or less perfectly the figures on the back of the mirror, is seen depicted on the screen. The explanation of this property has been the object of long and manifold discussion, from the thirteenth century down to the present day. Sir David Brewster and Sir Charles Wheatstone were of opinion that the phenomenon was due to a copy of the figures on the back being drawn on the polished face, but so skilfully concealed as to be invisible in ordinary lights. More recent theories ascribe the cause to the difference of density in the bronze plate; but Professors Ayrton and Perry have, ultimately, demonstrated that the phenomenon arises from inequality of curvature in the polished surface, the thicker portions (having the figures to the back) being *flatter* than the remainder of the convex surface.

Magna Charta. The great charter (of England).

Magna Charta of Hungary. Another name for the famous "Golden Bull" (*q. v.*).

Magna civitas, magna solitudo. (Lat.) A great city is a great desert.

Magna est veritas, et prævalebit. (Lat.) Great is truth, and it will prevail.

Magnanimous, The. (1) Alfonso V. of Aragon (1385–1458). (2) Chosroes or Khosru, twenty-first of the Sassanide dynasty (531–579).

Magnetic Statesman. James G. Blaine; an allusion to his personal charm of manner.

Magni Dei datum. (Lat.) The gift of the great God.

Magnificent, The. (1) Chosroes I. of Persia (d. 579). (2) Lorenzo de' Medici (fl. 1448–1492). (3) Robert of Normandy (d. 1035). (4) Soliman I., greatest of the sultans of Turkey (fl. 1493–1566).

Magni nominis umbra. (Lat.) The shadow of a great name.

Magnos inter opes inops. (Lat.) Poor in the midst of great wealth.

Magnum bonum. (Lat.) A great good; a plum, so called.

Magnum opus. (Lat.) "A great work."

Magnus Apollo. (Lat.) Great Apollo.

Magoogin. (Pseud.) John J. Jennings, in the St. Louis "Post-Despatch."

Magus of the North. (Pseud.) Johann Georg Hamann, German thinker and writer (1730–1788).

Mahadevi. In Hindu mythology "the great god," another name for the god Siva (*q. v.*). Similarly his consort, Durga, is styled *Mahadeva*, "the great goddess."

Mahomet's Stepping-stone. The stone upon which the prophet placed his foot when he mounted the beast Al Borak, on his ascent to heaven. It rose as the beast rose; but Mahomet, putting his hand upon it, forbade it to follow him, whereupon it remained suspended in mid-air, where the true believer, if he has faith enough, may still behold it.

Mai Conway. The stage-name of Mrs. Thomas Ryan.

Maiden, The. A nickname of Malcolm IV. of Scotland (fl. 1141–1165).

Maiden Assize. One in which there is no person to be brought to trial. In a maiden assize the sheriff of the county presents the judge with a pair of white gloves.

Maiden Queen. The same as Virgin Queen (*q. v.*).

Maiden Town. Edinburgh. An old legend has it that it was to this place the fair daughters of the Pictish monarchs were consigned for safety in time of war.

Maid of Bath. A sobriquet conferred on Miss Linley, a lovely and accomplished woman, who became the wife of Richard Brinsley Sheridan.

Maid of Norway. Margaret, daughter of Eric II. and of Margaret of Norway. She was proclaimed queen of Scotland on the death of Alexander III., and became betrothed to Edward I. of England, but died on her way thither.

Maid of Orleans. Jeanne d'Arc, or Joan of Arc (fl. 1412–1431).

Maid of Saragoza. Augustina, a maiden of Saragoza, who, when her lover fell during the siege by the French in 1808, sprang into his place and fought heroically.

Maillotins (lit., "small mallets"). A nickname applied to certain citizens of Paris who, in March, 1382, violently opposed the collection of some taxes imposed by the Regent, the Duc d'Anjou. They armed themselves with small iron maces, or mallets, which they purloined from the arsenals, and killed the collectors. Many were severely punished in 1383.

Main. (Fr.) The hand; as *Main droit*, or *M.D.*, the right hand; *Main gauche*, or *M.G.*, the left hand, in piano music.

Maine. This State takes its name from the French province of the same name, and was so called in compliment to Henrietta, queen of Charles I., of England.

Maine Law. As Maine was the first State of the Union to enact a stringent prohibitory law against the traffic in strong drink, the term has become since 1851 the synonym for all legislation of the kind. Several States, notably Iowa and Kansas, have since followed in Maine's footsteps. *See* LOCAL OPTION, NO LICENSE, HIGH LICENSE.

Main Plot. A conspiracy to make Arabella Stuart sovereign of England in place of James I., in 1603. Lord Cobham, Sir Walter Raleigh, and Lord Gray were sentenced to death for complicity in it, but were afterward reprieved. Others were punished; and on Oct. 29, 1618, Raleigh was executed.

Main, The Spanish. *See* SPANISH MAIN.

Maintien. (Fr.) Deportment; carriage.

Mai Richfield. The stage-name of Mrs. Thomas Ryan.

Maison d'arrêt. (Fr.) "House of custody." A prison.

Maison de détention. (Fr.) "House of detention." A prison.

Maison de santé. (Fr.) Private hospital.

Maison de ville. (Fr.) The city hall.

Maitland. (Pseud.) J. Bartlett.

Maître d'hôtel. (Fr.) House-steward.

Maj. Major.

Maj.-Gen. Major-General.

Majora canere. (Lat.) "To sing higher strains." To enter on matters of greater importance.

Major-domo. One who has the management of a household.

Major Jack Downing. (Pseud.) Seba Smith, American *littérateur* (1792–1868).

Major March. (Pseud.) O. B. Willcox, American soldier (b. 1823).

Major Muldoon. (Pseud.) William H. Macartney, American *littérateur*.

Major Penniman. Pen-name of C. W. Dennison, an American writer of the present day.

Major Spencer. A sobriquet bestowed on Miss William Loring Nuñez, who married General Spencer in 1877, presumably on account of her masculine Christian name. She is an author of note.

Mal. Malachi.

Malachi. (Pseud.) Sir Walter Scott, Scottish novelist (1771–1832).

Malachi Malagrowther. (Pseud.) Sir Walter Scott, Scottish novelist (1771–1832).

Malades imaginaires. (Fr.) Hypochondriacs; persons who fancy themselves ill.

Maladie du pays. (Fr.) Homesickness.

Maladresse. (Fr.) Want of management or tact.

Malady of Princes. War was so designated by Erasmus.

Mala fide. (Lat.) "With bad faith." Treacherously; falsely.

Mala fides. (Lat.) "Bad faith." Want of integrity.

Malagrida. An epithet applied by his political enemies to Lord Shelburne (fl. 1737–1805), who opposed the ministry and methods of Lord North.

Malakoff. (Pseud.) (1) Samuel Johnson, LL.D., English writer and lexicographer (1709–1784). (2) Dr. W. F. Johnson, in the New York "Times."

Malaprop, Mrs. A famous character in Sheridan's comedy, "The Rivals," and the type of a good-natured, pompous female ignoramus who is perpetually blundering in the use of words. "As headstrong as an allegory on the banks of the Nile," is one of her pet similes. *See* PARTINGTON, MRS.

Mal à propos. (Fr.) Ill-timed; impertinently.

Malgré nous. (Fr.) In spite of us.

Malum in se. (Lat.) A thing evil in itself.

Malus pudor. (Lat.) False shame.

Mambrino. (Pseud.) H. D. McKinney, correspondent at Janesville, Ohio, of the "Spirit of the Times," New York.

Mambrino's Helmet. A helmet of pure gold, which rendered the wearer invisible. It was taken possession of by Rinaldo, and stolen by Scaripante.

Mameluke Grip. A sword of peculiar make, adopted into the United States navy, and modelled on one presented to Commodore M. C. Perry by Mehemet Ali in 1829.

Mamie Sutton. The stage-name of Mrs. Fred Solomon.

Mammy. The negro nurse of Southern white children was called "mammy" (generally sounded *mawmer*). This last has invaded the North as the too frequent substitute for "mamma" among white children.

Man. Manassas.

Man about Town, The. (Pseud.) Articles in "The Star," New York, over the above signature are contributed by Charles E. File, P. McCann, William H. Muldoon, and other writers.

Man and a Brother. A negro. From a medallion by Wedgwood (1768), representing a negro in chains, with one knee on the ground, and both hands lifted up to heaven. This was adopted as a characteristic seal by the Antislavery Society of London.

Manchester of America. Lowell, Mass.; the seat of an enormous textile industry, like its English namesake.

Manchester of Belgium. Ghent.

Manchester of Prussia. Elberfeld. The specialty of Prussian Manchester is its "Turkey red." Krupp is the chief manufacturer there of steel.

Manchester Poet. Charles Swain (b. 1803).

Mandamus. (Lat.) "We command." A writ issued by the Court of Queen's Bench in name of the sovereign; so called from its initial word.

Manège. A riding-school.

Mange-tout. (Fr.) A spendthrift.

Manhattan. Another name for New York City. It is built on Manhattan Island.

Manhattan. (Pseud.) Joseph A. Scoville, English war correspondent (1815–1864).

Mania a potu. (Lat.) Madness caused by drunkenness.

Manibus pedibusque. (Lat.) "With hands and with feet." With all one's might.

Manière d'être. (Fr.) Manner; bearing.

Man in Claret. (Pseud.) Edward Sherman Gould (1808–1885), American, author of "The Sleep-rider," a work which created a literary sensation.

Man in the Moon. A popular personification of the marks seen upon the face of the queen of night, which are known to be caused by the inequalities of her surface, but which were thought to resemble the figure of an old man leaning on a staff and with a bundle of fagots on his back, for gathering which on Sunday he was confined to the moon. This is one of the oldest superstitions in the world.

Man is a Two-legged Animal without Feathers. Plato having defined man to be a two-legged animal without feathers, Diogenes plucked a cock, and bringing him into the school said, "Here is Plato's man." After which there was added to the definition, "with broad flat nails."

Manlian Discipline. Overstrained severity. Manlius Torquatus, the Roman consul, gave orders in the Latin war that no Roman, on pain of death, should engage in single combat; but one of the Latins provoked young Manlius by repeated insults, and Manlius

slew him. When the young man took the spoils to his father, Torquatus ordered him to be put to death for violating the commands of his superior officer.

Mano. (Ital.) The hand.

Mano dritta. (Ital.) The right hand.

Man of Bath. An appellation given to Ralph Allen, the friend of Pope, Warburton, and Fielding.

Man of Blood. (1) An epithet applied by the Puritans to Charles I., they having in mind 2 Sam. xxi. 7. (2) The name was also popularly applied to Thomas Simmons, an English murderer who was sent to the gallows at Hertford, March 7, 1808.

Man of Brass. Talus, the work of Hephæstus (Vulcan). He traversed the Isle of Crete thrice a year. Apollonius (*Argonautica*, iv.) says he threw rocks at the Argonauts, to prevent their landing. It is also said that when a stranger was discovered on the island, Talus made himself red-hot, and embraced the intruder to death.

> That portentous Man of Brass
> Hephæstus made in days of yore,
> Who stalked about the Cretan shore,
> And saw the ships appear and pass,
> And threw stones at the Argonauts.
> LONGFELLOW, *The Wayside Inn.*

Man of Chios. Homer, who lived at Chios, on the Ægean Sea.

Man of December. Napoleon III. was so called, in memory of the *coup d'état* which made him emperor on Dec. 2, 1852.

Man of Destiny. (1) A sobriquet applied to Napoleon I., who assumed to believe himself a chosen instrument of destiny, and thought that all his actions were guided by fate. (2) Grover Cleveland, President of the United States, 1884–1888. It was coined and bestowed in Buffalo, N. Y., in the spring of 1883, the occasion being a public banquet following the dedication of a soldiers' monument. Governor Cleveland and his staff were present. Congressman Farquhar was toastmaster for the occasion. When the time was reached for Governor Cleveland to respond to the State of New York, Mr. Farquhar said: "Ladies and Gentlemen, we will now have the pleasure of listening to some remarks on the glories and achievements attained by the Empire State by an appropriate character of New York, — 'the man of destiny,' — the present Governor of the State." Mr. Farquhar then continued his introduction by noting the quick and successive rise of Grover Cleveland to the position he then occupied, and prophesied still greater things in store for him. After that he was known as the "man of destiny."

Man of Iron. Prince Bismarck.

Man of Ross. John Kyrle, of Ross, in Herefordshire, whose praises are sung by Pope in his "Epistle on the Use of Riches."

Man of Sedan. Napoleon III., who "staked all and lost" at the battle of Sedan, Sept. 2, 1870.

Man of the People. A nickname popularly applied to Charles James Fox (fl. 1749–1806), a famous English orator and statesman.

Man-of-war. "A phrase applied to a line-of-battle ship, contrary to the usual rule in the English language by which all ships are feminine. It probably arose in the following manner: 'Men of war' were heavy armed soldiers. A ship full of them would be called a 'man-of-war ship.' In process of time the word 'ship' was discarded as unnecessary, and there remained the phrase 'a man-of-war.' " — TALBOT.

Man on Horseback, The. Gen. Georges Ernest Jean Marie Boulanger, the famous French soldier; so called from the fact that he is seldom seen in public except mounted on his favorite black charger.

Mano sinistra. (Ital.) The left hand.

Manton, Mr. The turf-name of the Dowager Duchess of Montrose, who owned a stud of race-horses. In 1888 she married Mr. Henry Milner.

Mantuan Swain. Virgil was so named.

Manu forti. (Lat.) With a strong hand.

Manu propria. (Lat.) With one's own hand.

Man without a Skin. Richard Cumberland the dramatist was so called by Garrick, because he was so extremely sensitive that he could not bear "to be touched" by the finger of criticism (1732–1811).

Man with the Sling. John Randolph. *See* JACK THE GIANT-KILLER.

Mar. March.

Marblehead Turkeys and Cape Cod Turkeys. Codfish. So called in Massachusetts. So Taunton Turkeys, Dig-

by Chickens (with Herrings), Albany Beef, and Welsh Rabbit (which some folk absurdly spell Rarebit!). Mutton stewed in a peculiar way is Welsh Venison in England.

Marbury's Case. A decision of the United States Supreme Court (1803), noted in American constitutional history, which established the power of that court to declare an act of Congress void for contravening the United States Constitution, and defined the extent to which members of the Cabinet are amenable to the courts.

Marcel. (Pseud.) William Francis Allen, in "The Nation."

March. Marchioness.

March and May, Field of. *See* FIELD OF MARCH AND MAY.

Marche (Fr.), **Marcia** (Ital.). A march.

Marchmont Needham. (Pseud.) Josiah Quincy, American orator and patriot (1744–1775).

March Newgate-fashion. To march two and two, as the prisoners were at one time conveyed to Newgate two and two together.

Falstaff. Must we all march?
Bardolph. Yea, two and two, Newgate-fashion.
    SHAKSPEARE, 1 *Henry IV.*, act iii. sc. 3.

Marco de St. Hilaire. (Pseud.) Émile Marc Hilaire de Saint-Hilaire, French writer (b. 1790).

Marcomannic War. A war carried on by the Marcobanni, under the leadership of Maroboduus, who made himself master of Bohemia, etc. Maroboduus was defeated by Arminius, and his confederation broken up (A. D. 20). In the second Christian century a new war broke out between the Marcomanni and the Romans, which lasted thirteen years. In A. D. 180 peace was purchased by the Romans, and the war for a time ceased.

Marcus Brutus. (Pseud.) Benjamin Pollard, in his letters to President Madison.

Marcus Cato. A reportorial personification of the Earl of Bath in the days when newspaper reports of Parliamentary proceedings were not legalized.

Mardi-Gras. Shrove-Tuesday; the last day of the Carnival, noted in Paris for the travesty of a Roman procession marching to offer an ox in sacrifice to the gods. The ox, which is always the "prize" beast of the season, is decorated with gilt horns and fillet round its head; mock priests with axes, etc., march beside it, a band with all sorts of tin instruments or instruments of thin brass follow; and lictors, etc., fill up the procession.

Mare clausum. (Lat.) A closed sea; a bay.

Mare magnum. (Lat.) The vast ocean.

Marg. Margin.

Margaret Mather. The stage-name of Mrs. Emil Haberkom.

Marg. Tran. Marginal translation.

Marguerite Saint-John. The stage-name of Mrs. G. M. Wood.

Maria dell' Occidente. (Pseud.) Maria Gowen Brooks, American poetess (1795–1845). Southey, who gave her the name, calls her the "most impassioned and imaginative of all poetesses."

Maria Harris. The stage-name of Maria Elizabeth Glossop.

Marian Douglas. (Pseud.) Annie Douglas Robinson, American poet (b. 1842), in various magazines and newspapers.

Marianites. Worshippers of Mary, the mother of Jesus. They said the Trinity consisted of God the Father, God the Son, and Mary the mother of God.

Marianne Farningham. (Pseud.) Mary Anne Hearne.

Marian Ward. The stage-name of Mrs. Tony Williams,

Marie Adair. The stage-name of Mrs. W. F. Loftus.

Marie Burroughs. The stage-name of Mrs. L. F. Massen.

Marie Giuri. The stage-name of Madame Rizzotti.

Marie Gordon. The stage-name of the first Mrs. John T. Raymond.

Marie Heath. The stage-name of Mrs. Warren W. Ashley.

Marie Jansen. The stage-name of Mrs. Barton Key, *née* Johnstone.

Marie Knowles. The stage-name of Ada Ringer.

Marie Milforde. The stage-name of Mary Fisher.

Marie Prescott. The stage-name of Mrs. Pertzel.

Marie Roseau. (Pseud.) Mary J. Reed, American poetess (b. 1830).

Marie Roze. The professional name of Mrs. Henry Mapleson, *née* Pousin, the celebrated *danseuse*.

Marie Stone. The stage-name of Mrs. W. H. Macdonald.

Marie Vogt. The stage-name of Mrs. James A. Seckener.

Marie Wainwright. The stage-name of Mrs. Louis James.

Marines. The sceptical phrase, "Tell that to the marines," is of English origin. In former times the "Jollies," or Royal Marines, were the butts of the sailors, from their ignorance of seamanship. "Jolly" was a sailor's nickname for a marine, who, in his opinion, bore the same relation to a "regular" as a jolly-boat or yawl to a ship. Another name given to a marine by the sailors was a "Gulpin;" that is, a person who would swallow anything that was told him. Hence arose the expression, "Tell that to the marines; the blue-jackets won't believe it," which was a common rejoinder to a stiff yarn. In Byron's poem, "The Island," written in 1823, the following lines occur:—

"'What cheer, Ben Bunting?' cried, when in full view,
Our new acquaintance Torquil; 'aught of new?'
But, whate'er betide, ah, Neivha! Now
Unman me not; the hour will not allow
A tear: 'I'm thine, whatever intervenes!'
'Right,' quoth Ben; 'that will do for the marines.'"

Marion Brent. The stage-name of Mrs. Edwin Elroy.

Marion Fiske. The stage-name of Mrs. T. J. Martin.

Marion Fleming. The stage-name of Mrs. F. S. Mordaunt.

Marion Harland. (Pseud.) Mary Virginia (Hawes) Terhune, American novelist (b. 1835).

Marion Manola. The stage-name of Mrs. Henry S. Mould, *née* Stevens.

Marion Ward. (Pseud.) Mrs. Harriet Marion Stephens.

Marjorie March. (Pseud.) Augusta Leibich, in her communications to the "Household," Brattleboro, Vt.

Mark Conway. (Pseud.) Frank Cahill, in the Philadelphia "Saturday Press."

Mark Hope. (Pseud.) Eustace Clare Grenville Murray.

Mark Littleton. (Pseud.) John Pendleton Kennedy, American statesman and author (1795–1870).

Mark Macrabin. (Pseud.) Allan Cunningham, Scottish critic and author (1785–1842).

Mark of Cain. McClintock and Strong's Cyclopædia says : " The words probably mean that Jehovah *gave a sign to* Cain, very much as signs were afterward given to Noah, Moses, Elijah, and Hezekiah. Whether the sign was perceptible to Cain alone, and given to him once for all in token that no man should kill him, or whether it was perceptible to others, and designed as a precaution to them, is uncertain ; the nature of the sign is still more uncertain." From this it would seem that the "mark" was a sign given by the Lord to clinch his promise that Cain should not be slain by the people of the earth.

Mark Quencher. (Pseud.) Charles M. Conolly.

Mark Rochester. (Pseud.) William Charles Mark Kent, *littérateur*.

Mark Twain. (Pseud.) Samuel Langhorne Clemens, American humorist (b. 1835).

Maroon. "The name given to revolted negroes in the West Indies and in some parts of South America. The appellation is supposed to be derived from Marony, a river separating Dutch and French Guiana, where large numbers of these fugitives resided. In many cases, by taking to the forests and mountains, they have rendered themselves formidable to the colonies, and sustained a long and brave resistance against the whites. When Jamaica was conquered by the English in 1655, about fifteen hundred slaves retreated to the mountains, and were called ' maroons.' They continued to harass the island till the end of the last century, when they were reduced by the aid of bloodhounds." — *Encycl. Americana.*

Marooning. (1) " To go marooning " is an expression used in the Southern States. It means to go on a picnic. The difference between a "marooning" party and a picnic is that the former is a party made up to pass several days on the shore or in the country, the latter is a party for a day. The expression is of course derived from the preceding noun. (2) The name given to the custom of punishing a refractory sailor by setting him ashore on a desert island. Alexander Selkirk was a "marooned " seaman.

Marprelate Tracts. *See* MARTIN MARPRELATE.

Marq. Marquis.

Marquis of Carabas. An antiquated nobleman, of unbounded pretensions, wealth, and vanity, who would like to restore the court usages of the reign of Louis XIV. The character is taken from Perrault's tale of " Puss in Boots."

Marrow Controversy. A bitter polemical warfare in Scotland between the Puritans and the Presbyterians, arising out of a book entitled "The Marrow of Modern Divinity," which was condemned by the General Assembly in 1720.

Marrow-men. A nickname given to twelve men who signed a remonstrance against the condemnation of the doctrines contained in " The Marrow of Modern Divinity."

Marseilles' Good Bishop. The Very Rev. H. F. X. de Belsunce, who during the plague of 1720–1722 performed valiant service in visiting and consoling the sick.

Marsh, The. Another name for " The Plain," or the lowest benches in the French National Assembly.

Marshal Forward. Blucher was thus nicknamed for his promptness and ready dash in the memorable campaign of 1813.

Mar's Insurrection. John, Earl of Mar, proclaimed James III. at Braemar, in Aberdeenshire, Sept. 6, 1715. He was defeated at the battle of Sheriffmuir with the Pretender, Feb. 4, 1716.

Mars of Portugal. Alfonso de Albuquerque, Viceroy of India (1452–1515).

Marsyas. In classic myth a Phrygian satyr who challenged Apollo to a contest in music. Being vanquished, he was flayed alive for his insolence.

Mar's Year. The year 1715, in which occurred the rebellion of the Earl of Mar.

> Auld uncle John wha wedlock's joys
> Sin Mar's year did desire.
> BURNS, *Halloween.*

Martian Laws are the laws collected by Martia, the wife of Guithelin, great-grandson of Malmutius, who established in Britain the " Malmutian Laws " (*q. v.*). Alfred translated both these codes into Saxon English, and called the Martian code " Pa Marchitle Lage." These laws have no connection with the kingdom of Mercia.

Martin Marprelate and Martin Priest. (Pseud.) John Ap Henry, English satirical writer (1559–1593).

Martin's Goose. The 11th of November, St. Martin's Day, was at one time the great goose-feast of France. The legend is that Saint Martin was annoyed by a goose, which he ordered to be killed and served up for dinner. As he died from the repast, the goose has been ever since "sacrificed" to him on the anniversary.

Martin's Summer, Saint. *See* SAINT MARTIN'S LITTLE SUMMER.

Martinus Scriblerus. (Pseud.) Alexander Pope, English poet and satirist (1688–1744).

Martlet. (Pseud.) Richard Bingham Davis, author of the "Drone Papers," in the "New York Magazine."

Martyred President. Abraham Lincoln (fl. 1809–1865), the sixteenth President of the United States. He was assassinated by Wilkes Booth, April 14, 1865. *See also* RAIL-SPLITTER.

Martyr to Science. Claude Louis, Count Berthollet (fl. 1748–1822), who died in his laboratory while testing in his own person the effects of carbonic-acid gas on the human organism.

Martyrs, Era of. *See* ERA OF MARTYRS.

Marvellous Boy. Thomas Chatterton, the youthful poet (fl. 1752–1770).

Mary Blake. (Pseud.) Mrs. Mary N. Blakeslee, a contributor to the "Century" on household affairs.

Mary Boeckel. The stage-name of Mrs. Samuel Reed.

Mary Densel. (Pseud.) Mrs. Mary Selden McCobb, in "Harper's Young People."

Mary Duff Gordon. (Pseud.) Mary Gordon Duffee, American author (b. 1840). She is a resident of Alabama, and writes on historical themes.

Mary E. Yates. The stage-name of Mrs. H. P. Madigan.

Mary Frances Clare. The religious name of Mary Frances Cusack.

Mary Jane. (Pseud.) W. J. Lampton, of the Washington "Critic."

Maryland. This State was so named in honor of Henrietta Maria, queen of Charles I. of England.

Mary Langdon. (Pseud.) Mrs. Mary H. Green Pike, American writer (b. 1827).

Mary Neville. (Pseud.) Mrs. Mary A. Foster, for several years a regular writer in the columns of the Cincinnati "Gazette" and the "Commercial."

Mary of Modena. The second wife of James II. of England, and mother of the "Pretender."

Mary Orme. (Pseud.) Mrs. Mary Sergeant Gove Nichols, American novelist and doctress (b. 1810).

Mary Pentland. The stage-name of Mrs. E. L. Tilton.

Mary Powell. (Pseud.) Mrs. Richard Rathbone, *littérateur*.

Mary Tucker. The stage-name of Mrs. Albert Clayton.

Mary Whittingham. The stage-name of Mrs. Skuse.

Mary Williams. The stage-name of Mrs. J. H. Barnes.

Masc. Masculine.

Mason and Dixon's Line. A line running along the parallel of lat. 39° 43′ 26.3″, and separating Pennsylvania from Maryland, drawn by two distinguished English astronomers and mathematicians, Charles Mason and Jeremiah Dixon. For about eighty years after 1691 there was constant dissension between the Lords Baltimore and the Penn family, the rival proprietors in Pennsylvania and Maryland, in regard to the position of the boundary-line between their colonial possessions. An agreement was come to in 1760, in accordance with which a party of surveyors commenced to make out the real boundary. The proprietors in London, not understanding the length of time required for such an undertaking, and growing impatient, sent out Mason and Dixon to hasten the survey in December, 1763, who completed it in 1767 all save 36′, this latter portion being surveyed in 1782 by Col. Alexander McLean and Joseph Neville. This line must not be confounded with that which separated the Cotton States from the Border Slave States as formerly designated, and was fixed by the Missouri Compromise as the northernmost limit of such Slave States as should be afterward admitted to the Union.

Mass. Massachusetts.

Massachusettensis. (Pseud.) David Leonard, American Tory, in Revolutionary War, and Chief-Justice of Bermuda (1740–1829).

Massachusetts. The name of this State is an Indian word, signifying "the country about the great hills."

Massachusetts. (Pseud.) Elias Haskett Derby, in the Boston papers.

Massachusetts Yankee. (Pseud.) Lyman Hotchkiss Baggs, in the "Anglo-American Times," London, 1876, and in the "Nation," New York, *circa* 1880.

Massacre of Wyoming. *See* Wyoming Massacre.

Master Adam. (Pseud.) Adam-Billaut, French poet (1602–1662).

Masterly Inactivity. The "Imperial Dictionary" attributes the phrase "masterly inactivity" to Sir J. Mackintosh, who said: "The Commons, faithful to their system, remained in a wise and masterly inactivity." Mr. Fletcher, assistant in the Watkinson Library, of Hartford, wrote to London "Notes and Queries" in 1879 that "it was in very common use in this country during the late civil war, as descriptive of the policy of some of our generals who were in favor of letting the 'rebellion die a natural death.'" Another authority insisted that Cowper must have originated the idea, if not the phrase, in these lines: —

"When admirals extoll'd for standing still
Or doing nothing with a deal of skill."

Then another remarks that "masterly inactivity" was easy to say after Cowper's line was written. In London "Notes and Queries," Sept. 17, 1859, a correspondent has this note: "This expression was used by the late John C. Calhoun in a debate in the Senate of the United States upon the acquisition of Cuba, in which he alleged that when the proper time came Cuba would gravitate toward the United States, and that in the mean while the policy of the United States was a masterly inactivity. I have lately heard that the phrase was used in the British House of Commons during the first French Revolution. The idea seems to be found in a sentence in one of the Hebrew prophets: 'His strength is to sit still.'"

Master of Court is, in England, the title given to a chief officer under a judge. His chief duties are to write minutes of procedure, and to tax bills of costs.

Master of Sentences. Pierre Lombard, a mediæval Schoolman (fl. 1100–1164).

Master of the Buckhounds. One of the ministers of the crown, to whose care is intrusted the management of the royal hunts. His emoluments amount to £1,700.

Master of the Ceremonies. An office instituted at all European courts for the direction of matters of state etiquette. It was established in England in 1603. The name is now extended to the director of the arrangements of a public ball.

Master of the Horse (Lat., *Magister Equitum*) among the Romans was from the earliest times the officer next in authority to a Dictator. In England the Master of the Horse is a minister of the crown, the third great officer of the royal household, intrusted with the direction of the royal stables, and privileged to ride next to the sovereign on state occasions. His salary is £2,500 a year.

Master of the Household. An officer of the royal household, charged with the choice, direction, and payment of the household servants. He holds office at the Queen's pleasure, and receives £1,158 a year.

Master of the Mint. A punning nickname for a gardener.

Master of the Rolls. (1) This is the title of the president of the Chancery division of the High Court of Justice. He formerly had the custody of the Rolls, or records. This he still has nominally. The Master of the Rolls ranks next to the Lord Chief-Justice of England. (2) A punning nickname for a baker.

Master of Trinity. A name by which Christopher Wordsworth, D.D. (fl. 1774–1846), a noted English scholar and divine, and brother of the poet Wordsworth, was often referred to. For many years he was Master of Trinity College, Cambridge University.

Masts, City of. *See* City of Masts.

Matchless Orinda. Katharine Phillips, an English poetess, "the first who wrote verse that people of her time talked about" (1631–1634).

Materfamilias. (Lat.) The mother of a family.

Materia medica. (Lat.) Substances used in the healing art.

Math. Mathematics; mathematician.

Mathilde Sessi. The stage-name of Baroness Erlanger, *née* Alexander.

Matilda Heron. The stage-name of Mrs. Robert Stoepfel.

Matilda Madison. The stage-name of Mrs. Denison.

Matinée. (Fr.) A morning party.

Matt. Matthew.

Matthew Bramble. (Pseud.) Andrew MacDonald, Scottish poet (1755–1788).

Matthew's Bible. An edition of the Scriptures which appeared in 1537, edited by the martyr Rogers, who used the unpublished MS. of Tyndale. *See also* TREACLE BIBLE.

Matthew Smith. (Pseud.) Charles Mordaunt, Earl of Peterborough (1658–1735).

Mattie Temple. The stage-name of Mrs. Henry Clark.

Mattie Vickers. The stage-name of Mrs. Charles S. Rogers.

Mattie Williams. The stage-name of Mrs. Wilbur M. Williams.

Matt Marling. (Pseud.) The sea-stories in the "Boys' and Girls' Weekly," New York, over this signature were written by Charles H. Webb and Alfred Trimble.

Maud Banker. The stage-name of Maud Adams.

Maud Branscombe. The stage-name of Mrs. Everard Stuart.

Maude Atkinson. The stage-name of Mrs. R. J. Johnston.

Maude Clifford. The stage-name of Mrs. E. V. Sinclair.

Maude Garrison. The stage-name of Jennie Neal.

Maude Goodwin. The stage-name of Mrs. George Richards.

Maude Granger. The stage-name of Mrs. Wm. R. Baxter, *née* Brainard.

Maude Mulle. The stage-name of Mrs. A. M. Bell.

Maude Oswald. The stage-name of Mrs. D. R. Hawley.

Maude Stuart. The stage-name of Mrs. Marble, *née* Maude Grubbs.

Maud Melville. The stage-name of Mrs. Oscar Anderson.

Maud Miller. The stage-name of Mrs. Loudon McCormick, daughter of Joaquin Miller.

Maul of Monks. *See* HAMMER, THE.

Maundy-Thursday. The Thursday of Holy Week. The name is derived from *mandatum*, the first word of the service chanted at the ceremony of washing the feet of pilgrims on that day, which is taken from John xiii. 34. This day is often erroneously called "Holy Thursday" (*q. v.*).

Maurice Barrymore. The stage-name of Maurice Kline.

Maurivaudage is analogous to our word "preciousness" as applied to the Oscar Wilde æsthetes, or "euphuism" as applied to the Sir Percy Shaftons of Queen Elizabeth's day; and it means a certain affected style of writing which was brought into fashion by Pierre Carlet de Marivaux in his unfinished novel of "Marianne" (1731).

Mauvaise honte. (Fr.) "False shame." Bashfulness.

Mauvaise langue. (Fr.) "An ill tongue." A slanderous person.

Mauvais goût. (Fr.) Bad taste.

Mauvais pas. (Fr.) "Bad step." An awkward fix; a dilemma.

Mauvais sujet. (Fr.) "A bad subject." A worthless fellow.

Mauvais ton. (Fr.) "Bad tone." Ill manners; vulgarity.

Maverick. The word "Maverick" is used in the cattle-ranges of the West to designate an unbranded and hence ownerless animal. The San Francisco "Maverick" gives this as the origin of the word: "A few years since Sam Maverick went from Massachusetts to Texas, where he entered largely into stock business. After buying several herds he neglected his range and left his stock to shift for themselves. Mr. Maverick, with humanitarian feeling, refrained from branding his young stock, believing in the implicit honesty of his neighbors. When the genuine stockmen of the region ran across an unbranded animal on the round up, they would say, ' There 's one of Maverick's; let 's brand it.' The word sprang into popularity, and its limited meaning was broadened and enlarged by constant use throughout the cattle-ranges and mining-camps of the frontier. If a man was unpronounced in his opinion on any subject, people would say, ' He holds Maverick views.' "

Max. Maxim.

Max Adeler. (Pseud.) Charles Heber Clark, an American humorist and author.

Max Eliot. (Pseud.) Mrs. Annie M. D. Eliot, in the Boston " Herald."

Maximum. The greatest.

Maximus in minimis. (Lat.) "Greatest in the least." Very great in very little things.

Max Mannering. (Pseud.) Josiah Gilbert Holland, in the " Springfield Republican," about 1852.

Max O'Rell. The pseudonym of Paul Blouët, the Franco-English *littérateur* and lecturer (b. 1848). He wrote " John Bull and his Island," " The Land of the Mounseer," " Jonathan and his Continent," etc.

Maxwell Gray. (Pseud.) Miss Uttiel, of Newport, Isle of Wight, author of " The Silence of Dean Maitland," a powerful novel published in 1888.

Max Werter. (Pseud.) Frank Smyth, in the " Capitol," Washington, D. C.

Mâyâ. In Hindu mythology " the personified will or energy of the Supreme Being, who by her created the universe."

May and December. A phrase frequently used to characterize the courting of a young girl by an old man. Chaucer has a poem called " January and May " (" The Merchant's Tale "), but January is so connected in the public mind with the new year that it symbolizes rather lusty youth than an old man in his dotage. December has therefore become the popular symbol for the mating of youth and age. There is an old ballad recounting the ill success of an old man's wooing, in which each verse ends with the refrain, —

" For May and December can never agree."

May Bowers. The stage-name of Mrs. Frank Bennett.

May Chalfaut. The stage-name of Mrs. Niemeyer, *née* Smith.

May Davenport. The stage-name of Mrs. William Seymour.

May-Day. This is peculiarly an English floral festival, and one observed for centuries among the rural population of " Merrie England." It is on the threshold of summer in the southern countries, and the hawthorn bush, popularly known as " The May," is usually in full bloom. In some parts of the island the young men go out very early to the woods, singing this quaint old song : —

" Come, lads, with your bills,
    To the woods we 'll away,

We 'll gather the boughs,
    And we 'll celebrate May.

" We 'll bring our load home,
    As we 've oft done before,
And leave a green bough
    At each pretty maid's door."

The May-pole, garlanded with flowers, and around which the village revels were held, was an important feature in English rustic life for hundreds of years, and is yet in some secluded corners. In some places the children and young women go about early in the morning hanging green boughs to the doors, singing this song, with variations. This is one form : —

" Here we come, poor Mayers all,
    And thus we do begin
To lead our lives in righteousness,
    Or else we die in sin.

" We have been rambling all this night,
    And almost all this day ;
And now returnèd back again,
    We have brought you a branch of May."

There is a May-pole yet standing at Ottley, in Yorkshire. Around these old May-poles used to be dancing and frolicking. The May-pole was like our liberty-poles, but was decorated with ribbons and garlands of flowers. The young people used to choose a Queen of May, who was honored as the lady of the day, wearing a crown of flowers. In the old times of the Saxons a king and a queen were both chosen, or else a lord and a lady. Tennyson's exquisite poem, " The Queen of the May," alludes to this charming custom. About sixty or seventy years ago there was a strange custom in vogue in London. The milkmaids used to come out on the 1st of May and call on all their customers, from whom they received a trifle of money, which was spent in finery. At about the same time, too, or perhaps in the latter part of the last century, the chimney-sweeps of the metropolis made it a practice on the 1st of May to parade the streets, togged out in tawdry finery, ribbons, and green boughs, whence the London name for May-Day, — " Sweeps' Day." " Jack-in-the-Green," with " Black Sal " and " Dusty Bob," with the second mentioned being usually a man dressed in woman's attire (probably a relic of the milkmaids), would go dancing and capering through the streets, the centre of an admiring rabble. Mrs. Elizabeth Montagu (who died in 1800) gave for many years, on May-Day, an entertainment at her house in Portman Square, to the chimney-sweepers of London. They were regaled with roast beef and plum-pudding, and a dance succeeded. Upon their departure each guest received a shilling from the mistress of the feast. It is said, though the statement is much doubted, that this entertainment was instituted to commemorate the circumstance of Mrs. Montagu having once found a son of her own, or that of a relation, among the sooty tribe. In allusion to this incident, perhaps, a story resembling the adventures of this lost child is pathetically related by Montgomery in " The Chimney-sweeper's Boy." Since 1876 the observance of Sweeps' Day has evinced signs of lapsing into "innocuous desuetude."

Mayfair. The district of London which bears this name is so called from a pleasure fair formerly held in the neighborhood. In the " Gentleman's Magazine," April, 1816, a Mr. Sharp gives an interesting account of the fair as he remembered it fifty years before. Duck-hunting, prize-fighting, donkey-racing, bull-baiting, and other brutal practices were among the chief amusements.

May Fielding. The stage-name of Mrs. Scovel.

May Irwin. The stage-name of Mrs. Keller.

May Kingston. (Pseud.) Sarah Lane.

May Meetings. A title applied to the annual gatherings, in May and June, of religious and charitable societies, to hear the annual reports, and appeals in behalf of continued or increased support.

May Miller. The stage-name of Mrs. Frank Hues.

May Niblo Drew. The stage-name of Mrs. Phillips Hanley.

May Olive. The stage-name of Mrs. S. T. Wheeler, formerly Mrs. Harry Thompson.

May-pole, The. A scurrilous sobriquet conferred on the Duchess of Kendal, mistress of George I., — so named because she was as tall and as thin as a May-pole.

May Rie. (Pseud.) Miss Mary Walsingham Crean, in the New Orleans newspapers.

May Riot. See HAYMARKET RIOT and BOMB CITY.

May Saville. The stage-name of Mrs. J. G. Saville.

May Smith. The stage-name of Mrs. A. R. Krause.

May Stembler. The stage-name of Mrs. A. D. Iasigi.

May Templeton. The stage-name of Mrs. James Reilly.

May Walk. See ANNIVERSARY DAY.

M. B. Bachelor of Medicine (*Medicinæ Baccalaureus*); Bachelor of Music (*Musicæ Baccalaureus*).

M. B. Drapier. (Pseud.) Jonathan Swift, English divine and satirist (1667–1745).

M. B. F. et H. Great Britain, France, and Ireland.

M. B. Waistcoat. A clerical waistcoat. " M. B." means " Mark (of the) Beast; " so called because, when these waistcoats were first worn by Protestant clergymen (about 1830), they were stigmatized as indicating a popish tendency.

He smiled at the folly which stigmatized an M. B. waistcoat. — MRS. OLIPHANT, *Phœbe, Jun.*

M. C. Member of Congress; Master of Ceremonies; Master Commandant.

Mch. March.

McLeod Case. A controversy between the United States and Canada, arising out of the incident of the destruction of the American steamer " Caroline " by the Canadian authorities (1837), in the course of which a man was killed. McLeod was arrested as one of the attacking party, and was indicted (1841) in New York State for murder; but he proved an alibi, and was acquitted. Also called the " Case of the ' Caroline.' "

M. C. S. Madras Civil Service.

M. D. *Medicinæ Doctor.* Doctor of Medicine.

Md. Maryland.

Mdpn. Midshipman.

M. E. Methodist Episcopal; military or mechanical engineer.

Me. Maine.

Me. (Pseud.) H. C. Bunner, in " Puck."

Meadow, The Bloody. See BLOODY MEADOW.

Meal-tub Plot. A pretended conspiracy against the Duke of York (James II.), concocted by Dangerfield in 1679, and by him falsely attributed to the Presbyterians. It was so named because the scheme of the pretended conspirators was hid in a meal-tub in the house of Dangerfield's mistress, who was named Collier. Dangerfield afterward confessed to the whole affair, was sentenced to fine, the pillory, and the lash May 30, 1685, but died two days later from injuries received in the execution of the sentence.

Mea maxima culpa. (Lat.) Through my very great fault.

Mech. Mechanic; mechanical.

Méchant écrivain. (Fr.) A mere scribbler.

Mecklenburg Declaration. What is known in United States history as the " Mecklenburg Declaration of Independence " was a document, dated May 31, 1775, signed and issued by prominent citizens of Mecklenburg County, N. C., asserting the independence of the British colonies in America. It antedated the adoption of the Declaration of Independence by Congress by nearly a year.

Med. Medicine.

Medea. In classic myth a famous sorceress, the daughter of Aëtes, King of Colchis, and of the Oceanid Idyia, or of Hecate. She married Jason, the leader of the Argonauts, and aided him in obtaining the Golden Fleece (*q. v.*).

Median Apples. Pome-citrons.

Medica manus. (Lat.) " The curative hand." Corrective skill.

Medicinal Days. The sixth, eighth, tenth, twelfth, sixteenth, eighteenth, etc., of a disease; so called because, according to Hippocrates, no " crisis " occurs on these days, and medicine may be safely administered.

Medicinal Hours. Hours proper for taking medicine, — namely, morning fasting, an hour before dinner, four hours after dinner, and bedtime.

Medicine for the Soul. Books; literature. Inscribed over the door of the library at Thebes.

Medio tutissimus ibis. (Lat.) You will succeed most safely in a middle course ; avoid all extremes.

Meditatione fugæ. (Lat.) In contemplation of flight.

Mediterranean Fund. *See* BARBARY PIRATES.

Mediterranean, Key of. *See* KEY OF THE MEDITERRANEAN.

Mediterranean of Brazil. The Amazon River.

Mediterranean of the North. The Baltic Sea.

Medusa. In classic myth one of the Gorgons. Her head was removed by Perseus, who gave it to Minerva. The latter placed it on her ægis, where it turned to stone all who gazed thereon.

Meek, The. *See* DÉBONNAIRE, LE.

Meeting-house. This term for a place of worship originated with the Puritans in America. In Elliot's " History of New England " it is stated that " the religious services of the Plymouth Church were held in the fort, upon the roof or deck of which were mounted the great guns; and it was in 1648 that a meeting-house was built. They held that a church was a body of Christians, and the place where they met was a 'meeting-house,' and so they called it by that name."

Meeting of the Waters. (1) The poetical name given by Moore to a picturesque locality in County Wicklow, Ireland. The junction here of two streams, the Avonbeg and the Avonmore, forms the Avoca, which, after a southeast course of six miles, enters the Irish Sea near Arklow. (2) The confluence of the Rhone and the Arno, near Avignon.

Megæra. In classic myth one of the Furies (*q. v.*).

M. E. G. H. P. Most Excellent Grand High Priest.

Me judice. (Lat.) " I being judge." In my opinion.

Melancholy Jacques. Jean Jacques Rousseau (fl. 1712–1777) was so named because of his frequent gloomy moods.

Mélange. (Fr.) A medley.

Melchior Gomez. Under this pseudonym Louis Jean Emmanuel Gonzales, the French feuilletonist and journalist (1815–1887), contributed to the Paris press. *See* RAMON GONERIL and CALIBAN.

Meleager. In classic myth one of the Argonauts, renowned for his skill in throwing the javelin.

Melibœan Dye. A rich purple; so called because Meliboea of Thessaly was famous for the *ostrum*, a fish used in dyeing purple.

> A military vest of purple flowed,
> Livelier than Melibœan.
> MILTON, *Paradise Lost.*

Melicertes. Son of Ino, a sea deity. Athamas imagined his wife to be a lioness, and her two sons to be lion's cubs. In his frenzy he slew one of the boys, and drove the other, named Melicertes, with his mother into the sea. The mother became a sea goddess, and the boy the god of harbors.

Melissa. (Pseud.) Jane Hughes Brereton, English poetess (1685–1740).

Mellifluous Doctor. Saint Bernard (fl. 1091–1153). His writings were called "a river of Paradise."

Mell Supper. A harvest supper; so called from the French *mêler* (to mix together), because the master and servants sit promiscuously at the harvest board.

Melpomene ("the singing one"). In classic myth one of the Nine Muses, specially invoked as the muse of tragedy.

Mem. Memorandum; remember (*memento*).

Member for Paris. (Pseud.) E. C. Grenville Murray, English writer (1828–1881).

Memento mori. (Lat.) Remember death.

Memnon. In classic myth a celebrated hero, the son of Tithonus and Eos, or Aurora, who led to Troy a host of Ethiopians, to support the cause of Troy after the fall of Hector. He was said to be clad in armor made by Hephæstus, or Vulcan, and killed Antilochus, son of Nestor, in single combat. He was killed in a duel with Ajax or Achilles. The river Paphlagonios flowed from his blood.

Memorabile nomen. (Lat.) "A memorable name." A remarkable person.

Memorabilia. (Lat.) Things to be remembered.

Memoria in æterna. (Lat.) In eternal remembrance.

Memorial Day. The custom of strewing flowers on the graves of dead soldiers originated among the women of the South, who during the civil war annually decorated the graves of their fallen heroes in that way. The beautiful custom was adopted throughout the country, and in 1868 and 1869 Gen. John A. Logan, as Commander-in-Chief of the Grand Army of the Republic, appointed May 30 for that purpose. Since that date the day has become a legal holiday in most of the States by legislative enactment. In all the national cemeteries the sight is a most impressive one. Decoration Day is not a national legal holiday. It is a legal holiday in the following States and Territories : California, Colorado, Connecticut, Dakota, Iowa, Illinois, Kansas, Kentucky, Massachusetts, Michigan, Nevada, New Hampshire, New Jersey, New York, Ohio, Oregon, Pennsylvania, Rhode Island, Utah, Vermont, Wisconsin, and Wyoming. A Memorial Day for the Confederate dead is also kept on April 26. Following is the text of the General Order referred to : —

"The 30th day of May, 1868, is designated for the purpose of strewing with flowers, or otherwise decorating, the graves of comrades who died in defence of their country during the late rebellion. We are organized for the purpose of preserving and strengthening those kind and fraternal feelings which have bound together the soldiers, sailors, and marines who united to suppress the late rebellion. What can aid more to assure this result than cherishing tenderly the memory of our heroic dead ? Their soldier lives were the reveille of freedom to a race in chains, and their deaths the tattoo of rebellious tyranny in arms. We should guard their graves with sacred vigilance. All that the consecrated wealth and taste of the nation can add to their adornment and security is but a fitting tribute to the memory of her slain defenders. Let no wanton foot tread rudely on such hallowed ground. Let pleasant paths invite the coming and going of reverent visitors and fond mourners. Let no vandalism of avarice or neglect, no ravages of time, testify to the present or to the coming generations that we have forgotten, as a people, the cost of a free and undivided republic. If other eyes grow dull, and other hands slack, and other hearts cold in the solemn trust, ours shall keep it well as long as the light and warmth of life remain. Let us then, at the time appointed, garland the passionless mounds with the choicest flowers of springtime ; let us raise above them the dear old flag they saved from dishonor ; let us, in this solemn presence, renew our pledges to aid and assist those whom they have left among us, a sacred charge upon a nation's gratitude, — the soldier's and sailor's widow and orphan."

Memoriter. By rote.

Ménage. (Fr.) Household.

Mending Fences. "A phrase sometimes used to signify that a politician is quietly laying plans and promoting his own interest. It originated as follows : Just before the Republican National Convention of 1880 John Sherman, one of the most prominent candidates for the Republican nomination, was visiting his farm at Mansfield, Ohio. One day while in a field with his brother-in-law, Colonel Moulton, engaged in replacing some rails of a fence, a reporter found him and sought some political news by inquiring what Sherman was doing. Colonel Moulton avoided the necessity of a direct reply by exclaiming, 'Why, you can see for yourself; he's mending his fences.'" — *American Political Dictionary*.

Menelaus. In classic myth king of Lacedæmon, the younger brother of Agamemnon, and husband of the famous Helen. The abduction of his wife by Paris is represented as the cause of the Trojan war.

Men in Buckram. Hypothetical men, existing only in the brain of the imaginer.

Mennonites. The followers of Simon Menno, a native of Friesland, who modified the fanatical views of the Anabaptists.

Men of Motley. Licensed fools; so called because of their dress.

Meno, or **Men.** (Ital.) Less so; as, *men. presto*, less quick; *men. forte*, less loud; *men. piano*, somewhat softer; *meno vivo*, with less spirit. (Mus.)

Mensa et thoro. From bed and board.

Mens agitat molem. (Lat.) Mind moves matter.

Mens sana in corpore sano. (Lat.) A sound mind in a sound body.

Mens sibi conscia recti. (Lat.) A mind conscious of rectitude.

Mentor. In classic myth a friend of Ulysses, in Ithaca. Minerva assumed his form to give directions to Telemachus, the son of Ulysses.

Mentor. (Pseud.) Josiah Quincy, American orator and patriot (1744–1775).

Men, Women, and Herveys. Lord Wharncliffe says, " The well-known sentence, almost a proverb, ' that this world consisted of men, women, and Herveys,' was originally Lady Montagu's." Wraxall says it was a saying of the Dowager Viscountess Townsend.

Meo periculo. (Lat.) At my own risk.

Merc. Mercury.

Mercator. (Pseud.) (1) Samuel Jones Lloyd, Lord Overstone, English economist (1796–1883). (2) William A. Brewer, in various newspapers of New York and Boston.

Mercurial Finger. The little finger.

The thumb, in chiromancy, we give Venus; The forefinger to Jove; the midst to Saturn; The ring to Sol; the least to Mercury.
BEN JONSON, *The Alchemist*.

Mercurius Rusticus. (Pseud.) Rev. Thomas Frognall Dibdin, LL.D., English bibliographer (1776–1847).

Mercury. In classic myth the god of speech, eloquence, the sciences, traffic, theft, and herds. All literary compositions were dedicated to him, and he was the scribe or clerk of the gods.

Mercury. (Pseud.) (1) George D. Baird, editor of " Cyclist and Athlete," New York. (2) L. C. Bruce, in " Turf, Field, and Farm," New York.

Mercutio. (Pseud.) William Winter, American poet and critic (b. 1836).

Mercutio of Actors. Lewis, an English comedian (fl. 1748–1811), who successfully aped the manners of a fop and of a gentleman.

Merlin. (Pseud.) Alexander Wilder, M.D., New York correspondent of the Boston " Daily Advertiser " from 1864–1870.

Merlin of England. William Lilly, the English " astrologer," was so named. He published two tracts over the pseudonym " Merlinus Anglicus."

Mero motu suo. (Lat.) Purely of his own accord.

Merope. In classic myth one of the Pleiades. Her star is less bright than her sisters', because she wedded a mortal.

Merop's Son. A nobody, a *terræ filius*, who thinks himself somebody. Thus Phaeton (Merop's son), forgetting that his mother was an earthborn woman, thought he could drive the horses of the sun, but, not being able to guide them, nearly set the earth on fire.

Merry as a Grig. A grig is a grasshopper. The cricket and the grasshopper are in most countries taken as types of a careless, happy existence. We have the related saying, " Merry as a cricket ; " and Tennyson, in " The Brook," speaks of —

" High-elbowed *grigs*, that leap in summer grass."

Merry England. A popular name for England. The word " merry " is used, not in its present sense, or in allusion to the gayety of the people, but according to its earlier meaning, *i. e.*, " agreeable," or pleasant. Thus Spenser speaks of " merry wind and weather," and we at this day often use the phrase, " merry month of May."

Merry Men of Mey. An expanse of broken water which boils like a witch's caldron on the southern side of the Stroma Channel. "Men" is a corruption of "main." The locality gives name to a novel by Robert Louis Stevenson, entitled "The Merry Men."

Merry Monarch. Charles II. of England.

Merse. Berwickshire was so called because it was the *merc*, or frontier, of England and Scotland.

Meru. In Hindu mythology a fabulous mountain in the centre of the world, 80,000 leagues high.

Merum sal. (Lat.) Pure salt; genuine Attic wit.

Mesopotamia. A popular designation among Londoners of thirty years ago of the new brick-and-mortar suburbs in the neighborhood of Warwick and Eccleston Squares. From the fact that the great firm of Cubitt & Son were the builders of the entire district, it was also known as Cubitopolis (*q. v.*).

Mess. & Docs. Messages and documents.

Messenger of Wandsbeck. Matthius Claudius (1743–1815), the German poet and prose-writer, was so named.

Messrs., or **MM.** Messieurs; gentlemen.

Messrs. Tag, Rag, and Bobtail. (Pseud.) Isaac Disraeli, author of "Curiosities of Literature" (1776–1848).

Mesto. (Ital.) Mournfully, sadly, pathetically. (Mus.)

Mestoso. (Ital.) Sadly, pensively. (Mus.)

Met. Metaphysics.

Metador. (Pseud.) William L. Alden, in the New York "Times."

Metal. Metallurgy.

Meta Lander. (Pseud.) Margaret Woods Lawrence, an American writer of the present day, author of "The Tobacco Problem" (1885), etc.

Meteor. Meteorology.

Meth. Methodist.

Methodist. This epithet is not, as is generally supposed, of modern origin. There was a sect called "Methodists," founded some thirty or forty years before the Christian era. It lasted more than three hundred years. Many of them were eminent physicians. The name was revived in Cromwell's time, by John Spencer, librarian of Zion College in the City of London, who published a book, in which he employs the word as one commonly in use to designate a certain class of religionists. He asks, "Where are now our Anabaptists, and plain pack-stuff Methodists, who esteem all flowers of rhetoric in sermons no better than stinking weeds?" Gale, also, in his "Court of the Gentiles," published in 1678, speaks of a religious sect called "the New Methodists;" and Dr. Calamy, in "The Ejected Ministers," says that those who stood up for God were called "Methodists." This was two generations before Wesley founded the sect now known as "Wesleyan Methodists."

Methuen Treaty. A commercial treaty between England and Portugal negotiated by Paul Methuen, in 1703, whereby the Portuguese wines were received at a lower duty than those of France. This treaty was abandoned in 1836.

Métif. In Louisiana this name denominates the child of a white man and a quadroon.

Metis. In classic myth the goddess of prudence. She was the daughter of Oceanus and Tethys, and the first wife of Jupiter.

Metonic Cycle. So called from its inventor, Meton, who flourished at Athens about 432 B.C., is a cycle of nineteen years, at the end of which time the new moons fall on the same days of the year, and eclipses recur in nearly the same order. This arises from the circumstance that nineteen solar years are nearly equal to 235 lunations, their average values being 6939.68835 and 6939.60249 days, respectively. *See* CALLIPPIC PERIOD.

Metropolis of Flora. Aranjuez, in Spain, is so called from its many beautiful gardens.

Metropolis of Tourists. Luzerne, in Switzerland, is so named.

Meum et tuum. (Lat.) Mine and thine.

Meuse, Ladies of the. *See* LADIES OF THE MEUSE.

Mex. Mexico, or Mexican.

Mexican Nightingale. A sobriquet bestowed on Señora Angela Peralta, a famous prima-donna and a native of Mexico. She died in 1883, aged about forty years.

Mexican Washington. A sobriquet conferred on B. P. Juarez, the Mexican statesman and president.

Mezza voce. (Ital.) With moderation as to tone; rather soft than loud. (Mus.)

Mezzo. (Ital.) In a middling degree or manner; as, *mezzo forte*, rather loud; *mezzo piano*, rather soft. (Mus.)

Mezzo termino. (Ital.) "A middle term." A sort of compromise.

Mfd. Manufactured.

Mfs. Manufactures.

Mg. Magnesium.

M. Goth. Mœso-Gothic.

M. H. S. (1) Massachusetts Historical Society. (2) Member of the Historical Society.

Mic. Micah.

M. I. C. E. Member of the Institution of Civil Engineers.

Mich. Michaelmas; Michigan.

Michael Angelo of America. Miguel Cabrera, artist, died in Mexico about 1730. His masterpieces, depicting the whole of the Virgin's life, are in the sacristy of the church of Tasco.

Michael Angelo of Battle Scenes. The painter Cerquozzi, a native of Rome (fl. 1600–1660), famous for his battle-pieces and shipwrecks.

Michael Angelo of Music. Johann Christoph von Glück, the German composer and conductor (fl. 1714–1787).

Michael Angelo of Sculptors. (1) Pierre Puget, a French sculptor (fl. 1623–1694). (2) Réné Michael Slodtz (fl. 1705–1764).

Michael Angelo Titmarsh. (Pseud.) William Makepeace Thackeray, English novelist and humorist (1811–1863).

Michaelmas Day. September 29. One of the four English quarter-days for the payment of rent.

Michael's Chair, St. The projecting stone lantern of a tower on St. Michael's Mount, Cornwall.

Michal, in the satire of "Absalom and Achitophel," by Dryden and Tate, is meant for Queen Catharine, wife of Charles II. As Charles II. is called David in the satire, and Michal was David's wife, the name is appropriate.

Michigan. This State derives its name from the lake, the Indian equivalent for "fish-weir" or "trap," which its shape suggested.

Miching Mallecho. A veiled rebuke; a bad deed probed by disguised means. To mich, or meech, means to skulk or shrink from sight. Michers are poachers or secret pilferers. *Malecho* is a Spanish word meaning an "evil action;" as a personified name it means a malefactor.

Mick. A term of reproach for an Irishman. It would seem to be a corruption of Mike, in its turn a nickname for Michael. A "mick" is a rowdy, a tough. We presume the name was first applied by some man, who, having in mind some particular ne'er-do-well Michael, likened his new acquaintance to him, calling him "a regular Mick."

Midas. In classic myth a Phrygian king, the son of Gordius and of Cybele. He was a pupil of Orpheus. The legend says that Bacchus granted his wish that whatever he touched might become gold, from which so great inconvenience ensued that he was glad to get himself relieved from the burden by washing, at the command of the god, in the river Pactolus, the sands of which became thenceforward productive of gold.

Middle Ages. A term which describes an epoch of no very definite period, but varies somewhat with almost every nation. Generally, it may be regarded as including a period of about one thousand years, or from the fifth to the end of the fifteenth century; or, if reckoned by events, as extending from the subversion of the Roman Empire, and the transfer of the Imperial dignity from Rome to Constantinople (A. D. 476), to the outbreak of the Reformation (A. D. 1520). Hallam, in his "History of the Middle Ages," says: "It is not possible to fix accurate limits to the Middle Ages; but though the ten centuries from the fifth to the fifteenth seem, in a general point of view, to constitute that period, a less arbitrary division was necessary to render the commencement and conclusion of an historical narrative satisfactory;" and he accordingly makes the period to extend "from the invasion of France by Clovis (A. D. 489) to that of Naples by Charles VIII. (1495)." For his purpose this might be advisable, but for common use there is little advantage in any such arbitrary restriction. The term must be accepted for convenience rather than precision, and to understand it as comprising one thousand years, from the end of the fifth to the beginning of the sixteenth century, is, for all ordinary purposes, sufficient.

Middle Kingdom, The. (Chinese, *Tchang-kooe.*) A name conferred on their country by the Chinese, who imagine that it is located in the middle of the earth.

Middle Passage. A term referring to the voyage across the Atlantic Ocean between the West Indies and Africa. It was once part of the nomenclature of the slave-trade.

Middlesex. (Pseud.) William Stevens Robinson, in the "Evening Post," New York.

Middle States. New York, New Jersey, Pennsylvania, and Delaware, in allusion to the fact that at the passage of the Constitution they were the central Commonwealths of the Federacy.

Midgard ("middle world"). In Scandinavian mythology the name given to the earth, as being between Asgard and Utgard.

Mid-Lent Sunday. *See* MOTHERING SUNDAY and PENNY-LOAF DAY.

Midlothian, Heart of. *See* HEART OF MIDLOTHIAN.

Midnight Judges. In the presidential election of 1800 the Federalists were defeated. In order to gain every possible advantage for their party, the Federalists in Congress constituted twenty-three new judgeships, although there was no necessity for such an increase. President John Adams was busy until after midnight on the last day of his term in signing judicial commissions, and the judges so commissioned were in contempt called "midnight judges."

Midnight Sun, Land of the. *See* LAND OF THE MIDNIGHT SUN.

Midsummer Day. June 24. One of the four quarter-days in England for the payment of rent.

Mignonette. (Pseud.) Emily H. Moore, *littérateur.*

Mike-apple. A fruit peculiar to New London County, Conn., where the legend as to its origin is common property. The Mike-apple, an amber-hued fruit, is peculiarly marked by a crimson red stain, varying in size and location, but always present, either on the skin or in the heart of the fruit. The parent tree of all those now so plentiful in the eastern part of the State originally stood on the farm of one Micah Rood, in the town of Franklin. When cut open, the red spot in the centre appears like a spot of blood. The legend runs to the effect that early in the eighteenth century a peddler, laden with costly wares, stopped at Rood's house one night; that the cupidity of the host was aroused, and that he stabbed the itinerant merchant to the heart, and buried him under the apple-tree in his orchard. The townsmen had no suspicion of the crime that had been committed in their midst, and Rood was never suspected. But the following year the blossoms of the apple-tree were splashed with red stains, and in the fall the hitherto mellow-skinned fruit bore a splash of blood-red color. The village children, as was their wont, begged for the windfalls, but the conscience-struck man bade them take of the best, saying that he wanted none of it, for the tree was cursed. The next year the same phenomenon appeared, and the now thoroughly terrified criminal declared openly that it was the peddler's blood, and by his own wild ravings first called the neighbors' attention to the matter. The story runs to the effect that Micah Rood remorsefully hanged himself to a bough of the self-same apple-tree under which he had buried the peddler. It should be remarked that the clot of blood does not affect the flavor of the fruit, which is one of the best early varieties. All Mike-trees are distinguished by blood-stained blossoms, and it is a part of the orthodox belief in this legend that the stain does not appear in the fruit from a grafted tree.

Mil. Military.

Milan Decree. The decree issued by Napoleon I., Dec. 27, 1807, at Milan, by which he declared the whole of the British dominions in a state of blockade, and forbade all countries trading in articles of British make.

Mileage Exposé. "On Dec. 22, 1848, Horace Greeley published a statement showing the distance by the shortest post-route from the residence of each member of Congress to Washington, the distance for which he received mileage, the amount paid him, and the excess over what he would have received on the basis of the shortest mail-route. The total of this excess for the Thirtieth Congress was $73,492.60, and the excess in miles was 183,031. Almost every Congressman had failed to make his journey as short as possible. Greeley's *exposé* caused considerable ill-feeling against him; its immediate effect was seen in the adoption of shorter routes by Congressmen in travelling, and several years later the rate of mileage was reduced one half, and constructive mileage was abolished by law." — BROWN AND STRAUSS.

Miles Pinkney. (Pseud.) Thomas Carre, English monk and religious writer (1600–1674).

Milky Way (the Galaxy). "This is that 'luminous zone or pathway, of singular whiteness, varying from four degrees to twenty degrees in width, which passes quite around the heavens. The Greeks called it Galaxy, on account of its color and appearance; the Latins, for the same reason, called it *Via Lactea*, or the Milky Way.'" — BURRITT. Astronomy develops the fact that this zone is composed of innumerable small stars, so many, indeed, that Dr. Herschel, with his best glasses, counted 558 stars in a single spot, without moving his telescope, and while he steadily gazed at one point, and the motion of the earth brought new ones to his telescopic vision, there passed in one quarter of an hour no less than 116,000 stars, and on another occasion, in forty-one minutes, no less than 258,000 stars. It is also a belief of astronomers that all the stars of the universe are arranged in clusters, or groups, which are called nebula, or starry systems, each of which contains many thousands of stars. Our sun, it is also said, belongs to the nebula of the Milky Way, and although at such an immense distance from other planets in that zone, is considered as near to any one of them as they are to one another. Of the character, motions, and peculiarities of the innumerable stars that form the Milky Way, little or nothing is known, although it appears that they are unequally dispersed and arranged into separate clusters; that various changes are taking place among the nebula, some increasing by accessions of stars, and others growing smaller by dissolution. More than 2,500 nebula have been observed.

Mill. (Pseud.) William M. Butler, in the Rochester "Post-Express."

Mill-boy of the Slashes. A nickname given to Henry Clay (fl. 1777–1852), the American orator and statesman, who was born near a place locally known as "The Slashes," in Hanover County, Va., where there was a mill to which he was often sent on errands when a boy.

Millie Mayfield. (Pseud.) M. S. S. Holmes, American author.

Millie Sackett. The stage-name of Mrs. Pike.

Millie Tournier. The stage-name of Mrs. Orinifo.

Milord Anglais. This French phrase has been greatly ridiculed in England. The "milord," however, is but the Celtic word "milwr," still in use in Brittany in the sense of "a gentleman, a cavalier." It is pronounced "milôr." It is allied to the Latin *miles*, a knight or soldier.

Milton of Germany. Friedrich G. Klöpstock (fl. 1724–1803), author of "The Messiah."

Mimir. The Norse god of wisdom, and most celebrated of the giants. The Vaner, with whom he was left as a hostage, cut off his head. Odin embalmed it by his magic art, pronounced over it mystic runes, and ever after consulted it on critical occasions.

Mimir's Well. In Norse mythology a well in which all wisdom lay concealed. It was at the root of the celestial ash-tree. Mimir drank thereof from the horn Gjallar. Odin gave one of his eyes to be permitted to drink of its waters, and the draught made him the wisest of the gods.

Min. Mineralogy; minute.

Minden Boys. An honorable nickname for the English Twentieth Regiment, because of its gallantry at the battle of Minden. It is also known as KINGSLEY'S STAND.

Minerva. In classic myth the name of a Roman goddess, by some identified with the Greek Athene, whom she greatly resembled. All the affairs of men were under her protection, and she was invoked alike by poets, painters, teachers, physicians, and all kinds of craftsmen. She had a temple at Rome on the Capitoline Hill, and another on the Aventine Hill.

Minerva Guernsey. The stage-name of Mrs. O. A. King.

Miniature Lake George. Greenwood Lake, situated in New York and New Jersey, forty miles N. N. W. of New York City. It is a favorite resort of health-seekers and sportsmen.

Minn. Minnesota.

Minnesota. The name of this State is an Indian word, meaning "whitish" or "sky-colored water."

Minnie Bertram. The stage-name of Mrs. Edward J. Cross.

Minnie Conway. The stage-name and also the maiden name of Mrs. Osmond Tearle.

Minnie Hauk. The professional name of Baroness von Hesse-Wartegg, the famous prima-donna.

Minnie Maddern. The stage-name of Mrs. Legrand White, *née* Davy.

Minnie Mayflower. (Pseud.) Mrs. Catherine Stratton Ladd.

Minnie McNeil. The stage-name of Mrs. Peter Dayton.

Minnie Myrtle. (Pseud.) The pen-name of Miss Minnie Theresa Dyer, who later became the wife of "Joaquin" Miller (*q. v.*).

Minnie Oscar Gray. The stage-name of Mrs. W. T. Stephens.

Minnie Palmer. The stage-name of Mrs. John R. Rogers.

Minos. The name of two mythological kings of Crete: (1) The son of Jupiter and Europa; (2) Grandson of the former and son of Lycastus and Ida. To the latter the "Laws of Midas" are described.

Minotaur. One of the most repulsive conceptions of the Grecian mythology was the son of Pasiphae and a bull, for which she had conceived a passion. It was half man, half bull, — a man with a bull's head. Minos confined him in the Cnossian Labyrinth, and there fed him with youths and maidens whom Athens supplied as an annual tribute.

Min. Plen. Minister Plenipotentiary.

Mintwood. (Pseud.) Miss Mary A. E. Wager, *littérateur.*

Mirabile dictu. (Lat.) Wonderful to tell.

Mirabile visu. (Lat.) Wonderful to be seen.

Mirabilia. (Lat.) Wonders.

Miracle Play. *See* PASSION PLAY.

Mir. for Mag. Mirror for magistrates.

Miriam. (Pseud.) Miss Maggie E. Heath, a well-known contributor to the Southern press.

Mise en scène. (Fr.) The getting up for the stage, or the putting in preparation for it.

Miss. Mississippi.

Miss Ada Clare. (Pseud.) Mrs. Jane McElhinney.

Miss Grundy. The journalistic pen-name of Miss Austine Snead, a society correspondent of the Washington "Post," who died in 1888.

Missing Link. The link between the monkey and man. According to Darwin, the present host of animal life began from a few elemental forms, which developed, and by natural selection propagated certain types of animals, while others less suited to the battle of life died out. Thus, beginning with the larvæ of ascidians (a marine mollusk), we get by development to fish lowly organized (as the lancelet), thence to ganoids and other fish, then to amphibians. From amphibians we get to birds and reptiles, and thence to mammals, among which comes the monkey, between which and man is a "Missing Link."

Mississippi. This State derives its name from the Natchez word for the great river forming its western border, which means "father of waters."

Mississippi Scheme. *See* LAW'S BUBBLE.

Miss Nancy. Applied to young men of affected speech and demeanor, and who ape superiority, walk gingerly, and dress effeminately. The allusion is to Miss Anna Oldfield, an actress who died in 1730. Her vanity was such that she desired on her death-bed that her remains should be laid "in state, dressed in a very fine Brussels lace head-dress, a holland shift with tucker and double ruffles of the same lace, new kid gloves, etc., etc." Pope alludes to her in the lines, —

"'Odious! in woollen? 't would a saint provoke,'
Were the last words that poor Narcissa spoke."

Miss Nancy King. A sobriquet fastened on William Rufus King.

Missouri. This State derives its name from the Indian word for the river, meaning "muddy water."

Missouri Compromise. The name generally given to an act of Congress passed in 1820, and intended to mollify the pro-slavery and anti-slavery parties, then struggling for national supremacy. By this act it was provided that Missouri should be admitted to the Union as a slaveholding State, but that slavery should never in the future be established in any State north of lat. 36° 30'.

Mistress of the Seas. The same as Sovereign of the Seas (*q. v.*).

Mistress of the World. Rome was anciently so called; for many centuries she was the recognized capital of Christendom.

Mit. (Ger.) With; as, *mit begleitung*, with an accompaniment. (Mus.)

Mithras. In Persian mythology a personification of the sun.

Mittens Willett. The stage-name of Mrs. Henry Aveling.

Mittimus. (Lat.) "We send." A warrant for the commitment of an offender.

Mjölnir. In Scandinavian mythology the name of Thor's celebrated hammer, a type of the thunderbolt. The word means "the crusher."

M. L. A. Mercantile Library Association.

Mlle. Mademoiselle.

MM. (1) Their Majesties. (2) Messieurs; Gentlemen. (3) Two thousand.

Mme. Madame.

M. M. S. Moravian Missionary Society.

M. M. S. S. *Massachusettensis Medicinæ Societatis Socius,* Fellow of the Massachusetts Medical Society.

Mn. Manganese.

M. N. A. S. Member of the National Academy of Sciences.

Mnemon. One of the signatures attributed to "Junius" (*q. v.*).

Mnemosyne. In classic myth the goddess of memory and the mother of the Nine Muses, whom she bore to Jupiter. The principal seat of her worship was at Eleutheræ, in Bœotia.

Mo. Molybdenum; Missouri; month.

Mod. Modern.

Moderado. (Span.) "A moderate." A conservative in politics.

Moderato. (Ital.) With moderation.

Moderato assai con melto sentimento. (Ital.) A very moderate degree of movement, with much feeling. (Mus.)

Moderator. One of the signatures commonly ascribed to Junius (*q. v.*).

Modern Antigone. Marie Thérèse Charlotte, Duchesse d'Angoulême, daughter of Louis XVI. (fl. 1778–1851). She received the nickname from her attachment for Louis XVIII., whose companion she was.

Modern Aristophanes. *See* ENGLISH ARISTOPHANES.

Modern Athens. (1) Edinburgh. It is the headquarters of learning in Scotland; as a literary town it is second only to London, and it is the seat of the supreme courts of Scotland. The good taste and culture of its people are marked. It contains a great university and many schools, and it is famed for the many distinguished men who have been born or who have resided there. Lastly, its topographical situation is very similar to that of its ancient namesake. (2) Boston, Mass. The city is famed alike for its institutions of learning and for the high order of the intelligence and culture of its citizens.

Modern Babylon. London. In point of size it is the greatest in the modern world, as Babylon is believed to have been of the ancient. But there is also an allusion in the term to the luxury and licentiousness common to both cities.

Modern Messalina. An epithet applied to Catherine II. of Russia (fl. 1729–1796), who, while a woman of great genius, was noted for her licentious character.

Modern Pythagorean. (Pseud.) Robert Macnish, M.D., LL.D., Scottish author (1802–1837).

Modern Rabelais. A title conferred on William Maguin (fl. 1794–1842), "the most remarkable magazine-writer of his time."

Modestus. The signature adopted by Sir William Draper in his newspaper controversy with "Junius."

Modjeska, Mme. The stage-name of Madame Charles Bozenta Chlapowsky, *née* Modrejewski.

Modoc. (Pseud.) J. E. P. Doyle, in the Cincinnati "Enquirer."

Modoc War. In 1872 an order was issued from Washington to remove the Modoc Indians from their lands on Lake Klamath, Ore., to a new reservation. They refused to go, and a body of United States troops were sent to coerce them into obedience. The Indians resisted, and maintained the war with vigor during the winter, and then retreated to an almost inaccessible region called the "lava beds." In 1873 they were surrounded, but not subdued. Demanding a conference, six members of the Peace Commission met the Indian chiefs, but in the midst of the deliberations the savages turned upon the white men, and shot in cold blood General Canby and Dr. Thomas, and dangerously wounded a third, Mr. Meacham. It was the 1st of June, 1873, before the United States troops under General Davis could force the Modocs to surrender. Captain Jack and other chiefs were courtmartialled, and executed in the following October.

Modus in rebus. (Lat.) "A measure in things." A medium in all things.

Modus operandi. (Lat.) The manner of operation; the way of setting about it.

Mœræ. In classic myth the Greek name for the Parcæ, or Fates.

Mohawk. (Pseud.) Dr. Nicholas Rowe, in the Chicago " Field."

Moina. (Pseud.) (1) Mrs. A. P. S. Dinnies, a charming poet of our own land and time. (2) Rev. A. J. Ryan.

Moke. In the United States a nickname for a negro; in England a nickname for a donkey.

Molière of Italy. Carlo Goldoni (fl. 1707–1793).

Molière of Spain. Leandro Fernandez Moratin (fl. 1760–1828).

Mollia tempora fandi. (Lat.) Occasions favorable for speaking.

Mollie Myrtle. (Pseud.) Miss Julia Bacon, a well-known American poet and story-writer.

Molly. *See* BETTY.

Molly Maguires. (1) "Stout, active young men dressed up in women's clothes, with faces blackened or otherwise disguised. This secret society was organized in 1843, to terrify the officials employed by Irish landlords to distrain for rent, either by grippers (bumbailiffs), process-servers, keepers, or drivers (persons who impound cattle till the rent is paid)." — W. S. TRENCH, *Realities of Irish Life.* (2) "A society in Pennsylvania, in character similar to the Ribbon Societies of Ireland, so far as they dealt with local agrarian troubles.

"'The Molly Maguires of the coal regions were composed almost entirely of Irishmen, and they kept the forms and practices of the secret societies of the old country. They combined against mine-owners and overseers as they had combined against landlords and agents, and from their combination came assassinations likewise, although with less excuse, — if there can be any excuse for assassination, — for they were not starved or evicted. Their crimes were worse, as their excuse was less; and the cruelty was as ferocious as the offence that caused it petty. In committing the murders the society took the course common in Ireland, and had it done by persons unknown in the section where the victims lived, and returns of courtesies were arranged by which murders were exchanged. They also pursued the same course in regard to terrorism of witnesses and to subornation of perjury, and consequently for a long time made trials a farce.' Murders were committed, and great quantities of coal and other property destroyed by incendiarism. In 1875 they terrorized over the whole country, threatened whole towns, and compelled the ordering out of the militia. On the withdrawal of the troops a series of the most cruel murders was committed, until at length, by strategy, ten of the members of the society were arrested for the crime. Notwithstanding the efforts made by the members, — who appeared to swear to an alibi, but were advised by counsel to go home and not be prosecuted for perjury, — all were convicted of murder, and on the 20th June, 1877, executed." — *Providence Journal.*

Moloch. The principal deity of the Ammonites, whose cult consisted chiefly of human sacrifices.

Molto. (Ital.) Very, extremely; as, *molto allegro*, very quick; *molto adagio*, extremely slow. (Mus.)

Momus. In classic myth a son of Night, and the personification of censure and mockery.

Mon ami. (Fr.) My friend.

Monarch of Moscow. The "great bell," weighing one hundred and ninety-three tons, twenty-one feet high, and twenty-one feet across.

Monarch of Mountains. Mont Blanc has been so named, though many other loftier peaks might fairly dispute the title.

Mon cher. (Fr.) My dear.

Monday, Blue, and Black. *See* BLUE MONDAY, BLACK MONDAY.

Monday Boanerges. Joseph Cook, the Boston lecturer, was so nicknamed by Judge Benjamin F. Burnham in his book "Elsmere Elsewhere." Mr. Cook was for several years famous for his Monday Lectures in Tremont Temple.

Monkey's Allowance. More kicks than pence. The allusion is to the monkeys carried about for show; they pick up the pence, but carry them to the master, who keeps "kicking" or ill-treating the poor creatures to urge them to incessant tricks.

Monk Lewis. Matthew Gregory Lewis (fl. 1773–1818); so named from his novel, "The Monk."

Monk of Westminster. Richard of Cirencester, the historian, who lived in the fourteenth century.

Monroe Doctrine. The name by which a famous maxim of United States policy, enunciated by James Monroe, President from 1817–1824, is popularly known. Briefly stated, it is "not to permit any European Power to interfere in restraining the progress of liberty in North or South America by exercising sovereignty on this continent." The foregoing sentiments were set forth in his seventh annual message, Dec. 2, 1823, as follows: "The citizens of the United States cherish sentiments the most friendly in favor of the liberty and happiness of their fellow-men on that side of the Atlantic. In the wars of the European Powers, in matters relating to themselves, we have never taken any part, nor does it comport with our policy to do so. It is only when our rights are invaded or seriously menaced that we resent injuries or make preparations for our defence. With the movements of this hemisphere we are of necessity more immediately concerned, and by causes which must be obvious to all enlightened and impartial observers. The political system of the allied Powers is essentially different in this respect from that of America. This difference proceeds from that which exists in their respective governments. And to the defence of our own, which has been achieved by the loss of so much blood and treasure, and matured by the wisdom of their most enlightened citizens, and under which we have enjoyed unexampled felicity, this whole nation is devoted. We owe it, therefore, to candor, and to the amicable relations existing between the United States and those Powers, to declare that we should consider any attempt on their part to extend their system to any portion of this hemisphere as dangerous to our peace and safety. With the existing colonies or dependencies of any European Power we have not interfered, and shall not interfere. But with the Governments who have declared their independence we have, on great consideration and on just principles, acknowledged we could not view any interposition for the purpose of oppressing them, or controlling in any other manner their destiny, by any European Power, in any other light than as the manifestation of an unfriendly disposition toward the United States."

Mons. Monsieur; Sir.

Monsieur. (1) Philippe, Duc d'Orléans (1674–1723), brother to Louis XIV., was called "Monsieur;" other gentlemen were only Monsieur this or that. (2) "Monsieur le Coadjuteur." Paul de Gondi, afterwards Cardinal de Retz (1614–1679). (3) "Monsieur le Duc." Henri Jules de Bourbon, eldest son of the Prince de Condé (1692–1740).

Monsieur de Paris. The popular sobriquet for the French public executioner. *See* JACK KETCH.

Monsieur le Grand. The Grand Equerry of France in the reign of Louis XIV.

Monsieur Prud'homme. A man of experience and great prudence, of estimable character and practical good sense.

Monsieur X. (Pseud.) Joseph Howard, New York journalist (b. 1842).

Mons Meg. "This was a large old-fashioned piece of ordnance, a great favorite with the Scottish common people; she was fabricated at Mons in Flanders, in the reign of James IV. or V. of Scotland. This gun figures frequently in the public accounts of the time, where we find charges for grease to grease Meg's mouth withal (to increase the loudness of the report), ribbons to deck her carriage, and pipes to play before her when she was brought from the castle to accompany the Scottish army on any distant expedition. After the Union there was much popular apprehension that the regalia of Scotland, and the subordinate palladium, Mons Meg, would be carried to England to complete the odious surrender of national independence. The regalia, sequestered from the sight of the public, were generally supposed to have been abstracted in this manner. As for Mons Meg, she remained in the Castle of Edinburgh till, by order of the Board of Ordnance, she was actually removed to Woolwich about 1757. The regalia, by special command, were brought forth from their place of concealment in 1818, and exposed to the view of the people, by whom they were looked upon with deep associations; and Mons Meg has been restored to the country where that which in every other place or situation was a mere mass of rusty iron becomes once more a curious monument of antiquity." — SCOTT.

Monster, The. An epithet popularly applied to Remick Williams, a villain who prowled about the London streets armed with a dirk, with which he shockingly wounded many women. He was tried and convicted July 8, 1790.

Mont. Montana.

Montaigne of Geneva. François de Bonnivard (1496–1570), a French historian, and the hero of Byron's "Prisoner of Chillon." *See* RABELAIS OF GENEVA.

Montana. A French word, — from *mont*, mountainous.

Montani semper liberi. (Lat.) Mountaineers are always freemen.

Monte Corno. *See* GREAT ROCK OF ITALY.

Montenegrins of Africa. The Abyssinians have been so named.

Montenegro of Africa. Abyssinia has been so named.

Montenegro of Sumatra. Acheen has been so named.

Montezuma's Realm. Mexico. Montezuma, the last emperor, was seized by Cortez, and compelled to acknowledge himself a vassal of Spain, 1519.

Montezuma's Watch. A curious stone, weighing twenty-four tons, of basaltic porphyry, in Mexico. This immense stone is cut into figures denoting the Mexican division of time, and may be termed their calendar.

Month of Sundays. A time that never comes; equivalent to Blue Moon (*q. v.*).

Months without an R. "It is unseasonable and unwholesome in all months that have not an *r* in their name to eat an oyster." — BUTLER, *Dyet's Dry Dinner.*

Montpellier of Australia. The city of Brisbane is so named on account of the salubrity of its climate.

Monumental City. Baltimore, Md. It contains the Washington and Battle monuments, and many others; whence its title.

Monumentum ære perennis. (Lat.) A monument more enduring than brass.

Moodus Noises. The local name for terrestrial disturbances occurring in the northern part of East Haddam, Conn., in and about the village of Moodus, at various times during the last two centuries. They were heard as recently as October, 1888. Just outside of the village streets the smooth flanks of a great hill, Mount Tom, rise into a rounded, grassy summit that grandly overlooks the distant Connecticut and miles of undulating country, field, and forest. The noises are produced in the mysterious interior of the mountain. The name "moodus" is a contraction of the old Indian word "Machimoodus" (place of noises), which was applied by them to the region about Mount Tom, the redmen believing that one of their mighty gods inhabited subterranean chambers in the hill, and that the unearthly sounds were the guttural expression of his displeasure. The noises were first heard by the white people as early as 1700, and they were no less awed by them than were the Indians. In 1729 the noises were most remarkable, and a description of them by local chroniclers may still be found in the annals of the river villages. A clergyman of that day writes wonderingly: "Whether there be anything diabolical in these things I know not; but this I know, that God Almighty is to be seen and trembled at." He adds: —

"I myself heard eight or ten sounds successively, and imitating small arms, in the space of five minutes. I have, I suppose, heard several hundred of them within twenty years, some more, some less, terrible. Oftentimes I have heard them to be coming down from the north, imitating slow thunder, until the sound came near, or right under, and then there seemed to be a breaking, like the noise of a cannon shot or severe thunder, which shakes the houses and all that is in them; they have, in a measure, ceased since that great earthquake [that of Lisbon]."

The noises are very peculiar. They begin oftenest with a deep, far-away quiver of the ground, which grows more profound and voluminous as the mighty pulsation rolls on through the caverns of earth, and the phenomenon culminates in a minute or so with a quick, sharp explosion, but at an unfathomable depth. Then, after a moment of subsidence, the mysterious shudder again vibrates through the giant frame of the hill, dying away in the hills and meadows eastward, and suggesting the sound of sullen waves breaking on a coast a great distance away. The sounds have been heard distinctly in Salem, an old witch-haunted town seven or eight miles distant, and so heavy have been the vibrations at times that window-glass jingled in all the wooden houses, the crockery rattled, and the metal sides of the bell in the village church belfry "sung" like a tuning-fork. The sounds were very weird and impressive when heard after nightfall by the superstitious folk of a hundred years ago, and they drew closer in a shuddering group about the billowing flame and smoke in their wide fire-places, and glanced affrightedly over their shoulders into the glowering dusk outside, fearful that the devil or an imp might be seen in the window making faces at them. The sounds were familiar occurrences, at irregular intervals, until early in the present century, when suddenly they ceased; and the story ran that an English necromancer, Dr. Steele, had unearthed a priceless carbuncle, which, imprisoned in Mount Tom, and groaning to be free, had been the cause of the noises, and that the rumbling would not be heard again until a new carbuncle had grown in the place of the old one.

Moon-cake Day (*Poh yueh shi Wo*). A great day for all loyal Chinamen. It falls on September 11 of each year. The festival lasts all day and night, and is celebrated by the eating of moon-cakes. These are supposed to be made in the shape of the moon, and are liberally mixed with seeds of various kinds. They are sold in packages by all the Chinese grocers in the various Chinese colonies in the United States at the rate of thirty cents per package, and the very poorest Chinaman in all Chinatown considers himself by religion bound to buy at least a single package. The Chinaman with a prosperous laundry buys from half a dozen to a dozen packages, and thus shows his great respect for the moon. But woe to any Chinaman born under the protection of the yellow dragon who does not eat, even if he cannot get a package, a single cake, vowing the while never-ending devotion to her lunar majesty! If he omits this tribute, the moon is sure to wreak vengeance on his head ere another moon-cake day comes around. So say all good Chinamen.

Moon Hoax. The "Moon Hoax" was published in the "Sun" of August 25, 26, 27, 28, 29, and 31, 1835. The full title of the series was: "Great Astronomical Discoveries lately made by Sir John Herschel, LL.D., F. R. S., etc., at the Cape of Good Hope;" and the articles purported to be extracts from and condensations of an account of those discoveries published in the Supplement to the July number of the Edinburgh "Journal of Science."

A little more than fifty years ago scientists were puzzled for a moment, journalists were un-duly excited, and the public minds of two continents were agitated by a marvellous tale of wonder, in the form of a literary hoax perpetrated by a young Englishman named Locke, and the editor of a popular magazine. Locke had been a reporter on the editorial staff of James Watson Webb's New York "Courier and Enquirer," and was, at the time we are considering, editor of the "Sun," the first "penny newspaper" ever issued from the press. . . . The publisher desired to have some new and startling feature for his journal to increase its circulation. Mr. Locke proposed, for a consideration, to prepare for it a sensational work of fiction that should have every semblance of truth, — in fact, a literary hoax. An agreement was made; and Lewis Gaylord Clark, then the editor of the "Knickerbocker Magazine," was called in for consultation. At that time the scientific world was much interested in the reports of remarkable discoveries made by Sir John Herschel at the Cape of Good Hope, with a newly constructed and powerful telescope. The Edinburgh "Scientific Journal" was then publishing full accounts of Herschel's astronomical discoveries at the Cape, and thinking men were prepared to accept as true almost any startling assertions of devotees of science, Locke and Clark devised the plan of a scientific romance, which Mr. Beach approved. Clarke agreed to furnish the *romance,* and Locke the *science.* The story was written with great care. It purported to be an account of Herschel's observations of the moon in the southern hemisphere. It declared that one great telescope (the construction of which was minutely described) brought the moon's surface within the apparent distance of eight miles of the earth, as seen with the naked eye. The topography of the satellite, its vegetation, and its animal life were all perceived with great clearness. Lofty mountains with rocky crags and peaks; magnificent foot-hills covered with large forest-trees, and valleys filled with rank verdure, delighted the eyes of astonished beholders. Strange-looking beasts and birds were seen, and the noblest inhabitants were specially revealed by the instrument. They were described as of fairly human form and feature, but in the general appearance of bats, having membranous wings with which they flitted about. The account of the habitations and the evident pursuits of these "man bats," and of the whole range of animated nature in our satellite, said to have been seen by Sir John, was given with so much graphic power and minuteness, and the telescope was described with such apparent scientific and mechanical accuracy, that the show of probability in every part of the narrative "deceived the very elect." The deception was more easily achieved by crediting the story to a supplement of the Edinburgh "Scientific Journal," an advanced copy (as alleged) having been received by the editor of the "Sun," and published as a "piece of interesting news." The wonderful narrative played upon the credulity and stimulated the speculations of scientific men everywhere. M. Arago, the eminent *savant,* proposed, in the French Academy, to send a deputation from that body to confer with the English astronomer at the Cape; and other scientific bodies in Europe were profoundly moved by the idea of the great discovery. Journalists everywhere were deceived. The New York "Daily Advertiser," one of the ablest of the "sixpenny" journals, declared that Sir John Herschel had "added a stock of knowledge to the present age that will immortalize his name, and place it high in the page of Science." The Albany "Advertiser" read, "with unspeakable emotions of pleasure and astonishment an article from the last Edinburgh 'Scientific Journal,' containing an account of the recent discoveries of Sir John Herschel at the Cape of Good Hope." Chagrined by the enterprise of the "Sun," an "obscure penny sheet" (as the large metropolitan newspapers described it), in getting the earliest copy of the "Supplement" alluded to, some newspapers resorted to positive lies as a covering for their mortification at being beaten in the strife for obtaining the earliest news by the despised little sheet. One otherwise respectable journal, piqued by the circumstances of the honor of having been the first to reveal the great event to our American people having been won by the "Sun," gravely assured its readers that it received the "Supplement" by the same mail, but was prevented from publishing the article on the day when it appeared in the "penny paper," only because of a "want of room." The newspapers throughout the country copied the article, and commented on it, some of them dishonestly withholding credit from the "Sun," leaving the inference that they had copied it from the famous "Supplement." Some of the grave religious papers made the "great discovery" a subject for pointed homilies on the "wonders of God's works more and more revealed to man." On the morning of the appearance of the article in the "Sun," the late Prof. James J. Mapes had occasion to start for Washington City on business. He had read and believed the marvellous story. He took a copy of the paper with him, and placed it in the hands of Professor Jones, of Georgetown College, to read in his presence. The learned professor read it with most absorbing interest and profound convictions of its truthfulness, until he came to some statements about the telescope which presented scientific impossibilities, when he dropped the paper and exclaimed, with tears starting from his eyes, "Oh, Professor Mapes, it's all a hoax! it's all a hoax!" The subject did not even become a "nine days' wonder." It was soon discovered that no such "Supplement" of the Edinburgh "Scientific Journal" had been issued, and that the whole story was a pure fiction. Locke was compelled to bear the honors and the penalties as sole author of the clever hoax, for it had been agreed that the hand of Clark should not be seen in the performance. The scientific men and the journalists who readily swallowed the bait never forgave Locke for this cruel infliction, for they were the butt of universal merriment for a long time. Their ire was unquenchable. Mr. Beach was satisfied with the result of the "conspiracy," for it gave the "Sun" a great business impetus. — LOSSING.

Moon of Bright Nights. A synonym for April; the moon of leaves, a synonym for May; the moon of strawberries is June; the moon of falling leaves is September; and the moon of snow-shoes is the synonym for November.

Moonrakers. A jocular nickname for the people of Wiltshire. The story goes that a woman of that county once took a hay-rake and tried to rake the moon from a river under the delusion that it was a cheese!

Moonshiners. Those who distil illicit whiskey and evade the payment of the government excise tax, their operations being carried on chiefly at night. The term arose in the mountains of North Carolina and Tennessee, where this practice is very common.

Moon's Men. Thieves or highwaymen, who ply their vocation by night.

Moral Gower. John Gower, the poet (fl. 1320–1402), is so named by Chaucer.

Morar. (Pseud.) Sir William A. Fraser, English writer.

Morceau. (Fr.) A morsel.

Mordente. (Ital.) A beat, or passing shake. (Mus.)

More majorum. (Lat.) After the manner of our ancestors.

More philosophico. (Lat.) After a philosophical manner.

More probato. (Lat.) After an approved manner.

More suo. (Lat.) After his own way.

Morey Letter. "About two weeks before the presidential election of 1880, a letter purporting to have been written by James A. Garfield, the Republican candidate, to H. L. Morey, of the Employers' Union, Lynn, Mass., was published. It was a short note relating to the Chinese question. It asserted the writer's belief that 'individuals or companies have the right to buy labor where they can get it the cheapest,' that our treaty with the Chinese Government should be 'religiously kept' until abrogated, and added that he was 'not prepared to say that it should be abrogated' just then. The letter appeared in a New York daily paper, and fac-similes were at once published in all the Democratic newspapers and circulated by Democratic campaign committees. It was thought that a large part of the labor vote of the country would be alienated from Garfield. Garfield at once declared the letter a forgery, but several prominent men familiar with his handwriting declared their belief in its authenticity. An employee of the paper that first published it was arrested on the charge of forging it, but the prosecution of the case was subsequently abandoned. In the judicial examination, however, evidence was produced to show that there was no such person as H. L. Morey, of Lynn. A witness that had sworn to the authenticity of the letter was subsequently convicted of perjury, and sentenced to eight years' imprisonment." — *Dictionary of American Politics.*

Morgan. *See* GOOD ENOUGH MORGAN, etc.

Morisonianism. The religious system of James Morison, the chief peculiarities being the doctrines of universal atonement, and the ability of man unaided to receive or reject the Gospel.

Morley, Mrs. A name assumed by Queen Anne of England in her private correspondence with Sarah, Duchess of Marlborough. *See* FREEMAN, MRS.

Morn. Morning.

Morna. (Pseud.) Mrs. Catherine Stratton Ladd.

Morning-Star of the Reformation. John Wycliffe (fl. 1324–1384).

Morpheus. In classic myth the son of Somnus (sleep), and the god of dreams. He is supposed to fashion the dreams that visit sleepers, and was depicted as an old man with wings, pouring somniferous vapor out of a vial or horn.

Mors. In classic myth the daughter of Erebus and Nox, and the personification of Death.

Mors omnibus communis. (Lat.) Death is common to all.

Morus Multicaulis Mania. The name popularly given to the wild spirit of speculation which passed over the United States in 1835, which led people by thousands to purchase and cultivate mulberry-trees, even at fabulous prices, with a view of rearing the silkworm. The craze soon died out, but not till heavy losses had been sustained. *Morus multicaulis* is the botanical name of the so-called Chinese mulberry-tree.

Mos., or mth. Months.

Mos majorum. (Lat.) The manner of ancestors.

Mos pro lege. (Lat.) Custom for law.

Mosso. (Ital.) Movement; as, *più mosso*, with more movement, quicker; *meno mosso*, slower. (Mus.)

Most Christian Doctor. (1) Jean de Gerson (fl. 1363–1429), an eminent and scholarly divine. (2) Nicholas de Cusa

(fl. 1401–1464), a German philosopher and a cardinal.

Most Christian King. (1) A title conferred by Pope Stephen III. in 755 on Pepin the Short of France. (2) The Council of Savonnières, in 859, conferred it on Charles the Bald. (3) Pope Paul II., in 1469, bestowed it on Louis XI. of France, since which it has been the peculiar title of the sovereigns of that country.

Most Erudite of the Romans. Marcus Terentius Varro, a man of universal erudition (fl. 116–27 B. C.).

Most Faithful Majesty. A title conferred by Pope Benedict XIV., in 1748, on John V. of Portugal.

Most Methodical Doctor. John Bassol (d. 1347), a famous Scotch philosopher, and a disciple of Duns Scotus.

Most Profound Doctor. Ægidius de Columna, a Schoolman of the fourteenth century, and a native of Sicily.

Most Resolute Doctor. Durand de St. Pourçain (d. 1332), a Dominican Schoolman and philosopher.

Mot d'ordre. (Fr.) Watchword.

Mot du guet. (Fr.) A watchword.

Motetto. (Ital.) A motet or piece of sacred music in several parts.

Mother and Head of all Churches. St. John Lateran of Rome. It occupies the site of the splendid palace of Plantius Lateranus, which escheated to the crown from treason, and was given to the Church by the Emperor Constantine. From the balcony of this church the Pope blesses the people of the whole world.

Mother Church of Christianity. The early Church at Jerusalem.

Mother Company. A nickname for the East India Company current among the peoples of India.

Mother Country. *See* OLD COUNTRY.

Mothering Sunday. Another name for Mid-Lent Sunday (*q. v.*), the fourth Sunday in Lent. The name arose from the fact that in the early days of Christianity it was considered incumbent on children to visit their parents and their mother church, taking with them some small offering. It is probable that this custom arose out of the pagan festival of Hilaria, celebrated by the Romans in honor of the mother of the gods on the Ides of March. During Lent a great quantity of bread, called "ayver" or "haver," consisting of oats, leavened and kneaded into large, thin, round cakes, which is placed over the fire in a griddle, is made and consumed in Westmoreland on Mothering Sunday. At Seville on this day there is a strange usage, evidently the relic of an ancient custom: "Children dressed very much after the fashion of English sweeps on May-day, wearing caps of gilt and colored paper and coats made of the crusade balls of the preceding year, parade the streets all day with drums and rattles, crying, ' Saw down the old woman !' At midnight parties of the commonalty parade the streets, knock at each door, repeat the same cries, and conclude by sawing in two the figure of an old woman representing Lent. This diversion is emblematical of Mid Lent." *See* PENNY-LOAF DAY.

Mother of Believers. Ayeshah, the second and favorite wife of Mahomet. Mahomet being the "Father of Believers," his wife of wives was "Mother of Believers."

Mother of Books. The city of Alexandria was so named, where was deposited the largest collection of books ever gathered together prior to the invention of printing.

Mother of Christian Missions. The city of Antioch. From thence (Acts xiii. 1–3) Paul started on his first missionary journey.

Mother of Cities. Balkh (the ancient Bactra), in Central Asia, so named by Orientals in allusion to its great antiquity. The modern town covers but a fraction of the surface embraced by the ancient city, the remains of which cover a space twenty miles in circumference.

Mother of Parliaments. England has been so named.

Mother of Presidents. Virginia is often so called. She has given six chief magistrates to the Union, — namely, Jefferson, Madison, Monroe, Tyler, Harrison, and Washington.

Mother of States. Virginia. Out of the original "Colony of Virginia" were formed Kentucky, Ohio, Indiana, Illinois, and West Virginia.

Mother of Teachers. Hamilton College, Clinton, N. Y., is so nicknamed.

Mother of the Camps. The Roman legions in Gaul so named Victoria, the mother of Victorinus, after the death of her son in 268.

Mother of the Gracchi. A hard, strong-minded, rigid woman, without one soft point or effeminate weakness.

Mother Shipton. Among the common people of England the name of Mother Shipton has for several centuries been regarded with awe, and by simple folk she is still looked on as a prophet. She flourished in the reign of bluff King Hal, and lived to a great age. She was born at Knaresborough, says tradition, and was generally regarded as a witch, the popular belief being that she sold her soul to the Evil One in return for the power of lifting the veil shrouding the future. But although universally believed to be a dealer in the black art, she died quietly in her bed near the village of Clifton, in Yorkshire, and in the churchyard near by a headstone bore this inscription:

> " Here lies she who never lied,
> Whose skill often has been tried;
> Her prophecies shall still survive,
> And ever keep her name alive."

It is said that each morning of her life was signalized by the utterance of some strange prediction of weal or woe to her neighbors or her country. Apart from the legendary flavor which is sure to surround such a unique character, enough is certainly known of her utterances to show that she at least must be credited with making a number of extremely accurate guesses at future events. Henry VIII., Elizabeth, and James I. did not disdain to consult her, either in person or by proxy. To Henry she foretold his suppression of the monasteries, his marriage with Anne Boleyn, Wolsey's downfall and death, and the fagot fires of Smithfield. To Elizabeth she predicted the execution of Mary Queen of Scots, and told of the coming to the throne of England of James VI., of Scotland, in the following couplet: —

> " From the cold North
> Every evil shall come forth."

In the reign of King James I. she sent word that —

> " Before the good folk of this kingdom be undone
> Shall Highgate Hill stand in the midst of London."

The superstitious king was so moved by this that he ordered all extension of the city by the addition of buildings on the north side to cease. To-day, if not

in the centre of the city, the march of
the brick and mortar brigade has already enclosed Highgate Hill, and the
close of the present century will doubtless see the second half of the prophecy
fulfilled. Among other oracular sayings Mother Shipton is credited with
the prediction that men would walk,
talk, and eat above the gilt ball and
cross of the dome of St. Paul's Cathedral, 404 feet from the ground. This
also came to pass in a manner unforeseen. For the purpose of a survey of
the city of London a scaffold and platform were actually erected a few years
ago over the cross of St. Paul's, on
which the topographical engineers spent
several days triangulating the chief
points. It is recorded that on the occasion of her last public utterance Mother
Shipton gave forth the following prediction, which has been thought to have
reference to the present century : —

" The time shall come when seas of blood
  Shall mingle with a greater flood;
  Great noise shall there be heard, great shouts
      and cries,
  And seas shall thunder louder than the skies.
  Then shall three lions fight with three, and
      bring
  Joy to a people, honor to a king.
  That fiery year as soon as o'er,
  Peace shall then be as before;
  Plenty shall everywhere be found,
  And men with swords shall plough the ground."

Motivo. (Ital.) The principal subject of an air or other musical composition.

Moto, or **Con moto.** (Ital.) With
agitation, anxiously. (Mus.)

Mot pour rire. (Fr.) A jest or joke.

Mots à double entente. (Fr.)
Words with a double meaning, usually
bad.

Mots d'argot. (Fr.) Slang; professional slang.

Motte Hall. (Pseud.) Miss Essie
B. Cheeseborough.

Mound City. St. Louis, Mo. In
the vicinity are many of those artificial
erections generally ascribed to the labors
of the "mound-builders."

Mountain City. (1) Another name
for Greenville, S. C. (2) Salt Lake City,
Utah.

Mountain Evangelist. The Rev.
Sam Jones, a Southern exhorter, who
conducted revival services throughout
the South in 1884-1886.

Mountain Meadow Massacre.
Early in September, 1857, a party of

immigrants, known as the "Arkansas
Company," arrived in Utah from the
East, on their way to California. A
Mormon named Laney, then living in
Utah, had given some food to two of
the immigrants, and this came to the
ears of certain leading "saints." For
this act Laney was murdered by an
"angel of death," at the instigation of
a Mormon "bishop." While the im-
migrant company were on their way
West, the Mormon leaders, among
whom were "Bishop" Dame, George
A. Smith (then first counsellor of the
church, and Brigham Young's right-
hand man), and another Mormon dignitary named Haight, as well as Lee,
conspired to massacre the entire outfit.
The "saints" claimed that immigrants
who had passed through Utah *en route*
to California had on several occasions
treated them and their people with indignities, had stolen or destroyed their
property, and had given the Mormons
just cause of complaint. The followers
of Young and his "bishops" and head
men had won over to their interests the
Indians residing near and among them,
and had sent out Mormon runners, who
gathered the Indians to the number of
several hundred to aid them in the butchery. Under the lead of the Mormons
the Indians attacked the immigrants,
killing some and wounding many more.
Then there was a lull in the fight. The
immigrants had defended themselves
behind their wagons and in pits thrown
up hastily in their camps. Then it was
urged among the Mormon leaders, who
held a council of war, that the immigrants be starved out; but the majority
were for carrying out orders, which
were said to have been dictated by
Brigham Young himself. It was arranged that there be a flag of truce, the
Indians to be kept quiet until this was
accomplished. The pilgrims responded
to this, and were advised by the Mormons to put away their arms in their
wagons and move to another point.
This they did. The road they were
to take was marked out, and the Mormons and Indians were secreted along
the trail behind rocks and within easy
range of the passing wagons. When
the unsuspecting company were driving
past they were halted by their Mormon
guides ; the Indians and the rest of the
Mormons rushed in upon them, and despatched them, man, woman, and child.
Only a few of the latter escaped. The

wagons of the victims were emptied, the bodies of the slain were stripped and left nude for the time, and later were thrown into shallow graves in a ravine near by. The remains were soon scented by the wolves, and were unearthed and made a horrid repast. When the military found the bones they gave them a decent burial, and some one carved on a rude stone raised over the graves, the words : " Vengeance is mine ! I will repay, saith the Lord." It was claimed by John D. Lee that Brigham Young knew of the massacre and permitted it.

Mountain of Fire. The Saracenic name for Mount Etna.

Mountain of Terrors. The Schreck-horn, in the Bernese Alps.

Mountain of Wealth. A fabulous El Dorado placed by the early Spanish adventurers in the country of the Esmeraldas, Brazil.

Mountain, Old Man of the. *See* OLD MAN OF THE MOUNTAIN.

Mount Caf. In Mohammedan mythology a mythical mountain supposed to encircle the earth like a ring.

Mourning, Field of. *See* FIELD OF MOURNING.

Mozis Addums. (Pseud.) Dr. George W. Bagby, who wrote the " Letters to Billy Ivins " in the " Southern Literary Messenger," a few years ago.

M. P. Member of Parliament; Member of Police.

M. P. C. Member of Parliament in Canada.

M. P. P. Member of Provincial Parliament.

M. P. S. Member of the Philological Society; Member of the Pharmaceutical Society.

M. Quad. (Pseud.) Charles B. Lewis, American *littérateur.*

M. R. Master of the Rolls.

Mr. Mister.

Mr. Absurd Knowless. A punning nickname conferred on Hansard Knollys, clergyman (1598–1691), by Cotton Mather, who denounced him as an Antinomian.

M. R. A. S. Member of the Royal Asiatic Society; Member of the Royal Academy of Science.

M. R. C. C. Member of the Royal College of Chemistry.

M. R. C. P. Member of the Royal College of Preceptors.

M. R. C. S. Member of the Royal College of Surgeons.

M. R. C. V. S. Member of the Royal College of Veterinary Surgeons.

M. R. G. S. Member of the Royal Geographical Society.

M. R. I. Member of the Royal Institution.

M. R. I. A. Member of the Royal Irish Academy.

Mr. Penn. (Pseud.) Stephen Colwell, American writer on trade and finance (1800–1871).

Mrs. Mistress.

Mrs. Alexander. (Pseud.) Mrs. Annie F. Hector, a well-known contemporary English novelist.

Mrs. Clara Moreton. (Pseud.) Mrs. Clara (Jessup) Moore, American novelist.

Mrs. Felix Summerly. (Pseud.) Mrs. Henry Cole, English writer (b. 1812).

Mrs. Freeman. (Pseud.) Sarah Jennings, Duchess of Marlborough (1660–1744).

Mrs. Gilman. (Pseud.) Hosea Ballou, American preacher (1771–1852).

Mrs. Glasse. (Pseud.) Sir John Hill, English writer and quack (1716–1775).

Mr. Shayback. (Pseud.) Rev. Samuel June Barrows.

Mrs. Horace Manners. (Pseud.) Algernon Charles Swinburne, in the London " Tatler."

Mrs. Josiah Allen, or Josiah Allen's Wife. (Pseud.) Marietta Holley.

M. R. S. L. Member of the Royal Society of Literature.

Mrs. Lovechild. (Pseud.) Lady Eleanor Fenn, story-writer for children (1744–1813).

Mrs. Manners. (Pseud.) Mrs. Cornelia H. (Bradley) Richards, American writer (b. 1822).

Mrs. Margaret Caudle. (Pseud.) Douglas W. Jerrold, English journalist and humorist (1803–1857).

Mrs. Markham. (Pseud.) Mrs. Elizabeth (Cartwright) Penrose, English writer of school histories (1790–1837).

Mrs. Mary Clavers. (Pseud.) Mrs. Caroline Matilda (Stansbury) Kirkland, American writer (1801–1864).

Mrs. Morley. (Pseud.) Queen Anne of England (1664–1714).

Mr. Sparrowgrass. (Pseud.) Frederick Swartwout Cozzens, American *littérateur* (1818–1869).

Mrs. Partington. (Pseud.) B. P. Shillaber, American humorous writer (b. 1814).

Mrs. Ramsbottom. (Pseud.) Theodore Edward Hook, English author and wit (1788–1841).

Mrs. Shayback. (Pseud.) Mrs. Catherine Isabel Barrows, wife of the foregoing.

M. S. Sacred to the memory (*Memoriæ Sacrum*); Master of the Sciences.

MS. *Manuscriptum.* Manuscript.

MSS. Manuscripts.

Mt. Mount, or mountain.

M. T. C. Marcus Tullius Cicero.

M. T. Jug. (Pseud.) Joseph Howard, New York journalist (b. 1842).

Mudo, El ("The Mute"). Juan Fernandez Ximenes Navarete (1526–1575) received this nickname from the fact that at the tender age of three a severe illness destroyed his hearing, and he also became dumb. It was happily said of this dumb artist by Lope de Vega that "no face he drew was dumb."

Mud-sill. Another name for the cross-ties used as a foundation for the rails in railroad building. In 1858 Senator Hammond, in referring to the working classes as the foundation of society and government, used the words, "the very mud-sill of society." The term spread, and was considered an equivalent for the working classes. During the civil war the Southerners, who had aristocratic tendencies, often referred to inhabitants of the manufacturing States of the North as "Northern mud-sills."

Mudsill Hammond. A sobriquet fastened on James Henry Hammond, American statesman (1807–1864). In March, 1858, he delivered a speech on the admission of Kansas, which gave great offence at the North, and earned him his nickname.

Mug-house Riot. A disturbance in Salisbury Court, Fleet Street, London, July 24, 1716, between Whigs and Tories. The riot was quelled by the Guards, and five of the rioters were hanged.

Mugwumps. A nickname originated by the New York "Sun" during the Presidential campaign of 1884, and applied to the Independents (*q. v.*). The word is said to be of Indian origin, and to mean "great lord."

Mulla. The river Awbeg, an affluent of the Blackwater in Ireland. Spenser coined the term, he having resided in its vicinity for many years, during which his "Faerie Queene," "Astrophel," and "Colin Clout" were composed.

Mulligan Letters. Two series of letters between James G. Blaine and Warren Fisher on certain business transactions. In 1876 charges of corruption were made against the former, in connection with legislation favoring the Little Rock and Fort Smith Railroad. The House of Representatives, of which Mr. Blaine was a member, passed a resolution to investigate these matters. The famous letters had been penned by Mr. Blaine in relation to this matter, and had passed into the possession of one Mulligan, the whilom clerk of Fisher. Mulligan went to the capital at the request of the investigating committee. Blaine sought an interview with him, and obtained possession of the letters, then went before the committee with them and with an explanatory statement. This occurred just before the meeting of the National Republican Convention. During the sitting of the convention Mr. Blaine had a sunstroke, and the investigation was dropped. When Mr. Blaine became a candidate for the Presidency in 1884 the old charges were revived, and another series of Mulligan letters was published. The friends of the statesman stoutly asserted their inability to see anything dishonorable in either series, while his opponents loudly proclaimed them to be perfect proof of guilt. However this may be, it is certain that many of the sentences, apart from the context, have a doubtful sound, and during the campaign of 1884 they were industriously disseminated and became part of the political nomenclature of the day. *See* TATTOOED MAN.

Mulmutine Laws. The code of Dunvallo Mulmutius, sixteenth king of the Britons (about B. C. 400). This code was translated by Gildas from British into Latin, and by Alfred into English. The Mulmutine laws obtained in this country till the conquest.

Multa docet fames. (Lat.) Hunger teaches many things.

Multum in parvo. (Lat.) "Much in little." A great deal in a small compass.

Mundane Era. Alexander fixed the Creation of the world at 5502 B. C. This reckoning remained in force till A. D. 284 (Alexandrian era 5786) but in 285 ten years were subtracted, and 5787 became 5786, to agree with the mundane era of Antioch, which dated the Creation at 5492 B. C.

Mundus edibilis. (Lat.) "The world eatable." All things in the world that are good for food.

Mundus vult decipi. (Lat.) The world wishes to be deceived.

Muni Tell. (Pseud.) Mrs. Alice McClure Griffin, an American poet.

Munkacszy. The professional name of the painter, whose real name is Michael Lieb, derived from the village of Munkacz, in Hungary, where he was born.

Murat of Russia. Michael Miloradowitch (fl. 1770–1820).

Murderers' Bible. A copy of the Scriptures issued in 1801, and so named from an error in Jude 16, the word "murderers" appearing instead of "murmurers."

Murim ("memory"). In Scandinavian mythology one of Odin's ravens. *See* HUGIN.

Murio-Celli, Mme. The professional name of Madame Ravin d'Elpeux.

Murray. (Pseud.) Robert Saunders, English writer (1727–1783).

Murray Hill. The fashionable locality of New York, answering to the London Belgravia (*q. v.*).

Mus. B. Bachelor of Music.

Mus. D. Doctor of Music.

Muses, The. In classic myth divinities to whom was ascribed the power of inspiring song, and who were supposed to look with especial favor on poets and musicians. Their names were Clio, Euterpe, Thalia, Melpomene, Terpsichore, Erato, Polyhymnia, Urania, and Calliope,— nine in all. The most widely spread account makes them the daughters of Zeus by Mnemosyne.

Mushroomopolis. Kansas City, Mo.

Music of the Spheres. The notion that the motions of the solar system must create harmonious sounds is as old as the classics. Among modern poets Shakspeare and Milton have most beautifully voiced this idea. The theory seems to have been that the daily progression of the planets must create sounds; and as each orb moves at stated speed the combined songs must harmonize.

Muspelheim. In Scandinavian mythology the realm of fire and heat. At Ragnarok, Sartur will bring flames from it and set fire to the universe.

Muss. A colloquial word, meaning "to throw into confusion, to muddle, to litter." As a noun it signifies rubbish, dirt, etc. A third meaning makes it do duty for a fight, a fracas, or a quarrel.

Mutanda. (Lat.) Things to be altered.

Mutatio elenchi. (Lat.) A changing of the argument,— commonly a sophistical one.

Mutatis mutandis. (Lat.) The necessary changes being made.

Mutato nomine. (Lat.) The name being changed.

Mutton. A courtesan, sometimes called a "laced mutton." "Mutton Lane," in Clerkenwell, was so called because it was a *suburra*, or quarter for harlots. The courtesan was called a "mutton" even in the reign of Henry III., for Bracton speaks of them as *oves*.

Mutton-eating King. Charles II. of England. The Earl of Rochester composed the following mock epitaph:

> "Here lies our mutton-eating king,
> Whose word no man relies on ;
> He never said a foolish thing,
> And never did a wise one."

Muttons. *See* REVENONS À NOS MOUTONS.

Mutual Admiration Society. A Parisian nickname popularly given to the Société d'Observation Médicale.

M. W. Most Worthy ; Most Worshipful.

M. W. G. C. P. Most Worthy Grand Chief Patriarch.

M. W. G. M. Most Worthy Grand Master ; Most Worshipful Grand Master.

M. W. P. Most Worthy Patriarch.

M. W. S. Member of the Wernerian Society.

My Eye and Betty Martin. The origin of this phrase is generally attributed to the mistake of a sailor, who, going into a Roman Catholic church, heard the words of a Latin prayer commencing *O mihi Beate Martine*, which he converted into "O my eye, Betty Martin." This story is most improbable, for there is no such public formulary in existence in the Roman Church; and supposing there were, the pronunciation would be "O mēhē beātay martenay," which has not the slightest resemblance to the other phrase. The following very much more probable origin was told to the boys at Shrewsbury School by Dr. Butler (afterward Bishop of Lichfield), when he was head-master: A number of gypsies were taken before a magistrate by a constable, who complained principally of a woman named Betty Martin. After he had given his evidence the woman rushed excitedly to him in court, and gave him a tremendous blow in the face, saying that what he had been telling the magistrate was "all my eye." The man's eye was fearfully discolored by the blow, and ever after he was teased by the populace calling after him, "My eye and Betty Martin."

Mylitta. The Greek name for Beltis, a goddess worshipped in Babylonia, Assyria, and Persia, corresponding to the Greek Aphrodite.

Mynheer Closh. A nickname for a Dutchman, akin to the Nicholas Frog of the French or the John Bull of the English.

My Pen. (Pseud.) Caleb Dunn, in "Puck."

Myra. (Pseud.) Mrs. A. W. Fairbanks, European correspondent of the Cleveland "Herald."

My Stars and Garters! This old lady's expletive was formerly much commoner than now. It is clearly an allusion to the star and garter of the order of knighthood, which is, of course, highly prized. Hence, when an old lady swore by her stars and garters, it is fair to presume that she swore by the most prized of her possessions.

Mysterious Bachelor. Dana Board man Clark.

Mystery. (Pseud.) Mrs. M. E. J. Westmoreland, a well-known Southern writer.

Mystical Babylon. A name of reproach by which Protestants often refer to the Roman Catholic Church. The term is taken from the 17th and 18th chapters of Revelation, where Saint John foretells the speedy overthrow of a world-power, which he likens to Babylon, once mighty, but now ruinous and desolate.

Myth. Mythology.

My Uncle. The term "uncle's," as applied to a pawnbroker's shop, is said to be a pun on the Latin word *uncus*, a hook. Pawnbrokers employed a hook to lift articles pawned before spouts were adopted. "Gone to uncus," therefore, is exactly tantamount to the modern phrase "up the spout." In French the concierge of a prison is called uncle, because the prisoners are "kept there in pawn" by government. In the seventeenth century a usurer was called "my uncle" in the Walloon provinces, because of his near connection with the spendthrifts, called, in Latin, *nepotes*, nephews.

N.

N. Nitrogen; north; number; noun; neuter; note.

N. A. North America.

Na. Natrium, or sodium.

Naboth's Vineyard. A fanciful title given by Charles Reade, the English novelist, to his house at Knightsbridge, London. The property consisted of a very pleasant dwelling situated on a lot running back to Hyde Park, and called by the late Lord Lytton the pleasantest house in London.

"Charles Reade lived there for many years, and it was the attempt of a so-called improve-

ment company to acquire the property which precipitated the memorable campaign which he conducted in Parliament and in print, and which resulted in the preservation of his pleasant home. It was in the heat of this struggle that he painted the name of Naboth's Vineyard on the property, although he was very much more fortunate than the Scriptural Naboth in saving his substance from the speculative Ahabs who assailed it."

Nadab, in Dryden's satire of "Absalom and Achitophel," is meant for Lord Howard, of Esrick or Escrick, a profligate who laid claim to great piety. Nadab offered incense with strange fire, and was slain by the Lord (Lev. x. 2):

and Lord Howard, while imprisoned in the Tower, is said to have mixed the consecrated wafer with a compound of roasted apples and sugar, called lamb's wool.

Naga. In Hindu mythology deified serpents, sons of Muni Kasyapa and of his wife Kadru; their king or ruler is Sesha, the sacred serpent of Vishnu.

Naglfar. In Scandinavian mythology a ship built by the giants out of dead men's nails. At Ragnarok the giants will embark on it to offer battle to the gods.

Nag's Head Consecration. *See* NAG'S HEAD STORY.

Nag's Head Story. Shortly after the consecration of Matthew Parker as Archbishop of Canterbury at Lambeth Palace by Bishops Barlow, Coverdale, Scory, and Hodgkins, in 1559, the Romish pamphleteers asserted that Parker and others had been consecrated at the Nag's Head Tavern, Cheapside, by Bishop Scory. But Bishop Burnet effectually proved the falsity of this "Nag's Head Story."

Nah. Nahum.

Naiads. In classic myth nymphs of the fresh-water lakes, rivers, and fountains. They were believed to possess the power of divination; hence soothsayers are sometimes called νυμφόληπτοι, "seized by the nymph."

Naïveté. Ingenuousness; simplicity.

Naked Truth. The fable says that Truth and Falsehood went bathing; Falsehood came first out of the water, and dressed herself in Truth's garments. Truth, unwilling to take those of Falsehood, went naked.

Namby-Pamby. This was Pope's nickname for Ambrose Phillips, the English poet and dramatist (1671–1749). The term is now a well-established English word, and thousands of persons use it without suspecting its origin.

Nameless City. Ancient Rome. This city possessed a name of much greater antiquity and of mysterious meaning, which it was death to pronounce, believed to have been Valentia, subsequently turned into the Greek Ρώμη, Rome.

N. Amer. North America.

Nanna. In Scandinavian mythology the wife of Baldur, the summer god, famed for her fidelity and piety.

Nanny-goats. The Twenty-third Welsh Fusiliers are so dubbed from the fact that "a goat always marches at the head of the regiment, a new one being presented every year in the name of the Queen."

Nap. Napoleon; Napoléonic.

Napier's Bones. Baron Napier and Mr. Henry Briggs, within a few years of each other, invented and perfected the indexes of the ratio of numbers, 1614–1618. The method of computing by the help of marked pieces of ivory was invented about the same time, and hence they were nicknamed "Napier's Bones."

Napoleon of Africa. Mirambo was the chief of a small district in East Africa, near Lake Tanganyika. For fifteen years he was the terror of the country for miles around, and many were the startling stories told of his prowess and daring. Stanley nicknamed him the "Napoleon of Africa." In general he was a good friend to the whites. He died in 1885.

Napoleon of Finance. Ferdinand Ward, a Wall-Street speculator, whose gigantic swindling operations astonished the moneyed world in 1884–1885.

Napoleon of Mexico. A sobriquet of Augusto Iturbide, Emperor of Mexico (fl. 1784–1824).

Napoleon of Oratory. W. E. Gladstone.

Napoleon of Peace. A sobriquet conferred on Louis Philippe, king of the French. During his reign (1830–1848) France made vast strides in the arts and industries.

Napoleon of the Drama. Alfred Bunn, lessee of Drury Lane Theatre (1819-1826), was so called; and so was Robert William Elliston, his predecessor (1774-1826, d. 1831).

Napoleon of the Indian Race. So Gen. O. O. Howard named Chief Joseph, of the Nez Percés Indian tribe.

Naraka. The hell of the Hindu system of mythology. The Purâna names twenty-eight divisions of Naraka, besides which, we are told, "there are hundreds and thousands of others in which sinners pay the penalty of their crimes."

Narcissa. The character of this name in Young's "Night Thoughts." was drawn from Elizabeth Lee, his stepdaughter.

Narcissus. In classic myth son of the river-god Cephissus and of the nymph Liriope, of Thespiæ in Bœotia. He was of extraordinary beauty, of which he was inordinately vain, and was punished by Nemesis by being made to fall in love with himself on seeing the reflection of his face in a fountain. He died from the excess of his passion, and on the spot where he fell sprang up the flower which bears his name.

Nard Almayne. The stage-name of Mrs. Nelson Decker, *née* Varley.

Narrowdale Noon. One o'clock P. M. The people living at the foot of the Narrowdale Hills, in Staffordshire, never see the sun for a quarter of the year. In summer-time it is one o'clock ere his disk appears over the summit. The phrase is colloquially used in the neighborhood to indicate something long deferred.

Nary Red. A contraction for "ne'er a red (cent)," alluding to the color of the copper cent.

In the course of a few weeks the new coin [the nickel cent] will be plentiful enough at par; the Spanish coins will go out of the hands of the brokers, just as they already have disappeared from ordinary circulation; and, as regards the old cents, there will be "nary red" to be seen, except such as will be found in the cabinets of coin collectors. — *Philadelphia Bulletin*.

N. A. S. National Academy of Sciences.

Nastrond. In Scandinavian mythology a pestilential swamp in the Norse hades, where the wicked will be punished in the future life.

Nat. Natural.

Natale solum. (Lat.) "Natal soil." One's native country.

Nath. Nathanael, or Nathaniel.

Nat. Hist. Natural History.

Natick Cobbler. Henry Wilson, American statesman (1812–1875). In 1840 he appeared in the political campaign as the supporter of William Henry Harrison, addressing more than sixty meetings, in which he was introduced as "The Natick Cobbler;" he followed the trade of shoemaking at the place named.

National Covenant. A bond of union drawn up at Edinburgh, in 1638, by the leading Presbyterian clergy, and signed by great numbers of persons in all walks of life. It embodied the Confession of Faith of 1580–1581, and was "binding on all who signed it to spare nothing which might serve or save their religion." The immediate cause of this outburst of popular feeling was the attempt of Charles I. to introduce Episcopacy and the Service Book into Scotland. *See* SOLEMN LEAGUE AND COVENANT.

National Hotel Poisoning. A mysterious disease which affected the guests of the National Hotel, Washington, D. C., in January and March, 1857. A special commission reported that the sickness was due to sewer gas. The event caused a great sensation, the time being that of Buchanan's inauguration, and rumors were rife among the Southern contingent that an attempt had been made to poison the president elect and his friends.

National Razor. The guillotine was so called in the first French Revolution.

Nation of Gentlemen. The Scotch were so dubbed by George IV. because of the hearty reception they accorded him on his visit in 1822.

Nation of Shopkeepers. From an oration purporting to have been delivered by Samuel Adams at the State House in Philadelphia, August 1, 1776.

To found a great empire for the sole purpose of raising up a people of customers may at first sight appear a project fit only for a nation of shopkeepers. — ADAM SMITH, *Wealth of Nations.*

And what is true of a shopkeeper is true of a shopkeeping nation. — TUCKER, Dean of Gloucester.

Let Pitt then boast of his victory to his nation of shopkeepers. — BERTRAND BARÈRE.

Nat. Ord. Natural order.

Nat Spencer. (Pseud.) Robert Saunders, English writer (1727–1783).

Nat Turner's Rebellion. In August, 1831, a slave revolt broke out in Southampton County, Virginia. It was led by Nat Turner, who believed himself inspired to do this, an eclipse of the sun in February of that year being the sign. The excitement of the supposed revelation, however, caused him to fall ill, and it was not until August that the design was executed. He and his fifty followers gave no quarter. The uprising was at once put down, however, and Turner was executed. About sixty whites and one hundred negroes lost their lives in the struggle.

Naut. Nautical.

Naut. Alm. Nautical Almanac.

Nb. Niobium.

N. B. North Britain; New Brunswick; North British. *Nota bene.* Mark well; take notice.

N. C. North Carolina.

N. E. New England; northeast.

Neapolitan Exile. Baron Poerio. One of the kings of Naples promised the people a constitution, but broke his word; whereupon a revolution broke out, and the baron, with many others, was imprisoned for many years in a dreadful dungeon near Naples. He was at length liberated and exiled to America, but compelled the captain to steer for Ireland, and landed at Cork, where he was well received.

Neb. Nebraska.

Nebo. A Babylonian deity, corresponding with the Greek Mercury and the Egyptian Thoth.

Nebraska. The name of this State is derived from the Indian *ne*, water, and *bras*, shallow, — " shallow water," — in reference to the Nebraska River, after which the State is named.

Nec bella nec puella. (Lat.) Neither beautiful nor a girl.

Ne cede malis. (Lat.) Yield not to misfortune.

Necessitas non habet legem. (Lat.) Necessity has no law.

Neck Verse. *See* BENEFIT OF CLERGY.

Nec pluribus impar. (Lat.) Not an unequal match for numbers.

Nec scire fas est omnia. (Lat.) It is not permitted to know all things.

Nectar. In classic myth the name given by the Greek poets and by the Romans to the beverage of the gods, their food being named ambrosia. But Sappho and Alcman reverse the order, and make nectar their food and ambrosia their drink.

Ned Buntline. (Pseud.) Edward Z. C. Judson, American novelist (1822–1886).

Née. (Fr.) Born.

Needs must when the Devil Drives. This proverb is of considerable antiquity. In " Johan the Husbande, Tyb his Wyfe, and Syr Jhan the Priest," printed by Rastall, 1533, it is mentioned as a proverb then current, in the following couplet: —

" There is a proverbe which trewe now preveth,
  He must nedes go that the dyvell dryveth."

Shakspeare uses it in " All 's Well that Ends Well," act i. sc. 3, where the clown says : —

" He must needs go that the devil drives."

Ne exeat. (Lat.) Let him not depart.

Nefasti dies. (Lat.) Days upon which no public business was transacted; also, unlucky days.

Ne fronti crede. (Lat.) Trust not to appearance.

Neh. Nehemiah.

n. e. i. *Non est inventus.* He is not found.

Nellie Amond. The stage-name of Mrs. S. W. Putnam.

Nellie Claire Ritchie. The stage-name of Mrs. Thomas C. Stephens.

Nellie Larkelle. The stage-name of Mrs. George W. Colligan (d. 1886).

Nellie Lingard. The stage-name of Mrs. F. M. Burbeck.

Nellie McHenry. The stage-name of Mrs. John Webster.

Nellie St. John. The stage-name of Mrs. Henry Van Auken.

nem. con., or **nem. diss.** *Nemine contradicente,* or *nemine dissentiente.* No one opposing; unanimously.

Nemean Lion. A lion of Argolis, slain by Hercules. In this word Shakspeare has preserved the correct accent :

" As hardy as the Nem'ean lion's nerve."
                              Hamlet, act i. sc. 5.

but Spenser incorrectly throws the accent on the second syllable, which is *e* short : —

" Into the great Neme'an lion's grove."

Nemesis. In classic myth daughter of Night, and the awful and mysterious avenger of wrong, who punishes and humbles haughty evil-doers in particular. Nemesis was originally " the personification of the moral feeling of right and a just fear of criminal actions, — in other words, of the conscience."

Nemesis. (1) One of the pen-names adopted by Junius. (2) James Neal, in the London press.

Nemine contradicente. (Lat.) " No one opposing." Without opposition; contracted into *nem. con.*

Nemine dissentiente. (Lat.) " No one dissenting." Without opposition; contracted into *nem. dis.*

Nemo. (Pseud.) Capt. Roland F. Coffin, an American writer of sea-stories (1836–1888).

Nemo me impune lacessit. (Lat.) " No one assaults me with impunity," — the motto of the Order of the Thistle.

Nemo mortalium omnibus horis sapit. (Lat.) No one is wise at all times.

Nemo repente fuit turpissimus. (Lat.) No man ever became a villain at once.

Nemo solus sapit. (Lat.) No one is wise alone.

Ne plus supra. (Lat.) Nothing higher than it.

Ne plus ultra. (Lat.) Nothing superior to it.

Neptune. In classic myth originally an ancient Roman god. When the Romans became a maritime power, and grew familiar with the mythology of the Greeks, they identified Neptune with the Grecian deity whom he most resembled. This was Poseidon, son of Cronos and of Rhea, and brother of Jupiter. On the partition of the universe among the sons of Cronos he obtained the sea as his portion, in the depths of which he had his palace, near Ægæ, in Eubœa.

Ne quid nimis. (Lat.) Pursue not an object too far; too much of one thing is good for nothing.

Nereids. In classic myth beautiful young maidens, the nymphs of the Mediterranean Sea as opposed to the Oceanides. They were fifty in number, and were daughters of Nereus and Doris.

Nereus. In classic myth a sea-god who ruled over the Mediterranean, and father of the Nereids.

Neri. *See* BIANCHI.

Nero, Golden House of. *See* GOLDEN HOUSE OF NERO.

Nero of the North. Christian II. of Denmark (fl. 1480–1559).

Nessus. In classic myth a centaur who, for offering violence to Dejanira, was slain by Hercules with a poisoned arrow.

Nessus's Shirt. Nessos (in Latin, *Nessus*), the centaur, carried the wife of Hercules over a river, and attempting to run away with her was shot by Hercules. As the centaur was dying, he told Dejanira that if she steeped in his blood her husband's shirt, she would secure his love forever. This she did; but when Hercules put the shirt on, his body suffered such agony that he rushed to Mount Œta, collected together a pile of wood, set it on fire, and rushing into the midst of the flames was burned to death.

Nestor. In classic mythology a Greek hero, who took part in the Trojan war, and famed for his justice, bravery, wisdom, and eloquence.

Nestor. (Pseud.) Sir Richard Steele, English essayist and dramatist (1671–1729).

Nestor Ironside. The pen-name of Sir Richard Steele, in the "Guardian" (1671–1729).

Nestor of English Scholarship. Dr. Kennedy (d. 1889), Professor of Greek at Cambridge.

Nestor of Europe. Leopold, King of Belgium (fl. 1790–1865).

Nestor of the Chemical Revolution. Lavoisier thus named Dr. Black (fl. 1728–1799).

Ne sutor ultra crepidam. (Lat.) Let the shoemaker stick to his last.

Ne tentes, aut perfice. (Lat.) Attempt not, or accomplish thoroughly.

Neth. Netherlands.

Netta Guion. The stage-name of Miss Elizabeth A. Cortelyou. There is also a Netta Guion, who was some time attached to Wallack's Theatre, in New York, but her family and professional names are identical, and should not be confused with the above.

Nettie Neale. (Pseud.) Miss Maggie E. Heath, a well-known contributor to the Southern press.

Neut. Neuter (gender).

Neutral Ground. A space between the Spanish lines and Gibraltar.

Nev. Nevada.

Nevada. The name of this State is a Spanish word, meaning "snow-covered," having reference to the snowy summits of the Sierras.

Neville Temple. (Pseud.) Hon. Julian Charles Henry Fane, English poet (b. 1830).

New Albion. In 1578 Sir Francis Drake visited the northwest coast of North America, and gave the name of New Albion to what was then known as California. Subsequently the former name was restricted to the country now comprised within the boundaries of the States of Oregon and Washington.

New Alexandre Dumas. A name conferred on Paul Henri Féval (1817–1887), the famous French novelist, on account of the power and imagination displayed in his books.

New Amsterdam. The name conferred on the present city of New York by its original Dutch settlers.

New Atlantis, The. An island imagined by Lord Bacon, where was established a philosophical commonwealth bent on the cultivation of the natural sciences.

New Christians. Certain Jews of Portugal, in the fifteenth century, who yielded to compulsion, and suffered themselves to be baptized, but in secret observed the Mosaic ceremonies.

New Connecticut. A nickname for the Western Reserve (*q. v.*).

New Departure. A term originating with Clement C. Vallandigham, the Ohio Democrat, shortly after the close of the civil war, when he advised his fellow Democrats to cease obstructing the Republican measures for reconstructing the States lately in rebellion. The term was soon caught up, and became current in a variety of ways.

New Dress-improver. A nickname conferred by the London " World " upon Oscar Wilde, the æsthete, on account of his writings in 1884–1885 upon the absurdities of modern attire, both male and female.

New England Farmer. (Pseud.) John Lowell, LL.D., American lawyer and political writer (1769-1840).

New England States. The same as Eastern States (*q. v.*).

New France. Canada was formerly thus named, having been first colonized by Frenchmen.

Newgate Fringe. A beard worn only under the chin, as the hangman's rope is fastened round the neck of those about to be hanged. Sometimes called the " Newgate Frill," and sometimes the "Tyburn Collar."

Newgate Knocker. A lock of hair, worn especially by costermongers, twisted towards the ear. It is supposed to remind one of the knocker on the prison door of Newgate. The *cow-lick* is a curl worn on the temples.

New Hampshire. This State was named after Hampshire, England.

New Hampshire Grants. The territory which now forms Vermont was claimed formerly by New Hampshire, which granted the land to settlers, whence the above name.

New Jersey. This State was named by one of the original proprietors, Sir George Carteret, after the island of Jersey, in the English Channel, of which he was sometime governor.

New Jerusalem. An allusion to the heavenly abode of the Redeemer. See the Book of Revelation.

New Learning. A term applied in the fifteenth and sixteenth centuries to the revival of the study of the Scriptures in the original tongues which contributed so greatly to the rise and spread of the Reformation.

New Lights. Religious revivalists in New England about the middle of the eighteenth century. George Whitefield (1714–1770), the Wesleyan, was one of their leading men, and it was his preaching in New England in 1770 which precipitated the long controversy between the conservative party and the Revivalists, or New Lights.

New M. New Mexico.

Newmarket of America. Monmouth Park Race-course, New Jersey.

New Mexico. The word " Mexico " is Aztec, meaning " habitation of the god of war."

New Moses. The later Greek writers thus styled Anastasius, a monk who dwelt on Mt. Sinai in the latter part of the seventh century.

New Netherlands. The collective name of the early Dutch settlements in what is now New York State.

New Orleans, Anniversary of the Battle of. This happens on January 8, and is a legal holiday in the State of Louisiana.

New Philosophy. Bacon's system was so named in the seventeenth century. It was propounded principally in his " Novum Organon," published 1620.

New Side. A party in the Presbyterian Church in America opposed to the " Old Side " party during the half century succeeding 1730. The " New Side " were those excluded from the reconstructed Synod of Philadelphia. *See* OLD SIDE.

New Sweden. The former name of the territory lying between the English colony of Virginia and the Dutch colony called New Netherlands. The Swedes founded a settlement here in 1627.

New Test., or **N. T.** New Testament.

Newton of Harmony. Jean Philippe Rameau (fl. 1683-1784) was so named. He wrote a " Dissertation on the Principles of Harmony."

New World, The. The Western Hemisphere. This name is of very early origin; for Ferdinand inscribed on the tomb of Columbus, "To Castile and to Leon Columbus gave a new world."

New World which is the Old. America, though the last to be discovered and peopled, is probably, geologically speaking, the oldest of the continents. The phrase occurs in Tennyson's poem "Locksley Hall."

New Year's Day. The practice of keeping holiday on the first day of the New Year is world-wide and of very ancient origin. Among the nations of antiquity it generally prevailed; and Egyptians, Persians, Hindus, Jews, Romans, Chinese, and Mohammedans were in accord in making it a day of special note in their calendars, though they differed as to the time from which they reckoned the beginning of the year. And as different nations have varied as to the commencement of the year, so have they as to the usages with which they commemorate its recurrence. The Jews regard it as the day on which God holds judgment, and also as the anniversary of the day on which Adam was created. Among the Romans, in the time of Numa, the day was dedicated to Janus, the double-faced deity, who faced the future while he looked back upon the past. The Romans offered him a cake of sifted meal, with incense, salt, and wine. They also did something in the way of their art or calling to begin the year industriously, that they might have good fortune through it. On this day, too, the magistrates went in procession to the Capitol, where they sacrificed to Jupiter; and as the people met and saluted in the street, they passed the mutual greeting, "Annum novum faustum felicemque tibi." "The old Roman year began in March," says M'Clintock; "and on the first day of that month the festival Ancylia was celebrated, when the 'salii,' or priests of Mars, carried the sacred shield in procession through the city, and the people spent the day in feasting and rejoicing. The Romans counted it lucky to begin any new enterprise or to enter upon any new office on New Year's Day. The same sacredness was attached to the first day of the year after the change took place in the Roman calendar that made January the commencing month instead of March; and Pliny tells us that on the 1st of January people wished each other health and prosperity, and sent presents to their friends. It was accounted a public holiday, and games were celebrated in the Campus Martius. The people gave themselves up to riotous excess, and various kinds of heathen superstition. The first Christian emperors kept up the custom, though it tolerated and afforded the opportunity for idolatrous rites. The Church, however, saw itself finally obliged to condemn these, prohibited Christians from joining in the social celebration, but ended by making it a religious festival. This principle was gradually adopted in the practice of the Western Church; and three days of penitence and fasting were opposed to the pagan celebration of January, until, the time being designated, the festival of Christ's circumcision was transferred to this season (the first day of January being the eighth day after the nativity), when a Jewish rite was opposed to the Pagan observances, and its reference to the circumcision of the heart by repentence, to heathen revelry." "On New Year's Day among the Druids was performed the famous ceremony of cutting the mistletoe. Beneath the oak where it grew preparations were made for a banquet and sacrifices, and for the first time two white bulls were tied by the horns. Then came one of the Druids, clothed in white, mounted the tree, and cut off the mistletoe with a golden sickle, receiving it into a white sagum, or cloak, laid over his hand. The sacrifices were next commenced, and prayers were offered to God to send a blessing upon his own gift, while the plant was supposed to bestow fertility on man and beast, and to be a specific against all sorts of poisons." The English New-Year superstitions are many and curious. Thus we are told that the first person to enter the house on a New Year's morning must be a man. Many Holderness folks tell some little chap to be ready to come in so soon as the old year is dead, and so secure good luck to the household. When the master enters his house for the first time in the new year, he must take something in which he did not take out. "A Hull friend told me he always emptied his pockets before he left home on New Year's morning, and put in some money and bread, which he procured at his mother's, and so reached his home armed with the necessaries of life. Some people place a sixpence on the door-step on New Year's Eve, and so soon as the clock strikes it is brought in. N. B. This, I need hardly say, is done in the country! You must never go out on New Year's Day until some one has come in, is the rule in some parts." At present the ringing in of the New Year from the belfry of churches is the only open demonstration of joy at the recurrence of the anniversary. This is now a custom also in other countries. In France it still subsists, uneclipsed by the popular observance of Christmas. Inasmuch as the Puritan element has always been unfriendly to the existence, much more to the multiplication, of holidays, so Pagans and Christians have ever shown a disposition to regard "the first day of the first month" with solemn interest, and to celebrate its return with religious ceremony. At New-Year parties in the country in England the young men have the privilege of kissing any of the opposite sex they can get hold of. When "Sir Roger de Coverley" is danced, the chief guests are expected to dance with the cook and butler. All peacock feathers must be thrown out before New Year's Day, or else you will have ill luck, says the local proverb. New Year's Day was celebrated among the New York Dutch by the calls of the gentlemen on their lady friends; it is perhaps the only distinctly Dutch custom that afterward came into widespread use in the United States. New Year's Day, and the church festivals kept alike by the Dutch and the English, brought an intermission of labor to the New York slaves, who gathered in throngs to devote themselves to wild frolics. The Brooklyn fields were crowded with them on New Year's Day, at Easter, at Whitsuntide, or "Pfingster," as the Dutch called it, and on "San Claus Day," — the feast of St. Nicholas. New Year's Day is a legal holiday in all the States except Arkansas, Delaware, Georgia, Kentucky, Maine, Massachusetts, New Hampshire, North Carolina, Rhode Island, and South Carolina, although in these its observance is well-nigh universal. In certain country districts of England to this day, on both Christmas and New Year's Eves, when the clock begins to strike twelve, the doors — especially the front and back — are

opened, that the bad spirits may pass out and the good ones pass in, and immediately the clock has struck twelve the doors are shut, as it is said, "to keep the good spirits in." Among the Saxons, New Year's Day was given to festivities; and they reckoned their age by the number of merrymakings which they had attended. In Herrick's "Noble Numbers" are three songs, with choruses, for this day, illustrating the religious ceremony, and drawing a consolation therefrom: —

"Come thou, and gently touch the birth
Of him who's Lord of heaven and earth,
And softly handle him: y'ad need,
Because the pretty babe does bleed.
Poore pittied child! who from thy stall
Bring'st in thy blood a balm that shall
Be the best New Year's gift to all."

On the first day of the year, Humboldt informs us, the primitive Mexicans carefully adorned their temples and houses, and employed themselves in various religious ceremonies. One — which at first was peculiar to this season, though subsequently it became of more frequent occurrence — was the offering up to the gods of a human sacrifice. The wretched victim, after having been flayed alive, was carried to the pyramidal summit of the sacred edifice which was the scene of these barbarities, and after his heart had been torn out by a priest in presence of assembled thousands, his body was consumed to ashes by being placed on a blazing funeral-pile. On New Year's Eve, say English wiseacres, you must take pieces of money, bread, wood, and coal, and a little salt; tie them up in a bundle, and lay them on the doorstep after twelve o'clock. Some one will then come, and you must ask his name. If he says "John Smith," he must not be admitted, because the initial letters of his name are curved; but if he says "Edward Thompson," admit him at once, as his initial letters are made up of straight lines; but he must bring the bundle in with him that was laid on the step. He must then wish you a happy New Year, and after receiving a gift, pass out by the back door. Then, behold! good luck is yours for another year. Among the ancient Persians prisoners were liberated and offenders forgiven on this day; and, in short, the Persian New Year's Day resembled the Sabbatical year of the Jews. A curious Oriental custom peculiar to this day may be mentioned. It is called by the

Arabs and Persians the "Game of the Beardless River," and consists in a deformed man, whose hair has been shaved and his face ludicrously painted with variegated colors, riding along the streets on an ass, and behaving in the most whimsical manner, to the great delight of the multitudes that follow him. Thus equipped, he rides from door to door, soliciting small pieces of money. A similar custom is still found in various parts of Scotland, under the name of "guizzarding." The New Year, being the eighth day after Christmas, was kept by some Christians as the festival of Christ's circumcision; and whilst almost universally celebrated with some kind of religious ceremony, all over the continent of Europe, in Britain, and in America, it is universally kept as a day devoted to social festivity. "The social observances of the first day of the new year," says McClintock, "appear to have been in substance the same in all ages. From the earliest recorded celebration we find notice of feasting and the interchange of presents as usages of the day. Suetonius alludes to the bringing of presents to the capital, and Tacitus makes a similar reference to the practice of giving and receiving New Year's gifts. Under the Cæsars these presents became such a source of personal profit to the sovereign, and so onerous to his subjects, that Claudius limited them by a decree. This custom was continued by the Christian kingdoms into which the Western Empire was divided. In England we find many examples of it, even as a part of the public expenditure of the court, so far down as the reign of Charles II.; and as all our antiquarian writers mention, the custom of interchanging presents was common in all classes of society." In Japan New Year's Day is devoted to calling upon friends and wishing them well; and one of the little customs belonging to this pleasant ceremony is the giving of the shells of a large kind of mussel called *awabi*. The reason for this seemingly worthless and not very elegant gift is that it is an emblem of the time, long ago, when their forefathers were so simple and frugal that their food was principally the mussels which they gathered on the rocks by the sea-shore. The shell bears a little warning, in this recollection, against the danger of too great delicacy and luxury.

New York. This State was named in honor of the Duke of York, brother of Charles II. of England.

N. F. Newfoundland.

N. G. New Granada; Noble Grand.

N. H. New Hampshire; New Haven.

N. H. H. S. New Hampshire Historical Society.

Ni. Nickel.

Niaiserie. (Fr.) Stillness.

Nibelungen Hoard. In Teutonic mythology a mythical mass of gold and precious stones, which Siegfried obtained from the Nibelungs, and gave to his wife Kriemhild as her marriage portion. It was guarded by Albric the dwarf. After the murder of Siegfried, his widow removed the hoard to Worms; here Sagan seized it, and buried it secretly beneath the Rhine, intending at a future time to enjoy it, "but that was ne'er to be." Kriemhild married Etzel with the view of avenging her wrongs. In time Gunther, with Hagan and a host of Burgundians, went to visit Etzel, and Kriemhild stirred up a great broil, in which a most terrible slaughter ensued.

Nic. Fitzerburtus. (Pseud.) Nicholas Fitzherbert, English Catholic writer (1550–1612).

Nicholas Frog. The Dutch are so named in Arbuthnot's satirical "History of John Bull."

Nicholas Spicer. (Pseud.) Col. Alban S. Payne, in "Turf, Field, and Farm."

Nicka-Nan Night. The night preceding Shrove-Tuesday is so called in Cornwall, England, because boys play impish tricks and practical jokes on the unwary.

Nidhogg. In Scandinavian mythology a hideous dragon, dwelling in Naströnd, who incessantly gnaws at the root of Yggdrasil (*q. v.*).

Niflheim. In Scandinavian mythology "the abode of clouds" was one of the nine separate abodes or homes of which the old Scandinavians conceived the world as consisting in the beginning of time. It is the kingdom of cold and darkness, and is separated from Muspelheim, the realm of light and heat, by a wide and deep chasm.

Nigger in the Woodpile. An expression indicating that something is hidden which does not appear at first sight, — that everything is not open and above-board. It arose in the South, and refers to the thievish propensities of the slaves.

Nightingale of the Twrch. So John Edwards, the author (1806-1887), was known among the Welsh in America, he having been born near the River Twrch, in Wales.

Nightmare of Europe. Napoleon I. was so named.

Night-soilers. An opprobrious name applied to the Free Soilers by their opponents.

Nihil ad rem. (Lat.) "Nothing to the thing" (point or purpose).

Nihil debet. (Lat.) "He owes nothing." A plea denying a debt.

Nihilists, Nihilism. Two words that have come into prominence in late years in connection with Russian politics. Primarily the word Nihilism (Fr. *nihilisme*, from the Latin *nihil, nihilum*, nothing) signifies "the doctrine that nothing can be known; scepticism carried to the denial of all knowledge and reality." The Nihilists of Russia have been justly described as those "who disbelieve in any permanent improvement in the social condition or progress of man; particularly a member of a secret association which is devoted to the destruction of the present form of [Russian] government without any hope or definite theory of substituting another." The nihilist spirit appears to have permeated every strata of Russian society. Its recruits are gathered from every social grade, alike from the nobles and the peasants. A series of political crimes of exceptional atrocity has marked the existence of a clique of assassins which for some years has baffled the utmost vigilance of the state police. Previous to the year 1878 the Nihilists contented themselves with the propagation of democratic ideas among the masses, urging the overthrow of the existing despotic government, but keeping pretty strictly within the ordinary line of socialistic agitation. In the year named, however, a new sect arose from the midst of the society referred to, calling themselves "Terrorists," and urging the most violent and sanguinary measures; and this group of men and women soon signalized themselves by a series of crimes of the gravest character. Assassination of those in power in Russia was their remedy for all social evils.

Their first crime was the fatal shooting of Prince Krapotkine, Governor of Kharkov, on Feb. 9, 1879, while he was returning home in a closed carriage. On the morning of April 2, 1879, as the Czar Alexander II. was walking near the Winter Palace, St. Petersburg, he was fired upon by Alexander Solovieff, who was soon after tried and executed. The pistol having failed, another weapon, dynamite, was called into requisition. No less than three attempts were made in 1879 to blow up the imperial train by undermining the roads over which it was expected to pass. A fourth attempt of a like character was made in the Winter Palace on Feb. 5, 1880. All of these were unsuccessful, though in three of them several persons were killed or injured. The diabolical schemes of the Nihilists were, however, at length successful, so far as the unfortunate Czar was concerned. On Sunday, March 13, 1881, as the emperor was returning in a sleigh from a review, two nitro-glycerine bombs were thrown from among the crowd. The first missile, thrown by a man named Roussakoff, shattered the sleigh without injuring the Czar; but the second, thrown by an accomplice after the Czar had alighted, wounded him so terribly that he died within two hours. The two principal criminals, with three or four accessaries, were hanged April 15.

Nihil quod tetigit, non ornavit. (Lat.) Whatever he touched, he embellished.

Nika Sedition. An episode at Constantinople in January, 532, is so named. A riot occurred, lasting nearly a week, during which about thirty thousand lives were lost, and Justinian was indebted for his life and his throne to the heroism of the Empress Theodosia. The Blues and the Greens, two circus factions, united for a day against the emperor, taking *Nika!* ("Overcome!") for a countersign or war-cry. But the Blues turned on the Greens, and massacred them.

Nikita, Mlle. The stage-name of Louise Nicholson.

Nil Admirari. Esq. (Pseud.) Frederick William Shelton, American writer and Protestant Episcopal clergyman (b. 1810).

Nil admirari. (Lat.) To wonder at nothing.

Nil desperandum. (Lat.) "Nothing is to be despaired of." Never despair.

Nillo. (Pseud.) A. A. Curtiss, American writer.

Ni l'un ni l'autre. (Fr.) Neither the one nor the other.

Nimis poeta. (Lat.) Too much a poet.

Nimium ne crede colori. (Lat.) Trust not too much to appearances.

N'importe. (Fr.) It matters not.

Nimrod. (Pseud.) (1) Charles J. Apperley, English writer on field sports (1777–1843). (2) John Hamilton Reynolds, English poet (1794–1852).

Nine Days' Wonder. This phrase is thought to have originated in some reference to the nine days during which Lady Jane Grey was styled Queen of England. Another authority attributes it to the nine days after birth during which a puppy remains blind. There is an old saw given in Bohn's "Handbook of Proverbs," "A wonder lasts nine days, and then the puppy's eyes are open."

Nine-killer. "The popular name of the Northern Butcher-bird (*Lanius septentrionalis*) of ornithologists. In Canada and the Eastern States it is sometimes called Mocking-bird. 'The name of "nine-killer,"' says Dr. DeKay, 'is derived from the popular belief that it catches and impales nine grasshoppers in a day.' " — *Natural History of New York.*

Nine-pins. The game that in England is known as "skittles." *See* TEN-PINS.

Nine Tailors make a Man. In North's "Church Bells of Leicestershire," the author, in speaking of tolling for the dead, says : "These tolls are called 'tellers,' and it has been suggested that the old saying, 'Nine tailors make a man,' is a corruption of 'Nine tellers mark a man,' meaning that three times three tolls or tellers are struck on the passing bell for a man." At Wimbledon it is still the custom to strike three times three for an adult male and three times two for a female on the tenor bell ; but for children under twelve the treble bell is used, and the strokes are twice three for a male, and twice two for a female.

Nine Worthies. Joshua, David, and Judas Maccabæus ; Hector, Alexander, and Julius Cæsar ; Arthur, Charlemagne, and Godfrey of Bouillon.

Nine Worthies of Ancient London. "(1) Sir William Walworth, fishmonger, who stabbed Wat Tyler, the rebel. Sir William was twice Lord Mayor, 1374, 1380. (2) Sir Henry Pritchard, who in 1356 feasted Edward III. with five thousand followers ; Edward, the Black Prince ; John, King of Austria ; the King of Cyprus ; and David, King of Scotland. (3) Sir William Sevenoke, who fought with the Dauphin of France, built twenty almshouses and a free school, 1418. (4) Sir Thomas White, merchant tailor, son of a poor clothier. In 1553 he kept the citizens loyal to Queen Mary, during Wyatt's Rebellion. Sir John White founded St. John's College, Oxford, on the spot where 'two elms grew from one root.' (5) Sir John Bonham, intrusted with a valuable cargo for the Danish market, and made commander of the army raised to stop the progress of the great Solyman. (6) Christopher Croker, famous at the siege of Bordeaux, and companion of the Black Prince when he helped Don Pedro to the throne of Castile. (7) Sir John Hawkwood, one of the Black Prince's knights, and immortalized in Italian history as 'Giovanni Acuti Cavaliero.' (8) Sir Hugh Caverley, famous for ridding Poland of a monstrous bear. (9) Sir Henry Maleverer, generally called 'Henry of Cornhill,' who lived in the reign of Henry IV. He was a crusader, and became the guardian of 'Jacob's Well.' The chronicle of these worthies is told in a mixture of prose and verse by Richard Johnson, author of 'The Seven Champions of Christendom,' 1592." — BREWER.

Ninus. In classic myth the son of Belus, husband of Semiramis, the reputed builder of Nineveh, and founder of the Assyrian Empire.

Niobe. In classic myth the daughter of Tantalus and sister of Pelops. She married Amphion, King of Thebes, and bore him six sons and six daughters. Proud of her offspring, she despised Latona, who had only two, — Apollo and Diana, and hindered the people from worshipping those two divinities ; whereupon Latona, enraged, moved her children to destroy all the children of Niobe with their arrows. After lying nine days in their blood, they were buried by the gods. Niobe wandered about disconsolate, and at last was changed into stone on Mount Sisyphus.

Niobe of Nations. Rome, the "lone mother of dead empires."

Ni. pri. Nisi prius.

Nisi Dominus, frustra. (Lat.) Unless the Lord be with us, all our toil is in vain.

Nitor in adversum. (Lat.) I strive against opposition.

Nitrate King. Col. John T. North, a native of Yorkshire, England. He went to South America twenty years ago, saw an opportunity, and embraced it. He amassed a fortune of from forty to sixty million dollars.

N. J. New Jersey.

Njord. In Scandinavian mythology the god of the north wind.

N. l. *Non liquet.* It does not appear.

N. lat. North latitude.

N. M. New measurement; New Mexico.

N. N. E. North-northeast.

N. N. W. North-northwest.

N. O. New Orleans.

No. *Numero.* Number.

Nobis judicibus. (Lat.) "With ourselves as judges." In our opinion.

Noble, The. (1) Charles III. of Navarre (fl. 1361–1425). (2) Soliman Tchelibi, Turkish prince at Adrianople (d. 1410).

Noble Buzzard. In Dryden's "Hind and Panther," this is Bishop Burnet, who attacked Dryden because of the great lewdness of his dramas.

Noble-soul. A name applied to Chosroes II., the most eminent of the Sassanide dynasty (d. 579).

Noblesse oblige. (Fr.) Rank has its obligations; nobility binds to noble obligations.

Noctes Ambrosianæ. While Lockhart was writing "Valerius," he was in the habit of taking walks with Professor Wilson every morning, and of supping with Blackwood at Ambrose's, a small tavern in Edinburgh. One night Lockhart said, "What a pity there has not been a short-hand writer here to take down all the good things that have been said!" and next night he produced a paper from memory, and called it "Noctes Ambrosianæ."

No Flint Grey. A sobriquet fastened on Charles Grey, the British soldier (1729–1807). On the night of Sept 21, 1777, he surprised General Wayne near Paoli Tavern, on the Lancaster Road. Grey approached stealthily, and ordered the flints to be taken from the muskets, attacked with the bayonet, defeating the Americans with great slaughter.

Nol. pros. *Nolle prosequi.* Unwilling to proceed.

Nolens volens. (Lat.) Whether he will or not.

Nolentes volentes. (Lat.) Whether they will or not.

No License. A party shibboleth during the temperance agitation in recent times in the United States, by which is denoted the total prohibition of the traffic in intoxicating liquors by refusal to license the sale of the same.

Noli me tangere. (Lat.) Do not touch me.

Noll. *See* GOLDY.

Nolle prosequi. (Lat.) "To be unwilling to proceed." In law, an acknowledgment or agreement on the part of a plaintiff in a suit that he will abandon it.

Nolo episcopari. (Lat.) I am not willing to be made a bishop (an old formal way of declining a bishopric).

No Man is a Hero to his Valet. This phrase is commonly attributed to Madame de Sévigné, but, on the authority of Madame Aisse, belongs to Madame Cornuel.

"Few men are admired by their servants." — MONTAIGNE.

"When Herodotus described Antigonus as the son of Helios (the sun), 'My valet-de-chambre,' said he, 'is not aware of this.'"

Nom., or **nom.** Nominative,

No Man's Land. (1) This is the strip of public land lying west of the Indian Territory, north of Texas, east of New Mexico, and south of Kansas. It does not belong to, and is not subject to the laws of, any of these States or Territories, and is a refuge for evil-doers of them all; hence its name, "No Man's Land." (2) The southern extremity of London Britain township, Chester County, Penn., extends in a narrow tongue between the boundary of Maryland and Delaware. Although this tongue is shown on the official maps of Chester County as belonging in Pennsylvania, many of the people living on it have always voted and paid their taxes in New Castle County, Del., the titles to their land and all legal papers being recorded in that State and county instead of Chester County, Penn. Some of the people dwelling on the narrow and pointed strip of land insist that they are not legally located in either Pennsylvania, Delaware, or Maryland. They refuse to pay taxes to either State, and do not vote. The strip is known locally as No-Man's Land.

Nom de guerre. (Fr.) "Name of war." A name of war; an assumed name on entering the army.

Nom de plume. (Fr.) "Name of pen." An assumed title, — as by a literary person.

Nomen et omen. (Lat.) "Name and omen." A name that is ominous.

Nominatim. (Lat.) By name; expressly.

Nominis umbra. (Lat.) The shadow of a name.

Non. (Ital.) An adverb of negation, generally associated with *troppo;* as *non troppo presto,* not too fast. (Mus.)

Nonchalance. Coolness.

Non compos mentis. (Lat.) "Not sound of mind." Not in his right senses.

Non con. Not content; dissenting (House of Lords).

Non cul. *Non culpabilis.* Not guilty.

Non deficiente crumena. (Lat.) If the money does not fail.

Nones and Ides.

On March the 7th, June, July,
October, too, the Nones you spy ;
Except in these, those Nones appear
On the 5th day of all the year.
If to the Nones you add an 8,
Of all the Ides you'll find the date.

Hence we have the 15th for the Ides of March, June, July, and October; and the 13th for every other month.

Non est disputandum. (Lat.) It is not to be disputed.

Non est inventus. (Lat.) He has not been found.

Non est tanti. (Lat.) It is not of so great value ; it is not worth while.

Non exercitus, neque thesauri, proesidia regni sunt, verum amici. (Lat.) Neither armies nor treasures are the safeguards of a state, but friends. The passage is from Sallust.

Non ex quovis ligno Mercurius fit. (Lat.) "Not out of every log a Mercurius is made." It is not every one can be trained to be a scholar.

Non libet. (Lat.) It does not please.

Non liquet. (Lat.) It is not clear or evident, — said of one undecided in mind.

Non mi ricordo. (Ital.) I do not remember.

Non multa, sed multum. (Lat.) Not many (things), but much.

Non nobis solum. (Lat.) "Not to us." The first words of the Latin version of the One Hundred and Fifteenth Psalm.

Non obst. *Non obstante.* Notwithstanding.

Non obstante. (Lat.) Notwithstanding.

Non omnia possumus omnes. (Lat.) We are not all able to do everything.

Non omnis moriar. (Lat.) I shall not wholly die.

Non passibus æquis. (Lat.) Not with equal steps.

Non pros. *Non prosequitur.* He does not prosecute.

Non quo, sed quomodo. (Lat.) Not by whom, but in what manner.

Non seq. *Non sequitur.* It does not follow.

Non sequitur. (Lat.) It does not follow ; it is not a necessary deduction.

Non sibi sed patriæ (Lat.) Not for himself, but for his country.

n. o. p. Not otherwise provided for.

No-Popery Riots. Disturbances at Edinburgh and Glasgow Feb. 5, 1779, and at London June 2–9, 1780. The latter are also known as the Gordon Riots, having been occasioned by the zeal of Lord George Gordon. During these disturbances most persons, to save their houses from being gutted, wrote on the doors " No Popery."

Nordica, Mlle. The professional name of Mrs. Gower, *née* Norton, the famous vocalist.

Norfolk Howards. Another name for bed-bugs ; derived from the fact that a gentleman named Bugg once gave notice that he should apply to Parliament for permission to change it to " Norfolk Howard." *See* B-FLATS.

Norman Reconciliation. *See* LA-MOURETTE'S KISS.

Norna. (Pseud.) Mrs. M. E. Brooks, *née* Aiken, an American poet.

Nornæ. The Parcæ (*q. v.*) of the Scandinavian mythology. They were three maidens, — Urd, Verdandi, and Skuld ; *i. e.*, Past, Present, and Future.

They sit by the Urdar-wells under the world-tree Yggdrasil, and there determine the fate of both gods and men.

Norrisian Professor. A Professor of Divinity in the University of Cambridge, England. This professorship was founded in 1760 by John Norris, Esq., of Whitton, in Norfolk.

Northamptonshire Poet. John Clare, son of a farmer at Helpstone (fl. 1793–1864).

North Britain. Scotland is often referred to by this name, it forming the northernmost part of the island of Britain.

North Carolina. This State was named in honor of Charles I. of England.

Northern Athens. See MODERN ATHENS (1).

Northern Bear, Northern Giant. Russia, in allusion to the size, power, and resources of the empire.

Northern Harlot. An epithet applied to Elizabeth Petrovna, Empress of Russia (fl. 1709–1761). She was also named " The Infamous."

Northern Herodotus. A sobriquet conferred on Snorri Sturleson (fl. 1179–1241), the Icelandic poet, chronicler, and lawmaker.

North German Confederation. See ZOLLVEREIN.

Northwest Conspiracy. By this name is known a plot that was hatched by Southern sympathizers at the North, during the civil war, for the purpose of aiding the South by an insurrection of large proportions. It takes its name from the section of the country in which it was formed. Illinois was probably the headquarters. In June, 1864, exposures in regard to it were made, arms seized, and leaders arrested. The execution of the design was thus thwarted.

Northwest Territory. By the terms of the treaty of 1783 Great Britain surrendered to the United States all the territory east of the Mississippi and south of the great lakes. Before Congress adjourned in 1787 the Northwest Territory was organized, it having, as a preliminary measure, been ceded to the Federal Government by Virginia, New York, Massachusetts, and Connecticut. Out of this noble domain the five great States of Ohio, Indiana, Illinois, Michigan, and Wisconsin were destined to be formed and added to the Union. See WESTERN RESERVE.

Nos. Numbers.

Nosce teipsum. Know thyself.

Noscitur e sociis. (Lat.) By his companions he is known.

Nose, Anthony's. See ANTHONY'S NOSE.

Nostradamus of Portugal. Gonsalo Annes Bandarra, a poet cobbler (d. 1556). His writings were placed under the ban of the Inquisition.

Nostro periculo. (Lat.) At his own risk.

Nota bene. (Lat.) " Mark well." Pay particular attention.

Notanda. (Lat.) " Deserving or requiring to be marked." Matters requiring notice.

Notion. " Notion," in the sense of small, trifling wares, is probably the word which, of all Americanisms, is regarded as the most absolutely American, both in origin and in usage. " Yankee notions " is a phrase known the world over. But so grave and didactic a poet as Young, than whom none could be less American, used it nearly one hundred and fifty years ago exactly in the sense in which it is now used in New England, —

" And other worlds send odors, sauce, and song,
And robes, and *notions* framed in foreign looms."
NIGHT THOUGHTS, *Night II.*

Notions, City of. See CITY OF NOTIONS.

Not lost, but gone before. These words are quoted in a collection of epitaphs by Pettigrew, published by Lackington early in the nineteenth century. The tomb on which they occur is that of Mary Angell, widow, who died at Stepney, 1693, aged seventy-two. The inscription runs thus : —

" To say an angel here interred doth lye
May be thought strange, for angels never dye.
Indeed some fell from heav'n to hell;
Are lost and rise no more.
This only fell from death to earth,
Not lost, but gone before.
Her dust lodged here, her soul, perfect in grace,
'Mongst saints and angels now hath took its place."

Notre Dame. (Fr.) Our lady.

Nottingham Poet. Philip James Bailey, author of " Festus " (b. 1816).

Notturno, Nocturne. A musical composition, either vocal or instrumental, suitable for evening performance.

Nous avons changé tout cela. (Fr.) We have changed all that.

Nous verrons. (Fr.) We shall see.

Nov. November.

Novalis. (Pseud.) Friedrich von Hardenberg, German philosopher (1772–1801).

Novanglus. (Pseud.) John Adams, second President of the United States (1735–1826).

Novendial Ashes. The ashes of the dead just consigned, or about to be consigned, to the grave. The Romans kept the body seven days, burned it on the eighth, and buried the ashes on the ninth.

Novendial Holiday. Nine days set apart by the Romans, in expiation of a shower of stones.

Novi homines. (Lat.) New men.

Novissima verba. (Lat.) The last words — as of a person just before death.

Novus homo. (Lat.) "A new man." A man who has risen from the ranks; the first one of a family that has been ennobled.

Nox. In classic myth the goddess of night.

Noyades. A series of wholesale "drownages" executed by Carrier, deputy of the Convention at Nantes, during the French Revolution. Priests, women, and children were packed into flat-bottomed boats, which were scuttled in the middle of the Loire. There were twenty-five of these "sentences of deportation executed vertically."

N. P. Notary Public.

N. P. D. North Polar Distance.

N. R. North River.

N. S. New Style (after 1752); Nova Scotia.

n. s. Not specified.

N. S. J. C. *Noster Salvator Jesus Christus.* Our Saviour Jesus Christ.

N. T. New Testament; Nevada Territory.

n. u. Name or names unknown.

Nudity Theatre. A name conferred on the Gayety Theatre, London, because of the character of the works — burlesques, farces, comic operas, etc. — produced there, in which the female characters were very slimly attired.

Nudum pactum. (Lat.) A verbal agreement only.

Nugæ canoræ. (Lat.) "Melodious trifles." Mere sing-song without meaning.

Nulla bona. (Lat.) No goods.

Nulla dies sine linea. (Lat.) "No day without a line," — that is, without doing something.

Nulla nuova, bona nuova. (Lat.) The best news is no news.

Nullification Movement. In United States history the name given to a movement in South Carolina in 1832, headed by John C. Calhoun, who proclaimed it as the sovereign right of a State to nullify by its own decree any act of the General Government which it deems unconstitutional.

Nulli secundus. (Lat.) Second to none.

Nullius filius. (Lat.) The son of nobody.

Nullius in bonis. (Lat.) "In the goods of no one." The property of nobody.

Num. Numbers; numeral.

Number of God. The number three has been so named, from its peculiar use in the Scriptures in connection with the Divine name. *See* NUMBER OF THE TRINITY.

Number of the Trinity. The number three, — also supposed to symbolize completeness. *See* NUMBER OF GOD.

Number of the World. The number four, from its frequent reference to the visible creation (Jer. xlix. 36; Ezek. vii. 2, xxxvii. 9; Dan. vii. 2, viii. 8; Matt. xxiv. 31; Mark xiii. 27; Isa. xi. 12; Rev. vii. 1, xx. 8; 1 Chron. ix. 24; Ps. cvii. 3; Luke xiii. 29; Zech. i. 18, ii. 6, vi. 1, 5).

Numbers. *See* BERNOUILLI'S NUMBERS; also distinguishing titles, as NUMBER OF GOD, NUMBER OF THE TRINITY, etc.

Nunc aut nunquam. (Lat.) Now or never.

Nunquam non paratus. (Lat.) Never unprepared.

Nutcrackers. The Third Foot of the English army, so called because at Albuera they cracked the heads of the Polish Lancers, then opened and retreated, but in a few minutes came again into the field, and did most excellent service. *See* OLD BUFFS.

Nutcrack Night. All Hallow Eve, when it is customary in some places to crack nuts in large quantities.

Nutmeg State. Connecticut. Its sons possess such a reputation for shrewd habits that they have been jocularly charged with manufacturing and selling nutmegs made of wood and colored to imitate the real article.

N. V. New Version.

N. V. M. Nativity of the Virgin Mary.

N. W. Northwest.

N. W. T. Northwest Territory.

N. Y. New York.

N. Y. H. S. New York Historical Society.

Nym Crinkle. (Pseud.) A. C. Wheeler, American journalist (b. 1825).

Nymphs. In classic myth, female divinities of inferior rank inhabiting the sea, streams, groves, meadows, pastures, grottos, fountains, hills, glens, trees, etc. There were several different classes of nymphs; *e. g.*, Oceanides, Nereids, Naiads, Oreades, Dryads, etc. (*q. v.*).

Nym Rugby. (Pseud.) Nugent Robinson, in the New York "Boys and Girls' Weekly."

N. Z. New Zealand.

O.

O. Ohio; oxygen.

Oak Barrens. Wild land that has been denuded of its more valuable timber, leaving only a scrub growth. The term is peculiar to the West. *See* PINE BARRENS.

Oak Openings. Grassy forest-glades are so named, though there may be no oaks near.

Oannes. A mythical deity of the Babylonians, half man, half fish.

Ob. *Obiit.* He or she died.

Obad. Obadiah.

Obadiah. A nickname for a Quaker. *See* AMINADAB.

Obelisk, The. Allen G. Thurman, of Ohio, was so named by the New York "World" during the campaign of 1888. *See* OLD ROMAN.

Oberon. In fairy mythology the king of the fairies. Titania was his wife.

Obiit. (Lat.) He or she died.

Obiter dicta. (Lat.) Things said by the way; casual remarks.

Obiter dictum. (Lat.) A thing said by the way.

Obligato, or **Obligati.** (Ital.) A part or parts of a piece indispensable to its proper performance, and which cannot therefore be properly omitted. (Mus.)

Obs. Obsolete; observatory; observation.

Observant Friars. Those friars who observe the rule of Saint Francis, — to abjure books, land, house, and chapel; to live on alms, dress in rags, feed on scraps, and sleep anywhere.

Obsta principiis. (Lat.) Resist the beginnings.

Obt., or **Obdt.** Obedient.

Occasional. (Pseud.) Col. Sanders D. Bruce, in "Turf, Field, and Farm."

Oceanidæ. In classic myth the ocean nymphs, three thousand in number, daughters of Oceanus.

Oceanus. In classic myth son of Cœlus and Terra, and the god of the great salt stream which the ancients thought surrounded the land. *See* OCEANIDÆ.

O'Connell's Tail. A nickname given in England at and after the Reform agitation of 1832 to a small body in Parliament who worked and voted at the dictation of Daniel O'Connell.

Oconomowoc. (Pseud.) James A. Henshall, a noted writer on pisciculture in the Western press.

Oct., or **8vo.** Octavo, eight pages.

Oct. October.

Octave Thanet. (Pseud.) Miss Alice French, of Davenport, Iowa, in her contributions to current literature.

Octavia Hensel. The stage-name of Lady Alice Seymour.

Odds and Ends. (Pseud.) Walter C. Quevedo, in the "Despatch," New York.

Oderint modo metuant. (Lat.) Let them hate, so long as they fear.

Odin. The chief deity of the Scandinavian mythology. As ruler of heaven his seat is Valaskjalf, from whence his two black ravens, Huginn (Thought), and Munin (Memory), fly daily forth to gather tidings of all that is being done throughout the world. As god of war he holds court in Valhalla, whither come all brave warriors after death.

Odin, Hall of. *See* HALL OF ODIN.

Odi profanum vulgus. (Lat.) I hate the vulgar throng.

Odium theologicum. (Lat.) "The bitter hatred of rival religionists. No wars so sanguinary as holy wars; no persecutions so relentless as religious persecutions; no hatred so bitter as theological hatred."

Odor of Sanctity. To die "in the odor of sanctity" did not mean simply "in good repute." It was a prevalent notion that the dead body of a saint positively emitted a sweet-smelling savor, and the dead body of the unbaptized an offensive smell.

Od rot 'em. *See* DRAT 'EM.

Odur. In Scandinavian mythology the husband of Freyja. He abandoned his wife when youth and beauty left her, and as a punishment he was changed to a statue.

Odysseus. The Greek form of Ulysses.

Œdipus. In classic myth the hero of a celebrated legend which, though of the most revolting nature in itself, has supplied both Euripides and Sophocles with themes for celebrated tragedies. He was the son of King Laius of Thebes, and of Jocasta. He solved the riddle of the Sphinx, unwittingly killed his own father, and married his mother, who bore him four children. When the incestuous connection was discovered, Jocasta hanged herself and Œdipus went mad and put out his own eyes.

Œnone. In classic myth a Phrygian nymph, espoused by Paris, who afterward deserted her for Helen.

O. F. Odd-Fellow, or Odd-Fellows.

Officier d'ordonnance. (Fr.) An orderly officer.

Officina gentium. (Lat.) "The workshop of the nations." The workshop of the world.

O. G. Outside Guardian.

Ogyges. The earliest king of Attica and Bœotia named in the Greek legends. In his time (1759 B. C.) a great flood took place, called the Ogygian Deluge, which desolated both countries.

Ogygia. In classic myth a fabulous island of surpassing loveliness in the Western Ocean, the abode of Calypso.

Ogygian Deluge. A flood which overran a part of Greece while Ogyges was king of Attica. There were two floods so called, — one in Bœotia, when Lake Copais overflowed its banks; and another in Attica.

Ohe! jam satis est. (Lat.) Hullo! there is now enough of this.

Ohio. The name of this State is the Shawnee name for "beautiful river," *i. e.*, the Ohio River.

Ohio Gong. A nickname given to William Allen, the Ohio statesman (1806–1879), in Washington, so powerful was his voice and so penetrating its tones.

O. H. M. S. On His or Her Majesty's Service.

Oil. In the days of the petroleum excitement in Pennsylvania the finding of oil meant fortune to the lucky prospector. Hence the phrase "struck oil" passed into current speech to signify sudden riches.

Oil on Troubled Waters. Mr. David M. Stone, of the "Journal of Commerce," traced the saying to its origin some seven years ago, and on March 31, 1882, published the result of his labors thus: —

"The phrase, so far as we can trace it, first occurs in Bede's 'Ecclesiastical History' (book iii. chapter xv.), written in Latin more than eleven hundred years ago (from 716 to 731 A. D.). The Venerable Bede is speaking of Bishop Aidan, who was permitted to work miracles. A priest called Vtta (Utta) was sent into Kent to fetch Eanflede, King Edwine's daughter, who was to be married to King Oswirra. He was to go by land, but to return by water. Before his departure Vtta visited the Bishop and besought his prayers for a prosperous journey. The Bishop blessed him, and, predicting for his return a great tempest and a contrary wind that should rise suddenly, gave him a pot of oil, saying: 'Remember that you cast into the sea this oyle that I give you, and anon, the winds being laid, comfortable fayer weather shall ensue on the sea, which shall send you againe with as pleausaunt a passage as you have wished.' The tempest came as predicted, the sailors essayed to cast 'ancar' in vain, the water began to fill the ship, and 'no thing but present death was looked for.' At the near approach of death came the thought of the Bishop and the pot of oil. Taking it in his hand the priest cast of the oil into the sea, when, as if by magic. it became quiet and calm, and the ship was delivered. Bede declares that he had it from 'a very creditable man, a priest of our Church, Cymmund by name, who saied that he had hearde it of Vtta, the priest, in whom the miracle was wrought.' Modern experiments show that it was no miracle, and we have no doubt the scene occurred precisely as described. This was the first recorded instance we can find of 'pouring oil on the troubled waters.' It is now a common metaphor, used of all efforts to allay commotion of any kind by smooth words of council in the interests of peace."

Oil Spot. (1) About ten miles to the south of the Sabine river, which forms the boundary between Texas and Louisiana, and about a mile from the shore, in the Gulf of Mexico there exists a natural phenomenon known to sailors as the "Oil Spot." In fine weather there is nothing remarkable to attract the attention of a stranger; but when an angry gale from the northeast sweeps the ocean this charmed natural harbor reveals itself. No visible boundary divides it from the tempestuous ocean around, but within a space two miles in length the waters remain perfectly calm, their only change being that they become turbid and red, as though oil-bearing mud were stirred up from below. We believe that no scientific examination of this "Oil Spot" has yet been made. Sailors who have here found refuge, state that the bottom is of a soft, soapy mud, into which they can easily push a pole to a considerable depth — a mud which, when applied to deck-scrubbing, is found to be exceedingly cleansing. (2) There is another so-called "Oil Spot" in New York Bay, off the point of Sandy Hook, so named by yachtmen from the fact that frequent calms occur within a small radius.

O imitatores, servum pecus! (Lat.) O imitators, a servile herd!

O Jiminy! This, which was a common interjectional remark in the last generation and is not yet quite extinct, is a corruption of *O Gemini*, a Latin invocation to the divine brothers Castor and Pollux.

O. K. These letters in America signify "all right." Their use, it is said, originated with old Jacob Astor, the millionnaire of New York. He was looked upon in commercial circles as a man of great information and sound judgment, and was a sort of general referee as to the solvency or standing of other traders. If a note of inquiry as to any particular trader's position came, the answer to which he intended to be satisfactory, he was accustomed to write across the note the letters "O. K.," and return it to the writer. The letters "O. K." he supposed to be the initials of "all correct," and in this sense they are now universally current in the States. Another account comes from a correspondent who says he re-

ceived it from James Parton: While at Nashville in search of material for his history, Mr. Parton found among the records of the court of which General Jackson had been judge a great many legal documents endorsed " O. R." which meant "Order recorded," but often so scrawlingly written that one could easily read it as O. K. If "Major Downing" noticed a bundle of papers thus marked upon President Jackson's table, documents perhaps from his former court, in which he still had interest, it is very easy to see how a punster could imagine it to be " O. K.," or " oll korrect." No doubt Seba Smith, who wrote under the *non de plume* of "Major Jack Downing," had much to do with creating the impression that President Jackson was unlettered and illiterate, whereas many existing personal letters, military reports, court opinions, and State papers show to the contrary.

Old and Bold. The Fifth Regiment of Foot (English).

Old Bachelor. (Pseud.) George William Curtis, American author and lecturer (b. 1824).

Old Bags. John Scott, Lord Eldon (fl. 1751–1838); so named from his habit of carrying home with him in a solicitor's bag the briefs of the cases pending before him.

Old Bandanna. Allen G. Thurman. *See* RED BANDANNA.

Old Bay Rum State. Massachusetts. This punning nickname was bestowed by Gen. Clinton B. Fisk in a speech at the anniversary of the National Temperance Association in New York, 1889, in allusion to the then recent rejection of a prohibition amendment by the voters of that State.

Old Bay State. Massachusetts, whose shores are washed by Cape Cod Bay. Prior to the adoption of the United States Constitution Massachusetts was known as "the Colony of Massachusetts Bay."

When first the pilgrims landed on the Bay State's iron shore,
The word went forth that slavery should one day be no more.
LOWELL.

Old Blizzard. "William Wing Loring (Loring Pasha), American soldier (1818–1886). In the spring of 1863, when General Grant was operating for the investment of Vicksburg, Loring was sent to Fort Pemberton, where he mounted two heavy siege guns that silenced the fire of the Federal gunboat *Chillicothe.* His exclamation, ' Give her a blizzard, boys ! ' on 'this occasion was the origin of the name ' Old Blizzard ' by which he was afterwards known."

Old Bona Fide. Louis XIV. of France was so named ; though why, it would be hard to say, for a more faithless monarch, when it suited his purpose, it would be difficult to name.

Old Brags. *See* SLASHERS.

Old Brains. A by-name attached to General Halleck during the war for the Union.

Old Buffs. A nickname for the Third Foot Regiment of the English army, from the color of its facings. It is also called "Nutcrackers (*q. v.*)." *See* RESURRECTIONISTS.

Old Bullion. A nickname conferred on Thomas H. Benton, the American statesman and financier (fl. 1782–1858), because of his steadfast advocacy of a gold and silver currency as a cure for the financial embarrassments in which the country was plunged after the lapsing of the United States Bank charter.

Old Cabinet. (Pseud.) R. Watson Gilder, American *littérateur* and editor.

Old Cartman. (Pseud.) Isaac S. Lyon, in the Newark " Daily Journal," about 1871.

Old Chalk. (Pseud.) Henry Chadwick, in the Brooklyn " Union."

Old Chickamauga. An appellation bestowed on General Stedman (d. 1883) for gallant conduct at that memorable action during the American civil war.

Old Colony. A name sometimes given to the southeastern part of the State of Massachusetts.

Old Corner Bookstore. The oldest bookstore in Boston, in the quaint building, erected in 1712, on the corner of Washington and School Streets. An ancient landmark, long known as the " Old Corner Bookstore," as it has been a book-stand since 1828, before which time it was used as an apothecary shop, and before that as a dwelling-house, for which it was originally erected by Thomas Crease.

Old Country. A term common in Australia and in the United States, usually applied to the British Isles.

Old Denmark. Christian Febiger (1746–1796), a gallant soldier in the American Revolution, was known by this nickname during his military career. He was born on the island of Fünen, Denmark.

Old Dessauer. A nickname conferred on Prince Leopold of Anhalt-Dessau (fl. 1676–1747), who may be termed the creator of the Prussian army.

Old Dominion. Virginia. In colonial days acts of Parliament relating to the Virginian settlements (which at that time included all the British dominions in North America) always designated them as the " Colony and Dominion of Virginia." In the maps of the time this colony was described as " Old Virginia," in contradistinction to the New England settlements, which were called " New Virginia." The transition from " Old Virginia " to " Old Dominion " would be an easy and a natural one.

Old Dreadnought. Edward Boscawen, a gallant English admiral (1711–1761), was so named by his sailors.

Old Elm. A famous tree on Boston Common, which stood near the " long walk," at the foot of Flagstaff Hill, and was in its day considered the " oldest inhabitant " of Boston. It was a tree of unknown age, and was believed to have stood there before the settlement of the town in 1630. It was already decrepit as long ago as 1755. It was over seventy-two feet high, and measured twenty-two and a half feet in circumference one foot above the ground. After resisting many a storm, it was blown down in the winter of 1876. An iron fence surrounds the spot where it stood.

Oldenburg Horn. A horn long in the possession of the reigning princes of the house of Oldenburg, but now in the collection of the king of Denmark. According to tradition, Count Otto of Oldenburg, in 957, was offered drink in this silver-gilt horn by a " wild woman " at the Osenberg. As he did not like the look of the liquor, he threw it away, and rode off with the horn.

Old Fogs. The Eighty-seventh English Regiment of Foot; so called from their war-cry, *Fag-au-Bealach* (" Clear the way !"), pronounced " Faug-a-Bollagh."

Old Fox. Marshal Soult was thus nicknamed by his soldiery because of his crafty manœuvres.

Old Fritz. A nickname given to Frederick the Great by his soldiery.

Old Gib. Another name for Gibraltar.

Old Glory. (1) The flag of the United States. (2) A nickname of Sir Francis Burdett (fl. 1770–1844).

Old Grog. Admiral Edward Vernon (fl. 1684–1757) was thus nicknamed on account of his practice of wearing a grogram cloak in rainy weather. The name "grog" was by this means given to the mixture of spirits and water which he introduced as a beverage for seamen.

Old Guard. The famous "306" delegates to the Republican Convention of 1880, who steadfastly voted for General Grant.

Old Harlo. (Pseud.) Rev. Charles Edwards Abbott.

Old Harry. The Devil.

Old Hickory. General Jackson. Parton says he was first nicknamed "Old Tough," next "Tough as Hickory," and lastly "Old Hickory," all in allusion to his powers of endurance. There are, however, several other derivations of the appellation. When war was declared against England in 1812, General Jackson, in command of twenty-five hundred men of the Tennessee militia, offered his services, and was ordered to convey his troops to New Orleans. The infantry marched across the country. Later, when the order came to dismiss his forces, he chose to conduct his company back to Tennessee before disbanding it. During his homeward march his men gave him the name "Hickory," to symbolize his endurance and toughness; and this in time was changed to "Old Hickory." There is another version of the origin of the name: During the Creek war he had a bad cold, and his soldiers made for him a shelter of hickory-bark. The next morning a tipsy soldier, not knowing who was under the bark, kicked it over. As the General, speechless with rage, struggled out of the ruins, the soldier yelled, "Hello, Old Hickory! Come out of your bark and take a drink!" When the soldiers saw Jackson shaking the bark from his uniform they gave three cheers for "Old Hickory," and the name stuck.

Old Humphrey. (Pseud.) George Mogridge, English religious writer for the young (1802–1854).

Old Hundred. The One Hundredth Royal Canadian Regiment is so nicknamed.

Old Hunkers. *See* HUNKERS.

Old Ironsides. A title popularly conferred on the United States frigate "Constitution," on account of her good fortune, the number of actions in which she bore a part, and the length of time she was in active service. She was in commission more than seventy years, having been launched in 1797.

Old Lady of Threadneedle Street. The Bank of England, situated in Threadneedle Street, London.

Old Landmarkism. The name given to the peculiar views held by James Robinson Graves (b. 1820), the eminent Baptist controversialist. He was the champion of "High Church" notions, so called.

Old Leather Man. A curious character, clad almost entirely in leather, who for thirty years tramped over portions of Eastern New York and Connecticut. He lived in a cave near Sing Sing where he was found dead in 1889. In his ceaseless wanderings he did occasional jobs of plumbing, never accepting anything but food or tobacco in return, while he always slept in barns. He was entirely harmless, and is said to have been made crazy by a love affair in France in 1856. As young and handsome Jules Bourglay he had won the heart of a wealthy leather merchant's daughter, and entered the merchant's employ to prove his worthiness. He speculated in leather, and when a crash in that commodity came his employer was impoverished and his own hopes were shattered. Poor Bourglay's mind was unhinged by the shock, and he left the country, determined to always do penance by wearing leather.

Old Man Eloquent. (1) Isocrates, the Greek orator. When he heard that Grecian liberty was extinguished by the battle of Chæronea, he died of grief. (2) John Quincy Adams.

Old Man of the Mountain. Another name for Profile Mountain in the Franconia Range, New Hampshire. It consists of a huge rock about one thousand feet in altitude, which, when viewed from the right position, has a marked likeness to a man's face.

Old Man of the Mountain. (Pseud.) Nathaniel P. Rogers, American journalist (1794–1846).

Old Man of the Sea. A term meaning a burden that cannot be shaken off, the allusion being to the tale of "Sindbad the Sailor" in the "Arabian Nights."

Old Mathematics. General Humphrey, a distinguished engineer, was so named during the civil war.

Old Merry. The pen-name of Edwin Hodder, a well-known writer for juvenile periodicals.

Old Noll. Oliver Cromwell was so named by the Cavaliers.

Old Noll's Fiddler. Sir Roger L'Estrange was so nicknamed by the Cavaliers because he performed on the bass viol at the musical parties held at John Hingston's house, at which Cromwell was frequently a guest.

Old North State. North Carolina.

Old Pam. See PAM.

Old Parr. Thomas Parr (fl. 1483–1635), who lived in the reigns of ten English monarchs, was married to a second wife when one hundred and twenty years old, and died aged one hundred and fifty-two years.

Old Pete. Gen. James Longstreet, the Confederate soldier.

Old Port School. Clergymen and gentlemen of the old school, who are stanch adherents of Church and State, old port and orthodoxy.

Old Private. The pen-name of the Rev. T. Gerrish, an American writer.

Old Put. The soldiers under his command thus dubbed Gen. Israel Putnam (fl. 1718–1790), a famous major-general in the Revolutionary War.

Old Q. The fifth Earl of March, who later became the Duke of Queensberry.

Old Q.'s Balcony. A famous balcony in Piccadilly, London, from which in this century's early years the wicked, worn-out Duke of Queensberry — "Old Q." — leered at the passers-by from under his parasol.

"From Primrose Balcony, long ages ago,
Old Q. sat at gaze; who now passes below?"

Here he would sit of an afternoon, his groom Jack Radford waiting mounted in the street below, ready to ride after and stop any friend that the Duke had a mind to speak to. From this porch he was hoisted out by a kind of inclined plane, and lowered to his dark-green *vis-à-vis* with its two long-tailed, black horses. While the porch still remained, the ghost of that colossal *roué*, that "emaciated libel on manhood," still seemed to haunt Piccadilly, and to take the air that blows from the Green Park.

Old Reliable. The nickname conferred on General Thomas in recognition of his steadfast bravery.

Old Roman. Allen Granbery Thurman, the Ohio statesman, was so named. See GLADSTONE OF AMERICA.

Old Rough and Ready. A popular nickname bestowed on Gen. Zachary Taylor, twelfth President of the United States.

Old Rowley. Charles II. was thus nicknamed after his favorite race-horse. There is still a "Rowley Mile" at the Newmarket race-course from the same origin.

Old Saddlebags. Joseph E. McDonald, an Indiana lawyer and United States Senator (b. 1819). He was dubbed "Old Saddlebags" because, in early life he followed the trade of a saddler, working thereat while fitting himself for the bar.

Old Sailor. (Pseud.) (1) Capt. Roland F. Coffin, an American writer of sea-stories, used this pen-name among others (1826–1888). (2) Matthew Henry Barker.

Old Si. (Pseud.) Samuel W. Small, sometime editor of the Atlanta "Constitution," but later a revival preacher.

Old Side. (1) A sect or faction in the Presbyterian Church in America during the half-century succeeding 1730. The "Old Side" party included the more intolerant members of the Synod of Philadelphia. See NEW SIDE. (2) A sect in Pennsylvania, Maryland, and Virginia, who opposed the tenets of the "New Lights," led by the Rev. George Duffield. See NEW LIGHTS.

Old Sleuth. The pen-name of Harland P. Halsey, the author of "detective" stories under the disguise of "Old Sleuth the Detective."

Old South. (Pseud.) Benjamin Austin, American political writer (1752–1820).

Old Stars. A nickname given by the men of his command to Gen. Ormsby McK. Mitchell (fl. 1810–1862), on account of his high reputation as a practical astronomer.

Old Stone. Henry Stone, a famous statuary and painter (d. 1653).

Old Stone Hammer. Thomas Metcalfe, Governor of Kentucky (1780–1855). He was a friend and follower of Henry Clay, and took pride in the fact that in early life he had pursued the trade of a mason, delighting in the above nickname.

Old Straws. (Pseud.) Joseph M. Field, in the New Orleans " Picayune."

Old Stubborn. The Forty-fifth Regiment of Foot in the English army is so dubbed.

Old Tecumseh. Gen. William T. Sherman's soldiery used thus to speak of him during the civil war.

Old Test., or **O. T.** Old Testament.

Old Three Stars. A nickname conferred on Gen. U. S. Grant, in allusion to the number of stars on his uniform indicating his army rank as Lieutenant-General. *See also* OLD UNITED STATES.

Old 'Un. (Pseud.) Francis Alexander Durivage, in " Turf, Field, and Farm."

Old United States. A by-name by which Gen. U. S. Grant was known throughout the Army of the Potomac, from the initials of his name. *See also* OLD THREE STARS.

Old Usufruct. The late Samuel J. Tilden was known by this nickname.

Old Wagon. The U. S. frigate " United States " was so named because she was such a slow sailer. After the War of 1812 she was substantially rebuilt, and much improved in this respect.

Old Wheel-Horse of Democracy. Samuel Medary, American editor (1801–1864). He was a stanch upholder of Democratic doctrines with tongue and pen.

Old World. The Eastern Hemisphere was so named in popular parlance subsequent to the discovery of the New World (*q. v.*) in 1492.

Oleander City. Galveston, Texas.

O lepidum caput! (Lat.) O you charming fellow!

Olive Berkely. The stage-name of Mrs. Olive Dickson.

Oliver Doud Byron. The stage-name of Oliver B. Doud.

Olive Rivers. The stage-name of Mrs. James Reynolds.

Oliver Oldschool. (Pseud.) Nathan Sargent, American author (1794–1875).

Oliver Optic. (Pseud.) William Taylor Adams, American writer of juvenile fiction (b. 1822).

Oliver Yorke. (Pseud.) Francis Mahony, Irish author and wit (1805?–1866.)

Olivia. (Pseud.) Mrs. Briggs, *littérateur*.

Olla Podrida. (Pseud.) Frank M. Pixley, in the San Francisco " Argonaut."

Olla podrida. (Span.) An incongruous mixture.

Olphar Hamst, Esq. (Pseud.) Ralph Thomas, English bibliographer (b. 1843).

Olym. Olympiad.

Olympus of Ethiopia. Mount Kilima, 18,200 feet high, in Eastern Africa, was so named by the Portuguese.

O. M. Old Measurement.

Oman's Sea. The Persian Gulf.

Om Mani Padma Hum. A celebrated sacred sentence in use among the Buddhists. They believe that it is possessed of untold virtues, and it is heard and seen everywhere. The people inscribe it on their flags, houses, and domestic utensils, and on trees, walls, columns, and gates; little children learn to lisp it before anything else; and, says one writer, " the traveller repeats this formula on his journey, the shepherd when guarding his flock, the housewife when attending to her domestic duties, the children when at play, and the monk when rapt in religious ecstasy." In fact, there is no condition or phase of human life in which its supposed miraculous powers are not appealed to. *See* ABRACADABRA.

Omne ignotum pro magnifico. (Lat.) Everything unknown is thought to be magnificent.

Omnes. (Lat.) All.

Omne solum forti patria. (Lat.) To a brave man every land is his country.

Omnia bona bonis. (Lat.) To the good all things are good.

Omnia vincit amor. (Lat.) Love conquers all things.

Omnibus Bill. The name generally given to a series of compromise measures embodied in one act and introduced in the United States Senate by Henry Clay, on Jan. 29, 1850. It provided for the admission of California, Utah, and New Mexico, for the abolition of the slave-trade in the District of Columbia, and for the more speedy and certain return of fugitive slaves. As a whole the bill did not pass, but most of its provisions became the law of the land through separate enactments.

Omnium gatherum. " Of all things a collection." A slang term in Latin form, of which *omnium* is the only Latin word, signifying generally "a heterogeneous collection of articles."

Omphale. In classic myth a queen of Lydia, to whom Hercules was bound for three years for the murder of Iphitus. He fell in love with her, and wore women's garments, while she donned his lion's skin.

Once in a Blue Moon. "Blue" is a favorite adjective in slang phrases. Schoolboys, in their own choice dialect, talk of "blue fear" and "blue funk." The indefinite period known as "once in a blue moon" is a favorite with Miss Braddon, if one may judge by her frequent use of the expression. The moon will doubtless not be blue until the Greek Calends, or, as they say in Ireland, till "Tib's Eve," whenever that may be. Swift, in his "Polite Conversation," a wonderful series of dialogues, crammed with the colloquialisms current in the early part of the last century, uses the strange expression, "to blush like a blue dog," meaning, not to blush at all. More than a century earlier, in the "Apologie for the School of Abuse," published in 1579, Stephen Gosson speaks with similar meaning of blushing "like a blacke dogge." Both expressions appear to be equally meaningless. To drink "till all is blue" is an old-established euphemism for getting very drunk. Ford in the "Lady's Trial," 1639, says, "He can drink till all is blue."

On dit. (Fr.) "They say." A flying rumor.

One-armed Phil. A by-name conferred upon Gen. Phil Kearney among the men in the ranks. He lost an arm in Mexico.

One half the world knows not how the other lives. This proverbial saying seems to have originated with Bishop Hall. It occurs in "Holy Observations," No. XVII., ed. 1837.

One Step from the Sublime to the Ridiculous. This saying is generally attributed to Napoleon. It is, however, to be found in the works of Thomas Paine, before Napoleon's time. Paine says: "The sublime and the ridiculous are often so nearly related that it is difficult to class them separately. One step above the sublime makes the ridiculous, and one step above the ridiculous makes the sublime again."

One Swallow does not make a Summer. This is an ancient Greek proverb, and may be found in Aristotle in this form: "One swallow maketh not a spring, nor a woodcock a winter." (Ethic. Nicom., lib. i.) In Attica the children were given a holiday when the swallow first appeared. Horace connects the zephyrs of spring with the arrival of the swallow. In Italy and Spain the proverb still runs, "one swallow does not make a spring." But in more northern latitudes the swallows appear later, and their proverbial literature denies that a single swallow makes a summer. In Northbrooke's "Treatise against Dancing," 1577, the proverb reads, "One swallow proveth not that summer is near." Shakspeare, in "Timon of Athens," act iii. scene 6, says, "The swallow follows not the summer more willing than we your lordship." Dr. Fowler gives the 15th of April as swallows' day.

Onety-oneth. A jocose by-name bestowed on the Eleventh Regiment of the Line in the army of England. *See* BLOODY ELEVENTH.

Onghill. (Pseud.) John Creswell, in the "World."

On Hand. This phrase in England is confined to the language of commerce. A corn merchant may say he "has no oats on hand," or a fishmonger when applied to for salmon may say he has none on hand. Americans give the phrase a far wider significance, as the following extract from the New York "Express" will show: "The anti-Sabbath meeting, so long talked of, has at length taken place in Boston. About three hundred females were on hand."

Onkel Adam. (Pseud.) Carl Anton Wetterbergh.

Only, The. Jean Paul Friedrich Richter (fl. 1763–1825), of whom Carlyle said: "In the whole circle of literature we look in vain for his parallel."

Only Aretino, The. A complimentary title given to Bernardo Accolti, an Italian lyric poet of the sixteenth century, intended to signify his superiority to his uncle, Francesco Accolti (d. 1483) and to Pietro Accolti, a famous contemporary versifier.

Onslow Yorke. (Pseud.) William Hepworth Dixon, English author (1821–1879).

Ont. Ontario.

On the Fence. This political phrase, which is very common, is said to have originated as follows : General Washington once asked a negro belonging to Judge Imlay, of New Jersey, whether his master was a Whig or a Tory. The reply was, " Massa on de fence ; him want to know which de strongest party."

On the Nail. To pay on the nail, — that is, at once. On the Bristol Exchange are four bronze pillars having expanded tops like tables ; they are called nails. On these " nails " the earnest money of bargains was formerly paid by merchants at the time the bargain was made. Hence to " pay on the nail " became synonymous with " paying ready money."

On to Berlin! *See infra.*

On to Richmond! The popular cry in the North just after the outbreak of the civil war, when it was believed that a ninety days' campaign would suffice to crush the rebellion. The disastrous first battle of Bull Run effectually silenced the cry. Similarly, at the outbreak of the Franco-Prussian War in 1870 the French raised the cry " On to Berlin ! " but they never crossed the Rhine.

Onus probandi. (Lat.) The burden of proving.

Onyx. (Pseud.) Elizabeth Stuart Phelps, in her " Silent Partner," published 1871.

O'Pake. (Pseud.) William M. Mallison, in the Brooklyn " Eagle."

Ope et consilio. (Lat.) With assistance and counsel.

Operæ pretium est. (Lat.) It is worth one's while.

Opera omnia. (Lat.) All the works.

Opimius. (Pseud.) W. H. Fitzhugh, American writer.

Opium War. The war of 1839 between England and China is so known to history. Opium was largely cultivated in India, and was introduced into China by English merchants in spite of the prohibition of the trade by the Chinese Government. England came to the aid of her merchants, and the infamous traffic was forced upon the weaker country.

Opportunists. A name given to French politicians (especially the ultra-liberals) who suspend agitation for their peculiar opinions till a suitable opportunity comes ; among them Gambetta was prominent, 1876–1878.

Opprobrium medicorum. (Lat.) The reproach of medical men ; said of a disease for which they have failed to find a remedy or remedies.

O. P. Riots (Old Prices Riots). " On the night of the 20th of September, 1808, Covent Garden Theatre was burned. A new theatre was built, and the opening announced for Sept. 18, 1809, one year after the fire. Much expense was incurred, and, to make the opening attractive, Mr. Kemble, Mrs. Siddons, and Madame Catalani were engaged. In order to cover expenses, the managers decided to increase the admission-prices, putting them one shilling advance for boxes and sixpence advance for the pit. This announcement created great dissatisfaction, and a war-cry was at once raised. The subject was discussed in clubs and coffee-houses. Newspapers took it up. Kemble and Covent Garden were as often discussed as Napoleon and France. The plays on the opening night were ' Macbeth,' and for an after-piece, ' The Quaker.' The house was crowded, especially the pit. As soon as the curtain rose, the noise began. ' Old prices forever ! ' rang through the house. Mr. Kemble tried to deliver an address in honor of the occasion, but could not be heard. The noise continued through the five acts of the play. Magistrates read the ' Riot Act ' on the stage. The next night the same scenes were repeated, with the addition of placards inscribed ' Old prices forever ! ' Constables seized the placard-bearers and carried them off. The next night more placards appeared. Mr. Kemble came forward and said, ' What do you want ? ' A Mr. Leigh replied, ' We want the old prices.' This started another tumult. Horns, whistles, and watchmen's rattles were heard in every part of the house, and dogs were brought in, whose barking and yelping added to the confusion. Placards inscribed

'Come forth, O Kemble,
Come forth, and tremble ! '

and

' Seventeen thousand a year goes pat
To Kemble, his sister, and Madame Cat,'

were shown through the house. On the fifth night the placards were marked ' O. P.' for the first time. Another placard was, —

'John Kemble alone is the cause of this riot :
When he lowers his prices, John Bull will be
quiet.'

On the sixth night Mr. Kemble announced that the theatre would be closed,
and a committee appointed to determine
whether the prices could be lowered.
This announcement was received with
applause, and a placard exhibited bearing the following :—

' Here lies the body of new price, an ugly brat
and base-born, who expired on Sept. 23, 1809,
aged six days. Requiescat in pace.'

A committee was appointed, made up of
well-known gentlemen, who, after conferring together, decided that the managers could not afford to return to the
old prices. So the theatre was reopened, and this announcement made.
The riots were then worse than ever.
Party feeling was shown everywhere.
Ladies appeared in the boxes with O. P.
on their bonnets; O. P. hats for men
were common ; some wore waistcoats
with O. embroidered on one lapel and P.
on the other; O. P. toothpicks were in
fashion ; O. P. handkerchiefs were waved
at the theatre, so also were O. P. flags ;
O. P. medals were worn. At a grand
dinner given at the Crown and Anchor
tavern to celebrate the victory of Mr.
Clifford, — a barrister who had espoused
the O. P. cause, been arrested, and by
some quibble of the law been released
after being fined five pounds, — Mr.
Kemble appeared, and a conference was
held. A treaty was signed which ended
the O. P. Riots and restored peace to
the drama. Mr. Kemble announced at
the theatre that night that the old prices
would be restored. This announcement
was greeted with applause ; and the next
night a placard was exhibited, inscribed
'We are satisfied.' The contest ended
on the 10th of December, after three
months of disgraceful tumult." — OLIVE
OLDSCHOOL, in *Lippincott*.

Ops. In classic myth the wife of
Saturn, and the goddess of plenty, fertility, and power.

Opt. Optics.

Opum furiata cupido. (Lat.) An
irresistible craving after wealth.

Or. Oregon.

Oracle of the Church. Saint Bernard (fl. 1091–1153).

Ora et labora. (Lat.) Pray and work.

Oran. (Pseud.) F. N. Otis, a former contributor to "Harper's Magazine."

Orange Lilies. A nickname for the
Thirty-fourth Regiment in the English
service.

Orange-Peel. A nickname given to
Sir Robert Peel when he was Chief-
Secretary for Ireland (1812–1818), because of his stanch anti-Catholic principles.

Ora pro nobis. (Lat.) Pray for us.

Oraquill. (Pseud.) Mary Borne-
mann, a San Francisco author.

Orator fit poeta nascitur. The orator is made by education, but a poet
must be born.

Orator Henley. The Rev. John
Henley (fl. 1692–1756), who for upward
of thirty years lectured on a variety of
topics in a fashionable London chapel.

Orator of the Human Race. *See*
ANACHARSIS CLOOTZ.

Orchard of Denmark. The island
of Falster, in the Baltic Sea ; so named
from its great fertility in fruit.

Orcus. In classic myth the lower
world of the Romans, the realm of the
dead; the same as the Greek hades.
Also, the name of its presiding deity,
and often used by the older poets as a
synonym for death.

Order reigns in Warsaw. General
Sebastiani announced the fall of Warsaw in the Chamber of Deputies, Sept. 16,
1831 : "Des lettres que je reçois de
Pologne m'annoncent que la tranquillité
règne à Varsovie." — DUMAS.

Ordinance of 1787. This Ordinance
created the first Territorial government
in this country ; namely, the Northwest
Territory, embracing Ohio and all that
portion of the United States of that date
north and west of the Ohio River. General St. Clair, ex-president of the Continental Congress, was the first governor.
The ordinance forbade slavery, and provided for the maintenance of public
schools largely by the proceeds of a portion of the public land. This ordinance
guaranteed many rights subsequently
guaranteed to the whole country through
the Constitution. The authorship of
the Ordinance is generally attributed to
Nathan Dane, but is claimed by others
for Rev. Dr. Cutler, who conceived a
vast scheme of colonization, if a satisfactory ordinance could be secured.

Ordinario. (Ital.) Usual; as *a tempo
ordinario*, in the usual time. (Mus.)

Oreades. In classic myth mountain
nymphs, attendants on Diana.

Oregon. The name of this State is an Indian word, meaning "river of the West," referring to the great river of the name.

Oregon Escort. A military company raised under act of Congress in 1862, under command of Capt. M. Crawford, for the purpose of protecting emigrants to California against hostile Indians.

Ore rotundo. (Lat.) "With round mouth." With swelling eloquence.

Orestes. In classic myth a son of Agamemnon and Clytemnestra; he was pursued by the Erinnyes, who drove him mad as a punishment for the murder of his mother.

Oriana. (1) A title given to Queen Elizabeth to celebrate her beauty and chastity at the age of sixty-eight! (2) Anne, Queen of James II., was so named by Ben Jonson.

Oriental Venice. Bangkok, in Siam; so named because a large number of its population dwell in floating houses.

Orig. Originally.

Origo mali. (Lat.) The source of the evil.

Origo malorum. (Lat.) The source of the evils.

Orion. In classic myth a mighty hunter, and reputed the handsomest man in the world. He was a son of Hyrieus, of Hyria, in Bœotia, or, say others, of Poseidon and Euryale, while others say that he was autochthonous, or earth-born. His stature was so great that when he waded through the deepest seas he was still a head and shoulders above the water, and when he walked on dry land his stature reached the clouds. After his death he was placed among the stars, where to this day a splendid constellation bears his name.

Orion. A magnificent constellation of about two thousand stars, seventy-eight of which are visible, situated midway between the poles of the heavens and directly over the earth's equator; coming to the meridian about January 23. It represents a man in the attitude of assaulting the Bull, having a sword in his belt, a huge club in his right hand, and a shield of lion's skin in his left. Two of the stars are of the first magnitude, four of the second, three of the third, and fifteen of the fourth. It is full of interest to the astronomer.

Orithyia. In classic myth a daughter of Erechtheus, whom Boreas abducted while she was walking near the river Ilissus.

Orlando. (Pseud.) James Hall, an Illinois editor and journalist.

Orleanists. Political partisans in France; so called from Louis Philippe, son of Louis Philippe, Duc d'Orleans, called Égalité, descended from Philippe, Duc d'Orleans, son of Louis XIII., born Oct. 6, 1773; married Nov. 25, 1809, Maria Amelia, daughter of Ferdinand I. (IV.), king of the two Sicilies (she died March 24, 1866); raised to the throne as king of the French August 9, 1830; abdicated Feb. 24, 1848; died in exile, in England, August 26, 1850. Heir — Louis Philippe, Count of Paris, born August 24, 1838.

Ornith. Ornithology.

Orphan of the Temple. Marie Thérèse Charlotte, Duchesse d'Angoulême, daughter of Louis XVI.; so called from the Temple, where she was imprisoned. She was called the "modern Antigone" by her uncle Louis XVIII.

Orpheus. In classic myth a son of Apollo, who bestowed on him the lyre which Hermes invented, and by its strains Orpheus moved men, beasts, the birds in the air, the fishes in the deep, the trees, and the rocks. He accompanied the Argonauts in their famous voyage; and the power of his music warded off all mishaps and disasters, rocking monsters to sleep, and stopping cliffs in their downward rush.

Orpheus C. Kerr. (Pseud.) Robert H. Newell, New York journalist (b. 1836).

Orpheus of Highwaymen. John Gay (fl. 1688-1732) was so named because of his "Beggars' Opera."

Orthodox City. Thessalonica (the modern Salonica) was so named. It was for centuries a bulwark of Christianity, but in 1430 was captured by Amurath II.

Orthodoxy is my Doxy; Heterodoxy is another man's Doxy. "'I have heard frequent use,' said the late Lord Sandwich, in a parliamentary debate on the Test Laws, 'of the words "orthodoxy" and "heterodoxy;" but I confess myself at a loss to know precisely what they mean.' 'Orthodoxy, my Lord,' said Bishop Warburton, in a whisper, — 'Orthodoxy is my doxy, —

heterodoxy is another man's doxy.'" — *Priestley's Memoirs.*

O. S. Old Style; outside sentinel.

Os. Osmium.

Os à ronger. (Fr.) "A bone to pick" or gnaw. Something to do.

Os durum. (Lat.) "A brazen face." A brazen-faced or impudent fellow.

Osiris. In Egyptian mythology a celebrated deity whose worship was universal throughout Egypt.

O si sic omnia! (Lat.) "Oh, if thus all things!" Oh that he had always done or spoken so!

Ossa. *See* PELION AND OSSA.

Os sublime. (Lat.) "A countenance sublime." A lofty aspect; a grand presence.

Ostend Manifesto. A state paper famous in American history. It was drawn up by Buchanan, Mason, and Soule, in 1854, and recommended the purchase of Cuba by the United States.

O. T. Old Testament; Oregon Territory.

O tempora! O mores! (Lat.) "Oh the times! Oh the manners!" Oh the altered times! Oh the laxity of men's manners!

Other One. A name used by his partisans to designate Napoleon I. during his exile in Elba.

Otium cum dignitate. (Lat.) "Ease with dignity." Dignified leisure; the pleasures of freedom from business, with dignity of social position.

Otium sine dignitate. (Lat.) "Ease without dignity." The pleasures of retirement from business without any dignity.

Ottava. (Ital.) An octave. (Mus.)

Ottava alta. (Ital.) To be played an octave higher. (Mus.)

Ottava bassa. (Ital.) To be played an octave lower. (Mus.)

O. U. A. Order of United Americans.

Ouida. (Pseud.) Louisa de la Rame, English novelist (b. 1840).

Oui-dire. (Fr.) Hearsay.

Our Mary. (1) A sobriquet bestowed on Mary Cecilia Ewen, *née* Taylor (1836–1866), a once famous American actress. (2) The same endearing title was bestowed on Mary Anderson, the celebrated Shakspearian impersonator (b. 1859).

Our own Correspondent. (Pseud.) James O. Noyes, M.D., American author and editor (b. 1829).

Our own Evarts. So New Yorkers refer to William M. Evarts.

Our Member for Paris. (Pseud.) Henry Labouchere, English journalist and author (b. 1831).

Our Tender. The pen-name of G. Hamlen, author of "Chats."

Outré. (Fr.) Preposterous; eccentric.

Over the Left. This expression, which is usually thought to be modern slang, is really sanctioned by the usage of two hundred years, as evidence by the following, written in 1682: "What the Protestant religon gets by lives and fortunes spent in the service of a Popish successor will be over the left shoulder." A morganatic wife is said to be married "over the left." In the records of the County Court at Hartford, Conn., it is stated that on Sept. 4, 1705, one James Steel brought an action against Beevel Waters, in which judgment was given for the plaintiff. On departing from court the said Waters addressing the court said, "God bless you, over the left shoulder." At the next sitting of the court Waters was fined £5 for contempt of court, against which he appealed. Pending the hearing, the court asked counsel of the ministers of two Hartford churches as to the meaning of the phrase; and those gentlemen decided, "1st, that the words were prophane;" and secondly, "that they carry great contempt in them, arising to the degree of an imprecation or curse." This opinion, which is still in existence, is signed "T. Woodbridge" and "T. Buckingham," and is dated March 7, 1705–6.

Ovid of France. Du Bellay, a French poet, one of the "Pleiads" (fl. 1524–1560).

Owen Meredith. (Pseud.) Edward Robert Bulwer, Lord Lytton, English poet (b. 1831).

Ox-eye. A cloudy speck which indicates the approach of a storm. Thomson alludes to this storm-signal in his "Summer."

Oxf. Oxford.

Oxf. Gloss. Oxford Glossary.

Oxford Blues. A nickname of the English Horse-Guards.

Oxon. *Oxonia, Oxonii.* Oxford.

Oxtail Soup, which is now such a favorite, was originally the humble fare of Protestant refugees who fled from France at the revocation of the Edict of Nantes, in 1685. In the extremity of want they purchased from the tanners of Bermondsey the oxtails, which were there sold with the hides, and made them into soup. Accident brought it under the notice of a philanthropic epi-cure, who was on a mission of charity to the homes of the poor foreigners; and he proclaimed its virtues, so that it very soon became a fashionable dish and source of revenue.

O yes! A corruption of the French *Oyez* ("Hear ye!"). The ancient term used by a crier to enjoin silence and attention.

Oz. Ounce.

P.

P. Phosphorus.

P. *Pondere.* By weight.

P., or p. Page; part; participle.

Pa., or Penn. Pennsylvania.

Pace tua. (Lat.) With thy leave or permission.

Pacific, The. (1) Amadeus VIII., Count of Savoy (fl. 1383–1451). (2) Frederick III., Emperor of Germany (fl. 1415–1493). (3) Olaus III., of Norway (fl. 1030–1093).

Pacification of Ghent. A compact between the north and south provinces of the Netherlands to resist the tyranny of Spain. Signed at Ghent in 1576.

Pacificator of the Occident. Manuel González, the Mexican soldier (b. 1820). After the overthrow of Lerdo, in 1878, the Congress gave him the rank of General of Division, thanked him, and bestowed the complimentary title "Pacificator of the Occident."

Pacific Blockade is a blockade enforced while there is no war existing between the blockading and the blockaded countries. It is hardly justified by international law, but is sometimes employed as a coercive measure by a powerful nation against a weak one.

Pacta conventa. (Lat.) Conditions agreed upon.

Pacte de famille. (Fr.) "Agreement of family." A family compact.

Pactum illicitum. (Lat.) An unlawful agreement or compact.

Padalon. In the Hindu mythology the abode of departed spirits, — hades.

Paddies Royal, or Royal Irish. The Eighteenth Regiment in the English army.

Paddington Fair. A slang phrase for a public execution. Tyburn, near London, where numberless executions formerly took place, is in Paddington parish, and such occasions, even down to our own day, were often scenes and occasions for holiday-making and revelry among the on-lookers.

Paddy. A nickname for an Irishman the world over; the equivalent of "Johnny Crapaud" for a Frenchman, "Sandy" for a Scotchman, etc. Patrick is merely a corruption of the Celtic *Padhrig.*

Paddywhack Almanac. In reply to a question, What is a Paddywhack Almanac? a correspondent of "Notes and Queries" says: "'Paddywhack' means 'An Irish wag,' as may be gathered from the words of the song : —

'I'm Paddywhack, from Ballynack,
    Not long ago turned soldier.'

Before the stamp duty of 1*s.* 3*d.* on each almanac was repealed in August, 1834, no regular almanacs were sold under 2*s.* 6*d.* each, 2*s.* 9*d.* being the usual price. A sheet almanac was, however, surreptitiously sold by hawkers, under the name of 'Paddy's Watch,' for about threepence, or was more frequently exchanged for some old garment or kitchen stuff. I have several times seen these in small houses before that period. As the possession of them was punishable, they were most frequently in such houses pasted inside a cupboard or pantry door, where they could be readily consulted. Besides a calendar, the 'Paddy's Watch' contained some predictions, after the manner of Partridge and Francis Moore, about the weather and general matters.

Though it is now over fifty years since I saw one, I have a perfect picture in my mind of it. The sheet of common paper was about twenty-four inches by eighteen inches, printed in the Catnach style, and the title, ' Paddy's Watch,' was in italics, — capitals and small letters. The term ' Watch ' was probably given to it to describe its reference to times and seasons, and to avoid the dangerous use of the word ' almanac,' which would have carried conviction of itself."

Pæon. In classic myth the physician to the gods, and the god of medicine.

Paganus Piscator. (Pseud.) Payne Fisher, English poet (1614–1693).

Painter of Nature. An honorary title conferred on Remi Belleau (fl. 1528–1577), one of the " Pleiad Poets." His " Song on April " is said to have been largely drawn upon by Spenser in his " Shepherd's Calendar."

Painter of the Graces. Andrea Appiani (fl. 1754–1817), an Italian artist famed for his beautiful frescos.

Paix des Dames. *See* LADIES' PEACE.

Paix Fourrée. *See* LAME AND UNSTABLE PEACE.

Pal. Palæontology.

Palaces, City of. *See* CITY OF PALACES.

Palæmon. In classic myth a surname of Melicertes, the son of Ino. He was the patron deity of shipwrecked voyagers.

Palamedes. In classic myth son of Nauplius, king of Eubœa, and of Clymene his wife. He invented measures, the scales, dice, and many other implements. Hence his name is often used as a sobriquet for a person possessed of mechanical genius.

Palatinates. Persecuted Protestants who emigrated from the Upper and Lower Palatinate in Germany, in the seventeenth century, to Pennsylvania.

Palatine Counties. *See* COUNTIES PALATINE.

Pale, The. Those portions of Ireland over which England ruled and English law was acknowledged after the invasion of 1172. It comprised the territory now included in the counties of Dublin, Meath, Carlow, Kilkenny, and Louth.

Pales. In Roman mythology the patron deity of shepherds, flocks, and cattle.

Palindrome. The palindrome has been erroneously described as a species of anagram. As the name implies, it indicates a sentence which reads alike backward or forward; as the word " madam." One of the best is that which the Lowell " Courier " claims to have originated : " No it is opposition." A palindrome in actual existence is the sign of a baker in Yreka, Siskiyou County, Cal., — " Yreka Bakery." Here is one of some length : " Snug & raw was I ere I saw war & guns." The last word would be slightly imperfect did we not use the ampersand for the conjunction " and," as is the following : " Lewd did I live & evil did I dwel." The flexible Latin language affords some fine palindromic phrases ; as, for example, " Signa te signa temera me tangis et angis," or " Roma tibi subito moribus ibit amor," or " Sator arepo tenet opera rotas." In English we have Adam's brief self-introduction to Eve in the garden of Eden, " Madam, I 'm Adam ; " and the famous Napoleonic palindrome, " Able was I ere I saw Elba."

Palladium. Among the ancient Greeks and Romans an image of Pallas, usually identified with Athene, upon the safe keeping of which, in a temple or shrine, the public weal was thought to depend. The Palladium of Troy is specially celebrated in classic story. According to the legend, it was thrown down from heaven by Zeus, and fell on the plain of Troy, where it was picked up by Ilus, the founder of the city, as a good omen. On its preservation the safety of Troy depended, and it was therefore stolen by Ulysses and Diomed.

Pallas. In classic myth a surname of Minerva (*q. v.*).

Pallida mors. (Lat.) Pale death.

Palmam qui meruit, ferat. (Lat.) Let him bear the palm who has gained it. (The palm was the emblem of victory.)

Palmetto State. South Carolina. On its coat-of-arms is a delineation of one of these trees, for the growth of which the State is famous.

Palm-Sunday. The last Sunday of Lent is so called from the custom of blessing branches of the palm-tree, or of other trees substituted in those countries in which palm cannot be procured, and of carrying the blessed branches in procession, in commemoration of the triumphal entry of our Lord into Jerusalem. The date of this custom is uncertain. The first writer in the West who expressly refers to it is the Venerable Bede. The usage certainly existed in the seventh century.

Pam, or **Old Pam**. A familiar appellation bestowed on Henry John Temple, Viscount Palmerston, the English statesman.

Pan. In the Greek mythology the chief god of pastures, forests, and flocks. He was outside of the principal deities, and his worship became widespread at a comparatively late date. The generally received account makes him the son of Penelope by Ulysses.

Pancake Day. *See* SHROVE-TUESDAY.

P. & O. Co. Peninsular and Oriental Steam Navigation Company.

Pandora. In classic myth the first mortal woman, created by Vulcan at the behest of Jupiter. The latter gave her a box filled with winged blessings, which would have been preserved for the human race, but which all flew out, save Hope, when her curiosity tempted her to raise the lid.

Panhandle, The. (1) A descriptive designation popularly given to the northern extremity of the State of West Virginia, a somewhat elongated strip of territory between the western frontier of Pennsylvania and the Ohio River. (2) The northwestern projection of Texas is sometimes called by the same name.

Pantagruel. Under this thinly veiled disguise Henri II. of France, is satirized by Rabelais in his cynical romance entitled " History of Pantagruel and Gargantua."

Pantagruelian Herb. Hemp; so named because from it ropes are made, while Pantagruel was the inventor of hanging in Rabelais's famous satire of the name.

Pan, The Great. *See* GREAT PAN.

Panther. *See* SPOTTED PANTHER.

Panurge. " A licentious and intemperate libertine, a coward, and a knave," the companion of Pantagruel, in Rabelais's immortal satire. The character was meant for an attack on Calvin, though some think that Cardinal Lorraine is meant.

Paper City. (1) Holyoke, Mass. (2) Said of cities in embryo, the names of which are put in maps and plans with their streets, public places, etc., laid down and named, — the work of speculators, who hope by these displays to attract settlers. *See* CITY.

Paper House, in theatrical language, is one where the stall and box occupants have not paid cash for their places, but have come in with orders.

Paper King. John Law, the promoter of the notorious Mississippi scheme (fl. 1671–1729).

Paper Marriages. Weddings of dons, who pay their fees in bank-notes.

Paphian Mimp. An expression of the lips, considered needful for " the highly genteel." Lady Emily told Miss Alscrip " the heiress " that it was acquired by placing one's self before a looking-glass, and repeating continually the words " nimini pimini," " when the lips cannot fail to take the right plie."

Paps of Jura. A fanciful name given to three peaks on the island of Jura in the Hebrides.

Pap Thomas. A nickname of endearment applied to Gen. George H Thomas by the men of his command during the civil war in the United States.

Par. Paragraph.

Paradise. The abode of the blest, according to many widely divergent religions. " Paradise " appears in the Old Testament as well as in the New, and scholars seem to agree that it found its way both to the Hebrew and the Greek from the Persian. It is thoroughly discussed in Smith's " Bible Dictionary." Perhaps a more comprehensive explanation is that of the very learned Dr. Adam Clark, which we present as follows : —

" The ' Garden of Eden,' mentioned Genesis ii. 8, is also called, from the Septuagint, the ' garden of Paradise.' The word ' Eden ' signifies pleasure and delight. Several places were thus called (see Genesis iv. 16; 2 Kings xix. 12; Isaiah xxxvii. 12; Ezekiel xxvii. 27, and Amos i. 5), and such places probably had this name from their fertility, pleasant situation, etc. In this light the Septuagint have viewed Genesis ii. 8, as they render the passage thus : ' God planted a paradise in Eden.' Hence the word has been translated into the New Testament, and is used to signify a place of exquisite pleasure and delight. From this the ancient heathens borrowed their ideas of the gardens of the Hesperides, where the trees bore golden fruit. And the gardens of Adonis, a word which is evidently derived from the Hebrew ' Eden ;' and hence the origin of sacred groves, gardens and other enclosures dedicated to the purposes of devotion, some comparatively innocent, others impure. The word ' paradise ' is not Greek, but is of Asiatic origin. In Arabic and Persian it signifies ' a garden, a vineyard,' and also the 'place of the blessed.' In the 'Kushuf ul Loghat,' a very celebrated Persian dictionary, the 'Jenet al Ferdoos' (Garden of Paradise) is said to have been 'created by God out of light, and that the prophets and wise men ascend thither.' In the 'Institutes of Menu,' chapter Œconomics, Institute 243, are the following words : 'A man habitually pious, whose offences have been expiated, is instantly conveyed, after death, to the higher world, with a radiant form, and a body of ethereal substance.' The 'state of the blessed' is certainly what our Lord means (Luke xxiii. 43) ; in what the 'locality' of that state consists, we know not. The Jews have a multitude of fables on the subject."

Paradise of Americans. *See* AMERICANS' PARADISE.

Paradise of Fools. Many systems of religion, — notably the Roman Catholic, the Mohammedan, and the Buddhist, — to avoid a theological difficulty, imagine a place between Paradise and Purgatory. They say there can be no sin without intention, so of course infants and fools cannot commit sin; but not being believers, they cannot be placed with the saints, so they are relegated to the " Paradise of Fools."

Paradise of the World. The natives of Congo so call their table-lands. To them the climate is salubrious, and travellers all agree that the scenery is beautiful.

Paradoxes, Country of. *See* COUNTRY OF PARADOXES.

Parallax. The signature of Samuel Birley Robotham, who taught that the earth is a circular plain over which the sun moves.

Parcæ. In classic myth the three goddesses, sometimes called the Destinies, who were believed to determine the course of human life, and represented, one holding the distaff, a second spinning, and the third cutting the thread. Their names were Clotho, Lachesis, and Atropos.

Parc aux Cerfs. The abode of disreputable characters. The phrase is derived from a château of the name in a secluded corner of the park at Versailles, where young maidens were inveigled for the licentious pleasures of Louis XV.

Par ci par la. (Fr.) Here and there; now and then.

Pardon Bell. The bell tolled after full service, to call those who wish to stay to the invocation of the Virgin for pardon.

Par excellence. (Fr.) " By excellence." By way of eminence; pre-eminently.

Par hasard. (Fr.) By chance.

Parian Chronicle. A register of the chief events in the history of ancient Greece for 1318 years, beginning with the reign of Cecrops and ending with the archonship of Diognetus. It is one of the Arundelian Marbles, and was found in the island of Paros.

Parian Verse. Ill-natured satire; so called from Archilochus, a native of Paros.

Pari passu. (Lat.) " With equal pace." In the same degree or proportion.

Pari ratione. (Lat.) " By equal reasoning." By parity of reasoning.

Paris. In classic myth the son of Priam and Hecuba, famed for his beauty. He married Œnone, daughter of the river deity Cebren. When the dispute arose between Juno, Minerva, and Venus, as to which of them was the most beautiful, Paris was made umpire, and awarded the palm to Venus, who had promised him the hand of Helen, as his wife. By running away with her he precipitated the Trojan war, in which he was killed by Philoctetes.

Paris of Eastern Europe. Vienna is so named.

Paris of Japan. The city of Kioto. *See* VENICE OF JAPAN.

Paris of the Ancient World. Corinth. Its people were devoted to pleasure, and so profligate that the name became a by-word.

Parke Richards. (Pseud.) Mrs. Laura R. Fewell, in " Godey's Lady's Book."

Parl. Parliament.

Par le droit du plus fort. (Fr.) By the right of the strongest.

Parliament. *See* ADDLED, BAREBONES', BLACK, DEVIL'S, DRUNKEN, DUNCES', GOOD, LONG, MAD, PENSIONER, RUMP, RUNNING, UNMERCIFUL, USELESS, AND WONDER-MAKING PARLIAMENTS.

Parliament Oak. A tree in Thoresby Park, England (on the site of Sherwood Forest); so named because under its spreading branches King John once held a Parliament of his barons. *See* SHAMBLES OAK.

Parliament of Love. In Provence, during the flourishing time of the Troubadours, Love was esteemed so grave and formal a part of the business of life, that a Parliament or High Court of Love was appointed for deciding such questions. " This singular tribunal was, it may be supposed, conversant with more of imaginary than of real suits; but it is astonishing with what cold and pedantic ingenuity the Troubadours of whom it consisted set themselves to plead and decide, upon reasoning which was not less singular and able than out of place, the absurd questions which their own fantastic imaginations had previously devised. There, for example, is a reported case, of much celebrity, where a lady sitting in company with three persons, who were her admirers, listened to one with the most favorable smiles, while she pressed the hand of the second, and touched with her own the foot of the third. It was a case much agitated and keenly contested in the Parliament of Love, which of these rivals had received the distinguishing mark of the lady's favor. Much ingenuity was wasted on this and similar cases, of which there is a collection, in the judicial form of legal proceedings, under the title of ' Arrêts d'Amour' (Adjudged Cases of the Court of Love)."

Parlor City. The name given by its admirers to Binghamton, N. Y. Finer homes and better kept lawns are seldom seen than line some of its streets.

Par manière d'acquit. (Fr.) By way of discharge; carelessly.

Par negotiis neque supra. (Lat.) Neither above nor below his business; equal to his position; the right man in the right place.

Par nobile fratrum. (Lat.) " A noble pair of brothers." Two just alike.

Parole d'honneur. (Fr.) Word of honor.

Par. Pas. Parallel passage.

Parsee Merchant. The pen-name of J. S. Moore, an American writer on economic questions.

Parsley Peel. The first Sir Robert Peel; so called from the great quantity of printed calico with the parsley-leaf pattern manufactured by him (1750–1830).

Pars magna. (Lat.) A great part; the mainspring or stay.

Parson Adams. In Fielding's novel of " Joseph Andrews," the ideal of a benevolent, simple-minded, eccentric country clergyman; ignorant of the

world, bold as a lion for the truth, and modest as a girl.

Parson Brownlow. (Pseud.) William Gannaway Brownlow, American political writer (1805–1877).

Parson Frank. (Pseud.) Rev. Francis Jacox, in various English magazines.

Parson Lot. (Pseud.) Rev. Charles Kingsley, English author (1819–1875).

Parson of the Islands. Joshua Thomas, a Maryland preacher, was so named.

Parson's Cause, The. A famous law case tried in 1763 before Judge Henry, father of Patrick Henry, in Virginia. The latter pleaded the case of the people "with such extraordinary eloquence and vehemence that the clergymen present rose and left the room, and Henry's father wept tears of triumph, while the people carried the young lawyer about on their shoulders."

Parson's Emperor. A nickname given to Charles IV. of Moravia. At the behest of Pope Clement VI. he was put up as a competitor of Louis IV., the rightful reigning sovereign.

Parsonus Rusticus. (Pseud.) Samuel Walton McDaniel, in the New York " Christian Messenger."

Pars pro toto. (Lat.) A part for the whole.

Parthenon of Gothic Architecture. A name bestowed on Amiens Cathedral by Viollet-le-Duc. Ruskin says that the style of the edifice is "pure, unadulterated, and unaccusable."

Parthenon of Western Europe. The Church of the Madeleine, in Paris. Its front is very similar to that of its ancient namesake in Athens.

Parthenope. (1) In classic myth one of the three sirens. She fell in love with Ulysses, and in her sorrow at his not returning her passion threw herself into the sea. Her body was cast up on the shore where Naples was built at a later epoch, and that city was anciently called by her name. (2) A poetic nickname for the city of Naples, after Parthenope, the siren, who flung herself into the sea for love of Ulysses, and was cast ashore in the Bay of Naples.

At last the Muses . . . scattered . . .
Their blooming wreaths from fair Valclusa's
            bowers [*Petrarch*].
To Arno [*Dante* and *Boccaccio*] . . . and the
            shore
Of soft Parthenope.
        AKENSIDE, *Pleasures of Imagination.*

Parthenope of Naples. Sannazaro, the Neapolitan poet, called "The Christian Virgil." Most of his poems were published under the assumed name of Actius Sincerus (1458–1530).

Particeps criminis. (Lat.) "A sharer of the crime." An accomplice in the guilt.

Particular Baptists. That branch of the Baptist Communion who limit the Sacrament of the Lord's Supper to those who have been the recipients of adult baptism. "Open Baptists" admit any baptized person to receive it.

Particularists. (1) Those who hold the doctrine of particular election and reprobation. (2) In American politics the Particularists were those Whigs who, in the early history of our Government, feared that the Federal Government would be unduly strengthened to the detriment of the independence of the States.

Partie carrée. (Fr.) "A party square." A party of two ladies and two gentlemen; a party of four.

Partington, Mrs. An American Mrs. Malaprop, famous for her solecisms; the character was created by B. P. Shillaber, the humorist (b. 1814), whose was the personality veiled behind the name.

Partington, Mrs., and her Mop. A gibe at those who attempted to frustrate progress of any sort, political or social.

The English newspapers once related that a Mrs. Partington had a cottage at Sidmouth, in Devonshire. In November, 1824, a heavy gale drove the sea-waves into her house, and the old lady labored with a mop to sop the wet up, till she was obliged to take refuge in the upper part of the house. The Rev. Sydney Smith, speaking on the Lords' rejection of the Reform Bill, October, 1831, compares them to Dame Partington with her mop, trying to push back the Atlantic. "She was excellent," he says, "at a slop or puddle, but should never have meddled with a tempest."

Parturiunt montes, nascetur ridiculus mus. (Lat.) The mountains are in labor, and will only produce a laughter-exciting mouse.

Parvenu millionnaire. (Fr.) "An upstart millionnaire." An upstart who is worth a million.

Parvis componere magna. (Lat.) To compare great things with small.

Pas. (Fr.) "Step." Precedence; action. Hence a dance; as, *pas seul,* a dance by one; *pas de deux,* a dance by two performers; a quickstep.

Pascarel. (Pseud.) Rev. B. E. Warner, in the "Springfield Republican."

Paschal Controversies. The Paschal Controversies arose in the middle of the second century, on the question of the proper date of keeping Easter. The term "pascha" was in the first ages of the Church applied to the anniversary of the Saviour's death. After a time Easter became included in this term, but at length the "pascha," as an ecclesiastical term, was confined to Easter alone, Good Friday being excluded. The churches in Asia Minor used to celebrate the Paschal Supper, or anniversary of the crucifixion, on the 14th day of the month of Nisan, the date of the Jewish Passover; and three days later they kept Easter, regardless of what day of the week it fell upon. The practice of Rome and the majority of the churches was always to keep Easter on the Sunday and the Paschal Supper on its eve. The former custom — called the "quartodeciman," from its being kept on the 14th day — was claimed as derived from Saint John and Saint Philip; the latter from Saint Peter and Saint Paul. About the year 158 Polycarp, bishop of Smyrna, visited Anicetus, bishop of Rome, and discussed this question with him in a friendly spirit, the result being that it was agreed that a difference of practice was allowable on this point. But about the year 196 Victor, bishop of Rome, sought to enforce uniformity of practice by threatening to cut off communion with the Asiatic churches unless they submitted to the Western custom. His efforts, however, were doomed to failure. Polycrates, bishop of Ephesus, writing on behalf of the Asiatics, refused to yield to Victor; and when the latter sought to cut off so large a body of people from Christian communion, he was opposed by many Western bishops, among others by Irenæus, bishop of Lyons. In the year 314 the Council of Arles decreed that Easter should in all places be kept "on one day and at one time;" but the council had no jurisdiction in the East, and therefore did not affect the Asiatics. But in the Council of Nicæa the bishops from Asia Minor consented to conform to the Western and more general custom of keeping Easter; and although individual congregations resisted this surrender, yet the controversy was then at an end, and by the sixth century all traces of the Quartodecimans had disappeared.

Paschal Lambs. A by-name given to the Second Foot Regiment in the English army.

Passe-partout. (Fr.) A master-key.

Passe-port de mer. (Fr.) "Passport of sea." A sea-passport; permission to travel by sea.

Passim. (Lat.) Everywhere; all through.

Passion-flower. The passiflora, or passion-flower, is a climbing plant, whose name is derived from a fancied resemblance between the parts of the fructification and the emblems of our Saviour's crucifixion. The five stamens have been compared to the five wounds of Christ: the three styles to the nails by which he was fixed to the cross; the columns which elevate the germ, to the cross itself, or to the pillar to which he was bound; and the rays of the nectary to the crown of thorns. All the species of this beautiful and numerous genus are natives of America. The flower was originally named Flos passiones, till altered by Linnæus. There are cuts in ancient books, drawn probably from description (like the hog in armor to represent the rhinoceros), in which the flower is made up of the above emblems. In reality, the flower of the passiflora consists of a calyx and corolla, each of five divisions consolidated into a cup, from within the rim of which spread several rows of filamentous processes, regarded by some as barren stamens; within these, from the sides of the cup, there proceed one or more elevated rings notched or undivided, variously developed in different species. In the centre of the flower stands a column or gynophore, with the sides of which five stamens are united, but spread freely from it beyond the apex, and bear five oblong horizontal anthers. At the apex of the column is the ovary, a one-celled case with three parietal polyspermous placentæ, and bearing three club-shaped styles at its vertex. Eventually a gourd-like fruit is produced, containing many seeds, each having its own fleshy aril and usually enveloped in a subacid mucilage. So much for the botanical description. The plants are chiefly valued, in the countries where they grow wild, on account of their fruit. The Passiflora lauriflora produces the water lemon of the West Indies; the P. maliformis bears the sweet calabash. Many varieties are cultivated in our gardens, especially the P. alata, quadrangularis, edulis, cœrulea, racemosa, soudoni, onychina, palmata, and filamentosa.

Passionists. Certain priests of the Roman Catholic Church, who mutually agreed to preach "Jesus Christ, and him crucified." The founder of this "congregation" was Paul Francis (1694–1775).

Passion Orator. A name conferred on John Urkhardt Andrews (1825–1883). He was a Virginian by birth and achieved notoriety as a leader of the draft riots in New York in 1863, in the course of which his fervid speeches did not a little to sway the mob. He was arrested and confined in Fort Lafayette and Sing Sing, and after his release practised law.

Passion Play. The modern drama arose in the rude attempts of minstrels and travelling buffoons to illustrate portions of Scripture at fairs in France, Italy, and England. Later, stories from the Bible were represented by the priests, and were the origin of sacred comedy. So early as the year 364 A.D., Gregory Nazianzen, a father of the early Church, is believed to have constructed a drama on the Passion, in order to counteract the evil tendencies and profanity of the heathen stage, which is perhaps the earliest example we have of the "miracle plays" which arose and attained such wide popularity during the next twelve hundred years. Fitzstephen, who died about the year 1190, states, in his life of Thomas à Becket, "that London had for its theatrical exhibitions holy plays, and the representations of miracles performed by holy confessors; and at Clerkenwell, where was situated the hospice of the Knights Templars, and where now stands the old Shakspearian Sadler's Wells Theatre, plays and "miracles" were performed by the parish clergy in the open fields in 1397. In fact, up to the end of the fifteenth century, the only dramatic representations were those in which sacred subjects formed the chief theme. In the earliest times to which we can trace these shows the actors were generally monks, friars, and other ecclesiastics; the representations were generally given in the churches, seldomer in the open air; and the aim was the religious training and instruction of the people by means of amusement. In these last respects the modern drama, whose rise we have just sketched, differed not at all from the first inception of the ancient Greek drama; and from the very earliest ages down to the time of Solon, religious feasts were accompanied by songs and dances. As is well known, there was in the early Christian Church, composed as it was of large numbers of heathen converts, a constant tendency to perpetuate heathen practices and observances, as witness the many customs surviving to-day whose origin can be traced back to a pagan parentage; and to prevent the introduction of the heathen theatre, with all its abuses, the Church may have felt itself forced to provide a dramatic entertainment in which sacred subjects took the place of those of mythology; a course that probably achieved the end aimed at. No doubt we can thus account for the custom which prevailed, even in apostolic times, of reading at Easter the narrative of the Passion, the various parts distributed among different personages; which later came to be accompanied by an interpolated dialogue and gestures, and also, probably, the readers officiated in what they considered appropriate dresses. So that even here we have a very close approach to the genuine passion play. In due time other days and feasts than Easter came to be devoted to these representations and as they grew in length and the number of persons engaged increased, ecclesiastics ceased to take any direct part in them, confining themselves simply to the training of others to the work, and, under the name of "mysteries," the plays were acted after the sermon. As a general rule, the mystery play was taken directly from the Biblical record, and the miracle plays from legendary subjects; for instance, the reported miraculous doings of some saint, as the legend of Saint Catherine; but this nomenclature has never been strictly adhered to, and the general character of both was about the same, each containing a nearly equal proportion of Biblical quotations and profane dialogues. The mysteries, strictly so-called, were representations, often of great length, requiring several days' performance of the Scripture narrative, which was usually followed most faithfully in its minutest details. The clergy, however, were soon entirely superseded by the laity, who formed themselves into companies and guilds for the purpose of representing mysteries, and very soon every considerable town had its fraternity for this purpose. This change from clergy to laity was eagerly welcomed, for the chief reason that hitherto the dialogue had been held in Latin, whereas the laity gave their representations in the vernacular; and in this way the mystery plays of the thirteenth and fourteenth centuries played no unimportant part in the development of the people's language. The most important of these guilds was the *Confrerie de la Passion et Resurrection de notre Seigneur* (" Brotherhood of the Passion and Resurrection of Our Lord "), which was composed of Paris artisans, citizens, and a few others of higher rank. By authority of King Charles VI. they were empowered to act "any mystery, whatsoever, either before the king or before his people, in any suitable place, either in the town of Paris itself or in its suburbs." Upon this they established themselves in the Hospital of the Holy Trinity, outside the Porte St. Denis; and there on public holidays they gave representations of pieces drawn from the New Testament, which were attended by crowds of the clergy, nobility, and those of humbler rank. In time, however, abuses crept in; and under cover of the miracle plays, gross immoralities were perpetuated, fully equal to the blasphemies of the pagan drama which originally they had superseded. So in 1799 a manifesto was issued by the prince-archbishop of Salzburg, in Germany, condemning them, and prohibiting their further performance, on the ground of the impious mixture of the sacred and profane, and the scandal arising from the exposure of sacred subjects to the ridicule of free-thinkers. This ecclesiastical prohibition was vigorously seconded by the civil authorities, and soon the passion play was a thing of the past. One exception was made, however, to the general suppression, — the sole miracle play that survives. In the year 1634 the village of Ober-Ammergau, in the Bavarian highlands, was devastated by a pestilence, and in their extremity the survivors vowed to perform every tenth year the Passion of Christ, if they should be spared, — a vow which has ever since been regularly observed. The town is situated in the valley of the Aumer, forty-six miles southwest of Munich; and the inhabitants, who number about a thousand, are chiefly engaged in the carving of wood. The performance lasts for twelve consecutive Sundays during the summer season, occurring every tenth year.

Passover. This is the first and most important of the three great annual festivals of the Jewish Church, the other two being Pentecost and the Feast of Tabernacles. It designates the paschal meal on the evening of the 14th of the month Nisan, which in turn commemorated the paschal sacrifice or passing over related in Exod. xii. 21, 27, 48. The following seven days are termed the "feast of unleavened bread." Nisan was the first month of the Hebrew sacred year, called Abib in the Pentateuch, and corresponds to the latter half of March and the first half of April.

Paston Letters. The first two volumes appeared in 1787, entitled "Original Letters written during the reigns of Henry VI., Edward IV., and Richard III., by various persons of rank;" edited by Mr., afterwards Sir, John Fenn. They are called "Paston" because chiefly written by or to members of the Paston family in Norfolk. They passed from the Earl of Yarmouth to Peter le Neve, antiquary; then to Mr. Martin, of Palgrave, Suffolk; were then bought by Mr. Worth, of Diss; then passed to the editor. Charles Knight calls them "an invaluable record of the social customs of the fifteenth century" (the time of the War of the Roses).

Pastorale. (Ital.) A soft and rural movement. (Mus.)

Patch. Another name for a fool; derived from the motley dress worn by licensed fools and jesters.

Patched-up Peace. The same as Lame and Unstable Peace (*q. v.*).

Paterfamilias. The father of a family.

Pater noster. (Lat.) Our Father, — the first words of the Lord's Prayer in Latin.

Pater patriæ. (Lat.) The father of one's country.

Pater Patrum. Gregory of Nyssa was thus saluted by the Council of Nice (332–395).

Pathfinder, The. Maj.-Gen. John Charles Fremont, U. S. A. (b. 1813), who conducted four expeditions across the Rocky Mountains in the days prior to the trans-continental railroads.

Pathol. Pathology.

Patient, The. Albert IV., Duke of Austria (fl. 1377–1404).

Pat. Of. Patent Office.

Patois. (Lat.) A provincial dialect.

Patres conscripti. (Lat.) Conscript fathers, — name applied to the Roman senators.

Patriarch of Dorchester. John White, a Puritan divine, much esteemed for his eloquence and piety (fl. 1564–1648).

Patriarch of Ferney. Voltaire was so named because he retired to the village of Ferney, near Geneva, from whence proceeded many of his works.

Patrick Fitzgibbons. (Pseud.) John W. McDonnell, in the "Daily News," New York.

Patrick, Free State of. *See* FREE STATE OF PATRICK.

Patrick Peale. (Pseud.) Gustav Anton von Seckendorf, author of many dramas and essays.

Patris est filius. (Lat.) He is the son of his father; a chip of the old block.

Patroclus. In classic myth a Grecian chief in the Trojan war, the companion and friend of Achilles. He was struck senseless by Apollo, and while in that condition was killed by Euphorbus and Hector.

Patron Saint of Queens. Saint Elizabeth of Hungary (fl. 1207–1231). She was herself a queen.

Patroon. A now obsolete name by which the old Dutch manorial proprietors in New York, New Jersey, and Pennsylvania were known.

Patsy Bolivar. A party of minstrels in Boston, about twenty years ago, had a performance in which they presented the scene of a country school. There was a little fellow named Patsy Bolivar, who sat in the corner, who was inoffensive, quiet, and generally well-behaved. The older boys took occasion to annoy the master in many ways; and when the pedagogue asked, in a rage, "Who did that?" the boys would answer, "Patsy Bolivar!" Then Patsy was chastised. As soon as that was over, some of the older boys would throw a wad of paper at the master's head, when, raging with anger, he would repeat the query, "Who was that?" Again the answer came, "Patsy Bolivar." The phrase, as many phrases have done, spread beyond the limits of the minstrel performance; and when a scapegoat was alluded to, it was in the name of " Patsy Bolivar," an inoffensive person who is always in trouble, brought about by mischievous associates, — the one who is always blamed for everything.

Patterson Aymar. (Pseud.) Charles Knight, in his articles in Knight's " Quarterly Magazine."

Patti Rosa. The stage-name of Jessie Buckingham.

Patty Lee. (Pseud.) Miss Alice Cary, contributor of sketches and essays to the " National Era," Washington, D. C.

Paucis verbis. (Lat.) In few words.

Paul Creyton. (Pseud.) John Townsend Trowbridge, American novelist (b. 1827).

Paul Hermes. (Pseud.) William Roscoe Thayer.

Paulianists. A sect of heretics; so called from Paulinus Samosatanus, elected bishop of Antioch in 262, the father of the Socinians.

Paulicians. A religious sect of the Eastern Empire, an offshoot of the Manichæans. It originated in an Armenian named Paul, who lived under Justinian II. Neander says they were the followers of Constantine of Mananalis, and were called Paulicians because the Apostle Paul was their guide. He says they rejected the worship of the Virgin and of saints, denied the doctrine of transubstantiation, and maintained the right of every one to read the Scriptures freely.

Pauline Brand. The stage-name of Pauline Hall.

Pauline Hall. The stage-name of Mrs. Frank White, *née* Schmittgall.

Pauline L'Allemand. The professional name of Pauline Elsasser, a well-known operatic soprano.

Pauline Lucca. The stage-name of Baroness von Walhofen.

Pauline Markham. The stage-name of Mrs. McMahon.

Paul of the Cross. Paul Francis (fl. 1694–1775), founder of the Passionist Fathers.

Paul Peebles. (Pseud.) Augustus Maverick, a well-known journalist.

Paul Pindar. (Pseud.) John Yonge Akerman, English numismatist (b. 1800).

Paul Prenaier. The professional name of Reginald Sperry, the prestidigitator.

Paul Preston. (Pseud.) Thomas Picton, American journalist (b. 1822), in the " Sunday Mercury," New York.

Paul Siegfolk. (Pseud.) Albert Mathews, American lawyer and writer (b. 1810).

Paul's Pigeons. The boys of St. Paul's School, London.

Paul's Walkers. Loungers who frequented the middle of St. Paul's, which was the Bond Street of London up to the time of the Commonwealth. Harrison Ainsworth describes these " walkers " in his novel entitled " Old Saint Paul's."

Pavonia. In old maps this name will be found to designate a region extending from Hudson County, N. J., to Perth Amboy. The name still survives in several places of local importance.

Pax. In Roman mythology the god of peace, the same as the Greek Irene.

Pax in bello. (Lat.) Peace in war.

Pax vobiscum. (Lat.) Peace be with you.

Paying through the Nose. Paying in driblets, or installments, and hence paying dearer than for cash. Grimm says that Odin had a poll-tax which was called in Sweden a nose-tax; it was a penny per nose, or poll.

Pays Latin. (Fr.) The Latin territory or district; the neighborhood of the University of Paris.

Payt. Payment.

P. B. Primitive Baptist.

P. B. *Philosophiæ Baccalaureus.* Bachelor of Philosophy.

Pb. *Plumbum.* Lead.

P. C. Conscript Fathers (*Patres Conscripti*); Senators; Privy Council; Privy Councillor.

P. C. P. Past Chief Patriarch.

P. C. S. Principal Clerk of Session.

P. D. *Philosophiæ Doctor.* Doctor of Philosophy.

Pd. Paid; Palladium.

P. E. Protestant Episcopal.

Peace. *See* LAME AND UNSTABLE, PERPETUAL, LADIES', etc.

Peace, City of. *See* CITY OF PEACE.

Peaceful, The. Kang-wang, the third ruler of the Thow dynasty of China (fl.

1098–1152). It was remarked that in this reign none were imprisoned or executed.

Peace, Isle of. *See* ISLE OF PEACE.

Peacemakers. *See* BLOODLESS LAMBS.

Peanut Politics. A name for political acts which have for their sole aim some petty partisan end.

Pearl Melville. The stage-name of Mrs. Walter S. Baldwin.

Pearl of the Antilles. Cuba. *See* QUEEN OF THE ANTILLES.

Pearl of the Atlantic. Madeira is so named.

Pearl Rivers. (Pseud.) (1) Mrs. A. M. Holbrook. (2) Mrs. E. J. P. Nicholson, in the New Orleans "Times-Democrat."

Peasant Bard. Robert Burns.

Peasant of the Danube. Louis Legendre (fl. 1756–1797), a member of the French National Convention, who bore a leading part in the Revolution.

Peasant Poet of Northamptonshire. John Clare (fl. 1793–1864), an English poet of good attainments but lowly birth.

Peasant War. In German history the name given to that great insurrection of the peasantry which broke out in the beginning of the year 1525. The rising was finally put down with much bloodshed, and it is supposed that more than 150,000 perished. *See* LEAGUE OF POOR CONRAD.

Peccavi. (Lat.) I have sinned.

Peculiar Institution. A common designation of slavery after it had become peculiar to the South. *See* TWIN RELIC.

Peculiar People. A sect formed in Essex, England, about 1845, whose principal tenet consisted in relying upon prayer instead of medical care in sickness. Some of the members were prosecuted for manslaughter in 1868, and at a later date others were fined or imprisoned for neglecting their sick.

Peeler. A colloquial English name for a policeman, after Sir Robert Peel, who established the Irish Constabulary. Singularly enough, however, this word "peeler" was in the sixteenth century a synonym for a thief. *See* BOBBY.

Peeping Tom. (Pseud.) Samuel Kettell, American editor and humorist (1800–1885), in the Boston "Courier." *See* TIMOTHY TITTERWELL.

Peep-o'-Day-Boys. A faction in Ireland prominent in the closing years of the last century, so named because, in the interest of Presbyterianism, they were wont to visit the residences of the "Defenders"—the Catholic faction—in search of arms and ammunition at about daybreak.

Pegasus. In classic myth a winged horse which arose with Chrysaor from the blood of the Gorgon Medusa when she was slain by Perseus. He afterward ascended to heaven, and was believed to carry the thunder and lightning of Zeus. According to later authors, however, he was the horse of Eos.

P. E. I. Prince Edward Island.

Peleg Arkwright. (Pseud.) D. L. Proudfit, American writer.

Pelian Spear. The lance of Achilles which wounded and cured Telephus; so called from Peleus, the father of Achilles.

Pelion and Ossa. Pelion was the classic name of a high wooded mountain in Thessaly; Ossa was a steep conical peak near by. According to the classic myth the Titans placed Pelion upon Ossa in order to scale Olympus, the abode of the gods.

Pellean Conqueror. Alexander the Great, who was born at Pella, in Macedonia.

Pelops. In classic myth grandson of Zeus and son of Tantalus; was slain by his father and served up at an entertainment which he gave to the gods in order to test their omniscience.

Penang Lawyer. A stout stick or club. Penang sticks come from Malaysia and Borneo, where club-law is best understood by the natives.

Penates. (Lat.) The household gods of the Romans.

Penchant. (Fr.) An inclination; a leaning toward.

Pendente lite. (Lat.) While the suit is pending; during the continuance of the law-suit.

Penelope. In Homeric legend the wife of Ulysses and mother of Telemachus. During the long absence of her husband she was beset by numerous suitors for her hand, whom she put off on the pretext that she must weave a shroud for the aged Laertes, her father-in-law. To prolong the time she unwove by night the portion she had completed by day. When her suitors discovered her device they became more urgent, but fortunately Ulysses returned in time to rescue his spouse from their pleadings.

Penetralia. (Lat.) Secret recesses.

Penholder. (Pseud.) Edward Eggleston, D.D., American preacher and novelist (b. 1837).

Peninsular War. The struggle maintained in Portugal and Spain by the English army under Sir Arthur Wellesley against the invading army of Napoleon I., between 1808–1812.

Peninsula State. Florida; so named on account of its shape.

Penitential Psalms. Seven of the Psalms of David, — vi., xxxii., xxxviii., li., cii., cxxx., and cxliii. of the Authorized Version, corresponding to Psalms vi., xxxi., xxxvii., l., ci., cxxix., cxlii. of the Vulgate. They are regarded as being especially expressive of sorrow for sin, and are accepted by Christians as forms of prayer suitable for repentant sinners.

Penn. Pennsylvania.

Penniless, The. Maximilian I. of Germany (fl. 1459–1519) was so named by the Italians.

Pennsylvania. This State takes its name from William Penn, and *sylvania*, meaning "forests, or woodlands."

Pennsylvania Farmer. John Dickinson (fl. 1732–1808), the American statesman and author, was so named. In 1768 he published "Letters from a Pennsylvania Farmer to the Inhabitants of the British Colonies."

Penny-loaf Day. Another name for Mid-Lent Sunday, also known as "Mothering Sunday" (*q. v.*). In commemoration of a wonderful dream, by which his life was saved during the siege of Newark-upon-Trent by the Parliamentary forces, and as a testimony to God for vouchsafing it, Alderman Hercules Clay, by his will, left £200 to the Corporation of Newark on condition that they should pay the interest of £100 to the vicar to preach an appropriate sermon every 11th of March; the interest of the other £100 to be spent in penny loaves for the poor. From this circumstance the day is locally known as "Penny-loaf Day."

Penny Weddings. or **Penny Bridals.** The name given to festive marriage services in Scotland at which the invited guests made contributions in money to pay the general expenses, and leave over a small sum which would assist the couple to commence housekeeping. The practice prevailed as late as the seventeenth century.

Pen Oliver. The pseudonym of Sir H. Thompson.

Pensioner Parliament. Another nickname for the Long Parliament (*q. v.*). It sat so long without a dissolution that the members were said to have a pension, or perpetual claim to membership.

Pent. Pentecost.

Pentecost. The second of the three great annual festivals of the Hebrews, the other two being the Feast of Tabernacles and the Passover. It fell on the 6th of the month Sivan, corresponding to our June. It is also called the Feast of Weeks, because it was celebrated seven complete weeks, or fifty days, after the Passover. It was a species of harvest festival, and commemorated the garnering of the later grains. *See also* WHIT-SUNDAY.

Penthesilea. In classic myth a queen of the Amazons. She fought against the Greeks at Troy, but was killed by Achilles.

Pentheus. In classic myth a king of Thebes. For ridiculing certain rites of Bacchus he was torn in pieces by his female relatives, they being for the time under the influence of the god.

People = RELATIONS. An American speaks of his "people," meaning his immediate kindred, where an Englishman would say "relations." The word "folk" is similarly used.

People of the Rock. The inhabitants of Arabia Petrea.

People's Friend. Dr. William Gordon, the philanthropist (fl. 1801–1849).

Peppercorn Rent. A merely nominal rental. The term is a familiar one in Great Britain, and instances of such a rent having been fixed are neither few nor far between. Thus Bermeton, in Durham, was held by the service of three grains of pepper yearly; Finchley, in Middlesex, by the annual rent of a pound of pepper; Highgate, in Denbigh, was leased for a term of five hundred years at the annual rent of one peppercorn; and for a fortieth part of one knight's fee in the manor of Leyham, in Suffolk, Philippa Ross rendered

" one capon, and the third part of one capon, and the third part of one pound of pepper."

Pequod War. The early history of Connecticut was marked by a struggle known as the " Pequod War." That stretch of country lying west of the Thames River was densely peopled with savages, and they looked with jealous eyes upon the occupancy of the choicest spots by the Saxon. In 1663 the crew of a small trading vessel was murdered on the banks of the Connecticut by the Indians. But an embassy was sent to Boston to apologize, a treaty was hastily concluded, and for a time peace reigned. But the compact was soon forgotten. Captain Oldham, while on a coasting voyage, was murdered, and a war began, into which all the slumbering hate and jealousy of the nation burst forth with fury. The Pequods endeavored to get the Narragansetts and Mohegans to join in a war of extermination against the English, but Roger Williams warned Sir Harry Vane in time to defeat the plot and frustrate the alliance. Repeated acts of violence stung the colony to madness. In the winter of 1636–1637 many murders happened in the vicinity of Saybrook. In April, 1631, nine persons were massacred in Wethersfield. On May 1 the towns of Connecticut declared war. Hartford, Saybrook, and Wethersfield sent each its quota of men, and Sir Harry Vane sent twenty soldiers from Boston. The little force sailed down the Thames, landed in Narragansett Bay, and proceeded to march into the heart of the Pequod country. On the 25th of May they drew near the Pequod fort, and at two o'clock in the morning the enemy were completely surprised. The cabins and wigwams were fired, and six hundred savages perished by sword and flame. A small remnant of the nation that were absent at the time were afterward chased and harried in the swamps and woods west of Saybrook, and were either hunted to death or were captured and distributed as servants among the Narragansetts.

Pequot. (Pseud.) Charles March, contributor to the New York "Tribune" and " Times " and to the Boston " Courier."

Per. Persia ; Persian.

Per, or **pr.** By the, or per lb.

Per ætatem. (Lat.) " By reason of one's age." On account of one's time of life.

Per ævum. (Lat.) Forever.

Per an. *Per annum.* By the year.

Per annum. (Lat.) " By the year." Yearly; annually.

Per aspera ad astra. (Lat.) Through trials to glory.

Per capita. (Lat.) " By the heads." Individually.

Per cent., Per centum. (Lat.) " By the hundred." Generally in the contracted form, "per cent."

Per conto. (Ital.) Upon account.

Per contra. (Lat.) Contrariwise.

Per curiam. (Lat.) By the court.

Perdendo, Perdendosi, or Perden. (Ital.) This term implies a gradual diminution, both in the quantity of tone and speed of movement. (Mus.)

Per diem. (Lat.) " By the day." Daily; every day.

Perdita. (Pseud.) Mrs. Mary Robinson, English poetess and actress (1758–1800).

Perdu. (Fr.) Lost.

Père de famille. The father of a family.

Père Duchêsne. The title assumed by Jacques Réné Hebert (fl. 1755–1794), one of the most unscrupulous and scurrilous characters of the French Revolution. He published an obscene sheet, which contained the grossest assertions against Marie Antoinette.

Peregrine Courtenay. (Pseud.) Winthrop Mackworth Praed, English poet and lawyer (1802–1839).

Peregrine Prolix. (Pseud.) Philip H. Micklin, *littérateur* (1786–1842).

Père La Chaise. (Fr.) " Father La Chaise." Eastern cemetery of Paris ; so called after a Jesuit named Lachaise.

Per far effetto. (Ital.) To do anything in style.

Per fas et nefas. (Lat.) " Through right and wrong." Justly or unjustly.

Perfectionists. A society founded by Father Noyes in Oneida, N. Y. They take Saint Paul for their law-giver, but read his epistles in a new light. They reject all law, saying the guidance of the Spirit is superior to all human codes. If they would know how to act in matters affecting others, they consult " public opinion," expressed by a committee; and the " law of sympathy " so expressed is their law of action. In material prosperity this society is unmatched by all the "communities" of North America.

Perfervidum ingenium. (Lat.) The very ardent disposition; as, *perfervidum ingenium Scotorum*, the warm or ardent temperament of the Scots.

Perfide Albion ("Faithless Albion"). An accusatory phrase coined by Napoleon I.

Per gradus. (Lat.) Step by step.

Peri. Perigee.

Peri (a fairy). In the Eastern mythology a being, the offspring of fallen spirits, which passes its existence in the enjoyment of every imaginable delight; enjoys immortality, but is eternally excluded from Paradise. The Peris stand midway between angels and demons, and may be of either sex. Like our own fairies, Peris, when of the female gender, are often of surpassing loveliness.

Periculum in mora. (Lat.) Danger in delay.

Per incuriam. (Lat.) Through carelessness.

Peris. The poetical name of Persia.

Perle Dudley. The stage-name of Mrs. Arthur P. Wilkinson, *née* Rous.

Per legem terræ. (Lat.) By the law of the land.

Perley. (Pseud.) Ben: Perley Poore, in Boston "Journal" and other newspapers.

Pernicibus alis. (Lat.) With swift wings.

Perpetual Edict. The decree issued by the Emperor Hadrian, approving and promulgating the legal code compiled by Salvius Julianus.

Perpetual Peace. A truce concluded Jan. 24, 1502, between the Scotch and English. Yet it was within a few years after that the battle of Flodden Field was fought.

Perpetuum mobile. (Lat.) Perpetual motion.

Per plures. (Lat.) By the majority.

Per saltum. (Lat.) By a leap or jump.

Per se. (Lat.) "By itself." Of itself.

Per se aut per alium. (Lat.) By himself or by another.

Persecutions, The Ten. In ecclesiastical history certain well-defined periods of persecution of the early Church are thus named and grouped.

The ten persecutions commonly regarded as general are the following: —

Under Nero, 64 A. D.	Under Septimius Severus,
Domitian, 95 A. D.	202 A. D.
Trajan, 107 A. D.	Maximus, 235 A.D.
Hadrian, 125 A. D.	Decius, 249 A. D.
Marcus Aurelius,	Valerian, 257 A.D.
165 A. D.	Diocletian, 303 A.D.

Persephone. In classic myth the Greek name of Proserpine (*q. v.*).

Perseus. A constellation in the northern hemisphere, representing Perseus, son of Jupiter and Danae, who slew Medusa, one of the three Gorgons, and cut off her head, which also forms part of this constellation, crowned with coiling snakes. Sixty-seven stars compose this constellation.

Perseus. In classic myth the son of Zeus and Danae, and grandson of Acrisius. He slew the Gorgon Medusa, and was deified as a hero in many parts of Greece and, say some, in Egypt also. In ancient sculptures the figure of Perseus much resembles that of Mercury.

Persian Alexander. Sandjar (fl. 1117–1158).

Persona ingrata. (Lat.) A disagreeable or objectionable person.

Perth, Five Articles of. Ever memorable in the ecclesiastical annals of Scotland, were, says Chambers, " five articles agreed upon in the meeting of the General Assembly of the Church of Scotland, convened at Perth by command of James I., on 25th August, 1618. These Articles enjoined kneeling at the Lord's Supper, the observance of Christmas, Good Friday, Easter, and Pentecost, and confirmation, and sanctioned the private administration of baptism and of the Lord's Supper. They were highly obnoxious to the Presbyterians of Scotland. They were, however, ratified by the Parliament on 4th August, 1621, — a day long remembered in Scotland as Black Saturday, — were enforced by the Court of High Commission, and became one of the chief subjects of contention between the king and the people.

Perugini, Signor. The professional name of John Chatterton.

Peruv. Peruvian.

Per varios casus. (Lat.) Through various chances or misfortunes.

Pestalozzi. (Pseud.) Bernard Peters, in the Brooklyn "Times," of which he has been editor for many years.

Pet. Peter; Petrine; Peter's Reports U. S. Circuit Court.

Pet Banks. In September, 1833, Roger B. Taney became Secretary of the United States Treasury, *vice* William J. Duane. Taney at once ordered that, after October 1, the public revenues should no longer be deposited with the National Bank, but with sundry State banks, which soon came to be known as "pet banks." Andrew Jackson was then President, and it was by his order this was done, but the Senate censured his action at its next session. *See* EX-PUNGING RESOLUTIONS.

Peter. (Pseud.) John Gibson Lockhart, British author, poet, and critic (1794–1854).

Peter Funk. A fellow employed at auctions to make fictitious bids on articles put up for sale in order to raise their price. The origin of the name lies in the fact that at one time it was the custom to give it as that of an ostensible purchaser when goods were really bought in by the auctioneer.

Peterloo Massacre. The name popularly given to the dispersal of a large meeting by yeomanry in St. Peter's Field, Manchester, England, Monday, July 16, 1819. Many were killed and wounded, and, the battle of Waterloo being then fresh in men's minds, the parody easily arose.

Peter Morris. (Pseud.) John Gibson Lockhart, British author, poet, and critic (1794–1854).

Peter Parley. (Pseud.) Samuel Griswold Goodrich, American writer of juvenile fiction (1793–1860).

Peter Pepperbox. (Pseud.) T. G. Fessenden, American author.

Peter Pindar. (Pseud.) John Wolcott, English physician and satiric poet (1738–1819).

Peter Plymley. (Pseud.) Sydney Smith, English divine and writer (1771–1845).

Peter Pomfret. (Pseud.) Richard Graves, English divine and author (1715–1804).

Peter Porcupine. (Pseud.) William Cobbett, English political writer (1762–1835).

Peter Query. (Pseud.) Martin Farquhar Tupper, English poet and novelist (b. 1810).

Peter Quince. (Pseud.) Isaac Story, American lawyer and author (1774–1851).

Peter Snooks. (Pseud.) John C. Moore, in the Boston "Journal."

Petit. Small; little.

Petit Bernard. Solomon Bernard, engraver, of Lyons (sixteenth century).

Petit bourgeois. (Fr.) "A little citizen." A second-rate citizen.

Petites affiches. (Fr.) Advertisements.

Petitioners and Abhorrers. Rival political factions in English affairs during the reign of Charles II., — the opponents and the advocates, respectively, of the right to petition the monarch.

Petition of Rights. A statement of certain rights and privileges of the subject obtained from King Charles I. during his third Parliament. It was so named because the Commons presented their grievances in the shape of a petition, refusing to accord the supplies until the prayer contained therein was granted.

Petitio principii. (Lat.) A begging of the question.

Petit littérateur. (Fr.) A petty man of letters; a dabbler in literature.

Petit maître. (Fr.) A fop; a coxcomb.

Petits soins. (Fr.) "Little cares." Little attentions.

Petrarch of England. Sir Philip Sidney was thus named by Raleigh.

Petrified City. Ishmonie, a ruined city of Upper Egypt. Its popular name arose from the fact that it contains a vast number of statues of human beings and animals in every possible posture, and which, according to a superstitious notion, were once living beings miraculously changed into stone.

Petroleum Vesuvius Nasby, Rev. (Pseud.) David Ross Locke, American humorous writer (b. 1833).

Petrus Firmianus. (Pseud.) Zacharie de Lisieux, mediæval writer (1582–1660).

Petticoat Insurrection. In Mobile, Ala., in 1706, the women generally threatened to rebel because they were dissatisfied with the diet, composed chiefly of Indian meal, on which they were compelled to subsist. This episode obtained the name of the Petticoat Insurrection.

Peu-à-peu. (Fr.) Little by little.

Peutingerian Table. The name given to a most interesting ancient document which exhibits the military roads of the Roman Empire, and indeed of the world known to the Romans. It is not, properly speaking, a map ; no regard being paid to geographic position or the extent of countries. The great lines of road are laid down in a narrow strip, as if nearly parallel, all proceeding from Rome as a centre; and as to rivers, it only appears whether they cross the road from left to right or from right to left of the traveller proceeding from Rome. The Mediterranean and other seas are represented by mere narrow channels. A small house is the mark for a town; important towns and military stations are distinguished by walls and towers. Rome, Constantinople, and Antioch are each represented by a circle, within which is a human figure seated; in the case of Rome the figure is crowned. Until very recently a portion of the only copy of this valuable relic of antiquity known to exist was evidently wanting, as it terminated abruptly on the west at the confines of Spain, and included only the eastern parts of Britain. In the east it traces roads through India to a number of places of trade as far as the mouths of the Ganges. It is on parchment, and as described in all the publications devoted to it, twenty-one feet in length and about one foot wide. It was found in the library of the Benedictine monastery at Tegernsee, in Upper Bavaria, in the fifteenth century, by Conrad Celtes, who bequeathed it to Conrad Peutinger, of Augsburg, a zealous antiquary, and one of the earliest authors on the Roman and other antiquities of Germany. Peutinger began to prepare a copy of it for publication, but died before he could accomplish his purpose, which, however, was partially executed by Mark Welser, in his " Fragmenta Tabulæ Antiquæ ex Peutingerorium Bibliotheca " (Venice, 1591). The ancient document itself remained in the hands of the Peutinger family, and attracted no further notice, till it was offered for sale in 1714, and purchased by Prince Eugene, who presented it to the Imperial Library of Vienna, in which it still remains.

Pewter Muggers was a name given to a faction of the Democratic party in New York City about 1828, in which year, with the help of the Adams men (the administration party) and the anti-Masons, they defeated the Tammany candidates for several important offices.

The name originated from the resort in Frankfort Street which the leaders of the faction patronized extensively.

Pfingster Montag. *See* Whit-Sunday.

P. Fisher, Esq. (Pseud.) William Andrew Chatto, English antiquary (b. 1805).

P. G. Past Grand.

Phædra. In classic myth a daughter of Minos, king of Crete, sister to Ariadne, and wife of Theseus.

Phaeton. In classic myth a frequent title of Helios, the sun-god, and subsequently employed as his name. Phaeton is also the name of a son of Helios, famed for his disastrous attempt to drive his father's chariot.

Phalaris. (Pseud.) One of the disguises attributed to Junius (*q. v.*).

Phantastes. (Pseud.) William Hazlitt, in the " New Monthly Magazine," 1822.

Phar. Pharmacy.

Phazma. (Pseud.) Matthew C. Field, American poet (1812–1844).

Ph. B. *Philosophiæ Baccalaureus.* Bachelor of Philosophy.

Ph. D. *Philosophiæ Doctor.* Doctor of Philosophy.

Phebe Davis. The stage-name of Mrs. Joseph R. Grismer.

Phelps and Gorham Purchase. An immense tract of land purchased from Massachusetts, in 1786, by Nathaniel Gorham and Oliver Phelps; their acquisition was situated in New York, on the Genesee River. They surveyed the land and sold it in small lots to speculators, but in 1790, Phelps and Gorham being unable to fulfill their contract, a part of the land reverted to Massachusetts.

Phil. Philip; Philippians; Philosophy; Philemon.

Phila., or Phil. Philadelphia.

Philadelphia Lawyer. " That beats a Philadelphia lawyer." " He knows as much as a Philadelphia lawyer." These are common sayings, whence it is to be inferred that the bar of the Quaker City are distinguished for their learning and shrewdness.

Philadelphia Stones. It is said that the walls of Philadelphia, in Turkey, were built of the bones of Christians killed in the Holy Wars. This idle tale has gained credit from the nature of the stones, full of pores and very light, not unlike petrified bones. Similar incrustations are found at Knaresborough and elsewhere.

Philalethes. (Pseud.) (1) Johann Nepomuk Maria Joseph, king of Saxony, who published in 1849 a German translation of Dante's "Divina Commedia." (2) Nicholas Amherst, in the "Evening Post," London.

Philalethes Iren. (Pseud.) Louis du Moulin, M.D., Professor of History at Oxford (1603–1680).

Philaretes. (Pseud.) John Gilbert Cooper, English author (1723–1769).

Philaretus. (Pseud.) Augustus Montagu Toplady, English Calvinistic divine (1740–1778).

Phileleutherus Lipsiensis. (Pseud.) Richard Bentley, English critic and classical scholar (1661–1742).

Philem. Philemon.

Philemon and Baucis. *See* BAUCIS.

Philemon Perch. Pseudonym of Col. R. M. Johnston, a Southern author, under which he published "The Dukesbury Tales."

Phililenia. (Pseud.) Sarah Wentworth Morton, American poetess (1752–1806).

Philip Quilibet. (Pseud.) George E. Pond, *littérateur*.

Philip Wharton. (Pseud.) J. P. Thompson, English writer.

Philisides. A poetical surname of Sir Philip Sidney, coined by himself from portions of the names *Philip* and *Sidney*, with a Latin termination. It occurs in his "Arcadia."

Philistines. A phrase applied by Matthew Arnold to the great middle class of Englishmen, whom he declares to be ignorant, vapid, narrow-minded, and barren of great thoughts or deeds.

Philoctetes. In classic myth son of Pœas and one of the Argonauts. At the death of Hercules he received from the dying hero some poisoned arrows ; and on the journey to Troy he accidentally wounded himself in the foot with one of these, and was treacherously left by his companions on the solitary isle of Lemnos to die. But in the tenth year of the war an oracle declared that Troy could not be captured without the arrows of Philoctetes ; and he at the solicitation of Ulysses repaired to Troy and fought nobly.

Philom. *Philomathes.* A lover of learning.

Philomath. *Philomathematicus.* A lover of the mathematics.

Philopater Irenæus. (Pseud.) Richard Beling, Irish Catholic writer (1613–1677).

Philopoliteius. (Pseud.) Sir John Skene, Scottish advocate and law-writer (1540–1617).

Philosopher, The. (1) Marcus Aurelius. (2) Leo VI., Emperor of the East. (3) Porphyry, the Antichristian.

Philosopher of China. Confucius.

Philosopher of Ferney. Voltaire ; so named from his château at that place.

Philosopher of Malmesbury. Thomas Hobbes.

Philosopher of Persia. Abou Ebn Sina, flourished in the eleventh century.

Philosopher of Sans Souci. Frederick the Great, who had a pleasure-seat of the name, where he spent many hours surrounded by his intimates.

Philosopher of the Unknown. An appellation assumed by Louis Claude de Saint-Martin, a French mystic (fl. 1743–1803).

Philosopher of Wimbledon. John Horne Tooke.

Philosophers of the Academic Sect. Plato, Speusippus, Xenocrates, Polemon, Crates, Crantor, Arcesilaus, Carneades, Clitomachus, Philo, Antiochus.

Philosophers of the Cynic Sect. Antisthenes, Diogenes of Sinope, Monimus, Onesicritus, Crates, Metrocles, Hipparchia, Menippus, Menedemus of Lampsacus.

Philosophers of the Cyrenaic Sect. Aristippus, Hegesias, Annicerus, Theodorus, Bion.

Philosophers of the Eleac Sect. Phædo, Plisthenes, Menedemus of Eretria.

Philosophers of the Eleatic Sect. Xenophanes, Parmenides, Melissus, Zeno of Tarsus, Leucippus, Democritus, Protagoras, Anaxarchus.

Philosophers of the Stoic Sect. Zeno, Cleanthes, Chrysippus, Zeno the Less, Diogenes of Babylon, Antipater, Panætius, Posidonius.

Phil. Trans. Philosophical Transactions.

Phineas Camp. (Pseud.) W. N. Duane, in his "Poems of the Mohawk Valley."

Phiz. (Pseud.) Hablot K. Browne, English caricaturist (1815–1882).

Phœbe. In classic myth sister to Phœbus and goddess of the moon; a surname of Diana.

Phœbus. In classic myth "the radiant," a title, and subsequently a name, of Apollo. It had reference both to the youthful beauty of the god and to the radiance of the sun when, latterly, Helios and Apollo became identified.

Phœnix. A fabled Egyptian bird, having human arms, and sacred to Osiris, and represented watching in the tamarisk-tree over his coffin. It visited Egypt after the death of its father, and entered the shrine particularly dedicated to it at Heliopolis, and there buried its parents, putting the body into an egg or case made of myrrh, and then closing up the egg. Another account is that the Phœnix, when about to die, made a nest for itself in Arabia, from which a new Phœnix sprang of itself. This bird proceeded to Heliopolis, and there burned and buried its father. But the more popularly known version is that the Phœnix burned itself, and a new and young Phœnix sprang from the ashes.

Phœnix. (Pseud.) Sir Henry Martin, English author.

Phœnix City. Atlanta, Ga.

Phœnix literarum. (Lat.) A Phœnix of literature.

Phren. Phrenology.

P. H. S. Pennsylvania Historical Society.

Phylactery. A charm, or amulet, among the ancients, especially the Jews, which, being worn bound on the arm or the forehead, was supposed to preserve people from certain diseases, evils, or dangers.

Phyllis. In classic myth daughter of Sithron, king of Thrace. Believing that her lover had deserted her, she hanged herself, and was changed by the gods into an almond-tree.

Physics. A by-name among the Pennsylvania Reserves, during the civil war, for General Crawford, who had been a surgeon at the beginning of his army career.

Piacere. (Ital.) Will, pleasure; as, *a piacere*, at the performer's pleasure in regard to time. (Mus.)

Piano, sempre staccato e marcato il basso. (Ital.) Soft, with the bass always well marked and detached. (Mus.)

Picayune. Something small, mean, or contemptible. The picayune is a Carib coin worth six and a quarter cents.

Piccadilly Butchers. The English regiment of Life-Guards was thus nicknamed, because on a certain occasion they charged down Piccadilly and killed some innocent spectators of a riot.

Picciola. (Pseud.) Angelina S. Mumford, American poetess (b. 1830).

Pickaway. (Pseud.) Allen O. Myers, in the Cincinnati " Enquirer."

Picket. (Pseud.) B. W. Tomlinson, in various Southern papers.

Picts' Workditch. The name applied to the remains of a fosse and double rampart, with round forts at intervals, in Roxburgh and Selkirk Counties, Scotland, which is supposed to have been a line of defence raised by the Britons against the invading Saxons. It is also named the Catrail and the Dividing Fence.

Pièce de position. (Fr.) Heavy gun.

Pièce de résistance. (Fr.) A solid joint of meat; a strong point.

Pie-crust Palmer. James Shedden Palmer, American naval officer (1810–1867), was popularly known by this sobriquet in allusion to his sallow complexion.

Pied-à-terre. (Fr.) " A foot on land." A temporary abode; a position.

Piedmont Region. The northwestern part of the State of Georgia is so named. The " Piedmont Fair " was held at Atlanta, Ga.

Pieds. (Fr.) The feet; as *Avec les pieds*, with the feet, in organ-playing. (Mus.)

Piepowder Court. An ancient tribunal at English fairs and markets to deal out justice in a rough and ready fashion to all applicants, called also the Court of Dusty Foot. Its jurisdiction was confined to petty offenders, — vagabonds, peddlers, or poachers. The court has long been obsolete.

Pierce Cutting. (Pseud.) Charles Hull Webb, author of stories and sketches in the " Boys and Girls' Weekly," New York.

Pierce Pungent. (Pseud.) J. McLennan, *littérateur*.

Pierre Loti. (Pseud.) Julien Viand (1850–1889), a famous French author and traveller.

Pig in a Poke. It is said that some wags at Northampton Market put a cat in a bag, or poke, and sold it to a countryman as a pig. Upon going to a tavern, to "have a drink" over the bargain, the buyer opened the bag, and of course the cat jumped out. This is stated to be the origin of the proverb, "You should never buy a pig in a poke," and also of "You have let the cat out of the bag." The word "poke" is still used for "sack" in the south of England.

Pig Iron. This is a mere play upon the word "sow." When iron is melted it runs off into a channel called a "sow," the lateral branches of which are called the "pigs." Here the iron cools, and is called "pig iron." "Sow" has nothing to do with "swine," but is from the Saxon *sawan*, "to scatter." Having "sow" for the parent channel, it required no great effort of wit to call the lateral grooves little "pigs."

Pilate Voice. A loud, ranting voice. In the old Mysteries all tyrants were made to speak in a rough, ranting manner.

Pile. The miner or the merchant who has grown rich is said to have "made his pile," — a phrase imported from the camp of the gold-hunter.

Pilgrim Fathers. Those who came over in the "Mayflower" and settled New England in 1620, landing at Plymouth Rock in Massachusetts Bay. The following are their names: John Carver, William Bradford, Edward Winslow, William Brewster, Isaac Allerton, Capt. Miles Standish, John Alden, Samuel Fuller, Christopher Martin, William Mullins, William White, Richard Warren, John Howland, Stephen Hopkins, Edward Tilly, John Tilly, Peter Brown, Richard Britteridge, George Soule, Richard Clark, Richard Gardiner, Francis Cook, Thomas Rogers, Thomas Tinker, John Ridgdale, Edward Fuller, John Turner, Francis Eaton, James Chilton, John Crackston, John Billington, Moses Fletcher, John Goodman, Degory Priest, Thomas Williams, Gilbert Winslow, Edward Margeson, John Allerton, Thomas English, Edward Dotey, Edward Leister. Howland was Carver's servant; Soule was Winslow's servant; and Dotey and Leister were servants of Hopkins. See PLYMOUTH ROCK. Their pastor's name was John Robinson. In 1607 these persecuted people left England and settled in Holland, where they lived about thirteen years, most of the time in the city of Leyden. Then they thought they would like to plant a colony in America, where they could worship God in their own way. These were the people whom we call "the Pilgrims," on account of their wanderings for the sake of religion and conscience. See FOREFATHER'S DAY.

Pillarites. See PILLAR SAINTS.

Pillar of Doctors. The honorary title conferred on William of Champeaux, the famous French philosopher and Schoolman of the twelfth century.

Pillar Saints. A class of anchoritical ascetics, called also Air Martyrs, Holy Birds, Pillarites, and Stylites, the last being their Greek name, from *stylos*, a pillar. They flourished chiefly in Syria during the early centuries of the Christian era, and Pillar Saints existed in the East so late as the twelfth century, when they were abolished. It is a noteworthy fact that this practice never obtained a foothold in the West; and when a certain Wulfilæius attempted to pose as a Stylite in Treves, the bishop quickly destroyed the pillar and expelled him from the city. The first and most widely famous of the Stylites was named Simeon, a Syrian monk, born about 390 A.D., who had been expelled from his monastery for the excess with which he indulged in the most rigid practices of mortification and abstinence. Of this phase of his career it is related that for nine years he never stirred from his narrow stone cell. On his expulsion he removed to an adjacent mountain, where he chained himself to a rock, and his reputation for sanctity became so widely noised abroad that great crowds of visitors made pilgrimages to the scene of his austerities. We are informed that, "incommoded by the pressure of the crowd, he erected a pillar on which he might stand, elevated at first six cubits and ending with forty. The top of the pillar was three feet in diameter, and surrounded with a balustrade. Here he stood day and night, in all weathers, loaded with chains. Through the night, till nine o'clock in the morning, he was constantly in prayer, often spreading his hands and bowing so low that his forehead touched his toes. A bystander once attempted to enumerate the number of these successive prostrations, and he counted till they amounted to twelve hundred and forty-four. At nine o'clock each day he commenced to address the admiring crowd below, to hear and answer their questions, to send messages and write letters, for he took concern in the wel-fare of the churches, and corresponded with bishops and even with emperors. Toward evening he suspended his intercourse with this world, and betook himself to his devotions till the following day. He generally ate but once a week, never reclined when he slept, and wore a long sheepskin robe and a cap of the same material. His beard was extremely long, and his frame terribly emaciated. In this manner he is reported to have spent thirty-seven years, and at last, in his sixty-ninth year, to have expired unobserved, in a praying attitude, in which no one ventured to disturb him till after three days, when Anthony, his disciple and biographer, mounting the pillar, found that his spirit had departed." There is a legend that his much-abused body emitted after death a ravishing perfume, and that innumerable miracles were performed at his shrine in the city of Antioch, whose patron saint he became. Such was the veneration in which his pillar was held that it was surrounded with chapels and monasteries for some centuries subsequent to his death. Of course, many imitators of Simeon arose in consequence of the adulation he received, and numbers took up their abodes on pillars of varying altitude, exposed to all the vicissitudes of a Syrian climate. A Stylite is mentioned as having lived in the sixth century, who ascended his perch in childhood nor descended till his death, when he was sixty-eight years of age.

Pill-Garlick. A half-contemptuous nickname for an unfortunate or a scapegoat. Webster derives it from *peeled* and *garlic*. There is an equivalent term in French. But whatever its origin the phrase has been long current in England among the common people to describe some one who has incurred some unforeseen responsibility, — "poor Pill-Garlick." In Morteux's "Don Quixote" (1743), the following lines occur : —

"A plague on ill-luck ! Now my Ready 's all
      gone,
To the wars poor Pill-Garlick must trudge."

Pindar Cockloft. (Pseud.) William Irving, in "Salmagundi."

Pindar of England. (1) Cowley, who was declared by George, Duke of Buckingham, to be "the Pindar, Horace, and Virgil of England." (2) Gray, according to his epitaph in Westminster Abbey.

Pindar of France. (1) Jean Dorat (fl. 1507–1588). (2) Ponce Denis Lebrun (fl. 1729–1807).

Pindar of Italy. Gabriello Chiabrera (fl. 1552–1637), a famous Italian poet whose imitations of Pindar's odes were exceedingly happy.

Pine Barrens. In the South, tracts of waste land from which the timber of utility has been cut, leaving only a growth of scrub or dwarf trees.

Pineries. Those regions east, west, north, or south where the valuable pine timber of commerce is cut.

Pine-tree Money. "Money coined in Massachusetts in the seventeenth century, and so called from its bearing a figure resembling a pine-tree." — WEBSTER.

Pine-Tree State. Maine. A large part of its surface is covered by pine forests.

Pinx., or **pxt.** *Pinxit.* He (or she) painted it.

Pinxit. (Lat.) He (or she) painted it.

Pious, The. (1) Ernest I., founder of the House of Gotha (fl. 1601–1674). (2) Robert Capet (fl. 971–1031). (3) Eric IX. of Sweden (d. 1161).

Pipe-Laying. "This term in political parlance means any arrangement by which a party makes sure of a certain addition to its legitimate strength in the hour of trial, — that is, the election. To 'lay pipe' means to bring up voters not legally qualified, or to make secret and perhaps discreditable plans to ensure success at the polls. The origin of the term arose from an accusation brought against the Whig party in New York City some years ago, of a gigantic scheme to bring on voters from Philadelphia. The accusation was made by a notorious Democrat, of not very pure political character, who professed to have derived his information from the agent employed by the Whigs for the service. This agent had actually been employed by certain leaders of the Whig party, but on a service deemed legitimate and proper in the art of electioneering. He, however, turned traitor, and, as was alleged by the Whigs, concocted a plot with the notorious Democrat to throw odium upon the Whigs. A mass of correspondence was brought forward in proof, consisting mainly of letters written by the agent to various parties in New York, apparently describing the progress and success of his operations. In these letters, as if for the purpose of concealment, the form of a mere business correspondence was adopted, — the number of men hired to visit New York and vote being spoken of as so many yards of pipe, — the work of laying down pipe for the Croton water being at that time in full activity. The Whig leaders were indicted on the strength of these pseudo revelations, and the letters were read in court; but the jury believed neither in them nor in the writer of them, and the accused were acquitted. The term 'pipe-laying,' however, was at once adopted as a synonym for negotiations to procure fraudulent votes." — INMAN AND BARTLETT.

Pipelet. A French sobriquet for a porter or a door-keeper; so named from a character of that name and station in Sue's " Mysteries of Paris."

Pis aller. (Fr.) A last shift; a makeshift.

Pisces (the Fishes). This constellation is now the first in order of the twelve constellations of the zodiac, and is usually represented by two fishes tied a considerable distance apart, at the extremities of a long undulating chord of ribbon. It occupies a large triangular space in the heavens, and its outline at first is somewhat difficult to be traced. The two Fishes and the chord between them make two sides of a large triangle, thirty and forty degrees in length, the open part of which is toward the northwest. This constellation is bounded north by Andromeda, west by Andromeda and Pegasus, south by the Cascade, and east by the Whale and the Triangles.

Pisistratus Brown. (Pseud.) William Black, English novelist (b. 1840).

Pisistratus Caxton. (Pseud.) Edward George Lytton, Bulwer-Lytton, English novelist (1805–1873).

Pitcher = JUG. " If a man asks for the milk-*jug*," says R. G. White, " be sure that he is British bred; if for the milk-*pitcher*, be equally sure that he is American."

Pitmen's Derby. The race for the time-honored Northumberland Plate, in England, which causes almost a general holiday among the coal-miners in the Newcastle district.

Pittsburg Phil. The turf-name of George Smith, a celebrated "plunger" on the American race-track.

Pitt's Mark. Another name for the printer's imprint at the end of English printed books, according to William Pitt's Act passed in the reign of George III.

Pitt's Pictures. Blind windows. In England, after the passage of the Window Tax in 1784 and 1797, advocated by William Pitt, hundreds of windows were bricked up, in order to save expense.

Più. (Ital.) An adverb of augmentation; as, *più presto*, quicker; *più forte*, louder; *più piano*, softer; *più tasto lente*, rather slow; *più lento*, slower. (Mus.)

Pixies. Devonshire Robin-Good-Fellows; said to be the spirits of infants who have died before baptism. The Pixy monarch holds court like Titania, and sends his or her subjects on their several tasks.

Pizzicato. (Ital.) To play with the finger. (Mus.)

P.-L. Poet-Laureate.

Pl., or Plur. Plural.

Place de Grève. (Fr.) " Place of strand," or shore. A square in Paris where executions formerly took place.

Place-maker's Bible. So named because of a remarkable typographical error occurring in Matt. v. 9: " Blessed are the place-makers." It appeared in 1562.

Placer, an American mining-term of Spanish origin, meaning at first simply pleasure at coming unawares to a rich gold-mine, has become familiar, and now means not only the driftsand which contains gold, but any good thing which promises a liberal return of profit. *See* BONANZA.

Plain, The. The Girondists in the French National Convention were so nicknamed because they sat on the " level floor, or plain," of the hall. *See* MOUNTAIN, THE.

Plain and Perspicuous Doctor. Walter Burleigh, the Schoolman and scholastic of the thirteenth and fourteenth centuries, was thus named by his admiring contemporaries.

Plantations. The British Government in old times used to make grants to all who were willing to *plant* colonies. Hence these colonies were called *plantations* at the North as well as at the South.

Platform. The American use of this word in the sense of a political plan, scheme, or design is justified by ancient use in England. In Lyly's " Alex. and Camp.," act v. sc. 4, Apelles is asked, " What peece of work have you now in hand ? " to which he replies, " None in hand, if it like your Majestie, but I am devising a platforme in my head." And in the " Discovery of the New World," quoted by Nares, " To procure himself a pardon went and discovered the whole platforme of the conspiracie." A very early example occurs in the following title of a tract in the Library of Queen's College, Cambridge : " A Survey of the pretended Holy Discipline, faithfully gathered by way of Historical Narration out of the Works and Writings of the principal favourers of that Platforme. 4to. London, 1593." Another example is in Patrick's " Parable of the Pilgrim," published in 1687, p. 206, where, speaking of persons changing their sect, the writer says, " He can soon quit the way wherein he was, and become religious, after the manner of this novel platform."

Plato of Germany. Friedrich Heinrich Jacobi (fl. 1743–1819).

Plato of the Puritans. John Howe, the nonconformist (fl. 1630–1706).

Plato's Year. A revolution of 25,000 years, in which period the stars and constellations return to their former places in respect to the equinoxes.

Plautus. (Pseud.) Alexander Wilder, Washington and Albany correspondent of the " Evening Post," New York, from 1859–1871.

Playground of Europe. Alpine Switzerland.

Playing with the Mouth. A gambler's phrase. If a dealer in any of the large gambling-houses sees a player thrust his forefinger into his mouth, he knows that it is a request for a loan when his money gives out. If a man is an old and heavy player, there is seldom any hesitancy in lending him a stack of chips, and a nod of the dealer's head is a sufficient indication that the gambler's credit is good. The action is known among the gamblers as " playing with his mouth ; " and when a man can successfully play in this way he is an honored man among his kind.

P. L. C. Poor-Law Commissioners.

Please the Pigs. This proverbial expression, ludicrous as it is in its present shape, had its origin in a deep religious feeling. It was formerly " please the pyx." The pyx was the box which contained the consecrated wafer, and was held in the greatest veneration as the symbol of the Almighty. The phrase, therefore, " If it please the pyx," was equivalent to " If it shall please God," or, in modern form, " D.V.," i. e. *Deo volente*, or God being willing.

Plebeian Child of the Revolution. Napoleon I. was so named. *See* HEIR OF THE REPUBLIC.

Plebeians of the Vegetable World. The great naturalist, Linnæus, so named the grasses. *See* PRINCES OF THE VEGETABLE WORLD.

Plebs. (Lat.) The common people.

Pleiades. In classic myth the seven daughters of Atlas Pleione, the daughter of Oceanus. After their death they were transformed into stars. But only six of the sisterhood are visible to the unaided eye, and the ancients believed that the seventh hid herself from shame that she alone of the seven had wedded a mortal, while each of her sisters had espoused different gods. Their names are Electra, Maia, Taygete, Alcyone, Celæno, Sterope, and Merope.

Pleiades of France. (1) Seven contemporary French poets in the sixteenth century, during the reign of Henri III.: Ronsard, Dorat, Du Bellay, Remi-Belleau, Jodelle, Baïf, and Thiard. (2) Seven other contemporary poets in the reign of Louis XIII.: Rapin, Commire, Larne, Santeuil, Ménage, Dupérier, and Petit. The Second Pleiad was vastly inferior in attainments to the First Pleiad.

Pleiad of Alexandria. Seven contemporary poets who flourished in the reign of Ptolemy Philadelphus: Callimachus, Apollonius of Rhodes, Aratus, Philiscus, Lycophron, Nicander, Theocritus.

Pleiad of Charlemagne. A group of *literati* in the reign of the great conqueror were so named : Alcuin, Angilbert, Adelard, Riculfe, Charlemagne, Varnefrid, and Eginhard.

Pleno jure. (Lat.) With full authority.

Plff. Plaintiff.

P.-L. G. Poor-Law Guardians.

Pliny of the East. Zakarija ibu Mohammed (fl. 1200–1283).

Plon-Plon. A ridiculous nickname attached to Prince Napoleon (b. 1822). It is a euphonious contraction of *Craint-plomb* (" Fear-bullet "), bestowed on him during the Crimean War.

Plot of Befort, or **Belfort.** A conspiracy organized by Amand Bazard (1791–1832), a French socialist, head of the French Carbonari, in 1820, with 200,000 members.

Plough Monday. The first Monday after the Epiphany. It was so named because it was the day upon which our ancestors were wont to return to their agricultural labors after the revels of Christmastide. On that day also the agricultural laborers of the north of England used to draw a plough from door to door and ask for " plough money " to buy drink.

Plover. (Pseud.) John S. Wise, in the " American Field."

Plum-duff. *See* DUFF.

Plumed Knight, or **White-Plumed Knight.** Titles applied to James G. Blaine, of Maine. Col. Robert G. Ingersoll, in his nominating speech at Cincinnati, in 1876, first called Mr. Blaine the " Plumed Knight."

Plupf. Pluperfect.

Pluto. In classic myth the third son of Chronos and Rhea, and brother of Zeus and Poseidon. He married Proserpine ; and at the tripartite division of the universe he obtained the sovereignty of the underworld, — " the realm of darkness and ghostly shades," — where he sits enthroned as a " subterranean Zeus."

Plymouth Brethren. A sect that protests against all sectarianism, and advocates the unity of the Church; some even go so far as to advocate a community of goods. So called from Plymouth, where they sprang into existence in 1830.

Plymouth Rock. On Dec. 22, 1620, the Pilgrim Fathers (*q. v.*) first set foot on a bare rock on the bleak coast of Massachusetts Bay, " while all around the earth was covered with deep snow." This rock became known as " Plymouth Rock," and is to New England what the Palladium was to ancient Troy, or the shield of Minerva to Athens. In course of time the rock became broken into two pieces. One part remained in its original position at Hedge's Wharf, Plymouth ; the other was taken to the centre of the town and surrounded by an iron railing. In 1880 this portion, which had been dragged into Plymouth by twenty yoke of oxen in 1774, and over which the Whigs erected a liberty-pole, was returned to its original position.

P. M. *Post meridiem.* Afternoon ; evening.

P. M. Postmaster ; Passed Midshipman.

P. M. G. Postmaster-General ; Professor of Music in Gresham College.

P. O. Post-Office.

Pobres vergonzantes. (Span.) The blushing poor ; namely, the poor who would rather conceal their griefs from an unfeeling world.

Poco. (Ital.) A little, rather, somewhat; as, *poco presto*, rather quick ; *poco piano*, somewhat soft; *poco più*, somewhat more; *poco meno*, somewhat less. (Mus.)

Poco à poco. (Ital.) Little by little, by degrees, gradually; as, *poco à poco crescendo*, louder and louder by degrees; *poco à poco diminuendo*, softer and softer by degrees. (Mus.)

Poco à poco, più di foco. (Ital.) With gradually increasing animation and fire. (Mus.)

Poco curante. (Ital.) " Little caring." Listless, negligent.

Poco di matto. (Ital.) " A little of a fool." Slight tinge of madness.

Podsnappery. Fossil etiquette, stiff-starched and extremely proper. Mr. Podsnap is a famous character in Dickens's " Our Mutual Friend."

> It may not be so in the Gospel according to Podsnappery . . . but it has been the truth since the foundations of the universe were laid. — *Our Mutual Friend.*

Poet. Poetical.

Poeta nascitur, non fit. (Lat.) A poet is born, not made.

Poet Laureate of Freemasonry. Robert Morris, author (b. 1818). He very early in life became an ardent Mason, and his pen has been actively employed in behalf of the order.

Poet Laureate of the Bees. " In a ' History of the Honey-Bee,' by W. H. Harris, published in London, in the first chapter occurs this passage : ' In our own country (England) Dr. John Evans, who has been called the Poet-Laureate of the Bees,' etc. In looking over an English Biographical Dictionary, I find that 'Dr. John Evans lived in 1802, and wrote much about bees.'"—OLIVE OLDSCHOOL, in *Lippincott.*

Poet of Greta Hall. Robert Southey (fl. 1774–1843), who lived at Greta Hall, in Keswick Vale.

Poet of Hygiene. Jean Baptiste Dumas (d. 1884), the eminent French chemist, was so nicknamed by the Emperor Louis Napoleon.

Poet of Low Hampton. William Miller, founder of the sect of Adventists, or "Millerites" (1782–1849). He was a quick and easy versifier, and resided at Low Hampton, N. Y.

Poet of Methodism. The Rev. Charles Wesley, the hymnologist.

Poet of Poets. Percy Bysshe Shelley.

Poet of the Excursion. William Wordsworth. His principal poem is named "The Excursion."

Poet of the poor. Rev. George Crabbe (fl. 1754–1832).

Poet of Wicomisco. Miss Amanda E. Dennis, whose magazine contributions, signed "Amanda," were published in 1888 under the title "Asphodels and Pansies."

Poets' Corner. A popular name given to a portion of the south transept of Westminster Abbey. Here are the tombs of many of the chief English poets, as well as monuments to many who are interred elsewhere.

Poet Scout, The. Capt. J. W. Crawford, who issued a volume of poems in New York in 1886.

Poet Squab. Rochester thus nicknamed Dryden, on account of his corpulency.

P. of H. Patron of Husbandry.

Pogonatus ("Bearded"). Constantine IV., Emperor of Rome (648–685).

Poi à poi tutti le corde. (Ital.) All the strings, one after another,—a musical expression used in playing the grand pianoforte.

Point d'appui. (Fr.) Point of support; a prop.

Poison. An American term for whiskey. "What's your poison?" is often heard as an invitation to drink.

Poisson d'Avril. (Fr.) An April fool.

Polacca (Ital.), **Polonaise** (Fr.). A slow Polish dance in three-quarter time.

Polar Star, or Pole-star. The present pole-star is the last one in the tail of the constellation of the Little Bear, near the north pole, which, owing to its position with relation to the earth, never sets, and is therefore of great use to mariners in ascertaining the latitude, etc. "The time taken for one revolution of the pole of the equator around that of the ecliptic, or, what is the same thing, for the first point of Aries (the Ram) to perform a complete circle around the ecliptic, is 25,800 miles; as a consequence it follows that the pole-star is not the same at different epochs. At present the (north) pole of the earth is approaching more nearly the direction of the bright star Polaris; but it will soon begin to recede from it, and some other star, coming more nearly in the direction, will be the polar star."—PLUMMER. The present one is of the second magnitude.

Polish Bayard. Prince Joseph Poniatowski (fl. 1763–1814), on account of his chivalrous bravery.

Polish Byron. Adam Mickiewicz (fl. 1798–1855).

Polish Franklin. The philosopher Thaddeus Czacki (fl. 1765–1813) was thus named.

Polish Succession. The so-called "War of the Polish Succession" began in 1733, and was closed by the definite treaty of Vienna, 1738.

Polish Voltaire. The author Ignatius Krasicki (fl. 1774–1801), a prolific writer of prose and poetry.

Poliuto. (Pseud.) F. B. Wilkie, American *littérateur* (b. 1830).

Pollini, Mme. The stage-name of Clara Poole.

Poll-men. A cant term in the English universities to indicate those who take no honors at "exams,"—the *hoi polloi,* "the many," as distinguished from the select few.

Polly Booth. The stage-name of Mrs. Frank Foster.

Polly Winner. The stage-name of Mrs. Edward P. Temple.

Polydore. In classic myth the youngest son of Priam and Hecuba. He was killed for his riches by Polymnestor, king of Thrace, who had been made his guardian.

Polyglot Bible. *See* COMPLUTEN-SIAN BIBLE.

Polyphemus. In classic myth the son of Poseidon and of the nymph Thoosa. He was the most famous of the fabulous Cyclops, who dwelt in the island of Sicily. He was of immense size, and had only one eye. When Ulysses landed on that island he was confined in the cave of Polyphemus, with twelve comrades, of whom this "tremendous cannibal" ate six. The others were hourly expecting the same fate; but Ulysses made the monster drunk, and then burned out his one eye with a blazing brand, and so escaped.

Pomona. Among the Latins the patron divinity of garden produce and of fruits.

Pomona. One of the pseudonyms commonly ascribed to Junius (*q. v.*).

Pompadours, or Saucy Pompeys. A nickname for the Fifty-sixth Regiment in the English army.

Pomp and Tortoise, The. A nickname for the Thirty-eighth Regiment of the line in the English army.

Pomposo. (Ital.) In a grand and pompous manner.

Ponce Pantolabus. (Pseud.) John Huntingdon, English writer (fl. 1542).

Pondere, non numero. (Lat.) By weight, not by number.

Pons asinorum. (Lat.) "The bridge of asses." The asses' bridge, — a name given to the fifth proposition of the first book of Euclid.

Ponsin, Mlle. The stage-name of Madame Henri Prévost.

Pontiac's War. During the French and Indian War (*q. v.*) Pontiac, a sagacious chief of the Ottawas, "who had been an early ally of the French, secretly confederated several of the Algonquin tribes, in 1763, for the purpose of expelling the English from the country west of the Alleghanies. After the fall of Montreal, Pontiac had professed an attachment to the English; and as there seemed safety for settlers west of the mountains, immigration began to pour its living stream over those barriers. Pontiac saw, in the future, visions of the displacement, perhaps destruction, of his race, by the pale-faces; and he determined to strike a blow for life and country. So adroitly were his plans matured, that the commanders of the western forts had no suspicion of his conspiracy until it was ripe, and the

first blow had been struck, in the month of June. Within a fortnight all the posts in possession of the English west of Oswego fell into his hands, except Niagara, Fort Pitt, and Detroit. Colonel Bouquet saved Pittsburg; Niagara was not attacked; and Detroit, after sustaining a siege of almost twelve months, was relieved by Colonel Bradstreet, who arrived there with reinforcements, in May, 1764. The Indians were speedily subdued, their power was broken, and the hostile tribes sent their chiefs to ask for pardon and peace. The haughty Pontiac refused to bow to the white people, and took refuge in the country of the Illinois, where he was treacherously murdered in 1769. This was the last act in the drama of the French and Indian War."—LOSSING.

Pontifex maximus. (Lat.) The chief priest, — a title of the Pope.

Pontius Pilate's Body-guard. The First Foot Regiment of the English army. When called *Le Regiment de Douglas,* and in the French service, they had a dispute with the Picardy regiment about the antiquity of their respective corps. The Picardy officers declared they were on duty on the night of the Crucifixion, when the Colonel of the First Foot replied, "If we had been on guard, we should not have slept at our posts."

Pony up. *See* LEGEM PONE.

Pool your Issues. A cry raised by Denis Kearney, the San Francisco "sand-lots orator," in which he counselled the laboring-men of California and other States to combine for mutual advantage and protection.

Poor Bernard. Claude Bernard, of Dijon, philanthropist (1588–1641).

Poor Man's Bible (*Biblia pauperum*). About threescore of pictures of Scriptural subjects, circulated in the Middle Ages to inculcate the leading events of Bible history, at a time when few could read.

Poor Richard. (Pseud.) Benjamin Franklin, American philosopher and statesman (1706–1790).

Poor Robin. (Pseud.) Robert Herrick, English poet and divine (1591–1674).

Pop. Population.

Pope of Philosophy. Aristotle has been so named in modern times on account of the reverence and universal homage with which his teachings are received.

Pope's Lyre. The stricter sects in the early Reformed Church so denominated the church organ.

Pope's Slave. So Cardinal Cajetan, in the sixteenth century, called the Church.

Poplicola. One of the signatures acknowledged by Junius, and the earliest he used.

Popularis aura. (Lat.) "Popular breath." Popular favor.

Popular Sovereignty. *See* SQUATTER SOVEREIGNTY.

Populus vult decipi. (Lat.) People wish to be deceived.

Porch, The. The philosophers of the Stoic sect (*q. v.*) were so named because Zeno, the founder, gave lectures in the Athenian picture-gallery called the Porch Poecile.

Porkopolis. A slang sobriquet for the city of Cincinnati, Ohio. More pork is here prepared and shipped than in any other city on the continent.

Port. Portugal, or Portuguese.

Portage, or Carry. A detour on land made around a rapid or waterfall.

Portamento. (Ital.) A gliding from one note to another. (Mus.)

Porte-crayon. The pen-name of David Hunter Strother (1817–1888), whose pen and pencil sketches of Southern life and character were familiar to readers of "Harper's Magazine" thirty years ago.

Porteous Mob. On April 15, 1736, one Captain Porteous commanded the guard at the execution, in Edinburgh, of Wilson, a notorious smuggler, who had aided a fellow-prisoner to escape. His unselfish conduct on that occasion earned for him much sympathy among the crowd of onlookers, who mercilessly hooted and pelted the soldiery. Fearing a rescue, Porteous ordered his men to fire on the mob, and seventeen persons were killed or wounded. He was found guilty of murder June 22, 1736, but was granted a reprieve. But the enraged populace broke into his prison, took out Porteous, and hanged him to a dyer's sign-post in the Grassmarket, Sept. 7, 1736. None of the rioters were ever apprehended.

Porterhouse Steak. It is not certain who first used this word; but the steak so-called was evidently the steak sold in the public houses where porter was sold. Porter is a dark-colored malt liquor, first made for and drank by porters. It is heavier than ale, and has tonic properties which ale has not. Probably, then, the large steak which is to the ordinary steak as porter is to ale, was sold in porter-houses, and so gained its name.

Portia. (Pseud.) Mrs. Abigail Smith Adams.

Portsmouth of the Steppes. The city of Bacu, on the Caspian Sea. It is a large shipping and commercial centre.

Portuguese Apollo. Luis Camoens.

Portuguese Cid. Nunez Alvarez Pereira, general and diplomatist (1360–1431).

Portuguese Livy. João de Barros.

Portuguese Mars. Affonso de Alboquerque.

Portuguese Nostradamus. *See* NOSTRADAMUS.

Portuguese Titian. Alonzo Sanchez Coello, the painter (fl. 1515–1590).

Poseidon. In classic myth the Greek name of Neptune (*q. v.*).

Posse comitatus. (Lat.) The power of the county; an armed force of a county which may be called out by the sheriff.

Possibile. (Ital.) Possible; as, *Il più forte possibile,* as loud as possible. (Mus.)

Post and Pan Houses. The name by which half-timbered houses are known in some parts of England. Halliwell says: "A post and pan house is one formed of uprights and cross-pieces of timber, which are not plastered over, but generally blackened, as many old cottages are in various parts of England." The timber in these structures is represented in the word "post." The Anglo-Saxon word *pan,* or *pane,* a piece or portion, refers to the filled-up interstices. We still use the word in the phrase "a pane of glass." "The knight showed me a pane of the wall, and said, 'Sir, see you yonder part of the wall, which is newer than all the remnant?'" — BERNERS.

Postage-stamps, Language of. Stamps on the left corner, upside down, "I love you;" on the left corner, crosswise, "I love another;" stamp on left corner, straight up and down, "Wish to be rid of your correspondence;" stamp placed at the bottom of right corner, crosswise, "No;" at the bottom of right corner, upside down, "Yes;" on the left lower corner, "Do you love me?" on the left lower corner, upside down, "I am displeased;" on the left lower corner, crosswise, "I wish to have your acquaintance;" on the right corner, up and down, "Business correspondence;" on the left side, in the centre, "Accept me as a lover;" left side, upside down, "I am engaged;" on the left side, in the centre crosswise, "Who cares?"

Post bellum auxilium. (Lat.) Help after the difficulty has been overcome, or the danger has passed away.

Posted. Among the colloquial terms derived from commerce none are more frequently heard than "posting" and "posted." The terms arise, of course, from accounts, which when fully entered on the ledger are said to be posted. As Americanisms, however, they are used to express full knowledge of any subject. A would-be farmer thus says: "I require much *posting* (information) before I can begin," and a scholar of various learning is reputed to be posted on all grave questions.

Poste restante. (Fr.) The department of a post-office at which letters lie till called for.

Post hoc. (Lat.) After this thing, matter, or circumstance.

Post hoc ergo propter hoc. (Lat.) "After this, therefore on account of this." Applied to a line of argument.

Post meridiem. (Lat.) "After midday." After noon; contracted into P. M.

Post mortem. (Lat.) After death.

Post obitum. (Lat.) After death.

Post prandium. (Lat.) After a meal.

Post tenebras lux. (Lat.) "After the darkness, light." After darkness comes light.

Postulata. (Lat.) Things assumed.

Potash Kettles. A term applied in the West to roundish elevations and depressions in the earth near the great lakes. They are attributed to the decay and washing away of the soft and easily decomposed limestone by which the ridges where they are found are probably underlaid.

Pot-de-Bière. A French nickname for an Englishman, literally "pot of beer," in reference to the frequency with which that measure of malt liquor is called for by the middle and lower classes.

Poteen, or Potheen, or Potteen. The name among the Irish peasantry for whiskey. The word *poitin* means "I drink," and *poitin* signifies "a small pot." *See* USQUEBAUGH.

Pot-hole. In many parts of the country are found circular holes of various diameters and depths, formed by the action of water in rolling a small bowlder in what was at first a natural depression of the rock. It is a common notion in the West that these were made by the Indians to pound corn in, whence they are often called "Indian mortars."

Pothooks. The Seventy-seventh English Regiment is thus dubbed because of the likeness of the two figures to pothooks and hangers of the copybooks.

Potpourri. (Fr.) A capriccio or fantasia on popular airs.

Potter's Field. "Potter's Field" was a piece of ground which, according to the statement in Matthew, xxvii. 7, was purchased by the priests with the thirty pieces of silver rejected by Judas, and converted into a burial-place for Jews not belonging to the city. Here is the passage: "And they took counsel and bought with them the potter's field to bury strangers in." With us the term "potter's field" denotes the ground where unidentified persons and the bodies of unclaimed paupers are buried; and the term undoubtedly had its origin in the transaction alluded to by Matthew.

Pot-wallopers. The popular nickname of a class forming the constituency of certain English boroughs whose qualification as householders or housekeepers was considered to be sufficiently well established by their boiling a pot within the limits of the borough over a fireplace erected in the open air.

Pound Party. A variation of the Surprise Party (*q. v.*), in which every person participating is supposed or expected to contribute a pound of something to the general stock. Frequently the unopened packages are auctioned off for the benefit of some charity.

Pour encourager les autres. (Fr.) By way of encouragement to others.

Pour faire de l'esprit. (Fr.) To show off one's wit.

Pour faire rire. (Fr.) To excite laughter.

Pour parler. (Fr.) An oral treaty; a consultation.

Pour passer le temps. (Fr.) To pass away the time; to while away the time.

Pour prendre congé. (Fr.) To take leave.

Pour toujours. (Fr.) "For always." Forever.

Poussin of England. Richard Cooper, painter and engraver (d. 1806).

Poussin of France. Gaspar Dughet, French painter (fl. 1613–1675).

Pouting-place of Princes. Leicester Square, London, was so named. George II., when Prince of Wales, quarrelled with his father, and retired to Leicester House; and his son Frederick, Prince of Wales, did likewise.

Pow-wow. This is the name given by the early chronicles to the feasts, dances, and other public doings of the red men, preliminary to a grand hunt, a council, a war expedition, or the like. It has been adopted in political talk, to signify any uproarious meeting for a political purpose, at which there is more noise than deliberation, more clamor than counsel.

Poynings Law. A statute confining all legislation in the Irish Parliament to matters first approved of by the king and the English Council. It was passed at Drogheda, Sept. 13, 1494, during the Lord Deputyship of Sir Edward Poynings, after whom it was named. It was repealed in 1782.

P. P. Parish Priest.

PP. *Patres.* Fathers.

Pp., or **pp.** Pages.

P. P. C. *Pour prendre congé.* To take leave.

P. P., Clerk of this Parish. (Pseud.) John Arbuthnot, British author, satirist, and physician (1675–1735).

Pph. Pamphlet.

P. Q. Previous question.

P. R. Prize ring; Porto Rico; the Roman people (*Populus Romanus*).

P. R. A. President of the Royal Academy.

Præcognita. (Lat.) Things previously known.

Præmia virtutis. (Lat.) The reward of virtue.

Præmoniti præmuniti. (Lat.) They who are forewarned are forearmed.

Præmonitus præmunitus. (Lat.) "Forewarned, forearmed." He who is forewarned of danger is better able to meet it.

Pragmatic Sanction. (1) The decree issued in 1713 by which Charles VI. of Germany settled his dominions on his daughter, Maria Theresa. Her succession was guaranteed by England, France, the States-General, and most of the European Powers, and she began to reign October, 1740, but a general European war followed. (2) That of Charles VII. of France, in 1438, setting bounds to the power of the pope in France. (3) That of Saint Louis, in 1268, forbidding Rome to levy tax or collect alms in France without the king's permission. (4) That of Germany, 1439, whereby the succession of the empire was secured to the House of Austria. (5) That of Naples, 1759, by which Carlos III. of Spain secured the succession to his third son.

Prairie. This term, equivalent to the steppes of Europe and Asia, and to the pampas of South America, is given to the vast stretches of grassy land in the far West. The word is from the French.

Prairie-dog. This is not a dog at all, but a marmot, deriving its colloquial name from its cry, like the sharp bark of a toy-terrier. *See* GOPHER.

Prairie-hen. The western American name for the pinnated grouse.

Prairie State. Illinois. The face of the State is mostly a level table-land, elevated from three hundred to eight hundred feet above the sea.

Prairie-wolf. This is an American variety of the genus *Lupus,* the size of a setter-dog, and living in a burrow in the earth. In the South and Southwest it bears the Spanish-American name of *coyote.*

Praise-God Barebone. This enthusiast's real name was Barbon. His baptismal name was undoubtedly "Praise-God." He was a leather-seller in Fleet Street, and was M. P. for London in the Parliament called, after him, the "Barebone's Parliament." He was imprisoned in the Tower in 1662; but whether he died there or was released, is not known. His son was a great builder and projector, and became "Dr. Barbon," but was generally known as "Damned Dr. Barebone," from the fact that he was christened "If-Christ-had-not-died-for thee-thou-hadst-been-damned." He built several houses in Red Lion Square, and in Essex Street, Strand, London.

Prajapati. In Hindu mythology a name of the god Brahma.

Pramnian Mixture. Any intoxicating draught; so called from the Pramnian grape, from which it was made. Circe gave Ulysses "Pramnian wine" impregnated with drugs, in order to prevent his escape from the island.

> And for my drink prepared
> The Pramnian mixture in a golden cup,
> Impregnating (on my destruction bent)
> With noxious herbs the draught.
> HOMER, *Odyssey.*

Prating Sophists. The Doctors of the Sorbonne were thus named by Budæus of Paris.

Prayer Cylinder. An instrument used by the Buddhists in worship. The phrase "turning-prayer" would better describe this appliance. It consists usually of a brass reel cased in wood or leather, to one end of which a handle is attached. Around the cylinder a strip of paper or cloth is wound, on which is written some sacred sentence, generally the "Om Mani." *See* OM MANI PADMA HUM. The cylinder being slowly turned from right to left, the number of revolutions made is considered to be equivalent to the recitation of so many prayers. The great monasteries have larger cylinders, and these are kept in constant motion by persons hired for the purpose, or by being placed over a running stream, like our mill-wheels.

P. R. C. *Post Romanum conditum.* From the building of Rome.

Preacher, The. Solomon, being the author of Ecclesiastes.

Preb. Prebend; prebendary.

Précieuse. (Fr.) A conceited or affected woman.

Précipité. (Fr.) Hurried, accelerated. (Mus.)

Pref. Preface; preferred.

Préfet. (Fr.) "A prefect." A superior magistrate in France.

Prep. Preposition.

Première. (Fr.) First; as, *première fois,* first time. (Mus.)

Premier pas. (Fr.) "First step." The beginning.

Pres. President.

Presb. Presbyterian.

Presbyterian True Blue. This allusion in "Hudibras" is to the blue apron which some of the Presbyterian preachers used to throw over their preaching-tub before they began to address the people. In one of the Rump songs we read of a person going to hear a lecture, and the song says: —

> "Where I a tub did view,
> Hung with an apron blue;
> 'T was the preacher's, I conjecture."

Prescriptum. (Lat.) (A thing) prescribed.

Preserver, The (" Soter "). A surname bestowed on Ptolemy I. of Egypt by the Rhodians, because he compelled Demetrius to raise the siege of Rhodes.

President Bates. (Pseud.) L. J. Bates, one of the editorial staff of the Detroit "Tribune."

Presidents, Mother of. *See* MOTHER OF PRESIDENTS.

Prestissimo. (Ital.) The most rapid degree of movement. (Mus.)

Presto. (Ital.) Very quick.

Pretender, The Old. James Francis Edward Stuart, son of James II. of England (fl. 1688–1766).

Pretender, The Young. Charles Edward Stuart, son of the Old Pretender (fl. 1720–1788). See *supra.*

Pretiosa supellex. (Lat.) Costly furniture.

Pretty. Among Southerners "pretty" is a word very often misused; for instance: "Isn't this a *pretty* day?" — and this error is a very general one. North Carolinians say the scenery is "pretty," — meaning "picturesque;" the day is "pretty," — meaning "fine;" and that a person's manners are "pretty," — meaning "well-bred."

Preux chevalier. (Fr.) A brave knight.

Priam. In classic myth king of Troy at the time of the Trojan War. He was the son of Laomedon and of Strymo or Placia. The epic poet gives him fifty sons and as many daughters. The best-known of these are Hector, Paris, Deiphobus, Helenus, Troilus, and Cassandra. One legend states that, being too old to bear any active part in the Trojan War, he was slain by Pyrrhus at the altar of Zeus Herkeios, when the Greeks stormed the city.

Pride of Gratz and Styria. The Johanneum; an institution in the city of Gratz, Austria, founded by Archduke John, in 1812, for the encouragement of the arts and manufactures of Styria. It is richly endowed in the various departments of science, art, mineralogy, antiquities, and coins, and has a chemical laboratory, a botanical garden, and a library.

Pride's Purge. When the Long Parliament (*q. v.*) showed some reluctance to condemn Charles I., it was *purged* of its unruly members by Colonel Pride, who, at the head of two regiments of infantry, imprisoned sixty, drove one hundred and sixty into the street, allowing only sixty of the most subservient to remain.

Prima donna. (Ital.) "The first lady." The chief female singer of the Italian opera.

Prima facie. (Lat.) On the first view of the matter.

Prima materia. (Lat.) The first material.

Prime Minister. The term "Prime Minister" seems to have originated in banter. It was first applied in this spirit to Sir Robert Walpole. On Feb. 11, 1712, that statesman is reported to have said in the House of Commons, "Having invested me with a kind of mock dignity and styled me a 'Prime Minister,' they [the Opposition] impute to me an unpardonable abuse of the chimerical authority which they only created and conferred."

Primi pensieri. (Ital.) The first thoughts.

Primo. (Ital.) First; as, *violino primo*, first violin; *tempo primo*, in the first or original time. (Mus.)

Primrose Campaign. During the English elections of 1885 the Duchess of Marlborough and Lady Churchill put forth strenuous efforts to compass the election of Lord Randolph Churchill to Parliament as representative of Birmingham. Three hundred ladies, nicknamed "Primrose Dames," made a house-to-house canvas of the voters; and Mr. John Bright, the rival candidate, referred to these endeavors in his speeches, as the "Primrose Campaign."

Primrose Day. April 19. The anniversary of the death of Lord Beaconsfield, on which the conservatives in England everywhere appear wearing the primrose, his favorite flower.

Disraeli's fondness for the primrose originated from the time when he was living in Highbury, London. Here he was much attached to a young lady residing in the same locality, who was the daughter of a gentleman of good property. At a ball, given at this gentleman's house, the young lady in question wore a wreath of primroses. A discussion arose between Mr. Disraeli and another gentleman as to whether the primroses were real or not. A bet of a pair of gloves was made, and on the young lady being consulted and the primroses examined, the bet was won by Mr. Disraeli. The primroses were real primroses, and the young lady gave two or three of them to the future Prime Minister, which he put in his buttonhole and kept and used to show long afterward. — *Letter to the Editor of the London "Spectator."*

Primrose League. The Primrose League of England has for its object the maintenance of religion, of the estates of the realm, and of the imperial ascendency of the British Empire. It works by means of habitations, of which there were 1,200 in 1886 in the United Kingdom, India, Africa, and the British Possessions generally. Its members are divided into knights, dames, and associates, by far the greater part belonging to the better class of society. The League's headquarters are at St. Margaret's Office, Victoria Street, Westminster. It rendered the Conservative party great assistance in the general election of 1885. Primrose Day is the anniversary of the death of Lord Beaconsfield, on April 19. Every member of the League must wear a bunch of primroses on that day in token of sympathy with and support of the objects of the League.

Primum mobile. (Lat.) "The first movement." The mainspring.

Primus inter pares. (Lat.) The first among equals.

Prin. Principally.

Prince Always in Front. (Ger. *Fürst Allezeit Voran.*) A nickname given by his soldiery to Prince Frederick Charles of Prussia (fl. 1828–1885), a gallant commander. *See* RED PRINCE.

Prince of Alchemy. Rudolph II., Emperor of Germany. He was also nicknamed "The German Trismegistus."

Prince of Artists. Albert Dürer (fl. 1471–1528) was so named by his admiring countrymen.

Prince of Coxcombs. Charles Joseph, Prince de Ligne (fl. 1735–1814).

Prince of Critics. Aristarchus of Byzantium.

Prince of Darkness. Satan.

Prince of Destruction. The conqueror Tamerlane.

Prince of Gossips. Samuel Pepys.

Prince of Grammarians. Apollonius of Alexandria.

Prince of Hypocrites. Tiberius Cæsar (fl. 42 B. C.–37 A. D.) was thus named because, while professing a great respect for virtue, he was a monster of lust and cruelty.

Prince of Liars. So Cervantes names Ferdinand Mendez Pinto, a Portuguese traveller of the sixteenth century, on account of the Munchausen-like tales which he told.

Prince of Painters. Parrhasius, the Athenian artist, so styled himself. He flourished in the fifth century B C.

Prince of Peace. The Messiah. (See Isa. ix. 6.)

Prince of Physicians. Avicenna, the Arabian, who flourished 980–1037.

Prince of Poets. Edmund Spenser is so styled on his monument in Westminster Abbey.

Prince of Spanish Poets. Garcilaso de la Vega was so named by Cervantes.

Prince of the Apostles. Saint Peter is so named. (See Matt. xvi. 18, 19.)

Prince of the Ode. Pierre de Ronsard, a French lyrist (fl. 1524–1585).

Prince of the Peace. Don Manuel de Godoy, Prime Minister to Charles IV. of Spain, because of the adroit way in which he separated Spain from England, and declared an offensive and defensive alliance with France.

Prince of the Power of the Air. Satan. (See Eph. ii. 2.)

Prince of the Sonnet. (1) Joachim du Bellay (fl. 1524–1560), a famous French poet. *See* PLEIAD. (2) Petrarch.

Princes of the Vegetable World. Linnæus, the naturalist, so named the different varieties of the palm-tree. *See* PLEBEIANS OF THE VEGETABLE WORLD.

Princess of the Plains. Wichita, Kansas.

Principia, non homines. (Lat.) Principles, not men.

Principiis obsta. (Lat.) Resist the first innovations.

Printer's Bible. Cotton Mather is authority for the statement that in a Bible issued before 1702 a blundering typographer made King David exclaim: " Printers have persecuted me without a cause " (Ps. cxix. 161).

Printer's Devil. The youngest apprentice in a printing-office, whose duty it is to do all the dirty jobs. The early printers were by many believed to practise the black art; Aldus Manutius had a negro boy for a body servant, and the superstitious townsfolk nicknamed this boy " the devil."

Prisoner of Chillon. François de Bonnivard, a French state prisoner confined for six years in the dungeon of the Château de Chillon by Charles III. of Savoy. Byron has immortalized him in his famous poem.

Prisoner of the Vatican. A commiserative title conferred on the Pope by his adherents subsequent to the occupation of the Papal territory by the Italian troops in 1870. They maintained that since the loss of his temporal power the Head of the Church was confined to the Vatican enclosure, and was virtually a prisoner.

Priv. Privative.

Privateer. The signature of Charles J. Foster, an American writer on sporting subjects. He was born in England in 1820; died in New York in 1883.

Private Miles O'Reilly. (Pseud.) Charles G. Halpine, American humorous writer and poet (1829–1868).

Pro aris et focis. (Lat.) " For altars and hearths." For our altars and our hearths; for God and our homes; for God and our country.

Prob. Problem.

Probatum est. (Lat.) It is proved.

Probitas laudatur et alget. (Lat.) Honesty is praised and is uncherished.

Pro bono publico. (Lat.) For the public good.

Proc. Proceedings.

Procès verbal. (Fr.) A written statement.

Procris. In classic myth daughter of Erechtheus, king of Athens, and wife of Cephalus, who shot her while hunting, in mistake. The gods changed her into a star.

Procrustes (" the stretcher "). In classic myth the surname of a notorious robber of Attica named Damastes or

Polypemon. According to the ancient legend he was wont to place all persons who fell into his hands upon a bed; if it was found either too long or too short for them, he stretched their limbs or cut them off till they fitted.

Proctor's Dogs, or Bull-dogs. The two "runners" or officials who accompany a university proctor in his rounds, to give chase to recalcitrant gownsmen.

Procul, O procul este, profani! (Lat.) Far, far hence, O ye profane!

Prodigal, The. Albert VI., Duke of Austria (fl. 1418–1453).

Prodigy of France. Guillaume Budé was so named by Erasmus.

Prodigy of Learning. Samuel Hahnemann, the German, was so named by Jean Paul Richter.

Pro et con. (Lat.) For and against. (*con.* for *contra.*)

Prof. Professor.

Profanum vulgus. (Lat.) "The profane common people." The rude multitude.

Pro forma. (Lat.) For form's sake.

Pro forma tantum. (Lat.) "For form only." For form's sake only.

Profound, The. Richard Middleton, the theologian (d. 1304).

Profound Doctor. (1) Thomas Bradwardine (d. 1349), Archbishop of Canterbury. (2) Richard Middleton (d. 1304), an English Schoolman.

Progne. In classic myth daughter of Pandion, king of Athens, sister of Philomela, and wife of Tereus. She was changed into a swallow by the gods.

Progresistas. A political party in Spain, headed by Espartero, Duke of Vittoria, and latterly by General Prim. After 1865 they adopted a policy of inaction in public affairs; by uniting with Unionists and Republicans in September, 1868, the Government was overthrown.

Progressive City. Atlanta, Ga.

Pro hac vice. (Lat.) On this occasion.

Prohibition Party. This party arose in Maine, where, in 1851, Neal Dow procured the passage of a law to prohibit the sale of intoxicating liquors as a beverage. In 1880–1881 Kansas did the same, and the party has considerable following in the Northwest States. Its votes for President in 1872 were 5,608, James Black being its candidate; and in 1876 it cast 9,223 for G. C. Smith. In 1880 the party polled 10,305 votes, in 1884, 150,369 votes, and in 1888, 246,406.

Proh pudor! (Lat.) "For shame!" Oh, for shame!

Pro libertate patriæ. (Lat.) For the liberty of one's country.

Pro loco et tempore. (Lat.) For the place and time.

Pro memoria. (Lat.) For a memorial.

Prometheus. In classic myth son of the Titan Iapetus and of Clymene. He made men of clay, and endued them with life by means of sacred fire which he purloined from heaven. For this offence he was chained to Mount Caucasus by Jupiter, where an eagle or a vulture devoured his liver by day, which grew again each night.

Prometheus. (Pseud.) Francis A. Steimer, in "Turf, Field, and Farm."

Promised Land. Canaan; that portion of Syria lying between the Jordan and the Mediterranean. It was frequently promised by Jehovah to the patriarchs (see Gen. xii. 7; xiii. 15; xxviii. 13; xxxv. 12), and finally bestowed on their descendants, the Israelites. *See* HOLY LAND.

Promise of Odin. *See* STANDING STONES OF STENNIS.

Pron. Pronoun; pronunciation.

Pronunciamento. (Lat.) A public declaration.

Prop. Proposition.

Propaganda fide. (Lat.) For propagating the faith.

Pro patria. (Lat.) For our country.

Prophecies of Mother Shipton. *See* MOTHER SHIPTON.

Prophet, The. (1) Mohammed. (2) Joachim, Abbot of Fiore (fl. 1130–1202).

Prophet Elm. An elm growing in Credenhill Court, belonging to the Eckley family. It is so called because one of the branches is said to snap off and thus announce an approaching death in the family.

Prophet of the Northwest. A title assumed by Louis David Riel (1844–1885), a Canadian half-breed insurgent. In 1870, and again in 1885, he engaged in insurrectionary operations against the Canadian Government, and in the latter year was captured, tried, and hanged as a traitor.

Prophet of the Syrians. Ephraem Syrus, who flourished in the fourth century.

Prophet's City. (In Arabic, *Medi-nat-al-Nebt.*) A name by which Medina, in Arabia, is often referred to. To this place Mohammed fled for refuge during the Hegira, July 16, 622, and here is his tomb.

Proprio motu. (Lat.) Of his own free will; spontaneously.

Propter hoc. (Lat.) "On account of this." By reason of this matter or circumstance.

Propter quod. (Lat.) "On account of which." On account of which thing or circumstance.

Pro rata. (Lat.) In proportion; proportionally.

Pro rege et patria. (Lat.) For king and country.

Pro rege, grege, lege. (Lat.) "For king, people, law." For the king, the people, and the law.

Pro re nata. (Lat.) According as circumstances require; for a special business; special.

Pro salute animæ. (Lat.) For the health of the soul.

Prose Homer of Human Nature. Henry Fielding, the novelist, was so named by Byron.

Proserpine. In classic myth daughter of Zeus and Demeter (Ceres), or of Styx. She was the queen of the underworld by virtue of her espousal of Pluto.

Prosperity Robinson. A nickname conferred on Frederick Robinson, afterward Viscount Goderich, because, just before the commercial crisis of 1825, he painted glowing pictures of the prosperity of the country. *See* ADVERSITY HUME.

Prot. Protestant.

Pro tanto. (Lat.) Just by so much.

Protector of Peru. A title conferred on José de San Martin (fl. 1778–1850), a South American patriot.

Protégé. (Fr.) A person taken charge of, or patronized; a ward, etc.

Pro tem. *Pro tempore.* For the time being.

Pro tempore. (Lat.) "For the time." For the time being.

Prot. Epis. Protestant Episcopal.

Protesilaus. In classic myth son of Iphides and husband to Laodamia. He fought at Troy, was killed by Hector, and his body sent home to Laodamia. She prayed to be allowed to converse with him for three hours only, and, her request being granted, when he expired a second time Laodamia died too.

Protestant Duke. James, Duke of Monmouth, executed on Tower Hill 1685. He embraced Protestantism, and became the idol of the English people, especially of the Nonconformists.

Protestant Pope. Clement XIV.

Proteus. In classic myth the guardian of the seal-flocks of Poseidon (Neptune), and possessed the gift of endless transformation. His favorite residence was, according to Homeric legend, the island of Pharos, off the mouth of the Nile; but according to Virgil, the island of Karpathos, between Crete and Rhodes.

Proud, The. (1) Otho IV., Emperor of Germany. (2) Tarquin II. of Rome. (3) Charles Seymour, Duke of Somerset (d. 1748), who would never suffer his own children to sit in his presence, and never deigned to address his servants.

Prov. Proverbs; Provost; Province.

Pro virili parte. (Lat.) To his utmost.

Prox. *Proximo.* Next (month).

P. R. S. President of the Royal Society.

Prs. Pairs.

Prudens futuri. (Lat.) Thoughtful of the future.

Prus. Prussia; Prussian.

Prussian Quadrilateral. The fortresses of Luxembourg, Coblentz, Sarrelouis, and Mayence.

P. S. Postscript (*Post scriptum*); Privy Seal.

Ps. Psalm, or Psalms.

P's, The Five. *See* FIVE P's.

Psyche ("breath," or "spirit"). A personification of the human soul devised by the later Greek poets. Her love for Cupid is regarded by critics as an allegory "of the progress of the human soul through earthly passion and misfortune to pure celestial felicity."

Pt. Part; pint; payment; point; port; platinum.

P.-T. Pupil-teacher.

p.-t. Post-town.

P. Th. G. Professor of Theology in Gresham College.

P. T. O. Please turn over.

p.-twp. Post-township.

Pub. Publisher; publication; published; public.

Pub. Doc. Public Documents.

Public Good, War of the. *See* WAR OF THE PUBLIC GOOD.

Publicola. (Pseud.) William Johnson Fox, English politician and writer (1786–1864).

Publius. (Pseud.) Alexander Hamilton, American statesman, orator, and general (1757–1804).

Pucelle, La. Another name for Jeanne D'Arc, "the Maid of Orleans."

Pudding-time. Formerly all English dinners commenced with pudding, as they still do in remote districts. Hence pudding-time meant dinner-time. A foreigner who in the seventeenth century visited England and published his experiences in French at the Hague, in 1698, speaks enthusiastically of English puddings. "Oh," says he, "what an excellent thing is an English pudding! To come at pudding-time is a proverbial phrase, meaning to come at the happiest moment in the world. Make a pudding for an Englishman and you will regale him, be he where he will."

Pugnis et calcibus. "With fists and heels." With all the might.

Pulteney. (Pseud.) Nicholas Amherst, *circa* 1726, as editor of the "Craftsman."

Pumpernickel. Under the nickname "His Transparency of Pumpernickel," the London "Times" satirized the petty German princelets.

Punica fides. (Lat.) "Punic or Carthaginian faith." Treachery. *See* FIDES PUNICA.

Punic Faith. Treachery.

Punic Wars. The name commonly given to the three great conflicts for supremacy waged between Rome and Carthage. The Latin word *punicus* or *panicus* was the name given by the Romans to the Carthaginians in allusion to their Phœnician descent.

Puppet Kings. *See* FAINÉANTS.

Purim. An annual Jewish festival "instituted by Mordecai, at the suggestion of Esther, to commemorate the wonderful deliverance of the Jews in Persia from the destruction with which they were threatened through the base designs of Haman." It occurs on the 13th and 14th of the month Adar, corresponding with the early part of our March. It is a festival of rejoicing and merry-making.

Puritan City. Boston, Mass., — a name referring both to its founders and to the supposed characteristics of its modern inhabitants.

Puritan Plato. John Howe, the Nonconformist (1630–1706).

Put none but Americans on guard to-night. This famous phrase occurred originally in one of General Washington's "Orders of the Day."

p.-v. Post-village.

P. W. P. Past Worthy Patriarch.

Pwt. Pennyweight; pennyweights.

Pxt. *Pinxit.* He (or she) painted it.

Pygmalion. In classic myth a grandson of Agenor. Having carved a beautiful statue, he fell so much in love with it that at his urgent request Venus gave it life.

Pygmies. In classic myth a nation of dwarfs, a span high, who dwelt on the banks of the Nile. Once a year, in spring-time, the Cranes attacked and defeated them.

Pylades. In classic myth a friend of Orestes, renowned for the constancy of his affection.

Pyramus. In classic myth the lover of Thisbe. On account of her supposed death he killed himself under a mulberry-tree. Thisbe, finding his corpse, killed herself in the same spot and with the same weapon, and the fruit of the mulberry has ever since been blood-red.

Pyrrhic Victory. Pyrrhus, king of Epirus, having defeated the Romans in a desperate battle in Calabria, is reported to have remarked, in compliment to the valor of his opponents, "Another such victory will ruin me!"

Pyrrhus. In classic myth the son of Achilles and Deïdamia, notorious for his cruelty at the siege of Troy. He was slain at Delphi by Orestes.

Python. In classic myth a huge serpent who sprang from the mud of the deluge of Deucalion. It was slain near Delphi by Apollo, and he founded the Pythian Games in honor of the victory.

Q.

Q. As it were (*quasi*); almost; queen; question.

Q. B. Queen's Bench.

Q. C. Queen's College; Queen's Counsel.

q. d. *Quasi dicat*, as if he should say; *quasi dictum*, as if said; *quasi dixisset*, as if he had said.

q. e. *Quod est.* Which is.

q. e. d. *Quod erat demonstrandum.* Which was to be proved,

q. e. f. *Quod erat faciendum.* Which was to be done.

q. e. i. *Quod erat inveniendum.* Which was to be found out.

Q. K. Philander Doesticks, P. B. (Pseud.) Mortimer M. Thompson, American humorous writer (1831–1865).

q. l. *Quantum libet.* As much as you please.

Q. M. Quartermaster.

q. m. *Quomodo.* How; by what means.

Q. Mess. Queen's Messenger.

Q. M. G. Quartermaster-General.

qp., or **q. pl.** *Quantum placet.* As much as you please.

qr. Quarter.

Q. S. Quarter Sessions.

q. s. *Quantum sufficit.* A sufficient quantity.

Qt. Quart.

Qu., or **qy.** *Quære.* Inquire; query.

Quad is a contraction of quadrangle. In some of the colleges at Oxford the students, when guilty of minor offences, are for a certain specified time not allowed to leave the college precincts. They may not pass beyond the quad or quadrangle. Hence to be "in quad" is equivalent to being a prisoner.

Quadragesima. The name of the Lenten season, or more properly of the first Sunday of Lent. It is so called by analogy with the three Sundays which precede Lent, and which are called, respectively, Septuagesima, 70th; Sexagesima, 60th; and Quinquagesima, 50th.

Quadrilateral, The. Four strong fortresses in northern Italy; namely, Peschiera, on an islet in the river Nun-cio; Mantua, also on the Nuncio; Verona; and Legnano, on the Adige. They are formidable works, since they mutually support one another, and form a barrier across the north plain of the river Po.

Quadrille. (Fr.) A French dance consisting of five consecutive movements, called *Le Pantalon, La Poule, L'Été, Le Trenise ou La Pastorelle*, and *La Finale*.

Quadroon. In Louisiana this term denotes the offspring of a white man and a griffin (*q. v.*).

Quadruple Alliance. (1) Between Germany, Spain, Denmark, Holland, in 1674, against France and the encroachments of Louis XIV. (2) England, France, Germany, and the United Provinces entered into an alliance, July 7, 1718, for the purpose of guaranteeing the succession of the then reigning families of England and France, and settling the partition of the Spanish monarchy. (3) Between England, France, Spain, and Portugal, in 1834, for the purpose of crushing the Carlists.

Quadruple Treaty. A compact concluded in London, April 22, 1834, by the ambassadors of England, Spain, Portugal, and France, and which guaranteed the throne to Isabella II. of Spain.

Quære. Query; inquiry.

Quaker. A nickname for a member of the Society of Friends.

It appears from the "Journal" of George Fox, who was imprisoned for nearly twelve months in Derby, that the Quakers first obtained the appellation by which they are now generally known in 1650, from the following circumstance: "Justice Bennet, of Derby," says Fox, "was the first to call us Quakers, because I bade him quake and tremble at the word of the Lord."

> Quakers (that, like lanterns, bear
> Their light within them) will not swear.
> BUTLER, *Hudibras.*

Quaker City. Philadelphia, which was planned and colonized by William Penn and other members of the Society of Friends.

Quaker Meadows Joe. Joseph McDowell, American Revolutionary soldier (b. 1756), was familiarly so named to distinguish him from his cousin of the same name.

Quaker Poet. (1) Bernard Barton (fl. 1784–1849), an English versifier of note, and a member of the Society of Friends. (2) John Greenleaf Whittier (b. 1807), the American poet, and also a member of the Society of Friends.

Quaker Soldier. Clement Biddle (1740–1814), a Philadelphia Friend who organized the famous "Quaker" Company of soldiers which performed such valiant service in the Revolution.

Quaker State. Pennsylvania. It was settled by members of the Society of Friends under William Penn.

Qualis ab incepto. (Lat.) The same as at the beginning.

Quamdiu se bene gesserit. (Lat.) As long as he shall conduct himself properly; during good behavior.

Quantum. (Lat.) "As much as." The amount; quantity.

Quantum libet. (Lat.) As much as you please.

Quantum meruit. (Lat.) As much as he deserved.

Quantum sufficit. (Lat.) "As much as is sufficient." Amply or quite sufficient; written in the contracted form *quant. suff.*

Quantum valeat. (Lat.) "As much as it may be worth." For what it is worth.

Quar. Quarterly.

Quarantine War. For several years prior to 1858 the people of Staten Island had labored to secure the removal of the Quarantine Hospital, and had persistently claimed that its presence endangered their lives and depreciated the value of their property. Failing to secure the desired object in a legal manner, they resolved to destroy the extensive and valuable property of the State, and thus compel a change in the location of the hospital. In the darkness of a September night a mob assembled in Tompkinsville, forcibly invaded the premises, and fired the obnoxious buildings. Everything of value was destroyed, and many of the inmates of the hospital barely escaped with their lives. A regiment of militia was at once ordered to Staten Island to preserve order and to occupy the State property, and then several regiments of the First Division guarded the Quarantine grounds until the close of the year 1858.

Quare impedit. (Lat.) Why he hinders.

Quarter. This phrase originated in an agreement between the Dutch and Spaniards that the ransom of an officer or soldier should be one quarter of his pay. Hence, to " beg quarter " was to offer a quarter of their pay for their safety, and to refuse quarter was to decline that composition as a ransom.

Quasi. (Lat.) "As if; as it were." In a manner; apparently.

Quasi. (Ital.) In the manner or style of ; as, *quasi allegretto*, like an allegretto. (Mus.)

Quasi dicas. (Lat.) As if you should say.

Quasimodo Sunday. The first Sunday after Easter; so called because the " Introit " of the day begins with these words : " Quasi modo geniti infantes."

Que. Quebec.

Queen Anne's Bounty. The produce of the first-fruits and tenths due to the crown, made over by Queen Anne to a corporation established in the year 1704, for the purpose of augmenting church livings under £50 a year.

Queen Anne's Fan. A polite name for the gesture which consists in putting one's thumb to one's nose with the fingers spread.

Queen Anne's War. The struggle between the English and French, in North America, about 1710. Incidents : the capture of Nova Scotia and New Brunswick and the depopulation of Acadia.

Queen City. Seattle, Washington Territory, on the shores of Puget Sound.

Queen City of the Hudson. Yonkers, N. Y.

Queen City of the Golden Gate. San Francisco.

Queen City of the Lakes. Buffalo, N. Y., — a city of commanding position on the great lakes, and of much commercial importance.

Queen City, Queen of the West. Names popularly given to Cincinnati at a time when its commercial supremacy in the West was undisputed by Chicago and St. Louis.

Queen of Bohemia. Miss Ada Clare (pseud. of Mrs. Jane McElhinney) has been so nicknamed.

Queen of Cities. Another of the many fanciful names given to ancient Rome.

Queen of Hearts. Elizabeth, daughter of James I., the unhappy queen of

Bohemia, who was so named in the Low Countries in consequence of her beauty and engaging manners.

Queen of Hearts. (Pseud.) Mrs. E. M. Patterson Keplinger, a well-known Southern poet.

Queen of Night. The moon; the sun being known poetically as the King of Day.

Queen of Queens. So Antony named Cleopatra.

Queen of Roads. The Appian Way, the oldest and best of all the Roman highways, has been so named. It led from Rome to Capua, and was commenced by the Decemvir Appius Claudius (B. C. 313).

Queen of Spain's Chair. A mountain of Spain, twelve miles from Gibraltar. During the last great siege the reigning queen ascended that mountain to behold the engagement, and declared she would never depart from it until the Spanish flag waved once more over Gibraltar.

Queen of Tears. Mary of Modena, the second wife of James II. of England, in allusion to the misfortunes she was called to endure — largely through her own foolish policy.

Queen of the Antilles. Cuba. It is the largest of the West Indian group, and presents the most beautiful and varied landscapes; while in fine harbors and in the great range of its vegetable products it ranks first among the islands of the Gulf of Mexico.

Queen of the Black Sea. The port of Odessa has been so named.

Queen of the East. (1) Antioch, a beautiful city, formerly the capital of Syria, and the place of residence of the Macedonian kings and Roman governors. (2) Batavia, in Java, the metropolis of the Dutch East Indian possessions.

Queen of the Eastern Archipelago. The island of Java, which bears the same relation to the East Indies as the Queen of the Antilles (*q. v.*) does to the West. It is the most fertile, the most salubrious, and the most picturesque member of the Malay Archipelago, and is, besides, the seat of the Dutch power in the East.

Queen of the Lakes. Windermere, the largest lake in England. On its shores may be seen the most beautiful scenery in the "lake country."

Queen of the North. Edinburgh, the largest city in North Britain.

Queen of the Plains. Denver, Col., is so named.

Queen of the Plaza. Adah Isaacs Menken, the famous actress (1835–1868), was so known during her sojourn in Havana.

Queen of the West. *See* QUEEN CITY.

Queen of the World. The city of Mero, in Turkestan, was once so named.

Queen of Weapons. The bayonet was so named by Lord Napier.

Queen's Bays. The Second Dragoon Guards; so named because they are mounted on bay horses only.

Queen's Day. November 17, the anniversary of the accession of Queen Elizabeth. It was first kept as a holiday in 1570, and is still observed at Westminster School and the Merchant Taylors' School, London.

Queen's Maries. Four young ladies of quality, of the same age as Mary afterwards "Queen of Scots." They embarked with her in 1548, on board the French galleys, and were destined to be her playmates in childhood, and her companions when she grew up. Their names were Mary Beaton, Mary Livingston, Mary Fleming, and Mary Seaton.

Queen's Own, The, or **Sleepy Queen's, The.** Nicknames bestowed upon the Second Regiment of Foot in the English army. *See also* PASCHAL LAMBS.

Queen-Square Hermit. Jeremy Bentham, the politico-economist (fl. 1748–1832), was so named. He resided for over half a century at No. 1 Queen Square, London.

Queen's Tobacco Pipe. This is the curious name given to a singularly shaped kiln which was at one time located at the corner of the great tobacco warehouses belonging to the London docks, on the Thames, England. This kiln consisted of a round brick stack or chimney, bulging out at its base so as to allow for an interior width of five feet. Inside were piled up damaged tobacco and cigars and contraband goods, such as tea, silks, manufactured tobacco, etc., which had been smuggled; books that were attempted evasions of the Copyright Act, etc., until a sufficient quantity had accumulated. Then it was set on fire and consumed. The total value of the goods and merchandise thus destroyed was enormous; and though the custom was widely criticised and stigmatized as wasteful and wrong, the Government continued, until recent years, periodically to fill and light the "Queen's Pipe." Now seized goods are sold at the annual "customs' sales" in London, where unclaimed merchandise, samples, etc., are disposed of by the authorities.

Queen's Weather. There is a tradition in England that Queen Victoria always enjoys good weather on the occasion of any public appearance or royal fête ; hence a fine sunshiny day.

Queerquill. (Pseud.) Mrs. Mary T. Waggamon, in the New York "Weekly."

Quellon. (Pseud.) Stephen Henry Bradbury, *littérateur* (d. 1865).

Quelque chose. (Fr.) "Something." A trifle ; a kickshaw.

Ques. Question.

Qui capit, ille facit. (Lat.) He who takes it, makes it.

Quid-nunc? (Lat.) "What now?" A newsmonger ; a political marplot or busybody.

Quid pro quo. (Lat.) One thing for another ; a mutual accommodation.

Quid rides? (Lat.) Why do you laugh?

Quids. A name given to the few supporters of Randolph when he seceded from the Republican party in 1805. The Latin phrase *tertium quid*, a "third something" (as distinguished from the two powerful parties), gave rise to the name.

Quietist. One who believes that the most perfect state of man is when the spirit ceases to exercise any of its functions, and is wholly passive. This sect has cropped up at sundry times ; but the last who revived it was Michael Molinos, a Spanish priest, in the seventeenth century.

Quiet Man, A. (Pseud.) Alexander Wheelock Thayer, in the Boston "Courier."

Quiet Observer. (Pseud.) Erasmus Wilson.

Quinquagesima Sunday. The Sunday before Lent. being the nearest Sunday to the fiftieth day before Easter.

Quintilians. Disciples of Quintilia, held to be a prophetess. These heretical Christians made the Eucharist of

bread and cheese, and allowed women to become priests and bishops.

Qui pense? (Fr.) Who thinks?

Quirinus. In classic myth the deified name by which Romulus, the reputed founder of Rome, was known.

Quis custodiet ipsos custodes? (Lat.) Who shall guard the keepers themselves?

Quis separabit? (Lat.) Who shall separate us?

Qui tam? (Lat.) "Who as well?" —the title given to a certain action at law.

Qui tam. Legal slang for a lawyer, —from the first two words in an action at law on a penal statute.

Qui transtulit sustinet. (Lat.) He who brought us hither, still preserves us.

Qui va là? (Fr.) Who goes there?

Quiver. (Pseud.) Timothy J. Dyson, in the "Union-Argus," Brooklyn, N. Y.

Qui vive? (Fr.) Who goes there? On the alert.

Quixote of the North. Charles XII. of Sweden (fl. 1682–1718), sometimes also called the Madman of the North.

Quoad. (Lat.) As long as; as far as ; as much as.

Quoad civilia. (Lat.) So far as regards civil rights and benefits. A Latin phrase used by a speaker or writer when he wishes to say something concerning some civil interest in a parish which cannot be affirmed of the spiritual or ecclesiastical interests.

Quoad hoc. (Lat.) As far as this.

Quoad omnia. (Lat.) As far as regards all things. A Latin phrase which, when applied to a parish in Scotland, as it often is, denotes that the parish exists in its original integrity, and that its affairs, both civil and ecclesiastical, are administered by its own civil and ecclesiastical authorities.

Quoad sacra. (Lat.) As far as regards sacred things. A Latin phrase which, when applied to a parish in Scotland, denotes that the district which is included within its boundaries has been erected into a parish *only* so far as regards its ecclesiastical interests ; its civil affairs, such as levying and administering poor-rates, continuing to be administered by the civil authorities of the parish or parishes from which it was disjoined.

Quoad ultra. (Lat.) As regards the rest; that is, in *law*, admitting a part and denying the rest.

Quoad valorem. (Lat.) As regards its real value.

Quo animo? (Lat.) With what intention?

Quocunque modo. (Lat.) In whatsoever way.

Quod avertat Deus. (Lat.) Which may God avert.

Quod erat demonstrandum. (Lat.) Which was to be demonstrated.

Quod erat faciendum. (Lat.) Which was to be done.

Quodlibet. (Lat.) A nice point; a subtlety.

Quod vide. (Lat.) Which see.

Quo jure? (Lat.) By what right?

Quondam. (Lat.) Former.

Quorum pars. (Lat.) "Of whom a part." A part of whom, — as of a nation, tribe, or race.

Quos Deus vult perdere prius dementat. (Lat.) Whom God wishes to destroy he first deprives of their reason.

Quot homines, tot sententiæ. (Lat.) As many men, so many opinions.

Quo warranto. (Lat.) By what warrant or authority.

q. v. *Quod vide*, which see; *quantum vis*, as much as you will.

R.

R. Reau; Reaumur (thermometer); take (*recipe*); Queen (*regina*); King (*rex*); river; rood; rod.

R. A. Royal Academy; Royal Academician; Royal Arch; Royal Artillery.

Rabelais of England. Swift, Sterne, and Thomas Amory have all been honored with this title. *See* MODERN RABELAIS.

Rabelais of Geneva. François de Bonnivard (1496–1570), a French historian, and the original of Byron's "Prisoner of Chillon." *See also* MONTAIGNE OF GENEVA.

Rabelais's Poison. Rabelais, being at a great distance from Paris, and without money to pay his hotel bill or his fare, made up three small packets of brick-dust. One he labelled "Poison for the King," another "Poison for Monsieur," and the third "Poison for the Dauphin." The landlord instantly informed against this "poisoner," and the Secretary of State removed him at once to Paris. When, however, the joke was found out, it ended only in a laugh.

Rabido ore. (Lat.) "With rabid mouth." With raving or railing invective.

Racehorse of the Mississippi. A name popularly given to the steamer "Robert E. Lee," noted for its speed.

Rachel. A nickname for a Quakeress. *See* AMINADAB.

Rachel Booth. The stage-name of Mrs. William Powers.

Rachelle Renard. The stage-name of Mrs. George J. Secor.

Racine of Italy. Metastasio (1698–1782).

Racine of Music. Antonio Gaspare Sacchini of Naples (1735–1786).

Radical. An extreme liberal in politics or religion. The term was first applied as a party name in England in 1818 to Henry Hunt, Major Cartwright, and others of the same clique, who wished to introduce radical reform in the representative system.

Radicals. The Southern name for Republicans, sometimes used reproachfully.

Rag and Famish. The Army and Navy Club; so christened by "Punch." The *rag* refers to the flag, and the *famish* to the bad cuisine.

Rag Baby. Paper money. In political cartoons during the Greenback agitation in the United States, the advocates of unlimited paper money were often depicted as nursing a rag doll, in allusion to the fact that the paper on which greenbacks are printed is made almost entirely from linen rags.

Ragged Regiment. The wan figures in Westminster Abbey, in a gallery over Islip's Chapel.

Rag Money. Paper money. *See* RAG BABY.

Ragnarok. In Scandinavian mythology the last day; the day of judgment; the period of the destruction of the universe; "the twilight of the gods;" — when men and gods are to perish in a shower of fire and blood.

Ragout. A highly seasoned dish.

Raid of Ruthven. The name given to the seizure of the person of James VI. of Scotland by William Ruthven, Earl of Gowrie, and several other nobles in 1582. They compelled the king to dismiss his favorites Arran and Lennox.

Railroad = RAILWAY. The "railroad," as Americans uniformly say, instead of "railway," as in England, has brought with it a number of terms peculiar to the New World. The English "station" becomes a "depot;" the "trucks" of the Old World are called "freight-cars," and we have "palace cars," and even "silver palace cars." *See* RAILS, SWITCH, etc.

Railroad City. Indianapolis, Ind. Upward of fifteen railroads centre there.

Railroad, The Underground. *See* UNDERGROUND RAILROAD.

Rails = METALS. The "rails" of American railroads are the "metals" of English lines.

Rail-splitter, The. A popular nickname for Abraham Lincoln, the sixteenth President of the United States (fl. 1809–1865), who in early life supported himself by that homely occupation. *See also* MARTYRED PRESIDENT.

Railway King. George Hudson, of Yorkshire (fl. 1800–1871), was thus named by the Rev. Sydney Smith. His operations were often on a colossal scale, though he died in comparative indigence.

Rainy-day Smith. A nickname bestowed on John Thomas Smith, the English antiquary (fl. 1766–1833).

Raise. "To raise," applied in England only to vegetables and animals, is used in America also in reference to men. Nothing is more common than the question, "Where were you raised?"

Raison d'être. (Fr.) Reason of its being or existence.

Raleigh's Conspiracy. *See* MAIN PLOT.

Ralph Iron. (Pseud.) Olive Schreiner, author of "The Story of an African Farm," published in 1888. She is a native of South Africa.

Ram Feast. May morning is so called at Holne, near Dartmoor, England, because on that day a ram is run down in the "Ploy Field." It is roasted whole with its skin and fur, close by a granite pillar. At mid-day a scramble takes place for a slice, which is supposed to bring luck to those who get it. This is a relic of Baal worship.

Ramie Austin. The stage name of Mrs. Dora Davidson.

Ramon Goneril. Under this pseudonym Louis Jean Emmanuel Gonzales, the French journalist and feuilletonist (1815–1887), contributed to the Paris press. *See also* MELCHIOR GOMEZ and CALIBAN.

Ramsay the Rich. A very old nickname for Ramsay Abbey, which used also to be named the "Crœsus of English Abbeys."

Ranch, Ranchman. The *rancho* was the farm of the Spaniard in Mexico, and the *ranchero* was the farmer himself. In the great West the term "ranch" indicates the home of the stock-raiser.

Rantipole. A nickname conferred on the late Napoleon III. in allusion to the many escapades of his youth.

Raphael of Cats. Godefroi Mind (fl. 1768–1814), a famous Swiss painter, noted for his delineations of cat life.

Raphael of France. Eustache Lesueur (fl. 1617–1655).

Rapids. This word is peculiar to New-World English, and serves to indicate the difference between a rapid descent or a series of descents in a river, and a waterfall or cascade.

Rapparee. An Irish brigand; so called because he was armed with a rapary, or half-pike.

Rara avis. (Lat.) "A rare bird." A prodigy, something very unusual.

Rare Ben. So Shakspeare named Ben Jonson, the early English dramatist.

Rationalist. One who depends wholly on his reason as the supreme authority in matters of religion; a disbeliever in revealed religion.

Raw Lobsters. As "lobster" is a sobriquet for an English soldier whose coatee is red, so at their first establishment about fifty years ago policemen were sarcastically called "raw lobsters," from the blue color of their uniform. The name was first given by the "Weekly Despatch" newspaper, which for years tried in vain to "write down" the new force. A raw lobster is dark blue, and turns red by being boiled.

Ray Samuels. The stage-name of Mrs. Nate Salsbury.

Ray Semon. The stage-name of Mrs. George A. Beane, Jr.

Rb. Rubidium.

R. C. Roman Catholic; a counterpart (*rescriptum*).

R. D. Rural Dean.

R. E. Reformed Episcopal; Royal Engineers.

Reading between the Lines. "The sagacious reader who is capable of reading between these lines what does not stand written, or is only implied." — GOETHE, *Autobiography*.

Readjusters. A political faction in Virginia, prominent from 1882–1885, led by General Mahone, who advocated a compromise with the creditors of the State holding its obligations incurred during the Civil War. The party carried several elections, and finally became merged in the Republican Party during the election of 1884. *See* REPUDIATION.

Ready, The. A slang ellipsis for "ready money."

Ready-money Spencer. The Rev. Elihu Spencer (1721–1784), a famous American Presbyterian clergyman, was so called, "from his facility in extempore address."

Rebecca Riots. Popular disturbances in Wales, 1843 and 1878, growing out of opposition to toll-gates and water-bailiffs.

Rebel Banker. John Morton, one of the earlier financial magnates of New York, was so styled by the British officers during the Revolution, on account of the large sums of money he loaned the Continental Congress.

Rebel Brigadiers. A sobriquet conferred by certain politicians at the North on those Southerners in Congress who had served in the Confederate armies.

Rebel Legislature. An Indiana legislature in 1862–1863 received this nickname because of its supposed sympathy with the Southern secessionists.

Rebellion to Tyrants is Obedience to God. From an inscription on the cannon near which the ashes of President John Bradshaw were lodged, on the top of a high hill near Martha Bay in Jamaica. — STILES. This suppositious epitaph was found among the papers of Mr. Jefferson and in his handwriting. It was supposed to be one of Dr. Franklin's spirit-stirring inspirations.

Rec. Recipe, or Recorder.

Recd. Received.

Réchauffé. (Fr.) "Heated again," as food. Stale; old.

Recitativo. (Ital.) A recitation or musical declamation.

Reckon. The Southern equivalent for the "guess" of New England and the "expect" of the Middle States.

Reconciliation Normande, La. *See* LAMOURETTE'S KISS.

Reconstruction. The measures adopted by the National Government after the close of the Civil War in the United States, looking to the restoration of the autonomy of the States lately in arms against its authority.

Recreative Religionists. The nickname given to an association of gentlemen who sought to diffuse a knowledge of natural religion by the aid of science, formed in London in 1866–1867. Sunday-evening lectures were given by eminent scientists at St. Martin's Hall, and sacred music was performed at stated intervals.

Rec. Sec. Recording Secretary.

Rect. Rector; receipt.

Recte et suaviter. Justly and mildly.

Rectus in curiâ. "Upright in the court." With clean hands.

Red Bandanna. The fact that Allen G. Thurman, the Democratic nominee for the Vice-Presidency in 1888, always used a bandanna handkerchief was made the occasion of the adoption of the Red Bandanna as a political emblem in that campaign.

Red Beard. (Barbarossa.) The surname of Frederick I. of Germany (fl. 1121–1190).

Red Becker. A sobriquet fastened on Herman Heinrich Becker (b. 1829) the German politician, on account of his extreme Radicalism.

Red Church Marriages. A system of "free marriages" established about 1875, by the Rev. E. F. Coke, vicar of the Red Church, Bethnal Green Road, London, to counteract the indifference to marriage rites among the London poor. The days set apart for these ceremonies are the regular Bank Holidays (*q. v.*), and the fees are next to nothing. Over 400 couples have been united annually since the free system was begun.

Red-Coats. A nickname for British soldiery, first conferred by the Americans in the war of Independence. *See* TOMMY ATKINS.

Red Comyn. Sir John Comyn of Badenoch, son of Marjory, sister of King John Baliol, so called from his ruddy complexion and red hair, to distinguish him from his kinsman "Black Comyn," whose complexion was swarthy and hair black. He was stabbed by Sir Robert Bruce in the church of the Minorites at Dumfries, and afterwards despatched by Lindesay and Kirkpatrick.

Red-Dog Money. A term applied, in the State of New York, to certain bank-notes which had on their back a large red stamp. The late General Banking-law of the State of New York, which was applied to all new banks as well as to those the charters of which were renewed, obliged the parties or individuals associated to deposit securities with the comptroller, and receive from him blank notes of various denominations, signed or bearing the certificate of the comptroller or officer authorized by him. These notes bore a *red stamp* on their backs. The free admission under this law of securities of a very questionable character induced many persons, both individually and collectively, to organize banks of issue; and as a natural consequence, a considerable portion of the circulating medium soon consisted of the notes of the free banks, bearing the red stamp. The community generally did not consider these notes as safe as those issued by the old banks, and stigmatized them as "red dogs," and the currency as "red-dog money." — BARTLETT.

Redeemed Captive. The Rev. John Williams (fl. 1644–1729), a New England clergyman who was captured by the French and Indians in 1704 and cleverly escaped in 1706. He published a book narrating his adventures under that title.

Redemptioners. *See* SOUL-DRIVERS.

Redemptionists. A Roman Catholic order, the priests of which devote themselves to the spiritual wants of the German people.

Red Hand, The. In coat armor is generally connected with some traditional tale of blood. " In Aston Church near Birmingham, England, is a coat-armorial of the Holts, the 'bloody hand' of which is thus accounted for: Sir Thomas Holt, some 200 years ago, murdered his cook in a cellar with a spit, and when pardoned for the offence, the king enjoined him, by way of penalty, to wear ever after a 'bloody hand' in his family coat. In the church of Stoke d'Abernon, Surrey, England, there is a red hand upon a monument, the legend of which is, that a gentleman shooting with a friend, was so mortified at meeting with no game, that he swore he would shoot the first live thing he met. A miller was the victim of this rash vow, and the 'bloody hand' was placed in his family coat to keep up a perpetual memorial of the crime."

Red Hand of Ireland. In an ancient expedition to Ireland, it was given out that whoever first touched the shore should possess the territory which he touched. O'Neil, seeing another boat likely to outstrip his own, cut off his left hand, and threw it on the coast.

Red-Headed Rooster of the Rockies. So Senator Belford of Colorado was known when in the United States Senate.

Redivivus. (Lat.) "That lives again." A copy or likeness of any one who lived before.

Red-Lattice Phrases. Ale-house talk. Red lattices or checkers were ordinary ale-house signs.

Red-Letter Day. In olden times, saints' days were regarded as lucky days and were marked on the calendar with red ink. From this sprang the term "red-letter day" to signify any auspicious or special occasion.

Redolet lucerna. (Lat.) "It is redolent of the lamp." It bears traces of laborious finishing.

Red Prince. Prince Frederick Charles of the House of Hohenzollern (fl. 1828–1885). *See* PRINCE ALWAYS IN FRONT.

Red Republicans. Those ultra republicans in France who scrupled not to shed blood in order to further their ends.

Red Rose. In the political nomenclature of England a popular designation of the House of Lancaster. A red rose was its emblem. Similarly the House of York was known as the "White Rose," for a like reason.

Red Shanks. A nickname for a Highlander, derived from a red buskin formerly worn, made of undressed deer hide.

Red Spinner. (Pseud.) William Senior, author of " Travel and Trout in the Antipodes," 1879. A well-known English sporting writer.

Red Tape. A phrase signifying official obstruction, or delay, or formality. From the red tape used in public offices for tying up documents, etc.

Red Terror. *See* REIGN OF TERROR.

Reductio ad absurdum. (Lat.) Reduction to an absurdity.

Red Wing. (Pseud.) Frederic Eugene Pond, in " Turf, Field and Farm."

Reef, City of the. *See* CITY OF THE REEF.

Reekie, Auld. *See* AULD REEKIE.

Ref. Reference ; Reformed ; Reformation.

Ref. Ch. Reformed Church.

Reformed Gambler. Jonathan H. Green (b. 1813), a famous character in the Southwestern States. He led a checkered career, reformed in 1842, and took to preaching and lecturing.

Reformed Minstrel. Robert Sutherland ("Bob Hart"), who in 1883 left the variety stage and became an evangelist. He died in 1888.

Refugitta. (Pseud.) Mrs. Constance Cary Harrison, a well-known contributor to Southern periodicals.

Reg. Register ; Regular.

Regenerator of Cookery. Carême, a celebrated French cook (fl. 1784–1833).

Regicides, The. A collective name for those who in any way took part in the trial and execution of Charles I. In American annals the term is particularly applied to Edward Whalley, William Goffe, and John Dixwell, who took refuge in Massachusetts and Connecticut, in 1661. These three had been condemned to death at the Restoration. John Dixwell changed his name to John Davids, and lived undiscovered in New Haven, where he had a wife and children. Goffe and Whalley were often pursued by crown officers, and at one time lived in a cave in West Rock, New Haven. Goffe died in New Haven, or Hartford, in 1670 ; Whalley died in Hadley, Mass., 1678.

Regina Klein. The stage-name of Baroness Gustav von Heine, of the Vienna Opera House.

Reginald Wolfe. (Pseud.) Thomas Frognall Dibdin, D.D., English bibliographer (1775–1847).

Region of Death. (*Marovsthulli.*) Thurr, near Delhi, fatal from some atmospheric influence, especially about sunset.

Reg. Prof. Regius Professor.

Regr. Registrar.

Regt. Regiment.

Reign of Terror. The name given to that period in the history of France when the revolutionary government, under the guidance of Maximilien Robespierre, supported itself by the pure operation of terror, exterminating with the guillotine all the enemies, or supposed enemies, of the dictatorship. In the year 1793 the Convention vested the government in a " Committee of Public Safety," — a body belonging to the party of the Mountain, of which Robespierre, Couthon, and St. Just became the triumvirate. This Committee, to which every other authority in the country was subjected, deliberated in secret, and the Convention sanctioned all its decrees. Louis XVI. had already been brought to the scaffold ; and on October 16, his queen, Marie Antoinette, after being subjected to every possible indignity, was beheaded ; the Princess Elizabeth sharing the same fate on the 10th of May, 1794. The execution of the Girondists followed, and that of the Duke of Orleans. This period was called the " Red Terror." The guillotine became the only instrument of government ; a look or gesture might excite suspicion, and suspicion was death. The calendar was remodelled, and all religious rites were suppressed. A section of the Mountain party became satiated with blood, and impatient of the control of Robespierre. On July 28, 1794, he was denounced in the Convention for his barbarities, and his death brought to a close this sanguinary era in French history.

Reipublicæ salus suprema lex. (Lat.) The immediate safety of the State is the highest law.

Rel. Religion.

Religio loci. (Lat.) The religion of the place.

Religio temporis. (Lat.) The religion of the time.

Religious City. An ancient name given to Athens by the old writers. It is said that there were thirty thousand temples, statues, and sacred places dedicated to the worship of the heathen gods.

Rem acu tetigisti. (Lat.) "You have touched the thing with the needle." You have touched the point exactly; you have hit the right nail on the head.

Remember the Alamo. *See* AL-AMO MASSACRE.

Remington Yonge. (Pseud.) Robert R. Doherty, an American author and editor.

Remis velisque. (Lat.) "With oars and sails." Putting forth every exertion.

Remus. The twin-brother of Romulus (*q. v.*). He was slain by his brother in a fit of passion, because when Romulus was building the walls of Rome, Remus, to show his contempt for the barriers, leaped over them.

Rena. (Pseud.) Mrs. M. L. R. Crossley, a miscellaneous writer.

Renaissance. A term often ambiguously used, but in general defining one portion of a long, but continuous, movement to preserve and advance European culture. It immediately succeeded the "Dark Ages" and the "Middle Ages." The word means "new birth." "The first of these three periods," says Palgrave, "we may date from the fall of the Western Empire roughly to the year 1100, during which time the barbarians in their youthful vigor first overthrew, and then were penetrated by, the ancient civilization. The second stage runs from that time to about 1350, and this may be called the first or general Renaissance. The Italian Renaissance, the modern movement, is the third."

Renaissant Period. That period in French history which began with the Italian wars in the reign of Charles VIII., and closed with the reign of Henry II.; but as everything was Italianized — the language, dress, architecture, poetry, prose, food, manners, etc., — it was a period of great national deformity.

Rencontre. (Fr.) An encounter.

Rep. Representative; Reporter.

Repeaters, Repeating. Voting "early and often" has been a frequent crime at popular elections in the United States, the perpetrators of this crime being dubbed "repeaters." *See* COLONIZATION.

Réponse sans réplique. (Fr.) An answer not admitting of a reply.

Reptile Bureaucracy. An epithet applied in Germany, in 1871 and subsequently, to certain journalistic writers in the pay of the Government.

Repts. Reports.

Republican Party, The, was organized during the administration of Mr. Pierce, 1853–1857. Its platform rested mainly on the prohibition of slavery in the Territories, declaring that freedom was the public law of the national domain; the prohibition of polygamy, which it classed with slavery as "the twin relic of barbarism;" and the admission of Kansas as a free State. In 1856, the party was in good working order and fairly divided the country with its Democratic competitor. In June of this year its convention met in Philadelphia, and nominated John C. Fremont for President. But the American party drew something from its strength, and though showing a popular vote of 1,341,264, it was defeated, the slave States — with the exception of Maryland, which voted for Mr. Fillmore, — going solidly for Mr. Buchanan, the Democratic candidate, who was elected with the aid of five free States, eleven of the latter voting for General Fremont. In 1860 the Republicans elected Abraham Lincoln, President. The sectional issue was still more strongly marked, and he received the electoral votes of all the free States except those of New Jersey, which were given to Mr. Douglas. On the announcement of his election the Southern States prepared to secede, South Carolina leading, followed by ten others. Mr. Lincoln was inaugurated March 4, 1861, General Scott carefully supervising the ceremony; and his address was conciliatory but firm. He asserted that there was no right to interfere with slavery in the States where it existed, and acknowledged that of the reclamation of fugitive slaves; but he expressed his determination to execute the laws and protect public property. April 12, 1861, South Carolina precipitated the war by firing on Fort Sumter, which was abandoned on the 14th; and on the 15th Mr. Lincoln made his first call for seventy-five thousand men. The cabinet at this time consisted of William H. Seward, John A. Dix (afterward succeeded by Salmon P. Chase), Simon Cameron (succeeded by Edwin M. Stanton), Gideon Welles, Caleb B. Smith, Montgomery Blair, and Edwin Bates. On Sept. 22, 1862, Mr. Lincoln issued his Emancipation Proclamation, which was essentially a war measure. The principles which it involved were confirmed by an amendment to the Constitution, adopted in 1865. In 1864 Mr. Lincoln was unanimously nominated by the Republicans, and was re-elected by an overwhelming majority. The war was brought to a close by the surrender of General Lee, April 9, 1865, and on the 14th Mr. Lincoln was assassinated, and died the next day. Andrew Johnson, the Vice-President, immediately succeeded him, and continued his Cabinet. Mr. Johnson had been a loyal Union man of Tennessee, and was chosen in view of the reconstruction of the South. He soon disagreed with the party, and came into actual conflict with Congress. He was impeached May 23, 1868, but acquitted May 16 and 26, for lack of one vote of two thirds for conviction. Chief-Justice Chase presided at this trial. In 1868, Ulysses S. Grant was elected President. His election was urged on the ground that the Republican party having successfully finished the war, maintained public credit, abolished slavery, and secured liberty, was the proper one to carry on the government. In May, 1872, the Liberal-Republicans met in Cincinnati and nominated Horace Greeley, which action was endorsed by the Democratic convention. The Republicans nominated General Grant, and re-elected him by a larger vote than that of the former term. In 1876 Rutherford B. Hayes, by the decision of the Presidential Electoral Commission (*q. v.*), was declared elected over Samuel J. Tilden, the Democratic candidate. It was during this administration that the resumption of specie payment took place, Jan. 1, 1879, and the reconstruction of the South went forward smoothly. In 1880, James A. Garfield was elected President, and died Sept. 19, 1881, from wounds inflicted July 2, and Chester A. Arthur, the Vice-President, took his place. In 1884, there arose a considerable defection from the party ranks, the seceders calling themselves Independent Republicans, and declining to vote for James G. Blaine, the regular nominee. As a result, Grover Cleveland, the Democratic candidate, was chosen President. In 1889, the party returned to power, having elected Benjamin Harrison in November, 1888, defeating Grover Cleveland.

Republican Queen. Sophie-Charlotte, wife of Frederick I. of Prussia.

Repudiation. Several of the Southern States of the American Union incurred enormous debts before and during the Civil War which they were totally unable to pay after its close. Some of them repudiated these debts entirely; others, as in Virginia (*see* READJUSTERS), sought to compound with their creditors.

Requiescat. (Lat.) May he (or she) rest.

Requiescat in pace. (Lat.) May he (or she) rest in peace; contracted into R. I. P.

Rerum primordia. (Lat.) The first elements of things.

Res adversæ. (Lat.) Adversity.

Res angustæ domi. (Lat.) Narrow circumstances at home; poverty.

Reserve, The Western. *See* WESTERN RESERVE.

Res est sacra miser. (Lat.) A suffering person is a sacred object.

Res gestæ. (Lat.) Deeds; exploits.

Residuary Legatee. (Pseud.) Henry Jackson Sargent, American poet (b. 1809).

Res incognitæ. (Lat.) "Things unknown." Matters of which we can have no knowledge.

Res judicata. (Lat.) A case that has been decided.

Res magna. (Lat.) A great or ample fortune.

Res, non verba. (Lat.) Deeds, not words.

Resolute, The. John Florio, the philologist (fl. 1545–1625), who was tutor to Prince Henry. According to Brewer, he was the "Holofernes" of Shakspeare.

Resolute Doctor. John Baconthorp, the English Schoolman (d. 1346).

Respice, aspice, prospice. (Lat.) "Look back, look at, look forward."

Look into the past, look at the present, look into the future.

Respice finem. (Lat.) "Look to the end." Consider well the consequences.

Resplendent, The. A name given to Ceylon by Hindu poets.

Respublica. (Lat.) The commonwealth.

Res secundæ. (Lat.) "Prosperous things." Prosperity.

Res severæ. (Lat.) Severe pursuits; business.

Restaurateur. (Fr.) A tavern-keeper who provides dinners, etc.

Restorationists. The followers of Origen's opinion that all persons, after a purgation proportioned to their demerits, will be restored to Divine favor and taken to Paradise.

Restorer of Parnassus. The Spaniards thus name their poet, Juan Melendez Valdez (fl. 1754–1817), who wrought great influence on his country's literature.

Résumé. (Fr.) An abstract or summary.

Resurgam. (Lat.) I shall rise again.

Resurrectionists. A by-name conferred on the Third Regiment of Foot in the English army, because some of its men were once detected in selling the bodies of the dead for medical dissection. *See also* OLD BUFFS.

Resurrection Pie is pie made of broken cooked meat.

Retardando. (Ital.) A retarding of the movement. (Mus.)

Retd. Returned.

Rett Winwood. (Pseud.) Frank Corey, in the New York "Weekly."

Returning Board. An institution peculiar to many of the Southern and Southwestern States, and having power to receive, canvass, and revise election returns. In Louisiana, in 1876, the State returning board gained a national notoriety from the manner in which it "counted out" Tilden and Hendricks. *See* ELECTORAL COMMISSION.

Rev. Reverend; Revelation (Book of); review; revenue; revise.

Revenons à nos moutons. (Fr.) Let us return to the matter in hand. The phrase comes from an old French comedy of the fifteenth century, entitled "L'Avocat Patelin," by Blanchet. A clothier, giving evidence against a shepherd who had stolen some sheep, is forever running from the subject to talk about some cloth of which Patelin, his lawyer, had defrauded him. The judge from time to time pulls him up by saying, "Well, well! and about the sheep? What about the sheep?"

Re vera. (Lat.) In the true matter; in truth.

Revocare gradum. (Lat.) To retrace one's steps.

Revocation of the Edict of Nantes. *See* EDICT OF NANTES.

Rex convivii. (Lat.) "The king of the banquet." The chairman at a feast.

Rex regum. (Lat.) King of kings.

Rex vini. (Lat.) "The king of wine." Master of the revels.

R. G. G. Royal Grenadier Guards.

R. H. A. Royal Horse Artillery; Royal Hibernian Academy.

Rhadamanthus. In classic myth son of Zeus and Europa and brother of Minos. He settled in Bœotia, and married Alcmene. He acquired so great a reputation for the exercise of justice, that after death he was appointed a judge in the under-world. "Rhadamanthus" is often used as a sobriquet for a judge.

Rhea. The same as Cybele (*q. v.*).

Rhesus. In classic myth a king of Thrace who marched to the assistance of the Trojans. He was killed by the Greeks on the instant of his arrival, because they sought to avert the fulfilment of a prophecy which stated that Troy should never be taken if the horses of Rhesus drank the waters of Xanthus or cropped grass on the Trojan plains.

Rhet. Rhetoric.

Rheta Mann. The stage-name of Mrs. Zell.

R. H. G. Royal Horse-Guards.

Rhineland. The dominions of Gunther, king of Burgundy.

Not a lord of Rhineland could follow where he flew.
Nibelungen Lied.

Rhode Island. This State was named from a fancied resemblance in contour to the Island of Rhodes, in the Mediterranean.

Rhody. General Burnside, when he rose to the command of a brigade, was thus nicknamed by his men in allusion to his native State.

Rhone of Christian Eloquence. Saint Hilary (300–367).

Rhone of Latin Eloquence. Saint Hilary is so called by Saint Jerome (300–367).

R. H. S. Royal Humane Society; Royal Historical Society.

Rhyming Chroniclers. Those writers in the thirteenth and fourteenth centuries who related the mythical and authentic history of England in verse. Layamon, Robert of Gloucester, and Robert of Brunne were the chief.

Rhyming to Death. In " I Henry VI." act i. sc. I, Thomas Beaufort, duke of Exeter, speaking about the death of Henry V., says : " Must we think that the subtle-witted French conjurors and sorcerers, out of fear of him, ' by magic verses have contrived his end '? " The notion of killing by incantation was at one time very common.

Irishmen . . . will not stick to affirme that they can rime either man or beast to death. — REG. SCOTT, *Discoverie of Witchcraft.*

R. I. Rhode Island.

Richard Brightwell. (Pseud.) John Frith, English reformer (d. 1553).

Richard D'Orsay Ogden. The stage-name of Richard Maxwell.

Richard Everett. (Pseud.) Col. Edward Ephram Cross, an American soldier (1832–1863), author of numerous poems and sketches.

Richard Haywarde. (Pseud.) Frederick Swartwout Cozzens, an accomplished American *littérateur.*

Richard Mansfield. The stage-name of Richard Rudersdorff, son of Madame Rudersdorff the singer.

Richard Roe. *See* JOHN DOE.

Richard Saunders. (Pseud.) Benjamin Franklin, American philosopher and statesman (1706–1790).

Richd. Richard.

Riddle of the Sphinx. A famous enigma of antiquity. The story runs that Juno sent a monster named the Sphinx to ravage the territory of Thebes. This monster had been taught riddles by the Muses, and she propounded one to the Thebans : " What is that which has one voice, is four-footed, two-footed, and at last three-footed ; " or, as some have it, " What animal is that which goes on four feet in the morning, on two at noon, and on three at evening ? " An oracle told the Thebans that they would not be delivered from her until they had

solved her riddle. They often assembled to try their skill, but as often failed, when the Sphinx always carried off and devoured one of their number. At length Œdipus (*q. v.*) came forward and gave the correct answer, " Man," who when an infant creeps on all fours, at manhood stands erect on two legs, and in old age hobbles about with the aid of a crutch.

Rien ne pèse tant qu'un secret. (Fr.) " Nothing weighs so much as a secret." There is nothing so troublesome to the mind as the possession of a secret.

Rigby, in Disraeli's " Coningsby," was a skit on John Wilson Croker.

Rigdum Funnidos. A sobriquet bestowed by Sir Walter Scott on his friend and partner, John Ballantyne (fl. 1776–1821), on account of his jovial, fun-loving disposition.

Right Arm of the Commonwealth. A descriptive term bestowed on the peninsula of Cape Cod; Mass., because of its peculiar shape.

Right away, Right off. In America these expressions mean " directly," *e. g.*, " I said I had never heard it, so she began right off and told me the whole thing." — *Story of the Sleigh Ride.* " Uncle John," said Nina, " I want you to get the carriage out for me right away." — MRS. STOWE, *Dred.* " I feel wonderfully consarned about that pain in your chest," said the widow to Mr. Crane. " It ought to be attended to right off, Mr. Crane, right off." — *Widow Bedott Papers.*

Right, Captain. *See* CAPTAIN RIGHT.

Right Here. If we happen to hear anybody say " rye cheer " we may know it is intended to mean " right here." For instance, a South Carolinian will say, " Where was he at last night ? " and his fellow-citizen will say, " He stayed rye cheer with me."

Right Smart. American for a good many, large, plenty, etc., *e. g.* " a right smart chunk of bacon." — OLMSTED'S *Texas,* p. 301. " I sold right smart of eggs this summer." — MRS. STOWE, *Dred,* vol. ii. p. 157. " She had right smart of life in her." — *Dred,* vol. i. p. 209. It is a pet Southern phrase, where one often hears of " a right smart lawyer," or " a right smart preacher."

Rigolo. (Pseud.) Napoleon L. Thieblin, journalist, war correspondent, and author of " Spain and the Spaniards " (d. 1888). *See* AZAMAT BATUK.

R. I. H. S. Rhode Island Historical Society.

Rimmon. A Syrian deity, thought to be the same as Baal.

Ring. Any clique or coterie of politicians or office-holders who hang together for the purpose of achieving their own selfish ends. The political annals of the United States have been prolific of such, notably the "Shepherd Ring" in Washington and the "Tweed Ring" in New York.

Ring Dropping. *See* GUINEA DROPPER.

Ringing. *See* BLAZE.

Ringing Island. (1) A poetical epithet applied to England in allusion to the sound of its numerous bells. The name can be traced back to Saxon times. (2) The Church of Rome. It is an island because it is cut off from the world; it is a ringing island because bells are incessantly ringing for religious services; it is entered only after four days' fasting, without which none in the Roman Church enter holy orders. — BREWER.

Ringlets. A nickname conferred on General Custer on account of his flowing curls.

Ring the Bells Backwards. To ring a muffled peal, to lament. Thus, John Cleveland, wishing to show his abhorrence of the Scotch, says : —

How! Providence! and yet a Scottish crew! . . .
Ring the bells backwards. I am all on fire;
Not all the buckets in a country quire
Shall quench my rage.
                    The Rebel Scot.

Risoluto, Risolumente. (Ital.) With boldness and resolution. (Mus.)

Ristori, Madame. The stage-name of Marchioness Capranica del Grillo.

Rita. (Pseud.) Mrs. Otto Booth-Daphne.

Ritenente, Ritenuto. (Ital.) A keeping back, a decrease in the speed of the movement. (Mus.)

Rivella. (Pseud.) Mrs. N. de la Riviere Manly.

River-bottoms. *See* BOTTOMS.

River of Paradise. Saint Bernard, Abbot of Clairvaux (1091–1153).

River of Swans. The Potomac, United States, America.

Riverside Visitor. (Pseud.) Thomas Wright, in "Good Words," "Sunday Magazine," etc.

Rixatur de lana caprina. (Lat.) He wrangles about goats' wool; goats have no wool — hence he disputes about trifles.

R. M. Royal Marines ; Royal Mail.

R. M. S. Royal Mail Steamer.

R. N. Royal Navy.

R. N. O. *Riddare af Nordstjerne.* Knight of the Order of the Polar Star.

R. N. R. Royal Naval Reserve.

Ro. Right-hand page (*recto*) ; Rhodium.

Road-Agent. A euphonious Americanism for a highwayman.

Roads, Queen of. *See* QUEEN OF ROADS.

Roaring-Boys. The riotous blades of Ben Jonson's time, whose delight it was to annoy the quiet folk of London.

Roaring Forties. A name given by sailor-men to the stormy belt of the North Atlantic lying between the fortieth and fiftieth parallels of north latitude.

Robber Synod. The Greeks so named a council convoked at Ephesus by Theodosius in 449, because of the intriguing and double-dealing which characterized its deliberations.

Robbing Peter to pay Paul. On or about Dec. 17, 1540, the Abbey Church of St. Peter, Westminster, London, was by royal patent advanced to the dignity of a cathedral ; ten years later, however, it was joined to the Diocese of London, and much of its property appropriated to the repairs of St. Paul's Cathedral. Hence it was said by a contemporaneous writer that "it was not meet to rob St. Peter's altar in order to build one to St. Paul."

Robe de chambre. (Fr.) A dressing or morning gown.

Robert B. Mantell. The stage-name of Robert Hudson.

Robert Burton. (Pseud.) Nathaniel Crouch, English historical writer (1681–1736).

Robert Doleman. (Pseud.) Robert Parsons, English Jesuit (1546–1610).

Robert G. Burton. The stage-name of Robert G. Hall.

Robert Heron. (Pseud.) John Pinkerton, Scottish poet, historian, and statesman (1758–1826).

Robert Macaire. A nickname for a Frenchman, derived from the fact that the name often appears as that of the hero in French plays.

Robert Merry. (Pseud.) J. N. Stearns, American writer.

Robertsons. James Robertson (1710–1788) was for many years barrack-master at New York, in which post he acquired a fortune by various methods of peculation and extortion. He paid for government supplies in clipped coins, which came to be known as "Robertsons," until the Chamber of Commerce resolved that such should be received only at their intrinsic value.

Robert the Devil. (1) Robert, First Duke of Normandy, so named on account of his ferocious cruelty and rapacity. (2) Robert Francis Damiens (fl. 1714-1757), who attempted to assassinate Louis XV.

Robert the Red (" Rob Roy "). A nickname given to Robert MacGregor, who assumed the name of Campbell when the clan MacGregor was outlawed in 1662. He is also named the Robin Hood of Scotland.

Robespierre's Weavers. "The fishwomen and female rowdies who joined the Parisian Guard, helped to line the avenues to the National Assembly in 1793, and screamed 'Down with the Girondists!'"

Robin Bluestring. Sir Robert Walpole was given this nickname, in the political squibs of his time, in allusion to the Blue Ribbon of the Garter which he wore.

Robin Hood of Scotland. *See* ROBERT THE RED.

Robt. Robert.

Robur et corporis et animi. (Lat.) Strength both of body and mind.

Rock. In most parts of America a stone, however small, is called a "rock." The following are singular instances of its use: — "Mr. M. had to carry rocks in his pocket to prevent the wind from blowin' him away." — *Major Jones's Travels.* "I see Arch Cooney walk down to the creek bottom, and then he began pickin' up rocks and slingin' 'em at the dogs." — *Mike Hooter, by a Missourian.* "On one occasion they threw a rock in at the window, hitting Mrs. Clem on the shoulder." — *Jonesborough (Tennessee) Whig.*

Rock, Captain. *See* CAPTAIN RIGHT, CAPTAIN ROCK.

Rock, Dome of the. *See* DOME OF THE ROCK.

Rock of Chickamauga. Gen. George H. Thomas, the famous Union general, was so named, because he prevented the utter rout of the Union army at the battle of Chickamauga, Sept. 19–20, 1863.

Rocks, City of. *See* CITY OF ROCKS.

Rock Scorpions. The colloquial and local name given to English children born on the rock or fortress of Gibraltar.

Rogation-Days. The Sunday, Monday, Tuesday, and Wednesday before Ascension-day, so called because on these days the Litanies are appointed to be sung or recited by the clergy and people in public procession.

Roger Bontemps. The personation of contentment with his station in life, and of the buoyancy of good hope.

Roger of Bruges. Roger van der Weyde, the famous painter (fl. 1455–1529).

Rogers' Slide. A steep declivity on Lake George, N. Y., famous in American annals as the scene of the escape of Robert Rogers, in 1757, who eluded his Indian captors by throwing his baggage down the icy side of the mountain and then walking away. The Indians believed that he had been killed, and so made no search.

Rogue's Island. A nickname applied to Rhode Island when that State refused to ratify the Constitution.

Roi Panade. *See* KING OF SLOPS.

Roland for an Oliver, A. To give "a Roland for an Oliver" is an old proverbial synonym for the matching of one bragging lie against another. Roland and Oliver were two of Charlemagne's most famous paladins, and some of the exploits of these worthies, as related by the old romancers, are as ridiculous as they are extravagant. Roland (*see* HORN OF FONTARABIA) received his death-wound at the hands of Oliver at the battle of Roncesvalles (778 A. D.).

Roland of the Army. A sobriquet of the Comte de Saint Hilaire (fl. 1760–1809), a French commander famed for his gallantry and heroism.

Rolla, Mlle. The stage-name of Mrs. Kate Rammelsberg, *née* Wheat.

Rollickers. A nickname for the Eighty-ninth English regiment. They are also dubbed Blaney's Bloodhounds or Blackguards.

Rom. Romans (Book of).

Roman, The. (1) Jean Dumont, the French painter (fl. 1700–1781). (2) Stephen Picard, the French engraver (fl. 1631–1721). (3) Giulio Pippi (fl. 1492–

1546). (4) Adrian van Roomen, the mathematician (fl. 1561–1615).

Roman Achilles. A surname of Sicinius Dentatus (fl. 405 B. C.), given to him by the populace on account of his prowess in battle.

Rom. Cath. Roman Catholic.

Romeo. (Pseud.) G. W. Fellowes.

Rome of Buddhism. The city of Lhasa, in Thibet. It is the "holy city" of the Buddhists in Asia.

Rome of Hindustan. The city of Agra, on the River Jumna. It was the seat of the Mohammedan Empire in India, and its ancient structures are on a scale of great magnificence.

Rome of Protestantism. The city of Geneva in Switzerland. Under the guidance of Calvin and his associates it became a stronghold of the Reformation.

Rome of the North. Cologne was so called (says Hope) in the Middle Ages, from its wealth, power, and ecclesiastical foundations.

Romulus. The legendary founder of the city of Rome. He was represented as the son of Mars and of a vestal named Silvia. Together with his twin brother, Remus, he was thrown into the Tiber by his uncle, but was washed ashore, nursed by a she-wolf, adopted by a shepherd, and finally became the founder and the first king of Rome. At death he was translated to the heavens by his father, Mars, where he was worshipped under the name of Quirinus. *See* REMUS.

Rondeau. (Fr.) **Rondo.** (Ital.) A musical composition of several strains or numbers, at the end of each of which the first part is repeated.

Rondino, Rondiletta, Rondinetto, or **Rondoletto.** (Ital.) A short rondo. (Mus.)

Roof of the World. Pameer, an extensive table-land of Central Asia, is so named by its natives. A part of the plateau is said to be 16,000 feet above the sea.

Roorback. In American political parlance a "roorback" is a story concocted and disseminated to damage the opposite side but which recoils upon its circulators.

In September, 1844, a Whig newspaper, "The Ithaca (N. Y.) Chronicle," received and printed what purported to be an "extract from Roorback's 'Tour through the Western and Southern States, in 1836;'" containing a description of a camp of slave-drivers on Duck River, and a statement that forty-three of the unfortunate slaves "had been purchased of the Honorable J. K. Polk, the present Speaker of the House of Representatives [and in 1844 a candidate for the Presidency], the mark of the branding iron, with the initials of his name, on their shoulders, distinguishing them from the rest." The pretended "extract" was copied into the "Albany Evening Journal," and by the Whig press throughout the country. A few days after its first appearance, the Democrats discovered that it was, in part, taken from G. W. Featherstonhaugh's "Tour," published in 1834, but that the name of "Duck River," and the quoted statement respecting Mr. Polk, had been interpolated by the correspondent of the "Chronicle." Thereafter, it was easy to reply to every charge preferred against the Democratic candidate, by pronouncing it "another roorback." The "Morey Letter," in the Garfield campaign, was another example of the "roorback."

Rooster. The campaign rooster of politics which ornaments the columns of partisan journals the day after a successful election has a strange origin as a party emblem. There was a Democratic editor in one of the towns of Indiana named Chapman. One of the Democratic managers of that date thought things were not going as prosperously for the party as they should go. He wrote to stir the politicians up, and among other things he said: "Tell Chapman to crow" and claim victory. This letter, by accident, fell into the hands of the Whigs. They printed it, and in the whole campaign, from one end of the country to the other, the words "Tell Chapman to crow" were ringing in derision. The "Boston Herald," which is pretty good authority, adds that the year following this episode the late Col. Charles G. Greene of the "Boston Post," when the Democrats began to win victories, turned the laugh upon the opponents of Democracy by getting out a cut of a rooster in earnest. That was the origin of the crowing fowl in American politics.

Rope of Ocnus. Profitless labor. Ocnus was always twisting a rope with unwearied diligence, but an ass ate it as fast as it was twisted.

Rosa. (Pseud.) Mrs. Rosa Vertner Jeffrey, English novelist.

Rosa Abbott. (Pseud.) Rosa Abbott Parker, author of the "Rosa Abbott Stories."

Rosa Graham. (Pseud.) Sarah L. Post, in the New York "Independent."

Rosa Hill. The stage-name of Mme. Réné Renaud.

Rosa Matilda. (Pseud.) Mrs. Charlotte Dacre Byrne.

Roscius of England. (1) Thomas Betterton. (2) David Garrick.

Roscius of France. Michael Boyron, or Boron (fl. 1653–1729).

Rose Coghlan. The stage-name of Mrs. Clinton Edgerly.

Rose Courtney Barnes. The stage-name of Mrs. John T. Raymond (*q. v.*), *née* Eytinge.

Rose Eytinge. The stage-name of Mrs. Cyril Searle.

Rose of England. The rose has figured prominently in the history of England, though it cannot be said to be the emblem of that country in the sense that the lily is of France. The famous " Wars of the Roses " — the struggle for supremacy between the rival houses of Lancaster and York — obtained the name from the fact that the former chose the red rose as its symbol, while the Yorkist party chose the white rose. It is said that this flower, being the symbol of silence, used to be placed over the confessionals in Rome to denote the secrecy that was therein supposed to prevail.

Rose Roberts. The stage-name of Mrs. Louis Calvert.

Rose Skerrett. The stage-name of Mrs. L. R. Shewell.

Rose Sydell. The stage-name of Mrs. Charles Emmett.

Rose Terry. (Pseud.) Rose Terry Cooke, an American poet and novelist.

Rose Vernon. The stage-name of Mrs. Luke Brant.

Rose-water Revolution. (Fr., *Révolution à l'eau des roses*), a name given to the bloodless upheaval whereby Tuscany, on April 27, 1859, deposed the Grand Duke Leopold, and proclaimed the annexation of the Duchy to Piedmont.

Rose Wood. The stage-name of Mrs. Lewis Morrison.

Rosicrucian. (Pseud.) W. Frothingham, American author.

Rosina Vokes. The stage-name of Mrs. Cecil Clay.

Rosin Bible. From an error in the same text (Jer. viii. 22), which gave its name to the Treacle Bible (*q. v.*): " Is there no rosin in Gilead? " This is the edition also known as the Douay Bible (*q. v.*).

Ross Neil. The pen-name of Miss Harwood, an American author (d. 1888). She wrote a play called " Loyal Love,"

which was performed with some success in New York.

Rosy. General Rosecrans was thus familiarly known to his soldiery.

Rota Club. The name given to a coterie which met at Miles's Coffee House, London (New Palace Yard), during the sway of Oliver Cromwell. Their scheme was that all the great State officials should be chosen by ballot, and that a certain proportion of the members of Parliament should be changed annually by rotation, whence was derived their nickname.

Rotten Cabbage Rebellion. An insurrection of the class of 1808 against the Faculty of Harvard College in 1807. The memory of this occurrence is still commemorated in the name of the " Rebellion tree " standing on the college grounds.

Rotten Row. The popular name corrupted from *Route en -Roi*, " the way of the king," for a famous driveway and promenade in Hyde Park, London, much frequented by fashionables during the season.

Roture. (Fr.) The commonalty.

Roturier. (Fr.) A commoner.

Roué. A profligate libertine. The name was first given to the notorious Duke of Orleans, Regent of France, and to his gay companions, with reference to whom he boasted that there was not one who did not deserve to be broken on the wheel; hence arose the nickname throughout France, Orleans *roués*, or wheels.

Rouge et noir. (Fr.) Red and black (the name of a game).

Rough and Ready. At the battle of Waterloo, Colonel Rough was selected by the Duke of Wellington to perform some service requiring energy and promptitude. " Rough and Ready," said the Duke when the Colonel cheerfully undertook the duty; and the Colonel thenceforth adopted the words as a motto, which is still borne by his family.

Rough Hewer. (Pseud.) Robert Yates, American author.

Rough Terror. The name given in 1874 in England to numberless assaults on women, children, and feeble persons, by "roughs" of the lower classes, and for "the repression of which the law seemed to be wholly inadequate."

Roundhead. This was a term of contempt applied to the Puritans in the time of Charles I., from their custom of cutting their hair close to the head; the Royalist party wearing theirs in ringlets.

Round Peg in a Square Hole. This witty saying in reference to misplaced talent is certainly earlier than the time of Sydney Smith, who is generally considered its author from his having used it in his "Lectures Delivered at the Royal Institution" (1824-1826). His words are: "If you choose to represent the various parts of life by holes upon a table of different shapes, some circular, some triangular, some square, some oblong, and the persons acting these parts by bits of wood of similar shapes, we shall generally find that the triangular person has got into the square hole, the oblong into the triangular, and a square person has squeezed himself into a round hole."

Roxbury Farmer. (Pseud.) John Lowell, LL.D., American lawyer and political writer (1769-1840).

Roy. (Pseud.) Nathaniel P. Willis's first literary efforts were published under this name in his father's paper.

Royal Irish. *See* PADDIES ROYAL.

Royalist Butcher. Blaise de Montluc (fl. 1502-1572), notorious for his cruel conduct toward the French Protestants during the reign of Charles IX.

Royal Keen. (Pseud.) F. F. Schrader, in the Western press.

Royal Martyr. Charles I. of England, beheaded Jan. 30, 1649.

Royal 'Prentice in the Art of Poesy. A self-assumed title of James I. of England, who composed a quantity of wretched and mediocre ballads, sonnets, etc.

Royal Psalmist. King David. He also is named "The Sweet Singer of Israel."

Royal Tigers. A nickname earned by the Sixty-fifth Regiment during its service in India.

R. P. Reformed Presbyterian; The King's Professor (*Regius Professor*).

R. R. Railroad.

R. R. Junc. Railroad Junction.

R. R. Sta. Railroad Station.

R. S. Recording Secretary.

Rs. To answer (*responsus*); Rupees.

R. S. A. Royal Society of Antiquaries; Royal Scottish Academy.

R. S. D. Royal Society of Dublin.

R. S. E. Royal Society of Edinburgh.

R. S. L. Royal Society of London.

R. S. S. *Regiæ Societatis Socius.* Fellow of the Royal Society.

R. S. V. P. *Répondez, s'il vous plaît.* Answer, if you please.

Rt. Hon. Right Honorable.

Rt. Rev. Right Reverend.

R. T. S. Religious Tract Society.

Rt. Wpful. Right Worshipful.

Ru. Ruthenium.

Ruat cœlum. (Lat.) Let heaven fall.

Rubbed Out. A Western euphuism for death.

Rubor efflorescens. (Lat.) The efflorescent or crimson blush.

Rudis indigestaque moles. (Lat.) A raw and confused mass.

Rufus (The Red.) (1) William II. of England. (2) Otho II. of Germany. (3) Gilbert Clare, Earl of Gloucester.

Ruhamah. (Pseud.) (1) Harriet M. Skidmore, in St. Louis "Globe Democrat." (2) Miss Lily Scudamore, in Washington "Republic."

Rump and Dozen. This was a favorite form of wager with our forefathers. A legal definition of its meaning was given in the King's Bench, *tempo* Lord Mansfield. An action, "Hussey *v.* Cricket" (Campbell's "Nisi Prius Cases," iii. 168), was brought upon a wager of a "rump and dozen," made upon the question as to which — plaintiff or defendant — was the older. The question as to whether the action was maintainable was argued before the full court, Mansfield, C. J., presiding. In giving judgment Mr. Justice Heath said: — "I am sorry this action has been brought, but I do not doubt that it is maintainable. Wagers are generally legal, and there is nothing to take this wager out of the common rule. We know very well privately that a 'rump and dozen' is what the witnesses stated, *viz.*, a good dinner and wine, in which I can discover no illegality."

Rump of a Rump. Another and a later name for the Rump Parliament of England (*q. v.*).

Rump Parliament. The "rump" or fag end of the Long Parliament (*q. v.*) during the Protectorate. It voted the arraignment of Charles I.

Rum, Romanism, and Rebellion. A historic phrase coined during the Presidential campaign of 1884. The Rev. Dr. Samuel Dickinson Burchard was considered to be peculiarly happy in making addresses on occasions when it was desired to entertain a miscellaneous audience. A few days before the election, the Republican managers called a "minister's meeting" in New York. About six hundred clergymen responded, and Dr. Burchard addressed them. In concluding he stigmatized the Democracy as the party of "Rum, Romanism, and Rebellion." The Republicans had made strenuous efforts to secure the Catholic vote, but these three alliterative words undid the work of months. The Democratic chieftains were quick to see their importance, and soon the whole country was placarded with posters headed "R. R. R.," with various fertile additions and variations, and ascribing to the Republican party and the party's candidate, J. G. Blaine, personal sentiments akin to those embodied in Dr. Burchard's phrase. The election hinged on New York State; the official count gave the State to the Democrats by only 1047 votes; the number of votes changed by Dr. Burchard's remark having been estimated at several thousand, it is easy to calculate the havoc wrought by an apparently innocuous sentence.

Run. Very expressive of American haste and hurry is the comparatively modern use of *to run,* in the sense of "to manage" or "to keep," when applied to any kind of business, from a gigantic hotel to a petty grocery. "Who runs this business now?" means, "Who is the manager?" The phrase "run on a bank" is not a pure Americanism, being often heard in England.

Run-about Raid. Murray's insurrection against Lord Darnley, so called from the hasty and incessant manner in which the conspirators posted from one part of the kingdom to another.

Running Parliament. A nickname for a Scottish Parliament, because it was continually shifted from place to place.

Running the Gauntlet. *See* GAUNTLET.

Running Thursday. December 13, 1688, in the early days of the reign of William III., when a rumor ran through the English coast-towns that the French and Irish had landed in force, and the people betook themselves to the country, running as for their lives.

Runnymede. (Pseud.) Benjamin Disraeli, Lord Beaconsfield (1805–1881).

Rupert of Debate. Lord Derby was thus nicknamed by Bulwer Lytton. *See also* HOTSPUR OF DEBATE.

Ruse contre ruse. (Fr.) A stratagem against a stratagem.

Ruse de guerre. (Fr.) A stratagem of war.

Rush Ellis. (Pseud.) Mrs. Alma Calder Johnson.

Rus in urbe. (Lat.) The country in the town.

Russ. Russia; Russian.

Russia, Key of. *See* KEY OF RUSSIA.

Russian Byron. A name bestowed by his compatriots on Alexander Sergeivitch Pushkin (fl. 1759–1837), the most distinguished poet Russia has produced during the present century.

Russian Ireland. The Baltic provinces of Russia, so named because they were for many years the scene of agrarian agitation and disaffection.

Russian Murat. The French so named Michael Miloradowitch (fl. 1770–1820), who gained immortal renown in the Napoleonic wars.

Rusticus abnormis sapiens. (Lat.) A rustic wise without rule; a peasant who is a philosopher without the principle derived from study.

Ruth Buck. (Pseud.) Mrs. Joseph Lamb, an American writer.

Rutherglen. The pen-name of Robert Macfarlane (d. 1883), a well-known journalist and author. He was born in Scotland, and from 1848–1865 was editor of the "Scientific American." He published a work of travel, "Rambles in Scotland," and was a frequent contributor to the "Scottish American."

Ruth Fairfax. (Pseud.) Mrs. Agnes Jean Stibbes, a well-known contributor to the "Banner of the South."

Ruthven, Raid of. *See* RAID OF RUTHVEN.

R. V. Revised Version.

R. W. Right Worthy.

R. W. D. G. M. Right Worshipful Deputy Grand Master.

R. W. G. R. Right Worthy Grand Representative.

R. W. G. S. Right Worthy Grand Secretary.

R. W. G. T. Right Worthy Grand Treasurer; Right Worshipful Grand Templar.

R. W. G. W. Right Worthy Grand Warden.

R. W. J. G. W. Right Worshipful Junior Grand Warden.

R. W. O. *Riddare af Wasare Ordare*, Knight of the Order of Wasa; *Riddare af Wasa Orden*, Knight of the Order of Wasa.

R. W. S. G. W. Right Worshipful Senior Grand Warden.

Ry. Railway.

Ryder, Prof. G. W. The professional name of Richard Grimm.

Ryehouse Plot. In 1683, at the same time that a scheme was formed in England among the leading Whigs to raise the nation in arms against Charles II., a subordinate scheme was planned by a few fiercer spirits of the party, including Colonel Rumsey, and Lieutenant-Colonel Walcot, two military adventurers, Goodenough, Under-Sheriff of London, Ferguson, an Independent minister, and several attorneys, merchants, and tradesmen of London — the object of which was to waylay and assassinate the king on his return from Newmarket. The deed was to be perpetrated at a farm belonging to Rumboldt, one of the conspirators, called the Ryehouse Farm, whence the plot got its name. It was defeated.

Ryswick, Peace of. A treaty concluded in 1697, at Ryswick, a Dutch village, between Delft and the Hague, which was signed by France, England, and Spain, on September 20, and by Germany, on October 30. It put an end to the sanguinary contest in which France and England had been engaged.

S.

S. South; saint; scribe; sulphur; Sunday; sun; series; a shilling (*solidus*).

S. A. South America; South Australia.

S. a. *Secundum artem.* According to art.

Sabbath Day's Journey. "A Sabbath day's journey, according to Dr. Adam Clarke, was 7½ furlongs, or about 1,650 yards. The Rabbins fix it at 2,000 cubits, which is about 1,350 yards. Josephus says that the Mount of Olives was five stadia, or 625 paces, from Jerusalem, which would make the allowable Sabbath day's journey about 1,050 yards." — CALMET.

Sabbathians. The disciples of Sabbathais Zwi (1641-1677), the most remarkable "Messiah" of modern times. At the age of fifteen he had mastered the Talmud, and at eighteen the Cabbala.

Sabbatical Year. One year in seven, when all land with the ancient Jews was to lie fallow for twelve months. This law was founded on Exodus xxiii. 10, etc.; Leviticus xxv. 2-7; Deuteronomy xv. 1-11.

Sabeans. An ancient religious sect; so called from Sabi, son of Seth. The Sabeans worshipped one God, but approached him indirectly through some created representative, such as the sun, moon, or stars.

Sabellians. A religious sect; so called from Sabellius, a Libyan priest of the third century. They believed in the unity of God, and said that the Trinity merely expressed three relations or states of one and the same God.

Sabine Berry. Juvenal thus alludes to the olive.

Sacer vates. (Lat.) The sacred prophet or bard.

Sacra indignatio. (Lat.) "Sacred indignation." Excessive indignation.

Sacred Band. A legion formed by Epaminondas (377 B. C.) for the defence of Thebes. It was revived in 1877.

Sacred City. The same as Holy City.

Sacred Fish. Greek, ἰχθύς ("a fish"), is compounded of the initial Greek letters: I[esous], CH[ristos], TH[eou], U[ios], S[oter] ("Jesus Christ, God's Son, Saviour "). Tennyson, describing the "Lady of the Lake," says :

> And o'er her breast floated the sacred fish.
> *Gareth and Lynette.*

Sacred Isle. The same as Holy Isle.

> O haste and leave this sacred isle,
> Unholy bark, ere morning smile.
> *Saint Senatus and the Lady.*

Sacred Wars. (1) A war undertaken by the Amphictyonic League for the defence of Delphi against the Cirrhæans. It occurred 595–587 B. C. (2) A war commenced by the Athenians for the purpose of recapturing Delphi from the Lacedæmonians, who had captured it from the Phocians 448–447 B. C. (3) The most famous of the sacred wars, in which the Phocians, who had seized Delphi 357 B. C., were attacked and conquered by Philip of Macedon. (4) The Crusades were so named.

Sadder and Wiser Man. This phrase is from the " Ancient Mariner " —

" A sadder and a wiser man
He rose the morrow morn."

Saddle-bag John. General Pope was thus nicknamed by the army in memory of his famous order about headquarters being on horseback.

Sadducees. A Jewish party which denied the existence of spirits and angels, and, of course, disbelieved in the resurrection of the dead ; so called from Sadoc (righteous man), the name of a rabbi three centuries before the birth of Christ.

Sadie Martinot. The stage-name of Mrs. Frederick Stinson, *née* Egins.

Sadie Wells. The stage-name of Mrs. William O'Day.

Saehrimnir. In Scandinavian mythology a boar whose flesh serves as food for the banquets in Valhalla. Every day it is served up at table, and by the next it is entirely renewed again.

S. Afr. South Africa.

Sage-hen State. The State of Nevada is popularly so named. The bird much abounds in the Rocky Mountain region, and feeds on the leaves of the sage-brush.

Sage of Auburn. William H. Seward was so named.

Sage of Chelsea. Thomas Carlyle, the English historian and essayist. During his long sojourn in London he resided in the same house in Cheyne Walk, Chelsea.

Sage of Monticello. Thomas Jefferson ; so named from the designation of his country seat and in allusion to his wise statesmanship and political foresight.

Sage of Wheatland. James Buchanan, President of the United States, was so named from his country-seat.

Sagittarius. Heinrich Schutz, also named " the Father of German music " (b. 1585), was a famous musician and critic. .

Sahara of the North. The inland plateau of Greenland.

Sailor-King. William IV. of England, who entered the navy as a middy and became Lord High Admiral in 1827.

Sain et sauf. (Fr.) Safe and sound.

Saint. Many kings and princes and rulers have been thus named : (1) Edward the Martyr. (2) Edward the Confessor. (3) Eric IX. of Sweden. (4) Ethelred I., King of Wessex. (5) Pope Eugenius I. (6) Pope Felix I. (7) Ferdinand III. of Castile and Leon. (8) Pope Julius I. (9) Lawrence Justiniani, Patriarch of Venice. (10) Pope Leo IX. (11) Louis IX. of France. (12) Olaus II. of Norway. (13) Stephen I. of Hungary. (14) Kang-he, the Chinese philosopher and emperor.

Saint-Amand. The pseudonym of Jean Amand Lacoste (1797–1885), the French dramatist. His best known play was " Robert Macaire."

St. Andrew's Day. November 30. Saint Andrew, the first disciple of Christ, and afterward an Apostle, was, like his brother Peter, a fisherman. Previous to his recognition of Christ as the Messiah he had been numbered among the disciples of John the Baptist. See John i. 40, 41. The career of Saint Andrew as an Apostle after the death of Christ is unknown. Tradition tells us that, after preaching the Gospel in Scythia, Northern Greece, and Epirus, he suffered martyrdom on the cross at Patræ, in Achaia, 62 or 70 A. D. A cross formed of beams obliquely placed is styled St. Andrew's Cross. Saint Andrew is the patron saint of Scotland ; he is also held in great veneration in Russia as the Apostle who, according to tradition, first preached the Gospel in that country. In both countries there is an order of knighthood named in his honor.

Saint Benjamin. (Pseud.) Richard Grant White, in his " New Gospel of Peace," New York, *circa* 1863–1866.

Saint Beuve of English Criticism. Matthew Arnold (1822–1888), the poet and essayist, was so named.

St. George's. The Eighth Regiment of Hussars (English) are thus nicknamed.

St. George's Day. April 23. He is the tutelary saint of England.

Saintine. (Pseud.) Joseph Xavier Boniface, French poet and playwright (1798–1865).

Saint Jerome. A nickname conferred on Senator Edmunds, the American statesman.

St. John's Day. December 27. There is a legend to the effect that a priest of Diana challenged Saint John to drink a cup of poison which he had prepared; upon which Saint John made on the vessel the sign of the cross, and emptied it without injury to himself. From this legend has arisen a custom, among the Roman Catholics, of drinking hallowed wine on St. John's Day to protect them from the effects of poison during the year.

St. Lubbock, or **St. Lubbock's Day.** The name given to the days on which the annual bank holidays occur in England, in allusion to the large part sustained by the firm of that name in the financial and banking affairs of the metropolis, and also to the fact that the act of Parliament establishing these holidays was passed largely through the instrumentality of Sir John Lubbock. *See* BANK HOLIDAYS.

St. Luke's Little Summer. St. Luke's Day, October 18. The idea is probably equivalent to that expressed by our term "Indian Summer."

Saintly City. St. Paul, Minn.

Saintly T's. A fanciful grouping of names of several worthies : — Sin Tander, Sin Tantony, Sin Tawdry, Sin Taustin, Sin Tedmund, and Sin Telders ; or, in plain English, Saint Andrew, Saint Anthony, Saint Audry, Saint Austin, Saint Edmund, and Saint Ethelred.

St. Martin's Little Summer. A period of mild weather occurring during the month of November throughout northern Europe, and corresponding to the "Indian Summer" of North America.

St. Michael's Chair. The projecting stone lantern of a tower erected on St. Michael's Mount, Cornwall, England. It is said that the rock received its name from a religious house built to commemorate the apparition of Saint Michael on one of its craggy heights.

St. Monday. A holiday observed by idle workmen and many merchants.

St. Nicholas's Day. Falls on December 6. He is the patron saint of children.

St. Partridge's Day. September 1, the first day of partridge shooting. So August 12 is called "St. Grouse's Day."

St. Patrick's Day. March 17 ; observed by the Irish in honor of the tutelary saint.

Saint-Simonism. The social and political system of Saint Simon (1760–1825). He proposed the institution of a European parliament, to arbitrate in all matters affecting Europe, and the establishment of a social hierarchy based on capacity and labor.

St. Stephen's Chapel. Properly the House of Commons, but sometimes applied to the two Houses of Parliament. So called by a figure of speech from St. Stephen's Chapel, built by King Stephen, rebuilt by Edward II. and III., and finally destroyed by fire in 1834. St. Stephen's Chapel was fitted up for the use of the House of Commons in the reign of Edward IV. The great council of the nation met before in the chapter-house of the abbey.

Saint Swithen. Tutor of King Alfred, and Bishop of Winchester. The monks wished to bury him in the chancel of the minster ; but the bishop had directed that his body should be interred under the open vault of heaven. Finding the monks resolved to disobey his injunction, he sent a heavy rain on July 15, the day assigned to the funeral ceremony, in consequence of which it was deferred from day to day for forty days. The monks then bethought them of the saint's injunction, and prepared to inter the body in the churchyard. Saint Swithen smiled his approbation by sending a beautiful sunshiny day, in which all the robes of the hierarchy might be displayed without the least fear of being injured by untimely and untoward showers.

Saint Tammany. The patron of democracy in the American States. His day is May 1. Tammany or Tammenund lived in the seventeenth century. He was a native of Delaware, but settled on the banks of the Ohio. He was a chief sachem of his tribe, and his rule was discreet and peaceful. His great maxim was, "Unite. In peace unite for mutual happiness, in war for mutual defence."

Sakuntala. A water-nymph and one of the most pleasing characters in the Hindu mythology.

Salad Days. Days of green youth, while the blood is still cool.

> . . . My salad days !
> When I was green in judgment, cold in blood.
> SHAKSPEARE, *Antony and Cleopatra.*

Sal Atticum. (Lat.) "Attic salt." That is, "wit."

Salchichon. A large Italian sausage. Thomas, Duke of Genoa, a boy of Harrow school, was so called, when he was thrust forward by General Prim as an "inflated candidate" for the Spanish throne.

Sales by Candle. A couple of centuries ago, it was customary to sell by "inch of candle." A lot being "put up" by the auctioneer, any bids were valid until the candle went out, when the last bidder was declared the purchaser. Upon this custom, Pepys, who was Secretary to the Admiralty, made the following curious entry in his "Diary," September 3, 1662 : — " After dinner we met and sold the 'Weymouth,' 'Successe,' and 'Fellowshippe' hulkes ; where pleasant to see how backward men are at first to bid, and yet when the candle is going out how they bawl, and dispute afterwards who bid the most. And here I observed one man cunninger than the rest, that was sure to be the last man and to carry it, and enquiring the reason he told me that just as the flame goes out the smoke descends, which is a thing I never observed before, and by that he do know the instant when to bid last."

Salic Law. The chapter of the Salian code regarding succession to salic lands, which was limited to heirs male, to the exclusion of females, chiefly because certain military duties were connected with the holding of those lands. In the fourteenth century females were excluded from the throne of France by the application of the Salic Law.

Salisbury Craigs. Rocks near Edinburgh, Scotland ; so called from the Earl of Salisbury, who accompanied Edward III. on an expedition against the Scots.

Salle. (Fr.) Hall.

Salle à manger. (Fr.) "A room for eating." A dining-hall.

Sallie A. Brock. (Pseud.) Mrs. Sarah A. Putnam, *née* Brock, author of "Kenneth my King" (1872).

Sallie Bridges. (Pseud.) Mrs. S. B. Stebbins, an American poet, in various periodicals.

Sallie Marks. The stage-name of Mrs. William Showles.

Sallie Shandley. The stage-name of Mrs. J. Stivers.

Sallust of France. César de Vichard, Abbé de St. Real, was so named by Voltaire (fl. 1639–1692).

Salmagundi. Irving's opening words in the publication bearing this name are, " As everybody knows, or ought to know, what a Salmagundi is, we shall spare ourselves the trouble of an explanation." In spite of this statement, the following definition of the word given here may not be out of place : " A mixture of minced veal, chicken, or turkey, anchovies or pickled herrings, and onions, all chopped together and served with lemon juice and oil." Hence in general the term is applied to any miscellany, or medley.

Saloon = PUBLIC-HOUSE. The corner public-house of English cities gives place, in America, to the more pretentious "saloon."

Salt, Salting. Western Americanisms. In the parlance of the mining-camp, "to salt" a worthless mine is to secretly place or scatter therein samples of rich ore for the purpose of effecting a sale. The rich ore is the "salt," and the practice is known as "salting a mine."

Salted Accounts. *See* COOKED ACCOUNTS.

Salt King. John Corbett, M. P., the owner of enormous salt-works at Droitwich, England.

Salt River. An imaginary stream up which a defeated candidate is supposed to be sent, and whence he is not expected to come back. The origin of the expression is as follows : Salt River, geographically, is a tributary of the Ohio. Its source is in Kentucky, and, being very crooked and difficult of navigation, it was in the early days a favorite stronghold for river-pirates. These highwaymen were in the habit of preying upon the commerce of the Ohio and rowing their plunder up Salt River, whence it was never recovered. Hence it came to be said of anything that was irrevocably lost, " It's rowed up Salt River." By an easy transition it was applied to unsuccessful candidates. "He has been rowed (or rode) up Salt River," or "We'll row him (or ride him) up Salt River next fall."

Saltwater Day. On the second Saturday of August in every year the inhabitants of New Jersey who reside within thirty or forty miles of the sea-coast make a pilgrimage thither. The occasion is one of general merrymaking, and is peculiarly a New Jersey insti-tution.

Salus populi suprema est lex. (Lat.) The safety and welfare of the people is the highest law.

Salvia Dale. (Pseud.) Alice Dal-sheimer, American poet (1845–1880), in the daily papers of New Orleans, her native city.

Salvo jure. (Lat.) "With uninjured right." Saving the right.

Salvo pudore. Without offence to modesty.

Sam. Samuel.

Sam. In the political phraseology of the United States, a popular synonym for the Know-Nothing or Native Ameri-can party. The word contains, of course, as allusion to "Uncle Sam," the per-sonification of the government of the United States.

Sam Adams Regiments. On the morning after the famous "Massacre" of March 5, 1770, Samuel Adams was appointed chairman of a committee to communicate the votes of the Boston town-meeting to the governor and coun-cil. More than five thousand persons were present at this meeting, which was held at the Old South Meeting-house, and all the neighboring streets were crowded. Lieutenant-Governor Hutch-inson, with the council and Colonel Dal-rymple, commander of two regiments, sat in the old State House at the head of King Street. When Adams presented the demand of the town-meeting that the soldiers should be removed to the castle in the harbor, Hutchinson at first disclaimed any authority in the matter; but Adams reminded him that as acting-governor of Massachusetts he was com-mander-in-chief of all troops within the province. Hutchinson consulted awhile with Dalrymple, and at length replied that the Colonel was willing to remove one of the regiments in order to appease the indignation of the people. The com-mittee, led by Adams, returned to the church with this message, and as they proceeded through the crowded street, Adams, bowing to right and left, passed along the watchword: "Both regiments or none!" When the question was put

to vote in the church, five thousand voices shouted: "Both regiments or none!" Armed with this ultimatum, Adams returned to the State House, and warned Hutchinson that if he failed to remove both regiments before night-fall he did so at his peril. Hutchinson was as brave and as obstinate as Adams, but two regiments were powerless in presence of the angry crowd that filled Boston, and before sunset they were removed to the castle. These troops were ever afterward known in Parlia-ment as the "Sam Adams Regiments."

Sam Clover. (Pseud.) Nugent Robinson in the "Boys' and Girls' Weekly," New York.

Samian Letter. The letter Y, used by Pythagoras as an emblem of the path of virtue and of vice. Virtue is like the stem of the letter. Once devi-ated from, the further the lines are ex-tended the wider the divergence be-comes.

> When reason, doubtful like the Samian letter,
> Points him two ways, the narrower the better.
> 						POPE, *The Dunciad.*

> Et tibi quæ Samios diduxit litera ramos.
> 						PERSIUS, *Satires.*

Samian Sage. Pythagoras, born at Samos (sixth century B. C.).

> 'Tis enough
> In this late age, adventurous to have touched
> Light on the numbers of the Samian Sage.
> 						THOMSON.

Sammy the Publican. Samuel Ad-ams (1722–1803) carried on a brewery in Boston after his father's death, which, in connection with the fact that he was tax-collector of Boston, gained him the above nickname from the wits of the town.

Samosatian Philosopher. Lucian of Samosata.

Sample-Room. A name for a liquor saloon, supposed to embody the fiction that patrons enter only to "sample" or try the beverages within. This, and the kindred term, "Shades" (*q.v.*), is prob-ably an outgrowth of the temperance agitation, which sought to render vulgar drinking in "bar-rooms" and "saloons."

Sam Slick. (Pseud.) Thomas Chandler Haliburton, English humor-ous writer (1796–1865).

Samson of England. Thomas Top-ham (fl. 1710–1753), the son of a Lon-don carpenter. His feats of strength bordered on the marvellous.

Samson's Crown. An achievement of great renown, which costs the life of the doer thereof. Samson's greatest exploit was pulling down the "grand stand" occupied by the chief magnates of Philistia, at the feast of Dagon. By this deed "he slew at his death more than [*all*] they which he slew in his life." — Judges xvi. 30.

Samuel A. Bard. (Pseud.) Ephraim George Squier, American archæologist (b. 1821).

Samuel Blotter. (Pseud.) Charles Henry Doe (b. 1838), an American author and journalist, in stories in the "Galaxy" and "Knickerbocker Magazine."

Samuel Prior. (Pseud.) John Galt, Scottish author (1779–1839).

Sancta Clara. (Pseud.) Christopher Davenport, English Catholic friar (1598–1680).

Sanctum Sanctorum. (Lat.) The holy of holies. *Sancta sanctorum*, the holy places of the holy places. *Sanctum*, the contracted form, has the familiar meaning, "a place for private use," and into which all persons or visitors are not admitted indiscriminately, as the study of a literary man, the private apartment of an editor, a laboratory, etc.

Sand. (1) An Americanism whose meaning is the same as "grit" (*q. v.*). A man with "sand in his craw" is supposed to be very plucky. (2) A second colloquial use of the word makes it stand for money, but though very common in the States it is doubtful if it is a pure Americanism. It is used by G. P. R. James in his novel, "Philip Augustus" ch. xix. De Courcy, while ruefully gazing on his poorly clad warriors, sees a laden ass approach. He inquires of the driver what he brings. The driver says, "Sand for De Courcy." To this the knight says, "You must mistake." "Not so," replies the driver, in a low tone, "it is a thousand marks of silver, the price of a ring sent by the hermit Bernard." De Courcy is at once relieved. He orders all the armorers to bring the arms they have ready, and exclaims, "A thousand marks of silver! By the Lord that lives, I will equip an army." The epoch is about 1200 A. D. and James wrote the novel about 40 or 50 years ago.

Sand-boys. The aristocratic English Grenadier Guards are thus nicknamed. *See also* TOWROWS.

Sand-hillers. A class of people in Georgia, and South Carolina. They are said to be the descendants of the poor whites, who, being deprived of work by the introduction of slave labor, took refuge in the pine woods that cover the sandy hills of those States, where they have since lived in a miserable condition.

Sand Lots. Waste lands on the outskirts of San Francisco much frequented by the rougher element in the population of the city, and where meetings of a semi-political character are often held. Denis Kearney, prominent a few years ago as a "labor" agitator, first won notoriety there, and was dubbed the "Sand-Lots Orator."

Sandy Hook. (Pseud.) Alexander Jones, American writer.

Sang-froid. Coolness; self-possession.

Sanglier des Ardennes. Guillaume de la Marck (fl. 1446–1485), who was driven from Liege for the murder of its bishop, and afterwards beheaded for his crime by the Archduke Maximilian.

San Jacinto, Anniversary of Battle of. This is a legal holiday in Texas, and falls on April 21.

Sankey's Horse. The Thirty-ninth Regiment of Foot is so dubbed because on one occasion Colonel Sankey mounted the men on horses. It is also known as Green Linnets.

Sans. (Fr.) Without.

Sansc. Sanscrit.

Sans cérémonie. (Fr.) "Without ceremony." In a homely, friendly way.

Sans Culottes ("without breeches"). The name given by the aristocratic party, during the French Revolution, to the rabble.

Sans Culottides. The five complementary days added to the twelve months of the Revolutionary calendar. Each month being made to consist of thirty days, the odd days were named in honor of the *sans culottes*, and made idle days, or holidays.

Sans doute. (Fr.) "Without doubt." Undoubtedly.

Sans façon. (Fr.) "Without ceremony." Unceremonious.

Sans peur et sans reproche. (Fr.) Without fear and without reproach.

Sans rime et sans raison. (Fr.) Without rhyme and reason.

Sans souci. (Fr.) "Without care." Free and easy.

Sans tâche. (Fr.) Stainless.

Santa Claus. The children's Christmas deity is known in the United States by this name, the Dutch form *Santa Klaas* being simply the abbreviation of Nicholas, a patron saint of unquestionable Holland ancestry.

Sapere aude. (Lat.). "Dare to be wise." Follow steadily the pursuit of knowledge, however formidable the difficulties which may lie in your path.

Sapientem pascere barbam. (Lat.) To cultivate a philosophic beard — long flowing beards having been supposed to indicate wisdom among the Romans.

Sapientium octavus. (Lat.) The eighth of the Wise Men (who were seven in number), said ironically of an individual of pretentious wisdom.

Sappho of Toulouse. Clemencé Isaure (fl. 1463–1513), a wealthy and benevolent lady of Toulouse who composed a bewitching "Ode to Spring."

Sappho's Leap. Cape Ducato, on Santa Maura, one of the Ionian isles, is so named. It was anciently called Leucadia (from the Greek λευκός, "white,") because of its snowy cliffs, and is famed in classic story as the spot from which the poetess Sappho, "the tenth muse," was said to have cast herself into the sea.

Sarah Bernhardt. In private life this French tragedienne is known as "Mme. Damala," which hints at her relations with the Duc d'Aumale.

Sarah Hildreth. The stage-name of Mrs. Benjamin Butler.

Sarah Stevens. The stage-name of Mrs. John C. Heenan.

Sarah Trenchard. The stage-name of Mrs. H. T. Chanfrau, *née* Fulton.

Sara Palma, Signora. The professional name of Mrs. Atkins Newell, *née* Von Hyeck.

Saraswati. In Hindu mythology the wife of the god Brahman, and the goddess of speech, of eloquence, of music and the arts, and the inventress of the Sanscrit tongue.

Saratoga. *See* EUROPEAN SARATOGA, WESTERN SARATOGA.

Saratoga of the West. Manitou, Col., a well-known "Springs" and summer resort.

Sard. Sardinia.

Sardanapalus of China. Cheo-tsin (fl. B. C. 1154–1022), who shut himself

in his palace and fired it that he might not fall into the hands of Woo-wung.

Sardonic Smile. An expression as old as Homer. It means literally to "grin like a dog," and bears reference to the hideous contortion of the facial muscles produced by eating the *sardonian*, a plant of Sicily, which was said to screw up the face of the eater, giving it a horrible appearance.

The island of Sardinia, consisting chiefly of marshes or of mountains, has, from the earliest period to the present, been cursed with a noxious air, an ill-cultivated soil, and a scanty population. The convulsions produced by its poisonous plants gave rise to the expression of "sardonic smile," which is as old as Homer. (Odyssey, xx. 302). — MAHON, *History of England*.

Sardonius risus. (Lat.) "Sardonic laughter." Unnatural or forced laughter.

Sarmatia. A modern poetical name for Poland. The ancient Sarmatia extended between the Don and the Vistula, and was the habitat of the Sarmatæ, a powerful Slavic race.

Sartor resartus. (Lat.) The tailor mended.

Sarum. Salisbury.

S. A. S. *Societatis Antiquariorum Socius.* Fellow of the Society of Antiquaries.

Sass. In New England "garden sass" means any kind of small vegetables. *See* TRUCK (1).

Sat. Saturday.

Satanic School. A name given by Southey, in his "Vision of Judgment," to a class of writers then thought to be subversive of all preconceived notions of morality and religion, and of the restraints of society. Under the name were included Byron, Shelley, Moore, Bulwer, Rousseau, Victor Hugo, Paul de Kock, and Georges Sand.

Sat cito, si sat bene. (Lat.) Done quickly enough, if well enough.

Satis eloquentiæ, sapientiæ parum. (Lat.) Eloquence enough, but little wisdom.

Satis superque. (Lat.) "Enough and more." Enough and more than enough.

Satis verborum. (Lat.) Enough of words.

Sat pulchra, si sat bona. (Lat.) Fair enough, if good enough.

Saturday, Black. *See* BLACK SATURDAY.

Saturday, Fatal. *See* FATAL SATURDAY.

Saturn. In classic mythology an ancient Roman divinity who presided over agriculture and who blessed the labors of the sower. His reign constituted the " Golden Age " of which the later poets sang as the era of ideal human happiness, and in memory of which the famous *Saturnalia* were thought to have been founded. In honor of the god the Italian peninsula received the name of *Saturnia*, or " land of plenty."

Saturnalia. *See* SATURN.

Saturnia. An ancient name for the Italian peninsula. *See* SATURN.

Satyrs. In classic myth a race of woodland deities who figure in great numbers in the train of Bacchus, their leader being the typsy Silenus. They are depicted as " robust in frame, with broad snub noses, large pointed ears like those of animals, bristly and shaggy hair, rough skin, little horny knobs on their foreheads, and short tails." The Romans identified them with the Fauni of their own mythology.

Sauces piquantes. (Fr.) Piquant sauces.

Saucy Greens. A nickname for the Thirty-sixth Regiment in the English army.

Saucy Pompeys. *See* POMPADOURS.

Saucy Worcesters. The Twenty-ninth Regiment in the English army is thus nicknamed.

Saul. Oliver Cromwell is alluded to under this name in Dryden's satire " Absalom and Achitophel."

Sauve qui peut. (Fr.) Save himself who can.

Savages. A self-bestowed nickname on the members of the Savage Club, in London, which was founded by some literary men about 1857, intended to signify freedom from conventionalism on the part of the members. " On some occasions," says Mr. Sala, " they gave a war-whoop."

Savanna. A term applied particularly to the prairies of the Southern States.

Savey, or Savvey. A Spanish word used interrogatively throughout the South and Southwest, an abbreviation of the Spaniard's " Quien Sabe ? "

Savid. (Pseud.) James Davis.

Savoir. (Fr.) Learning; scholarship.

Savoir-faire. (Fr.) Dexterity; management; wits.

Savoir-vivre. (Fr.) Good breeding; manners.

Sax. Saxon; Saxony.

Sax. Chron. Saxon Chronicle.

Saxe Holm. (Pseud.) (1) Miss Rush Ellis. American novelist (b. 1858). (2) Mrs. Helen Hunt Jackson (d. 1885).
" The mystery concerning the personality of the ' Saxe Holm Stories ' was well sustained for a number of years, but it is now generally believed they were the product of more than one pen."

Saxon. The pen-name of W. H. Noyes, sometime editor of the New York " Hotel Mail."

Saxon Milton. Caedmon.

Saxon Siberia. A portion of the mountain district of the Erz-Gebirge, in Saxony, is so named on account of the severity of its climate in winter.

Saxon Switzerland. A popular name for the hilly region in the kingdom of Saxony to the southeast of the city of Dresden. The scenery is strangely picturesque, but the peaks attain no great elevation.

Sb. Stibium, or antimony.

S. B. C. Southern Baptist Convention.

S. C. South Carolina; a decree of the Senate (*Senatus Consultum*).

Sc. *Sculpsit.* He (or she) engraved it.

Sc., or scil. *Scilicet.* Namely.

Scalchi, Madame. The professional name of the Countess Lolli, a famous contralto operatic singer.

Scandal, Hill of. *See* HILL OF SCANDAL.

Scandal of Astronomers. A nickname given to comets by Professor Proctor (d. 1888), in allusion to the difficulties experienced by scientists in determining accurately their origin, composition, etc.

Scandalum magnatum. (Lat.) Scandal of the great.

Scandinavia. In classic and mediæval times the name given to the great peninsula of Northern Europe, including Norway and Sweden. The name is frequent in modern poetry.

Scan. Mag. *Scandalum magnatum.* Scandal of the great.

Scapin. *See* JUPITER SCAPIN.

S. caps. Small capitals.

Scarborough Warning. A blow first, then a warning. In Scarborough robbers used to be dealt with in a very summary manner, by a sort of lynch law. Another origin is given of this phrase : It is said that Thomas Stafford, in the reign of Queen Mary, seized the castle of Scarborough, not only without warning, but even before the townsfolk knew he was afoot.

Scarlet Woman. In Protestant controversial writings a term of reproach for the Church of Rome, and intended to symbolize its vices and corruptions. Of course the allusion is to Rev. xvii., where the phrase occurs.

Scavenger's Daughter. An instrument of torture invented by Sir William Skevington, Lieutenant of the Tower in the reign of Henry VIII. "Scavenger" is a corruption of "Skevington." " To kiss the scavenger's daughter," to suffer punishment by this instrument of torture, to be beheaded by a guillotine or some similar instrument.

Sc. B. Bachelor of Science.

Schellenburg. (Pseud.) Johann Karl August Musäus, German author (1735–1787).

Scherzando, Scherzante, Scherzo, Scherzoso, or Scherz. (Ital.) In a light, playful, or sportive manner. (Mus.)

Schmalkald League. The name given to the defensive alliance concluded provisionally for nine years at Schmalkenden, in 1531, between the Protestant princes of Germany. The object of this formidable compact was the common defence of the religious and political freedom of the Protestants against Charles V. and the Catholic powers.

Schnake. (Pseud.) Carl Hauser, in the German reprint of " Puck."

Schol. *Scholium.* A note.

Scholastic, The. (1) Anselm of Laon (fl. 1050–1117). (2) Epiphanius, an Italian scholar of the ninth century.

Scholastic Doctor. Anselm of Laon (d. 1117), a famous French schoolman.

Schoolmaster Abroad. This phrase originated in a speech of Lord Brougham. The passage in which it occurred is subjoined : " Let the soldier be abroad if he will ; he can do nothing in this age. There is another personage abroad, a person less imposing — in the eyes of some, perhaps, insignificant. The schoolmaster is abroad ! and I trust to him, armed with his primer, against the soldier in full military array."

Schr. Schooner.

Scienter. (Lat.) Knowingly.

Sci. fa. *Scire facias.*

Scilicet. (Lat.) That is to say; to wit.

Scio's Blind Old Bard. Homer.

Scire facias. Cause it to be known.

Scironian Rocks, between Megara and Corinth. So called because the bones of Sciron, the robber of Attica, were changed into these rocks when Theseus hurled him from a cliff into the sea. It was from these rocks that Ino cast herself into the Corinthian bay.

Sclav. Scalvonic.

Scot. Scottish ; Scotland.

Scotia. The Latin name of Scotland, often used by her poets. The word is said to be derived from Queen Scota, the wife of a king of Ireland, who is thought to have invaded Scotland in 258 A. D. Previous to this event the land was known as Caledonia (*q. v.*).

Scottish Hogarth. David Allan, the artist (fl. 1744–1796).

Scottish Homer. William Wilkie, the author of " The Epigoniad " (fl. 1721–1772).

Scottish Sidney. Robert Baillie (executed 1684) was so named.

Scottish Solomon. James VI. of Scotland and I. of England.

Scottish Teniers. Sir David Wilkie, the painter (fl. 1785–1841).

Scottish Theocritus. Allan Ramsay, the poet (fl. 1685–1758).

Scotty. (Pseud.) C. H. Urquhart, in the Chicago " Times."

Scourers. A class of dissolute young men, often of the "upper ten," who infested the streets of London in the seventeenth century, and thought it capital fun to break windows, upset sedan-chairs, beat quiet citizens, and molest young women. These young blades called themselves at different times, Muns, Hectors, Scourers, Nickers, Hawcabites, and Mohawks, or Mohocks.

Scourge of Christians. Noureddin-Mahmûd of Damascus (fl. 1116–1174).

Scourge of God. (1) Attila, king of the Huns. (2) Genseric, king of the Vandals.

Scourge of Princes. Pietro Aretino (fl. 1492–1556) was so named on account of his satires.

Scourge of the Spaniards. Jacques Jean David Nau, a French buccaneer (1634–1671). He waged bitter war on the Spaniards in the Antilles.

Scout. A collegian's servant at Oxford, whose duties and privileges correspond to those of the Cambridge Gyp (*q. v.*).

Scr. Scruple.

Scrambling Committee. A nickname given to those Irish "patriots" who, in the Parliament of 1755, under the Duke of Devonshire as viceroy, became notorious for their rapacity and intrigue in search of "spoils."

Scrape an Acquaintance. Hadrian went once to the public baths, and, seeing an old soldier scraping himself with a potsherd for want of a flesh-brush, sent him a sum of money. Next day the bath was crowded with potsherd scrapers; but the emperor said when he saw them, "Scrape on, gentlemen, but you will not scrape an acquaintance with me."

Scratch, Scratching. To erase the name of a nominee to office from the party ticket. *See* HAW-EATER.

Scrip. Scripture.

Scripsit (Lat.) Wrote it.

Scrub Race for the Presidency. The presidential contest of 1824 was so called. The candidates, John Quincy Adams, Andrew Jackson, William H. Crawford, and Henry Clay, being all of the same party, the contest was merely a personal one; the truth of the comparison implied in the name is obvious.

Scrutator. (Pseud.) (1) John Loveday, D. C. L., in his contributions to the "Gentleman's Magazine." (2) John S. Rarey, American horse-tamer and writer (1825–1866).

Sculp. *Sculpsit.* He (or she) engraved it.

Sculpsit. (Lat.) Engraved it : placed after the engraver's name in prints.

Scylla and Charybdis. Two geographical sobriquets frequently met in ancient and modern literature. Scylla (Gr. Σκύλλα) is a rocky cape on the west coast of South Italy, jutting out boldly into the sea so as to form a small peninsula just at the northern entrance to the Straits of Messina. About the beginning of the fifth century B. C. a fort was built upon the rock (which is about two hundred feet high, and much hollowed out below by the action of the waves), and in course of time a small town grew up, straggling down the slopes toward the sea. The navigation at this place was looked upon by the ancients as attended with immense danger, which, however, seems to have been much exaggerated, for at the present day the risk is not more than attends the doubling of any ordinary cape. Charybdis (modern name Galofaro) is a celebrated whirlpool in the Straits of Messina, nearly opposite the entrance to the harbor of Messina in Sicily, and in ancient writings always mentioned in conjunction with Scylla. The navigation of this whirlpool is, even at the present day, considered to be dangerous, and must have been exceedingly so to the open ships of the ancients.

Thus, when I shun Scylla, your father, I fall into Charybdis, your mother.
Merchant of Venice, act iii.

Scylla and Charybdis of Scotland. The "Swalchie whirlpool" and the "Merry Men of Mey," a bed of broken water which boils like a witch's caldron, on the south side of the Stroma Channel. *See* MERRY MEN.

S. D. *Salutum dicet.* Sends health.

S. E. Southeast.

Se. Selenium.

Sea. (Pseud.) Capt. Roland F. Coffin, an American writer of sea stories (1836–1888).

Seacoal. The signature of William C. Hudson, an American journalist and correspondent.

Sea-girt Isle. England.

This precious stone set in the silver sea.
SHAKSPEARE, *Richard III.*

Sea, Lion of the. *See* LION OF THE SEA.

Seal of Confession. From very early times, so early, it is said, as the fourth and fifth centuries, the "seal of confession" in the Church was held to be inviolable, and no priest could be called upon, under any circumstances, to reveal facts which had been confided to him under its sanction. To this the case of treason was an exception in England, even in Roman Catholic times.

In Roman Catholic countries the privileges of the confessional remain unaltered; and several of the Protestant Churches of Germany having sanctioned the practice of confession, the privilege of secrecy has been extended to it, as a necessary consequence, by the civil power. In those States, however, in addition to imposing far lighter penalties upon clergymen who break the seal, the duty of doing so is enforced in all cases in which the confession has reference to a future crime. In England no special privilege whatever is extended to the Roman Catholic confessional; and the question as to how far a confession made to a clergyman for the purpose of obtaining spiritual comfort and consolation is protected, was long considered doubtful. The rule has, however, been settled for some time that no clergymen, of any religious persuasion, are entitled to the same privilege as legal advisers; though it has often been advocated as advisable to extend the rule to clergymen, including Roman Catholic priests. By a statute of the State of New York, ministers of the Gospel, and priests of every denomination, are forbidden to disclose confessions made to them in their professional character; and a similar statute exists in Missouri. It has been decided in England that communications to a medical man, even in the strictest professional confidence, are not protected from disclosure; but a contrary rule has been adopted in several of the States of America. — ALDEN.

Sea of Darkness. So the Atlantic was called in the fifteenth century.

Sea of Lot. See LAKE OF LOT.

Sea of Sedge. The Red Sea. The Red Sea so abounds with sedge that in the Hebrew Scriptures it is called "The Weedy or Sedgy Sea." Milton refers to it when he says the rebel angels were as numberless as the

. . . scattered sedge
Aflote, when with fierce winds Orion armed
Hath vexed the Red Sea coast.
　　　　　　　　　　Paradise Lost.

Sea of Stars. The source of the Yellow River, in Thibet, is so called because of the unusual sparkle of the waters.

Like a sea of stars,
The hundred sources of Hoangho.
　　SOUTHEY, *Thalaba the Destroyer.*

Searcher, The. A nickname given to Dr. Robert Fludd, the scientist (fl. 1574–1637), on account of his investigations in the sciences.

Seas, Sovereign of the. See SOVEREIGN OF THE SEAS.

Sec. Secretary; second.

Secessia, or Secesh. A slang name applied to those States that, in 1861, seceded from the American Union, thus precipitating the Civil War.

Sec. Leg. Secretary of Legation.

Sec. leg. *Secundum legem.* According to law.

Second Augustine. Thomas Aquinas, the Schoolman (fl. 1224–1275). See ANGELIC DOCTOR.

Seconda vol a molto crescendo. (Ital.) Much louder the second time of playing. (Mus.)

Second Rome. Aquiljar, a town of Austria. In the time of the Romans it was the entrepôt and commercial centre of northern and western Europe, and the Emperor Augustus often resided

there. It was taken and burned by Attila, at which time its population was reckoned at 100,000.

Second Washington. Benito Juarez (b. 1807), the Mexican patriot and statesman, has been so named by his countrymen.

Sec. reg. *Secundum regulam.* According to rule.

Secrétaire des commandements. (Fr.) A private secretary.

Secret de la comédie. (Fr.) "Secret of the comedy." Everybody's secret.

Sect. Section.

Secundum artem. (Lat.) "According to art or rule." Scientifically; in an artistic manner.

Secundum naturam. (Lat.) "According to nature." In a natural manner.

Secundum ordinem. (Lat.) "According to order." In an orderly manner.

Secundum usum. (Lat.) "According to usage." In a manner established by custom.

Securus judicat orbis terrarum. (Lat.) Secure in the judgment (*i. e.,* approval) of the round world.

Sedan Day. The anniversary of the battle of Sedan, Sept. 1, 1870, is observed as a holiday in many parts of Germany.

Se De Kay. (Pseud.) Charles D. Kirke, American *littérateur.*

Sedition Foundry. The office of the "Massachusetts Spy," in Boston (established 1770), a paper which advocated the cause of the patriots with great vigor and boldness, and was styled by the royalists "the sedition foundry."

Seekers. The Quakers, or Friends, were originally so named from their "seeking the truth."

Seeley Register. (Pseud.) M. V. Victor, American author.

Segne, Segnito. (Ital.) Now follows, or as follows. For example: *Segne il coro,* the chorus now follows; *Segne la finale,* the finale now follows. (Mus.)

Segne senza interruzione. (Ital.) Go on without stopping. (Mus.)

Segne subito senza cambiare il tempo. (Ital.) Proceed directly, and without changing the tone. (Mus.)

Segno. (Ital.) A sign; as, *al segno,* return to the sign; *dal segno,* repeat from the sign. (Mus.)

Selene. The Greek name of the goddess of the moon, the same as the Latin *Luna;* later she was identified with Artemis. The most common accounts make her the daughter of Hyperion and of Theia, and sister of Helios (the sun). She had many daughters, one of whom was called Erse (the dew).

Self-denying Ordinance. A resolution passed in the English Parliament, April 3, 1645, which ordained that no member should hold any civil or military office or command conferred by either of the Houses or by authority derived from them.

Selina Dolaro. The stage-name of Mrs. Isaac Belasco, *née* Simmons.

Selon les règles. (Fr.) According to rule.

Sem. It seems (*semble*); seminary.

Semele. In classic myth the mother of Bacchus (*q. v.*).

Semel in anno. (Lat.) Once in the year.

Seminole War. This struggle between the American Indians and the United States arose from an attempt on the part of the government to remove the tribe to a new domain west of the Mississippi. Hostilities began in 1835, and continued until 1839. Osceola, the Seminole chief, an able and daring leader, denied the validity of a previous treaty ceding the lands in dispute to the United States, and was captured and thrown into prison. But, professing to acquiesce, he was set at liberty, and immediately entered into a war of extermination against the whites. The war was waged with great bitterness on both sides till 1837, when Osceola was again captured, and died in jail in 1838. Although the loss of their leader was a great blow, the Indians continued to fight with great obstinacy until 1839, when the chiefs sent in their submission and signed a treaty; but, as in the case of the Cherokees, their removal to the West was undertaken with much reluctance.

Semiramis of the North. (1) Margaret of Sweden, Denmark, and Norway (fl. 1353–1412). (2) Catherine II. of Russia (fl. 1729–1796).

Semper avarus eget. (Lat.) The miser always suffers want.

Semper fidelis. (Lat.) Always faithful.

Semper idem. (Lat.) "Always the same" (person, character, or disposition).

Semper paratus. (Lat.) "Always prepared." Always ready.

Sempre. (Ital.) Always; as *Sempre forte*, always loud; *Sempre più forte*, continually increasing in force. (Mus.)

Sempre piano e ritenuto. (Ital.) Always more and more soft, and falling off in the degree of movement. (Mus.)

Sempre più decrescendo e più rallentando. (Ital.) Gradually softer and slower. (Mus.)

Sempre più forte, . . . ff mo. (Ital.) Louder and louder to the *fortissimo*. (Mus.)

Sen. Senate; senator; senior.

Senator Bob Hart. A sort of professional nickname given to Robert Sutherland, once a "negro minstrel," but who later became an evangelist. He died in 1888.

Senatus consultum. (Lat.) A decree of the senate.

Sen. Doc. Senate Document.

Seneca. (Pseud.) W. W. Pasko in "Truth," New York.

Senectus. (Pseud.) Gideon Granger, American lawyer (1767–1822).

Senex. (Pseud.) James Anderson, author of numerous essays in the "Bee."

Senior Soph. A third-class man in a University.

Se non è vero, è ben trovato. (Ital.) If it be not true, it is well feigned.

Sentinel. W. H. Bogart, who was long known as a newspaper correspondent under this signature, which suggested the title of a little book of reminiscences which he published, "Who Goes There?" He died in 1888, aged 78.

Senza. (Ital.) Without; as, *Senza organo*, without the organ; *Senza rigore*, without regard to exact time; *Senza replica*, without repetition. (Mus.)

Separatists. Another name for the Puritans, first bestowed in England.

Sept. September; Septuagint.

September Massacres. In the French Revolution a fearful massacre took place in Paris, Sept. 2–5, 1792. The prisons were broken open, and many of the prisoners confined therein for political reasons, among them a bishop and one hundred priests, slaughtered. The agents in this wholesale butchery were nicknamed Septembrizers, and their victims are estimated by various writers at from 1200 to 4000.

Septembrizers. *See* SEPTEMBER MASSACRES.

Septuagesima Sunday. The third Sunday before Lent, being the nearest Sunday to the seventieth day before Easter (from the Latin meaning "seventieth ").

Seq. *Sequentia*, following; *sequitur*, it follows.

Sequitur. (Lat.) "He (she or it) follows." A consequence.

Ser. Series.

Seraphic Doctor. John Fidanza Bonaventure (fl. 1221-1274).

Seraphic Saint. Saint Francis of Assisi, the founder of the Franciscan Order.

Serapis. The Greek name of an Egyptian deity introduced into Egypt in the time of Ptolemy I., and to whom, it is said, the Romans and Egyptians erected forty-two temples in various parts of Egypt. He would seem to have been a union of Osiris and Apis, and resembled the Pluto of the classic myth in that he was a judge of the dead and a ruler in Hades.

Serbonian Bog. An impassable morass; a Slough of Despond.

> A gulf profound as that Serbonian bog
> Betwixt Damiata and Mount Casius old,
> Where armies whole have sunk.
> *Paradise Lost.*

Serg. Sergeant.

Serg.-Maj. Sergeant-Major.

Seriatim. (Lat.) In order; successively.

Sero venientibus ossa. (Lat.) The bones for those who come late.

Serpent-bearer. A constellation in the mid-heavens, whose centre is very nearly over the earth's equator, opposite to Orion, and directly south of Hercules. It represents a man with a venerable beard, having both hands clenched in the folds of an enormous serpent, which is writhing in his grasp, and contains seventy-four stars, none of which are of the first magnitude. This constellation is also called Æsculapius, the god of medicine.

Servant of the Servants of God. A title adopted by Pope Gregory I. in his official documents, and retained by his successors.

Servile Wars. The name given to various risings of slaves against their masters in ancient times. The chief were, the rising of the gladiators in Italy, under Spartacus, 73-71 B. C.; and the insurrections in Sicily, 134-132, and 102-99 B. C.

Servt. Servant.

Servum pecus. (Lat.) "A slavish herd." A servile body of imitators.

Sesha. In Hindu mythology the mighty monarch of the serpent race on which Vishnu reclines on the primeval waters. He has a thousand heads, and his crest is ornamented with gems. Coiled up, Sesha is the emblem of eternity, and is often called *Ananta*, "the eternal."

Sess. Session.

Seth, in George Eliot's "Adam Bede," was a portraiture of her uncle, Samuel Evans.

Seven against Thebes. In classic myth Adrastus, Amphiaraus, Capaneus, Hippomedon, Parthenopæus, Polynices, and Tyndæus, who led an expedition designed to place Polynices on the throne of Thebes, from which he had been driven by his brother. It resulted in failure; but a second effort, led by their sons, the Epigoni, was crowned with success.

Seven-and-Sixpennies. A nickname for the Seventy-sixth English Regiment, taken from the two figures which make the number.

Seven Champions of Christendom. "(1) Saint George of England, seven years imprisoned by the Almidor, the black king of Morocco. (2) Saint Denys of France, who lived seven years in the form of a hart. (3) Saint James of Spain, seven years dumb out of love to a fair Jewess. (4) Saint Anthony of Italy, with the other champions, was enchanted into a deep sleep in the Black Castle, and was released by Saint George's three sons, who quenched the seven lamps by water from the enchanted fountain. (5) Saint Andrew of Scotland, who was guided through the Vale of Walking Spirits by the Walking Fire, and delivered six ladies who had lived seven years under the form of milk-white swans. (6) Saint Patrick of Ireland, immured in a cell where he scratched his grave with his own nails. (7) Saint David of Wales, slept seven years in the enchanted garden of Ormandine, but was redeemed by Saint George." — BREWER.

Seven Churches of Asia. Those of Ephesus, Smyrna, Pergamos, Thyatira, Sardis, Philadelphia, and Laodicea, to the "angels," *i. e.*, ministers, of which John was commanded to write in the Book of Revelation.

Seven Cities, The. Egypt, Jerusalem, Babylon, Athens, Rome, Constantinople, and either London or Paris. They are often grouped under this title, as embodying wealth, antiquity, greatness, and magnificence.

Seven Days' War. (1) The name given to the short, but sharp, struggle for German supremacy between Prussia and Italy and Austria in the Spring of 1866. Austria relinquished the Quadrilateral (*q. v.*) to France, and France gave it to Italy. (2) A popular name applied to the English military manœuvres in the autumn of 1871, when several thousand troops were massed about the metropolis.

Seven Deadly Sins. These are pride, wrath, envy, lust, gluttony, avarice, and sloth.

Seven Dials. The Seven Dials in London is a place where seven streets branch off; namely, (1) Great Earl Street; (2) Little Earl Street; (3) Great St. Andrew's Street; (4) Little St. Andrew's Street; (5) Great White Lion Street; (6) Little White Lion Street; (7) Queen Street.

Seven-hilled City. Rome, the ancient capital of Italy. At the time of its founding its site embraced seven considerable eminences, most of which, however, have been so abraded in the lapse of ages as to be now scarcely recognizable.

Seven Sages of Greece. Thales, Solon, Chiton, Pittacus, Bias, Cleobulus, Periander.

Seven Sleepers of Ephesus. In the year 249 of our era, the Emperor Decius assumed the government of the Roman Empire, which then held sway over the fairest lands of Europe, Asia, and Africa, and over many millions of people. Scarcely had he donned the purple garment of the emperors, when he commenced a persecution of the Christians throughout his dominion, — the seventh in respect of time, but in ferocity and cruelty the equal of that memorable one under the savage Diocletian. All civil magistrates were enjoined to destroy Christianity by threatening Christians with the cruelest of punishments should

they persist in their faith. The governors of the various provinces promulgated the decree, and commanded that, by a certain day, every disciple of the hated sect should appear before a certain officer and publicly renounce his faith. If he refused or neglected to appear, he was to be condemned to suffer the most hideous tortures. Decius wished to avoid the extreme penalty of death, but every other physical terror was, if necessary, to be resorted to. The prisons could not contain those who were arrested; thousands died from overcrowding in the jails, under the torturer's diabolical skill, or from exposure. Fortunately, the troubles which menaced Rome on her frontiers distracted attention from interior affairs, and by the year 251 the Decian persecution may be said to have ended. During its height, however, many persons fled from their homes. Among these fugitives was a party from the city of Ephesus, seven of whom — by name Malchus, Maximian, Denis, Martinian, John, Serapion, and Constantine — hid themselves in a cave a few miles outside the gates. Weary and panting, they fell into a deep slumber, although the vicinity was being scoured by the Roman legionaries. They were soon discovered by the pursuing soldiery, who blocked up the cave's mouth, hoping to starve them to death. Time passed on. The troubles of the Christians came to an end; the imprisoned were liberated, and the clergy returned to their flocks; but the unfortunates in the hillside cave were forgotten. But a miraculous hand cared for them. Their slumbers, begun in 251, remained unbroken till the reign of the Emperor Theodosius, in 447, — nearly two hundred years. When they awoke from this long sleep they imagined they had spent but a single night in the cave. They were hungry, and to procure provisions to carry with them on their journey, one of their number, Maximian, volunteered to endeavor to enter the city unperceived and purchase what was needed. So he departed. Ancient cities did not alter much in appearance with the lapse of time, and the few changes by the wayside did not attract his attention; but he could not fail to notice that, to the passers-by, he seemed an object of curious, but not unkindly, interest. But on entering the city, what was Maximian's amazement to see, elevated in triumph on the highest pinnacles of some magnificent buildings, the very cross that, only a few hours before, he had seen the object of contempt and blasphemy! And in niches by the side of the chief streets in Ephesus were smaller crosses, before which many stopped to murmur a prayer or to make a reverential gesture. A question here and there soon attracted a crowd, and when his wonderful story became known, half the city set out at his side to visit his companions and the scene of the miracle. Meantime the other six, supposing the persecution still in progress, had awaited their friend's return with anxiety; and when, at length, they heard the tramp of many feet and the hoarse murmur of many voices, they exclaimed, "All is lost!" and embraced each other for the last time, believing that Maximian had been captured, and that the fierce soldiery were coming to lead them away prisoners. They were soon undeceived. In a few moments a hundred stout arms had torn down the crumbling stones placed in the cave's mouth two centuries before, and in triumphal procession the Seven Sleepers were conducted into the city of Ephesus. The legend has it that a short time after they all died at the same instant, as if their lives were all controlled by the same mysterious power. The Church has perpetuated their story and the legend by setting apart, as sacred to their memory, one day in each year, — the 27th of June.

Seven Sorrows of Mary. (1) Simeon's prophecy; (2) The flight into Egypt; (3) Jesus missed; (4) The betrayal; (5) The crucifixion; (6) The taking down from the cross; and (7) The ascension. Her Seven Joys were: (1) The annunciation; (2) The visitation; (3) The nativity; (4) The adoration of the Magi; (5) The presentation in the Temple; (6) Finding the lost Child; and (7) The assumption.

Seventh Heaven. The height of happiness. The Cabbalists maintained that there are seven heavens, each rising in happiness above the other, the seventh being the abode of God and the highest class of angels.

Seventh of March Speech. "In January, 1850, Henry Clay introduced into Congress the series of resolutions that subsequently led to the Compromise of 1850 (*q. v.*). During the debate on these resolutions, Daniel Webster delivered an extraordinary speech, in which he opposed the views of the abolitionists and of all who in any way desired to restrict slavery. The one great aim of his speech was to smooth over differences between North and South. It has been charged that this speech was a virtual recantation of his political opinions for the purpose of aiding his presidential aspirations. The speech was delivered March 7, 1850." — *Dictionary of American Politics.*

Seven Towers. A State prison in Constantinople, near the Sea of Marmora. It stands at the west of the Seraglio.

But then they never came to the Seven Towers.
BYRON, *Don Juan.*

Seven Virtues. (1) Faith; (2) Hope; (3) Charity; (4) Prudence; (5) Justice; (6) Fortitude; and (7) Temperance. The first three are called the "holy virtues."

Seven Weeks' War. That between Prussia and Austria, from June 17 to August 23, 1866.

Seven Wonders of the Peak (Derbyshire): The three caves called the Devil's Arse, Pool, and Eden; St. Anne's Well, which is similar in character "to that most dainty spring of Bath;" Tideswell, which ebbs and flows, although so far inland; Sandy Hill, which never increases at the base nor abates in height; and the forest of the Peak, which bears trees on hard rocks.

Seven Wonders of the World were, in ancient times, reckoned to be the Pyramids of Egypt, the Hanging Gardens of Semiramis at Babylon, the Temple of Diana at Ephesus, the Statue of Jupiter at Athens by Phidias, the Mausoleum, the Colossus at Rhodes, and the Pharos of Alexandria. This cycle of seven wonders originated among the Greeks after the time of Alexander the Great, and they were described in a special work by Philo of Byzantium.

Seven Wonders of Wales. (1) Snowdon; (2) Pystyl Rhaiadr waterfall; (3) St. Winifred's Well; (4) Overton churchyard; (5) Gresford church bells; (6) Wrexham steeple; (7) Llangollen bridge.

Seven Words on the Cross. (1) "Father, forgive them, for they know not what they do;" (2) "To-day shalt thou be with me in paradise;" (3) "Woman, behold thy son;" (4) "My God, my God, why hast thou forsaken me?" (5) "I thirst;" (6) "It is finished!" (7) "Father, into thy hands I commend my spirit."

Seven Years' War. The conflict known by this name in European history was that maintained by Frederick the Great of Prussia against Austria, Russia, and France from 1756 to 1763. He gained Silesia.

Sexagesima Sunday. (From the Latin, meaning "sixtieth.") The second Sunday before Lent, it being the nearest Sunday to the sixtieth day before Easter.

Sextans (the Sextant). "Urania's sextant," a modern constellation made by Hevelius out of stars between the Lion on the north and Hydra on the south, and containing forty-one very small stars. It represents a sextant, an astronomical instrument resembling a quadrant.

S. G. South Georgia; Solicitor-General.

S. G. O. The literary signature of Rev. Lord Sydney Godolphin Osborne.

Shades. Wine-vaults. The Briggton Old Bank, in 1819, was turned by Mr. Savage into a smoking-room and gin-shop. There was an entrance to it by the Pavilion Shades, and Savage took down the word "Bank," and inserted instead the word "Shades."

Shades of Death. *See* WYOMING, MASSACRE OF.

Shak. Shakspeare.

Shakspeare of Divines. Jeremy Taylor.

Shakspeare of Eloquence. Mirabeau.

Sham Abram. *See* ABRAM MAN and ABRAHAM NEWLAND.

Shambles Oak. A tree in Thoresby Park, England (a part of what was once Sherwood Forest); so named from its hollow trunk having been made a butcher's shop, so to speak, in which were hung up and dressed the sheep and deer killed in the neighboring forest by those who, in times past, set property rights in game at defiance. *See* PARLIAMENT OAK.

Shamrock of Ireland. For long years the shamrock has been the emblem of Ireland. The story of the incident that led to its being chosen as the national symbol is quite poetical, and is

certainly "good enough to be true." It is said that the good Saint Patrick, about the year 432, was preaching to the rude islanders, many of whom had adopted the Christian faith. Some of its dogmas, however, the apostle found extremely difficult to render intelligible to his uncultured hearers. This was notably the case with the doctrine of the Trinity. On one occasion the preacher was holding forth in a field, and looking down he spied the three-leaved shamrock at his feet. Stooping and plucking a single stalk, he held it up before his auditors, telling them that there they might behold an illustration of "Trinity and Unity." Whether the story be true or no, certain it is that for centuries the shamrock has been known as the "Trinity flower."

Shanty. One of the few French words which have become naturalized in American speech is the *chantier*, thoroughly adopted in the shape of "shanty." Originally used by *voyageurs* and Canadian immigrants, it is universally employed to designate a slight wooden shed or shelter.

Shawmut. (Pseud.) Rev. Nathan Henry Chamberlain, in the Boston "Transcript."

Shays's Rebellion. When the Revolutionary War closed, the Federal Government was burdened with a heavy debt, and Congress recommended that it be portioned out among the several States, each to raise its quota by a direct tax. Much dissatisfaction ensued in certain States, and in 1787 a portion of the citizens of Massachusetts openly rebelled, being led by Daniel Shays, who committed various overt acts. The militia was called out, and though some of the insurgents were sentenced to death all were eventually pardoned.

Shebang. The name of a college student's sanctum, of a low drinking-den, and of a cheap theatre or variety show. The word is thought to be a corruption of the French *cabane*, and is common throughout the United States.

Sheep-dog. A lady-companion, who occupies the back seat of the barouche, carries wraps, etc., goes to church with the lady, and "guards her from the wolves," as much as the lady wishes to be guarded, but no more.

Sheep of the Prisons. A cant term in the French Revolution for a spy under the jailers.

Shell City. Mobile, Ala.

Shelley's Case. The decision in 1581, by all the judges of England, of the case of Nicholas Wolfe against Henry Shelley, in ejectment, involving questions upon the law of common recoveries. It is chiefly celebrated for a precise and clear statement by defendant's counsel of a previously well-established rule of law concerning the effect of the word " heirs " in certain conveyances, since known as the rule in Shelley's case. This rule, which is now regarded as a rule of interpretation rather than a rule of law, is to the effect that wherever there is a limitation to a man, which if it stood alone would convey to him a particular estate of freehold, followed by a limitation to his heirs or to the heirs of his body (or equivalent expressions), either immediately or after the interposition of one or more particular estates, the apparent gift to the heir or heirs of the body is to be construed as a limitation of the estate ; that is to say, not a gift to the heir, but a gift to the person first named of an estate of inheritance, such as his heir may take by descent.

Shell out. In many parts of the world shells (cowries) are used for money; hence the words mean, " Out with your shells (or money)."

She P. Billaber. (Pseud.) Benjamin P. Shillaber, in the "Boston Journal," Dec. 22, 1880, "Lines to Bismarck."

Shepherd Lord. Henry, tenth Lord Clifford, whose mother sent him from home to be brought up among shepherds, that he might escape the fury of the Yorkists. At the accession of Henry VII. he was restored to his rank and possessions.

Shepherd of Banbury. Supposed to be Dr. John Campbell, author of a weather-guide purporting to be by " John Claridge, Shepherd," and published in 1744.

Shepherd of Salisbury Plain. David Saunders, a moral writer noted for his practical wisdom and piety.

Shepherd of the Ocean. So Spenser named Sir Walter Raleigh in his poem " Colin Clout 's come home again."

Shepherd's Sun-dial. The scarlet pimpernel, which opens at seven in the morning, and closes at a little past two. When rain is at hand, it does not open at all.

Sherrill Kerr. (Pseud.) Miss Julia Magruder, in various publications.

Sherwood Bonner. (Pseud.) Mrs. Kate Sherwood McDowell, *née* Bonner, author of " Dialect Tales " (1883).

Sherwood Ryse. (Pseud.) Alfred B. Starey, in " Harper's Young People."

She-wolf of France. Isabella le Bel, wife of Edward II.

Shibboleth. A pass-word. The Ephraimites quarrelled with Jephthah, and Jephthah gathered together the men of Gilead and fought with Ephraim. There were many fugitives, and when they tried to pass the guard told them to say " Shibboleth," which the Ephraimites pronounced " Sibboleth," and by this test it was ascertained whether the person wishing to cross the river was a friend or a foe. In the Sicilian Vespers (*q. v.*), a word was given as a test of nationality. Some dried peas (*ciceri*) were shown to a suspect ; if he called them *cheecharee*, he was a Sicilian, and allowed to pass ; but if *siseri*, he was a Frenchman, and was put to death. In the great Danish slaughter on St. Bryce's Day (November 13), 1002, according to tradition, a similar test was made with the words " Chichester Church," which, being pronounced hard or soft, decided whether the speaker were Dane or Saxon.

Shinney = HOCKEY. The word " shinney," denoting a stick with a crook to it, used by boys to strike a ball with, and also applied to the game itself, is from the North of Ireland. It was in common use in the United States fifty years ago, but it is not so extensively employed to-day.

Shinplasters. Paper money; greenbacks (*q. v.*).

Ship of State. A poetical apostrophe of the political fabric of the United States. It was used by Longfellow.

> Sail on, O ship of State !
> Sail on, O Union, strong and great !
> Humanity with all its fears,
> With all the hope of future years,
> Is hanging breathless on thy fate.
> *The Building of the Ship.*

Ship of the Desert. A camel. *See* FLEET OF THE DESERT. The origin of this saying is in George Sandys's "Paraphrase of the Book of Job," 1610. It occurs in the couplet : —

> " Three thousand camels his rank pastures fed,
> Arabia's wandering ships, for traffic bred."

Ship's Husband. A part owner, or other person appointed as manager to look after and provide stores, provisions, or assistance for a ship when in port.

Ship-swallower, The. The Goodwin Sands, off the town of Deal, in the English Channel.

Shipton, Mother. *See* MOTHER SHIPTON.

Shirley Dare. (Pseud.) Mrs. S. C. D. Power, an American writer.

Shirley Penn. Literary pseudonym of Miss Sarah J. Clarke, an American author.

Shirt of Nessus. A source of misfortune from which there is no escape; a fatal present; anything that wounds the susceptibilities. *See* NESSUS'S SHIRT.

Shivering Mountain. A popular name given to Mam Tor, an eminence on the Peak, in Derbyshire, so called because of its rapid wasting away through the action of the elements. The rock falls off in flakes, or "shivers," and dust.

Shoe City. Lynn, Mass. Here are very extensive manufactures of shoes.

Shoe Pinches. We all know where the "shoe pinches;" we each of us know our own special troubles.

> *Lord Foppington.* Hark thee, shoemaker, these shoes . . . don't fit me.
> *Shoemaker.* My lord, I think they fit you very well.
> *Lord Fop.* They hurt me just below the instep.
> *Shoem.* No, my lord, they don't hurt you there.
> *Lord Fop.* I tell thee they pinch me execrably.
> *Shoem.* Why, then, my lord —
> *Lord Fop.* What! Wilt thou persuade me I cannot feel?
> *Shoem.* Your lordship may please to feel what you think fit, but that shoe does not hurt you. I think I understand my trade. — SHERIDAN, *A Trip to Scarborough.*

Shoestring District. The Sixth Congressional District of Mississippi, as laid out in 1874, is so called because it consists of a narrow strip extending along the Mississippi River almost the entire length of the State.

Shoe the Gray Goose. To undertake a difficult and profitless business. John Skelton says the attempt of the laity to reform the clergy of his time is about as mad a scheme as if they attempted to shoe wild geese.

> What hath laymen to doe,
> The gray goose to shoe?
> J. SKELTON, *Colyn Clout.*

Sholto and Reuben Percy. (Pseud.) Thomas Byerley, editor of the London "Star," and Joseph Clinton Robertson, editor of the "Philosophical Magazine."

Short-haired. The "horny-handed sons of toil" in our city politics are so named; though perhaps the term better fits the "toughs," those who from motives of convenience and policy keep their heads closely clipped. They are opposed to the "Silk Stockings," or well-to-do.

Short-lived Administration. In the political annals of England, the name given to a ministry formed by the Hon. William Pulteney, which retired from office Feb. 12, 1746, after only two days' tenure.

Short Sixes. The Sixth Regiment of Foot in the English service. *See* GURE'S GEESE.

Shot in the Locker. Lockers are compartments in ships of war for the reception of the shot. They are placed at the base of the mainmast, so that the weight of their contents may help to steady the motion of the ship. When a sailor, to express being without money, says he "has n't a shot in the locker," it is equivalent to saying that he is like a ship which has expended all her ammunition.

Shoulder-breaker. Sapor II., king of Persia, who dislocated the shoulders of all the Arabs captured in battle.

Shout of Stentor. Stentor was a Grecian warrior or herald who served in the Trojan war, and whose voice, according to Homer, was as loud as the combined tones of fifty men. *See* HORN OF FONTARABIA.

> The eloquence of the ancient Greeks can no more be heard again than the shout of Stentor or the blast of the dread horn of Fontarabia. — *Digest of Ancient and Modern History.*

Show Sunday. That Sabbath in early spring when the Royal Academy in London is opened to the friends of the artists for a private view of the annual exhibition.

Shrove-Tuesday. This is the day before Ash Wednesday (*q. v.*), and throughout Italy and other Catholic countries is held as a Carnival (*carnovale,* "farewell to flesh") or festival time. In its broadest sense "Shrovetide" includes the two or three days just before the beginning of Lent. Shrove-Tuesday is always the seventh Tuesday before Easter. It may occur any Tuesday between the 2d of February and the 8th of March. The name "Shrove-Tuesday" arose from the ancient practice in the Church of

Rome of confessing sins, and being shriven or shrove, that is, obtaining absolution, or forgiveness of sins, from the priests on that day. In Scotland Shrove-Tuesday is called " Fasten E'en," but is little thought of in that country. Shrove-Tuesday is also known in England as " Pancake Day," owing to the well-nigh universal custom of serving pancakes for dinner thereon. Says the " Water Poet," writing about this latter custom : " Shrove-Tuesday, at whose entrance in the morning all the whole kingdom is in quiet, but by the time the clock strikes eleven, which (by the help of a knavish sexton) is commonly before nine, there is a bell rung called pancake-bell, the sound whereof makes thousands of people distracted, and forgetful of either manners or humanity. Then there is a thing called wheaten flour, which the cooks do mingle with water, eggs, spice, and other tragical, magical enchantments, and they put it by little and little into a frying-pan of boiling suet, where it makes a confused, dismal hissing (like the Lernian snakes in the reeds of Acheron), until at last, by the skill of the cook, it is transformed into the form of a flip-jack, called a pancake, which ominous incantation the ignorant people do devour very greedily." Young ladies sometimes try tossing a pancake, because of the old superstition that the first person who comes to the house after she has tossed it will be her husband. Shrove-Tuesday is a legal holiday in Louisiana and in the cities of Mobile, Montgomery, and Selma, Ala.

S. H. S. *Societatis Historiæ Socius.* Fellow of the Historical Society.

Shuck. The outer covering of the spike or fruit of the maize plant. This name is peculiar to the South. In the Western and Northern States the equivalent term is " husk." So, a certain rural gathering is in the South a " shucking bee," and in the other localities named a " husking bee."

Shute. *See* CHUTE.

Si. Silicon.

Siberia, Saxon. *See* SAXON SI-BERIA.

Sibyl. The name anciently given to several prophetic women of mystical history. Some writers mention only four, — the Cytherean, the Samian, the Egyptian, and the Sardian ; but others increase the number to ten, the

Babylonian, the Libyan, the Delphian, the Cimmerian, the Cumæan, the Trojan, the Phrygian, the Tiburtian, the Samian, and the Erythrean. The history of the Cumæan sibyl, by far the most famous, is as follows : She came from the East, and appearing before King Tarquin the Proud, offered him nine books for sale. The price demanded appeared to the monarch exorbitant, and he refused to purchase them. She then went away, destroyed three, and, returning, asked as much for the remaining six as for the nine. This was again refused, whereupon she destroyed three more, and once again offered to sell him the rest, but without any abatement of the original price. Tarquin was struck by her pertinacity, and bought the books, which were found to contain advices regarding the religion and policy of the Romans. They were preserved in a subterranean chamber of the temple of Jupiter on the Capitoline, and were originally intrusted to two officials (*duumviri sacrorum*) appointed by the senate, who alone had the right to inspect them. The number of keepers was afterward increased to ten (*decemviri*), and finally, by Sulla, to fifteen (*quindecemviri*). In the year 84 B. C., the temple of Jupiter having been consumed by fire, the original Sibylline books or leaves were destroyed, whereupon a special embassy was despatched by the senate to all the cities of Greece, Italy, and Asia Minor, to collect such as were current in those regions. This being done, the new collection was deposited in the temple of Jupiter after it had been rebuilt.

Sibyl. (Pseud.) Mrs. Sallie M. D. Martin, in various Southern periodicals.

Sibylline Books. (1) The three surviving books of the Sibyl Amalthæa were preserved in a stone chest underground in the temple of Jupiter Capitolinus, and committed to the charge of custodians chosen in the same manner as the high priests. The number of custodians was at first two, then ten, and ultimately fifteen. *See* SIBYL. (2) A collection of poetical utterances in Greek, made of Jewish, Pagan, and Christian sibyllists, and compiled in the second century A. D. It is in eight books and relates to Jesus Christ.

Sibylline Leaves. The Sibylline prophecies were written in Greek, upon palm-leaves.

Sic. Doubtful.

Sicilian Anacreon. Giovanni Meli (1740–1815) was so named by his admirers.

Siciliano. (Ital.) A movement of a slow, pastoral character, in six-eight time. (Mus.)

Sicilian Vespers. The name given to a sanguinary massacre of the French, who conquered Sicily in 1266, begun at Palermo on March 30, 1282. The trouble commenced on Easter Monday through indignities offered to a bridal party by some French soldiery; the aggressor was instantly stabbed, and in a few minutes two hundred Frenchmen were slaughtered. The populace ran through the city shouting, "Let the French die!" About eight thousand perished.

Sic in originali. (Lat.) So it stands in the original.

Sic itur ad astra. (Lat.) Such is the way to immortality.

Sick, applied in England solely to nausea, is in America used for any kind of indisposition.

Sick Man of the East. Turkey. The phrase originated with the Czar Alexander I. of Russia, and alludes to the wide-spread belief that the rule of the Moslem in Europe is doomed to speedy extinction.

Sic passim. (Lat.) So in many places; here and there.

Sic sedebat. (Lat.) "Thus he sat." In his ordinary sitting posture.

Sic semper tyrannis. (Lat.) So be it ever to tyrants.

Sic transit gloria mundi. (Lat.) "Thus passes away the glory of the world." So earthly glory passes away.

Sicut ante. As before.

Sic volo, sic jubeo. (Lat.) Thus I will, thus I order.

Sic volumus. (Lat.) Thus we will it.

Sic vos non vobis. (Lat.) Thus you do not labor for yourselves. The origin of the phrase is this: Virgil wrote a distich in praise of Cæsar, which was claimed by a poet named Bathyllus; Virgil, angry, wrote beneath the distich the lines: —

"Hos ego versiculos feci, tulit alter honores ;
 Sic vos non vobis —
 Sic vos non vobis —
 Sic vos non vobis —
 Sic vos non vobis — "

Cæsar asked Bathyllus if he could finish the lines, but he could n't. Virgil then stepped up and said he could. So he finished them thus : —

" — fertis aratra boves ;
  — mellificatis apes ;
  — vellera fertis oves ;
  —nidificatis aves."

The translation of the five lines is : " These lines made I, another steals my honors ; so you for others, oxen, bear the yoke ; so you for others, bees, store up your honey ; so you for others, sheep, put on your fleece ; so you for others, birds, construct your nests."

Si Deus nobiscum, quis contra nos? (Lat.) If God be with us, who can stand against us?

Sidney Cowell. The stage-name of Mrs. Raymond Holmes.

Sidney Hyde. (Pseud.) Miss Mary Caroline Pike.

Sidney Luska. (Pseud.) Henry Harland, a well-known novelist, author of " As it was Written," " Mrs. Peixada," " The Yoke of the Thorah," etc.

Sidney's Sister, Pembroke's Mother. Mary Herbert, *née* Sidney, Countess of Pembroke (d. 1621).

Underneath this sable hearse
Lies the subject of all verse —
Sidney's sister, Pembroke's mother.
Death, ere thou hast killed another
Fair and good and learned as she,
Time shall throw his dart at thee.
                    WM. BROWNE.

Sidonian Tincture. Purple dye, Tyrian purple. The Tyrians and Sidonians were world-famed for their purple dye.

Not in that proud Sidonian tincture dyed.
    PHINEAS FLETCHER, *The Purple Island.*

Sidrophel. William Lilly, the astrologer.

Quote Ralph, " Not far from hence doth dwell
A cunning man, hight Sidrophel,
That deals in destiny's dark counsels,
And sage opinions of the moon sells ;
To whom all people, far and near,
On deep importances repair."
                    BUTLER, *Hudibras.*

Siècle d'or. (Fr.) " The age of gold." The Golden Age.

Siegfried. In Teutonic mythology the hero of the first part of the " Nibelungenlied." He was the youngest son of Siegmund and Sieglind, king and queen of the Netherlands, and was born in Rhinecastle called Xanton. He married Kriemhild, Princess of Burgundy, and sister of Gunther. Gunther

craved his assistance in carrying off
Brunhild from Issland, and Siegfried
succeeded by taking away her talisman
by main force. This excited the jealousy of Gunther, who induced Hagan,
the Dane, to murder Siegfried. Hagan
struck him with a sword in the only
vulnerable part (between the shoulder-
blades), while he stooped to quench his
thirst at a fountain.

Sieve and Shears. A method of discovering a thief. The *modus operandi* is
as follows : A sieve is nicely balanced
by the points of shears touching the
rim, and the shears are supported on
the tips of the fingers while a passage
of the Bible is read, and the apostles
Peter and Paul are asked whether so-
and-so is the culprit. When the thief's
name is uttered, the sieve spins round.
Theocritus mentions this way of divination in his " Idyll," iii., and Ben Jonson
alludes to it.

Sif. In Scandinavian mythology the
wife of Thor, and famed for the beauty
of her hair, which Loki cut off while
she was asleep. Thor compelled him
to get her a new head-covering of spun
gold, which he obtained from the
dwarfs.

Sighs, Bridge of. *See* BRIDGE OF
SIGHS.

Sigma. (Pseud.) Lucius Manlius
Sargent, in the Boston Evening " Transcript."

Signalement. (Fr.) The written
description of a person.

Signers, The. A group of worthies
whose names are perpetuated in American history, who signed the Declaration
of Independence, July 4, 1776. John
Hancock, President of the Continental
Congress, heads the list, and the document, as first published, on July 2, bore
only his name ; but two days afterwards
the whole having been agreed to, it was
signed by all the delegates and read to
the assembled people. The names of
the " Signers " are as follows, grouped
geographically : New Hampshire : Josiah Bartlett, William Whipple, Matthew
Thornton. Massachusetts Bay : Samuel Adams, John Adams, Robert Treat
Paine, Elbridge Gerry. Rhode Island :
Stephen Hopkins, William Ellery. Connecticut : Roger Sherman, Samuel Huntington, William Williams, Oliver Wolcott. New York : William Floyd, Philip
Livingston, Francis Lewis, Lewis Morris.
New Jersey : Richard Stockton, John

Witherspoon, Francis Hopkinson, John
Hart, Abraham Clark. Pennsylvania :
Robert Morris, Benjamin Rush, Benja-
min Franklin, John Morton, George
Clymer, James Smith, George Taylor,
James Wilson, George Ross. Dela-
ware : Cæsar Rodney, George Read,
Thomas M'Kean. Maryland : Samuel
Chase, William Paca, Thomas Stone,
Charles Carroll of Carrollton. Virginia :
George Wyeth, Richard Henry Lee,
Thomas Jefferson, Benjamin Harrison,
Thomas Nelson, Jr., Francis Lightfoot
Lee, Carter Braxton. North Carolina :
William Hooper, Joseph Hewes, John
Penn. South Carolina : William Rut-
ledge, Thomas Hayward, Jr., Thomas
Lynch, Jr., Arthur Middleton. Georgia :
Button Gwinnett, Lyman Hall, George
Walton.

Sign of the Sabre Cuts. A modern
euphemism signifying the outbreak of
hostilities between nations or parties,
akin to the " split arrow " of Saxon
times. It is related that when the
formal declaration of war by France
reached Berlin in July, 1870, Count
Bismarck was staying for a few days at
Varzin. The news was communicated
to him by a telegram, which was put
into his hands just as he was returning
from a drive. He at once sprang into
his carriage to go to the railway station,
and on his way through the village of
Wussow he saw the parish minister
standing at the door of his manse. " I
said nothing to him," ejaculated Bismarck, in relating the story long afterward to some friends, " but I just made
a sign as of two sabre cuts crosswise,
and he quite understood."

Signor Abacrombi. (Pseud.) James
Abercrombie, Baron Dunfermline.

Signor Scovello. The professional
name of Edward Scovell.

Siguna. In Scandinavian mythology
the wife of Loki (*q. v.*).

Silent, The. William I., Prince of
Orange (fl. 1533–1584).

Silent City. A cemetery. *See* CITY
OF THE DEAD.

Silent City. Amyclæ was a city in
Upper Calabria, said to have been peopled by a colony from the more ancient
town of Amyclæ in Laconia. The
Amycli were distinguished among ancient poets by the epithet of " taciti," or
silent, — some say, because the city
was built by the Lacedæmonians, who
adopted the system of Pythagoras and

recommended silence; while others explain that a law was enacted in this place — for the prevention of false rumors by which the people were alarmed — prohibiting any person to report the approach of an enemy. This law was, in the end, the cause of the ruin of the city, for the Dorians arrived unexpectedly and took the city. To this circumstance Silenus refers, — "Quasque evertare silentia Amyclæ." Virgil also alludes to this city in the Æneid, book x., line 564.

Silent Man, The. A nickname conferred on Gen. U. S. Grant because of his laconic mode of speech when in public life. Amid his intimates, however, he would on occasion prove himself to be both a fluent and interesting talker.

Silent One, The. Count von Moltke, the Prussian soldier (b. 1800), on account of the infrequency of his speaking in Parliament. It is a common saying, in reference to his linguistic attainments, that "Von Moltke is silent in eight languages."

Silent Sister, The. A name which has been bestowed on Trinity College, Dublin, the slight influence on modern thought exercised by which is out of all proportion to its great endowments and resources.

Silent South. A phrase indicating the thinking portion of the Southern people, as contrasted with the old Bourbon fire-eating class.

Silent Week. Holy Week, the interval between Palm Sunday and Easter Sunday, was so named in the monasteries of ancient times.

Silenus. In classic myth the son of Pan and Gæa (the earth), is generally depicted as the chief of the Satyrs, or Sileni, and as the inseparable companion of Bacchus. He was noted for his wisdom and prophetical powers. He had a temple at Elis.

Silk Stocking. The well-to-do or aristocratic members of a political party are so nicknamed in contradistinction to the Short-haired (*q. v.*).

Silly Billy. A nickname conferred on the Duke of Gloucester, one of the sons of George III., on account of the weakness of his intellect.

Siloa. A diminutive of Siloam, a pool near Jerusalem.

Or if Sion-hill
Delight the more, and Siloa's brook that flowed,
Fast by the oracle of God.
MILTON, *Paradise Lost.*

Siluria. The region including the shires of Hereford, Monmouth, Radnor, Brecon, and Glamorgan, famous for its cider and perry.

From Siluria's vats high sparkling wines
Foam in transparent floods.
THOMSON, *The Seasons.*

Silurist, The. Henry Vaughan, the British poet (fl. 1621–1695); so named because he was born among the Silures, or people of South Wales.

Silvanus. In classic myth a Roman deity who presided over woods, forests, and streams.

Silver Age. One of the four periods into which human history was divided by the classic poets. It was ruled by Jupiter, and was marked by the revolution in the seasons and the division and cultivation of land. It was preceded by the Golden, and followed by the Brazen, Age.

Silver-fork School. A name conferred on those novelists and essayists whose works abound in descriptions of "high life," and who are "sticklers for etiquette and the graces of society." Theodore Hook, Lady Blessington, Mrs. Trollope, and Lord Lytton were included in this classification.

Silver-Grays. This term originated in the State of New York, and was applied to the conservative portion of the Whig party. At a political convention in that State, certain measures proposed not being agreeable to many, they at once withdrew. As they left the meeting, it was observed that many were men whose locks were silvered by age, which drew forth the remark from some one present, "There go the silver-grays!" They were the Conservatives of their day, and were opposed to the Woolly Heads (*q. v.*).

Silver Mountain. In Assyrian mythology this corresponds to the Grecian Olympus. The epithet "silver" was doubtless suggested by some snowy, inaccessible peak, the supposed dwelling-place of the gods.

Silverpen. (Pseud.) Eliza Meteyard, English novelist (b. 1822).

Silver Streak, The. A poetical designation of the English Channel. *See* SLEEVE, THE.

Silver Thames. The river Thames is thus often alluded to by old English writers.

Silver-tongued, The. (1) William Bates, the Puritan divine (fl. 1625–

1699). (2) Anthony Hammond, the poet (fl. 1668–1738). (3) Henry Smith, the preacher (fl. 1550–1600). (4) Joshua the Sylvester, translator of Du Bartas (fl. 1563–1618).

Silver-tongued Orator of New Hampshire. William Hazeltine Gove (1817–1876). He was a famous stump-speaker.

S. I. M. Society for the Increase of the Ministry.

Simeon Toby. (Pseud.) Rev. George F. Trask, *littérateur* (1797–1875).

Simile simili gaudet. (Lat.) Like is pleased with like.

Similia similibus curantur. (Lat.) Like things are cured by like things.

Simon Snuggs. (Pseud.) Berd H. Young, in the New York "Clipper."

Si monumentum quæris, circumspice. (Lat.) "If a monument you seek, look around." If you seek a monument for him, look around you at his works, — Sir C. Wren's epitaph in St. Paul's.

Simple, The. Charles III. of France (fl. 879–929). ·

Simplex munditiis. (Lat.) Simple in neatness; unaffectedly neat.

Sin' al fine. (Ital.) To the end. (Mus.)

Sine die. (Lat.) Without naming a day for another meeting; postponing indefinitely.

Sine invidia. (Lat.) Without envy.

Sine odio. (Lat.) "Without hatred." Without any feeling of animosity.

Sine qua non. (Lat.) "Without which not." An indispensable condition; a thing absolutely necessary.

Sinews of War. Money is called τὰ νεῦρα τοῦ πολέμου in Libanius; and Cicero, in his "Philippics," speaks of "nervos belli, infinitam pecuniam."

He who first called money the sinews of the State seems to have said this with especial reference to war. — PLUTARCH.

Sing. Singular.

Singing Sibyl. Mrs. M. V. Victor (fl. 1830–1885), who at the age of sixteen was known as the "Singing Sibyl" of the "Home Journal." She wrote many poems and stories, and contributed to a long list of periodicals.

Single-Speech Hamilton. Rt. Hon. W. G. Hamilton, who was Chancellor of the Exchequer in Ireland, spoke but once in Parliament (Nov. 13, 1755), but

that was "a masterly torrent of eloquence which astonished every one."

Singular Doctor. William of Occam, the schoolman (d. 1347).

Sinistra. (Ital.) The left hand.

Sink-holes. Abrupt indentations in the soil, from the bottom of which mineral springs frequently issue.

Sinon. In classic myth the cunning Greek who induced the Trojans to drag the famous wooden horse into their city.

Sioux Falls Constitution. An instrument drawn up by the people of Southern Dakota, in 1885, and which was embodied in the constitution submitted to popular vote for the admission of the Territory of Dakota as two States, in 1889.

Sioux War. In 1876 occurred a struggle between the United States and the Sioux Indians, known to history by the above name. In 1867 the tribe had signed a treaty by which they engaged to relinquish all their territory south of the Niobrara River, and retire to a new reservation in Dakota, called the Black Hills, by Jan. 1, 1876. In the mean time gold was discovered in the reservation, and hordes of adventurers flocked into the Black Hills. This circumstance gave the Sioux a pretext for making incursions into the surrounding country, burning, stealing, and murdering all who opposed them. A large force of regulars was despatched under Generals Terry and Crook to drive them back upon their reservation, and the savages were crowded back upon the Big Horn Mountains. Generals Custer and Reno were sent forward to discover the exact location of the enemy, and found them encamped along the left bank of the Little Horn River. Without waiting for reinforcements Custer charged upon the Indians, June 25, and was immediately surrounded by a force many times exceeding his own. The details of the fight are not known, for every man, including Custer himself, fell in the fight. Reinforcements were hurried forward, and soon the Indians were so hardly pressed that the remaining bands, under Sitting Bull and Crazy Horse, escaped across the Canadian border. Negotiations were opened with the Indians through a commission headed by General Terry. Pardon for past offences was offered conditional upon future good behavior, but the proposal was rejected with scorn by Sitting Bull and his chiefs. Negotiations were abruptly broken off, and the Indians returned to their camp in the British dominions north of Milk River.

Si quæris peninsulam amœnam, circumspice. (Lat.) "If thou seekest a beautiful peninsula, behold it here." The motto of Michigan.

Sirens. In classic myth beautiful maidens who sat on the shore of a certain island or headland in the southwest coast of Italy, and sang with bewitching sweetness songs that allured the passing sailor to draw near, only to meet his death. *See* ORPHEUS. There is a close resemblance between the Sirens and the Mermaidens of Northern mythology.

Sirens of the Ditch. Frogs were so named by Tasso.

Sirius (the dog star). A very bright star of the first magnitude in the constellation of the Great Dog. In ancient times the rising and setting of Sirius was watched with much solicitude. The Thebans determined the length of the year by the number of its risings. To the Egyptians it was ominous of agricultural prosperity or blighting drought, since it foretold to them the overflow of the river Nile, when they sowed their grain. The Romans annually sacrificed a dog to Sirius, to court its favor. The Eastern nations looked to its rising as the precursor of great heat on the earth, hence to that portion of the year the ancients gave the name of "dog-days." It is with us overhead in the daytime during the dog-days, and so invisible, and is at night in the lower hemisphere, but is visible to us about midwinter.

Sir Jack Brag. A nickname bestowed on Sir John Burgoyne (1723–1792), for his boastful swaggering ways.

Sir Jawbone. A nickname fastened on Sir George Bowen, in 1885–1886, Governor of Hong Kong. Sir George, who was rather devoid of tact, thought that he had hit off a very neat compliment to Li-Hung-Chang, the eminent statesman, by dubbing him "the Chinese Bismarck;" but whether it was that Li didn't appreciate it, or took the full measure of Sir George, he retaliated by speaking of Sir George as "Sir Jawbone," by which name he will ever live in the memory of Hong Kong.

Sir John Edgar. (Pseud.) Sir Richard Steele, English essayist and dramatist (1671–1729).

Sir Morgan Odoherty. (Pseud.) William Maginn, Irish author (1793–1842).

Sir Oracle. A dictatorial prig; a dogmatic pedant.

> I am sir Oracle,
> And when I ope my lips, let no dog bark.
> SHAKSPEARE, *Merchant of Venice.*

Sir Thomas Fitz-Osborne. (Pseud.) William Melmouth, English miscellaneous writer (1710–1799).

S. Isl. Sandwich Islands.

Sister Isle, The. Ireland has been so named with reference to England.

Sisters of the West. (Pseud.) Mrs. Eleanor Percy Lee (b. 1819) and Mrs. Catherine Ann Warfield (b. 1822), American poets.

Siste, viator. (Lat.) Stop, traveller.

Sisyphus. In classic mythology the founder and king of Ephyra and the father of Odysseus. On account of his colossal wickedness he suffered a singular punishment in the lower world. He was condemned to roll an immense bowlder from the bottom to the summit of a hill, which, whenever it reached the top, rolled down again, and the task of Sisyphus began anew.

Siva. In Hindu mythology the name of the third deity in the Hindu triad, wherein he represents the principle of destruction.

Si vis pacem, para bellum. (Lat.) If you wish peace, prepare for war.

Six Bourgeois of Calais. The half-dozen devoted citizens who, at the capture of their city by Edward III. of England in 1347, offered themselves as hostages. Their lives were spared through the intercession of Queen Philippa. In 1885 a monument was erected to their memory, consisting of a group with Eustache de Saint-Pierre, the leader, in the centre.

Six Boy Kings. Edmund, Edred, Edwy, Edgar, Edward, and Ethelred, of England; so named for their youth at the time of their accession.

Sixes and Sevens. This phrase is of considerable antiquity. Shakspeare and Bacon use it, and their example has been followed by Arbuthnot and Swift. Many speculations as to its origin have been made. Some have thought it an allusion to Job's troubles (Job v. 19); others think it is in some way connected with six working days out of the seven days in a week; and the editor of "Notes and Queries" connects it with the proverbially unlucky number thirteen. Nares (p. 467) thinks it was originally "taken from the game of tables or backgammon, in which to leave single men exposed to the throws of *six* or *seven* is to leave them negligently, and under the greatest hazard, since there are more chances for throwing those numbers than for any other."

Six Months' War. The war between Prussia and France. Napoleon III. left St. Cloud, July 28, 1870, and Paris capitulated Jan. 28, 1871.

Six Nations. *See* IROQUOIS.

Sixpenny War. The O. P. (old prices) riot of Covent Garden in 1809. *See* O. P. RIOTS.

Six-stringed Whip. The "Six Articles" often mentioned in the ecclesiastical history of England, in the sixteenth century, were articles imposed by Act of Parliament in 1539, when Henry VIII., being displeased with some of the bishops most favorable to the Reformation, their opponents for a time regained the ascendency. These articles asserted the doctrine of transubstantiation, declared communion in both kinds not to be necessary, condemned the marriage of priests, enjoined the continued observance of vows of chastity, and sanctioned private masses and auricular confession. The act imposing them was popularly called "the six-stringed whip."

Sixteen-string Jack. John Rann, the notorious highwayman, equally famous for his foppery. He wore sixteen tags, eight at each knee. Hanged in 1774.

S. J. Society of Jesus.

S. J. C. Supreme Judical Court.

Skedaddle. This word is generally thought to be an Americanism, but it has been long commonly used in Scotland in the sense of spilling, as, " You will skedaddle that milk." The American use of the word has, however, classical authority.

Skidbladnir. In Scandinavian mythology the name of a vessel built by the gods and given to Frey. When its sails were set it had always a fair wind.

Skin-and-Bone. The by-name given to General Mahone, of the Confederacy, by his soldiery.

Skr. Sanskrit.

Sky-lark. A lark with the " skies " or " 'scis." The Westminster boys used to style themselves Romans, and the " town," Volsci; the latter word was curtailed to " 'sci " (sky). A row between the Westminsterians and the town roughs was called a " 'sci-lark " or a lark with the Volsci.

S. L. Solicitor at Law (Scot.).

Slashers, The, or **Old Brags, The.** A nickname for the Twenty-eighth Regiment in the English army, because of the boasting indulged in by the men when they recount the deeds of their predecessors.

S. lat. South latitude.

Slate. The cut-and-dried programme of a political faction or party in the United States is named "the slate." To "smash the slate" is to defeat it.

Slave Coast. *See* GUINEA COAST.

Slave Code. Those laws, written and unwritten, which existed in the Southern States for the government of the negro slaves. They were wiped out of existence with the abolition of slavery.

Sleep, Twin Brother of. *See* TWIN BROTHER OF SLEEP.

Sleepy Queen's, The. *See* QUEEN'S OWN.

Sleeve, The. The meaning of the French name for the English Channel, " La Manche," so called from its shape. *See* SILVER STREAK.

Sleipnir. In Scandinavian mythology the name of Odin's horse, who carries his rider over sea and land.

Slentando. (Ital.) Slacken the time. (Mus.)

Sling. A sling is an American drink composed of equal parts of spirit and water. A "rum sling" is, accordingly, half rum and half water. Probably the original of sling was the diminutive "ling" as in duckling. A "ginling" would in that case mean a small or weakened glass of gin. This, it is but right to say, is altogether conjectural.

Slip. "Slip" has acquired a new meaning in America. It means an opening between two wharves or in a dock; hence many localities in the city of New York bear such names as "Peck Slip," etc.

S. M. State Militia; short metre; Sergeant-Major; Sons of Malta.

Small-beer Poet. So William Cobbett dubbed William Thomas Fitzgerald, a rhymester (fl. 1759–1829), who was also pilloried by Byron in "English Bards and Scotch Reviewers."

Small Potatoes. Any thing or any body small, mean, or petty. *See* PICA-

YUNE. The complete phrase is "Small potatoes and few in a hill."

Smalls. *See* LITTLE-GO.

Smart. *See* CLEVER and RIGHT SMART.

Smart Chance. "Smart chance," "smart piece," "smart sprinkle," are American provincialisms, implying a good deal or a large quantity. It is an Old English form of speech. In the villages round Guildford in Surrey, fifty years ago, a "smart lot" was the usual expression for a good many. A "smart lot of apples" and similar phrases were very common, and may possibly still survive.

Smart Money. Money paid by a person to obtain exemption from some disagreeable office or duty. It used to be paid for exemption from military service.

Smectymnus. A word composed of the initials of certain writers against episcopacy in the seventeenth century,— Stephen Marshall, Edmund Calamy, Thomas Young, Matthew Newcomen, William Spurston, — who were antagonized by Bishop Hall, in 1640, in his "Divine Right of Episcopacy."

Smelfungus. So Sterne nicknamed Smollett on account of a volume of travels' published in 1766, which contained jaundiced and distorted accounts of what he saw by the way.

Smile. To "smile" is the Americanism, once immensely popular from Maine to California, used to denote the act of drinking liquor. "Let's smile" was a universally understood talisman.

Smile, Sardonic. *See* SARDONIC SMILE.

Smiling Island, The. Ischia, in the Bay of Naples. The soil is very fertile, and the island is one lovely garden.

S. M. Lond. Soc. *Societatis Medicæ Londoniensis Socius.* Member of the London Medical Society.

S. M. Lond. Soc. Cor. *Societatis Medicæ Londonensis Socius Correspondens.* Corresponding Member of the London Medical Society.

Smoky City. *See* IRON CITY.

Smorzando. (Ital.) Diminish or smother the sounds. (Mus.)

S. n. *Secundum naturam.* According to nature.

Sn. *Stannum.* Tin.

Snacks. In Wadd's "Memorabilia," he gives a brief account of the plague in London, in which he states that the important office of body-searcher was held by a man named Snacks. During the height of the plague his business increased so fast that he gave to any one who would assist in the hazardous business half the profits. Thus those who joined him were said to "go with Snacks;" and hence arose the expression "going snacks," meaning "dividing the spoil."

Snoggins. (Pseud.) Henry M. Putney, in the Manchester, N. H., "Mirror" (1860–1870).

Snowdonia. The district which contains the mountain range of Snowdon, Wales.

Snow King. Gustavus Adolphus of Sweden (fl. 1594–1632).

Snuffed out. A California euphemism for death.

Soave. (Ital.) In a soft, sweet, and delicate style. (Mus.)

Society for the Repeal of the Union. An Irish association was formed for this object under the leadership of Daniel O'Connell in 1829.

Socinianism. An Italian heresy of the sixteenth century, denying the Divine Trinity, the deity of Christ, the personality of the Devil, the atonement of Christ, and the eternity of future punishment.

Soc. Isl. Society Islands.

Socius Ejectus. (Pseud.) Thomas Baker, English antiquary (1656–1740).

Sœurs de charité. (Fr.) Sisters of Charity.

S. of Sol. Song of Solomon.

Soft Money. Paper money as distinguished from "hard money," or specie; a term in colloquial use in the United States. *See* GREENBACKERS.

Soft Shells. *See* HARD SHELLS.

Soi-disant. (Fr.) Self-styled; pretended.

Soirée. (Fr.) An evening party.

Sojer. A sailor-man's epithet for an idler or an incompetent fellow. The antipathy between soldiers and sailors is well established; a sailor can apply no more opprobrious name to another than that of "sojer." As a verb, the word, of course, means shirking duty.

Sol. In classic mythology a surname of Apollo.

Sol. Solomon; solution.

Solamen curarum. (Lat.) A solace or consoler of one's cares.

Solar City. The same as CITY OF THE SUN (*q. v.*).

Soldier of the Andes. Juan Espinosa, South American general (1804–1871).

Soldiers' Friend. (1) Frederick, Duke of York, second son of George III. (fl. 1763–1827), who was in command of the English troops in the Netherlands during the French Revolution. In every possible way he strove to ameliorate the hardships of the rank and file, for which he was publicly thanked by Parliament in 1814. (2) Count Leo Schwabe, who died at Beachmont, Mass., 1889, was widely known as the "Soldiers' Friend." On soldiers and sailors in distress or sickness he expended a large fortune; and no emergency was called to his attention without being met at once by a liberal donation. His first contribution of this character is recorded in Hadley's "Massachusetts in the Rebellion," the occasion referred to being that of Count Schwabe's visit to Commodore Tatnall in Connecticut during the days when the call came for three months' men.

"To the Connecticut troops," says Hadley, "he gave a full supply of hospital stores, his first contribution to the wants of the army. Since then, like the dew of heaven, his generosity has fallen upon every camp and almost every hospital cot in the vast arena of the Union arms."

Solemn Doctor. Henry Goerhals (fl. 1227–1293), the famous scholastic, was so named by the Sorbonne.

Solemn League and Covenant. A league between England and Scotland solemnly adopted by the Parliament, Sept. 25, 1643, accepted by Charles II., August 16, 1650, but repudiated by him after the Restoration, in 1661, declared to be illegal by Parliament, and ordered to be burned. It consisted of six articles, and was aimed chiefly at the preservation of the Reformed Church and the suppression of papacy.

Sol.-Gen. Solicitor-General.

Solid Doctor. Richard Middleton. *See* PROFOUND DOCTOR.

Soli Deo gloria. (Lat.) Glory to God alone.

Solid South, Solid North. The phrase "Solid South" denotes a political solidarity dominated by the Democratic party such as obtained in ante-bellum days. It came into vogue about ten years after the close of the war, and was confronted by a portion of the newspaper press with a "Solid North," based on a survival of the old war feeling. John Singleton Mosby, American soldier (b. 1833), was the first to use the phrase "Solid South," in a letter to the New York "Herald," in 1876, supporting the candidacy of R. B. Hayes for the Presidency.

Solitaire. (Pseud.) John S. Robb, in the Western press.

Solomon Abrabanel. (Pseud.) William Arnall.

Solomon Bell. (Pseud.) William Joseph Snelling, an American writer.

Solomon of France. (1) Charles V. (fl. 1337–1380). (2) Saint Louis (Louis IX.) (fl. 1215–1270).

So long. This phrase, so often heard in the United States for "good-by," is a pure Americanism, and according to Bartlett is used by Louisianians in that sense.

Solon of Parnassus. Boileau (fl. 1636–1711), was so named by Voltaire because of his magnificent "Art of Poetry," a work unparalleled before or since.

Sommersett's Case. A famous habeas corpus case in England in 1772, before Lord Mansfield, brought on behalf of Thomas Sommersett, a negro. It established the principle that a slave brought upon English soil became thereby free. Also called the "Negro Case."

Somnus. In classic myth the deity who personified Sleep, the son of Nox and Erebus.

Song of Degrees. The fifteen Psalms, cxx. to cxxxiv.; so called because they are prophetic of the return or "going up" from captivity. Some think there is a connection between these Psalms and the fifteen steps of the Temple porch.

Song of Roland. Roland was the renowned nephew of Charlemagne, slain in the pass of Roncesvalles. At the battle of Hastings, Taillefer advanced on horseback before the invading army, tossing his truncheon, and gave the signal for the attack by singing this famous song.

Sonica. (Pseud.) Robert W. McAlpine, in the New York "Sun."

Son of Jupiter Ammon. Alexander the Great was so named. His father, Philip, claimed descent from Hercules and consequently from Jupiter. By the Libyan priesthood (*see* AMMON) he was saluted as the son of Ammon.

Son of Perdition. (1) Judas Iscariot. See John xvii. 12. (2) Antichrist.

Son of Saint Louis, ascend to Heaven. This phrase is generally believed to have been used by the Abbé Edgeworth, the confessor of Louis XVI., at the instant the axe fell which deprived that ill-fated monarch of his head. The Abbé always said he did not use the words, and it is now known that the phrase was invented for him by the editor of " Le Républicain Français."

Son of the Devil. Ezzelino (fl. 1215–1259), chief of the Ghibellines and Governor of Vicenza, was so named on account of his infamous cruelties.

Son of the Last Man. *See* LAST MAN. Charles II. of England was so named by the Covenanters because, as they said, his father, Charles I., would be the " Last Man " to sit on the throne of England.

Sons of Han. The Chinese are so named. Han was the founder of the twenty-sixth dynasty (206–220 A.D.), from whom their modern history begins.

Sons of Thunder (Boanerges). James and John, the sons of Zebedee. *See* Mark iii. 17.

Sophie Croizette. The stage-name of Baroness Stern, the famous French actress.

Sophie Eyre. The stage-name of Mrs. Lonsdale, *née* Ryan.

Sophie May. (Pseud.) (1) Miss Rebecca Clarke, American writer, author of the " Little Prudy " stories, whose fame equals that of Miss Alcott's " Little Women." (2) Sophie Frederika Elizabeth Meyer.

Sophie Menter. The stage-name of Frau Popper.

Sophie Sparkle. (Pseud.) Jennie E. Hicks.

Sorehead. One who " kicks against the pricks " of party discipline, or who inveighs against party action and refuses to abide thereby.

Sorrow, China's. *See* CHINA'S SORROW.

Sorrowful Stone. *See* ELEUSINIAN MYSTERIES.

Sostenuto, or **Sost.** (Ital.) Sustained, continuous in regard to tone. (Mus.)

Sothic Year. The Persian year consists of 365 days, so that a day is lost in four years, and the lost bits in the course of 1,460 years amount to a year. This period is called a sothic period, and the reclaimed year made up of the bits is called a sothic year, from Sothis (the dog-star), at whose rising it commences.

Sotto voce. (Ital.) In an undertone. (Mus.)

Soul-drivers. About 1670 fifteen hundred bond-servants, called "redemptioners," were sold into Virginia. In Pennsylvania the men who took these unfortunate creatures about the country, and hawked them to the farmers, were called " Soul-drivers."

Sour, Soured. The humorous son of the West speaks of the discontented settler as a man who has " soured " on his section. The jilted lover " sours " on his former flame, and to lose money by the failure of a bank has " soured " the stockholders.

Southampton's Wise Men. In the early part of the present century the people of Southampton cut a ditch for barges between Southampton and Redbridge ; but as barges could go without paying dues through Southampton Water, the ditch or canal was never used. This wise scheme was compared to that of the man who cut two holes through the wall, one for the great cat and the other for its kitten.

South Britain. England and Wales, as distinguished from Scotland, popularly called North Britain.

South Carolina. This State derived its name from Charles I. of England.

Southern Gael. John Locke, a well-known Irish poet, journalist, and Nationalist resident in America (d. 1889).

Southern Gate of the Sun. The sign Capricornus, or winter solstice ; so called because it is the most southern limit of the sun's course in the ecliptic.

Southern Scott. Lord Byron called Ariosto the Sir Walter Scott of Italy.

South Sea. The Pacific Ocean. The name, " Mar del Sur," was bestowed by Vasco Nunez de Balboa, in 1513, because from the spot where he obtained his first view of the great expanse of water only its southern aspect was visible. The name is still often applied in literature, though with special reference to that part south of the equator.

South-Sea Bubble. The South Sea Company was established in 1710, and collapsed in 1720, ruining thousands. At first rashly managed, dishonesty soon became a part of its methods, and the estates of the directors, to the value of £2,000,000, were confiscated in 1721, and sold. Shares issued at £100 rose to £1,000, and scarcely a person in public life but was more or less deeply involved.

Souvenir. (Fr.) " Remembrance." A keepsake.

Sovereign of the Seas. A name by which England is often alluded to, with reference to her supremacy upon the ocean.

S. P. *Sine prole.* Without issue.

Sp. Spain; Spanish.

Spain, Garden of. *See* GARDEN OF SPAIN.

Spanish Brutus. Alphonso Perez de Guzman (fl. 1258–1320).

Spanish Ennius. Juan de Mena, the poet (fl. 1412–1456).

Spanish Fury. In 1576, the city of Antwerp was seized by the Spanish soldiery; eight thousand citizens were murdered in cold blood, and one thousand buildings burned. This act is known to history as "the Spanish Fury," or "the Fury of Antwerp."

Spanish Horaces. The brothers Argensola, whose Christian names were Lupercia and Bartolome.

Spanish Jack. A noted felon who was executed at Maidstone, England, April 18, 1756, for stealing. His real name was Bli Gonzales, which upon conversion he changed to John Symmonds.

Spanish Main. Among English voyagers and colonists of two or three centuries ago this name indicated the northeast coast of South America, from the Mosquito Coast to the Leeward Islands. A mistaken idea has prevailed among authors that this term referred to the Caribbean Sea, in the sense of main ocean; but the Caribbean Sea, though a part of the Atlantic, is not the main ocean, being almost a land-locked sea. The term has reference to the mainland, or continent.

Spanish Match. The name given to the projected marriage of Philip of Spain and Mary of England, in 1554.

Spanish Succession. What is known to European history as the War of the

Spanish Succession was a struggle which commenced May 4, 1702, and ended March 13, 1713, between England, France, Austria, and the United Provinces to determine the succession to the throne of Spain left vacant by the death of Charles II.

Spanish Tyrtæus. An honorary title conferred on Manuel José Quintana (fl. 1772–1857), the Spanish poet and orator.

Spanish Victor Hugo. José Zorilla (b. 1829), poet-laureate of Spain.

Spare the Rod and Spoil the Child. This saying is frequently erroneously attributed to Solomon. It is, however, from "Hudibras," and is to be found in Part II., canto 1, verse 45. What Solomon really did say was, "He that spareth the rod hateth his son" (Proverbs xiii. 24).

Sparse. This word has been said to be an Americanism, but it is not so. It is an old English word, and is to be found as a verb in the past tense in "Sternhold and Hopkins' Psalms," A. D. 1611. The tenth verse of the Forty-fourth Psalm is paraphrased thus : —

" Thou mad'st us fly before our foes
And so were over-trod,
Our enemies rob'd and spoyl'd our goods
When we were spars't abroad."

This evidently points to the word "disperse" (which in country places is usually pronounced as though written "disparse") as the origin of "sparse." Anything dispersed or scattered would of course be "sparsely" localized.

Spartan Broth. Sorry fare.

The promoters would be reduced to dine on Spartan broth in Leicester Square. — *Daily News,* Feb. 25, 1879.

Spartan Dog. A bloodhound.

O Spartan dog !
More fell than anguish, hunger, or the sea !
SHAKSPEARE, *Othello.*

S. P. A. S. *Societatis Philosophicæ Americanæ Socius.* Member of the American Philosophical Society.

Spasmodic School. So Professor Aytoun dubs a certain class of modern English writers, such as Carlyle, Bailey, Alexander Smith, Sydney Dobell, and others, whose style is, he thinks, marked by "spasmodic or forced conceits."

Speak by the Card. "Card" was the original name for the mariner's compass. Shakspeare ("Macbeth" i. 3) has —

" All the quarters that they know
I' the shipman's card."

Hence to "speak by the card" meant to speak with absolute correctness, true to a single point.

Speaker's Eye. The rule in the House of Commons is that the member whose rising to address the House is first observed by the speaker shall be allowed precedence. At all other times the members are known by the names of the places they represent, as "the right honorable member for Derby," etc., but when called upon by the speaker he names them, as "Mr. Gladstone," etc. The custom of leaving the speaker to call on the members originated on Nov. 25, 1640, when, a number of members rising together, "the confusion became intolerable." At last, "the House determined for Mr. White, and the speaker's eye was adjudged to be evermore the rule."

Spectas et spectaberis. (Lat.) You will see and be seen.

Spectator. (Pseud.) Henry Walter Bellew, in the Calcutta "Englishman."

Spellbinders. The name given to members of a Republican organization during the Harrison campaign in 1888. A "Spellbinder" is a person who holds other persons spellbound. A member of the Republican National Committee, noticing that the speakers, in reporting to the committee, invariably said that they had held their audiences "spellbound," gave them the name of "Spellbinders." The New York "Sun" applied the name to the Republican leaders who, soon after the election, held a jubilation at Delmonico's.

Speranza. (Pseud.) Lady Wilde, Irish poet (b. 1806).

Spero meliora. (Lat.) I hope for better times, or things.

Spes mea Christus. (Lat.) Christ is my hope.

S. P. G. Society for the Propagation of the Gospel.

Sp. gr. Specific gravity.

Sphinx. In mythology a monster usually represented as possessing the winged body of a lion and the face and bust of a young woman, though other forms are frequent. *See* RIDDLE OF THE SPHINX. The word "sphinx" signifies "squeezer" or "strangler."

Sphinxland. Egypt has been so named.

Spikes. (Pseud.) Randolph Botts, a miscellaneous writer, a resident of Albany, N. Y.

Spindles, City of. *See* CITY OF SPINDLES.

Spiral Groove. (Pseud.) Wilson Macdonald, in "Turf, Field, and Farm."

Spirito, or **Con Spirito.** (Ital.) With spirit. (Mus.)

Spiritoso. (Ital.) With great spirit. (Mus.)

Spirits and Crimps. People in England in the eighteenth century whose trade it was to entrap and fraudulently persuade men and women to go to the Virginia colonies.

Spirituel. (Fr.) Intellectual; witty.

Spitting-pot. Peter Pindar, in a letter to the elder Disraeli, calls Boswell "Johnson's Spitting-pot," in allusion to his well-known receptivity of the great lexicographer's smallest sayings.

Spittle Sermons. Sermons preached formerly at the Spittle, London, in a pulpit erected expressly for the purpose. Subsequently they were preached at Christchurch, City, on Easter Monday and Tuesday.

Splendide mendax. (Lat.) Nobly false; untruthful for a good object, hence, *ironically*, egregiously false.

Spoils. The pecuniary rewards of office contingent upon a victory at the polls. William M. Marcy was the author of the famous phrase "To the victors belong the spoils," and upon which axiom the government of the United States had always been conducted until the appearance of the "Civil Service Reform" agitation, whose advocates denounced what they termed the "Spoils System." *See* CIVIL SERVICE REFORM.

Spoke in his Wheel. To "put a spoke in his wheel" is to thwart or hinder a man in his design. Richardson thinks it meant to put a spike in the nave so as to prevent the wheel from turning. A more probable derivation refers it to a time when wheels were made of solid discs of wood without radiating bars. Such wheels are still in use on Dartmoor for vehicles called "three-wheeled buts." There are no shafts, and consequently the horse has no check on the vehicle in descending hills. To remedy this, the front wheel of the three has some holes bored through it, and the speed is checked by putting a stout bar of wood, locally called a "spoke," through one of the holes, thus effectually blocking it. Mr. Cobden totally misunderstood the meaning of the word. Writing, in 1852, as to W. J. Fox's candidature for Oldham, he says, " If I can put a spoke in Fox's wheel, when in Lancashire, I shall be right glad to do so." — *Life of Sir Joshua Walmsley.*

Spolia opima. (Lat.) In ancient Rome, the arms and baggage taken in personal conflict by a victorious general from the opposing leader.

Sponte sua. (Lat.) Of one's own free will; of one's own accord.

Sport of Kings. Hunting has been so named.

Spotted Panther. In Dryden's " Hind and Panther," the latter stands for the Church of England, covered with spots or blemishes of error, while the Church of Rome is depicted as being as pure as the lily-white hind.

Spout, Up the. *See* GONE UP.

S. P. Q. R. *Senatus Populusque Romani.* The Senate and the people of Rome.

Spread-eagle Oratory. A colloquial term for stump speaking in vogue in the United States, and which is thus defined by a writer in the " North American Review," November, 1858. " A compound of exaggeration, effrontery, bombast, and extravagance, mixed metaphors, platitudes, defiant threats thrown at the world, and irreverent appeals to the Almighty."

Springers. A nickname given to the Sixty-second Regiment in the English army.

S. P. R. L. Society for the Promotion of Religion and Learning.

Spy in Washington. *See* GENEVESE TRAVELLER.

Spy Wednesday. The Wednesday immediately preceding Good Friday, when Judas bargained to become the paid spy of the Sanhedrim.

sq. ft. Square foot, or square feet.

sq. in. Square inch, or inches.

sq. m. Square mile, or miles.

sq. r. Square rod, or rods.

Squadron Volante. *See* FLYING SCOTCH SQUADRON.

Squatter. One who does not pre-empt land in the legal way, but "squats " on the spot that happens to suit him.

Squatter Sovereignty. In American political nomenclature a phrase meaning " popular sovereignty." It was

much used by Stephen A. Douglas, who claimed to have invented it, but Charles Sumner retorted that the expression could be found in Milton's " Paradise Lost," where we are told that " Satan sat like a toad squat by the ear of Eve."

Squint-eyed. The surname (Guercino) conferred on Giovanni Francesco Barbieri, the great painter (fl. 1590– 1666).

sq. yd. Square yard.

Sr. Sir ; senior ; strontium.

S. R. I. *Sacrum Romanum Imperium.* Holy Roman Empire.

S. R. S. *Societatis Regiæ Socius.* Fellow of the Royal Society.

S. S. Sunday-school.

SS. Saints.

SS., or ss. *Scilicet.* To wit.

Ss. Half (*semis*); Sessions.

S. S. C. Solicitor before the Supreme Court (Scotland).

S.-S.-E. South-southeast.

S.-S.-W. South-southwest.

St. Saint; street; strait.

Staccato. (Ital.) In a detached, abrupt manner. (Mus.)

Staircase Wit. A belated retort ; a rejoinder not made at the apposite time, but given as a parting shot when one is going away.

Stalwarts. In its first inception this term denoted those Republicans who were disgusted with the pacificatory measures of President Hayes toward the South. It was coined by James G. Blaine. But, in 1880, those who at Chicago favored the nomination of General Grant and opposed that of Mr. Blaine appropriated it to themselves. In the State of New York the faction fight was especially bitter, and the opponents of the Stalwarts were known as Half-breeds and Featherheads (*q. v.*).

Stammerer, The. (1) Louis II. of France (fl. 846–879). (2) Michael II., Emperor of the East (d. 829). (3) Notger of St. Gall (fl. 830–912).

Stamp Act. In 1765 the British Parliament imposed a direct tax upon the colonies. The object was to defray the expenses of the French, or border, war from 1755 to 1763. It was claimed that the colonies ought to foot the bill, as it was waged in their interest. But they protested, and when war came, that direct tax or stamp act was one of the grievances complained of. It was, however, repealed in 1766. "No taxation without representation," was the position taken.

Stamp-Act Congress. A congress of delegates from nine of the colonies which met in New York City in October, 1765.

Stampede. (Pseud.) Jonathan F. Kelly, American humorist.

Standing Stones of Stennis. "The Standing Stones of Stennis, in the Orkneys, as by a little pleonasm this remarkable monument is termed, furnish an irresistible refutation of the opinion of such antiquaries as hold that the circles, usually called Druidical, were peculiar to that race of priests. There is every reason to believe that the custom was as prevalent in Scandinavia as in Gaul or Britain, and as common to the mythology of Odin as to Druidical superstition. There is every reason to think that the Druids never occupied any part of the Orkneys; and tradition, as well as history, ascribes the Stones of Stennis to the Scandinavians. Two large sheets of water, communicating with the sea, are connected by a causeway, with openings permitting the tide to rise and recede, which is called the Bridge of Broisgar. Upon the eastern tongue of land appear the Standing Stones, arranged in the form of a half circle, or rather a horseshoe, the height of the pillars being fifteen feet and upwards. Within this circle lies a stone, probably sacrificial. One of the pillars, a little to the westward, is perforated with a circular hole, through which loving couples are wont to join hands when they take the Promise of Odin. The enclosure is surrounded by barrows, and on the opposite isthmus, advancing towards the Bridge of Broisgar, there is another monument of Standing Stones, which in this case is completely circular. They are less in size than those on the eastern side of the lake, their height running only from ten or twelve to fourteen feet. This western circle is surrounded by a deep trench drawn on the outside of the pillars; and there are four tumuli, or mounds of earth, regularly disposed around it. Stonehenge excels this Orcadian monument; but that of Stennis is the only one in Britain which can be said to approach it in consequence. All the northern nations marked by those huge enclosures the places of popular meeting, either for religious worship or the transaction of public business of a temporal nature. The 'Northern Popular Antiquities' contain a particular account of the manner in which the Helga Fels, or Holy Rock, was set apart by the Pontiff Thorolf for solemn occasions." — SCOTT.

Stans pede in uno. (Lat.) Standing on one foot.

Star City. Lafayette, Ind.

Stare super vias antiquas. (Lat.) "To stand upon the ancient paths." Not readily to yield to bold innovations.

Star-eyed Goddess of Reform. This phrase was coined by Henry Watterson, editor of the Louisville "Courier-Journal," when he apostrophized a tariff reduction as "the Star-eyed Goddess of Revenue Reform."

Stark. (Ger.) Forte, loud; as *Mit starken Stimmen.* (Mus.)

Star of the North. The State of Minnesota is sometimes alluded to by this title, because of the motto on its coat of arms, *L'Étoile du Nord.*

Star Sisters. Pauline, Lucille, and Helen Western, American actresses. Pauline died in 1877.

Starvation Dundas. A nickname given to Henry Dundas, first Lord Melville, who is said to have been the coiner of the word "starvation" in a debate in Parliament in 1775, on the American colonies.

Starving Time, The. "When Capt. John Smith went back to England, in 1609, there were nearly five hundred white people in Virginia. But the settlers soon got into trouble with the Indians, who lay in the woods and killed every one that ventured out. There was no longer any chance to buy corn, and food was soon exhausted. The starving people ate the hogs, the dogs, and the horses, even to the skins. Then they ate rats, mice, snakes, toadstools, and whatever they could get that might stop their hunger. A dead Indian was presently eaten; and as their hunger grew more extreme, they were forced to consume their own dead. Starving men wandered off into the woods and died there; their companions, finding them, devoured them as hungry wild beasts might have done. This was always afterward remembered as 'the Starving Time.'" — EGGLESTON.

Stat. Statute.

Stated Salary. *See* CALL.

State of Camden and Amboy. New Jersey was so called by a statesman of national reputation because of the monopolistic privileges enjoyed by the railroad known by that name until the passage of the " New Jersey General R. R. Act."

State of Franklin. An old name of Tennessee, under which it was organized in 1785.

State Rights. The doctrine of State Rights maintains as its postulate that the States of the Union are sovereign States, and that the mutual union thereof is dissolvable at the pleasure of any of them. The Southern States based their right to secede, in 1861, upon the doctrine of State Rights.

State, Ship of. *See* SHIP OF STATE.

Stat magni nominis umbra. (Lat.) He stands the shadow of a mighty name.

Status in quo. (Lat.) " The state in which." The condition of affairs formerly existing. Or simply, *status quo,*

Status quo ante bellum. (Lat.) " The state in which before the war." The condition of matters that existed before the war commenced.

Statute of Frauds. An enactment (29 Charles II. chap. 3, 1677) entitled " An act for prevention of frauds and perjures."

Stay Law. A statute enacted in Massachusetts, in 1878, which limits and restricts the payment of money to depositors, and was framed to provide against a " run " on the savings banks. Under this law the commissioners, whenever they deem it expedient, can grant the bank authority to pay its depositors only such proportion of their deposits, and at such times, as the bank can pay without affecting its solvency or subjecting it to great loss.

S. T. B. *Sacræ Theologiæ Baccalaureus.* Bachelor of Sacred Theology.

S. T. D. *Sacræ Theologiæ Doctor.* Doctor of Divinity.

Steady Habits, Land of. *See* LAND OF STEADY HABITS.

Steamboat King. Oliver Newberry, the shipbuilder (1789–1860).

Steelbacks, or **Black Cuffs.** Nicknames conferred on the Fifty-eight Regiment in the English army.

Steel Pen. A sobriquet conferred on Colonel Penn, of the British army, for gallantry and bravery during the Abyssinian campaign.

Steenie. A diminutive for Stephen, and conferred by James I. on George Villiers, Duke of Buckingham, on account of his beautiful face. The reference is to Acts vi. 15 (*q. v.*).

Stella. (1) The lady whom Sir Philip Sidney addressed by this name was Lady Penelope Devereux. (2) Dean Swift so named his pupil, Hester Johnson.

Stella Fox. The stage-name of Mrs. Charles H. Boyle.

Stella Marion. The stage-name of Mrs. C. H. Boyle, *née* Fox.

Stella Rees. The stage-name of Mrs. William W. Allen.

Stemmata quid faciunt? (Lat.) What do pedigrees avail ?

Stentor. *See* SHOUT OF STENTOR.

Stephen Adams. (Pseud.) Michael Maybrick, an eminent vocalist and songwriter of London, England, author of " Nancy Lee," a song that for a time enjoyed very great popularity.

Stepney Papers. A voluminous collection of political letters (1692–1706), between Mr. Stepney, the British minister, and ambassadors at various European Courts, the Duke of Marlborough, and other public characters of the time. It is very valuable, as this was the period called the " Seven Years' War."

Stepniak. The pen-name of a famous revolutionary Russian writer whose real appellation is Michael Dragomanoff. He was born in 1841. He published a number of works exposing the inner workings of the police-spy system of Russia. He was popularly classed as a Nihilist.

Ster., or **Stg.** Sterling.

Steropes. One of the Cyclops (*q. v.*).

Stet. (Lat.) Let it stand.

Stewing in their own Gravy. This historical phrase, applied by Bismarck to the French, was not new, though it may in his case have been original. In the " London Spy," published 1716, is a description of a hot-air bath at the Hummums in Covent Garden, in which the writer says, " He relieved us out of our purgatory, and carried us to our dressing-rooms, which gave us much refreshment after we had been stewing in our own gravy."

Stheno. In classic myth one of the three Gorgons (*q. v.*).

Stigmata, Stigmatization, or **Bloody Sweat.** Stigmata are wounds resembling those received by our Lord at his crucifixion. "When fully developed they consist of one in the palm of each hand, one on the dorsum of each foot, each indicating the place where a nail was driven in the act of nailing Christ to the cross, and one on the side, showing the effect of the Roman soldier's spear-thrust. Sometimes, in addition to these, there are signs upon the forehead, corresponding to the lacerations caused by the thorns. Stigmatization is the technical ecclesiastical term for the formation of such resemblances." The word hæmidrosis (Greek αἷμα, blood, and ἱδρόω, I perspire) is the technical medical name for a morbid ·condition which has frequently been described by medical men. Cases of this bloody sweat have been described in which the greater part of the body was affected; in others only certain parts.

Görres acknowledges that in all Christian antiquity no known examples of stigmatization occurred. They are peculiar to the later eras of Christian history. Roman Catholicism has usually enumerated about eighty instances; but in 1873 Dr. Imbert Gourbeyre, professor in the School of Medicine of Clermont-Ferrand, in Belgium, and a writer attached to that religious system, enlarged the series so that it now comprehends one hundred and fifty-three cases, of which eight are living and known to him. Of all these instances that of Francis Bernadone, canonized as Saint Francis d'Assisi, in Italy, is the first and most commanding. Born in 1186 and dying Oct. 4, 1226, he is said to have received the stigmata in 1224. In the solitude of Monte Alverno, a part of the Apennines bestowed on him by Count Orlando, of Cortona, and a favorite place of retirement, he thrice opened the Scriptures where they detail the Passion of the Lord. This was interpreted to mean that in some way he was to be brought into mysterious conformity with the death of the Redeemer. While praying, he experienced a most passionate desire to be crucified with Christ, and saw, or imagined he saw, a seraph with six wings; two were arched over the head, two veiled the body, and two were stretched for flight. Amid these wings appeared the likeness of the Crucified. Joy filled the soul of Francis, but grief also pierced his heart like a sword. The vision vanished, but left him in an indescribable condition of delight and awe. His body, like wax, exhibiting the impression of the seal, now showed the stigmata. Each hand and foot was pierced in the middle by a nail. The heads of the nails, round and black like nails of iron, were on the palms of the hands and forepart of the feet. The points of the nails, which appeared on the other side, were bent backward on the wounds they had made. Though somewhat movable, they could not be drawn out. Saint Clare tried, but failed, to do it after his death. From a deep-red wound of three fingers' breadth

in his left side, as if he had been pierced by a lance, the sacred blood then and frequently afterward flowed upon his tunic. These wounds never gangrened nor suppurated, nor did he try to heal them. Hands and feet could be used as aforetime, but walking became so difficult that on subsequent journeys he usually rode on horseback. Countless miracles were ascribed to these wounds. — WHEATLEY.

Stile, Essex. *See* ESSEX STILE.

Stinkomalee. A slang epithet applied by Theodore Hook to London University. At the time of its coining, an acrimonious discussion was proceeding in Parliament about Trincomalee, in Ceylon; the institution in question happened to be at loggerheads with King's College and other universities because it received students of all beliefs.

Stirrup. (Pseud.) Henry J. Brent, in the "Spirit of the Times."

Stir-up-Sunday. The last Sunday in Trinity. It is a school-boy's term taken from the first words of the Collect for the day, and which, being about four weeks from Christmas, are supposed to indicate the near approach of the bustle and fun of the holiday season.

Stockholm Blood Bath. On the 10th and 11th of November, 1520, Christian II. of Denmark caused so many of his opponents to be executed that it took two days to complete the bloody work; hence the name.

Stonehenge. (Pseud.) John Henry Walsh, M. R. C. S., English medical writer (b. 1826).

Stone Jug. This is not so absurd a name for a jail as many suppose. The Greek word κέραμος signifies both an earthen jug and a jail. Homer uses it in both senses (Iliad, v. 387 and ix. 469).

Stone of the Broken Treaty. Limerick. About a century and a half ago England made a solemn compact with Ireland. Ireland promised fealty, and England promised to guarantee to the Irish people civil and religious equality. When the crisis was over England handed Ireland over to a faction that has ever since bred strife and disunion.

Stonewall Jackson. Thomas J. Jackson, one of the Confederate commanders in the Civil War (fl. 1826–1863). There are a number of stories as to the origin of this nickname, one being that it was conferred because his command was recruited in the "stone wall" country of Virginia. But the most authentic is to the effect that General Bee, of South Carolina, to encourage his own men, cried "Look at Jackson's men! they stand like a stone wall!"

Stonewall Jackson's Commissary. "When I was with General Lee's army at Winchester in the autumn of 1862, the soldiers of every camp laughingly spoke of Pope as 'Stonewall Jackson's Commissary,' so entirely had Jackson, in the 'Pope Campaign,' depended upon capturing from that general everything he required for his men." — GENERAL WOLSELEY, in *North American Review*.

Stool of Repentance. The stool so called was an elevated seat on which persons stood in Scottish churches who had been guilty of certain offences against chastity. — L'ESTRANGE.

Stoop = DOORSTEP, or PORCH. The stoop, as designating the place between the steps leading up to the house and the door, is a genuine Americanism due to the Dutch, for the burghers loved to sit on their *stoeps* (seats) smoking their pipes. Now "stoop" is the name for any covered or open porch in front of a house.

Stop-watch Critics. Those who judge by "rule-o'-thumb" so to speak. It is related of one of these gentry that, when he was asked about the merits of a certain speech, he gravely stated that the orator consumed so many seconds at each pause, and that he had timed him with a stop-watch.

Store is the universal equivalent for the English "shop."

Storm and Stress Period. In the literary history of Germany a period of wonderful industry and of an intellectual outbreak (1750–1830) against the bonds of a labored and artificial literary spirit. It took its name from a drama by Klinger, whose tragedies reflected the ferment of the time.

Storm King. The name by which Prof. James P. Espy (1785–1860), one of the earliest meteorologists in this country, was known. His weather forecasts received wide attention, and he was an authority on storms and atmospheric disturbances.

Stormy Cape. The same as CAPE OF STORMS (*q. v.*).

Stormy Petrel of Politics. John Scott, Earl of Eldon (1751–1838). So called because he was in the habit of hastening up to London when any rumor of a dissolution of the Cabinet reached him. He did so at the death of Lord Liverpool under the expectation that the king would call on him to form a ministry, but the task was assigned to Canning. Again, when Canning died he was in full expectation of being sent for, but the king applied to Lord Goderich. Again, when Lord Goderich resigned, Eldon felt sure of being sent for, but the king asked Wellington to form a ministry.

Stot, The. James Stuart, the Scottish traveller (1776–1849), figures in the "Noctes Ambrosianæ" under this name. "Stot" means "a steer."

Stowe Nine Churches. The name given to the hamlet of Stowe, Northamptonshire, England. The tradition is that the people of this hamlet wished to build a church, and made nine ineffectual efforts to do so, for every time the church was finished the Devil came by night and knocked it down.

S. T. P. *Sacræ Theologiæ Professor.* Professor of Divinity.

Str. Steamer.

Straight-tongue. Henry Benjamin Whipple, the Protestant Episcopal bishop (b. 1822), is so called by the Indians, of whom he has large numbers in his diocese of Minnesota.

Strait City, The. Detroit, Mich., situated on the stream or strait that joins Lakes Erie and St. Clair. The word "Detroit" is French, and signifies "strait."

Strawberry Day. A Southern custom consists in the setting apart by extensive strawberry-growers of the proceeds of the first day's pickings to the sick and poor. The fame of this pleasant "movable feast" has been sung by Susan Coolidge.

Strawboots. *See* BLACK HORSE.

Straws. (Pseud.) J. M. Field, an American writer.

Straws, Jr. (Pseud.) Kate Field, in the "Springfield Republican."

Street Arabs. *See* ARABS.

Strike, but Hear. "Eurybiades lifting up his staff as if he was going to strike, Themistocles said, 'Strike if you will, but hear.'" — PLUTARCH, *Life of Themistocles*.

Striped Pig. A New England synonym for a glass of liquor. To avoid a very stringent liquor law, a citizen of Dedham erected a booth, hung out a placard announcing "the striped pig now on exhibition," and then served free drinks to those who paid for admission. The same ruse was repeated in Boston, during the severe winter of 1844, when the harbor was frozen over, and a sort of fair was held on the ice.

Strix. (Pseud.) George W. Howes, in the " Evening Post," and the "Dial," New York.

Strong-bow. Richard de Clare, Earl of Strigul, Chief-Justice of Ireland (d. 1176).

Struck Oil. *See* OIL.

Stuart Leigh. (Pseud.) Mrs. M. B. D. Clarke.

Stuarts' Fatal Number. This number is 88. James III. was killed in flight near Bannockburn, 1488. Mary Stuart was beheaded, 1588 (New Style). James II. of England was dethroned, 1688. Charles Edward died, 1788. James Stuart, the " Old Pretender," was born, 1688, the very year that his father abdicated.

Stump. In a country, newly reclaimed from the forest, tree-stumps remain for years a conspicuous feature of the landscape. Such often furnished a convenient platform for political speakers, and hence "to take the stump " or to " stump the country " signifies a travelling from place to place, speaking and canvassing for votes. Such a man is known as a "stump speaker."

Stupid Boy. Saint Thomas Aquinas. *See* DUMB OX.

Stylites. *See* PILLAR SAINTS.

Styx. In classic mythology a river of Hades, around which it flowed seven times, and over which Charon conveyed the shades of the departed. As a goddess, Styx was the daughter of Oceanus and Tethys, dwelling in a grotto at the entrance of Hades.

Su., Sun, or **Sund.** Sunday.

Sua cuique voluptas. (Lat.) Every one has his own peculiar pleasure.

Suaviter in modo, fortiter in re. (Lat.) Gentle in manner, firm in action.

Subito. (Ital.) Quickly.

Subj. Subjunctive.

Sub judice. (Lat.) " Before the judge." Under consideration.

Sublime Porte. The synonym by which is designated the government of the Sultan of Turkey. It is the French equivalent of *Bab-i-Humayoon*, " the high gate." The term contains an allusion to the Oriental custom of transacting public business at the principal gate of the city or palace, and from this practice the Sultan's government is popularly styled in Turkey " the Sultan's gate."

Sub pœna. (Lat.) " Under a penalty." A summons to attend a court as a witness.

Sub rosa. (Lat.) " Under the rose." Privately; secretly.

Sub silentio. (Lat.) In silence.

Subst. Substantive.

Subtle Doctor. Duns Scotus, the schoolman (fl. 1265–1308).

Succedaneum. (Lat.) A substitute.

Sucker State. Illinois, whose inhabitants are pretty generally dubbed " suckers " by their fellow-citizens of neighboring States. The following is the commonly received origin of the epithet: A writer in the " Providence Journal " says, — " The western prairies are full of the holes made by the crayfish, which burrows to reach the water beneath the soil. In the early days of the country's settlement travellers armed themselves with slender hollow reeds, which they thrust, when thirsty, into these natural reservoirs, and thus easily supplied their longings by sucking the water through reed or pipe." But another version is, that the mines in Northern Illinois and Southern Wisconsin were worked by men who went South when winter came, and returned about the time that suckers appeared in the brooks in spring time in Illinois, and that badgers showed themselves in Wisconsin; and that from this they were called " Suckers " and "Badgers," and gave their nicknames to the two States.

Suck the Monkey. Captain Marryat says that rum is sometimes inserted in cocoa-nuts for the private use of sailors, and as cocoa-nut shells are generally fashioned into the resemblance of a monkey's face, sucking the rum from them is called " sucking the monkey."

Sugar-camp. In the Northern States and in Canada, a gathering in the maple grove for the purpose of making sugar, which is obtained from syrup drained from " tapping" the sugar maple.

Sugar-lip. Hafiz, the Persian poet.

Sugar Loaf, The. The popular name given to a conical hill rising abruptly from the Hudson River at the northern entrance to the Highlands, about fifty-seven miles from New York City.

Sugar-orchard. A grove of sugar-maple trees is thus called in the Northern States and Canada.

Suggestio falsi. (Lat.) The suggestion of a falsehood.

Su-Goth. Suio-Gothic.

Sui generis. (Lat.) "Of its own kind." Of a kind peculiar to itself.

Suit of Hair. In the Middle and Southern States of America the hair of the head is called a "suit" of hair. Dr. J. S. Cartwright, of New Orleans, in describing a "strong-minded woman," says, *inter alia*, "She had a thick suit of black hair, and although she had reached her fortieth year it had not begun to turn gray, so active was her capillary circulation." — *Boston Medical and Surgical Journal*, Oct. 18, 1854. "The face of this gentleman was strikingly marked by a suit of enormous black whiskers that flowed together and united under his chin." — *Margaret*, p. 289.

Sultan's Gate. *See* SUBLIME PORTE.

Sum. Sumner's Reports United States Circuit Court.

Summer Capital of America. Long Branch, N. J., a famous watering-place. It is situated on a broad plateau and bluff overlooking the Atlantic, thirty-one miles south of New York. The beach is one of the finest in the world, and the drives are excellent. In the vicinity are Seabright, Monmouth Beach, Atlanticville, Pleasure Bay, Oceanic, Red Bank, Monmouth Park Race Course, Elberon, Deal Beach, and the village of Deal.

Summer, St. Martin's Little. *See* ST. MARTIN'S LITTLE SUMMER.

Summum bonum. (Lat.) "The highest good." The thing most desirable.

Sum of all Villanies. John Wesley so named the slave-trade.

Sun, City of the. *See* CITY OF THE SUN.

Sunday Saint. One who observes the ordinances of religion, and goes to church on a Sunday, but is worldly, grasping, and dishonest the following six days.

Sundowner. They call the tramp in Australia a "sundowner," because he always reaches a cattle or sheep ranch at sundown, too late for work and just in time for supper and bed. There is nothing in the name, however, as the animal is the same in the antipodes as he is here — a cumberer of the earth who is more worthless than a coyote or a jack rabbit.

Sun, Land of the. *See* LAND OF THE SUN.

Sunless Summer. The name given, in England, to the summer of 1888, when it was established that so cool a season had not been known in thirty years. It rained nearly every day, and there was less than a week of uninterrupted sunshine.

Sunset Cox. A sobriquet conferred on Samuel Sullivan Cox (1824–1889), author, lecturer, and legislator. The foundation of this name is as follows. In the "Ohio Statesman" of May 19, 1853, appeared the following brilliant description by Mr. Cox of the setting of the sun, headed "A Great Old Sunset:" —

"What a peculiar sunset was that of last night! How glorious the storm and how splendid the setting of the sun! We do not remember ever to have seen the like on our round globe. The scene opened in the west, with a whole horizon full of a golden interpenetrating lustre which colored the foliage and brightened every object in its own rich dyes. The colors grew deeper and richer, until the golden lustre was transfused into a storm-cloud full of finest lightning, which leaped in dazzling zigzags all around and over the city. The wind arose with fury, the slender shrubs and giant trees made obeisance to its majesty. Some even snapped before its force. The strawberry beds and grassplats 'turned up their whites' to see Zephyrus march by. As the rain came and the pools formed and the gutters hurried away, thunder roared grandly, and the fire-bells caught the excitement and rang with hearty chorus. The south and east received the copious showers, and the west all at once brightened up in a long polished belt of azure, worthy of a Sicilian sky. Presently a cloud appeared in the azure belt in the form of a castellated city. It became more vivid, revealing strange forms of peerless fanes and alabaster temples, and glories rare and grand in this mundane sphere. It reminds us of Wordsworth's splendid verse in his 'Excursion:' —

'The appearance instantaneously disclosed
Was of a mighty city, boldly say
A wilderness of buildings, sinking far
And self withdrawn into a wondrous depth,
Far sinking into splendor without end.'

But the city vanished only to give place to another isle, where the most beautiful forms of foliage appeared, imaging a paradise in the distant and purified air. The sun, wearied of the elemental commotion, sank behind the green plains of the west. The great 'eye in heaven,' however, went not down without a dark brow hanging over its departing light. The rich flush of unearthly light had passed, and the rain had ceased, when the solemn church bells pealed, the laughter of children, out and joyous after the storm, is heard with the carol of birds, while the forked and purple weapon of the skies still darted illumination around the Starling College, trying to rival its angles and leap into its dark windows."

Sun-up, Sun-down are American-isms for sunrise and sunset. "One would think that such a horse as that might get over a good deal of ground atwixt sun-up and sun-down."—Cooper's *Last of the Mohicans*, p. 50.

Sup. Supreme; supplement; super-fine.

Sup. Ct. Superior Court.

Superb. A sobriquet attached to the name of General Hancock during the Civil War from a remark made by General Meade at Gettysburg when the Second Corps repulsed Longstreet's brigade.

Superb, The. In the Middle Ages Genoa was thus named. *See* BEAUTIFUL, THE.

Super-Grammaticam. Sigismund, Emperor of Germany (fl. 1367-1437). The story goes that at the Council of Constance, in 1414, he defended himself against some solecism by declaring: "I am King of the Romans and above grammar."

Super visum corporis. (Lat.) Upon a view of the body.

Suppressio veri, suggestio falsi. (Lat.) A suppression of the truth is the suggestion of a falsehood.

Supra. (Lat.) Above.

Supt. Superintendent.

Surg. Surgeon; Surgery.

Surg.-Gen. Surgeon-General.

Surprise-party. A social gathering, in which the family visited is not forewarned, being therefore "surprised," and on this account the visitors bring their own refreshments.

Surprise Plot. *See* BYE PLOT.

Surprisers. The Forty-sixth Regiment of Foot in the English army is so nicknamed because one of their commanders was continually trying to steal a march on the enemy.

Surtur. In Scandinavian mythology a giant who is to set fire to the universe at Ragnarok (*q. v.*).

Surv. Surveyor.

Surv.-Gen. Surveyor-General.

Surya. In Hindu mythology the god of the sun. He was the ancestor of a royal race called "the solar race."

Sus. Susannah.

Susan Coolidge. (Pseud.) Miss Woolsey, American writer.

Susan Woods. A sobriquet applied to Col. Charles Robert Woods, U. S. A.

(1827-1885), when he was in the West Point Academy, and which clung to him all through his army career.

Susie Wilde. The stage-name of Mrs. Mark Adams.

Suum cuique. (Lat.) "His own to every one." Let every one have his own.

S. v. *Sub verbo.* Under the word, or title.

S. W. Southwest.

Sw. Swiss.

Swaddlers. A derisive nickname formerly given to the Methodists.

Swamp Angel. An eight-inch two-hundred-pounder Parrott rifled gun, mounted by the Federal troops in a morass on Morris Island, Charleston Harbor, in 1863. On August 22 and 23 the city of Charleston, five and one half miles distant, was shelled, the gun bursting at the thirty-sixth shot. After the war the "Swamp Angel" was sold for old metal, and conveyed to Trenton, N. J.; but having been identified, it was set up on a granite pedestal at the corner of Perry and Clinton Streets in that city.

Swan of Avon. Shakspeare.

Swan of Cambray. Fénelon, Archbishop of Cambray, and author of "Telemaque" (1651-1715).

Swan of Lichfield. Anna Seward, an English writer of considerable merit (1747-1809). Her writings, prose and poetical, are now nearly forgotten.

Swan of Mantua. Virgil, who was born at Mantua (B. C. 70-29).

Swan of Meander. Homer, who lived on the banks of the Meander, in Asia Minor (fl. B. C. 950).

Swan of Padua. Count Francesco Algarotti (1712-1764).

Swe. Sweden; Swedish; Swedenborg; Swedenborgian.

Sweating Sickness. A terribly fatal epidemic or plague which visited Europe in 1485, 1506, 1517, 1528, 1551. Death resulted in the cases of those attacked in four or five hours.

Swedish Nightingale. Jenny Lind, afterwards Madame Goldschmidt.

Sweeps' Day. *See* MAY DAY.

Sweet Singer of Israel. *See* ROYAL PSALMIST.

Sweet Singer of the Temple. George Herbert, the poet (fl. 1593-1633), author of "The Temple: Sacred Poems and Private Ejaculations."

Sweet William. William Henry Draper, the Canadian jurist (1801–1877), was so named on account of his eloquent and persuasive style of address.

Swinging round the Circle. In the spring of 1865 Andrew Johnson became President. The Civil War had just closed and reconstruction was in order. It became evident that the President was not in harmony with the party which had elected him. In the summer of 1866 Governor Morton, of Indiana, made a powerful speech in opposition to the President, and it was resolved to do something to counteract its influence. The corner-stone of the monument to Stephen A. Douglas was to be laid in Chicago, September 2. It was decided that the President, accompanied by Secretary Seward and others, should attend, and on the route address the people in defence of his views on the question of reconstruction. The trip was called by himself, "swinging around the circle." The unfriendly press took it up, and made such derisive use of the term, saying that he had "swung round the entire circle of offices from alderman to President," that it proved very damaging to his influence with the people during the rest of his administration.

Switch = SHUNT. Americans say they "switch" a train where their English cousins speak of "shunting" one.

Switchman = POINTSMAN. The "switchman" or "switch-tender" of American railroads is the "pointsman" of English roads.

Switz. Switzerland.

Switzerland of America. (1) The White Mountains. (2) The region around Mauch Chunk, Glen Onoko, and the Switchback Railroad, Penn.

Switzerland, Saxon. *See* SAXON SWITZERLAND.

Sword of Damocles. Damocles, the courtier of Dionysius the Elder, envied the condition of his master; he was invited by his master to assume the position he so much envied. Accordingly he was set down before a gorgeous banquet, but in mid-air above his seat was a glittering sword suspended by a hair. Afraid to move, lest the slightest jar should cause it to fall, Damocles passed the allotted time in a torment of fear. The phrase is used to denote impending or dreaded disaster.

Sydney. (Pseud.) Miss Molly Elliot Seawell, in the New York "Mail and Express."

Sydney A. Story, Jr. (Pseud.) Mrs. Mary H. Pike, American story-writer (b. 1827).

Sydney Dare. (Pseud.) Mrs. Martha J. Cochrane, in "Harper's Young People."

Sydney Yendys. (Pseud.) Sydney Dobell, English poet (fl. 1824–1874).

Sykesey. A name conferred by the New York regiments on General Sykes in the late Civil War.

Sylvan Scribe. (Pseud.) Seloftus D. Forbes, in "Turf, Field, and Farm."

Sylvanus Urban. (Pseud.) The editor of "The Gentleman's Magazine."

Sylvester's Eve. The last night of the old year. "In Germany on *Sylvesterabend* — the eve of St. Sylvester, the last night of the year — you shall wake and hear a chorus of voices singing hymns, like the English waits at Christmas or the Italian *pifferari.*"

Symmes's Hole. An imaginary aperture in the earth's crust near 82° north latitude, imagined by Captain John Cleves Symmes (1780–1829) to communicate with the interior of the planet, which he thought was inhabited with animal and plant life, and lighted by two subterranean suns, Pluto and Proserpine. Humboldt states that Symmes repeatedly and publicly invited him and Humphry Davy to descend to the earth's interior by this hole.

Symplegades. In classic myth two floating rocks in the Euxine Sea, which, when driven together by the winds, crushed all between them. When, however, the *Argo* passed between them in safety, the rocks became fixed as islands.

Syn. Synonym; synonymous.

Syr. Syriac.

Syrinx. In classic myth a nymph who was beloved by Pan. At her own request she was changed into a reed, out of which Pan made his flute.

T.

T. Territory; all together (*tutti*).

T., or **tom.** Tome; volume.

Ta. Tantalum (Columbium).

Tab. Table; tabular.

Tabernacles, Feast of. The third of the three great annual Jewish festivals, the other two being the feasts of Passover and Pentecost. Every Israelite was commanded to live in "tabernacles" or booths during its continuance. In the Pentateuch it is called the Feast of Ingathering, because it celebrated the completion of the harvest season. It is kept from the 15th to the 22d of the month Tishri, corresponding to our October. It is the most joyful of the Jewish national festivals.

Table d'hôte. (Fr.) An ordinary at which the master of the hotel presides.

Tablets of Moses. A variety of Scotch granite, composed of felspar and quartz, so arranged as to present, when polished, the appearance of Hebrew characters on a white ground.

Tabula rasa. (Lat.) "A tablet smoothed." A smoothed tablet — referring to the wax-covered tablets of the ancients for writing on with the pointed iron tool called a *stylus*. The writing was effaced by simply smoothing the wax-covered surface; hence, 'a mere blank.'

Tacet. (Lat.) He (or she) is silent.

Tædium vitæ. (Lat.) "The weariness of life." The burden of existence.

Taffy. A sobriquet for a Welshman, the equivalent of John Bull for an Englishman, and Sandy for a Scotchman. It is derived from Davy, or David, a very common Welsh name, which in that tongue becomes Tafy, or Taffy.

Tagliere, Signor. The professional name of George Tyler.

Tag, Rag, and Bobtail. The rabble; the English equivalent for the French *sans culottes*. This proverbial saying is doubtless an old hunting expression to signify a herd of deer. In Prescott's " Philip the Second," quoted by Strype and Hollingshead, is the following: " They hunted the deer, and were so greedy of their destruction that they killed them rag and tag with hands and swords." The word "tegg" or "tag" signifies, according to Bailey, " a doe in the second year of her age." " Rag " the same writer defines as " a herd of young colts," but other old writers have "ræg" to signify a herd of deer at rutting time. " Bobtail" means a fawn just after it has been weaned. " Tag " and " bobtail " are used in the same sense when speaking of sheep, but "rag" does not seem known in this connection. The complete original sense of the phrase "rag, tag, and bobtail" seems to have been a collection of sheep or deer, of all sorts, mixed indiscriminately.

Taking a Sight. This is the schoolboy's name for the act which Ingoldsby describes in the lines —

" The Sacristan he said no word to indicate a doubt,
But he put his thumb unto his nose and he spread his fingers out."

It is by no means a modern practice. In Rabelais (book ii. chap. xix.) we read, " Panurge suddenly lifted up in the air his right hand and put the thumb thereof into the nostril of the same side, holding his four fingers straight out." Marryat, in his " Jutland," says, " Some of the old coins found in Denmark represent the god Thor, and what do you imagine he is doing? Why, applying his thumb to the end of his nose, with his four fingers extended in the air." *See* QUEEN ANNE'S FAN.

Talent of the Academy. So Plato called Aristotle.

Tale quale. (Lat.) Such as it is.

Talisman, Gate of the. *See* GATE OF THE TALISMAN.

Tallapoosa Treaty. The name given to a supposititious compact believed to have been arranged by Gen. B. F. Butler and Mr. William E. Chandler, on the United States steamer " Tallapoosa," during the Presidential canvass of 1884.

Talvi. (Pseud.) Mrs. (Theresa Albertina Luise Von Jakob) Robertson, German novelist (1797–1870).

Tammany Ring. The name given to a corrupt gang of politicians, who for years plundered the treasury of the

City of New York. Most of the members of this clique were connected with Tammany Hall, the headquarters of the city Democracy. The frauds were exposed in 1871–1872, and some of the criminals prosecuted. *See* SAINT TAMMANY.

Tammany, Saint. *See* SAINT TAMMANY.

Tam of the Cowgate, Sir Thomas Hamilton, the Scottish lawyer, whose residence was in the Cowgate, Edinburgh. He died in 1563.

Tan. Tangent.

Tan-Ku. The professional name of George W. Bailey, prestidigitator.

Tantalus. In classic myth a character noted for the torments he suffered in the lower world because he divulged the divine counsels of Zeus, his father, by whom they had been communicated as secrets. "He was afflicted with an insatiable thirst, and was immersed up to his chin in a lake of water, which receded whenever he bent his head to drink; clusters of fruit hung suspended within his reach, but they ever eluded his grasp; and in addition he was kept in constant terror lest a huge rock, suspended above his head, and ever threatening to fall, should crush him."

Tant mieux. (Fr.) So much the better.

Tant pis. (Fr.) So much the worse.

Tapis. (Fr.) The carpet.

Tap-up Sunday. The Sunday immediately preceding the fair which is held October 2, of each year, on St. Catherine's Hill, near Guilford, England, and so named because at it any person without a license to sell liquor may "tap" or sell malt liquor on the hill for that day only.

Tariff of Abominations. The name given to the act enforcing the tariff of 1828, which "was the first extreme application of the protective system in Federal legislation."

Tarik, Hill of. *See* HILL OF TARIK.

Tartarrax. In Lincoln, Neb., every Fourth of July, there is a sort of carnival, known as the "Carnival of King Tartarrax." The story of Tartarrax and Coronado is old; it has come down to us through the legends of the Indians and the fanciful and fragmentary efforts of the old Spanish historians, and has

been dressed up and rewoven by the historians of a later day. It is a story of surpassing interest, full of dramatic possibilities, and above all is the exclusive property of Nebraska, and especially of Lincoln; for Quivera, the fabled realm of this mighty Indian monarch, embraced the territory of which Lincoln is now the chief city. Coronado's visit to this king, three hundred and fifty years ago, took him from the city of Mexico up along the mountain regions to where Santa Fé now stands, northwesterly across the plains of the Indian Territory, Kansas, and Nebraska, and landed him within a few miles of this city. Hence it is especially appropriate that the carnival of King Tartarrax be held in "the ancient capital of his realm."

Tartars of America. Mounted guerillas organized by Jacinto Monagas, the South American soldier, in the war for independence under Bolivar.

Tartarus. In classic myth the infernal regions, the abode of lost spirits.

Tasselburg. Alton, Ill.

Tasting Death. The rabbis say there are three drops of gall on the sword of Death: one drops in the mouth and the man dies; from the second the pallor of death is suffused; from the third the carcass turns to dust.

Tasto solo. (Ital.) Play without chords. (Mus.)

Taswert. (Pseud.) John Allan Stewart, in the Springfield, Mo., "Times."

Tatianists. The disciples of Tatian, who, after the death of Justin Martyr, "formed a new scheme of religion; for he advanced the notion of certain invisible æons, branded marriage with the name of fornication, and denied the salvation of Adam."

Tattooed Man. "During the Presidential campaign of 1884 a New York illustrated paper published a cartoon which represented the Republican candidate, James G. Blaine, in the rôle of Phryne before the Athenian judges. His robe was removed, and he appeared tattooed with the names of the scandals with which his enemies tried to connect him. This was regarded as an excellent conceit, and from it arose the name of 'tattooed man,' so often applied to Blaine." — BROWN AND STRAUSS.

Taurus (the Bull). A constellation of the northern hemisphere, representing the head and shoulders of a furious bull, and the second sign of the zodiac, Aries, the Ram, being first. It is found between Perseus and the Charioteer on the north, the Twins on the east, and Orion and the river Po on the west. It contains 141 visible stars, including the two beautiful clusters of the Pleiades and Hyades, the first on the shoulder and the latter in the face of the Bull. *See* PLEIADES.

Tawny, The. Alexander Bonvicino, the historian (fl. 1514-1564).

Tax on Fools. The name given by Count Cavour to the Italian lottery.

T. C. D. Trinity College, Dublin.

.T. E. Topographical Engineers.

Te. Tellurium.

Teacher of Germany. Philip Melanchthon, the famous reformer, was often so named.

Teanlay Night. All-Hallow Eve, the last night of October, the night before All-Saints Day, when bonfires and candles were formerly kindled throughout England for succoring the souls in purgatory.

Tearless Battle. A fight between the Lacedæmonians and the Arcadians and Argives, 367 B. C., in which the latter were disastrously defeated, while not a Spartan bit the dust. Hence, says Plutarch, it was known among the Greeks as the Tearless Battle.

Tears, Gate of. *See* GATE OF TEARS.

Tears, Vale of. *See* VALE OF TEARS.

Tears, Villa of. *See* VILLA OF TEARS.

Tea-Water Pump. A famous pump in the early days of the history of New York. In Mrs. Lamb's "History of the City of New York," we find several allusions to the "Tea-Water Pump." At page 349 this entry appears: One of the springs which supplied the fabulously reported unfathomable depths of the remarkable lake (the Fresh Water Pond) bubbled forth near the present junction of Chatham and Roosevelt Streets, where was erected the famous "Tea-Water Pump" which supplied the city with wholesome drinking water; the various wells in the lower part of the town affording only a miserable and brackish substitute for water. Regarding some complaints about obstructions, there is the following explanation on page 424: Complaints were made that the water carts obstructed Chatham Street when drawn up in a row to receive water from the "Old Tea-Water Pump" for the supply of the city, and an order went forth causing the spout of said pump to be raised some two feet and lengthened so as to deliver the water at the outer part of the walk and allow persons to walk under it without inconvenience. On page 727, there are some further items which cannot fail to be interesting to readers of the present day when they contrast their expensive and extensive water supply with that of the "good old days." The population had reached 270,000, and the great human tide was flowing from the Old World in a resistless and almost overpowering current. From the brackish wells and the "Old Tea-Pump" to the practical operation of the Manhattan Water Works in Reade Street, which managed to distribute very poor water pumped from wells through the lower part of the city, in hollow logs, the citizens had always been restricted in their water supply, and the more people the less water. The situation in time became absolutely appalling.

Tecumseh. *See* OLD TECUMSEH.

Teetotal. The word "teetotal" had its origin through a stuttering temperance orator, who urged on his hearers that nothing less than "te-te-te-total" abstinence would satisfy temperance reformers. Some one at once adopted the word "teetotal," and it sprang into general use.

Teian Poet. Anacreon, who was born at Teos, in Ionia (fl. 563-478 B. C.).

Te judice. (Lat.) You may judge.

Telamon. In classic myth an Argonaut, and the first to scale the walls of Troy when Hercules took that city in the reign of Laomedon.

Telemachus. In classic myth the only son of Ulysses and Penelope. At the fall of Troy he went in quest of his father, accompanied by Minerva in the form of Mentor.

Tellus. In classic myth a Roman deity, the personification of the productive earth ; the same as Terra.

Tel maître, tel valet. (Fr.) Like master, like man.

Tema. (Ital.) A subject, or theme. (Mus.)

Tempest, The. A title conferred on Andoche Junot (fl. 1771-1813), one of the Napoleonic generals, because of his bravery and reckless impetuosity.

Tempest in a Teapot. The famous insurrectionary movement in Geneva was so named in contempt by Paul, Grand Duke of Russia. This phrase is also one of the modifications of an old proverb which can be traced as far back as the time of Cicero, who quotes it as a common saying, — *e. g., Gratidius excitabat fluctus in simpulo, ut dicitur* (Gratidius raised a tempest in a ladle, as the saying is). — *De Legibus,* iii. 16. Athenæus, who wrote in the third century, makes the flute-player Dorian ridicule Timotheus, who undertook to imitate a storm at sea on the zither, by saying, — " I have heard a greater storm in a boiling pot." The French form, *une tempête dans une verre d'eau* (a tempest in a glass of water), was first applied to the disturbances in the Republic of Geneva near the end of the seventeenth century, and is variously attributed to the Austrian Duke Leopold, to Paul, Grand Duke of Russia, and to the French author and jurist, Linguet. Balzac, in his " Curé de Tours," assigns the authorship, without any apparent evidence, to Montesquieu. The English phrase is an evident reminiscence of the French, "teapot" being substituted for the sake of alliteration, but it is doubtful who first gave it currency. Lord North is said to have applied the phrase to the outbreak of the American colonists against the tax on tea ; but Lord Chatham is also said to have characterized a London riot in the same terms.

Templeton. (Pseud.) The pen-name of George H. Monroe, an American journalist and correspondent.

Tempo, or A tempo. (Ital.) In time. An expression used after some relaxation in the measure, to indicate a return to the original movement. (Mus.)

Tempo giusto. (Ital.) In strict time. (Mus.)

Tempo primo. (Ital.) In the first, or original, time. (Mus.)

Tempora mutantur, et nos mutamur in illis. (Lat.) The times change, and we change with them.

Tempus edax rerum. (Lat.) Time is the consumer of all things.

Tempus fugit. (Lat.) Time flies.

Tempus omnia revelat. (Lat.) Time reveals all things.

Ten Alcott. (Pseud.) Charles Adiel Lewis Totten, American inventor (b. 1851), in his " Gems, Talismans, and Guardians " (1887).

Ten-cent Jimmy. A nickname conferred on James Buchanan. It was affirmed by John Davis (1787–1854) in a speech that Buchanan was in favor of reducing the wages of American workmen to ten cents a day.

Tenete sino alla fine del suono. (Ital.) Keep the keys down as long as the sound lasts. (Mus.)

Tenn. Tennessee.

Tennessee. The name of this State is an Indian word meaning " river of the big bend."

Tennessee Bond Cases. A name given to seventeen causes decided by the United States Supreme Court in 1885, wherein it was held that the statutory lien upon railroads created by act of the Tennessee Legislature, Feb. 11, 1852, was for the benefit of the State, and not of the holders of State bonds issued under that act.

Tennessee, Little. *See* LITTLE TENNESSEE.

Tennis Ball of Fortune. Pertinax, the Roman Emperor, was thus named. He was a charcoal peddler, a schoolmaster, a soldier, and lastly emperor. Finally he was dethroned and murdered.

Ten-strike. A law against the game of " Ninepins " (*q. v.*) having been evaded by the addition of a tenth pin, the man who bowled over the whole number was said to make a " ten-strike." So the phrase " to make a ten-strike " passed into current phraseology to indicate a lucky stroke.

Tenth Day Excitement. Oct. 24–25, 1844, when, so said the Millerites, the world was to come to an end. This was the grand culmination of the fanatical excitement caused by the preaching of William Miller and his dupes.

Tenth Muse. (1) Sappho. (2) Juana Inez de la Cruz, a Mexican poet (1651–1695). (3) Anne Bradstreet, the New England poet (1612–1672), whose works were re-issued in London under the title " The Tenth Muse lately sprung up in America."

Ten Thousand. What is known in ancient history as "the retreat of the Ten Thousand " was the retreat of the Greek auxiliaries of Cyrus, under Xenophon, in which they succeeded in reaching the sea, 401–400 B. C.

Ten Thousand. *See* UPPER TEN.

Tenuto. (Ital.) To be held its full length. (Mus.)

Ter. Territory.

Terence of England. Richard Cumberland, the British bard (fl. 1732–1811), was so named by Goldsmith.

Teresa Carreño. The professional name of Madame Tagliapetra.

Teres atque rotundus. (Lat.) Smooth and round.

Terminus ad quem. (Lat.) "The boundary to which." The end of one's journey.

Terminus a quo. (Lat.) "The boundary from which." The starting-point.

Terpsichore. In classic myth one of the Muses. She presides over dancing.

Terrace City. Yonkers, N. Y.

Terræ filius. (Lat.) A son of the earth — applied snobbishly to a man of obscure or humble birth.

Terræ motus. (Lat.) "Motion of the earth." An earthquake; a commotion.

Terra firma. (Lat.) "The solid ground." The shore or land as distinguished from the sea or water.

Terra incognita. (Lat.) "A land unknown." A land or district of country one has not visited or entered before.

Terrapin Policy. The name given to the course of action which resulted in the "Embargo of 1807," or "Jefferson's Embargo," an act passed by Congress in December, 1807, forbidding the departure of vessels from American ports. It was the one unfortunate act of Jefferson's administration, which was otherwise very popular. While American ships rotted in port, English ships picked up the trade they had lost. The above name is an allusion to the terrapin's habit of pulling its head and feet into its shell when frightened.

Terrible, The. Ivan IV. of Russia (fl. 1529–1584) was so named. Though an able executive, he was notorious for his cruelty.

Terror of the World. Attila.

Terrors, Mountain of. *See* MOUNTAIN OF TERRORS.

Terry Alts. Riotous bands who infested Clare County, Ireland, after the Union, perpetrating many outrages.

Terry Finnegan. (Pseud.) James McCarroll, American editor and *littérateur* (b. 1814).

Tertium quid. (Lat.) A third something.

Testis. One of the pseudonyms commonly attributed to Junius (*q. v.*).

Tête-à-tête. (Fr.) A conversation between two parties.

Tethys. In classic myth daughter of Cœlus and Terra, and mother of the Oceanides and the river-gods.

Tex. Texas.

Texan Independence, Anniversary of. This falls on March 2, and is a legal holiday in Texas.

Texas. This State took its name from the Tachies, a tribe of Indians, whose descendants, the Inies, now reside in the Indian Territory. The word "Texas" signifies "friends."

Text. Rec. *Textus Receptus.* The Received Text.

t. f. Till forbid.

Th. Thorium.

Th., or Thurs. Thursday.

Thalia. In classic myth one of the Muses. She presided over comedy.

Thammuz. The name under which the Phœnicians and Syrians adored Adonis.

Thamyris. In classic myth a poet of Thrace whose unbounded conceit led him to believe that he could surpass the Muses in song. In punishment for his presumption he was deprived of sight and of the power to sing. He is usually depicted with a broken lyre.

Thanelian. (Pseud.) N. W. Coffin, in the Boston "Journal."

Thanksgiving Day. There are only three distinctively and generally observed American national festivals, — Independence Day, Memorial Day, and Thanksgiving Day. Christmas and New Year's, though as heartily honored, are exotics. The two first named are indigenous to our institutions, and redolent of our soil. Of these, Independence Day, though coeval with, and commemorative of, our national natal day, boasts only a respectable antiquity of little more than a century. But Thanksgiving Day carries us backward more than two centuries and a half, —

back to the days of bluff Governor
Bradford, and to the first struggling
colony of stern and heroic Pilgrims, —
thus springing Minerva-like, full grown
from the very cradle of our Commonwealth,

"Where Freedom spread her banner wide,
    And cast her soft and hallowed ray."

The first observance of a day of thanksgiving, formally recommended by the
civil authorities, occurred in Leyden,
Holland, Oct. 3, 1575, it being the first
anniversary of the deliverance of that
city from siege. In July, 1623, a day of
fasting and prayer was appointed in the
infant colonies of New England, on account of drought. Rain came abun-
dantly while they were praying; and
the Governor appointed a day of thanksgiving, which was observed with religious
exercises. The Charlestown record
shows a similar change of fast day into
thanksgiving, in 1631, on account of the
arrival of supplies from Ireland. Dr.
Franklin tells us that, in a time of great
despondency among the first settlers of
New England, it was proposed in one
of their public meetings to proclaim a
fast. An aged farmer rose and spoke
of their provoking Heaven with their
complaints, and of the many mercies
they had received, and of the cause they
had for thanksgiving. He then made a
motion that instead of appointing a day
of fasting, they should appoint a day of
thanksgiving. To this the assembly
readily agreed. The first Thanksgiving
Day was kept amid circumstances most
unpropitious, and with gaunt Famine
hovering over the rude and cheerless
dwellings of that little colony. The
summer of 1621, following the landing
at Plymouth, yielded but a scanty harvest, and unless speedy supplies came
from Europe the sturdy colonists fore-
saw that they would be reduced to the
point of starvation. Yet, amid such
surroundings as these, we learn from
the old chronicles that Governor Bradford, "the harvest being gotten in, sent
four men out on fowling, so that we
might, after a more speciall manner, rejoice together after we had gathered the
fruit of our labor." And thus,

"While sickness lurked, and death assailed,
    And foes beset on every hand,"

the first Governor of New England instituted the American Harvest Home;
and thus, amid peril and privation such
as we of to-day can but poorly appreciate, was celebrated the first New Eng-

land Thanksgiving. The old colonial
records also tell of the appointment of
thanksgiving days, for various causes,
in the Massachusetts Colony, in the
years 1633, 1634, 1637, 1638, and 1639.
In Plymouth Colony similar observances
took place in 1651, 1668, and 1680, when
the tenor of the proclamation seems
to indicate that it had then become a
settled yearly custom. Massachusetts
Bay was the first of the colonies to appoint an annual thanksgiving by the
proclamation of the English governor.
During the Revolution, Thanksgiving
Day was a national institution, being
annually recommended by Congress ;
but after the general thanksgiving for
peace, in 1784, there was no national appointment until 1789, when Washington,
by request of Congress, recommended
a day of thanksgiving for the adoption
of the Constitution. Washington issued a second proclamation of thanksgiving, in 1795, on account of the suppression of insurrection. President
Madison, by request of Congress, recommended a thanksgiving for peace, in
1815. But the official recommendation
of a day for the giving of thanks was
mainly confined to New England until
the year 1817, after which date it was
regularly appointed by the governor of
New York. We find that the Dutch
governors of the New Netherlands proclaimed thanksgiving days in 1644,
1645, 1655, and 1664; and, in 1755 and
1760, a day was similarly designated by
the English governor of New York.
In 1855 Governor Johnson, of Virginia,
recommended a day of thanksgiving;
but in 1857 Governor Wise, when requested to do so, publicly declined, on
the ground that he was not authorized
to interfere in religious matters. During the Civil War, in 1863 and 1864,
President Lincoln issued proclamations
recommending annual thanksgivings.
Since then a proclamation has been
issued annually by the President as well
as by the governors of the several
States and the mayors of the principal
cities. Custom fixes the time as the
last Thursday in November; but up to
1864 there was no uniformity as to the
date of the observance, and Presidents
and governors were bound by no fixed
rules in setting apart a day, and each
State had its own Thanksgiving. The
Puritan Christmas, as it has been called,
is essentially a country, not a town festival, and those only really enjoy it

whose national birds are raised, fed, and fattened on their own lands, and whose pumpkins grow on their own vines.

"Like most things that come to stay," says a writer in the "Century," "the autumn thanksgiving feast of New England grew so gradually that its development is not easily traced. Days occasionally set apart for thanksgiving were known in Europe before the Reformation, and were in frequent use among Protestants afterward. The early New Englanders appointed fasts and thanksgivings on proper occasions without reference to the season. Some of the first thanksgivings were for harvests, for the safe arrival of ships with provisions, and for the success of the arms of the Protestants in Germany. There were also fast-days and thanksgiving days kept by single churches, and private fasts and private thanksgivings set apart by individuals, and observed in retirement. Public thanksgiving for the harvest, and for the other blessings of a year that was near its end, occurred frequently in the autumn, and easily became customary. Christmas and other church-festivals had been severely put down; the very names of the months were at first changed to numeral designations, 'not out of any peevish humor of singularity, . . . but of purpose to prevent the Heathenish and Popish observation of Dayes, Moneths, and Yeares, that they may be forgotten among the people of the Lord.' But custom is stronger than precept, and when the Thanksgiving holiday became annual, it borrowed many of the best and most essential features of the English Christmas. It was a day of family reunion, on which the Puritans ate turkey and pumpkin-pies instead of boars' heads and plumpudding. Thanksgiving Day was long in settling down to its present fixity of season; it is even on record that one prudent town took the liberty of postponing its celebration of the day for a week, in order to get molasses with which to sweeten the pumpkin-pies."

Whenever appointed, Thanksgiving Day is a legal holiday in all the States.

Thaumaturgist (Miracle-worker). A name given to many saints and divines: Apollonius of Tyana, Saint Bernard of Clairvaux, Francis d'Assisi, Gregory of Neo-Cæsarea, Saint Isidore, Blaise Pascal, Proclus, Simon Magus, Sospitra, Saint Vincent de Paul, J. Joseph Gassner, and Prince Alexander of Hohenlohe.

Theban Bard, or **Theban Eagle.** Pindar, the classic poet.

Theban Legion, The, was composed of Christians who submitted to martyrdom rather than attack their brethren during the persecution of Maximian, about 286 A.D. Their leader, Maurice, was canonized.

The Empire, it is Peace. An exclamation of Napoleon III. at a public banquet at Bordeaux, Oct. 9, 1852.

The Guard Dies, but never Surrenders. "This phrase, attributed to Cambronne, who was made prisoner at Waterloo, was vehemently denied by him. It was invented by Rougemont, a prolific author of *mots*, two days after the battle, in the 'Independent.'" — FOURNIER.

The King is Dead! Long Live the King! The death of Louis XIV. was announced by the captain of the bodyguard from the window of the state apartment. Raising his truncheon above his head, he broke it in the centre, and throwing the pieces among the crowd, exclaimed in a loud voice, "Le Roi est mort!" then, taking another staff, he flourished it in the air as he shouted, "Vive le Roi!"

Themaninthemoon. (Pseud.) Rev. John Eagles, English writer and artist (1784–1855).

Themis. In classic myth the goddess of Justice. She was a daughter of Cœlus and Terra.

Theo. Theodore.

Theodore de la Guard. The penname under which Nathaniel Ward (d. 1652) published his "Simple Cobler of Agawam in America," 1646–1647. This literary disguise was merely a slight veiling of his own name, "Theodore" being the Greek equivalent of the Hebrew name Nathaniel, and "de la Guard" the French of the English Ward.

Theo Gift. (Pseud.) Mrs. Dora Henrietta Boulger, *née* Havers, author of "Lil Lorimer," etc.

Theol. Theology; theological.

Theoph. Theophilus.

Theophilus Marcliffe. (Pseud.) William Godwin, author of "Caleb Williams" (1756–1836).

Theophilus Secundus. (Pseud.) Robert Isaac Wilberforce, English divine and author (1802–1857).

Theophilus South. (Pseud.) Edward Chitty, English law writer (b. 1807).

Theresa Newcomb. The stage-name of Mrs. T. J. Jackson.

Theresa Vaughn. The stage-name of Mrs. W. A. Mestayer.

Thermidorians. Those who took part in the *coup d'état* which effected the fall of Robespierre, with the desire of restoring the legitimate monarchy. So called, because the Reign of Terror was brought to an end on the 9th Thermidor of the second Republican year (July 27, 1794).

Thermometer of Zeal. This instrument is said to have been invented in the reign of Henry VIII., but to have been first put to eminent use by a gentleman of later times, who lived in his vicarage to a good old age; and, after having seen several successors of his neighboring clergy either burned or banished, departed this life with the satisfaction of having never deserted his flock, and died Vicar of Bray. " As this glass," the narrator continues, "was first designed to calculate the different degrees of heat in religion, as it raged in Popery, or as it cooled and grew temperate in the Reformation, it was marked at several distances after the manner of an ordinary thermometer is to this day; namely, extreme heat, sultry heat, very hot, hot, warm, temperate, cold, just freezing, frost, hard frost, great frost, extreme cold. The new markings proposed are in the following order : Ignorance, persecution, wrath, zeal, church, moderation, lukewarmness, infidelity, ignorance."

Thermopylæ of America. Fort Alamo, Texas, is so named in allusion to the heroic defence of it made, in 1836, by a small body of Texans against a force of Mexicans ten times their number. During the subsequent struggle for independence the Texan war cry was, "Remember the Alamo !" the Mexicans having murdered the six defenders of the fort whom they found alive on its surrender.

Thersites. In classic myth the most ill-looking and the most abusive of the Greeks before Troy. He was killed by Achilles for deriding his grief for Penthesilea. The name is used to denote a backbiter or a calumniator.

Theseus. In classic myth son of Ægeus and king of Athens. Next to Hercules he was the most renowned of the heroes of antiquity.

Thess. Thessalonians.

Theta. (Pseud.) William Thorne, English scholar (1558–1629).

Thetis. In classic myth a sea-nymph. She was daughter of Nereus and Doris, wife of Peleus, and mother of Achilles.

Theuerdank ("dear thanks"). Maximilian I., of Germany (fl. 1459–1519), was so named.

Thieves' Candles. A widespread superstition among the ignorant in Europe that candles made from the fat of a human being render the bearers invisible.

Thieves' Synod. The name bestowed on the ecclesiastical council at Ephesus in 431, and in which the Eutychian doctrines respecting the Incarnation were affirmed, because the opposers of these tenets were either silenced or excluded.

Thieves' Vinegar. A kind of aromatic vinegar for a sick-room, consisting of the dried tops of rosemary, sage leaves, lavender flowers, and bruised cloves, steeped in acetic acid and boiling water. It derives its name and popularity as a disinfectant from a story that four thieves who plundered dead bodies during a plague with perfect security from contagion attributed their immunity from risk to the use of this decoction.

Third Founder of Rome. The Roman general, Caius Marius, was so named on account of his oft-repeated triumphs over the enemies of his country.

Thirty Tyrants of Athens. The thirty magistrates appointed by Sparta over Athens at the termination of the Peloponnesian War. But their reign of terrorism was overthrown by Thrasybulus, after the lapse of one year, in 403 B. C.

Thirty Tyrants of Rome were those military usurpers "who endeavored, in the reigns of Valerian and Gallienus (253–268), to make themselves independent princes. The number thirty must be taken with great latitude," says Brewer, "as only nineteen are given, and their resemblance to the thirty tyrants of Athens is extremely fanciful." They were —

In the East.	Illyricum.
(1) Cyriades.	(11) Ingenuus.
(2) Macrianus.	(12) Regillianus.
(3) Balista.	(13) Aureolus.
(4) Odenathus.	
(5) Zenobia.	

In the West.	Promiscuous.
(6) Posthumus.	(14) Saturninus in Pontus.
(7) Lollianus.	(15) Trebellianus in Isauria.
(8) Victorinus and his mother Victoria.	(16) Piso in Thessaly.
(9) Marius.	(17) Valens in Achaia.
(10) Tetricus.	(18) Æmilianus in Egypt.
	(19) Celsus in Africa.

Thirty Years' War. That long series of conflicts between the Catholics and Protestants in Germany in the first half of the seventeenth century. It began in 1618, and ended with the Peace of Westphalia in 1648.

Thisbe. *See* PYRAMUS.

Thistle of Scotland. "There is much obscurity as to the circumstances under which the thistle was adopted as its emblem by the Scottish nation, but the following is a tradition: Queen Scotia had led her troops in a well-fought field, and when the day was won retired to the rear to rest from her toils. She threw herself upon the ground, when, as ill-luck would have it, an envious thistle had elected to grow at the very spot selected for her repose. Whether the fair Amazon fought in the national costume I know not, but the spines of the offending herb were sufficiently powerful to penetrate the skin in a very painful manner. A proverbial philosopher (not Mr. Tupper, I think) has declared that 'he that sitteth on nettles riseth up quickly,' and the same remark holds good of thistles. Queen Scotia sprang up and tore the thistle up by the roots. She was about to cast it from her with a military but unladylike expression, when it struck her that the prickly plant would henceforth be ever associated in her mind with the glorious victory which she had just gained. Her intention was changed. She placed the thistle in her cask, and it became the badge of her dynasty." The earliest written mention of the thistle as the badge of Scotland occurs in the reign of James III. during the fifteenth century. But there is very little doubt that centuries before this the thistle had been recognized as the Scottish emblem. The Order of the Thistle, a badge of knighthood akin to that of the Bath in England, is said to have been founded by King Achaius I. in the year 809. Many have wondered how a plant of so forbidding and unattractive an aspect came to be selected as an emblem of royalty. Here is the story: During one of the then frequent incursions of the Danes to the coast of Britain they planned a night attack on the camp of the Scottish King. Advancing stealthily toward the sleeping soldiery, several of the foremost invaders trod unexpectedly upon a bed of thistles. The Danes were barefooted, and the sudden pain caused so many of them to cry out that the Scots were alarmed in time, and successfully drove back the enemy. In memory of this deliverance they adopted the thistle as the national emblem.

Thomas Brown, the Younger. (Pseud.) Thomas Moore, Irish poet (1779–1852).

Thomas Ingoldsby. (Pseud.) Richard Harris Barham, English divine and humorous writer (1788–1845).

Thomas Maitland. (Pseud.) Robert Buchanan, British poet (b. 1809).

Thomas Reynold, Physition. (Pseud.) Eucharius Rhodion, English writer (1540-1598).

Thomas, the Rhymer. By this name Thomas Learmont, a Scottish "rhyming chronicler" who flourished in the time of Alexander III., is best known.

Thor. In Scandinavian mythology the son of Odin and Frigga, and the god of War. He was the defender of the gods against the attacks of the giants. His chief weapon was his hammer Mjölnir (*q. v.*).

Thorough Doctor. William Varro, the English mediæval scholastic, was thus named.

Thos. Thomas.

Thoth. In Egyptian mythology the god of Eloquence.

Though lost to Sight to Memory dear. The authorship or origin of this familiar line has long been a literary puzzle. A writer in "Harper's Bazar" says, "It originated with Ruthven Jenkyns, and was first published in the 'Greenwich Magazine for Marines,' in 1701 or 1702." The entire poem was as follows: —

"Sweetheart, good-bye! that fluttering sail
   Is spread to waft me far from thee;
And soon before the favoring gale
   My ship shall bound upon the sea.
Perchance all des'late and forlorn
   These eyes shall miss thee many a year;
But unforgotten every charm —
   Though lost to sight, to mem'ry dear.

"Sweetheart, good-bye! one last embrace!
   O cruel fate, two souls to sever!
Yet in this heart's most sacred place
   Thou, thou alone, shalt dwell forever.
And still shall recollection trace
   In Fancy's mirror, ever near,
Each smile, each tear; that form, that face —
   Though lost to sight, to mem'ry dear."

Three Bad K's. The Greeks so named the Karians, Kretans, and Kikilians. The Romans retained the expression, though they spelled the words with a C.

Three Bishoprics. The three cities of Lorraine, Metz, and Verdun, each of which was at one time under the lordship of a bishop. They were united to the kingdom of France by Henri II., in 1552.

Three Calendars. Three royal princes, disguised as begging dervishes, the subject of three tales in the "Arabian Nights."

Three Chapters. Three books, or parts of three books, — one by Theodore of Mopsuestia, one by Theodoret of Cyprus, and the third by Ibas, Bishop of Edessa. These books were of a Nestorian bias, on the subject of the Incarnation and two natures of Christ. The Church took up the controversy warmly, and the dispute continued during the reign of Justinian and the popedom of Vigilius. In 553 the "Three Chapters" were condemned at the general Council of Constantinople.

Three Estates of the Realm. The nobility, the clergy, and the commonalty. In the collect for Gunpowder Treason, the English thank God for "preserving the king and the three estates of the realm;" from which it is quite evident that the sovereign is not one of the three estates, as nine persons out of ten suppose. These three estates are represented in the two Houses of Parliament. *See* FOURTH ESTATE.

Three-fingered Jack. The famous negro robber, who was the terror of Jamaica in 1780. He was hunted down in 1781.

Three F's. The phrase "fixity of tenure, fair rents, and free sale," was much used in Parliamentary discussions of Irish affairs in 1880–1882. Sir Stafford Northcote retorted that the three F's were rightly to be described as "fraud, force, and folly," and they were strenuously opposed by Lord Dufferin and others.

Three Kings' Day. Epiphany, or Twelfth Day; designed to commemorate the visit of the three kings, or Wise Men of the East, to the child Jesus.

Three Kings of Cologne. The name given to the three Magi who came from the East to worship the infant Christ. Tradition current in Cologne gives their names as Kaspar, Melchior, and Balthasar.

Three K's. Messrs. Kingsley, Kinsella, and Keeney, prominent citizens of Brooklyn, N. Y., were so nicknamed. They were jointly interested in many civic enterprises, and all three died within a year of each other, 1884–1885.

Three-Mile-Point Controversy. A local quarrel in 1837 between J. Fenimore Cooper, the novelist, and the people of Cooperstown regarding the ownership of part of the Cooper estate on Otsego Lake. For many years the public had used the Point, until they had come to consider it as their own; and when Cooper sought to define his rights a storm of abuse arose. The courts, however, sustained him.

Three-State Boundary Stone, The, lies at the junction of the States of Rhode Island, Massachusetts, and Connecticut.

Three-tailed Bashaw. A *beglerbeg*, or prince of princes among the Turks, having a standard of three horse-tails borne before him. The next in rank is the bashaw, with two tails, and then the bey, who has only one horse-tail.

Three Wonders of Babylon. The Palace, the Hanging Gardens, and the Tower of Babel.

Thro'. Through.

Throne of Jamsheed, The. Persepolis; so named by its Persian founders. Jamsheed removed the seat of government from Balkh thither.

Thumb Bible. An edition published at Aberdeen in 1693. It measured one inch square, and half an inch thick, and was called "Verbum Sempiternum."

Thumb, Tom. *See* TOM THUMB.

Thunder and Lightning. Stephen II. of Hungary (fl. 1100–1131).

Thunderbolt of Italy. Gaston de Foix, nephew of Louis XII. (fl. 1489–1512).

Thunderer, The. A nickname given to the "Times," of London, based on the following sentence beginning an article by Captain Sterling: "We thundered forth, the other day, an article on the subject of social and political reform."

Thundering Legion. A Roman legion that dispersed the Marcomanni in 179 A. D. The story goes that a thunderstorm was sent in answer to the prayers of certain Christians in its ranks.

Thunders of the Vatican. The anathemas of the Pope, which are issued from the Vatican.

Ti. Titanium.

Tib's Eve. A phrase current in Ireland, and meaning a day that never comes, — equivalent to the "Greek Calends." *See* ONCE IN A BLUE MOON.

Tichborne Dole. When Lady Mabella was dying, she requested her husband to grant her the means of leaving a charitable bequest. It was to be a dole of bread, to be distributed annually on the Feast of the Annunciation, to any who chose to apply for it. Sir Roger, her husband, said he would give her as much land as she could walk over while a billet of wood remained burning. The old lady was taken into the park, and managed to crawl over twenty-three acres of land, which was accordingly set apart, and is called "The Crawls" to this hour. When the Lady Mabella was taken back to her chamber she said: "So long as this dole is continued the family of Tichborne shall prosper; but immediately it is discontinued the house shall fall, from the failure of an heir male. This," she added, "will be when a family of seven sons is succeeded by one of seven daughters." The custom began in the reign of Henry II., and continued till 1796, when, singularly enough, the baron had seven sons and his successor seven daughters; and Mr. Edward Tichborne, who inherited the Doughty estates, dropping the original name, called himself Sir Edward Doughty.

Tick. A slang term for credit. In the seventeenth century the word "ticket" was given to any written acknowledgment of a debt, and hence any one subsisting on credit was said to "live on tick."

Tiddy Doll. A nickname given to Richard Grenville, Lord Temple (fl. 1711–1770), in the pasquinades of his time.

Tiger Lily. (Pseud.) Mrs. Lily Devereux Blake.

Tiger of Alica. A sobriquet bestowed on Manuel Losada, a Mexican bandit (1825–1873), on account of his cruelties.

Tiger of Honduras. Santos Guardiola, soldier and sometime President of Honduras (1812–1862). His daring and cruelty in the petty wars of Central America earned him his nickname.

Tiger of Tacayuba. A sobriquet conferred on Gen. Leonardo Marquez, a Mexican officer under Santa Anna (b. 1818). He obtained the title on account of some violent political and military reprisals.

Tigers, The. The Seventeenth Regiment of Foot in the English service.

Tillie Pfeiffer. The stage-name of Mrs. Edward Fuber.

Tim. Timothy.

Timber = FOREST. The word "timber" is used throughout the West for any woodland or forest growth. Hence "to take to the timber" is to hide in the forest. See LUMBER. The phrase "Presidential timber" is also used of men considered available for that high office. As none but the tallest and straightest trees are selected by the woodsman's axe, so only the most eminent men are likely to be talked of for the highest office in the gift of the people.

Timeo Danaos et dona ferentes. (Lat.) I fear the Greeks even when they bring gifts.

Time of Memory. An English law term, signifying time commencing with the beginning of the reign of Richard I.

Tim Linkinwater. (Pseud.) Mr. Waldo, in the New Orleans "Picayune."

Timon's Banquet. Nothing but covers and warm water. Being shunned by his friends in adversity, he pretended to have recovered his money, and invited his false friends to a banquet. The table was laden with covers, but when the contents were exposed, nothing was provided but lukewarm water.

Timothy Hairbrain. (Pseud.) James Anderson, editor of the "Bee" (1790), and author of numerous essays therein over the above signature.

Timothy Quill. (Pseud.) Arthur Warren, English correspondent of the Boston "Herald."

Timothy Templeton. (Pseud.) Charles Baker Adams, American naturalist (1814–1853).

Timothy Tickler. (Pseud.) Robert Syme, Scottish lawyer and writer (b. 1795).

Timothy Titcomb. (Pseud.) Josiah Gilbert Holland, M.D., American author (1819–1881).

Timothy Titterwell. Samuel Kettell, American editor and humorist (1800–1885), in the Boston "Courier." See PEEPING TOM.

Timpani. (Ital.) The kettle-drums. (Mus.)

Tine = PRONG. Our American custom of calling the prong of a fork a tine is a Lincolnshire peculiarity, and came over with our fathers. The more general word "prong" is indeed driving it out, and the word "tine" is understood in Lincolnshire alone of all England.

Tinker's Dam. " A dam of dough or other suitable material constructed by a tinker to confine his molten solder to the business in hand. Inasmuch as when a tinker's dam has once served its purpose it possesses little or no value, the phrase has come to be a frequently used and almost universally understood synonym for worthlessness." The foregoing explanation refutes the current notion that the expression savors of profanity.

Tin Pocket. A curious taunt among the people of the northwest of Ireland. When it was intended to convey to any person, in the strongest possible manner, that his pride in his family circumstances was only that of an upstart, the common expression for this was: " Your grandmother was Doherty ——, and wore a tin pocket." The origin of this saying was as follows: The northern part of the county of Donegal, particularly the district of Innishowen, is largely peopled by persons of the name of Doherty and O'Doherty. In past times one of the best means of smuggling poteens into Londonderry and other towns in the vicinity was by a tin flask carried by the women in their pockets. Hence the expression.

Tippecanoe. A nickname conferred on Gen. William Harrison in the political campaign which resulted in his election as President of the United States, in allusion to the victory gained by him over the Indians, Nov. 6, 1811, at the junction of the Tippecanoe and Wabash Rivers.

Tippecanoe and Tyler too. The refrain of a popular campaign song in 1840. " Tippecanoe " was a nickname of General Harrison in allusion to his victory over the Indians at that place in Indiana.

The author of this song was Alexander Coffman Ross, a merchant of Zanesville, Ohio (1812–1883). He sang in a church choir, and in the Presidential canvass of 1840 was a member of a Whig glee-club. A friend having suggested that the tune " Little Pigs " would be a suitable chorus for a political song, Ross set himself to compose the song, and one Sunday during sermon-time produced " Tippecanoe and Tyler too." This was sung by his glee-club at a mass-meeting in Zanesville, and at once became popular. When he went to New York in September to buy goods, he sang it at a great meeting in Lafayette Hall, the audience took up the chorus, after the meeting it was repeated by crowds in the streets and about the hotels, and thenceforth it was the most successful song of a canvass in which General Harrison was said to have been sung into the White House. From a boy Mr. Ross was interested in scientific inventions, and he is said to

have produced the first daguerreotype ever made in this country. He was one of the most enterprising business men in Zanesville, and accumulated a large property.

Tipperary. A nickname enjoyed by the Ninety-eighth English Regiment. The name was won in India, where an English general, seeing the regiment go roystering to the charge, exclaimed, " Magnificent Tipperary ! "

Tipton Slasher. The nickname given to an old-time English prize-fighter whose real name was William Perry.

Tiresias. In classic myth a blind soothsayer of Thebes, who lived to a great age, and who figures extensively in the legendary history of Greece.

Tissue Ballots. In the Presidential election of 1876, great frauds were perpetrated at the ballot-boxes in South Carolina, the boxes being stuffed with bogus ballots printed on tissue paper.

Tit. Titus.

Titan. In classic myth son of Cœlus and Terra, elder brother of Saturn, and father of the giants (Titans) who tried to deprive Saturn of the sovereignty of heaven, and who were, by the thunderbolts of Jupiter, hurled into Tartarus.

Titania. Wife of Oberon and queen of the fairies.

Tithonus. In classic myth a son of Laomedon, king of Troy. Aurora became enamored of him, and persuaded the gods to make him immortal ; but as she forgot to ask also for perpetual youth, he became old and ugly, and she changed him into a cicada.

Titian of Portugal. Alonzo Sanchez Coello (fl. 1515–1590).

Titus A. Brick. (Pseud.) C. E. File, in the New York " Star."

Tityre Tus (long *u*). The name assumed in the seventeenth century by a clique of young blades of the better class, whose delight was to break windows, upset sedan-chairs, molest quiet citizens, and rudely caress pretty women in the streets at night-time. These brawlers took successively many titular names, as Muns, Hectors, Scourers, afterwards Nickers, later still Hawcabites, and lastly Mohawks or Mohocks. " Tityre tus " is meant for the plural of " Tityre tu," in the first line of Virgil's first Eclogue : " Tityre, tu patulæ recubans sub tegmine fagi," and meant to imply that these blades were men of leisure and fortune, who " lay at ease under their patrimonial beech-trees." *See* SCOURERS.

Tityus. In classic myth a giant, son of Jupiter and Terra. His body was so vast that it covered nine acres of ground.

Tl. Thallium.

T. O. Turn over.

Toad-eater. "This slang phrase for a fawning, obsequious sycophant was first applied to a gluttonous parasite famous for his indiscriminate praise of all viands set before him. To test his powers of stomach and complaisance one of his patrons had a toad cooked for him, which he both ate and praised in his usual way." — OGILVIE. Another authority says it is "a metaphor taken from a mountebank's boy eating toads in order to show his master's skill in expelling poison." — *Adventures of David Simple*, 1744.

Tob. Tobit.

Tobacco City. Lynchburg, Va. Tobacco is one of the chief staples of trade.

Tobia Gorrio. The anagrammatic pen-name under which Arrigo Boito wrote his libretto of Ponchielli's opera, " Gioconda."

Tobias Guarnerius. (Pseud.) Alexander Dimitry (1805–1883), author of several short stories under this name. His son, Charles Patton Dimitry (b. 1837), contributed to current literature under the name "Tobias Guarnerius, Jr." *See* BRADDOCK FIELD.

Toby, M. P. The signature of Mr. H. W. Lucy, an English journalist.

Toga virilis. (Lat.) The manly robe — a garment assumed by the Roman youth when they reached fourteen years of age.

To get to go. "To get to go" is essentially a Georgia expression. They say: "Do don't fail to come to-night," and the reply is, "I've tried to get to go three weeks, now, so I reckon I'll be there t'night." The expression "Do don't" is heard in Georgia and South Carolina, but rarely elsewhere.

To kalon. (Gr.) "The beautiful." The chief good.

Toledo War, in United States history, was a dispute between Ohio and Michigan, concerning a boundary line, which cost the pioneers of that region fully $250,000.

Toleration Act. A Parliamentary statute, in 1689, which stopped the persecution of Protestant Dissenters in England.

Toler King. The pen-name of Mrs. Arthur H. Noyes.

Tolmen, Constantine. *See* CONSTANTINE TOLMEN.

Tom. Volume.

Tomb of all the Capulets. *See* CAPULETS.

Tom Folio. Thomas Rawlinson, the bibliomaniac (fl. 1681–1725).

Tom Folio. (Pseud.) Joseph E. Babson, in the Boston "Transcript."

Tom Fool. A popular nickname for a fool, or a foolish person, — probably arising from the name of some jester of forgotten fame.

Tom Moore of France. *See* ANACREON OF THE TEMPLE.

Tommy Atkins. A sobriquet for the British soldier. The term arose from a little pocket-book, or ledger, at one time served out to British soldiers, in which were to be entered the name, age, date of enlistment, length of service, wounds, medals, etc., of each individual. The War Office sent with each little ledger a form for filling it in, and the "M or N" selected, instead of the legal "John Doe" and "Richard Roe," was "Tommy Atkins." The books were instantly so named, and it was not many days before the soldier himself was dubbed "Tommy Atkins."

Tommy Shop. A place where wages are paid to workmen, who are expected to lay out a part of the money for the good of the shop. "Tommy" means bread or a penny roll, or the food taken by a workman in his handkerchief; it also means goods in lieu of money.

Tom Noddy. A popular name for a silly person.

Tom Styles. A fictitious character used by lawyers in their writs of ejectment, commonly coupled with the name John O'Noakes (*q. v.*). *See* JOHN DOE.

Tom Thumb, General. The professional pseudonym of Charles Sherwood Stratton, a famous dwarf, born at Bridgeport, Conn., 1838; died there July 15, 1883.

Tom Tidler's Ground. The ground or tenement of a sluggard. The expression occurs in Dickens's "Christmas Story," 1861. "Tidler" is a contraction of "the idler," or "t'idler." There is an English schoolboy game so called, which consists in this: Tom Tidler stands on a heap of stones, gravel, etc.; other boys rush on the heap crying

"Here I am on Tom Tidler's ground," and Tom bestirs himself to keep the invaders off.

Tontine System. The Tontine system was devised by Lorenzo Tonti, a Neapolitan, who introduced it into France about 1650. A certain number of persons subscribe to a general fund. Each draws an annuity according to his age; the annuity of the survivors increases as each member dies. The last survivor receives the total annuity during his life. This is the general plan, altered and improved on since it was originated.

Tony Hart. The stage-name of Anthony Cannon.

Topeka Constitution. In American history a document drawn up by a Kansas pro-slavery convention, in 1855.

Topog. Topography; topographical.

Topsy Venn. The stage-name of Mrs. E. J. Cornell.

To-Remain Bible. This was published in Cambridge, England, in 1805. The editor wrote on the margin of a proof the words "to remain" respecting a comma which the printer thought should be omitted. The latter, however, settled any doubts he may have had on the subject by inserting the words "to remain" in the passage in question (Gal. iv. 29), so that it read : "persecuted him that was born after the spirit to remain even so it is now."

Tories. A term first given to a political party about 1678. Dr. Johnson defines a Tory as one who adheres to the ancient constitution of the State and the apostolical hierarchy of the Church of England. The Tories long maintained the doctrines of "divine heredity, indefeasible right, lineal succession, passive obedience, prerogative, etc." "Tory" was probably an Irish word signifying savage. It was first applied to Irish brigands, who robbed "in the king's name," and from them it was transferred to all those who were devoted to the support of the king.

Tory Terrier. A nickname conferred on Lord Randolph Churchill (b. 1850), Secretary of State for India, in 1885, in the Salisbury cabinet, on account of his aggressive manners.

Tot homines, quot sententiæ. (Lat.) So many men, so many minds.

Totidem verbis. (Lat.) In just so many words.

Toties quoties. (Lat.) As often as; as many times as.

Totis viribus. (Lat.) "With the whole strength." With all the strength he can muster.

Toto cœlo. (Lat.) "By the whole heavens." As opposite as the poles.

Toto corde. (Lat.) With the whole heart.

Totum. (Lat.) The whole.

Toujours prêt. (Fr.) Always ready.

Tour à tour. (Fr.) By turns.

Tour d'adresse. (Fr.) A sleight-of-hand trick.

Tour de force. (Fr.) A feat of strength, or skill.

Tours de page. (Fr.) School-boys' tricks.

Tous frais faits. (Fr.) Clear of all expenses; all expenses paid.

Tout-à-fait. (Fr.) Entirely; wholly; exactly.

Tout bien ou rien. (Fr.) The whole or nothing.

Tout ensemble. (Fr.) "All together." Whole appearance; the whole taken together; general effect.

Tout le monde. (Fr.) "All the world." Every one; everybody.

Townley Mysteries. Certain religious dramas, so called because the manuscript containing them belonged to P. Townley. These dramas are supposed to have been acted at Widkirk Abbey, in Yorkshire. In 1831 they were printed for the Surtees Society, under the editorship of the Rev. Joseph Hunter and J. Stevenson.

Town Listener. (Pseud.) Leander Richardson, in the New York "World."

Town, Lud's. See LUD'S TOWN.

Towrows. A nickname conferred on the aristocratic Grenadier Guards. See also SANDBOYS.

Tp. Township.

T. Pym. (Pseud.) Clara Creed, a writer for the young.

Tr. Transpose; translator; translation; trustee; a shake (*trillo*).

Track = LINE. The road-bed of a railroad, which we name the "track," is called the "line" in England.

Trade Dollar. During the period of suspension of specie payments, early in 1873, Congress authorized the coinage of a silver piece containing 420 grains of silver, for use in trade with China and Japan. That coin was designated a "trade dollar," and was never designed for circulation in this country. It is not a legal tender, although intrinsically more valuable than the standard dollar. When silver became a currency in general use, about 1879, the "trade dollar" came into circulation, often proving very annoying to business. The government never accepted it as a deposit, or payment, and, in 1883, all the banks of the country which had not already refused to take it, did so, thus banishing it from the channels of traffic.

Trades Unions. The First Dragoon Guards.

Trans. Translator; translation; transactions; transpose.

Trans-Atlantic. The pen-name of Thomas Mooney (1806–1888), an Irish agitator and journalistic correspondent.

Translator General. An honorary title conferred on Philemon Holland (d. 1636), and who rendered into English most of the classic poets of antiquity.

Transubstantiation. A doctrine of the Roman Catholic Church that the bread and wine in the Lord's Supper are actually changed into Christ's flesh' and blood.

Tre. (Ital.) Three; as, *à tre*, for three voices or instruments. (Mus.)

Treacle Bible. "A copy of the Scriptures issued in 1568, and so named from its rendering of Jer. viii. 22: 'Is there no treacle in Gilead?' But this is not the only passage where the word occurs. There are three instances of it, which are as follows in Matthew's Bible, 1537: 'I am heauy and abashed, for there is no more tryacle at Galaad.' — Jer. viii. 22. 'Go vp (O Galaad) and brynge tryacle vnto the daughter of Egipte.' — Jer. xlvi. 11. 'Juda and the lande of Israel occupyed with thee, and brought vnto thy markettes, wheat, balm, hony, oyle, and triacle.' — Ezek. xxvii. 17. Becke's Bible, 1549, the Bishops' Bible, and others have 'tryacle' in the same passages." — *Notes and Queries.*

Treas. Treasurer.

Treasury of Sciences. Bokhara, Asia, an Asiatic centre of learning. It has one hundred and three colleges with ten thousand students, besides a host of schools and three hundred and sixty mosques.

Tree. The practice common to hunted game, of seeking refuge in the branches of a tree, led to the phrase "to tree" one's self, or to "tree" game. In an opossum chase, the dogs often mistake the tree up which the creature has sought safety, and are then said to be "barking up the wrong tree," a phrase which has come to be applied to similar blunders in real life. The phrase "up a tree," meaning "in a predicament," is also of the same origin.

Tree of the Universe. *See* YGG-DRASIL.

Tremando, or Tremolo. (Ital.) It implies the repetition of a note or chord with great rapidity, so as to produce a tremulous kind of motion. (Mus.)

Tremont. The early name by which Boston, Mass., was known. It arose from the three hills on which the city is built. It has also been called "Tri-mount," or "Trimountain."

Trencher Cap. The mortar-board cap worn at college; so called from the trenchered or split boards which form the top.

Trencher Friends. Persons who cultivate the friendship of others for the sake of sitting at their board, and the good things they can get.

Trencher Knight. A table knight; a suitor from cupboard love.

Tria juncta in uno. A Latin phrase meaning "three joined in one." It is the motto of the Order of the Bath, and was probably at the first institution of the Order adopted in allusion to faith, hope, and charity. It is now thought to signify the three classes of those admitted into the Order, or perhaps to the three crowns which are the armorial ensign of the Order.

Tribes, City of the. *See* CITY OF THE TRIBES.

Trilby. (Pseud.) Vicomtesse de Peyronney, French novelist and writer (b. 1841).

Trillo. (Ital.) A rapid alternation of two notes. (Mus.)

Trimmers. A name of reproach affixed to various members of the two great English parties during and after the Revolution of 1688. Halifax, the "chief of trimmers," rather gloried in the title, affirming that "everything good trims betwixt extremes."

Trin. Trinity.

Trinculo. (Pseud.) Andrew C. Wheeler, in the New York "Leader."

Trinity Day. Trinity Sunday is the Sunday following Whit-Sunday. The festival of the Holy Trinity was instituted by Pope Gregory IV. in 828, on his ascending the papal throne, and is observed by the Latin and Protestant Churches on the Sunday next following Pentecost, or Whitsuntide. The observance of the festival was first made obligatory by the Council of Arles in 1260, and was appointed to be held on the present day by Pope John XXI. in 1334.

Trinity Flower. *See* SHAMROCK.

Trinity Jones. The sobriquet conferred on William Jones, of Nayland (fl. 1726–1800), who wrote a masterly treatise in defence of the doctrine of the Trinity.

Trinity of the Anti-Corn Laws League. John Bright, Richard Cobden, and Villiers, three able British statesmen.

Triple Alliance. (1) A treaty entered into, in 1688, by England, Sweden, and the United Provinces for the purpose of thwarting the ambitious designs of Louis XIV. of France. (2) A convention or treaty, in 1718, between England, the United Provinces, and the Duke of Orleans, Regent of France, with the object of hindering the schemes of Spain.

Triple Tree. The gallows. Early English writers allude to it as the "three trees." Harman, in his "Caveat," 1573, says, "Repentaunce is never thought upon until they clyme three trees with a ladder."

Triptolemus. In classic myth a favorite of Ceres, who taught him husbandry.

Trismegistus ("thrice greatest"). The surname conferred on Hermes, the Egyptian philosopher.

Trissotin ("thrice foolish"). The name of a poet and coxcomb in Molière's comedy, "Les Femmes Savantes." Under this character Molière satirized the Abbé Cotin, a personage who affected to unite in himself the rather inconsistent characters of a writer of poems of gallantry and of a powerful and excellent preacher. His dramatic name was originally "Tricotin," which, as too plainly pointing out the individual, was softened into "Trissotin."

We hardly know any instance of the strength and weakness of human nature so striking and so grotesque as the character of this haughty, vigilant, resolute, sagacious blue-stocking [Frederick the Great], half Mithridates and half "Trissotin," bearing up against a world in arms, with an ounce of poison in one pocket, and a quire of bad verses in the other. — MACAULAY.

Triton. In classic myth son of Neptune and Amphitrite ; a powerful sea deity who at the bidding of his father blows through his shell to rouse or calm the ocean.

Triumvirate. In English history the Duke of Marlborough controlling foreign affairs, Lord Godolphin controlling Council and Parliament, and the Duchess of Marlborough controlling the Court and Queen.

Triumvirate, The Great, of American politics was the offensive and defensive alliance between Calhoun, Clay, and Webster.

Trivia. In classic myth a name given to Diana, in allusion to the fact that her temples were often erected where three roads met.

Troilus. In classic myth son of Priam and Hecuba. He was slain by Achilles.

Troja fuit. (Lat.) Troy has been.

Trottoir. (Fr.) A sidewalk ; a pavement or foot-path.

Trs. Trustees.

Truce of God. A very curious mediæval custom. It was decreed by a synod convened at Roussillon, in 1027, that none should attack his enemy between Saturday evening at nones, and Monday morning at the hour of prime. Similar regulations were adopted in England, in 1042, though sometimes Wednesday and Friday were designated as the time for the truce. The Truce of God was confirmed by many church councils.

Truck = VAN or DRAY. The vehicle known as a "truck" in the cities of the United States is the "van" or "dray" of the English.

Truck = VEGETABLES. Kitchen-garden produce in America is known as "truck," "garden-truck," or "garden-sass." *See* GREENS.

Truck = LITTER or RUBBISH. Another meaning of the Americanism "truck" is its equivalent use for the English words "lumber," "litter," or "rubbish," of any sort.

Truditur dies die. (Lat.) One day treads on the heels of another.

True Blue. Of genuine or high degree in origin or character. *See* BLUE BLOOD.

Truepenny. "Hamlet says to the Ghost, 'Art thou there, Truepenny?' Then to his comrades, 'You hear this fellow in the cellarage?' And again, 'Well said, old mole; canst work?' Truepenny means 'earth-borer' or 'mole' — an excellent word to apply to a ghost ' boring through the cellarage ' to get to the place of purgatory before cock-crow. Miners use the word for a run of metal or metallic earth, which indicates the presence and direction of a lode." — BREWER.

True Thomas. Thomas the Rhymer was so called from his prophecies, the most noted of which was the prediction of the death of Alexander III. of Scotland, made to the Earl of March in the castle of Dunbar the day before it occurred.

Trusta. (Anagrammatic pseud.) Mrs. Elizabeth Stuart Phelps, American writer (1815–1852).

Tub Conspiracy. "During John Adams's administration the Federalists were, or pretended to be, afraid of plots against the Government, on the part of the French agents in America. In 1799 the Department of State pretended to have information of the departure for the United States of secret agents of France, having in their possession documents dangerous to our peace. The vessel was boarded immediately on its arrival at Charleston, S. C. Four men and a woman, passengers on board, were arrested as the spies, and two tubs, in a false bottom of which the papers were said to be hidden, were seized. The passengers turned out to be no spies, and the papers were not compromising." — *Dictionary of American Politics.*

Tuebor. (Lat.) I will defend.

Tues., or Tu. Tuesday.

Tuft-hunter, Tuft-hunting. A "tuft" was the name given to noblemen at the English universities, so named because of the silk gowns and tasselled caps they alone wore. Hence those who toadied to them were dubbed "tuft-hunters." The phrase has been extended to those who carried the same practice into the world or public life.

Tulcan Bishops. Certain Scotch bishops appointed by James I., with the distinct understanding that they were to hand over a fixed portion of the revenue to the patron. A tulcan is a stuffed calf-skin, placed under a cow that withholds her milk. The cow, thinking the tulcan to be her calf, readily yields her milk to the milk-pail.

Tulip Mania. A reckless mania for the purchase of tulip-bulbs in the years 1634–1637. A root of the species called "Viceroy" sold for £250; "Semper Augustus," more than double that sum. The tulips were grown in Holland, but the mania which spread over Europe was a mere stock-jobbing speculation.

Tumble-down Dick is a sobriquet originally applied to Richard Cromwell after his fall.

Tuneful Nine. The nine Muses. *See* MUSES.

Tune the Old Cow died of. Many people use this expression without any definite idea of its meaning or origin. It seems to have come to us from over the sea. In Scotland and the north of Ireland the saying is very common in the mouths of the peasantry. It arose out of an old song: —

"There was an old man and he had an old cow,
   And he had nothing to give her;
So he took out his fiddle and played her a tune:
   'Consider, good cow, consider;
This is no time of year for the grass to grow;
   Consider, good cow, consider.'"

The old cow died of hunger; and when any grotesquely melancholy song or tune is uttered, the north-country people say: "That is the tune the old cow died of." Hence it has passed into a proverb, meaning "a homily in place of alms."

Tunkers. A politico-religious sect of Ohio. They came from a small German village on the Eder. They believe all will be saved, are Quakers in plainness of dress and speech, and will neither fight nor go to law. Both sexes are equally eligible for any office. Celibacy is the highest honor, but not imperative. "Tunker" means "to dip a morsel into gravy," "a sop into wine;" and as they are Baptists this name has been given them.

Tunnel City. North Adams, Mass., near the famous Hoosac Tunnel.

Tun of Heidelberg. A great wine-vat at Heidelberg. The first was begun in 1343, and was made to contain twenty-one pipes. Another, begun in 1589 and finished in three years, had a diameter of eighteen feet and held 128 English hogsheads. In 1664 a third was made to hold six hundred hogsheads, and was destroyed by the French four years later. The one which at present is mouldering away, and, according to Longfellow, is "next to the Alhambra one of the most magnificent ruins of the Middle Ages," was begun in 1751, and was capable of holding 283,000 bottles. For nearly twenty years it was kept steadily replenished. At every vintage the grape-growers used to meet and dance on its top. It was twenty-four feet high, and thirty-six feet in its longest diameter. The biggest vats, however, have never figured in history. In one English brewery there is a cask said to be capable of holding twice as much as the tun of Heidelberg. It is thirty-six feet in diameter and forty feet high.

Tu quoque. (Lat.) "Thou also." You are as bad yourself, — a term in mutual recriminations.

Tur. Turkey.

Turkey, Block Island. *See* BLOCK ISLAND TURKEY.

Turkey Talk, or **To Talk Turkey.** To act or speak in a straightforward and an honest manner. Two men, an Indian and a white man, agreed to hunt together for a day, and to divide the spoils. When the time came, there was no difficulty in apportioning the smaller birds and animals, — one of a kind to each. At last they reached the last pair, — a crow and a turkey. "Now," says the white man, with a great show of fairness; "you may have the crow, and I'll take the turkey; or I'll take the turkey, and you may have the crow." "Huh!" says the Indian, "why you no talk turkey to me?"

Turncoat. The name of "turncoat" took its rise from one of the first dukes of Savoy, whose dominions lying open to attacks from both France and Spain, was obliged to temporize, and fall in with that Power that was most likely to distress him, according to the success of their arms against one another. So being frequently obliged to change sides, he humorously got a coat made that was blue on one side and white on the other, and might be indifferently worn either side out. While in the Spanish interest he wore the blue side out, and the white side was the badge for the French. Hence he was called "Emmanuel the Turncoat," to distinguish him from other princes of the same name of that house.

Turnip-hoer. A nickname conferred on George I. of England. It was said that when he first arrived at the capital he threatened to convert St. James's Park into a turnip-field.

Turpentine State. North Carolina, which annually sends vast quantities of turpentine to market.

Tutor et ultor. (Lat.) The protector and avenger.

Tutti. (Ital.) All the voices, or instruments, or both. (Mus.)

Tutto è buono che vien da Dio. (Ital.) All is good which comes from God.

Tuum est. (Lat.) It is your own.

Tweed Case. The proceedings against William M. Tweed and others, known as the Tweed Ring (*q. v.*), for frauds perpetrated while they were municipal officers of New York, by which they obtained over six million dollars from the county of New York. In a civil case it was decided by the Court of Appeals of New York, in 1874 (People *v.* Ingersoll, 58 N. Y. 1), that an action for money fraudulently obtained from a county could not be brought in the name of the people of the State. This was subsequently remedied by statute, and a judgment obtained. In a criminal case, Tweed was found guilty on twelve counts for similar offences in one indictment, and was separately sentenced to one year's imprisonment on each, with the direction that service of one sentence should not begin until the completion of service on a prior sentence. After completing the term of his first sentence, a writ of habeas corpus was served on his jailer, and the Court of Appeals, in 1875 (People *ex rel.* Tweed *v.* Liscomb, 60 N. Y. 559), decided that, under the statutes conferring the power to sentence, cumulative sentences in such cases were not lawful, and discharged him; but he was immediately imprisoned in default of bail in preceding civil suits. Other minor decisions on questions of procedure are also included under this term.

Tweedledum and Tweedledee. The lines in which these words occur were written by Byrom, the inventor of a system of stenography, in 1725, when a musical charlatan named Bononcini was fashionable and Handel was neglected. They were published in "Byrom's Remains" by the Chetham Society, and are as follows: —

"Some say compared to Bononcini
That Mynheer Handel's but a ninny;
Others aver that, to him, Handel
Is scarcely fit to hold a candle.
Strange all this difference should be
'Twixt Tweedledum and Tweedledee."

Tweed Ring. A corrupt gang of New York politicians who, headed by William M. Tweed and others, plundered the city of millions of dollars from 1868–1872. Many arrests were made; some of the thieves were forced to disgorge; and "Boss" Tweed himself died in prison. *See* TWEED CASE.

Twelfth-Day, Twelfth-Night. The 6th of January, the twelfth day after Christmas (*see* EPIPHANY), also called "Little Christmas," has long been celebrated as a social festival in England, bringing to a close the merrymakings of the Christmas cycle. On Twelfth-Night, throughout England the Christmas holly and mistletoe are burned to the accompaniment of roasting nuts and merry pranks. The word "Epiphany," which has been given to the season, ushered in by the 6th of January, signifies "a manifestation," and denoted, among the heathen Greeks, a festival held in commemoration of the appearance of a god in any particular place. The word subsequently passed into the usage of the Christian Church, and was used to designate the manifestation or appearance of Christ upon the earth to the Gentiles, — with special reference to the day on which he was seen and worshipped by the wise men who came from the East. The custom of wassailing the fruit trees on the eve of Twelfth-Day, by the Devonshire farmers, was a very old one. They would proceed to their orchards in the evening, accompanied by their farm servants, who carried with them large pitchers or milkpails filled with cider. In each orchard one tree was selected as the representative of the rest, and saluted with a certain form of words; they would then immerse cakes in cider and hang them on the apple-tree; after which they sprinkled the tree, pronounced their incantation, danced right merrily round it, and then went home to feast. This was done in order that the trees might bear much fruit, as we learn from the following old verse: —

"Wassail the trees that they may bear
You many a plum and many a pear;
For more or less fruits they will bring
As you do give them wassailing."

On Twelfth-Night there is a curious custom in vogue in Drury Lane Theatre, London, known as "Cutting the Baddeley Cake." *See* BADDELEY CAKE.

Twelve Labors of Hercules. These were imposed upon Hercules (*q. v.*) by his kinsman Eurystheus, in the following order: (1) To slay the Nemean lion. (2) To destroy the hydra which lurked in the wood and marsh of Lerna. (3) To overtake and capture a swift stag, possessing antlers of gold and feet of brass, and owned by Diana. (4) To capture alive the wild boar which infested the neighborhood of Erymanthus. (5) To cleanse the Augean stables. (6) To kill the hideous flesh-eating birds that hovered over the country near Lake Stymphalis, in Arcadia. (7) To capture alive the mad bull belonging to Minos, king of Crete, and bring it bound to Eurystheus. (8) To secure the brood-mares, which fed on human flesh, belonging to Diomedes, king of the Bistones, in Thrace. (9) To seize the girdle of Hippolyta, the Amazonian queen. (10) To kill the monster Geryon, and lead his herds to Argos. (11) To obtain possession of certain apples concealed in the garden of the Hesperides. (12) To bring from the nether world the triple-headed dog, Cerberus. All of these feats the hero performed, and they gave rise to many other exploits scarcely less wonderful.

Twelve Tables. A famous code of laws, called the "Laws of the Twelve Tables," was promulgated in Rome about 450 B. C.

Twilight of the Gods. *See* RAGNAROK.

Twin Brother of Sleep. Death has been euphemistically so named.

Twin Cities of the Northwest. St. Paul and Minneapolis, Minn.

Twin Relic. Polygamy has been called "the twin relic of barbarism," coupling it with slavery, and indicating that it was comparable therewith in iniquity.

Two Kings of Brentford. There is an old quip about "two kings of Brentford smelling at one nosegay," said of persons who were once rivals, but have become reconciled. The allusion is to an old farce called "The Rehearsal," by the Duke of Buckingham. The two kings of Brentford enter hand in hand; and the actors, to heighten the absurdity, used to make them enter "smelling at one nosegay."

Twopenny Trash. A nickname given to William Cobbett's "Weekly Political Register," in 1816, after he reduced its price from twelve and one half pence to twopence. Its sale was enormously increased.

Tyburnia. A Latinized form of Tyburn, a former suburb of London, now built over, and including Portman and Devonshire Squares and their surrounding streets, to which fashionable district the above popular name has been given.

The elegant, the prosperous, the polite Tyburnia, the most respectable district of the habitable globe. — THACKERAY.

Tydæus. In classic myth a son of Œneus, king of Calydon, and father of Diomedes. *See* SEVEN AGAINST THEBES.

Tyndaridæ. Another name for Castor and Pollux (*q. v.*).

Tyneman ("losing man"). A so-briquet bestowed on Archibald, fourth Earl of Douglas, on account of his many disastrous defeats in battle.

Typ. Typographer.

Typhon. In classic myth a giant who breathed forth fire, and who was killed by a thunderbolt from Jupiter, and buried under Mount Ætna.

Tyr. In Scandinavian mythology son of Odin and younger brother to Thor. He was a fighting god, and the especial deity of champions and heroes.

Tyrant of the Chersonese. Miltiades.

Tyrrel's Case. A noted decision in English law (1558), in which after Parliament, by the statute of uses, had thought to put an end to the holding of land in the name of one person to the use of another, the courts introduced the doctrine of a use upon a use, leading to the present law of trusts.

U.

U. Union; uranium.

U. B. United Brethren.

Uberrima fides. (Lat.) Boundless trust, or faith.

Ubi jus incertum, ibi jus nullum. (Lat.) Where the law is uncertain, there is no law.

Ubi libertas, ibi patria. (Lat.) Where liberty dwells, there is my country.

Ubi mel, ibi apes. (Lat.) Where there is honey, there will be found bees.

Ubi supra. (Lat.) "Where above." It will be found mentioned above.

Ubique. Under this pen-name Parker Gillmore, the American author, wrote "Prairie and Forest."

U. C. Upper Canada.

U. C. *Urbe condita*. Year of Rome.

U. Donough Outis. (Pseud.) Richard Grant White, American critic (1822–1885).

U. E. I. C. United East India Company.

Ugly = ILL-TEMPERED. As strange a perversion of a word as can be found in the long list of Americanisms, is the use of the word "ugly" for "ill-tempered" or "angry."

U. G. R. R. Underground Railroad.

U. J. C. *Utriusque Juris Doctor*. Doctor of Both Laws.

U. K. United Kingdom.

U. K. A. Ulster King-at-Arms.

Ullur. In Scandinavian mythology a god who presided over duels, archery, and hunting.

Ult. Last (*ultimo*); of the last month.

Ultima ratio. (Lat.) The last resource.

Ultima ratio regum. (Lat.) The last resource of kings — that is, war.

Ultima Thule. At the dawn of modern history, when Southern Europe began to turn its eyes toward the hitherto unknown lands lying westward and northward, "Thule" stood at successive epochs for the then farthest known land. Thus, the Latin phrase, "Ultima Thule" means "Uttermost Thule," and in it men fabled their superstitious beliefs respecting the wild north. Norway, Iceland, and Foula (the westernmost of the Shetland group) bore the title in turn.

Ultimus Romanorum. (Lat.) The last of the Romans.

Ultramontanists (from *ultra montes*, beyond the mountains). A term originally applied in France to those who upheld the extreme authority of the Pope in opposition to the freedom of the Gallican church, which had been secured by various bulls, and especially by the concordat of July 15, 1801. Ultramontanists now are those who maintain the official infallibility of the Bishop of Rome.

Ulysses. In classic myth a son of Laertes, king of Ithaca, husband of Penelope, and father of Telemachus. He was distinguished above all the Greeks at the siege of Troy for valor, craft, and eloquence. On his way back to Ithaca he was beset by innumerable perils, and at length reached home alone after twenty years' absence.

Ulysses, The. Albert III., Margrave of Brandenburg, was so named. *See also* ACHILLES.

Ulysses of the Highlands. Sir Evan Cameron, Lord of Lochiel (d. 1719), was thus named.

Un. (Ital.) A; as, *un poco*, a little.

Un air noble. (Fr.) "A mien noble." A distinguished appearance.

Una voce. (Lat.) "With one voice." Unanimously.

Un bel esprit. A wit; a virtuoso.

Uncle Adam. (Pseud.) George Moyridge.

Uncle Blue Jacket. The pen-name of Maurice Wurts McEntee (d. 1883), an American journalist and miscellaneous writer. He was sometime editor of the Kingston, N. Y., "Freeman."

Uncle Dick. A familiar appellation bestowed on Gov. Richard Oglesby of Illinois.

Uncle Esek. (Pseud.) Henry W. Shaw, in the "Bric-a-Brac" department in the "Century."

Uncle Philip. (Pseud.) Francis Lister Hawks, D. D., American divine and author (1798–1866).

Uncle Sam. A synonym for the government of the United States. "Immediately after the last declaration of war with England, Elbert Anderson, of New York, then a contractor, visited Troy, on the Hudson, where was concentrated, and where he purchased, a large quantity of provisions, — beef, pork, etc. The inspectors of these articles at that place were Messrs. Ebenezer and Samuel Wilson. The latter gentleman (invariably known as 'Uncle Sam') generally superintended in person a large number of workmen, who, on this occasion, were employed in overhauling the provisions purchased by the contractor for the army. The casks were marked 'E. A. — U. S.' This work fell to the lot of a facetious fellow in the employ of the Messrs. Wilson, who, on being asked by some of his fellow-workmen the meaning of the mark (for the letters U. S., for United States, were then almost entirely new to them), said 'he did not know, unless it meant Elbert Anderson and "Uncle Sam" Wilson.' The joke took among the workmen, and passed currently; and 'Uncle Sam' himself, being present, was occasionally rallied by them on the increasing extent of his possessions. . . . Many of these workmen, being of a character denominated 'food for powder,' were found, shortly after, following the recruiting drum and pushing toward the frontier lines, for the double purpose of meeting the enemy and of eating the provisions they had lately labored to put in good order. Their old jokes accompanied them, and before the first campaign ended this identical one first appeared in print; it gained favor rapidly till it penetrated, and was recognized, in every part of the country, and will no doubt continue so while the United States remain a nation." — FROST.

Uncle Will. (Pseud.) Prof. William Wells, Ph. D., LL. D., American writer (b. 1820).

Underground Railroad. (1) A popular and half-humorous synonym for the numberless methods by which fugitive slaves from the Southern States were aided in escaping to the North, or to British territory during the Anti-slavery agitation. It was often contracted to U. G. R. R. (2) In 1882–1885, after the passage by Congress of the "Chinese Bill," which excluded Chinamen from entering the United States, the same phrase was applied to the various routes and devices by which its provisions were eluded by the wily Celestials.

Undertakers. In the political annals of the Irish Parliament, in the last century, a body of place-hunters were thus nicknamed, because they bargained with the government slavishly to perform its behests.

Under the Rose. This phrase is said to have originated in Birmingham. A Jacobite Club, established in the early part of the eighteenth century, met in a room the ceiling of which was ornamented by the figure of an open rose. It was one of the rules of the Club that everything which took place there "under the rose" was to be kept a profound secret. Perhaps, however, the founders of the Club placed the rose on the ceiling in allusion to the Latin phrase *sub rosa.*

Un fait accompli. (Fr.) An accomplished fact.

Unfortunate Peace. The peace of Cateau-Cambresis, signed April 2, 1559.

Unguibus et rostro. (Lat.) "With nails and beak." Tooth and nail; with our whole powers.

Unit. Unitarian.

United Irishmen. A political society which met secretly to establish a republic, and became active in 1795. Theobald Wolf Tone, the founder, was captured by Sir John Warren in the "Hoche," one of six frigates destined to support the rebellion, in October, 1798. He anticipated his punishment by suicide in prison, November, 1798.

Univ. University.

Universal Doctor. (1) Alain de Lille (fl. 1114–1203). (2) Thomas Aquinas (fl. 1227–1274).

Universalist. One who believes in the future restoration of all men to eternal felicity.

Universe, Hub of the. *See* HUB OF THE UNIVERSE.

Univt. Universalist.

Unlikists. *See* ANOMŒANS.

Unmerciful Parliament. Held in the reign of Richard II., and thus named by the people of England on account of its tyrannical and high-handed proceedings.

Uno ictu. (Lat.) "With one stroke." At one blow.

Uno impetu. (Lat.) "With one onset." At one effort.

Unpleasantness, The Late. *See* LATE UNPLEASANTNESS, THE.

Unready, The. Ethelred II. of England.

Un sot à triple étage. (Fr.) An egregious blockhead.

U. P. United Presbyterian.

Upas-tree. During the latter part of the eighteenth and far into the present century, the upas-tree was a standard illustration of that species of dangers which must not be approached, "the belief being that the poisonous emanations from the tree were so pernicious as to be fatal to the life of any living creature, including man, that came near it." Pereira, in his "Materia Medica," says of it: "This is the celebrated Autsjar, or, Upas Poison-tree of Java, rendered notorious, principally in consequence of certain gross falsehoods concerning it, about 1780 by a person of the name of Foersch, said to have been a surgeon in the service of the Dutch East India Company. Malefactors, says this person, when they receive sentence of death, are offered the chance of life, if they will go to the upas-tree for a box of poison; and although every precaution is taken to avoid the injurious influence of the emanations of the tree, yet of seven hundred criminals who went to collect the poison, scarcely two out of twenty returned. Foersch further adds that for fifteen or eighteen miles around this tree no living animal of any kind has ever been discovered." But Horsfield and Leschinault proved that these statements were purely fabulous; that, on the contrary, birds roost in its branches, and that while a poisonous juice may be obtained by tapping the tree and boiling the sap, the tree is absolutely harmless. But scarcely had the upas-tree declined in favor, in consequence of this exposure, when there sprung up in its place the equally deadly Judas-tree. Gerard, an old English writer who flourished in the sixteenth century, says that the name was whimsically bestowed on the juniper-tree, on a variety of which the traitorous disciple was said to have hanged himself. The tree is valuable as an ornament, partly for its pleasant form, and partly for its pretty pink blossoms. But by perfervid writers and speakers, this tree has been described as "bearing most beautiful flowers which are especially alluring to bees, to whom its nectar is deadly poison, in proof of which they aver that the ground beneath it at its period of bloom is covered with bees and insects that have succumbed to its deadly effect." But these notions are, as has been well said, entirely erroneous, and can have arisen only in the brain of some mendacious dreamer, who saw in the name "Judas-tree" something forbidding and abhorrent. The Judas-tree and the upas are twin monstrosities that may be relegated to the misty realm of the unreal. Darwin, in his "Loves of the Plants," has perpetuated Foersch's fable when he says : —

"On the blasted heath
Fell Upas sits, the hydra tree of death."

It is probable that the fable of the blighting influence of the upas-tree has been derived from the fact that there is in Java a small tract of land on which nothing can live. This is caused, not by the "fell upas," but by emanations of carbonic acid gas, which are constantly exuding from the soil. At the same time it is quite true that the juice of the upas is a deadly poison.

Up a Tree. *See* TREE.

Upper-crust. The *crême de la crême* of society. The name originated with Thomas Chandler Haliburton in his "Sam Slick in England," where he says : "I want you to see Peel, Stanley, Graham, Shiel, Russell, Macaulay, Old Joe, and so on. They are all upper-crust here." The idea seems to be that of a coterie higher and more select than the Upper Ten Thousand (*q. v.*).

Upper Ten Thousand. The aristocracy. A phrase coined by N. P. Willis in speaking of the fashionables of New York, who at the time of which he wrote did not number more than ten thousand. *See* FOUR HUNDRED.

Up to the Hub. This is a proverbial expression in America, signifying "to the utmost," or "to the extreme point." The allusion is to a vehicle sunk in the mud to the "hub" of the wheels, which is as far as it can go. " 'For my part,' said Abijah, grimly, 'if things was managed my way I should n't commune with nobody that did n't believe in election up to the hub.' " — MRS. STOWE, *Dred*, vol. i. p. 311.

Urania. In classic myth one of the Muses. She presided over Astronomy.

Uranus. In classic myth husband of Tellus and father of Saturn. He was one of the oldest of the gods.

Ursa Major. *See* GREAT BEAR.

Ursa Minor (The Little Bear). A constellation of the northern hemisphere, containing twenty-four stars, of which the seven principal ones form a figure resembling that in the Great Bear, only the "dipper" is reversed and about half as large. The first star in its

handle is the present polar star, and the others revolve constantly about it. All the stars in the group being situated near the pole of the heavens, seem to move very slowly around it in circles so small that they never sink below the horizon. *See* POLAR STAR.

U. S. United States.

u. s. *Ut supra*, or *uti supra*. As above.

U. S. A. United States Army; United States of America.

Used up. This familiar expression for "tired" or "exhausted" took its rise in America. The first known use of the phrase in print occurs in Sam Slick's "Human Nature," p. 192, "Well, being out, night arter night, she got kinder used up."

Useless Parliament. Was convened by Charles I., June 18, 1625; removed to Oxford on August 1 ; and dissolved August 12, having accomplished nothing save to call down the displeasure of the monarch.

U. S. M. United States Mail; United States Marines.

U. S. M. A. United States Military Academy.

U. S. M. C. United States Marine Corps.

U. S. N. United States Navy.

U. S. N. A. United States Naval Academy.

Usque ad aras. (Lat.) "Even to the altars." To the last extremity.

Usque ad nauseam. (Lat.) "Even to sickness." Till absolutely sickening.

Usque ad satietatem. (Lat.) "Even to satiety." To an extent to create disgust.

Usquebaugh. A colloquial name in Ireland and Scotland for whiskey, but in reality it is much stronger than the common spirit known by that name. The word "usquebaugh" means "water of life." There is also a compound of brandy, raisins, cinnamon, lemon, sugar, and water, known by the same name. *See* POTEEN.

U. S. S. United States Senate.

Usus loquendi. (Lat.) "The usage of speaking." The usage in speech.

U. T. Utah Territory.

Utah. An Indian word, meaning "contented people."

Utgard. In Scandinavian mythology the same as Jotunheim, the abode of the giants.

Utgard-Loki. In Scandinavian mythology the king of the giants and of Utgard. *See* LOKI.

Utica Crib. A name given to the State Lunatic Asylum at Utica, N. Y.

Utile dulci. (Lat.) "The useful with the sweet." The useful combined with the pleasant.

Ut infra. (Lat.) As below.

Uti possidetis. (Lat.) As you now possess, — that is, the condition of the combatants on the conclusion of war; the opposite of *status quo ante*.

Utraquists. The followers of Huss were so called, because they insisted that both the elements should be administered to all communicants in the Eucharist.

Ut supra. (Lat.) As above.

V.

V. Village; vanadium; five, or fifth; violin.

V., or **vid.** *Vide.* See.

V., or **vs.** Against (*versus*); in such a verse (*versiculo*).

Va. Virginia.

Vade mecum. (Lat.) "Go with me." An indispensable hand-book or pocket companion.

Vae victis. (Lat.) Woe to the vanquished.

Val. Value.

Valdarfer. (Pseud.) Joseph Haslewood, English bibliographer (1769–1833).

Vale. "Be in good health." Farewell.

Valeat quantum. (Lat.) "It may be effective so far." This may be taken for what it is worth.

Vale, Ladies of the. *See* LADIES OF THE VALE.

Valentine's Day. February 14. Saint Valentine is said to have been a bishop who suffered martyrdom under the Roman emperor, Claudius, or else under Aurelian in 271. Like many another semi-Christian custom, the day set apart to the memory of Saint Valentine in the Christian Calendar is an old pagan festival, upon which our ancestors believed that the birds chose their mates for the coming year. This, at least, is the commonly received version of our modern custom of "choosing a valentine" on the 14th of February, and of sending a *billet-doux* or a fancy "valentine" through the mail to some favored one.

Valentine Vox. (Pseud.) John Henry Walsh.

Vale of Baca. A valley of tears; this world is so named in Psalm lxxxiv. 6, because of the sin and sorrow therein.

Vale of Tears, or **Valley of Baca.** This world.

Our sources of common pleasure dry up as we journey on through the Vale of Baca. — SCOTT, *Antiquary.*

Valérie. (Pseud.) Madame Wilhelmine Josephine Simonin Fould.

Valerius. One of the pen-names commonly attributed to Junius (*q. v.*).

Valet-de-chambre. (Fr.) A servant who assists in dressing.

Valhalla, in Scandinavian mythology, is the palace of immortality, inhabited by the souls of heroes slain in battle.

Valiant, The. Jean IV. of Brittany (fl. 1389–1442).

Valiant Lion. Alep Arslan, son of Togrul Bey, the Perso-Turkish monarch (d. 1072).

Valkyries (Choosers of the Slain). In Teutonic mythology the twelve nymphs of Valhalla. They were mounted on swift horses, and held drawn swords in their hands. In the *mêlée* of battle they selected those destined to death, and conducted them to Valhalla, where they waited upon them, and served them with mead and ale in cups of horn called skulls. The chief were Mista, Sangrida, and Hilda.

Valleria, Madame. The professional name of Mrs. Hutchinson.

Valse. (Fr.) A waltz.

Val Versatile. (Pseud.) Harry Enton, in the Baltimore "Sun."

Van. (Pseud.) David W. Bartlett, in the Springfield "Republican."

Van Augustine. (Pseud.) John G. Abbott, in letters of travel to the Boston "Journal."

Vandoo. Throughout the Middle States, especially in the rural portion, the "vandoo" signifies an auction sale of goods and chattels. It is, of course, a corruption of *vendue.*

Vandyck of England. William Dobson, painter (fl. 1610–1647).

Vandyck of Sculpture. Antoine Coysevox (fl. 1640–1720).

Vandyke Brown. (Pseud.) Frederick J. Prouting, editor of the "Berkshire Bell."

Van Saxon. (Pseud.) Mrs. Evangeline M. Simpson, author of "Marplot Cupid," 1883.

Vantage Loaf. *See* BAKER'S DOZEN.

Varangian Guard. Saxon mercenaries who performed valiant service for Alexius Comnenus in the East. The etymology of the name is uncertain, though the German *fort-ganger,* i. e., "forth-goer," "wanderer," "exile," seems the most probable. The term occurs in various Italian and Sicilian documents, anterior to the establishment of the Varangian Guards at Constantinople, and collected by Muratori; as, for instance, in an edict of one of the Lombard Kings, " Omnes Warengangi, qui de exteris finibus in regni nostri finibus advenerint, seque sub scuto potestatis nostræ subdiderint, legibus nostris Longobardorum vivere debeant; " — and in another: " De Warengagis nobilibus, mediocribus, et rusticis hominibus, qui usque nunc in terra vestra fugiti sunt, habeatis eos." With regard to the origin of the Varangian Guard, the most distinct testimony is that of Ordericus Vitalis, who says, " When therefore the English had lost their liberty, they turned themselves with zeal to discover the means of throwing off the unaccustomed yoke. Some fled to Suevo, king of the Danes, to excite him to the recovery of the inheritance of his grandfather, Canute. Not a few fled into exile in other regions, either from the mere desire of escaping from under the Norman rule, or in the hope of acquiring wealth, and so being one day in a condition to renew the struggle at home. Some of these, in the bloom of youth, penetrated into a far distant land, and offered themselves to the military service of the Constantinopolitan Emperor, — that prince against whom Robert Guiscard, Duke of Apulia, had then raised all his forces. The English exiles were favorably received, and opposed in battle to the Normans, for whose encounter the Greeks themselves were too weak. Alexius began to build a town for the English, a little above Constantinople, at a place called Chevelot; but the trouble with the Normans from Sicily still increasing, he soon recalled them to the capital, and intrusted the principal palace with all its treasures to their keeping. This was the method in which the Saxon English found their way to Ionia, where they still remain, highly valued by the Emperor and the people."

Variæ lectiones. (Lat.) Various readings.

Variazioni. (Ital.) Variations upon an air or theme. (Mus.)

Variorum notæ. (Lat.) The notes of various authors or editors.

Varuna. In Hindu mythology the ruler of the ocean.

Vastus animus. (Lat.) " A vast mind." An insatiable disposition.

Vat. Vatican.

Vatican of Buddhism. Mandalay, in Burmah.

V. C. Vice-Chancellor ; Victoria Cross ; Vice-Chairman.

V. D. L. Van Diemen's Land.

V. D. M. *Verbi Dei Minister.* Minister of God's Word.

Ve. In Scandinavian mythology one of the three gods who created the universe, and a brother of Odin and Vili.

Veda, Land of the. *See* LAND OF THE VEDA.

Vehmgericht. The secret tribunals of Westphalia, for the preservation of public peace, suppression of crime, and maintenance of religion. The judges were enveloped in mystery ; they had their spies ; their judgments were certain, but no one could discover the executioner. These tribunals flourished from the twelfth to the sixteenth century.

Velis et remis. (Lat.) " With sails and oars." With the utmost speed possible.

Veloce, or Con velocita. (Ital.) In a rapid time. This term is sometimes used to signify that a particular passage is to be played as quickly as possible. (Mus.)

Veluti in speculum. (Lat.) As in a mirror.

Ven. Venerable.

Venerable Doctor. (1) William of Champeaux. (2) Peter of Clugny.

Venerable Initiator. William of Occam (d. 1347), the famous English mediæval schoolman.

Venial Sin. A sin that weakens but does not destroy the person's sanctity; a doctrine of the Roman Catholic Church; a sin that can be forgiven.

Venice, Little. *See* LITTLE VENICE.

Venice of France. Amiens. *See* LITTLE VENICE.

Venice of Japan. The city of Osaka. *See* PARIS OF JAPAN.

Venice of the East. Soo-Choo-Foo, a town of China, has been so named. It contains an immense floating population, is intersected by numerous canals, and is celebrated throughout China for its magnificence and beauty.

Venice of the West. Glasgow, in Scotland, — a name for which it is difficult to see any reason.

Veni Vidi. (Pseud.) Mrs. Jennie Cunningham Croly, in her correspondence with various journals. *See* JENNIE JUNE.

Veni, Vidi, Vici. " I came, I saw, I conquered." Cæsar's despatch to the Roman Senate announcing his conquest of Britain.

The classic *Veni, vidi, vici* of Cæsar, says Abraham Hayward, has fallen from the lips of many imitators. Thus, John Sobieski, after raising the siege of Vienna in 1683, announced his victory over the Moslem in a despatch to the Pope as follows : "I came; I saw; God conquered!" (*Je suis venu. j'ai vu, Dieu a vaincu.*) Cardinal Richelieu signified his approval and acceptance of a work dedicated to him in the curt despatch : " I have received, read, approved " (*Accipi, legi, probavi*).

Venomous Preacher. Robert Traill (fl. 1642–1716).

Ventis secundis. (Lat.) " With prosperous winds." Uniformly successful.

Venus. In classic myth the goddess of love and beauty, said to have sprung from the foam of the sea. By the Romans she was looked on as the mother of their race.

Venusberg. In Teutonic mythology the mountain of delight and love, where Lady Venus holds her court. Human beings occasionally are permitted to visit her, as Heinrich von Limburg did, and the noble Tannhauser ; but as such persons run the risk of eternal perdition, Eckhardt the Faithful, who sat before the gate, failed not to warn them against entering.

Ver. Verse.

Verbatim et literatim. (Mid. Lat.) Word for word and letter for letter.

Verbum sat sapienti. (Lat.) A word is enough for a wise man.

Verdad es verde. (Span.) Truth is green.

Veritas vincit. (Lat.) Truth conquers.

Vérité sans Peur. (Pseud., " Truth without Fear.") Frederick James Prouting, in various English periodicals.

Vermilion Sea. The Gulf of California is sometimes so named, in allusion to the scarlet *infusoria* which infest its waters.

Vermont. The name of this State is from the French words *verts monts*, meaning " Green Mountains."

Vermont of the West. Iowa has been so named because, like its Eastern namesake, it was for many years solidly Republican in politics.

Vernona Jarbeau. The stage-name of Mrs. Jefferson F. Bernstein.

Vernon Lee. The pen-name of Violet Paget.

Ver non semper viret. (Lat.) The spring is not always green.

Versailles of Poland. The palace of the Counts of Braniski, in the town of Bialystok.

Versus. (Lat.) Against.

Vertu. (Fr.) " Virtue." Taste ; art ; skill.

Vesta. In classic myth daughter of Rhea and Saturn, and sister of Ceres and Juno. She was the goddess of Fire.

Vestigia nulla retrorsum. (Lat.) No going back.

Veteran Observer. (Pseud.) E. D. Mansfield, American journalist (1800–1880).

Veto. (Pseud.) Theodore Sedgwick, Jr., in the New York " Evening Post."

Veto, Monsieur and Madame. Louis XVI. and Marie Antoinette were so dubbed by the Republicans because the Constituent Assembly accorded the king the right to veto any decree submitted to him.

Vetus. (Pseud.) Edward Sterling, Irish soldier and journalist (1773–1847).

Vexata quæstio. (Lat.) A vexed or disputed question.

V. G. Vicar-General.

v. g. *Verbi gratiâ.* As for example.

V. Hugo Dusenberry. (Pseud.) Henry C. Bunner, in the New York " Puck."

VI. Six, or sixth.

VII. Seven, or seventh.

VIII. Eight, or eighth.

Via. (Lat.) By way of.

Via Dolorosa (Way of Pain). The road leading from the Mount of Olives to Golgotha which our Lord traversed on the way to his crucifixion. It is about a mile in length.

Via media. (Lat.) The middle way or course.

Viator. (Pseud.) J. H. Bright, American poet (1804–1837).

Vicarious Atonement. The sufferings and death endured by Jesus Christ in the place of sinful men, that they might escape from deserved punishment.

Vice. (Lat.) In the room of.

Vice-Emperor. A name sometimes used with reference to Eugene Rouher (1813–1884), who was prime-minister of France under Napoleon III.

Vice-Pres., or **V.-P.** Vice-President.

Vice versa. (Lat.) The terms being exchanged; reversely.

Victoria Temple. The stage-name of Mrs. W. J. Mason, *née* Nathanson.

Victorious, The. Chosroes II.

Victorious City. Cairo, in Egypt. The term has reference to the signification of its Arabic name, — *El Kahvia,* the Victorious.

Vide. (Lat.) See.

Vide et crede (Lat.) See and believe.

Videlicet. (Lat.) To wit; namely.

Vidette. (Pseud.) (1) Jefferson E. P. Doyle, in the " Globe Democrat." (2) J. J. Elliott, in the New Orleans " Picayune."

Vide ut supra. (Lat.) " See as above." See the preceding statement.

Vidi. (Pseud.) William C. Conant, New York correspondent for the religious press in other parts of the United States from 1870 until 1887.

Vi et armis. (Lat.) " By force and arms." By main force.

Vieux Moustache. (Pseud.) George Gordon.

Vieux routier. (Fr.) A shrewd old man; an old stager.

Vigilant. (Pseud.) (1) R. Mitchell, in the London " Sportsman." (2) F. W. Vosburg, in the New York " Spirit of the Times."

Vigilant and Wizard. (Pseud.) John Corlett, the " racing prophet," in the London " Sporting Times."

Vigilantes, Vigilance Committees. Self-appointed law-and-order leagues in the primitive settlements of the West, to award and mete out punishment to evil-doers. When the ordinary political institutions fail to afford protection to persons and property, the people sometimes resort to a voluntary, secret, and temporary organization called Vigilance Committee. The most notable instance was in San Francisco, in the early days of mining, when the criminal class seemed to have their own way, and resort to extraordinary and illegal remedies was necessary.

Among those who hastened to California after the discovery of gold, in 1849, were many lawless characters, who soon caused a reign of terror. The Territory became a State, in 1850, but the laws seemed powerless to restrain the commission of crime. To alter this condition of affairs large numbers of the best citizens, irrespective of party, banded together in San Francisco and other places in 1851, under the name of Vigilance Committees took the law into their own hands, and by their vigorous actions gradually restored the country to a safe and peaceable state. In 1856 they were again forced to administer the law. They held trials and administered justice as seemed to them right. — *American Political Dictionary.*

Vigoroso. (Ital.) Vigorously; with energy. (Mus.)

Villanies. *See* SUM OF ALL VIL-LANIES.

Villa of Tears (Port., *Quinta das lagrimas*). A name popularly bestowed on a house in the suburbs of Coimbra, Portugal, the scene of the death of Inez de Castro.

Vincit amor patriæ. (Lat.) Love of country prevails.

Vincit, qui se vincit. (Lat.) " He conquers, who himself conquers." Self-conquest is the true victory.

Vinculum matrimonii. (Lat.) The bond of matrimony.

Vindex. (Pseud.) (1) Edmund Henry Barker. (2) One of the signatures used by Junius (*q. v.*). (3) John Loveday, D. C. L., in his contributions to the " Gentleman's Magazine."

Vinegar Bible. An edition which appeared in 1717, and was so named from the headline of the 20th chapter of Luke, which reads, "The Parable of the Vinegar," instead of "The Parable of the Vineyard." This edition was gotten up in splendid style by J. Basket, an Oxford printer, but so plentifully was it bestrewn with errors that it was christened "a basketful of errors."

Vineyard Controversy. A paper war provoked by the Hon. Daines Barrington who entered the lists to overthrow all chroniclers and antiquaries from William of Malmesbury to Samuel Pegge, respecting the vineyards of Domesday-book. He maintained that the vines were currants, and the vineyards currant-gardens.

Vinland. A name given by certain Scandinavian voyagers of the tenth century to a part of the North American coast of pleasant aspect and abounding in wild grapes. The locality is thought by many to be somewhere on the coast of Massachusetts or Rhode Island, though very respectable authorities maintain that these early voyagers sailed no farther south than Labrador or Newfoundland.

Vintie Valdeau. The stage-name of Mrs. James Wheeler.

Viola. (Pseud.) (1) Mrs. Fanny M. Downing, an American writer for children. (2) Mrs. Laura M. Hawley Thurston, an American poet and contributor to the Western newspapers. (5) *See* FRANK DASHMORE.

Violated Treaty, City of the. *See* CITY OF THE VIOLATED TREATY.

Violet Cameron. The stage-name of Mrs. De Bensaude.

Violet Corporal. After the banishment of the great Napoleon to Elba his adherents in France adopted the violet and wore it publicly as a party badge. In consequence thereof Napoleon himself was openly toasted under the nicknames of "Corporal Violet," or "Father Violet," coupled with the wish that he might return, in the spring of 1815, and confound his enemies.

Violet-crowned, The. A nickname applied to Athens, "first by Pindar; and the learned pundits who comment on him see in the epithet an allusion to the violet crowns offered to the god at the Dionysiac festivals. It soon became a stock phrase, and, according to Aristophanes, every stump-orator could win over his audience by judicious use of 'violet-crowned city,' or 'ancient violet-crowned Athens.'"

Violetta Colville. The stage-name of Mrs. C. R. Andrews.

Virgil of England. *See* HORACE OF ENGLAND.

Virgin Chimes. The first chimes rung after twelve o'clock on Christmas-eve; also the first chimes rung on a peal of bells newly consecrated.

Virginia. This State received its name in honor of Queen Elizabeth, the so-called "Virgin" Queen.

Virginia. (Pseud.) Mrs. Virginia E. Davidson, in "Southern Opinion," published at Richmond, Va.

Virginia Buchanan. The stage-name of Mrs. Benton Parker.

Virginia Coupon Cases. The generic name under which are known a number of suits determined by the United States Supreme Court, in 1884, enforcing a Virginia statute which declared coupons on bonds of that State receivable in payment of State taxes, notwithstanding the repeal of that statute.

Virginia Francis. The stage-name of Virginia F. Bateman.

Virginia Gabriel. (Pseud.) Mrs. Constance Crane Marsh, an American poet.

Virginia Influence. "By this name is known the influence wielded by the State of Virginia, headed by Jefferson, Madison, Monroe, Taylor, Tazewell, the Randolphs, and others, from the adoption of the Constitution until about 1824. It arose largely from the unanimity of its people on national subjects, owing to a certain clannish feeling among them. The lead taken by the State in opposition to Hamilton's view of the Constitution caused it to be regarded as the head of that opposition, and therefore of the Republican party. This 'Virginia Influence' was a distinct factor in national politics. After John Adams, all the presidents until John Quincy Adams, in 1825, were from Virginia." — BROWN AND STRAUSS.

Virginia Melville. The stage-name of Mrs. J. J. Murray.

Virginia Rebel. *See* BACON'S REBELLION.

Virginia Ross. The stage-name of Mrs. Edward J. Conolly.

Virgin Modesty. So Charles II. dubbed the Earl of Rochester (John Wilmot) because he blushed so easily.

Virgin Queen. Elizabeth of England (fl. 1533–1603), was so named in allusion to the fact that she was never married, though there are sundry reasons for doubting the aptness of the sobriquet.

Virtus in arduis. (Lat.) Virtue (or valor) in difficulties.

Virtus semper viridis. (Lat.) "Virtue always green." Virtue is ever green and blooming.

Virtute officii. (Lat.) By virtue of office.

Vis-à-vis. (Fr.) Face to face.

Visc. Viscount.

Vishni. In Hindu mythology the second person of the holy triad, or *trimurti.*

Vis inertiæ. (Lat.) "The strength of inactivity." The power by which matter in rest or in motion resists any change in its state.

Vis medicatrix naturæ. (Lat.) The healing or curative power of Nature.

Vis motrix. (Lat.) The motive or moving power.

Vis poetica. (Lat.) Poetic genius.

Vis vitæ. (Lat.) "The power (or *force*) of life." The vital powers.

Vita brevis, ars longa. (Lat.) Life is short, but art is long.

Vitalis. (Pseud.) Erik Sjoberg, Swedish poet (1794–1828).

Vitruvius of England. Inigo Jones (fl. 1572–1652).

Viva. (Pseud.) Miss Eva Williams, in the Jersey City "Evening Journal."

Vivace, Vivamente, or **Con vivacita.** (Ital.) With briskness and animation. (Mus.)

Vivant rex et regina! (Lat.) Long live the king and queen!

Vivat regina! (Lat.) Long live the queen!

Vivat respublica! (Lat.) Long live the republic!

Vivat rex! (Lat.) Long live the king!

Viva voce. (Lat.) By word of mouth; by the living voice.

Vive la bagatelle. (Fr.) Success to trifling.

Vive la reine! (Fr.) Long live the queen!

Vive la république! (Fr.) Long live the republic!

Vive l'empereur! (Fr.) Long live the emperor!

Vive le roi! (Fr.) Long live the king!

Vive l'impératrice! (Fr.) Long live the empress!

Vive ut vivas. (Lat.) "Live that you may live." Live uprightly, that you may live long and enjoy life.

Vive, vale. (Lat.) Farewell, and be happy.

Vivian. (Pseud.) George Henry Lewes, in the London "Leader," about 1852.

Vivian Reynolds. The stage-name of Mrs. Snyder.

Vivida vis animi. (Lat.) The vigorous force of mind.

Vivo, or **Con vivezza.** (Ital.) Animated, lively. (Mus.)

Viz., or **vl.** *Videlicet.* To wit; namely; that is to say.

Vo. *Verso.* Left-hand page.

Voce. (Ital.) The voice. (Mus.)

Voce di petto. (Ital.) The chest or natural voice. (Mus.)

Voce di testa. (Ital.) The head voice. (Mus.)

Voilà. (Fr.) "Behold there." Behold; there is or there are.

Voilà tout. (Fr.) That's all.

Voilà une autre chose. (Fr.) That's quite a different matter.

Vol. Volume.

Volens et potens. (Lat.) Willing and able.

Volgo gran bestia. (Ital.) The mob is a great beast.

Voll. (Ger.) Full; as, *mit volle Orgel,* full organ. (Mus.)

Volta. (Ital.) Time of playing a movement, — as, *prima volta,* the first time of playing; *seconda volta,* the second time of playing. (Mus.)

Voltaire of Germany. Johann Wolfgang von Goethe.

Voltaire of Poland. Ignatius Krasicki (fl. 1774–1801).

Volti subito. (Ital.) Turn the leaf quickly. (Mus.)

Volventibus annis. (Lat.) "With revolving years." In the course of years.

Von Boyle. (Pseud.) Acland Boyle, in "Scribner's Magazine."

Von Vohning. (Pseud.) Mrs. A. W. M. Howard.

Vox et præterea nihil. (Lat.) "A voice and nothing besides." Sound without sense.

Vox populi. (Lat.) "The voice of the people." The popular voice.

Vox populi vox Dei. (Lat.) The voice of the people is the voice of God.

Vox stellarum. (Lat.) The voice of the stars.

V. R. *Victoria Regina.* Queen Victoria.

V. S. Veterinary Surgeon.

Vt. Vermont.

Vul. Vulgate (Version).

Vulcan. In classic myth son of Jupiter and Juno, and husband of Venus. He was the god of fire, and the patron of smiths and metal-workers. He was named Hephæstus by the Greeks.

Vulgo. (Lat.) "Among the people." Commonly; usually.

Vulnus immedicabile. (Lat.) An irreparable injury.

Vultus est index animi. (Lat.) The countenance is the index of the mind.

VV. Violins. (Mus.)

Vyvian Joyeuse. (Pseud.) Winthrop Mackworth Praed, in "Knight's Quarterly Magazine."

W.

W. Wolfram, or tungsten; west.

Wager of Battle. One of the forms of ordeal or appeal to the judgment of God, in the old Norman courts. It consisted of a personal combat between the plaintiff and defendant, in the presence of the court itself. It was abolished by act of Parliament in the reign of George III.

Wagoner Boy. Thomas Corwin, the American statesman, was so named. In early life he drove a team laden with supplies for General Harrison, then engaged with his army on the northern frontier.

Waif Woodland. The pseudonym under which Mrs. Caroline Blair, *née* Pease (1816–1869), contributed to the "Ladies' Repository" for many years.

Walcheren Expedition. A well-devised scheme, ruined by the stupidity of the agent chosen to carry it out. Lord Castlereagh's instructions were "to advance instantly in full force against Antwerp," but Lord Chatham wasted his time and strength in reducing Flushing. Ultimately, the commander did get possession of the island of Walcheren, but seven thousand men died of malaria, and as many more were permanently disabled.

Walk Chalks. To "walk chalks" is an ordeal used on board ship as a test for drunkenness. Two parallel lines are chalked for some distance upon the deck, and if the supposed delinquent can walk from one end to the other without overstepping either he is pronounced to be sober.

Walking Gallows. Edward Hepenstall, who is referred to by Sir Jonah Barrington as "the Walking Gallows," was thus described in the Dublin "Irish Magazine" in 1810:—

"This notorious officer was a Goliath in stature and a Nero in feeling. When Hepenstall met a peasant who could not give a satisfactory account of himself, he knocked the poor fellow down with a blow from his fist, which was quite as effectual as a sledge-hammer, and then, adjusting the noose around the man's neck, drew the rope over his own shoulders and trotted along, the victim's legs dangling in the air and his tongue protruding until death at last ended the torture. These details, incredible as they may now seem, are authenticated by several witnesses and were admitted by Hepenstall himself on the trial of Hyland, when Lord Norbury complimented the giant on having done no act which was not creditable to him as a zealous, loyal, and efficient officer."

Walking Leaves. The "walking and climbing leaves" of Australia were, for over half a century, among the best attested of natural wonders. A party of sailors, wandering inland, sat down to rest under a tree. A gust of wind shook to earth several dead and brown leaves. These, after remaining prone on the ground for a few minutes, proceeded to show signs of life and crawl toward the trunk, which they ascended, and attached themselves to their respective twigs! Hence the sailor-men, who promptly ran away, said the spot was bewitched. But the simple fact turned out to be that the so-called "leaves" were really leaf-shaped insects, having long, pendulous legs, which could be folded out of sight, and possessing the chameleon-like power of varying their color to correspond with that of the foliage they were clinging to. Upon being shaken to the ground, instinct taught them to seek the shelter of the friendly leaves again as soon as possible.

Walking Library. Longinus (fl. 213–273), the Roman philosopher and rhetorician, was so named on account of his great erudition.

Walking Polyglot. (1) Maria Gætana Agnesi (1718–1799), a woman remarkable for her varied attainments, and famous for her familiarity with ancient and modern languages. She was a native of Milan, and succeeded her father as professor of mathematics in the University of Bologna. (2) *See* BRIAREUS OF LANGUAGES.

Walking Stewart. John Stewart, the English traveller (d. 1822), who on foot made tours of Hindustan, Persia, Nubia, Abyssinia, Arabia, Europe, and the United States.

Walking-sticks. A satirical nickname bestowed, in 1878, on candidates for election to the House of Commons nominated and controlled by political or trade associations.

Wall. "To go to the wall" or "to be driven to the wall." These expressions mean that when a man in a fight is in extremity he places his back to the wall, so that it is only necessary to defend himself in front; his enemies cannot come behind him. Figuratively, it signifies the last chance.

Wall. Wallace's Supreme Court Reports.

Wallabout. A certain waterside district in Brooklyn, the site of the Government Navy Yard. The name originated not from any "wall about" the place, but from its being settled by Walloon emigrants, who came over in 1623, and first settled in New Amsterdam, and afterward moved over to Rapelje's tract, where the Navy Yard now is. There were so many Walloons there that the place was called "Waal-bogt," — the "Walloon's Bay," — in time corrupted into "Wallabout."

Wallace of Persia. Nadir Shah, a famous Persian ruler (fl. 1688–1747). Under his rule the country grew and prospered, many abuses were swept away, and foreign foes were vanquished.

Wallace Peck. (Pseud.) Charles T. Walter, an American author, who wrote "A Story of the Puritans" (1889), etc.

Walled Kingdom. China.

Waller's Plot. A scheme of Waller, the poet, to disarm the London militia and admit the Royalists, May, 1643. The plot was discovered and frustrated in June and July of the same year. Waller turned informer, and was permitted to emigrate.

Wall of Antonine. A turf entrenchment raised by the Romans from Dunglass Castle, on the Clyde, to Caer Ridden Kirk, near the Frith of Forth, under the direction of Lollius Urbicus, legate of Antoninus Pius, A. D. 140.

Wall Street of Boston. State Street is so named.

Wall, The Devil's. *See* DEVIL'S WALL.

Walraven. (Pseud.) James Otis Kaler, in "Frank Leslie's Newspaper."

Walsingham. (Pseud.) Clinton Stewart, in the New York "Herald."

Walter Aimwell. (Pseud.) William Simonds, American author (1822–1859), in the "Aimwell Stories."

Walter Barrett, Clerk. (Pseud.) Joseph A. Scoville, miscellaneous essayist (1810–1864).

Walter Bentley. The stage-name of Walter Begg.

Walter Maynard. (Pseud.) William Beale.

Walter Scott of Belgium. Hendrik Conscience (1812–1885).

Walter Scott of Hungary. The sobriquet given to Baron Miklos Nicholas Josika (fl. 1796–1865), a remarkable Hungarian novelist and man of letters.

Walter Scott of Italy. So Byron called Ariosto.

Wanderer, The. (Pseud.) Matthew Henry Barker.

Wandering Jew, The. For upward of five centuries the Wandering Jew was regarded by many throughout Christendom as a being of flesh and blood, and his thrilling tale as veritable history, — a belief kept alive until so recently as the last century by periodic reappearances of various individuals, rank impostors, claiming to be the hoary wanderer. For the origin of the legend of the Wandering Jew we must go to the Scriptures, and to the words of the Master himself. In Matt. xvi. 28, we are told: "Verily I say unto you, There be some standing here which shall not taste of death, till they see the Son of Man coming in his kingdom." So Mark ix. 1. In Luke ix. 26, 27, the coming of the kingdom refers to the judgment-day, where the same thought is expressed as follows: "For whosoever shall be ashamed of me and of my words, of him shall the Son of Man be ashamed, when he shall come in his own glory, and in his Father's, and of the holy angels. But I tell you of a truth there be some standing here, which shall not taste of death till they see the kingdom of God." Again, in John xxi. 21-23: "Peter seeing him [the Beloved Disciple] saith to Jesus, Lord, and what shall this man do? Jesus saith unto him, If I will that he tarry till I come, what is that to thee? Follow thou me. Then went this saying abroad among the brethren, that that disciple should not die: yet Jesus said not unto him, He shall not die; but If I will that he tarry till I come, what is that to thee?" "There can be no doubt," says Baring-Gould, "in the mind of an unprejudiced person, that the words of the Lord do imply that some one or more of those then living should not taste death till He came again. We may not insist on a literal interpretation, but it is certainly compatible with ,the power and attributes of the Lord to have fulfilled His words to the letter. We are also to remember that mysterious witnesses are to appear in the last, great, eventful days of earth's history, and bear testimony to the Gospel truth before an anti-christian world. One of these has been often conjectured to be Saint John the Evangelist, and the other has been variously conjectured to be Elias, or Enoch, or the Wandering Jew." While the tradition that "the disciple whom Jesus loved" should not die obtained credence in the Christian Church, we are presented, as its corollary, with the story of an enemy of the Redeemer sentenced by Divine Justice, or compelled by remorse, to ceaseless wanderings until His second coming. But, like many another, this legend appears in diverse forms. The earliest extant mention of the story by a Christian writer is in the "Book of the Chroni-

cles of the Abbey of St. Albans," — the "Historia Major," — continued by the Benedictine historian, Matthew Paris, who died in the year 1259. This account he claims to have received from an Armenian bishop, to whom the Wandering Jew had related his weird history. He records that in the year 1228 "a certain archbishop of Armenia Major came on a pilgrimage to England, to see the relics of the saints and visit the sacred places of the kingdom, as he had done in others; he also produced letters of recommendation from his Holiness the Pope to the religious men and prelates of the churches, in which they were enjoined to receive and entertain him with due reverence and honor. On his arrival he went to St. Albans, where he was received with all respect by the abbot and monks; at this place, being fatigued with his journey, he remained some days to rest himself and his followers, and a conversation was commenced between him and the inhabitants of the convent by means of their interpreters, during which he made many inquiries concerning the religion and the religious observances of this country, and related many strange things concerning Eastern lands. In due course he was asked whether he had ever seen or heard anything of Joseph, a man of whom there was much talk in the world, who, when our Lord suffered, was present and spoke to him, and who is still alive in evidence of the Christian faith. In reply to which a knight in his retinue, who was his interpreter, said, speaking in French: 'My lord well knows that man, and a little before he took his way to the western countries the said Joseph sat at the table of my lord the archbishop, in Armenia, and he has often seen and held converse with him.' He was then asked about what had passed between Christ and the same Joseph, to which he replied: 'At the time of the suffering of Jesus Christ He was seized by the Jews and led into the Hall of Judgment before Pilate, the governor, that He might be judged by him on the accusation of the Jews; and Pilate, finding no cause of adjudging Him to death, said to them: "Take Him, and judge Him according to your law." The shouts of the Jews, however, increasing, he at their request released unto them Barabbas, and delivered Jesus to them to be crucified. When, therefore, the Jews were dragging Jesus forth, and had reached the door, Cartaphilus, a Roman porter of the hall in Pilate's service, as Jesus was going out of the door, impiously struck Him on the back with his hand, and said in mockery, " Go quicker, Jesus; why do you linger?" And Jesus, looking back on him with a severe countenance, said to him, " I am going, but you will wait till I return." And according as our Lord had said, this Cartaphilus is still awaiting His return. At the time of our Lord's suffering he was thirty years old, and when he attains the age of a hundred years he always returns to the same age as he was when our Lord suffered. He places his hope of salvation on the fact that he sinned through ignorance, — for the Lord, when suffering, prayed for his enemies in these words: " Father, forgive them, for they know not what they do." ' " Such is the earliest written form of the legend, told with all the circumstantiality one would expect to find were the person claiming to be the Wanderer so in fact. The Wandering Jew is not heard from again in a circumstantial manner for nearly three hundred years. In 1505 we catch a glimpse of him in Bohemia, where a person claiming to be Cartaphilus assists a poor weaver, named Kokot, to reclaim a treasure buried sixty years before by the grandfather of Kokot in the presence of the Jew. About this time various places in the Low Countries were, it was claimed, visited by this restless one. A few years later he turns up in the East, and is assumed to be Elijah. About this time, too, he appears to one Fadhillah, near the city of Elvan, under the name of Zerib Bar Elia. The Arabs having captured the place, Fadhillah, a Moslem warrior, at the head of three hundred horsemen, encamps in a defile between two mountains. At the hour of sunset he falls on his knees at his prayers, and is astonished to hear every word of his supplication repeated in a loud and distinct voice. At first he thought this phenomenon was the result of an echo, but at length he cried out: " O thou! whether thou art of the angel ranks, or whether thou art of some other order of spirits, it is well; the power of God be with thee. But if thou art a man, then let mine eyes light upon thee, that I may rejoice in thy presence and society!" The words were

scarcely out of his mouth when a venerable man stood before him, white with age, carrying a rough staff, and much resembling a holy dervish. In answer to Fadhillah's questions as to who he was and whence he came, the stranger answered: " Bassi Hadhret Issa, I am here by command of the Lord Jesus, who has left me in this world that I may live therein until He comes a second time to earth. I wait for this Lord, who is the Fountain of Happiness, and in obedience to His command I dwell beyond yonder mountain." Being asked by Fadhillah when the Lord Christ would appear, he replied: " At the end of the world, at the last judgment." Fadhillah next inquired of the signs heralding the approach of that momentous event; "whereupon Zerib Bar Elia gave him an account of the general, social, and moral dissolution which would be the climax of this world's history," saying that " when there shall be no difference in sex between men and women, when the blood of innocents shall be shed, when abundance of food shall not lessen its price, when the poor beg alms without finding anything to live on, when love to man shall be lost, when the Holy Scriptures shall be put into songs, when the temples dedicated to the true God are filled with idols, — then be sure that the day of judgment is near." The year 1547 brings in its train the next well-attested account of the appearance of the Wandering Jew and of his mournful tale. The narrative is chiefly derived from the learned Dr. Paulus von Eitzen, who subsequently became bishop of Schleswig. He was accustomed to tell, how, "when he was young, having studied at Wittenberg, he returned home to his parents in Hamburg, in the winter of 1547, and that on the following Sunday in church he observed a tall man, with his hair hanging over his shoulders, standing barefoot during the sermon over against the pulpit, listening with the deepest attention to the discourse; and whenever the name of Jesus was mentioned, bowing himself profoundly and humbly, with sighs and beatings of the breast. He had no other clothing in the bitter cold of winter except a pair of hose which were in tatters about his feet, and a coat with a girdle which reached to his heels; while his general appearance was that of a man of fifty years. And many people, some of high degree and title, have seen this same man in England, France, Italy, Hungary, Persia, Spain, Poland, Moscow, Lapland, Sweden, Denmark, Scotland, and other places. Everybody wondered over the man. Now, after the sermon, the said Doctor inquired diligently where the stranger was to be found; and when he had sought him out he inquired of him privately whence he came, and how long that winter he had been in the place. Thereupon the stranger replied modestly that he was a Jew by birth, a native of Jerusalem, by name Ahasuerus, by trade a shoemaker; he had been present at the crucifixion of Christ, and had lived ever since, travelling through various lands and cities, the which he substantiated by accounts he gave; he related also the circumstances of Christ's transference from Pilate to Herod, and the final crucifixion, together with other details not recorded in the evangelists and historians; he gave accounts of the changes of governments in many countries, especially of the East, through several centuries, and moreover he detailed the labors and deaths of the holy apostles of Christ most minutely." Now when Dr. Paulus von Eitzen heard this with profound astonishment, on account of its incredible novelty, he inquired further, in order that he might obtain more accurate information. Then the man answered that he had lived in Jerusalem at the time of the crucifixion of Christ, whom he had regarded as a deceiver of the people and a heretic; he had seen Him with his own eyes, and had done his best along with others to bring this deceiver, as he thought Him, to justice and to have Him put out of the way. When the sentence had been pronounced by Pilate, Christ was about to be dragged past his house. Then he ran home and called together his household to have a look at Christ and see what sort of a person He was. This having been done, he had his little child on his arm, and was standing in his doorway to see the concourse go by. " As, then, Christ was led past, bowed under the weight of the heavy cross, He tried to rest a little and stood still a moment; but the shoemaker, in zeal and rage and for the sake of obtaining credit among the other Jews, drove the Lord Christ forward, and told Him to hasten on His way. Jesus, obeying, looked at him and said: ' I shall stand and rest, but thou shalt go on till the last day !' " At these words the man set down the child, and unable to remain where he was, followed Christ and saw 'how cruelly He was crucified, how He suffered, how He died. As soon as this had taken place, it came upon him suddenly that he could no more return to Jerusalem, nor see again his wife and child, but must go forth into foreign lands, one after another, like a mournful pilgrim. When, years after, he returned to Jerusalem, he found it ruined and utterly razed, — so that not one stone was left standing on another, and he could not recognize former localities. In the year 1575 the Secretary Christopher Krause and Master Jacob von Holstein, Legates to the Court of Spain, were sent into the Netherlands to pay the soldiers serving his Majesty in that country. They related, on their return home to Schleswig, and confirmed with solemn oaths, that they had come across the same mysterious individual at Madrid, in Spain, — in appearance, manner of life, habits, clothing, just the same as when he had been seen at Hamburg. They said they had spoken with him, and that many people of all classes had conversed with him, and found him to speak good Spanish. In the year 1599, in December, a trustworthy person wrote from Brunswick to Strasburg that the same-mentioned strange person had been seen alive at Vienna, and that he had started for Poland, and that he purposed going on to Moscow. This Ahasuerus was at Lubeck in 1601; also, about the same date, in Revel, in Livonia, and in Cracow. In Moscow he was seen by many, and addressed by numbers. From the beginning of the seventeenth century scarcely a decade passes without mention of the reappearance of the hoary Wanderer. The year 1604 finds him at Paris, and it would seem as if all Europe at that time rang with his fame. Says Rudolph Botoreus, writing from that city: "I fear lest I be accused of giving ear to old wives' fables, if I insert in these pages what is reported all over Europe of the Jew coeval with our Saviour Christ. . . . I may say that he who appeared not in one century only, and in Spain, Italy, and Germany, was also in this year seen and recognized as the same individual who had appeared in Hamburg, anno 1566." Of this Hamburg visit J. C. Bulenger says: "It was reported at this time that a Jew of the era of Christ was wandering without food and drink, having for a thousand and odd years been a vagabond and an outcast, condemned by God to rove, because he, of that generation of vipers, was the first to cry out for the crucifixion of Christ and the release of Barabbas; and also because, soon after, when Christ, panting under the burden of the rood, sought to rest before his workshop (he was a cobbler), the fellow ordered Him away with acerbity. Thereupon Christ replied: 'Because thou grudgest me such a moment of rest I shall enter into my rest, but thou shalt wander restless.' At once frantic and agitated, he fled through the whole earth, and on the same account to this day he journeys through the world." The mysterious Jew next shows himself in Naumberg, where he was again noticed in church, attentive to the sermon, and, as at Hamburg,. he being questioned after the service told anew his marvellous tale. Among the events of the year 1633 is the reappearance of the Jew at Hamburg. In 1640 he turns up at Brussels under a new name. Says Baring-Gould: "In the year aforesaid two citizens living in the Gerbertstrasse, in Brussels, were walking in the Sonian Wood, when they encountered an aged man, whose clothes were in tatters and of an antiquated appearance. They invited him to go with them to a house of refreshment, and he went with them, but would not seat himself, remaining standing to drink. When he came before the doors with the two burghers he told them a great deal, but they were mostly stories of events which had happened many years before. Hence the burghers gathered that their companion was Isaac Laquedem, the Jew who had refused to permit our blessed Lord to rest for a moment on his doorstep, and they left him, full of terror." In 1642 the Jew was reported at Leipsic; and on Whit-Sunday, 1658, "about six of the clock, just after evensong," he appeared suddenly in Stamford, England, and prescribed successfully for a sick man. "For many a long day," we are told, "there was war, hot and fierce, among the divines of Stamford as to whether the stranger were an angel or a devil." In 1644 John Paul Marana, the famous "Turkish Spy," then in Paris, and writing to a friend, Ibrahim Haly Sheik, in

the East, pens what deserves to rank as the most realistic portraiture of the Jew on record. Marana says that his name was Michob Ader, and that he was an officer in the Court of Judgment in Jerusalem when Christ was condemned. "He had seen Jesus hang upon the cross, had often been in the company of Mohammed at Ormuz, in Persia, was in Rome when Nero set fire to the city and stood triumphing on the top of a hill to behold the flames, heard Vespasian lament the destruction of Solomon's Temple, saw Saladin's return from his conquests in the East, was the intimate friend of Godfrey de Bouillon, Bajazet, and Soliman the Magnificent, and told many remarkable passages concerning these famous men whereof our histories are silent. He knew Tamerlane the Scythian, and told me he was so called because he halted on one leg. He pretends also to have been acquainted with Scanderbeg, the valiant and fortunate Prince of Epirus. He remembers the ancient caliphs of Babylon and Egypt, the empire of the Saracens, and the wars in the Holy Land. He says he has washed himself in the two headsprings of the river Nile, which arise in the southern part of Ethiopia; that its increase is occasioned by the great rains in Ethiopia, which swell all the rivers that fall into the Nile, and cause that vast inundation, — to discover whose origin has so much puzzled philosophy. I tell thee, if this man's pretences be true, he is so full of choice memories, and hath been witness to so many grand transactions for the space of centuries of years, that he may not unfitly be called a Living Chronology, — the Prothonotary of the Christians' Hegira, or principal recorder of that which, they esteem the last epocha of the world's duration. By his looks we would take him for a relic of the old world, or one of the long-haired fathers before the Flood. To speak modestly, he might pass for the younger brother of Time." On July 22, 1721, the Wanderer presented himself at the gates of the city of Munich, in Bavaria. But prior to this, about the end of the seventeenth century or the opening of the eighteenth, "a man calling himself Michob Ader, and claiming to be the Wandering Jew, attracted attention in England, and was listened to by the ignorant or despised by the educated. He contrived to thrust himself into the notice of the nobility, who, half in jest, half in curiosity, questioned him and paid him as they might a juggler. He declared that he had been an officer of the Sanhedrim, and that he had struck Christ as He left the Judgment Hall of Pilate. He remembered all the Apostles, and described their clothes, their personal appearance, and their peculiarities. He spoke many languages, claimed the power of healing the sick, and asserted that he had travelled nearly all over the world. Those who heard him were perplexed by his familiarity with foreign tongues and places. Oxford and Cambridge sent professors to question him, and to discover the imposition, if any. An English nobleman conversed with him in Arabic, and the mysterious stranger told his questioner, in that language, that historical works were not to be relied on. And on being asked his opinion of Mohammed, he replied that he had been acquainted with the father of the prophet, and that he had dwelt at Ormuz. As for Mohammed, he believed him to have been a man of intelligence; once, when he heard the prophet deny that Christ was crucified, he answered abruptly by telling him that he was a witness to the truth of that event." After appearing abruptly at various places in Denmark and Sweden, he vanished. In the following century, in the years 1818, 1824, and 1830, various personages claiming to be the Wanderer appeared in England, and made many converts or dupes. It is perhaps needless to remark that these "reappearances" have totally ceased in recent times. That the story of the Wandering Jew is a pure myth none can now doubt. With this view of the case, we must conclude that those personages who from time to time claimed to be the hoary Jew were rank impostors. "Whether the allegory of Ahasuerus, or this ever-restless being, is to be understood as a type of the anti-christian spirit of scepticism, or whether, in a more concrete sense, it is meant to typify the ever-wandering, homeless, yet still unchanged Jewish people, is a question for critics to decide." While there have not been wanting expounders who claimed for the Jew a real existence, the weight of opinion accepts the mythical and allegorical view. Even Mr. Baring-Gould, perhaps the most devout and considerate of all who have written thereon,

admits the shadowy basis on which the story rests.

Wandering Jew of Ancient Greece. *See* ARISTEAS.

Warbler of Poetic Prose. Sir Philip Sidney (fl. 1554–1586) was so named by Cowper. *See* ENGLISH PETRARCH.

Wardrow's Regiment. *See* INVALIDS.

Warhawk. (Pseud.) William Palmer, English special correspondent.

War-horse. Rear-Admiral J. W. A. Nicholson, U. S. N. (1821–1887), was so nicknamed.

Warming-pans. A scurrilous nickname for the Jacobites. It arose in this way, says Brewer: Mary of Este, the wife of James II., never had, it was claimed, a living child; but on one occasion a child, introduced to her in a warming-pan, was substituted for her own dead infant. This "warming-pan child" was the Pretender.

War of 1812. The conflict between the United States and Great Britain which began June 18, 1812, and ended Feb. 17, 1815.

War of Liberation. The struggle of the Germans, in 1813, to throw off the French yoke.

War of the Barons. An insurrection against Henry III., 1262, headed by the barons, led by Simon de Montfort.

War of the Public Good. A struggle between Louis XI. of France and the dukes of Bourbon, Brittany, and Burgundy. It was ended by the treaty of Conflans, 1465.

War of the Three Henries. The war between Henry III. of France, Henry of Navarre, and Henry, Duke of Guise, occasioned by the efforts of the last-named to bar Henry of Navarre from his rightful succession to the French throne.

Warrington. (Pseud.) William Stevens Robinson, a well-known journalist and author, in various New England journals from 1856 to 1871.

Wars of the Roses. The internal struggle in England between the rival houses of York and Lancaster, 1452–1486, the badges of the respective parties being a white and a red rose.

Wars of the Two Janes. The conflict between Jane of Flanders and Jane of Penthièvre, who, in the fourteenth century, waged ceaseless war against each other during the captivity of their respective husbands.

Warwick. (Pseud.) F. B. Otterson, English writer.

Wash. Washington.

Washee-Washee. A vulgar sobriquet for a Chinaman in many parts of the United States, growing out of the fact that so many of the Celestials embark in the laundry business on coming to America.

Washington of Colombia. Simon Bolivar.

Washington's Birthday. A general holiday throughout the United States, February 22, in honor of the natal day of "the Father of his Country," George Washington. It is a legal holiday in all States except Alabama, Arkansas, Florida, Illinois, Indiana, Iowa, Kansas, Maine, Missouri, North Carolina, Ohio, Oregon, Tennessee, and Texas.

Wash-out. Like the term "crevasse" (*q. v.*), this also signifies a break in an embankment; but while a "crevasse" has reference to a river dike, a "wash-out" applies more especially to a railway embankment, and also to the dropping out of the bottom of a canal.

Wash. Ter. Washington Territory.

Watch-Night. The Kingswood colliers, who had been accustomed on the last day of the year to

> " . . . pass the guilty night
> In revelry and frantic mirth,"

in drunkards' debaucheries, when converted, wisely converted their customs also, and these meetings were changed into religious festivals. Wesley caught up the idea and carried it throughout Great Britain. This was the origin of "Watch-Night," so named because of the beautiful custom of sitting up with one's friends to watch "the Old Year out and the New Year in." But the custom is not peculiar to English-speaking peoples, and possesses a far greater antiquity than that indicated above. In many countries the night of New-Year's Eve, — "St. Sylvester's Eve," — was celebrated with great festivity, which was prolonged till after twelve o'clock, when the New Year was ushered in with congratulations, complimentary visits, and mutual wishes for a "Happy New Year." This is an ancient Scottish custom, which also prevails in many parts of Germany, where the form of wish — " Prosst [for the Latin *prosit*] Neujahr " (" May the

New Year be happy ") — sufficiently attests the antiquity of the observance.

Watering-pot of America, The. Utica, N. Y. A few years ago the Utica Driving Park was first opened for running and trotting races. For some reason, not yet understood, whenever an unusually large crowd attended, it rained from first to last. Whenever the races were postponed, the rain was likewise put off, and as often as the horses were called a shower — not called — also came on. Eventually the sun smiled on the races, and the association has been smiling ever since; yet to this day, far and near, horsemen know Utica only as "the Watering-pot of America."

Water-poet, The. John Taylor, the English poet (fl. 1580-1654), who was totally devoid of book-learning, and who for many years followed the occupation of a Thames waterman.

Watling Street. An old Roman military road leading across England from east to west. It began at Dover, ran through Canterbury to London, and thence across country to Chester. Many portions of it still exist as a public highway, and the part that passed through London still retains its name.

> Fram south-est to north-west (that is sum del grete)
> Fram Dover into Chestre go'th Watling Strete.
> ROBERT OF GLOUCESTER.

See also ERMINAGE STREET, IKENILD STREET, and FOSSE, THE.

Wattie. (Pseud.) Walter Chisholm.

Watts of Wales. William Williams (fl. 1717-1791), a noted Welsh hymnologist.

Waverly. (Pseud.) A. J. Wilson, an English tricyclist, author of articles in the Springfield "Wheelmen's Gazette."

Wayne Hovey. (Pseud.) George William Johnson.

Wayward Sisters. A name conferred on the seceding Southern States. It originated in General Scott's letter of March 3, 1861, in which occurred the sentence : " Say to the seceding States, ' Wayward sisters, go in peace.' "

W. B. M. Women's Board of Missions.

W. B. M. I. Women's Board of Missions of the Interior.

W. C. Western Central (London Postal District).

W. C. A. Women's Christian Association.

We are Dancing on a Volcano. In the midst of a *fête* given by the Duke of Orleans to the King of Naples, in 1830, a few days before the events of the three days of July, M. de Salvandy said to the Duke, *Nous dansons sur un volcan.*

Weaver's Beef. The sprat, a small and exceedingly cheap fish caught in English waters, and much esteemed by the poor. *See also* ALBANY BEEF and BLOCK ISLAND TURKEY, for similar terms current on the hither side the Atlantic.

Wed. Wednesday.

Wedge of Republicanism. A name given by modern writers to the territory occupied by France and Switzerland, which projects from the Atlantic into the very heart of the European continent.

Wednesday, Spy. *See* SPY WEDNESDAY.

Week of Indulgences. Another name for Holy Week, the week before Easter.

Weeks, Feast of. *See* PENTECOST.

Weeping Philosopher. Heraclitus.

We have met the Enemy and they are Ours. Commodore Perry's laconic despatch to Gen. W. H. Harrison announcing the victory on Lake Erie, 1813.

Weissnichtwo ("I know not where.") Almost the same as the Scottish Kennaquhair (*q. v.*). A place in Carlyle's "Sartor Resartus," generally supposed to represent London, spoken of as containing a university, in which Herr Teufelsdröch is professor.

Well-Beloved. Charles VI. of France (fl. 1368–1422).

Well-born, The. "A term of contempt applied to the Federalists. The term was used by John Adams during the discussion preceding the adoption of the Constitution. 'The rich, the well-born, and the able will,' wrote he, 'acquire an influence among the people that will soon be too much for simple honesty and plain sense in a House of Representatives.'" — BROWN AND STRAUSS.

Well-founded Doctor. Ægidius de Columna (d. 1316).

Wellington's Colonels. A collective nickname conferred popularly on Charles, William, and George Napier,

three brothers who performed gallant service in the Peninsular War.

Well-languaged Daniel. Samuel Daniel (fl. 1562–1619), the English poet, was so named by William Browne (fl. 1590–1645).

We love him for the Enemies he has made. This famous phrase was said of Grover Cleveland, then governor of New York, by Gen. E. S. Bragg, on the occasion of Cleveland's nomination for the Presidency at Chicago, in July, 1884. The full text of the General's speech was as follows: —

"Gentlemen of the Convention, it is with feelings of no ordinary pride that I fill the post that has been assigned to me to-day. Grim and gray personally fighting the battles of the Democratic party, I stand to-day to voice the sentiment of the young men of my State when I speak of Governor Cleveland. His name is upon their lips; his name is in their hearts; and he is the choice, not only of that band of young men, but he is the choice of all those who desire for the first time as young men to cast their votes in November for the candidate nominated by this Convention. They love him, gentlemen, and they respect him, not only for himself, for his character, for his integrity and judgment and iron will, but they love him most for the enemies that he has made."

Wench. A term in vogue in the Southern States for a negro woman. But "wench" for a "maid or girl" is pure Staffordshire, and remained so in this country, but only applicable to a negress. That famous line in "Othello"

"O ill-starr'd wench, pale as thy smock,"

has sometimes been rendered by an affected actor,

"O ill-starr'd wretch, pale as thy sheets."

Still, it is probable that wench never was commonly applied to a lady of high degree, for in the "Canterbury Tales" we find, —

"I am a gentlewoman, and no wench."

Wesley Brooke. (Pseud.) George Lunt, American lawyer and author (b. 1807).

Western Reserve, The. When, by the treaty of 1783, Great Britain relinquished the territory south of the great lakes and east of the Mississippi, disputes arose among the States of Virginia, New York, Massachusetts, and Connecticut as to the right of occupancy in that locality. The difficulty was finally settled by the cession of the whole to the Federal Government, but Connecticut reserved a tract of nearly 4,000,000 acres on Lake Erie. That State finally disposed of this in small lots to colonists, and so accumulated a magnificent school-fund. *See* NORTHWEST TERRITORY.

Western Saratoga. Waukesha, Wis.

Westminster Abbey of the Florentines. The Church of Santa Croce, in Florence, where Michael Angelo Buonarotti and many others equally eminent are entombed.

West. Res. Coll. Western Reserve College.

Wet Bobs. *See* DRY BOBS.

Wets and Drys. In 1886 the question of prohibition of the liquor traffic was prominent in Southern politics in the United States, those who opposed restriction being nicknamed the "Wets," and those in favor of it being called "Drys."

w. f. Wrong fount.

W. F. M. S. Women's Foreign Missionary Society.

Wharncliffe Meetings. The stated meetings of British public companies are held and regulated by standing orders of the House of Lords, introduced by Lord Wharncliffe about 1846. Hence the nickname.

Whatshisname. (Pseud.) E. C. Massey.

What will Mrs. Grundy say? This question occurs in Morton's comedy, "Speed the Plough," where Farmer Ashfield, annoyed at his wife's continually bringing up the name of a neighbor's wife and her doings, in contrast with theirs, exclaims petulantly: "Be quiet, woolye? always ding, dinging Dame Grundy into my ears, — 'What will Mrs. Grundy say? what will Mrs. Grundy think?' Caunst thee be quiet? Let ur aloane and behave thyself pratty?" — Act i. sc. i.

Wheat. Wheaton's Supreme Court Reports.

Wheeler Compromise. A name given to the final adjustment of the Louisiana difficulty in 1876–1877, promoted by William A. Wheeler.

Wheeling Bridge Case. The case of Pennsylvania *v.* Wheeling and Belmont Bridge Co., decided by the United States Supreme Court (in 1851 and 1855), concerning a railroad bridge across the Ohio River at Wheeling, Va. After holding, in 1851, by a divided court, that a bridge, though entirely within the jurisdiction of the State that authorized its construction, could be enjoined as a nuisance by the courts

of the United States if it obstructed interstate navigation, the court held, in 1855, that Congress, under the constitutional power to regulate commerce between the States, may determine what shall or shall not be deemed an obstruction to navigation, and may declare a bridge, when erected, to be a lawful structure so as to avoid the effect of its having been judicially declared a nuisance.

When at Rome, do as the Romans do. Saint Augustine was in the habit of dining upon Saturday as upon Sunday; but, being puzzled with the different practices then prevailing (for they had begun to fast at Rome on Saturday), consulted Saint Ambrose on the subject. Now at Milan they did not fast on Saturday, and the answer of the Milan saint was this: "When I am here, I do not fast on Saturday; when at Rome, I do fast on Saturday."

Where the Shoe Pinches. Plutarch relates the story of a Roman being divorced from his wife. "This person, being highly blamed by his friends, who demanded, Was she not chaste? was she not fair? holding out his shoe, asked them whether it was not new and well-made. 'Yet,' added he, 'none of you can tell where it pinches me.'"

Whf. Wharf.

Whigs. (1) During the seventeenth century, when the Scotch were contending for liberty against the oppression of the crown, one of the popular clubs of the day inscribed upon its banners this appropriate and Christian motto, "We hope in God." Sometimes only the initial letter of each word, "W. H. I. G.," was used. In this way the word "Whig" was formed, which is thus seen to be an abbreviation of this declaration of trust and hope. Those who were designated by this term, at first in derision, were the friends and defenders of the people against tyranny. In the reign of Charles II., in England, the name "Whig" was a term of reproach given by the court party to their antagonists for holding the principles of the "Whigs," or fanatical Covenanters in Scotland; and in return the name "Tory" was given to the court party, comparing them to the Tories, or popish robbers, in Ireland. The distinction arose out of the discovery of the Meal-tub plot in 1678. Upon bringing up the Meal plot before Parliament, two parties were formed: those who doubted the plot styled those who believed in it Whigs; these styled their adversaries Tories. The Whigs brought about the revolution of 1688–1689, and established the Protestant succession. They were chiefly instrumental in obtaining the abolition of the slave trade and slavery, the repeal of the Test and Corporation Acts, Catholic emancipation, parliamentary and municipal reform, the repeal of the Corn Laws, and similar measures. The Whig Club was established by Charles James Fox. (2) The Whig Party in America. During the administration of Andrew Jackson the opposition took definite shape under the leadership of Henry Clay and Daniel Webster. This was afterward known as the Whig party, though when Mr. Clay was their candidate in 1832, they went by the name of National Republicans. It was joined by Federalists, and its active principles were the advocacy of the United States Bank, a protective tariff, and internal improvements by the general government. And it opposed the system adopted by Jackson of removal from office on account of political opinions, which he had justified on the plea that "to the victors belong the spoils." Its first success was in 1840, when Gen. William H. Harrison was elected President and John Tyler Vice-President; but the fruits of the victory were lost by the course of Mr. Tyler after his accession to the presidency at the death of General Harrison when only a month in office. The "spoils" system proved too attractive for the virtue of the incoming party, and was adopted. The country was agitated during Mr. Tyler's administration over the annexation of Texas, and on that issue Mr. Clay was defeated, and the Whig Party lost the position it nominally held. In 1848 the Whigs nominated and elected President, Zachary Taylor, a popular general in the Mexican War. The slavery question was now constantly intruding itself, and both parties were trying to avoid its difficulties. Mr. Clay, on May 9, 1850, brought forward a series of compromises known as the Omnibus Bill, of which the concessions made to Texas, the admission of California as a free State, and a more stringent Fugitive Slave Law were the chief features. During its consideration General Taylor died, and Millard Fillmore became President, July 9, 1850.

The bill was passed complete September 18, but did not satisfy the growing sentiment against slavery and the slave power. There was little heart in the party; and the death of Mr. Clay, June 28, and of Mr. Webster, Oct. 24, 1852, tended still further to its decline. In 1852 it put forward Gen. Winfield Scott as its candidate, but not even his splendid military reputation could save it from defeat. The slavery issue now overbalanced all else. A new party arose, — the Republican, — and the Whig party disappeared.

Whipping-post, The. *See* ITINERANT DEY OF NEW JERSEY.

Whiskey Insurrection. An outbreak in Pennsylvania, in 1794, arising from an effort to enforce an excise law passed in 1791, imposing a tax on domestic distilled liquors.

Whiskeytown. Peoria, Ill.

Whispering Jimmie. A nickname given to General Ketcham, of New York, in Congress, because of his habit of whispering into everybody's ear what he had to say.

Whistle Drunk. In the Middle Ages drinking-vessels were often made with a whistle at the side, which came into use when the tankard was empty, in order that the drawer of the liquor might know that more was desired. "Whistle drunk" meant that a man was so far gone that he could no longer blow the whistle as a signal for more liquor. *See* CHAMPION OF THE WHISTLE.

White Blythe, Jr. (Pseud.) Solon Robinson, American miscellaneous writer (b. 1803).

White Brethren. A sect in the beginning of the fifteenth century. Mosheim says that a certain priest came from the Alps, clad in white, with an immense concourse of followers, also dressed in white linen. They marched through several provinces, following a cross borne by their leader. Boniface X. ordered their leader to be burned, when the multitude dispersed.

White Caps. (1) A rebellious party of zealous Mohammedans, put down by Kienlung, the Chinese emperor, in 1758. (2) A vigilance organization which appeared in some of the Western States in 1886–1889.

White Devil of Wallachia. George Castriota was so called by the Turks (1404–1467).

White Horse of Berkshire. During the latter half of the ninth century the warlike Danes — "the sea-wolves of the North" — constantly ravaged and pillaged the fairest portions of southern and eastern England. In the year 867, while King Ethelred was on the throne, they landed in the Humber in great force from a fleet of three hundred vessels, marched inland, plundering and burning, and took the city of York. Proceeding southward, they worsted the Saxons at Merton, but near Oxford they were met by a strong army under Alfred, the king's brother. The Danes here received such a decided defeat that they were glad to enter into a treaty with the victors and to hastily return to their own land. For some years thereafter the kingdom was not molested by these barbarous marauders. The country folk were so overjoyed at this hardly won victory over their fierce foes that they proceeded to carve on a neighboring hill-side a monument, which endures to this day. This is a figure of a galloping horse, 510 feet long, known as the White Horse of Berkshire, while the valley which it overlooks is still known as the Vale of White Horse. Seen from a distance, against the dark background of herbage, it looks as though a giant, standing in the valley, had amused himself by sketching in white crayons on the face of a slope 200 feet above; but the lines that appear so slender from afar are really deep and broad trenches cut in the yellowish-white clay soil. These ditches are 18 feet wide and 6 feet deep; the horse's eye is 6 feet long, and his ears measure 45 feet. At a distance of sixteen miles across country, in ordinary weather, the White Horse can be seen; and it is fully as interesting a monument of former times, though not as ancient, as the Druidical temple of Stonehenge on Salisbury Plain. Once a year the people for fifty miles round gather on the spot to cleanse the trenches from weeds and all vegetable growth; for on the clearness and sharpness of its outlines, seen at a distance, does the distinctness of the figure largely depend. These meetings form a sort of rural carnival; many hands make light work; the great trenches are carefully trimmed and scoured, for the Berkshire folk take great pride in what is certainly the largest horse in the world. This labor of love ended, they engage in all kinds of rustic games, and then part until next year's gathering reunites them. Perhaps the unintermitted observance of this simple rural festival for a thousand years of eventful history is even more remarkable than the strange monument which is thus annually renewed.

White Horse of the Peppers. A sprat to catch a mackerel. After the battle of the Boyne, the estates of many of the Jacobites were confiscated, and given to the adherents of William III. Among others, the estate of the Peppers was forfeited, and the Orangeman to whom it was awarded went to take possession. "Where was it, and what was its extent?" These were all-important questions; and the Orangeman was led up and down, hither and thither, for several days, under pretence of showing the estates to him. He had to join the army by a certain day, but was led so far afield that he agreed to forego his claim if supplied with the means of reaching his regiment within the given time. Accordingly, the "white horse," the pride of the family, and the fastest animal in the land, was placed at his disposal, the king's grant was revoked, and the estate remained in the possession of the original owner.

White House. The name of the residence of the Chief Executive of the United States in Washington. It is derived from the fact of the Virginia freestone of which it is built being painted white to conceal the discoloration caused by weather and smoke.

White Lady of Avenel. A spirit mysteriously connected with the Avenel family, as the Irish banshee is with true Milesian families. She announces good or ill fortune, and manifests a general interest in the family to which she is attached, but to others she acts with considerable caprice; thus she shows unmitigated malignity to the sacristan and the robber. Any truly virtuous mortal has commanding power over her.

> Noon gleams on the lake,
> Noon glows on the fell;
> Awake thee, awake,
> White maid of Avenel!
> SIR W. SCOTT, *The Monastery.*

White League. A secret political organization formed in New Orleans, in 1874, for the overthrow of negro and carpet-bag ascendency. A riot occurred Sept. 14, 1874, in which over a hundred negroes were killed.

White Liner. A term applied in Louisiana at the close of the Civil War to those who were determined to prevent the exercise of the ballot by the newly enfranchised negroes.

White Man's Grave. Sierra Leone, from the deadly nature of its climate to Europeans.

White-plumed Knight. *See* PLUMED KNIGHT.

White Queen. Mary, Queen of Scots, because she wore white mourning for her husband.

White Rose. *See* RED ROSE.

White Rose of England. So Perkyn Warbeck, the pretender, was always addressed by Margaret of Burgundy, sister of Edward IV.

White Rose of Raby. Cicely, wife of Richard, Duke of York, and mother of Edward IV. and Richard III.

Whites. *See* BIANCHI.

White Sheep. A nickname given to the Turcomans who conquered Persia in 1468, and persecuted the Shütes.

White-stoned, The. Moscow is popularly so named, in allusion to the ramparts around the old city, which are of a snowy-white limestone.

White Terror. *See* REIGN OF TERROR.

Whit-Sunday. This is literally "White-Sunday," a festival appointed to commemorate the descent of the Holy Ghost upon the Apostles; the newly baptized persons or catechumens are said to have worn white garments on that day. It is a movable feast, being always exactly seven weeks after Easter. By some it is called Pentecost. Whit-Monday is a general holiday throughout England and in some parts of the Continent. The Germans name this "Pfingster Montag," and keep high holiday thereon.

Whittington's Priory. Holloway Prison, London, has been so nicknamed. It is a fortress-like structure, much used for civil offenders, and hard by is the eminence famed in the old story of Whittington and his cat. In 1885, when the London journalist, Edmund Yates, was confined therein for libelling Lord Lonsdale in the columns of the London "World," he dated a number of articles written while in prison from "Whittington's Priory."

W. H. M. A. Women's Home Missionary Association.

Who Stole the Mutton? This was a common street jeer flung on policemen when the force was first organized, and arose thus: The first case the force had to deal with was the theft of a leg of mutton; but they wholly failed to detect the thief, and the laugh turned against them.

Who's Who? Administration. The administration formed by the Earl of Derby, in February, 1852. It contained so many little-known names that the country was at a loss to know "who" the members were or why they had been selected; whence the nickname.

Whyte Tye. (Pseud.) Lewis Wingfield, a London correspondent and journalist.

W. I. West Indies.

Wicked Bible. So named from the fact that the negative was omitted from the Seventh Commandment (Exod. xx. 14), for which the printer was fined £500. It bears date 1631–1632. Archbishop Laud called in the whole edition, and appropriated the fine to the "purchase of a fount of Greek type."

On the 8th of May, 1632, Richard Barker and Martin Lucas, the printers, were summoned before the Court of High Commission for having in the edition of the Bible printed by them in the previous year made grievous errors and used very bad paper. The Bishop of London (William Laud) "shewed that this would undoe the trade, and was a most dishonorable thing; that they of the Church of Rome are soe carefull, that not a word or letter is to be found amisse in their Ladie's Psalter and other superstitious bookes; and that we should not (*sic*) be so carefull in printeing the sacred Scriptures, and that they in Holland, at Amsterdam, had gott up an English presse, and had printed the Bible in better paper, and with a better letter, and can undersell us 18d in a bible." The unhappy printers tried to excuse themselves through their advocates, and offered submission and amendment, but the Court refused to listen. The case therefore came on again on the 14th of June, when the printers moved the Court to pass by the errors as being faults of the workmen; but the royal advocate required a legal defence and the regular hearing of the cause, when Laud "would have the Church sett upright in her reputacian, that we are as carefull in printeing the Bible as they are of their Jesus' psalter, and whereas the Printers say this is stirred up by the malice of one man against them; the Bishop saith he stirred not till the Bible was sould into his house, bought by his footman; and he saith the printeing is soe bad and the paper too, that, if it be not mended shortlie, they wilbe put downe by those of Amsterdam and their trade spoyled, and the two grossest errors, vizt., 'shalt commit adultery,' and 'great asse': for 'shalt not commit adultery,' and 'greatnesse.' The Arch Bishop of Canterbury (Abbot) saith, that the Printers that print for his Matie have a very profitable place, and therefore should be more carefull. I knew the tyme when greater care was had about printeing, the Bibles especiallie, good compisetors and the best correctors were gotten being grave and learned men, and the paper and letter rare and faire every way of the best; but now the paper is naught, the composers boyes, and the correctors unlearned. There is a former and he makes the benefit, and careth for nothing about it. They heertofore spent their whole time in printeing, but these looke to gaine, gaine, gaine, nothing els : if it be good to bribe, to give hundreds, thousands, what to do? not to benefitt the people, but to make a gaine, then they are to be commended : Well, let them looke to it, and let the cause proceed, saith the Arch-Bishop, London. There was a great deale to doo betweene you of this Citty and those of Cambridge heertofore about the priviledge of printeing the Bible and Psalmes which they of Cambridge claymed ; then the Bible was exactlie printed, now you have forced the Cambridg printer to an agreement, now noe Bible is right printed." (Rawlinson MS., printed Camden Society, N. S. 39.) This case was ultimately remitted to the Star Chamber, where the printers were fined £500 and the edition of 1,000 erroneous copies was ordered to be burned. — *The Bookworm.*

Wide Awakes. In the presidential campaign which resulted in the choice of Abraham Lincoln, the "Wide Awakes" gave an immense impetus to the Republican cause. The first club was organized in Hartford, Conn., in the spring of 1859, but it was not until after the Chicago convention of the next year that such clubs became general. They enlisted the sympathies of a great many young men who had never before cast a ballot for president. Each had an oilcloth cap and cape, and carried a torch swung upon a short pole. The processions which they formed marched in the evening, with their lamps burning. There were at least five hundred thousand " Wide Awakes " during that campaign. Some lingering traces of the organization survived, and the Democracy attempted to get up a similar series of popular demonstrations; but for the most part the " Wide Awakes " were confined to the Republican campaign of 1860.

Widow Priscilla P. Bedott. (Pseud.) Mrs. Frances Miriam Whitcher, *née* Berry, author of " The Widow Bedott Papers," New York, *circa* 1867.

Widows' Pianos. Inferior instruments sold as bargains ; so called from the ordinary advertisement announcing that " a widow lady is compelled to sell her piano, for which she will take halfprice."

Widow's Port. A wine sold for port, but of quite a different family. As a widow retains her husband's name after the husband is taken away, so this mixture of potato-spirit and some inferior wine retains the name of port, though every drop is taken from it.

Wild Boar of the Ardennes. William, Count of Lamarck, was so nicknamed, because of the ferocity of his temper and the delight he took in hunting the forest of Ardennes. He died 1485.

Wild Cat. In a general way the term applied to depreciated paper money before the war, but more particularly to the notes of the banks of the State of Michigan, which had on their face the picture of a panther. It was applied to the bills of these banks by those who had suffered loss by taking them. It was one of several opprobrious epithets justly given to the money issued by banks doing business under State charters, as well as to the banks themselves.

Wilhelm. (Pseud.) William A. Brewer, in various American newspapers.

Wilibald Alexis. (Pseud.) Wilhelm Haring, German novelist (1798–1871).

Wilkes's Number 45. On April 23, 1763, the " North Briton " newspaper, edited by John Wilkes, M. P., for Aylesbury, issued the above number, in which the king, George III., was charged with uttering falsehood in his speech from the throne. Wilkes and others concerned were arrested and committed to the Tower. " Number 45 " was declared by Parliament to be a " scandalous and seditious libel," and ordered to be burned by the common hangman. A riot ensued at the burning in Cheapside.

Will Adams. (Pseud.) John Neal.

Will Honeycomb. (Pseud.) William Cleland, Scottish poet and soldier (1660–1689).

William. (Pseud.) Jeremiah Evarts, American editor (1781–1831).

William and Robert Whistlecraft. (Pseud.) John Hookham Frere, English diplomatist and writer (1769–1846).

William Churne. (Pseud.) F. E. Paget, English minister and religious writer (b. 1806).

William Herbert. The stage-name of William Eden.

William Hickling. (Pseud.) Benjamin F. DeCosta.

William Mestayer. The stage-name of William Hoppe.

William Terriss. The stage-name of Arthur Lewin.

William Wastle. (Pseud.) John Gibson Lockhart, British author, poet, and critic (1794–1854).

Williwaws. A sailor-man's name for violent squalls peculiar to the Terra del Fuego Islands.

Will Watson. The stage-name of Jeremiah Stivers.

Will Wildwood. (Pseud.) Frederick Eugene Pond, in "Turf, Field, and Farm."

Wilmot Proviso. An amendment to a bill placing $2,000,000 at the disposal of President Polk with which to negotiate a treaty of peace with Mexico. The amendment was introduced in the House of Representatives, August 8, 1846, by David Wilmot, of Pennsylvania, and provided that slavery should not exist in any territory that might be acquired under the said treaty. It did not become a law.

Wilt. "To wilt" appears to be a genuine Americanism denoting the stage in the life of a flower between drooping and withering. The imaginative phrase, "He wilted right down," is an expression peculiar to the New World.

Winds, Sale of. It is well known that in the Middle Ages the Laplanders drove a profitable trade in selling winds to mariners. The King of Sweden, the same Eric quoted by Mordaunt, was, says Olaus Magnus, "in his time held second to none in the magician art; and he was so familiar with the evil spirits whom he worshipped, that what way soever he turned his cap, the wind would presently blow that way. For this he was called Windy-cap." "It is perhaps less notorious," says Sir Walter Scott, "that within the present century such a commodity might be purchased on British ground, where it was likely to be in great request. At the village of Stromness, on the Orkney main island, called Ponoma, lived in 1814 an aged dame, called Bessie Millis, who helped out her subsistence by selling favorable winds to mariners. He was a venturous master of a vessel who left the roadstead of Stromness without paying his offering to propitiate Bessie Millis; her fee was extremely moderate, being exactly sixpence, for which, as she explained herself, she boiled her kettle and gave the bark the advantage of her prayers, for she disclaimed all unlawful arts. The wind

thus petitioned for was sure, she said, to arrive, though sometimes the mariner has to wait some time for it. The woman's dwelling and appearance were not unbecoming her pretentions; her house, which was on the brow of the steep hill on which Stromness is founded, was only accessible by a series of dirty and precipitous lanes, and for exposure might have been the abode of Æolus himself, in whose commodities the inhabitant dealt. She herself was dried up like a mummy. A clay-colored kerchief, folded round her head, corresponded in color to her corpse-like complexion. Two light-blue eyes that gleamed with a lustre like that of insanity, an utterance of astonishing rapidity, a nose and chin that almost met together, and a ghastly expression of cunning, gave her the effect of Hecate. She remembered Gow, the pirate, who had been a native of these islands, and in which he closed his career. Such was Bessie Millis, to whom the mariners paid a sort of tribute with a feeling betwixt jest and earnest."

Windward Isles. Another name for Barbadoes, St. Vincent, Grenada, Tobago, and St. Lucia, West Indies. They are so named in distinction from the Leeward Isles (*q. v.*) with reference to the Trade-winds.

Windy City. Chicago, Ill. The gales from Lake Michigan are frequent and furious.

Winter King. Frederick V., Elector Palatine (fl. 1596–1632). He was chosen King of Bohemia by the Protestants in 1619, and was defeated and dethroned in 1620.

Winter Queen. Elizabeth, daughter of James I. of England, and wife of the foregoing.

Winton. Winchester.

Wiped out. A Western euphemism for death.

Wire-pulling. In politics the scheming and figuring of place-seekers is called "wire-pulling," and those who manipulate are called "wire-pullers." Just when the term was first employed cannot be determined. It certainly dates back to the summer of 1848. It has always had a strong coloring of disrepute, referring particularly to those who manage to live off the public by being serviceable to their party in the use of unscrupulous means, especially in controlling caucuses and conventions.

Wirt. (Pseud.) William Francis Williams, in the New York "Evening Post."

Wis. Wisconsin.

Wisconsin. The name of this State is an Indian word meaning "a wild or rushing channel."

Wisd. Wisdom (Book of).

Wise, The. (1) Albert II., Duke of Austria (fl. 1289–1358). (2) Alfonso of Leon and Castile (fl. 1203–1285). (3) Aben-Ezra, the Spanish rabbi (fl. 1119–1174). (4) Charles V. of France (fl. 1337–1380). (5) Che-Tsou, founder of the fourteenth Chinese dynasty (fl. 1278–1325). (6) Comte de las Casas (fl. 1766–1842). (7) Frederick, Elector of Saxony (fl. 1463–1554). (8) John V. of Brittany (fl. 1389–1442).

Wisest Man of Greece. Socrates.

Witchcraft Delusion. The name given to the Salem excitement in 1691–1692, when so many innocent persons were arrested, tried, or executed on suspicion of witchcraft.

Witchfinder. Matthew Hopkins, who flourished in the seventeenth century, travelled up and down the eastern counties of England pretending to discover witches. Being tested by his own rule, he was cast into a river and floated, when he was declared to be a wizard, and put to death.

Witling of Terror. Bertrand Barère, a prominent actor in the Reign of Terror. *See* ANACREON OF THE GUILLOTINE.

Wittenberg Monk, The. Martin Luther, the great Reformer. In Wittenberg he lived, preached, and was buried.

Wizard of Kinderhook. Martin Van Buren.

Wizard of the North. (1) A sobriquet given to Sir Walter Scott by John Wilson. (2) John Scott, a famous horse-trainer, was so named by his patrons.

Wk. Week.

W. M. Worshipful Master.

Wm. William.

W. M. S. Wesleyan Missionary Society.

W. N. C. T. U. Women's National Christian Temperance Union.

W. N. W. West-northwest.

Woden. The Scandinavian form of Odin (*q. v.*).

Wolf, The. So Dryden calls the Presbytery, in his "Hind and Panther."

Wolfe's Own. The Sixty-seventh Regiment in the English army is thus named, after the general who vanquished Montcalm on the Heights of Abraham.

Wolfland. A former nickname for Ireland, pointing to the popular notion that wolves formerly abounded there.

Wolverine State. Michigan; so named from the fact that wolverines formerly infested the State in great numbers.

Woman Capet, The. *See* MADAME DEFICIT.

Wonderful Doctor. Roger Bacon.

Wonder-making Parliament. Another nickname for the Unmerciful Parliament (*q. v.*). By aiding the designs of the Duke of Gloucester, it foiled the King.

Wonders of the World. *See* SEVEN WONDERS OF THE WORLD.

Wonder-worker. Gregory of Neo-Cæsarea.

Wood. Woodbury & Minot's U. S. Circuit Court Reports.

Wooden Horse. In classic myth a gigantic image of a horse made of wood by the Greeks and filled with armed men, which the Trojans were induced to take into their city. At night the Greeks made their way out, unlocked the gates of Troy, and admitted their waiting friends. By this stratagem the Greeks gained possession of the city.

Wooden-legged Commissary. Sir Brook Watson, the English soldier (1735–1807). In 1749, while bathing in the harbor of Havana, his right leg was bitten off by a shark. In 1758 he served at the siege of Louisburg with General Wolfe, where he was known by the above nickname.

Wooden Spoon. The last of the honor men, *i. e.*, of the Junior Optimes, in Cambridge University, England. Sometimes two or more "last" men are bracketed together, in which case the group is termed the "spoon bracket." It is said that these men are so called because in days of yore they were presented with a wooden spoon, while the other honor men had a silver or golden one, a spoon being the usual *prix de mérite* instead of a medal.

Wooden Walls of England. Another name for the English navy — in these days of iron and steel ships somewhat of a misnomer. The expression "wooden walls" is of great antiquity, having been used by Themistocles with reference to the fleet of Athens.

Wooden Wedge. Last in the classical tripos. When, in 1824, the classical tripos was instituted at Cambridge, England, it was debated by what name to call the last on the list. It so happened that the last on the list was Wedgewood, and the name was accepted and moulded into Wooden-wedge.

Wood's Halfpence. Money coined, for circulation in Ireland, by one Wood by virtue of a patent issued 1722–1723. Against this project Dean Swift raised such a storm of opposition, by his "Drapier's Letters" (*q. v.*), that Wood was banished from the realm.

Woolly Heads. That faction of the old Whig Party which espoused the cause of negro liberation, being closely affiliated with the abolition party of Garrison and Wendell Phillips.

Woolwich Infant. An experimental gun cast at Woolwich Arsenal in May, 1874. It weighed 80 tons, was 27 feet long, carried a projectile weighing 1,650 pounds, and consumed a charge of powder weighing 300 pounds.

Workditch, The Picts'. *See* PICTS' WORKDITCH.

Worth a Jew's Eye. This is a common proverbial synonym for a large sum. Its meaning is not very obvious, but it probably arose in the days of King John, who extorted large sums of money from the Jews under threats of mutilation. It is on record that John had the whole of the teeth of one Jew, at Bristol, drawn before he would satisfy the monarch's rapacity. The "ransom" for an eye would probably be greater than for teeth, and so it became proverbial. There is another probable origin. In the "Merchant of Venice" (act ii. sc. 5) Shylock has just been telling his daughter Jessica that a mask or procession is to pass the house, and, as he is going out, she is on no account to look out of the window, upon which Launcelot, very slyly, advises Jessica, notwithstanding the parental prohibition, to look out, for —

"There will come a Christian by
Will be worth a Jewess' eye."

That is, there will be some one coming by, whom, Jewess though you be, you will find worth looking at. As no reference to the proverb earlier than

the time of Shakspeare is known, this speech entirely misunderstood may have been the origin of the saying.

Wpful. Worshipful.

W. S. Writer to the Signet.

W. S. W. West-southwest.

W. T. Washington Territory.

Wt. Weight.

W. Tirebuck. The literary signature of W. Sharp.

W. Va. West Virginia.

Wycliffe Lane. (Pseud.) Mrs. E. Jenings.

Wyo. Wyoming.

Wyoming. An Indian word, meaning "wide plain."

Wyoming Massacre. "During the Revolutionary War a large number of families settled in the valley of Wyoming, Luzerne Co., Penn., which from its seclusion could not well be protected from hostile arms. The greater portion of the able-bodied men were on duty with General Washington, when, on June 30, 1778, a body of four hundred British troops and seven hundred Seneca Indians invaded the valley. On July 3, the battle of Wyoming was fought between this force and about three hundred settlers, chiefly old men and boys, who were defeated and with the women and children driven into Forty Fort. Uncertain of their fate, — for the invaders were sweeping like a dark storm down the Susquehanna, — the night of the battle-day was a terrible one for the people in the fort. But their agony of suspense was ended the following morning, when the leader of the invaders, contrary to the expectations of those who knew him, agreed upon humane terms of surrender. The gates of the fort were thrown open, and most of the families returned to their homes in fancied security. They were doomed to terrible disappointment and woe. Brant, the great Indian leader, was not there to restrain his savage bands, and their thirst for blood and plunder soon overcame all their allegiance to their white commander. Before sunset they had scattered over the valley; and when night fell upon the scene the blaze of more than twenty dwellings cast its lurid glare over the paradise of yesterday. The cries of the murdered went up from almost every house and field; and when the moon arose, the terrified inhabitants were fleeing to the Wilkesbarre Mountains and the dark morasses of the Pocono beyond. In that vast wilderness between the valley and the Delaware, appropriately called the Shades of Death, many women and children who escaped the hatchet perished by hunger and fatigue. The 'Wyoming Massacre,' as it has been appropriately called, stands out in bold relief as one of the darkest crimes perpetrated during the War for Independence." — LOSSING.

Wy. Ter. Wyoming Territory.

X.

X., or **Xt**. Christ.

X. Ten, or tenth.

XC. Ninety.

XI. Eleven.

XII. Twelve.

XIII. Thirteen.

XIV. Fourteen.

XIX. Nineteen.

XL. Forty.

XV. Fifteen.

XVI. Sixteen.

XVII. Seventeen.

XVIII. Eighteen.

XX. Twenty.

XX., XXX., XXXX. *See* DOUBLE *X*.

XXX. Thirty.

Xariffa. (Pseud.) Mrs. M. A. Townsend, an American poet.

Xavier. (Pseud.) Joseph Xavier Boniface, English critic (b. 1797).

Xenette. (Pseud.) Miss Pamela S. Vining, an American writer for the magazines.

XLers. A by-name for the Fortieth Foot Regiment in the English army.

Xmas., or **Xm**. Christmas.

Xn., or **Xtian**. Christian.

Xnty., or **Xty**. Christianity.

Xper., or **Xr**. Christopher.

Xtian. Christian ; Christians.

X Y Z Scandal. During the ambassadorship of John Marshall to the court of France, Talleyrand and the French ministers tried to get a bribe of the American envoys in payment for a treaty which was to be made with the United States. They failed, however, and their attempt forms one of the most scandalous pages in the history of French diplomacy in regard to the United States. When Adams sent the documents in the case to Congress, the letters X, Y, and Z were substituted for the names of Talleyrand's emissaries. Hence these papers have ever since been known as the " X Y Z despatches," and the episode as the " X Y Z scandal."

Y.

Y. Yttrium.

Y^e. The ; thee.

Y^m. Them.

Y^n. Then.

Y^r. Their.

Y^s. This.

Y^t. That.

In such contractions as y^e, y^m, y^n, y^r, y^s, and y^t, for "the," "them," "then," "their," "this," and "that," the "y" is simply an arbitrary modern form of an old MS. contraction for "th," and should be so pronounced.

Yama. In Hindu mythology the lord of hell, and the tormentor of the wicked.

Yamstocks. The inhabitants of St. Helena are so named because of their fondness for yams — a monstrous variety of the sweet potato.

Yankee. The theories as to the origin of the word "Yankee" are numerous. Dr. William Gordon, in a history of the American war published in 1789, said it was a cant word in Cambridge, Mass., as early as 1713, and was used to denote especial excellence, as "a yankee good horse," "yankee good cider," etc. He supposed it was originally a byword in the college, and being taken by students into other parts of the country, was applied to New Englanders as a term of slight reproach, and gradually obtained general currency throughout New England. Thierry says it was a corruption of Jankin, a diminutive of John, which was a nickname given by the Dutch colonists of New York to their neighbors in the Connecticut settlements. Aubury, an English writer, says it is derived from a Cherokee word *eankke*, which signifies "coward and slave." This epithet was bestowed on the inhabitants of New England by the Virginians for not assisting them in a war with the Cherokees, and they have always been held in derision by it. Another theory, and one which is regarded the most probable, is that of Mr. Heckewelder, that the Indians, in endeavoring to pronounce the word "English," or "Anglais," made it "Yengees" or "Yangees," and this originated the term. There is no doubt that the name was given by the Indians to the English colonists; from them it was adopted by the British, who applied it generally to New Englanders only. Europeans subsequently applied it to all natives of the United States; and during the war the Southerners dubbed all inhabitants of the Northern States by the epithet; but it properly belongs solely to native New Englanders.

Yankee, A. (1) Richard Grant White, author and critic (fl. 1821–1885), wrote under this pen-name a series of letters to the London "Spectator" during the Civil War. (2) J. K. Mitchell, physician (1798–1858), in his poem "Saint Helena," published 1821.

Yankee Farmer. John Lowell, LL.D., American lawyer and political writer (1769–1840), in the periodical literature of his day. Other pen names which he used were "Citizen of Massachusetts," "Layman," and "Massachusetts Lawyer."

Yankee Hill. The sobriquet of George Handel Hill, American actor (1809–1849), during his appearance at Drury Lane Theatre, London, 1836.

Yankee Notions. *See* NOTION.

Yarborough Hand. A hand at whist in which there is no card above a nine. The name is derived from a certain Lord Yarborough, who used to offer the attractive, but really very safe, wager of £100 to £1 that a hand of this sort would not be dealt.

Yazoo Fraud. The name popularly given to a sale of lands situated in Western Georgia, in 1789, to certain companies by a venal legislature. The transaction occasioned widespread excitement, which was only allayed by a decision of the United States Supreme Court in 1810.

Yd. Yard.

Year of Wonders. The year 1666, memorable for the great fire of London and for the English victories over the Dutch. Dryden wrote a poem, "Annus Mirabilis," in which both events are set forth.

Year without a Summer. The year 1816 was so named. So cloudy were the skies that crops refused to ripen and fruit-trees bore no fruit.

Yellow Envelope. *See* BLUE ENVELOPE.

Yellow Jack. The scourge of the countries bordering on the Gulf of Mexico, yellow fever, is thus nicknamed. *See* BRONZE JOHN.

Yellow Jackets. A military company commanded by Capt. Spier Spencer, which served throughout the campaign which ended in the battle of Tippecanoe, Nov. 7, 1811.

Yggdrasil. In Norse mythology the ash-tree, whose roots run in three directions: one to the Asa-gods in heaven, one to the Frost-giants, and the third to the under-world. Under each root is a fountain of wonderful virtues. In the tree, which drops honey, sit an eagle, a squirrel, and four stags. At the root lies the serpent, Nithhogg, gnawing it; while the squirrel, Ratatoskr, runs up and down to sow strife between the eagle at the top and the serpent.

Y. M. C. A. Young Men's Christian Association.

Y. M. C. U. Young Men's Christian Union.

Ymir. In Scandinavian mythology the progenitor of the giant race and the first of all beings. He is considered as the type of chaos.

Yom Kippur. "The day of Atonement," the great Jewish religious anniversary, falls on October 9. This fast day has done more to bring Jews together in their ancient faith than all of the rest of their holy days. Of course the Sabbath is calculated to make a separate people of the Hebrews all over the world, but we see how less and less, yearly, this day of rest is observed by the Jews dwelling and doing business in the busy marts of Europe and America; whereas Yom Kippur, which only exacts one day in the year for exclusive worship, has always been a sacred charge which very few of those who outwardly still profess Judaism neglect to observe. The warranty for this so-called day of atonement is found in the Bible and reads as follows : —

"And the tenth day of the seventh month ye shall have an holy convocation ; and ye shall afflict your souls, ye shall not do any work therein."

And again we find as a command: —

"And this shall be an everlasting statute unto you, to make an atonement for the children of Israel for all their sins, once a year."

This latter command was for the Highpriest. There is no other religion, be it Christian, Mohammedan, Buddhist, or Confucian, that has a similar festival. The great object is, of course, that once a year one day out of the 365 shall be set apart for no other purpose than to commune with God, confess the errors of life, and perchance resolve to amend them. Considering that this command was given during the wanderings of the Hebrews in the wilderness, nearly 4,000 years ago, the strict observance of it by this people at this distant day, all over the world, and in many countries, even under dangerous and difficult circumstances, may well awaken our admiration. If we choose to give the subject any thought at all, we cannot fail to be impressed with the grandeur not only of the sublime command, but of the people who observe it.

Yorick. (Pseud.) James Warner Ward (1807–1873), in "Home-made Verses and Stories in Rhyme" (1857).

Yorkshireman's Coat of Arms. A flea, a fly, and a flitch of bacon. These are facetiously said to represent a Yorkshireman's coat of arms, and indicate, that a flea will suck any one's blood, like a Yorkshireman; a fly will drink out of any one's cup, like a Yorkshireman; and a flitch of bacon is no good till it is hung, neither is a Yorkshireman.

York's Tall Son. William Trotter Porter (1809–1858), American journalist, was so named because of his great stature, — six feet four inches.

Yorktown Celebration. The centennial observance in 1883 of the surrender of Cornwallis at Yorktown, Va., 1783.

You All, or **You Alls.** "You all," or, as it should be abbreviated, "y'all," is one of the most ridiculous of all the Southernisms we can call to mind. It usually means two or more persons, but is sometimes used when only one person is meant. For instance, a caller, on taking her departure, says : " Y'all must come to see us." She means that the lady upon whom she is calling and her husband may call.

Young America. A popular nickname for American youth, intended to embody a personification of their supposed characteristics.

Young Buffs. The Thirty-first Regiment in the English service is so nicknamed.

Young Chevalier. Charles Edward Stuart, the Young Pretender (fl. 1720–1788).

Young Cupid. See BEAU D'ORSAY.

Young Europe. France, Germany, Spain, Ireland, Poland, Italy, Switzerland, etc. Political coteries which sprang into life throughout Europe in consequence of the ferment resulting from the French Revolution of 1830.

Young Hotspur. Ralph Isaacs Ingersoll, statesman (1788–1872). During his congressional career he was one of the most conspicuous debaters on the Democratic side, and the press called him " Young Hotspur."

Young Roscius. William Henry West Betty, who acted mature parts while yet in his teens. It is said that in fifty-six performances he realized £30,000. He died in 1874, aged eighty-four. In his maturer years he evinced none of the dramatic fervor and aptitude which made his youth so noteworthy.

Young Thieves. A nickname bestowed on the Forty-fourth East Essex Regiment in the English army.

Young Un. (Pseud.) George P. Burnham and Francis Alexander Durivage in "Stray Subjects Arrested and Bound over " (1848). See OLD UN.

Young Yale Movement. A successful effort about 1869, led by William Walter Phelps, which resulted in giving the alumni a voice in the government of the institution.

Yr. Year.

Yrs. Years ; yours.

Y. W. C. A. Young Women's Christian Association.

Z.

Zach. Zachary.

Zadkiel. (Pseud.) Lieutenant Morison, R. N., English author.

Zarzel. The professional name of Mrs. George O. Starr, *née* Richter.

Zech. Zechariah.

Zena Clifton. (Pseud.) Mrs. Lilian T. R. Messenger, in the Memphis "Avalanche."

Zenith City of the Unsalted Seas. Duluth, Minn., was thus named by Proctor Knott in a famous speech in Congress a few years ago.

Zeph. Zephaniah.

Zephyrus. In classic myth a son of Æolus and Aurora, and the lover of Flora; a personification of the west wind.

Zeus. The Greek name of Jupiter (*q.v.*), king of gods and men. According to the most common mythology, he was the son of Cronos and Rhea, brother of Poseidon and Hera, the latter of whom was also his wife. Crete, Dodona, and Arcadia were the places where the worship of Zeus was most cultivated; and although, originally, the inhabitants of these places may not have looked upon themselves as worshippers of the same god, yet, in process of time, all the local gods revered under the name of Zeus were at last merged into one great Hellenic divinity; a process which was carried still further when he was identified with the Jupiter of the Romans, and the Ammon of Libya.

Zimri. Under this title Dryden satirized the Duke of Buckingham in his "Absalom and Achitophel."

Zina Richard. The stage-name of Mrs. Louis Merante.

Zn. Zinc.

Zoe, Mlle. The professional name of Mrs. Benjamin Yates.

Zoilus. John Dennis was satirized by Pope and Swift under this name. He was called "the best-abused man in England."

Zollverein. (German "Customs Union.") A league of twenty-two independent German States for purposes of commerce and defence, as follows: Prussia, Saxony, Mecklenburg-Schwerin, Mecklenburg-Strelitz, Oldenburg, Saxe-Weimar, Brunswick, Anhalt, Saxe-Meiningen, Saxe-Coburg-Gotha, Saxe-Altenburg, Lippe-Detmold, Waldeck, Schwarzburg-Rudolstadt, Schwarzburg-Sondershausen, Reuss (Younger Line), Schaumburg-Lippe, Reuss (Elder Line), and the free cities, Hamburg, Lubeck, and Bremen, and Upper Hesse. It was also known as the North German Confederation.

Zoöl. Zoölogy.

Zoöphilus. (Pseud.) Edward Blyth, in "Land and Water," and in "The Field."

Zr. Zirconium.

Zu-zu. A common name in the Union army for the "Zouaves," during the late Rebellion.

My love is a " Zu-zu " so gallant and bold;
He 's rough, and he 's handsome, scarce nineteen
　　years old.
　　　　　　　　　Comic Song.

Once again ! — the hours are fleeting ;
　Drinking is the soldier's trick ;
Hark ! the drum the roll-call 's beating, —
　Scatter, " Zoo-zoos," " double quick ! "
　　　　　　Song, The Zoo-zoo's Toast.